STAR WARS

FOURTH EDITION

OVER 40,000 COLLECTIBLES LISTED FROM AROUND THE WORLD

SUPER COLLECTOR'S WISH BOOK

IDENTIFICATION & VALUES

OVER 16,000 PHOTOS!

Geoffrey T. Carlton

COLLECTOR BOOKS
A Division of Schroeder Publishing Co., Inc.

Cover design by Beth Summers
Book design by Geoffrey T. Carlton and Tamara Carlton
Cover photography by Charles R. Lynch

COLLECTOR BOOKS
P.O. Box 3009
Paducah, Kentucky 42002-3009
www.collectorbooks.com

The current values in this book should be used only as a guide. They are not intended to set prices, which vary from one section of the country to another. Auction
prices as well as dealer prices vary greatly and are affected by condition as well as
demand. Neither the author nor the publisher assumes responsibility for any losses
that might be incurred as a result of consulting this guide.

Searching for a Publisher?

We are always looking for people knowledgeable within their fields. If you
feel that there is a real need for a book on your collectible subject and have a
large comprehensive collection, contact Collector Books.

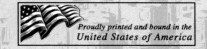

Proudly printed and bound in the
United States of America

Contents

Fourth Edition Design

Every edition of the *Star Wars Super Collector's Wish Book* is designed with new layouts and different photo selections. This allows each book the ability to stand on its own merit. Each edition also contains unique focuses and features, providing owners of previous editions an expanded library of references to draw upon. Previous editions may be sought from www.collectorbooks.com.

Reference Photographs

Photographs in this guide are included solely for identification purposes and may not be reproduced. It is important to note that they are not in scale with one another. Completely different sized pieces may be printed next to each other and appear to be the same size. Photos should be viewed individually and not comparitively.

Photo References to Previous Editions

To continue showing new images of collectibles from around the world, not every item or set shown in previous editions has been included in the current edition. To aid users of this guide, any item which has been pictured in previous editions that were not included in the current edition will have a reference indicating the most recent edition and page number the photos appeared on. For example, the Jabba the Hutt ceramic bank by Sigma is not pictured in this edition. Its photo caption says [3:116] which indicates it can be seen in the third edition, page 116. Photos are referenced all the way back to the first edition.

Contacting the Author

Geoffrey Carlton runs a collecting site at www.StarWarsGuide.net and may be reached via e-mail at info@StarwarsGuide.net.

Introduction

The Star Wars collectibles covered by this book are not individually unique. They are mass produced with prices and availability subject to the whims and desires of investment speculators, dealers, fans, and collectors.

The selling price of any given collectible can skyrocket during the clamoring and interest at the time of its initial release only to plateau and plummet once any mania turns to focus on the next marketing spotlighted piece. Hundreds of collectibles illustrate this principle by having sold for a lot of money initially, but now aren't even worth their original retail price. Not every piece of Star Wars merchandise is a diamond to be polished for an easy profit. On the other hand, a select few turn out to be pure platinum.

Sellers and buyers each need to understand whether the going price for an item is due to popularity (short term) or desirability (prolonged duration). It means the difference of whether sales should be approached impulsively, or if patience will prove more profitable for the interested party.

Some collectors buy extra pieces to resell which helps to finance their own habits. This brings up the question of who is a collector and who is a dealer? A true collector buys for long-term holding, perhaps 10 to 30 years. Dealers buy for the short-term, no more than 10 to 30 weeks. Many dealers also collect. Few collectors routinely deal.

Calculating values is tricky, which is why a printed guide is essential. As with any other investment choice, the strategy is the classic "buy low; sell high." So should the value of an item be calculated based upon the lowest it can obtained for by a nondescript buyer, or would it make more sense to report the value on the highest amount an established dealer could get for the piece? The debate has raged for years and often depends on whether the point of view is that of the buyer or that of the seller. Values expressed in this book are median, providing a baseline for buyers and sellers to adjust according to market, availability, and special grading considerations.

A determining factor to be made when establishing a specific price is whether or not the collectible is "investment grade." For every mass-produced item distributed some become damaged, some acquire wear, some are opened for use or display, and a percentage remains sealed for the posterity of collecting. Of the last group of items most are "hobby grade." Only a small percentage of those are truly investment grade. Investment grade collectibles have the ability to command a price greater than their published value. To illustrate, a vintage action figure with a value of a couple hundred dollars could double or triple in price if it receives a top score from a professional grading house. Its increase in value has no effect on the value of equivalent-condition action figures that have not been professionally graded.

Adding to the confusion about values is online trade and auction sites. It's rare to hear a person complain that they paid too much in a situation where they got to offer their own price to the seller. All too often when a bid is placed on an item, somebody else who values the item even more places a higher bid. The purpose of this type of transaction is for the buyer to obtain items at less than they are worth. Sellers may sacrifice the profit of true value for the sake of a quick turn of inventory, or to try to minimize their own losses on items. Items posted at below their value and receiving no bid whatsoever don't reduce the value of all alike pieces, it simply indicates current lack of the auction community's interest in the movement for that piece, or a flaw in the system such as when items are miscategorized or incorrectly identified.

Star Wars is a volatile market for speculation and acquisition. The property is too fast paced to capture more than a snapshot of the market. New merchandise is released every month worldwide for collectors and fans to search out. There is a huge secondary market right below the retail level who seems to specialize in obtaining the highest demand goods, marking it up, and turning it around quickly to the public who become concerned when items are released and cannot be found immediately at the retail level. When the next wave of merchandise is released, the previous is all but forgotten as focus shifts the newer goods. By the time a third additional wave or series is released, the true value of the original items is revealed — a value based on desirability instead of popularity.

It is this value, the durable value of items once out of the population's eye that the *Star Wars Super Collector's Wish Book* reports. Less than investment grade conditioned items can be found for a lower street price. Professionally graded items have the ability to go for a higher price. Ultimately though, the calculation of a selling price of an item is definitely based upon the foundation of its recorded value.

Address Books

PPA01 PPA02 PPA03 PPA04 PPA05 PPA06 PPA07 PPA08 PPA09 PPA10 PPA11

PPA12 PPA13 PPA14 PPA15

Address Books

____Episode I with Notepad [PPA01] 15.00

EPI:TPM tabbed address books.
____Adventures [PPA02] 3.00
____Heroes [PPA03] 3.00
____Jedi Battles [PPA04] 3.00

Episode I 3D magnetic phone books.
____Jar Jar Binks [PPA05] 5.00
____Queen Amidala [PPA06] 5.00
____Yoda [PPA07] 5.00

Antioch
____Art, "The Glove of Darth Vader" [PPA08] 5.00

Day Runner
Telephone books, 6-ring binder.
____Jar Jar Binks 12.00
____Queen Amidala 12.00
____Qui-Gon Jinn 12.00

Telephone books, bound spine.
____Jar Jar Binks [PPA09] 4.00
____Queen Amidala [PPA10] 4.00
____Qui-Gon Jinn [PPA11] 4.00

Letts
____Princess Leia [PPA12] 5.00
____Queen Amidala [PPA13] 3.00
____Stormtrooper [PPA14] 8.00

Yukari
Address book with scheduler and 1978 – 79 pocket calendar. Various colors.
____Droids / space battle [PPA15] 30.00
____Tatooine / Hildebrandt art [3:99] 30.00

Advertising: Displays

____ROTJ painting competition flyer [AD01] 22.00

12"x12" cardboard hanging displays.
____Anakin Skywalker 6.00
____Darth Maul 6.00
____Jar Jar Binks 6.00
____Queen Amidala 6.00

20th Century Fox
____EPI: Darth Maul DVD [AD02] 15.00

____EPII:AOTC Yoda, "Unlock the Saga" [3:100] 55.00
____Imperial Invasion video re-launch flyer [3:100]. 3.00
____Shuttle Tydirium hanging display with character danglers [AD03] 115.00

20th Century Fox, Japan
7.25"x10.25", 1 sheet flyers in the style of vintage movie posters. 25th anniversary premiums.
____Star Wars [3:100] 6.00
____Empire Strikes Back [3:100] 6.00
____Return of the Jedi, advance [3:100] 6.00
____Return of the Jedi [3:100] 6.00

20th Century Fox, Mexico
AOTC invitations.
____Anakin and Padme [AD04] 10.00
____Jango Fett [AD05] 10.00
____SW:SE video standee [2:71] 25.00

Advanced Graphics
Star Wars Celebration II. Holocron CubiCard.
____Bounty Hunters [2:71] 2.00
____Skywalker Family 2.00
____Villains [AD06] 2.00

Star Wars Celebration II.
____Single sheet flyer featuring Holocron Cubicard, 8.5"x11" 1.00

Agfa
____Poster: free frisbee or yo-yo with film purchase [AD07] 11.00

Applause
____Episode I 3-D shelf display [3:100] 50.00

At-A Glance
____Hexagonal dump with double-corrugated die-cut header for posters 11.00

Australia Post
____25th Anniversary souvenir stamp sheet ad 1.00

Avon
____Jedi Knights tin card set flyer [2:71] 2.00

Avon, Mexico
____AOTC products, 1-sheet flyer [3:100] 6.00

Bantam/Spectra
____"Star Wars Where the Adventure Continues," R2-D2 shaped 5.00

Bimbo
____Star Cards window poster [3:100] 25.00

Brooklyn Museum of Art
____Magic of Myth, April 5-July 7, 2002 ....2.00

Burger Chef
____Burger Chef Funmeal tray, table tent 30.00

Burger King
____ESB Glasses Coming Soon C-3PO and R2-D2 [3:100]...185.00
____ESB Glasses counter display [3:100] 280.00
____ESB Glasses standee C-3PO and R2-D2 [3:100] 300.00

____ESB Super Scene premium display [3:100] 200.00
____Flyer: Play the Star Wars Team game! 5.00
____ROTJ Glasses counter display [3:100] 225.00
____ROTJ Glasses counter display, Darth Vader-shaped [3:100] 200.00
____ROTJ Glasses standee Darth Vader [AD08] 400.00
____ROTJ Glasses, hanging [AD09] 100.00
____Star Wars Glasses counter display [AD10] 385.00
____SW Posters Collect All Fours, 2-piece hanging [3:100] 650.00
____Translite display for ROTJ glasses [3:101].........54.00

Butterfly Originals
____Pencil Top Eraser counter display [3:101] 12.00
____ROTJ pen display, cardboard box with die-cut header, 36 count pens [3:101] 8.00
____Royal Guard standee [2:72] 50.00
____Vending machine header, pencil toppers and paper protectors [AD11] 18.00

Cedco Publishing
____2002-2003 17-month Locker Calendar 1.00
____2003 Classic Poster Art Datebook 2-sided flyer 1.00
____2003 EPII AOTC Daily Calendar 1.00
____Episode II calendars for 2003..............................2.00

Celebration III
____Exhibitor packet [AD12] 15.00

Children's Museum of Indianapolis
____Art of the Starfighter 1.00

Chupa Chups
Classic trilogy countertop displays to hold product.
____Fantasy Balls [3:101] 5.00
____Pen Pops [3:101] 5.00
____Port-a-Chups [3:101] 5.00
____Port-a-Chups counter display island [3:101]......35.00

Clarks
____Handbill flyer advertising Clarks shoe line [AD13]..26.00
____Handbill flyer with Clarks shoe line prices [2:72] 7.00
____Order form for Clarks shoe line [2:72] 11.00

Coca-Cola
____"Match Star Wars Pairs And You Could Win A Cash Prize" bottlecap game promotion [3:101] 24.00
____Bottle hanger for SW cap game [3:101] 11.00

Code 3 Collectibles
____Millennium Falcon / X-wing, Free Poster inside [AD14] 2.00

Colgate
____Colgate SW:EPI retail toothbrush cardboard display [AD15] 14.00

Collector Books
Flyers, 2-sided.
____1st edition 2.00
____2nd edition 2.00
____3rd edition 2.00

Dark Horse Comics
____3"x5" card for X-Wing Rogue Squadron 4.00

AD01 AD02 AD03 AD04 AD05 AD06 AD07

| AD08 | AD09 | AD10 | AD11 | AD12 | AD13 |

Deka
____Flyer for plastic merchandise [AD16] 11.00
____Return of the Jedi display header, "For kids of all ages" 35.00

Del Rey
____Cloak of Deception 11"x11" flyer 2.00
____Vector Prime ad: "You Know Where the Star Wars Saga has been…" 3.00

Disney / MGM
2004 Star Wars Weekends. 1 page flyer, "Complete your Jedi Training," "Construct Your Own Lightsaber."
____Blue [AD17] 5.00
____Green 5.00
____Purple 5.00
____Red 5.00

Dixie / Northern Inc.
____Dixie Cups, Darth Vader header [2:72] 65.00

DK Publishing
____Jango Fett POP 125.00
____Visual Dictionary 2-page brochure 2.00

Duncan Heinz
____ESB poster dump [3:101] 95.00

Electronic Boutique
____Official Offer Guide with free keychain and poster offer 2.00

Encuntros
2004 flyers, EPIII.
____Anakin 14.00
____Obi-Wan Kenobi 14.00
____Obi-Wan vs. Vader [AD18] 12.00

Estes
____Star Wars EPI catalog..2.00

Factors, Etc.
____Earrings, upright [AD19] 75.00
____Pendant and necklace countertop display rack, rotating [3:101] 33.00

Fan Club
____Order form for ink-revealing pens and keychain [3:101] 30.00

Fernandes
One-sheet flyers.
____Character Series Guitar Knob Collection [2:72]...5.00
____Character Series Guitar Strap Collection [2:72]...5.00
____Character Series Star Wars Guitar Collection, Vader and Stormtrooper [2:72] 5.00
____Character Series Star Wars Guitar Collection, Vader, Stormtrooper, and Boba Fett [2:72]...........5.00
____Character Series Trading Guitar Pick Collection [3:101] 8.00
____Character series 4-page products 2.00

Forbidden Zone
____Forbidden Zone poster promoting SW Exhibition 9/10-9/30/98 [2:72]...28.00

Frigo
____La Guerra de las Galaxias [2:72] 22.00

Frito Lay
____Can You Resist framed game cards, promo [2:72]...45.00
____Clone Trooper oversized puzzle game piece 9"x9" [AD20]..20.00
____EPI floor sticker, 18"x24" [AD21] 15.00
____Experience the Adventure stand-up, 60"x35" [AD22] 60.00

Fundimensions
____Duel at Death Star shelf talker tag [3:101].........85.00

GE Consumer Finance
____Star Wars VISA Application brochure 10.00

Golden Villa
____News 31 – center spread advertisement for EPII:AOTC charity screening in Singapore...........8.00

Gym Dandy
____Scout Walker Command Tower counter display [AD23] 35.00

H.E. Harris and Company
____Display bin and 2-piece header for stamp collecting set...64.00

Hallmark
____2002 Ornament Wish List, 11"x17", b/w 2.00

Hamilton Collection
____Brochure for wall-mount plate holder [2:73].........3.00

Harrod's
Sculpted face in 26"x27"x13" black plastic.
____Darth Vader [3:101] 175.00
____Stormtrooper 175.00

Hasbro
____Padme Amidala hanging banner [2:73] 18.00
____Action Figure free standing display, EPIII:ROTS [AD25] 25.00
____EPII lightsaber counter display [3:101]................7.00
____Fan Choice Figure #4 ballot 2.00
____OTC Action Figure floor display, 24 figure..........45.00
____OTC Action Figure shelf talker 8.00

CommTech counter displays with amplified speaker.
____1st release – red [AD24] 75.00
____2nd release – green 85.00

EPII:AOTC. Action figure header displays.
____Anakin / Amidala / R2-D2 and C-3PO [2:73]......35.00
____Clone trooper / Mace Windu [2:73] 35.00
____Obi-Wan / Jango [2:73] 35.00

Hasbro, Mexico
Hanging pegboard banners.
____POTJ, Obi-Wan [2:73] 18.00
____Saga, Obi-Wan [2:73] 14.00
____Ed Poder De Los Jedi [2:73] 30.00

Hollywood Chewing Gum
____AOTC 8.5"x11" folded brochure [2:73] 16.00

K F C
____8 piece meal / flying topper menu topper (straight bottom, shaped top) outdoor advertising, made of corrugated plasticized cardboard 26.00
____Cup toppers vertical sign outdoor advertising, made of corrugated plasticized cardboard 17.00
____EPI pre-release maketing plan [2:74].................77.00
____Jar Jar / kid's meal toys vertical sign outdoor advertising, made of corrugated plasticized cardboard 24.00

Kenner
____"The Force" Lightsaber 12-saber retail display [AD26] 295.00

| AD14 | AD15 | AD16 | AD17 | AD18 | AD19 | AD20 |

| AD21 | AD22 | AD23 | AD24 | AD25 | AD26 |

Advertising: Displays

AD27 AD28 AD29 AD30 AD31 AD32 AD33

AD34 AD35 AD36 AD37 AD38 AD39 AD40 AD41

____Collect all 21 counter display [3:101] 275.00
____Collect all 21 hanging bell [2:73] 650.00
____Collect all 21 header [3:101] 190.00
____Diecast Spacecraft counter display [3:102] 400.00
____Ewoks counter display, holds 8 Woklings 55.00
____Fold-out showing 9 original POTF2 OC figures, tri-logo [2:73] 19.00
____Get a Free Boba Fett Action Figure header [3:102] 260.00
____Get a Free Boba Fett Action Figure header, shows rocket-firing Fett [3:102] 275.00
____Laser Rifle and Laser Pistol [AD27] 2,400.00
____Micro Collection, 3-sided hanging [3:102] ..1,250.00
____Star Wars Lightsaber 35" Inflated [AD28] 400.00
____The Ewoks counter display, holds 2 large Ewok packages 55.00
____Toy advertisement (magazine), full page glossy 1979 [2:73] 6.00
____Toy Center header [2:74] 285.00
____Toy Galaxy hanging bell [2:74] 350.00
____Twelve Exciting Figures counter display [3:102] 450.00

Kinder
1 sheet flyers for Star Wars Hipperium chocolate eggs.
____Dark Laser [3:102] 5.00
____Luke Eiwalker / floor display 5.00
____Luke Eiwalker, Hippoda, Erzwo Hippo / counter display [3:102] 8.00

Kotobukiya
____Flyer, ArtFX models: Vader, Clone Trooper, Anakin, 1-sided 3.00

LucasArts
____Flyer, Galaxies 60 day pre-paid cards 5.00
____Jedi Power Battles, Coming in April standee [2:74] 35.00
____SOTE Nintendo oversized display box [AD29] ..15.00

Lucasfilm
Episode II promotion flyers.
4.25"x5.5".
____www.AcklayComeHome.com [AD30] 3.00
____www.DroidTutor.com [AD31] 3.00
____www.KaminoRentals.com [AD32] 3.00
____www.OutlanderClub.com [AD33] 3.00
____www.PurpleLightsaber.com [AD34] 3.00
____www.uSeekYoda.com [AD35] 3.00
8.5"x11".
____www.AcklayComeHome.com [AD36] 5.00

____www.DroidTutor.com [AD37] 5.00
____www.KaminoRentals.com [AD38] 5.00
____www.OutlanderClub.com [AD39] 5.00
____www.PurpleLightsaber.com [AD40] 5.00
____www.uSeekYoda.com [AD41] 5.00

M1
____Cellphone M1 Top-Up cards countertop display [AD42] 35.00

Marvel Comics
____The Force That Has Taken America By Storm…, one sheet flyer [2:74] 6.00

Masterfoods USA
____M&M Choose Dark Chocolate shelf talker 8.00
____Star Wars Mpire code redemption instruction flyer 3.00

MBNA
____Flyer for chome Jango Fett premium 5.00

Meiji
____Xylish gum dispenser box with flap, counter holder [AD43] 5.00

Metal Box Ltd.
____Metal Collector Cards, A New Hope – One page color flyer [2:74] 3.00

MPC
____MPC plastic model squadron promotes ROTJ model ships, newsprint from comic books [2:74] 4.00

N.S.W. Building Society Ltd.
____Folder for SW savings account 14.00
____Folder for SW savings account, ewok 14.00

Natural Balance
____Floor display, Luke, Leia, Chewbacca, Wicket, Yoda, R2-D2 [3:102] 43.00

Omni Cosmetics
____Bath Collection counter display [3:102] 125.00
____R2-D2 bath soap display rack [3:102] 135.00
____Vader / Royal Guards bath products [3:103] 350.00

Oral-B
____Toothbrush display header, R2-D2 and C-3PO [2:74] 60.00

Orquesta Pops De Mexico
____2004 Julio flyer 5.00

Palitoy
Enter the ROTJ Competition promotion.
____AT-AT Toy Display [AD44] 995.00
____Entry brochure [AD45] 25.00

Parker Bros.
____ROTJ game cartridge advertisement, glossy from publication [2:74] 1.00

Pepperidge Farms
____Free Tumbler display, 23"x30" [2:74] 80.00

Pepsi Cola
____"Join the celebration," shelf talker, Boba Fett [3:103] 11.00

Episode I: The Phantom Menace.
____"Collect all 24 Star Wars cans," shelf talker, Jar Jar [2:74] 5.00
____"Find Yoda, Win Cash," cooler sign [2:74] 5.00
____"Find Yoda, Win Cash," shelf talker, Yoda [2:74] 5.00
____"Find Yoda, Win Cash," window sign [2:74] 10.00
____Darth Maul 3-D wall hanger [AD47] 16.00
____Pole sign, "Look for a Limited Edition can" [2:74] 15.00
____Rotating Death Star 30.00
____Vader / Death Star, Join The Celebration 3D stand-up 52"x47" [AD48] 60.00

Pepsi Cola, Japan
____Counter mat promotion, EPI bottle caps [3:103] 16.00

Pepsi Cola, Mexico
Episode I: The Phantom Menace.
____Jar Jar Binks, Pepsi / Mountain Dew [2:74] 10.00

Pepsi Cola, UK
____Win a Star Wars Family Holiday to the USA flyer [AD49] 3.00

Pepsico, Inc.
____SW:SE invitation [2:75] 12.00

Pez Candy, Inc.
____Advertising sticker, Europe [2:75] 7.00
____Handbill, candy dispensers [2:75] 1.00

AD42 AD43 AD44 AD45 AD47 AD48 AD49

| AD50 | AD51 | AD52 | AD53 | AD54 | AD55 | AD56 |

____Star Wars fun and games dispenser cardboard dump with header card [3:103] 10.00
____Star Wars fun and games dispenser header card only 6.00

Pizza Hut
____"Collect Them All!" (toys) 4"x6" plasticized card for table-top display [1:49]..2.00
____"Don't Leave Coruscant Without Them" two-sided counter standee (6 toys / cup toppers) 35.00
____"Take A Piece Of Coruscant Home" (cup toppers) 4"x6" plasticized card for table-top display [3:103]..2.00
____Building-shaped header card, "Welcome to Coruscant, Your senate box is being prepared" 69.00
____Kids Pack with mini-transforming playsets 3.00
____Micromachine heads, one-sheet flyer [3:103] 8.00

Pizza Hut, Australia
____Star Wars Works free with isa Works, hanging sign [3:103] 45.00

Pizza Hut, UK
____EPI: Exclusive Star Wars Meal Deal offers brochure / menu [AD50] 5.00
____SW:SE menu flyer 5.00

Presto Magix / American Publishing
____Rubdown transfer counter display, ESB [3:103] 17.00

Rarities Mint
____Silver and gold coins brochure [2:75] 12.00

Rawcliffe
____Counter sign: "Coming to this store May 3, 1999" [AD51] 4.00
____Episode II keychain flyer..2.00

Safeway
Entry forms.
____Win a Star Wars family holiday to the USA 5.00

Scholastic
____Jedi Quest / Born to Be A Bounty Hunter, 2-sided 1.00

Sigma
____ESB display for ceramic figures [AD52] 150.00

Smart Buddy
____EPIII:ROTS cellphone downloadable content pamphlet 2.00
____Jollibee value meal / cellphone content downloadable content flyer 1.00

Sonrics
____Counter display, 18 packages [3:103] 24.00

Sony Classical
____EPII:AOTC soundtrack display tower 35.00

Sony Ericsson
____Be the Envy of the Empire flyer 1.00

Star Jars
____Advertising flyer, one-sheet color 8.5"x11" [3:103] 4.00

Suncoast
____The Epic Continues at Booth 500, SWCII red 1.00

Super Live Adventure
____Super Live Adventure stand-up [AD53]............150.00

Taco Bell
Feel the Force game.
____Darth Vader THX dangler [3:103] 10.00
____R2-D2 premium display [3:103].......................150.00

Tambola
____Chocolate Egg countertop display [3:103]............5.00

The LEGO Group
____Enter The Lego Galactic Challenge Building Contest padded poster [2:74] 16.00
____Mural, Episode I and classic trilogy, 49"x 5.5" 12.00
____Naboo Fighter 19"x13" [2:74] 45.00
____Star Wars 2-sided window sticker.....................15.00
____Star Wars Galactic Challenge building contest, official entry form 1.00
____Toy Fair promotion: 4"x5"x2" box with Luke and Vader figures and sound chip, labelled "Building a New Galaxy in 1999" 77.00

Theatrical
____ESB poster, 22"x28", printed materials at refreshment stand 625.00

Thomas Salter
Rub down Action Transfers.
____Display for POS, complete 215.00

Topps
____1977 One-sheet flyer, "Topps Introduces 15 cent Star Wars Movie Photo Cards!" [3:103].....................24.00
____Return of the Jedi widevision cards flyer [2:75] 8.00
____ROTS Cards sales sheet / brochure 15.00

Total
____Topps Store Saver Star Wars point promotion brochure [AD54] 5.00

Toys R Us
____Naboo Sweepstakes hanging poster [2:75]..........3.00

Toys R Us, UK
____X-Wing Fighter Tour poster 10.00

Tricon Global Restaurants, Inc.
Translites.
____EPI: 2.99 Cup Toppers [3:103] 25.00
____Mediallion collection page and official rules 8.5"x11" 6.00

Wallace Berrie and Co.
____Pendant and necklace countertop display rack, Darth Vader [3:103] 85.00

Walmart
____EPII:AOTC Jedi Challenge advertisement 3.00

Wells
____Battle Droid ice pop counter display [AD55] 8.00

Williams
____EPI Pinball Tips and Tricks [AD56] 5.00

Wizards of the Coast
____TCG SWCII Events 1.00

Wonder Bread
____16 Free trading cards, shelf talker [2:75] 24.00

Yves Saint Laurent
____One Love, Queen Amidala cover [2:75]..............13.00

Air Fresheners

C and D Visionaries, Inc.
____ANH Poster [A1R01] 2.00
____Clone Trooper Collage [A1R02] 2.00
____Darth Vader – Fighting [A1R03] 2.00
____Darth Vader vs. Luke [A1R04].............................2.00
____Darth Vader with Lightsaber [A1R05] 2.00
____Jabba and Leia [A1R06] 2.00
____Light Saber Fight [A1R07] 2.00
____R2-D2 and C-3PO [A1R08] 2.00
____Sith Lord [A1R09] 2.00
____Star Wars logo [A1R10] 2.00
____Yoda Collage [A1R11]...2.00
____Yoda [A1R12] 2.00

Albums: Collecting

Argentina.
____1977 Card Collector [CA01] 27.00
____O Retorno de Jedi card album [CA02] 15.00

Brazil.
____El Regreso I Jedi sticker album [CA03] 15.00

Mexico.
____2005 Lottery ticket collecting album [CA04] 10.00
____Movieshots binder [CA05] 25.00

| A1R01 | A1R02 | A1R03 |

| A1R04 | A1R05 | A1R06 | A1R07 | A1R08 | A1R09 | A1R10 | A1R11 | A1R12 |

Albums: Collecting

CA01

CA02

CA03

CA04

CA05

CA06

CA07

CA08

CA09

CA10

CA11

CA12

CA13

CA14

CA15

CA16

CA17

CA18

CA19

CA20

CA21

CA22

CA16

CA17

CA18

CA19

CA20

CA21

CA22

Activa Consumer Promotions Corp.
Canada. Winnipeg Free Press.
____Holds 20 pin set 10.00

Agence Generale d'Edition
France.
____L'Empire Contre-Attaque [CA06] 25.00

Burger King
____Super Scene sticker album [CA07] 12.00

Cedibra
Brazil.
____Star Wars [CA08] 16.00

Costa
Argentina.
____Holds 40 square stickers [CA09] 15.00

Dark Horse Comics
____Special Collectors Album [CA10] 8.00

DinaMics
____DinaMics sticker album [CA11] 11.00

Eskimo, Japan
____AOTC mail-in premium for Lucky Card 50.00

FKS, UK
____Empire Strikes Back, C-3PO [CA12] 25.00

General Mills
____Wallet for holding 3.25"x4.5" cards, brown with gold border and Star Wars logo; clear plastic foldouts to hold 18 cereal premium cards [CA13] 15.00

K F C, Mexico
____EPI:TPM Sticker collection sheet [CA14] 8.00

Merlin Publishing Internat'l Ltd.
____Episode I Sticker Collection album 4.00
____Sticker Collection plus free Saga wallchart 8.00

Panini, Germany
____Star Wars [CA15] 18.00

Panini, Italy
____Star Wars [CA16] 25.00

Topps
____Episode I Widevision cards 18.00
____ROTJ Sticker Album [CA17] 8.00

Topps, UK
EPII:AOTC card binders with exclusive trading card.
____Anakin Skywalker [CA18]....................................35.00
____Count Dooku [CA19] 35.00
____Jango Fett [CA20] 35.00
____Obi-Wan Kenobi [CA21] 35.00

Walkers
UK. Produced with Pepsi to collect premium stickers.
____EPI:TPM Sticker collection sheet [2:135] 5.00
____Tazo Collector's Force Pack [CA22] 7.00

Answering Machines

Tiger Electronics
____Royal Naboo Starship [AMS01] 50.00

Arcade: Pinball Machines

A. Hankin and Co.
____Empire Strikes Back [2:344] 2,300.00

Data East
____Star Wars [2:344]..................................1,950.00

Sega
____SW:SE Trilogy [2:344]...................................3,800.00

Williams
____Star Wars Episode I [2:344] 3,900.00
____Star Wars Episode I, The Final Collector Series, limited to 100 ....6,500.00
____Star Wars Special Edition 3,600.00

Arcade: Slot Machines

Promatic
German.
____Star Wars, plays in Euros [VSL01]...............8,500.00

Arcade: Video Games

Atari
____Empire Strikes Back [NA01] 1,100.00
____Return of the Jedi [NA02] 1,000.00
____Star Wars [NA03] 1,800.00
____Star Wars, cockpit case [NA04]...................2,250.00

AMS01

VSL01

NA01

NA02

NA03

NA04

NA05

NA06

Art: Lithography

AF01	AF02	AF03	AF04	AF05	AF06

AF07	AF08	AF09

Sega
Coin operated. Value includes coinbox intact.
____Star Wars Racer, cockpit case [NA05] 2,250.00
____Star Wars Trilogy [NA06] 3,400.00
____Star Wars Trilogy, cockpit case 4,725.00

Art: Animation Cels

"The Great Heep" feature.
____Any scene 175.00

Droids cartoon series.
____Animation elements 65.00
____Any scene 175.00

Ewoks cartoon series. Many original animation elements of varying quality and detail were distributed to Fan Club members in 2004.
____Animation elements 35.00
____Any scene without background 175.00

Acme Archives
Clone Wars character keys by Genndy Tartakovsky.
____Anakin Skywalker, limited to 1,000.............65.00
____ARC Captain, limited to 750......................95.00
____Asajj Ventress, limited to 1,250 ....85.00
____C-3PO, limited to 1,000 ....45.00
____Count Dooku, limited to 1,250 ....85.00
____Darth Sidious, limited to 1,000..................85.00
____General Grievous, limited to 1,000 [AF01]..65.00
____Mace Windu, limited to 1,000 ....65.00
____Obi-Wan, limited to 750 [AF02] 95.00
____Padme Amidala 65.00
____R2-D2, limited to 1,000 ....45.00
____Shaak Ti, limited to 1,250 ....45.00
____Yoda, limited to 1,000................................135.00

Clone Wars model sheets by Genndy Tartakovsky.
____General Grievous, limited to 300 ....300.00
____Yoda, limited to 300 [AF03] 300.00

Disney / MGM
____Defend-ears of the Kingdom [AF04] 350.00

Royal Animation Art
Limited edition cel series.
____Droids: Battle Cruiser 85.00
____Droids: Best Friends [AF05] 85.00
____Droids: Stranded [AF06] 85.00
____Ewoks: Celebration [AF07] 85.00
____Ewoks: The Big Hug [AF08] 85.00
____Holiday Special: Boba Fett: Bounty Hunter, limited to 5,000 [3:103]....................................85.00

Warner Bros.
____Star Warners [AF09] 275.00

Art: Crystal and Glass

Cards, Inc.
____Jedi Starfighter....................................45.00
____Yoda 45.00

Code 3 Collectibles
____Millennium Falcon, satin lined case, ordering gift at San Diego Comic-Con 2003 [ATC01] 75.00

Disney / MGM
Star Wars Weekends logo, crystal.
____2004..250.00
____2005, limited to 75.............................250.00
____2006, limited to 75 [3:326].................250.00

Stiefelmayer-Contento
Laser engraved 3D glass cubes. 3 inches. (9cm x 5cm x 5cm).
____AT-RT with driver 75.00
____Darth Vader.......................................75.00
____Yoda 75.00

Laser engraved 3D glass cubes. 5 inches. (13cm x 9cm x 7.5cm).
____ARC-170 [ATC02].............................200.00
____AT-RT Driver [ATC03] 200.00
____Darth Vader [ATC04] 200.00
____R2-D2 [ATC05].................................200.00
____The Emperor [ATC06]........................200.00
____Yoda [ATC07] 200.00

Art: Lithography

EPIII:ROTS.
____Portfolio of 10 prints [LTG01].....................80.00
____Empire Strikes Back by Billy Dee Williams, 30"x30", limited to 1,000 [LTG02] 125.00
____EPIII:ROTS, Best Buy exclusive for EPIII DVD preorder [LTG03] 35.00

20th Century Fox
____Episode I: Premium for pre-ordering EPI video [LTG04] 11.00
____Special Edition Video Covers, free with purchase of SW:SE [LTG05]...12.00
____THX Video Covers, free with purchase of THX SW classic trilogy [LTG06] 15.00

Animated Animations
Coruscant Skyline framed giclee. 34 1/4" x 13". Limited to 1,000 pieces.
____Night in the Galactic Capital 365.00
____Sunset on the Republic 365.00

Cards, Inc.
____Star Wars Movie Poster Lithograph Collection, A3 sized, limited to 6,000..................................60.00

Disney / MGM
Star Wars Weekends.
____May 2000 [LTG07] 49.00
____May 2001 [LTG08] 49.00

ATC01	ATC02	ATC03	ATC04	ATC05	ATC06	ATC07

LTG01	LTG02	LTG03	LTG04	LTG05	LTG06

LTG07	LTG08	LTG09	LTG10	LTG11	LTG12	LTG13

Art: Lithography

____May 2003 [LTG09] 49.00
____May 2005 [LTG10] 49.00

Gifted Images Publishing
____Darth Vader from box artwork of Topps SW Galaxy cards, 23.5"x30" signed by the artist, 500 produced numbered 560.00
____Luke and Yoda signed by the artist, 500 produced numbered 410.00

Lucasfilm
____Darth Vader ceoncept, McQuarrie art, 100lb. linen, 18"x24" 100.00
____Fett "Like Father, Like Son," 17"x25", limited to 350 [LTG12] 100.00

Manga
ANH, ESB, ROTJ comic cover trio, 18"x24"
____Framed, unlimited 100.00
____Signed and framed, limited to 500 ....170.00
____Unlimited [LTG13] 30.00

Official Pix
____10 Characters, QVC exclusive............................135.00

Score Board
____Yoda sitting at his desk by Michael Whelan, 18"x17" signed, 850 produced 130.00

Star Struck
____ROTJ lithograph: 3 X-wings flying toward Death Star II with planets all around, signed and numbered, 3,000 produced 325.00

Art: Metal

____Battle Droid [3:104] 40.00
____Captain Tarpals [3:104] 45.00
____Jango Fett [3:104] 35.00

Bolt Gallery
____Battle Droid, 20", 9 lbs. [3:104] 100.00
____Battle Droid, 9", 4 lbs. [3:104] 50.00
____Boba Fett, 24", 20lbs. [3:104] 275.00
____C-3PO, 18", 13 lbs. [3:104] 140.00
____Darth Vader, 24", 25lbs. [3:104]............................275.00
____R2-D2, 10", 15 lbs. [3:104] 100.00
____R2-D2, 8", 3 lbs. [3:104]............................40.00

PPD01

Art: Portfolios

____Star Wars Episode I: The Phantom Menace [PPD01]............................40.00
____Star Wars Episode I: The Phantom Menace, deluxe [PPD02]............................135.00

Aardvark-Vanaheim Press
____Star Wars: A Collection of Ten Prints, unlicensed, approx 250 produced 145.00

Ballantine
Art portfolios featuring the work of Ralph McQuarrie.
____Empire Strikes Back [PPD03]............................25.00
____Return of the Jedi [PPD04] 25.00
____Star Wars [PPD05] 45.00

Black Falcon
____McQuarrie Empire Strikes Back concept prints in Dath Vader folder, sealed with pewter medallion [PPD06] 375.00

Chronicle Books
____The Art of Ralph McQuarrie (art box) [PPD07]............................30.00

Classico
____Star Wars [PPD08] 18.00

Zanart Publishing Inc.
Set of eight 11"x14".
____Trilogy moviecards [PPD09] 35.00
____Vehicle blueprints [PPD10]............................55.00

Art: Prints

Cards, Inc.
A3 size, lenticular with COA.
____Jedi Rescue 3D, limited to 2,000............................40.00
____Turn to the Dark Side, limited to 6,000, QVC exclusive............................25.00

Art prints with COA in storage tin.
____Revenge of the Sith, art 65.00
____Star Wars Saga, art 65.00

Crystal Art Gallery International
16"x20" posters by Trends International, framed.
____Anakin Skywalker [2:77] 12.00
____Battle of Geonosis [2:77] 12.00

Galoob
Art work by Ralph McQuarrie, signed, limited to 1,500 and numbered. Toy Fair exclusive.
____Death Star 45.00
____Hoth 45.00
____Star Wars [AH01] 45.00
____Yavin 45.00

Gifted Images Publishing
____Darth Vader by Ken Steacy, 23.5"x30", limited to 500............................475.00

Icarus
Textured prints are mounted in 5.5"x7.5" silver wooden frames with sealed brown paper backing.
____Boba Fett 28.00
____C-3PO and R2-D2 [AH02] 28.00
____Chewbacca 28.00
____Darth Vader............................28.00
____Luke Skywalker 28.00
____Yoda 28.00

Lucasfilm
Giclee. A Destiny Unfolds, hand signed.
____20.5"x13.5", limited to 200 [AH03] 850.00
____41"x27", limited to 200 ....1,250.00

Giclee. Anakin vs. Asajj, 20"x27".
____Framed, limited to 350 total 300.00
____Matted and framed, ltd. to 350 [AH04] ....5 6 0 . 0 0

Giclee. Boba Fett: Bounty Hunter, 26"x17", framed.
____Canvass, limited to 100 [AH05] 800.00
____Paper, limited to 350 ....500.00

Giclee. Clone Wars.
____16"x20" matted, hand numbered, limited to 500 [AH06] 125.00

Giclee. Darth Vader, 26"x17", framed.
____Canvass, limited to 100 [AH07] 800.00
____Paper, limited to 350 ....500.00

Giclee. Yoda, 26"x17", framed.
____Canvass, limited to 100 ....800.00
____Paper, limited to 350 ....500.00

Paizo Publishing / Fan Club
____Episode II, Attack of the Clones, 30"x24", hand signed and numbered, limited to 500 [AH08] 50.00

Star Struck
____X-Wing Fighters and Death Star II by Michael David Ward, limited to 3000 ....225.00

starwars.com
In 2003 the official Star Wars site offered 13 themed galleries of approximately 12 images in each gallery. Fans could order the images from an online merchandiser in a variety of formats. Considering the number of galleries, images available, and formats to choose from there are literally thousands of combinations that could have been made.

The galleries were comprised of images of Bounty Hunters, Clone Wars, Creatures, Droids, Holiday Art, Jedi, Logos and Emblems, Padme, Poster Art, Princess Leia, Rebels, Sith, and Vehicles.

____8"x10" high-quality glossy prints............................10.00
____8"x10" high-quality matte prints............................10.00
____16"x20" high-quality glossy prints............................17.00
____16"x20" high-quality matte prints 17.00
____20"x24" high-quality glossy prints............................19.00
____20"x24" high-quality matte prints 19.00
____20"x30" high-quality glossy prints............................20.00
____20"x30" high-quality matte prints 20.00

PPD02

PPD03

PPD04

PPD05

PPD06

PPD07

PPD08

PPD09

PPD10

Willitts Designs

Art work by Ralph McQuarrie, 18"x12", signed, limited to 2,500 and numbered. Mounted in frame with lighted film clip.

____Cloud City of Bespin [AH09] 179.00
____Darth Vader's Arrival [AH10] 179.00
____Death Star Main Reactor [AH11] 179.00
____Jabba the Hutt [AH12] 179.00
____Luke and Darth Vader Duel [AH13] 179.00
____Millennium Falcon [AH14] 179.00
____Rebel Attack on Death Star [AH15]...................179.00
____Rebel Celebration [AH16] 179.00
____Rebel Patrol of Echo Base [AH17] 179.00
____Speeder Bike Chase [AH18] 179.00
____The Battle of Hoth [AH19] 179.00
____The Cantina on Mos Eisley [AH20] 179.00
____The Rancor Pit [AH21] 179.00

Zanart Publishing Inc.

____Darth Vader by Williamson, signed, limited to 500 ....225.00
____Luke Skywalker, X-Wing Pilot by Williamson, signed, limited to 500 [3:105] 75.00
____Millennium Falcon w/Han and Chewie. Darth Vader w/Tie Fighter. Luke w/X-Wing. Blueprints used as background. Framed and signed. 65.00
____Stormtroopers by Williamson, signed, limited to 500...175.00

Art: Prints – ChromeArt

O.S.P. Publishing Inc.

____Star Wars SE Trilogy, QVC exclusive..................45.00

Zanart Publishing Inc.

11"x14" matted. Technical drawings.

____A-Wing 20.00
____AT-AT 20.00
____AT-ST 20.00
____B-Wing 20.00
____Star Destroyer 20.00
____Tie Fighter 20.00
____X-Wing 20.00
____Y-Wing 20.00

1995 THX video cover art.

____Star Wars / Darth Vader 12.00
____Empire Strikes Back / Stormtrooper [2:78] 12.00
____Return of the Jedi / Yoda [2:78].........................12.00

Shadows of the Empire. Limited to 4,500 each.

____Prince Xizor 12.00
____Shadows of the Empire 12.00

Art: Prints – ChromeArt

International video cover art. Limited to 10,000 each.

____Star Wars, video box art [AK01]..........................12.00
____Empire Strikes Back [AK02] 12.00
____Return of the Jedi [AK03]....................................12.00

Movie Poster Art.

____Star Wars [2:78] 12.00
____Star Wars Special Edition [AK04].......................12.00
____The Empire Strikes Back [2:78] 12.00
____Return of the Jedi...12.00

____Bounty Hunters [AK05]..12.00
____AT-AT Attack 12.00
____B-Wing Battle 12.00
____Dark Forces cover art [2:78]...............................12.00
____Darth Vader, art [2:78] 12.00
____Darth Vader, photo [2:78] 12.00
____Escape from Hoth [AK06] 12.00
____Space Battle [AK07]..12.00

AH01

AH02

AH03

AH04

AH05

AH06

AH07

AH08

AH09

AH10

AH11

AH12

AH13

AH14

AH15

AH16

AH17

AH18

AH19

AH20

AH21

Autographs

| AK01 | AK02 | AK03 | AK04 | AK05 | AK06 | AK07 |

Autographs

Prices listed are what the actual signature is "worth," if on an 8"x10" photograph or action figure. Add $10.00 to the price if the item is an 11"x14" or 16"x20" auto-graphed photo. Officially licensed photographs are pre-ferred more than non-licensed items. Deduct $10.00 from the price if the photograph is grainy, out-of-focus, or an obviously fan-made/amateur photograph from screen captures or other artwork.

"Premium-signed" items, such as official one-sheet posters, should be considered more valuable if signed on more recent items later than 1995 (i.e., an Episode I poster). Autographs on original vintage posters actually decrease the value of the entire piece, especially if on Original Trilogy material.

The addition of a character name is preferable, but does nothing to affect value. Some individuals – such as Carrie Fisher and Mark Hamill – do not write their char-acter names or use shortened abbreviations (like "PLO" for Princess Leia Organa). Quotes or other messages do not affect value, but should only be written if the indi-vidual actually uttered the line. Personalization will usu-ally deduct value from the piece unless the individual is deceased.

In the following listings, "!" indicates the individual is deceased.

Episode I: The Phantom Menace

___August, Pernilla	45.00
___Austen, Don	25.00
___Best, Ahmed	50.00
___Blake, Jerome [ATG01]	25.00
___Blessed, Brian	30.00
___Bonfils, Khan	25.00
___Bourriague, Michonne [ATG02]	25.00
___Bronagh, Gallagher	25.00
___Brown, Ralph	25.00
___Burtt, Ben	35.00
___Candice, Orwell	25.00
___Capurro, Scott	25.00
___Carson, Silas [ATG03]	25.00
___Celia, Imrie	30.00
___Chanchani, Dhruv	45.00
___Chiang, Doug	30.00
___Clarke, Gin	60.00

___Coleman, Rob	30.00
___Coppola, Roman	25.00
___Coppola, Sofia	35.00
___Cottrell, Michaela	25.00
___Coulier, Mark	25.00
___Cristina da Silva, Karol	25.00
___Davies, Oliver Ford	30.00
___Duncan, Lindsay	25.00
___Eason, Phil	30.00
___Easton, C. Michael	25.00
___Ellis, John	25.00
___Fensom, John	30.00
___Friedman, Ira	20.00
___Gillard, Nick	25.00
___Green, Jenna	45.00
___Greenaway, David	30.00
___Griffiths, Ray	15.00
___Hamill, Nathan	30.00
___Hindes, Nifa	25.00
___Hindes, Nishan	25.00
___Jackson, Samuel L.	100.00
___Joti, Dipika O'Neill	40.00
___Knightley, Keira	25.00
___Knoll, John	30.00
___Lloyd, Jake	20.00
___Lloyd, Madison	30.00
___Longworth, Toby	25.00
___Macleod, Lewis	25.00
___Madsen, Dan	25.00
___McCallum, Rick	40.00
___McGregor, Ewan	100.00
___Neeson, Liam	250.00
___Park, Ray [ATG04]	25.00
___Portman, Natalie	150.00
___Proops, Greg	30.00
___Quarshie, Hugh	25.00
___Ruscoe, Alan [ATG05]	25.00
___Sanders, Chris	25.00
___Sansweet, Steve	25.00
___Secombe, Andrew	25.00
___Serafinowicz, Peter	30.00
___Shapi, Hassani	25.00
___Shay, Jeff	25.00
___Silk, Marc	25.00
___Simpson, Christian	25.00
___Smee, Katherine	30.00
___Smith, Clarence	25.00
___Smith, Paul Martin	25.00
___Speirs, Steven	25.00
___Stamp, Terence	40.00

___Taylor, Benedict [ATG06]	25.00
___Taylor, James	30.00
___Taylor, Michelle	25.00
___Towner, Margaret	30.00
___Tyger, Lucas	75.00
___Udall, Megan	50.00
___Wagner, Danny	25.00
___Walpole, Oliver	50.00
___West, Dominic	25.00
___Williams, Dwayne	25.00
___Wilson, Liz	25.00
___Wood, Matthew	25.00
___Woods, Bob	25.00

Episode II: Attack of the Clones

___Allen, Amy [ATG07]	25.00
___Bowers, David	25.00
___Boyle, Steven	25.00
___Byrne, Rose	25.00
___Christensen, Hayden	75.00
___Clay, William	25.00
___Csokas, Marton	25.00
___Dharker, Ayesha	25.00
___Doran, Matt	25.00
___Easton, C. Michael	20.00
___Edgerton, Joel	30.00
___Falk, Ron	25.00
___Jensen, Zachariah [ATG08]	25.00
___Knoll, Alex	25.00
___Krishan, Nalini [ATG09]	25.00
___Laga'aia, Jay	25.00
___Lee, Christopher	75.00
___Logan, Daniel	20.00
___Lucas, Jett	50.00
___Lucas, Katie	50.00
___McGrath, Alethea	30.00
___Morrison, Temuera [ATG10]	30.00
___Owen, Rena [ATG11]	25.00
___Oyaya, Mary [ATG12]	25.00
___Phelan, Anthony	25.00
___Piesse, Bonnie [ATG13]	25.00
___Porter, Susie	25.00
___Rowan, Matt	25.00
___Sanchez, Juan	25.00
___Sauers, Steve	25.00
___Scott, P. Kevin	25.00
___Segura, Veronica	25.00
___Shepherd, Steve John	25.00
___Sloan, Matt	25.00
___Smits, Jimmy	30.00

| ATG01 sample | ATG01 sample | ATG01 sample | ATG01 sample | ATG02 sample | ATG03 sample | ATG04 sample |

| ATG05 sample | ATG05 sample | ATG05 sample | ATG06 sample | ATG07 sample | ATG08 sample | ATG09 sample |

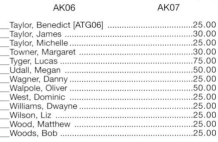

____Taylor, Bodie 25.00
____Thompson, Jack 30.00
____Truswell, Chris 30.00
____Walsman, Leanna 25.00
____Watkin, Ian 25.00
____Wong, Eric 25.00
____Yiamkiati, Phoebe..25.00

Episode III: Revenge of the Sith
____Acord, David 25.00
____Akindoyeni, Tux 30.00
____Alexander, Coinneach 25.00
____Blundell, Graeme 25.00
____Brooks, Jill 25.00
____Canning, Josh 25.00
____Castle-Hughes, Keisha 25.00
____Chan, Kee 25.00
____Chionchio, Dominique 25.00
____Coleman, Rob 35.00
____Cooke, Ben 25.00
____Cope, Robert 25.00
____Daraphet, Mimi 25.00
____David, Fay 25.00
____Davies, Paul 25.00
____De Souza Correa, Caroline 25.00
____Dench, Axel 25.00
____Eager, Malcolm 25.00
____Ferguson, Nicholas 25.00
____Finlay, Sandi 25.00
____Foster, Lawrence 25.00
____Foy, Steven 25.00
____Freer, Chantal 25.00
____Guyett, Roger 25.00
____Hidalgo, Pablo 15.00
____Hinksman, Luke 25.00

____Jackson Mendoza, Rebecca 25.00
____Jackson, Peter 25.00
____Karvan, Claudia 25.00
____Khazzouh, Julian 25.00
____Kingma, Michael 25.00
____Kirby, Christopher 25.00
____Koffi, Gervais 25.00
____Levi, Olive 25.00
____Lewin, Janet 25.00
____Louez, Jacqui 25.00
____Lucas, Amanda 50.00
____Lucas, George 250.00
____Lucas, Jett 50.00
____Lucas, Katie 50.00
____MacPhee, Jason 25.00
____McCallum, Mousy 25.00
____Moore, T.V. 25.00
____Mooy, Hayley 25.00
____Nichol, Rohan 25.00
____Nicholson, Paul 25.00
____Noble, Trisha 25.00
____Nyamwasa, Lily 25.00
____O'Reilly, Genevieve 25.00
____Oates, Kenji 25.00
____Owens, Warren 25.00
____Prestoe, Jeremy 25.00
____Pygram, Wayne 25.00
____Ream, Denise 25.00
____Rowan, Matt 25.00
____Rowling, Kyle 30.00
____Roxburgh, Hamish 25.00
____Shaunessy, Lisa 25.00
____Simpson, Christian 25.00
____Spence, Bruce 30.00
____Spence, Paul 25.00

____Stiff, David 25.00
____Stringer, Holly 25.00
____Thompson, Sandy 25.00
____Ware, Colin 25.00
____Wetherill, Marty 25.00
____Williams, Aliyah 25.00
____Wingate, Keira 25.00
____Wright, Kristy 25.00
____Yamaguchi, Masa 25.00

Episode IV: A New Hope
____Ashley, Graham 75.00
____Austin, Mark 25.00
____Baker, Kenny [ATG14] 25.00
____Baker, Rick 35.00
____Beswick, Doug 25.00
____Blake, Paul [ATG15] 25.00
____Brown, Phil! [ATG16] 35.00
____Burnett, Ted! 300.00
____Byrne, Eddie 25.00
____Chapman, John 20.00
____Cushing, Peter! 250.00
____Daniels, Anthony [ATG17] 45.00
____De Aragon, Maria [ATG18] 25.00
____Diamond, Fraser 50.00
____Diamond, Peter! [ATG19] 65.00
____Diamond, Warwick 45.00
____Eddon, Sadie 30.00
____Fisher, Carrie [ATG20] 75.00
____Ford, Harrison 200.00
____Fraser, Shelagh! 50.00
____Goffe, Rusty [ATG21] 25.00
____Guinness, Alec! 150.00
____Hagon, Garrick [ATG22] 25.00
____Hall, Nelson 25.00

ATG10 sample | ATG11 sample | ATG12 sample | ATG13 sample | ATG14 sample | ATG15 sample | ATG16 sample

ATG17 sample | ATG18 sample | ATG19 sample | ATG19 sample | ATG19 sample | ATG20 sample | ATG21 sample

ATG22 sample | ATG23 sample | ATG24 sample | ATG25 sample | ATG26 sample | ATG27 sample | ATG28 sample

ATG29 sample | ATG30 sample | ATG31 sample | ATG32 sample | ATG33 sample | ATG34 sample | ATG35 sample

Autographs

____Hamill, Mark [ATG23] 75.00
____Harris, Alan 30.00
____Henderson, Don! 60.00
____Henley, Drewe 50.00
____Hewett, Christine [ATG24] 30.00
____Hootkins, William! [ATG25] 50.00
____Jones, James Earl 75.00
____Klaff, Jack 30.00
____Kurtz, Melissa [ATG26] 25.00
____Kurtz, Tiffany L. 25.00
____Lawson, Denis 65.00
____LeParmentier, Richard [ATG27] 25.00
____MacInnes, Angus [ATG28] 25.00
____Mayhew, Peter [ATG29] 25.00
____McCrindle, Alex! 200.00
____Peterson, Lorne 25.00
____Prowse, David [ATG30] 25.00
____Purvis, Jack! 200.00
____Rimmer, Shane 25.00
____Schofield, Leslie 30.00
____Sinden, Jeremy! 75.00
____Sumner, Peter 30.00
____Sylla, John 25.00
____Sylla, Tom 25.00
____Tierney, Malcolm 30.00
____Tippett, Phil 30.00
____Tucker, Burnell 35.00

Episode V: Empire Strikes Back

____Boa, Bruce [ATG31] 50.00
____Bulloch, Jeremy [ATG32] 30.00
____Bush, Morris 200.00
____Capri, Mark 25.00
____Chancer, Norman 25.00
____Colley, Ken [ATG33] 25.00
____Culver, Michael 30.00
____Dicks, John 25.00
____Duff, Norwich 25.00
____Edmonds, Mike [ATG34] 25.00
____Frandy, Michael A. 25.00
____Glover, Julian [ATG35] 25.00
____Harte, Jerry 25.00
____Hassett, Ray 25.00
____Hollis, John! [ATG36] 50.00
____Hudson, Susie 30.00
____Johns, Milton 25.00
____Jones, Mark 25.00
____Kahn, Brigitte 25.00
____Liston, Ian [ATG37] 25.00
____Maguire, Oliver 25.00

____Malcolm, Christopher 30.00
____McKenzie, Jack 25.00
____McQuarrie, Ralph 30.00
____Morton, John [ATG38] 25.00
____Mullen, Kathryn 30.00
____Munro, Cathy 75.00
____Nelson, C. Andrew 25.00
____Oldfield, Richard 25.00
____Oz, Frank 50.00
____Parsons, Chris [ATG39] 25.00
____Ratzenberger, John 35.00
____Revill, Clive 25.00
____Scobey, Robin 35.00
____Sheard, Michael! [ATG40] 40.00
____Weed, Harold / Howie 30.00
____Williams, Billy Dee [ATG41] 50.00
____Williams, Treat 30.00
____Wingreen, Jason 45.00

Episode VI: Return of the Jedi

____Altman, John 25.00
____Anderson, Franki 25.00
____Apostalos, Margo 25.00
____Arbogast, Annie 50.00
____Armstrong, Ray 25.00
____Baker, Eileen 25.00
____Ballan, Michael Henbury 25.00
____Barclay, David Alan [ATG42] 30.00
____Bareham, Adam 30.00
____Bell, Bobby 25.00
____Bell, Patty 25.00
____Bennett, Alan 25.00
____Bennett, Sarah 25.00
____Berk, Ailsa 25.00
____Betts, Pamela 25.00
____Bies, Don [ATG43] 30.00
____Blackner, Danny 25.00
____Blakiston, Caroline [ATG44] 25.00
____Bowley, Linda 25.00
____Brooke, Paul 25.00
____Burroughs, Peter 25.00
____Busby, Jane 65.00
____Carrington, Debbie Lee 25.00
____Carter, Michael [ATG45] 25.00
____Charlton, Maureen 25.00
____Chew, Dalyn 25.00
____Coppen, Willie 25.00
____Corrie, Sadie 25.00
____Cottrell, Mike 35.00
____Cox, Tony 25.00

____Crawford, Sean 40.00
____Crowley, Dermot 35.00
____Cumming, John 25.00
____Cunningham, Andy 100.00
____D'Agostino, Jean 20.00
____Davenport, Claire! 60.00
____Davis, Warwick [ATG46] 25.00
____De Jesus, Luis 25.00
____Dixon, Debbie 25.00
____Dixon, Malcolm 30.00
____Dry, Tim 25.00
____Fernandez, Margarita 25.00
____Fondacaro, Phil 25.00
____Fondacaro, Sal 25.00
____Friel, Tony 25.00
____Frishman, Daniel 25.00
____Fushille-Burke, Celia 25.00
____Ghavan, John 25.00
____Gilden, Michael 25.00
____Grand, Isaac! 45.00
____Grant, Paul 25.00
____Green, Lars 25.00
____Green, Lydia 25.00
____Grizz, Pam 25.00
____Hall, Nelson 25.00
____Hattrick, Graeme 30.00
____Herbert, Philip 25.00
____Herd, Andrew 25.00
____Home, Gerald [ATG47] 30.00
____Jackson, J.J. 25.00
____Jones, Glynn 25.00
____Jones, Richard 25.00
____Jones, Trevor 25.00
____Lahr, Larin 30.00
____Lay, Karen 25.00
____Lim, Swee 40.00
____Lummiss, John 25.00
____MacLean, Nancy 25.00
____Mandell, Peter 25.00
____Mannion, Tom 35.00
____Marquand, Richard! 100.00
____McDiarmid, Ian 100.00
____McRae, Hilton 30.00
____Miller, George 25.00
____Miller, Pip 30.00
____Morris, Carole 25.00
____Ngoh, Mercedes [ATG48] 20.00
____Nicholls, Stacy 25.00
____Nunn, Chris 25.00
____O'Laughlin, Barbara 25.00

ATG36 sample   ATG37 sample   ATG38 sample   ATG39 sample   ATG40 sample   ATG41 sample   ATG42 sample

ATG43 sample   ATG44 sample   ATG45 sample   ATG46 sample   ATG47 sample   ATG48 sample   ATG49 sample

ATG50 sample   ATG51 sample   ATG52 sample   ATG53 sample   ATG54 sample   ATG55 sample   ATG56 sample

Backpacks and Carrybags

BCL01

BCL02

BCL03

BCL04

BCL05

BCL06

BCL07

BCL08   BCL09   BCL10

___ Oliver, Jonathan 30.00
___ Orenstein, Brian 25.00
___ Parker Jr., Harrell 25.00
___ Pedrick, John 25.00
___ Pennington, Michael 30.00
___ Perkins, April 25.00
___ Phillips, Ronnie 25.00
___ Philpott, Toby 25.00
___ Purvis, Katie 25.00
___ Quinn, Mike [ATG49] 25.00
___ Read, Carol 25.00
___ Read, Nicholas 25.00
___ Reynolds, Diana 25.00
___ Robertson, Barry 25.00
___ Rodgers, Daniel 25.00
___ Romano, Chris 25.00
___ Rose, Timothy M. [ATG50] 25.00
___ Roy, Deep 30.00
___ Shackelford, Dean 25.00
___ Shah, Kiran 25.00
___ Shaw, Sebastian 500.00
___ Silla, Felix 25.00
___ Spriggs, Linda 25.00
___ Staddon, Gerald 25.00
___ Staddon, Josephine 25.00
___ Star, Tony 30.00
___ Taylor, Femi [ATG51] 25.00
___ Thompson, Kevin 25.00
___ Wall, Kendra 25.00
___ Watts, Robert 30.00
___ Wheeler, Brian 25.00
___ Wilhelm, Butch 25.00
___ Williamson, Simon 25.00

___ Allston, Aaron 10.00
___ Baksa, Shannon [ATG52] 40.00
___ Brooks, Terry 15.00
___ Denning, Troy 15.00
___ Freeborn, Stuart [ATG53] 150.00
___ Freeling, Cynthia [ATG54] 35.00
___ Holland, Barrie 15.00
___ Kurtz, Gary, [ATG55] 50.00
___ Luceno, James 25.00
___ Stackpole, Michael 10.00
___ Traviss, Karen 10.00
___ Zahn, Timothy 25.00

Disney / MGM
Autograph cards, Star Wars Weekends, May 2000.
___ Baker, Kenny, hand-signed 40.00
___ Baker, Kenny, pre-printed [3:109] 15.00
___ Bulloch, Jeremy, hand-signed 45.00
___ Bulloch, Jeremy, pre-printed [3:109] 20.00
___ Fisher, Carrie, hand-signed 75.00
___ Fisher, Carrie, pre-printed [3:110] 20.00

___ Lloyd, Jake, hand-signed 60.00
___ Lloyd, Jake, pre-printed [3:110] 15.00
___ Mayhew, Peter, hand-signed 45.00
___ Mayhew, Peter, pre-printed [3:110] 20.00
___ McCaig, Ian, hand-signed [3:110] 25.00
___ McCaig, Ian, pre-printed 10.00
___ Prowse, David, hand-signed [3:110] 50.00
___ Prowse, David, pre-printed 20.00
___ Quarshie, Hugh, hand-signed [3:110] 25.00
___ Quarshie, Hugh, pre-printed 20.00

Autograph cards, Star Wars Weekends, May 2001.
___ Baker, Kenny, hand-signed [3:110] 40.00
___ Baker, Kenny, pre-printed 15.00
___ Brown, Phil, hand-signed [3:110] 30.00
___ Brown, Phil, pre-printed 15.00
___ Bulloch, Jeremy, hand-signed 40.00
___ Bulloch, Jeremy, pre-printed [3:110] 20.00
___ Chiang, Doug, hand-signed 25.00
___ Chiang, Doug, pre-printed [3:110] 10.00
___ Davis, Warwick, hand-signed 30.00
___ Davis, Warwick, pre-printed [3:110] 15.00
___ Fisher, Carrie, hand-signed 75.00
___ Fisher, Carrie, pre-printed [3:110] 20.00
___ Mayhew, Peter, hand-signed [3:110] 45.00
___ Mayhew, Peter, pre-printed 20.00
___ Quinn, Mike, hand-signed [3:110] 30.00
___ Quinn, Mike, pre-printed 10.00

Autograph cards, Star Wars Weekends, May 2003.
___ Bourriague, Michonne, hand signed 20.00
___ Bourriague, Michonne, pre-printed 20.00
___ Bulloch, Jeremy, hand-signed 45.00
___ Bulloch, Jeremy, pre-signed [3:110] 20.00
___ Morrison, Temuera, hand-signed 55.00
___ Morrison, Temuera, unsigned [3:110] 10.00

Official Pix
___ Darth Vader: David Prowse / James Earl Jones, 11"x14", limited to 100 [ATG56] 145.00
___ Hayden Christensen as Darth Vader, limited to 200 ...... 300.00

Awards

Hasbro
___ "Hand and Hand into the new Millennium," Mr. Potato Head and C-3PO figures 250.00
___ Hasbro / Star Wars, X-Wing etched lucite with pilot Luke figure 95.00

Pepsico, Inc.
___ 1997 SW:SE Congratulations, lucite 125.00

Backpack Tags

Betty Crocker
EPII:AOTC fruit snack premiums.
___ Anakin Skywalker [BCL01] 4.00
___ Mace Windu [BCL02] 4.00
___ Obi-Wan Kenobi [BCL03] 4.00
___ Yoda [BCL04] 4.00

Hasbro
Backpack Heroes.
___ Boba Fett [BCL05] 10.00
___ Darth Tater [BCL06] 10.00
___ Darth Vader [BCL07] 10.00
___ Han Solo [BCL08] 10.00
___ Luke Skywalker [BCL09] 10.00
___ Yoda [BCL10] 10.00

Backpacks and Carrybags

Celebration III.
___ Gray and Black [LB01] 25.00
___ Darth Maul [LB02] 10.00
___ Darth Vader and Star Destroyer [LB03] 10.00
___ EPI:TPM canvass 10.00
___ Epic duel in front of Vader, red and yellow [LB04] 10.00
___ ESB, Millennium Falcon flees Imperial Star Destroyer [LB05] 12.00
___ Imperial black, Darth Vader embossed rubber flap [LB06] 14.00
___ Jedi vs. Sith, Obi-Wan / Darth Maul [LB07] 10.00
___ ROTJ Millennium Falcon over Death Star II [LB08] 10.00
___ X-Wings over Yavin [LB09] 12.00
___ Yoda face on black pack [LB10] 17.00

LB01

LB02

LB03

LB04

LB05

LB06

LB07

LB08

LB09

LB10

LB11

LB12

LB13

LB14

LB15

LB16

Backpacks and Carrybags

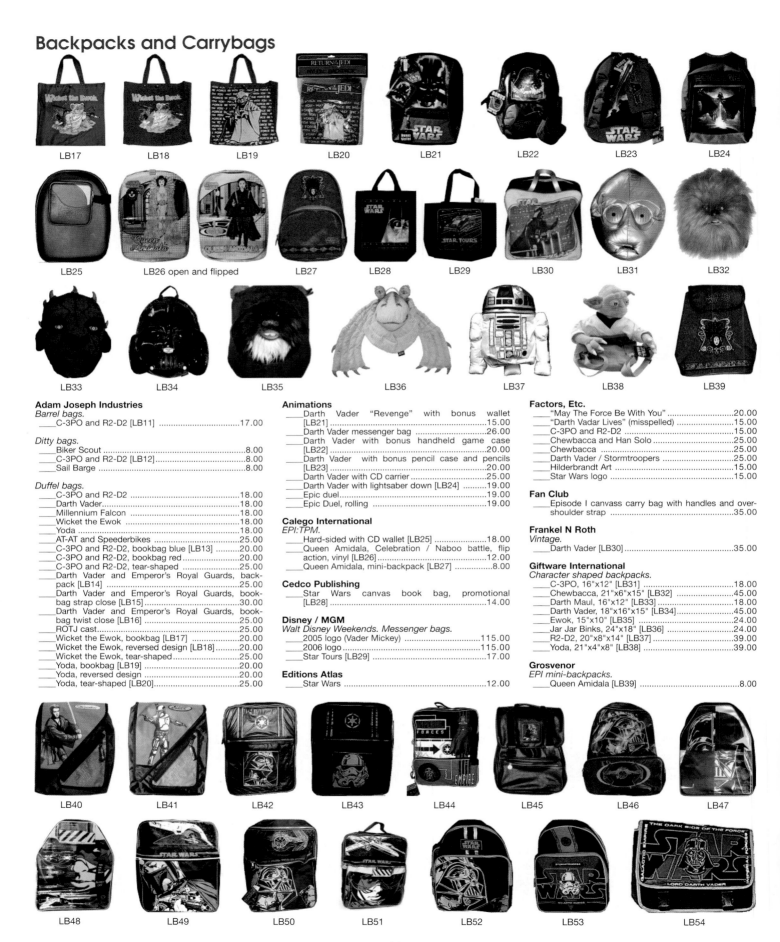

LB17   LB18   LB19   LB20   LB21   LB22   LB23   LB24

LB25   LB26 open and flipped   LB27   LB28   LB29   LB30   LB31   LB32

LB33   LB34   LB35   LB36   LB37   LB38   LB39

Adam Joseph Industries
Barrel bags.
____C-3PO and R2-D2 [LB11] 17.00

Ditty bags.
____Biker Scout 8.00
____C-3PO and R2-D2 [LB12]..............................8.00
____Sail Barge 8.00

Duffel bags.
____C-3PO and R2-D2 ....18.00
____Darth Vader..18.00
____Millennium Falcon 18.00
____Wicket the Ewok 18.00
____Yoda 18.00
____AT-AT and Speederbikes 25.00
____C-3PO and R2-D2, bookbag blue [LB13] 20.00
____C-3PO and R2-D2, bookbag red......................20.00
____C-3PO and R2-D2, tear-shaped 25.00
____Darth Vader and Emperor's Royal Guards, back-
    pack [LB14] 25.00
____Darth Vader and Emperor's Royal Guards, book-
    bag strap close [LB15].................................30.00
____Darth Vader and Emperor's Royal Guards, book-
    bag twist close [LB16] 25.00
____ROTJ cast..25.00
____Wicket the Ewok, bookbag [LB17] 20.00
____Wicket the Ewok, reversed design [LB18]..........20.00
____Wicket the Ewok, tear-shaped.........................25.00
____Yoda, bookbag [LB19] 20.00
____Yoda, reversed design 20.00
____Yoda, tear-shaped [LB20]...............................25.00

Animations
____Darth Vader "Revenge" with bonus wallet
    [LB21]...15.00
____Darth Vader messenger bag 26.00
____Darth Vader with bonus handheld game case
    [LB22]...20.00
____Darth Vader with bonus pencil case and pencils
    [LB23]...20.00
____Darth Vader with CD carrier 25.00
____Darth Vader with lightsaber down [LB24] 19.00
____Epic duel...19.00
____Epic Duel, rolling 19.00

Calego International
EPI:TPM.
____Hard-sided with CD wallet [LB25] 18.00
____Queen Amidala, Celebration / Naboo battle, flip
    action, vinyl [LB26].....................................12.00
____Queen Amidala, mini-backpack [LB27] 8.00

Cedco Publishing
____Star Wars canvas book bag, promotional
    [LB28] 14.00

Disney / MGM
Walt Disney Weekends. Messenger bags.
____2005 logo (Vader Mickey) 115.00
____2006 logo 115.00
____Star Tours [LB29] 17.00

Editions Atlas
____Star Wars 12.00

Factors, Etc.
____"May The Force Be With You" 20.00
____"Darth Vadar Lives" (misspelled) 15.00
____C-3PO and R2-D2 ....15.00
____Chewbacca and Han Solo 25.00
____Chewbacca 25.00
____Darth Vader / Stormtroopers 25.00
____Hilderbrandt Art 15.00
____Star Wars logo 15.00

Fan Club
____Episode I canvass carry bag with handles and over-
    shoulder strap 35.00

Frankel N Roth
Vintage.
____Darth Vader [LB30] 35.00

Giftware International
Character shaped backpacks.
____C-3PO, 16"x12" [LB31] 18.00
____Chewbacca, 21"x6"x15" [LB32] 45.00
____Darth Maul, 16"x12" [LB33] 18.00
____Darth Vader, 18"x16"x15" [LB34] 45.00
____Ewok, 15"x10" [LB35] 24.00
____Jar Jar Binks, 24"x18" [LB36] 24.00
____R2-D2, 20"x8"x14" [LB37] 39.00
____Yoda, 21"x4"x8" [LB38] 39.00

Grosvenor
EPI mini-backpacks.
____Queen Amidala [LB39] 8.00

LB40   LB41   LB42   LB43   LB44   LB45   LB46   LB47

LB48   LB49   LB50   LB51   LB52   LB53   LB54

LB55 open and flipped   LB56 open and flipped   LB57   LB58   LB59   LB60   LB61

LB62   LB63   LB64   LB65   LB66   LB67   LB68   LB69

LB70   LB71   LB72   LB73   LB74   LB75   LB76   LB77

EPII mini-backpacks.
   ____Anakin Skywalker [LB40] 8.00
   ____Jango Fett [LB41] 8.00

LucasArts
   ____Star Wars Galaxies, messenger bag 50.00

Pyramid
Backpacks: classic trilogy. Dark Side collection, nylon with embossed rubber artwork.
   ____Boba Fett 16.00
   ____Darth Vader 16.00
   ____Luke Skywalker 16.00
   ____Stormtrooper 16.00

Backpacks: classic trilogy. Destroyer collection, vinyl with metallic trim and inset artwork.
   ____Boba Fett 16.00
   ____Darth Vader [LB42] 16.00
   ____Luke Skywalker 16.00
   ____Stormtrooper [LB43] 16.00

Backpacks: classic trilogy. Hi-Tech collection, nylon with allover artwork.
   ____Boba Fett 16.00
   ____Darth Vader [LB44] 16.00
   ____Stormtrooper 16.00
   ____Yoda 16.00

Backpacks: classic trilogy. Imperial collection, nylon with rubber patch.
   ____Boba Fett 16.00

   ____Darth Vader [LB45] 16.00
   ____Stormtrooper 16.00

Backpacks: classic trilogy. Interactive collection, lights and battle sounds.
   ____Darth Vader / Tie Fighter [LB46] 19.00
   ____Darth Vader, breathes [LB47] 19.00
   ____Luke Skywalker / X-Wing Fighter [LB48] 19.00

Backpacks: classic trilogy. Pilot collection, vinyl with schematic artwork.
   ____Boba Fett / Slave I [LB49] 16.00
   ____Darth Vader / Tie Fighter [LB50] 16.00
   ____Luke Skywalker / X-Wing Fighter [LB51] 16.00

Backpacks: classic trilogy. Star Class collection, vinyl with inset artwork.
   ____Boba Fett 16.00
   ____C-3PO 16.00
   ____Darth Vader [LB52] 16.00
   ____Stormtrooper [LB53] 16.00

Backpacks: classic trilogy. Zoom collection, vinyl with allover artwork.
   ____Boba Fett 16.00
   ____Darth Vader [LB54] 16.00
   ____Luke Skywalker 16.00

Backpacks: EPI:TPM. Flip down art flap, velcro strap, vinyl.
   ____Darth Maul / Qui-Gon Jinn [LB55] 15.00
   ____Starfighters [LB56] 15.00

Backpacks: EPI:TPM.
   ____Anakin Skywalker and Sebulba [LB57] 12.00
   ____Anakin Skywalker in podracer gear with checker-board, vinyl [LB58] 12.00
   ____Anakin in podracer gear, canvas [3:112] 12.00
   ____Anakin in podracer gear, vinyl [LB59] 12.00
   ____Canvass carry bag with handles and over-shoulder strap, black or blue [LB60] 16.00
   ____Darth Maul art [LB61] 7.00
   ____Darth Maul bust, canvas [LB62].........................12.00
   ____Darth Maul full-body, canvas [LB63] 12.00
   ____Darth Maul shoulderbag [LB64] 12.00
   ____Darth Maul [LB65] 12.00
   ____Jar Jar Binks, vinyl [LB66] 12.00
   ____Jedi vs. Sith art [LB67] 7.00
   ____Jedi, vinyl [LB68] 12.00
   ____Obi-Wan lenticular 10.00
   ____Podracing art [LB69] 7.00
   ____Queen Amidala [LB70] 18.00
   ____Queen Amidala, mini [LB71] 8.00
   ____Starfighters, vinyl [LB72] 12.00

Backpacks: EPII:AOTC. Plastic with stationary supplies in outer pouch.
   ____Anakin Skywalker Jedi, side pockets 18.00
   ____Heroes, side pockets 18.00
   ____Jango Fett [LB73]..14.00
   ____R2-D2 and C-3PO [LB74] 14.00

Backpacks: EPII:AOTC.
   ____Anakin Skywalker's destiny, red. gray, and black [LB75] 16.00

LB78   LB79   LB80   LB81   LB82

LB83   LB84   LB85   LB86   LB87

Backpacks and Carrybags

____Anakin Skywalker blue and orange, side pockets 18.00
____Anakin Skywalker destiny, side pockets [LB76] 18.00
____Anakin Skywalker 15.00
____Heroes 15.00
____Jango Fett 15.00
____Jango Fett, blue and gray [LB77] 16.00
____Villains 15.00
____Yoda 15.00

Duffel bags: classic trilogy. Dark Side collection, nylon with embossed rubber artwork.
____Boba Fett 20.00
____Darth Vader 20.00
____Luke Skywalker 20.00
____Stormtrooper 20.00

Duffel bags: classic trilogy. Destroyer collection, vinyl with metallic trim and inset artwork.
____Boba Fett 20.00
____Darth Vader 20.00
____Luke Skywalker 20.00
____Stormtrooper [LB78] 20.00

Duffel bags: classic trilogy. Hi-Tech collection, nylon with allover artwork.
____Boba Fett 20.00
____Darth Vader 20.00
____Stormtrooper [LB79] 20.00
____Yoda 20.00

Duffel bags: classic trilogy. Imperial collection, nylon with rubber patch.
____Boba Fett 20.00
____Darth Vader 20.00
____Stormtrooper 20.00

Duffel bags: classic trilogy. Star Class collection, vinyl with inset artwork.
____Boba Fett 20.00
____C-3PO 20.00
____Darth Vader 20.00
____Stormtrooper 20.00

Duffel bags: classic trilogy. Zoom collection, vinyl with allover artwork.
____Boba Fett [LB80] 20.00
____Darth Vader 20.00
____Luke Skywalker [LB81] 20.00

Duffel bags: EPI:TPM.
____Anakin Skywalker [LB82] 12.00
____Darth Maul [LB83] 12.00
____Jedi vs. Sith [LB84] 12.00
____Jedi vs. Sith [LB85] 12.00
____Pod Racing [LB86] 12.00

Scholastic
____Star Wars Junior sign-up bonus [LB87] 14.00

Badges

SW Celebration II passes.
____Associate [ACC01] 35.00
____Exhibitor 40.00
____Licensee [ACC02] 100.00
____Press [ACC03] 50.00
____Staff [ACC04] 30.00

____VIP Guest [ACC05] 175.00
____Star Wars Weekends staff badge 35.00

SW Celebration III passes.
____4-day Adult Darth Vader.....................................10.00
____4-day Child, Anakin Skywalker, animated 10.00
____Exhibitor [ACC06] 15.00
____Friday Adult, Padme..12.00
____Friday Child, Padme animated...........................12.00
____Saturday Adult, Yoda 10.00
____Saturday Child, Yoda animated 10.00
____Sunday Adult, Obi-Wan 12.00
____Sunday Child, Obi-Wan animated 12.00
____Thursday Adult, Mace Windu 15.00
____Thursday Child, Mace Windu animated..............15.00
____VIP 15.00
____Volunteer...15.00

501st Legion
____Droid Hunt, Celebration III game badge 10.00

Fan Club
Collectible badges are similar size, shape, design as celebration passes. Fan Club exclusives.
____#1 Imperial / Mara Jade [3:112] 4.00
____#2 Rebel / Jek Porkins [3:112] 4.00
____#3 Bounty Hunter / Aurra Sing [3:112] 4.00
____#4 Tatooine / Wuher the bartender [3:112]...........6.00
____#5 Imperial / Darth Vader [3:112] 4.00
____#6 Jedi Council / Mace Windu [3:112] 4.00

SW Celebration passes.
____All access Sebulba 133.00
____Backstage Pit Droid 35.00
____Exhibitors Jar Jar 25.00
____Friday Obi-Wan Kenobi 12.00
____Saturday Qui-Gon Jinn 8.00
____Staff C-3PO 82.00
____Sunday Anakin Skywalker 8.00
____Three Day Darth Maul 10.00
____VIP guest Queen Amidala 68.00
____Volunteer Battle Droid 30.00

SW Celebration II passes.
____3-day adult [ACC07]..35.00
____3-day child [3:113] 35.00
____Friday adult [ACC08] 25.00
____Friday child [3:113] 25.00
____Saturday adult [ACC09] 25.00
____Saturday child [3:113] 25.00
____Sunday adult [ACC10] 25.00
____Sunday child [3:113] 25.00

SW Celebration pass replicas. "Star Wars Insider — Limited Edition" printed on back.
____All access Sebulba [3:113] 6.00
____Backstage Pit Droid [3:113] 8.00
____Exhibitors Jar Jar [3:113] 6.00
____Exhibitors Jar Jar, signed by Ahmed Best..........50.00
____Friday Obi-Wan Kenobi [3:113] 6.00
____Saturday Qui-Gon Jinn [3:113] 6.00
____Staff C-3PO [3:113] 6.00
____Staff C-3PO, signed by Anthony Daniels 44.00
____Sunday Anakin Skywalker [3:113] 6.00
____Three Day Darth Maul [3:113].............................6.00
____VIP guest Queen Amidala [3:113] 23.00
____Volunteer Battle Droid [3:113].............................6.00

K B Toys
____EPI Premere Weekend Commerative Badge, May 19-23, 1999 [3:113]...8.00

Marin County
____Marin County Star Wars summit '96 [3:113] 7.00

Mexico Collector Convention 2001 July
July 2001, Mexico City.
____Comite Organizador, Darth Vader art [3:112] 15.00
____Domingo, red R2 art [3:112] 4.00
____Expositor, Watto art [3:112] 10.00
____Sabado, R2-D2 art [3:112] 4.00
____Staff, stormtrooper art [3:112] 10.00
____Tres Dias, Boba Fett art [3:112] 7.00
____Viernes, blue R2 art [3:112] 4.00
____VIP, Yoda image [3:112] 15.00

Mexico Collector Convention 2002
____Domingo / Mace Windu [ACC11]........................10.00
____Expositor / Watto [ACC12] 10.00
____Invitado VIP / Yoda [ACC13] 15.00
____Organizador / Lightsaber [ACC14] 15.00
____Sabado / Obi-Wan [ACC15].................................10.00
____Seguridad / Super Battle Droid [ACC16] 15.00
____Staff / Clone Trooper [ACC17] 10.00
____Tres Dias / Jango Fett [ACC18] 10.00

Mexico Collector Convention 2003
____Boba Fett / Dos Dias [3:113] 12.00
____Chewbacca / Domingo [3:113] 12.00
____Darth Vader / Organizador [3:113] 35.00
____Gamorrean Guard / Seguridad [3:113] 12.00
____Han Solo / Sabado [3:113]...................................12.00
____Jawa / Expositor [3:113] 12.00
____Lobot / Prensa [3:113] 35.00
____Stormtrooper / Staff [3:113] 12.00
____Yak Face / Fan Club [3:113] 12.00
____Yoda / Invitado VIP [3:113]..................................12.00

Mexico Collector Convention 2004
____Fan club [ACC19] 5.00
____Pase Jedi [ACC20] 10.00
____Prensa [ACC21] 15.00

Bags

____Celebration II convention fan bag 5.00
____Celebration III convention fan bag 5.00
____Space battle, flat paper [BRF04] 3.00

EPIII:ROTS.
____Clone Trooper [BRF01] 5.00
____Darth Vader [BRF02] 5.00
____Yoda [BRF03] 5.00

Baleno
EPIII:ROTS.
____Plastic carrybag [BRF05] 5.00

Cingular
EPIII:ROTS.
____Plastic carrybag [BRF06] 4.00

Disney / MGM
____Use In Case of Space Sickness [BRF07] 10.00

Forbidden Planet
____Micromachines promo [BRF08]...........................5.00

Target
EPIII:ROTS.
____Plastic carrybag 3.00

ACC01   ACC02   ACC03   ACC04   ACC05   ACC06 badge and name tag   ACC07   ACC08

ACC09   ACC10   ACC11   ACC12   ACC13   ACC14   ACC15   ACC16   ACC17   ACC18   ACC19   ACC20   ACC21

BRF01

BRF02

BRF03

BRF04

BRF05

BRF06

BRF07

BRF08

Virgin Atlantic
Air sickness bags. 24 in set. Only 4 are Star Wars theme.
____Know Your Lightsaber [BRF09] 8.00
____Lightsaber Etiquette [BRF10] 8.00
____Seating Jedi and Sith [BRF11] 8.00
____The Art of Jedi Combat [BRF12] 8.00

Bags: Drawstring

Grosvenor
____C-3PO and R2-D2 [3:113] 5.00

BRF09

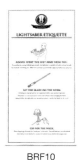
BRF10

BRF11

BRF12

BRF09 back

Bags: Gift

____B-Wing fighter attack [3:113] 7.00
____Space battle above second Death Star [3:113]...7.00
____X-Wings [3:113]...7.00

Die-cut top.
____Chewbacca [3:113]...8.00
____Darth Vader with stormtroopers [3:113] 8.00
____Darth Vader 7.00
____R2-D2 [3:113] 6.00

Shopping-style.
____Droids, R2-D2 and C-3PO [3:113] 22.00

Expressions
Gift box.
____Yoda / Darth Vader 5.00

Fan Club
____Star Wars Celebration..6.00

Hallmark
Classic trilogy.
____Join the Dark Side 6.00

Episode I: The Phantom Menace.
____Jedi vs. Sith 4.00

Episode II: Attack of the Clones.
____Large 6.00
____Small approx. 8"x9.5" 3.00

Episode III: Revenge of the Sith.
____Darth Vader 4.00
____Yoda / Darth Vader 5.00

Balloons

Anagram International
Mini mylar balloons on sticks.
____Darth Maul 5.00
____Jar Jar Binks...5.00
____Naboo fighter 5.00
____R2-D2 ....5.00

Mylar helium balloons.
____"Happy Birthday" Darth Vader and Millennium Falcon [3:114]...4.00
____"Happy Birthday" R2-D2 and C-3PO [PFB01]...5.00
____"Happy Birthday Young Jedi" [PFB02] 4.00
____Anakin Skywalker in podracer [PFB03] 4.00
____C3PO jumbo shaped 27"x21" 10.00

____C3PO mini shaped 10"x12" [PFB04] 5.00
____Classic trilogy characters [PFB05] 4.00
____Darth Maul jumbo shaped 30"..........................10.00
____Darth Maul mini shaped 12" [PFB06]..................5.00
____Darth Maul [PFB07] 4.00
____Darth Vader / Millennium Falcon (no message) [PFB08]..4.00
____Darth Vader mini shaped 12" [PFB09] 5.00
____Darth Vader, super shape...............................15.00
____Droids, May The Force Be With You [PFB10]..7.00
____Jar Jar Binks [PFB11]..4.00
____Jar Jar Binks, shaped [PFB12].............................4.00
____Naboo Space Battle [PFB13] 5.00

PFB01

PFB02

PFB03

PFB04

PFB05

PFB06

PFB07

PFB08

PFB04

PFB05

PFB06

PFB07

PFB08

PFB09

PFB10

PFB04 PFB05 PFB06 PFB07 PFB08 PFB09 PFB10 PFB11

PFB12 PFB13 PFB14 PFB15 PFB16 PFB17 PFB18 PFB19

PFB20 PFB21 PFB22 PFB23 PFB24 PFB25 PFB26 PFB27

Balloons

BND01	BND02	BND03	BND04	BND05	BND06	BND07

BND08	BND09

____Queen Amidala, super shape [PFB14] 5.00
____R2-D2 mini shaped 12" [PFB15] 5.00
____R2-D2, air walker [PFB16] 15.00
____Yoda, round with ears [PFB17] 8.00

Ariel
Characters or vehicles in assorted colors.
____8-pack [PFB18] 25.00
____AT-AT 3.00
____C-3PO 3.00
____Chewbacca 3.00
____Darth Vader 3.00
____Millennium Falcon 3.00
____R2-D2 ....3.00
____Stormtrooper.......................................3.00

Drawing Board Greeting Cards, Inc.
Balloon multi-packs, assorted colors.
____ESB, 10-pack [PFB19] 8.00

____ROTJ 4-pack punch balloons 10.00
____ROTJ 5-pack...8.00
____ROTJ 6-pack, Ewoks, K-Mart excl. [PFB20] 10.00
____ROTJ, 10-pack [PFB21] 8.00

Overbreak LLC
Hover Discs, EPIII:ROTS.
____Darth Vader [PFB22]...........................10.00
____General Grievous 10.00
____Saga hoverblimp [PFB23] 12.00
____Yoda 10.00

Party Express
Mylar helium balloons, 18" round.
____Episode II [PFB24] 5.00
____Episode III [PFB25] 5.00
____Saga [PFB26] 5.00
____Darth Vader 42" jumbo [PFB27] 8.00

Bandages

Curad
30 sterile bandages in character box.
____C-3PO [BND01] 8.00
____Jar Jar Binks [BND02] 9.00

EPI:TPM. 30 sterile bandages in character box. Collector's Edition.
____Anakin Skywalker [BND03].....................8.00
____Darth Maul [BND04] 8.00
____Jar Jar Binks [BND05] 8.00
____Queen Amidala [BND06].........................8.00

EPII:AOTC. 30 sterile bandages. Lenticular card front (removable).
____EPII heroes [3:114] 6.00
____Jango Fett [BND07] 6.00
____Saga villains [BND08] 6.00
____Yoda [BND09] 6.00

Bank Books

N.S.W. Building Society Ltd.
"Passbook Savings Account"
____C-3PO and R2-D2 ....42.00
____Wicket..42.00

Banks

Episode I characture sculpts. PVC, approximately 5 1/2" in height. Large coin slots.
____Battle Droid [PEB01] 10.00
____Darth Maul [PEB02] 10.00
____Darth Sidious [PEB03] 10.00
____Darth Vader [PEB04] 10.00
____Jar Jar Binks [PEB05] 10.00

Spain.
____Droids, cylinder 15.00

U.K.
____Chewbacca [PEB06] 45.00
____Darth Vader [PEB07] 45.00

PEB01	PEB02	PEB03	PEB04	PEB05	PEB06	PEB07	PEB08

PEB09	PEB10	PEB11	PEB12	PEB13	PEB14	PEB15	

PEB16	PEB17	PEB18	PEB19	PEB20	PEB21

| PEB22 | PEB23 | PEB24 | PEB25 | PEB26 | PEB27 | PEB28 |

| PEB29 | PEB30 | PEB31 | PEB32 | PEB33 | PEB34 | PEB35 | PEB36 |

Action
____Jeff Gordan pedal car with trailer, limited to 2,508 [PEB08]....................................35.00
____2005 #5 Kyle Busch 1:24 clear window 45.00

Adam Joseph Industries
Ewoks.
____Princess Kneesaa [PEB09]..........................25.00
____Wicket [PEB10]..25.00

Return of the Jedi.
____Darth Vader [PEB11] 45.00
____Emperor's Royal Guard [PEB12] 45.00
____Gamorrean Guard [PEB13]........................125.00
____R2-D2 [PEB14] 45.00

Applause
U.S. releases sold without boxes.
____Darth Maul on Sith Speeder 8.00
____Jar Jar Binks [PEB16] 8.00

Applause, UK
Boxed banks.
____Darth Maul on Sith Speeder [PEB15] 10.00
____Jar Jar Binks 10.00

Comic Images
EPIII:ROTS ceramic.
____Darth Vader helmet [PEB17] 25.00
____Yoda [PEB18] 25.00

Commonwealth Savings
____Darth Vader [PEB19] 35.00
____R2-D2 figural, dark blue..............................35.00
____R2-D2 figural, light blue [3:115]..................35.00
____R2-D2 figural, white [PEB20] 35.00

Kinnerton Confectionery
Originally packaged with candy included.
____Darth Maul ceramic [PEB21] 26.00
____Darth Vader, ceramic [PEB22] 24.00
____R2-D2 [PEB23] 7.00

Merit
____Return of the Jedi coin sorter [PEB24] 85.00

Metal Box Ltd.
____Darth Vader with combination dials [PEB25]......30.00
____ESB, octagonal [PEB26] 18.00
____Yoda with combination dials [PEB27] 30.00

NECA
____EPII Heroes, tin [PEB28]...............................15.00
____EPII Villains, tin [PEB29] 15.00
____R2-D2, AOTC limited to 5,000 [PEB30]..............35.00

Northlight Productions, Ltd.
____R2-D2 [PEB31]..275.00

NTD Apparel Inc.
Plastic bust bank with t-shirt inside.
____Anakin Skywalker [PEB32].............................18.00
____Darth Maul [PEB33] 18.00
____Jar Jar Binks [PEB34] 18.00

Pepsi Cola
EPI:TPM soda can body with slit top. Pepsi Cola premiums.
____R2-D2 [PEB35] 6.00
____Set of 24 on Pepsi wall display stand 95.00

Pepsi Cola, Mexico
SW:SE soda can body with slit top. Pepsi Cola premiums.
____Darth Vader 7.00
____Stormtrooper [PEB36].....................................7.00

Reliable, Canada
____R2-D2 [PEB37] 65.00

Roman Ceramics
Ceramic coin banks, vintage.
____C-3PO [PEB38]..75.00
____Darth Vader [PEB39] 90.00
____R2-D2 [PEB40] 45.00

Roy Lee Chin
____Darth Vader ceramic [PEB41] 14.00

Sigma
____Chewbacca [PEB42] 40.00
____Darth Vader [PEB43] 125.00
____Jabba the Hutt [3:116] 27.00
____Yoda [PEB44] 40.00

Takara
____R2-D2 pocket coin dispenser [PEB45] 50.00

Thinkway
Electronic, Obi-Wan, Darth Maul, and Qui-Gon interact when combined.
____Darth Maul [PEB46] 32.00
____Obi-Wan Kenobi [PEB47]..............................32.00
____Qui-Gon Jinn [PEB48] 32.00

Electronic, talking with music, bi-language package.
____C-3PO and R2-D2 [PEB49] 15.00

Electronic, talking with music.
____C-3PO and R2-D2 [3:116] 12.00
____Darth Vader ROTS package [PEB50].................25.00
____Darth Vader [PEB51] 12.00

Plastic bust coin banks.
____C-3PO..17.00
____Darth Vader [PEB52] 18.00

Thinkway, Canada
Plastic bust coin banks, bi-language package.
____C-3PO [PEB53]..17.00
____Darth Vader [3:116] 17.00

| PEB37 | PEB38 | PEB39 | PEB40 |

| PEB41 | PEB42 | PEB43 | PEB44 | PEB45 | PEB46 | PEB47 | PEB48 |

Banks

PEB49

PEB50

PEB51

PEB52

PEB53

PEB54

PEB55

PEB56

BAR01 closed and open

BAR02 closed and open

BAR03 closed and open

BAR04 front and bottom

Unlicensed
____R2-D2 in bag with POTF2 hanger card 14.00

Vinolos Romay
____Darth Vader [PEB54] 35.00
____R2-D2 [PEB55] 30.00
____Yoda [PEB56] 35.00

Banners: Advertising

20th Century Fox
Pre-release theater banners.
____Episode I:TPM [3:116] 265.00
____Episode II:AOTC [3:116] 240.00
____Episode III:ROTS 240.00

20th Century Fox, Mexico
AOTC.
____Jango Fett, no text [3:116] 135.00
____Jango Fett, Preventa De Boletos 23 De Junio [3:116] 185.00
____Padme, Estreno Lunes 10 De Julio [3:116] 185.00
____Pre-release theater banner 270.00

Fan Club
____Star Wars original trilogy DVD art, 39"x27" limited to 2,500 ....20.00

Movie City
____EPI: The Phantom Menace [3:116] 35.00
____EPIV: A New Hope [3:116] 35.00
____EPV: The Empire Strikes Back [3:116] 35.00
____EPVI: Return of the Jedi [3:116] 35.00

Nestlé, Mexico
____EPII cereal advertisement banner (Anakin and Clone Trooper) [3:116] 90.00

Barware

Unique Concepts
Sculpted barware exclusive pewter collectibles.
____C-3PO foil knife [BAR01] 65.00
____Darth Vader corkscrew [BAR02] 75.00
____R2-D2 bottle opener [BAR03] 65.00
____Yoda wine cork [BAR04] 70.00

Bath Mats

Jay Franco and Sons
20"x30".
____Anakin Skywalker [RUG01] 16.00
____Naboo Space Battle [RUG02] 14.00

Bathroom Sets

Avon, Mexico
EPII:AOTC toothbrush and cup with holder.
____Movie Scenes [BTH01] 12.00
____Padme Amidala [BTH02] 12.00
____Padme Amidala makeup bag [BTH03] 10.00

Cosrich Group, Inc.
____Bubbling Bath Set: bubble bath, Yoda pouf, pouf hanger, lip balm with zipper pull, 3 giant bath fizzies [BTH04] 10.00
____Groom n' Go Bath Set: body soap, shampoo, squirting play razor [BTH05] 10.00

Jay Franco and Sons
____Toothbrush holder, soap dish, tumbler all featuring space battle scenes [BTH06] 16.00

Beachpads

Bibb Co.
____SW: Galaxy design [CBZ01] 45.00
____SW: Space Fantasy design 45.00

Bedding: Bedcovers

Bibb Co.
Star Wars.
____Aztec Gold 25.00
____Galaxy [2:89] 25.00
____Jedi Knights 25.00
____Lord Vader 25.00
____Space Fantasy 25.00

Empire Strikes Back.
____Boba Fett (J.C. Penney) 25.00
____Boba Fett 25.00
____Darth's Den 25.00
____Darth Vader and Yoda 25.00
____Ice Planet 25.00
____Lord Vader's Chamber 25.00
____Lord Vader 25.00
____Yoda 25.00

Return of the Jedi.
____Jabba the Hutt, Ewoks, etc. 25.00
____Logos from all 3 films 25.00
____Luke and Darth Vader Duel, AT-ST, etc. 25.00
____Star Wars Saga 25.00

Bedding: Blankets

EPIII:ROTS camping mat / blanket.
____Black [CBL01] 25.00
____White [CBL02] 25.00

EPIII:ROTS fleece blanket sack 50"x60".
____Jedi [CBL03] 25.00

Stadium blankets.
____Vader in flames, Celebration III exclusive 75.00
____Rebel Alliance 16.00

Bibb Co.
Star Wars.
____Aztec Gold 15.00

RUG01

RUG02

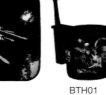

BTH01

BTH02

BTH03

BTH04

BTH05

BTH06

CPZ01

CBL01

CBL02

CBL03

____Galaxy	20.00
____Jedi Knights	20.00
____Lord Vader	20.00
____Space Fantasy [2:89]	15.00

Empire Strikes Back.

____Darth's Den	25.00
____Boba Fett	30.00
____Boba Fett, J.C. Penney exclusive	25.00
____Ice Planet	15.00
____Lord Vader's Chamber	25.00
____Lord Vader	25.00
____Spectre	15.00
____Yoda	30.00

Return of the Jedi.

____Jabba the Hutt, Ewoks, etc.	20.00
____Logos from all 3 films	20.00
____Luke and Darth Vader duel, AT-ST, etc.	20.00
____Star Wars saga	20.00

Springs Industries, Inc.

____Darth Vader no-sew fleece throw	25.00

The Northwest
Multi-layered woven jacquard blankets and throws.

____Anakin Skywalker and pod race [2:89]	28.00
____Darth Maul [2:89]	20.00
____Darth Maul and SW logo [2:89]	35.00
____Episode I logo [2:89]	28.00
____Jar Jar Binks [2:89]	20.00
____Jedi [2:89]	20.00
____Jedi vs. Sith [2:89]	20.00
____Naboo fighters [2:89]	20.00
____Naboo space battle and SW logo [2:89]	28.00
____R2-D2 [2:89]	20.00
____Star Wars fighters [2:89]	20.00
____The Dark Side [2:89]	20.00

Bedding: Comforters

EPIII:ROTS.

____Galactic Heroes [CMF01]	30.00

Caprice
Quilt cover sets.

____EPI Space Battle	35.00
____EPII Speeder Chase	35.00
____EPIII Darth Vader	35.00
____EPIII Epic Battle	35.00

Character World Ltd.

____EPII:AOTC Heroes and Villains [2:89]	45.00

Dan River, Inc.
EPII:AOTC designs, reversable. Available in twin and full size only.

____Lightsabers	39.00

Westpoint Stevens
Classic Trilogy.

____Characters	26.00

EPI:TPM.

____Pod Racing [2:89]	46.00
____Space Battle [2:89]	26.00

Bedding: Pillowcases

2-pack of characters.

____Han and Chewbacca [CPC01]	18.00
____Luke and Leia [2:89]	18.00
____Yoda and Obi-Wan Kenobi [2:89]	18.00

Return of the Jedi.

____Ewok village	10.00
____Pillow sham [CPC02]	35.00
____Tatooine Skiff / Chewbacca with Droids	10.00

Star Wars.

____Poly cotton	25.00
____Character Study, 2-sided	6.00
____ESB 2-sided, heroes and villains	24.00

Bibb Co.
Empire Strikes Back.

____Boba Fett / Darth Vader [CPC03]	35.00

Bedding: Pillows

____C-3PO / R2-D2 [CPC04]	30.00
____Chewbacca / Yoda [CPC05]	26.00

Sheet designs.

____ESB [CPC06]	20.00
____ROTJ	45.00

Dan River, Inc.
EPII:AOTC designs.

____Lightsabers pillow sham	15.00

Westpoint Stevens

____Space Battle pillow sham [CPC07]	14.00
____Space Battle pillowcase [CPC08]	10.00

Bedding: Pillows

16" square.

____Darth Vader / Yoda [PIL02]	15.00

EPII:AOTC. Bed pillows.

____Anakin and Obi-Wan in Speeder / Obi-Wan and Jedi Starfighter	15.00

Japan.

____Yoda	35.00

Square.

____Chewbacca [2:344]	5.00
____Han Solo [2:344]	7.00
____Darth Vader, shaped	18.00

CMF01

CPC01 front and rear

CPC02

CPC03 front and rear

CPC04 front and rear

CPC05 front and rear

Box for CPC03-CPC05

CPC06

CPC07

CPC08

PIL01

PIL02 front and rear

PIL03 front and rear

PIL04

PIL05 front and rear

PIL06

PIL07

PIL08

PIL09

PIL10

PIL11

25

Bedding: Pilows

Adam Joseph Industries
Die-cut.
____Darth Vader......................................26.00
____Jabba the Hutt [PIL01]........................26.00
____R2-D2...26.00

Bibb Co.
____C-3PO and R2-D2 / Darth Vader 15" square,
     quilted [2:344]................................24.00

Dan River, Inc.
Episode II: Attack of the Clones.
____Anakin wielding lightsaber / Star Wars logo
     [PIL03]..14.00
____R2-D2 [PIL04]....................................8.00
____Republic Gunship / Slave I [PIL05]..............8.00

Liebhardt, Inc.
16" square.
____Anakin [PIL06]...................................8.00
____Darth Maul [PIL07]..............................8.00
____Jar Jar [PIL08].................................8.00
____Queen Amidala [PIL09]...........................8.00
____Qui-Gon [PIL10].................................8.00
____Space Battle [PIL11]............................8.00

Bedding: Sheets

ROTS.
____Galactic Heroes 30.00
____Classic trilogy bed linen 20.00
____Trilogy Home Collection 20.00

Bibb Co.
Empire Strikes Back packaging.
____Boba Fett (J.C. Penney)........................22.00
____Boba Fett 22.00
____Darth's Den 20.00
____Ice Planet 16.00
____Lord Vader's Chamber 18.00
____Lord Vader 20.00
____Spectre 16.00
____Yoda 22.00

Return of the Jedi packaging.
____Jabba the Hutt, Ewoks, etc. 20.00
____Logos from all 3 films 16.00
____Luke and Darth Vader Duel, AT-ST, etc..........18.00
____Star Wars Saga 18.00

Star Wars packaging.
____Aztec Gold 12.00
____Galaxy 10.00
____Jedi Knights 12.00
____Lord Vader 20.00
____Space Fantasy 15.00

Black Falcon
____Empire Strikes Back............................15.00

Dan River, Inc.
____Episode II, Lightsabers twin size 24.00

Hayjax Manufacturing
____Ewoks twin sheet set 28.00

Westpoint Stevens
____Episode I twin sheet set [2:90].................22.00
____Star Wars twin sheet set [2:90] 24.00

Bedskirts

____Space Battle, EPI [2:90] 17.00
____Starships, classic trilogy 17.00

Belt Buckles

Brass lettering.
____C-3PO [BB01]....................................18.00
____R2-D2 [BB02]....................................18.00
____Star Wars [BB03] 24.00

Star Wars.
____C-3PO and R2-D2 [BB04] 35.00

Basic Tool and Supply
____C-3PO R2-D2 [BB05].............................35.00
____Darth Vader, Oval [BB06] 35.00
____Star Wars logo [BB07]..........................35.00
____X-Wing fighter with Star Wars logo [BB08] 35.00

BB01   BB02

BB03   BB04   BB05   BB06   BB07   BB08

BB09   BB10   BB11   BB12   BB13   BB14

BB15   BB16   BB17   BB18   BB19   BB20

BB20   BB21   BB22   BB23   BB24   BB25

BB26   BB27   BB28   BB29   BB30   BB31

BB32   BB33   BB34   BB35   BB36   BB37

Hot Topic
____Boba Fett helmet, sculpted 35.00
____Darth Vader helmet, sculpted [BB09] 35.00
____Star Wars logo [BB10] 25.00
____Star Wars logo, cut out [BB11] 30.00
____Stormtrooper helmet, sculpted 35.00

Leather Shop
____C-3PO and R2-D2 [BB12] 24.00
____Darth Vader [BB13]...................................24.00
____Darth Vader, oval with name on either side of helmet [BB14]...30.00
____Darth Vader, oval with name under helmet [BB15]..30.00
____May The Force Be With You [BB16] 24.00
____R2-D2 [BB17] 24.00
____Star Wars logo [BB18] 30.00
____X-Wing fighter with Star Wars logo [BB19] 30.00

Lee Co.
____C-3PO and R2-D2, enameled rectangle [BB20]..16.00
____Darth Vader, oval enameled [BB21] 16.00
____Darth Vader, oval [BB22] 23.00
____Droids pewter [BB23].................................25.00
____Empire Strikes Back logo, enameled [BB24]......16.00
____Jabba the Hutt, rectangle enameled [BB25] 16.00
____Jabba the Hutt, rectangle [BB25] 23.00
____Return of the Jedi logo, enameled [BB26] 16.00
____Star Wars logo, enameled [BB27] 26.00
____Yoda, circle enameled 16.00
____Yoda, circle [BB28] 23.00

Unlicensed
____Star Wars logo, enamel filled [BB29] 12.00

Prismatic logo, black background, red and black detail.
____Sawtooth [BB30] 10.00
____Stars [BB31] 10.00

Star Wars characters on black prism sticker.
____C-3PO and R2-D2 ....15.00
____Darth Vader [BB32]...................................15.00
____Darth Vader, 2 line name [BB33] 15.00
____Luke and Leia [BB34].................................15.00

Swirled sun background.
____C-3PO [BB35]..10.00
____Star Wars logo [BB36] 10.00
____Star Wars logo gold tone trim [BB37] 15.00

Belt Packs

The Phantom Menace.
____Anakin Skywalker [3:118] 4.00
____Darth Maul 10.00
____Jedi [3:118] 4.00

Disney / MGM
____Star Tours with logo [3:118] 11.00

Pyramid
Dark Side collection, nylon with embossed rubber artwork.
____Boba Fett 12.00
____Darth Vader..12.00
____Luke Skywalker 12.00
____Stormtrooper 12.00

Destroyer collection, vinyl with metallic trim and inset artwork.
____Boba Fett 12.00
____Darth Vader 12.00
____Luke Skywalker 12.00
____Stormtrooper 12.00

Hi-Tech collection, nylon with allover artwork.
____Boba Fett 12.00
____Darth Vader 12.00
____Stormtrooper 12.00
____Yoda 12.00

Imperial collection, nylon with rubber patch.
____Boba Fett 12.00
____Darth Vader 12.00
____Stormtrooper 12.00

Pilot collection, vinyl with schematic artwork.
____Darth Vader / Tie Fighter 12.00
____Luke Skywalker / X-Wing Fighter.....................12.00

Star Class collection, vinyl with inset artwork.
____Boba Fett 12.00
____C-3PO...12.00
____Darth Vader 12.00
____Stormtrooper 12.00

Zoom collection, vinyl with allover artwork.
____Boba Fett...12.00
____Darth Vader..12.00
____Luke Skywalker 12.00

Q-Stat
U.K. The Phantom Menace.
____Podracing [3:118] 10.00
____Queen Amidala [3:118] 10.00
____Sith Lord [3:118] 10.00

Belts

American Supply
____Star Wars designs 12.00

El Buen Equipaje
Dark vinyl with enameled character buckle.
____AT-ST 16.00
____Baby Ewoks 16.00
____C-3PO..16.00
____Chewie 16.00
____Darth Vader 16.00
____Jabba 16.00
____Speederbike 16.00
____Wicket 16.00
____Yoda 16.00
____Dark vinyl silk screened with ESB logo, tie fighter, Luke, Leia, R2-D2, Tie fighter art.....................12.00

Hot Topic
____Star Wars art, b/w vinyl, adult sizes [AB01]........25.00

Lee Co.
Fabric, Droids, pewter buckle with R2-D2, C-3PO, and landspeeder.
____Blue [AB02]..35.00
____Spaceships, robots, planets [AB03]..................35.00

Fabric, Ewoks.
____Ewoks with Wicket buckle [AB04] 35.00

Fabric, SW, magnetic clasp buckle.
____Blue with white logo [AB05]..........................20.00
____White with blue logo [AB06]..........................20.00

Fabric, ROTJ, character buckle with 2-line text.
____Darth Vader, brown and white, red and yellow [AB07]...15.00
____Darth Vader, red and white [AB08]....................15.00
____Jabba the Hutt, blue belt with brown lettering [AB09]...15.00
____Wicket the Ewok, yellow and brown belt with yellow lettering [AB10] 15.00

AB01

AB02

AB03

AB04

AB05

AB06

AB07

AB08

AB09

AB10

AB11

Belts

AB12

AB13

AB14

AB15

AB16

AB17

AB18

AB19

AB20

AB21

AB22

Fabric, ROTJ, rectangular buckle with 2-line logo.
____White belt with blue lettering [AB11] 12.00

Fabric, ROTJ, rectangular buckle with 2-line text.
____Blue and white belt with white and red lettering
[AB12] 12.00
____Red and blue belt with blue and red lettering
[AB13] 12.00
____White and brown belt with red and yellow lettering
[AB14] 12.00
____Yellow and brown belt with brown and yellow lettering
[AB15] 12.00

Fabric, ROTJ, character buckle with 2-line text.
____Wicket the Ewok, tan belt with blue lettering
[AB16] 15.00

Vinyl, SW, Darth Vader, Luke, Leia, Droids, SW logo.
____Blue [AB17] 25.00
____Brown [AB18] 25.00

Vinyl, ROTJ, Skiff, Ewoks, Jabba, and ROTJ logo art.
____Brown [AB19] 20.00

Nishimura Seni Kogyo
Star Wars designs.
____Leather 20.00
____Vinyl with brass buckle....................................12.00
____Vinyl with movie photos 15.00

Textile Artesa
____Star Wars designs 10.00

The Leather Shop
Star Wars.
____Logo on enameled brass buckle, boxed
[AB20] 18.00
____Logo on enameled brass buckle, hanging
tag..15.00

Empire Strikes Back.
____Darth Vader 3D bust on enameled brass
buckle 15.00
____Empire Strikes Back Logo on enameled brass
buckle 10.00
____Yoda 3D on round brass buckle 16.00

Return of the Jedi.
____Circular portraits and logo screened on
belt 12.00
____Embossed with logo on rectangular enameled brass
buckle 14.00
____Jabba the Hutt 3D on rectangular brass
buckle 16.00

Droids.
____Screened logo and droids in landspeeder..........10.00
____Space emblems and 3D droid busts on brass
buckle 15.00
____Space emblems and 3D droid busts on pewter
buckle 16.00
____C-3PO and R2-D2 on enameled brass buckle,
boxed 18.00
____C-3PO and R2-D2 on enameled brass buckle, hang-
ing tag..15.00

____Darth Vader on enameled brass buckle,
boxed 18.00
____Darth Vader on enameled brass buckle, hanging
tag..15.00
____Han and Chewbacca, Droids and Luke, Leia and Darth
Vader [AB21]...20.00
____Obi-Wan and Darth Vader pattern 20.00
____Oval Darth Vader buckle [AB22] 15.00

Bicycle Accessories

Adie
____Bell and Bottle set [BA01] 12.00
____Horn, Darth Vader sculpted [BA02] 10.00
____Seat (saddle) cover, EPIII art [BA03] 15.00

Bicycles

Australia. EPIII:ROTS.
____Darth Vader 145.00

Dynacraft
____Darth Maul, boys, 16" [B01]...............................85.00
____Jar Jar, boys, 12" [B02] 75.00
____Queen Amidala, girls, 12" 75.00

Huffy
____Baba Ewok, Baga, and Princess Kneesaa first bike,
girls [B03]..135.00
____C-3PO and R2-D2 first bike, boys 225.00
____Princess Kneesa high rise, girls 175.00
____X-Wing first bike, boys/girls [B04]...................185.00

EPIII:ROTS.
____Darth Vader, boys, 16" [B05] 79.00

Kenner
____Speeder Bike pedal vehicle [B06] 860.00

Lord and Taylor
____Rebel Assault, chrome [B07] 350.00

BA01

BA02

BA03

B01

B02

B03

B04

B05

B06

B07

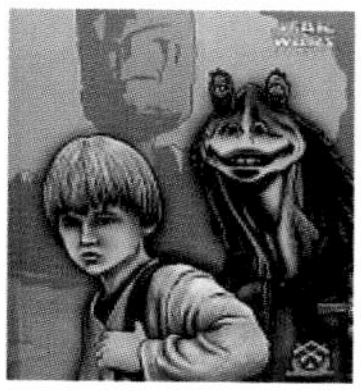
SUB01

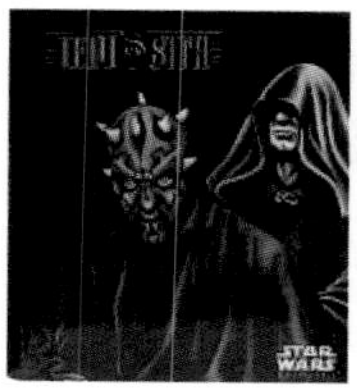
SUB02

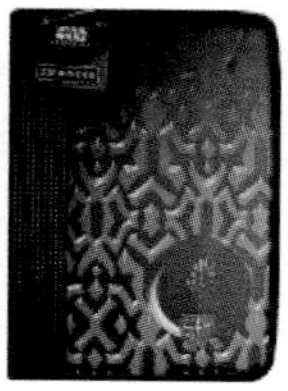
SUB03

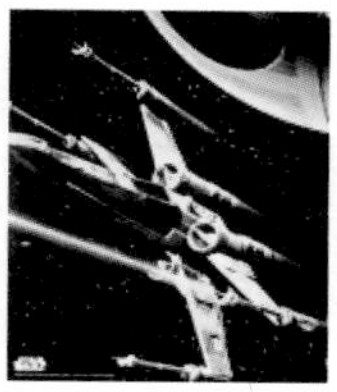
SUB04

SUB05

SUB06

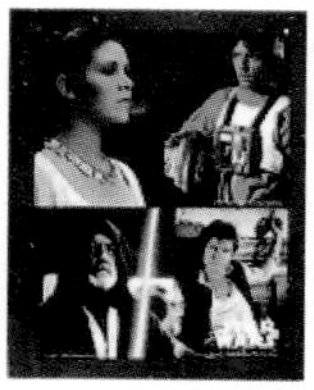
SUB07

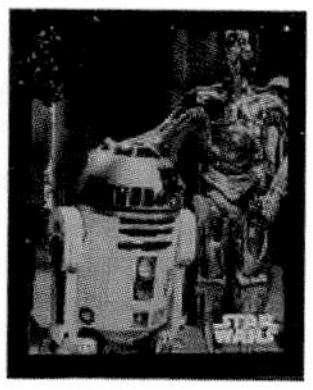
SUB08

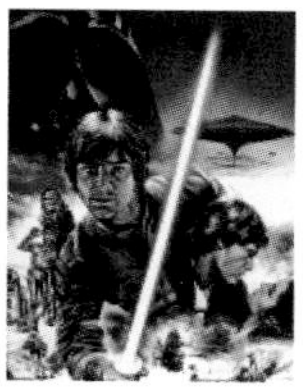
SUB09

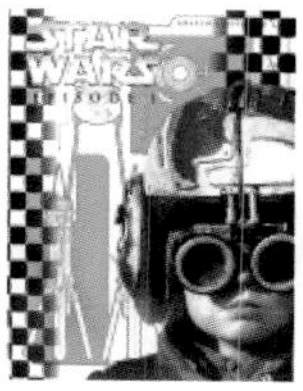
SUB10

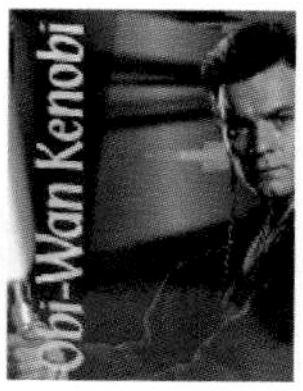

SUB11

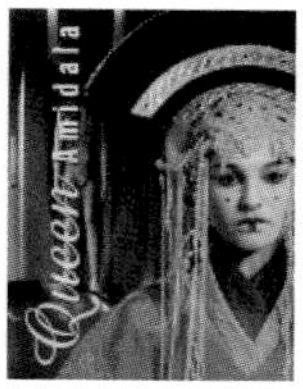
SUB12

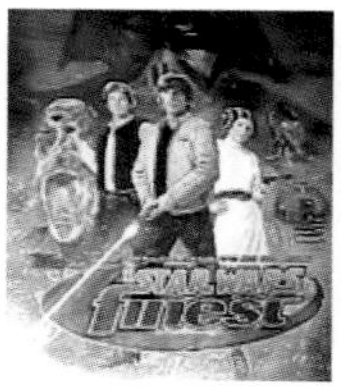
SUB13

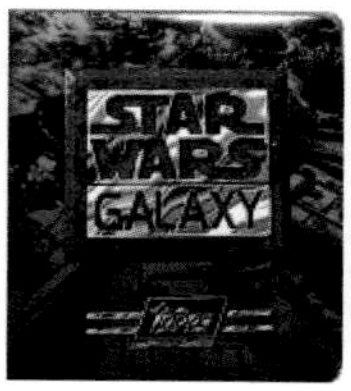

SUB14

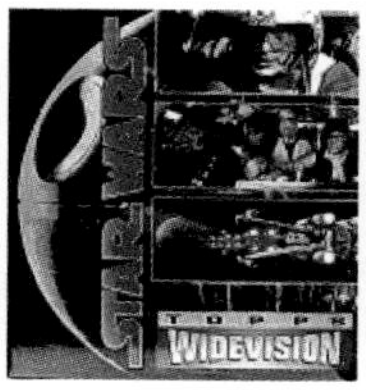
SUB15

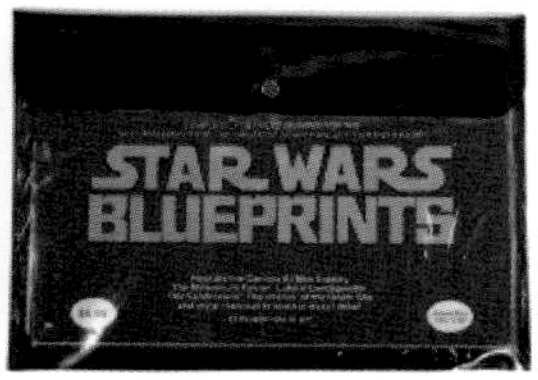

PPB01

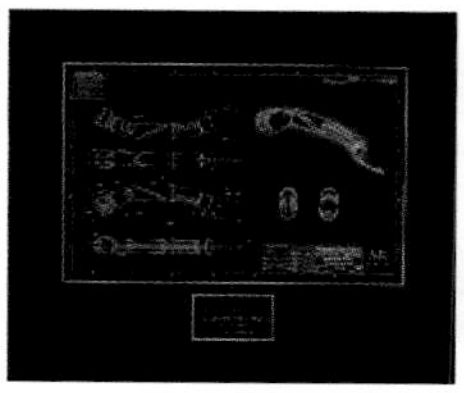
PPB02

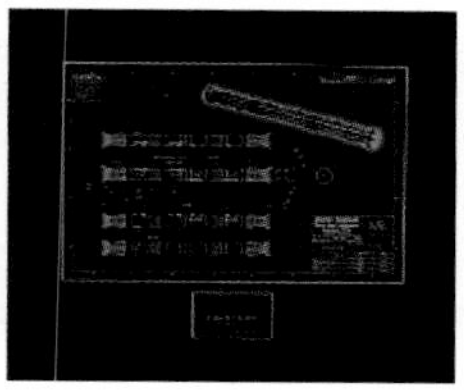
PPB03

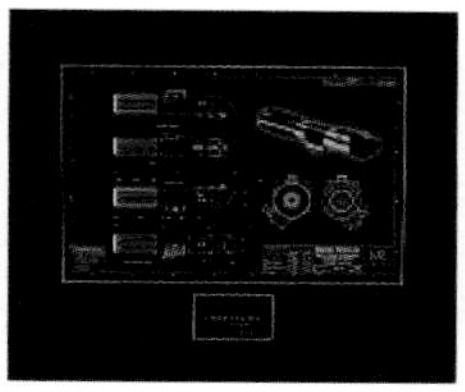
PPB04

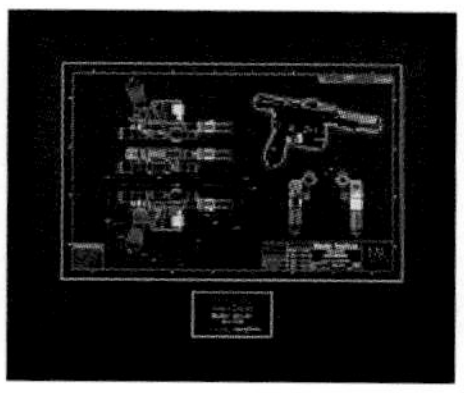
PPB05

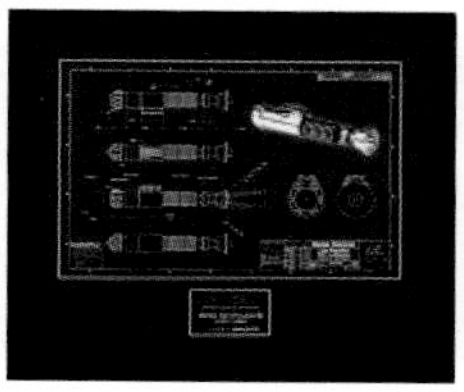
PPB06

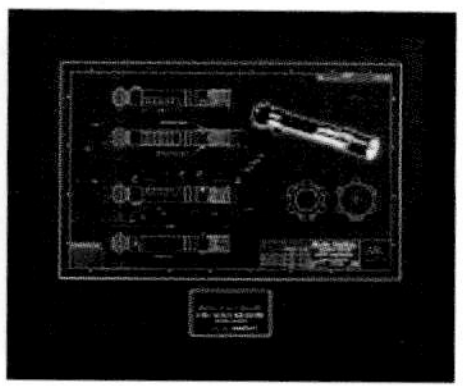
PPB07

Binders

Animations
____Darth Vader lightsaber up 10.00
____Darth Vader..10.00

Cards, Inc.
____Medalionz storage binder (folder) 10.00

Impact, Inc.
____Anakin Skywalker 4.00
____Anakin, Jar Jar / Tatooine [SUB01] 4.00
____Darth Maul, Darth Sidious / Jedi vs. Sith [SUB02]..4.00
____Jar Jar 4.00
____Queen Amidala 4.00
____Qui-Gon Jinn...4.00
____R2-D2 / C-3PO 4.00
____Sith [SUB03] 4.00

Letraset
____X-Wing pursues Tie fighter over Death Star [SUB04] 19.00

Mead
____Darth Vader, blue zippered [SUB05] 12.00
____Darth Vader, gray zippered [SUB06] 12.00

Vintage.
____Ben Kenobi, Han Solo, Luke Skywalker, Princess Leia [SUB07] 30.00
____C-3PO and R2-D2 [SUB08] 30.00
____Darth Vader / Ben Kenobi 30.00
____Han and Chewbacca / Stormtroopers................30.00

Merlin Publishing Internat'l Ltd.
2-ring binders.
____Empire Strikes Back [SUB09] 9.00
____Star Wars 9.00

Q-Stat
____Anakin's Podracer / Sebulba's Podracer [SUB10] 12.00
____Obi-Wan Kenobi [SUB11] 10.00
____Queen Amidala [SUB12] 12.00

Stuart Hall
____2-1B, Bounty Hunters, Probot, Ugnaught 15.00
____C-3PO and R2-D2 ....15.00
____Darth Vader and Stormtroopers.........................15.00
____Luke on Dagobah..15.00
____Yoda 15.00

Topps
____SW Finest [SUB13]..44.00
____SW Galaxy [SUB14] 40.00
____SW Widevision, incl. promo card [SUB15] 46.00

Blueprints

____Millennium Falcon 15.00
____Star Destroyer 15.00

Ballantine
____Blueprints, 15 in plastic pouch ROTJ sticker 24.00
____Blueprints, 15 in plastic pouch [PPB01] 24.00

Master Replicas
Artist proofs, limited to 1,000.
____Count Dooku lightsaber...................................175.00
____Darth Maul lightsaber 175.00
____Darth Vader lightsaber 175.00
____Han Solo blaster 175.00
____Luke Skywalker lightsaber...............................175.00
____Obi-Wan Kenobi lightsaber 175.00

Matted, framed, limited to 5,000.
____Count Dooku lightsaber [PPB02]........................75.00
____Darth Maul lightsaber [PPB03]...........................75.00
____Darth Vader lightsaber [PPB04] 75.00
____Han Solo blaster [PPB05] 85.00
____Luke Skywalker lightsaber [PPB06]....................85.00
____Obi-Wan Kenobi lightsaber [PPB07] 85.00

Bobble Heads

____Darth Vader [BBH01] 25.00
____Yoda [BBH02]...25.00

EPIII:ROTS. Mini.
____Darth Vader [BBH03] 15.00
____Yoda [BBH04]...15.00

Cards, Inc.
EPIII:ROTS.
____C-3PO [BBH05] 25.00
____Clone Trooper [BBH06] 25.00
____Darth Vader [BBH07] 25.00
____General Grievous [BBH08]...................................25.00
____R2-D2 [BBH09]..25.00
____Yoda [BBH10] 25.00

Wizards of the Coast
Limited edition of 4,000.
____Boba Fett [BBH11]...28.00
____C-3PO with R2-D2 [BBH12].................................28.00
____Darth Vader [BBH13] 28.00

Book Covers

Butterfly Originals
____Jabba the Hutt and Speeder Bikes [PPE01] 14.00

Factors, Etc.
____Original Fan Club logo [3:123] 6.00

Impact, Inc.
____Episode I 4-pack of book covers [PPE02] 7.00

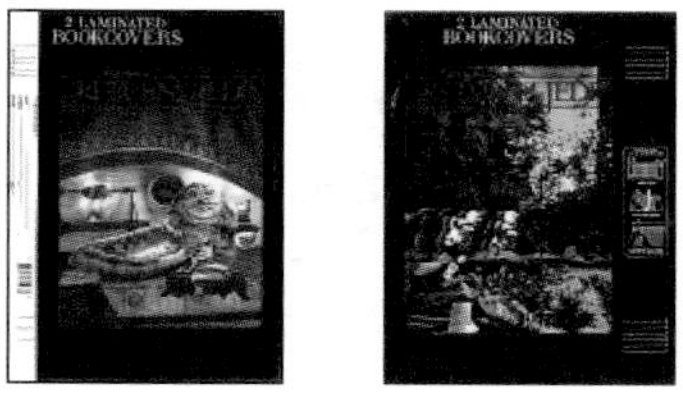
PPE01 front and back

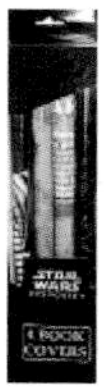
PPE02

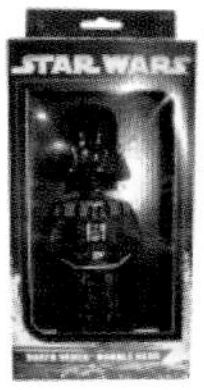
BBH01

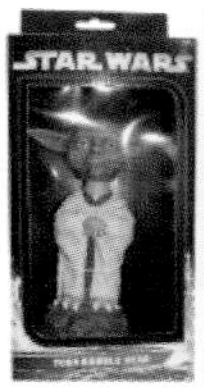
BBH02

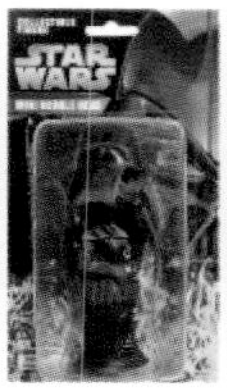
BBH03

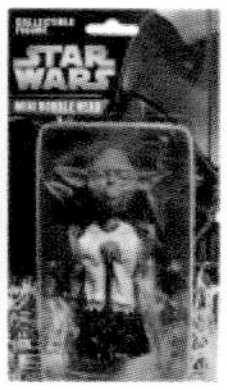
BBH04

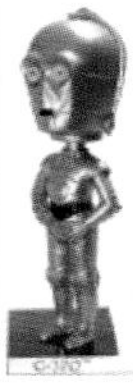
BBH05

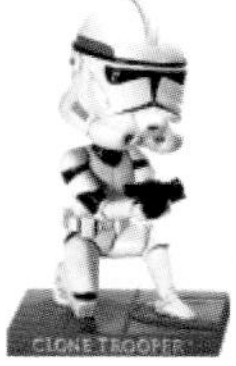
BBH06

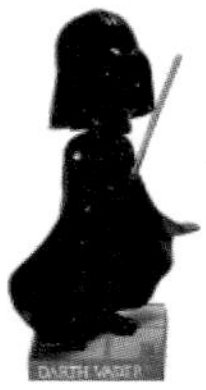
BBH07

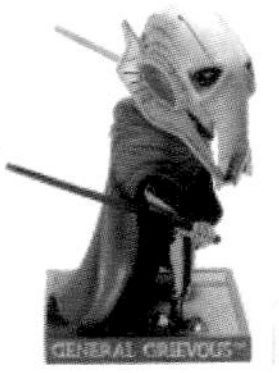
BBH08

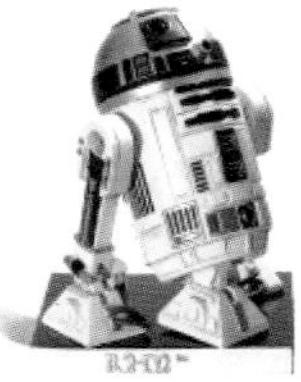
BBH09

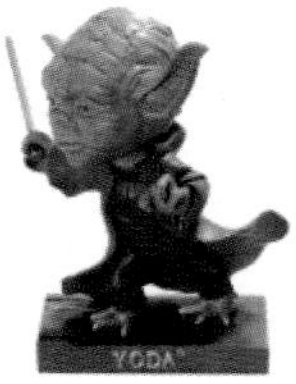
BBH10

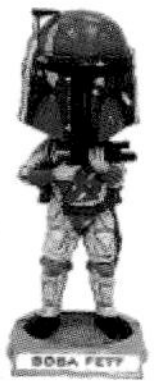
BBH11

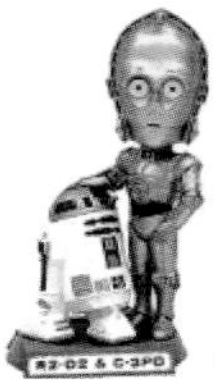
BBH12

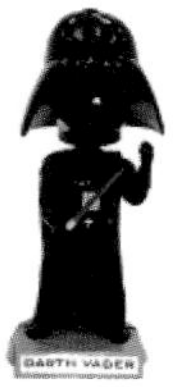
BBH13

Bookcases

FUB01   HOB01   HOB02

Bookcases

American Toy and Furniture Co.
____Return of the Jedi bookcase [FUB01]..............130.00

Bookends

Gentle Giant Studios
____Mos Eisley Cantina, Han Solo and Greedo [HOB01] 165.00

Sigma
Ceramic.
____Chewbacca and Darth Vader [HOB02] 225.00

Booklets and Catalogs

Borders, Inc.
____Special edition collector's catalog, 8-page pamphlet of SW titles 5.00

Burger Chef
____Fun'n Games Booklet (and Kenner catalog) [CL01] 8.00

Butterick
____Halloween Catalog [2:236] 9.00

Collector Books
____2003 Spring, Star Wars Super Collector's Wish Book 2nd Ed. on cover [3:225] 3.00

Collectors Gallery West
____Illustrated listing of original Star Wars comic strip artwork 5.00

Decopac
EPIII:ROTS cakes.com catalog insert pages.
____Darth Vader voice converter 3.00
____Yoda light-up saber 3.00

Estes / Cox
____Mini-Catalog Activity book [3:225] 2.00

Fantasia Katalog
Germany.
____2002, Kinder SW Hippo cover, hardcover 28.00
____2002, Kinder SW Hippo cover, paperback 10.00

Galoob
____The Star Wars Universe 3.00

Hallmark
____2002 Dream Book..2.00

Hasbro
____1999 Toyline, interactive CD with Green SW label 65.00

Mini-Catalog included with products.
____Obi-Wan deluxe cover, Saga [3:225] 2.00

J C Penney
____1978 JC Penney toy flyer [2:236] 7.00

Kenner
____1980 products, includes ESB toys [2:236] 12.00
____1983 products, includes ROTJ toys [2:236] 12.00
____1984 Pre-Toy Fair...100.00
____1986 products, includes Droids 2nd series images 65.00
____Preschool, Your Child's Favorite Playmates [3:225] 5.00
____Star Wars Collection 1997 with checklist.............5.00

Star Wars mini-catalog included with products.
____12" figures cover, "Cash Refunds..." [CL02] 15.00
____Death Star Battle [CL03].......................................5.00
____Logo / Starfield [CL04]...12.00
____X-Wing over Yavin [CL05]......................................5.00
____X-Wing with pink info-box [CL06] 5.00

Empire Strikes Back mini-catalog included w/products.
____ESB logo [CL07] 5.00
____Luke and Yoda [CL08] 5.00

Collections, Return of the Jedi mini-catalog included with products.
____Jabba the Hutt [CL09] 5.00
____Jabba the Hutt, Paploo, and Lumat added........10.00
____Vader on DSII, Chief Chirpa, Logray, Jabba blacked out [CL10] 5.00
____Vader on DSII, red cape Bib Fortuna.................15.00

Collections, Star Wars mini-catalog included with products.
____Hoth trench, gray border [CL11]...........................5.00
____Hoth trench, silver border [CL12] 3.00

POTF2 mini-catalog included with products.
____Kenner is Fun! [3:225]..5.00

Star Wares
____1997 January 2.00

The LEGO Group
____Shop-At-Home catalog, Summer 1999 (Podrace, space battle, and TPM character figures on cover) 4.00
____Shop at Home Attack of the Clones 5.00

Toys R Us
____1997 Star Wars Special Edition toys [3:225] 8.00
____Star Wars Collection 1998 with checklist.............5.00

Booklists

Bantam Books
____1996 Darth Vader / Shadows of the Empire [3:123] 3.00
____1996, "...await you in the exciting and ever-expanding universe of Star Wars" [3:123] 2.00
____1997 "The Adventure Continues" / Lightsaber [3:123] 3.00

Del Rey
____The Time Line [3:123] 3.00

Bookmarks

20th Century Fox
EPIII:ROTS.
____Darth Vader, "Rise Lord Vader" 3.00
____Epic Duel...3.00
____Yoda 3.00

20th Century Fox, Thailand
EPIII:ROTS.
____Anakin / Epic Duel 2.00
____Anakin holding Padme 2.00
____Anakin, Padme / Padme 2.00
____Bail Organa, Obi-Wan, Anakin, Yoda 2.00
____C-3PO...2.00
____Darth Vader 2.00
____Droids / Anakin (dark side) 2.00
____General Grievous 2.00
____Grievous' bodyguard 2.00
____Jedi ... captured 2.00
____Mace Windu 2.00
____Obi-Wan / Epic Duel 2.00
____Obi-Wan Kenobi 2.00
____Obi-Wan, Anakin, Padme 2.00
____Wookie rage 2.00
____Yoda 2.00

A.H. Prismatic
Each bookmark shows 3 hologram images.
____B-Wing, Millennium Falcon, Tie Fighter [BKM02] 5.00
____Millennium Falcon, Darth Vader, Star Destroyer..5.00
____X-Wing Fighter, Tie Interceptor, Imperial AT-AT 5.00

American Library Association
____"Read, You Will!" Yoda, EPI [BKM01]....................2.00
____Darth Vader, Conquer the Information Universe [BKM03] 4.00

Antioch
Book cover art with tassel.
____The Courtship of Princess Leia [BKM04] 4.00
____The Crystal Star [BKM05].......................................4.00
____The Glove of Darth Vader [BKM06] 4.00
____The Lost City of the Jedi 4.00
____Truce at Bakura [BKM07] 4.00
____Zorba the Hutt's Revenge [BKM08] 4.00

Classic trilogy character bookmark with bead on tassel.
____Luke and Leia [BKM09] 4.00
____R2-D2 and C-3PO [BKM10] 4.00

Classic trilogy character bookmark with tassel.
____Ben Kenobi [BKM11] 4.00
____Chewbacca..4.00
____Darth Vader [BKM12] 4.00

CL01

CL02

CL03

CL04

CL05

CL06

CL07   CL08

CL09

CL10

CL11

CL12

BKM01   BKM02   BKM03   BKM04   BKM05   BKM06   BKM07   BKM08   BKM09   BKM10   BKM11   BKM12   BKM13   BKM14

BKM15   BKM16   BKM17   BKM18   BKM19   BKM20   BKM21   BKM22   BKM23   BKM24   BKM25   BKM26   BKM27   BKM28

____Han Solo [BKM13] 4.00
____Lando Calrissian [BKM14] 4.00
____Luke Skywalker [BKM15] 4.00
____MosEisley Cantina [BKM16] 4.00
____Princess Leia Organa [BKM17] 4.00
____SW: Special Edition [BKM18] 4.00
____Yoda [BKM19] 4.00

Classic trilogy die-cut character bookmark.
____Boba Fett [BKM20] 4.00
____C-3PO [BKM21] 4.00
____Chewbacca 3.00
____Darth Vader [BKM22] 4.00
____Han Solo 4.00
____Jawa [BKM23] 4.00
____R2-D2 [BKM24] 4.00
____Stormtrooper 3.00
____Tusken Raider [BKM25] 4.00
____Yoda [BKM26] 4.00

Prequel trilogy character with bead on tassel.
____Anakin Skywalker [BKM27] 4.00
____Clone Trooper [BKM28] 4.00
____Destroyer Droid [BKM29] 4.00
____Jango Fett [BKM30] 4.00
____Jar Jar Binks [BKM31] 4.00
____Queen Amidala, Coruscant [BKM32] 4.00
____Queen Amidala, travel gown [BKM33] 4.00
____R2-D2 [BKM34] 4.00
____Sith Villains [BKM35]..4.00

Prequel trilogy character bookmark with tassel.
____Anakin Skywalker's destiny [BKM36] 4.00
____Anakin Skywalker [BKM37]...............................4.00
____C-3PO [BKM38] 4.00
____Count Dooku [BKM39] 4.00
____Darth Maul [BKM40] 4.00
____Obi-Wan Kenobi, EPI [BKM41] 4.00
____Obi-Wan Kenobi, EPII [BKM42] 4.00

____Padme Amidala [BKM43] 4.00
____Qui-Gon Jinn [BKM44] 4.00
____Sith Lords [BKM45] 4.00
____Zam Wesell [BKM46] 4.00

Prequel trilogy die-cut character bookmark.
____Darth Maul [BKM47] 4.00
____Jar Jar Binks [BKM48] 4.00
____Queen Amidala [BKM49] 4.00
____Rune Haako [BKM50] 4.00
____Sebulba [BKM51] 4.00

Prequel trilogy Gallery Edition bookmarks.
____Battle Droids [BKM52] 5.00
____Podrace [BKM53] 5.00
____Starfighters [BKM54]..5.00

Prequel trilogy with punch out page clip.
____Anakin Skywalker [BKM55]...............................5.00

BKM29   BKM30   BKM31   BKM32   BKM33   BKM34   BKM35   BKM36   BKM37   BKM38   BKM39   BKM40   BKM41   BKM42

BKM43   BKM44   BKM45   BKM46   BKM47   BKM48   BKM49   BKM50   BKM51   BKM52   BKM53   BKM54   BKM55   BKM56

BKM57   BKM58   BKM59   BKM60   BKM61   BKM62   BKM63   BKM64   BKM65   BKM66   BKM67   BKM68   BKM69   BKM70

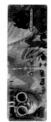

Bookmarks

BKM71 BKM72 BKM73 BKM74 BKM75 BKM76 BKM77 BKM78 BKM79 BKM80 BKM81 BKM82 BKM83 BKM84 BKM85 BKM86 BKM87

PPG01 PPG02 PPG03 PPG04 PPG05 PPG06 PPG07 PPG08

PPG09 front and rear   PPG10   PPG11   PPG12

____Darth Vader [BKM56] 5.00
____Jar Jar Binks [BKM57] 5.00
____Queen Amidala [BKM58] 5.00
____Trade Federation Droids [BKM59] 5.00

Cards, Inc.
____Anakin Skywalker [BKM60]...................5.00
____Clone Trooper [BKM61] 5.00
____Darth Vader [BKM62] 5.00
____General Grievous [BKM63] 5.00
____Obi-Wan Kenobi [BKM64] 5.00
____Yoda [BKM65] 5.00

Dark Horse Comics
____"May The Horse Be With You" [BKM66] 3.00
____"Submit to the Dark Side of the Horse!" [BKM67] 3.00
____Darth Vader 3.00
____The Saga Continues / Graphic Novel Chronology 2.00

Del Rey
____Star Wars, Episode I Characters [BKM68] 2.00

Fantasma
3D bookmarks, 2"x6".
____Darth Vader and Luke Skywalker [BKM69] 3.00
____Darth Vader [BKM70] 3.00

Random House
____#01 Luke Skywalker [BKM71].................4.00
____#02 Darth Vader [BKM72].....................4.00
____#03 Princess Leia (Boushh) [BKM73].......4.00
____#04 R2-D2 [BKM74] 5.00
____#05 C-3PO [BKM75]..............................5.00

____#06 Lando Calrissian [BKM76].............4.00
____#07 Chewbacca [BKM77].....................4.00
____#08 Yoda [BKM78] 5.00
____#09 Ben Kenobi [BKM79] 4.00
____#10 Han Solo [BKM80].........................4.00
____#11 Boba Fett [BKM81] 5.00
____#12 Wicket the Ewok [BKM82]...............4.00
____#13 Emperor's Royal Guard [BKM83] 4.00
____#14 Stormtrooper [BKM84] 4.00
____#15 Jabba the Hutt [BKM85] 4.00
____#16 Admiral Ackbar [BKM86] 4.00

Rye by Post
Film cell bookmark.
____A New Hope 5.00
____Attack of the Clones............................5.00
____Return of the Jedi 5.00
____The Empire Strikes Back 5.00
____The Phantom Menace 5.00

Smithsonian Institute
____Darth Vader, Yoda, Luke, promotes "The Magic of Myth" display, with plastic case [BKM87] 6.00

Bookplates

Antioch
____C-3PO and R2-D2 [PPG01] 8.00
____Dark Empire, 10 pack on hanger card [PPG02]..6.00
____Dark Empire, 30 pack boxed 9.00
____Darth Vader, Boba Fett, Luke in X-Wing gear, 3 of each [PPG03]...........................5.00

____Hildebrandt Art [PPG04]....................8.00
____Jedi vs. Sith, Podrace, Naboo Space Battle, 3 of each 5.00
____Obi-Wan, Darth Maul, Qui-Gon, 3 of each..........5.00

Hunters, Inc.
Australia. EPIII:ROTS.
____School Book Labels, characters 8.00

Introduct
Holland.
____ROTJ scenes 8.00

MAUCCI S.A.
Argentina. Packets of 6 different designs.
____Characters, art [PPG05] 5.00
____Darth Vader [PPG06].........................5.00
____McQuarrie concept art [PPG07] 5.00
____Starships [PPG08]..............................5.00

Random House
____C-3PO and R2-D2 [PPG09] 10.00
____Darth Vader [PPG10].......................10.00
____Wicket the Ewok [PPG11] 10.00
____Yoda [PPG12] 10.00

Books: Activity

Japan releases.
____ROTJ activity book.............................35.00
____The Star Wars Book of Masks 26.00
____The Star Wars Iron-On Transfer Book [BKA01]..17.00

BKA01   BKA02   BKA03   BKA04   BKA05   BKA06   BKA07

Books: Activity

Ballantine
____Star Wars Iron-On Transfer Book [BKA02] 50.00

Collins
____Punch-Out and Make It Book (SW) 15.00

Dalmation Press
____Power of the Empire [BKA03]..............................6.00

Books to color with stickers.
____Droids [BKA04] 6.00
____In a Galaxy Far, Far Away [BKA05]......................6.00

DK Publishing
Ultimate sticker books.
____Clone Wars [BKA06]...12.00
____Revenge of the Sith [BKA07] 12.00
____Star Wars Episode I [BKA08]..............................8.00
____Star Wars [BKA09]..8.00
____Star Wars (revised) [BKA10]............................12.00

____You Can Draw Star Wars Characters [BKA11]...20.00

Editora Abril
____Guerra Nas Estrelas [BKA12]............................18.00

Editorial Norma
____Punch-Out and Make It Book (SW) 15.00

Fabbri Editori
____Giochi Galattici Puzzles and Games [BKA13] 6.00

Fun Works
____Millennium Falcon Punch-Out book [BKA14]........8.00

General Mills, Canada
____1 Star Wars [3:125]...10.00
____2 Empire Strikes Back [3:125] 10.00
____3 The Rebel Alliance [3:125] 10.00
____4 Imperial Forces [3:125] 10.00
____5 Jabba the Hutt [3:125] 10.00
____6 The Green Moon of Endor [3:125] 10.00
____7 The Rescue of Han Solo [3:125] 10.00
____8 The Battle of the Empire [3:125] 10.00

Golden Books
____A More Wretched Hive, The Mos Eisley Cantina scratch and sniff [3:125].................................12.00
____Royal Rescue, galactic search [3:125]...............11.00
____Tell-a-Story stickerbook [3:125] 4.00
____The Rebel Alliance vs. The Imperial Forces 4.00
____The Training of a Jedi Knight [3:125] 4.00

Lego / Walmart
____Jedi Challenge [3:125] 6.00

Oberon
____The R2-D2 Quiz Book / C-3PO Puzzle Book [BKA15]..35.00

Random House
____Revenge of the Sith big sticker book [BKA16] 8.00

Classic trilogy, vintage.
____Artoo Detoo's Activity book [3:125] 7.00
____Chewbacca's Activity book [3:125] 7.00
____Darth Vader's Activity book [3:125] 7.00
____Dot-to-Dot Fun, ROTJ [BKA17] 4.00
____ESB mix or match storybook [BKA18]................15.00

____How to Draw Star Wars Heroes, Creatures, Spaceships, and Other Fantastic Things [BKA19]...15.00
____Luke Skywalker's Activity book 7.00
____Mazes, ROTJ [BKA20] 5.00
____Monster Activity book, ROTJ [BKA21] 5.00
____Picture Puzzle Book, ROTJ [BKA22] 4.00
____Punch-Out and Make It Book (ESB) [BKA23]..15.00
____Punch-Out and Make It Book (ROTJ) [BKA24]..15.00
____Punch-Out and Make It Book (SW) [BKA25]..15.00
____Star Wars Word Puzzles [BKA26] 5.00
____The Star Wars Book of Masks [BKA27].............32.00
____Things to Do and Make [BKA28] 5.00
____Winter Dot-to-Dot [BKA29] 18.00
____Word Puzzle Book, ROTJ [BKA30]........................4.00
____Yoda's Activity book [BKA31] 9.00

Episode I: The Phantom Menace.
____Galactic Puzzles and Games [BKA32] 4.00
____Jedi Punch-Outs, full-color backdrop included [BKA33]..4.00
____Lightsaber Marker Activity book, includes blue marker [BKA34]...4.00
____Lightsaber Marker Activity book, includes green marker 4.00
____Lightsaber Marker Activity book, includes red marker 4.00
____Mask punch-out book [BKA35] 8.00
____Micro Vehicle Punch-Outs [BKA36] 4.00
____Podracer Punch-Outs [BKA37].............................9.00
____Posters to Color, mail-in premium [BKA38]........12.00
____Queen Amidala Paper Doll Book [BKA39] 5.00

BKA08 BKA09 BKA10 BKA11 BKA12 BKA13 BKA14
BKA15 BKA16 BKA17 BKA18 BKA19 BKA20 BKA21
BKA22 BKA23 BKA24 BKA25 BKA26 BKA27 BKA28
BKA29 BKA30 BKA31 BKA32 BKA33 BKA34 BKA35

Books: Activity

BKA36

BKA37

BKA38

BKA39

BKA40

BKA41

BKA42

BKA43

BKA44

Episode II: Attack of the Clones.
____Big Sticker Book [BKA40].....................................7.00
____Jedi Activity Book [BKA41].............................6.00
____Jedi Training and Trials Quiz Book, blue lightsaber
pen 7.00
____Jedi Training and Trials Quiz Book, green lightsaber
pen 7.00
____Jedi Training and Trials Quiz Book, purple lightsaber
pen [BKA42]...7.00
____Jedi Training and Trials Quiz Book, red lightsaber
pen 7.00
____Padme Amidala paper doll book [BKA43] 3.99
____Ship Schematics Punch-Out Book [BKA44] 4.00

Sandylion
____My Sticker Tote includes over 100 stickers 7.00

Scholastic
____Anakin's Activity Magazine 2.00
____Obi-Wan's Activity Magazine 2.00

Books: Art

Japan releases.
____N.Olai Original Sketch Collection.......................40.00
____The Return of the Jedi Sketchbook....................28.00

Amber
____Gwiezdne Wojny (Art of Star Wars) [3:126] 18.00

Ballantine
____The Art of Return of The Jedi, 1994 cover, paperback
[BKB01] 18.00
____The Art of Return of The Jedi, 1997 Special Edition
section, paperback [BKB02] 20.00
____The Art of Return of The Jedi, hardcover 60.00
____The Art of Return of The Jedi, paperback 25.00
____The Art of Star Wars, 1994 cover, paperback 18.00
____The Art of Star Wars, 1997 Special Edition section,
paperback [BKB03] 20.00
____The Art of Star Wars, hardcover [BKB04] 50.00
____The Art of Star Wars, paperback 25.00
____The Art of The Empire Strikes Back, 1994 cover,
paperback [BKB05] 18.00
____The Art of The Empire Strikes Back, 1997 Special
Edition section, paperback [BKB06] 20.00
____The Art of Empire Strikes Back, hardcover 60.00
____The Art of Empire Strikes Back, paperback 25.00
____The ESB Sketchbook [BKB07]...........................12.00
____The Illustrated Star Wars Universe, Cloud City cover
[BKB08] 40.00
____The Illustrated Star Wars Universe, Sandcrawler cover
[BKB09] 40.00
____The Return of the Jedi Sketchbook [BKB10] 12.00
____The Star Wars Sketchbook [BKB11] 12.00

Bandai
Japan releases.
____Star Wars Book of Blueprints 35.00

Bantam Books
____The Illustrated Star Wars Universe 25.00

Benford Books
____Art of Dave Dorman, numbered and signed,
hardcover 80.00
____Art of Dave Dorman, paperback [BKB13] 25.00

Cartoon Network
____Clone Wars, A Collection of Sketches from Cartoon
Network [BKB12] 6.00

Dark Horse Comics
____Panel to Panel 20.00

Del Rey
____Art of Star Wars: Attack of the Clones
[BKB14] 35.00
____Art of Star Wars : Episode I the Phantom Menace
[BKB15] 23.00
____The Art of the Brothers Hildebrandt [BKB16] 25.00
____The Art of The Phantom Menace [BKB17] 29.00

Topps
____The Art of Star Wars Galaxy [BKB18] 20.00
____The Art of Star Wars Galaxy II,
paperback [3:126] 20.00
____The Art of Star Wars Galaxy II, foil cover,
paperback 25.00
____The Art of Star Wars Galaxy, QVC exclusive with card
sheet...25.00

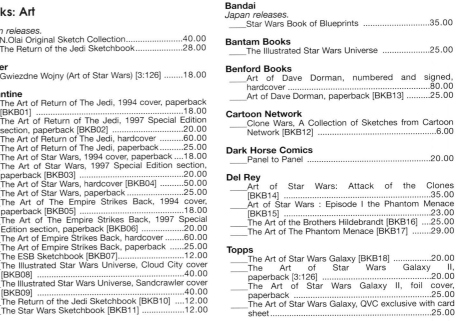

BKB01

BKB02

BKB03

BKB04

BKB05

BKB06

BKB07

BKB08

BKB09

BKB10

BKB11

BKB12

BKB13

BKB14

BKB15

BKB16

BKB17

BKB18

BKB19

Underwood-Miller Inc.
____The Art of Star Wars Galaxy, limited edition (bound and boxed) [BKB19] 175.00

Books: Audio – Cassette

Bantam Books
____Before the Storm 15.00
____Children of the Jedi 14.00
____Courtship of Princess Leia.....................18.00
____Crystal Star..14.00
____Dark Apprentice 15.00
____Dark Empire [2:98] 12.00
____Dark Empire II [2:98].............................16.00
____Dark Empire trilogy in Millennium Falcon collector's box [2:98] 46.00
____Dark Force Rising.....................................14.00
____Dark Saber 15.00
____Han Solo Omnibus: The Paradise Snare, the Hutt Gambit, Rebel Dawn [2:98] 30.00
____Heir to the Empire [2:98] 15.00
____Hutt Gambit [2:98] 16.00
____Jedi Academy Omnibus [2:98]..............24.00
____Jedi Search [2:98]......................................14.00
____Last Command [2:98].................................14.00
____Mandalorean Armor [2:98] 14.00
____Nightlily, the Lovers Tale.........................12.00
____Paradise Snare [2:98] 18.00
____Planet of Twilight [2:98] 18.00
____Rogue Planet, abridged [2:98] 25.00
____Shadows of the Empire [2:98].................18.00
____Shield of Lies 18.00
____Showdown at Centerpoint 18.00
____Slave Ship [2:98] 18.00
____Specter of the Past 18.00
____Star Wars sampler, 6 stories [2:98] 8.00
____Star Wars: Episode I..................................40.00
____The New Rebellion [2:98] 14.00
____The Phantom Menace, unabridged [2:98] 17.00
____Thrawn Omnibus [2:98] 30.00
____Truce at Bakura 17.00
____Tyrant's Test 17.00
____X-Wing 05: Wraith Squadron [2:98] 18.00
____X-Wing 06: Iron Fist [2:98] 14.00
____X-Wing 07: Solo Command [2:98] 18.00
____X-Wing 08: Isard's Revenge [2:98]..........15.00
____X-Wing 09: Starfighters of Adumar 18.00

Griffin
____The Science of Star Wars, unabridged 25.00

Highbridge Company
____Soldier for the Empire [2:98] 15.00

Random House
____Ambush at Corellia/Assault at Selonia/Showdown at Centerpoint, abridged 30.00
____Cloak of Deception, abridged [2:98] 26.00
____Dark Journey 18.00
____Darth Maul Shadow Hunter 15.00
____Star Wars Episode 2, abridged 20.00
____Star Wars Episode 2, unabridged 50.00
____Survivor's Quest, abridged.....................20.00
____The Approaching Storm, abridged [2:98] 26.00

____Yoda, Dark Rendezvous: A Clone Wars Novel, abridged 20.00

New Jedi Order.
____01 Vector Prime [2:98] 18.00
____02 Dark Tide I: Onslaught [2:98] 16.00
____03 Dark Tide II: Ruin [2:98]...................18.00
____04 Agents of Chaos 1: Hero's Trial [2:98] 18.00
____05 Agents of Chaos 2: Jedi Eclipse [2:98].........18.00
____06 Balance Point [2:98] 18.00
____07 Edge of Victory I: Conquest [2:98] 18.00
____08 Edge of Victory II : Rebirth [2:98] 18.00
____09 Star by Star, abridged......................18.00
____10 Dark Journey [2:98]...........................26.00
____11 Enemy Lines I: Rebel Dream 18.00
____12 Enemy Lines II: Rebel Stand............18.00
____13 Traitor..18.00

Books: Audio – CD

Bantam Books
____Nightlily, the Lovers Tale.......................14.00
____Rogue Planet [2:99] 30.00
____Shadows of the Empire [2:99] 20.00
____Star Wars: Episode I [2:99].................28.00
____We Don't Do Weddings, The Band's Tale 14.00

Penguin Audiobooks
____Crimson Empire [2:99] 24.00
____Dark Forces : The Collector's Trilogy [2:99].......50.00

Random House
____Dark Nest I, The Joiner King, abridged 20.00
____Dark Nest II, The Unseen Queen, abridged........20.00
____Dark Nest III, The Swarm War, abridged 20.00
____Shatterpoint, abridged............................30.00
____Star Wars Cloak of Deception, abridged...........20.00
____Star Wars Dark Empire, abridged 20.00
____Star Wars Dark Lords of the Sith, abridged 20.00
____Star Wars Episode 2, abridged 25.00
____Star Wars Episode 2, abridged 50.00
____Star Wars Labyrinth of Evil, abridged 20.00
____Star Wars Tales of the Jedi, abridged 20.00
____Star Wars, Revenge of the Sith, abridged.........17.00
____Star Wars, Revenge of the Sith, unabridged......20.00
____Star Wars: Episode I, unabridged limited edition boxed set 160.00
____Star Wars: Episode I, unabridged 40.00
____Survivor's Quest, abridged.....................30.00
____Tatooine Ghost, abridged.......................20.00
____The Approaching Storm, abridged [2:99] 30.00
____The Complete Star Wars Trilogy, the original radio dramas 55.00
____Yoda, Dark Rendezvous: A Clone Wars Novel, abridged 20.00

Clone Wars Novels.
____Jedi Trial, abridged.................................20.00
____Medstar I, Battle Surgeons, abridged 20.00
____Medstar II, Jedi Healer, abridged.........20.00
____The Cestus Deception, abridged 20.00

Legacy of the Force.
____1 Betrayal 30.00

Books: Coloring

____2 Bloodlines 30.00
____3 Tempest 30.00
____4 Exile 30.00

New Jedi Order.
____12 Enemy Lines II, Rebel Stand, abridged 20.00
____14 Destiny's Way, abridged....................20.00
____15 Force Heretic I: Remnant, abridged 20.00
____16 Force Heretic II: Refugee, abridged 20.00
____17 Force Heretic III: Reunion, abridged.............20.00
____18 The Final Prophecy, abridged...........20.00
____19 The Unifying Force, abridged 20.00

Books: Coloring

Episode II flip books.
____Anakin and Amidala 4.00
____Heroes and Villains 4.00

Collins
____Droid Colouring Book of the Future [3:127]........19.00
____Ewok Fun Colouring Book [3:127] 19.00

Dalmation Press
____Balance of the Force [BKC01] 5.00
____Beware the Dark Side with 8 milky crayons [BKC02]..8.00

Golden Books
____A Galaxy of Creatures, Characters, and Droids [BKC03] 5.00
____An Ewok Adventure [BKC04] 4.00
____Galactic Adventures [3:127] 2.00
____Heroes and Villains [BKC05].................2.00
____Invisible Forces [BKC06]...........................9.00
____Join the Jedi [3:128] 4.00
____Mark and See Magic [BKC07] 8.00
____Posters to Color 6.00

Kenner
Empire Strikes Back.
____C-3PO and Chewbacca 7.00
____Chewbacca and Princess Leia [BKC08] 7.00
____Chewbacca, Han, Lando, Leia [3:128] 7.00
____Darth Vader and Stormtroopers [3:128] 7.00
____Luke [3:128] 7.00
____R2-D2 [BKC09] 7.00
____Yoda [BKC10] 7.00

Return of the Jedi.
____Lando as Skiff Guard 5.00
____Lando [BKC11] 5.00
____Luke with lightsaber [BKC12] 5.00
____Max Rebo band [BKC13] 5.00
____Wicket's World [BKC14] 7.00
____Wicket and Kneesaa 5.00
____Wicket the Ewok [BKC15] 5.00
____Wicket, Kneesaa, and Logray..................6.00

Star Wars.
____C-3PO and Luke 15.00
____Chewbacca and Luke 15.00
____Chewbacca 15.00
____R2-D2 [3:128] 15.00

BKC01	BKC02	BKC03	BKC04	BKC05	BKC06	BKC07
BKC08	BKC09	BKC10	BKC11	BKC12	BKC13	BKC14

Books: Coloring

BKC15

BKC16

BKC17

BKC18

BKC19

BKC20

BKC21

BKC22

BKC23

BKC24

BKC25

BKC26

BKC27

BKC28

Kenner, Canada
____Wicket's World 10.00
____Wicket the Ewok 10.00

Lucas Books
____Episode II 4.00

Oral-B
____Dental Health Adventure Book, 4/83 [BKC16]....12.00
____Dental Health Adventure Book, 8/83 ....16.00

Random House
____Attack of the Clones, Movie Scenes to Color, Anakin / Amidala [BKC17]...4.00
____Attack of the Clones, Movie Scenes to Color, Villains / Heroes...4.00
____Battles To Color, TPM [BKC18] 4.00
____Droids, Creatures, and Vehicles [BKC19]............3.00
____EPI Anakin's Adventures To Color [BKC20] 3.00
____EPI Heroes and Villains [BKC21] 3.00
____EPI Jedi Missions [BKC22].................................3.00
____Giant Coloring Fun [BKC23]...............................12.00
____Jar Jar's Coloring Fun [BKC24]...........................3.00
____Jedi Knights and Heroes [BKC25].......................4.00
____Podracer! [BKC26]...4.00
____Queen Amidala [BKC27].......................................4.00
____The Phantom Menace [BKC28] 4.00

Books: Cooking

Chronicle Books
____Darth Malt and More Galactic Recipes [BKX01]..17.00

____Star Wars Party Book [BKX02] 18.00
____Wookiee Cookies [BKX03] 28.00

Enterprise Incidents
____The Alien Cook [3:128]......................................16.00

Books: E-Book

Ballantine
New Jedi Order.
____Dark Tide: Ruin 5.00
____Recovery [3:128] 3.00
____Vector Prime 5.00
____Ylesia [3:128]...5.00

Del Rey
____A Forest Apart [3:128] 3.50
____Darth Maul: Saboteur [3:128] 3.00
____Fool's Bargain 5.00

J L J Marketing
____Star Wars Online Directory..............................20.00

Books: Educational

Cortexia Publishing
____Teaching, Learning, and Star Wars 18.00

Golden Books
____Han Solo's Rescue from Jabba the Hutt, math grades 2-3 [BKE01]...7.00

____Luke Skywalker's Battle with Darth Vader, reading grades 2-3 [BKE02] 7.00
____Princess Leia's Escape from the Death Star, spelling grades 2-3 [BKE03] 7.00

Super shape books.
____Chewbacca the Wookiee [2:100] 5.00
____Han Solo, Rebel Hero [3:129].............................5.00
____Luke Skywalker, Jedi Knight [3:129]....................6.00
____Princess Leia, Rebel Leader [3:129] 5.00
____R2-D2 and C-3PO, Droid Duo [3:129] 5.00

Longman Publishers
____Star Wars, easy reading edition 14.00

Random House
____C-3PO's Book About Robots [3:129].................12.00
____Ewok: ABC Fun 10.00
____Ewok: Learn-to-Read 10.00
____Spelling Workbook 5.00
____The Star Wars Book About Flight [3:129] 12.00
____The Star Wars Question and Answer Book About Computers, softcover [3:129] 12.00
____The Star Wars Question and Answer Book About Space, hardcover [3:129] 20.00

Star Wars learning fun books.
____Grade 1 Simple Adding and Subtracting [BKE04]...5.00
____Kindergarten Learning Word Sounds [BKE05] 5.00
____Preschool – kindergarten Counting Numbers 1-20...5.00
____Preschool – kindergarten Learning Shapes [BKE06] 5.00

BKX01

BKX02

BKX03

BKE01

BKE02

BKE03

BKE04

BKE05

BKE06

BKE07

BKE08

BKE09

BKE10

BKE11

____Preschool – kindergarten Writing Letters A to Z [BKE07]...5.00
____Preschool – kindergarten Writing Numbers 1 to 10 [3:129]..5.00

Attack on Reading series.
____Comprehension 1 [BKE08]......................10.00
____Comprehension 2 [3:129]......................10.00
____Study Skills [BKE09]...............................10.00
____Teacher's Guide....................................20.00
____Word Study [BKE10].............................10.00

Workbooks.
____ABC Readiness [3:129].............................5.00
____Addition and Subtraction 5.00
____Early Numbers [3:129]..............................5.00
____Multiplication [BKE11]...............................5.00
____Reading and Writing [3:129]......................5.00

Scholastic
____The Star Wars Question and Answer Book About Space, softcover [3:129] 14.00

Books: Galaxy of Fear

Galaxie de la Peur
____Armee de Terreur [2:101] 8.00
____La Cite des Morts [2:101] 8.00
____La Monstre Cache [2:101] 8.00

Bantam Books
____01 Eaten Alive [2:101]..............................8.00
____02 City of the Dead [2:101].....................8.00
____03 Planet Plague [2:101]..........................8.00
____04 The Nightmare Machine [2:101] 8.00
____05 The Ghost of the Jedi [2:101] 8.00
____06 Army of Terror [2:101] 8.00
____07 The Brain Spiders [2:101] 8.00
____08 The Swarm [2:101] 8.00
____09 Spore [2:101].......................................8.00
____10 The Doomsday Ship [2:101] 8.00
____11 Clones [2:101] 8.00
____12 Hunger [2:101] 8.00

Sperling and Kupfer
La Galassia del Terrore.
____La Citta Dei Morti 8.00
____Mangiati VIVI..8.00

VGS
____Lebendig begraben / Stadt det Toten 12.00

Books: Game Guides

____Battle Masters Guide 8.00
____Defender of the Empire: Official Secrets and Solutions...10.00
____Jedi Knight Strategy Guide [BKF01]........14.00
____Secrets of Shadows of the Empire [BKF02] 12.00
____Shadows of the Empire: Official Strategy Guide [BKF03]...16.00
____Star Wars Nintendo Hint Book (Special Offer)..15.00
____Super Empire Strikes Back Official Game Secrets [2:102]...10.00
____Super ROTJ Official Game Secrets 10.00
____Super Star Wars Official Game Secrets.............12.00
____Tie Fighter Collector's CD-Rom: The Official Strategy Guide [2:102].............................12.00
____Tie Fighter: The Official Strategy Guide [BKF04]..12.00
____X-Wing Collector's CD-Rom: The Official Strategy Guide......................................15.00
____X-Wing vs. Tie Fighter Strategy Guide 18.00
____X-wing: The Official Strategy Guide....................12.00

BradyGames Strategy Guides
____Tie Fighter: Authorized Strategy Guide [BKF05]..10.00

Infotainment World Books
____Rebel Assault II: Official Player's Guide..............12.00

LucasArts
____Dark Forces: Official Players Guide [BKF06]......18.00

Nintendo
____Episode I: Pod Racer, Official Nintendo Players Guide [2:102] 15.00

Prima Publishing
____Bounty Hunter [BKF07]...........................15.00
____Demolition, Prima's Official Strategy Guide [BKF08] 13.00
____Empire at War [BKF09]............................18.00
____EPI: The Phantom Menace, Prima's Official Strategy Guide [BKF10] 15.00

Books: Graphic Novels

____Episode I: Pod Racer, Prima's Official Strategy Guide [BKF11]....................................15.00
____Galactic Battlegrounds, Prima's Official Strategy Guide 20.00
____Galaxies Map Atlas (Expanded).........................18.00
____Galaxies: An Empire Divided (console) 18.00
____Gungan Frontier, Prima's Official Strategy Guide [BKF12]..18.00
____Jedi Power Battles, Prima's Official Strategy Guide [BKF13]..15.00
____Knights of the Old Republic [BKF14]......15.00
____Lego Star Wars 2: The Original Trilogy 18.00
____Masters of Teras Kasi [BKF15]................15.00
____Rebel Assault: The Official Insider's Guide 14.00
____Star Wars Galaxies: The Complete Guide [BKF16] 18.00
____Star Wars: Battlefront [BKF17].................20.00
____Star Wars: Force Commander, Prima's Official Strategy Guide [BKF18] 16.00
____Starfighter, Prima's Official Strategy Guide [BKF19]..15.00
____X-Wing Alliance, Prima's Official Strategy Guide [BKF20]..15.00

Star Wars Galaxies: Prima's Official Strategy Guides.
____An Empire Divided, w/giant poster [BKF21] 25.00
____Collector's Guide 30.00
____Map Atlas 20.00
____Quick Reference Guide 10.00
____Space Expansion 20.00

Books: Graphic Novels

Parody theme.
____Star Jaws 8.00

Dark Horse Comics
____Star Wars, The Comics Companion 25.00

Dark Forces.
____Jedi Knight [BGN01]................................25.00
____Rebel Agent [BGN02].............................25.00
____Soldier For the Empire [BGN03] 28.00

Marvel Books
____Star Wars [BGN04].....................................8.00
____Empire Strikes Back [BGN05] 8.00
____Return of the Jedi [BGN06] 8.00

BKF01	BKF02	BKF03	BKF04	BKF05	BKF06	BKF07
BKF08	BKF09	BKF10	BKF11	BKF12	BKF13	BKF14
BKF15	BKF16	BKF17	BKF18	BKF19	BKF20	BKF21

Books: Graphic Novels

| BGN01 | BGN02 | BGN03 | BGN04 | BGN05 | BGN06 | BGN07 | BGN08 |

Titan Books

____Episode II 14.00
____Jango Fett [BGN07] 5.00
____Zam Weseli [BGN08] 5.00

Boxed set, Special Collector's Edition.
____EPII, Jango Fett, Zam Wesell 20.00

Books: Guides

____All About the Star Wars 37.00
____Force of Star Wars [BKG01] 36.00
____Geonosis and the Outer Rim Worlds 30.00
____Inside the Worlds of Star Wars Episode II
[BKG02] 22.00
____Kiddie Meal Collectibles, Darth Maul cover
[BKG03] 16.00

____Star Wars Encyclopedia [BKG04] 50.00
____The Ultimate Visual Guide [BKG05] 45.00
____The World of Star Wars 12.00

Antique Trader Books
____Galaxy's Greatest Collectibles [BKG06].............25.00

Back Bay Books
____Unauthorized SW Companion: The Complete Guide
to the SW Galaxy 18.00

Ballantine
____A Guide to the Star Wars Universe [BKG07] 12.00
____A Guide to the Star Wars Universe, 2nd edition
[BKG08] 18.00
____A Guide to the Star Wars Universe, 3rd edition
[BKG09] 15.00
____Galactic Phrase Book and Travel Guide
[BKG10]...8.00

____The Essential Guide to Alien Species [BKG11] ..19.00
____The Essential Guide to Characters [BKG12] 16.00
____The Essential Guide to Characters, condensed ..8.00
____The Essential Guide to Droids [BKG13]............18.00
____The Essential Guide to Planets and Moons
[BKG14] 18.00
____The Essential Guide to Vehicles and Vessels
[BKG15] 16.00
____The Essential Guide to Vehicles and Vessels, con-
densed 8.00
____The Essential Guide to Weapons and Technology
[BKG16] 18.00

Beckett
____Collectibles from a galaxy far, far away
[BKG17] 20.00
____Everything you need to know about Collecting Star
Wars [BKG18]...20.00
____Official Price Guide to SW Memorabilia 20.00

| BKG01 | BKG02 | BKG03 | BKG04 | BKG05 | BKG06 | BKG07 |

| BKG08 | BKG09 | BKG10 | BKG11 | BKG12 | BKG13 | BKG14 |

| BKG15 | BKG16 | BKG17 | BKG18 | BKG19 | BKG20 | BKG21 |

| BKG22 | BKG23 | BKG24 | BKG25 | BKG26 | BKG27 | BKG28 |

Chronicle Books
____Anakin Skywalker, The Story of Darth Vader [3:130] 75.00
____Aurra Sing Masterpiece Edition [3:130] 125.00
____C-3PO: Tales of the Golden Droid [3:130] 55.00
____Star Wars Poster Book, The 85.00
____The Action Figure Archive [BKG19] 30.00
____Wildlife of Star Wars: A Field Guide [BKG20] 40.00

Collector's Guide
____Irwin Toys: Canadian Star Wars Connection 27.00

Collector Books
Star Wars Super Collector's Wish Book.
____1st edition [BKG21] 35.00
____1st edition signed at Celebration 2 ....35.00
____2nd edition [BKG22] 35.00
____3rd edition 35.00
____3rd edition signed at Celebration 3 ....35.00
____4th edition 35.00
____4th edition signed at Celebration 4 ....35.00

Del Rey
____New Essential Chronology [BKG23] 25.00
____New Essential Guide to Alien Species [BKG24] 25.00
____New Essential Guide to Droids [BKG25] 25.00
____New Essential Guide to Vehicles and Vessels [BKG26] 25.00
____The New Essential Guide to Characters 25.00

DK Publishing
____Complete Locations, Inside the Worlds of the Entire Saga 40.00

____Complete Visual Dictionary [BKG27] 40.00
____EPI: Cross Sections [BKG37] 22.00
____EPI: Cross Sections, inside metal box with combination lock, 500 produced for promotional purposes [3:131] 360.00
____EPI: The Visual Dictionary [BKG38] 17.00
____EPII: Incredible Cross-Sections [BKG28] 20.00
____EPII: Visual Dictionary [BKG29] 20.00
____EP III: Incredible Cross-Sections [BKG30] 20.00
____EPIII: Visual Dictionary [BKG31] 20.00
____Inside the Worlds of Star Wars Episode I [BKG32] 22.00
____Inside the Worlds of SW Trilogy [BKG33] 26.00
____SW: Incredible Cross-Sections [BKG34] 35.00
____SW: The Visual Dictionary [BKG35] 35.00
____The Complete Locations of Star Wars [BKG36] 22.00

Fabbri Editori
____Episodio I Guida Al Film [BKG39] 12.00

Fantasia Verlag
____Star Heroes #1 ....10.00
____Star Heroes #2 ....10.00
____Star Heroes #3 ....10.00
____Star Heroes #4 ....25.00

Front Back Books
____Star Wars Vintage Action Figures [BKG40] 35.00

FunFax
Data files.
____Episode I [3:131] 8.00
____Star Wars [3:131] 8.00

Henderson Publishing
Data Files.
____Star Wars [3:131] 18.00

Funfax Missions.
____1: Star Wars 5.00
____2: Empire Strikes Back 5.00
____3: Return of the Jedi 5.00

Microfax series.
____#01: Darth Vader 2.00
____#02: C-3PO and R2-D2 ....2.00
____#03: Galactic Empire 2.00
____#04: Jabba the Hutt and Bounty Hunters 2.00
____#05: Princess Leia 2.00
____#06: Luke Skywalker..2.00
____#07: Millennium Falcon 2.00
____#08: Obi-Wan Kenobi 2.00
____#09: Han Solo and Chewbacca 2.00
____#10: Imperial Fleet 2.00
____#11: Rebel Fleet 2.00
____#12: Rebel Alliance 2.00
____Mini-Binder [3:131] 5.00

Krause Publications
____Star Wars Collectibles Price Guide [BKG41] 30.00
____Star Wars Collector's Pocket Companion [3:131] 12.00
____Warman's Star Wars Field Guide [BKG42] 12.00

Little, Brown
____The Unauthorized Star Wars Compendium: The Complete Guide to the Movies, Comic Books, Novels, and More [BKG43] 20.00

BKG29	BKG30	BKG31	BKG32	BKG33	BKG34	BKG35
BKG36	BKG37	BKG38	BKG39	BKG40	BKG41	BKG42
BKG43	BKG44	BKG45	BKG46	BKG47	BKG48	BKG49
BKG50	BKG51	BKG52	BKG53	BKG54	BKG55	BKG56

Books: Guides

Lucasbook
____Revenge of the Sith scrapbook [BKG44] 5.00

Planeta
Episode I: The Phantom Menace.
____Incredible Cross-Sections [BKG45] 24.00
____Visual Dictionary [BKG46] 24.00

Random House
____Attack of the Clones Scrapbook [BKG47] 8.00
____EPI:TPM Scrapbook [BKG48] 12.00
____Price Guide to SW Collectibles [BKG49] 14.00
____Secrets of the Sith Movie Scrapbook [BKG50] 7.00

Reeds
____Darth Vader mini-book [3:131] 4.00
____Han Solo mini-book [3:131] 4.00
____Princess Leia mini-book 4.00

Running Press
____Star Wars Collectibles: A Pocket Guide
[BKG51] 7.00
____Tie Fighter: A Pocket Manual [BKG52].................6.00
____What's What: A Pocket Guide to the The Phantom
Menace [3:131] 6.00
____Who's Who: A Pocket Guide to the Characters of The
Phantom Menace [3:131] 6.00
____Who's Who: A Pocket Guide to the Characters of the
Star Wars Trilogy [BKG53] 9.00
____X-Wing: A Pocket Manual [BKG54] 6.00

Schiffer Publishing
____Collecting SW Toys 1977 – 1997: An Unauthorized
Practical Guide [BKG55] 30.00

Scholastic
Star Wars Trilogy Scrapbooks.
____Complete [3:131] 10.00
____The Galactic Empire [3:131] 8.00
____The Rebel Alliance [3:131] 8.00

Tomart
____Tomart's Price Guide to Wordwide Star Wars
Collectibles [3:131]...30.00
____Tomart's Price Guide to Wordwide Star Wars
Collectibles, 2nd edition hardcover [BKG56]......75.00
____Tomart's Price Guide to Wordwide Star Wars
Collectibles, 2nd edition..30.00

VGS
____Episode I Die Risszeichnungen [3:131] 35.00

WSOY
____Episodi I Kuvitettu Opas [3:131] 35.00

Books: Jedi Apprentice

Bonnict
____Den morka rivalen..5.00

Fabbri Editori
____Il rivale oscuro..5.00

Scholastic
____01 The Rising Force [2:104] 5.00
____02 The Dark Rival [2:104] 5.00
____03 The Hidden Past [2:104] 5.00
____04 The Mark of the Crown [2:104] 5.00
____05 The Defenders of the Dead [2:104] 5.00
____06 The Uncertain Path [2:104] 5.00
____07 The Captive Temple [2:104] 5.00
____08 The Day of Reckoning [2:104] 5.00
____09 The Fight for Truth [2:104] 5.00
____10 The Shattered Peace [2:104] 5.00
____11 The Deadly Hunter [2:104] 5.00
____12 The Evil Experiment [2:104] 5.00
____13 The Dangerous Rescue [2:104] 5.00
____14 The Ties That Bind [2:104] 5.00
____15 The Death of Hope [2:104] 5.00
____16 The Call to Vengeance [2:104].......................5.00
____17 The Only Witness [2:104] 5.00
____18 The Threat Within [2:104] 5.00

____Special Edition 1: Deceptions [2:104] 7.00
____Special Edition 2: The Followers [2:104] 7.00

Books: Jedi Quest

Scholastic
____01 The Way of the Apprentice [3:132] 5.00
____02 The Trail of the Jedi [3:132] 5.00
____03 The Dangerous Games [3:132] 5.00
____04 The Master of Disguise [3:132] 5.00
____05 The School of Fear [3:132] 5.00
____06 The Shadow Trap [3:132] 5.00
____07 The Moment of Truth [3:132] 5.00
____08 The Changing of the Guard.............................5.00
____09 The False Peace 5.00
____10 The Final Showdown 5.00

Books: Journals – Blank

Antioch
____20th Anniversary with Rystall bookmark and 2 wallet
cards [PPJ01] 18.00
____Episode I limited edition journal, free bookmark and
bookplate, 50,000 produced [PPJ02] 11.00
____Episode II cloth coverd, limited to 25,000 ....12.00
____Episode II heroes with bookmark 9.00
____Space Battle with bookmark 10.00
____Star Wars poster art with bookmark [PPJ03] 10.00
____The Courtship of Princess Leia with bookmark
[PPJ04] 10.00
____The Crystal Star with bookmark [PPJ05].............10.00
____Trade Federation journal, free bookmark and book-
plate, 50,000 produced [PPJ06] 10.00
____Truce at Bakura with bookmark [PPJ07] 10.00

*EPI:TPM. Free bookmark and bookplate, 50,000 pro-
duced.*
____Queen Amidala [PPJ08] 10.00
____Qui-Gon Jinn [PPJ09] 10.00
____Sith [PPJ10] 11.00

Ballantine
____My Jedi Journal [PPJ11] 18.00

Chronicle Books
____Star Wars Logbook [PPJ12]...............................14.00

Heyne
____Star Wars Timer, 365 Tag [PPJ13] 26.00

Random House
____Anakin Skywalker, A Jedi's Journal [PPJ14] 9.00

Tokyo Queen
____Darth Vader cover, C-3PO on back [PPJ15] 24.00

Books: Junior Jedi Knights

Boulevard
____01 The Golden Globe [2:105] 8.00
____02 Lyric's World [2:105] 6.00
____03 Promises [2:105] 6.00
____04 Anakin's Quest [2:105] 6.00
____05 Vader's Fortress [2:105] 6.00
____06 Kenobi's Blade [2:105]..................................6.00

PPJ01

PPJ02

PPJ03

PPJ04

PPJ05

PPJ06

PPJ07

PPJ08

PPJ09...

PPJ09

PPJ10

PPJ11

PPJ12

PPJ13

PPJ14

PPJ15

BKV01

BKV01   BKV03   MB01   MB02   MB03   MB04   MB05   MB06

Books: Make Your Own Adventure

Bantam Books
___Star Wars [BKV01] 6.00
___Empire Strikes Back [BKV02] 6.00
___Return of the Jedi [BKV03].................................6.00

West End Games
___Jedi's Honor [3:132] 12.00
___Scoundrel's Luck [3:132] 12.00

Books: Music

___Music from ROTJ and 20 movie gems, for trumpet [MB01] 6.00
___Star Wars plus 12 giant pop chart winners [MB02] 4.00
___Top Pops, easy play piano [MB03].......................5.00

Alfred Publishing
___Episodes I, II & III Instrumental Solos Book and CD (Alto Sax Edition) [MB04] 18.00

Fox Fanfare Music
___Star Wars Picture Book 15.00
___Star Wars Saga Book..24.00
___Star Wars 15.00
___The Empire Strikes Back 12.00

Warner Bros Publications
___Music from Star Wars Episode I 10.00
___Music from the Trilogy for flute [MB05] 10.00
___Phantom Menace Clarinet Songbook with CD...12.00
___Phantom Menace Tenor Sax Songbook with CD...12.00
___Phantom Menace Trumpet Songbook with CD...12.00
___Selections from Star Wars for Guitar [MB06] 15.00

Books: Non-Fiction

___Famous Spaceships and How to Model Them [BKZ01]...36.00
___Flying Solo, hardcover with slipcase, limited to 2,000, signed by Jeremy Bulloch 55.00

___ROTJ Official Colletor's Album [BKZ02]...............8.00
___Sci-Fi Now [BKZ03] 12.00
___The Making of The Phantom Menace, Limited First Edition..27.00
___The Making of The Phantom Menace, Special Collector's Limited Edition 35.00

German releases.
___The Making of Return of the Jedi 24.00
___The Star Wars Album 24.00

Japan releases.
___George Lucas Museum 45.00
___Industrial Light and Magic 27.00
___Star Wars: From Concept to Screen to Collectible..35.00
___The George Lucas Exhibition..............................45.00
___The Making of Return of the Jedi 25.00
___The Star Wars Album 24.00

Netherlands release.
___The Star Wars Album 25.00

Abrams
___Dressing a Galaxy: The Costumes of Star Wars 50.00
___Dressing a Galaxy: The Costume of Star Wars Limited Edition with DVD 295.00
___George Lucas The Creative Impulse: Lucasfilm's First Twenty Years 40.00
___George Lucas: The Creative Impulse.................35.00
___George Lucas: The Creative Impulse.................40.00
___George Lucas: The Creative Impulse, 2nd edition [BKZ04]..35.00
___Monsters and Aliens from George Lucas [BKZ05]..25.00
___The Cinema of George Lucas 50.00

Ballantine
___Making of Return of the Jedi [BKZ06] 16.00
___Once Upon A Galaxy, The Making of Empire Strikes Back [BKZ07] 22.00
___Star Wars, Star Trek and 21st Century Christians 26.00

Bantam Books
___The Magic of Myth, hardcover............................35.00
___The Magic of Myth, trade paperback [BKZ08] ..24.00

Benbella Books
___Star Wars on Trial [BKZ09]................................18.00

British Film Institute
___Big Picture: Hollywood Cinema from "Star Wars" to "Tiantic" (Paperback) 25.00

Chronicle Books
___Aliens and Creatures (postcard book) [BKZ10]...16.00
___Behind the Scenes (postcard book) [BKZ11]...16.00
___From Star Wars to Indiana Jones: The Best of Lucasfilm Archives, hardcover 45.00
___From Star Wars to Indiana Jones: The Best of Lucasfilm Archives, trade paperback [BKZ12]...25.00
___Star Wars Chronicles II 175.00
___Star Wars Chronicles [BKZ13]...........................175.00
___Star Wars Scrapbook: The Essential Collection [BKZ15]...35.00
___Star Wars: From Concept to Screen to Collectible, hardcover [BKZ14]...35.00
___Star Wars: From Concept to Screen to Collectible, paperback 25.00
___The Toys (postcard book) [BKZ16] 16.00

Citadel
___Empire Building: The Remarkable Real Life Story of SW [BKZ17] 16.00

Continuum Publishing Group
___Using the Force: Creativity, Community and Star Wars Fans [BKZ18] 30.00

Del Rey
___Industrial Light and Magic: Into the Digital Realm [BKZ19]...75.00
___Industrial Light and Magic: The Art of Special Effects..75.00
___Star Wars: The Making of Episode III 35.00
___The Art of Star Wars: Episode III 35.00

DK Publishing
___Classic Gift Pack (Visual Dict., Cross-Sections, Ultimate Sticker book, Power of Myth book, calendar)...65.00
___EPI Gift Pack (Visual Dict., Cross-Sections, Ultimate Sticker book, Power of Myth book, Calendar) ..65.00
___The Power of Myth [BKZ20]...............................14.00

Facts on Demand
___The Incredible Internet Guide to Star Wars [BKZ21]...12.00

BKZ01   BKZ02   BKZ03   BKZ04   BKZ05   BKZ06   BKZ07   BKZ08

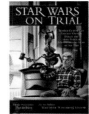

BKZ09   BKZ10   BKZ11   BKZ12   BKZ13   BKZ14

BKZ15   BKZ16   BKZ17   BKZ18   BKZ19   BKZ20

Books: Non-Fiction

 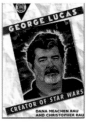      

| BKZ21 | BKZ22 | BKZ23 | BKZ24 | BKZ25 | BKZ26 | BKZ27 | BKZ28 |

 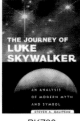     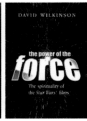 

| BKZ29 | BKZ30 | BKZ31 | BKZ32 | BKZ33 | BKZ34 | BKZ35 | BKZ36 |

Fictioneer Books, Ltd.
____David Anthony Kraft's Comics Interview Super Special: SW 18.00

Franklin Watts
____George Lucas: Creator of Star Wars, paperback [BKZ22] 7.00
____George Lucas: Creator of Star Wars, hardcover 16.00

Griffin
____Science of Star Wars, hardcover 22.00
____Science of Star Wars, paperback [BKZ23] 15.00

Hachette
____The Star Wars Album 24.00

Harry N. Abrams, Inc.
____Dressing a Galaxy: The Costumes of Star Wars 50.00
____Dressing a Galaxy: The Costumes of Star Wars, limited edition with DVD 295.00

Henry Holt and Company
____A Galaxy Not So Far Away [BKZ24] 15.00

Hobby Japan
____The Modeling of Star Wars [BKZ25] 35.00

Humanics Trade Group
____Tao of Star Wars [BKZ26]...............................18.00

Insight Editions
____Sculpting a Galaxy [BKZ27]..........................300.00

Lucas Books
____Making of Episode I: The Phantom Menace [BKZ28]..25.00
____Making of Episode I: The Phantom Menace, limited 1st edition...40.00

Marvel Comics
____The Star Wars Album 20.00

National Geographic
____Star Wars Where Science Meets Imagination, hardcover...45.00
____Star Wars: Where Science Meets Imagination [BKZ29]..18.00

Open Court Publishing
____Star Wars And Philosophy, paperback 18.00
____The Journey of Luke Skywalker: An Analysis of Modern Myth and Symbol [BKZ30]...................20.00

Orbit
____The Making of Return of the Jedi 24.00

Peter Lang Pub Inc
____Finding the Force of the Star Wars Franchise: Fans, Merchandise, and Critics, hardcover...................85.00
____Finding the Force of the Star Wars Franchise: Fans, Merchandise, and Critics, paperback [BKZ31] ..30.00

Random House
____Attack of the Clones Postcard Book 4.00

____Star Wars, The Making of the Movie, step-up [BKZ32]..12.00
____Stars of Star Wars...6.00

Samuel French Trade
____Skywalking: the Life and Films of George Lucas [BKZ33]...15.00
____Skywalking: the Life and Films of George Lucas; updated edition 1997 ....17.00

Sphere
____Once Upon A Galaxy, The Making of Empire Strikes Back 22.00

Starlog
____Starlog Salutes Star Wars, 10th Anniversary souvenir program 15.00

The World Book
Year books.
____1978 Motion Pictures [BKZ34]...................12.00
____1980 Special report and games.................10.00
____1981 Motion Pictures 10.00
____1984 Motion Pictures 10.00

Trafalgar Square
____The Power of the Force, The spirituality of the Star Wars films [BKZ35]..15.00

Wisdom Publications
____The Dharma of Star Wars, paperback 12.00

Xlibris Corporation
____Star Wars: The New Myth, hardcover [BKZ36]...35.00
____Star Wars: The New Myth, paperback................25.00

Books: Novels

____Star Wars Chronology, hardcover 30.00
____Star Wars Chronology, trade paperback 16.00
____Star Wars Trilogy Omnibus Edition 10.00
____Star Wars Trilogy Omnibus Edition, 10th anniversary edition 15.00

Belgium.
____Episode III: De wraak van de Sith 6.00

Finland releases.
____Imperiumin Vastaisku (ESB) 15.00
____Jedin Paluu (ROTJ)..15.00
____Mustan Lordin Paluu (Splinter of the Mind's Eye)...15.00
____Tahtien Sota (SW) 15.00

France releases.
____L'Empire Contre-Attaque, hardcover (ESB)........25.00
____L'Empire Contre-Attaque, paperback (ESB) 14.00
____L'Heritier de l'Empire, paperback (Heir to the Empire)..8.00
____La Bataille des Jedi, paperback (Dark Force Rising)...8.00
____La Guerre des Etoiles, paperback (SW)..............14.00
____Le Retour du Jedi, paperback (ROTJ) 14.00

____Les Derniers Ommand, paperback (The Last Command) 8.00

Japan releases.
____Return of the Jedi, hardcover 20.00
____Return of the Jedi, Darth Vader on cover, paperback 30.00
____Return of the Jedi, droids and ewok on cover, paperback 25.00
____Splinter of the Mind's Eye, hardcover [BKN01] ..20.00
____Star Wars, hardcover [3:133] 20.00
____Star Wars, Hildebrant cover, paperback 25.00
____Star Wars, space battle cover, paperback..........20.00
____The Empire Striles Back, hardcover [3:133] 20.00

Korea releases.
____Heir to the Empire 25.00

Netherland releases.
____De terugkeer von de Jedi, illustrated paperback (ROTJ)..22.00
____De terugkeer von de Jedi, Jabba cover, paperback (ROTJ)..20.00
____De terugkeer von de Jedi, paperback (ROTJ) 18.00
____De Wraak van Han Solo 15.00
____Gevangenen aan de Oerwoudplaneet (Splinter of the Mind's Eye) [BKN02]....................................20.00
____Han Solo in Stars' End [3:133]..........................15.00
____Strijd tussen de sterren, Falcon cockpit cover, paperback (SW) [3:133] 22.00
____Strijd tussen de sterren, paperback (SW) 20.00
____Wraak uit het heelal, Dagobah cover, paperback (ESB) 20.00
____Wraak uit het heelal, paperback (ESB) 18.00

Poland.
____Atak Klonow 6.00
____Krysztalowa Gwiazda 6.00
____Przed Burza 6.00
____Stadkobiercy Mocy...6.00
____Utracona Fortuna 6.00
____Zagubieki 6.00

Russia.
____Empire Strikes Back, hardcover 15.00
____Return of the Jedi, hardcover 15.00
____The Courtship of Princess Leia, paperback..........5.00

Singapore releases.
____Return of the Jedi, McQuarrie cover, paperback 18.00

Spain releases.
____El Imperio Contra ataca, softcover (ESB) 15.00
____El Ojo de la Mente 15.00
____El Retorno del Jedi (ROTJ)................................15.00
____La Guerra de las Galaxis, paperback (SW) 12.00
____La Guerra de las Galaxis, softcover (SW) 15.00

Taiwan releases.
____Heir to the Empire...6.00
____The Last Command 6.00

Arnoldo Mondadori
Italy releases.
____Guerre Stellari, hardcover (SW) 20.00

____Guerre Stellari, softcover with slipcase (SW)......45.00
____Han Solo Guerriero Stellare 25.00
____L'imperio Colpisce Ancora, hardcover (ESB)......20.00

Ballantine

Empire Strikes Back.
____Hardcover 16.00
____Hardcover Special Edition cover art [3:134] 12.00
____Paperback [3:134]..6.00
____Paperback classic edition [BKN04] 6.00
____Paperback illustrated edition [BKN03]................10.00
____Paperback medallion art cover [3:134].................6.00
____Paperback special edition art cover [3:134]..........6.00

Han Solo Adventures.
____Paperback classic edition [3:134]......................8.00
____Paperback compilation 8.00

Han Solo and the Lost Legacy.
____Hardcover 15.00
____Paperback [BKN08] 6.00
____Paperback classic edition [BKN07] 4.00

Han Solo at Stars' End.
____Hardcover 15.00
____Paperback [BKN10] 6.00
____Paperback classic edition [BKN09] 6.00

Han Solo's Revenge.
____Hardcover 15.00
____Paperback [BKN06] 6.00
____Paperback classic edition [BKN05] 6.00

Lando Calrissian Adventures.
____Paperback classic edition [3:134].......................8.00
____Paperback compilation 8.00

Lando Calrissian and the Flamewind of Oseon.
____Hardcover 35.00
____Paperback [BKN11] 6.00

Lando Calrissian and the Mindharp of Sharu.
____Hardcover 35.00
____Paperback [BKN12] 6.00

Lando Calrissian and the Starcave of Thonboka.
____Hardcover 35.00
____Paperback [BKN13] 6.00

Return of the Jedi.
____Hardcover Special Edition cover art [3:134] 12.00
____Hardcover, book club edition [BKN14] 20.00
____Paperback..6.00
____Paperback classic edition [BKN15] 6.00
____Paperback illustrated edition [3:134] 10.00
____Paperback medallion art cover [3:134]..................6.00
____Paperback special edition art cover [3:134]..........6.00

Rogue Planet.
____Hardcover 12.00
____Paperback [BKN16] 7.00

Splinter of the Mind's Eye.
____Hardcover 15.00
____Paperback [BKN18] 6.00
____Paperback classic edition [BKN17] 6.00

Star Wars Trilogy.
____Hardcover special edition art [BKN19] 10.00
____Paperback [BKN20]..6.00
____Paperback boxed set [3:134] 28.00
____Paperback classic edition [3:134] 12.00

Star Wars.
____Hardcover [3:134] 15.00
____Hardcover 1976 ....12.00
____Hardcover Special Edition cover art [3:134] 12.00
____Hardcover with gold dust jacket 80.00
____Hardcover [BKN21] 15.00
____Paperback "Over 5 Million in Print" red medallion [3:134] 6.00
____Paperback "Over 5 Million in Print" yellow medallion [3:134] 6.00
____Paperback "The Year's Best Movie" [BKN22].......6.00
____Paperback 1st edition: 1976 [BKN23] 35.00
____Paperback classic edition [BKN24] 6.00
____Paperback medallion art cover [3:134]..................6.00
____Paperback special edition art cover 6.00

The Exploits of Han Solo.
____Paperback boxed set [3:135] 24.00

Ballentine

____Dark Lord: The Rise of Darth Vader, hardcover 25.00
____Dark Nest I: The Joiner King [BKN25] 8.00
____Dark Nest II: The Unseen Queen [BKN26] 8.00
____Dark Nest III: The Swarm War [BKN27] 8.00
____Star Wars Trilogy with introduction by George Lucas, paperback 20.00
____Star Wars Trilogy, 25th Anniversary Collectors Edition, hardcover 35.00

Bantam Books

____Ambush at Corellia [3:135] 7.00
____Ambush at Corellia, signed 34.00
____Assault on Selonia [3:135] 7.00
____Before the Storm [3:135] 8.00
____Black Fleet Crisis Trilogy, hardcover compilation..21.00
____Bounty Hunter Wars: 01 Mandalorian Armor [BKN28]..7.00
____Bounty Hunter Wars: 02 Slave Ship [BKN29]..7.00
____Bounty Hunter Wars: 03 Hard Merchandise [BKN30]..7.00

____Champions of the Force [3:135].............................6.00
____Children of the Jedi, hardcover [3:135] 25.00
____Children of the Jedi, hardcover, book club edition 12.00
____Children of the Jedi, paperback 6.00
____Corellian Trilogy, hardcover compilation [3:135]..16.00
____Corellian Trilogy, paperback boxed set 24.00
____Courtship of Princess Leia, hardcover................25.00
____Courtship of Princess Leia, hardcover, book club edition 10.00
____Courtship of Princess Leia, paperback [BKN31]..6.00
____Crystal Star, hardcover...25.00
____Crystal Star, hardcover, book club edition..........10.00
____Crystal Star, paperback [BKN32] 6.00
____Dark Apprentice [3:135] 6.00
____Dark Force Rising, hardcover 24.00
____Dark Force Rising, paperback [3:135] 8.00
____Dark Force Rising, signed and numbered, hardcover with slipcover..175.00
____Darksaber, hardcover..20.00
____Darksaber, hardcover, book club edition 12.00
____Darksaber, paperback [3:135] 5.00
____Heir to the Empire, hardcover 25.00
____Heir to the Empire, paperback [3:135] 8.00
____Heir to the Empire, signed and numbered, hardcover with slipcover..175.00
____Hutt Gambit [3:135] 7.00
____I, Jedi, hardcover 25.00
____I, Jedi, paperback [BKN33]....................................7.00
____Jedi Academy Trilogy, hardcover compilation ...14.00
____Jedi Acadamy Trilogy, paperback boxed set......20.00
____Jedi Search [3:135] 6.00
____Last Command, hardcover 24.00
____Last Command, paperback [BKN34] 8.00
____Last Command, signed and numbered, hardcover with slipcover..175.00
____New Rebellion, hardcover 22.00
____New Rebellion, hardcover, book club edition 12.00
____New Rebellion, paperback [BKN35].......................6.00
____Paradise Snare [3:135] 8.00
____Planet of Twilight, hardcover book club edition 10.00
____Planet of Twilight, hardcover [BKN36] 20.00
____Planet of Twilight, paperback 4.00
____Rebel Dawn [3:135] 7.00
____Shadows of the Empire, hardcover 23.00
____Shadows of the Empire, hardcover, book club edition 15.00
____Shadows of the Empire, paperback [BKN37] 17.00

BKN01 BKN02 BKN03 BKN04 BKN05 BKN06 BKN07 BKN08 BKN09

BKN10 BKN11 BKN12 BKN13 BKN14 BKN15 BKN16 BKN17 BKN18

BKN19 BKN20 BKN21 BKN22 BKN23 BKN24 BKN25 BKN26 BKN27

Books: Novels

BKN28 BKN29 BKN30 BKN31 BKN32 BKN33 BKN34 BKN35 BKN36

BKN37 BKN38 BKN39 BKN40 BKN41 BKN42 BKN43 BKN44 BKN45

BKN46 BKN47 BKN48 BKN49 BKN50 BKN51 BKN52 BKN53 BKN54

____Shield of Lies [3:135] 8.00
____Showdown at Centerpoint [3:136] 7.00
____Specter of the Past, hardcover 28.00
____Specter of the Past, paperback [3:136] 9.00
____Star Wars: Episode I TPM, hardcover, Anakin Skywalker cover [3:136] 25.00
____Star Wars: Episode I TPM, hardcover, Darth Maul cover [3:136] 25.00
____Star Wars: Episode I TPM, hardcover, Obi-Wan Kenobi cover [3:136] 25.00
____Star Wars: Episode I TPM, hardcover, Queen Amidala cover [3:136] 25.00
____Tales from Jabba's Palace [BKN38] 8.00
____Tales from Mos Eisley Cantina [BKN39] 8.00
____Tales from the Empire [BKN40] 9.00
____Tales from the New Republic [BKN41] 6.00
____Tales of the Bounty Hunters [BKN42] 8.00
____Thrawn Trilogy, paperback boxed set 32.00
____Truce at Bakura, hardcover 25.00
____Truce at Bakura, hardcover, book club edition ..10.00
____Truce at Bakura, paperback [3:136] 6.00
____Tyrant's Test [3:136] 8.00
____Vision of the Future, hardcover 28.00
____Vision of the Future, paperback [3:136] 9.00

X-Wing: Rogue Squadron.
____1 Rogue Squadron [3:135] 6.00
____2 Wedge's Gamble [3:135] 6.00
____3 The Krytos Trap [3:135] 6.00
____4 The Bacta War [3:135] 6.00
____5 Wraith Squadron [3:135] 8.00
____6 Iron Fist [3:135] 7.00
____7 Solo Command [3:135] 8.00
____8 Isard's Revenge [3:135] 7.00
____9 Starfighters of Adumar [3:135] 7.00

Bantam Books, Brazil
____Ala-X 6.00
____Amanecer Rebelde 6.00
____La Maniobra Hutt 6.00

Blanvalet
____Episode I, hardcover [3:136] 24.00
____Episode I, paperback [3:136] 12.00

Cimino
____The SW Diaries, 84-page paperback with CD-ROM..25.00

Del Rey
____Allegiance, hardcover.........................25.00

____Cloak of Deception, hardcover [3:136] 26.00
____Cloak of Deception, paperback 7.00
____Coruscant Nights: Jedi Twilight 8.00
____Dark Lord: The Rise of Darth Vader, paperback [BKN43] 8.00
____Darth Plagueis, hardcover 26.00
____Darth Maul: Shadow Hunter, paperback [BKN44] 7.00
____Darth Maul: Shadow Hunter, hardcover 26.00
____Episode I: The Phantom Menace autographed, ltd to 5,000. Red foil Darth Maul on book, slipcase 65.00
____Episode II authgraphed, limited to 500, Suncoast exclusive [3:136] 130.00
____Episode II: Attack of the Clones, hardcover 1st art [BKN45] 25.00
____Episode II: Attack of the Clones, hardcover 2nd art 20.00
____Episode II: Attack of the Clones, paperback [BKN46] 7.00
____Episode II autographed, limited edition, silver foil Vader on slipcase 140.00
____Episode III: Revenge of the Sith, hardcover 25.00
____Episode III: Revenge of the Sith, paperback 8.00
____Jedi Trail 25.00
____Labyrinth of Evil, hardback 25.00
____Labyrinth of Evil, paperback..............................8.00
____Medstar I: Battle Surgeons 7.00
____Medstar II: Jedi Healer 7.00
____Outbound Flight, hardcover 25.00
____Outbound Flight, paperback [BKN47] 8.00
____Path of Destruction, Darth Bane, hardcover [BKN48] 25.00
____Republic Commando: Hard Contact 8.00
____Republic Commando: Triple Zero [BKN49] 8.00
____Shatterpoint, hardcover 26.00
____SW: Episode I TPM, paperback [BKN50]..............6.00
____Survivor's Quest 7.00
____Survivor's Quest, hardcover 26.00
____Survivor's Quest [BKN51] 25.00
____Tatooine Ghost, hardcover...............................26.00
____Tatooine Ghost, paperback [BKN52] 8.00
____The Approaching Storm, hardcover [3:137]........26.00

Clone Wars novels.
____Yoda, Dark Rendezvous 8.00
____Yoda: Dark Rendezvous, hardcover 25.00

Legacy of the Force.
____1 Betrayal, hardcover [BKN53] 25.00
____2 Bloodlines, paperback......................................8.00
____3 Tempest, paperback 8.00
____4 Exile, paperback 8.00

New Jedi Order.
____01 Vector Prime, hardcover 22.00
____01 Vector Prime, paperback [BKN54] 8.00
____02 Dark Tide I: Onslaught [BKN55]....................8.00
____03 Dark Tide II: Ruin [BKN56].............................8.00
____04 Agents of Chaos I: Hero's Trial [BKN57] 8.00
____05 Agents of Chaos 2: Jedi Eclipse [BKN58].......8.00
____06 Balance Point, hardcover 24.00
____06 Balance Point, paperback [BKN59]...................7.00
____07 Edge of Victory I: Conquest [BKN60] 8.00
____08 Edge of Victory II: Rebirth [BKN61].................8.00
____09 Star by Star, hardcover (misprinted timeline, page 1) 28.00
____09 Star by Star, hardcover book club edition 10.00
____09 Star by Star, hardcover [BKN62]...................26.00
____09 Star by Star, paperback................................7.00
____10 Dark Journey, paperback [BKN63] 7.00
____11 Enemy Lines I: Rebel Dream, paperback [BKN64] 7.00
____12 Enemy Lines II: Rebel Stand, paperback [BKN65] 7.00
____13 Traitor, paperback [BKN66] 7.00
____14 Destiny's Way, hardcover [BKN67] 26.00
____14 Destiny's Way, paperback 7.00
____15 Force Heretic I: Remnant [BKN68] 7.00
____16 Force Heretic II: Refugee, paperback 7.00
____17 Force Heretic III: Reunion, paperback...............7.00
____18 The Final Prophecy [BKN69] 7.00
____19 The Unifying Force, hardcover [BKN70] ...35.00
____19 The Unifying Force, paperback.......................7.00

Editora Record
Brazil releases.
____Guerra nas Estrelas (SW) 15.00
____O Imperio Contra-Ataca (ESB)..........................15.00
____O Retorno de Jedi (ROTJ) 15.00

Europa-America
Portugal releases.
____A Guerra das Estrelas, paperback (SW) 14.00
____A Ressureicao Da Force Negra [3:137] 10.00
____O Imperio Contra-Ataca, paperback (ESB) 14.00
____O Imperio Contra-Ataca, softcover (ESB) 18.00
____O Regresso de Jedi, paperback (ROTJ) 14.00
____O Regresso de Jedi, softcover (ROTJ) 18.00
____Treguas Em Bakura [3:137] 10.00

FF
____Star Wars: A New Hope [3:137] 16.00
____Star Wars: Empire Strikes Back [3:137].............16.00
____Star Wars: Return of the Jedi...........................16.00

Fleu Ve Noir
____Le defi du tyran [3:137]............................8.00
____Un piege nomme Krytos [3:137]..........................8.00

Fredholis Forlag
Norway release.
____Evighetens oye (Splinter of the Mind's Eye) 20.00
____Imperiet slar tilbake, paperback (ESB) 15.00
____Jedi Ridderen Vender Tilbake, paperback (ROTJ)..15.00
____Stjerne Krigen, paperback (SW)........................15.00

Futura
____Return of the Jedi 8.00
____Return of the Jedi, junior edition, paperback........8.00

G.K. Hall and Co.
____Specter of the Past, large print [3:137] 26.00

Guild America Books
____Star Wars Tales hardcover 6.00

Guild America
Hardcover story re-release.
____Enemy Lines [3:137].......................................30.00
____The Corellian Trilogy [3:137]...............................30.00

Heyne
____Der Hinterhalt [3:137] 6.00
____Der Pakt von Bakura [3:137]...............................6.00
____Palpatines Auge [3:137] 6.00
____Schatten Der Vergangenheit [3:137]......................6.00
____Showdown auf Centerpoint [3:137] 6.00

Kozmosz Konyvek
Hungary releases.
____A Birodalom visszavag (ESB)............................15.00
____A Jedi visszater (ROTJ) 15.00
____Csillagok haboruja (SW)...................................17.00

Lucasbook
Japan releases.
____Cloak of Deception [3:137]...............................12.00
____Shadow Hunter [3:137] 12.00
____The Approaching Storm [3:137]..........................12.00
____Truce at Bakura [3:137] 12.00

MacDonald Film Tie-In
____Return of the Jedi, hardcover 12.00

Martinez Roca
____El Courtejo de la Princesa Leia [3:137] 6.00
____Estrella de Cristal [3:137] 6.00
____La Nueva Rebelion [3:137] 6.00
____La Tregua de Bakura [3:137]...............................6.00
____Los Hijos de los Jedi [3:137] 6.00
____Sombras del Imperio [3:137] 6.00

Triloga de Academia Jedi.
____1 ....6.00
____2 El Dicipulo de la Fuerza Oscura [3:137] 6.00
____3 Campeones de la Fuerza [3:137] 6.00

Triloga de Corellia.
____1 ....6.00

____2 ....6.00
____3 Ajuste de Cuentas en Centralia [3:137]..............6.00

Trilogia de la Flota Negra.
____1 ....6.00
____2 Escudo de Mentiras [3:137]..............................6.00
____3 La Prueba del Tirano [3:137] 6.00

Minotaur
Yugoslavia releases.
____Zvezdani Ratovi (SW) 26.00

MsfX
____Aanval op Selonia [3:137] 6.00
____De droom van de Jedi [3:137] 6.00
____De Jedi Academe 6.00
____De Macht van de Duistere Kant [3:138] 6.00
____Het Laatste Bevel [3:138] 6.00
____Hinderlaag op Corellia [3:138] 6.00
____Wapenstilstand bij Bakura 6.00

Pocket
____Assaut sur Solonia [3:138] 6.00
____Bras de fer sur Cernterpoint [3:138].....................6.00
____Traquenard sur Corellia [3:138] 6.00

Random House
____Labrynth of Evil, hardcover [BKN71] 20.00
____Rogue Planet, hardcover [3:138] 26.00
____Shatterpoint, paperback [BKN72] 6.00
____Star Wars Trilogy, compilation[3:138] 8.00
____The Cetus Deception, hardcover [BKN73] 20.00

Clone Wars novels.
____Jedi Trial [BKN74] 8.00

Star Wars Galaxies.
____The Ruins of Dantooine [3:138] 8.00

Roman Presses de la Citie
____L'Etoile De Cristal [3:138] 6.00
____La Nouvelle Rebellion [3:138] 6.00
____Le Sabre Noir [3:138] 6.00

Scholastic
____Jedi Quest – Path to Truth [3:138] 13.00
____Legacy of the Jedi [3:138] 7.00
____Secrets of the Jedi 7.00
____The Phantom Menace Collector's Edition, foil slipcase [3:138]...12.00

Science Fiction Book Club
____Bounty Hunter Wars (Mandalorian Armor / Slave Ship / Hard Merchandise), hardcover 1999 ....9.00
____Han Solo Trilogy (The Paradise Snare / The Hutt Gambit / Rebel Dawn), hardcover 1998...............7.00
____Republic Commando: Hard Contact and Triple Zero [BKN75]..50.00

New Jedi Order.
____02/03 Dark Tide (Onslaught / Ruin), hardcover 7.00
____04/05 Agents of Chaos (Hero's Trial / Jedi Eclipse), hardcover 7.00
____07/08 Edge of Victory (Conquest / Rebirth), hardcover 7.00

____10 Dark Journey, hardcover 7.00
____11/12 Enemy Lines (Rebel Dream / Rebel Stand), hardcover10 Dark Journey, hardcover 7.00
____13 Traitor, hardcover 7.00
____15/16/17 Force Heretic (Remnant / Refugee / Reunion), hardcover 7.00
____18 The Final Prophecy, hardcover 7.00

Sony Library
Japan releases, New Jedi Order.
____(Force Heretic I: Remnant) [3:138] 16.00
____(Force Heretic I: Remnant)b [3:138] 16.00
____(Force Heretic II: Refugee) [3:138] 16.00
____(Force Heretic II: Refugee)b [3:138] 16.00
____(Force Heretic III: Reunion)...............................16.00
____(Force Heretic III: Reunion)b.............................16.00
____1 (Vector Prime) [3:138] 16.00
____1 (Vector Prime)b [3:138] 16.00
____2 (Dark Tide I: Onslaught) [3:138] 16.00
____2 (Dark Tide I: Onslaught)b [3:138] 16.00
____3 (Dark Tide II: Ruin) [3:138]............................16.00
____3 (Dark Tide II: Ruin)b [3:138] 16.00
____4 (Agents of Chaos 1: Hero's Trial) [3:138] 16.00
____4 (Agents of Chaos 1: Hero's Trial)b [3:138] 16.00
____5 (Agents of Chaos 2: Jedi Eclipse) [3:138].........16.00
____5 (Agents of Chaos 2: Jedi Eclipse)b [3:138]. ...16.00
____6 (Balance Point) 16.00
____7 (Edge of Victory I: Conquest) [3:138] 16.00
____8 (Edge of Victory II: Rebirth) 16.00
____9 (Star by Star) 16.00
____10 (Dark Journey) 16.00
____11 (Enemy Lines I: Rebel Dream).......................16.00
____12 (Enemy Lines II: Rebel Stand) 16.00
____13 (Traitor)...16.00
____14 (Destiny's Way) 16.00
____15 (Force Heretic I: Remnant) 16.00
____16 (Force Heretic II: Refugee) 16.00
____17 (Force Heretic III: Reunion) 16.00
____18 (The Final Prophecy) 16.00
____19 (The Unifying Force) 16.00

Japan releases.
____(Spectre of the Past) [3:138] 16.00
____(Spectre of the Past)b [3:138] 16.00
____(Vision of the Future) [3:138] 16.00
____(Vision of the Future)b [3:138] 16.00

Sperling and Kupfer
____L'Erede Dell'Impero [3:138]..............................6.00
____L'Ultima Missione [3:138] 6.00

BKN55 BKN56 BKN57

BKN58 BKN59 BKN60 BKN61 BKN62 BKN63 BKN64 BKN65 BKN66

BKN67 BKN68 BKN69 BKN70 BKN71 BKN72 BKN73 BKN74 BKN75

Books: Novels

 BKO01
 BKO02
 BKO03
 BKO04
 BKO05
 BKO06
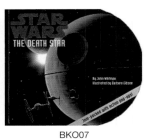 BKO07

 BKO08
 BKO09
 BKO10
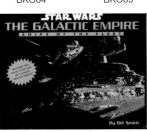 BKO11
 BKO12
 BKO13

____La Stella Di Cristallo [3:138] 6.00
____La Trilogia Classica [3:138] 6.00

Sphere
____Empire Strikes Back, paperback 8.00
____Han Solo at Stars' End [3:138] 7.00
____Splinter of the Mind's Eye [3:139] 7.00
____Star Wars, paperback Greatest Film of the
Century 8.00
____Star Wars, paperback Spectacular Motion
Picture [3:139] 8.00

Tidena Forlag
Sweden releases.
____Stjarnornas Krig, paperback (SW) 20.00

VGS
____Der Kristallstern [3:139] 6.00

Wilhelm Goldmann
German releases.
____Das Imperium schlagt zuruck, paperback
(ESB) 8.00
____Das Imperium schlagt zuruck, paperback 2nd cover
(ESB) [3:139]..................................14.00
____Das Imperium schlagt zuruck, paperback 2nd cover
revised (ESB) 18.00
____Die neuen Abenteuer des Luke Skywalker, paperback
(Splinter of the Mind's Eye) 10.00
____Die Ruckkehr der Jedi-Ritter, paperback
(ROTJ) [3:139] 8.00
____Die Star Wars Saga [3:139] 10.00
____Han Solo auf Stars' End, paperback 10.00
____Han Solo und das verlorene Vermachtnis, paperback
(Han Solo and the Lost Legacy) 10.00

 BKO14
 BKO15

____Han Solos Abenteuer 10.00
____Han Solos Rache, paperback (Han Solo's
Revenge)..10.00
____Krieg der Sterne (Star Wars) [3:139].............8.00
____Lando Calrissian Rebell Des Sonnensystems 10.00
____Palast der Dunklen Sonnen 10.00
____Sturm Uber Tatooine 10.00

WSOY
____Jedin Etsinta [3:139] 6.00
____Keisarin Kasky [3:139] 6.00

Books: Pop-Up / Action / Flap

Bandai
Japan releases.
____Star Wars [BKO01] 45.00

Collins
____Star Wars Pop-Up 18.00

Dark Horse Comics
____Battle of the Bounty Hunters [BKO02]...........26.00

Editorial Roma
Spain releases.
____Droids, Capturados 18.00
____Droids, La Desaparacion de C-3PO [BKO03].....18.00
____Droids, Las Adventuras de Mungo Babab
[BKO04] 18.00
____Droids, Trigon [BKO05].......................18.00
____Ewoks, Amenaza sobre la Aldea 18.00
____Ewoks, Asha 18.00
____Ewoks, Fuego en el Bosque 18.00
____Ewoks, Latara................................18.00

Flammarion
France releases.
____La Guerre des Etoilles (SW) 18.00

Fun Works
Shiny, shimmer books.
____Heroes in Hiding 6.00
____Star Wars, shimmer [BKO06] 8.00

Flip books. Classic trilogy mini-series.
____Empire Strikes Back [2:111] 4.00
____Return of the Jedi [2:111] 4.00
____Star Wars [2:111] 4.00

Little, Brown
Pop-Up books.
____Death Star [BKO07] 15.00
____Jabba's Palace [BKO08] 20.00
____Millennium Falcon [BKO09] 18.00
____Mos Eisley Cantina [BKO10] 20.00

Ships of the Fleet series.
____Galactic Empire [BKO11] 12.00
____Rebel Alliance [BKO12] 12.00

Random House
____Anakin Skywalker [BKO13] 8.00
____EPI Great Big Flap Book [BKO14] 14.00
____Han Solo's Rescue, hardcover 8.00
____Han Solo's Rescue, softcover 14.00
____Jar Jar Binks [BKO15] 8.00
____Return of the Jedi Pop-Up, shuttle Tydirium cover
[3:139]...18.00
____Return of the Jedi Pop-Up, star destroyer cover
[BKO16]...18.00
____Star Wars Lift the Flap [BKO17]...............12.00
____Star Wars Pop-Up [BKO18] 16.00
____The Empire Strikes Back Panorama [BKO19] ...23.00
____The Empire Strikes Back Pop-Up [BKO20] 16.00
____The Ewoks Save The Day, hardcover [BKO21] 8.00
____The Ewoks Save The Day, softcover 12.00

Sperling and Kupfer
Italy releases.
____Guerre Stellari (SW) 15.00

Books: Poster

Scholastic
Pull-out poster books.
____Star Wars [2:112] 6.00
____Empire Strikes Back [2:112] 6.00
____Return of the Jedi [2:112] 6.00

Books: Science Adventures

Scholastic
____Emergency in Escape Pod Four (pages 45 – 46 miss-
ing, pages 55 – 56 appear twice) 7.00
____Emergency in Escape Pod Four [2:112]........5.00
____Journey Across Planet-X [2:112] 5.00

 BKO16
 BKO17
 BKO18
 BKO19
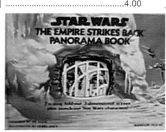 BKO20
 BKO21

Books: Scripts

Japan release screenplays.
____Episode I, Illustrated..........35.00
____Star Wars..........26.00
____Empire Strikes Back..........26.00
____Return of the Jedi..........26.00

Ballantine
National Public Radio Dramatizations.
____Star Wars..........12.00
____Empire Strikes Back [BKR01]..........12.00
____Return of the Jedi [BKR02]..........12.00

____Annotated Scripts [BKR03]..........25.00
____ESB Notebook, illustrated script [BKR04]..........29.00

D.S.P. Publishing, Inc.
____SW Trilogy Original Movie Scripts Collector's Edition [BKR05]..........40.00

Del Rey
Complete Script with Special Edition Scenes.
____Star Wars [BKR10]..........22.00
____Empire Strikes Back [BKR07]..........22.00
____Return of the Jedi [BKR09]..........22.00

Illustrated Screenplays.
____Star Wars [BKR11]..........14.00
____Empire Strikes Back [BKR06]..........14.00
____Return of the Jedi [BKR08]..........14.00

Lucas Books
____Episode I: The Phantom Menace [BKR12]..........12.00
____Episode I: The Phantom Menace, the Illustrated Screenplay [BKR13]..........16.00

Lucasbook
Japan releases.
____Episode I: The Phantom Menace, the Illustrated Screenplay [BKR14]..........12.00

Premiere
____Star Wars..........15.00
____Star Wars Trilogy, boxed set..........50.00
____Empire Strikes Back..........15.00
____Empire Strikes Back, recalled for typographical errors..........75.00
____Return of the Jedi..........15.00
____Return of the Jedi, recalled for typographical errors..........75.00

Virgin Books, UK
Complete illustrated scripts.
____A New Hope..........20.00
____Empire Strikes Back [BKR15]..........20.00
____Return of the Jedi..........20.00

Books: Star Wars Adventures

Scholastic
Episode I: The Phantom Menace.
____#01 Search for the Lost Jedi game book..........3.00
____#01 Search for the Lost Jedi..........4.00
____#02 The Bartokk Assassins game book..........3.00
____#02 The Bartokk Assassins..........4.00
____#03 The Fury of Darth Maul game book..........3.00
____#03 The Fury of Darth Maul..........4.00
____#04 Jedi Emergency game book..........3.00
____#04 Jedi Emergency..........4.00
____#05 The Ghostling Children game book..........3.00
____#05 The Ghostling Children..........4.00
____#06 Hunt for Anakin Skywalker game book..........3.00
____#06 Hunt for Anakin Skywalker..........4.00
____#07 Capture Arawynne game book..........3.00
____#07 Capture Arawynne..........4.00
____#08 Trouble on Tatooine game book..........3.00
____#08 Trouble on Tatooine..........4.00
____#09 Rescue in the Core game book..........3.00
____#09 Rescue in the Core..........4.00
____#10 The Festival of Warriors game book..........3.00
____#10 The Festival of Warriors..........4.00
____#11 Pirates From Beyond the Sea game book..........3.00
____#11 Pirates From Beyond the Sea..........4.00
____#12 The Bongo Rally game book..........3.00
____#12 The Bongo Rally..........4.00
____#13 Danger on Naboo game book..........3.00
____#13 Danger on Naboo..........4.00
____#14 Podrace to Freedom game book..........3.00
____#14 Podrace to Freedom..........4.00
____#15 The Final Battle game book..........3.00
____#15 The Final Battle..........4.00

Episode II: Attack of the Clones.
____#01 Hunt the Sunrunner game book..........3.00
____#01 Hunt the Sunrunner..........4.00
____#02 Cavern of Screaming Skulls game book..........3.00
____#02 Cavern of Screaming Skulls..........4.00
____#03 The Hostage Princess game book..........3.00
____#03 The Hostage Princess..........4.00
____#04 Jango Fett vs. Razor Eaters game book..........3.00
____#04 Jango Fett vs. Razor Eaters..........4.00
____#05 The Shape-Shifter Strikes game book..........3.00
____#05 The Shape-Shifter Strikes..........3.00
____#06 The Warlords of Balmorra game book..........3.00
____#06 The Warlords of Balmorra..........3.00
____#07 The Ghostling Children game book..........2.00
____#07 The Ghostling Children..........2.00
____#08 Hunt for Anakin Skywalker game book..........2.00
____#08 Hunt for Anakin Skywalker..........2.00
____#09 Capture Arawynne game book..........2.00
____#09 Capture Arawynne..........2.00
____#10 Trouble on Tatooine game book..........2.00
____#10 Trouble on Tatooine..........2.00
____#11 Danger on Naboo game book..........2.00
____#11 Danger on Naboo..........2.00
____#12 Podrace to Freedom game book..........2.00
____#12 Podrace to Freedom..........2.00
____#13 The Final Battle game book..........2.00
____#13 The Final Battle..........2.00

Books: Story

____Beyond the Stars, Tales of Adventure in Time and Space..........7.00
____Crossfire [3:140]..........6.00
____Ewoks Annual [3:140]..........16.00
____The Maverick Moon, UK cover [3:140]..........12.00

Droids series, U.K.
____#1 The White Witch [BKS01]..........15.00
____#2 Escape into Terror [BKS02]..........15.00
____#3 The Trigon Unleashed [BKS03]..........15.00

Ewoks series, U.K.
____#1..........15.00
____#2..........15.00
____#3 Sun Star Against Shadow Stone [BKS04]..........15.00

Japan
____ESB photo storybook..........35.00

20th Century Fox
____Caravan of Courage [BKS05]..........32.00

Ballantine
____Star Wars Album..........32.00
____Star Wars Storybook, hardcover..........12.00

Brown Watson
____Annual No. 1 hardcover..........5.00

Chronicle Books
____Attack of the Clones, mini hardcover..........8.00
____Empire Strikes Back, mini hardcover [1:78]..........8.00
____Return of the Jedi, mini hardcover [1:78]..........8.00
____Star Wars, mini hardcover [1:78]..........8.00
____The Phantom Menace, mini hardcover [1:78]..........8.00
____The Queen's Amulet [BKS06]..........14.00

Collins
____Star Wars Storybook, with dust jacket..........27.00

Fernandez Editores
____El Imperio Contraataca [3:140]..........7.00
____El Regreso Del Jedi [3:140]..........7.00
____Una Nueva Esperanza [3:140]..........7.00

Fun Works
Toy bound into book's spine.
____Darth Vader's Mission: The Search for the Secret Plans [3:140]..........8.00
____Han Solo's Rescue Mission [3:140]..........8.00
____Luke Skywalker's Race Against Time [3:140]..........8.00
____R2-D2's Mission: A Little Heroes Journey [3:140]..........8.00

Futura
____Return of the Jedi, "Special Junior Edition" [3:140]..........14.00

Golden Books
____A Droid's Tale soundstory [3:140]..........24.00
____A New Hope (with tattoos) [BKS07]..........5.00
____A New Hope [BKS08]..........5.00
____Adventure in Beggar's Canyon [3:140]..........5.00
____Empire Strikes Back [3:141]..........5.00
____Empire Strikes Back (with tattoos) [3:141]..........5.00
____Escape from Jabba's Palace [3:141]..........5.00
____Journey to Mos Eisley [3:141]..........5.00
____Meltdown on Hoth [BKS09]..........5.00
____Pilots and Spacecraft (glow in the dark pages) [BKS10]..........5.00
____Rebel Heroes and Galactic Villains [BKS11]..........7.00
____Return of the Jedi..........5.00

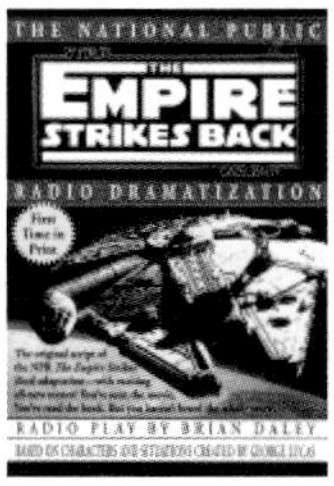

BKR01

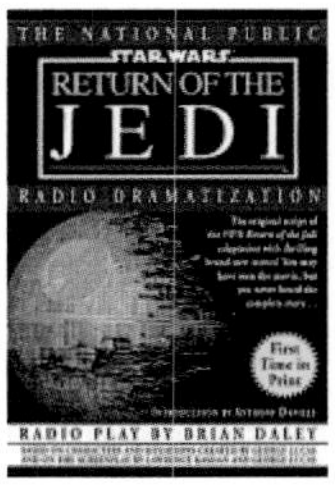

BKR02

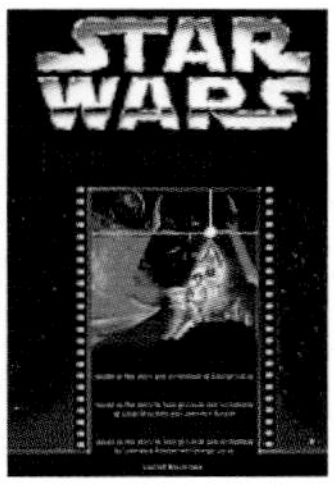

BKR03

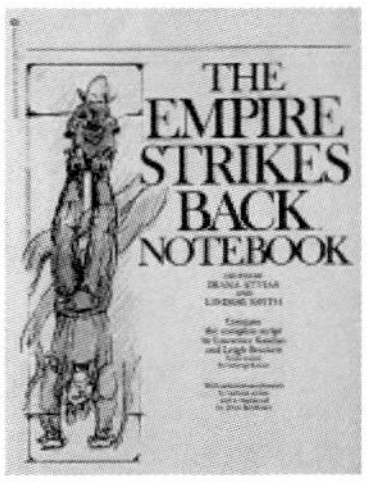

BKR04

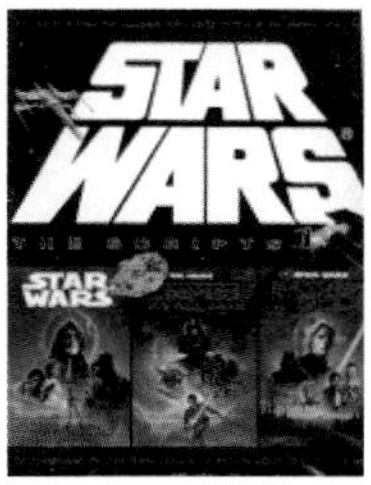

BKR05

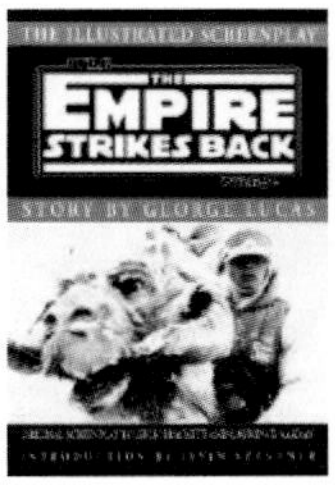

BKR06

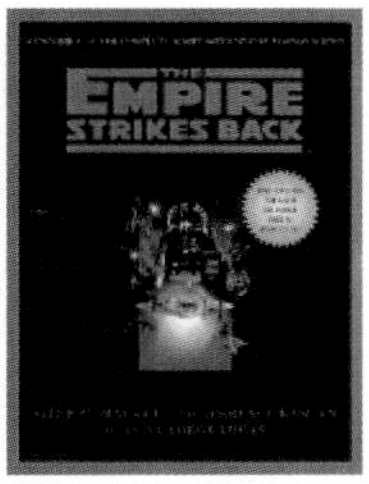

BKR07

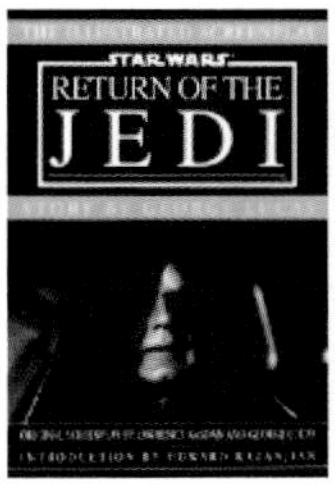

BKR08

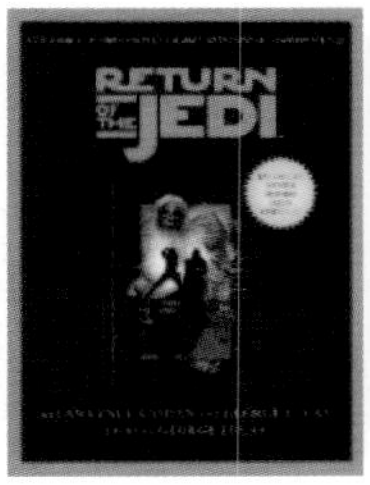

BKR09

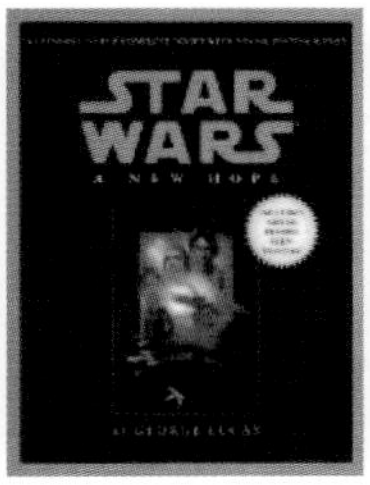

BKR10

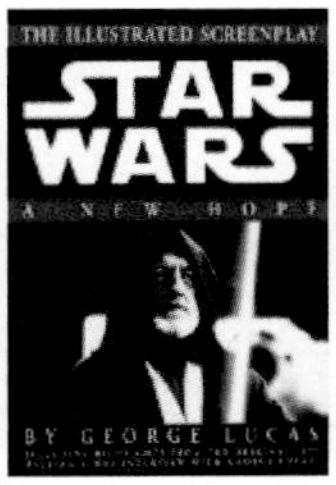

BKR11

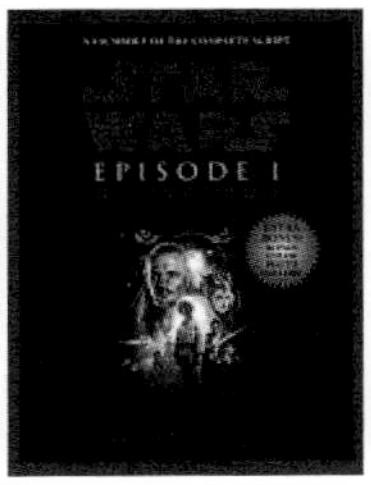

BKR12

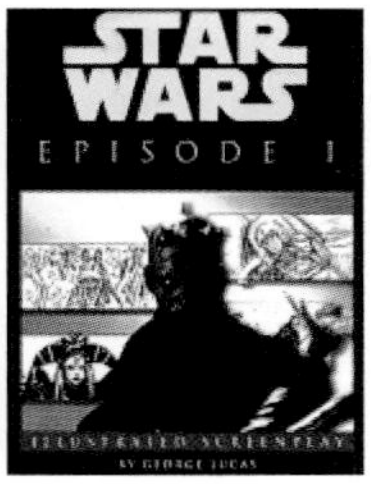

BKR13

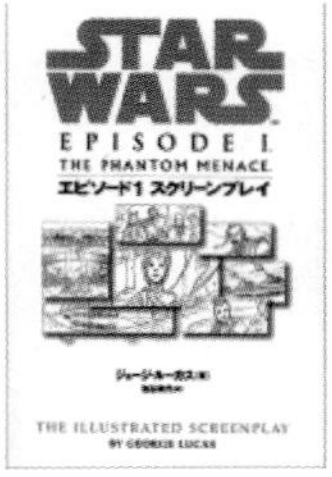

BKR14

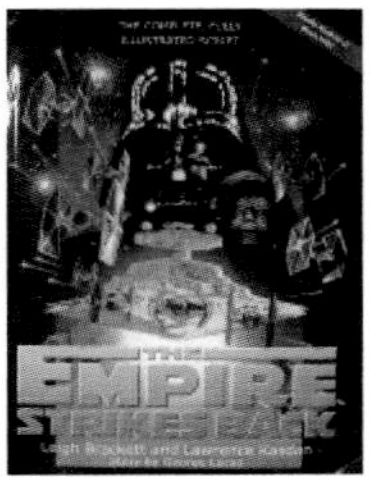

BKR15

Books: Story

BKS01

BKS02

BKS03

BKS04

BKS05

BKS06

BKS07

BKS08

BKS09

BKS10

BKS11

BKS12

BKS13

____Return of the Jedi (with tattoos) [3:141] 5.00
____SW: The Greatest Battles, includes 3D glasses [BKS12] 6.00
____The Hoth Adventure [BKS13] 5.00

Keibunsha
____Return of the Jedi picture book with dust jacket 24.00

Marvel Books
____Return of the Jedi Storybook [3:141]...............10.00
____Star Wars, Four New Adventures [BKS14] 14.00
____World of Fire, Star Wars 2 [1:78] 12.00

Phidal
____Anakin a la conquete de la liberte [3:141] 5.00
____Attention, Jar Jar [3:141] 5.00
____Je suis un droide [3:141] 5.00
____Je suis un Jedi [3:141] 5.00

Publications International
____Episode I play-a-sound [3:141] 14.00
____Episode I, R2-D2 play-a-sound 8.00
____Star Wars play-a-sound [3:141] 11.00

Random House
____Anakin: Apprentice [BKS15] 4.00
____Attack of the Clones Movie Storybook [BKS16]...............24.00
____Battle in the Arena [BKS17] 5.00
____Droid Dilemma 12.00
____Droids 10.00
____Empire Strikes Back Storybook, hardcover [3:141]...............12.00
____Empire Strikes Back, classic [3:141] 7.00

____EPI TPM Movie Storybook 8.00
____Escape from the Monster Ship [3:141] 16.00
____Fuzzy as an Ewok [BKS18] 10.00
____How the Ewoks Saved the Trees, hardcover [BKS19]...............15.00
____How the Ewoks Saved the Trees, softcover 8.00
____I am a Bounty Hunter [3:141] 5.00
____I am a Droid [3:141] 5.00
____I am a Jedi [3:141] 5.00
____I am a Jedi Apprentice [3:141] 4.00
____I am a Pilot [3:141] 5.00
____I am a Queen [3:141] 5.00
____Jango Fett: Bounty Hunter [3:141] 4.00
____Luke's Fate [BKS20] 5.00
____Luke's Fate, "Brand New" on cover [BKS21].......6.00
____Luke's Fate, brown cover [BKS22] 6.00
____Return of the Jedi Storybook, hardcover [3:141]...............12.00
____Revenge of the Sith movie storybook [BKS23]...............7.00
____School Days, Ewoks 12.00
____Shiny as a Droid [BKS24]...............10.00
____Skywalker Family Album [BKS25] 4.00
____Star Wars Storybook Trilogy 10 year anniversary [3:142]...............12.00
____Star Wars Storybook, hardcover 12.00
____The Adventures of R2-D2 and C-3PO...............12.00
____The Adventures of Teebo [BKS26]...............25.00
____The Baby Ewoks' Picnic Surprise [3:142] 4.00
____The Ewok Who Was Afraid [BKS27] 12.00
____The Ewoks' Hang-Gliding Adventure [3:142] 4.00
____The Ewoks and the Lost Children [BKS28] 12.00
____The Ewoks Join the Fight [BKS29]...............5.00
____The Lost Prince, hardcover 20.00
____The Lost Prince, softcover [BKS30]...............14.00

____The Maverick Moon [3:142] 4.00
____The Mystery of the Rebellious Robot [3:142].......4.00
____The Pirates of Tarnoonga [3:142] 20.00
____The Red Ghost [BKS31]...............6.00
____The Ring, Witch, and the Crystal [BKS32] 6.00
____The Shadow Stone [BKS33]...............8.00
____The White Witch — A Droid Adventure [BKS34]...............14.00
____The Wookiee Storybook [BKS35]...............12.00
____Three Cheers for Kneesaa [BKS36] 6.00
____Wicket and the Dandelion Warriors [BKS37] 8.00
____Wicket Finds a Way [BKS38] 4.00
____Wicket Goes Fishing [BKS39]...............8.00

Step-Up Movie Adventures 1995.
____Star Wars 5.00
____The Empire Strikes Back 5.00
____Return of the Jedi 5.00

Step-Up Movie Adventures 2004.
____Return of the Jedi [BKS40] 8.00
____Star Wars [BKS41] 8.00
____The Empire Strikes Back [BKS42] 8.00

Step-Up Movie Adventures.
____Star Wars 10.00
____The Empire Strikes Back 12.00
____Return of the Jedi [3:142]...............12.00

Scholastic
____Episode I: The Phantom Menace 7.00
____Episode II: Attack of the Clones...............6.00

Journals.
____Anakin Skywalker [3:142] 5.00

BKS14

BKS15

BKS16

BKS17

BKS18

BKS19

BKS20

BKS21

BKS22

BKS23

BKS24

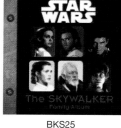
BKS25

BKS26

BKS27

BKS28

| BKS29 | BKS30 | BKS31 | BKS32 | BKS33 | BKS34 | BKS35 |

| BKS36 | BKS37 | BKS38 | BKS39 | BKS40 | BKS41 | BKS42 |

____Captive to Evil by Princess Leia [3:142] 5.00
____Darth Maul [3:142] 6.00
____Hero for Hire by Han Solo [3:142] 5.00
____Queen Amidala [3:142] 6.00
____The Fight for Justice by Luke Skywalker [3:142] 5.00

Star Wars Junior.
____Obi-Wan's Bongo Adventure [3:142] 2.00
____Podrace! [3:142] 2.00

Storybooks, hardcover Trilogy.
____A New Hope 8.00
____The Empire Strikes Back 8.00
____Return of the Jedi 8.00

Storybooks, hardcover.
____Star Wars [3:142] 8.00
____Empire Strikes Back [3:142] 8.00
____Return of the Jedi [3:142] 8.00

Storybooks, softcover.
____Star Wars Storybook [3:142] 5.00
____Empire Strikes Back [3:142] 8.00
____Return of the Jedi Storybook [3:142] 8.00
____Star Wars Treasury, all 3 in a slipcase 28.00

St. Michaels Press
____Return of the Jedi [3:142]..................................25.00

Books: Technical

Starlog
Star Wars Technical Journals.
____Compilation, hardcover 35.00
____Vol. 1: Tatooine..10.00
____Vol. 1: Tatooine, foil cover 15.00
____Vol. 1: Tatooine, special edition insert 12.00
____Vol. 2: Imperial Forces [1:80] 10.00
____Vol. 2: Imperial Forces, special edition insert. 12.00
____Vol. 3: Rebel Forces [1:80] 10.00
____Vol. 3: Rebel Forces, special edition insert 12.00

Books: Trivia

____From The Blob to Star Wars – The Science Fiction Movie Quiz Book [BKU01] 4.00

____Revenge of the Sith trivia quest [BKU02].............6.00

Ballantine
____425 Questions and Answers about Star Wars and Empire Strikes Back..18.00
____Diplomatic Corps Extrance Exam [BKU03] 12.00
____I'd Just as soon Kiss a Wookiee: The Quotable Star Wars [2:116] 4.00
____I'd Just as soon Kiss a Wookiee: The Quotable Star Wars, condensed 2.00
____The Jedi Master's Quizbook [BKU04] 8.00

Carol Publishing
____The Jedi Academy Entrance Exam: Tantalizing Trivia from the Star Wars Trilogy [2:116] 12.00

FunFax
Quiz Quest.
____Empire Strikes Back [BKU05]................................4.00
____Return of the Jedi [BKU06]..................................4.00
____Star Wars [BKU07] 4.00

Kensington
____Ultimate Unauthorized Star Wars Trilogy Challenge [BKU08] 12.00

Lucasbook
____Attack of the Clones Trivia Challenge [BKU09] 5.00

Summersdale Publishing
____The Unofficial Book of Star Wars Trivia [BKU10] 17.00

Books: Young Jedi Knights

Berkley
____1 Heirs to the Force [2:116] 7.00
____2 Shadow Acadamy [2:116] 7.00
____3 The Lost Ones [2:116] 7.00
____4 Lightsabers [2:116] 7.00
____5 Darkest Knight [2:116] 7.00
____6 Jedi Under Seige [2:116] 7.00
____7 Shards of Alderaan [2:116] 6.00
____8 Diversity Alliance [2:116] 6.00
____9 Delusions of Grandeur [2:116]..........................6.00
____10 Jedi Bounty [2:116] 6.00
____11 The Emperor's Plague [2:116] 6.00
____12 Return to Ord Mantell [2:116] 6.00
____13 Trouble on Cloud City [2:116] 6.00

____14 Crisis at Crystal Reef [2:116] 6.00
____Set of books 1-3, boxed 18.00

Books recompiled under combined names.
____Books 1 – 3, "Jedi Shadow" 8.00
____Books 4 – 6, "Jedi Sunrise" 8.00

Hardcover compilations.
____Books 1 – 6, Rise of the Shadow Academy 14.00
____Books 7 – 11, Fall of the Diversity Alliance 14.00
____Books 12 – 14, Under Black Sun.......................14.00

Omnibus Editions.
____Books 01 – 06 ....14.00
____Books 07 – 11 ....14.00
____Books 12 – 14 ....14.00

VGS
____Allianz der Vergessenen [2:116] 8.00
____Angriff auf Yavin [2:116] 8.00
____Gefangen auf Ryloth [2:116]................................8.00

Books: Young Reader

Bantam Books
#1 The Glove of Darth Vader.
____First edition 6.00
____Gold foil logo [3:143] 4.00
____Hard cover with library binding 16.00
#2 The Lost City of the Jedi.
____First Edition [3:143] 6.00
____Gold foil logo [3:143] 4.00
____Hard cover with library binding 16.00
#3 Zorba the Hutt's Revenge.
____First edition [3:143] 6.00
____Gold foil logo [3:143] 4.00
____Hard cover with library binding 16.00
#4 Mission from Mount Yoda.
____First Edition 6.00
____Gold foil logo [3:143] 4.00
____Hard cover with library binding 16.00
#5 Queen of the Empire.
____First edition [3:143] 8.00
____Gold foil logo. 4.00
____Hard cover with library binding 16.00
#6 Prophets of the Dark Side.
____First edition [3:143] 8.00
____Gold foil logo. 4.00
____Hard cover with library binding 16.00

         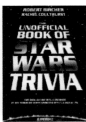

| BKU01 | BKU02 | BKU03 | BKU04 | BKU05 | BKU06 | BKU07 | BKU08 | BKU09 | BKU10 |

Books: Young Reader

BKY01

BKY02

BKY03

BKY04

BKY05

BKY06

BKY07

BKY08

BKY09

BKY10

BKY11

BKY12

BKY13

BKY14

BKY15

BKY16

BKY17

BKY18

BKY19

BKY20

BKY21

BKY22

BKY23

BKY24

BKY25

BKY26

____Books 1 – 3, boxed set 25.00

Barnes and Noble
____Books 1 – 3, hardcover compilation [3:143] 10.00
____Books 4 – 6, hardcover compilation [3:143] 10.00

Bullseye Books
____Star Wars: A New Hope [BKY01] 6.00
____Star Wars: Empire Strikes Back [BKY02] 6.00
____Star Wars: Return of the Jedi [BKY03]..................6.00

Cartwell Books
____Boba Fett: The Fight to Survive, hardcover........10.00

Del Rey
____Marvel Comics Illustrated Version of Star Wars....6.00

DK Publishing
____Galactic Crisis! 6.00
____Journey Through Space [BKY04]..........................4.00
____Obi-Wan's Foe [BKY05] 6.00
____Star Pilot 6.00
____What is a Wookiee? [BKY06] 4.00

Pocket Junior
____La reine de l'Empire [3:143] 7.00
____La vengeance de Zorba le Hutt [3:143] 7.00
____Le destin du Prince Jedi [3:143]...........................7.00
____Le Prophete Supreme du Cote Obscur [3:143] 7.00
____Le Prophete Supreme du Cote Obscur, non-text cover 5.00

Random House
____Anakin's Fate [BKY07] 5.00
____Anakin's Pit Droid [BKY08].....................................4.00
____Anakin's Race for Freedom [3:144] 4.00
____Anakin to the Rescue [BKY09]...............................5.00
____Dangers of the Core [BKY10].................................5.00
____Darth Maul's Revenge [BKY11] 5.00
____Jar Jar's Mistake [BKY12].......................................5.00
____Obi-Wan's Foe 6.00
____Queen in Disguise [BKY13] 5.00
____Watch Out Jar Jar! [3:144] 4.00

Classic Star Wars.
____A New Hope [3:144] 4.00
____Empire Strikes Back [3:144] 4.00
____Return of the Jedi [3:144].......................................4.00

Scholastic
____Boba Fett: Crossfire [BKY14]..............................10.00
____Legacy of the Jedi / Secrets of the Jedi [BKY15]..8.00
____Star Wars, young reader edition...........................4.00

Boba Fett / Clone Wars Novels.
____1 The Fight to Survive [BKY17] 6.00
____2 Crossfire [BKY18] 6.00
____3 Maze of Deception [BKY19] 6.00
____4 Hunted [BKY20]..6.00
____5 A New Threat [BKY21]...6.00
____6 Pursuit [BKY22] 6.00

Junior Novelizations.
____A New Hope 8.00
____Empire Strikes Back 8.00
____Return of the Jedi 8.00
____Revenge of the Sith [BKY16] 6.00
____Shadows of the Empire [3:143] 8.00

Star Wars Missions.
____1: Assault on Yavin Four [2:117]............................3.00
____2: Escape from Thyferra [2:117] 3.00
____3: Attack on Delrakkin [2:117] 3.00
____4: Destroy the Liquidator [2:117] 4.00
____5: The Hunt for Han Solo [2:117] 4.00
____6: The Search for Grubba the Hutt [2:117]............4.00
____7: Ithorian Invasion [2:117] 4.00
____8: Togorian Trap [2:117] 4.00
____9: Revolt of the Battle Droids [2:117] 4.00
____10: Showdown in Mos Eisley [2:117] 4.00
____11: Bounty Hunters vs. Battle Droids [2:117].........4.00
____12: The Vactooine Disaster [2:117].........................4.00
____13: Prisoner of the Nikto Pirates [2:117] 4.00
____14: The Monsters of Dweem [2:117] 4.00
____15: Voyage to the Underworld [2:117] 4.00
____16: Imperial Jailbreak [2:117] 4.00
____17: Darth Vader's Return [2:117] 4.00
____18: Rogue Squadron to the Rescue [2:117]..........4.00

The Last of the Jedi.
____1 The Desperate Mission [BKY23] 6.00
____2 Dark Warning [BKY24]..6.00
____3 Underworld [BKY25] 6.00
____4 Death on Naboo [BKY26] 6.00
____5 A Tangled Web...6.00
____6 Return of the Dark Side...6.00

Sphere
Young reader editions.
____Empire Strikes Back [3:144]................................17.00
____Star Wars [3:144] 23.00

Bottle Cap Accessories

Pepsi Cola, Japan
____A New Hope cap stage, holds 5 ....35.00
____Empire Strikes Back cap stage, holds 5 ....35.00
____Return of the Jedi cap stage, holds 5 ....35.00
____The Phantom Menace cap stage, holds 5..........35.00
____Vehicles and Starships cap stage, holds 5 ....35.00

Cap stages.
____EPI: Tatooine [3:145] 135.00
____EPII: Arena [3:145] 75.00
____EPIII: Death Star 150.00

Episode I concealment bags.
____3D hologram magnets 4.00
____Anakin Skywalker 3.00
____Artoo-Detoo 3.00
____Darth Maul 3.00
____Jar Jar Binks..3.00
____Obi-Wan Kenobi [2:118] 3.00
____Queen Amidala 3.00
____Yoda 3.00

Episode II concealment bags.
____Anakin Skywalker 3.00
____Barris Offee 3.00
____Boba Fett 3.00
____C-3PO...3.00
____Chancellor Palpatine...3.00
____Clone Trooper 3.00
____Count Dooku..3.00
____Kitt Fisto [2:118] 3.00
____Mace Windu 3.00
____Obi-Wan Kenobi 3.00
____Padme Amidala [2:118]...3.00
____R2-D2 ....3.00
____Shaak Ti [2:118] 3.00
____Super Battle Droid [2:118] 3.00
____Yoda [2:118] 3.00
____Zam Wesell 3.00

Episode III concealment bags.
____Anakin Skywalker (Jedi) 3.00
____Anakin Skywalker (Podracer) 3.00
____Battle Droid..3.00
____C-3PO...3.00
____Chewbacca...3.00
____Darth Vader 3.00
____Emperor Palpatine 3.00

_____General Grievous 3.00
_____Han Solo 3.00
_____Luke Skywalker......................................3.00
_____Padme Amidala.....................................3.00
_____Princess Leia 3.00
_____R2-D2 ....3.00
_____Stormtrooper 3.00
_____Yoda 3.00

Bottle Caps

China. Iced Tea pets. 6-packs in window boxes.
_____C-3PO, R2-D2, Chewbacca, Han Solo, Princess Leia,
Luke Skywalker [BTL01]............................35.00
_____Anakin Skywalker, Darth Maul, Darth Vader, Yoda, The
Emperor, Padme Amidala [BTL02].....................35.00

Coca-Cola, Canada
_Bottle caps featuring Star Wars characters, peel-off
game pieces underneath._
_____C-3PO, Coca-Cola [BTL03] 5.00
_____C-3PO, Coke [BTL04]......................................6.00
_____Star Cruiser [BTL05] 8.00

Coca-Cola, Japan
Random scenes under Coca-Cola, Fanta, Sprite caps.
_____C-3PO and R2-D2, tatooine [BTL06] 9.00
_____C-3PO, oil bath [3:145]...................................9.00
_____C-3PO, Tatooine [3:145] 9.00
_____Darth Vader, blockade runner [3:145]..................9.00
_____Detention block [3:145]...................................9.00
_____Escape Pod [3:145]..9.00
_____Han Solo, Death Star [3:145] 9.00
_____Han Solo, posed [3:145].................................9.00
_____Jawa [3:145] 9.00
_____Luke Skywalker [3:145] 9.00
_____Luke, landspeeder [3:145] 9.00
_____Millennium Falcon [3:145]................................9.00
_____Obi-Wan Kenobi, duel [3:145] 9.00
_____Obi-Wan Kenobi, tractor beam [BTL07]...............9.00
_____Princess Leia and C-3PO, Yavin [BTL08].............9.00
_____Princess Leia, regal [3:145]..............................9.00
_____Princess Leia, Yavin [3:145] 9.00
_____PRIZE [3:145]..25.00
_____Quad Turrets, destroying Tie fighter [3:145].........9.00
_____R2-D2, canyon [3:145] 9.00
_____Space Battle [3:145] 9.00
_____Stormtrooper, mounted [3:145] 9.00
_____Tie Fighter, firing [3:145] 9.00
_____Tusken Raider, attacking [3:145]........................9.00
_____X-Wing and Vader's Tie Fighter [3:145] 9.00
_____X-Wing, firing under Death Star [3:145] 9.00
_____Yavin ceremony [3:145]...................................9.00
_____Yavin Rebel hanger 9.00

Coca-Cola, Mexico
Random scenes under Coca-Cola, Boing, Fanta caps.
_____Artoo-Deetoo [3:145] 5.00
_____Artoo-Deetoo escapa [3:145] 5.00
_____Artoo-Detoo Y See-Threepio [3:145] 5.00
_____Busqueda de Artoo-Deetoo [3:145] 5.00
_____Chewbacca [3:145]...5.00
_____Combate Galactico [BTL09] 5.00
_____Darth Vader [BTL10].......................................5.00
_____Darth Vader escapa [3:145] 5.00
_____Grand Moff Tarkin [3:145] 5.00
_____Han Solo [BTL11]...5.00
_____Han Solo y Chewbacca [BTL12].........................5.00
_____Jawas [3:145]...5.00
_____Jawas y Artoo-Deetoo [3:145] 5.00
_____Kenobi y Threepio [3:145] 5.00
_____La Guerra De Las Galaxias [BTL13].....................10.00
_____Luke en su nave [3:145] 5.00
_____Luke Skywalker [3:145] 5.00
_____Luke y Threepio [3:145] 5.00
_____Nave Imperial [BTL14] 5.00
_____Obi-Wan Kenobi [3:145] 5.00
_____Princess Leia [3:145].......................................5.00
_____Princess Leia y Luke [3:145] 5.00
_____Princess Leia y Vader [3:145] 5.00
_____See-Threepio [3:145] 5.00
_____Stormtroopers [3:145] 5.00
_____Stormtroopers atacan [3:145] 5.00
_____Stormtroopers en el desierto [3:145] 5.00
_____Tarkin y Vader [3:145] 5.00
_____Triunfo de la Alianza [3:145] 5.00
_____Tusken Raider [3:145] 5.00
_____Tusken Raider y la Bestia [3:145] 5.00
_____Tusken Raider y Luke [3:145] 5.00
_____Vader y Stormtroopers [3:145] 5.00

Pepsi Cola
_____EPI:TPM prmotion, twist-on [3:146] 1.00
_____EPI:TPM prmotion, Yoda $20 winner [3:146]......20.00

Pepsi Cola, Japan
EPII:AOTC. Set 1 Star Wars.
_____5-pack, sealed [3:146] 25.00
_____C-3PO and R2-D2 ....8.00
_____Han Solo 8.00
_____Luke Skywalker Tatooine 8.00
_____Obi-Wan Kenobi (aged) 8.00
_____Princess Leia 8.00

EPII:AOTC. Set 2 Star Wars.
_____5-pack, sealed [3:146] 25.00
_____Darth Vader 8.00
_____Grand Moff Tarkin 8.00
_____Greedo 8.00
_____Jawa 8.00
_____Tie fighter pilot 8.00

EPII:AOTC. Set 3 Empire Strikes Back.
_____5-pack, sealed [3:146] 25.00
_____Han Solo in carbonite 8.00
_____Lando Calrissian 8.00
_____Princess Leia Hoth 8.00
_____Yoda 8.00

EPII:AOTC. Set 4 Empire Strikes Back.
_____5-pack, sealed [3:146] 25.00
_____Boba Fett 8.00
_____Bossk 8.00
_____IG-88 ....8.00
_____Luke Skywalker jedi 8.00
_____Snowtrooper 8.00
_____Stormtrooper 8.00

EPII:AOTC. Set 5 Return of the Jedi.
_____5-pack, sealed [3:146] 25.00
_____Admiral Ackbar 8.00
_____Chewbacca 8.00
_____Emperor Palpatine 8.00
_____Luke Skywalker X-wing pilot 8.00
_____Wicket 8.00

EPII:AOTC. Set 6 Return of the Jedi.
_____5-pack, sealed [3:146] 25.00
_____Bib Fortuna 8.00
_____Gamorrean Guard 8.00
_____Jabba the Hutt 8.00
_____Oola 8.00
_____Speederbike trooper 8.00

EPII:AOTC. Set 7 Phantom Menace.
_____5-pack, sealed [3:146] 25.00
_____Anakin Skywalker padawan 8.00
_____C-3PO unfinished 8.00
_____Obi-Wan Kenobi 8.00
_____Queen Amidala travel gown 8.00
_____Qui-Gon Jinn 8.00

EPII:AOTC. Set 8 Phantom Menace.
_____5-pack, sealed [3:146] 25.00
_____Battle Droid 8.00
_____Darth Maul 8.00
_____Destroyer Droid 8.00
_____Jar Jar Binks 8.00
_____Pit Droid 8.00

EPII:AOTC. Set 9 Vehicles.
_____5-pack, sealed [3:146] 25.00
_____Darth Vader's Tie fighter 8.00
_____Death Star II 8.00
_____Millennium Falcon 8.00
_____Tie fighter 8.00
_____X-Wing 8.00

BTL01   BTL02

BTL03   BTL04   BTL05   BTL06 top   BTL06   BTL07   BTL08

BTL09 top   BTL09   BTL10   BTL11   BTL12   BTL13   BTL14

Bottle Caps

BTL15   BTL16   BTL17   BTL18   BTL19   BTL20   BTL21   BTL22

BTL23   BTL24   BTL25   BTL26   BTL27   BTL28   BTL29   BTL30   BTL31   BTL32   BTL33

EPII:AOTC. Set 10 Vehicles.
5-pack, sealed [3:146] 25.00
Landspeeder 8.00
Naboo fighter 8.00
Royal Starship..8.00
Slave I 8.00
Star Destroyer...8.00

Episode I: The Phantom Menace.
Anakin Skywalker [3:147] 3.00
Anakin Skywalker podracer [3:147]............3.00
Anakin Skywalker podracer head [3:147] 4.00
Anakin Skywalker podracer head with moveable arms [3:147]....................................15.00
Battle Droid [3:147] 3.00
Boss Nass [BTL15] 3.00
Boss Nass, head [BTL16] 4.00
Boss Nass, head w/moveable arms [BTL17] 15.00
C-3PO [3:147] 3.00
Captain Tarpals, head [3:147] 4.00
Captain Tarpals, head with moveable arms [3:147]..15.00
Chancellor Velorum [3:147]......................3.00
Darth Maul, head [BTL18]........................4.00
Darth Maul, head with moveable arms [BTL19]..15.00
Darth Maul, Jedi duel [BTL20] 3.00
Darth Maul, Tatooine [3:147] 3.00
Darth Sidious [3:147] 3.00
Darth Vader [3:147] 4.00
Darth Vader, head [3:147] 4.00
Jar Jar Binks [BTL21] 3.00
Jar Jar Binks, head [BTL22] 5.00
Jar Jar Binks, head with moveable arms [BTL23]...15.00
Ki-Adi-Mundy [3:147] 3.00
Mace Windu [3:147] 3.00
Mace Windu, head [3:147] 4.00
Mace Windu, head with moveable arms [3:147].......................................15.00
Nute Gunray [3:147] 3.00
Nute Gunray, head [3:147] 5.00
Nute Gunray, head with moveable arms [3:147].......................................15.00
Obi-Wan Kenobi Jedi duel [3:147] 3.00

Obi-Wan Kenobi Tatooine [3:147]...........................3.00
Padme [3:147].......................................3.00
Princess Leia as Jabba's Prisoner [3:147] 2.00
Queen Amidala battle dress [3:147] 3.00
Queen Amidala Coruscant [3:147] 3.00
Queen Amidala Naboo [3:147] 3.00
Queen Amidala, head [3:147] 4.00
Queen Amidala, with moveable arms [3:147] 15.00
Qui-Gon Jinn [3:147]..............................3.00
R2-D2 [3:147] 12.00
R2-D2 with moveable arms [3:147] 24.00
Sebulba [3:147] 3.00
Sebulba, head [3:147] 5.00
Sebulba, head with moveable arms [3:147] 15.00
Senator Palpatine [3:147] 3.00
Tusken Raider [3:147] 2.00
Watto [3:147] 3.00
Watto, head [3:147] 4.00
Watto, head with moveable arms [3:147] 15.00
Yoda [3:147] 3.00
Yoda, head [3:147] 12.00
Yoda, head with moveable arms [3:147] 15.00

Episode II: Attack of the Clones.
Anakin Skywalker [3:147] 8.00
Anakin Skywalker / Darth Vader, 7-11 exclusive [3:147] 8.00
Anakin Skywalker bust [3:147] 8.00
Battle Droid [3:147] 8.00
Boba Fett [3:147] 8.00
C-3PO [3:147] 8.00
C-3PO bust [3:147] 8.00
Captain Typho [3:147] 8.00
Chancellor Palpatine [3:147] 8.00
Clone trooper [BTL24] 8.00
Clone trooper bust [BTL25] 8.00
Count Dooku [3:147] 8.00
Count Dooku bust [3:147] 8.00
Darth Sidious [3:147] 8.00
Dexter Jettster [3:147] 8.00
Dexter Jettster bust [3:147] 8.00
Genosian warrior [3:147].........................8.00
Genosian warrior bust [3:147] 8.00
Jango Fett [BTL26] 8.00
Jango Fett / Clone, 7-11 exclusive [BTL27]..........8.00

Jango Fett bust [BTL28] 8.00
Jar Jar Binks senator [3:147] 8.00
Kitt Fisto [3:147] 8.00
Kitt Fisto bust [BTL29] 8.00
Lama Su [3:147] 8.00
Luminara Unduli [3:147] 8.00
Luminara Unduli bust [3:147] 8.00
Mace Windu [3:147] 8.00
Mas Amedda [3:147]..............................8.00
Mas Amedda bust [3:147] 8.00
Obi-Wan Kenobi [3:147] 8.00
Obi-Wan Kenobi bust [BTL30] 8.00
Orn Free Ta [3:147] 8.00
Padme Amidala arena escape [3:147] 8.00
Padme Amidala senator [3:147] 8.00
Plo Koon [3:147] 8.00
Plo Koon bust [BTL31] 8.00
Poggle the Lesser [3:147] 8.00
R2-D2 [3:147] 8.00
RIC-920 [3:147] 8.00
Royal Imperial Guard [3:147] 8.00
Royal Imperial Guard bust [BTL32] 8.00
Saesee Tiin [3:147] 8.00
Saesee Tiin bust [BTL33] 8.00
Shaak Ti [3:147] 8.00
Shaak Ti bust [3:147] 8.00
Super Battle Droid [3:147] 8.00
Taun We [3:147] 8.00
Taun We bust [3:147] 8.00
Tusken female [3:147].............................8.00
Wat Tambor [3:147] 8.00
Yoda [3:147] 8.00
Zam Wesell [3:147] 8.00
Zam Wesell bust [3:147] 8.00

Episode III: Revenge of the Sith.
Anakin Skywalker (Jedi) 8.00
Anakin Skywalker (podracer) 8.00
Anakin Skywalker, head only 15.00
AT-AT Driver...8.00
Battle Droid 8.00
Battle Droid, head only 15.00
Boba Fett 8.00
C-3PO 8.00
C3PO, head only 15.00

BTL34   BTL35   BTL36   BTL37   BTL38   BTL39   BTL40

BTL41   BTL42   BTL43   BTL44   BTL45   BTL46   BTL47

BTL48　　BTL49　　BTL50　　BTL51　　BTL52　　BTL53　　BTL54

BTL55　　BTL56　　BTL57　　BTL58　　BTL59　　BTL60　　BTL61

____Chewbacca with C3PO 8.00
____Chewbacca, head only 15.00
____Clone Trooper 8.00
____Clone Trooper, head only 15.00
____Commander Bly 8.00
____Count Dooku 8.00
____Darth Maul 8.00
____Darth Maul, head only 15.00
____Darth Vader 8.00
____Darth Vader, head only 15.00
____Emperor Palpatine 8.00
____Emperor Palpatine, head only 15.00
____Fugrin Dan 8.00
____Gamorrean Guard 8.00
____General Grievous 8.00
____General Grievous Guard 8.00
____General Grievous, head only 15.00
____Han Solo 8.00
____Han Solo, head only 15.00
____Jabba the Hutt 8.00
____Janga Fett 8.00
____Jar Jar Binks 8.00
____Jawa 8.00
____Lando Calrissian 8.00
____Luke Skywalker with Yoda 8.00
____Luke Skywalker, head only 15.00
____Mace Windu 8.00
____Max Rebo 8.00
____Obi-Wan Kenobi (Jedi) 8.00
____Obi-Wan Kenobi (old) 8.00
____Obi-Wan Kenobi, head only 15.00
____Padme Amidala..8.00
____Padme Amidala, head only 15.00
____Pit Droid 8.00
____Princess Leia 8.00
____Princess Leia, head only 15.00
____Qui-Gon Jinn 8.00
____R2-D2 ....8.00
____Sandtrooper 8.00
____Scout Trooper 8.00
____Sebulba 8.00
____Senator Bail Organa 8.00
____Stormtrooper, head only 15.00
____Super Battle Droid 8.00
____Tarfful 8.00
____Teebo 8.00
____Tie Fighter Pilot...8.00
____Tie Fighter Pilot, head only 15.00
____Watto 8.00
____Yoda 8.00
____Yoda, head only 15.00

Pepsi Cola, Mexico
Clario.
____1 Jar Jar Sonriendo [BTL34].................................1.00

____2 R2-D2 [3:148]...1.00
____3 Jar Jar Sacando La Lengua [3:148] 1.00
____4 Boss Nass En Su Trono [BTL35] 1.00
____5 C-3PO [3:148] 1.00
____6 Anakin Skywalker [BTL36] 1.00
____7 Qui-Gon [3:148] 1.00
____8 R2-D2 [3:148] 1.00
____9 Jar Jar [3:148] 1.00
____10 Mace Windu [3:148] 1.00
____11 Boss Nass [3:148] 1.00
____12 Reina Amidala [3:148] 1.00
____13 Obi-Wan [3:148] 1.00
____14 Captain Panaka [3:148] 1.00
____15 Anakin Skywalker [3:148] 1.00
____16 Padme (handmaiden) [3:148] 1.00
____17 Reina Amidala [BTL37] 1.00
____18 Padme (Tatooine) [3:148] 1.00
____19 Qui-Gon En Batalla [BTL38] 1.00
____20 Shmi Y Qui-Gon [BTL39] 1.00
____21 C-3PO Y R2-D2 [3:148] 1.00
____22 Qui-Gon Y Jar Jar [3:148] 1.00
____Yoda 1 (facing right) [3:148] 3.00
____Yoda 2 (facing left) [BTL40] 3.00

EPI:TPM. Lenticular motion caps.
____1 Jar Jar Sonriendo [3:148] 1.00
____2 R2-D2 [3:148]...1.00
____3 Jar Jar Sacando La Lengua [3:148] 1.00
____4 Boss Nass En Su Trono [3:148].........................1.00
____5 C-3PO [3:148] 1.00
____6 Anakin Skywalker [3:148] 1.00
____7 Qui-Gon [BTL41] 1.00
____8 R2-D2 [3:148] 1.00
____9 Jar Jar [BTL42] 1.00
____10 Mace Windu [BTL43] 1.00
____11 Boss Nass [3:148] 1.00
____12 Reina Amidala [3:148] 1.00
____13 Obi-Wan [3:148] 1.00
____14 Captain Panaka [BTL44] 1.00
____15 Anakin Skywalker [3:148] 1.00
____16 Padme (handmaiden) [BTL45] 1.00
____17 Reina Amidala [BTL46] 1.00
____18 Padme (Tatooine) [3:148] 1.00
____19 Qui-Gon En Batalla [3:148] 1.00
____20 Shmi Y Qui-Gon [3:148] 1.00
____21 C-3PO Y R2-D2 [3:148] 1.00
____22 Qui-Gon Y Jar Jar [3:148] 1.00
____23 Yoda 1 (facing right) [3:148]............................1.00
____24 Yoda 2 (facing left) [BTL47] 1.00
____25 Androide De Batalla [BTL48] 1.00
____26 Watto [3:148] 1.00
____27 Darth Sidious Y Darth Maul [BTL49] 1.00
____28 Watto [3:148] 1.00
____29 Darth Sidious [3:148] 1.00
____30 Sebulba [BTL51] 1.00

____31 Nute Gunray Y Rune Haako [BTL52] 1.00
____32 Qui-Gon Y Darth Maul [3:148]........................1.00
____33 Senador Palpatine [3:148] 1.00
____34 Darth Maul Y Obi-Wan [BTL53].......................1.00
____35 Darth Maul 1 (face only, Tatooine) [3:148] 1.00
____36 Darth Maul 3 (face only, Jedi duel) [3:148] 1.00
____37 Darth Maul 3 (lightsaber drawn) [BTL54]..........1.00

Ladio.
____1 Androide De Batalla [BTL55] 1.00
____2 Watto [3:148] 1.00
____3 Darth Sidious Y Darth Maul [BTL56] 1.00
____4 Watto [3:148] 1.00
____5 Darth Sidious [BTL57] 1.00
____6 Sebulba [BTL58] 1.00
____7 Nute Gunray Y Rune Haako [3:148] 1.00
____8 Qui-Gon Y Darth Maul [BTL59]..........................1.00
____9 Senador Palpatine [3:148] 1.00
____10 Darth Maul Y Obi-Wan [BTL60]........................1.00
____Darth Maul 1 (face only, Tatooine) [3:148] 3.00
____Darth Maul 3 (face only, Jedi duel) [3:148]...........3.00
____Darth Maul 3 (lightsaber drawn) [BTL61] 3.00

Bottle Openers

____Celebration 3 logo, magnetic back [B1T01] 20.00

Bottle Toppers

Pepsi Cola, Japan
____C-3PO, Musical with movement [BTT01] 25.00

Bowling Ball Bags

Brunswick / Strike Ten
____Darth Vader [BWB01] 45.00

Bowling Balls

Brunswick / Strike Ten
____Boba Fett 85.00
____C-3PO [BWL01] 85.00
____Darth Maul [BWL02]..85.00
____Darth Vader 85.00
____Padme/ Leia [BWL03]..85.00
____Stormtrooper 85.00
____Yoda 85.00

B1T01

BTT01 Flap Closed and Flap Open

BWB01

BWL01

BWL02

BWL03

Boxes: Ceramic

HOC01

HOC02

HOC03

HOC04

TIC01

TIC02

TIC03 Lid

TIC04 Lid

TIC05 Lid

TIC06 Lid

TIC07

TIC08

TIC09

TIC10

Boxes: Ceramic

Limoges
7cm tall porcelain boxes, FAO Schwarz exclusives.
____Queen Amidala [HOC01] 245.00
____Yoda [HOC02] 245.00

Sigma
____Stormtrooper ceramic box [HOC03] 55.00
____Yoda in Backpack ceramic box [HOC04] 65.00

Boxes: Plastic

3D Arts
Hologram foil on lid, 2" square.
____C-3PO and R2-D2 ....7.00
____Darth Vader 7.00
____Millennium Falcon..7.00
____X-Wing Fighter 7.00

A.H. Prismatic
Hologram foil on lid, 2" square.
____AT-AT 7.00
____B-Wing 7.00
____Darth Vader's Tie Fighter 7.00
____Darth Vader..7.00
____Imperial Cruiser...7.00
____Millennium Falcon..7.00
____Tie Interceptor...7.00
____X-Wing Fighter 7.00

Boxes: Tin

Butterscotch candy tins from the U.K.
____Anakin Skywalker [3:407] 6.00
____Darth Maul [3:407] 6.00
____Obi-Wan Kenobi [3:407] 6.00
____Qui-Gon Jinn [3:407].......................................6.00

Chein Industries
____ROTJ Round Cookie Tin with lid 23.00

Carry-all rectangular tins with handles and lid.
____Ewoks [TIC01] 14.00
____ROTJ [TIC02] 17.00

Mini-tins, 3.5" high.
____C-3PO and R2-D2 [TIC03] 8.00
____Darth Vader 8.00
____Ewoks 8.00
____Han Solo, Luke Skywalker, and Princess Leia [TIC04] 8.00
____Jabba the Hutt [TIC05] 8.00
____Max Rebo Band [TIC06] 8.00

Trinket tins, 1" high.
____C-3PO and R2-D2 ....4.00
____Darth Vader 4.00
____Ewoks 4.00
____Han Solo, Luke Skywalker, and Princess Leia 4.00
____Jabba the Hutt 4.00
____Max Rebo Band 4.00

Frito Lay
EPII:AOTC. 4 Big Grab bags of snack chips inside.
____1 of 3, The Life of Anakin [TIC07].....................8.00
____2 of 3, Jedi Heroes [TIC08]..............................8.00
____3 of 3, Droids and Clones [TIC09] 8.00

Masterfoods USA
____Sith and Jedi collector tin set [TIC10] 14.00

Heart shaped tins filled with M&M minis.
____Chewbacca, "I'd Just As Soon Kiss A Wookiee"...5.00
____Yoda, "A Happy Valentines Day You Will Have" 5.00

Round tins with lenticular characters, filled with M&M minis.
____Anakin / Darth Vader [TIC11] 8.00
____Yoda / General Grievous [TIC12] 8.00

Metal Box Ltd.
Medium sized tins.
____Chewbacca [TIC13] 9.00
____Darth Vader [TIC14] 9.00
____Han Solo 9.00
____Luke Skywalker 9.00
____Princess Leia tin 9.00
____Probot tin [TIC15] 9.00
____Star Destroyer tin [TIC16] 9.00
____Yoda tin [TIC17] 9.00

Oval tins.
____Cloud City [TIC18] 18.00

TIC11 Image 1 and 2

TIC12 Image 1 and 2

TIC13

TIC14

TIC15

TIC16

TIC17

TIC18

TIC19

TIC20

TIC21

TIC22

TIC23

TIC24

TIC25

TIC26

TIC27

TIC28

POP01

POP02

POP03

POP04

POP05

Buttons

BSC01

BS01

BS02

BS03

BS04

BS05

BS06

BS07

BS08

BS09

Small sized tins.
- ____AT-AT [TIC19] 7.00
- ____Boba Fett [TIC20] 7.00
- ____Darth Vader and Luke Skywalker Duel [TIC21] 7.00
- ____Lando Calrissian [TIC22] 7.00
- ____Luke on Tauntaun [TIC23] 7.00
- ____Yoda tin [TIC24] 7.00

Space trunks.
- ____Droids / Probot [TIC25] 20.00
- ____Luke Skywalker [TIC26] 20.00

Movistar
Argentina. Tin canisters for Nokia 1100 series phones.
- ____Darth Vader [TIC27] 5.00
- ____Yoda [TIC28] 5.00

Buckets: Food

Plastic popcorn pails. Theater promotions.
- ____Star Wars Special Edition [POP01] 7.00
- ____SW:SE trilogy scenes [POP02] 22.00

Frito Lay
EPII:AOTC. Four Big Grab bags of snack chips inside.
- ____1 of 3, The Life of Anakin [POP03] 5.00
- ____2 of 3, Jedi Heroes [POP04] 5.00
- ____3 of 3, Droids and Clones [POP05] 5.00

Bumper Stickers

- ____Darth Vader Lives [BS01] 8.00
- ____I'm a SW fan, honk if you R2 [BS02] 5.00
- ____I saw Star Wars at Mann's Chinese Theater 6.00
- ____Star Wars exhibition in Space World [3:154] 7.00
- ____Star Wars Lives, R2-D2 [BS03] 6.00
- ____Star Wars Logo [BS04] 5.00

Creation Entertainment
- ____10th Anniversary bumper sticker [BS05] 8.00

Dark Horse Comics
- ____Starfighter Corssbones 3.00

Disney / MGM
- ____My Other Vehicle is an X-Wing [BS06] 8.00

Fantasma
- ____Star Wars logo on holographic foil 5.00

Hot Topic
- ____May The Force Be With You [BS07] 5.00
- ____My other transport is the Millennium Falcon [BS08] 8.00
- ____Use the Force [BS09] 5.00

Business Cards

Oral-B
- ____Membership / Dental Appt. [BSC01] 10.00

Buttons

- ____20-pack, Die Ruckkehr der Jedi-Ritter 75.00
- ____Darth Vader's Tie Fighter attacking [BT01] 4.00
- ____Droids: On Video Now [BT02] 8.00
- ____First 10 Years, pewter 25.00
- ____Happy EMPIRE Day [BT03] 12.00

BT01

BT02

BT03

BT04

BT05

BT06

BT07

BT08

BT09

BT10

BT11

BT12

BT13

BT14

Buttons

BT15   BT16   BT17   BT18   BT19   BT20   BT21

BT22   BT23   BT24   BT25   BT26   BT27   BT28

BT29   BT30   BT31   BT32   BT33   BT34   BT35   BT36   BT37

BT38   BT39   BT40   BT41   BT42   BT43   BT44   BT45   BT46

____Ice Capades and Ewoks with light-up eyes, 2.25" 8.00
____Ice Capades and Ewoks, 3.5" [BT04] 5.00
____May The Force Be With You, Saturday March 10th [BT05] 8.00
____Star Wars Books On Sale Now [BT06]..................3.00
____Star Wars Sandpeople [BT07] 9.00
____starwarscards.net [BT08] 3.00
____Super Collector's Wish Book [BT09] 3.00
____Yoda for President 4.00

EPII:AOTC.
____Star Wars [BT10]...................................5.00
____Star Wars Coming April 23 [BT11].....................10.00
____Train to be a Jedi May 18th 10:99am to Noon [BT12] 10.00

Tenth anniversary.
____C-3PO and R2-D2 [BT13]............................6.00

____Darth Vader [BT14] 6.00
____Leia and Luke [BT15] 6.00
____The First Ten Years, black round [BT16]................8.00
____The First Ten Years, silver rectangle [BT17] 6.00

U.K.
____Darth Vadar Lives (misspelled) [BT18] 8.00

20th Century Fox
____Space Balls, May The Schwartz Be With You [BT19] 8.00
____The Star Wars Trilogy, March 28, 1985 [BT20] 25.00

Classic trilogy video pre-release employee buttons.
____Continue the Adventure on Video [BT21].............6.00
____Special Edition Trilogy [BT22].......................7.00
____Special Edition Trilogy, Aug 26 [BT23] 7.00
____Trilogy Video Re-Release Aug 29 [BT24] 7.00

EPII DVD pre-release employee buttons.
____Yoda, "Unlock the Saga..." [BT25] 5.00

EPIII DVD.
____The saga is complete. Own it on DVD. [BT26]......8.00

Episode I DVD pre-release employee buttons. "The Saga Begins on DVD October 16!"
____Darth Maul [BT27] 10.00
____Maul and Kenobi duel [BT28] 10.00
____Queen Amidala [BT29] 10.00

Episode I video pre-release employee buttons.
____Darth Maul, "Ask me how to reserve..." [BT30]..10.00
____EPI: "The One To Own On Video" [BT31].............5.00

A.H. Prismatic
Holograms, series 1.
____AT-AT 4.00

BT47   BT48   BT49   BT50   BT51   BT52   BT53   BT54   BT55

BT56   BT57   BT58   BT59   BT60   BT61   BT62

BT63

BT64

BT65

BT66

BT67

BT68

BT69

BT70

BT71

BT72

BT73

BT74

BT75

BT76

BT77

BT78

BT79

BT80

BT81

BT82

BT83

BT84

BT85

BT86

BT87

BT88

BT89

BT90

____ B-Wing 4.00
____ Darth Vader's tie fighter 5.00
____ Darth Vader 4.00
____ Imperial Cruiser [BT32] 4.00
____ Millennium Falcon 4.00
____ Millennium Falcon with SW logo 4.00
____ Tie Interceptor...4.00
____ X-Wing Fighter 4.00

Holograms, series 2.
____ C-3PO and R2-D2 [BT33] 4.00
____ Darth Vader 4.00
____ Millennium Falcon [BT34] 4.00

Adam Joseph Industries
Ewoks.
____ Baby Ewoks [BT35] 3.00
____ Ewok Daydreaming [BT36]........................3.00
____ Ewok Flying Glider [BT37] 3.00

____ Ewok Lessons [BT38] 3.00
____ Ewok Village in Snow [BT39] 3.00
____ Ewok with Basket on Head [BT40]..............3.00
____ Kneesaa and Wicket Feed Baga [BT41] 3.00
____ Princess Kneesaa [BT42] 3.00
____ Wicket and R2-D2 [BT43] 3.00
____ Wicket on a Vine [BT44] 3.00
____ Wicket Tells a Story [BT45] 3.00
____ Wicket the Ewok [BT46] 3.00

Return of the Jedi.
____ Chewbacca [BT47] 5.00
____ Darth Vader 5.00
____ Emperor's Royal Guard [BT48] 5.00
____ Gamorrean Guard [BT49] 5.00
____ Heroes on Endor [BT50] 5.00
____ Jabba the Hutt [BT51] 5.00
____ Max Rebo [BT52] 5.00
____ R2-D2 and C-3PO [BT53]...........................5.00

____ Revenge art...6.00
____ Return of the Jedi logo [BT54] 5.00
____ Revenge of the Jedi logo [BT56] 12.00
____ Yoda [BT55]...6.00

Burger King
____ "Ask Me For Your ROTJ Glasses" [BT57] 12.00

Burger King, UK
EPIII:ROTS. Play the Choose Your Destiny game.
____ Blue [BT58] 5.00
____ Red [BT59] 5.00

C and D Visionaries, Inc.
____ Adventure... Excitement... A Jedi craves not these things [BT60]..2.00
____ Boba Fett [BT61]..3.00
____ Chewbacca [BT62] 5.00
____ Clone Helmet [BT63]..................................5.00

BT91

BT92

BT93

BT94

BT95

BT96

BT97

BT98

BT99

BT100

BT101

BT102

BT103

BT104

BT105

BT106

BT107

BT108

Buttons

BT109   BT110   BT111   BT112   BT113   BT114   BT115

BT116   BT117   BT118   BT119   BT120   BT121   BT122

BT123   BT124   BT125   BT126   BT127   BT128   BT129

____Clone Trooper [BT64] 5.00
____Darth Vader Sith Lord [BT65] 5.00
____Do... or do not. There is no try. Art. [BT66] 3.00
____Do... or do not. There is no try.'Photo. [BT67] 3.00
____Jedi [BT68] 5.00
____Look at me... Judge me by my size do you? [BT69] 3.00
____May The Force Be With You [BT70] 3.00
____My ally is The Force... and a powerful ally it is [BT71] 3.00
____R2-D2 and C-3PO [BT72]...................................3.00
____Size Matters Not -Yoda [BT73] 3.00
____Use The Force [BT74] 3.00
____Who's Your Daddy? [BT75]..................................3.00
____Yoda [BT76] 5.00
____You have failed me for the last time [BT77] 3.00

Large.
____Boba Fett [BT78]...3.00

____I'd just as soon kiss a wookiee [BT79].................3.00
____Princess Leia captive [BT80] 3.00

Small.
____5-pack set on Yoda backer card [BT81] 10.00

CHOZ F.M.
____Star Wars NPR promotional [BT82] 5.00

Coca-Cola
____Things Go Better... [BT83] 18.00
____Y A Rien Comme Un Coke [BT84]......................24.00

Dark Horse Comics
____Ask Me About Star Wars Comics! [BT85] 5.00

Disney / MGM
____A short time ahead... Star Tours [BT86] 8.00
____Star Tours and Disney-MGM logos 4.00

____Star Tours and Disney-MGM logos with C-3PO and R2-D2 [BT87] 6.00
____Star Tours Flight Test Team [BT88] 17.00
____Star Tours logo [BT89] 5.00
____Star Tours logo w/C-3PO and R2-D2 [BT90]........5.00
____Star Tours logo, 3" glow-in-dark 6.00
____Star Wars Weekends – May 2000 [BT91].............8.00
____Star Wars Weekends – May 2001 [BT92].............8.00

3D Holographic buttons.
____R2-D2 and C-3PO [BT93] 25.00
____Star Tours Shuttle [BT94] 25.00

DK Publishing
____Ask me about the SW EPI books... [BT95] 5.00

Factors, Etc.
____"May The Force Be With You" [BT96] 5.00
____"May The Force Be With You" [BT97] 6.00

BT130   BT131   BT132   BT133   BT134   BT135   BT136   BT137

BT138   BT139   BT140   BT141   BT142   BT143   BT144   BT145

BT146   BT147   BT148   BT149   BT150   BT151   BT152   BT153

BT154   BT155   BT156   BT157   BT158   BT159   BT160

BT161   BT162   BT163   BT164   BT165   BT166   BT167   BT168

BT169   BT170   BT171   BT172   BT173   BT174   BT175

BT176   BT177   BT178

____"May The Force Be With You" Kenner logo 20.00
____Ben (Obi-Wan) Kenobi (1977-80) [BT98] 6.00
____Boba Fett 8.00
____C-3PO (1977-80) [BT99] 6.00
____C-3PO and R2-D2 ....7.00
____Chewbacca [BT100] 7.00
____Darth Vader (photo) (1977 – 80) [BT101] 6.00
____Darth Vadar Lives (misspelled) [BT102] 10.00
____Darth Vader [BT103] 7.00
____Darth Vader mirrored keychain (1977 – 80) 8.00
____Darth Vader mirrored necklace (1977 – 80) 8.00
____Han Solo and Chewbacca [BT104] 6.00
____Luke Skywalker [BT105] 7.00
____Princess Leia [BT106] 6.00
____R2-D2 (1977-80) [BT107] 6.00
____R2-D2 and C-3PO with logo [BT108] 10.00

Fan Club
____Artoo [BT109] 8.00
____Ben Kenobi [BT110] 8.00
____Chewbacca [BT111] 8.00
____Darth Vader [BT112] 8.00
____George Lucas [BT113] 8.00
____Han Solo [BT114] 8.00
____Jawa [BT115] 8.00
____Luke [BT116] 8.00
____Moff Tarkin [BT117] 8.00
____Official Member [BT118] 10.00
____Princess Leia [BT119] 8.00
____Stormtrooper [BT120] 8.00
____Threepio [BT121]...8.00
____Tusken raider [BT122] 8.00

Fox Video
Star Wars Trilogy for the first time on DVD 9.21
____Darth Vader [BT123]...10.00
____Heroes [BT124]...10.00

Hungry Jacks
____Episode III: Revenge of the Sith [BT125] 5.00

K B Toys
____Destination EPI, employee button [BT126] 8.00

Kenner
____The Kenner Star Wars Convention, 2" round [BT127] 34.00

Kenner, POTF
____Biker Scout..15.00

Kinnerton Confectionery
Starfield background.
____C-3PO and R2-D2 [BT128].....................................3.00
____Darth Vader [BT129]...3.00
____The Force Will Be With You Always 3.00

LucasArts
____Battle Front 2, on 11.01.05 [BT130] 5.00

Mister Badges
____2-pack of random buttons 21.00
____C-3PO 4.00
____C-3PO and white protocol droid 4.00
____Chewbacca 4.00
____Darth Vader 4.00
____Darth Vader and Stormtrooper 4.00
____Han Solo 4.00
____Luke as pilot 4.00
____Luke as pilot, close-up 4.00
____Luke in Millennium Falcon gunwell 4.00
____Luke with gun drawn 4.00
____Millennium Falcon 4.00
____Princess Leia..4.00
____R2-D2 ....4.00
____Star Destroyer 4.00
____X-Wing 4.00
____Yoda 4.00
____Yoda and Luke 4.00

Return of the Jedi photo buttons. Originally sold on card and loose.
____AT-ST 4.00
____Darth Vader 4.00
____Emperor's Royal Guard..4.00
____Gamorrean Guard 4.00
____Jabba the Hutt 4.00
____Jabba the Hutt, close-up 4.00
____Luke and Leia 4.00
____Millennium Falcon 4.00
____Stormtrooper..4.00
____Wicket the Ewok 4.00

Present Needs Ltd.
____Baby Ewoks 6.00
____Darth Vader and Royal Guard 6.00
____May The Force Be With You..................................4.00

Scholastic
____Darth Maul, lenticular [BT131] 3.00

Skywalkers
____Don't Give In To The Dark Side [BT132] 11.00

Star Badges
____Admiral Ackbar..15.00
____Bib Fortuna...15.00
____C-3PO [BT133]..15.00
____Chewbacca 15.00
____Darth Vader 15.00
____Gamorrean Guard 15.00
____Jabba the Hutt 15.00
____R2-D2 [BT134]..15.00
____Shuttle Tydirium 15.00
____Yoda 15.00

Super Live Adventure
Japan.
____Trilogy characters [BT135] 14.00

Takara
____C-3PO and R2-D2 ....45.00
____Star Wars logo, black on silver [BT136].............35.00
____Star Wars logo, silver on black 35.00
____Stormtroopers stop landspeeder [BT137] 45.00

Tapper Candies
____Guest of Honor Ribbon, lights up [BT138]............3.00

Touchline
____Admiral Ackbar 7.00
____C-3PO 7.00
____Chewbacca 7.00
____Darth Vader 7.00
____Ewok 7.00
____Jabba the Hutt 7.00
____R2-D2 ....7.00
____Stormtrooper..7.00

Wal-mart
____48 Hours of the Force, April 2nd and 3rd [BT139] 10.00

Yujin
1" buttons dispensed in capsules with insert.
____01. Luke Skywalker..2.00
____02. Chewbacca [BT140]...2.00
____03. Jawa 2.00
____04. Qui-Gon Jinn 2.00
____05. Boba Fett 2.00
____06. Mace Windu 2.00
____07. Stormtrooper...2.00
____08. Han Solo in Carbonite 2.00
____09. Princes Leia 2.00
____10. X-Wing Fighter 2.00
____11. Try not. Do or do not. There is no Try. 2.00
____12. Training to be a Jedi will not be easy. 2.00
____13. Mandalorian emblem 2.00
____14. Bantha skull..2.00
____15. (Mystery button) 2.00
____16. Han Solo [BT141]...2.00
____17. Obi-Wan Kenobi 2.00
____18. Anakin Skywalker podracer 2.00
____19. Lando Calrissian [BT142] 2.00
____20. Jar Jar [BT143] 2.00
____21. Yoda 2.00

Buttons

| BTS01 | BTS02 | BTS03 | BTS04 | BTS05 | BTS06 | BTS07 | BTS08 | BTS09 |

| BTS10 | BTS11 | BTS12 |

____22. AT-AT Driver 2.00
____23. The Kiss (ESB) [BT144]................2.00
____24. Death Star 2.00
____25. Darth Vader on Bespin 2.00
____26. May the Force Be With You 2.00
____27. The Force is Strong with This One. [BT145] 2.00
____28. Rebel emblem 2.00
____29. Imperial emblem 2.00
____30. ESB poster art 2.00
____31. Darth Vader 2.00
____32. Princess Leia on Hoth [BT146]........2.00
____33. C-3PO EPI [BT147].......................2.00
____34. Salicious Crumb 2.00
____35. Battle Droid [BT148] 2.00
____36. Tusken Raider [BT149] 2.00
____37. Queen Amidala [BT150] 2.00
____38. C-3PO and R2-D2 ....2.00
____39. Millennium Falcon cockpit 2.00
____40. Biker Scout [BT151] 2.00
____41. It's a wonder you're still alive. 2.00
____42. I have a very bad feeling about this. [BT152] 2.00
____43. Rebel emblem [BT153] 2.00
____44. Anakin's podracer emblem..............2.00
____45. (Mystery button) 2.00
____46. C-3PO [BT154] 2.00
____47. R2-D2 [BT155] 2.00
____48. Darth Maul [BT156] 2.00
____49. Jabba the Hutt [BT157] 2.00
____50. Obi-Wan Kenobi [BT158] 2.00
____51. TIE Fighter Pilot [BT159] 2.00
____52. IG-88 [BT160] 2.00
____53. Stormtrooper [BT161]....................2.00
____54. TIE Fighter [BT162] 2.00
____55. Boba Fett [BT163] 2.00

____56. "Wars not make one great" [BT164] 2.00
____57. "Concentrate on the moment..." [BT165]........2.00
____58. Rebel Alliance Emblem [BT166] 2.00
____59. Republic Emblem [BT167] 2.00
____60. (Mystery button) 2.00
____61. Jango Fett [BT168] 2.00
____62. Anakin Skywalker [BT169] 2.00
____63. Obi-Wan Kenobi [BT170] 2.00
____64. Padme Amidala [BT171] 2.00
____65. Boba Fett [BT172] 2.00
____66. Zam Wesell [BT173] 2.00
____67. Count Dooku [BT174] 2.00
____68. Clone Trooper 2.00
____69. Yoda 2.00
____70. Super battle droid [BT175] 2.00
____71. Begun this Clone War has. [BT176] 2.00
____72. The dark side clouds everything. [BT177] 2.00
____73. Republic emblem [BT178] 2.00
____74. Lightsaber 2.00
____75. (Mystery button) 2.00

Buttons: Sewing

Birchcroft
Porcelain, hand painted. Set 1.
____Darth Maul [BTS01] 5.00
____Freedon Nadd [BTS02] 2.00
____Naga Sadow [BTS03] 2.00
____Palpatine [BTS04] 5.00
____Too-Onebee [BTS05] 5.00
____Wicket [BTS06] 5.00

Porcelain, hand painted. Set 2.
____C-3PO [BTS07] 5.00
____Darth Vader [BTS08] 5.00
____Han Solo [BTS09] 5.00
____Leia Organa [BTS10]..5.00
____R2-D2 [BTS11] 5.00
____Yoda [BTS12] 5.00

Cake Decorating Supplies

____C-3PO look-alike cupcake topper [BR01] 2.00
____R2-D2 look-alike cupcake topper [BR02] 2.00

Decopac
____Chewbacca / Han Solo..7.00

Cake topper kits.
____Darth Maul figure / Jedi vs. Sith edible image 8.00
____Darth Vader figurine / Vader backpack tag 12.00
____Luke and R2D2 with candy stars and moons 7.00

____Obi-Wan and Jango Fett / Kamino scene 15.00

EPI:TPM edible images.
____Jedi vs. Sith 6.00

EPII:AOTC edible images.
____Classic 6.00
____Collage 6.00
____Heroes 6.00
____R2-D2 and C-3PO 6.00

EPIII:ROTS.
____Cake skirts [BR03] 3.00

Episode II: Attack of the Clones.
____Bakery promo kit 50.00

Wilton
Cake top figures, Empire Strikes Back "Put Ons."
____C-3PO and R2-D2 [BR04] 12.00

Cake top figures, Star Wars "Cake Tops."
____C-3PO and R2-D2 [BR05] 15.00
____Darth Vader and Stormtrooper [BR06]................12.00

Cake Pans

Wilton
____Boba Fett [BP01] 75.00
____C-3PO [BP02]...50.00
____Darth Vader [BP03]...65.00
____R2-D2 [BP04] 50.00

Cake decorating kits, boxed.
____Darth Vader [BP05]..30.00
____Darth Vader, free book [BP06] 40.00
____R2-D2 [BP07]..30.00
____R2-D2, free book 40.00

Cakes

Memory Lane Cakes, Ltd.
____Darth Vader, package only [3:157] 8.00

Calculators

Industrial Light and Magic
____Employee calculator [3:157]..............................35.00

Tiger Electronics
____A-Wing, solar, 3 sound FX [CC01] 18.00

BR03

| BR01 | BR02 | BR04 | BR05 | BR06 | BP01 | BP02 |

    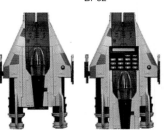

| BP03 | BP04 | BP05 | BP06 | BP07 | CC01 Closed and Open |

PED01

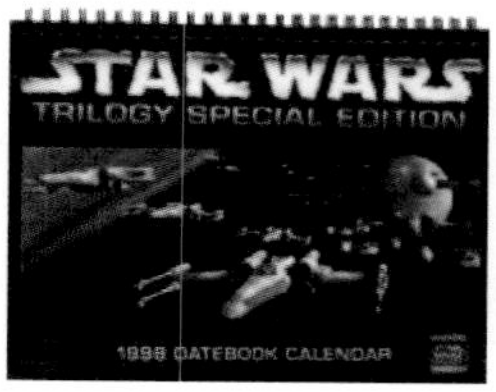

PED02

PED03

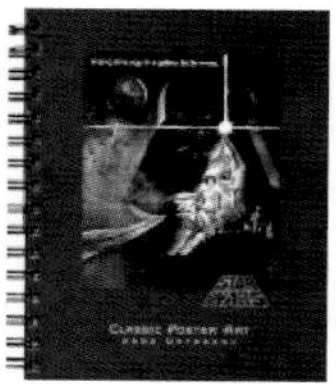
PED04

PED05

PED06

PED07

PED08

PLN01

PLN02

PLN03

PLN04

PLN05

PLN06

PLN07

PLN08

PLN09

PLN10

PLN11

PLN12

PLN13

PLN14

PLN15

PLN16

PLN17

PLN18

Calendar Datebooks

Antioch

____1996 Star Wars "Book of Days" [PED01] 14.00

Cedco Publishing

____1996 Wide Image 12.00
____1997 Art of Star Wars [2:262] 10.00
____1998 Trilogy Special Edition [PED02] 10.00
____1999 May The Force Be With You 14.00
____2000 Star Wars Episode I 7.00
____2002 Star Wars Style (Architecture, Vehicles, Fashion, Accessories) 8.00
____2003 Classic Poster Art [PED03] 16.00
____2003 Classic Poster Art, spiral bound [PED04] 4.00
____2003 Imperial Forces 8.00
____2003 Rebel Alliance 8.00
____2004 Star Wars [PED05] 16.00

Day Runner

____2 Year Monthly Planner, Obi-Wan and Qui-Gonn Jinn on cover [PED06] 6.00

Ink Group

____1999 Diary Weapons and Vehicles [PED07] 10.00

Trielle Corporation

____1997 Diary, includes early sketches of the characters and ideas [PED08] 9.00

Calendar Planners

Cedco Publishing

____2002 – 03 Vehicles and Vessels [PLN01] 12.00
____2003 – 04 Aliens and Creatures [PLN02] 12.00
____2005 – 2006 Darth Vader 12.00

Day Runner

Academic monthly planning calendar with assignment pages July 1999 – July 2000, 8.5"x11"

____Anakin Skywalker 7.00
____Darth Maul 7.00
____Obi-Wan Kenobi 7.00
____Queen Amidala 7.00

Academic monthly planning calendars with assignment pages July 1999 – July 2000, 5.5"x8.5"

____Anakin Skywalker 4.00
____Darth Maul 4.00
____Queen Amidala 4.00

Dated assignment books.

____Anakin Skywalker 8.00
____Darth Maul 8.00
____Jedi 8.00

Monthly planners, 5.5"x8.5"

____Anakin Skywalker 5.00
____Darth Maul monthly planner [PLN03] 5.00
____Obi-Wan Kenobi [PLN04] 5.00
____Queen Amidala [PLN05] 5.00

Student planners.

____Darth Maul [PLN06] 13.00
____Jar Jar Binks [PLN07] 13.00
____Obi-Wan Kenobi 13.00
____Queen Amidala [PLN08] 13.00
____Queen Amidala (travel gown) 13.00
____Qui-Gon Jinn [PLN09] 13.00

Two-year monthly planner Jan 2000 – Dec 2001.

____Darth Maul 6.00
____Obi-Wan Kenobi 6.00
____Queen Amidala 6.00

Weekly planners. Assignments Aug 1999 to July 2000.

____Queen Amidala 6.00

Letts

____Luke Skywalker [PLN10] 2.00

Address book, datebook, and notepad.

____Classic Trilogy [PLN11] 6.00
____Queen Amidala [PLN12] 6.00

Mead

Student day planners.

____Darth Vader [PLN13] 8.00
____Darth Vader inset art [PLN14] 8.00
____Technology design with SW logo [PLN15] 8.00
____Technology design with SW logo on velcro latch [PLN16] 8.00
____Yoda inset art [PLN17] 8.00

Q-Stat

EPI:TPM address book, datebook, and notepad.

____Jar Jar Binks [PLN18] 6.00

Calendars

Poster wall calendars, 19"x35".

____2002 Art of Star Wars Episode I [PPC01] 24.00
____2002 Darth Vader: Reflections of Darkness [PPC02] 24.00

Thailand. Classic Trilogy poster pocket calendar cards.

____Empire Strikes Back 10th anniversary 2.00
____Empire Strikes Back 1982 re-release 2.00
____Empire Strikes Back public radio broadcast 2.00
____Empire Strikes Back style A 2.00
____Empire Strikes Back style A advance 2.00
____Empire Strikes Back style B 2.00
____Empire Strikes Back style C art 2.00
____Le Retour Du Jedi 2.00
____Return of the Jedi 10 anniversary advance 2.00
____Return of the Jedi 10th anniversary 2.00
____Return of the Jedi 1985 re-release 2.00
____Return of the Jedi horizontal 2.00
____Return of the Jedi style A in red 2.00
____Return of the Jedi style B 2.00
____Star Wars 10th anniversary 2.00
____Star Wars concert 2.00
____Star Wars lobby poster art [PPC03] 2.00
____Star Wars program art 2.00
____Star Wars public radio broadcast 2.00
____Star Wars style D 2.00

Thailand. Classic Trilogy SE pocket calendar cards.

____A New Hope [3:158] 2.00
____Empire Strikes Back [3:158] 2.00
____Return of the Jedi [3:158] 2.00

Thailand. EPI:TPM pocket calendar cards.

Characters / Pepsi logo.

____Anakin Skywalker [PPC04] 2.00
____C-3PO [3:158] 2.00
____Darth Maul [3:158] 2.00
____Jar Jar Binks [3:158] 2.00
____Queen Amidala [3:158] 2.00
____Qui-Gon Jinn [3:158] 2.00
____Sebulba [3:158] 2.00
____Watto [3:158] 2.00
____Yoda [3:158] 2.00

Characters.

____Anakin Skywalker [3:158] 2.00
____Darth Maul [PPC05] 2.00
____Movie Poster [3:158] 2.00
____Obi-Wan Kenobi [3:158] 2.00
____Queen Amidala [3:158] 2.00
____Qui-Gon and Obi-Wan [3:158] 2.00
____Qui-Gon Jinn [3:158] 2.00
____Yoda, Qui-Gon, and Obi-Wan [3:158] 2.00

Colleges.

____Confrontations [3:158] 2.00
____Entire cast [3:158] 2.00
____Heroes on Tatooine [3:158] 2.00
____Heroes over Naboo [3:158] 2.00
____Jedi vs. Sith on Tatooine [PPC06] 2.00
____Quartet of Destiny [3:158] 2.00
____Tatooine Duel / Podracing [3:158] 2.00

Thailand. EPIII:ROTS pocket calendar cards.

Characters.

____Anakin Skywalker [PPC07] 2.00
____Clone Trooper [PPC08] 2.00
____Epic Duel / Jedi [PPC09] 2.00
____General Grievous [PPC10] 2.00
____Mace Windu [PPC11] 2.00
____Yoda [PPC12] 2.00

Colleges.

____Anakin [PPC13] 2.00
____Darth Vader [PPC14] 2.00

Calendars

| PPC01 | PPC02 | PPC03 | PPC04 | PPC05 | PPC06 | PPC07 | PPC08 | PPC09 | PPC10 |

| PPC11 | PPC12 | PPC13 | PPC14 | PPC15 | PPC16 | PPC17 | PPC18 | PPC19 | PPC20 |

____Darth Vader lightsaber down [PPC15] 2.00
____Epic Duel / Darth Vader [PPC16] 2.00
____EPIII Conflict [PPC17]......................................2.00
____Jedi [PPC18] 2.00
____Obi-Wan [PPC19] 2.00
____Sith [PPC20] 2.00

20th Century Fox
____1999 Movie release desktop calendar [1:89]......16.00

Abrams
____1991 Lucasfilm [PPC21] 8.00

Andrews and McNeel
____1995 Trilogy 3D [PPC22] 11.00

Antioch
____1995 Trilogy 10.00

Ballantine
____1978 Star Wars [PPC23] 16.00
____1979 Star Wars [PPC24] 15.00
____1980 SW Poster Art [PPC25] 18.00
____1981 Empire Strikes Back [PPC26] 12.00
____1984 Return of the Jedi [PPC27] 16.00

Bay Street Publishing
____1998 Trilogy Special Edition [PPC28] 14.00
____1999 Darth Vader Reveals Anakin Skywalker [PPC29]...11.00
____2003 Attack of the Clones, 18 month [PPC30] ..14.00
____2003 SW Heroes and Villains..............................12.00

____2004 SW Heroes and Villains [PPC31] 12.00
____2005-2006 Darth Vader [PPC32] 8.00
____2005-2006 Revenge of the Sith [PPC33] 8.00
____2006 Poster Calendar [PPC34] 15.00

Bonbon Buddies
____Milk chocolate advent calendar 10.00

Cadbury
Advent 3-D.
____Jedi-Sith Duel, EPI [PPC35] 8.00

Capital
____1995 Distributing [PPC36] 8.00

Cedco Publishing
____1990 Trilogy [PPC37] 14.00
____1991 Trilogy [PPC38] 16.00
____1996 Wide Image 14.00
____1997 Art of Star Wars 11.00
____1997 Star Wars 20th Anniversary [PPC39] 14.00
____1998 Art of Star Wars: Classic Characters [PPC40]..16.00
____1998 Trilogy Special Edition, Han and Jabba on cover 8.00
____1999 Daily Wisdom of Star Wars........................12.00
____1999 Darth Vader Reveals Anakin Skywalker [PPC41]..14.00
____1999 Empire Strikes Back [PPC42] 14.00
____1999 May The Force Be With You [PPC43].......11.00
____1999 Star Wars 14.00
____1999 Weapons and Technology [PPC44] 15.00

____2003 Daily box calendar [PPC45] 12.00
____2003 Daily Character A-Z...............................12.00
____2003 Daily Episode II: Attack of the Clones 14.00
____2003 Droids locker calendar [PPC46] 10.00
____2003 Episode II, 18-month [PPC47] 15.00
____2003 Heroes and Rebels [PPC48] 14.00
____2003 Scum and Villainy [PPC49] 14.00
____2003. Daily Characters, Creatures, Droids 14.00
____2004 Art of Episode II [PPC50] 14.00
____2004 Classic Adventures [PPC51] 14.00
____2004 Daily Characters, Creatures, Droids [PPC52]..14.00
____2005 Star Wars Evolutions: Characters.............12.00
____2005 Star Wars Evolutions: Vehicles 12.00
____2006 Revenge of the Sith 12.00
____2006 The Complete Saga 12.00

Chronicle Books
____1997 Vehicles with blueprints 16.00

Code 3 Collectibles
____2004 1-sheet with lift-up panels [PPC53] 5.00

Cosmic Cat Creations
Fan Made.
____2005 The Year of the Crumb [PPC54] ....N/V

Day Runner
14"x16" laminated wipe-off 1-month blank wall calendar.
____Darth Maul [PPC55] 7.00
____Jar Jar Binks, horizontal [PPC56].........................7.00

| PPC21 | PPC22 | PPC23 | PPC24 | PPC25 | PPC26 |

 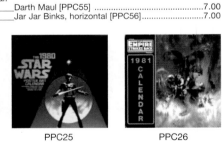

| PPC27 | PPC28 | PPC29 | PPC30 | PPC31 | PPC32 |

| PPC33 | PPC34 | PPC35 | PPC36 | PPC37 | PPC38 | PPC39 | PPC40 |

| PPC41 | PPC42 | PPC43 | PPC44 | PPC45 | PPC46 | PPC47 |

| PPC48 | PPC49 | PPC50 | PPC51 | PPC52 | PPC53 | PPC54 |

  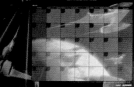  

| PPC55 | PPC56 | PPC57 | PPC58 | PPC59 |

____Jar Jar Binks, vertical 7.00
____Jedi 7.00
____Naboo fighters [PPC57] 7.00
____Obi-Wan Kenobi 7.00
____Queen Amidala [PPC58]...7.00
____Qui-Gon Jinn 7.00
____Watto, horizontal [PPC59] 7.00
____Watto, vertical 7.00

24"x35" laminated, 2-sided sheet.
____Jar Jar Binks 6.00
____Naboo Fighter 6.00
____Obi-Wan Kenobi 6.00
____Podrace 6.00
____Queen Amidala 6.00

Golden Turtle Press
____1997 Collector's Edition [PPC60]......................14.00
____1999 EPI 20-month wall calendar [PPC61] 18.00

____2000 Characters of Episode I [PPC62] 12.00
____2000 Han Solo cover [PPC63] 5.00
____2000 Mos Eisley Cantina Regulars [PPC64] 14.00
____2000 Yoda cover [PPC65]....................................5.00
____2001 Bounty Hunters [PPC66]...........................15.00
____2001 Jedi Forces [PPC67] 14.00
____2001 Podrace [PPC68]......................................14.00
____2002 Good vs. Evil [PPC69]...............................13.00

1999 18-month mini wall calendars.
____Darth Maul [PPC70] 5.00
____Jar Jar Binks [PPC71]...5.00
____Obi-Wan Kenobi [PPC72] 5.00
____Queen Amidala [PPC73] 5.00

2001 12-month mini wall calendars.
____Bounty Hunters [PPC74].......................................7.00
____Heroes [PPC75] 7.00
____Vehicles [PPC76]..7.00

____Villains [PPC77]..7.00

52 week engagement calenders.
____2000 Episode I [PPC78]......................................12.00
____2002 Star Wars Style [PPC79] 15.00

Flip animation, trivia calendars, boxed.
____2000 Podracer cover [PPC80] 7.00
____2001 Tie Fighters cover [PPC81] 8.00
____2001 X-Wings cover [PPC82]...............................8.00
____2002 Saga scenes cover [PPC83] 13.00

Hallmark
____1996 Star Wars 8.00
____1998 Return of the Jedi [PPC84] 7.00

Hallmark, Australia
____2000 Episode I, millennium collection [PPC85] 8.00
____2003 Episode II [PPC86].......................................8.00

| PPC60 | PPC61 | PPC62 | PPC63 | PPC64 | PPC65 | PPC66 |

| PPC67 | PPC68 | PPC69 | PPC70 | PPC71 | PPC72 | PPC73 |

| PPC74 | PPC75 | PPC76 | PPC77 | PPC78 | PPC79 |

Calendars

PPC80

PPC81

PPC82

PPC83

PPC84

PPC85

PPC86

PPC87

PPC88

PPC89

PPC90

PPC91

PPC92

PPC93

PPC94

PPC95

PPC96

PPC97

PPC98

PPC99

PPC100

PPC101

PPC94

PPC95

PPC96

PPC97

PPC98

PPC99   PPC100   PPC101

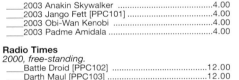
PPC102   PPC103   PPC104   PPC105   PPC106   PPC107

galleries, images available, and formats to choose from there are literally thousands of combinations that could have been made.

The galleries were comprised of images of Bounty Hunters, Clone Wars, Creatures, Droids, Holiday Art, Jedi, Logos and Emblems, Padme, Poster Art, Princess Leia, Rebels, Sith, and Vehicles.

____10"x15" glossy 15.00
____10"x15" matte 15.00
____20"x30" glossy 20.00
____20"x30" matte 20.00

Thomas Foreman and Sons
____1982 Star Wars / Empire Strikes Back 18.00

Calling Cards: Telephone

____Anakin Skywalker [3:161] 5.00
____C-3PO and R2-D2 [TPC01] 5.00
____Darth Maul [TPC02] 5.00
____Jar Jar Binks [3:161] 5.00
____Lucas Legacy 15.00
____Queen Amidala [3:161] 5.00
____Qui-Gon Jinn [3:161] 5.00
____ROTJ Chewbacca [3:161] 6.00
____Star Wars SE, promotion for pre-ordering SE Videos [3:161] 6.00
____Yoda [3:161] 5.00

$10.00, 250 fixed minutes, THX vido cover art.
____ANH / Vader [3:160] 14.00
____ESB / Stormtrooper [3:160] 14.00
____ROTJ / Yoda [3:160] 14.00

EPII:AOTC.
____Heroes top-up [TPC03]..............................6.00

Taiwan. Comic book and novel art.
____Dark Empire 1 ....5.00

Ink Group
____1998 – 2000 Star Wars Episode I 20 month calendar [PPC87]..18.00
____1998 Classic Commerative [PPC88] 14.00
____1998 The Battles [PPC89] 10.00
____1999 Heroes and Villains [PPC90] 10.00
____2000 Aliens and Creatures [PPC91] 10.00
____2000 EPI Collector's edition [PPC92] 8.00
____2000 EPI: The Adventures [PPC93] 8.00
____2002 Darth Vader: Reflections in Darkness [PPC94]..10.00
____2002 The Art of Star Wars Episode I 8.00
____2003 Attack of the Clones [PPC95] 8.00

Day-to-day calendars, boxed.
____1998 [PPC96] 8.00
____1999 C-3PO and X-Wings cover [PPC97] 7.00
____2000 Anakin / Podracing cover [PPC98] 8.00

Kinnerton Confectionery
Advent calendar, 26 chocolates with SW punch-out on back.
____Mask [PPC99].......................................10.00
____Mobile [PPC100] 10.00

Landmark
____1995 Trilogy.......................................6.00

Major Cineplex
EPII:AOTC pocket calendar cards.

____2003 Anakin Skywalker 4.00
____2003 Jango Fett [PPC101] 4.00
____2003 Obi-Wan Kenobi 4.00
____2003 Padme Amidala 4.00

Radio Times
2000, free-standing.
____Battle Droid [PPC102] 12.00
____Darth Maul [PPC103] 12.00
____Darth Maul with Sith Probes Droids [PPC104] ..12.00
____Jar Jar [PPC105] 12.00
____Obi-Wan Kenobi [PPC106]............................12.00

Random House
____1984 Return of the Jedi with Ewok stickers [PPC107]..16.00

Shooting Star Press
____1997 20th Anniversary 10.00

Slow Dazzle Worldwide
____1999 A New Hope / Star Wars 5.00
____1999 Empire Strikes Back 5.00
____1999 Return of the Jedi 5.00

starwars.com
In 2003 the official Star Wars site offered 13 themed galleries of approximately 12 images in each gallery. Fans could order the images from an online merchandiser in a variety of formats. Considering the number of

TPC01

TPC02

TPC03

TPC04

TPC05

TPC06

TPC07

TPC08

| TPC09 | TPC10 | TPC11 | TPC12 | TPC13 | TPC14 | TPC15 | TPC16 | TPC17 |

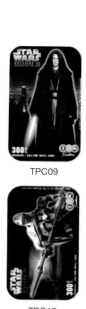

| TPC18 | TPC19 | TPC20 | TPC21 | TPC22 | TPC23 | TPC24 | TPC25 |

____Dark Empire 2 ....5.00
____Empire's End 5.00
____Empire's End 2 ....5.00
____Heirs to the Force 5.00
____Luke Skywalker..5.00

Taiwan. Movie collage art.
____EPI: characters 5.00
____EPI: heroes 5.00
____EPI: Phantom Menace 5.00
____EPII: Geonosis Jedi..5.00
____EPIII: Epic Duel / Obi-Wan 5.00
____EPIII: Epic Duel / Yoda 5.00

1-2-Call
300 units, ruler.
____Anakin vs. Obi-Wan [TPC04] 6.00
____Darth Vader [TPC05]..6.00
____Epic Duel [TPC06]..6.00
____Yoda [TPC07]..6.00

EPIII:ROTS Call Time Refill Card. 300 Baht. Series 2.
____Anakin Skywalker / Darth Vader [TPC08].............6.00
____Clone Commander 6.00
____Clone Trooper 6.00
____Darth Vader 6.00
____General Grievous 6.00
____Grievous' bodyguard 6.00
____Jedi Starfighters 6.00
____R2-D2 and C-3PO 6.00

EPIII:ROTS Call Time Refill Card. 300 Baht.
____Anakin (dark side) [TPC09] 5.00
____Anakin (Jedi) [TPC10] 5.00
____Anakin vs. Obi-Wan [TPC11] 5.00

____Clone Commander [TPC12] 5.00
____Clone Trooper (Order 66) [TPC13] 5.00
____Clone Trooper (standing) [TPC14] 5.00
____Darth Vader [TPC15]..5.00
____Darth Vader (reaching) [TPC16] 5.00
____General Grievous [TPC17] 5.00
____Grievous' bodyguard [TPC18] 5.00
____Obi-Wan Kenobi [TPC19] 5.00
____Yoda [TPC20] 5.00

EPIII:ROTS. Thailand.
____Forty different images, each 5.00

7-11, Japan
____1000 Minutes, contest premium [TPC21] 35.00

BT
ROTJ calling cards with collectible folders.
____01 Return of the Jedi image 15.00
____02 Return of the Jedi image 15.00
____03 Star Destroyer / DSII 15.00
____04 Inside DSII 15.00
____05 B-Wing Attack 15.00
____06 Boba Fett 15.00

Celcom
Gold EPII lenticular cards with folder for Malaysia.
____Anakin and Padme [TPC22] 30.00
____Heroes [TPC23] 30.00
____Sith [TPC24] 30.00
____Villains [TPC25]...30.00

Silver EPII lenticular cards with folder for Malaysia.
____Anakin and Padme...30.00
____Heroes 30.00

____Sith 30.00
____Villains..30.00

Disney / MGM
____C-3PO / Starspeeder 3000, mirrored [TPC26] 8.00

Entel
Bolivia. EPIII:ROTS. BS-30 prepaid.
____Anakin Skywalker [TPC27] 5.00
____Clone Trooper [TPC28] 5.00
____Epic Duel / Darth Vader [TPC29] 5.00
____Epic Duel / Emperor [TPC30] 5.00
____General Grievous [TPC31] 5.00
____Jedi Starfighter [TPC32] 5.00
____Obi-Wan Kenobi [TPC33] 5.00
____R2-D2 and C-3PO [TPC34] 5.00
____Wookies [TPC35] 5.00
____Yoda [TPC36] 5.00

Globalcall
____$10 Star Wars: Episode I collage [3:161] 7.00

GTI
$5 cards.
____B-Wing Fighter 8.00
____Darth Vader on Second Death Star 8.00
____Gamorrean Guard 8.00
____Imperial Star Destroyer 8.00
____Luke Skywalker in Landspeeder [TPC37] 8.00
____R2-D2 on Dagobah 8.00
____Speeder Bike Trooper [TPC38] 8.00
____Yoda [TPC39] 8.00
$10 cards.
____A-wing 15.00

| TPC26 | TPC27 | TPC28 | TPC29 | TPC30 | TPC31 | TPC32 | TPC33 |

| TPC34 | TPC35 | TPC36 | TPC37 | TPC38 | TPC39 | TPC40 | TPC41 |

Calling Cards: Telephone

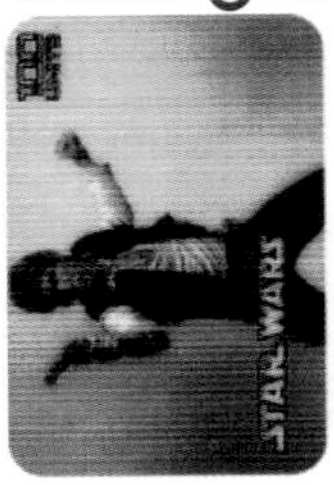
TPC42

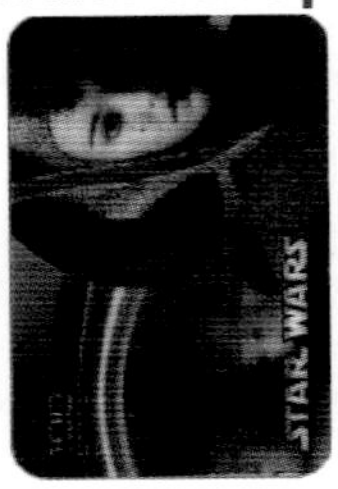
TPC43

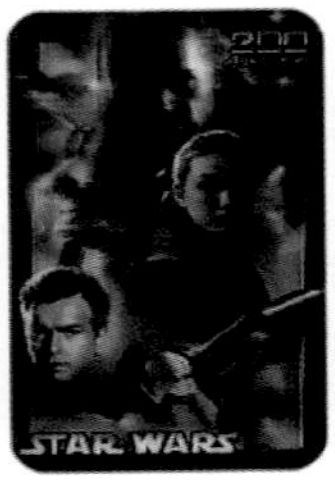
TPC44

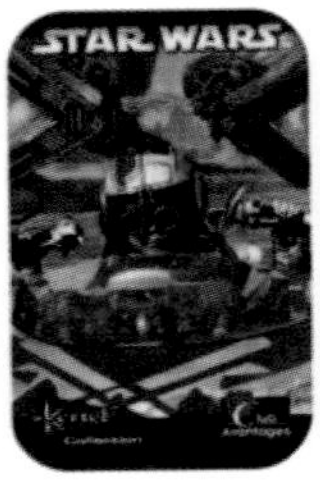
TPC45

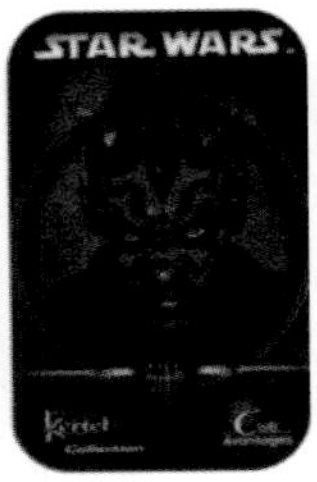
TPC46

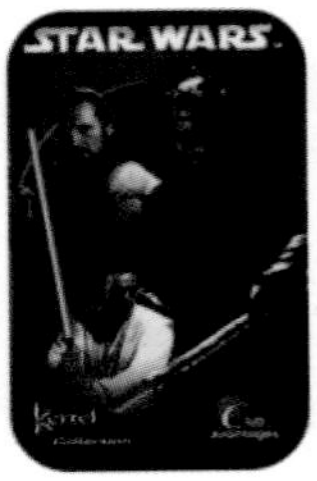
TPC47

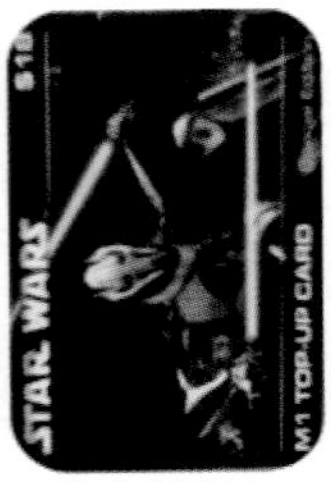
TPC48

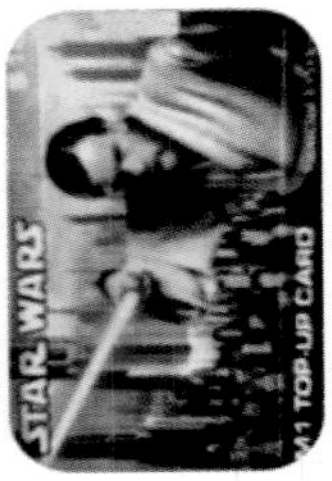
TPC49

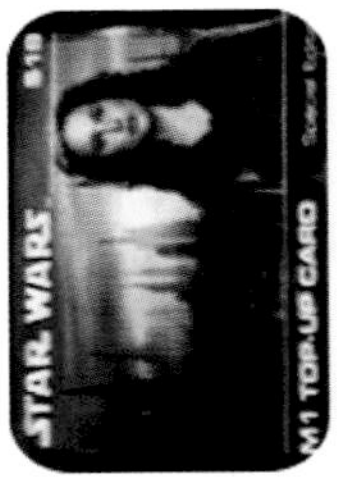
TPC50

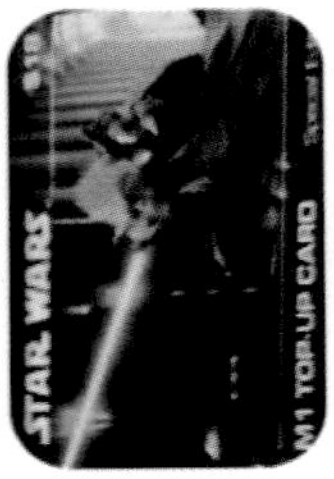
TPC51

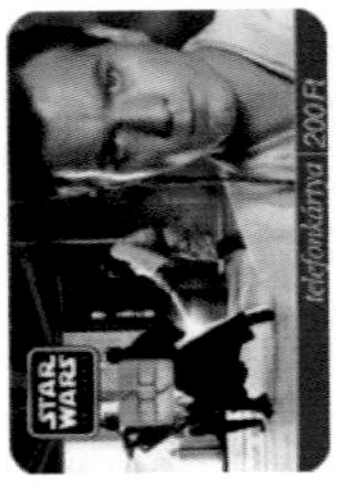
TPC52

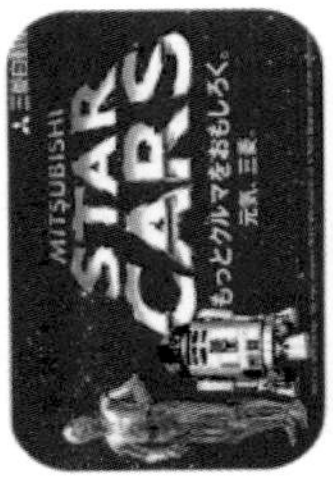
TPC53

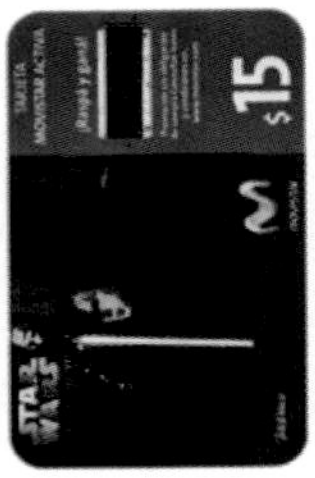
TPC54

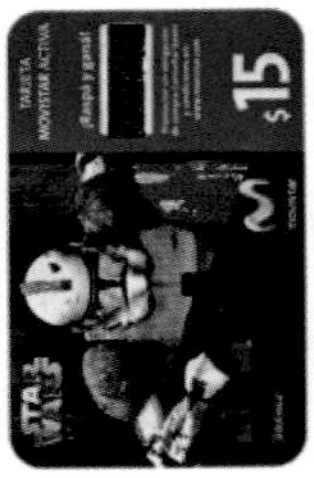
TPC55

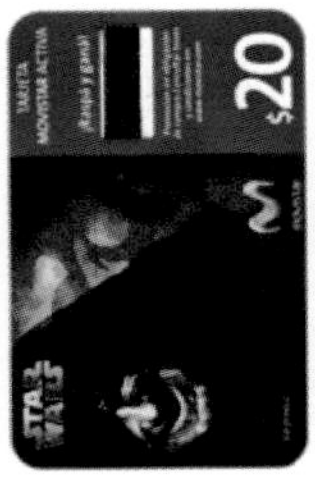
TPC56

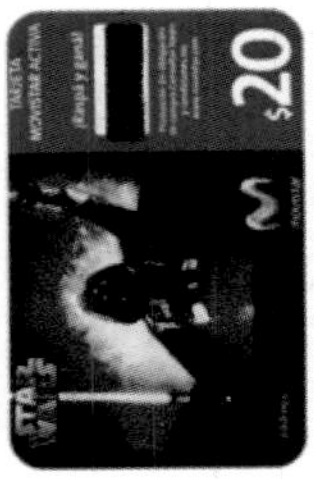
TPC57

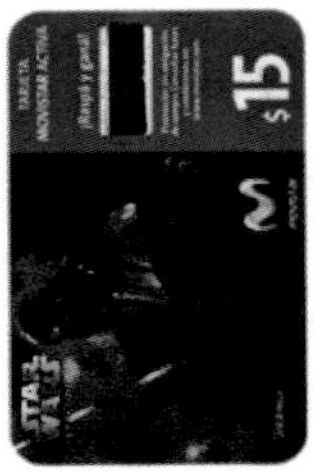
TPC58

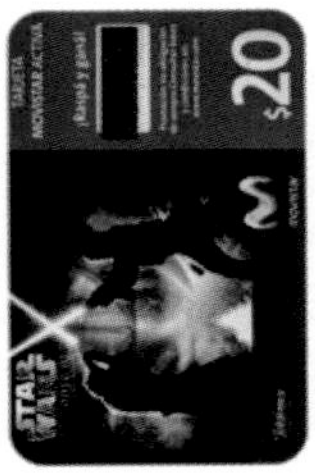
TPC59

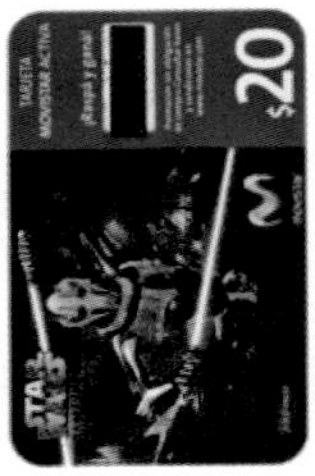
TPC60

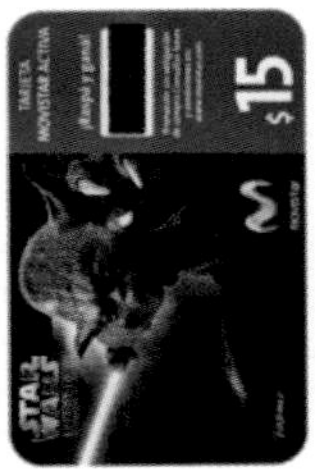
TPC61

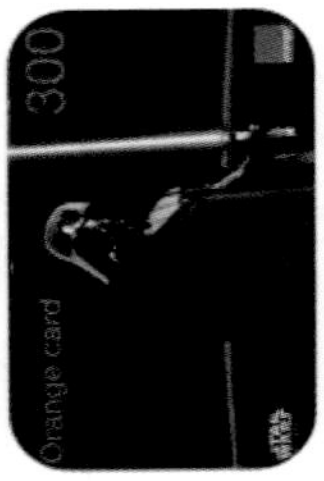
TPC62

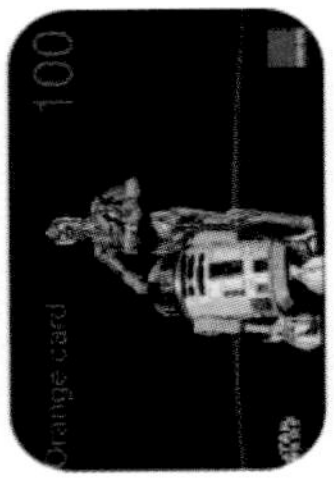
TPC63

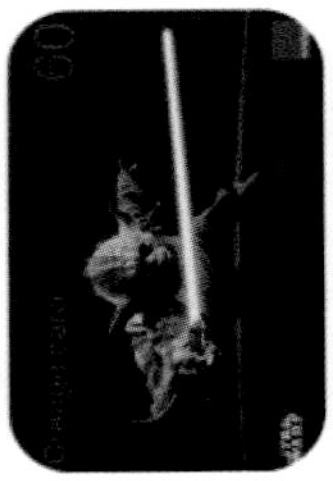
TPC64

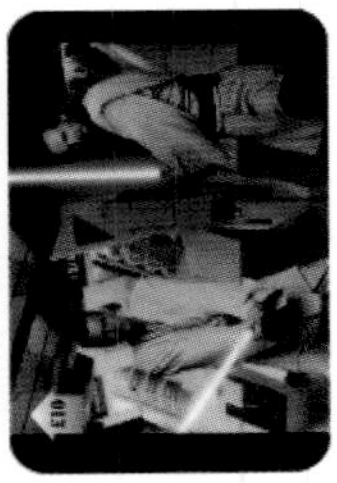
TPC65

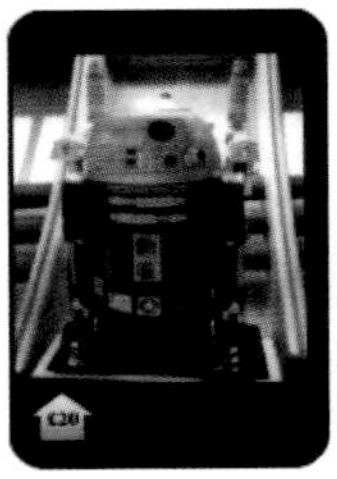
TPC66

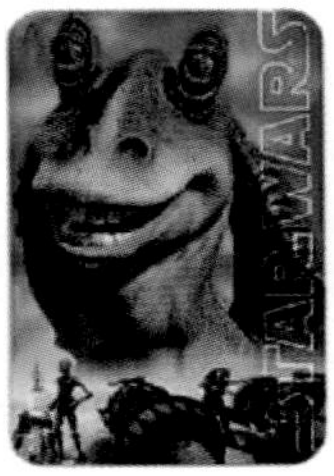
TPC67

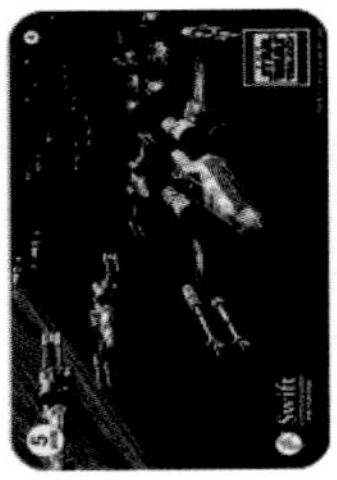
TPC68

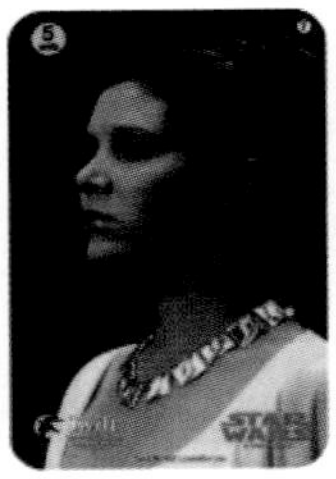
TPC69

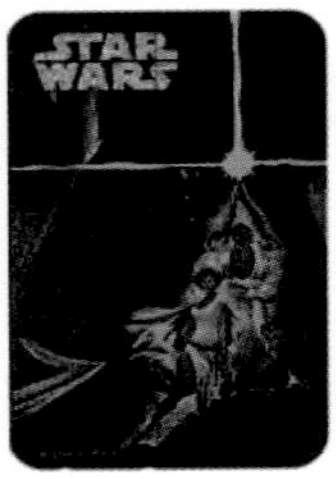
TPC70

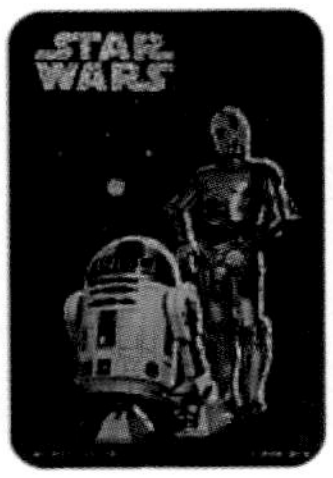
TPC71

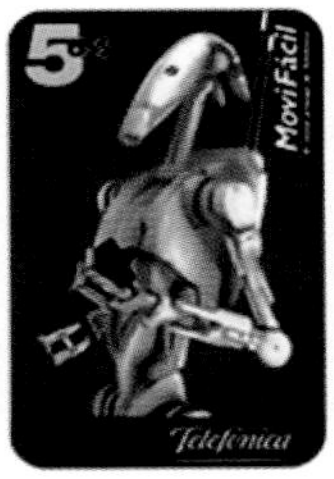
TPC72

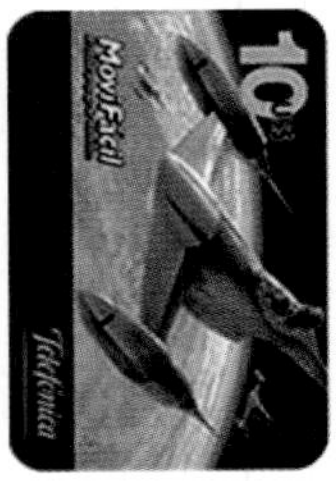
TPC73

____ANH Ben 15.00
____ANH ceremony 15.00
____AT-AT 15.00
____B-wings 15.00
____Darth Vader at Cloud City 15.00
____Emperor 15.00
____Han and Chewbacca 15.00
____Jabba and Bib Fortuna 15.00
____Luke and Yoda 15.00
____Millennium Falcon 15.00
____TIEs and X-wing 15.00

$20 cards.

____Ceremonial droids 18.00
____Ceremonial Leia 18.00
____Rebels on Hoth 18.00
____ROTJ ceremony 18.00
____ROTJ duel 18.00
____TIE bomber 18.00

Intelcom

50 Unit cards, 3D.

____ANH desert C-3PO and Luke [3:161] 4.00
____ANH jawas [3:161] 4.00
____ANH Leia and Luke [TPC40] 4.00
____ANH lightsaber duel [3:161] 4.00
____ANH Vader choking rebel [3:161] 4.00
____ANH X-wings [3:161] 4.00
____ESB AT-AT 4.00
____ESB Chewie and Leia [3:161] 4.00
____ESB finale scene [3:161] 4.00
____ROTJ AT-AT [3:161] 4.00
____ROTJ B-wings [3:161] 4.00
____ROTJ Boushh and frozen Han [3:161] 4.00
____ROTJ Death Star and star destroyer [3:161] 4.00
____TPM Naboo fighter [TPC41] 4.00
____TPM Royal Starship [3:161] 4.00

100 Unit cards, 3D.

____ANH Han promo shot [TPC42] 7.00
____ANH R2-D2 [3:161] 7.00
____ANH Stormtrooper promo shot [3:161] 7.00
____ESB Fett [3:161] 7.00
____ESB Yoda [3:161] 7.00
____TPM Anakin [3:161] 7.00
____TPM Battle Droid and Federation Tanks [3:161] 7.00
____TPM Darth Maul / Lightsaber Battle [3:161] 7.00
____TPM Jar Jar [3:161] 7.00
____TPM Obi-Wan Kenobi [3:161] 7.00
____TPM Queen Amidala [TPC43] 7.00
____TPM Qui-Gon Jinn [3:161] 7.00
____TPM Watto [3:161] 7.00

200 Unit cards, 3D.

____ESB intl video artwork [3:161] 8.00
____TPM characters [TPC44] 8.00

Kertel

____Anakin Skywalker [TPC45] 5.00
____Darth Maul [TPC46] 5.00
____Jedi vs. Sith [TPC47] 5.00

M1

EPIII:ROTS. Top Up cards, special edition.

____General Grievous [TPC48] 8.00
____Obi-Wan Kenobi [TPC49] 8.00
____Padme [TPC50] 8.00
____Yoda [TPC51] 8.00

Matav

____Anakin Skywalker [3:161] 11.00
____Obi-Wan Kenobi [TPC52] 11.00
____Queen Amidala [3:161] 14.00
____Qui-Gon Jinn [3:161] 11.00

Mitsubushi

____C-3PO and R2-D2 [TPC53] 12.00

Movistar

Argentina. EPIII:ROTS.

____Anakin Skywalker / Darth Vader [TPC54] 5.00
____Anakin Skywalker / Darth Vader 5.00
____Chewbacca 5.00
____Clone Trooper [TPC55] 5.00
____Darth Sidious [TPC56] 5.00
____Darth Vader (helmet) 5.00
____Darth Vader reaching [TPC57] 5.00
____Darth Vader standing [TPC58] 5.00
____Epic Duel, blue [TPC59] 5.00
____Epic Duel, red 5.00
____General Grievous 5.00
____General Grievous with lightsabers [TPC60] 5.00
____Obi-Wan Kenobi 5.00
____Yoda jumping 5.00
____Yoda reaching [TPC61] 5.00
____Yoda standing 5.00

Guatemala. EPIII:ROTS.

____Anakin and Obi-Wan 5.00
____Chewbacca 5.00
____Clone Trooper 5.00
____Darth Vader 5.00
____Darth Vader and Anakin 5.00
____R2-D2 and C-3PO 5.00
____Yoda 5.00

Venezuela. EPIII:ROTS.

____Clone Trooper 5.00
____Epic Duel 5.00
____Mace Windu 5.00
____Yoda 5.00

CAM01

CAM02

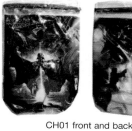
CAM03

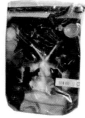
CH01 front and back

CH02

CH03

BC01

BC02

BC03

BC04

HOA01

LCV01

LCV02

LCV03

LCV04

Orange
Dominican Republic.
____Darth Vader 300 units [TPC62]		20.00
____Droids 100 units [TPC63]		20.00
____Yoda 60 units [TPC64]		15.00

PPS Ltd.
____Anakin and Obi-Wan [3:161] 2.00
____Battle Droid Army [3:161] 2.00
____Obi-Wan and Qui-Gon [TPC65] 2.00
____Obi-Wan Kenobi [3:161] 2.00
____Queen Amidala [3:161] 2.00
____Qui-Gon, Jar Jar, and Anakin [3:161] 2.00
____R2 unit, blue [TPC66] 2.00
____R2 unit, red [3:161] 2.00

Singapore Telecom
____Jar Jar Binks [TPC67] 6.00
____Obi-Wan Kenobi [3:161] 6.00
____Watto [3:161]..6.00

Swift Communications International
____1 Millennium Falcon over Mos Eisley [3:161] 14.00
____2 Millennium Falcon over Bespin [3:161]............14.00
____3 Millennium Falcon / Death Star II [3:161] 14.00
____4 X-Wings in formation [TPC68] 14.00
____5 Heroes on Hoth [3:161] 14.00
____6 Yoda in hut [3:161] 14.00
____7 Princess Leia, Yavin celebration [TPC69]........14.00
____8 Cloud City welcome [3:161] 14.00
____9 Emperor's throne room [3:161] 14.00
____10 Heroes in 3863827 [3:161] 14.00
____11 Chewbacca and R2 [3:161] 14.00
____12 Logray [3:161] 14.00
____13 Obi-Wan and Vader duel [3:161]...................14.00
____14 X-Wing and medical frigate [3:161] 14.00
____15 Millennium Falcon docked [3:161] 14.00
____16 "Help me Obi-Wan Kenobi..." [3:161]............14.00
____17 Preparing Han for carbon freeze [3:161] 14.00
____18 Battle above death Star II [3:161].................14.00
____19 Ronto in Mos Eisley [3:161] 14.00
____20 Cloud City residents [3:161] 14.00
____21 Shuttle landing on Death Star II [3:161] 14.00
____22 Luke, Han, and Chewbacca entering Yavin ceremony [3:161]..14.00
____23 Cloud cars outside Leia's window [3:161]...14.00
____24 Bib Fortuna and Boushh [3:161]....................14.00
____25 Cantina patron reports disturbance [3:161]...14.00
____26 Millennium Falcon lands on Cloud City [3:161]...14.00
____27 Emperor in his throne room [3:161] 14.00
____28 Jabba and Han in Mos Eisley [3:161]............14.00
____29 Wampa's meal disturbed [3:161] 14.00
____30 Imperial welcome [3:161] 14.00

Teleca
Star Wars anniversary set.
____ANH movie poster art [TPC70] 10.00
____Anniversary 10.00
____C-3PO and R2-D2 [TPC71] 10.00
____Darth Vader 10.00
____Falcon above Death Star II 10.00
____Han and Chewbacca 10.00
____Yoda 10.00

Telefonica
____Anakin Skywalker [3:161] 5.00
____Battle Droid [TPC72]...5.00
____C-3PO [3:161] 5.00
____Jedi Knights [3:161] 5.00
____Naboo Fighter [TPC73] 5.00

Cameras

Celebration 3.
____Characture art [CAM01] 10.00

Kellogg NA Co.
____Disposable, 12 exposure [CAM02] 10.00

Tiger Electronics
Picture Plus image camera.
____Darth Maul with background 35.00
____Darth Maul without background [CAM03] 25.00

Can Holders

____EPIII inflatable bottle cozy [CH01]......................14.00

Pepsi Cola
Mail-in premiums, Japan exclusives.
____Battle Droid [CH02] 65.00
____R2-D2 [CH03] 95.00

Candles

Unique
____SW:EPI with classic logo [BC01] 5.00

Wilton
____Chewbacca Cake Candle [BC02]..........................7.00
____Darth Vader Cake Candle [BC03].........................7.00
____R2-D2 Cake Candle [BC04] 7.00

Candlestick Holders

Sigma
____Yoda candlestick holder, ceramic [HOA01] 65.00

Candy Covers

Chupa Chups
Port-a-Chups lollipop covers, hanging.
____C-3PO [LCV01]..2.00
____Chewbacca [LCV02] 2.00
____Darth Vader [LCV03]...2.00
____Stormtrooper [LCV04]...2.00

Candy Jars

Audus Noble Blyth
Plastic lolly jar with character sculpt on lid.
____Darth Maul [JC01]..8.00
____Darth Vader [JC02]..12.00
____R2-D2 and C-3PO [JC03] 12.00

Galerie Chocolates
____C-3PO [JC04] 30.00
____Darth Vader [JC05]..20.00

Candy Molds

Suckers.
____3: Chewbacca, R2-D2, Darth Vader [2:133] 12.00
____3: Yoda x 3 [2:133] 10.00
____4: C-3PO x 4 [2:133] 12.00
____4: Chewbacca x 2, Darth Vader x 2 [2:133]........14.00
____6: Bib Fortuna, Gamorrean Guard, Jabba, Squid Head, Luke, Leia as Boushh [2:133] 25.00

JC01   JC02   JC03   JC04   JC05

Candy Molds

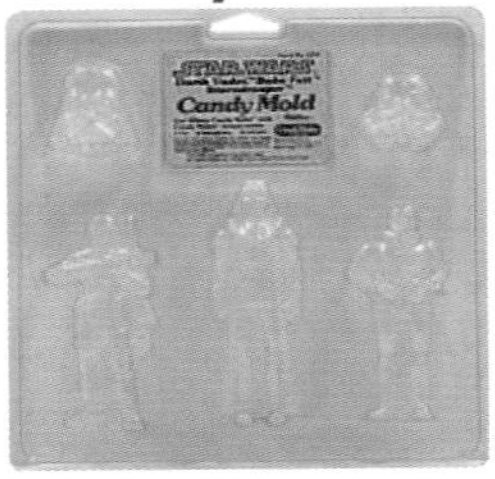
BM01

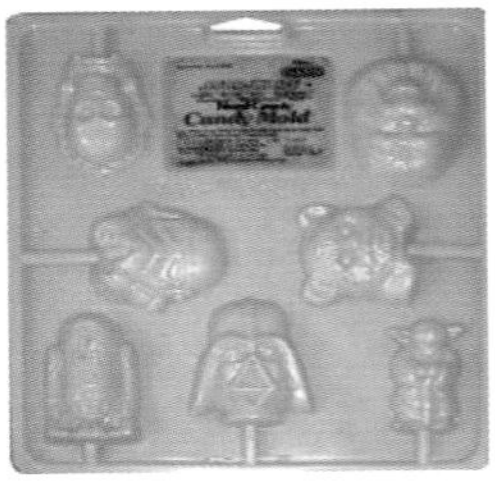
BM02

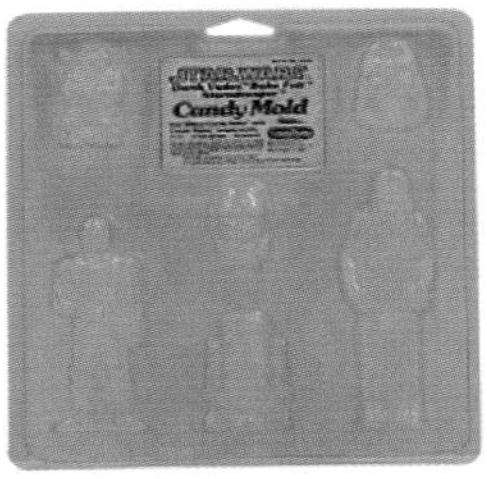
BM03

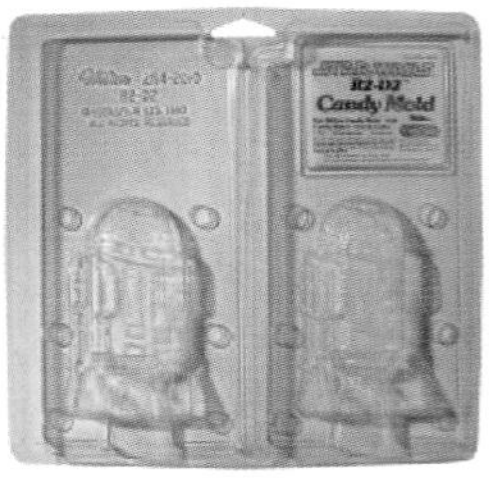
BM04

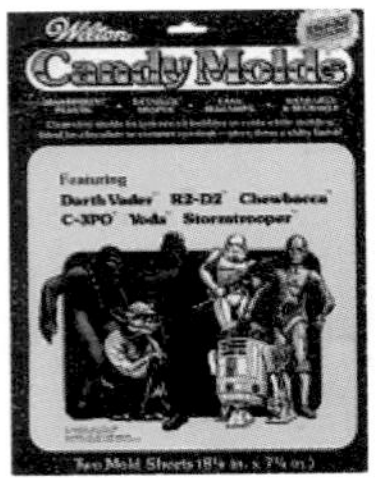

BM05

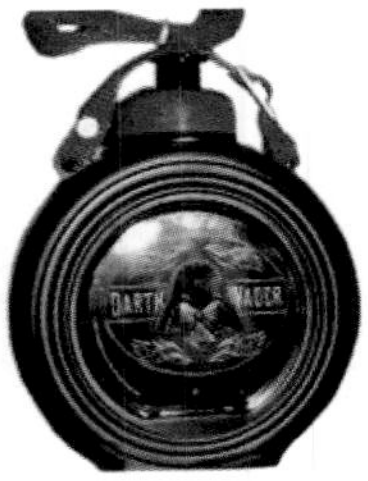
CNT01

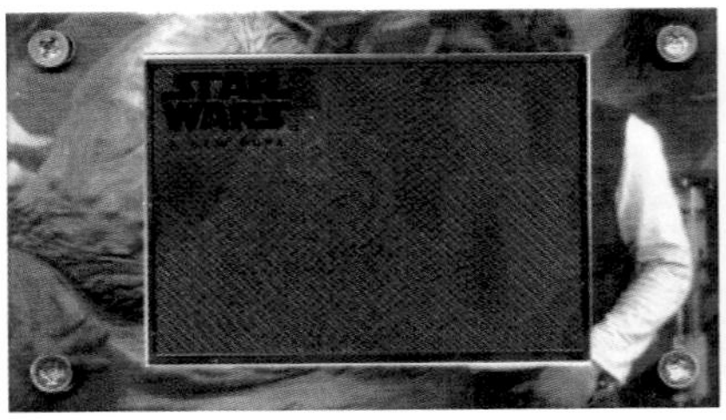
PMC01

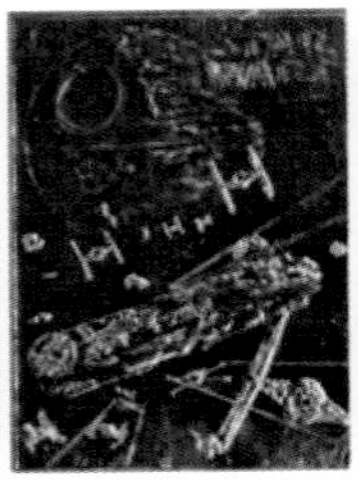
PMC02

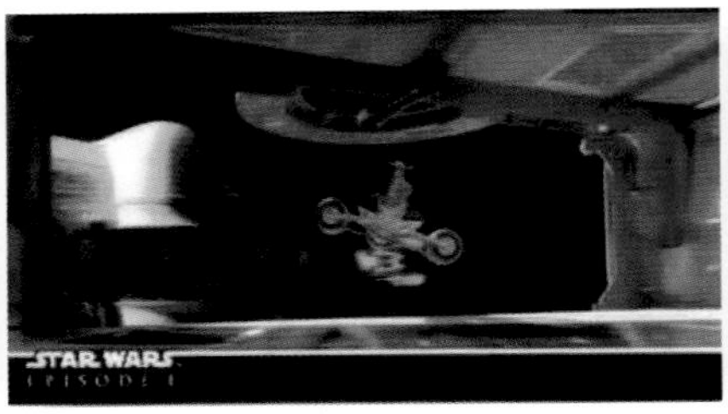

TE301 Card #1

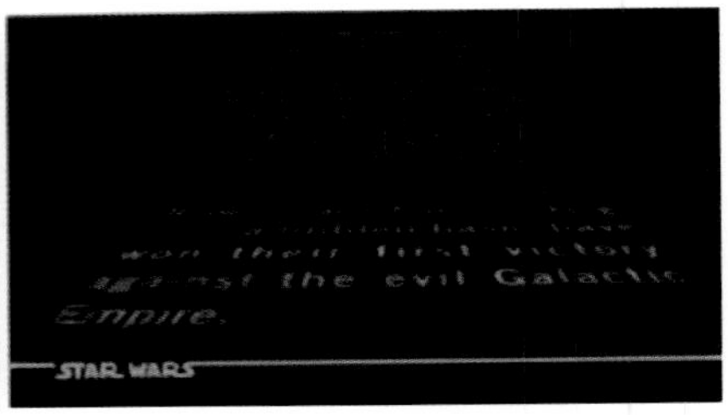

DI301 Card #2

____6: C-3PO, Chewbacca, Darth Vader x 2, Stormtrooper x 2 [2:133] 18.00
____6: Ewok x 6 [2:133]....12.00
____6: Yoda x 6 [2:133] 12.00

Wilton
____Boba Fett, Darth Vader, Stormtrooper [BM01] 20.00
____C-3PO, Chewbacca, Darth Vader, R2-D2, Stormtrooper, Ewok, and Yoda suckers [BM02] 20.00
____C-3PO, Chewbacca, R2-D2, Yoda candy, C-3PO and Chewbacca suckers [BM03] 20.00
____Chewbacca, C-3PO, R2-D2, Yoda 20.00
____R2-D2, large [BM04]....15.00
____Two mold sheets featuring Darth Vader, R2-D2, Chewbacca, C-3PO, Yoda, Stormtrooper [BM05] 45.00

Canteens

____Darth Vader [CNT01] 17.00

Card Holders: Business

Japan.
____Jedi Training Acadamy / EPII AOTC [3:166] 14.00

Cards: 24k Gold

Authentic Images
Acrylic holder and padded storage box. A New Hope images. Limited to 1,997 per image.
____Ben Kenobi, Darth Vader, Han and Jabba [PMC01], Leia and Vader, Luke, each 85.00

Acrylic holder and padded storage box. Empire Strikes Back images. Limited to 1,000 per image.
____Boba Fett, Darth Vader, Emperor Palpatine, Luke, Yoda, each 85.00

Acrylic holder and padded storage box. Return of the Jedi images. Limited to 1,000 per image.
____Darth Vader unmasked, Droids, Jabba's court, Jedi spirits, Luke vs. Boba Fett, each 85.00

24k gold ingot image.
____Trilogy Movie Poster, 5,000 produced....170.00

Score Board
23k gold. Limited to 10,000 per image. (Images in 2nd edition, page 163.)
____Bounty Hunters, Darth Vader, Millennium Falcon [PMC02], each 40.00
____Shadows of the Empire 35.00
____SW Trilogy movie poster, set of 3 in mini storage binder sleeve 89.00

Cards: 3D, TPM

Topps
46 numbered cards, 1 promotional card, 2 multi-motion cards. (Images in 2nd edition, page 94. Checklist in 3rd edition, page 166.)
____Cards 1 – 46, each 1.00
____Cards 1 – 46, set 25.00
____Multi-motion cards, each 10.00
____Promo card, each 8.00
____Unopened card packets, each 7.00

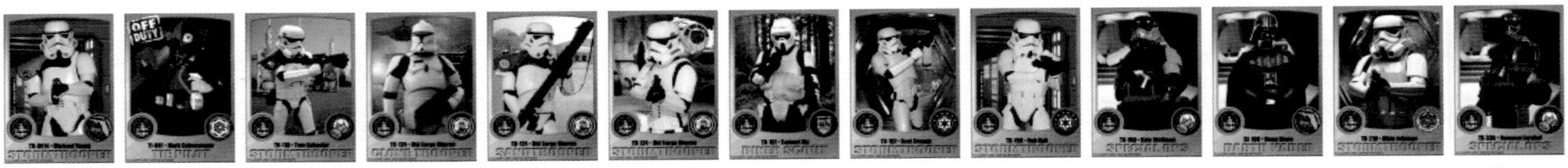
TK01 TK02 TK03 TK04 TK05 TK06 TK07 TK08 TK09 TK10 TK11 TK12 TK13

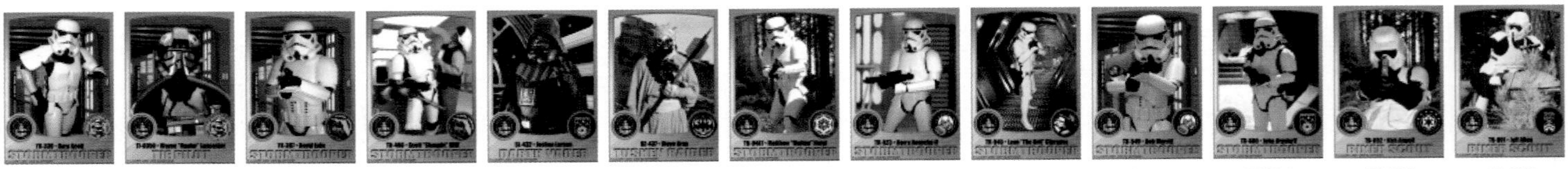
TK14 TK15 TK16 TK17 TK18 TK19 TK20 TK21 TK22 TK23 TK24 TK25 TK26

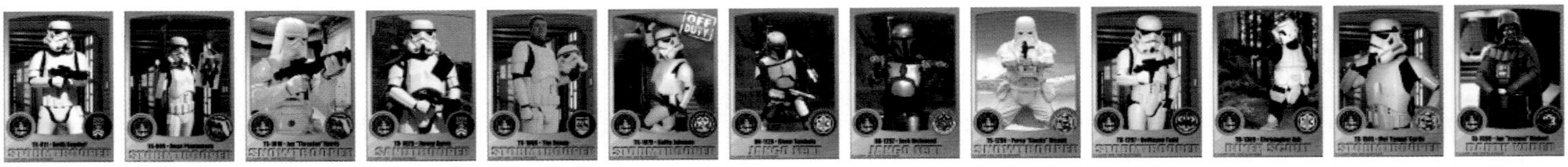
TK27 TK28 TK29 TK30 TK31 TK32 TK33 TK34 TK35 TK36 TK37 TK38 TK39

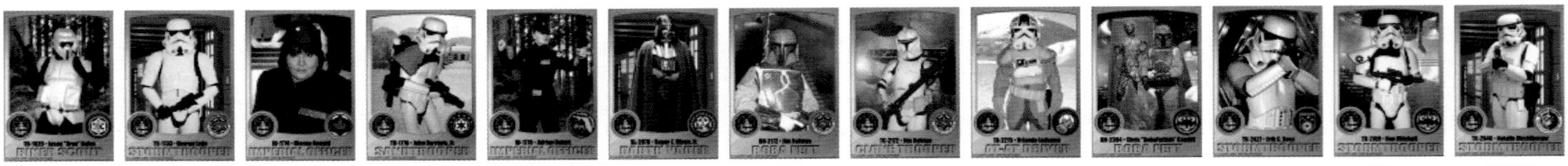
TK40 TK41 TK42 TK43 TK44 TK45 TK46 TK47 TK48 TK49 TK50 TK51 TK52

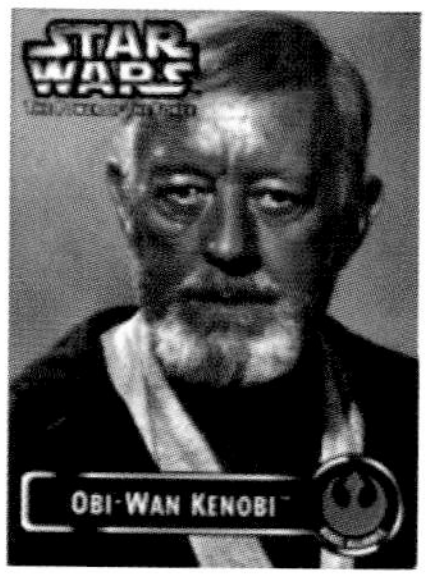

OA01 sample

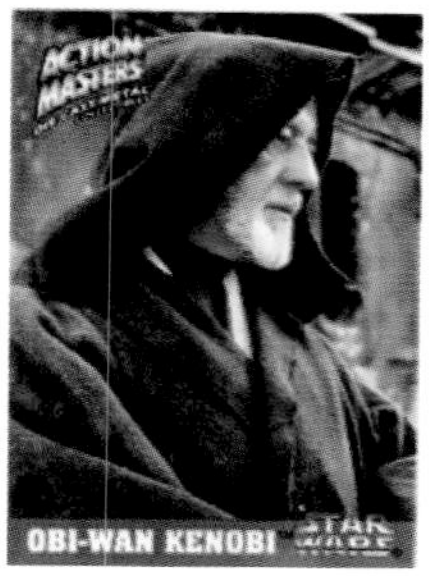

OA02 sample

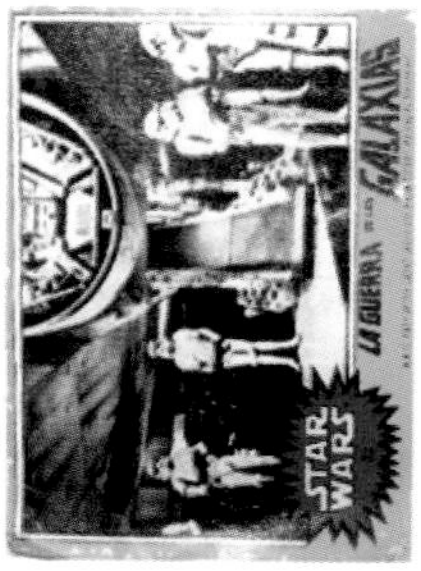

OV01 sample

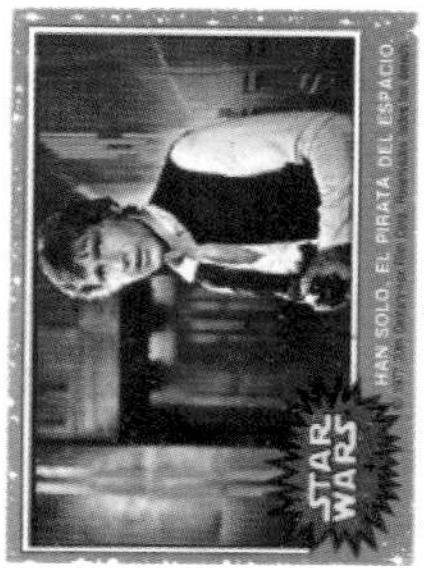

OV02 sample

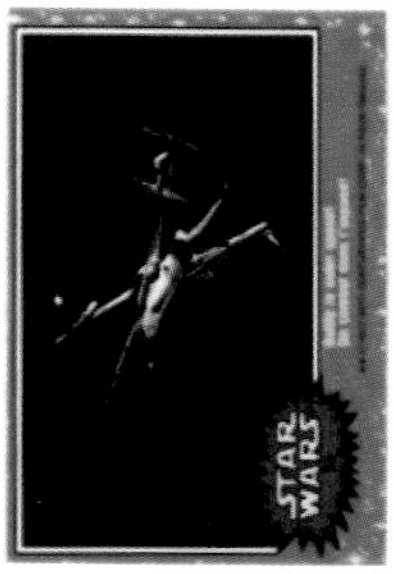

OV03 sample

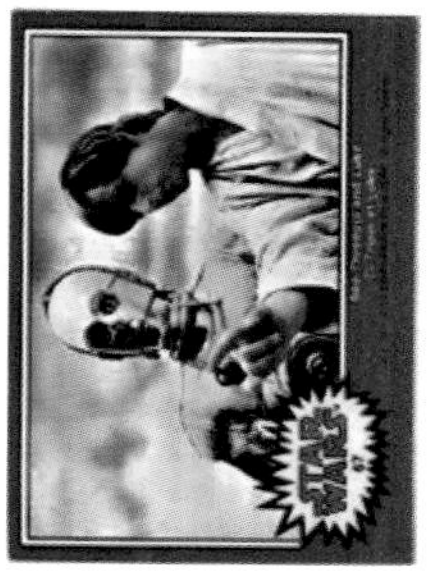

OV04 sample

Cards: 3Di

Topps
63 numbered cards, 4 promotional cards, 1 bonus card, 1 multi-motion cards. (Images in 2nd edition, page 95. Checklist in 3rd edition, page 166.)

____Bonus card with envelope 4.00
____Cards 1 – 63, each 1.00
____Cards 1 – 63, set 25.00
____Multi-motion card 6.00
____Promo cards, each 6.00
____Unopened card packets, each 7.00

Cards: 501st

501st Legion
100 unnumbered trading cards given away by 501st members at Star Wars Celebration III. (Checklist at www.StarWarsCards.net)

____Cards [TK01-TK100], each 2.00
____Cards, set 85.00

Cards: Action Masters

Kenner
Action Masters. 25 cards, unnumbered. Distributed inside 4-packs, 6-packs, and single packs of Action Master figures. (Images in 2nd edition, page 167 and 3rd edition, page 165. Checklist in 3rd edition, page 164.)

____Cards from 1st packaging [OA01], each 1.00
____Cards from POTF2 packaging [OA02], each 1.00

Cards: ANH

Argentina. Guerra de las Galaxias. 66 numbered blue border cards, no stickers.

____Cards 1 – 66 [OV01], each 1.50
____Cards 1 – 66, set 66.00
____Unopened card packets, each 10.00

Laboratorios y Agencias Unidas
Mexico. Spanish text. Series 1. 66 numbered blue border cards, no stickers.

____Cards 1 – 66 [OV02], each 1.50
____Cards 1 – 66, set 75.00
____Unopened card packets, each 11.00

O-Pee-Chee, Canada
English and French text. Series 1. 66 numbered blue border cards, 11 numbered stickers.

____Cards 1 – 66 [OV03], each 1.50
____Cards 1 – 66, set 75.00
____Stickers 1 – 11, each 5.00
____Unopened card packets, each 8.00

English and French text. Series 2. 66 numbered red border cards, 11 numbered stickers.

____Cards 67 – 132 [OV04], each 1.50
____Cards 67 – 132, set 75.00
____Stickers 12 – 22, each 5.00
____Unopened card packets, each 8.00

English and French text. Series 3. 132 numbered orange border cards, 11 numbered stickers.

____Cards 133 – 265 [OV05], each 1.50
____Cards 133 – 265, set 125.00
____Stickers 13 – 33, each 4.00
____Unopened card packets, each 10.00

Pacosa Dos/Internacional
187 numbered cards. White borders, no text. (Images in 3rd ed., pg. 168. Checklist in 3rd ed., pg. 167.)

____Cards 1 – 187 [OV06], each 1.00
____Cards 1 – 187, set 55.00
____Unopened card packets, each 18.00

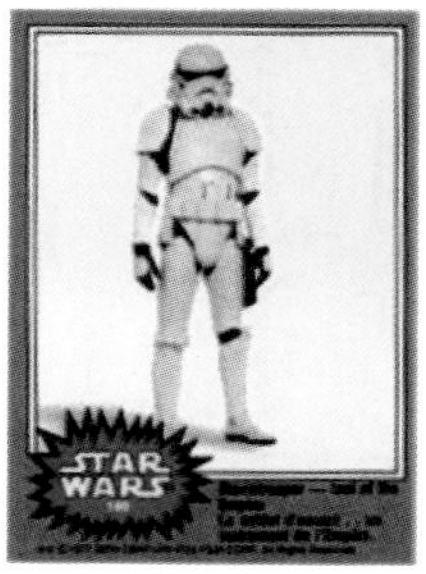

OV05 sample

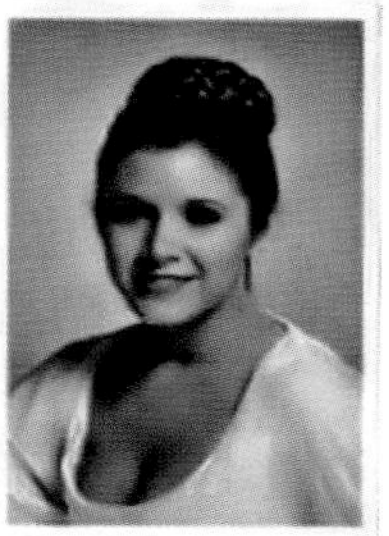

OV06 sample

Scanlens
72 numbered cards. (Checklist in 3rd ed. pg. 170.)

____Cards 1 – 72, each 1.50

Topps
Series 1. 66 numbered blue border cards, 11 numbered stickers. (Images in 2nd edition, page 166. Checklist in 3rd edition, page 170.)

____Cards 1 – 66 [OV07], each 1.50
____Cards 1 – 66, set 75.00
____Stickers 1 – 11 [OV08], each 5.00
____Unopened card packets, each 8.00

Series 2. 66 numbered red border cards, 11 numbered stickers. (Images in 2nd edition, page 167. Checklist in 3rd edition, page 170.)

____Cards 67 – 132 [OV09], each 1.50
____Cards 67 – 132, set 75.00
____Stickers 12 – 22 [OV10], each 5.00
____Unopened card packets, each 8.00

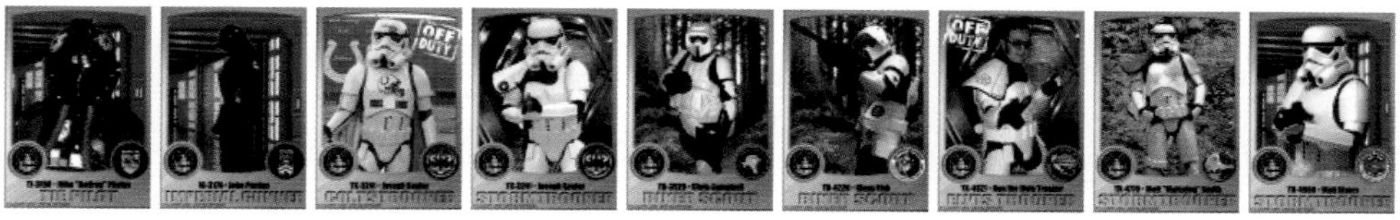

TK53 TK54 TK55 TK56 TK57 TK58 TK59 TK60 TK61

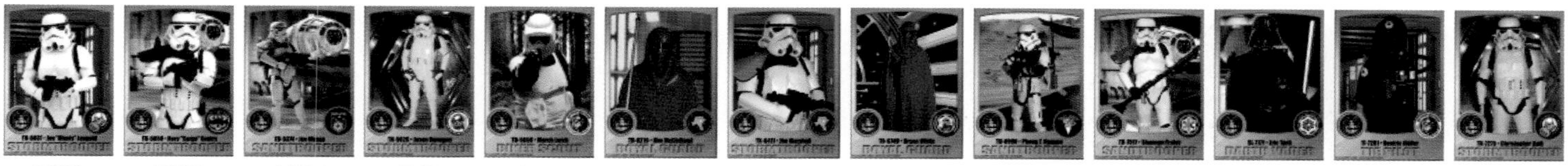

TK62 TK63 TK64 TK65 TK66 TK67 TK68 TK69 TK70 TK71 TK72 TK73 TK74

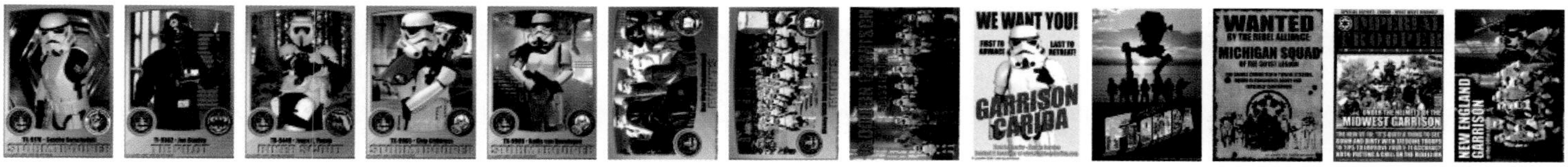

TK75 TK76 TK77 TK78 TK79 TK80 TK81 TK82 TK83 TK84 TK85 TK86 TK87

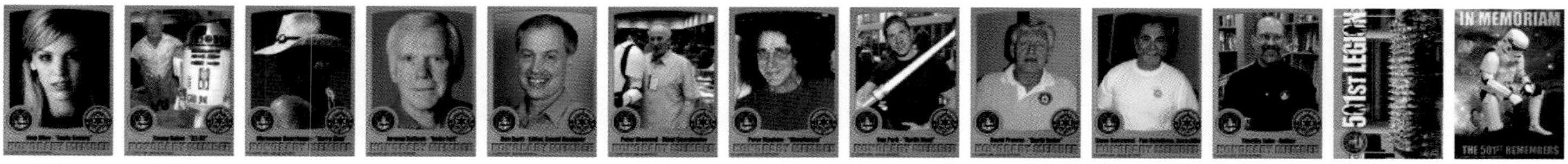

TK88 TK89 TK90 TK91 TK92 TK93 TK94 TK95 TK96 TK97 TK98 TK99 TK100

Cards: ANH

OV07 sample

OV08 sample

OV09 sample

OV10 sample

OV11 sample

OV12 sample

OV13 sample

OV14

OV15 sample

OV16 sample

OV17 sample

OV18 sample

Series 3. 66 numbered yellow border cards, 11 numbered stickers. (Images in 2nd edition, page 168. Checklist in 3rd edition, page 171.)
____Cards 133 – 198 [OV11], each 1.50
____Cards 133 – 198, set 75.00
____Stickers 23 – 33 [OV12], each 5.00
____Unopened card packets, each 8.00

Series 4. 66 numbered green border cards, 11 numbered stickers. (Images in 2nd edition, page 169. Checklist in 3rd edition, page 171.)
____Cards 199 – 264 [OV13], each 1.50
____Cards 199 – 264, set 75.00
____Cards #207 original X-rated version [OV14] 36.00
____Stickers 34-44 [OV15], each.................................5.00
____Unopened card packets, each 8.00

Series 5. 66 numbered orange border cards, 11 numbered stickers. (Images in 2nd edition, page 170. Checklist in 3rd edition, page 172.)
____Cards 265 – 330 [OV16], each 1.50
____Cards 265 – 330, set 75.00
____Stickers 45 – 55 [OV17], each 5.00
____Unopened card packets, each 8.00

Topps, U.K.
Series 1. 66 numbered blue border cards, no stickers. (Checklist in 3rd edition, page 172.)
____Cards 1 – 66, each 1.50
____Cards 1 – 66, set 75.00

Series 2. 66 numbered red border cards, no stickers. Numbered 1a – 66a. (Checklist at: www.StarWarsCards.net)
____Cards 1a – 66a, each 1.50
____Cards 1a – 66a, set 75.00
____Unopened card packets, each 8.00

Yamakatsu Corporation
Japan. Set of 36 unnumbered blue border cards, text on back. (Images in 3rd edition, page 172. Checklist in 3rd edition, page 173.)
____Cards [OV18], each..2.50
____Cards, set 75.00
____Unopened card packets, each 8.00

Cards: AOTC

20th Century Fox
Germany. Episode 2 opening-day cinema foil cards. 4 numbered cards. (Images in 3rd edition, page 173. Checklist in 3rd edition, page 173.)
____Cards [CA101], each 14.00

7-11
Japan. 16 unnumbered cards, 3 winner cards. (Images in 3rd ed., pg. 173. Checklist in 3rd ed., pg. 173.)
____Cards [CA102], each..4.00
____Winner cards [CA103], each.................................4.00

Black Diamond
Canada. Set of 12 numbered Connector Cards. First six produced by Cheesestrings, last six produced by Black Diamond. (Images in 3rd edition, page 174. Checklist in 3rd edition, page 174.)
____Cards 7 – 12 [CA101], each 1.00

Cheesestrings
Canada. Set of 12 numbered Connector Cards. First six produced by Cheesestrings, last six produced by Black Diamond. (Images in 3rd edition, page 174. Checklist in 3rd edition, page 174.)
____Cards 1 – 6 [CA105], each 1.00

Eskimo
Japan. 30 numbered cards, 1 lucky winner card. Ice cream premiums. (Images in 3rd edition, page 174. Checklist in 3rd edition, page 174.)
____Cards 1 – 30 [CA106], each 2.00
____Lucky Winner card [CA107] 45.00

Habib's Restaurant
Brazil. 8 unnumbered cards. (Images in 3rd edition, page 174. Checklist in 3rd edition, page 174.)
____Cards [CA108], each..3.00

Mainland Food
New Zealand. 18 numbered cards. (Images in 2nd edition, page 172. Checklist in 3rd edition, page 174.)
____Cards 1 – 18 [CA109], each 3.00

CA101 sample

CA102 sample

CA103 sample

CA104 sample

CA105 sample

CA106 sample

CA107 sample

CA108 sample

CA109 sample

CA110 sample

CA111 sample

CA112 sample

CA113 sample

CA114 sample

CA115 sample

Topps
100 cards plus 6 promotional, 5 mega-sized foil, 5 panaramic fold out, 8 prismatic foil, 10 silver foil cards. (Images in 2nd edition, page 173. Checklist in 3rd edition, page 174.)
Cards 1 – 100 each
____Cards 1 – 21 (characters) [CA110], each 0.25
____Cards 22 – 90 (movie scenes) [CA111], each 0.25
____Cards 91 – 100 (behind-the-scenes) [CA112], each 0.25
____Cards 1 – 100, set 18.00
____Mega-sized foil cards, each 25.00
____Panaramic fold-out cards [CA113], each 5.00
____Prismatic foil cards [CA114], each 2.00
____Promo cards P1-P5, each 5.00
____Promo card P6 ....8.00
____Silver foil cards [CA115], each 1.00
____Unopened card packets, each 4.00

Collector tins. Contains 7 packs of random movie cards, 1 mega-foil card. (Checklist in 3rd ed. pg 175.)
____Unopened tin with card intact, each 25.00

Topps, UK
10 foil cards, 1 card in collector binder. (Checklist in 3rd edition, page 175.)
____Binder card...14.00
____Foil cards, each 8.00

Cards: Bend-Ems

Just Toys
28 cards numbered alphabetically A – BB. Images taken from Star Wars Galaxy series of cards. (Images in 2nd edition, page 175. Checklist in 3rd edition, page 175.)
____Cards A – Z and AA – BB, each 3.00

Cards: Card Game

Hungary. Return of the Jedi matching game. Title card, 24 'matching pairs'. (Images in 3rd edition, page 175. Checklist in 3rd edition, page 175.)
____Cards [LU01], each 2.00

Cards: Ceramic

Hamilton Collection
12 unnumbered ceramic cards. (Images in 3rd edition, page 176. Checklist in 3rd edition, page 176.)
____Cards [OVV01], each 20.00

Score Board
3 unnumbered cards, limited to 5,000 each. Star Wars, Empire Strikes Back, Return of the Jedi. (Images in 3rd edition, page 176. Checklist in 3rd edition, page 176.)
____Cards, each 35.00

Cards: Chile

Lider
Chile. 30 numbered cards. Episode I. (Images in 2nd edition, page 175. Checklist in 3rd edition, page 176.)
____Cards [CDC01], each 1.00

Cards: Chrome Archives

Topps
90 chrome foils cards, 4 clear chrome cards, 9 double-sided cards, 2 promotional cards. (Images in 2nd edition, page 176. Checklist in 3rd edition, page 176.)
____Cards 1 – 90, each 1.00
____Cards 1 – 90, set 35.00
____Clear chrome cards, each 6.00
____Double-sided cards, each 4.25
____Promotional cards, each...3.00
____Unopened card packets, each 5.00

Cards: Clone Wars

Topps
90 cards, 2 autograph cards, 10 battle motion cards, 3 promo cards, 10 stickers.
____Cards 1 – 9, characters [CCW01], each 0.25
____Cards 10 – 71, chapter scenes, each 0.25
____Cards 72 – 73, EPIII previews, each 0.25
____Cards 74 – 89, Dark Horse gallery, each 0.25
____Cards 90, Checklist 0.25
____Cards 1 – 90, set 25.00
____Autograph card: Anthony Phelan (Lama Su) 15.00
____Autograph card: Jack Thompson (Cliegg Lars) 15.00
____Battle Motion cards B1 – B10, each 5.00
____Promo cards P1 – P3, each 5.00
____Stickers 1 – 10, each 5.00
____Unopened card packets, each 6.00

Cards: DinaMics

DinaMics
168 numbered cards. (Images in 3rd edition, page 178. Checklist in 3rd edition, page 178.)
____Cards 1 – 168 [OC01], each..................................1.00
____Cards 1 – 168, set 40.00

Cards: ESB Giant Photo

Topps
30 numbered cards. Oversized. (Images in 2nd edition, page 178. Checklist in 3rd edition, page page 179.)
____Cards 1 – 30 [OOA01], each 1.75
____Cards 1 – 30, set 25.00
____Unopened card packets, each 5.00

Cards: ESB

200 white bordered ESB cards with several Star Trek cards mistakenly printed into the set. Produced with two different logos; 1 large text and the other small text. Text is in Greek using the Greek alphabet. (Images in 3rd edition, page 188. Checklist in 3rd edition, page 188.)
____Cards 1 – 200, large text logo [OE01], each 1.50
____Cards 1 – 200, large text logo, set 165.00
____Cards 1 – 200, small text logo [OE02], each 1.50
____Cards 1 – 200, small text logo, set 150.00
____Unopened packet of cards 17.00

Agence Generale d'Edition
L'Empire Contre-Attaque. 225 cards. (Checklist in 3rd edition, page 179.)
____Cards 1 – 225, each 1.00
____Cards 1 – 225, set 75.00
____Unopened card packets, each............................12.00

Coca-Cola, Hong Kong
Sprite cards. 6 unnumbered cards. (Images in 3rd edition, page 180. Checklist in 3rd edition, page 180.)
____Cards [OE03], each..5.00

Editorial Fher
El Imperio Contrataca. 225 cards. (Images in 3rd edition, page 180. Checklist in 3rd edition, page 180.)
____Cards 1 – 225 [OE04], each 1.00
____Cards 1 – 225, set 85.00
____Unopened card packets, each............................12.00

FKS
U.K. 225 cards. (Checklist in 3rd edition, page 180.)
____Cards 1 – 225, each 1.00
____Cards 1 – 225, set 65.00
____Unopened card packets, each 7.00

O-Pee-Chee, Canada
Series 1. English / French text. 132 red border cards, 33 stickers.
____Cards 1 – 132, each 1.00
____Cards 1 – 132, set 50.00
____Stickers 1 – 33, each 5.00
____Unopened card packets, each 7.00

Series 2. English / French text. 132 blue border cards, 33 stickers.
____Cards 133 – 264, each 1.00
____Cards 133 – 264, set 50.00
____Stickers 34 – 66, each 5.00
____Unopened card packets, each 7.00

Series 3. English / French text. 88 blue border cards, 22 stickers. Similar to Topps series 3.
____Cards 265 – 352, each 1.00
____Cards 265 – 352, set 30.00
____Stickers 67 – 88, each 5.00
____Unopened card packets, each 7.00

Scanlens
132 cards. (Checklist in 3rd edition, page 182.)
____Cards 1 – 132, each 1.20
____Cards 1 – 132, set 60.00

Topps
Rack packs.
____3 wax packs 16.00
____51 random cards 14.00

Series 1. 132 red border cards, 33 stickers. (Images in 2nd edition, page 179. Checklist in 3rd ed., pg. 183.)
____Cards 1 – 132 [OE05], each 0.75
____Cards 1 – 132, set 35.75
____Stickers 1 – 33 [OE06], each 0.75
____Unopened card packets, each 5.00

Series 2. 132 blue border cards, 33 stickers. (Images in 2nd edition, page 181. Checklist in 3rd ed., pg. 183.)
____Cards 133 – 264 [OE07], each 0.75
____Cards 133 – 264, set 35.00
____Stickers 34 – 66 [OE08], each 0.75
____Unopened card packets, each 5.00

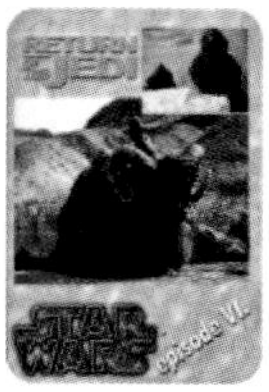
LU01 sample

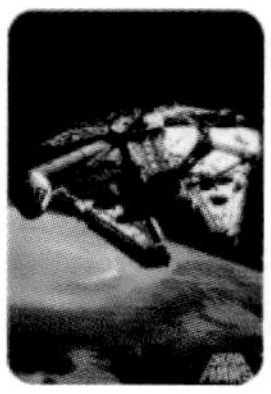
OVV01 sample

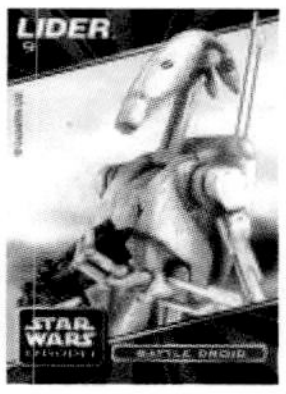

CDC01

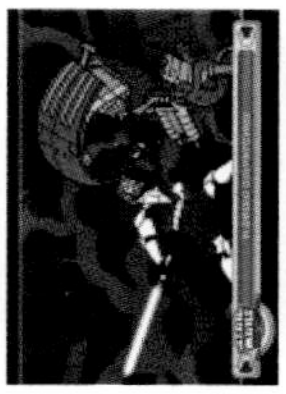
CCW01 sample

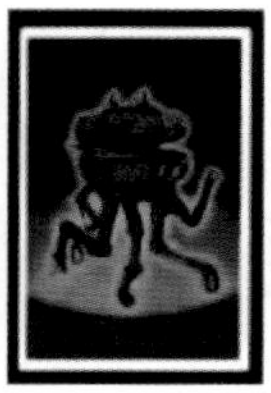
OC01 sample

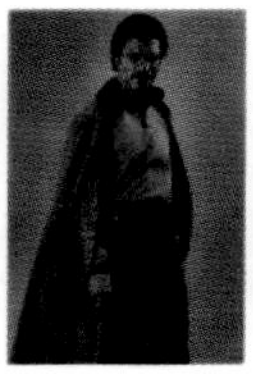
OOA01 sample

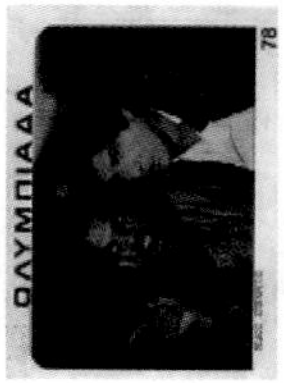
OE01 sample

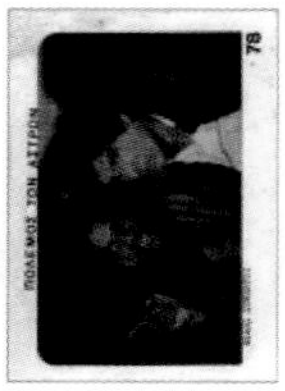
OE02 sample

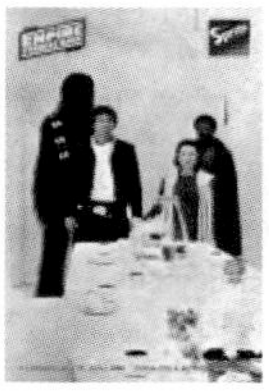
OE03 sample

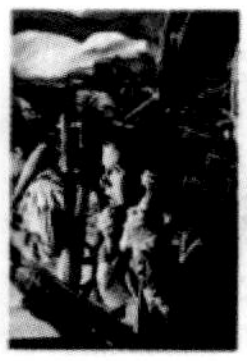
OE04 sample

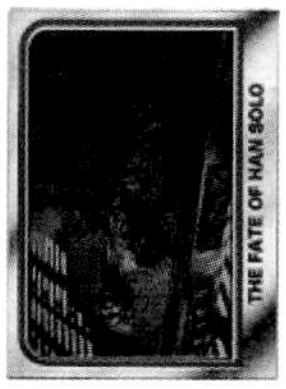

OE05 sample

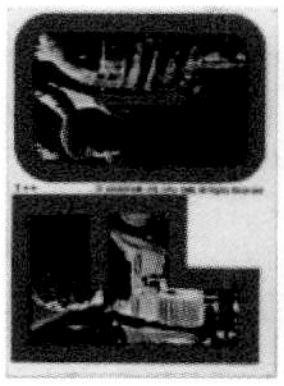
OE06 sample

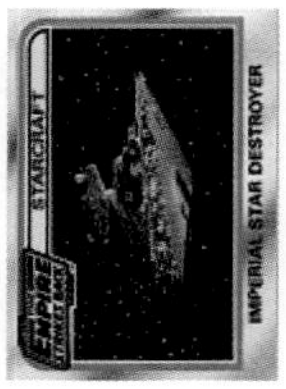

OE07 sample

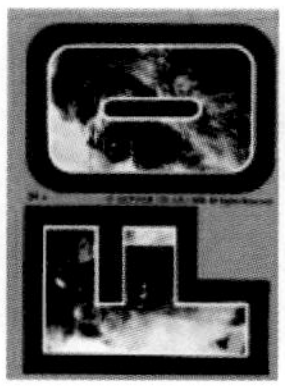
OE08 sample

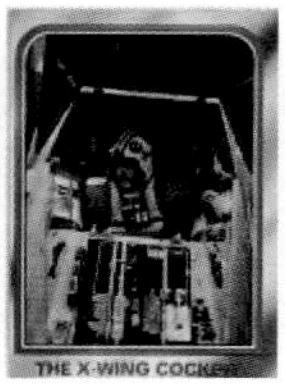
OE09 sample

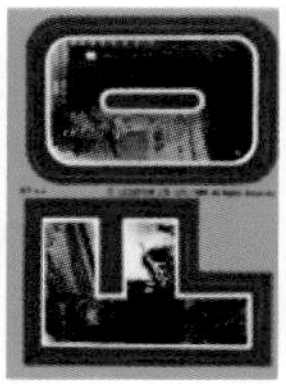
OE10 sample

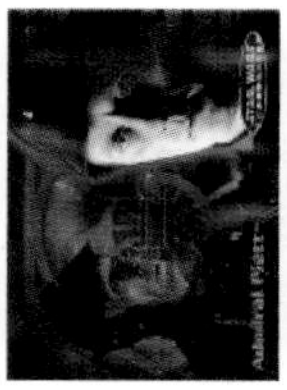
BCE01 sample

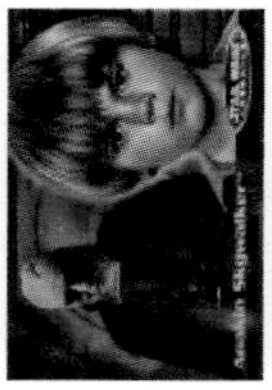
BCE02 sample

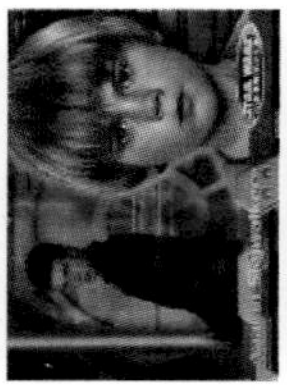
BCE03 sample

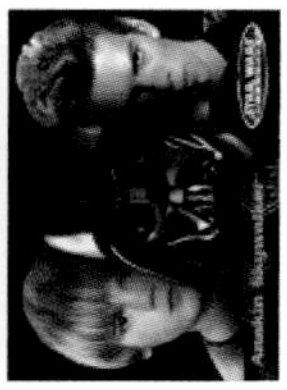
BCE04 sample

Cards: ESB

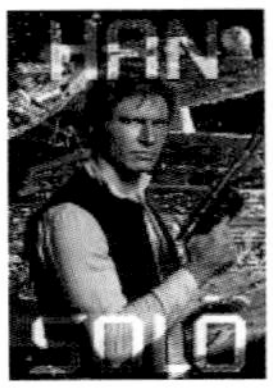
PRF01 sample

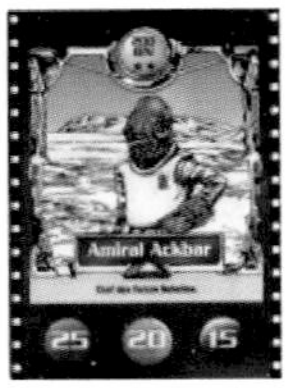
OD01 sample

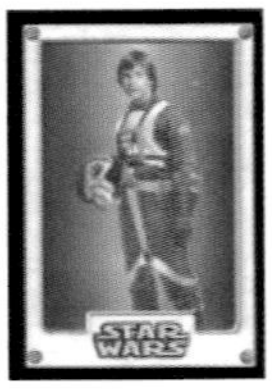
OD02 sample

Series 3. 88 yellow border cards, 22 stickers. (Images in 2nd edition, page 183. Checklist in 3rd edition, page 184.)

Cards 265 – 352 each

____Cards 265 – 353 [OE09], each 0.60
____Cards 265 – 353, set 0.60
____Stickers 67 – 88 [OE10], each 0.75
____Unopened card packets, each 5.00

Cards: Evolution

Topps

90 cards, 3 checklist cards, 12 set "A" insert cards, 8 set "B" insert cards, 4 promotional cards, 25 hand-signed autograph cards.

____Cards 1 – 90 [BCE01], each 1.00
____Cards 1 – 90, set 22.00
____Checklist cards C1 – C3, each 3.00
____Insert cards A1 – A12 [BCE02], each 2.00
____Insert cards B1 – B8 [BCE03],each 3.00
____Promo cards P1 – P2, each 4.00
____Promo card P3, Alphacon exclusive. Autographed and numbered, limited to 250 ....125.00
____Promo card P3, Alphacon exclusive. Limited to 5,000 ....24.00
____P4 Darth Vader, convention "Connections" exclusive [BE04] 10.00
____Unopened card packets, each 6.00

Autographed cards, 100 signed of each

____C-3PO / Anthony Daniels 1,200.00
____Princess Leia Organa / Carrie Fisher 1,000.00

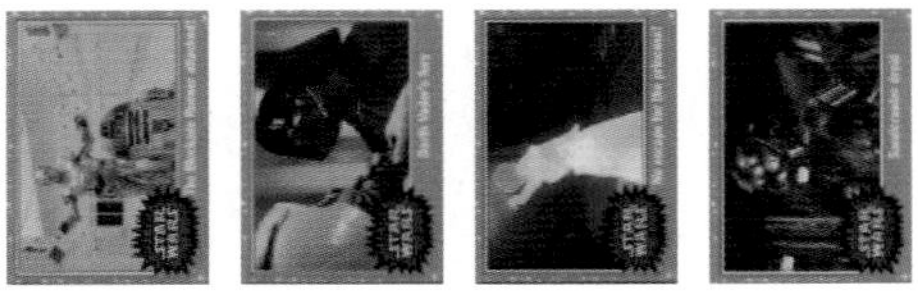
OS01 OS02 OS03 OS04

Autographed cards, 300 signed of each

____Lando Calrissian /Billy Dee Williams 425.00

Autographed cards, 400 signed of each

____Chewbacca / Peter Mayhew 200.00
____Senator Palpatine / Ian McDiarmid 200.00

Autographed cards, 1,000 signed of each

____Admiral Ackbar / Tim Rose 35.00
____Admiral Ozzel / Michael Sheard 35.00
____Admiral Piett / Kenneth Colley 35.00
____Aurra Sing / Michonne Bourriague 45.00
____Boba Fett / Jeremy Bulloch 75.00
____Captain Needa / Michael Culver 35.00
____Darth Vader, voice / James Earl Jones 75.00
____General Crix Madine / Dermot Crowley 35.00
____Greedo / Paul Blake 35.00
____Lyn Me / Dalyn Chew 30.00
____Moff Jerjerrod / Michael Pennington 35.00
____Mon Mothma / Caroline Blakiston 30.00
____Nien Nunb / Mike Quinn 30.00
____Oola / Femi Taylor 40.00
____Owen Lars / Phil Brown 45.00
____R2-D2 / Kenny Baker 60.00
____Rystall / Mercedes Ngoh 45.00
____Sebulba, voice / Lewis MacLeod 45.00
____Watto, voice / Andrew Secombe 45.00
____Wicket W. Warrick / Warwick Davis 40.00

Cards: Evolution Update Edition

Topps

90 cards, "A" insert cards, set "B" insert cards, promotional cards, autograph cards.

____Cards 1 – 90, each 1.00
____Cards 1 – 90, set 35.00
____Cards Etched foil puzzles, each 2.00
____Cards Galaxy crystal, each 2.00
____Cards Insert set A, each 4.00
____Cards Insert set B,each 6.00
____Cards Promotional, each 4.00

Autograph cut cards, limited to one of each

____George Lucas ....N/V
____Grand Moff Tarken / Peter Cushing ....N/V
____Obi-Wan Kenobi / Alec Guinness ....N/V

Autograph cards, level "A", odds 1:2,005

____Anakin Skywalker / Hayden Christensen 235.00
____Darth Vader / James Earl Jones 270.00

Autograph cards, level "B", odds 1:231

____Governor Tarkin / Wayne Pygram 85.00
____Jabba the Hutt / David Barclay 45.00
____Jabba the Hutt / Bob Keen 52.00
____Jabba the Hutt / John Coppinger 50.00
____Jabba the Hutt / Mike Edmonds 48.00
____Jabba the Hutt / Mike Quinn 45.00
____Jabba the Hutt / Toby Philpott 48.00

Autograph cards, level "C", odds 1:81

____Admiral Motti / Richard LeParmentier 45.00
____Aurra Sing / Michonne Bourriague 40.00
____Greedo / Maria de Aragon 40.00
____Sly Moore / Sandi Finlay 46.00
____Tarfful / Michael Kingma 48.00

Autograph cards, level "D," odds 1:259

____Barriss Offee / Nalini Krishan 44.00

Autograph cards, level "E," odds 1:48

____Biggs Darklighter / Garrick Hagon 39.00
____Kit Fisto / Zach Jensen 37.00
____Plo Koon / Matt Sloan 40.00
____Saesee Tiin / Jesse Jensen 37.00

Cards: Fanclub

Skywalkers

7 unnumbered cards. 1 Membership card, 6 character cards. (Images and checklist in 3rd edition, page 186.)

____Character cards, each 8.00
____Membership 11.00

Cards: French

Biscuiterie Nantaise

40 unnumbered cards. 36 character cards, 4 planet cards. (Images in 3rd edition, page 187. Checklist in 3rd edition, page 186.)

____Character cards, each 2.00
____Planet cards, each 2.00
____Cards, set 65.00

Dyna Mart

200 cards, 150 sticker cards. Classic trilogy and EPI images.

____Cards 1 – 200, each 0.50
____Cards 1 – 200, set 35.00
____Sticker cards s1 – s150, each 0.50
____Sticker cards s1 – s150, set 50.00

Merlin Publishing Internat'l Ltd.

125 cards. Scenes from all 3 classic trilogy films. (Images in 2nd edition, page 186. Checklist in 3rd edition, page 186.)

____Cards 1 – 35, ANH scenes, each 2.00
____Cards 36 – 70, ESB scenes, each 2.00
____Cards 71 – 105, ROTJ scenes, each 2.00
____Cards 106 – 115, characters, each 2.00
____Cards 116 – 124, vehicles, each 2.00
____Card 125, checklist 2.00
____Cards 1 – 125, set 70.00
____Unopened card packets, each 5.00

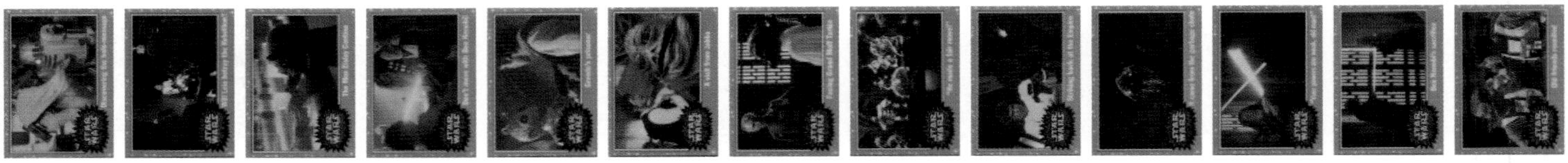
OS05 OS06 OS07 OS08 OS09 OS10 OS11 OS12 OS13 OS14 OS15 OS16 OS17

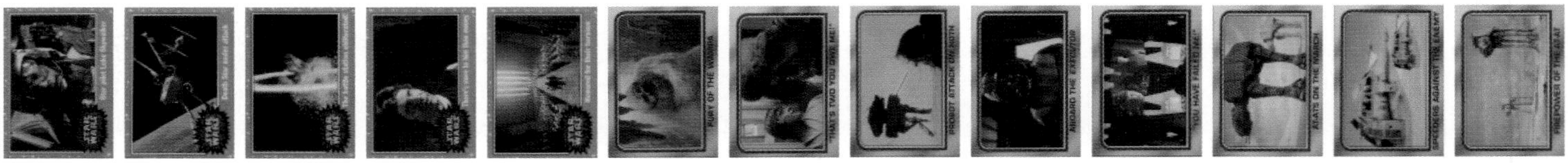
OS18 OS19 OS20 OS21 OS22 OS23 OS24 OS25 OS26 OS27 OS28 OS29 OS30

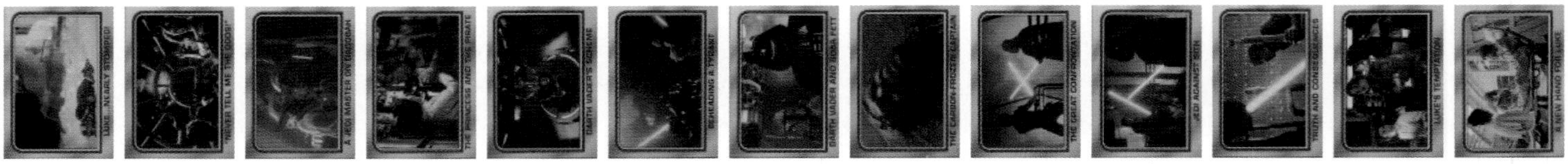
OS31 OS32 OS33 OS34 OS35 OS36 OS37 OS38 OS39 OS40 OS41 OS42 OS43

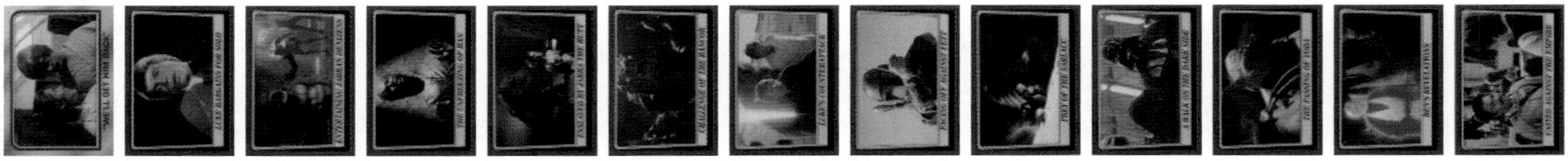
OS44 OS45 OS46 OS47 OS48 OS49 OS50 OS51 OS52 OS53 OS54 OS55 OS56

Cards: German

Merlin Publishing Internat'l Ltd.
125 cards. Scenes from all 3 classic trilogy films. (Checklist in 3rd edition, page 187.)
____Cards 1 – 35, ANH scenes, each..........................2.00
____Cards 36 – 70, ESB scenes, each 2.00
____Cards 71 – 105, ROTJ scenes, each 2.00
____Cards 106 – 115, characters, each 2.00
____Cards 116 – 124, vehicles, each 2.00
____Card 125, checklist..2.00
____Cards 1 – 125, set 70.00
____Unopened card packets, each 5.00

Cards: Giant Movie Pin-Ups

Topps
Set of movie theater poster cards. Only cards #5 and #8 are Star Wars related.
____Card #5: Star Wars 6.00
____Card #8: The Empire Strikes Back 6.00

Cards: Heritage

Topps
120 cards, 6 etched foil cards (hobby set), 6 promo cards, 30 stickers (retail set). (Checklist at www.StarWarsCards.net)
____Cards 1 – 22 SW [OS01-OS22], each 0.25
____Cards 23 – 44 ESB [OS23-OS44], each 0.25
____Cards 45 – 66 ROTJ [OS45-OS66], each 0.25
____Cards 67 – 88 TPM [OS67-OS88], each 0.25
____Cards 89 – 110 AOTC [OS89-OS110], each 0.25
____Cards 111 – 119 ROTS [OS111-OS119], each 0.25
____Card 120 Checklist [OS120].................................0.25
____Cards 1 – 120, set 25.00
____Hobby etched foil cards 1 – 6, each 0.25
____Promo cards 1 – 6, each [OS121] 0.25
____Stickers 1 – 10, green, Anakin puzzle, each 1.00
____Stickers 11 – 20, yellow, Obi-Wan puzzle, each...1.00
____Stickers 21 – 30, blue, droids puzzle, each 1.00

Cards: Italian

Merlin Publishing Internat'l Ltd.
Italy. 124 cards plus checklist. Scenes from all 3 classic trilogy films. (Checlist in 3rd edition, page 190.)
____125 Check List 2.00
____Cards 1 – 35 ANH scenes, each 2.00
____Cards 36 – 70 ESB scenes, each 2.00
____Cards 71 – 105 ROTJ scenes, each 2.00
____Cards 106 – 115 characters, each 2.00
____Cards 116 – 124 vehicles, each 2.00
____Cards125 checklist 2.00
____Cards 1 – 125, set 38.00
____Unopened card packets, each 5.00

Cards: Japan

Topps
72 cards plus 6 chase cards. Scenes from all 3 classic trilogy films. (Checklist in 3rd edition, page 191.)
____Cards 1 – 24 ANH scenes, each 1.75
____Cards 25 – 48 ESB scenes, each 1.75
____Cards 49 – 72 ROTJ scenes, each 1.75
____Cards 1 – 72, set 64.00
____Cards Chase 1 – 6, each 8.00
____Unopened card packets, each 8.00

Cards: Mastervision

Topps
36 cards, 4 unnumbered promotional cards. (Images in 2nd ed., pg. 191. Checklist in 3rd ed., pg. 191.)
____Cards 1 – 36, each 2.00
____Cards 1 – 36, set 25.00
____Promotional cards, each......................................8.00
____Unopened card packets, each 6.00

Cards: Misc.

____Married with Children parody [2:192] 6.00

Fan Made
____Star Wars Super Collector's Wish Book, 3rd edition. Celebration III exclusive 2.00

Blockbuster Video
50 video game promotional card series.
____#35 Super Star Wars 4.00

Comic Images
____Card #29 of the "Lost Worlds by William Stout" set features Luke, his tauntaun, and a fleet of Twin Pod Cloud Cars on Hoth; artwork for a Varese Sarabond record album of 1980 ....9.00

Gentle Giant Studios
____2005 Fan Club promo for Bust-Ups......................3.00

Packaging Parodies
____Bar Wars parody [2:192].......................................3.00

Runnin Bare QSL Cards
Story of Star Wars. Numbered story cards, 3"x5" hand drawn art. Images in 2nd edition, page 192. Checklist in 3rd edition, page 191.)
____Cards 1 – 15, each 3.00

Sci-Fi Expo and Toy Show
Parody of Topps vintage series 4 to commerate attending actors.
____P1 Garrick Hagon (Biggs) [2:192] 12.00
____P2 Peter Mayhew (Chewbacca) [2:192]..............12.00

The LEGO Group
Background/character card included with mini-figures. (Images in 3rd edition, page 191.)
____Cards, each..1.00

Topps
____Gummy Award card, ltd. to 1,000 [3:191] 23.00
____Truce at Bakura cover art, Waldenbooks with novel purchase [2:192]..15.00

Convention cards.
____Millennium Falcon, B/W art 10.00
____Cards SD1-SD2, 5"x6", each.............................20.00
____Star Wars Galaxy Magazine, large......................10.00

OS57	OS58	OS59	OS60	OS61	OS62	OS63	OS64	OS65	OS66	OS67	OS68	OS69
OS70	OS71	OS72	OS73	OS74	OS75	OS76	OS77	OS78	OS79	OS80	OS81	OS82
OS83	OS84	OS85	OS86	OS87	OS88	OS89	OS90	OS91	OS92	OS93	OS94	OS95
OS96	OS97	OS98	OS99	OS100	OS101	OS102	OS103	OS104	OS105	OS106	OS107	OS108
OS109	OS110	OS111	OS112	OS113	OS114	OS115	OS116	OS117	OS118	OS119	OS120	OS121

Cards: Misc.

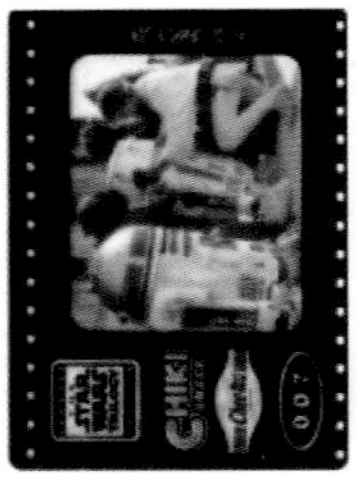
OVQ01 sample

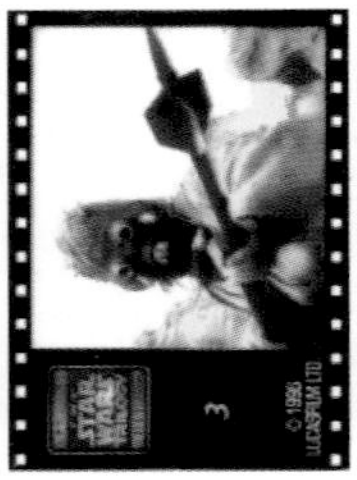
OVQ02 sample

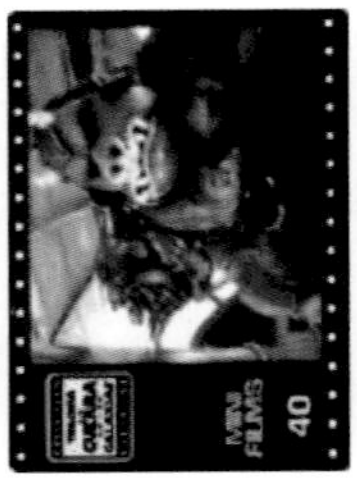
OVQ03 sample

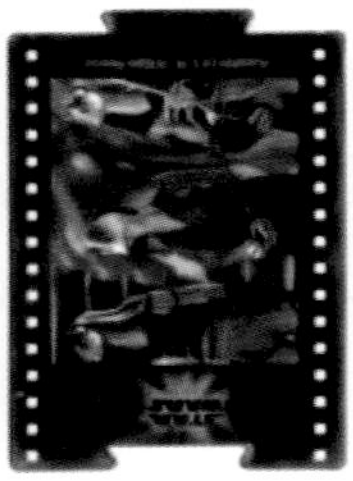
CME01 sample

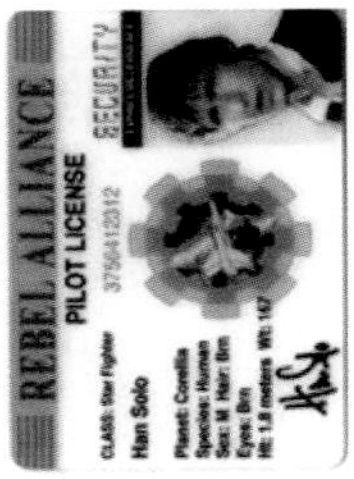
OVZ01 sample

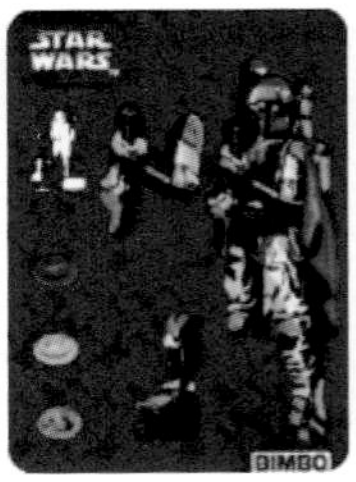
PR01 sample

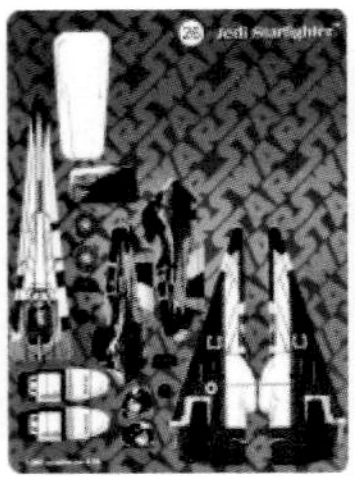
PR02 sample

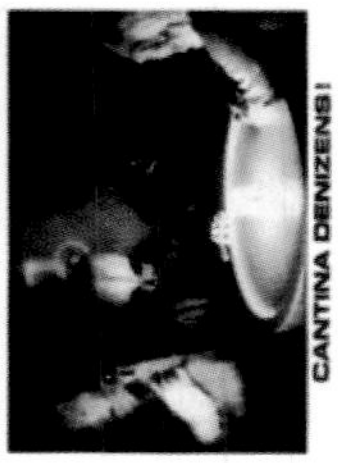
PR03 sample

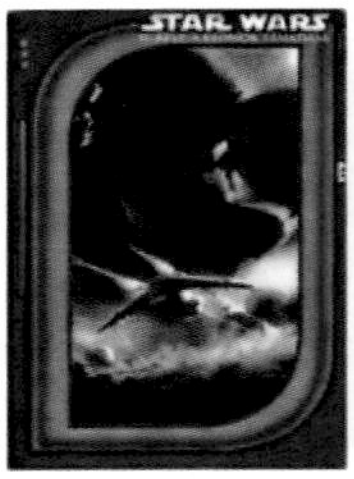
PR04 sample

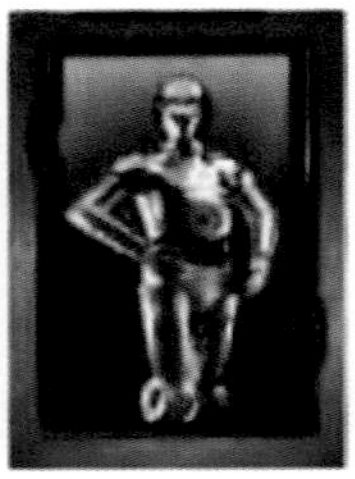
PR05 sample

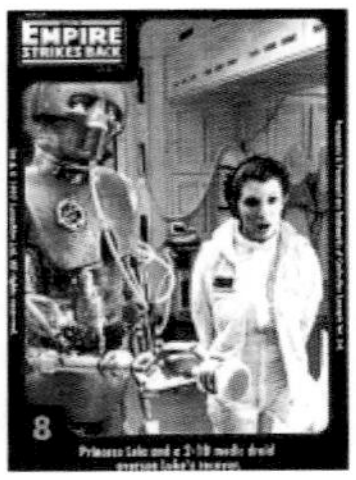
PR06 sample

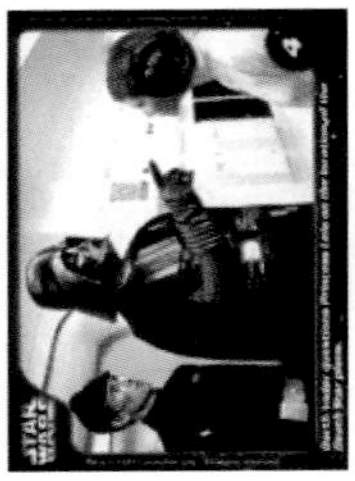
PR07 sample

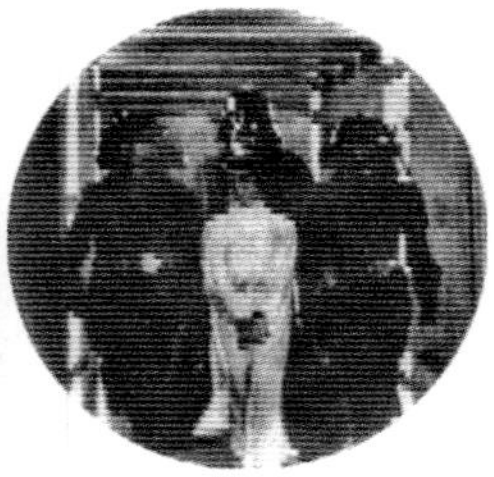
PR08 sample

Dark Horse Comic cards.
____DH1 War Droids 10.00
____DH2 Boba Fett 10.00
____DH3 Millennium Falcon 10.00

Cards: Movie Shots

Movie Shots
Belgium. 50 miniature single frame film scenes from all 3 classic trilogy movies. (Checklist in 3rd ed., pg. 192.)
____Cards 1 – 8 ANH scenes, each 1.60
____Cards 9 – 14 ESB scenes, each.............................1.60
____Cards 15 – 20 ROTJ scenes, each 1.60
____Cards 21 – 27 ANH scenes, each 1.60
____Cards 28 – 38 ESB scenes, each 1.60
____Cards 39 – 50 ROTJ scenes, each 1.60
____Cards 1 – 50, set 40.00

Indonesia. 100 miniature frame films from all 3 classic trilogy movies. (Checklist in 3rd edition, page 192.)
____Cards 1 – 34 ANH scenes [OVQ01], each 1.60
____Cards 35 – 68 ESB scenes, each 1.60
____Cards 69 – 100 ROTJ scenes, each 1.60
____Cards 1 – 100, set 55.00

Mexico. 40 miniature single frame film scenes from all 3 SE classic trilogy movies. (Images in 2nd edition, page 193. Checklist in 3rd edition, page 193.)
____Cards 1 – 13 ANH scenes [OVQ02], each 1.00
____Cards 14 – 26 ESB scenes, each 1.00
____Cards 27 – 39 ROTJ scenes, each 1.00
____Card 40 SW:SE Logo 1.00
____Cards 1 – 40, set 25.00

Netherlands. 50 miniature single frame film scenes from all 3 SE classic trilogy movies. (Checklist in 3rd edition, page 192.)
____Cards 1 – 15 ANH scenes, each 1.75
____Cards 16 – 32 ESB scenes, each 1.75
____Cards 33 – 50 ROTJ scenes, each 1.75
____Cards 1 – 50, set 40.00

Spain. 50 miniature single frame film scenes from all 3 special edition classic trilogy movies. (Images in 2nd edition, page 194. Checklist in 3rd edition, page 193.)
____Cards 1 – 15 ANH scenes, each 1.60
____Cards 16 – 32 ESB scenes ,each 1.60
____Cards 33 – 50 ROTJ scenes [OVQ03], each 1.60
____Cards 1 – 50, set 35.00

Cards: Movie Shots, TPM

Pelis
40 miniature single frame film scenes from Episode I. (Images in 2nd edition, page 195. Checklist in 3rd edition, page 193.)
____Cards 1 – 40 [CME01], each 2.00
____Cards 1 – 40, set 70.00

Cards: Pilot Licenses

5 different characters. (Images and checklist in 3rd edition, page 193.)
____Cards [OVZ01], each 8.00

Cards: Premiums

21 trading cards given away at Celebration III during collector panels. (Checklist at www.StarWarsCards.net)
____Cards 1 – 21, each 3.00
____Cards 1 – 21 [PR09-PR29], set 75.00

Mexico. 19 unnumbered punch-out bread cards. 10 classic characters, 15 prequel characters, 4 vehicles. (Images and checklist in 3rd edition, page 193.)
____Classic characters [PR01], each...........................3.00
____Prequel characters, each 3.00
____Vehicles [PR02], each 3.00

Burger Chef
12 unnumbered cut-apart cards from Funmeal box.
____Cards [PR30 – PR41], each 2.00

Burger King
36 cut-apart cards distributed in sheets of 6. Some sheets cut apart at store to make sheets of 3. Value of cards should take into account precision and quality of cuts since all were made by hand. (Images in 3rd edition, page 196. Checklist in 3rd edition, page 194.)
____6 card cut-apart sheets, each 8.00
____3 card cut-apart sheets, each 5.00
____Individual cut-apart cards [PR03], each................1.00

Chio
Hungary. 40 unnumbered chip / crisp cards from EPII:AOTC. (Images 2nd edition, page 196. Checklist in 3rd edition, page 194.)
____Cards [PR04], each...2.00
____Cards, set 46.00

Poland. 38 unnumbered chip / crisp cards from EPII:AOTC. (Images in 2nd edition, page 196. Checklist in 3rd edition, page 194.)
____Cards [PR05], each...2.50
____Cards, set 50.00

Confection Concepts
45 Empire Strikes Back cards. Dark blue borders with puzzle scenes on back. (Images in 2nd edition, page 197. Checklist in 3rd edition, page 194.)
____Cards 1 – 45 [PR06], each 0.85
____Cards 1 – 45, set 65.00

50 Star Wars cards. Dark blue borders with puzzle scenes on back. (Images and checklist in 3rd edition, page 195.)
____Cards 1 – 50 [PR07], each 0.85
____Cards 1 – 50, set 65.00

Dark Horse Comics
6 classic characters on cut-apart sheet. 2 cards per sheet. (Images and checklist in 3rd edition, page 196.)
____Uncut sheet of 2 [PR42], each 5.00
____Individual cards, each..1.00

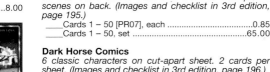

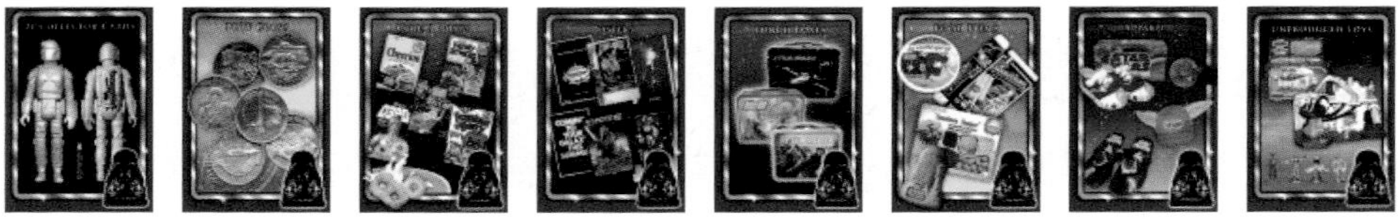
PR09 PR10 PR11 PR12 PR13 PR14 PR15 PR16

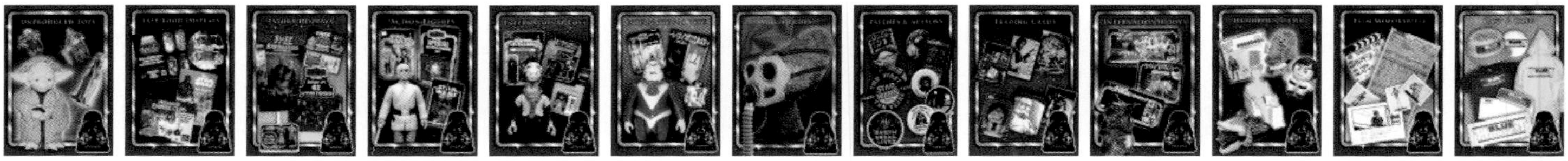
PR17 PR18 PR19 PR20 PR21 PR22 PR23 PR24 PR25 PR26 PR27 PR28 PR29

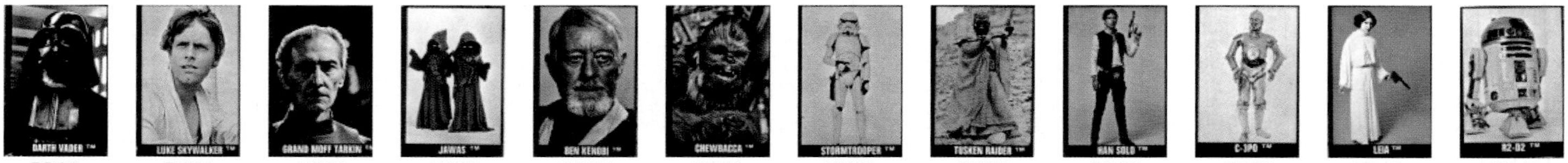
PR30 PR31 PR32 PR33 PR34 PR35 PR36 PR37 PR38 PR39 PR40 PR41

PR42 sample front / rear | PR43 sample front and rear | PR44 sample front and rear | PR45 sample | PR46 sample

PR47 sample | PR48 sample | PR49 sample | PR50 sample | PR51 sample

PR52 sample | PR53 sample | PR54 sample | PR55 sample | PR56 sample | PR57 sample | PR58 sample | PR59 sample

Dixie / Northern Inc.
8 large cards. Set of 4 Rebel and 4 Empire (Image and checklist in 3rd edition, page 196.)
____Empire cards [PR43], each 8.00
____Rebel cards, each...8.00

24 story cards. Cut-apart strips of 4 cards. (Images and checklist in 3rd edition, page 196.)
____Cards 1 – 24 each 2.00
____Uncut strips [PR44], each 10.00

Doo Wap
France. 12 cards in 4 brochures. Each brochure has cut-apart strips of 3 cards. (Images and checklist in 3rd edition, page 197.)
____Brochures [PR47], each 4.00
____Cards cut apart, each..1.00

Doritos
20 3D motion discs distributed in chip bags. (Images in 2nd ed., pg. 198. Checklist in 3rd edition, page 197.)
____Discs 1 – 20 [PR08], each 1.25

Doritos/Cheetos
6 3D motion cards, 2 bonus cards. (Images in 2nd edition, page 198. Checklist in 3rd edition, page 197.)
____3D motion cards [PR45], each 1.50
____3D motion bonus cards, each 3.00

Energizer
3 unnumbered lightsaber duel lenticular cards. (Images in 2nd edition, page 199. Checklist in 3rd edition, page 197.)
____Cards [PR46], each..5.00

Evercrisp
Argentina. 30 classic trilogy characters and ships. (Image and checklist in 3rd edition, page 197.)
____Cards 1 – 30 each 1.00
____Cards 1 – 30, set 20.00

Fanta
Thailand. 12 unnumbered cards. SW:SE scenes. (Images and checklist in 3rd edition, page 197.)
____Cards [PR48], each..3.00

Fernandes
Guitar Pick Collection checklists. 4 checklists per series. (Images and checklist in 3rd edition, page 197.)
____Series 1 classic characters [PR49], each.............2.50
____Series 2 prequel characters [PR50], each 2.50

Freegels
Brazil. 50 cards made of plastic. (Images and checklist in 3rd edition, page 197.)
____Cards 1 – 23 photos [PR51], each 1.00
____Cards 24 – 50 art, each 3.00

Fromagerie Bel
France. 10 unnumbered cards from EPI:TPM. (Images in 2nd edition, page 199. Checklist in 3rd edition, page 198.)
____Cards [PR52], each..2.00

General Mills
18 cards distributed in cereal. (Images and checklist in 3rd edition, page 198.)
____Cards 1 – 6 yellow border [PR53], each 2.00
____Cards 7 – 12 blue border [PR54], each 2.00
____Cards 13 – 18 red border [PR55], each 2.00

Gummi
4 unnumbered 2" squares from EPI:TPM.
____Cards, each..2.00

Hollywood Chewing Gum
France. 20 chewing gum box peel-away cards. (Images in 2nd edition, page 199. Checklist in 3rd edition, page 198.)
____Cards 1 – 20 each 2.00

Kellogg
10 Stick'R Cards. Stickers are adhered to trading cards for backing. (Images and checklist in 3rd edition, page 198.)
____Cards 1 – 10, each 5.00

Australia. Ewok Adventure Collect-a-Prize game pieces. Three different Ewoks to complete using four pieces, each. (Images and checklist in 3rd ed. pg 198.)
____Cards A1 – A4 (Ewok 1), each 6.00
____Cards B5 – B8 (Ewok 2), each 6.00
____Cards C9 – C12 (Ewok 3), each 6.00

Canada. 10 Stick'R Cards. (Set numbers 1 – 10 are listed as sticker premiums.) (Images in 3rd edition, page 199. Checklist in 3rd edition, page 198.)
____Cards 11 – 20 PR57], each 7.00

Canada. 16 unnumbered cut-out cards. 4 on each of 4 different unnumbered box panels.
____Individual cards cut apart, each 1.00
____Uncut box panel with 4 cards, each 14.00

PR60 sample | PR61 sample | PR62 sample

Canada. Oversized 3D cards attached to the front of cereal boxes.
____Cards, each...2.00

France. 14 unnumbered cards from EPIII:ROTS.
____Cards, each...2.00

Kent
Turkey. 27 cards distributed individually in packets of gum. (Images and checklist in 3rd edition, page 199.)
____Cards 1 – 27 [PR58], each 1.00

Masterfoods USA
4 unnumbered Mpire cards.
____Cards [PR59], each..5.00

Meiji
Japan. 30 EPI:TPM cards distributed in chip packets. (Images and checklist in 3rd edition, page 199.)
____Cards 1 – 30 [PR60], each 1.00

Myojo Foods Ltd.
Japan. 30 Star Wars trilogy cards. (Images and checklist in 3rd edition, page 199.)
____Cards 1 – 30 [PR61], each 2.50

Natur
Chile. 36 cards distributed in gum. Scenes from ESB and ROTJ. (Images and checklist in 3rd edition, page 200.)
____Cards 1 – 36 [PR62], each 1.00

Nestlé
Asia. 6 unnumbered lenticular scenes. (Images in 2nd edition, page 199. Checklist in 3rd edition, page 200.)
____Cards [PR62 – PR68], each 2.00

Cards: Premiums

PR63   PR64   PR65   PR66   PR67   PR68

PR69 sample   PR70 sample   PR71 sample   PR72 sample   PR73 sample   PR74 sample   PR75 sample   LHB01 sample

PR76   PR77   PR78   PR79   PR80   PR81   PR82   PR83   PR84   PR85   PR86   PR87   PR88

Chile. 5 unnumbered cards, packaged in Estrellitas and Gold candy. (Images and checklist in 3rd edition, page 200.)
  ____Cards, each...2.00

Mexico. 6 unnumbered lenticular scenes. (Images in 2nd edition, page 199. Checklist in 3rd edition, page 200.)
  ____Cards, each...2.00

Pacosa Dos/Internacional
Droids. Set of 224 cards.
  ____Cards 1 – 224, each 4.00

Pepsi Cola
Mexico. 24 unnumbered cards showing Hasbro toys. (Images in 2nd edition, page 200. Checklist in 3rd edition, page 201.)
  ____Cards [PR69], each...3.00

Pepsico
Argentina. 30 cards. Classic trilogy characters and ships. (Images in 3rd edition, page 200. Checklist in 3rd edition, page 201.)
  ____Cards 1 – 30, each 1.00

Quaker
Guatemala. 8 cards, 3D images from EPI:TPM. (Images and checklist in 3rd edition, page 201.)
  ____Cards [PR71], each...3.00

Quality Bakers
10 cards from classic trilogy. (Images in 2nd edition, page 200. Checklist in 3rd edition, page 201.)
  ____Cards 1 – 10 [PR72], each 1.25

Sonrics
Gamesa. Set of 30 cards showing images from all three classic trilogy movies. (Images in 2nd edition, page 200. Checklist in 3rd edition, page 201.)
  ____Cards 1 – 30 [PR73], each 1.75

30 cards, 3 multi-part cut-away scenes, 10 background cards. (Images in 2nd edition, page 201. Checklist in 3rd edition, page 201.)
  ____Background cards, each 2.00
  ____Cards 1 – 30, each 1.80
  ____Cut-away cards, each...4.00

Taco Bell
  ____Princess Leia 3D flip card [3:202].........................2.00

Topps
10 cards included in packages with candy head dispensers. (Checklist in 3rd edition, page 202.)
  ____Cards 1 – 10 [PR76 – PR85], each.........................1.50

Packed in with Hope Industries trilogy watches. (Checklist in 3rd edition, page 202.)
  ____Movie poster cards [PR86 – PR88], each 4.00

Wonder Bread
16 cards distributed inside bread. (Images in 2nd edition, page 201. Checklist in 3rd edition, page 202.)
  ____Cards 1 – 16 [PR74], each 2.00

York
6 round unnumbered cards, distributed under peanut butter jar caps. (Images in 2nd edition, page 201. Checklist in 3rd edition, page 202.)
  ____Cards [PR75], each...4.00

Cards: Role Playing

Scholastic
Adventures game, EPII. 3"x3" cards. (Images in 3nd edition, page 203. Checklist in 3rd edition, page 202.)
  ____Cards [LHB01], each..0.25

West End Games
Distributed inside books and games. (Checklist in 3rd edition, page 203.)
  ____Cards, each...0.50

Cards: ROTJ

Cromy
Argentina. 240 cards.
  ____Cards 1 – 240, each 1.00
  ____Cards 1 – 240, set 115.00
  ____Unopened card packets, each 6.00

Lamy
Japan.
  ____Unopened card packets, each...........................22.00

Monty Factories
100 yellow bordered cards. (Images in 2nd edition, page 202. Checklist in 3rd edition, page 203.)
  ____Cards 1 – 100 [OJ01], each 1.00
  ____Cards 1 – 100, set 75.00
  ____Unopened card packets, each 9.00

O-Pee-Chee, Canada
Canada. Series 1. 132 red border cards, no stickers. Bilingual: English/French.
  ____Cards 1 – 132, each 1.00
  ____Cards 1 – 132, set 45.00
  ____Unopened card packets, each 4.00

Pacosa Dos/Internacional
200 mini-cards with plain white borders and no text on the card fronts.
  ____Cards 1 – 200 [OJ02], each 1.00
  ____Cards 1 – 200, set 100.00
  ____Unopened card packets, each 11.00

Scanlens
132 cards. (Checklist in 3rd edition, page 204.)
  ____Cards 1 – 132, each 1.15
  ____Cards 1 – 132, set 100.00
  ____Unopened card packets, each 6.00

Topps
  ____Rack-Pack of 45 movie cards 12.00

Series 1. 132 red border cards, 33 stickers. (Images in 2nd edition, page 204. Checklist in 3rd ed., pg. 204.)
  ____Cards 1 – 132 [OJ03], each 1.00
  ____Cards 1 – 132, set 70.00
  ____Stickers 1 – 33 [OJ04], each 1.25
  ____Unopened card packets, each 5.00

Series 2. 88 blue border cards, 22 stickers. (Images in 2nd ed., pg. 206. Checklist in 3rd edition, page 205.)
  ____Cards 133 – 220 [OJ05], each 1.00
  ____Cards 133 – 220, set 45.00
  ____Stickers 34 – 45 [OJ06], each 1.25
  ____Unopened card packets, each 5.00

OJ01 sample   OJ02 sample   OJ03 sample   OJ04 sample   OJ05 sample   OJ06 sample

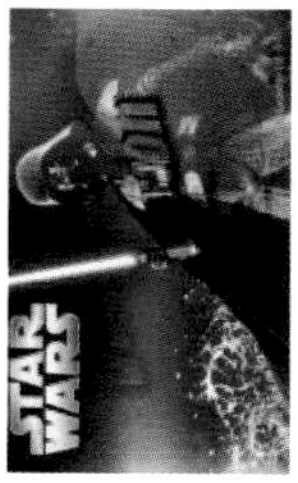

PRS01

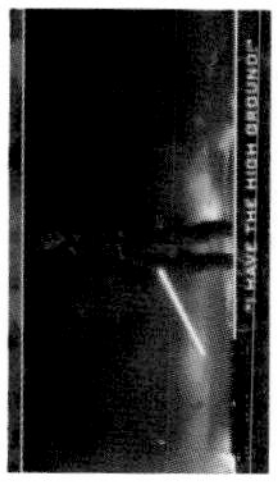

PRS02 sample

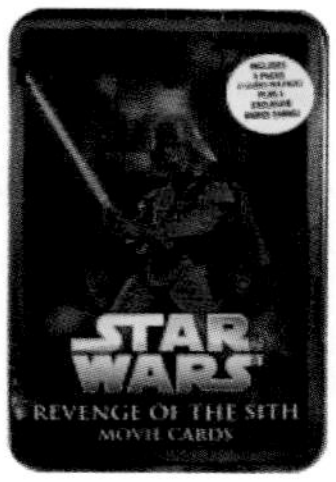

PRS03

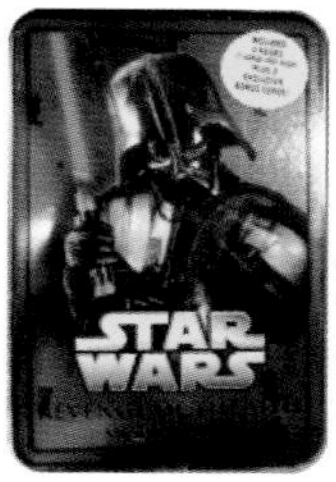

PRS04

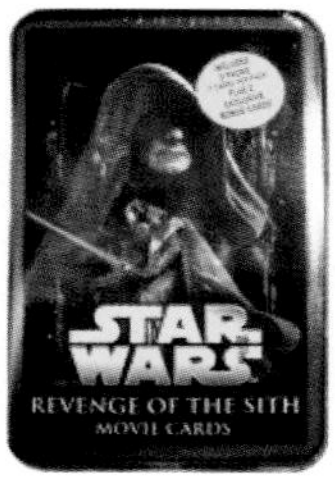

PRS05

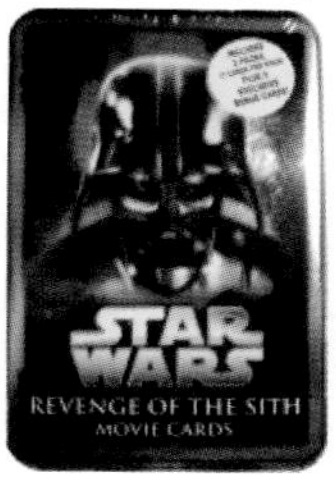

PRS06

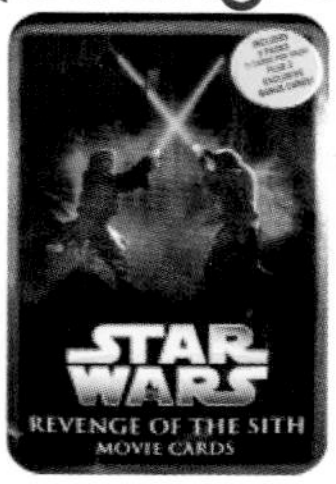

PRS07

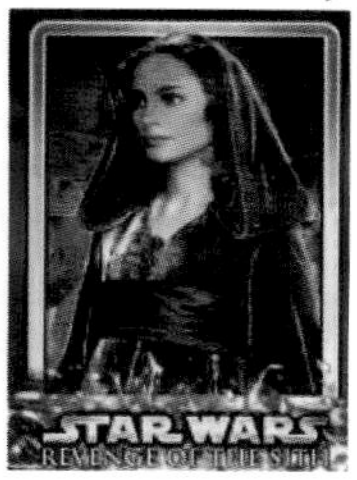

PRS08 sample

Cards: ROTS

16 cards. Distributed through Safeway. Sold numerically in packets of four cards each.

____Cards 1 – 16, each 1.00

Mello Smello

____Darth Vader, lenticular promotes Vivid Vision [PRS01] 3.00

Topps

____Lenticular poster card, 10"x8" 15.00

90 cards, 6 etched foil puzzle cards, 3 lenticular morphing cards, 5 promo cards, individually unique artist sketch cards.

____Cards 01 – 15, Characters, each 0.25
____Cards 16 – 21, Alliances, each 0.25
____Cards 22 – 72, Storyline [PRS02], each 0.25
____Cards 73 – 76, Planets, each 0.25
____Cards 77 – 81, Hardware, each 0.25
____Cards 82 – 86, Production Art, each 0.25
____Cards 87 – 89, Behind-the-Scenes, each 0.25
____Card 90, Checklist 0.25
____Cards 1 – 90, set 25.00
____Cards P1 – P5, Promotion cards, each 5.00
____Collector tin, 3 packs, and 2 bonus cards [PRS03-PRS07], each 10.00
____Unopened card packets, each 3.00

<u>*Hobby set.*</u>

____Cards F1 – F6, Etched Foil Puzzle cards, each 4.00
____Cards M1 – M3, Lenticular Morphing cards 5.00

<u>*Retail set.*</u>

____Bonus cards A – F, each..3.00
____Embossed foil cards 1 – 10, each 3.00
____Hologram cards 1 – 3 ....3.00
____Stickers 1 – 10 ....3.00
____Story cards 1 – 6, each 3.00
____Tattoos1 – 10, each 3.00

Topps, UK

Flix-pix. 68 lenticular and 3D cards.

____Cards 01 – 13, characters [PRS08], each 0.75
____Cards 14 – 21, vehicles 0.75
____Cards 22 – 29, connections, each 0.75
____Cards 30 – 37, Jedi versus Sith, each 0.75
____Cards 38 – 67, Revenge of the Sith, each 0.75
____Card 68, Title Card 0.75
____Cards 1 – 68, set 65.00
____Unopened card packets, each 5.00

Cards: Signing

Comicon: Dallas

____Zachariah Jensen / Kit Fisto [OAS01] 5.00

Dark Horse Comics

Unnumbered convention signing cards. (Checklist in 3rd edition, page 206.)

____Cards unsigned, each..6.00

Topps

Value for cards is unsigned.

____1995 San Diego Comic Con, limited to 5,000 [OAS02] 12.00

Cards: SOTE

Topps

100 cards, 7 promotional cards, 1 autographed prom-otional card. (Images and checklist in 3rd ed., pg. 206.)

____Cards 1 – 100 [ON01], each 1.00
____Cards 1 – 100, set 1.00
____Promotional cards 1 – 7, each 5.00
____Promotional cards 7 signed, only available via mail-in redemption 35.00
____Redemption "Winner" card 15.00
____Reservation Coupon 1.15
____Unopened card packets, each 5.00

Cards: Star Wars Galaxy Magazine

Topps

9 cards, numbered in two sets.

____Cards C1 – C4, each 4.00
____Cards SWGM1 – SWGM4, each 4.00

Cards: SW Finest

Topps

90 cards plus promotional, foil, matrix, and oversized chase cards. (Images in 2nd edition, page 207. Checklist in 3rd edition, page 207.)

____Cards 1 – 90 [OBA01], each..................................1.00
____Cards 1 – 90, set 55.00
____Foil cards F1 – F6, each 4.00
____Matrix cards 1 – 4, each 8.00
____Oversized card 5.00
____Oversized refractor card 5.00
____Promo binder card 15.00
____Promo cards SWF1 – SWF3....................................4.50
____Unopened card packets, each 5.00
____Refractor sheet of 90 uncut chromium cards, gold metallic printing on back. Ltd. to 250 ....225.00

Cards: SW Galaxy I

Topps

140 cards, promotional cards, foil chase cards. (Images in 2nd ed., pg. 208. Checklist in 3rd ed., pg. 208.)

____Cards 1 – 140 [OGX01],each 1.00
____Cards 1 – 140, set 25.00
____Foil cards 1 – 6, each 3.40
____Promo cards, each 9.00
____Promo cards, uncut sheet 48.00
____Unopened card packets, each 7.00
____Millennium Falcon factory set, limited to 10,000..95.00

Cards: SW Galaxy II

Topps

135 cards, promotional, foil chase cards. (Images in 2nd ed., pg. 210. Checklist in 3rd ed., pg. 209.)

____Cards 141 – 275 [OGY01], each............................1.00
____Cards 141 – 275, set 25.00
____Foil cards 7 – 12, each 3.00
____Promo binder card 7.00
____Promo cards P1 – P2, P4 – P6, each......................4.00
____Promo card P3 banned from release ....N/V
____Promo cards, unnumbered, each 8.00
____Promo cards, overiszed, each 8.00
____Unopened card packets, each 5.00
____Deluxe factory set, includes collector's tin 65.00

Cards: SW Galaxy III

Topps

90 cards plus promotional, embossed, lenticular, and foil chase cards. (Images in 2nd edition, page 212. Checklist in 3rd edition, page 209.)

____Cards 276 – 365 [OGZ01], each............................1.00
____Cards 276 – 365, set 30.00
____Cards 276 – 365 first day printing, each 3.00
____Cards 276 – 365 first day printing, set 90.00
____Embossed cards E1 – E6, each 3.00
____Foil cards 13 – 18, each 4.00
____Lenticular cards L1 – L12, each 3.00
____Promo cards oversized, each 9.00
____Promo cards P1 – P8, each 8.00
____Promo cards unnumbered, each 5.00
____Unopened card packets, each 5.00

Cards: Sweden

Nellba

Set 1. 125 cards. Available in both "Stjarnornas Krig" and with English scene description. (Images in 2nd edition, page 213. Checklist in 3rd edition, page 210.)

____Cards 1 – 125, each 1.50
____Cards 1 – 125, set 70.00
____Unopened card packets, each............................14.00

Set 2. 125 cards. Available in both "Stjarnornas Krig" and with English scene description. (Images in 2nd edition, page 214. Checklist in 3rd edition, page 210.)

____Cards 201 – 326 [OLA01 – OLA02], each 1.50
____Cards 201 – 326, set 70.00
____Unopened card packets, each............................14.00

Cards: TCG (Trading Card Game)

The trading card game (TCG) play decks were built from cards purchased in random booster packs. During the years the game had a large active play goup, values of individual cards varied depending on the scarcity of the card and amount of influence the card had to offer in stronger or popular play strategies.

The most desired cards had values of $10 – $20 each with some of the rarest cards reaching nearly $100 in value. The most common of the cards rarely exceeded $0.10 to $0.25 in value. The addition of foil chase cards also increased card values.

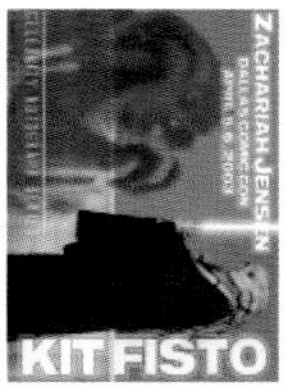

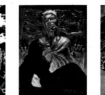

OAS01

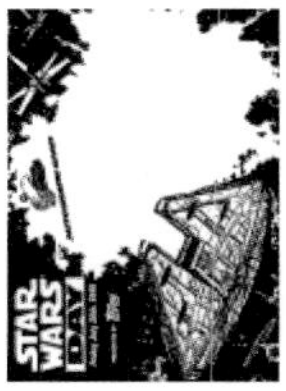

OAS02

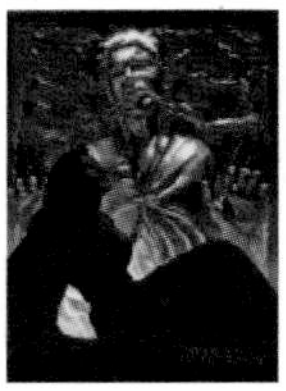

ON01 sample

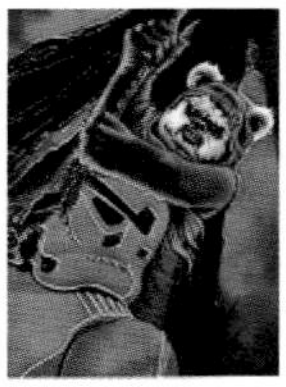

OBA01 sample

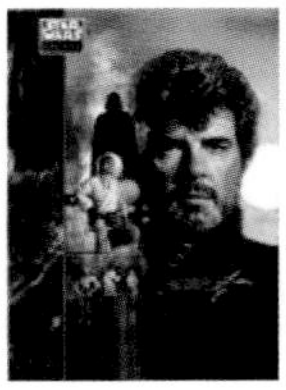

OGX01 sample

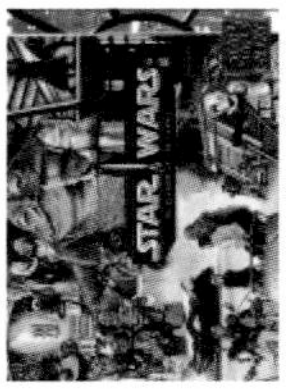

OGY01 sample

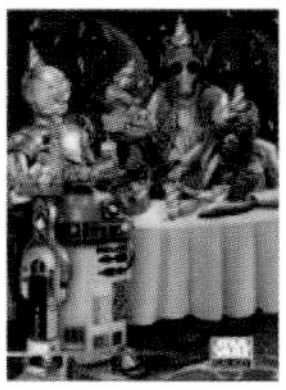

OGZ01 sample

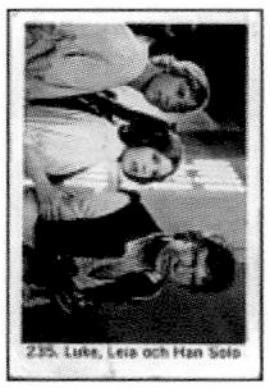

OLA01 sample

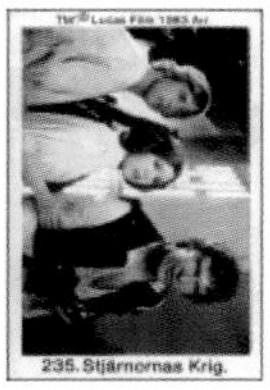

OLA02 sample

Cards: TCG (Trading Card Game)

EJK01

EJK02

EJK03

EJK04

EJK05

EJK06

EJK07

EJK08

EJK09

EJK10

EJK11

EJK12

Since the development for the trading card game has ended, the value of the cards has plunged as only a core of dedicated gamers and collectors who find the card art curious has any interest.

Trading card game cards are often found at auction in large quantites and without specific card listings due to the hundreds of cards and card variations that exist.

A brief description of each set is provided here. At the time of this book's publishing, complete card sets can be found at the manufacturer's site (www.Wizards.com) by performing a site search for "star wars."

Collectors may pick up cards as novelties. Gamers usually pay more, but only for specific cards they desire to complete a specific strategy for play.

Decipher.
Jedi Knights. 173 cards total.
Cards counted by rarity.
C (40), F (32), PL (6), PR (4), P (1), RS (50), US (1), U (39)
Cards counted by type.
Character – Alliance Hero (8), Character – Alliance (16), Character – Empire Dark Hero (8), Character – Empire (22), Character – Independent (18), Event (36), Force (10), Location (8), Starship (15), Theme (8), Weapon (24)

Jedi Knights, Master of the Force. 140 cards total.
Cards counted by rarity.
C (40), R (39), RS (21), U (40)
Cards counted by type.
Character – Alliance Hero (2), Character – Alliance (19), Character – Empire Dark Hero (2), Character – Empire (15), Character – Independent (7), Event (30), Force – Black (4), Force – Blue (14), Force – Green (2), Force – Orange (2), Jedi Power (10), Sith Power (6), Starship (15), Theme (8), Weapon (4)

Jedi Knights, Master of the Force. 140 cards total.
Cards counted by rarity.
C (40), R (39), RS (21), U (40)
Cards counted by type.
Character – Alliance Hero (2), Character – Alliance (19), Character – Empire Dark Hero (2), Character – Empire (15), Character – Independent (7), Event (30), Force – Black (4), Force – Blue (14), Force – Green (2), Force – Orange (2), Jedi Power (10), Sith Power (6), Starship (15), Theme (8), Weapon (4)

Jedi Knights, Scum and Villainy. 140 cards total.
Cards counted by rarity.
C (40), R (30), RS (30), U (40)
Cards counted by type.
Character – Alliance Hero (4), Character – Alliance (7), Character – Empire Dark Hero (4), Character – Empire (17), Character – Independent (6), Event (27),

Force (18), Jedi Power (11), Sith Power (9), Starship (15), Theme (8), Weapon (14)

Wizards of the Coast
A New Hope. 180 cards total.
Cards counted by rarity.
Common (60), Uncommon (61), Rare (59)
Cards counted by type.
Battle (38), Character (63), Ground (28), Mission (27), Space (24)

Attack of the Clones. 180 cards total.
Cards counted by rarity.
Common (60), Uncommon (60), Rare (60)
Cards counted by type.
Battle (37), Character (60), Ground (30), Mission (25), Space (28)

Battle of Yavin. 105 cards total.
Cards counted by rarity.
Common (34), Uncommon (36), Rare (35)
Cards counted by type.
Battle (19), Character (39), Ground (21), Mission (7), Space (19)

Empire Strikes Back. 210 cards total.
Cards counted by rarity.
Common (70), Uncommon (69), Rare (71)
Cards counted by type.
Battle (38), Character (58), Ground (28), Location (27), Mission (27), Space (32)

Jedi Guardians. 105 cards total.
Cards counted by rarity.
Common (34), Uncommon (36), Rare (35)
Cards counted by type.
Battle (13), Character (42), Ground (18), Mission (15), Space (17)

Return of the Jedi. 109 cards total.
Cards counted by rarity.
Common (40), Uncommon (29), Rare (40)
Cards counted by type.
Battle (15), Character (41), Ground (19), Location (15), Mission (4), Space (15)

Revenge of the Sith. 110 cards total.
Cards counted by rarity.
Common (40), Uncommon (30), Rare (40)
Cards counted by type.
Battle (17), Character (35), Equipment (8), Ground (13), Location (7), Mission (9), Space (21)

Rogues and Scoundrels. 105 cards total.
Cards counted by rarity.
Common (35), Uncommon (35), Rare (35)
Cards counted by type.
Battle (11), Character (45), Ground (11), Location (12), Mission (6), Space (20)

Sith Rising. 90 cards total.
Cards counted by rarity.
Common (29), Uncommon (30), Rare (31)
Cards counted by type.
Battle (14), Character (36), Ground (17), Mission (9), Space (14)

The Phantom Menace. 90 cards total.
Cards counted by rarity.
Common (30), Uncommon (30), Rare (30)

Cards counted by type.
Battle (7), Character (31), Ground (20), Location (12), Mission (6), Space (14)

Cards: Thailand

Pepsi Cola
4 unnumbered cards. One for each classic trilogy movie, plus one SW:SE logo. (Images in 3rd edition, page 211. Checklist in 3rd edition, page 210.)
____Cards, each..5.00

Cards: Tin

Metallic Images
A New Hope. 20 cards. Distributed as a set inside a collector's tin. (Images in 2nd edition, page 215. Checklist in 3rd edition, page 210.)
____Cards 1 – 20 with tin [CTS01] 40.00
____Promo card P1 ....15.00

Bounty Hunters. 6 cards. Distributed as a set inside a collector's tin. (Images in 2nd edition, page 215. Checklist in 3rd edition, page 211.)
____Cards 1 – 20 with tin [TBH01] 25.00

Dark Empire. 6 cards showing covers from Dark Empire comics. Distributed as a set inside a collector's tin. (Images in 2nd edition, page 215. Checklist in 3rd edition, page 211.)
____Cards 1 – 6 with tin [OF01] 15.00

Dark Empire II. 6 cards showing covers from Dark Empire II comics. Distributed as a set inside a collector's tin. (Images in 2nd edition, page 215. Checklist in 3rd edition, page 211.)
____Cards 1 – 6 with tin [OF101] 10.00

Empire Strikes Back. 20 numbered cards. Distributed as a set inside a collector's tin. Continued numbering from the A New Hope set. (Images in 2nd edition, page 215. Checklist in 3rd edition, page 211.)
____Cards 21 – 40 with tin [OG01] 40.00
____Promo card P2 ....15.00

Jedi Knights. 7 cards. Distributed as a set inside a collector's tin. Avon exclusive. (Images in 2nd edition, page 216. Checklist in 3rd edition, page 211.)
____Cards 1 – 7 with tin [OM01] 15.00

Ralph McQuarrie Art. 20 numbered cards. Distributed as a set inside a collector's tin. (Images in 2nd edition, page 216. Checklist in 3rd edition, page 211.)
____Cards 1 – 20 with tin [OM101] 65.00

Return of the Jedi. 20 numbered cards. Distributed as a set inside a collector's tin. Continued numbering from the Empire Strikes Back set. (Images in 2nd edition, page 216. Checklist in 3rd edition, page 211.)
____Cards 41 – 60 with tin [OZ01] 40.00
____Promo card P3 ....15.00

Shadows of the Empire. 6 cards showing covers. Distributed as a set inside a collector's tin. (Images in 2nd ed., pg. 216. Checklist in 3rd ed., page 211.)
____Cards 1 – 6 with tin [ONE01] 18.00

CTS01 sample

TBH01 sample

OF01 sample

OF201 sample

OG01 sample

OM01 sample

OM101 sample

OZ01 sample

ONE01 sample

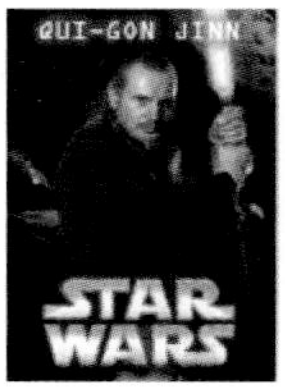

CRD01 sample

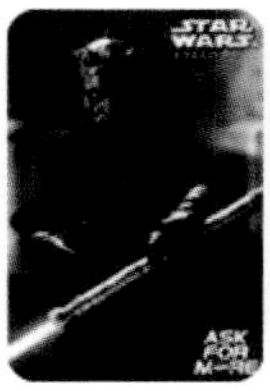
CRD02 sample

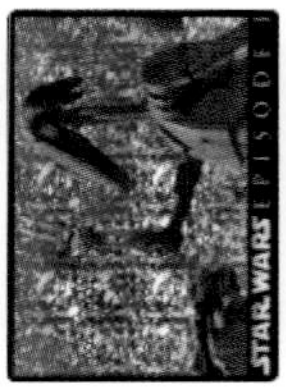
CRD03 sample

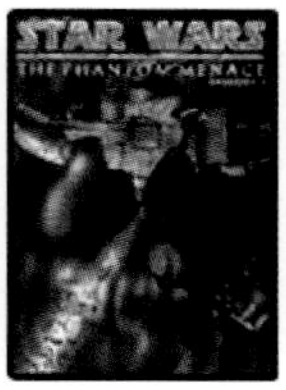

CRD04 sample

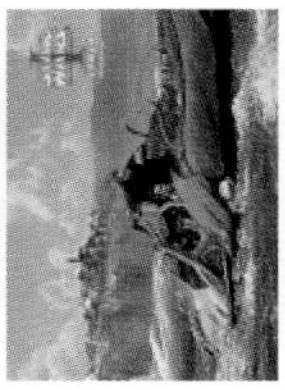
CRD05 sample

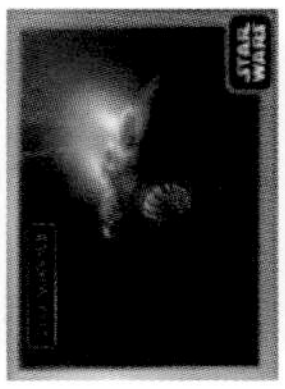
CRD06 sample

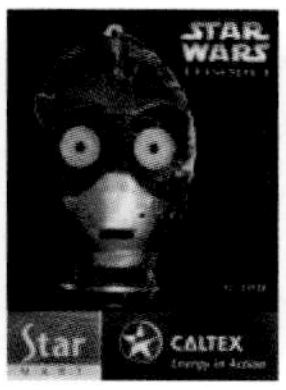

CRD07 sample

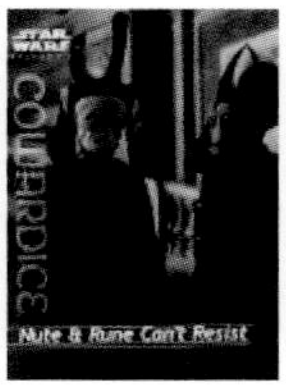

CRD08 sample

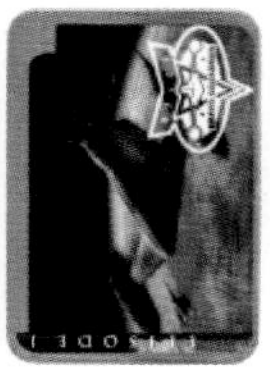
CRD09 sample

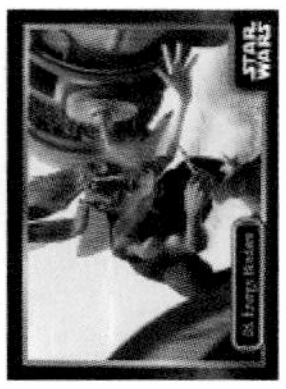
CRD10 sample

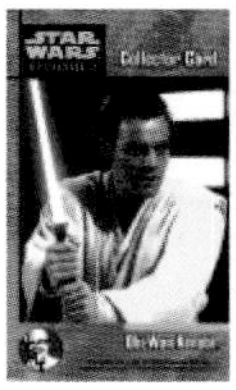
CRD11 smpl.

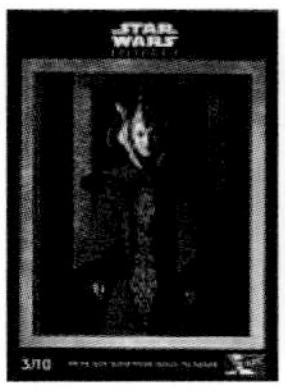
CRD12 sample

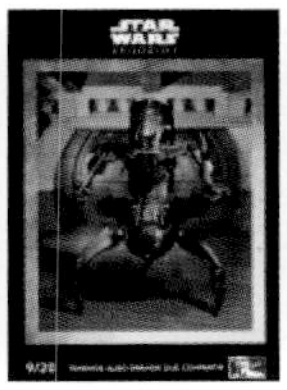
CRD13 sample

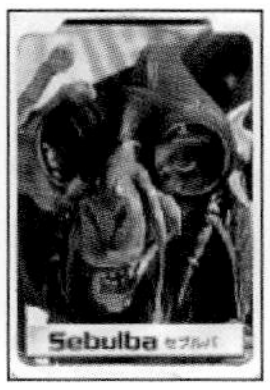

CRD14 sample

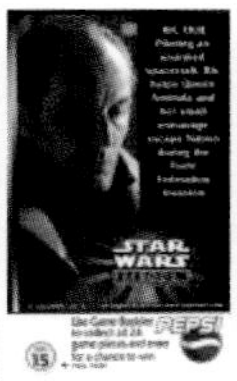
CRD15 smpl.

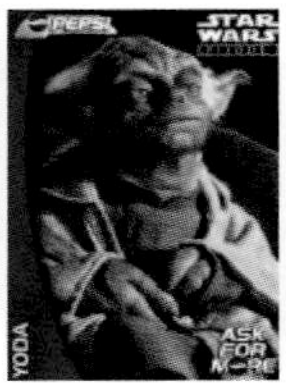

CRD16 sample

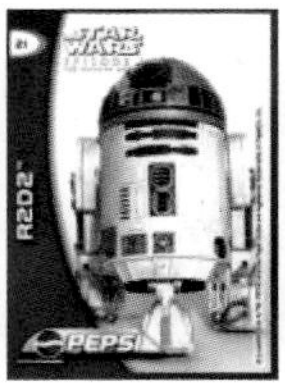

CRD17 sample

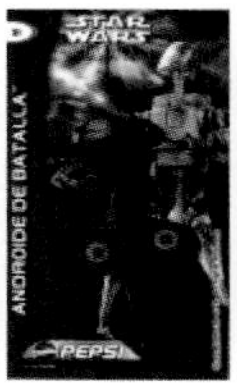

CRD18 smpl.

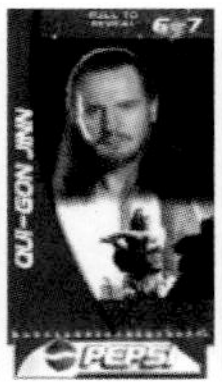

CRD19 smpl.

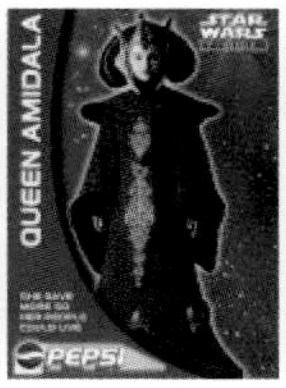

CRD20 sample

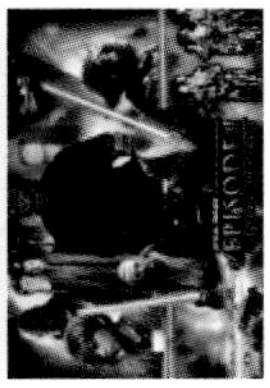
CRD21 sample

Cards: TPM

Hungary. 20 unnumbered cards. (Images and checklist in 3rd edition, page 212.)
____Cards [CRD01], each 3.00
____Cards, set 35.00

Japan. 8 unnumbered cards. Has Pepsi "Ask for More" logo, but not produced by Pepsi. (Images and checklist in 3rd edition, page 212.)
____Cards [CRD02], each 1.00

Prismatic series 1. 36 unnumbered cards. (Images in 2nd ed., pg. 216. Checklist in 3rd ed., pg. 212.)
____Cards [CRD03], each 0.50
____Cards, set 9.00

Prismatic series 2. 36 unnumbered cards. (Images in 2nd ed., pg. 217. Checklist in 3rd ed., pg. 212.)
____Cards [CRD04], each 0.50
____Cards, set 11.00

20th Century Fox
4 cards. *Walmart exclusive, used to view new scenes on DVD at the store during the promotional release of Episode I. (Images in 2nd edition, page 217. Checklist in 3rd edition, page 212.)*
____Cards 1 – 4 [CRD05], each....................................3.00

Bluebird
18 cards "medium" in size. (Checklist in 3rd edition, page 212.)
____Cards 1 – 18, each 1.00
____Cards 1 – 18, set 30.00

18 cards "mini" in size. Numbering continued from medium-sized set. (Checklist in 3rd edition, page 213.)
____Cards 19 – 36, each 1.00
____Cards 19 – 36, set 20.00

30 cards "large" in size. (Images in 2nd edition, page 216. Checklist in 3rd edition, page 213.)
____Cards 1 – 30 [CRD06], each.................................1.50
____Cards 1 – 30, set 15.00

Caltex
South Africa. 4 unnumbered cards. (Images and checklist in 3rd edition, page 213.)
____Cards [CRD07], each 5.00

Family Toy Warehouse
3 unnumbered lenticular cards. (Images and checklist in 3rd edition, page 213.)
____Cards, each..2.00

Frito Lay
12 unnumbered cards. Characters with an associated trait description. (Images in 2nd edition, page 218. Checklist in 3rd edition, page 213.)
____Cards [CRD08], each. 1.00

Harmony
Australia. (Images and checklist in 3rd ed., pg. 213.)
____Cards 1 – 24 [CRD09], each.................................3.00
____Cards 1 – 24, set 26.00

iKon
61 red and black bordered cards. (Images in 2nd edition, page 218. Checklist in 3rd edition, page 213.)
____Cards 1 – 61 [CRD10], each.................................0.50
____Cards 1 – 61, set 38.00

Interlace4D
6 unnumbered oversized lenticular cards. (Checklist in 3rd edition, page 214.)
____Cards, each..5.00

KFC
5 unnumbered character cards. (Images in 2nd edition, page 219. Checklist in 3rd edition, page 214.)
____Cards [CRD11], each 1.75

Australia. 10 character cards. (Images in 2nd edition, page 219. Checklist in 3rd edition, page 214.)
____Cards 1 – 10 [CRD12], each.................................1.20
____Cards 1 – 10, set 10.00

Mexico. 20 character cards. (Images in 2nd edition, page 219. Checklist in 3rd edition, page 214.)
____Cards 1 – 20 [CRD13], each.................................1.50
____Cards 1 – 20, set 24.00
____Collecting envelope 5.00

U.K. *20 character cards. (Images in 2nd edition, page 219. Checklist in 3rd edition, page 214.)*
____Cards 1 – 20, each 1.50
____Cards 1 – 20, set 24.00

Meiji
30 characters cards. (Image and checklist in 3rd edition, page 214.)
____Cards 1 – 30 [CRD14], each.................................3.00
____Cards 1 – 30, set 55.00

Pepsi Cola
24 cards showing Pepsi cans with characters. Game piece attached. (Images in 2nd edition, page 219. Checklist in 3rd edition, page 215.)
____Cards 1 – 24 [CRD15], each.................................1.00
____Cards 1 – 24, set 25.00
____Collector Card Game Booklet 5.00

Australia. 12 unnumbered 3" circular carton cut-outs. (Images and checklist in 3rd edition, page 215.)
____6-pack 5.00
____12-pack 7.00
____15-pack 9.00
____Cards cut apart, each 0.50

Europe / general release. 9 unnumbered character cards. (Images in 2nd edition, page 219. Checklist in 3rd edition, page 215.)
____Cards [CRD16], each 1.50

Germany. *45 numbered scenes with character names. (Images in 2nd edition, page 220. Checklist in 3rd edition, page 215.)*
____Cards 1 – 45 [CRD17], each.................................1.00
____Cards 1 – 45, set 30.00

Hong Kong. 7 unnumbered cards marked "Galactic Passport." (Images in 3rd edition, page 215. Checklist in 3rd edition, page 216.)
____Cards, each..3.00

Mexico. Set of 96 cards. (Images in 3rd edition, page 214. Checklist in 3rd edition, page 216.)
____Cards 1 – 96 [CRD18], each.................................1.00
____Cards 1 – 96, set 70.00

Netherlands. 26 square 2"x2" character cards. (Images in 2nd ed., pg. 220. Checklist in 3rd ed., pg. 216.)
____Cards 1 – 26, each 2.00
____Cards 1 – 26, set 45.00

U.K. 7 pop-up cards. (Images and checklist in 3rd edition, page 216.)
____Cards 1 – 7 [CRD19], each....................................2.00

4 unnumbered cards. Cardbacks make Darth Maul image. (Images and checklist in 3rd edition, page 216.)
____Cards, each..6.00

Smith's Snackfood
Dutch. 26 unnumbered cards featuring characters and trait description. (Image in 3rd edition, page 216)
____Cards 1 – 26, each 1.00
____Cards 1 – 26, set 18.00

Topps
7-packs of movie cards in collectible tin. Includes 1 mega-size foil card. (Checklist in 3rd edition, page 216.)
____Sealed tins, each 24.00

Unif
Thailand. 6 unnumbered cards. Promotes drink products. (Images and checklist in 3rd ed., pg. 216.)
____Cards [CRD20], each 5.00

Walkers
25 unnumbered character cards. (Images in 2nd edition, page 221. Checklist in 3rd edition, page 217.)
____Cards [CRD11], each 1.00

Cards: TV Week

TV Week
Set of 4 cards advertising Special Edition videos. (Images in 2nd edition, page 222. Checklist in 3rd edition, page 217.)
____Cards 1 – 4 [OH01], each......................................3.50

Cards: UK

Merlin Publishing Internat'l Ltd.
125 cards, 3 promotional cards. (Checklist in 3rd edition, page 217.)
____Cards 1 – 35 ANH, each...1.60
____Cards 36 – 70 ESB, each 1.60
____Cards 71 – 105 ROTJ, each 1.60
____Cards 106 – 115 characters, each 1.60
____*Cards* 116 – 124 vehicles, each 1.60
____*Card* 125 checklist 1.60
____Cards 1 – 125, set 75.00
____Promotion cards P1 – P3, each 6.50

Walkers
8 unnumbered Tazos. (Images in 2nd edition, page 222. Checklist in 3rd edition, page 217.)
____Cards [OCU01], each 4.00

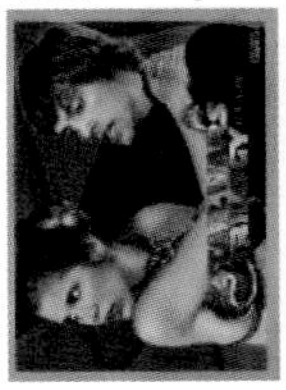
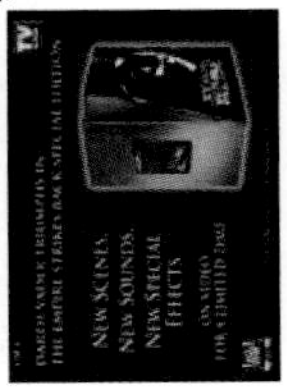
OH01 front / rear sample

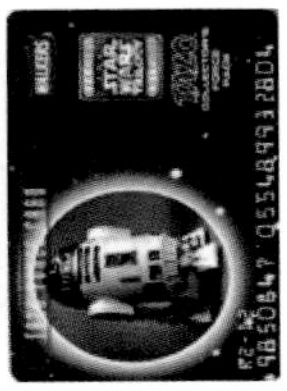
OCU01 sample

Cards: Vehicle

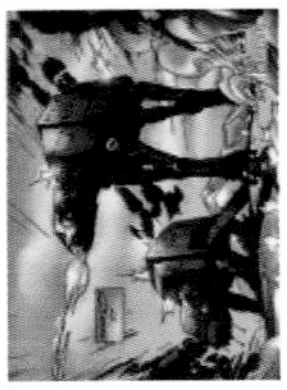
OAV01 sample

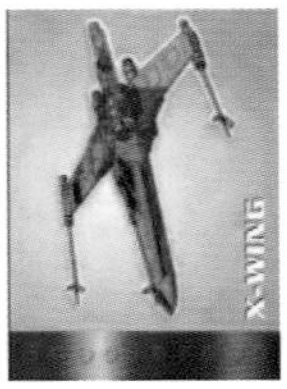
OAV02 sample

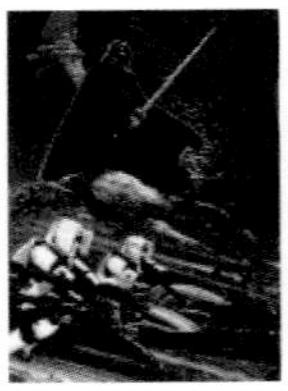
OAV03

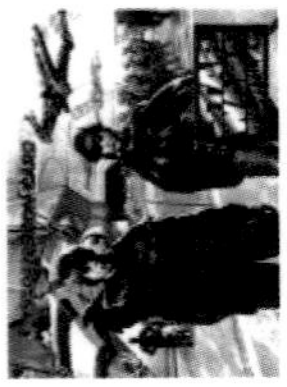
OAV04

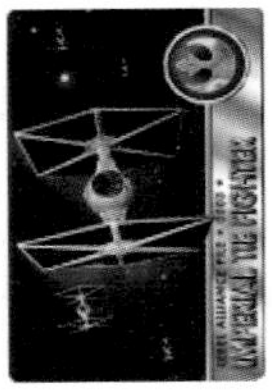
IDC01 sample

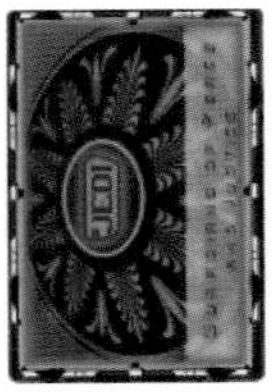
IDC02 sample

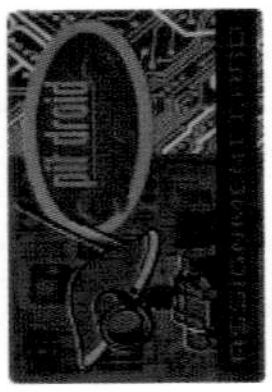
IDC03 sample

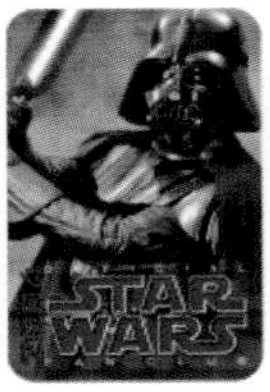
IDC04 sample

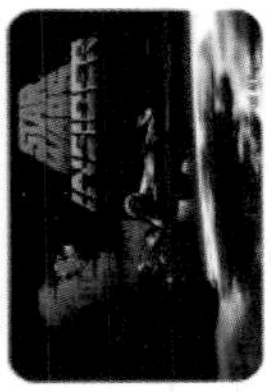
IDC05 sample

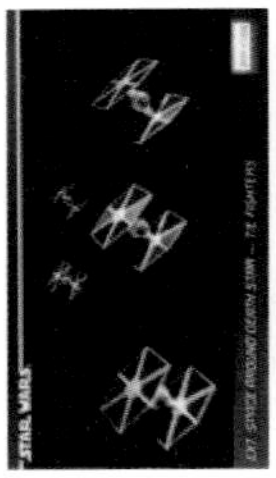
OTA01 sample

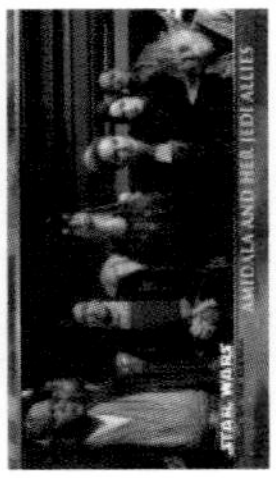
CA201 sample

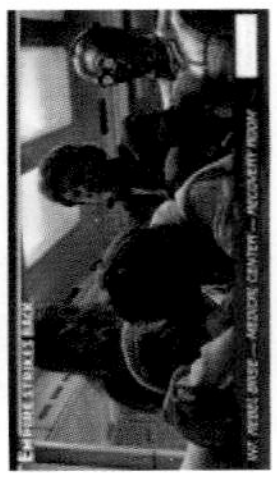
OI01 sample

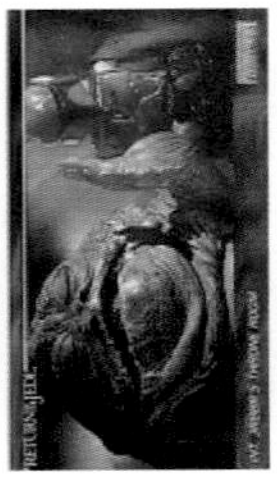
OR01 sample

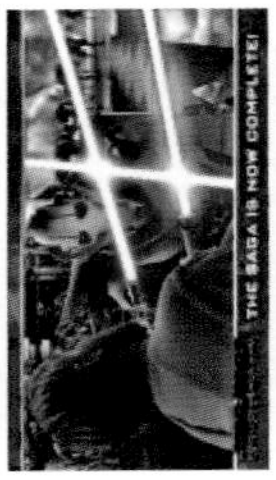
P1R01 sample

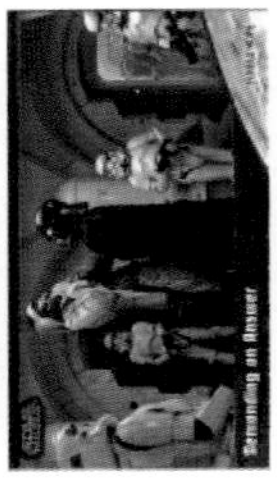
OT01 sample

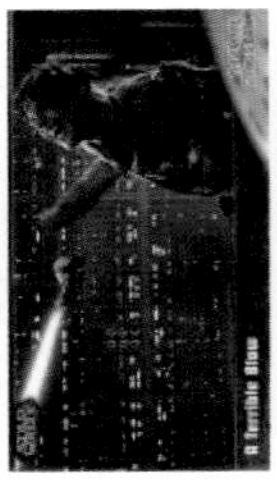
OT02 sample

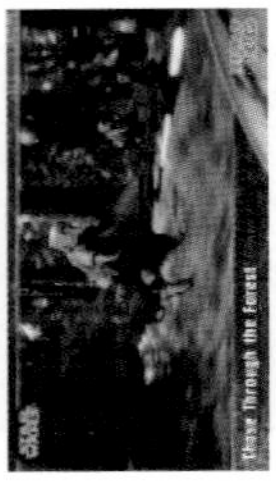
OT03 sample

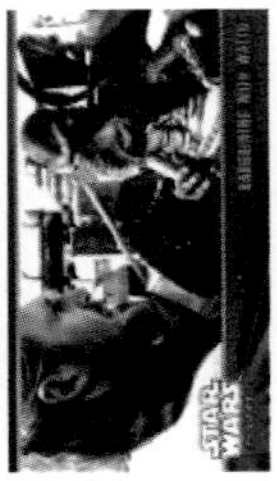
TW301 sample

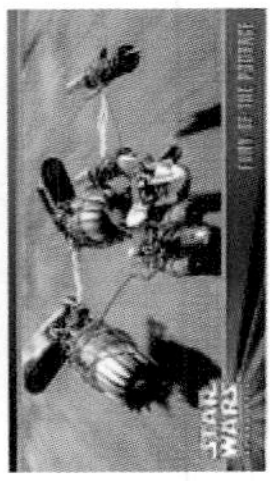
TW101 sample

Cards: Vehicle

Topps
72 cards, 6 promotional cards, 4 chase cards, 1 redemption card, 1 redeemed card. (Images in 2nd edition, page 223. Checklist in 3rd edition, page 217.)
____Cards 1 – 72 [OAV01], each 1.00
____Cards 1 – 72, set 75.00
____Chase cards C1 – C4 [OAV02], each 4.00
____Promo cards 1 – 2, each 3.50
____Promo card P1 limited to 3,200 [OAV03]............85.00
____Promo card P1 refractor, limited to 350 ....360.00
____Promo card P2 limited to 1,600 ....115.00
____Promo card P2 refractor, limited to 175 ....340.00
____Redeemed card, oversized 3D...........................29.00
____Redemption card [OAV04] 26.00
____Redemption card bonus envelope 4.00

Cards: Wallet

Antioch
Classic trilogy characters and vehicles. (Images in 2nd edition, page 417. Checklist in 3rd edition, page 218.)
____Cards [IDC01], each 5.00

Episode I: The Phantom Menace images. (Images in 2nd edition, page 417. Checklist in 3rd edition, page 218.)
____Cards [IDC02 – IDC03], each 5.00

Paizo Publishing
Fan Club Membership cards 2003 and 2004. (Images in 3rd edition, page 218.)
____Cards [IDC04], each 7.00

Star Wars Insider
Space battle images.
____Card, each [IDC05] 5.00

Cards: Widevision

Blockbuster Video, Mexico
Mexico. Revenge of the Sith. 3 unnumbered cards.
____Cards, each...5.00

Topps
A New Hope. 120 cards, 10 chase cards, 4 Kenner cards, 7 promotional cards. (Images in 2nd edition, page 224. Checklist in 3rd edition, page 218.)
____Cards 1 – 120 [OTA01], each 1.00
____Cards 1 – 120, set 35.00
____Chase cards C1 – C10, each 5.00
____Kenner cards K1 – K4, each 10.00
____Promo binder card #00...5.00
____Promo card 5"x7" 4.00
____Promo cards SWP0-SWP6, each.............................6.00
____Unopened card packets, each 5.00

Attack of the Clones. 80 cards, 23 hand signed autograph cards, 1 hand signed chase card, 2 promo cards. (Checklist in 3rd edition, page 219.)
____Cards 1 – 80 [CA201], each 0.35
____Cards 1 – 80, set 40.00
____Promo cards P1 and S1, each 6.00

Cards, autograph.
____Ahmed Best, Jar Jar Binks voice.........................35.00
____Alethea Mcgrath, Jocasta Nu 25.00
____Amy Allen, Aayla Secura 25.00
____Andrew Secombe, Watto voice 25.00
____Ayesha Dharker, Queen Jamillia 25.00
____Bodie Taylor, Clone Trooper 40.00
____Bonnie Piesse, Beru Whiteson.............................75.00
____Daniel Logan, Boba Fett 85.00
____David Bowers, Mas Amedda 25.00
____Frank Oz, Yoda 120.00
____Jay Laga'aia, Captain Typho 25.00
____Jesse Jensen, Saesee Tiin......................................65.00
____Joel Edgerton, Owen Lars 50.00
____Kenny Baker, R2-D2..30.00
____Leeanna Walsman, Zam Wesell 30.00
____Mary Oyaya, Luminara Unduli 25.00
____Matt Doran, Elan Sleazebaggano 25.00
____Matt Sloan, Plo Koon 25.00
____Nalini Krishan, Barriss Offee 25.00
____Rena Owen, Taun We voice 25.00
____Ronald Falk, Dexter Jettster 25.00
____Silas Carson, Ki Adi Mundi 45.00
____Silas Carson, Nute Gunray.....................................80.00
____Zachariah Jensen, Kit Fisto 65.00

Empire Strikes Back. 144 cards, 10 chase cards, 8 promotional cards. (Images in 2nd edition, page 226. Checklist in 3rd edition, page 219.)
____Cards 1 – 144 [OI01], each......................................1.00
____Cards 1 – 144, set 35.00
____Chase cards C1 – C10, each 5.00
____Promo card #0 ....5.00
____Promo card 5"x7" 6.00
____Promo cards P1 – P6, each 4.25

Return of the Jedi. 144 cards, 9 promotional cards, 10 chase card, 1 redemption card, 1 redeemed card. (Images in 2nd ed, pg 228. Checklist in 3rd edition, page 220.)
____Cards 1 – 144 [OR01], each 1.00
____Cards 1 – 144, set 35.00
____Chase cards C1 – C10, each 5.00
____Promo card #0 ....6.00
____Promo card #0, 5"x7" 4.25
____Promo card DIII...8.00
____Promo cards P1 – P6, each 6.50
____Redemption card 3-D offer 14.00
____Redemption card bonus envelope 4.00

Revenge of the Sith. 80 cards, 10 chrome art cards (hobby set), 10 chrome art cards (retail set), 10 flix pix cards, 5 autograph cards.
____Cards 1 – 80 [P1R01], each 0.50
____Cards 1 – 80, set 20.00
____Chrome art cards H1 – H10, each 3.00
____Chrome art cards R1 – R10, each 5.00
____Flix pix cards 1 – 10, each 10.00

Autograph cards.
____Amy Allen (Aayla Secura) 1:66 ....35.00
____Matthew Wood (General Grievous) 1:435 ....125.00
____Michael Kingma (Tarfful) 1:66.............................45.00
____Peter Mayhew (Chewbacca) 1:328 ....65.00
____Samuel L. Jackson (Mace Windu) 1:2795........550.00

Collector tins. 6 different images.
____Sealed tins, each 18.00

Special Edition hobby set. 72 cards plus 2 holographic, 6 laser cut cards. (Checklist in 3rd edition, page 221.)
____Cards 1 – 72, each 1.00
____Cards 1 – 72, set 20.00
____Holographic cards H1 – H2, each 5.00
____Laser cut chrome cards C1 – C6, each 8.00

Special Edition retail set. 72 cards plus 5 Galoob chase, 4 Kenner chase, 6 laser cut, 8 promo cards. (Images in 2nd ed., pg. 230. Checklist in 3rd ed., pg. 221.)
____Cards 1 – 72 [OT01 – OT03], each 1.00
____Cards 1 – 72, set 20.00
____Galoob chase cards G1 – G5, each 9.00
____Kenner chase cards H1 – H4, each 9.00
____Laser cut cards C1 – C6, each 11.00
____Promo cards P1 – P8, each 4.00

The Phantom Meance series 1. 80 cards. (Images in 2nd edition, page 232. Checklist in 3rd ed., pg. 222.)
____Cards 1 – 80 [TW301], each 0.50
____Cards 1 – 80, set 20.00

The Phantom Menace series 1. Hobby sets: 40 bonus cards, 8 chrome cards. (Checklist in 3rd ed., pg. 222.)
____Bonus cards X1 – X40, each 2.00
____Bonus cards X1 – X40, set......................................35.00
____Chrome cards C1 – C8, each 9.00

The Phantom Menace series 1. Retail sets: 10 mirror cards, 5 unnumbered oversized cards, 16 stickers, 3 trivia cards, 2 promo cards. (Checklist in 3rd ed., pg 222.)
____Mirror cards F1 – F10, each 9.00
____Oversized cards, each 4.00
____Promo cards 0 – 000, each 4.00
____Promo cards SW1 – SW9, each.................................4.00
____Sticker cards S1 – S16, each 6.00
____Trivia cards H1 – H3, each 3.00

The Phantom Menace series 2. 80 cards. (Images in 2nd ed., pg. 234. Checklist in 3rd ed., pg. 223.)
____Cards 1 – 80 [TW101], each 0.50
____Cards 1 – 80, set 18.00

The Phantom Meance series 2. Hobby special sets: 4 chrome cards, 6 foil cards, 3 oversized box cards. (Checklist in 3rd edition, page 223.)
____Chrome cards HC1 – HC4, each 11.00
____Foil embossed cards HE1 – HE6, each 14.00
____Oversized cards, each 4.00

The Phantom Meance series 2. Retail special sets: 4 chrome cards, 6 foil cards. (Checklist in 3rd edition, page 223.)
____Chrome cards C1 – C4, each 5.00
____Foil embossed cards E1 – E6, each 14.00

CCG (Collectible Card Game)

Decipher.
Young Jedi, Battle of Naboo. 158 cards total.
Cards counted by rarity.
C (61), R (30), SS (10), SRF (6), URF (4), U (39), VRF (8)
Cards counted by type.
Dark Side: Battle (11), Characters (38), Effects (5), Foil (9), Locations (3), Starships (4), Weapons (9)
Light Side: Battle (15), Characters (33), Effects (5), Foil (9), Locations (3), Starships (4), Weapons (10)

CCG (Customizable Card Game)

| E1D01 | E1D02 | E1D03 | E1D04 | E1D05 | E1D06 | E1D07 | E1D08 | E1D09 |

| E1D10 | E1D11 | E1D12 |

Young Jedi, Battle of Naboo Enhanced. 12 cards total. [E1D01 – E1D12]
<u>Cards counted by rarity.</u>
PM (12)
<u>Cards counted by type.</u>
Dark Side Character (6), Light Side Character (6)

Young Jedi, Boonta Eve Podrace. 60 cards total.
<u>Cards counted by rarity.</u>
C (18), R (18), UR (2), U (22)
<u>Cards counted by type.</u>
Dark Side: Battle (4), Characters (17), Effects (3), Objetive (1), Starship (1), Weapons (4)
Light Side: Battle (4), Characters (15), Effects (3), Objective (1), Starship (1), Weapons (6)

Young Jedi, Duel of Fates. 60 cards total.
<u>Cards counted by rarity.</u>
C (19), R (18), UR (2), U (21)
<u>Cards counted by type.</u>
Dark Side: Battle (11), Characters (10), Effects (5), Starships (1), Weapons (3)
Light Side: Battle (9), Characters (11), Effects (7), Starships (1), Weapons (2)

Young Jedi, Jedi Council. 158 cards total.
<u>Cards counted by rarity.</u>
C (60), R (30), SS (10), SRF (6), URF (4), U (40), VRF (8)
<u>Cards counted by type.</u>
Dark Side: Battle (15), Characters (35), Foil (9), Locations (3), Starships (3), Weapons (14)
Light Side: Battle (13), Characters (39), Foil (9), Locations (3), Starships (3), Weapons (12)

Young Jedi, Menace of Maul. 158 cards total.
<u>Cards counted by rarity.</u>
C (60), CF (8), R (30), RF (4), SS (10), U (40), UF (6)
<u>Cards counted by type.</u>
Dark Side: Battle (14), Characters (36), Foil (9), Locations (3), Starships (3), Weapons (14)
Light Side: Battle (18), Characters (33), Foil (9), Locations (3), Starships (3), Weapons (13)

Young Jedi, Menace of Maul Enhanced. 6 cards total.
<u>Cards counted by rarity.</u>
PM (6)
<u>Cards counted by type.</u>
Dark Side: Characters (3)
Light Side: Characters (3)

Young Jedi, Reflections. 101 cards total.
<u>Cards counted by set.</u>
Battle of Naboo Enhanced (12), Battle of Naboo (7), Boonta Eve Podrace (12), Duel of Fates (10), Jedi Council (6), Menace of Maul Enhanced (6), Menace of Maul, Premium (1), Reflections (41)
<u>Cards counted by type.</u>
Dark Side: Armed and Dangerous (6), Combo Battle (7), Double Impact (7), Foil (30)
Light Side: Armed and Dangerous (7), Combo Battle (7), Double Impact (7), Foil (30)

CCG (Customizable Card Game)

The customizable card game (CCG) play decks were built from cards blindly purchased in random booster packs. During the years the game had a large active play goup, values of individual card varied depending on the scarcity of the card and amount of influence the card had to offer in stronger or popular play strategies.

Most of most desired cards had values of $10 – $20 each with some of the rarest cards reaching nearly $100 in value. The most common of the cards rarely exceeded $0.10 to $0.25 in value, each. The addition of foil highlights to chase cards also increased card value in proportion to the value of the non-foil version of the card. The cards also enjoyed international release, allowing collectors to locate and treasure foreign cards for their set.

Since the development for the customizable card game ended, the value of the cards have dropped in value to only a fraction of the amount they used to command. Only a small core of gamers and collectors who find the cards to be curious has any interest.

Customizable card game cards are often found at auction in large quantites and without specific card listings due to the hundreds of cards and card variations that exist.

Collectors may pick up inexpensive cards as novelties. Gamers usually are willing to pay more, but only for specific cards they desire to complete a specific strategy for play.

A complete checklist for the CCG cards may be found in the second edition from page 135 to page 161.

Decipher
1st Anthology. 6 cards total. [EH01]
<u>Cards counted by rarity.</u>
Preview (6)
<u>Cards counted by type.</u>
Character (2), Effect (2), Starship (2)

2nd Anthology. 6 cards total. [EM01]
<u>Cards counted by rarity.</u>
Preview (6)
<u>Darkside cards counted by type.</u>
Character (2), Location (2), Starship (2)

3rd Anthology. 6 cards total. [EH301]
<u>Cards counted by rarity.</u>
Preview (6)
<u>Cards counted by type.</u>
Character (1), Effect (2), Objective (2), Starship (1)

A New Hope. 162 cards total. [EA01]
<u>Cards counted by rarity.</u>
C1 (10), C2 (42), C3 (2), R1 (30), R2 (24), U1 (30), U2 (24)
<u>Cards counted by type.</u>
Automated Weapon (2), Character Weapon (5), Character: Alien (24), Character: Alien/Rebel (1), Character: Droid (10), Character: Imperial (10), Character: Rebel (7), Creature Vehicle (1), Death Star Weapon (1), Device (10), Effect (19), Epic Event (2), Immediate Effect (4), Location (17), Lost Interrupt (13), Shuttle Vehicle (2), Starship Weapon (2), Starship (11), Swamp Creature (1), Transport Vehicle (1), Used Interrupt (11), Used qor Lost Interrupt (5), Utinni Effect (3)

Cloud City. 180 cards total. [EB01
<u>Cards counted by rarity.</u>
C (50), R (80), U (50)
<u>Cards counted by type.</u>
Character: Alien (15), Character: Droid (1), Character: Imperial (6), Character: Rebel (5), Character Weapon (4), Character: Alien (2), Combat Vehicle (2), Device (7), Effect (27), Epic Event (1), Imm. Effect (5), Location

Sector (4), Location: Site (15), Location: System (2), Lost Interrupt (38), Starship (5), Used Interrupt (21), Used or Lost Interrupt (20), Utinni Effect (3)

Coruscant. 189 cards total.
<u>Cards counted by rarity.</u>
C (60), R (69), U (60)
<u>Cards counted by type.</u>
Character: Alien (13), Character: Darth Maul (2), Character: Droid (5), Character: Jedi Master (8), Character: Republic (38), Character Weapon (6), Effect (24), Immediate Effect (2), Location: Site (22), Location: System (8), Lost Interrupt (10), Objective (4), Political Effect (3), Starship: Capital (3), Starship: Starfighter (3), Used Interrupt (19), Used or Lost Interrupt (1), Used or Lost Interrupt (7), Used or Starting Interrupt (2)

Dagobah. 180 cards total. [EC01]
<u>Cards counted by rarity.</u>
C (50), R (80), U (50)
<u>Cards counted by type.</u>
Character: Alien (3), Character: Droid (2), Character: Imperial (12), Character: Jedi Master (1), Character: Rebel (1), Character Weapon (6), Creature (8), Device (7), Effect (40), Immediate Effect (3), Jedi Test (5), Location: Sector (4), Location: Site (14), Location: System (5), Lost Interrupt (21), Mobile Effect (3), Starship Weapon (1), Starship (8), Used Interrupt (15), Used or Lost Interrupt (12), Utinni Effect (5)

Death Star II. 182 cards total. [EO01]
<u>Cards counted by rarity.</u>
C (50), R (78), U (50), UR (2), XR (2)
<u>Cards counted by type.</u>
Admiral's Orders (10), Characters: Imperial (23), Characters: Jedi Master / Imperial (1), Characters: Rebel (26), Effects (16), Epic Events (1), Events (14), Interrupts (13), Jedi Tests (1), Locations: Sector (3), Locations: Site (7), Locations: System (2), Starships (49), Weapons (12)

Empire Strikes Back. 60 cards total.
<u>Cards counted by rarity.</u>
C (54), PM (6)
<u>Cards counted by type.</u>
Automated Weapon (4), Character Weapon (3), Character: Alien (2), Character: Droid (4), Character: Imperial (9), Character: Rebel (8), Device (3), Effect (2), Location (10), Lost Interrupt (10), Used Interrupt (3), Vehicle (2)

Endor. 180 cards total. [EQ01]
<u>Cards counted by rarity.</u>
C (50), R (80), U (50)
<u>Cards counted by type.</u>
Artillery Weapon (1), Auto. Weapon (1), Character: Imperial (1), Character: Alien (14), Character: Droid (1), Character: Imperial (24), Character: Rebel (18),

| EH01 sample | EM01 sample | EH301 sample | EA01 sample | EB01 sample | EC01 sample | EO01 sample | EQ01 sample | EE01 sample |

CCG (Customizable Card Game)

EF01 sample   EI01 sample   EG01 sample

Character Weapon (6), Combat Vehicle (11), Effect (27), Epic Event (1), Location: Site (18), Location: System (4), Lost Interrupt (12), Objective (2), Starship: Starfighter (3), Transport Vehicle (1), Used Interrupt (20), Used or Lost Interrupt (11), Used or Starting Interrupt (2), Vehicle Weapon (2)

Hoth. 162 cards total. [EE01]
Cards counted by rarity.
C1 (10), C2 (42), C3 (2), R1 (30), R2 (24), U1 (30), U2 (24)
Cards counted by type.
Artillery Weapon (5), Automated Weapon (4), Character Weapon (3), Character: Imperial (9), Character: Rebel (20), Combat Vehicle (8), Creature Vehicle (1), Device (8), Effect (12), Epic Event (1), Immediate Effect (1), Location (19), Lost Interrupt (15), Mobile Effect (2), Snow Creature (1), Starship Weapon (1), Starship (3), Used Interrupt (20), Used or Lost Interrupt (7), Utinni Effect (6), Vehicle Weapon (3)

Jabba's Palace. 180 cards total. [EF01]
Cards counted by rarity.
C (50), R (80), U (50)
Cards counted by type.
Character: Alien (69), Character: Droid (3), Character: Rebel (1), Character: Alien (19), Character: Droid (2), Character Weapon (7), Creature (3), Device (4), Effect (14), Immediate Effect (2), Location: Site (7), Location: System (4), Location: Site (6), Lost Interrupt (10), Mobile Effect (2), Transport Vehicle (3), Used Interrupt (15), Used or Lost Interrupt (5), Used or Starting Interrupt (2), Vehicle Weapon (2)

Jabba's Palace sealed deck. 20 cards total.
Cards counted by rarity.
PR(20)
Cards counted by type.
Characters: Alien (4), Effects (6), Locations: Site (4), Objectives (2), Vehicles: Transport (2), Weapons: Character (2)

Jedi Pack. 11 cards total.
Cards counted by rarity.
PR (11)
Cards counted by type.
Aliens (2), Effects (2), Game Aids (1), Imperials (2), Interrupts (1), Locations (1), Vehicles (2)

CD01   CW01

Official Sealed Deck Premiums. 18 cards total.
Cards counted by rarity.
PM (18)
Cards counted by type.
Character: Alien (2), Character: Imperial (1), Character: Rebel (1), Effect (2), Location: Site (2), Location: System (2), Starship (6), Used or Lost Interrupt (2)

Premiere Enhanced. 6 cards total. [EI01]
Cards counted by rarity.
PM (6)
Cards counted by type.
Character: Imperial (2), Character: Rebel (4)

Premiere Two-Player Into Set Premiums. 6 cards total.
Cards counted by rarity.
PM (6)
Cards counted by type.
Location: Site (2), Character: Imperial (1), Character: Rebel (1), Effect (2)

Premiere Limited. 324 cards total. Black border images. [EG01]
Cards counted by rarity.
C1 (20), C2 (86), C3 (2), R1 (60), R2 (48), U1 (60), U2 (48)
Cards counted by type.
Automated Weapon (7), Character Weapon (13), Character: Alien (26), Character: Droid (14), Character: Imperial (14), Character: Rebel (15), Creature Vehicle (1), Device (17), Effect (43), Location (37), Lost Interrupt (58), Starship Weapon (5), Starship (16), Transport Vehicle (7), Used Interrupt (40), Utinni Effect (11)

Premiere Unimited. 324 cards total. White border images.
Cards counted by rarity.
C1 (20), C2 (86), C3 (2), R1 (60), R2 (48), U1 (60), U2 (48)
Cards counted by type.
Automated Weapon (7), Character Weapon (13), Character: Alien (26), Character: Droid (14), Character: Imperial (14), Character: Rebel (15), Creature Vehicle (1), Device (17), Effect (43), Location (37), Lost Interrupt (58), Starship Weapon (5), Starship (16), Transport Vehicle (7), Used Interrupt (40), Utinni Effect (11)

Rebel Leaders. 2 cards total.
Cards counted by rarity.
PM (2)
Cards counted by type.
Character: Rebel (2)

Reflections. 114 cards total.
Cards counted by rarity.
SRF (25), URF (2), VRF (87)
Cards counted by set.
A New Hope (16), Cloud City (16), Dagobah (18), Hoth (13), Jabba's Palace (10), Premiere (25), Special Edition (16)

Reflections 2. 45 cards total.
Cards counted by rarity.
SRF (15), URF (10), VRF (20)
Cards counted by type.
Admiral's Order (2), Character: Alien (6), Character: Alien/Imperial (1), Character: Dark Jedi Master / Imperial (1), Character: Droid (3), Character: Imperial (3), Character: Rebel (6), Device (2), Effect (3), Lost Interrupt (3), Objective (2), Starfighter (4), Used Interrupt (3), Used or Lost Interrupt (15)

Reflections 3. 106 cards total.
Cards counted by rarity.
P (100), Pv/SRF (6)
Cards counted by type.
Character: Alien (4), Character: Darth Maul (1), Character: Imperial (1), Character: Jedi Master (2), Character: Rebel (3), Character: Republic (3), Character Weapon (6), Defensive Shield (34), Effect (19), Epic Event (2), Imm. Effect (5), Location: Site (5), Lost

Interrupt (8), Objective (2), Starship: Starfighter (1), Used Interrupt (DS) (1), Used Interrupt (8), Vehicle: Combat (1)

Special Edition. 324 cards total.
Cards counted by rarity.
C (80), F (44), R (120), U (80)
Cards counted by type.
Character: Alien (61), Character: Droid (6), Character: Imperial (9), Character: Rebel (22), Character Rebel (1), Character Weapon (8), Combat Vehicle (4), Creature Vehicle (4), Creature (6), Device (4), Effect (45), Immediate Effect (6), Location: Site (41), Location: System (11), Lost Interrupt (11), Mobile Effect (1), Objective (10), Starship: Capital (6), Starship: Squadron (2), Starship: Starfighter (12), Starship Weapon (4), Starship (1), Transport Vehicle (6), Used Interrupt (31), Used or Lost Interrupt (8), Used or Starting Interrupt (2), Utinni Effect (2)

Tatooine. 99 cards total.
Cards counted by rarity.
C (30), R (39), U (30)
Cards counted by type.
Character: Alien (19), Character: Darth Maul (2), Character: Droid (4), Character: Jedi Master (2), Character: Republic (4), Character Weapon (3), Creature Vehicle (1), Device (1), Effect (17), Epic Event (4), Immediate Effect (2), Location: Site (8), Lost Interrupt (10), Lost or Starting Interrupt (2), Podracer (5), Used or Lost Interrupt (13)

Theed Palace. 129 cards total.
Cards counted by rarity.
C (40), R (49), U (30)
Cards counted by type.
Admiral's Order (4), Character: Alien (11), Character: Dark Jedi Master (2), Character: Darth Maul (1), Character: Droid (15), Character: Jedi Master (3), Character: Republic (20), Character Weapon (2), Effect (15), Immediate Effect (2), Location: Site (6), Lost Interrupt (4), Objective (2), Starship: Capital (2), Starship: Starfighter (12), Starship Weapon (2), Used Interrupt (1), Used or Lost Interrupt (4), Vehicle: Combat (6), Vehicle: Creature (2), Vehicle: Transport (1), Vehicle Weapon (4)

CD-Players

Tiger Electronics
____Darth Maul [CD01] 98.00

CD Wallets

American Covers
____"Darth Vader / Boba Fett" [CW02].....................17.00
____Episode I Collage [CW03] 18.00

Animations
____Darth Vader [CW04] 20.00

Class of 77
____Darkside [CW05] 20.00

World Wide Licenses Ltd.
____Darth Maul [CW06]..16.00
____Space Battle [CW07]...16.00
____Star Wars logo on metal plate [CW08] 14.00
____Star Wars logo on metal plate, double wallet
[CW01] 19.00

Cellphone Accessories

Mascot straps.
____C-3PO...14.00
____Darth Vader..14.00

CW02   CW03   CW04   CW05   CW06   CW07   CW08

C2S01a   C2S01b   C2S01c   C2S01d   C2S01e   C2S01f   C2S02   C2S03   C2S04

Cellphone Straps

Nokia
3220 "Orange" model.
____ 6 Lenticular character skins [C2S01] 15.00
____ Chewbacca fur with bandolier [C2S02] 8.00
____ Darth Vader light-up phone holder [C2S03] 15.00
____ Hard side storage case, black [C2S04] 10.00
____ Hard side storage case, silver 10.00

Cellphone Faceplates

____ Podracer / Jar Jar Binks [CFP01] 16.00
____ Podracer / R2-D2 and C-3PO [CFP02] 16.00

Replacement covers for Nokia 3210 and 5100 phones.
____ Darth Maul / movie poster art [CFP03] 25.00

Replacment covers for Nokia 3210 and 5100 phones.
____ Darth Maul / Tatooine [CFP04].........................25.00
____ Queen Amidala [CFP05].....................................25.00
____ Queen Amidala [CFP06].....................................25.00
____ Yoda [CFP07]..25.00

Theme stickers to cover faceplates.
____ Empire / Vader Super Seal [CFP08] 7.00

Dextra Accessories Ltd.
____ Yoda for 3310 phone [CFP09] 20.00

Image Communications, Ltd.
Episode I: The Phantom Menace.
____ Anakin Skywalker 24.00
____ Darth Maul [CFP10] 24.00
____ Jar Jar Binks 24.00
____ Obi-Wan Kenobi 24.00
____ Queen Amidala..24.00

MPC Ltd.
Replacment covers for Nokia 3310 and 3330 phones.
____ Anakin / Vader 25.00
____ C-3PO [CFP11]..25.00
____ Clone Trooper [CFP12]..25.00
____ Darth Vader [CFP13] 25.00
____ Jango Fett [CFP14] 25.00
____ Obi-Wan Kenobi [CFP15]......................................25.00
____ Padme Amidala [CFP16] 25.00
____ R2-D2 ....25.00
____ Stormtrooper [CFP17] 25.00
____ The Dark Lords..25.00
____ Yoda [CFP18] 25.00

Nokia
Active Xpress-on Active Covers.
____ Anakin Skywalker for 3510 phone [CFP19] 25.00
____ Jango Fett for 3510 phone [CFP20] 25.00
____ Yoda for 3510 phone [CFP21] 25.00

Sony Ericsson
EPIII:ROTS.
____ Darth Vader / Epic Battle [CFP22] 10.00
____ General Grievous [CFP23] 10.00
____ Han and Chewbacca / R2-D2 and C-3PO
[CFP24]..10.00
____ Yoda / Anakin and Obi-Wan [CFP25]..................10.00

Cellphone Graphics

Cingular
Cellular phone downloadable.
____ C-3PO with R2-D2 ....5.00
____ Chewbacca 5.00
____ Darth Vader 5.00
____ Han Solo 5.00
____ Luke Skywalker..5.00
____ Princess Leia with R2 ....5.00

Cellphone Ringtones

Cingular
____ Binary Sunset 5.00
____ C3PO...5.00
____ Chewbacca 5.00

____ Imperial March 5.00
____ Lightsaber 5.00
____ Luke 5.00
____ Main Theme 5.00
____ Obi-Wan 5.00
____ R2D2 ....5.00
____ Rebel Blaster...5.00

Cellphone Straps

____ Tennis shoe, "Dunk Low S3 Jedi" [CPS01] 8.00

Bear Wars Part I.
____ Black 6.00
____ Blue 6.00
____ Green 6.00
____ Pink [CPS02] 6.00
____ Red 6.00
____ White 6.00

Japan, classic trilogy.
____ Chewbacca [CPS03] 12.00
____ Han Solo [CPS04] 12.00
____ Luke Skywalker [CPS05] 12.00
____ Princess Leia [CPS06] 12.00
____ Stormtrooper [CPS07] 12.00

Japan, EPI.
____ Anakin Skywalker [CPS08]...................................10.00
____ Darth Sidious [CPS09] 10.00
____ Jar Jar Binks [CPS10] 12.00
____ Ric Ollie [CPS11] 10.00

CFP01   CFP02   CFP03   CFP04   CFP05   CFP06   CFP07   CFP08

CFP09   CFP10   CFP11   CFP12   CFP13   CFP14   CFP15   CFP16   CFP17   CFP18

CFP19   CFP20   CFP21   CFP22   CFP23   CFP24   CFP25

Cellphone Straps

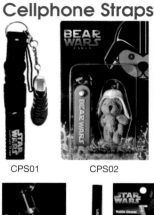         

| CPS01 | CPS02 | CPS03 | CPS04 | CPS05 | CPS06 | CPS07 | CPS08 | CPS09 | CPS10 | CPS11 | CPS12 |

| CPS13 | CPS14 | CPS15 | CPS16 | CPS17 | CPS18 | CPS19 | CPS20 | CPS21 | CPS22 | CPS23 |

| CPS24 | CPS25 | CPS26 | CPS27 |

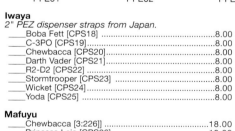

| PFE01 | PFE02 | PFE03 | PFE04 | PFE05 |

Japan. EPIII:ROTS.
____Darth Vader, black strap, blue light-up eyes 10.00
____Darth Vader, black strap, green light-up eyes 10.00
____Darth Vader, black strap, red light-up eyes 10.00
____Darth Vader, black strap, white light-up eyes [CPS12]..10.00
____Darth Vader, black strap, yellow light-up eyes ..10.00
____Darth Vader, red strap, light-up eyes 10.00
____Lightsaber, light-up red [CPS13] 10.00

1-2-Call
EPIII:ROTS. Round medals hanging off straps.
____Anakin vs. Obi-Wan 10.00
____Clone Trooper [CPS14]......................................10.00
____Darth Vader..10.00
____Yoda 10.00

Heart Art Collection, Ltd.
EPIII:ROTS. Mobile Cleaners.
____Darth Vader [CPS15] 10.00
____R2-D2 and C-3PO [CPS16] 10.00
____Yoda [CPS17] 10.00

Iwaya
2" PEZ dispenser straps from Japan.
____Boba Fett [CPS18] 8.00
____C-3PO [CPS19]...8.00
____Chewbacca [CPS20]...8.00
____Darth Vader [CPS21]...8.00
____R2-D2 [CPS22] 8.00
____Stormtrooper [CPS23] 8.00
____Wicket [CPS24] 8.00
____Yoda [CPS25] 8.00

Mafuyu
____Chewbacca [3:226]] 18.00
____Princess Leia [CPS26] 18.00

Sony Ericsson
____Darth Vader helmet in crystal.............................18.00
____Darth Vader helmet, metal [CPS27] 14.00

Cellphones

Mobistar
____Samsung 450 Star Wars tempo 350.00

Nokia
____EPI, boxed [3:226] 275.00

Centerpieces

Drawing Board Greeting Cards, Inc.
____Cloud City [PFE01]...15.00
____Darth Vader and Luke Duel [PFE02] 15.00
____Ewoks in Forest [PFE03] 12.00

Party Express
____Classic, neon [PFE04]...8.00
____EPI:TPM party table centerpiece [PFE05] 6.00

Unique
____Episode I: The Phantom Menace 6.00

Certificates

Lego / Walmart
____Jedi Challenge [3:227] 10.00
____Jedi Lightsaber Building Contest [3:227]............12.00

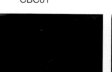    

| CBC01 | CBC02 | CBC03 | CBC04 | CBC05 |

| CBC06 | CBC07 | CBC08 | CBC09 | CBC10 |

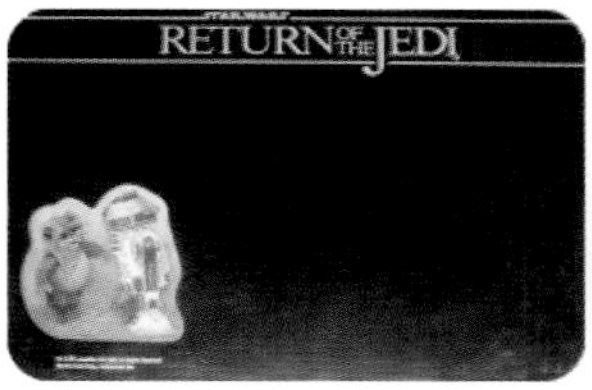

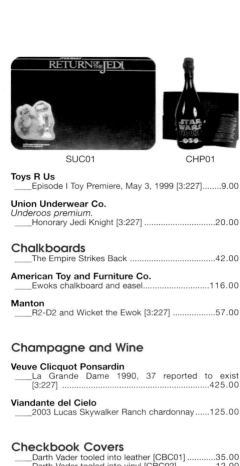

SUC01

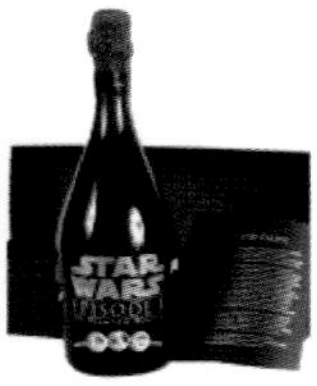

CHP01

Toys R Us
____Episode I Toy Premiere, May 3, 1999 [3:227]........9.00

Union Underwear Co.
Underoos premium.
____Honorary Jedi Knight [3:227] 20.00

Chalkboards
____The Empire Strikes Back 42.00

American Toy and Furniture Co.
____Ewoks chalkboard and easel............................116.00

Manton
____R2-D2 and Wicket the Ewok [3:227] 57.00

Champagne and Wine

Veuve Clicquot Ponsardin
____La Grande Dame 1990, 37 reported to exist [3:227] 425.00

Viandante del Cielo
____2003 Lucas Skywalker Ranch chardonnay......125.00

Checkbook Covers
____Darth Vader tooled into leather [CBC01] 35.00
____Darth Vader tooled into vinyl [CBC02]................12.00
____Star Wars logo set against starfield on blue vinyl [CBC03] 10.00

Clone Wars.
____Yoda, leather [CBC04] 35.00

The Anthony Grandio Company
____25th Anniversary, vinyl [CBC05]..........................15.00
____Boba Fett vector art, leather 35.00
____Boba Fett vector art, leather autographed 65.00
____Darth Vader EPIII, leather....................................45.00
____Darth Vader holographic foil, stamped vinyl 9.00
____Darth Vader vector art, leather............................35.00
____Imperial logo, leather [CBC06]............................45.00
____Path to the Dark Side, vinyl 9.00
____Rebellion logo, leather [CBC07]..........................45.00

Celebration 3 exclusives.
____Darth Vader, leather [CBC08] 30.00

Clone Wars.
____Heroes [CBC09] 25.00
____Sepratist [CBC10]...25.00

Checks

Kenner
____Refund for out-of-stock action figure poster 5.00

Pepsi
____Prize check for finding Gold Yoda can 25.00

The Anthony Grandio Company
25th anniversary, 24 designs.
____A-Wing Fighters [CHK01] 1.00
____B-Wing fighters [CHK02] 1.00
____Darth Vader's TIE Fighter [CHK03] 1.00
____Jedi Starfighter [CHK04].......................................1.00
____Medical Frigate [CHK05]..1.00
____Millennium Falcon [CHK06] 1.00
____Millennium Falcon escapes the Death Star [CHK07]...1.00
____Millennium Falcon evades TIE Fighters [CHK08]...1.00
____Naboo Fighter [CHK09] 1.00
____Naboo Royal Starship [CHK10] 1.00
____Naboo Starship [CHK11] 1.00
____Shuttle Tyderium [CHK12] 1.00
____Sith Infilterator [CHK13] 1.00
____Slave I – Jango boarding [CHK14] 1.00
____Slave I [CHK15]...1.00
____Solar Sailer [CHK16] 1.00
____Star Destroyer [CHK17] 1.00
____Super Star Destroyer [CHK18] 1.00
____TIE Bomber [CHK19] 1.00
____Trade Federation Fighter [CHK20] 1.00
____Trade Federation Landing Ship [CHK21] 1.00
____X-Wing squadron [CHK22] 1.00
____X-Wings attack Death Star [CHK23] 1.00
____Y-Wing Fighter [CHK24] 1.00

Alliance, 2 characters.
____Galactic Empire...1.00
____Rebel Alliance 1.00

Characters, 9 characters.
____C-3PO 1.00
____Chewbacca 1.00
____Darth Vader 1.00
____Han Solo 1.00
____Luke Skywalker..1.00
____Obi-Wan Kenobi 1.00
____Princess Leia..1.00
____R2-D2 ....1.00
____Yoda 1.00

Cigar Bands

Morrita
Sets produced with 5 different background colors.
____1 Han Solo [3:228] 2.00
____2 Obi-Wan Kenobi [3:228] 2.00
____3 Darth Vader [3:228] 2.00
____4 Han Solo [3:228] 2.00
____5 Luke Skywalker [3:228] 2.00
____6 C-3PO [3:228] 2.00
____7 Yoda [3:228]...2.00
____8 Obi-Wan Kenobi [3:228] 2.00
____9 R2-D2 C-3PO [3:228] 2.00
____10 Boba Fett [3:228]...2.00
____11 R2-D2 C-3PO [3:228] 2.00
____12 Luke Skywalker [3:228] 2.00
____13 R2-D2 [3:228]..2.00
____14 Ewok [3:228] 2.00
____15 Jawa [3:228]...2.00
____16 Emperor [3:228]...2.00
____17 Luke Skywalker [3:228] 2.00
____18 Chewbacca [3:228] 2.00
____19 Star Wars [3:228]...2.00
____20 Luke / Leia [3:228]..2.00
____21 Lando Calrissian [3:228] 2.00
____22 Yoda [3:228]...2.00
____23 C-3PO [3:228] 2.00
____24 Leia Organa [3:228] 2.00

Gold design and 5 different background colors.
____1 Han Solo [3:229] 2.00
____2 Obi-Wan Kenobi 2.00
____3 Darth Vader 2.00
____4 Han Solo 2.00
____5 Luke Skywalker 2.00
____6 C-3PO [3:229] 2.00
____7 Yoda 2.00
____8 Obi-Wan Kenobi 2.00
____9 R2-D2 C-3PO 2.00
____10 Boba Fett 2.00
____11 R2-D2 C-3PO 2.00
____12 Luke Skywalker 2.00
____13 R2-D2...2.00
____14 Ewok 2.00
____15 Jawa...2.00
____16 Emperor 2.00
____17 Luke Skywalker 2.00
____18 Chewbacca 2.00
____19 Star Wars 2.00
____20 Luke / Leia...2.00
____21 Lando Calrissian 2.00
____22 Yoda 2.00
____23 C-3PO 2.00
____24 Leia Organa 2.00

Murillo
EPI sets produced with 5 different background colors: blue, white, red, yellow, or green.
____1 Heroes (art) [3:229] 2.00
____2 Royal Starship in the Tatooine desert (cartoon) [3:229] 2.00
____3 Darth Maul (cartoon) [3:229] 2.00
____4 Queen Amidala (art) [3:229].......................................2.00
____5 Trade Federation Battleship (cartoon) [3:229] 2.00
____6 Qui-Gon and Obi-Wan with lightsabers (cartoon) [3:229] 2.00
____7 Heroes in Shmi's home (cartoon) [3:229] 2.00
____8 Jabba the Hutt (cartoon) [3:229] 2.00
____9 Watto in the pod race hanger (cartoon) [3:229] 2.00
____10 Darth Maul releases probe droids (cartoon) [3:229] 2.00

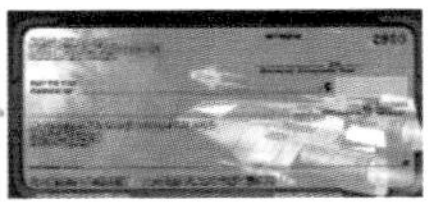

CHK01

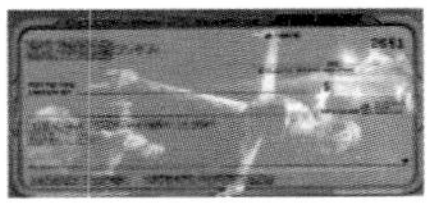

CHK02

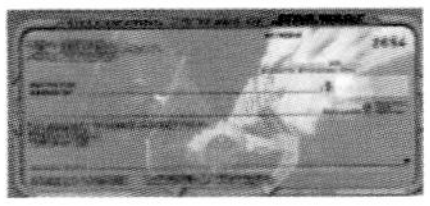

CHK03

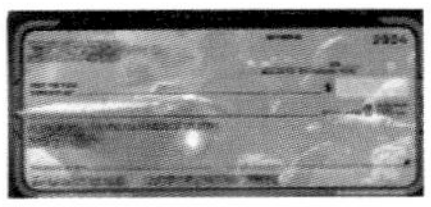

CHK04

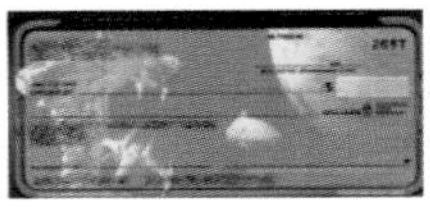

CHK05

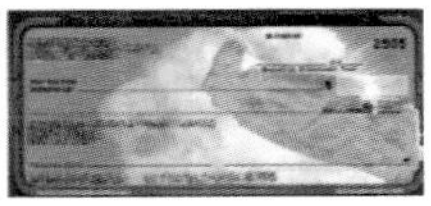

CHK06

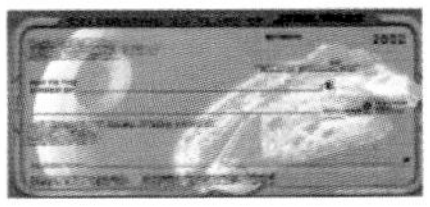

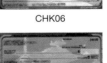

CHK07

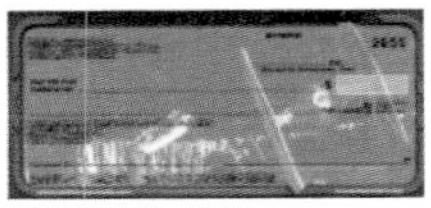

CHK08

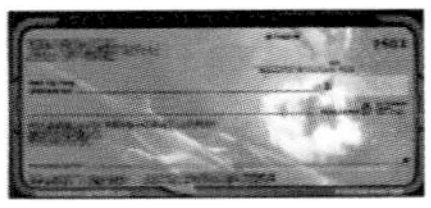

CHK09

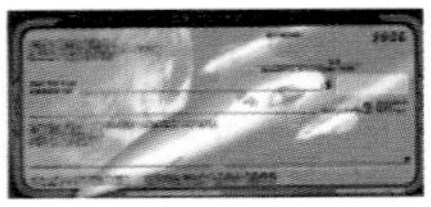

CHK10

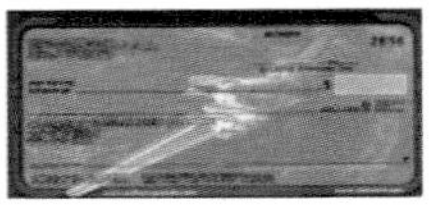

CHK11

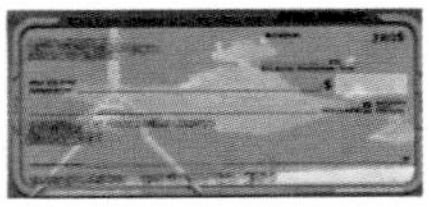

CHK12

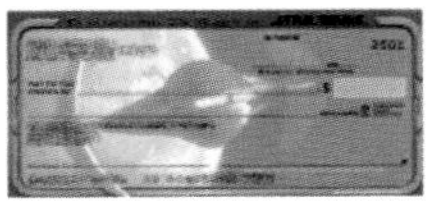

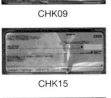

CHK13

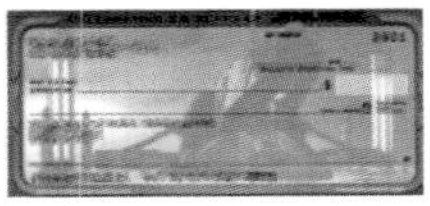

CHK14

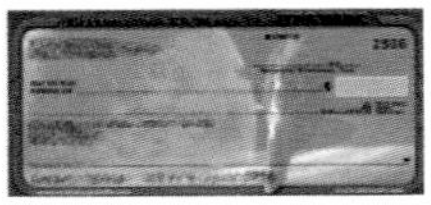

CHK15

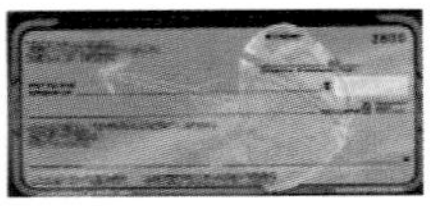

CHK16

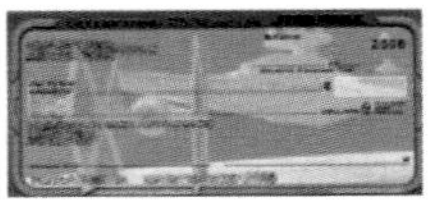

CHK17

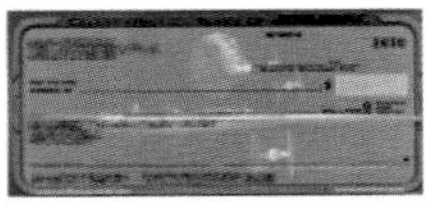

CHK18

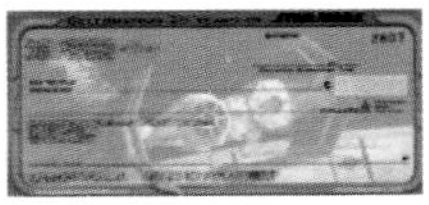

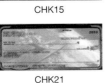

CHK19

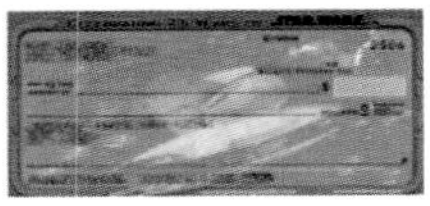

CHK20

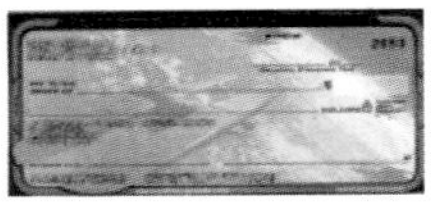

CHK21

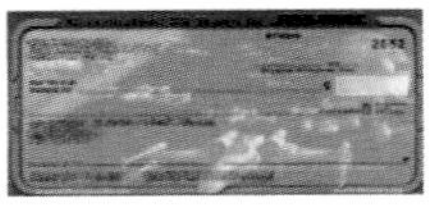

CHK22

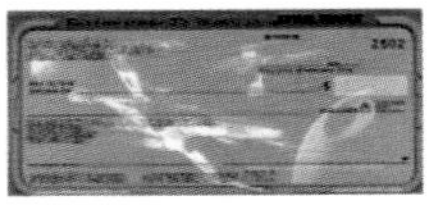

CHK23

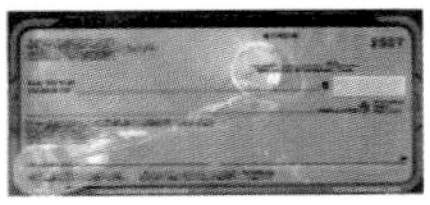

CHK24

Clip Boards

CPB01

CLP01

CSN01

CSN02

CSN03

CSN04

CSN05

CSN06

CSN07

CSN08

Clip Boards

____EPIII:ROTS 12.00

Reding Stationary

____Empire Strikes Back, R2-D2 [CPB01] 35.00

Clippos

Cadbury

____Anakin Skywalker [2:239] 4.00
____Darth Maul [CLP01] 4.00
____Jar Jar Binks [2:239] 4.00
____Queen Amidala [2:239] 4.00

Clips, Snack Chip

Pepsi, Japan

____Anakin Skywalker [CSN01] 15.00
____C-3PO [CSN02] 15.00

____Chewbacca [CSN03] 15.00
____Darth Vader [CSN04] 15.00
____Jango Fett [CSN05] 15.00
____R2-D2 [CSN06] 15.00
____Stormtrooper [CSN07] 15.00
____Yoda [CSN08] 15.00

Concealment bags.
____Darth Vader 3.00

Clocks

____C-3PO and R2-D2 ....20.00
____C-3PO and R2-D2 portable clock radio 35.00
____Darth Maul alarm clock, round [TAC01]..............23.00
____Darth Maul vs. Qui-Gon Jinn alarm 35.00
____Darth Maul with lightsaber pendulum, plays SW Main
Theme [TAC02] 27.00
____Darth Vader projection alarm 45.00
____EPI Battleship alarm clock, sculpted Naboo Fighter
flies over, digital display [TAC03] 18.00
____Lightsaber battle alarm clock [TAC04]...............25.00
____Mpire, projection, limited to 2,400....................125.00

9"x11" battery powered.
____Empire Strikes Back Special Edition 36.00
____Return of the Jedi Special Edition 36.00
____Star Wars Special Edition 36.00

Australia.
____Darth Vader twin bell alarm 35.00

EPIII:ROTS.
____Darth Vader alarm, Belgium 45.00
____Darth Vader, approx 30cm, Belgium 15.00
____Yoda travel alarm, Japan [TAC05] 25.00

Bradley Time

____3-way "Anywhere" clock, C-3PO and R2-D2
[TAC06] 37.00
____C-3PO and R2-D2 battery-operated quartz clock
[TAC07] 65.00
____C-3PO / R2-D2 cube clock radio [TAC08]..........38.00
____C-3PO / R2-D2 wind-up talking clock, ESB 45.00
____C-3PO / R2-D2 wind-up talking clock, SW 65.00
____Droids and Tie Fighter battery-operated quartz clock
[TAC09] 75.00
____Droids and Tie Fighter battery-operated quartz clock,
KB Toys exclusive package [TAC10] 75.00

TAC01

TAC02

TAC03

TAC04

TAC05

TAC06

TAC07

TAC08

TAC09

TAC10

TAC11

TAC12

TAC13

TAC14

TAC15

TAC16

TAC17

TAC18

| TAC19 | TAC20 | TAC21 | TAC22 | TAC23 | TAC24 | TAC25 |

____Space Battle Scene and 2nd Death Star, black frame under glass..45.00
____Super Live Adventure Clock, digital tabletop clock [TAC11] 75.00

Clicks
Retro alarm clocks.
____Darth Vader..20.00
____Darth Vader, brown clock face and hands [TAC12] 20.00

Clock-Wise
____Death Star battle (ROTJ) artwork, beveled glass quartz clock 19.00

Humbrol
____Mold and Paint Glow in the Dark Clock, Jango Fett [TAC13] 35.00

Micro Games of America
____Darth Vader AM/FM clock radio [TAC14]...........32.00

NECA
____Attack of the Clones wall clock, limited to 5,000 [TAC15] 30.00

Nelsonic
Mini-clocks.
____Darth Maul on Sith Speeder [TAC16]..................16.00
____Jar Jar Binks [TAC17]..25.00
____Naboo Fighter [TAC18].......................................25.00
____Queen Amidala [TAC19]......................................34.00
____Qui-Gon Jinn [TAC20] 34.00

Pepsi Cola
____R2-D2 Alarm Clock (Pepsi promo) [TAC21]........38.00

Pepsi Cola, Thailand
____Boba Fett 30.00

Spearmark Int.
____Darth Vader digital alarm [TAC22] 35.00

Welby Elgin
Battery-operated wall clock, ESB.
____C-3PO and R2-D2 ....40.00
____Darth Vader and Stormtroopers [TAC23] 45.00

Zeon
____Animated talking clock [TAC24] 25.00
____Jar Jar travel alarm [TAC25] 25.00

| TAC26 | TAC27 | TAC28 | TAC29 |

____Podrace Viewscreen [TAC26]..............................15.00
____R2-D2 travel alarm [TAC27] 25.00

Wall clocks.
____Jedi / Sith [TAC28] 23.00
____Space Battle [TAC29] 23.00
____Space Battle, 3D wall clock alt package 23.00

Clothes Hooks

____Boba Fett 25.00
____C-3PO...25.00
____Darth Vader..25.00
____Emperor's Royal Guard 25.00

Clothing: Aprons

____Art smock, plastic 35.00

Barco
Pizza Hut Episode I employee aprons.
____Anakin [APR01]..24.00
____Dark Maul [APR02]..24.00
____Queen Amidala [APR03].......................................24.00

Clothing: Bibs, Baby

Hot Topic
____Yoda: Good Food, Hmm? [APS01] 10.00

Clothing: Boots

____Anakin Skywalker [SHB01] 8.00
____Darth Maul, attacking [SHB02].............................8.00
____Darth Maul, face [SHB03]......................................8.00
____Darth Vader / Luke Skywalker [SHB04] 8.00
____Ewoks, vinyl [SHB05] 45.00
____Podracing [3:144] 8.00
____Stormtrooper / Star Wars [SHB06] 10.00

Clothing: Caps

____20th Anniversary [AC01]......................................14.00
____Jedi white front with blue bill 12.00
____R2-D2 and C-3PO [AC02] 8.00
____Star Wars clone logo [AC03] 14.00
____Star Wars early logo, gray 14.00
____Star Wars logo with trimmed bill [AC04] 18.00
____Ten year anniversary, black with gold lettering and trim [AC05]..25.00
____Ten year anniversary, black / silver [AC06] 20.00
____The Empire Strikes Back [AC07] 10.00

Episode I: The Phantom Menace.
____Anakin Skywalker [AC08] 8.00
____Darth Maul [AC09] 8.00
____Naboo Bravo Sqadron [AC10] 8.00

Star Wars Special Edition.
____Silver logo on black cap [AC11]...........................10.00
____Star Wars Trilogy, silver and red thread on black cap [AC12] 8.00

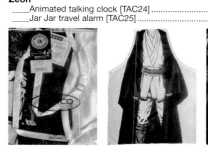

| APR01 packaged and open | APR02 | APR03 packaged and open | APS01 | SHB01 |

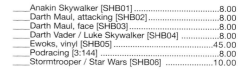

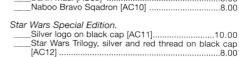

| SHB02 | SHB03 | SHB04 (both lenticular images shown) | SHB05 | SHB06 |

Clothing: Caps

AC01 · AC02 · AC03 · AC04 · AC05 · AC06

AC07 · AC08 · AC09 · AC10 · AC11 · AC12 · AC13 · AC14

501st Legion
____Imperial emblem, TK id embroidered on back [AC13] ....N/V

Applause
____Logo on tan cap with black trimmed bill [AC14] 8.00

Episode I: The Phantom Menace.
Baseball caps.
____Darth Maul [AC15] 7.00
____Jar Jar Binks [AC16] 7.00
____Podrace, featuring Anakin Skywalker, black with red bill [AC17] 7.00
____Podrace, featuring Anakin Skywalker, sky blue [AC18] 7.00
____R2-D2 [AC19] 7.00
____Star Wars EPI, silver logo[AC20] 10.00
____Star Wars logo strip down front, "Podracer" embroidered 7.00
____SW:EPI blue bill with lightsaber [AC21] 7.00
____SW:EPI blue cap with silver threading [AC22] 7.00
____The Dark Side, Darth Maul's red face on black cap, red and white text on yellow bill [AC23] 7.00

Bucket hats.
____Darth Maul with red band [AC24] 10.00
____Star Wars logo, Episode I [AC25]...........................7.00

B/W Character Merchandising
____ESB black and silver 18.00

Bossini
Attack of the Clones.
____Black [AC26] 8.00
____White [AC27] 8.00

Burger King
Argentina. Character caps. Only available with the purchase of a kids meal.
____Chewbacca [AC28] 35.00
____R2-D2 [AC29] 35.00
____Yoda [AC30] 35.00

Chase Authentics
____M&M Dale Jarrett with Mpire Anakin and Padme [AC31] 25.00
____Nascar Jeff Gordon, Space Battle [AC32]..........24.00

DeAgostini
____Twenty Fifth Anniversary logo on black cap, SW Fact File premium [AC33]...12.00

Disney / MGM
Star Wars Weekends.
____2001 R2-D2 projecting hologram Mickey [AC34]..18.00
____2005 Darth Vader / Mickey 18.00
____2006 Darth Vader, embroidered 18.00
____2006 Imperial emblem, embroidered.................18.00

Dixie / Northern Inc.
Mail-in premium.
____Mesh with characters and ESB logo 15.00

Drew Pearson Marketing
____Boba Fett [AC35] 8.00
____C-3PO [AC36] 8.00
____Chewbacca [AC37] 8.00
____Clone Trooper, orange on blue [AC38]................15.00
____Darth Vader [AC39] 8.00
____Darth Vader, mesh [AC40] 8.00
____Jabba the Hutt [AC41] 8.00
____Obi-Wan Kenobi [AC42] 8.00
____R2-D2 [AC43] 8.00
____Sith, black letters on red [AC44] 14.00
____Star Wars logo in red on black with silver lightsaber on bill [AC45] 8.00
____Star Wars, black and blue [AC46] 20.00
____Star Wars, blue and gold [AC47] 20.00
____Star Wars, orange and black [AC48] 20.00

EPIII:ROTS.
____Sith [AC49] 20.00
____Star Wars logo blue [AC50] 20.00
____Star Wars logo yellow [AC51] 20.00

Factors, Etc.
____Embroidered logo, stars on bill [AC52] 30.00

Fan Club
____Attack of the Clones [AC53]...............................15.00
____Episode I black cap with silver logo[AC54] 14.00
____Episode I bucket hat 14.00
____SW Fan Club 20.00
____SW Fan Club, black with embroidered logo patch...18.00

AC15 · AC16 · AC17 · AC18 · AC19 · AC20 · AC21 · AC22

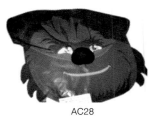

AC23 · AC24 · AC25 · AC26 · AC27 · AC28

AC29 · AC30 · AC31 · AC32 · AC33 · AC34 · AC35

| AC36 | AC37 | AC38 | AC39 | AC40 | AC41 | AC42 | AC43 |

| AC44 | AC45 | AC46 | AC47 | AC48 | AC49 | AC50 |

Fresh Caps Ltd.

____"Star Wars Celebration" embroidered on back cap, slide buckle 43.00
____3-D plastic Vader head on cap bill.....................14.00
____Boba Fett [AC55] 9.00
____Darth Vader...10.00
____Glitter X-wing 7.00
____Podrace [AC56]...8.00
____Return of the Jedi [AC57] 7.00
____Stormtrooper [AC58] 10.00
____Stormtrooper, "Freeze you Rebel scum" black cap with THX-style character on front, quotation on back 8.00
____Stormtrooper, "Freeze you Rebel scum" black cap with quotation on front 8.00
____SW EPI logo, dark green cap, slide buckle 10.00
____SW EPI logo, olive green cap, slide buckle........10.00
____Vader, "Never underestimate the darkside" black cap with THX-style character on front, quotation on back [AC59] 8.00
____Vader, "Never underestimate the darkside" black cap with THX-style character on front, quotation on front..8.00
____X-Wing / Star Wars [AC60] 7.00
____Yoda, "May the force be with you" black cap with THX-style character on front, quotation on back 8.00
____Yoda, "May the force be with you" black cap with THX-style character on front, quotation on front..8.00

Frito Lay
____Episode II logo [AC61] 18.00

General Mills
____Mesh with battle scene and SW logo [AC62] 35.00
____Mesh with ESB logo and characters [AC63] 10.00

Home Game Inc.
____Queen Amidala [AC64]......................................12.00

Jedicon
____1997 Jedicon, black with silver text [AC65] 15.00

Kelloggs
____"C-3PO's The Force" [AC66] 50.00

KFC
Australia. Employee mystery caps.
____C-3PO [AC67]...34.00
____Jar Jar Binks [AC68].......................................34.00
____Queen Amidala [AC69].....................................34.00
____Sebulba [AC70]..34.00
____Watto [AC71] 34.00

LucasArts
____Jedi Acadamy logo 17.00
____Star Wars Galaxies...18.00
____X-wing embroidered logo, knit...........................23.00

M&M World
____Dark Side lineup adult hat 18.00
____Jedi lineup adult hat...18.00

Mexico Collector Convention 2003
____POTF-style logo, embroidered / crew 150.00
____POTF-style logo, patch 25.00

Millennium Collection
____Rebel Logo / "May The Force..." [AC72] 17.00

Pepsi Cola
____Episode I logo [AC73]..8.00
____Nascar #24, with EPI logo 8.00

Pizza Hut
Australia. Employee mystery caps.
____C-3PO [AC74]...34.00
____Jar Jar Binks [AC75].......................................34.00
____Queen Amidala [AC76].....................................34.00
____Sebulba [AC77] 34.00
____Watto [AC78] 34.00

Sales Corp. of America
____"JEDI" corduroy with stars on bill 12.00
____Admiral Ackbar [AC79] 9.00
____Darth Vader and Royal Guards [AC80] 12.00
____Darth Vader and Royal Guards, blue [AC81] 12.00
____Gamorrean Guard [AC82]..................................10.00
____Jabba the Hutt [AC83] 10.00
____Luke and Darth Vader 10.00
____Luke and Darth Vader Duel [AC84] 12.00
____ROTJ Hi-C premium cap [AC85]........................25.00
____ROTJ logo [AC86]..10.00

Super Live Adventure
____Star Wars [AC87]...18.00

Thinking Cap
____ESB logo...10.00
____Imperial with metal rank insignia [AC88] 24.00

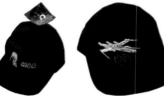      

| AC51 | AC52 | AC53 | AC54 | AC55 | AC56 | AC57 | AC58 |

| AC59 | AC60 | AC61 | AC62 | AC63 | AC64 | AC65 |

| AC66 | AC67 | AC68 | AC69 | AC70 | AC71 | AC72 | AC73 |

Clothing: Caps

AC74 AC75 AC76 AC77 AC78 AC79 AC80 AC81

AC82 AC83 AC84 AC85 AC86 AC87 AC88

AC89 AG01 AG02 AG03 AG04 AG05 AG06 AG07

AG08 AG09 AG10

____SW Rebel Forces 18.00
____Yoda ears [AC89] 25.00

Clothing: Earmuffs

Rayman/Ridless Products Group
____ROTJ Earmuffs 36.00

Clothing: Gloves

____Darth Vader [AG01] 30.00
____Stormtrooper [AG02] 30.00

Drew Pearson Marketing
____"Vader" 6.00
____Darth Vader, blue 6.00

Handcraft Mfg. Corp.
____Darth Maul, fleece [AG03] 12.00
____Star Wars logo, fleece [AG04] 12.00

Rubies
ROTS.
____Darth Vader gauntlets [AG05] 12.00

Sales Corp. of America
Gloves.
____C-3PO [AG06] 12.00
____Chewbacca [AG07] 12.00
____Darth Vader [AG08] 12.00
____R2-D2 [AG09] 14.00

Mittens.
____C-3PO..10.00
____Chewbacca 10.00
____Darth Vader [AG10] 10.00
____Paploo 8.00
____R2-D2 ....11.00
____Wicket 8.00

Tomokuni
Japan.
____X-Wing 25.00

Clothing: Hats

____Star Wars jester hat [PH01] 15.00
____Star Wars stocking cap [PH02] 10.00

Classic trilogy knit hats.
____Darth Vader [PH03]...........................8.00

Drew Pearson Marketing
____"Sith Lord" 10.00
____Darth Vader, blue 10.00

Fresh Caps Ltd.
____Anakin Skywalker, Podrace [PH04] 8.00
____Episode I, black with stripes and round logo on front
    [PH05] 7.00
____Episode I, blue, stripes, round logo on front 7.00
____Jar Jar [PH06] 8.00
____Podracing crew cap [PH07] 8.00
____Star Wars [PH08] 8.00
____Star Wars crew cap [PH09] 8.00
____Star Wars Episode I crew cap [PH10] 8.00

Grossman
____C-3PO, knit [PH11].............................10.00
____Chewbacca, knit [PH12].......................15.00
____Gamorrean Guard, knit [PH13]..............10.00
____Paploo (Ewok), knit 10.00
____R2-D2, knit [PH14] 10.00
____ROTJ logo, knit [PH15] 10.00
____Wicket (Ewok), knit [PH16]..................10.00

Sales Corp. of America
Return of the Jedi cuffed knit hats.
____Black with red text [PH17] 20.00
____Patch logo [PH18] 20.00
____Red with black text [PH19] 20.00
____White with red text [PH20] 20.00

PH01 PH02 PH03 PH04 PH05 PH06 PH07

PH08 PH09 PH10 PH11 PH12 PH13 PH14 PH15

PH16   PH17   PH18   PH19   PH20   AJ01   AJ02

AJ03   AJ04   AJ05   AJ06   AJ07   AJ08   AJ09

AJ10   AJ11   AJ12   AJ13   AJ14   AJ15   AL01

Clothing: Jackets

____X-Wing fighter [AJ01]....................................275.00
____X-Wing Rogue Squadron, leather bomber [AJ02]...350.00

Rain jackets.
____Anakin Skywalker 8.00
____Darth Maul [AJ03]....................................14.00
____Jar Jar Binks [AJ04]................................14.00
____Sith Lord [AJ05] 14.00
____Star Wars Episode I [AJ06] 14.00

Adam Joseph Industries
Rain jackets.
____C-3PO and R2-D2, blue.....................25.00
____Darth Vader and Royal Guards, silver 25.00
____Darth Vader and Royal Guards, yellow 25.00

Baltro Italiana
____Star Wars, wool 65.00

Bright Red Group
____"Darth Vadar Lives" patch (misspelled), black with white trim, unlined [3:279] 25.00
____"Darth Vadar Lives" patch (misspelled), red with white trim, quilted windbreaker 25.00
____"MTFBWY" patch, white with black trim, quilted windbreaker 25.00
____Solid color with white trim, quilted wind breaker 15.00
____SW logo patch, blue with white trim, quilted windbreaker...30.00
____SW logo patch, blue with white trim, unlined [3:279]..25.00

Disney / MGM
____Star Tours crew member jacket [3:279] 125.00

Star Wars Weekends.
____2006 Poster art applique 35.00

Fan Club
____10th Anniversary [AJ07]....................................175.00

____Boba Fett embroidered denim [AJ08] 165.00
____Darth Vader's Helmet embroidered denim 135.00
____Han Solo's vest [AJ09].....................................125.00
____Luke Skywalker's fatigue jacket [AJ10] 150.00
____Podracing jacket 59.00

Galoob
____1999 Toy Design Team [AJ11] 575.00

Home Game Inc.
____Battle Above Death Star II [AJ12] 14.00

Hot Topic
____Stormtrooper skull and crossbones, black with white striped sleeves 40.00

Lucasfilm
Cast and Crew.
____Episode I [AJ13]..225.00

Star Wars Celebration II
____Darth Maul embroidered [AJ14] 400.00

Tiger Electronics
____Electronic Toy Design Team, Maul art [AJ15] 185.00

Clothing: Leg Warmers

Reknown
____SW high socks 8.00

Sales Corp. of America
____"Jedi," black and red [AL01] 10.00
____"Jedi," black, red, and white 10.00
____C-3PO 10.00
____Chewbacca 12.00
____Darth Vader 12.00
____Ewok, blue and white..10.00
____Ewok, pink and white 10.00
____R2-D2 ....12.00
____Return of the Jedi logo, applique 14.00

Clothing: Neckties

Star Wars Galaxy style artwork.
____Boba Fett [AQ01]..20.00
____Stormtrooper, black tie with yellow surface [AQ02]..20.00
____Stormtrooper, blue tie with red surface [AQ03]..20.00

Fan Club
____15th anniversary, scenes from trilogy, 35mm plastic film [AQ04] 35.00

Marks and Spencer
____Battle Droids repeating [AQ05] 19.00
____Darth Maul icons repeating [AQ06] 17.00
____Darth Maul in front of repeating pattern of probe droids [AQ07]...17.00
____Jar Jar Binks making faces, square icons [AQ08]..19.00
____Jedi icon between crossed sabers [AQ09] 17.00
____Naboo fighter icons repeating [AQ10] 19.00
____R2-D2 icons repeating [AQ11] 19.00

Episode I: The Phantom Menace.
____C-3PO [AQ12] 18.00

Ralph Marlin and Co.
Polyester/blend.
____Anakin Skywalker in podracer gear [AQ13]........15.00
____ANH 1995 international video artwork [AQ14]..12.00
____ANH style "A" poster art (Vader's lightsaber extends along length of tie) [AQ15] 12.00
____AT-AT McQuarrie art [AQ16] 15.00
____Battle Above Naboo [AQ17]................................15.00
____Battle Droid art over Federation tank [AQ18] 15.00
____Bounty hunters artwork [AQ19].........................15.00
____Darth Maul (name and drawings) [AQ20]............12.00
____Darth Maul line-art bust over repeating name [AQ21]..15.00
____Darth Maul photo over Tatooine duel scene [AQ22]..15.00
____Darth Vader line art [AQ23] 15.00

AQ01   AQ02   AQ03   AQ04   AQ05   AQ06   AQ07   AQ08   AQ09   AQ10   AQ11   AQ12

Clothing: Neckties

AQ13 AQ14 AQ15 AQ16 AQ17 AQ18 AQ19 AQ20 AQ21 AQ22 AQ23 AQ24 AQ25 AQ26 AQ27 AQ28 AQ29 AQ30 AQ31 AQ32

AQ33 AQ34 AQ35 AQ36 AQ37 AQ38 AQ39 AQ40 AQ41 AQ42 AQ43 AQ44 AQ45 AQ46 AQ47 AQ48 AQ49 AQ50 AQ51 AQ52 AQ53

AQ54 AQ55 AQ56 AQ57 AQ58 AQ59 AQ60 AQ61 AQ62 AQ63 AQ64 AQ65 AQ66 AQ67 AQ68 AQ69 AQ70 AQ71 AQ72 AQ73

____Darth Vader video art (same as 1995 ANH video release) [AQ24] 14.00
____Death Star Assault (McQuarrie art of TIE chasing X-wing) [AQ25] 12.00
____Death Star Rising (X-wings attack Death Star) 16.00
____Droids line art and square photo on sage green [AQ26] 10.00
____ESB 1995 international video artwork [AQ27] 12.00
____Gold and black Darth Vader helmet repeating pattern 12.00
____Han and Chewbacca line art and square photo on navy [AQ28] 15.00
____Invasion Army, battle droids on STAPs and tanks [AQ29] 15.00
____Jar Jar Binks over bubble pattern on blue background [AQ30] 15.00
____Jar Jar Binks pictured above Anakin's podracer [AQ31] 15.00
____Jar Jar posed over repeating name [AQ32]........15.00
____Jedi Obi-Wan Kenobi [AQ33]........................18.00
____Jedi Obi-Wan Kenobi Jedi Master [AQ34]..........18.00
____Jedi Qui-Gon Jinn [AQ35] 15.00
____Qui-Gon Jinn [AQ36] 15.00
____Qui-Gon Jinn Jedi Master [AQ37] 15.00
____Race to Freedom [AQ38] 15.00
____ROTJ 1995 international artwork [AQ39]............18.00
____Sith Darth Maul (photos of character) [AQ40]...18.00
____Sith Lord [AQ41]..15.00
____Sith, The Dark Side [AQ42] 15.00
____Space Battle (Naboo fighters) [AQ43] 18.00
____Starfighters (TPM) [AQ44] 15.00
____Stormtrooper video art (same as 1995 ESB video release) [AQ45] 15.00
____SW characters (character photos and SW logo at bottom) [AQ46] 16.00
____SW Characters II (from top to bottom: Han, Ben, Leia, Luke, Vader) [AQ47] 14.00
____SW Original Illustration (McQuarrie SW novel cover artwork of Vader looming over Luke and Leia) 14.00

____T.I.E. tie (3 TIEs in trench) [AQ48] 15.00
____TPM characters [AQ49] 16.00
____Yoda line art and square Luke/Yoda photo on emerald [AQ50]...16.00
____Yoda video art (same as 1995 ROJ video release) [AQ51]..15.00
____Young Skywalker [AQ52] 15.00

Silk.

____All Character Icons (character vignettes repeating pattern in green, orange, red, black, and blue) [AQ53]..16.00
____Anakin Skywalker icons repeating [AQ54]..........19.00
____Battle Droid icons repeating [AQ55] 19.00
____Cantina (on orange tie).................................16.00
____Darth Maul face repeating, silk [AQ56] 12.00
____Darth Vader from SW novel cover artwork repeating pattern, limited edition in tin [AQ57] 14.00
____Imperial vehicles "blueprints" [AQ58] 11.00
____Jar Jar Binks icons repeating – black [AQ59]...19.00
____Jar Jar Binks icons repeating - navy [AQ60] 19.00
____Jedi icons repeating – black [AQ61] 19.00
____Jedi icons repeating – navy [AQ62] 19.00
____Jedi vs. Sith pattern repeating [AQ63]................19.00
____Jung Poster Art [AQ64] 16.00
____Rebel Alliance Blueprint [AQ65] 14.00
____Silver and black Darth Vader helmet repeating pattern 18.00
____Sith, The Dark Side pattern repeating [AQ66]..19.00
____Starfighter blueprints – black [AQ67].................19.00
____Starfighter blueprints – navy [AQ68] 19.00
____Starfighter blueprints – olive [AQ69] 19.00
____SW Vehicles - black [AQ70].............................14.00
____SW Vehicles (multicolor line drawings on black tie) [AQ71]...12.00
____TPM Ships repeating [AQ72] 14.00
____Yoda artwork 32.00

Tie Mart

____Episode I logos on space background [AQ73]..10.00

Clothing: Nightgowns

Penshield Ltd.
____Empire Strikes Back................................35.00

Wilker Bros.
____Darth Vader and Death Star..............................10.00
____Darth Vader and Luke Skywalker.......................10.00
____Darth Vader...10.00
____Luke Skywalker and Princess Leia 10.00
____Luke Skywalker and Yoda................................12.00
____Princess Kneesaa...15.00
____R2-D2 and C-3PO...10.00
____R2-D2, C-3PO, and Starfield 10.00
____Yoda...15.00

Clothing: Outfits, 2-Piece

Giant Manufacturing
____Anakin Skywalker [CMC01] 16.00
____Clone Trooper No. 214736184505196 [CMC02] 16.00
____Droids [CMC03] 16.00
____Jango Fett Bounty Hunter [CMC04] 16.00
____Jedi Knight Yoda [CMC05] 16.00
____R2-D2 [CMC06] 16.00
____Yoda [CMC07] 16.00

Kids Headquarters
____Anakin Skywalker, dark blue/gray, shirt-and-shorts set..14.00
____Bravo Squadron polyester black over black, shirt-and-pants set..16.00
____Bravo Squadron polyester blue over blue, shirt-and-pants set..16.00
____Darth Maul black polyester over white nylon, shirt-and-pants set...16.00
____Darth Maul, gray/black, shirt-and-shorts set......14.00
____Darth Maul, white/black, shirt-and-shorts set..14.00

CMC01 CMC02 CMC03 CMC04 CMC05 CMC06 CMC07 CMC08 ALS01

____Droids sweats, gray and blue over blue, shirt-and-pants set....................................16.00
____Droids, yellowith dark blue, shirt-and-shorts set....................................14.00
____Jar Jar (4 faces), blue/gray, shirt-and-shorts set....................................14.00
____Jar Jar nylon jogger, green over blue, shirt-and-pants set....................................16.00
____Jar Jar sweats, gray and blue over blue, shirt-and-pants set....................................16.00
____Jar Jar, light blue/dark blue, shirt-and-shorts set....................................14.00
____Jedi duel, black/gray, shirt-and-shorts set 14.00
____Jedi vs. sith, gray/blue/dark blue, shirt-and-shorts set....................................14.00
____Jedi vs. sith, red/gray, shirt-and-shorts set........14.00
____Naboo starfighter embroidered on knit polo shirt, shirt-and-shorts set....................................14.00
____Naboo starfighter, dark blue/gray, shirt-and-shorts set....................................14.00
____Naboo starfighter, white polyester over black nylon, shirt-and-pants set....................................16.00
____Pit droid, yellow with dark blue, shirt-and-shorts set....................................14.00
____Pit Droids, blue shirt, red shorts [CMC08].........14.00
____Podracing, gray/red, shirt-and-shorts set 14.00
____R2-D2, Pit Droid, C-3PO knit shirt and sweat pants set....................................17.00

Clothing: Overalls

Bibb Co.
____Toddler suit....................................12.00

Kids Headquarters
____Jar Jar overalls and long sleeve shirt set 18.00
____Pit Droid [ALS01] 18.00

Liberty Trouser Co.
____Short pants sun suit....................................12.00
____Star Wars overalls 12.00

Clothing: Pajamas

____C-3PO with droids background and pants [APJ01] 14.00

____Darth Vader, Snowtroopers, AT-AT's, 2-piece red with black [APJ02]....................................12.00
____Jar Jar Binks [APJ03]....................................14.00
____Jar Jar Binks emerging from Naboo swamp [APJ04]....................................14.00
____Jar Jar, 1-piece sleeper [APJ05]....................................8.00
____Jedi, 2-piece [APJ06] 8.00

EPIII: ROTS.
____Darth Vader / Revenge [APJ07] 15.00
____Star Wars Jedi [APJ08] 15.00
____Star Wars Revenge of the Sith [APJ09].............15.00

Ame
____Anakin Skywalker with Vader background, includes cape [APJ10] 18.00
____Jango Fett [APJ11] 18.00
____Jedi Starfighter [APJ12] 18.00

American Marketing Enterprises, Inc.
2 cotton sleepwear sets.
____Darth Vader and "Vader" 25.00

Big Dog
____Empire Bites Back, parody [APJ13]....................17.00
____Return of the Dogi, parody [APJ14]....................17.00

Bing Harris Sargood
____Return of the Jedi....................................20.00

Harley, Inc.
____Star Wars 20.00

Long Eddies
____Anakin Skywalker, long sleeves and legs [APJ15]....................................16.00
____Darth Vader and Luke Skywalker [APJ16] 18.00
____Jedi vs. Sith, long sleeves and legs [APJ17]......16.00

Marks and Spencer
____Star Wars 20.00

PCA Apparel
____Darth Vader, 100% polyester with velcro-attaching cape 29.00
____Jedi vs. Sith white T-shirt tops with blue shorts....................................18.00
____Lightsaber duel T-shirt tops with black shorts ..18.00
____STAPs and battle droids button front red and white tops....................................18.00

Penshiel
Empire Strikes Back designs.
____Darth Vader and Luke 20.00
____Image collage....................................20.00

Return of the Jedi designs.
____Darth Vader, Jabba the Hutt, and Luke 20.00
____Image Collage....................................20.00

Reknown
____Star Wars 20.00

Wilker Bros.
____"Darth Vader Lives" 20.00
____Admiral Ackbar....................................20.00
____Baby Ewoks 23.00
____Biker Scouts 25.00
____Boba Fett 30.00
____Boba Fett and Darth Vader 30.00
____Boba Fett, C-3PO, Chewbacca, and R2-D2 ......22.00
____C-3PO and Darth Vader....................................21.00
____C-3PO and Ewoks 20.00
____C-3PO and Luke Skywalker 20.00
____C-3PO and R2-D2....................................22.00
____C-3PO, R2-D2 and X-Wing 23.00
____C-3PO, R2-D2, and Chewbacca 20.00
____C-3PO, R2-D2, and Emperor's Guards 23.00
____Cantina Band 24.00
____Chewbacca 20.00
____Chewbacca and Millennium Falcon....................22.00
____Darth Vader....................................21.00
____Darth Vader and Death Star 22.00
____Darth Vader and Emperor's Guards [APJ18] 25.00
____Darth Vader and Luke Skywalker....................................23.00
____Droopy McCool 23.00
____Ewoks in Village 20.00
____Gamorrean Guards....................................20.00
____Han Solo and Chewbacca 22.00
____Han Solo and Darth Vader 21.00
____Jabba the Hutt 20.00
____Jabba the Hutt and Bib Fortuna 20.00
____Jabba the Hutt and Boba Fett 24.00
____Latara 21.00
____Luke Skywalker and Princess Leia 20.00
____Luke Skywalker on Tauntaun [APJ19] 20.00
____Max Rebo 25.00
____Papaloo on Speeder Bike 20.00
____Princess Kneesaa....................................20.00
____Princess Kneesaa on swing 20.00
____Princess Kneesaa skipping rope 20.00

APJ01   APJ02   APJ03   APJ04   APJ05   APJ06   APJ07

APJ08   APJ09   APJ10   APJ11   APJ12   APJ13

APJ14   APJ15   APJ16   APJ17   APJ18   APJ19

Clothing: Pajamas

AP01 AP02 AP03 CPT01 CPT02

CPT03 CPT04 CPT05

____Stormtrooper 20.00
____Stormtrooper and R2-D2 ....20.00
____Wicket and Princess Kneesaa in bush 20.00
____Wicket and Princess Kneesaa on skateboard....20.00
____Wicket and Princess Kneesaa on teeter-totter ..20.00
____Wicket and Princess Kneesaa on vine 20.00
____Wicket and Princess Kneesaa playing musical instruments 20.00
____Wicket and Princess Kneesaa tug-of-war 20.00
____Wicket and Princess Kneesaa with flowers........20.00
____Wicket and R2-D2 ....20.00
____Wicket in basket................................20.00
____Wicket on vine..................................20.00
____Wicket the Ewok................................20.00
____Wicket with balloons 20.00
____Wicket with butterfly net 20.00
____Wicket with walking stick 20.00
____Wiley the Ewok................................20.00
____Yoda 20.00
____Yoda and Luke Skywalker 20.00

Clothing: Pants

____Shorts: Luke "Use the Force" / Droids "We're Doomed" [AP01] 6.00

Bibb Co.
____Shorts, gym 14.00

Star Wars jeans.
____Chambray..10.00
____Corduroy..10.00

Gans Enterprises
Denim jeans.
____Darth Vader and droids........................8.00
____Darth Vader, Ewok, Jedi logo 10.00

Giant Manufacturing
____Sport shorts, black with red piping [AP02] 14.00

Harley, Inc.
Variety, any style.
____Pants 14.00
____Shorts 8.00

Liberty Trouser Co.
Jeans, SW with over-all pattern.
____Brown 16.00
____Navy blue 16.00
____Royal blue......................................16.00

Shorts with ROTJ logo.
____Fleece 12.00
____Gym 10.00

Shorts, SW with overall pattern.
____Brown 10.00
____Navy blue 10.00
____Royal blue......................................10.00

Mr. Seb Sportswear
____Shorts, athletic with Jedi logo 10.00

Reknown
____Short pants......................................18.00

Webundies
____Darth Vader / Death Star louge pants [AP03] 18.00

Clothing: Ponchos

Adam Joseph Industries
Rain ponchos.
____C-3PO and R2-D2, blue [CPT01]....................17.00
____Darth Vader and Royal Guards, silver [CPT02]..17.00
____Darth Vader and Royal Guards, yellow 17.00

B/W Character Merchandising
____Rain cape, plastic ESB..........................31.00

Ben Cooper
____C-3PO [CPT03]..................................18.00
____Darth Vader [CPT04] 18.00
____Yoda [CPT05] 25.00

Pyramid
____Darth Maul rain poncho 6.00
____Jedi vs. Sith rain poncho 6.00

Clothing: Robes

____Darth Vader [ABR01] 20.00

Vintage.
____Empire Strikes Back print with red trim [ABR02]..18.00
____Return of the Jedi, Dath Vader and Royal Guards [ABR03]..18.00

Mr. Australia Garments
____C-3PO's head......................................34.00
____C-3PO..34.00
____Darth Vader and Stormtroopers..................34.00
____Han and Chewbacca 34.00
____Luke on Tauntaun................................34.00
____R2-D2, gray 34.00
____R2-D2, red 34.00
____Yoda 34.00

Wilker Bros.
____"May The Force Be With You" 20.00
____Darth Vader......................................30.00

   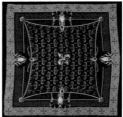

ABR01 ABR02 ABR03 AS01

Clothing: Scarves

Grossman
____C-3PO 8.00
____Chewbacca 7.00
____Darth Vader 7.00
____R2-D2 ....8.00
____ROTJ logo 7.00
____Wicket 7.00

Ralph Marlin and Co.
____Queen Amidala, 22"x22" silk fashion [AS01]......15.00

Clothing: Shirts

____"All I Need To Know About Life I Learned From Star Wars" [ATS01]..24.00
____Anakin / Podracer line drawing polo [ATS02]........8.00
____Bart Wars [ATS03] 16.00
____C-3PO and R2-D2 on black shirt with red sleeves [ATS04] 8.00
____C-3PO and R2-D2, shadowed [ATS05]........8.00
____Clone Wars characters, Star Wars Celebration 3 [ATS06]..15.00
____Darth Maul sweatshirt, black with red stripes circling sleeves [ATS07]..................................18.00
____Darth Vader / Space Battle over DSII long sleeves [ATS08] 10.00
____Darth Vader / Space Battle over DSII short sleeves [ATS09] 10.00
____Darth Vader sweatshirt, blue with gray sleeves, blue cuffs [ATS10] 11.00
____Darth Vader, lightsaber, Death Star, neon colors [ATS11] 15.00
____Darth, purple and silver [ATS12] 7.00
____EPI characters / Pepsi logo on sleeve................15.00
____Jeff Gordon 24, Pepsi / Lays / EPI [ATS13]........24.00
____Join the Celebration, SW:SE 26.00
____Podracing on Tatooine, blue and red [ATS14] 10.00
____R2-D2 / C-3PO / Pit Droids [ATS15] 14.00
____R2-D2 / C-3PO / Star Wars [ATS16] 12.00
____Sith Happens, Vader's chestbox [ATS17] 18.00
____Size Matters Not, Yoda art..........................20.00
____Stormtrooper [ATS18]..........................12.00
____Stormtrooper, infant jumper [ATS19] 17.00
____Stormtrooper, toddler size [ATS20] 17.00
____The Star Wars Trilogy SE [ATS21] 18.00
____Trade Federation fighters attacking Naboo fighters [ATS22]..16.00
____Vader, Sith Lord [ATS23] 12.00

Black character drawing on white t-shirt.
____Princess Leia [ATS24]..........................20.00
____Stormtrooper..................................20.00

EPI:TPM images on black t-shirt, 2-sided.
____Darth Maul, The Darkside [ATS25]....................10.00
____Jar Jar Binks [ATS26]..........................10.00
____Jedi vs. Sith [ATS27] 10.00
____Naboo space battle [ATS28] 10.00
____Sebulba / STAP [ATS29]......................10.00

EPIII:ROTS.
____R2-D2 blue sleeveless [ATS30] 15.00

Episode II: Attack of the Clones.
____C-3PO R2-D2, droids background [ATS31]........14.00
____Droid Army [ATS32]..........................14.00
____Yoda, Anakin/Padme / movie logo [ATS33]........20.00

Return of the Jedi yellow t-shirt with applique.
____Admiral Ackbar [ATS34] 8.00
____R2-D2 and Wicket [ATS35]..................8.00

ROTS.
____Anakin vs. Obi-Wan – epic duel navy shirt [ATS36]..10.00
____Anakin vs. Obi-Wan – epic duel yellow shirt [ATS37] 10.00

ATS01

ATS02

ATS03

ATS04

ATS05

ATS06

ATS07

ATS08

ATS09

ATS10

ATS11

ATS12

____Darth Vader silouette art [ATS38] 10.00
____Imperial Domination with cog [ATS39]................10.00
____Jedi stafighter and ARC-170's [ATS40] 10.00
____Star Wars logo (clones) [ATS41].......................10.00
____Star Wars tri-fighters [ATS42]............................10.00
____Star Wars Vader b/w [ATS43]..............................10.00
____Stormtrooper skill and crossbones on brown shirt
 [ATS44]...10.00
____Vader helmet in flames b/w [ATS45] 10.00
____Vader overlooking lava [ATS46] 10.00
____Yoda – Justice [ATS47]..10.00
____Yoda – lightsaber action [ATS48] 10.00

Star Wars, rebel alliance print.
____Blue [ATS49] 14.00
____Purple [ATS50] 14.00

All Out Fan
____A Jedi's Strength Flows From the Force
 [ATS51] 10.00

____Boba Fett [ATS52] 10.00
____ESB, vintage fanclub logo [ATS53] 10.00
____Powrot JEDI [ATS54] 10.00
____Stormtrooper [ATS55]..10.00

Amate Textile
El Regreso del Jedi.
____Baby Ewoks 20.00
____Biker Scouts 20.00
____Darth Vader and Luke 20.00
____Darth Vader and Luke duel 20.00
____Han, Luke, and Leia 20.00
____Vader's Helmet, Star Wars logo, dogfight 24.00

American Marketing Enterprises
____Boba Fett, artwork 15.00
____Bounty Hunters, artwork...7.00
____Chewbacca, artwork..7.00
____Droids and red sky, artwork 7.00
____Emperor 7.00

____Empire Villains, artwork 7.00
____ESB Vader with crossed lightsabers, artwork 7.00
____Han Solo, artwork..7.00
____Jawa with big wrench, artwork...............................7.00
____Luke and Leia swinging, artwork 7.00
____Movie Poster "A," artwork 7.00
____Rancor...7.00
____Vader, artwork..7.00
____Yoda, artwork...7.00

Barrett Sportswear
____SW trilogy for Musicland, Sci-Fi Channel and
 Suncoast Video 35.00

Big Dog
____Attack of the Bones [ATS56] 18.00
____Dog Wars, polo [ATS57]..12.00
____Dog Wars, sweatshirt [ATS58]..............................30.00
____Grrrl Power [ATS59] 18.00
____Return of the Dogi [ATS60] 12.00

ATS13 front and rear

ATS14

ATS15

ATS16

ATS17

ATS18

ATS19

ATS20

ATS21

ATS22

ATS23

ATS24

ATS25 front and rear

ATS26

ATS27 front and rear

ATS28 front and rear

ATS29 front and rear

ATS30

ATS31

ATS32

Clothing: Shirts

ATS33 front and rear   ATS34   ATS35   ATS36   ATS37

ATS38   ATS39   ATS40   ATS41   ATS42   ATS43

ATS44   ATS45   ATS46   ATS47   ATS48   ATS49

____South Bark Wars, "Oh my Gawd, he killed Kenny!" [ATS61] 15.00
____Southbark Wars, gray or white shirt [ATS62]......12.00
____The Empire Bites Back, parody [ATS63] 12.00
____The Panting Menace, Bark Maul [ATS64]..............8.00
____Yo Quiero nar un Jadog mastor [ATS65] 12.00
____Yodog: It's not the size of the dog in the fight... [ATS66] 18.00

Bing Harris Sargood
____Return of the Jedi..15.00

Bossini
____Darth Vader / Star Destroyer [ATS67] 12.00
____Luke / Hoth [ATS68] 12.00
____Luke and Leia / Anakin and Padme [ATS69] 12.00
____R2-D2 and C-3PO [ATS70] 12.00
____Stormtrooper [ATS71] 12.00
____Super Battle Droid [ATS72] 12.00

Burger King
EPIII:ROTS.
____Darth Vader [ATS73] 25.00

Changes
____Han Solo blasting stormtroopers [ATS74] 10.00

Coca-Cola, Hong Kong
EPIII:ROTS.
____Anakin Skywalker [ATS75] 25.00
____Anakin vs. Obi-Wan tank top [ATS76] 25.00
____Darth Vader [ATS77] 25.00

Creative Conventions
____10th anniversary SW Convention 25.00

Disney / MGM
____2003 Star Wars Weekends, Mickey and Yoda [ATS78] 25.00
____Clone Trooper, orange 2-sided [ATS79] 15.00

____Star Tours [ATS80] 10.00
____Star Tours, The adventure is real [ATS81] 15.00
____Star Wars lightsaber, 2-sided [ATS82] 15.00
____Stormtrooper punching through Imperial logo [ATS83] 25.00

Star Wars Weekends.
____2004 Mickey / ANH poster.................................25.00
____2004 Mickey and Minnie / ANH poster [ATS84] 25.00
____2005 Darth Vader / Mickey 25.00
____2005 Darth Vader / Mickey babydoll b/w [ATS85] 25.00
____2006 Vader / Yoda glittered t-shirt....................15.00
____2006 Vader / Yoda polo 25.00
____2006 Vader / Yoda t-shirt 15.00

Drew Pearson Marketing
Classic Trilogy Collection sports jerseys.
____Baseball: Vader 77 ....125.00

ATS50   ATS51   ATS52   ATS53   ATS54   ATS55

ATS56   ATS57   ATS58   ATS59   ATS60   ATS61

ATS62   ATS63   ATS64   ATS65   ATS66   ATS67

ATS68   ATS69   ATS70   ATS71   ATS72   ATS73

ATS74   ATS75   ATS76   ATS77   ATS78   ATS79

ATS80   ATS81   ATS82 front and rear   ATS83   ATS84

____Baseball: Yoda 80 ....125.00
____Basketball: Fett 80..............................100.00
____Basketball: Vader 77 ....100.00
____Football: Fett 80 ....125.00
____Football: Vader 77 ....125.00
____Football: Yoda 80 ....125.00

ELMS Marketing
____Star Wars Episode I, Battle Droid [ATS86] 18.00

Factors, Etc.
____"Darth Vader Lives" 10.00
____"May The Force Be With You" 10.00
____C-3PO...10.00
____C-3PO and R2-D2 ....10.00
____C-3PO and R2-D2 on sand 10.00
____C-3PO, glitter 10.00
____Chewbacca 10.00
____Chewbacca, glitter 10.00

____Darth Vader...10.00
____Darth Vader and Obi-Wan Kenobi 10.00
____Darth Vader and X-Wing Fighter 10.00
____Darth Vader, glitter 10.00
____Han Solo...10.00
____Han Solo and Chewbacca 10.00
____Jawas..10.00
____Jawas, glitter 10.00
____Luke Skywalker 10.00
____Luke Skywalker, glitter 10.00
____Millennium Falcon, glitter [ATS87] 10.00
____Princess Leia 10.00
____Princess Leia, glitter...............................10.00
____R2-D2 ....10.00
____R2-D2, glitter [ATS88].............................10.00
____Star Wars logo 10.00
____Star Wars logo, glitter 10.00
____Stormtrooper on Dewback.......................10.00
____Stormtrooper, glitter 10.00
____X-Wing and Tie Fighter Dogfight 10.00

Fan Club
____1987 "First Ten Years" [ATS89] 35.00
____EPII:AOTC clone design / fan club logo 15.00
____Episode I, long sleeve, black with white logo embroidered 24.00
____Episode I, short sleeve, black or white with logo embroidered across chest 24.00
____Episode I, 3-button polo, tan 44.00
____Episode I, denim, long sleeve 47.00
____Official Star Wars Fan Club Member [ATS90] 35.00

Freeze
____"Lord Vader" TIE fighter blueprints 12.00
____"Star Wars, May The Force Be With You" silver and black on black shirt 12.00
____Boba Fett and Darth Vader on black shirt 12.00
____Darth Vader and small red plasticized square on black shirt 12.00
____Darth Vader on gray shirt [ATS91] 12.00

ATS85   ATS86   ATS87   ATS88   ATS89   ATS90

ATS91 front and rear   ATS92   ATS93   ATS94   ATS95

ATS96   ATS97   ATS98   ATS99   ATS100

Clothing: Shirts

ATS101 front and rear

ATS102 front and rear

ATS103

ATS104

ATS105

ATS106

ATS107

ATS108

ATS109

ATS110

ATS111

ATS112

ATS113

ATS114

ATS115

ATS116

____Droids and green framing on black shirt 12.00
____Droids and small blue plasticized square 12.00
____Droids, reflective silver / gold on black shirt 12.00

Giant Manufacturing
____3-D Jar Jar Binks head 16.00
____Anakin (with lightsaber) [ATS92]..........................20.00
____Anakin Skywalker's destiny [ATS93] 14.00
____Anakin Skywalker [ATS94] 14.00
____Anakin Skywalker (Anakin's destiny) [ATS95] 12.00
____Anakin Skywalker running on half brown, half black shirt 14.00
____Astroid chase, superimposed on Jango's helmet [ATS96] 14.00
____Bantha Skull [ATS97] 20.00
____Bounty Hunter, baseball jersey [ATS98]..............14.00
____C-3PO and R2-D2 [ATS99] 14.00
____C-3PO and R2-D2, green neon border [ATS100] 14.00

____Celebration III Darth Vader black [ATS101] 30.00
____Celebration III Darth Vader red [ATS102] 30.00
____Chewbacca, Mommy's Little Monster [ATS103] 15.00
____Darth Maul "Sith" 14.00
____Darth Maul action pose in green glowing ink 14.00
____Darth Maul and horizontal pattern stripe............14.00
____Darth Maul black spiral tie-dye 14.00
____Darth Maul face and horizontal flames 14.00
____Darth Maul green lettering, tattoo pattern all over...14.00
____Darth Maul on black and red diagonal tie-dye..14.00
____Darth Star (crossed sabers Vader and Death Star) on black shirt...14.00
____Darth Vader [ATS104]...14.00
____Darth Vader / Anakin Skywalker, baseball jersey [ATS105] 14.00
____Darth Vader / Anakin Skywalker 14.00

____Darth Vader silver helmet, "Darth Vader" on sleeve [ATS106] 14.00
____Darth Vader, "Don't push mu buttons" [ATS107] 15.00
____Darth Vader, "Menace to Society," kids sizes only [ATS108] 14.00
____Darth Vader, "Never Underestimate the Dark Side" [ATS109] 14.00
____Darth Vader, classic art helmet [ATS110]...........12.00
____Darth Vader, gray with movie scenes [ATS111] 14.00
____Death Star Battle art [ATS112] 20.00
____Droids, baseball jersey [ATS113] 14.00
____Emperor Palpatine [ATS114] 20.00
____Empire Strikes Back "The Saga Continues" 20.00
____Empire Strikes Back poster art [ATS115]...........20.00
____EPI "line up" 14.00
____EPI "the Emperor" 14.00
____Episode II with clone trooper [ATS116] 14.00

ATS117

ATS118

ATS119

ATS120

ATS121

ATS122

ATS123

ATS124

ATS125

ATS126 front and rear

ATS127

ATS128 front and rear

ATS129

ATS130

ATS131

ATS132

ATS133

ATS134　　ATS135　　ATS136　　ATS137　　ATS138　　ATS139

ATS140　　　　ATS141 front and rear　　　ATS142　　ATS143

ATS144　　ATS145　　ATS146　　ATS147　　ATS148　　ATS149　　ATS150

____Episode II with gunship [ATS117] 14.00
____Executive Order Sixty-Six [ATS118]....................20.00
____Jango Fett [ATS119] 14.00
____Jango Fett in front of Clone trooper army, baseball jersey [ATS120]...14.00
____Jango Fett with scene of Jango vs. Obi-Wan [ATS121]...12.00
____Jar Jar Binks with long tongue on green and blue tie-dye shirt...14.00
____Jedi Starfighter [ATS122] 14.00
____Jedi starfighter with picture of Obi-Wan [ATS123]...12.00
____Jedi, Anakin's Speeder [ATS124] 14.00
____Jedi, Yoda, Obi-Wan and Anakin, baseball jersey [ATS125]...14.00
____Luke Skywalker Jedi, anime [ATS126]...............12.00
____Mos Eisley Cantina [ATS127] 14.00
____Obi-Wan vs. Jango with movie scenes on back [ATS128] 14.00

____Pod race scene in large SW logo on red tie-dye shirt..14.00
____Podracer on blue and brown tie-dye shirt..........14.00
____Princess Leia, "Princess," kids sizes only [ATS129] 14.00
____Queen Amidala on dark blue tie-dye 14.00
____Queen Amidala on pink and red tie-dye 14.00
____R2-D2 and C-3PO chracture art [ATS130].........20.00
____R2-D2 tank top [ATS131] 15.00
____Return of the Jedi poster art 15.00
____Sith Happens [ATS132] 20.00
____Sith Lord photo on dark blue shirt.....................14.00
____Sith, Darth Maul on black and red V tie-dye 14.00
____Slave I vs. Jedi Starfighter, cross-fire [ATS133]..14.00
____Slave I vs. Jedi Starfighter, pursuit [ATS134]......12.00
____Star Wars Death Star Attack [ATS135] 12.00
____Star Wars Death Star Trench orange, anime [ATS136] 12.00

____Star Wars EPIII:ROTS Vader lava art [ATS137] 15.00
____Star Wars logo on starfield [ATS138].................20.00
____Star Wars poster art [ATS139] 20.00
____Star Wars, Darth Vader on back [ATS140]..........17.00
____Star Wars, Luke as x-wing pilot, anime style [ATS141]...14.00
____SW orange oval on horizontal double-sided lightsaber...14.00
____SW yellow oval 14.00
____TPM "Jedi shadow" tie-dye 14.00
____TPM "new band" on black shirt..........................14.00
____TPM lightsaber duel in large SW logo 14.00
____TPM space battle in horizontal strip 14.00
____TPM space battle in large SW logo 14.00
____Wicket, Daddy's Little Ewok [ATS142] 15.00
____X-wing battles tie fighter [ATS143].....................14.00
____X-Wings and Tie Fighters, "Star Wars" on sleeve [ATS144] 14.00

ATS151　　ATS152　　ATS153　　ATS154　　ATS155　　ATS156

ATS157　　ATS158　　ATS159　　ATS160　　ATS161　　ATS162

ATS163　　ATS164　　ATS165　　ATS166　　ATS167　　ATS168　　ATS169

Clothing: Shirts

ATS170 ATS171 ATS172 ATS173 ATS174 ATS175

ATS176 ATS177 ATS178 ATS179 ATS180 front and rear

ATS181 front and rear ATS182 ATS183 ATS184

____X-Wings escape the Death Star, "Star Wars" on sleeve
[ATS145] 14.00
____Yoda block letters, Yoda art in oval, "JEDI MASTER"
on dark green shirt 18.00
____Young Vader, two-tone dyed 14.00

Baby one-piece.
____Chewbacca, Mommy's Little Monster
[ATS146] 15.00
____Darth Vader, Star Wars Celebration 3
[ATS147] 15.00
____Princess Leia [ATS148].................................15.00

Thin polyester. Front and back printed identically.
____Droids in front of starfield [ATS149] 18.00
____Jango Fett [ATS150]....................................18.00
____Naboo starfighters [ATS151] 18.00
____Villains in front of starfield [ATS152]..................18.00

Hanes
____"Star Wars" metalized oval logo 18.00
____"JEDI" in huge lettering with scenes in the letters, on
brick red shirt 18.00
____"Star Wars," Darth Vader, and lightsaber battle on
black shirt 18.00
____20th Anniversary logo on black sweatshirt 28.00
____Darth Vader's head with glow-in-the-dark "X-ray" fea-
tures on black shirt 18.00
____Darth Vader and "Join the Dark Side" 18.00
____Darth Vader, "The Empire wants you" 18.00
____Rancor on white shirt..................................18.00
____Space battle on black shirt [ATS153].................18.00

Harley, Inc.
Star Wars designs.
____Polo shirts...23.00
____T-shirts 20.00
____Tank tops 25.00

Hasbro
____Star Wars Episode III, pre-release convention ..65.00

Hi-C
____ROTJ: T-Shirt premium from Hi-C 25.00

Hot Topic
____Chewie [ATS154] 18.00
____I (heart) Darth Vader 18.00
____Jabba the Hutt, "Original Gangsta"
[ATS155]..18.00
____Princess Leia characture [ATS156] 20.00
____Princess Leia pink toddler long-sleeve
[ATS157] 15.00
____Size Matters Not, toddler size 18.00
____Speak softly, but carry a big blaster 18.00
____Star Wars logo x 4 ....18.00
____Stormtrooper / Jolly Roger [ATS158] 18.00
____The Force is strong in this one 18.00

____Who's Your Daddy, toddler size 18.00
____Yoda [ATS159] 18.00
____Yoda, "Judge Me by My Size Do You?" 18.00
____Yoda, "Pull My Finger" [ATS160] 18.00

Babydoll style.
____Artoo, silver trim and highlights [ATS161] 12.00
____Chewbacca, "I'd Just As Soon Kiss A Wookiee"
[ATS162]..19.00
____Ewok [ATS163] 18.00
____Luke [ATS164] 19.00
____Princess Leia, "Somebody Has To Save Our Skins"
[ATS165]..19.00
____Solo [ATS166] 19.00
____Wicket [ATS167] 18.00

Ringer style t-shirt.
____Boba Fett characture [ATS168] 18.00
____Chewbacca, "let the wookiee win"
[ATS169]...18.00
____Darth Vader classic [ATS170]..........................14.00
____Imperial AT-AT Walker [ATS171] 18.00
____Stormtrooper characture [ATS172] 18.00
____Yoda, "There is no try... only do" [ATS173] 18.00
____Yoda, "Y'all Better Recognize!" [ATS174] 18.00

ILM
Pre-EPI production crew only, "ILM Dept. of Defense"
____"Loose Lips Sink Starships" [ATS175].................45.00
____The Empire is Watching 45.00

In Advance
____ANH style "C" poster art on black shirt
[ATS176]..12.00
____Blue Darth Vader helmet and Luke on black shirt (blue
Vader and crossed lightsabers on back) 12.00
____C-3PO head fills up orange shirt 14.00
____Darth Vader and "The Galactic Empire Wants You" on
gray shirt...12.00
____Darth Vader and "The Galactic Empire Wants You" on
white shirt 12.00
____Darth Vader and saber and blue window on black
shirt 12.00
____Darth Vader and saber and blue window on gray shirt
(long sleeve, with SW logo on sleeve) 12.00
____Darth Vader and saber and blue window on white shirt
(long sleeve, with SW logo on sleeve) 12.00
____Darth Vader and star destroyer and "Join the Empire
and See the Universe" on black shirt 12.00
____Darth Vader helmet fills up black shirt................14.00
____Darth Vader, 2 stormtroopers, and blueprint on black
shirt (short sleeve, with Imperial emblem on sleeve)
[ATS177]..12.00
____Darth Vader, Death Star II, Falcon [ATS178] 12.00
____Darth Vader, Death Star II, Falcon (long
sleeve)..12.00
____Darth Vader, Death Star II, star destroyer, yellow sun
on black shirt (long sleeve) 12.00

____Darth Vader, fighters, and exploding TIE (blue Vader
and crossed lightsabers on back) 12.00
____Darth Vader, fighters, and exploding tie on black shirt
(nothing on back) 12.00
____Darth Vader, star destroyer, and 2 stormtroopers on
dark blue shirt 12.00
____Droids and twin suns on white shirt 12.00
____Droids in orange glow 12.00
____Fett head fills up brown shirt 15.00
____Luke and Yoda and ROTJ logo on gray shirt 12.00
____Stormtrooper head fills up green shirt 15.00
____TIEs and X-wing in trench (XRS logo on
back)..12.00
____TIEs shooting an X-wing over the Death Star
surface 12.00
____Yoda head fills up black shirt...........................15.00

J E M Sportswear
____"SW Darth / Maul" 2-sided black shirt 14.00
____"SW EPI" Darth Maul eyes on black shirt 14.00
____Anakin Skywalker on gray shirt 14.00
____Darth Maul's eyes / "At last..." 2-sided black
shirt 14.00
____Droid fighters on tie-dyed dark gray shirt 14.00
____Jar Jar's head on blue shirt 14.00
____Jedi vs. Sith on tie-dyed dark gray shirt 14.00
____Lightsaber battle on black shirt 14.00
____Naboo space battle tie-dyed dark blue
shirt 14.00
____TPM characters on black shirt.........................14.00
____TPM villains on black shirt 14.00

KFC
Episode I: The Phantom Menace.
____Defeat the Dark Side, green crew shirt
[ATS179] 15.00

KFC, Australia
*Employee mystery caps, Episode I pre-release. Blue
shirt with a question mark and character face.*
____C-3PO [ATS180] 34.00
____Jar Jar Binks 34.00
____Queen Amidala 34.00
____Sebulba [ATS181].......................................34.00
____Watto 34.00

Kids Headquarters
____Anakin blue knit shirt, short sleeves 14.00
____Darth Maul button front red with short black sleeves
[ATS182]..14.00
____Jedi vs. Sith red [ATS183]..............................8.00
____Jedi vs. Sith white with short black sleeves 14.00
____Sith Lord black knit shirt, short sleeves.............14.00

Knitwear, Inc.
____"Sith Lord" all-over print 12.00
____"EPI Darth Maul The Dark Side," with rubber oval logo
on sleeve 12.00

____Black shirt with SW diagonal gray, EPI red; SW white embroidered on sleeves....................15.00
____Darth Maul "The darkside".................................15.00

Kortex
____Darth Vader, "May The Force Be With You" 24.00

Return of the Jedi designs.
____Baby Ewoks and Wicket, white sleeveless 26.00
____Baby Ewoks, blue sleeveless...............................26.00
____Baby Ewoks, white tanktop 26.00
____Han Solo and Millennium Falcon.......................24.00
____Luke Skywalker and Stormtrooper 24.00
____R2-D2 and C-3PO...24.00
____Return of the Jedi, white on blue.......................24.00
____Speederbike, white with red sleeves 24.00
____Wicket and R2-D2, blue sleeveless 24.00
____Wicket, blue tanktop 24.00
____Wicket, white sleeveless 24.00

Lee Sportswear
____Darth Maul black baseball jersey with red striped sleeves [ATS184] 12.00
____Darth Maul button-up [ATS185] 12.00
____Darth Maul red baseball jersey with black striped sleeves [ATS186] 12.00
____Denim, long sleeve, Star Wars over pocket, Qui-Gon, Obi-Wan, and Darth Maul embroidered on back [ATS187] 24.00
____Episode I, long sleeve, Fan Club exclusive [ATS188] 30.00
____Jedi / Sith button-up baseball style [ATS189] 12.00
____Star Wars, Qui-Gon, Darth Maul, Obi-Wan [ATS190] 12.00

Liquid Blue
____Anakin's Podracer [2:382] 15.00
____Astroid Field, 2-sided [2:382]............................15.00
____Boba Fett [2:382] 15.00
____Chewbacca [2:382] 15.00
____Darth Maul 15.00
____Darth Maul Silhouette, 2-sided [2:382] 15.00
____Death Star Battle [2:382].....................................15.00
____Death Star II [2:382] 15.00
____Droids [2:382] 15.00
____Droids on Tatooine [2:382] 15.00
____Episode I Teaser [2:382]......................................15.00
____Heroes [2:382] 15.00
____Jabba's Palace [2:382] 15.00
____Jar Jar Binks [2:382] 15.00
____Jedi Council [2:382]..15.00
____Jedi Master [2:382]...15.00
____Lightsaber Duel, 2-sided [2:383] 15.00
____Millennium Falcon [2:383] 15.00
____Mos Espa, 2-sided [2:383] 15.00
____Planet Hoth, 2-sided [2:383] 15.00
____Podracer...15.00

____Podracer Canyon 15.00
____Podracer with logo [2:383] 15.00
____Queen Amidala [2:383]...15.00
____Sand People [2:383] 15.00
____Sebulba's Podracer [2:383] 15.00
____Slave I [2:383]..15.00
____Space Battle, 2-sided [2:383] 15.00
____STAP with Battledroid [2:383]..............................15.00
____Star Wars Poster, 2-sided [2:383] 15.00
____Star Wars Space Battle, 2-sided [2:383] 15.00
____Stormtroopers [2:383] 15.00
____Submarine Chase, 2-sided 15.00
____Tie Fighters 15.00
____Watto [2:383] 15.00
____Yoda 15.00

LucasArts
____AT-AT blueprint, Rebel Strike 20.00
____Bantha skull sweatshirt, Bounty Hunter 30.00
____Jedi Starfighter, puck wrapped [ATS191] 15.00
____Knights of the Old Republic sweatshirt 40.00
____Tie Fighter [ATS192] 10.00
____X-Wing polo 35.00

Star Wars Galaxies.
____Concept art 16.00
____Wookiee raging..20.00

Lucasfilm
____Revenge of the Sith hooded sweatshirt 45.00
____Revenge of the Sith t-shirt...................................18.00
____Revenge of the Sith t-shirt, Hyperspace logo sleeve [ATS193] 45.00

M&M World
____Dark Side character line up 18.00
____Jedi character line up...18.00
____Join me and together we can rule M-Pire 18.00
____Storm Trooper character line up 18.00

Melanie Taylor Kent Ltd.
____Hollywood Blvd. Artwork 14.00

Mexico Collector Convention 2003
____Polo, POTF style logo 35.00
____T-shirt, POTF style logo 25.00
____T-shirt, POTF style logo, staff.............................95.00

Mondragon
Die Ruckkehr der Jedi-Ritter.
____C-3PO, R2-D2, Wicket with star background 16.00
____Vader's helmet and the duel 16.00
____Woklings 16.00

MSD International
Star Wars.
____SW gray letters with red outline.........................18.00
____SW logo with red and silver letters 18.00

L'Empire Contre-Attaque.
____C-3PO and R2-D2 ....20.00
____Yoda 20.00

Le Retour Du Jedi.
____Red letters on cream 16.00
____Red letters on white 16.00

NTD Apparel Inc.
____Jabba the Hutt Presents: Podracing [ATS194]......7.00

Patty Marsh Productions
____Ewoks "Color-Me" 25.00

Pepsi Cola
____Episode I, polo [ATS195] 26.00

Perfect Fit
____C-3PO, ESB 24.00

Pizza Hut, Australia
Employee mystery caps, Episode I pre-release. Red shirt with a question mark and character face.
____C-3PO [ATS196] 34.00
____Jar Jar Binks 34.00
____Queen Amidala 34.00
____Sebulba [ATS197] 34.00
____Watto 34.00

Playthings
____Han, Chewbacca, Luke, Leia 16.00

Reknown
____C-3PO and R2-D2, angled background 15.00
____C-3PO and R2-D2, round background 15.00
____Hildebrandt Bros. Art 15.00
____Star Wars logo 15.00

Royal Prints
____Ironed-on decal on 100% cotton shirt, sealed in poly-bag with header [ATS198] 35.00

Seio Insatsu Co.
____Return of the Jedi designs..................................18.00

Taco Bell
____"Play The Feel The Force Game" 35.00

The LEGO Group
____EPII mini figures on black [ATS199]....................35.00
____EPII Republic gunship [ATS200] 26.00
____Yoda, Celebration II exhibitor [ATS201] 75.00

Thunder Creek
____I did it all for the Wookie 15.00

Thyrring Agency
____Return of the Jedi designs..................................18.00

ATS185

ATS186

ATS187

ATS188

ATS189

ATS190

ATS191

ATS192

ATS193

ATS194

ATS195

ATS196

ATS197

ATS198

ATS199

ATS200

ATS201

ATS202

ATS203

Clothing: Shirts

SHH01

SHH02

SHH03

SHH04

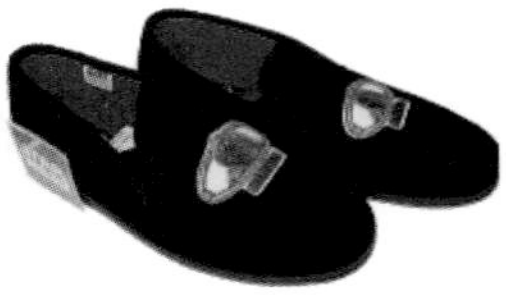
SHH05

SHH06

SHH07

SHH08

SHH09

SHH10

SHH11

Top Textiles Ltd.
____Mos Espa Arena, tank top [ATS202] 8.00

Tour Champ
____Jawas, SW Galaxy art [ATS203] 15.00

Tsurumoto Room Co.
____Star Wars designs, silk screened........................35.00

Uniprints
____Chewbacca 12.00
____Darth Vader..12.00
____ESB: Logo 12.00
____ESB: Probe Droid 12.00
____ESB: Tauntaun 12.00
____ESB: X-Wing Fighter 12.00
____ESB: Yoda 12.00
____Ewoks with ROTJ logo..10.00
____Han Solo..12.00
____Luke Skywalker 12.00
____Millennium Falcon 12.00
____ROTJ: C-3PO and R2-D2 ....14.00
____ROTJ: Stormtrooper and AT-ST Vehicle 14.00
____Star Wars Cast, main characters........................12.00
____SW: Logo 12.00
____SW: Tie Fighter..12.00
____SW: X-Wing Fighter 12.00
____Wicket on Vine 10.00
____Wicket the Ewok 10.00
____Wicket W. Warrick 12.00

Wright and Co.
Return of the Jedi designs.
____Black logo on white 16.00
____Ewoks..18.00
____Logo, Darth Vader, and red circle on white 18.00
____Speederbike 18.00
____Stormtrooper 23.00
____Yoda 18.00

Yagi Shoten Co.
____Darth Vader..22.00
____ESB logo..22.00
____Millennium Falcon 22.00

Clothing: Shoes, Sandals, Slippers

Australia. Slippers.
____Yoda 10.00

Sandals, vintage.
____X-Wing / Tie Fighter flip-flops [SHH01] 18.00

Sandals.
____Anakin Skywalker flip flops [SHH02] 8.00

Slippers.
____Anakin Skywalker and Sebulba [SHH03]............10.00
____Darth Maul [SHH04] 10.00
____Darth Maul, Tatooine [SHH05] 10.00
____Darth Vader, lights when you walk......................15.00

Buster Brown and Co.
____Anakin Skywalker / Darth Vader, black and blue, laceless elastic [SHH06] 20.00
____Anakin Skywalker / Darth Vader, white and blue, velcro fasteners [SHH07] 20.00
____Anakin Skywalker open heel [SHH08] 18.00
____Anakin Skywalker, destiny lace-up black-and-silver [SHH09] 10.00
____Anakin Skywalker, destiny lace-up white [SHH10] 20.00
____Clone Trooper [SHH11] 15.00
____Clone Trooper foil [SHH12] 15.00
____Darth Vader with lightsaber [SHH13] 15.00
____Darth Vader with lightsaber [SHH14] 15.00
____Darth Vader, helmet only, velcro 15.00
____Darth Vader, helmet with flames, white 20.00
____Droids: C-3PO and R2-D2, flashes 15.00
____Yoda, saber flashes [SHH15] 15.00

Sandals.
____Anakin Skywalker / Darth Vader [SHH16] 14.00
____Darth Vader sandals [SHH17] 15.00
____Droids sandals, blue..12.00
____Jedi Starfighter [SHH18] 16.00
____Star Wars logo in hyperspace with Imperial logo on strap [SHH19] 7.00

Slippers.
____Anakin's Destiny [SHH20] 8.00
____Darth Vader with lightsaber, velcro fastener, black and red..10.00
____Jango Fett, flashing red LEDs [SHH21] 8.00
____Vader, gray 10.00

Clarks
____"May The Force Be With You" 35.00
____C-3PO..28.00
____Chewbacca 28.00
____Darth Vader [SHH22] 28.00
____Darth Vader Lives 25.00
____Luke Skywalker 28.00
____Princess Leia 28.00
____R2-D2 ....28.00
____Reflective [SHH23] 16.00
____Reflective with B/W stripes [SHH24] 20.00
____Stormtrooper 28.00
____Tie Fighter..38.00
____Tusken Raider..28.00

Sandals.
____Cosmic Rambler..14.00
____Landspeeder 16.00
____Solar Racer..12.00
____Star Rider 12.00

Slippers.
____Star Wars logo 12.00

Converse
____Stormtrooper punch-out flip-flops [SHH25] 55.00

Footzee
Slippers.
____C-3PO and R2-D2 [SHH26] 16.00

Kid Nation
____Anakin Skywalker pod racing white x-trainer 17.00
____Anakin Skywalker pod racing white, velcro........15.00
____Anakin Skywalker water shoes 10.00
____Anakin Skywalker water shoes red/blue/black [SHH27] 10.00

SHH12

SHH13

SHH14

SHH15

SHH16

SHH17

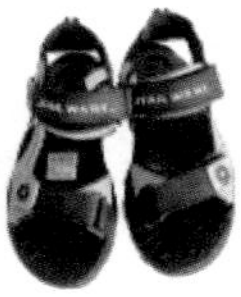
SHH18

SHH19

SHH20

SHH21

SHH22

SHH23

SHH24

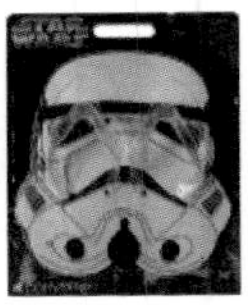
SHH25

SHH26

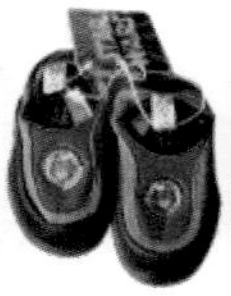
SHH27

SHH28

SHH29

SHH30

SHH31

SHH32

SHH33 SHH34 SHH35 SHH36 SHH37 SHH38 SHH39 SHH40

SHH41 SHH42 SHH43 SHH44 SHH45 SHH46

____Bespin gantry multi-motion image, black 2-strap velcro, court shoes 18.00
____Darth Maul "The Dark Side" athletic 14.00
____Darth Maul athletic black/silver/blue 14.00
____Darth Maul black hiker with blue trim [SHH28] ..16.00
____Darth Maul black x-trainer with white and silver trim [SHH29] 17.00
____Darth Maul black/silver/blue 14.00
____Darth Maul tennis with black and red sole and red design inside [SHH30] 18.00
____Darth Vader and his TIE fighter, white/blue/black high-tops, velcro [SHH31] 16.00
____Darth Vader repeating pattern, black upper / white under, slip-on shoes 10.00
____Darth Vader with Imperial insigina hiking boot, black 21.00
____Darth Vader with Imperial insigina on toe, black shoes, velcro 15.00
____Darth Vader, black shoes, velcro [SHH32] 12.00
____EPI logo on black and gray suede court shoe ..14.00
____Podracing, white/blue/green 14.00
____Star Wars canvas sneakers, black/white 14.00
____Stormtrooper, black below trooper, white shoes, velcro 10.00
____Stormtrooper, white shoes, strings [SHH33] 12.00
____Stormtrooper, white shoes, velcro 11.00

Sandals.
____Anakin Skywalker heavy sandals, dark tan 14.00
____Anakin Skywalker sandals, blue [SHH34] 12.00
____Anakin Skywalker, slip-ons [SHH35] 10.00
____Darth Maul black sport sandal [SHH36] 12.00
____Darth Maul face-bottom sandals [SHH37] 13.00
____Darth Maul flip-flops, black 10.00
____Darth Maul heavy sandals, black/red [SHH38] 14.00
____Darth Vader, Death Star [SHH39] 12.00
____Droids sandals, blue and silver, elastic back [SHH40] 9.00
____Pod racing black sport sandal 12.00

Slippers.
____Chewbacca with sculpted head on toe 10.00
____Darth Maul with hooded sculpted head on toe of slippers [SHH41] 8.00
____Darth Vader, gray 10.00
____Jar Jar Binks with sculpted head on toe 8.00
____Naboo fighter [SHH42] 7.00
____Podracing gray, velcro 8.00
____R2-D2 [SHH43] 7.00

Marks and Spencer
Slippers, adult sizes.
____C-3PO / R2-D2 lenticular [SHH44] 25.00

Stride Rite
____C-3PO and R2-D2 ....50.00
____Darth Vader 50.00
____Ewoks [SHH45] 46.00
____Millennium Falcon 65.00
____X-Wing Fighter [SHH46] 65.00

Slipper socks.
____C-3PO and R2-D2 [SHH47] 8.00
____Darth Vader [SHH48] 8.00
____Wicket the Ewok [SHH49] 6.00
____Yoda [SHH50] 8.00

Slippers.
____Darth Vader 16.00
____Ewoks 12.00

Clothing: Socks

____R2-D2 [AE01] 7.00

Episode I header card.
____The Dark Side, Darth Maul [AE02] 16.00

R2-D2 header card.
____Yoda 12.00

American Supply
____Star Wars designs 12.00

British Home Stores
____Socks and Mug Set [AE03] 24.00

Charleston Hosiery
Empire Strikes Back.
____Boba Fett 18.00
____Darth Vader [AE04] 18.00
____R2-D2 ....18.00
____Snowspeeder [AE05] 18.00
____Stormtrooper [AE06] 18.00
____Yoda 18.00

Return of the Jedi.
____C-3PO and R2-D2 [AE07] 18.00

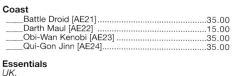

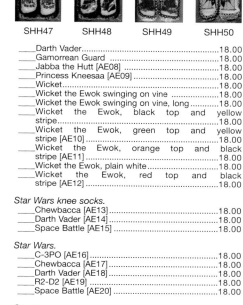

SHH47 SHH48 SHH49 SHH50

____Darth Vader 18.00
____Gamorrean Guard 18.00
____Jabba the Hutt [AE08] 18.00
____Princess Kneesaa [AE09] 18.00
____Wicket 18.00
____Wicket the Ewok swinging on vine 18.00
____Wicket the Ewok swinging on vine, long 18.00
____Wicket the Ewok, black top and yellow stripe 18.00
____Wicket the Ewok, green top and yellow stripe [AE10] 18.00
____Wicket the Ewok, orange top and black stripe [AE11] 18.00
____Wicket the Ewok, plain white 18.00
____Wicket the Ewok, red top and black stripe [AE12] 18.00

Star Wars knee socks.
____Chewbacca [AE13] 18.00
____Darth Vader [AE14] 18.00
____Space Battle [AE15] 18.00

Star Wars.
____C-3PO [AE16] 18.00
____Chewbacca [AE17] 18.00
____Darth Vader [AE18] 18.00
____R2-D2 [AE19] 18.00
____Space Battle [AE20] 18.00

Coast
____Battle Droid [AE21] 35.00
____Darth Maul [AE22] 15.00
____Obi-Wan Kenobi [AE23] 35.00
____Qui-Gon Jinn [AE24] 35.00

Essentials
UK.
____Character freeze mug and sock set [AE25] 18.00
____Star Wars - X-Wing [AE26] 10.00
____Jedi [AE27] 8.00

AE01 AE02 AE03 AE04 AE05 AE06 AE07 AE08 AE09 AE10 AE11 AE12

AE13 AE14 AE15 AE16 AE17 AE18 AE19 AE20 AE21 AE22 AE23 AE24

Clothing: Socks

AE25 AE26 AE27 AE28 AE29 AE30 AE31 AE32 AE33 AE34 AE35 AE36 AE37

AE38 AE39 AE40 AE41 AE42 AE43 AE44 AE45 AE46 AE47 AE48 AE49 AE50 AE51 AE52 AE53

AE54 AE55 AE56 AE57 AE58 AE59 AE60 AE61 AE62 ASP01 hanger styles ASP02 hanger styles

____R2-D2 [AE28] 8.00
____Star Wars logo [AE29]..8.00
____Vader [AE30] 8.00
____Vader (art) 10.00

Handcraft Mfg. Corp.
____Darth Maul, Jedi duel pose [AE31].........................5.00
____Darth Maul, lightsaber ignited on white background [AE32] 5.00
____Darth Maul, Sith Lord [AE33] 5.00
____Darth Maul, Tatooine pose [AE34] 5.00
____Jar Jar, face above Star Wars logo [AE35]............5.00
____Jar Jar, walking [AE36] 5.00
____Story Socks, Battle above Naboo [AE37] 8.00

High Point Knitting, Inc.
____Anakin [AE38] 5.00
____Anakin / Darth Vader [AE39] 5.00
____Darth Vader [AE40] 5.00
____Yoda [AE41]...5.00

Clone Wars.
____Yoda, dark side [AE42] 6.00
____Yoda, light side [AE43] 6.00

Ladybird
UK. Glow-in-the-dark.
____Clone Trooper [AE44] 10.00
____Darth Vader [AE45]..10.00
____Darth Vader [AE46] 8.00
____Evil Vader [AE47]...8.00
____Jedi [AE48] 8.00
____Star Wars logo [AE49]..8.00

Marks and Spencer
Classic trilogy.
____C-3PO [AE50] 8.00
____R2-D2 [AE51] 8.00
Episode I.
____2-pack: SW logo, The Dark Side [AE52] 18.00
____Darth Maul [AE53]..8.00
____Star Wars logo [AE54]..8.00
____The Dark Side [AE55] 8.00

Master Footwear
____Ewoks designs 15.00

Quality Socks
____Anakin Skywalker [AE56] 6.00
____C-3PO [AE57] 6.00
____Darth Maul [AE58]...6.00
____Jar Jar Binks [AE59] 6.00
____R2-D2 [AE60] 6.00

Totes
____Darth Maul [AE61] 20.00
____Lightsaber on gray 12.00
____R2-D2 on black [AE62]...15.00

Clothing: Suspenders

Lee Co.
Striped with badge.
____ C-3PO and R2-D2 die-cut [ASP01] 18.00
____Darth Vader helmet die-cut or sculpted..............20.00
____Yoda face [ASP02] 15.00

Textile Artesa
____Star Wars designs 14.00

Clothing: Swimming Attire

EPI:TPM
____Darth Maul Sith Lord, SW logo [SWA01]............10.00
____Darth Maul bust [SWA02].....................................10.00
____Darth Maul close-up [SWA03] 10.00
____Naboo Fighter [SWA04] 10.00

EPIII:ROTS.
____Darth Vader with lightsaber [SWA05]...................10.00
____Vader [SWA06] 10.00

Episode II: Attack of the Clones.
____Droids [SWA07] 10.00
____Jango Fett [SWA08] 10.00
____Star Fighters [SWA09] 10.00
____Yoda [SWA10]...10.00

Clothing: Undergarments

____"Feel the Force" Darth Vader [AU01] 8.00
____C-3PO boxers [AU02] 14.00
____Darth Vader / Dark Side [AU03]...........................20.00
____Darth Vader, purple silk [AU04] 25.00

SWA01 SWA02 SWA03 SWA04 SWA05

SWA06 SWA07 SWA08 SWA09 SWA10

AU01   AU02   AU03 front   AU03 rear   AU04

AU05   AU06   AU07   AU08   AU09 front

AU09 rear   AU10 front   AU10 rear   AU11   AU12

AU13   AU14   AU15   AU16   AU17   AU18

____Hildebrandt Art [AU05] 20.00
____Vader, silk [AU06] 20.00

Ame
____C-3PO and R2-D2 [AU07] 12.00
____C-3PO pointing and R2-D2 [AU08] 12.00
____Jedi print...12.00
____R2-D2 ....12.00

American Marketing Ent., Inc.
____Darth Vader, black [AU09] 8.00
____Darth Vader, red [AU10] 8.00

Big Dog
____Dog Wars charcoal boxers [AU11]....................17.00
____Epawsode One icons [AU12] 20.00

Bloopers
Re-marketed irregular clothing.
____Darth Maul, boys boxers [AU13] 8.00

Briefly Stated
Boxer shorts.
____Darth Maul, adult [AU14] 12.00
____Darth Maul, childrens [AU15] 9.00
____Droids, childrens 9.00
____Hoth Scene, childrens 9.00
____Jar Jar pictured with patch, adult [AU16] 12.00
____Jar Jar text, adult [AU17] 12.00
____Naboo Space Battle, adult [AU18].....................12.00
____Naboo Space Battle, childrens 9.00
____Sebulba, adult 12.00
____Sith Lord, adult 12.00
____Space Battle, childrens...9.00
____Stormtroopers, childrens 9.00

Fruit of the Loom
____Anakin Skywalker pkg., 3 boys briefs [AU19] 5.00
____Anakin Skywalker pkg., New Space Prints, 3 boys
briefs [AU20]...5.00
____C-3PO pkg., 3 toddler boys briefs [AU21] 5.00

____Darkside / Jedi vs. Sith boxers [AU22].................2.00
____Darth Maul, 3 toddlers boys boxers [AU23]..........8.00
____EPI logo pkg., 2 boys briefs [AU24] 5.00
____Jar Jar pkg., 3 toddler girls panties [AU25] 5.00
____Lightsaber green pkg., 5 printed boys briefs 6.00
____Lightsaber red pkg., 5 printed boys briefs 6.00
____Queen Amidala pkg., 3 girls panties [AU26] 5.00
____R2-D2 shaped box, 5 printed boys briefs 15.00

EPIII: ROTS.
____Darth Vader 2 pk. boxer briefs [AU27] 6.00
____Epic Battle 2 pk. boxer briefs [AU28] 6.00
____Yoda 2 pk. briefs [AU29]......................................6.00

Hanes
____Anakin Skywalker pkg., 3 boys briefs [AU30] 5.00
____Yoda pkg., 3 boys glow briefs [AU31] 8.00

Long Eddies
____Darth Vader and Luke thermal underwear..........10.00

AU19   AU20   AU21   AU22   AU23   AU24   AU25   AU26   AU27   AU28   AU29   AU30

AU31   AU32   AU33   AU34   AU35   AU36   AU37

Clothing: Undergarments

AU38

AU39

AU40

AU41

AU42

AU43

AU44

AU45

AU46

AU47

AU48

AU49

AU50

AU51

Marks and Spencer
Episode I: The Phantom Menace, adult sizes.
____Darth Maul [AU32] 15.00
____Obi-Wan Kenobi [AU33] 15.00
____Sith Lord / The Darkside [AU34] 15.00

Ralph Marlin and Co.
Boxer shorts.
____Darth Vader pattern, silk [AU35] 27.00
____Spaceship pattern w/logo, cotton [AU36] 25.00
____Spaceship pattern, cotton 23.00

Short Eddies
T-shirt and boxer shorts sets, childrens.
____Darth Vader 14.00
____Space Battle..14.00

Smiley 2000
____Darth Vader parody [AU37] 20.00

Union Underwear Co.
Underoos, thermal.
____Darth Vader 20.00
____Han Solo, thermal 20.00
____R2-D2 [AU38] 20.00
____Wicket..20.00
____Yoda 20.00

Underoos.
____Boba Fett [AU39] 15.00
____C-3PO [AU40] 15.00
____Chewbacca [AU41] 15.00
____Darth Vader [AU42]...................................15.00
____Ewoks [AU43]...15.00
____Han Solo [AU44]..15.00
____Luke Skywalker [AU45] 18.00
____Luke Skywalker, flight suit [AU46] 15.00
____Princess Leia [AU47] 15.00
____Priness Leia, ROTJ [AU48]..........................45.00
____R2-D2 [AU49]...15.00
____Wicket [AU50]...15.00
____Yoda [AU51] 15.00

Woolworths
____3-pack Boys Slips, Darth Vader designs 10.00

Clothing: Visors

B/W Character Merchandising
____ESB black and silver 10.00

Drew Pearson Marketing
____Count Dooku 12.00
____Jedi Starfighter red and black 14.00
____Jedi Starfighter, tan 12.00
____Jedi, red 12.00

Factors, Etc.
____Star Wars, May the Force Be With You 35.00

Clothing: Warm-Up Suits

Hot Topic
Infant body suits.
____Darth Vader, "Who's Your Daddy?" 18.00
____Yoda, "Size Matters Not" 18.00

Sales Corp. of America
Boys: hooded with shorts.
____Admiral Ackbar 10.00
____Darth Vader and Royal Guards 14.00
____Darth Vader...10.00
____Luke and Darth Vader dueling 10.00
____ROTJ logo 10.00

Boys: with pants.
____Admiral Ackbar 10.00
____Darth Vader and Royal Guards 12.00
____Darth Vader...10.00
____Luke and Darth Vader dueling 10.00
____Paploo 10.00
____ROTJ logo 8.00

Girls.
____Max Rebo Band 10.00
____Wicket and Paploo 10.00
____Wicket and R2-D2 ....10.00
____Wicket..10.00

Toddlers.
____Baby Ewoks 10.00
____Wicket and Baby Ewoks 10.00
____Wicket and Paploo 10.00
____Wicket and R2-D2 ....10.00

Toddlers: hooded fleece.
____Wicket and Paploo 10.00
____Wicket and R2-D2 ....10.00

Clothing: Wrist Bands

C and D Visionaries, Inc.
____Anakin (logo) [WB01] 5.00
____Boba Fett [WB02] 5.00
____Clone Trooper [WB03]...............................5.00
____Sith [WB04] 5.00
____Star Wars logo black and silver [WB05]...............5.00
____Star Wars logo on green [WB06] 5.00
____Vader (logo) [WB07] 5.00
____X-Wing Squadron [WB08]...........................5.00
____Yoda, Use the Force [WB09] 5.00

Leather.
____Darth Vader...8.00

Coasters

____Celebration at Celebration 3 [CST01] 10.00

Black Falcon
Empire Strikes Back.
____Black print [CST02] 65.00
____Blue print [CST03] 65.00

Coca-Cola, Hong Kong
EPIII:ROTS. Round, boxed.
____Anakin Skywalker 12.00
____C-3PO and R2-D2 [CST04] 12.00
____Darth Vader [CST05] 12.00
____Yoda 12.00

WB01

WB02

WB03

WB04

WB05

WB06

WB07

WB08

WB09

CST01

CST02

CST03

CST04

CST05

CST06

CST07

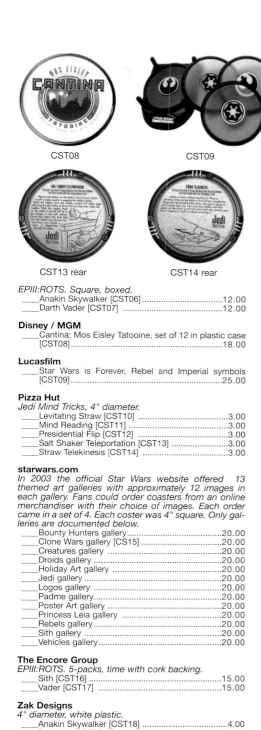

CST08

CST09

CST10-CST4 front

CST10 rear

CST11 rear

CST12 rear

CST13 rear

CST14 rear

CST15 sample

CST16-17 package

CST16

CST17

CST18

CST19

CST20

CST21

EPIII:ROTS. Square, boxed.
____Anakin Skywalker [CST06] 12.00
____Darth Vader [CST07] 12.00

Disney / MGM
____Cantina: Mos Eisley Tatooine, set of 12 in plastic case
[CST08] 18.00

Lucasfilm
____Star Wars is Forever, Rebel and Imperial symbols
[CST09] 25.00

Pizza Hut
Jedi Mind Tricks, 4" diameter.
____Levitating Straw [CST10] 3.00
____Mind Reading [CST11] 3.00
____Presidential Flip [CST12] 3.00
____Salt Shaker Teleportation [CST13] 3.00
____Straw Telekinesis [CST14] 3.00

starwars.com
In 2003 the official Star Wars website offered 13 themed art galleries with approximately 12 images in each gallery. Fans could order coasters from an online merchandiser with their choice of images. Each order came in a set of 4. Each coster was 4" square. Only galleries are documented below.
____Bounty Hunters gallery 20.00
____Clone Wars gallery [CS15] 20.00
____Creatures gallery 20.00
____Droids gallery 20.00
____Holiday Art gallery 20.00
____Jedi gallery 20.00
____Logos gallery 20.00
____Padme gallery 20.00
____Poster Art gallery 20.00
____Princess Leia gallery 20.00
____Rebels gallery 20.00
____Sith gallery 20.00
____Vehicles gallery 20.00

The Encore Group
EPIII:ROTS. 5-packs, time with cork backing.
____Sith [CST16] 15.00
____Vader [CST17] 15.00

Zak Designs
4" diameter, white plastic.
____Anakin Skywalker [CST18] 4.00
____Darth Maul [CST19] 4.00
____Jar Jar Binks [CST20] 4.00
____Queen Amidala [CST21] 4.00

Coin Purses

____Queen Amidala treasure keeper look-alike
[PET01] 5.00

Applause
Treasure Keepers.
____Jar Jar Binks [PET02] 6.00
____Queen Amidala [PET03] 8.00
____R2-D2 [PET04] 6.00
____Yoda [PET05]....................................6.00

Touchline
3" round with split, any color. Sold loose.
____Admiral Ackbar [PET06] 10.00
____C-3PO [PET07] 10.00
____Chewbacca [PET08] 10.00
____Darth Vader [PET09]............................10.00
____Ewok [PET10] 10.00
____Jabba the Hutt [PET11] 10.00
____R2-D2 [PET12] 10.00
____Stormtrooper [PET13] 10.00

Coins: Action Figure

Just Toys
Bend-Ems premiums.
____Millennium Falcon [C01].........................12.00
____Tie Fighter [C02] 12.00
____X-Wing Fighter [C03] 12.00

Kenner
Droids.
____A-Wing Pilot 35.00

____Boba Fett [C04] 65.00
____C-3PO [C05] 12.00
____Jann Tosh [C06] 10.00
____Jord Dusat [C07] 10.00
____Kea Moll [C08] 10.00
____Kez-Iban [C09] 10.00
____RD-D2 [C10] 12.00
____Sise Fromm [C11] 10.00
____Thall Joben [C12] 10.00
____Tig Fromm [C13]................................10.00
____Uncle Gundy [C14] 10.00

Ewoks.
____Dulok Scout [C15] 10.00
____Dulok Shaman [C16] 10.00
____King Gorneesh [C17] 10.00
____Logray..17.00
____Urgah Lady Gorneesh [C18] 10.00
____Wicket [C19] 17.00

Power of the Force 2.
____C-3PO 15.00
____Chewbacca 5.00
____Emperor Palpatine 5.00
____Han Solo 5.00
____Luke Skywalker...................................5.00
____Princess Leia [C20] 5.00
____Snowtrooper 5.00

Power of the Force.
____2-1B [C21] 100.00

PET01

PET02

PET03

PET04

PET05

PET06

PET07

PET08

PET09

PET10

PET11

PET12

PET13

Coins: Action Figure

A-Wing Pilot [C22]	10.00
Amanaman [C23]	17.00
Anakin Skywalker [C24]	70.00
AT-AT [C25]	100.00
AT-ST Driver [C26]	15.00
B-Wing Pilot [C27]	12.00
Barada [C28]	10.00
Bib Fortuna [C29]	150.00
Biker Scout [C30]	15.00
Boba Fett [C31]	305.00
C-3PO [C32]	15.00
Chewbacca [C33]	25.00
Chief Chirpa [C34]	35.00
Creatures [C35]	70.00
Darth Vader [C36]	18.00
Droids (R5-D4 and Power Droid) [C37]	58.00
Emperor's Royal Guard [C38]	55.00
Emperor [C39]	30.00
EV-9D9 [C40]	10.00
FX-7 [C41]	75.00
Gamorrean Guard [C42]	40.00
Greedo [C43]	102.00
Han Solo, Carbon Freeze [C44]	10.00
Han Solo, Rebel [C45]	20.00
Han Solo, Rebel Fighter [C46]	125.00
Han Solo, Rebel Hero [C47]	125.00
Hans Solo, Rebel (misspelling) [C48]	250.00
Hoth Stormtrooper [C49]	225.00
Imperial Commander [C50]	46.00
Imperial Dignitary [C51]	15.00
Imperial Gunner [C52]	15.00
Jawas [C53]	22.00
Lando Calrissian, Rebel General (Cloud City) [C54]	67.00
Lando Calrissian, Rebel General (Falcon) [C55]	10.00
Logray [C56]	32.00
Luke Skywalker, Jedi Knight [C57]	20.00
Luke Skywalker, Jedi Knight on Dagobah [C58]	95.00
Luke Skywalker, Jedi with X-Wing [C59]	25.00
Luke Skywalker, Rebel Leader [C60]	35.00
Luke Skywalker, Rebel Leader (Scout Bike) [C61]	10.00
Luke Skywalker, Rebel Leader (Stormtrooper armor) [C62]	26.00
Luke Skywalker, Rebel Leader (Stormtrooper armor, no eyes) [C63]	12.00
Luke Skywalker, Rebel Leader (Tauntaun) [C64]	141.00
Lumat [C65]	12.00
Millenium Falcon (misspelling) [C66]	175.00
Millennium Falcon [C67]	80.00
Obi-Wan Kenobi [C68]	15.00
Paploo [C69]	11.00
Princess Leia, Boushh [C70]	149.00
Princess Leia, Rebel Leader (Endor Fatigues) [C71]	15.00
Princess Leia, Rebel Leader (R2-D2) [C72]	73.00
R2-D2 [C73]	16.00
Romba [C74]	10.00
Sail Barge [ ]	225.00
Sail Skiff [C75]	255.00
Sail Skiff without Star Wars logo	175.00
Star Destroyer Commander [C76]	78.00
Stormtrooper [C77]	50.00
Teebo [C78]	30.00
Tie Fighter Pilot [C79]	40.00
Tusken Raider [C80]	150.00
Warok [C81]	10.00
Wicket [C82]	15.00
Yak Face [C83]	100.00
Yoda [C84]	26.00
Zuckuss [C85]	165.00

C01 front / rear   C02   C03   C04   C05   C06   C07

C08   C09   C10   C11   C12   C13   C14   C15

C16   C17   C18   C19   C20   C21   C22   C23

C24   C25   C26   C27   C28   C29   C30   C31

C32   C33   C34   C35   C36   C37   C38   C39

C40   C41   C42   C43   C44   C45   C46   C47

C48 C49 C50 C51 C52 C53 C54 C55

C56 C57 C58 C59 C60 C61 C62 C63

C64 C65 C66 C67 C68 C69 C70 C71

C72 C73 C74 C75 C76 C77 C78 C79

C80 C81 C82 C83 C84 C85 C86 front / rear

____63rd: Jedi Knight, prototype only, aluminum or bronze
finish [C86] 750.00

Toy Fair
____Darth Vader, Toy Fair exclusive 25.00

Coins: Minted

California lottery scratch-off coins.
____C-3PO [CPM01] 20.00
____Darth Vader [CPM02] 15.00
____Luke Skywalker [CPM03] 15.00
____Princess Leia [CPM04].....................................15.00
____R2-D2 [CPM05] 15.00
____Yoda [CPM06] 20.00

Germany.
____Darth Vader, limited to 9,999 [CPM07] 35.00

Japan.
____EPII: Young Jedi / Lord of the Sith [CPM08] 45.00
____EPIII: Darth Vader / ROTS [CPM09]....................45.00

20th Century Fox
EPIII:ROTS.
____Star Wars Episode III, give-away with DVD, Target
exclusive [CPM10] 15.00

Cards, Inc.
Medalionz, bronze.
____Collector's set with display box, limited to
2,000 ....100.00

Medalionz, gold.
____Anakin Skywalker 8.00
____Anakin Skywalker vs. Count Dooku 8.00
____Anakin Skywalker vs. Obi-Wan [CPM11] 8.00
____ARC-170 Fighter..8.00
____Battle Droid 8.00
____C-3PO and R2-D2 ....8.00
____Clone Trooper 8.00
____Count Dooku 8.00
____Darth Sidious 8.00
____Darth Sidious vs. Yoda 8.00
____Darth Vader 8.00
____Droid Tri-Fighter 8.00
____Evil Separatists 8.00

____Galactic Republic emblem 8.00
____General Grievous 8.00
____Jedi Knights emblem 8.00
____Jedi Starfighter 8.00
____Mace Windu 8.00
____Obi-Wan Kenobi 8.00
____Padme Amidala..8.00
____Republic Cruiser 8.00
____Sith Lords emblem 8.00
____Yoda 8.00

Medalionz, silver.
____Anakin Skywalker 4.00
____Anakin Skywalker vs. Count Dooku [CPM12] 4.00
____Anakin Skywalker vs. Obi-Wan [CPM13] 4.00
____ARC-170 Fighter..4.00
____Battle Droid 4.00
____C-3PO and R2-D2 ....4.00
____Clone Trooper 4.00
____Count Dooku...4.00
____Darth Sidious [CPM14] 4.00
____Darth Sidious vs. Yoda [CPM15] 4.00
____Darth Vader [CPM16] 4.00
____Droid Tri-Fighter [CPM17]...................................4.00

CPM01 CPM02 front CPM02 rear CPM03 CPM04 CPM05 CPM06

Coins: Minted

CPM07 front

CPM07 rear

CPM08 front

CPM08 rear

CPM09

CPM10 front

CPM10 rear

CPM11

CPM12

CPM13

CPM14

CPM15

CPM16

CPM17

CPM18

CPM19

CPM20

CPM21

CPM22 front

CPM22 rear

____Evil Separatists 4.00
____Galactic Republic emblem 4.00
____General Grievous [CPM18] 4.00
____Jedi Knights emblem 4.00
____Jedi Starfighter 4.00
____Mace Windu 4.00
____Obi-Wan Kenobi 4.00
____Padme Amidala [CPM19] 4.00
____Republic Cruiser [CPM20] 4.00
____Sith Lords emblem 4.00
____Yoda 4.00

Medalionz, special edition / oversized.
____Yoda, TheCollectorZone.com exclusive, limited to 500
[CPM21] 50.00

Catch a Star Collectibles
____15th Anniversary, silver, limited to 5,000
[CPM22] 135.00

Disney / MGM
2001 R2-D2 projecting hologram Mickey.
____Limited to 1200 [CPM23]...................100.00
2003 Jedi Mickey and Yoda.
____Week 1 nickel silver, limited to 500 [CPM24]......80.00
____Week 2 bronze, limited to 500 ....80.00
____Week 3 gold, limited to 1000 [CPM25] 65.00
____Week 5 fine silver, limited to 500 ....95.00
2004 Jedi Mickey and Leia Minnie.
____Framed set of 5, includes exclusive x-wing coin, limit-
ed to 250 [CPM26]...250.00
____Week 1 bronze, limited to 1000 ....45.00
____Week 2 nickel silver, limited to 1000 [CPM27]....45.00
____Week 3 gold, limited to 1000 ....45.00
____Week 4 fine silver, limited to 1000 ....45.00
2005 Darth Vader and Mickey.
____Framed set of 5, limited to 250 [CPM28] 250.00
____Framed set of 6, includes exclusive 2000 coin, limited
to 250 [CPM29] 250.00

____Sterling .999, 1 Troy oz. [CPM30] 75.00
____Week 1 gold limited to 1,000 [CPM31] 45.00
____Week 2 bronze, limited to 1,000 ....45.00
____Week 3 silver overlay, limited to 1,000 ....45.00
____Week 4 nickel silver, limited to 1,000.................45.00
2006 Darth Vader & Yoda.
____Bronze, limited to 1,000 [CPM33] 45.00
____Framed set of 5 [CPM32] 175.00
____Gold, limited to 1,000.......................................45.00
____Nickel silver, limited to 1,000 ....45.00
____Sterling .999, 1 Troy oz. 250.00

Echo Base Toys
____Boba Fett, limited to 250 [CPM35] 45.00
____Queen Amidala, limited to 250 [CPM36] 35.00

Franklin Mint
____20th Anniversary commerative medal, 24k gold on
sterling silver, limited edition [CPM37]................85.00

CPM23

CPM24

CPM25

CPM26

CPM27

CPM28

CPM29

CPM30

CPM31

CPM32

CPM33

CPM35

CPM36

CPM37 front

CPM37 rear

CPM38

CPM39

CPM40

CPM41

Coins: Minted

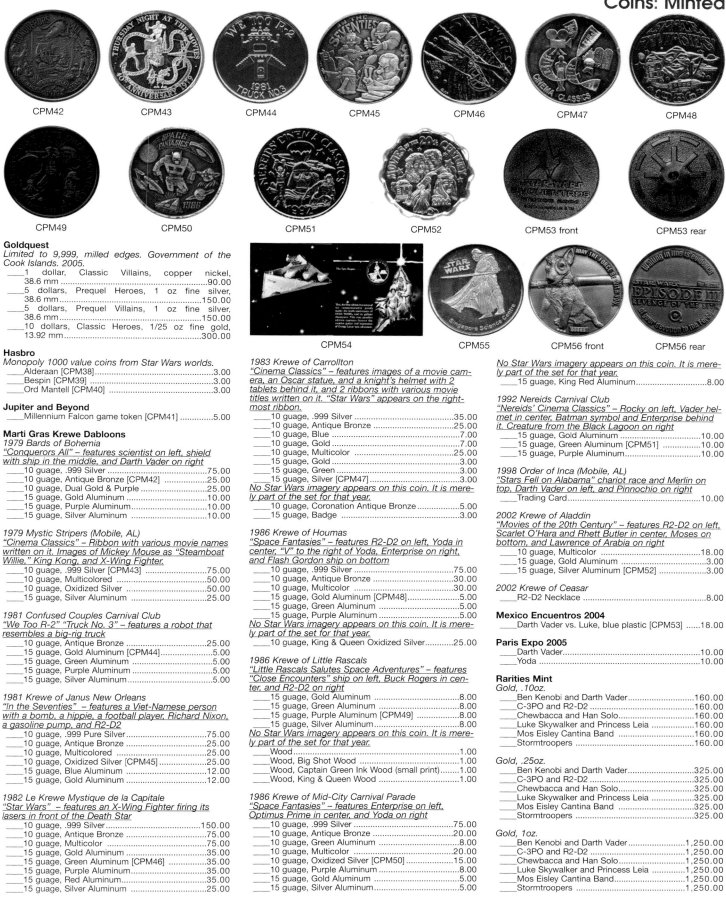

CPM42   CPM43   CPM44   CPM45   CPM46   CPM47   CPM48

CPM49   CPM50   CPM51   CPM52   CPM53 front   CPM53 rear

CPM54   CPM55   CPM56 front   CPM56 rear

Goldquest
Limited to 9,999, milled edges. Government of the Cook Islands. 2005.

____1 dollar, Classic Villains, copper nickel, 38.6 mm 90.00
____5 dollars, Prequel Heroes, 1 oz fine silver, 38.6 mm 150.00
____5 dollars, Prequel Villains, 1 oz fine silver, 38.6 mm 150.00
____10 dollars, Classic Heroes, 1/25 oz fine gold, 13.92 mm 300.00

Hasbro
Monopoly 1000 value coins from Star Wars worlds.

____Alderaan [CPM38].......................................3.00
____Bespin [CPM39] 3.00
____Ord Mantell [CPM40] 3.00

Jupiter and Beyond
____Millennium Falcon game token [CPM41] 5.00

Marti Gras Krewe Dabloons
1979 Bards of Bohemia
"Conquerors All" – features scientist on left, shield with ship in the middle, and Darth Vader on right

____10 guage, .999 Silver 75.00
____10 guage, Antique Bronze [CPM42] 25.00
____10 guage, Dual Gold & Purple 25.00
____15 guage, Gold Aluminum 10.00
____15 guage, Purple Aluminum................................10.00
____15 guage, Silver Aluminum 10.00

1979 Mystic Stripers (Mobile, AL)
"Cinema Classics" – Ribbon with various movie names written on it. Images of Mickey Mouse as "Steamboat Willie," King Kong, and X-Wing Fighter.

____10 guage, .999 Silver [CPM43] 75.00
____10 guage, Multicolored 50.00
____10 guage, Oxidized Silver 50.00
____15 guage, Silver Aluminum 25.00

1981 Confused Couples Carnival Club
"We Too R-2" "Truck No. 3" – features a robot that resembles a big-rig truck

____10 guage, Antique Bronze 25.00
____15 guage, Gold Aluminum [CPM44].......................5.00
____15 guage, Green Aluminum 5.00
____15 guage, Purple Aluminum..............................5.00
____15 guage, Silver Aluminum 5.00

1981 Krewe of Janus New Orleans
"In the Seventies" – features a Viet-Namese person with a bomb, a hippie, a football player, Richard Nixon, a gasoline pump, and R2-D2

____10 guage, .999 Pure Silver 75.00
____10 guage, Antique Bronze 25.00
____10 guage, Multicolored 25.00
____10 guage, Oxidized Silver [CPM45]...................25.00
____15 guage, Blue Aluminum 12.00
____15 guage, Gold Aluminum 12.00

1982 Le Krewe Mystique de la Capitale
"Star Wars" – features an X-Wing Fighter firing its lasers in front of the Death Star

____10 guage, .999 Silver....................................150.00
____10 guage, Antique Bronze 75.00
____10 guage, Multicolor 75.00
____15 guage, Gold Aluminum 35.00
____15 guage, Green Aluminum [CPM46] 35.00
____15 guage, Purple Aluminum..............................35.00
____15 guage, Red Aluminum...............................35.00
____15 guage, Silver Aluminum 25.00

1983 Krewe of Carrollton
"Cinema Classics" – features images of a movie camera, an Oscar statue, and a knight's helmet with 2 tablets behind it, and 2 ribbons with various movie titles written on it. "Star Wars" appears on the right-most ribbon.

____10 guage, .999 Silver 35.00
____10 guage, Antique Bronze 25.00
____10 guage, Blue 7.00
____10 guage, Gold 7.00
____10 guage, Multicolor 25.00
____15 guage, Gold 3.00
____15 guage, Green 3.00
____15 guage, Silver [CPM47]..................................3.00
No Star Wars imagery appears on this coin. It is merely part of the set for that year.
____10 guage, Coronation Antique Bronze 5.00
____15 guage, Badge 3.00

1986 Krewe of Houmas
"Space Fantasies" – features R2-D2 on left, Yoda in center, "V" to the right of Yoda, Enterprise on right, and Flash Gordon ship on bottom

____10 guage, .999 Silver 75.00
____10 guage, Antique Bronze 30.00
____10 guage, Multicolor 30.00
____15 guage, Gold Aluminum [CPM48].....................5.00
____15 guage, Green Aluminum 5.00
____15 guage, Purple Aluminum 5.00
No Star Wars imagery appears on this coin. It is merely part of the set for that year.
____10 guage, King & Queen Oxidized Silver............25.00

1986 Krewe of Little Rascals
"Little Rascals Salutes Space Adventures" – features "Close Encounters" ship on left, Buck Rogers in center, and R2-D2 on right

____15 guage, Gold Aluminum 8.00
____15 guage, Green Aluminum 8.00
____15 guage, Purple Aluminum [CPM49] 8.00
____15 guage, Silver Aluminum 8.00
No Star Wars imagery appears on this coin. It is merely part of the set for that year.
____Wood 1.00
____Wood, Big Shot Wood 1.00
____Wood, Captain Green Ink Wood (small print)........1.00
____Wood, King & Queen Wood 1.00

1986 Krewe of Mid-City Carnival Parade
"Space Fantasies" – features Enterprise on left, Optimus Prime in center, and Yoda on right

____10 guage, .999 Silver 75.00
____10 guage, Antique Bronze 20.00
____10 guage, Green Aluminum 8.00
____10 guage, Multicolor 20.00
____10 guage, Oxidized Silver [CPM50]...................15.00
____10 guage, Purple Aluminum 8.00
____15 guage, Gold Aluminum 5.00
____15 guage, Silver Aluminum 5.00

No Star Wars imagery appears on this coin. It is merely part of the set for that year.
____15 guage, King Red Aluminum.............................8.00

1992 Nereids Carnival Club
"Nereids' Cinema Classics" – Rocky on left, Vader helmet in center, Batman symbol and Enterprise behind it. Creature from the Black Lagoon on right

____15 guage, Gold Aluminum 10.00
____15 guage, Green Aluminum [CPM51] 10.00
____15 guage, Purple Aluminum..............................10.00

1998 Order of Inca (Mobile, AL)
"Stars Fell on Alabama" chariot race and Merlin on top, Darth Vader on left, and Pinnochio on right

____Trading Card...10.00

2002 Krewe of Aladdin
"Movies of the 20th Century" – features R2-D2 on left, Scarlet O'Hara and Rhett Butler in center, Moses on bottom, and Lawrence of Arabia on right

____10 guage, Multicolor 18.00
____15 guage, Gold Aluminum 3.00
____15 guage, Silver Aluminum [CPM52] 3.00

2002 Krewe of Ceasar
____R2-D2 Necklace 8.00

Mexico Encuentros 2004
____Darth Vader vs. Luke, blue plastic [CPM53] 18.00

Paris Expo 2005
____Darth Vader...10.00
____Yoda 10.00

Rarities Mint
Gold, .10oz.
____Ben Kenobi and Darth Vader...........................160.00
____C-3PO and R2-D2 ....160.00
____Chewbacca and Han Solo............................160.00
____Luke Skywalker and Princess Leia 160.00
____Mos Eisley Cantina Band 160.00
____Stormtroopers 160.00

Gold, .25oz.
____Ben Kenobi and Darth Vader...........................325.00
____C-3PO and R2-D2 ....325.00
____Chewbacca and Han Solo............................325.00
____Luke Skywalker and Princess Leia 325.00
____Mos Eisley Cantina Band 325.00
____Stormtroopers 325.00

Gold, 1oz.
____Ben Kenobi and Darth Vader...........................1,250.00
____C-3PO and R2-D2 ....1,250.00
____Chewbacca and Han Solo............................1,250.00
____Luke Skywalker and Princess Leia 1,250.00
____Mos Eisley Cantina Band 1,250.00
____Stormtroopers 1,250.00

Coins: Minted

CCP01 front / rear

CCP02 front / rear

CCP03 front / rear

CCP04 front / rear

LEC01

LEC02

CLG01

CLG02

CLG03

TOC01

TOC02

TOC03

TOC04

TOC05

TOC06

TOC07

Silver, 1oz.
____Ben Kenobi and Darth Vader 50.00
____C-3PO and R2-D2 ....50.00
____Chewbacca and Han Solo 50.00
____Luke Skywalker and Princess Leia [CPM54] 50.00
____Luke Skywalker and Princess Leia, 15th anniversary 65.00
____Mos Eisley Cantina Band 50.00
____Stormtroopers 50.00

Silver, 5oz.
____Ben Kenobi and Darth Vader............................175.00
____C-3PO and R2-D2 ....175.00
____Chewbacca and Han Solo..................................175.00
____Luke Skywalker and Princess Leia 175.00
____Mos Eisley Cantina Band 175.00
____Stormtroopers 175.00

Singapore Mint
____Darth Vader, Singapore Science Center, limited to 20,000 [CPM55] 35.00

CB01

CB02 sample

CB03 sample

Target
____"Waiting in line is evidence of your devotion to the force, May 19, 2005" [CPM56] 50.00

Coins: Premiums

Nestlé
Cereal premiums from Nestl'e cereals in Spain.
____Chewbacca / 50 / Kashyyyk [CCP01] 14.00
____Darth Vader / 1000 / Death Star [CCP02] 14.00
____Luke Skywalker / 500 / Tatooine [CCP03] 14.00
____Princess Leia / 10000 / Alderaan [CCP04] 14.00

Collectors Box

____EPI: Collector's Art Book, Visual Dictionary, 3 posters [LEC01] 34.00
____SW Trilogy paperback (discounted), SE CCG card pack, announcement of Tomart's 1999 Star Wars book [LEC02] 25.00

Cologne

Avon, Mexico
Cologne for kids.
____Anakin and Amidala [CLG01] 8.00
____Jedi Starfighter [CLG02]......................................10.00
____Padme Amidala, wrist compact [CLG03] 14.00
____Roll-On 8.00

Combs

Adam Joseph Industries
Comb-n-Keepers.
____Landspeeder 10.00
____Max Rebo Band 12.00
____Princess Kneesaa 8.00
____Wicket and Princess Kneesaa 12.00

Pop-Up Combs.
____C-3PO and R2-D2 ....10.00
____Darth Vader..10.00
____Princess Leia as Jabba's Prisoner......................16.00

Comic Books

____Star Rats [CB01] 5.00

France releases.
____L'Empire Contre-Attaque issues 1-2, each 5.00
____La Guerre des Etoiles issues 1-2, each 5.00
____Le Retour du Jedi issues 1-2, each 5.00

Blackthorne Publishing
(Images in 2nd edition, page 243. Checklist in 3rd edition, page 235.)
____01 Star Wars 3D issues 1-3 [CB02], each 12.00

Bruguera
(Images in 2nd edition, page 243.)
____El Imperio Contraataca 25.00
____Issues 1-15 [CB03], each 35.00
____Issues Especial 1 – 4, each 34.00

Carlsen
____Del Af Thrawns Haevn 15.00
____Del Af Trilogy 15.00
____Der Kampf Der Droiden [CB04] 10.00

Chikara Comics
____Pop Parody #1, "Episode Uno, The Parody Menace" [CB05] 5.00

Comics Forum
(Images in 2nd edition, page 244. Checklist in 3rd edition, page 235.)
____El Retorno Del Jedi, graphic novel 16.00
____Issues 1 – 16 [CB06], each 10.00

Delcourt
____L'Ultime Commandment Vol. 1 [CB07]..................8.00
____L'Ultime Commandment Vol. 2..............................8.00
____Le Retour Du Jedi 10.00

CB04 sample

CB05

CB06 sample

CB07 sample

CB08 sample

CB09

CB10

CB11

CB12

CB13 sample

CB14 sample

CB15 sample

CB16

CB17 sample

CB18

CB19 sample

CB20 sample

CB21 sample

CB22 sample

CB23 sample

Dino
____Crimson Empire issues 1 – 6 [CB08], each 8.00

Entity Comics
____Fart Wars, parody [CB09] 4.00
____Return of One-Eye, parody [CB10] 4.00

Epic Comics
____Samurai Cat [CB11] 7.00

Fan Made
____The Norm, Night of the Wookiee [CB12] 3.00

Feest Comics
____Das Goldene Zeitalter Der Sith I – III, each 6.00
____Das Letzte Kommando Teil I – III, each 6.00
____Der Sith-Krieg Teil I – III, each 6.00
____Der Untergang Der Sith I – III, each 6.00
____Die Dunkle Seite Der Macht Teil I – III, each 6.00
____Die Lords von Sith Teil I – III [CB13], each 6.00
____Luke Skywalker Teil I – III, each 6.00

Classic Star Wars.
____Band 6 – 9 [CB14], each 6.00

Foom
____Star Wars [CB15] 15.00

Hasbro
____Clone Wars Short Stories Collection [CB16] 8.00

Magic Press
____Il Ritorno de lo Jedi 14.00

Mala Stripoteka
Serbia.
____Vol. II, No. 1 – 7 [CB17], each 10.00

Manga
____A New Hope, issues 1 – 4, each 14.00
____Empire Strikes Back, issues 1 – 4, each 14.00
____Return of the Jedi, issues 1 – 4, each 14.00
____Star Wars Episode I: The Phantom Menace
[CB18] 28.00

Cine-Manga.
____EPI: The Phantom Menace 15.00
____EPII: Attack of the Clones 15.00
____EPIII: Revenge of the Sith 15.00

Mundicomics
____Issues 1 – 9 [CB19], each 18.00

Planeta DeAgostini Comics
____Issues 1 – 4 Una Nueva Esperanza [CB20], ea. ..5.00
____Issues 5 – 8 El Imperio Contraataca, each 5.00
____Issues 9 – 12 El Retorno Del Jedi, each 5.00

Super Heros Collection
France releases.
____La Guerre Des Etoiles [CB21] 35.00

Surco
____Issues 1 – 6 [CB22], each 25.00

Telecomic
____Issue 24 Ewoks and Droids [CB23] 19.00
____Issues 25 – 26: Droids 16.00
____Issue 27: Ewoks and Droids 19.00

YPS
____Der Stormtrooper des Imperiums 43.00

Comic Books: Dark Horse

Dark Horse Comics
____A New Hope: Special Edition issues 1 – 4, ea. 6.00
____Boba Fett #1/2 Gold Foil Edition 18.00
____Boba Fett #1/2 Wizard mail-away 12.00
____Boba Fett Agent of Doom 3.00
____Boba Fett Bounty on Bar-Kooda 6.00
____Boba Fett Murder Most Foul (double-sized) 6.00
____Boba Fett Twin Engines of Destruction 8.00
____Boba Fett When The Fat Lady Swings 6.00
____Boba Fett: Enemy of the Empire   issues 1-4,
[CBD01] each 3.00
____Bounty Hunters #1: Scoundrel's Wages..............5.00
____Bounty Hunters #2: Kenix Kil 5.00
____Chewbacca issues 1-4 [CBD02], each................5.00
____Classic Star Wars issues 1-20 ....6.00
____Classic Star Wars, The Early Adventures issues
1 – 9 [CBD04], each 5.00
____Classic Star Wars: The Vandelhelm Mission 5.00
____Clone Wars Adventures 1 – 6, each....................7.00
____Clone Wars Adventures vol. 1-current, each 6.00
____Crimson Empire issues 1 – 6 [CBD05], each........7.00
____Crimson Empire II issues 1 – 6 [CBD06], each 6.00
____Dark Empire #1 Wizard Ace edition 16.00
____Dark Empire issues 1 – 6 [CBD07], each.............25.00
____Dark Empire 2nd printing issues 1 – 3, each 5.00
____Dark Empire II issues 1 – 6 [CBD08], each 7.00
____Dark Empire II. Platinum edition 1 – 6, each........8.00
____Dark Empire. Gold edition issues 1 – 6, each 22.00
____Dark Empire. Platinum edition 1 – 6, each 16.00
____Dark Force Rising issues 1 – 6 [CBD09], each 4.00
____Dark Horse Classics: Dark Empire 1 – 6, each 4.00
____Dark Horse Comics #7: "Beginning an All New Star
Wars Adventure" 5.00
____Darth Maul issues 1 – 4 [CBD10], each 5.00
____Devil Worlds issues 1 – 2 [CBD11], each.............6.00
____Droids issues 1 – 6 [CBD12], each......................5.00
____Droids: 2nd series 1 – 8 [CBD13], each 5.00
____Droids: Special Edition 8.00
____Droids: The Constancia Affair, KB Toys excl........4.00
____Droids: The Protocol Offensive (Co-Written with
Anthony Daniels) 8.00
____Empire's End 1 – 2 [CBD14], each 4.00
____Empire #1 – current [CBD15], each 4.00
____EPI:TPM. Glow-in-the-dark features on photo covers,
limited to 15,000, any cover, each 25.00
____EPI:TPM. Holofoil logo on photo covers, limited to
15,000, any cover, each 25.00
____Episode I: The Phantom Menace #1/2 ....12.00
____Episode I: The Phantom Menace 1 – 4, each 3.00
____Episode I: The Phantom Menace, art cover, any,
each 3.00
____Episode I: The Phantom Menace, photo cover, any,
each 3.00
____Episode II Attack of the Clones issues 1 – 4, art cover,
each 4.00
____Episode II Attack of the Clones issues 1 – 4, photo
cover, each 4.00
____Exclusives issues 1 – 4 Hasbro / Toys R Us exclusive
[CBD16], each...5.00
____Free Comic Book Day: 2002-present, each..........5.00
____General Grievous issues 1 – 4, each 3.00
____Han Solo at Stars' End issues 1 – 3, each............3.00
____Handbook: Crimson Empire. 3.00
____Handbook: Star Wars, Vol. 3 Dark Empire 5.00

Comic Books: Dark Horse

____Handbook: X-Wing Rogue Squadron...................4.00
____Heir to the Empire issues 1 – 6, each 4.00
____Infinities A New Hope issues 1 – 4 [CBD17],
each 5.00
____Infinities Empire Strikes Back issues 1 – 4 [CBD18],
each 5.00
____Infinities Return of the Jedi issues 1 – 4, each 5.00
____Jabba the Hutt Betrayal 4.00
____Jabba the Hutt The Dynasty Trap 4.00
____Jabba the Hutt The Gaar Suppoon Hit
[CBD19]...4.00
____Jabba the Hutt The Hunger of Princess
Nampi 4.00
____Jabba the Hutt The Jabba Tape 4.00
____Jango Fett, Open Seasons issues 1 – 4 [CBD20],
each 4.00
____Jedi: Aayla Secura 5.00
____Jedi: Count Dooku 5.00
____Jedi: Mace Windu 5.00
____Jedi: Shaak Ti 5.00
____Jedi: Yoda 5.00
____Jedi Acadamy: Leviathan issues 1 – 4 [CBD21],
each 4.00
____Jedi Council: Acts of War issues 1 – 4 [CBD22],
each 3.00
____Jedi Quest issues 1 – 4 [CBD23], each 3.00
____Jedi vs. Sith issues 1 – 6, each 3.00
____Knights of the Old Republic issues 1-current,
each 3.00
____Last Command issues 1 – 6, each......................4.00
____Manga: Empire Strikes Back issues 1 – 4, ea. ...12.00
____Manga: Return of the Jedi issues 1 – 4, each......10.00
____Manga: Star Wars issues 1 – 4, each 14.00
____Manga: The Phantom Menace 1 – 2, each 10.00
____Mara Jade: By The Empreror's Hand issues 1-6
[CBD24], each...5.00
____Obsession issues 1 – 5 [CBD25], each...............3.00
____Qui-Gon and Obi-Wan. Last Stand on Ord Mantell
issues 1 – 3 [CBD26], each 3.00
____Qui-Gon and Obi-Wan. The Aurorient Express issues
1 – 2, each 3.00
____Republic issues 46 – 83 [CBD27 – CBD28], ea. ..3.00
____Revenge of the Sith issues 1 – 4, each 3.00
____River of Chaos issues 1 – 4 [CBD29] 6.00
____Sergio Aragonis Stomps Star Wars 14.00
____Shadow Stalker 4.00
____Shadows of the Empire issues 1 – 6 [CBD30],
each 4.00
____Shadows of the Empire: Evolution issues 1 – 5
[CBD31], each...4.00
____Splinter of the Mind's Eye issues 1 – 4 [CBD32],
each 4.00
____Star Fighter Crossbones issues 1 – 3 [CBD33],
each 3.00
____Star Wars #0: Luke and Leia cover 14.00
____Star Wars #0: Princess Leia cover 11.00
____Star Wars issues 1 – 45 [CBD34], each 8.00
____Star Wars Tales issues 1 – 25, art cover [CBD35],
each 7.00
____Star Wars Tales issues 1 – 25, photo cover,
each 7.00
____Tag and Bink are Dead issues 1 – 2 [CBD36] 7.00
____Tag and Bink, The Return Of... issues 1 – 2..........3.00
____Tales from Mos Eisley 4.00
____Tales of the Jedi issues 1 – 5, each 6.00
____Tales of the Jedi: Dark Lords of the Sith issues 1 – 6,
each 6.00
____Tales of the Jedi: Dark Lords of the Sith Ashcan
Special Edition for Topps 10.00
____Tales of the Jedi: Redemption issues 1 – 5 [CBD37],
each 4.00

CBD01 #4   CBD02 #4   CBD03 #12   CBD04 #2   CBD05 #3   CBD06 #5   CBD07 #3   CBD08 #4   CBD09 #6   CBD10 #2

CBD11 #1   CBD12 #3   CBD13 #5   CBD14 #2   CBD15 #2   CBD16 #2   CBD17 #2   CBD18 #4   CBD19   CBD20 #2

Comic Books: Dark Horse

CBD21 #3 | CBD22 #3 | CBD23 #1 | CBD24 #2 | CBD25 #2 | CBD26 #1 | CBD27 #81 | CBD28 #56 | CBD29 #4 | CBD30 #6

CBD31 #3 | CBD32 #4 | CBD33 #1 | CBD34 #11 | CBD35 #3 | CBD36 #2 | CBD37 #4 | CBD38 #4 | CBD39 #4 | CBD40 #2

____Tales of the Jedi: The Fall of the Sith Empire #1 (Wizard excl. signed by Kevin Anderson) 25.00
____Tales of the Jedi: The Fall of the Sith Empire issues 1 – 5, each 4.00
____Tales of the Jedi: The Freedon Nadd Uprising issues 1 – 2, each 3.00
____Tales of the Jedi: The Golden Age of the Sith #0 ....6.00
____Tales of the Jedi: The Golden Age of the Sith issues 1 – 5, each 4.00
____Tales of the Jedi: The Sith War issues 1 – 6, each 4.00
____Underworld: The Yavin Vassilika issues 1 – 5, each 3.00
____Union issues 1 – 4 [CBD38], each 4.00
____Vader's Quest issues 1 – 4 [CBD39], each..........3.00
____X-Wing Rogue Squadron #1/2 Movie Ed. 18.00
____X-Wing Rogue Squadron #1/2 Platinum ed. 14.00
____X-Wing Rogue Squadron #1/2 mail-away 10.00
____X-Wing Rogue Squadron (cereal give-away) 4.00
____X-Wing Rogue Squadron issues 1 – 35 [CBD40], each 8.00

Graphic novels.

____Jango Fett..........6.00
____Zam Wesell 6.00

Trade paperbacks.

____A Long Time Ago ... #1 – #7, each 30.00
____A New Hope (reprints Marvel Comics 1 – 3) 12.00
____A New Hope (reprints Marvel Comics 4 – 6) 12.00
____A New Hope: Special Edition..........10.00
____Boba Fett: Death, Lies, and Trechery 14.00
____Boba Fett: Enemy of the Empire (reprints issues 1 – 4) 12.00
____Bounty Hunters 13.00
____Chewbacca 13.00
____Classic Star Wars..........16.00
____Classic Star Wars, The Early Adventures (reprints issues 1 – 9) 17.00
____Classic Star Wars, The Rebel Storm 16.00
____Clone Wars (reprints issues 1 – 6) with 2 Gentle Giant mini bust-ups including exclusive amber Chewbacca 25.00
____Clone Wars volume 1 – 9, each..........15.00
____Crimson Empire (reprints issues 1 – 6) 18.00
____Crimson Empire II Council of Blood 18.00
____Dark Empire 22.00
____Dark Empire II (reprints issues 1 – 6) 18.00
____Dark Empire II, 2nd edition 20.00
____Dark Empire, 2nd printing 18.00
____Dark Force Rising (reprints issues 1 – 6)..........18.00
____Darth Maul 13.00
____Droids (reprints issues 1 – 6, plus Dark Horse and Star Wars Galaxy Magazine stories) 18.00
____Droids: 2nd Series (reprints issues 1 – 8)..........8.00
____Droids: Rebellion 16.00
____El Imperio Volumen 1 ....15.00
____Emissaries to Malastare..........16.00
____Empire's End (reprints issues 1 – 2) 6.00
____Empire 13.00
____Empire Strikes Back (reprints Marvel Comics 39 – 41)..........12.00
____Empire Strikes Back (reprints Marvel Comics 42 – 44)..........12.00
____Empire Strikes Back: Special Edition 10.00
____Empire Vol. 1 (reprints issues 1 – 6) with Gentle Giant Darth Vader bust-up..........25.00
____Empire vol. 1 – 6, each 18.00
____Episode I: Adventures (reprints short stories 1 – 4)..........13.00
____Episode I, The Phantom Menace..........14.00
____Episode III, Revenge of the Sith 14.00
____Han Solo at Stars' End..........16.00
____Heir to the Empire (reprints issues 1 – 6)..........20.00
____Honor and Duty 18.00
____Jabba the Hutt: The Art of the Deal..........10.00
____Jango Fett Open Season..........14.00
____Jedi Academy: Leviathan (reprints issues 1 – 4)..........12.00
____Jedi Council: Acts of War..........13.00
____La Guerra De Los Clones Adventuras vol. 1 ......15.00
____La Guerra De Los Clones: La Defensa de Kamino 15.00
____Last Command (reprints issues 1 – 6) 15.00
____Mandatory Retirement 13.00
____Mara Jade: By The Empreror's Hand (reprints issues 1 – 6) 13.00
____Outlander – The Exile of Sharad Hett 15.00
____Return of the Jedi (reprints Marvel Comics issues 1 – 2)..........10.00
____Return of the Jedi (reprints Marvel Comics issues 3 – 4)..........10.00
____Return of the Jedi: Special Edition 10.00
____Riteof Passage 15.00
____Shadows of the Empire (reprints 1 – 6) 18.00
____Splinter of the Mind's Eye (reprints 1 – 4) 15.00
____Star Wars Trilogy Boxed Set (comic book adaptation) 28.00

CBM01 #1 | CBM02 #6 | CBM03 #6 | CBM04 #8 | CBM05 #10 | CBM06 #4 | CBM07 #1 | CBM08 #2 | CBM09 #3

CBM10 #1 | CBM11 #2 | CBM12 #3 | CBM13 #4 | CBM14 #5 | CBM15 #6 | CBM16 #7 | CBM17 #8 | CBM18 #9 | CBM19 #10

CBM20 #2 | CBM21 #17 | CBM22 #78 | CBM23 #94 | CBM24 #97 | CBM25 #101 | CBM26 #106 | CBM27 #109 | CBM28 #112

CBM29 #115	CBM30 #119	CBM31 #124	CBM32 #132	CBM33 #139	CBM34 #140	CBM35 #150	CBM36 #154	CBM37 #164

CBM38 #166	CBM39 #170	CBM40 #1	CBM41 #9	CBM42 #18	CBM43 #21	CBM44 #25	CBM45 #53	CBM46 #111

____Star Wars, Prelude to Rebellion (reprints issues 1 – 6)...15.00
____Star Wars: Infinities – A New Hope 13.00
____Star Wars: Tales, Vol. 1 – 5, each 20.00
____Tag and Bink...18.00
____Tales of the Jedi – Redemption 15.00
____Tales of the Jedi (reprints issues 1 – 5) 16.00
____Tales of the Jedi: Dark Lords of the Sith Book 1 (reprints issues 1 – 6) 18.00
____Tales of the Jedi: The Fall of the Sith Empire (reprints issues 1 – 6) 18.00
____Tales of the Jedi: The Freedon Nadd Uprising (reprints issues 1 – 2) 6.00
____Tales of the Jedi: The Golden Age of the Sith (reprints issues 1 – 5) 18.00
____Tales of the Jedi: The Sith War 18.00
____The Stark Hyperspace War 15.00
____Twilight 13.00
____Underworld 15.00
____Union (reprints issues 1 – 4)............................14.00
____X-Wing Rogue Squadron Omnibus Vol. 1 ....20.00
____X-Wing Rogue Squadron Omnibus Vol. 2 ....20.00
____X-Wing Rogue Squadron, Battleground Tatooine 12.00
____X-Wing Rogue Squadron, In the Empire's Service (reprints issues 1 – 4) 12.00
____X-Wing Rogue Squadron, The Phantom Affair (reprints issues 1 – 4) 12.00
____X-Wing Rogue Squadron, Warrior Princess 14.00
____Infinities Empire Strikes Back 14.00
____Infinities Return of the Jedi 14.00
____Infinities Star Wars (reprints issues 1 – 4) with Gentle Giant Stormtrooper bust-up..................25.00

Comic Books: Marvel

Marvel Comics
____3-Pack, Star Wars issues 7 – 9, reprints 19.00
____4-Pack, Return of the Jedi issues 1 – 4 ....26.00

____Droids issues 1 – 8 [CBM01 – CMB02], each 7.00
____Ewoks issues 1 – 14 [CBM03 – CBM05], each..10.00

____Marvel Age #10, Star Wars cover.........................7.00
____Marvel Movie Showcase #1, Star Wars (reprints of SW issues 1 – 6)..6.00
____Return of the Jedi issues 1 – 4 [CBM06], each 8.00
____Star Wars annuals #1 – #3 [CBM07 – CBM09], each 15.00
____Star Wars triple comic, any issue, each...............3.50

Star Wars Special Edition, oversized.
____Issues 1 – 2, each...9.00

Star Wars.
____#1, July 1977, 35 cent cover with barcode......330.00
____Issue 1 [CBM10]...62.00
____Issues 2 – 6 [CBM11-CBM15], each 24.00
____Issues 7 – 38 [CBM16-CBM19], each 17.00
____Issues 39 – 44 (ESB), each 22.00
____Issues 45 – 67, each 16.00
____Issue 68 (Origin: Boba Fett).............................34.00
____Issues 69 – 80, each..8.00
____Issues 81 – 106, each..6.00
____Issue 107 ....24.00

Marvel Comics, UK
____Star Wars Weekly Summer Special 4.00

Star Wars Weekly.
____Issue 1...55.00
____Issues 2 – 20 [CBM20-CBM21], each 20.00
____Issues 21 – 35, each 10.00
____Issues 36 – 50, each 5.00
____Issues 51 – 117 [CBM22-CBM29], each 2.50

Empire Strikes Back Weekly.
____Issues 118 – 139 [CBM30-CBM33], each 2.50

Empire Strikes Back Monthly.
____Issues 140 – 158 [CBM34-CBM36], each 2.50

Star Wars Monthly.
____Issues 159 – 171 [CBM37-CBM39], each 2.50

Return of the Jedi Weekly.
____Issues 1 – 155 [CBM40-CBM46], each 5.00

Computers

Alienware
____Darkside design [P2C01] 1,565.00
____Lightside design [P2C02]..........................1,565.00

Computers: Dust Covers

World Wide Licenses Ltd.
____Darth Maul, for monitor and keyboard [DCC01] 16.00

Computers: Mice

____Anakin Skywalker, sculpted [CM01]...................35.00
____EPII with Anakin / Vader mousepad 10.00

American Covers
3D sculpted mice.
____C-3PO [CM02] 35.00
____Darth Vader [CM03].......................................35.00
____Stormtrooper [CM04]......................................35.00

World Wide Licenses Ltd.
____Anakin Skywalker [CM05]................................11.00
____Darth Maul [CM06]...16.00
____Jar Jar Binks [CM07] 12.00

P2C01 right / left

P2C02 right / left	DCC01	CM01	CM02	CM03	CM04

CM05	CM06	CM07	CM08	CM09	CM10	CM11	CM12

Computers: Mice

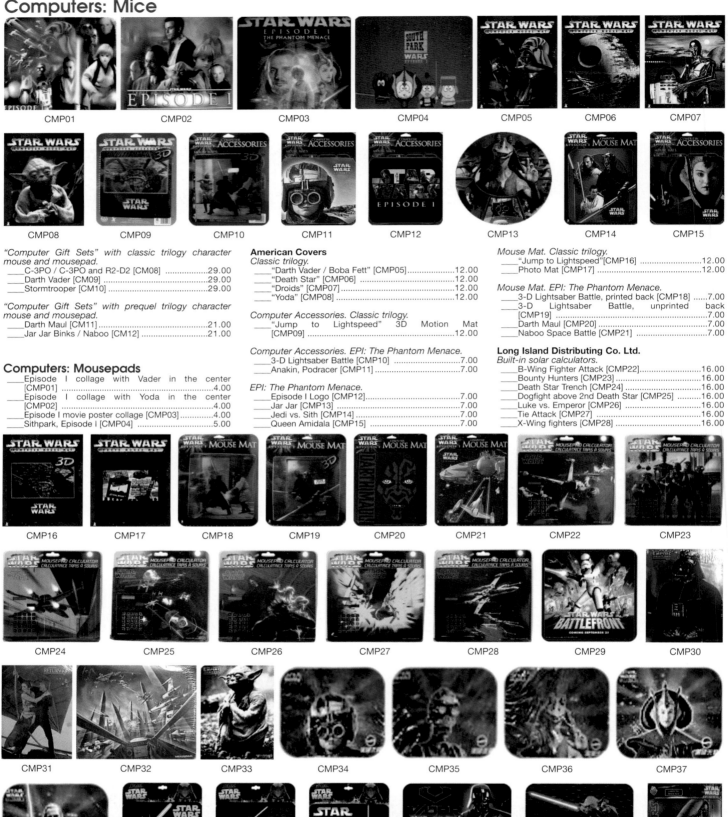

CMP01 CMP02 CMP03 CMP04 CMP05 CMP06 CMP07

CMP08 CMP09 CMP10 CMP11 CMP12 CMP13 CMP14 CMP15

"Computer Gift Sets" with classic trilogy character mouse and mousepad.
____C-3PO / C-3PO and R2-D2 [CM08] 29.00
____Darth Vader [CM09] 29.00
____Stormtrooper [CM10] 29.00

"Computer Gift Sets" with prequel trilogy character mouse and mousepad.
____Darth Maul [CM11] 21.00
____Jar Jar Binks / Naboo [CM12] 21.00

Computers: Mousepads
____Episode I collage with Vader in the center [CMP01] 4.00
____Episode I collage with Yoda in the center [CMP02] 4.00
____Episode I movie poster collage [CMP03].............4.00
____Sithpark, Episode I [CMP04] 5.00

American Covers
Classic trilogy.
____"Darth Vader / Boba Fett" [CMP05]...................12.00
____"Death Star" [CMP06] 12.00
____"Droids" [CMP07]...12.00
____"Yoda" [CMP08] 12.00

Computer Accessories. Classic trilogy.
____"Jump to Lightspeed" 3D Motion Mat [CMP09] 12.00

Computer Accessories. EPI: The Phantom Menace.
____3-D Lightsaber Battle [CMP10] 7.00
____Anakin, Podracer [CMP11] 7.00

EPI: The Phantom Menace.
____Episode I Logo [CMP12].......................................7.00
____Jar Jar [CMP13] 7.00
____Jedi vs. Sith [CMP14] 7.00
____Queen Amidala [CMP15] 7.00

Mouse Mat. Classic trilogy.
____"Jump to Lightspeed"[CMP16] 12.00
____Photo Mat [CMP17] 12.00

Mouse Mat. EPI: The Phantom Menace.
____3-D Lightsaber Battle, printed back [CMP18] 7.00
____3-D Lightsaber Battle, unprinted back [CMP19] 7.00
____Darth Maul [CMP20] 7.00
____Naboo Space Battle [CMP21] 7.00

Long Island Distributing Co. Ltd.
Built-in solar calculators.
____B-Wing Fighter Attack [CMP22]...........................16.00
____Bounty Hunters [CMP23] 16.00
____Death Star Trench [CMP24] 16.00
____Dogfight above 2nd Death Star [CMP25] 16.00
____Luke vs. Emperor [CMP26] 16.00
____Tie Attack [CMP27] 16.00
____X-Wing fighters [CMP28] 16.00

CMP16 CMP17 CMP18 CMP19 CMP20 CMP21 CMP22 CMP23

CMP24 CMP25 CMP26 CMP27 CMP28 CMP29 CMP30

CMP31 CMP32 CMP33 CMP34 CMP35 CMP36 CMP37

CMP38 CMP39 mousepad 1 / mousepad 2 CMP40 CMP41 CMP42 CMP43

CS01	CS02	CS03	CS04	CS05	CS06	CS07	CS08

LucasArts
____Battlefront, promo [CMP29] 5.00
____Star Wars Galaxies, 8" round 8.00

Mousetrak
____Bounty Hunters 14.00
____C-3PO and R2-D2 ....14.00
____Dark Forces 14.00
____Darth Vader [CMP30] 14.00
____Leia and Luke on Jabba's sail barge [CMP31] 14.00
____Millennium Falcon 14.00
____Rebel Assault [CMP32] 14.00
____Yoda [CMP33] 14.00

Pepsi Cola, Singapore
Episode I, lenticular.
____Anakin Skywalker [CMP34] 10.00
____C-3PO [CMP35] 10.00
____Jar Jar Binks [CMP36] 10.00
____Queen Amidala [CMP37] 10.00
____Qui-Gon Jinn [CMP38] 10.00

Rawcliffe
Anime style characters.
____2-pack Darth Vader and Yoda [CMP39] 20.00
____Luke and Leia [CMP40] 10.00

EPIII:ROTS.
____Darth Vader [CMP41] 10.00
____Yoda [CMP42] 10.00

starwars.com
In 2003 the official Star Wars site offered 13 themed galleries of approximately 12 images in each gallery. Fans could order the images from an online merchandiser on a variety of products. Considering the number of galleries and images available, there are well over one hundred varieties of mouse pads that could have been made.

The galleries were comprised of images of Bounty Hunters, Clone Wars, Creatures, Droids, Holiday Art, Jedi, Logos and Emblems, Padme, Poster Art, Princess Leia, Rebels, Sith, and vehicles.
____Bounty Hunters gallery, each 11.00
____Clone Wars gallery, each 11.00
____Creatures gallery, each..................................11.00
____Droids gallery, each.......................................11.00
____Holiday Art gallery 11.00
____Jedi gallery 11.00
____Logos gallery 11.00
____Padme gallery...11.00
____Poster Art gallery 11.00
____Princess Leia gallery 11.00
____Rebels gallery 11.00
____Sith gallery 11.00
____Vehicles gallery..11.00

World Wide Licenses Ltd.
____Battle Droid with Trade Federation tank [CMP43] 9.00
____Darth Maul 9.00

Computers: Software

America On-Line
____Episode II CD: footage, images, sound tracks, AOL client [CS01] 18.00
____Episode III CD: games, AOL client 9.0 ....15.00

USB01	USB02	USB03	USB04

LucasArts
____Episode I Insider's Guide [CS02] 17.00
____Star Wars: Behind the Magic for Win95/98 ....35.00
____Star Wars: Behind the Magic for Win95/98 (French Version) [CS03] 17.00

Pepsi Cola
____Essential Guide to Star Wars: Episode I, limited edition [CS04]...14.00

Simon and Schuster Interactive
____SW Trilogy Moviebook software on CD-ROM for Macintosh...40.00
____SW Trilogy Moviebook software on CD-ROM for Windows...40.00

SLC Interactive
____The Art of Drew Struzan multimedia [CS05] 45.00

Sound Source Interactive
____Star Wars Audio Clips [CS06] 35.00
____Star Wars Audio Clips (special offer) 15.00
____Star Wars Trilogy Entertainment Utility, Limited Edition [CS07] 25.00
____Star Wars Visual Clips (Macintosh Only) [CS08]...45.00
____Star Wars Visual Clips add-on (special offer) 20.00

Computers: USB Drives

256MB brushed steel.
____C-3PO...50.00
____Darth Vader...50.00
____Jedi...50.00
____R2-D2...50.00

Computers: Wrist Rest

American Covers
____Jedi vs. Sith [WR01].......................................12.00
____Podrace [WR02]..12.00
____Scenes from ESB [WR03] 14.00

Condoms

____Star Condoms, parody....................................13.00

Confetti

Party Express
____Star Wars [C1F01]..5.00

WR01

WR02

WR03

Construction Paper

Stuart Hall
____Biker Scout pad [PPH01] 17.00

Containers: Figural

Applause
____Darth Maul [AFC01] 18.00
____R2-D2 [AFC02] 18.00

Kelloggs
Mail-in "cookie jar" premiums.
____C-3PO [AFC03] 10.00
____Darth Vader [AFC04] 10.00
____R2-D2 [AFC05] 10.00

Cookie Jars

Cards, Inc.
____Boba Fett [CJ01] 75.00
____C-3PO [CJ02]...75.00
____Chewbacca [CJ03]..75.00
____Clone Shock Trooper [CJ04] 75.00
____Clone Special Ops Trooper [CJ05] 75.00
____Clone Trooper [CJ06] 75.00
____Clone Trooper Commando [CJ07] 75.00
____Darth Maul [CJ08] 75.00
____Darth Vader [CJ09] 75.00
____Death Star [CJ10] 75.00
____General Grievous [CJ11] 75.00
____R2-D2 [CJ12] 75.00
____Stormtrooper [CJ13].......................................75.00
____Yoda bust [CJ14] 75.00
____Yoda full [CJ15] 75.00

Crabby Onion
____Darth Vader, ceramic [CJ16] 45.00

Roman Ceramics
____C-3PO, ceramic figure [CJ17] 275.00
____R2-D2, ceramic figure [CJ18] 245.00

Sigma
____Darth Vader and Droids, ceramic 2-sided hexagonal [CJ19]..125.00

Star Jars
____Ben Kenobi [CJ20]...200.00

CND01	C1F01	PPH01	AFC01	AFC02	AFC03	AFC04 lid on / lid off	AFC05

Cookie Jars

CJ01 CJ02 CJ03 CJ04 CJ05 CJ06 CJ07 CJ08

CJ09 CJ10 CJ11 CJ12 CJ13 CJ14 CJ15 CJ16

CJ17 CJ18 CJ19 front / rear CJ20 CJ21 CJ22 CJ23

CJ24 CJ25 CO01 CO02 CO03 CO04 CO05 CO06

____C-3PO [CJ21]..200.00
____Chewbacca [CJ22] 200.00
____Jabba the Hutt [CJ23] 275.00
____Princess Leia [CJ24] 200.00
____Wicket the Ewok [CJ25] 275.00

____R2-D2 cooler SE [CO05] 250.00
____R2-D2 cooler ROTS [CO06] 300.00

Pepsi Cola, Japan
____R2-D2 cooler 85.00

____Chewbacca, glow-in-dark dome round "glows" sticker [CK07]..18.00
____Darth Vader [CK08] 24.00
____Darth Vader and Luke Skywalker Duel [CK09]..18.00
____Darth Vader, glow-in-dark dome [CK10] 18.00
____Darth Vader, helmet and shoulders [CK11] 24.00
____Ewok Hut [CK12] 18.00
____Jabba's Palace [CK13] 18.00
____Jabba the Hutt [CK14] 18.00
____Luke on Tauntaun [CK15]...............................24.00
____Luke on Tauntaun, glow-in-dark dome [CK16]..18.00
____Max Rebo Band [CK17] 18.00
____Millennium Falcon "May The Force Be With You"..23.00
____Paploo, Wicket, C-3PO and Artoo-Detoo [CK18]..18.00
____Star Wars logo, Millennium Falcon, Tie Fighters, X-Wing [CK19] 22.00

Coolers

Bluebird
____Cool Bag, Darth Vader art [CO01] 21.00
____Cool Bag, stormtrooper art [CO02] 18.00

Kooler Kraft
____R2-D2, approx 2.5' tall, given away as Pepsi promotion [CO03] 75.00

Pepsi Cola
____MMT with Battle Droid can holders [CO04] 315.00

Cork Boards

Manton Cork
____AT-AT, glow-in-dark dome [CK01] 18.00
____Boba Fett, Darth Vader, Stormtroopers [CK02]..26.00
____C-3PO and R2-D2, 2-piece set [CK03] 28.00
____C-3PO and R2-D2, glow-in-dark dome [CK04]..18.00
____C-3PO, Chewbacca, Han, Leia, Luke, R2-D2 [CK05]..24.00
____Chewbacca, glow-in-dark dome [CK06] 18.00

CK01 CK02 CK03 CK04 CK05 CK06 CK07 CK08 CK09

CK10 CK11 CK12 CK13 CK14 CK15 CK16 CK17

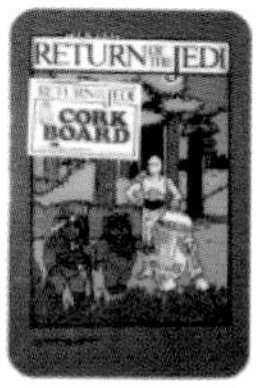
CK18

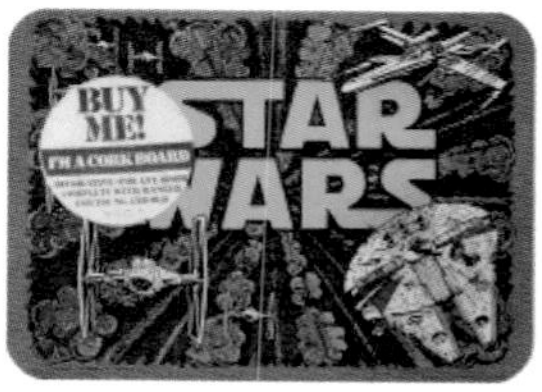
CK19

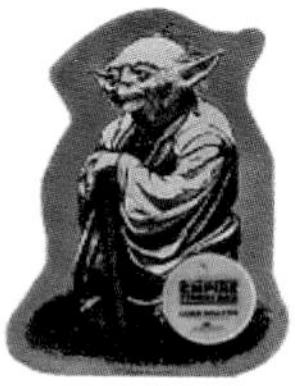
CK20

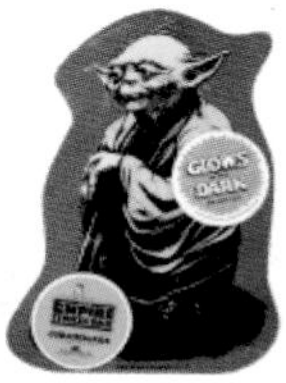
CK21

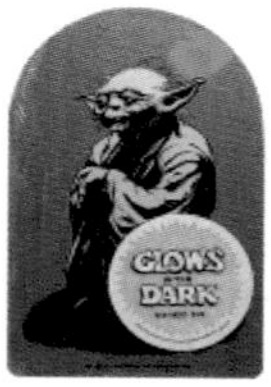
CK22

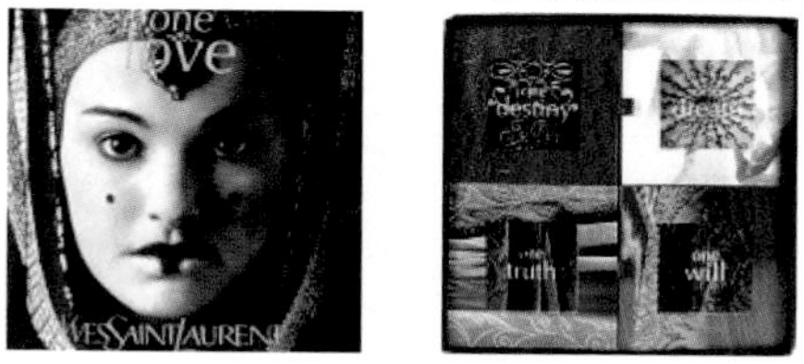
CSC01 cover and open

____Yoda [CK20] 24.00
____Yoda, glow-in-dark [CK21]...................................25.00
____Yoda, glow-in-dark dome [CK22].........................18.00

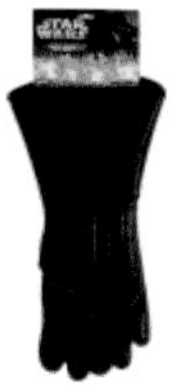
CTA01

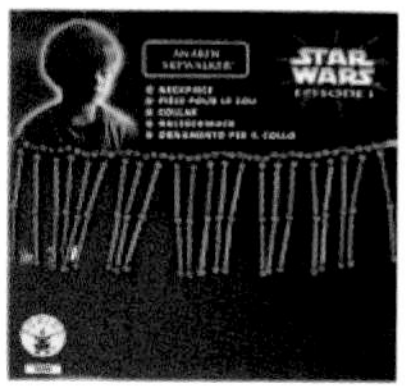
CTA02

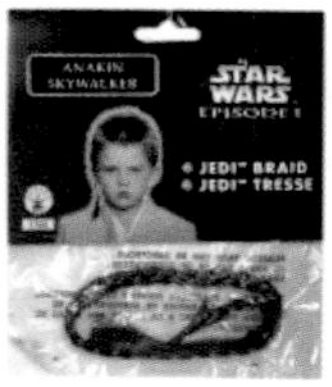
CTA03

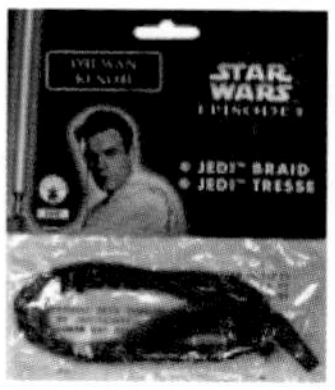
CTA04

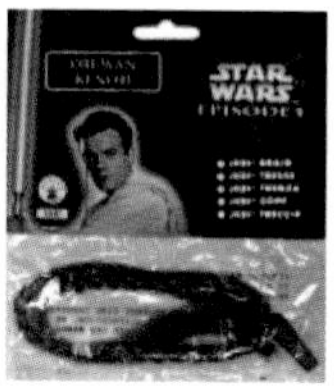
CTA05

Cosmetics

Yves Saint Laurent
____One Love, Queen Amidala [CSC01] 165.00

Costume Accessories

Rubies
____Anakin glove [CTA01] 15.00
____Anakin Skywalker neckpiece [CTA02] 4.00
____Jedi Braid, Anakin Skywalker's, clip-on [CTA03] 3.00
____Jedi Braid, Obi-Wan Kenobi's, clip-on [CTA04] 3.00
____Queen Amidala super deluxe headpiece with attached wig and braids 48.00

Canada. Jedi braids, clip-on.
____Anakin Skywalker 3.00
____Obi-Wan Kenobi [CTA05] 3.00

Costumes

Acamas
____C-3PO..28.00
____Chewbacca 28.00
____Darth Vader..28.00
____Gamorrean Guard 28.00
____Klattu 28.00
____Luke Skywalker 28.00
____Princess Leia 28.00
____Stormtrooper 28.00
____Wicket...28.00
____Yoda 28.00

Ben Cooper
____Admiral Ackbar, Revenge......................................85.00
____Admiral Ackbar, ROTJ [CT01] 26.00
____Boba Fett, ESB [CT02]..35.00
____Boba Fett, ROTJ 35.00
____C-3PO (Golden Robot), ESB 16.00
____C-3PO (Golden Robot), SW [CT03] 25.00
____Chewbacca, ESB [CT04] 20.00
____Chewbacca, ROTJ 30.00
____Chewbacca, SW [CT05] 25.00
____Gamorrean Guard, Revenge 85.00
____Gamorrean Guard, ROTJ [CT06] 28.00
____Klattu, Revenge 85.00
____Klattu, ROTJ 25.00
____Lord Darth Vader, ESB 20.00
____Lord Darth Vader, ROTJ 30.00
____Lord Darth Vader, SW [CT07] 25.00
____Luke Skywalker (X-Wing Pilot), ESB [CT08] 18.00
____Luke Skywalker (X-Wing Pilot), ROTJ 30.00
____Luke Skywalker (X-Wing Pilot), SW 20.00
____Luke Skywalker, ESB 16.00
____Luke Skywalker, ROTJ 30.00
____Luke Skywalker, SW [CT09] 25.00
____Princess Leia, ESB [CT10] 35.00
____Princess Leia, ROTJ..30.00
____Princess Leia, SW [CT11]......................................35.00
____R2-D2, ESB 20.00
____R2-D2, ROTJ 35.00
____R2-D2, SW [CT12] 30.00
____Stormtrooper, ESB [CT13] 25.00
____Stormtrooper, ROTJ..28.00
____Stormtrooper, SW [CT14]......................................23.00
____Wicket, Revenge 95.00
____Wicket, ROTJ [CT15] 30.00
____Wicket, ROTJ tots [CT16] 70.00
____Yoda, ESB [CT17]..35.00
____Yoda, ROTJ 35.00

3-piece disguise kits.
____Chewbacca, SW [CT18] 22.00

Fun suits.
____Chewbacca 40.00
____Darth Vader..40.00

Cheryl Playthings Ltd.
____C-3PO [2:257]..35.00

Croner Toys
____Stormtrooper, childrens size [2:257] 35.00

Len Hunter Trading
____Darth Vader mask, vest, cape, lightsaber 7.00

Rubies
____C-3PO Adult: Mask and jumpsuit 65.00
____C-3PO Child Box Set: 3/4 mask and jumpsuit [CT19] 48.00
____C-3PO Child Deluxe: Over-the-head mask and jumpsuit w/attached boot tops 78.00
____C-3PO Child: PVC mask and jumpsuit 25.00
____Darth Vader Adult: Mask, cape and jumpsuit 74.00
____Darth Vader Child Better Box Set: 3/4 mask, cape, jumpsuit and lightsaber [CT20] 57.00
____Darth Vader Child Box Set: PVC mask, jumpsuit and lightsaber 44.00
____Darth Vader Child Set: 3/4 mask, cape, jumpsuit and cape 40.00
____Darth Vader Child: PVC mask and jumpsuit 26.00
____Darth Vader Deluxe: Overhead mask, cape, chestpiece and jumpsuit with attached boottops 100.00
____Darth Vader: cape and chest armor, mask, lightsaber...20.00
____Stormtrooper Boxed Set: 3/4 mask and jumpsuit [CT21] 46.00
____Yoda Deluxe: Mask, robe and waist sash 55.00

Classic trilogy.
____C-3PO childrens size 12.00
____C-3PO, adult 55.00
____C-3PO, children's deluxe 35.00
____Chewbacca, adult...70.00
____Chewbacca, children's deluxe 35.00
____Chewbacca, childrens size 12.00
____Darth Vader, adult..60.00
____Darth Vader, children's deluxe [2:257] 35.00
____Darth Vader, childrens size..................................12.00
____Jabba the Hutt, children's deluxe 35.00
____Princess Leia, adult [2:257] 45.00
____Princess Leia, children's deluxe..........................25.00
____Stormtrooper, adult 55.00
____Stormtrooper, children's deluxe [2:257] 40.00
____Stormtrooper, childrens size [2:257] 12.00
____Tusken Raider, children's deluxe 40.00
____Yoda, adult 60.00
____Yoda, children's deluxe 25.00

Episode I: The Phantom Menace.
Anakin Skywalker.
____Actionwear: PVC mask and jumpsuit 25.00

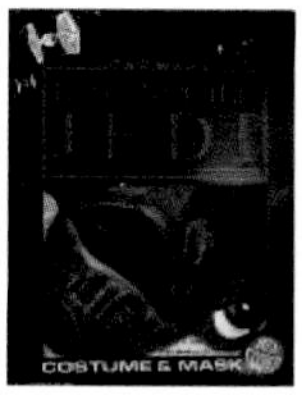
CT01

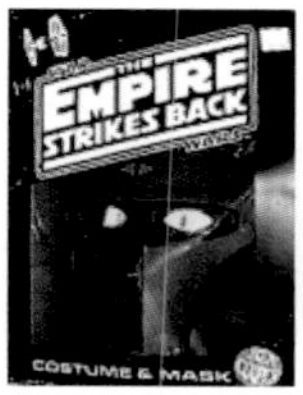
CT02

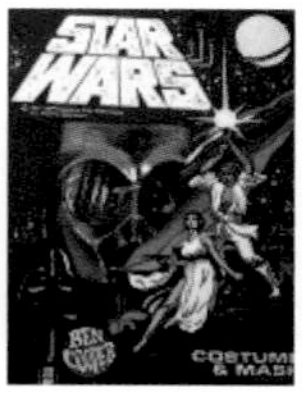
CT03

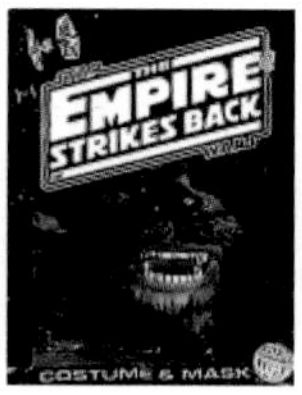
CT04

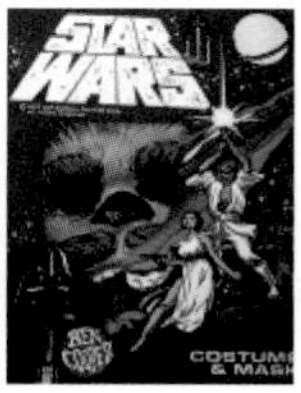
CT05

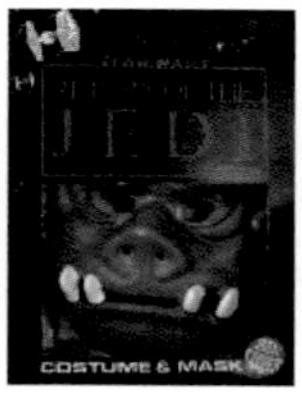
CT06

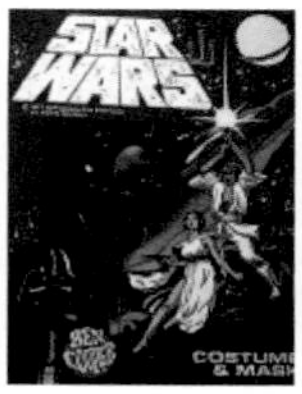
CT07

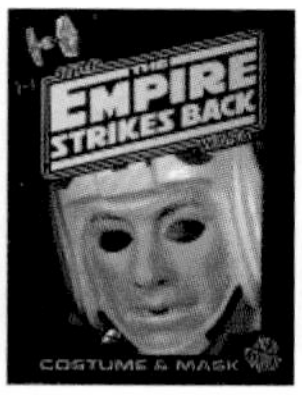
CT08

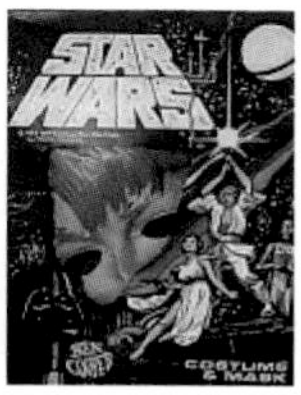
CT09

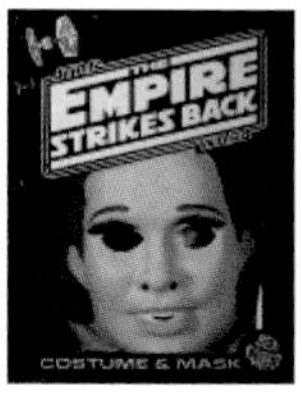
CT10

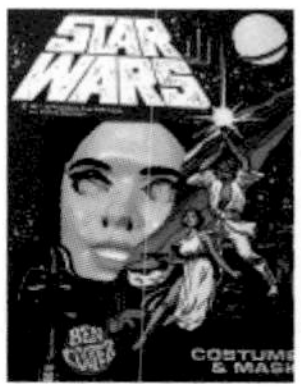
CT11

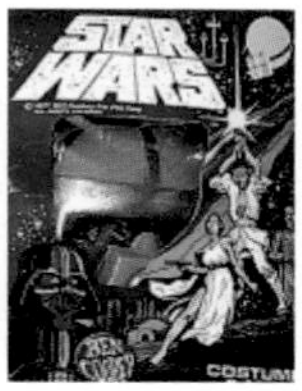
CT12

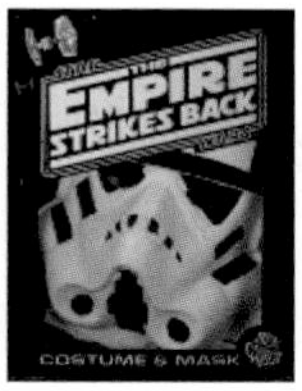
CT13

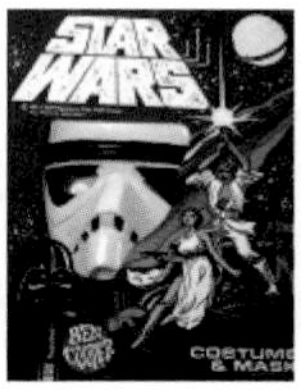
CT14

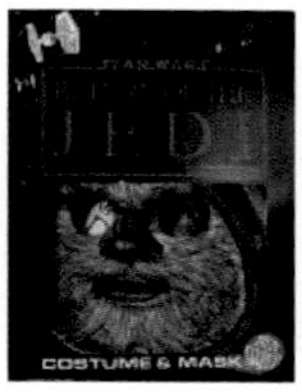
CT15

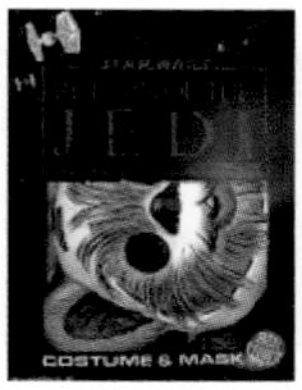
CT16

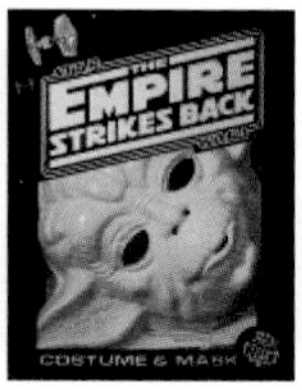
CT17

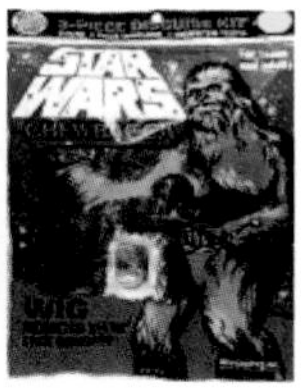
CT18

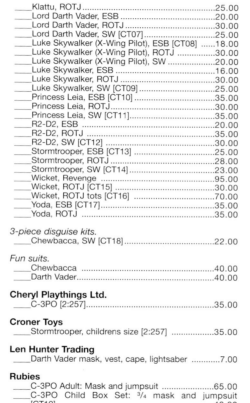

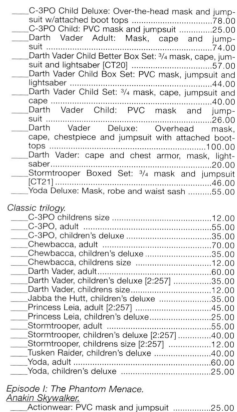

Costumes

CT19

CT20

CT21

CT22

CT23

CT24

CT25

CT26

CT27

CT28

CT29

CT30

CT31

CT32

CT33

CT34

CT35

CT36

CT37

CT38

____Deluxe actionwear: PVC helmet, tunic, pants with attached boot tops, belt....................................38.00
____Jedi Apprentice childrens deluxe: tunic, shirt, pants with attached boot tops, printed vinyl belt 40.00
____Jedi Apprentice childrens super deluxe: tunic, shirt, pants with attached boot tops, sash, rubber 3D belt 60.00
____Jedi Apprentice childrens: tunic, pants with attached boot tops 20.00
____Podrace childrens deluxe: PVC headpiece, tunic, pants with attached boot tops, printed vinyl belt 40.00
____Podrace children's super deluxe: vinyl headpiece, tunic, pants with attached boot tops, belt.........60.00
____Podrace childrens: PVC headpiece, tunic, pants with attached boot tops..20.00

Darth Maul.
____Actionwear deluxe: PVC mask, hooded tunic, pants with attached boot tops, molded 3D rubber belt 38.00
____Actionwear: PVC mask and jumpsuit [CT22]......25.00
____Adult deluxe: mask, hooded tunic, pants with attached boot tops, rubber 3D belt 50.00
____Adult super deluxe: latex mask, hooded tunic, pants with attached boot tops, sashes, rubber 3D belt 80.00
____Adult: PVC mask, hooded tunic, pants with attached boot tops, belt [CT23] 25.00
____Childrens blister card costume kit: PVC mask, lightsaber, hooded cloak, belt 14.00
____Childrens boxed costume kit: PVC mask, lightsaber, hooded cloak, belt [CT24] 16.00
____Childrens deluxe: mask, hooded tunic, pants with attached boot tops, belt [2:257].........................45.00
____Childrens super deluxe: vinyl 3/4 mask, hooded tunic, pants with attached boot tops, sashes, rubber 3D belt 75.00
____Childrens: PVC mask, hooded tunic, pants with attached boot tops..20.00

Jar Jar Binks.
____Actionwear: PVC mask and jumpsuit 25.00
____Adult: PVC mask, tunic, pants...........................30.00
____Childrens deluxe: PVC mask, jumpsuit with attached shoe covers 40.00
____Childrens: PVC mask, tunic, pants 20.00
____Deluxe actionwear: PVC mask, tunic, pants [CT25] 38.00

Jedi robe.
____Adult 20.00
____Adult deluxe 30.00
____Children's 15.00
____Children's deluxe 25.00

Obi-Wan Kenobi.
____Actionwear: PVC mask and jumpsuit 25.00
____Adult deluxe: tunic, shirt, pants with attached boot tops, sash, rubber 3D belt 60.00
____Adult: tunic, pants with attached boot tops, belt 35.00
____Children's blister card costume kit: PVC mask, lightsaber, hooded cloak, belt 14.00
____Children's boxed costume kit: PVC mask, lightsaber, hooded cloak, belt 16.00
____Children's deluxe: tunic, shirt, pants with attached boot tops, printed vinyl belt 40.00
____Children's super deluxe: tunic, shirt, pants with attached boot tops, sash, rubber 3D belt 60.00
____Children's: tunic, pants with attached boot tops...20.00
____Deluxe actionwear: tunic, pants with attached boot tops, molded 3D rubber belt 38.00

Queen Amidala.
____Actionwear: PVC mask and dress 25.00
____Adult deluxe: PVC headpiece, dress 40.00
____Adult supreme: headpiece, velvet dress, lights 80.00
____Adult: PVC headpiece, dress 20.00
____Children's deluxe: PVC headpiece, dress [2:257]...35.00
____Children's super deluxe: headpiece, dress, lights 55.00
____Children's supreme: headpiece, velvet dress, lights 70.00
____Children's: PVC headpiece, dress 20.00
____Deluxe actionwear: PVC headpiece, dress, make-up kit [CT26] 38.00

Qui-Gon Jinn.
____Actionwear: PVC mask and jumpsuit 25.00
____Adult deluxe: tunic, shirt, pants with attached boot tops, sash, rubber 3D belt 60.00
____Adult: tunic, pants with attached boot tops, belt 35.00
____Children's blister card costume kit: PVC mask, lightsaber, hooded cloak, belt 14.00
____Children's boxed costume kit: PVC mask, lightsaber, hooded cloak, belt 16.00
____Children's deluxe: tunic, shirt, pants with attached boot tops, printed vinyl belt 40.00
____Children's super deluxe: tunic, shirt, pants with attached boot tops, sash, rubber 3D belt 60.00
____Children's: tunic, pants with attached boot tops...20.00
____Deluxe actionwear: tunic, pants with attached boot tops, molded 3D rubber belt 38.00

Episode II: Attack of the Clones.

Amidala.
____Mask, blaster and shawl [CT27] 20.00

Anakin Skywalker.
____Basic boxed: PVC mask and jumpsuit 26.00
____Basic: PVC mask and jumpsuit 24.00
____Boxed kit: PVC mask, hooded cloak, belt and lightsaber [CT28] 38.00
____Boxed set: Tunic pants with attached boot tops and lightsaber 56.00
____Costume kit: hooded cloak, belt, mask and light saber [CT29] 32.00
____Deluxe: Tunic pants with attached boot tops [2:257]...36.00
____Deluxe: Tunic with attached shirt, belt and pants with attached boot tops...78.00
____Deluxe: Tunic with attached shirt, pants with attached boot tops and belt 52.00

Clone Trooper.
____Adult: Jumpsuit with attached boot tops and mask 70.00
____Adult deluxe Adult: Jumpsuit with armor, gloves and 2-piece helmet...100.00
____Boxed: Jumpsuit and PVC mask........................26.00
____Deluxe: Jumpsuit with armor, gloves and helmet..82.00
____Large boxed set: Jumpsuit, mask and blaster [CT30] 45.00
____Jumpsuit and mask 36.00

Count Dooku.
____Adult basic: Cloak with clasp.............................86.00
____Boxed: Cloak with clasp, belt and light saber...38.00
____Cloak with clasp, belt, light saber [CT31] 32.00

Jango Fett.
____Adult ultra deluxe: 2-piece injection molded mask with eye piece, jumpsuit with latex molded body armor, detailed molded belt and Jango gloves 75.00
____Adult: Jumpsuit w/attached boot tops and mask 70.00
____Boxed: Mask, chestpiece and blaster 38.00
____Boxed basic: PVC mask and jumpsuit [CT32] 26.00
____Child: Mask, chestpiece and blaster [CT33] 32.00
____Deluxe: 2 Pc. PVC mask, jumpsuit with molded body armor and gloves 82.00
____Deluxe child: 2-piece PVC mask, jumpsuit with molded body armor, molded belt and gloves [2:257] 95.00
____Large boxed: PVC mask & jumpsuit, attached boot tops..56.00
____Jumpsuit and mask 24.00
____PVC mask and jumpsuit, attached boot tops [2:257]...36.00

Jedi Cloak.
____Child [CT34] 25.00

Jedi Knight.
____Adult Kit: Hooded Cloak, belt, Jedi braid and light saber [CT35] 44.00
____Boxed Set, Child: Tunic, pants w/attached boot tops and light saber [CT36] 56.00
____Boxed Set: Hooded Cloak, belt, Jedi braid and light saber [CT37] 38.00
____Boxed Set: Jumpsuit and PVC mask [CT38]......26.00
____Kit: Cloak, belt, braid and light saber [CT39] 32.00
____Shirt, pants w/attached boot tops and belt........70.00

Jedi Robe.
____Adult 40.00
____Adult Deluxe 70.00
____Child Deluxe 46.00

Mace Windu.
____Boxed set: Hooded Cloak, mask, belt and light saber [CT40] 38.00
____Boxed set: Jumpsuit and PVC mask [CT41] 26.00
____Deluxe: Shirt, pants w/attached boot tops 36.00
____Kit: Cloak, belt, mask and light saber [CT42] 32.00
____Kit: Jumpsuit and mask 24.00
____Large Boxed Set: Tunic, pants and light saber [CT43] 56.00

Obi-Wan Kenobi.
____Box Set: Hooded Cloak, mask, belt and light saber [CT44] 38.00
____Child: Tunic, pants, belt and boot tops [2:257]...33.00
____Kit: Cloak, belt, mask and light saber [CT45] 32.00
____Kit: Jumpsuit and mask 24.00
____Shirt, pants with attached boot tops 36.00

Padme Amidala.
____Adult Basic: Jumpsuit with attached boot tops..70.00
____Basic Boxed Costume: PVC Mask and jumpsuit [CT46] 26.00
____Basic Costume: PVC Mask and jumpsuit 24.00
____Boxed Costume Kit: Mask, blaster and shawl [CT47] 38.00
____Child Deluxe: Jumpsuit with attached boot tops, belt and shawl 73.00
____Deluxe Costume: Jumpsuit with attached boot tops, belt and shawl 82.00
____Jumpsuit with attached boot tops, belt and shawl 36.00
____Large boxed: Jumpsuit with attached boot tops, belt with separate gun and shawl [CT49] 56.00
____Mask, blaster and shawl [CT48] 32.00

Episode III: Revenge of the Sith.

Anakin Skywalker.
____Children's accessory kit 15.00
____Children's deluxe: tunic with attached shirt, pants with attached boot tops, and belt 40.00

CT39

CT40

CT41

CT42

CT43

CT44

CT45

CT46

CT47

CT48

CT49

CT50

CT51

CT52

CT53

CT54

CT55

MUK01

MUK02

MUK03

C-3PO.
____Children's deluxe: over-the-head mask and jumpsuit with attached boot tops 65.00

Chewbacca.
____Adult deluxe: fur body suit, high quality latex mask, sash, and pouch 100.00
____Adult supreme: bodysuit and mask covered with hand-layered multicolored fur, latex hands, bandoleer and pouch 650.00
____Children's deluxe: fur body suit, latex mask, sash and pouch 70.00

Clone Trooper.
____Adult deluxe: jumpsuit with EVA pieces and deluxe helmet...75.00
____Children's deluxe: jumpsuit with EVA body pieces and deluxe helmet 75.00

Count Dooku.
____Adult robe 50.00

Darth Vader.
____Adult deluxe: injection molded helmet and mask, cape, belt, jumpsuit with molded EVA collar, boot tops, and chest piece 80.00
____Adult supreme: jumpsuit with faux leather pants and sleeves, cape, injection molded pieces (collar, shoulder guards, boot tops, chest piece and belt), ABS mask and helmet set, gloves with gauntlets...1,250.00
____Children's accessory kit 15.00
____Children's deluxe: injection molded helmet and mask, cape, belt, jumpsuit with molded EVA collar, boot tops, and chest piece 50.00

Jango Fett.
____Adult deluxe: 2-piece PVC mask, jumpsuit with molded body armor, molded belt and gloves 75.00
____Children's deluxe: 2 piece PVC mask, jumpsuit with molded body armor, molded belt, and gloves....60.00

Jedi Knight.
____Children's deluxe: tunic with attached shirt, pants with attached boot tops and belt 40.00

Jedi Robe.
____Adult 50.00
____Childre's 35.00

Obi-Wan Kenobi.
____Children's deluxe: tunic with attached jacket, pants with attached boot tops and belt........................40.00

Padme Amidala.
____Children's deluxe: shawl, jumpsuit with attached boot tops and belt 30.00

Yoda.
____Children's deluxe 50.00

Pet costumes. Headpiece and jumpsuit.
____Darth Vader, cape with belt 25.00
____Princess Leia 25.00
____Princess Leia captive 25.00
____Yoda 25.00

ROTS.
____Count Dooku accessory kit [CT50] 25.00
____Darth Vader, boxed [CT51].................................30.00
____Darth Vader, child's mask and cape [CT52]........25.00
____Jedi accessory kit [CT53]....................................25.00
____Mace Windu, boxed [CT54] 30.00
____Obi-Wan accessory kit [CT55] 25.00
____Yoda's hands 20.00

Toddler fleece costumes. Sizes: Newborn (1 – 6 mos.), Infant (6 – 12 mos.) Headpiece and romper.
____Chewbacca with underleg snap enclosure and attached sash and belt 25.00
____Darth Vader with detachable cape and underleg snap enclosure 25.00
____Princess Leia with robe and attached belt 25.00
____Yoda with hooded robe 25.00

Costumes: Make-Up Kits

Rubies
____Darth Maul 7.00
____Darth Maul Deluxe [MUK01] 12.00
____Queen Amidala [MUK02] 7.00
____Queen Amidala w/Jewelry [MUK03] 12.00

Costumes: Masks and Helmets

____C-3PO [MA01]...7.00
____Chewbacca [MA02] 15.00
____Darth Vader [MA03] 20.00
____Darth Vader [MA04]...7.00
____Gamorrean Guard [MA05] 15.00
____Stormtrooper [MA06] 7.00

Altmann's Armor
____AT-AT Driver [MA07]..225.00
____Boba Fett [MA08]..225.00
____Darth Vader [MA09] 300.00
____Imperial Fleet Officer [MA10]...........................175.00
____Imperial Gunner [MA11]....................................225.00
____Imperial Scout Trooper [MA12] 250.00
____Imperial Stormtrooper [MA13]..........................225.00
____Rebel [MA14] 175.00
____Royal Guard [MA15] 200.00
____X-Wing Pilot [MA16]..250.00

Limited to 500, numbered.
____Darth Vader 575.00
____Stormtrooper 350.00

Ben Cooper
____Admiral Ackbar, adult [MA17] 9.00
____Admiral Ackbar, child [MA18] 7.00
____C-3PO [MA19]..5.00
____C-3PO, 1977 [MA20] 8.00
____Chewbacca, 1977 adult [MA21] 9.00
____Chewbacca, 1977 child [MA22] 7.00
____Chewbacca, adult [MA23] 8.00
____Chewbacca, children's [MA24] 5.00
____Darth Vader, mouth breather [MA25] 7.00
____Darth Vader, mouth breather smile [MA26] 7.00
____Darth Vader, nose breather [MA27] 9.00
____Gamorrean Guard [MA28]......................................9.00
____Klaatu, adult [MA29] 8.00
____Klaatu, child [MA30] 7.00
____Princess Leia, Hoth [MA31] 8.00
____Stormtrooper [MA32] 5.00
____Stormtrooper, 1977 [MA33] 8.00
____Tusken Raider, 1977 [MA34]..................................8.00
____Wicket, adult [MA35]...8.00
____Wicket, child [MA36]...8.00
____Yoda [MA37] 10.00

Cesar
____C-3PO...35.00

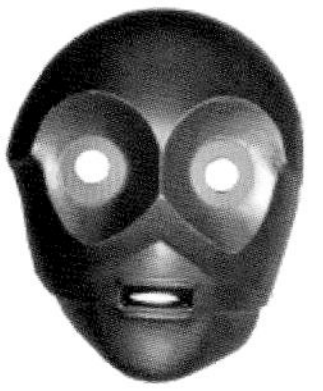

MA01

MA02

MA03

MA04

MA05

MA06

MA07

MA08

MA09

MA10

MA11

MA12

MA13

MA14

Costumes: Masks and Helmets

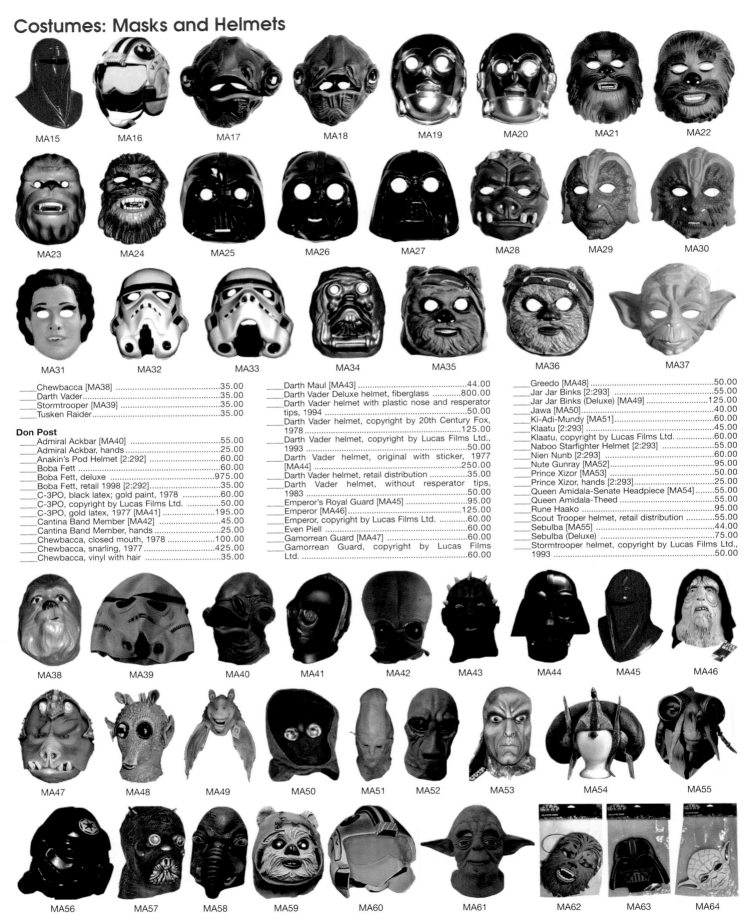

MA15   MA16   MA17   MA18   MA19   MA20   MA21   MA22

MA23   MA24   MA25   MA26   MA27   MA28   MA29   MA30

MA31   MA32   MA33   MA34   MA35   MA36   MA37

____Chewbacca [MA38] 35.00
____Darth Vader...35.00
____Stormtrooper [MA39] 35.00
____Tusken Raider...35.00

Don Post
____Admiral Ackbar [MA40] 55.00
____Admiral Ackbar, hands 25.00
____Anakin's Pod Helmet [2:292] 60.00
____Boba Fett..60.00
____Boba Fett, deluxe 975.00
____Boba Fett, retail 1998 [2:292]...........................35.00
____C-3PO, black latex; gold paint, 1978 ....60.00
____C-3PO, copyright by Lucas Films Ltd. 50.00
____C-3PO, gold latex, 1977 [MA41] 195.00
____Cantina Band Member [MA42] 45.00
____Cantina Band Member, hands 25.00
____Chewbacca, closed mouth, 1978 ....100.00
____Chewbacca, snarling, 1977 ....425.00
____Chewbacca, vinyl with hair 35.00

____Darth Maul [MA43] 44.00
____Darth Vader Deluxe helmet, fiberglass 800.00
____Darth Vader helmet with plastic nose and resperator tips, 1994 ....50.00
____Darth Vader helmet, copyright by 20th Century Fox, 1978 ....125.00
____Darth Vader helmet, copyright by Lucas Films Ltd., 1993 ....50.00
____Darth Vader helmet, original with sticker, 1977 [MA44] 250.00
____Darth Vader helmet, retail distribution 35.00
____Darth Vader helmet, without resperator tips, 1983 ....50.00
____Emperor's Royal Guard [MA45] 95.00
____Emperor [MA46]...125.00
____Emperor, copyright by Lucas Films Ltd. 60.00
____Even Piell 60.00
____Gamorrean Guard [MA47] 60.00
____Gamorrean Guard, copyright by Lucas Films Ltd. 60.00

____Greedo [MA48] 50.00
____Jar Jar Binks [2:293] 55.00
____Jar Jar Binks (Deluxe) [MA49] 125.00
____Jawa [MA50]..40.00
____Ki-Adi-Mundy [MA51]..60.00
____Klaatu [2:293]..45.00
____Klaatu, copyright by Lucas Films Ltd. 60.00
____Naboo Starfighter Helmet [2:293] 55.00
____Nien Nunb [2:293]...60.00
____Nute Gunray [MA52]..95.00
____Prince Xizor [MA53]...50.00
____Prince Xizor, hands [2:293]...............................25.00
____Queen Amidala-Senate Headpiece [MA54]........55.00
____Queen Amidala-Theed 55.00
____Rune Haako 95.00
____Scout Trooper helmet, retail distribution 55.00
____Sebulba [MA55]...44.00
____Sebulba (Deluxe) 75.00
____Stormtrooper helmet, copyright by Lucas Films Ltd., 1993 ....50.00

MA38   MA39   MA40   MA41   MA42   MA43   MA44   MA45   MA46

MA47   MA48   MA49   MA50   MA51   MA52   MA53   MA54   MA55

MA56   MA57   MA58   MA59   MA60   MA61   MA62   MA63   MA64

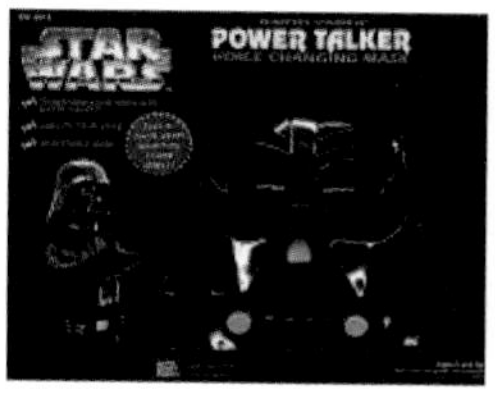

MA65

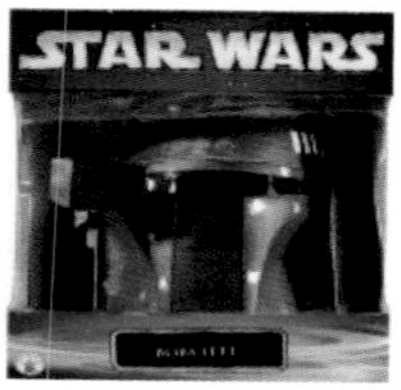

MA66

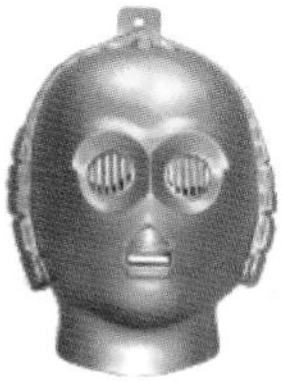
MA67

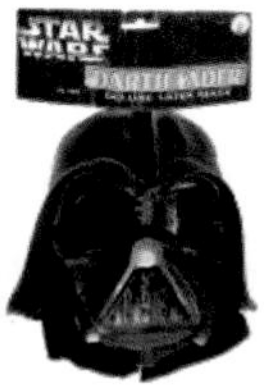
MA68

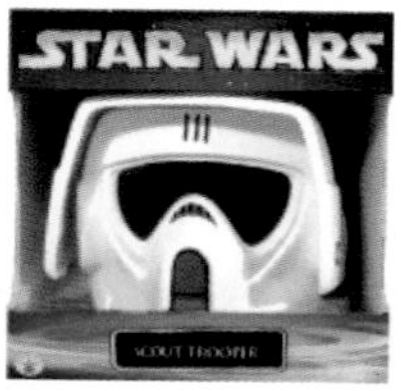

MA69

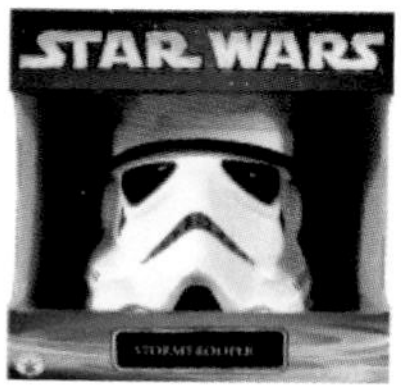

MA70

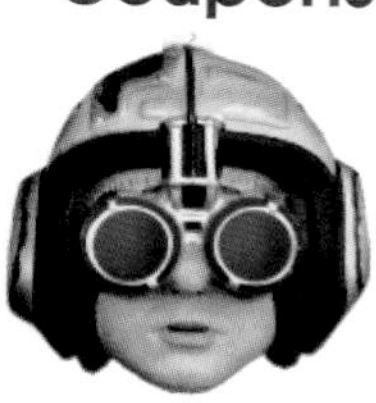
MA71

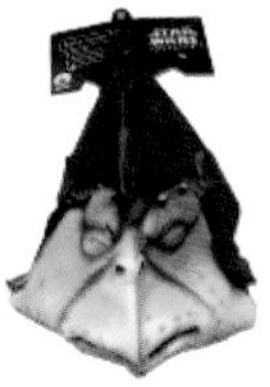
MA72

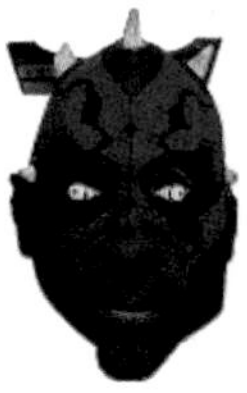
MA73

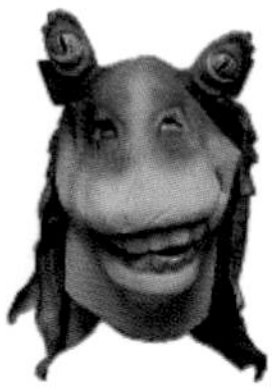
MA74

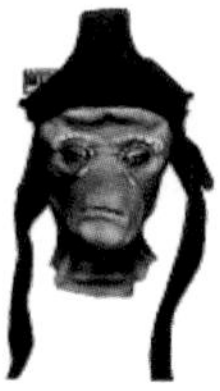
MA75

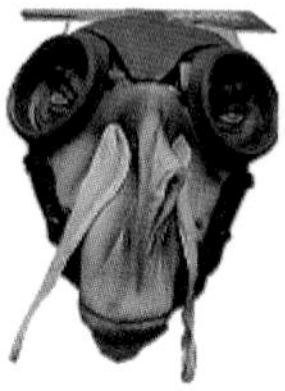
MA76

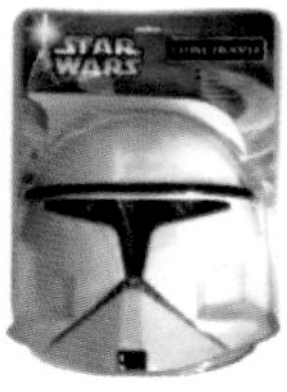
MA77

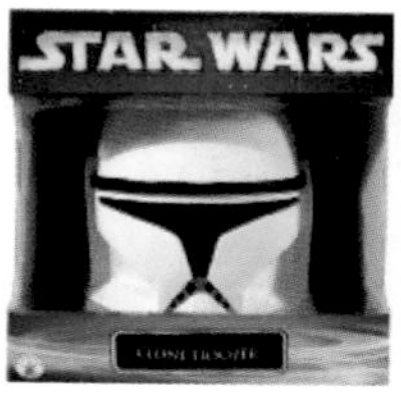

MA78

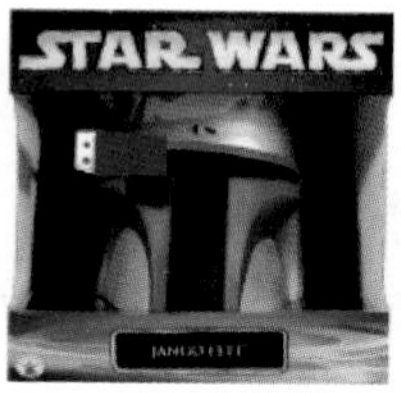

MA79

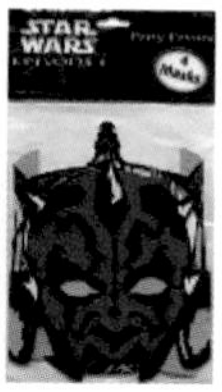
MA80

____Stormtrooper helmet, lighter eye lenses 1978 ....85.00
____Stormtrooper helmet, molded band 45.00
____Stormtrooper helmet, original 1977....................100.00
____Stormtrooper helmet, painted eyes, 1988 ....55.00
____Stormtrooper helmet, retail distribution, 1998 [2:293] 35.00
____Tie Pilot Helmet 110.00
____Tie Pilot Helmet and Chest Plate....................1,200.00
____Tie Pilot Helmet, retail 1998 [MA56] 40.00
____Tusken Raider [MA57] 40.00
____Tusken Raider, 1977 ....125.00
____Tusken Raider, copyright by Lucas Films Ltd., 1993 ....50.00
____Ugnaught 75.00
____Watto [MA58] 44.00
____Weequay....................95.00
____Wicket, molded fur [MA59] 85.00
____Wicket, real fur 70.00
____X-Wing Pilot [MA60]....................110.00
____Yoda [MA61]....................40.00

Galerie Chocolates
Collector masks.
____Chewbacca [MA62] 7.00
____Darth Vader [MA63]....................7.00
____Yoda [MA64] 7.00

Kelloggs, Canada
____Clone trooper, cereal premium....................16.00

Micro Games of America
____Power Talker, Darth Vader mask with microphone and belt-clipped speaker [MA65] 36.00

Party Express
____4 Darth Vader masks, bagged 8.00

Rubies
____Boba Fett collector's 95.00
____Boba Fett collectors edition....................75.00
____Boba Fett deluxe vinyl 35.00
____Boba Fett vinyl adult [MA66] 45.00
____Boba Fett, covers head, flexible rubber 23.00
____C-3PO deluxe....................60.00
____C-3PO injection molded 100.00
____C-3PO vinyl 30.00
____C-3PO, children's [MA67] 5.00
____C-3PO, covers head, flexible rubber 35.00
____C-3PO, PVC childrens 4.00
____Chewbacca deluxe: sculpted latex 55.00
____Chewbacca supreme: latex, hand-layered multicolored long hair fur 125.00
____Chewbacca, children's PVC 4.00
____Chewbacca, covers head, flexible rubber 23.00
____Darth Maul deluxe 20.00
____Darth Vader deluxe: two-piece mask and helmet, injection molded plastic 35.00
____Darth Vader one-sided plastic, child 5.00
____Darth Vader super deluxe mask and helmet: injection molded ABS, cast from original Lucasfilm molds 1,335.00
____Darth Vader, children's PVC 4.00
____Darth Vader, covers head, 2-piece molded plastic 18.00
____Darth Vader, covers head, flexible rubber [MA68] 23.00
____Emperor Palpatine deluxe 45.00
____Scout Trooper [MA69] 45.00
____Scout trooper helmet collectors edition 85.00
____Stormtrooper collector's....................95.00
____Stormtrooper covers head, flexible rubber 23.00
____Stormtrooper injection molded [MA70] 55.00
____TIE fighter helmet collectors edition 75.00
____Tusken Raider, covers head, flexible rubber 23.00
____X-Wing fighter helmet 75.00
____Yoda 30.00
____Yoda deluxe overhead latex, adult....................60.00
____Yoda, covers head, flexible rubber 23.00

Episode I: The Phantom Menace.
____Anakin Skywalker, childrens [MA71]....................5.00
____Boss Nass deluxe overhead latex, adult 43.00
____Boss Nass vinyl 3/4, adult [MA72]....................22.00
____Darth Maul deluxe overhead latex, adult..........43.00
____Darth Maul PVC, adult 5.00
____Darth Maul PVC, childrens 5.00
____Darth Maul vinyl 3/4, adult [MA73] 22.00
____Darth Maul vinyl 3/4, childrens....................8.00
____Jar Jar Binks deluxe overhead latex, adult 40.00
____Jar Jar Binks vinyl 3/4, adult [MA74]....................18.00
____Jar Jar Binks vinyl 3/4, childrens 8.00
____Jar Jar Binks, adult....................5.00
____Jar Jar Binks, childrens 5.00
____Nute Gunray deluxe overhead latex, adult 45.00
____Nute Gunray vinyl 3/4, adult [MA75] 26.00
____Queen Amidala, childrens....................5.00
____Sebulba deluxe overhead latex, adult 43.00
____Sebulba vinyl 3/4, adult [MA76]....................20.00
____Watto deluxe overhead latex, adult 36.00
____Watto vinyl 3/4, adult....................18.00

Episode II: Attack of the Clones.
____Anakin Skywalker, PVC children 12.00
____Clone Trooper 2-piece deluxe 35.00
____Clone Trooper 2-piece injection molded [MA77] 60.00
____Clone Trooper 3/4 PVC [MA78] 18.00
____Clone Trooper collector's 95.00
____Geonosian latex 50.00
____Jango Fett injection molded deluxe [MA79] 75.00
____Jango Fett, PVC children....................14.00
____Jango Fett, PVC children 2-piece 32.00
____Kit Fisto latex 60.00
____Mace Windu, PVC childrens 10.00
____Obi-Wan Kenobi, PVC childrens 10.00
____Padme Amidala PVC childrens 10.00
____Plo Koon latex 75.00
____Saesee Tiin latex 60.00

Tapper Candies
____Party Mask 4-pack [MA80]....................3.00

Coupons

Cinnabon
____Princess Bunhead, free Cinnamon roll [COU01] ..5.00

Del Rey
____$2 rebate, Unifying Force [COU02] 0.50

Hasbro
____Top Trumps, buy 1 get 1 free, incl. Star Wars [COU03] 1.00

K B Toys
____Coupon, $3 off packaged with promo TCG card [COU04] 3.00

Kelloggs
____C-3PO cereal, 25 cents off [COU05] 4.00

Natural Balance
____$1 off vitamins [COU06] 4.00

Pizza Hut, Australia
____EPI: Get Into It coupon booklet [COU07] 10.00

Target
____April 4th Collection Edition Darth Vader with Lava Reflection Figure line placeholder ticket 6.00
____ROTS coupons and product catalog in Death Star mailer 2.00

Toys R Us
____EPIII:ROTS reservation coupon 2.00

Walkers
____Free single packet of chips SW:SE [COU08] 2.00

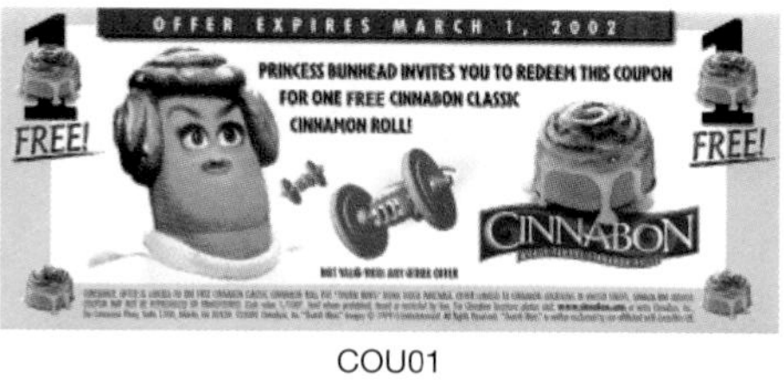

COU01

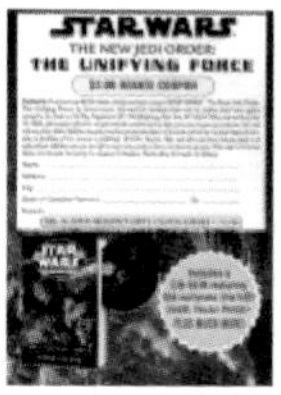

COU02

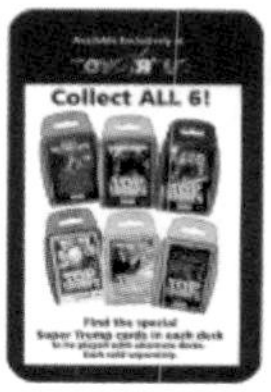

COU03

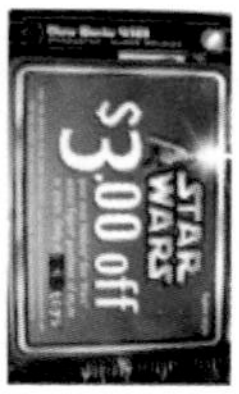

COU04

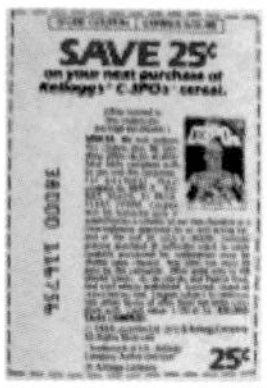

COU05

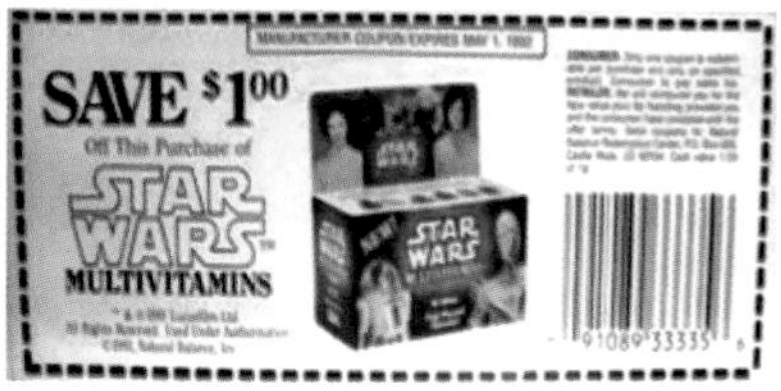

COU06

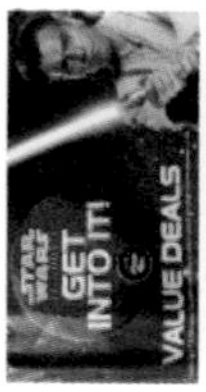

COU07

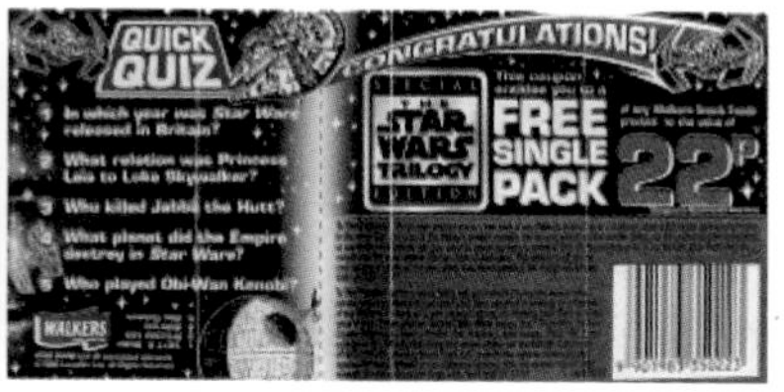

COU08

Crackers

CKS01

CKS02

CKS03

FK01

FK02

FK03

FK04

FK05

FK06

FK07

FK08

COL01

COL02

COL03

COL04

COL05

COL06

COL07

COL08

COL09

COL10

COL11

Crackers

United Kingdom.
____TPM, package of 6. [CKS01] 25.00

Boots
____TPM, package of 6. [CKS02] 25.00

Brite Sparks Ltd.
____TPM single gift cracker, any [CKS03] 10.00

Crafts: Art Kits

Funtastic Pty. Ltd.
____C-3PO art kit [FK01] 8.00
____Darth Maul color and paint center [FK02] 24.00

DOD01

DOD02

DOD03

Hasbro
____R2-D2 Art Center [FK03] 14.00
____Star Wars Ultimate Art Kit [FK04] 9.00

Q-Stat
____Jar Jar Binks [FK05] 15.00

Rose Art Industries
____A New Hope Sand Art [FK06]...........................9.00
____Activity Case, ANH [FK07] 10.00
____Star Wars Fun Kit [FK08] 8.00

EPIII:ROTS.
____Fuzzy t-shirt kit...10.00

Crafts: Coloring Sets

Craft House
Star Wars Mega-Fuzz coloring sets.
____AT-AT [COL01]...7.00
____Darth Vader [COL02]...7.00
____Death Star Battle [COL03] 5.00
____Luke and Leia [COL04]..7.00

Craft Master
____Color N' Clean Machine [COL05] 35.00

Rose Art Industries
____A New Hope: 3-D Crayon by Number [COL06] 7.00
____Deluxe Light-Up Drawing Desk [COL07] 18.00
____Designer Desk [COL08] 16.00

____Droid Factory [COL09] 12.00
____Light Up Drawing Desk [COL10] 12.00

EPIII:ROTS.
____Activity Roller Desk [COL11] 25.00
____Lite Up Tracing Desk 15.00

Crafts: Doodle Kits

Trends International Corp.
Episode I.
____3-D Doodle Kit [DOD01] 6.00
____Doodle Bag [DOD02] 8.00
____Doodle Clings with 6 Markers [DOD03] 8.00
____Jar Jar Binks Velvet Doodle 11"x15" plus 6 color pens [DOD04]..7.00
____Podrace doodle poster, six markers, bonus magnet, bonus full-color movie poster [DOD05] 14.00

Episode II.
____Doodles with six markers [DOD06] 6.00

Crafts: Figure Makers

Hasbro, UK
____Star Wars [FGM01]..15.00

Humbrol
____3D Plaster Mold and Paint Set, EPII [FGM02]....15.00
____Badge and Magnet figure molding set, EPII [FGM03] 30.00

Mako
Plaster character casting sets.
____8 classic trilogy characters [FGM04] 35.00
____Darth Vader [FGM05] 8.00
____Luke Skywalker [FGM06] 8.00

Supercast
____Badge & Magnet molding set, EPI [FGM07] 27.00
____Heroes 3D plaster molding set [FGM08] 24.00
____Villains 3D plaster molding set [FGM09] 24.00

DOD04

DOD05

DOD06

FGM01

FGM02

FGM03

FGM04

FGM05

FGM06

FGM07

FGM08

FGM09

CRL01

CRL02

CRP01

CRP02

CRP03

CRP04

CRP05

CRP06

CRP07

CRP08

CRP09

CRP10

CRP11

CRP12

CRP13

CRP14   CRP15   CRP16

CRF01

CRF02

CRF03

CRF04

CRF05

CRF06

Crafts: Latchhook Kits

Leewards Creative Crafts
____C-3PO and R2-D2 rug 24"x36" 35.00
____C-3PO rug 35.00
____Chewbacca rug, 20"x27" 35.00
____Darth Vader pillow, 15"x15" (head only) 35.00
____Darth Vader rug, 20"x27" (full figure) 35.00
____R2-D2 pillow, 15"x15" 35.00
____R2-D2 rug, 20"x27" [CRL01] 35.00
____Stormtrooper rug 24"x36" 35.00
____Yoda rug 20"x27" [CRL02] 35.00

Crafts: Paint-By-Number

Craft House
____AT-ST and Speeder Bike [CRP01] 5.00
____Darth Vader and Boba Fett [CRP02] 6.00
____Luke and Han [CRP03] 3.00

Craft Master
____Battle on Hoth [CRP04] 16.00
____Boba Fett 16.00
____C-3PO and R2-D2 [CRP05] 16.00
____Chase Through Astroids [CRP06] 16.00
____Darth Vader [CRP07] 16.00
____Ewok Gliders 16.00
____Ewok Village [CRP08] 16.00
____Han Solo and Princess Leia [CRP09] 16.00

____Jabba the Hutt [CRP10] 16.00
____Lando Calrissian and Boushh [CRP11] 16.00
____Luke Skywalker [CRP12] 16.00
____Max Rebo band [CRP13] 16.00
____Wicket and Baga [CRP14] 16.00
____Yoda [CRP15] 16.00

Rose Art Industries
____A New Hope [CRP16] 8.00

Crafts: Paintable Figures

Craft Master
____Admiral Ackbar [CRF01].................................20.00
____Boba Fett [CRF02] 20.00
____C-3PO and R2-D2 [CRF03] 20.00
____Han Solo [CRF04] 20.00
____Luke on Tauntaun [CRF05].............................20.00
____Princess Leia [CRF06] 20.00
____Wicket [CRF07] 20.00
____Yoda [CRF08] 20.00

Hasbro
3D Figure Painters.
____Darth Maul [CRF09] 9.00
____Obi-Wan Kenobi [CRF10] 9.00
____Qui-Gon Jinn [CRF11] 9.00

Lili Ledy
____Wicket the Ewok [CRF12] 45.00

Crafts: Poster Art Kits

Craft Master
____Dagobah & Yoda / Battle on Hoth [CRA01]........40.00
____Darth Vader 3D [CRA02] 35.00
____Darth Vader Lives [CRA03] 25.00
____Galactic dogfight / Forces [CRA04]...................25.00
____Heroes and Villains / Aliens [CRA05] 28.00

Kenner
____Playnts, 5-poster set [CRA06] 50.00

Merlin Publishing Internat'l Ltd.
____Star Wars, 4 posters w/crayons [CRA07] 12.00

Q-Stat
Episode I: The Phantom Menace.
____Anakin Skywalker [CRA08]...............................10.00
____Darth Maul [CRA09] 10.00
____Queen Amidala [CRA10] 10.00

Rose Art Industries
____A New Hope, 4 Exciting Scenes [CRA11] 8.00

EPIII:ROTS Fuzzy poster art 6"x9" with 3 pens.
____Darth Vader [CRA12]..5.00
____Droids [CRA13] 5.00

EPIII:ROTS.
____Fuzzy posters 11"x15" [CRA14] 8.00
____Fuzzy super value set [CRA15] 20.00

CRF07

CRF08

CRF09

CRF10

CRF11

CRF12

CRA01

CRA02

CRA03

CRA04

CRA05

CRA06   CRA07   CRA08

CRA09

CRA10

CRA11

CRA12   CRA13

CRA14   CRA15

Crafts: Sewing Kits

CRK01

CRS01

CRS02

CRS03

CRS04

CRS05

CRS06

CRS07

CRS08

CRS09

CRS10

CRS11

CRS12

CRS13

CRY01

CRC01

CRC02

CRC03

CRC04

CRC05

CRC06

CRC07

CRC08

CWR01

CWR02

CWR03

Crafts: Sewing Kits

Craft Master
____Wicket and Friends, "Sew 'N Show Cards"
[CRK01] 17.00

Crafts: Sun Catcher Kits

Fundimensions
Makeit and Bakeit kits.
____Darth Vader [CRS01] 12.00
____Gamorrean Guard [CRS02] 12.00
____Jabba the Hutt [CRS03].....................12.00
____R2-D2 [CRS04]....................................12.00

Leewards Creative Crafts
The Empire Strikes Back.
____C-3PO [CRS05] 28.00
____Darth Vader [CRS06] 28.00
____Darth Vader, head [CRS07] 28.00
____IG-88 [CRS08] 28.00
____Luke on Tauntaun [CRS09] 28.00
____Luke Skywalker [CRS10] 28.00
____Millennium Falcon [CRS11] 28.00
____Princess Leia 28.00
____R2-D2 and Yoda [CRS12]...................28.00
____Snowspeeder [CRS13] 28.00
____Stormtrooper 28.00
____X-Wing Fighter 28.00

Crayons

Funtastic Pty. Ltd.
____Logo on technical background. Included in art kits
[CRY01], each 0.50

Rose Art Industries
EPIII:ROTS.
____16-pack 5.00

Credit and ATM Cards

GE Consumer Finance
VISA cards.
____Darth Vader [CRC01] 35.00
____R2-D2 and C-3PO [CRC02] 35.00
____X-Wings over Yavin [CRC03] 35.00

MBNA
Galactic Rewards Mastercard.
____Darth Vader [CRC04] 50.00
____Logo only [CRC05]..............................60.00
____Yoda [CRC06]......................................50.00

Siam Commercial Bank
ATM cards, Thailand.
____Darth Vader [CRC07] 15.00
____Yoda [CRC08].....................................15.00

Crowns: Paper

Burger King, Argentina
EPIII:ROTS.
____Movie Scenes [CWR01] 15.00

Burger King
EPIII:ROTS.
____Heroes [CWR02] 5.00
____Heroes and Villains 5.00
____Lightsabers [CWR03] 5.00

Cup Toppers

KFC
Classic trilogy characters. SW:SE promotion.
____R2-D2, SW:SE promotion [CUT01] 12.00
____Stormtrooper [CUT02] 10.00

EPI: Character topper with matching cup.
____Boss Nass [CUT03] 4.00
____Capt. Tarpals [CUT04] 4.00
____Queen Amidala [CUT05] 4.00
____R2-D2 [CUT06] 4.00

Pizza Hut
EPI: Character topper with matching cup.
____Jar Jar Binks [CUT07].........................4.00
____Mace Windu [CUT08]..........................4.00
____Nute Gunray [CUT09] 4.00
____Yoda [CUT10] 4.00

Taco Bell
Classic trilogy characters. SW:SE promotion.
____C-3PO [CUT11] 11.00
____Darth Vader [CUT12] 11.00

EPI: Character topper with matching cup.
____Anakin Skywalker [CUT13] 4.00
____Darth Maul [CUT14] 4.00
____Sebulba [CUT15]................................4.00
____Watto [CUT16] 4.00

Cups: Disposable

Burger King
EPIII:ROTS.
____Anakin, Obi-Wan, and Yoda plastic [PFL01] 3.00
____Hot, Starships [PFL02] 3.00
____King size, Chewbacca and Tarfful plastic
[PFL03] 3.00

CUT01

CUT02

CUT03

CUT04

CUT05

CUT06

CUT07

CUT08

CUT09

CUT10

CUT11

CUT12

CUT13

CUT14

CUT15

CUT16

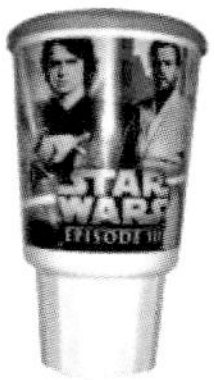
PFL01
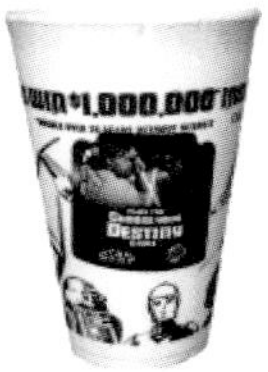
PFL02
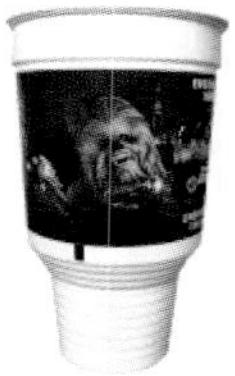
PFL03
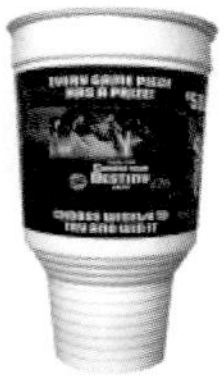
PFL04
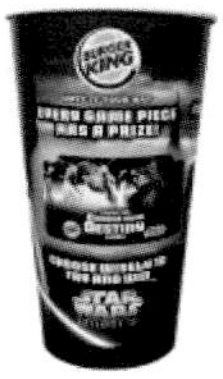
PFL05
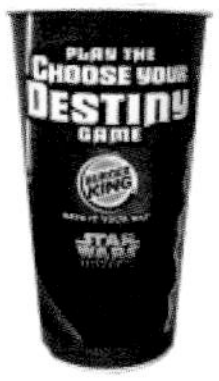
PFL06
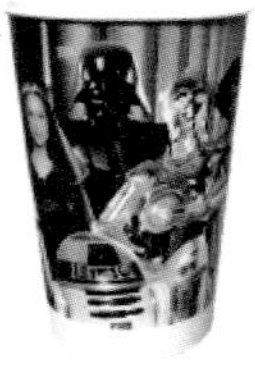
PFL07
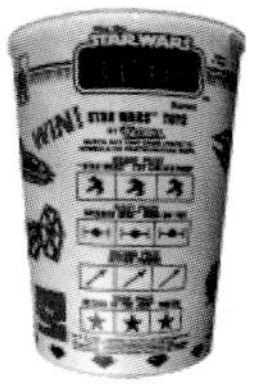
PFL08
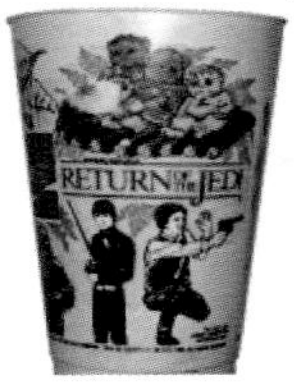
PFL09
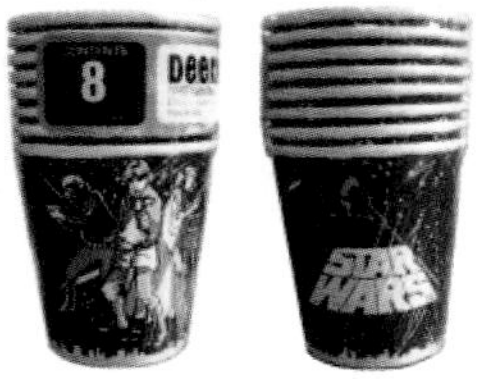
PFL10 front / rear

____King size, Palpatine and Anakin plastic [PFL04] 3.00
____Large, Obi-Wan and Anakin [PFL05] 3.00
____Medium, Darth Vader [PFL06] 3.00
____Small, Saga characters [PFL07] 3.00

Coca-Cola / 7-11
____Darth Vader 2.00
____Stormtrooper 2.00
____Yoda 2.00

Coca-Cola
____Advertises Kenner Toys with game piece attached, theater promotion [PFL08] 26.00

Coca-Cola, Australia
____Return of the Jedi [PFL09] 5.00

Deeko
____8-pk. Illustrated Star Wars scenes [PFL10] 14.00

Dixie / Northern Inc.
Star Wars characters.
____Ben (Obi-Wan) Kenobi [3:252] 0.50
____C-3PO [PFL11] 0.50
____Chewbacca [PFL12] 0.50
____Death Star Droid [3:252] 0.50
____Grand Moff Tarkin [3:252] 0.50
____Greedo [3:252] 0.50
____Hammerhead [3:252] 0.50
____Han Solo [3:252] 0.50
____Lord Darth Vader [3:252] 0.50
____Luke Skywalker [3:252] 0.50
____Princess Leia Organa [3:252] 0.50
____R2-D2 [3:252] 0.50
____The Jawas [3:252] 0.50
____The Stormtrooper [3:252] 0.50
____Tusken Raiders [3:252] 0.50
____Walrus-Man [3:252] 0.50

Star Wars scenes.
____Battle above Death Star [3:252] 0.50
____C-3PO, Luke and Ben watch and listen to Princess Leia's message. [3:252] 0.50
____Darth Vader and Obi-Wan Kenobi duel to the death with their lightsabers. [3:252] 0.50
____Darth Vader orders the torture robot to commence in its prime function! [3:252] 0.50
____General Dodonna explains the Rebel strategy to destroy the Death Star. [3:252] 0.50
____Han, Ben, Luke and Chewie look in awe as their ship is dragged toward the Death Star! [3:252] 0.50
____Imperial guards fire upon the Millennium Falcon as it makes a hasty departure. [3:252] 0.50
____Luke and Ben are stopped by Imperial Soldiers at the Mos Eisley spaceport. [3:252] 0.50
____Luke and C-3PO were looking for R2-D2 in the desert when the the Tusken Raiders appeared! [3:252] 0.50
____Luke practices with the lightsaber using a small robot "seeker" for a target. [3:252] 0.50
____The cantina, where many space pilots often spend their leisure time. [3:252] 0.50
____The Jawas dragged R2-D2 back to their enormous sandcrawler. [3:252] 0.50
____The planet Alderaan is destroyed by the Death Star! [3:252] 0.50
____The Rebel Blockade Runner tries to outrun the Imperial Star Destroyer. [3:252] 0.50
____The sandcrawler is the enormous Jawa transport that scours the Tatooine deserts. [3:252] 0.50
____Trapped in the garbage compactor...as the walls begin to move in! [3:252] 0.50

Star Wars vehicles.
____Blockade Runner [3:252] 0.50
____Imperial Star Destroyer [3:252] 0.50
____Luke's Landspeeder [3:252] 0.50
____Millennium Falcon [PFL13] 0.50
____Rebel X-Wing Fighter [3:252] 0.50
____TIE Fighter [3:252] 0.50
____TIE Fighter (Vader's) [3:252] 0.50
____Y-Wing Fighter [3:252] 0.50

Empire Strikes Back characters.
____Artoo-Detoo [3:252] 0.50
____Boba Fett [PFL14] 0.50
____Chewbacca [3:252] 0.50
____Darth Vader 0.50
____Han Solo [3:252] 0.50
____Lando Calrissian [3:252] 0.50
____Lobot 0.50
____Luke Skywalker [3:253] 0.50
____Obi-Wan Kenobi [3:253] 0.50
____Princess Leia Organa [3:253] 0.50
____See-Threepio [3:253] 0.50
____Wampa Ice Creature [3:253] 0.50
____Yoda 0.50

Empire Strikes Back scenes.
____"Don't worry, they won't follow us through this asteroid field!" Han exclaimed. 0.50
____"Easy, girl, it's just another meteorite!" Luke said reassuringly. [3:253] 0.50
____"I must admit," C-3PO muttered, "There are times I don't understand human behavior." [PFL15] 0.50
____"Luke, I will complete your training and we will rule the galaxy together." 0.50
____"Perhaps you are not as strong as the emperor thought." [3:253] 0.50
____"You fixed us all pretty good, some friend Lando!" [3:253] 0.50
____Darth Vader assembles a group of bounty hunters on the bridge of his ship. [3:253] 0.50
____Han skillfully pilots the Falcon around the huge Imperial destroyer. [3:253] 0.50
____Luke's only chance against the Wampa ice creature is his lightsaber. 0.50
____Luke's tauntaun senses danger when suddenly a huge claw knocks him down. [3:253] 0.50
____Luke finds Cloud City suspiciously friendly...until his fated meeting with Darth Vader. [3:253] 0.50
____The crew of the Millennium Falcon was imprisoned and tortured while in Cloud City. 0.50
____The Falcon sped through the crevice, pursued by a titanic space slug. 0.50
____The fearsome Imperial stormtroopers and their leader Darth Vader. 0.50
____The Imperial walkers were heading for the Rebel base. [3:253] 0.50
____The looming figure of Darth Vader appeared out of the darkness. 0.50
____Yoda began to teach Luke the ways of the Jedi! [3:253] 0.50

Empire Strikes Back vehicles.
____Boba Fett's ship Slave I [3:253] 0.50
____Imperial Star Destroyer [3:253] 0.50
____Imperial TIE Fighter [3:253] 0.50
____Imperial Walker 0.50
____Imperial Walker Scout 0.50
____Millennium Falcon [3:253] 0.50
____Rebel Armored Snowspeeder [3:253] 0.50
____Rebel Cruiser 0.50
____Rebel Transport 0.50
____Rebel X-Wing fighter [3:253] 0.50

Return of the Jedi characters.
____Admiral Ackbar and the Mon Calamari [3:253] 0.50
____Bounty Hunters [3:253] 0.50
____Droopy McCool / Max Rebo / Sy Snootles [3:253] 0.50
____Emperor's Royal Guards and Darth Vader [3:253] 0.50
____Galactic Emperor 0.50
____Gamorrean Guard / Gargan / Squid Head [3:253] 0.50
____Gamorrean Guard / Hermi Odle / Salacious Crumb [3:253] 0.50
____Han Solo / Luke Skywalker / Lando Calrissian 0.50
____Han Solo Frozen / Han Solo and Princess Leia [3:253] 0.50
____Jabba the Hutt / Bib Fortuna / Chewbacca and Boushh [3:253] 0.50
____Kieeoo / Wicket W. Warrick / R2-D2 and Wicket [PFL16] 0.50
____Oola / Gargan / The Mole [3:253] 0.50
____Paploo / Wicket W. Warrick / R2-D2 and Wicket 0.50
____Princess Leia / Jabba the Hutt / Salacious Crumb / Bib Fortuna [3:253] 0.50
____R2-D2 / C-3PO [3:253] 0.50
____The Emperor [3:253] 0.50
____The Rancor / Luke Skywalker 0.50
____The Skiff / The Sarlacc Pit 0.50
____Yak Face / Salacious Crumb / C-3PO / Ree Yees 0.50

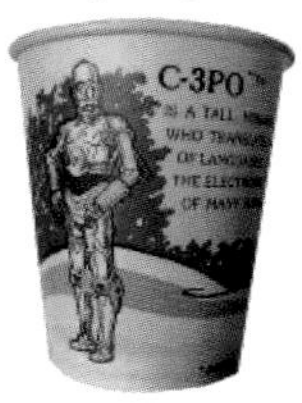
PFL11
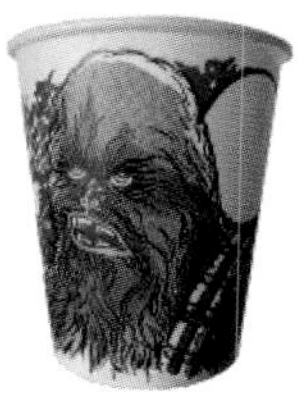
PFL12
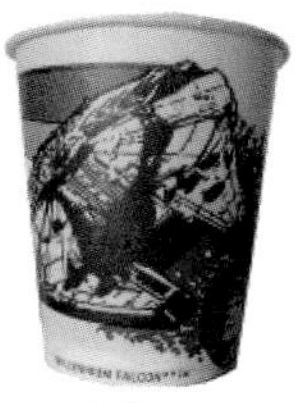
PFL13
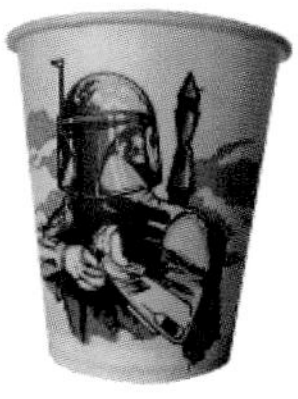
PFL14
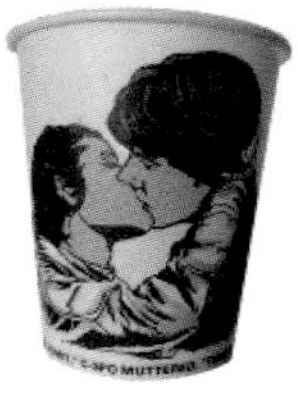
PFL15
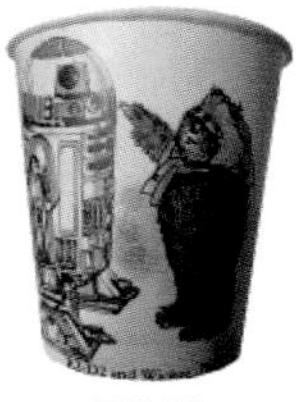
PFL16
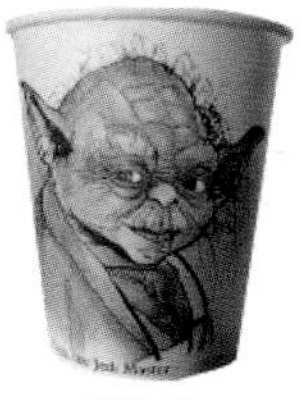
PFL17
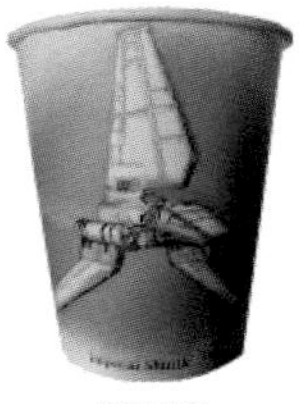
PFL18
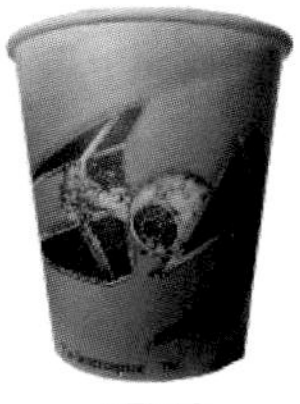
PFL19

PFL20
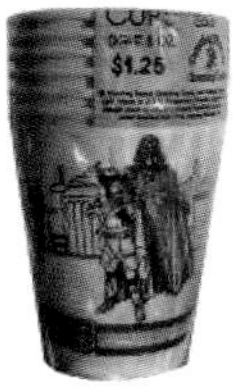
PFL21
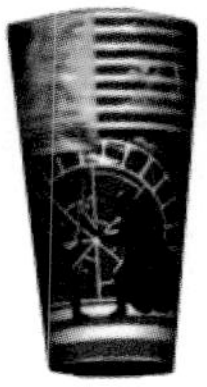
PFL22
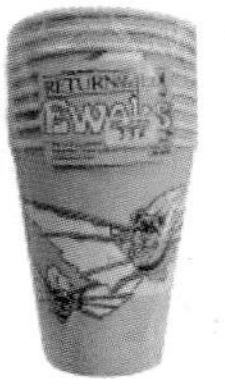
PFL23
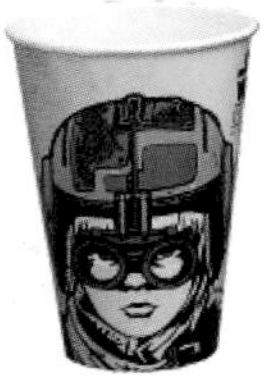
PFL24
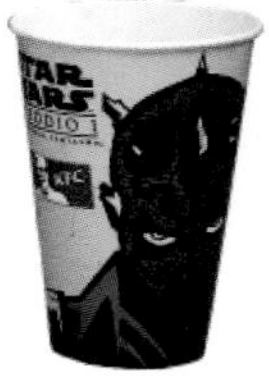
PFL25
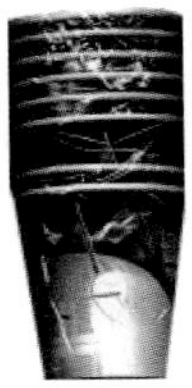
PFL26
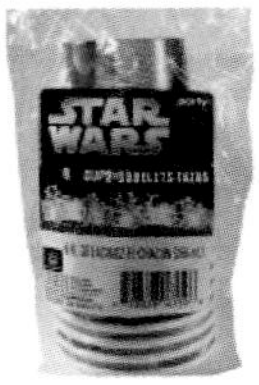
PFL27
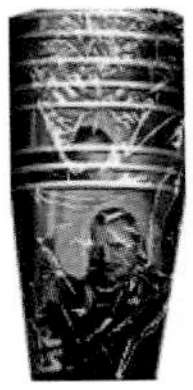
PFL28
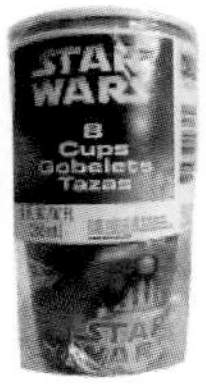
PFL29
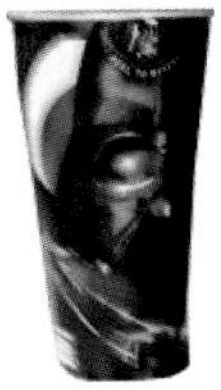
PFL30
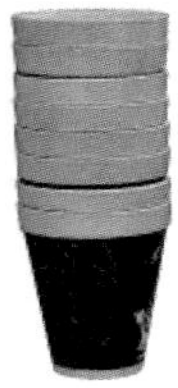
PFL31

Cups: Disposable

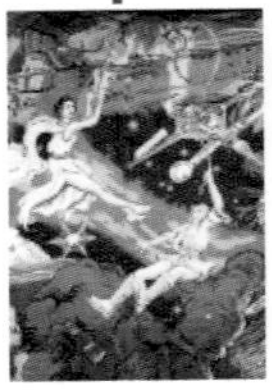

CCR01

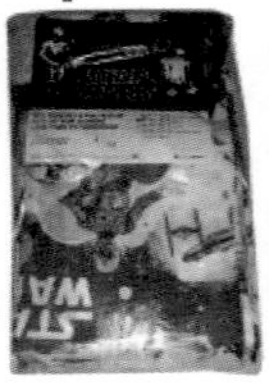

CCR02

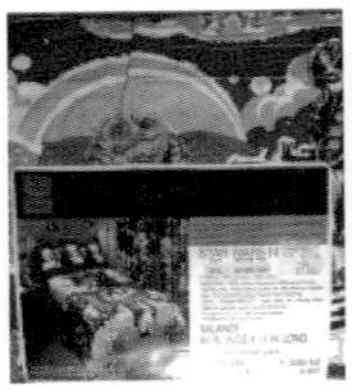

CCR03

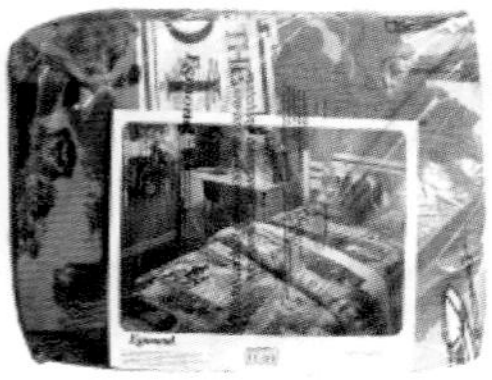

CCR04

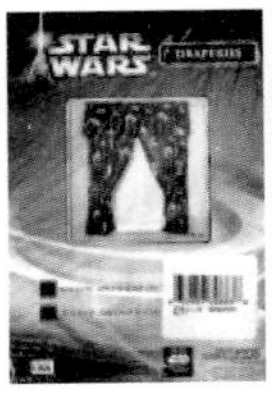

CCR05

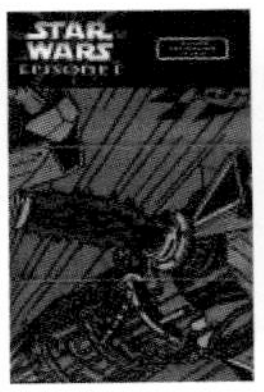

CCR06

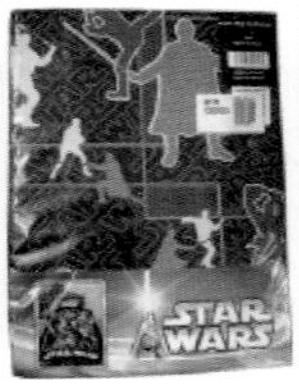

CCR07

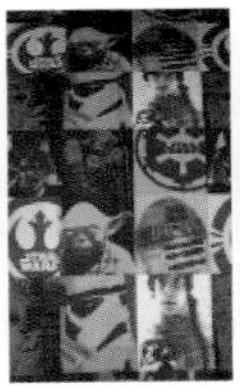

CCR08

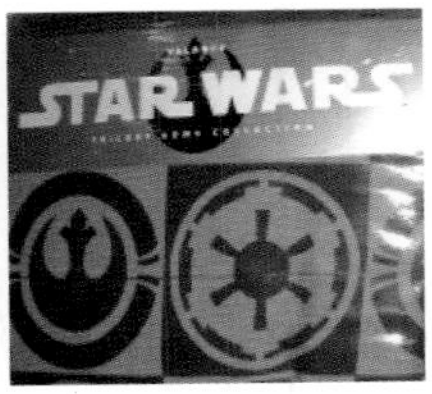

CCR09

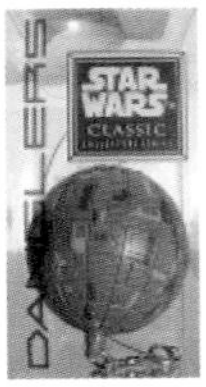

DA01

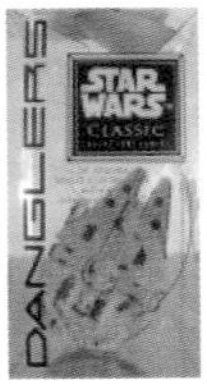

DA02

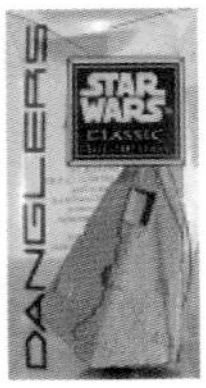

DA03

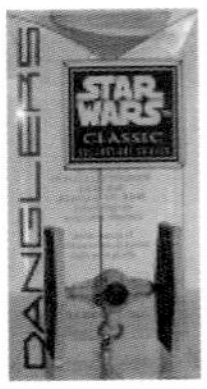

DA04

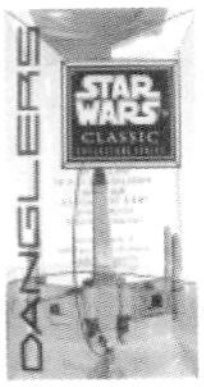

DA05

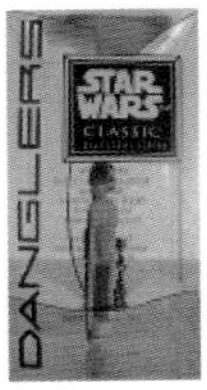

DA06

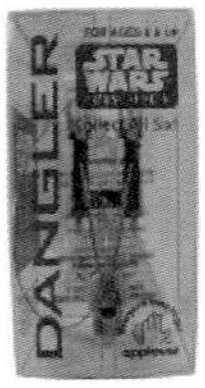

DA07

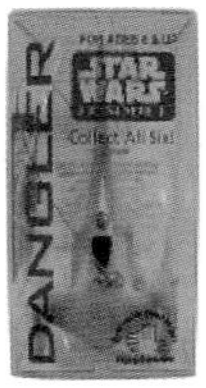

DA08

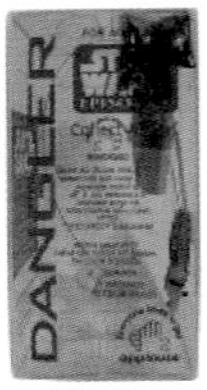

DA09

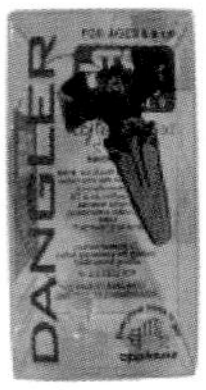

DA10

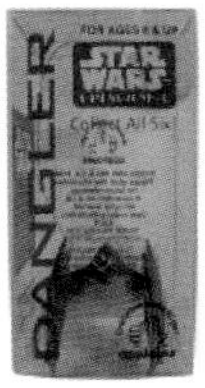

DA11

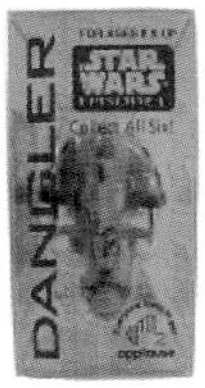

DA12

____Yoda, The Jedi Master / Luke Skywalker [PFL17] 0.50

Return of the Jedi vehicles.
____A-Wing [3:253] 0.50
____B-Wing 0.50
____Imperial Shuttle [PFL18] 0.50
____The Sail Barge....................0.50
____The Skiff 0.50
____Tie-Interceptor [PFL19] 0.50

Saga characters.
____Ben (Obi-Wan) Kenobi 0.50
____Han Solo 0.50
____Lando Calrissian 0.50
____Yoda the Jedi master 0.50

Saga IQ tests.
____Darth Vader 0.50
____Luke Skywalker....................0.50

Saga scenes.
____"I must admit," C-3PO muttered, "there are times I don't understand human behavior." 0.50
____Darth Vader and Obi-Wan Kenobi duel to the death with their lightsabers. 0.50
____Luke and C-3PO are looking for R2-D2 in the desert when the tusken raider appears. 0.50
____Luke's tauntaun senses danger and is suddenly attacked by a hoth wampa. 0.50
____The cantina, where many space pilots often spend their leisure time. (Hammerhead / 2 Jawas)..........0.50
____The cantina, where many space pilots often spend their leisure time. (Walrusman / Jawa) 0.50
____The Falcon speeds through the crevice, pursued by a titanic space slug. 0.50

Saga vehicles.
____Imperial star destroyer 0.50
____Rebel X-wing....................0.50
____Rebel Y-wing....................0.50

Drawing Board Greeting Cards, Inc.
____Classic Characters, 8-pack [PFL20] 10.00
____Cloud City, 8-pack [PFL21] 10.00
____Darth Vader and Luke Duel, 8-pack [PFL22]......10.00
____Ewoks Hang-Gliding, 8-pack [PFL23] 8.00

KFC
____Boss Nass 16oz. 2.00
____Boss Nass 20oz. 2.00
____Boss Nass 32oz. 2.00
____Jar Jar Binks 16oz. 2.00
____Jar Jar Binks 20oz. 2.00
____Jar Jar Binks 32oz. 2.00
____Jedi 16oz. 2.00
____Jedi 20oz. 2.00
____Jedi 32oz. 2.00
____Queen Amidala 16oz. 2.00
____Queen Amidala 20oz. 2.00
____Queen Amidala 32oz. 2.00

KFC, Mexico
EPI: The Phantom Menace.
____Anakin Skywalker [PFL24] 6.00
____Darth Maul [PFL25] 6.00

Party Express
8-packs.
____Anakin, Obi-Wan, Jango, Count Dooku 2.00
____Dogfight over Death Star [PFL26] 6.00
____Episode III [PFL27] 3.00
____Qui-Gon Jinn, Obi-Wan Kenobi, Jedi vs. Sith [PFL28] 4.00
____Star Wars Saga [PFL29] 8.00

Pepsi Cola, Holland
____SW:SE "Peel to Reveal" promotion [PFL30] 5.00

Quela
____Vader neon, 8-pack styrofoam [PFL31] 8.00

Curtains

Look-alike characters.
____Orange space scenes [CCR01] 15.00

Bibb Co.
Star Wars.
____Aztec Gold [CCR02] 16.00
____Galaxy....................18.00
____Jedi Knights 20.00
____Lord Vader 20.00
____Space Fantasy 16.00

Empire Strikes Back.
____Boba Fett 22.00
____Boba Fett, J.C. Penney exclusive 24.00
____Darth's Den....................20.00
____Ice Planet 16.00
____Lord Vader's Chamber 20.00
____Lord Vader 20.00
____Spectre 18.00
____Yoda 20.00

Return of the Jedi.
____Jabba the Hutt, Ewoks, etc. 20.00
____Logos from all 3 films....................18.00
____Luke and Darth Vader Duel, AT-ST, etc.....................20.00
____Star Wars Saga 16.00
____Valance [CCR03] 25.00

Esmond
____Return of the Jedi [CCR04] 45.00

KIDS Home Fashions
____Lightsabers draperies [CCR05] 25.00

Westpoint Stevens
____Character study drapery with tiebacks 45.00
____EPI: Podracers, valance [CCR06] 17.00
____EPII: Hanger Duel [CCR07] 35.00
____Logos and characters, 3x3 image pattern [CCR08] 15.00
____Rebel and Imperial logos, valance [CCR09] 18.00

Curtains: Drapes

____EPI Naboo space battle scenes [2:263]....................18.00
____Star Wars, pleated top 18.00

Black Falcon
____Empire Strikes Back, pleated top 10.00
____Return of the Jedi, pleated top 15.00

Danglers

Applause
Classic trilogy.
____Death Star [DA01] 7.00
____Millennium Falcon [DA02] 7.00
____Star Destroyer [DA03] 7.00
____Tie Fighter [DA04] 7.00
____X-Wing Fighter [DA05] 7.00
____Y-Wing Fighter [DA06] 7.00

Episode I: The Phantom Menace.
____Anakin's Podracer [DA07] 6.00
____Naboo Starfighter [DA08] 6.00
____Sebulba's Podracer [DA09]....................6.00
____Sith Infilterator [DA10]....................6.00
____Trade Federation Droid Fighter [DA11]....................6.00
____Trade Federation Tank [DA12] 6.00
____Unopened box of 12 [2:262] 73.00

Decals

C and D Visionaries, Inc.
____C-3PO and R2-D2 [DE01]....................5.00
____Darth Vader 3.00
____Darth Vader, "Who's Your Daddy?" [DE02] 5.00
____Darth Vader, "You Have Failed Me For The Last Time" [DE03] 5.00
____Han Solo 3.00
____Join the Dark Side [DE04] 5.00
____Luke Skywalker....................3.00
____Princess Leia, "I don't know where you get your delusions, laser brain!" [DE05] 5.00

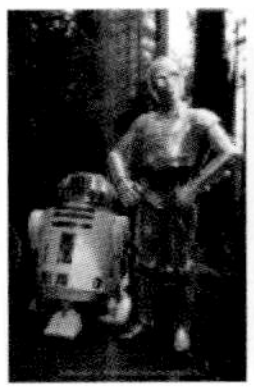

DE01

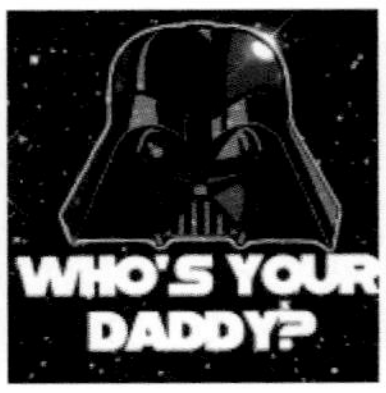

DE02

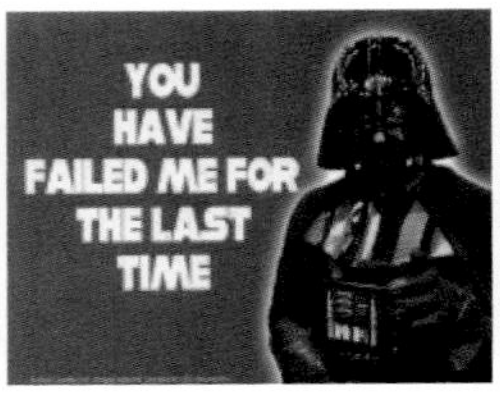

DE03

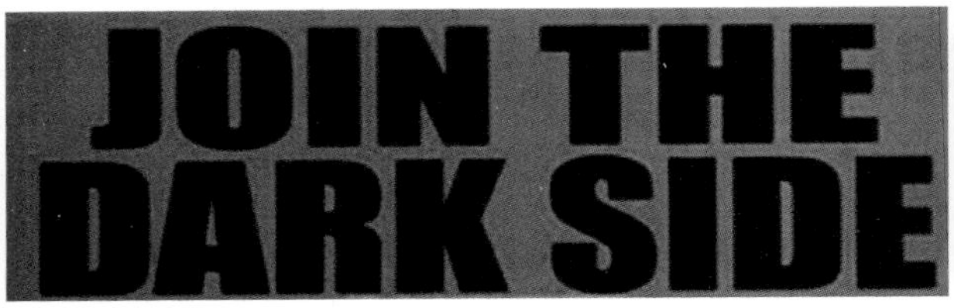

DE04

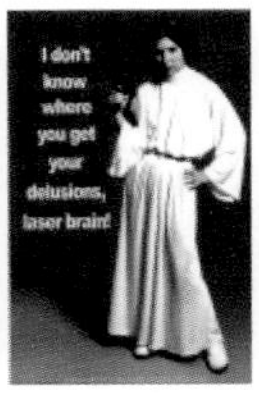

DE05

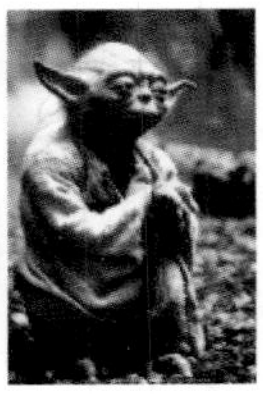

DE06

DE07 DE08 DE09 DE10 DE11 DE12

DE13 DE14 DE15 DE16

DE17 DE18 DE19 DE20 DE21 DE22 DE23 DE24

DE25 DE26 DE27 DE28 DE29 DE30 DE31 DE32 DE33 DE34 DE35 DE36

____R2-D2 and C-3PO 3.00
____Star Wars, white letters on blue background........5.00
____Yoda [DE06] 5.00
____Yoda, "Do... or do not." [DE07] 5.00

Vinyl cut.
____Boba Fett [DE08] 7.00
____C-3PO [DE09] 7.00
____Chewbacca [DE10] 7.00
____Darth Vader [DE11] 7.00
____Join the Dark Side [DE12] 5.00
____May The Force Be With You ... Always [DE13] 5.00
____"My other transport..." [DE14] 5.00
____Sand People [DE15] 7.00
____Stormtrooper...7.00
____Yoda [DE16] 7.00
____Yoda fighting 7.00

Disney / MGM
____Jedi Training Acadamy 8.00
____Star Tours, 3"x4", glows [DE17] 5.00

Fan Club
____Bounty Hunters, 4"x5" 12.00
____Star Wars cling [DE18] 8.00
____The First 10 Years, 4"x5" [DE19] 5.00
____Yoda, 4"x5" [DE20]...10.00

Image Marketing
____C-3PO and R2-D2 [DE21]....................................8.00
____Darth Vader [DE22]..8.00
____Millennium Falcon under Attack [DE23] 8.00
____Yoda [DE24] 8.00

Liquid Blue
Series 1, red header.
____#1 Queen Amidala [DE25] 3.00
____#2 Anakin Skywalker [DE26]................................3.00
____#3 Jar Jar Binks [DE27] 3.00
____#4 Darth Maul [DE28] 3.00
____#5 Qui-Gon Jinn [DE29] 3.00
____#6 Obi-Wan Kenobi [DE30]..................................3.00
Series 2, blue header.
____#1 Jedi vs. Sith [DE31] 3.00
____#2 Jedi [DE32] 3.00
____#3 Anakin's Podracer [DE33] 3.00
____#4 Battle Droid [DE34] 3.00
____#5 Naboo Space Battle [DE35] 3.00
____#6 Federation Droid Fighter [DE36] 3.00

Deodorant

Avon, Mexico
____Heroes roll-on [WET01] 10.00
____Jedi 2-pack: roll-on and talc powder [WET02] ..15.00

Desktop Organizers

Grosvenor
____R2-D2 desk tidey [DTO01].................................12.00

Impact, Inc.
____Trade Federation Tank organizer [DTO02] 18.00

Diaries

Antioch
____Queen Amidala diary, inset photo [DR01] 8.00
____Queen Amidala diary, photo framed [DR02]..........8.00

Charles Letts and Co.
____Star Wars, limited to 8,000 [DR03] 14.00

Ink Group
____Episode I 2000 Diary [DR04] 16.00

Letts
____Darth Vader [DR05]...7.00
____Han Solo [DR06]..7.00
____Millennium Falcon under Attack [DR07]...............5.00

Q-Stat
____Queen Amidala diary [DR08] 8.00

WET01 WET02 DTO01

DTO02 DR01 DR02 DR03 DR04 DR05 DR06 DR07 DR08

Dishes: Bowls

DIB01

DIB02

DIB03

DIB04

DIB05

DIB06

DIB07

DIB08

DIB09

DIB10

DIB11

Dishes: Bowls

Deka
Star Wars.
____14oz. [DIB01] 15.00
____20oz. [DIB02] 15.00

Empire Strikes Back.
____14oz. [DIB03] 12.00
____20oz. [DIB04] 12.00

Return of the Jedi.
____14oz. [DIB05] 12.00
____20oz. [DIB06] 12.00

General Mills
25th anniversary, mail-in premiums.
____Heroes, blue-rimmed [DIB07] 5.00
____Villains, red-rimmed [DIB08] 5.00

Kelloggs
____R2-D2 electronic, mail-in premium 15.00

Sigma
____The World of Star Wars Fantasy Childset [DIB09] 20.00

Spearmark Int.
____Vader and Stormtroopers [DIB10] 7.00

Zak Designs
____Podracer, white with scene in bottom and black rim [DIB11] 4.00

Dishes: Cups

7-Eleven Inc.
EPIII:ROTS. Lenticular slurpee cups with Vader topper.
____Darth Vader [CU09].............................5.00
____Epic Duel..5.00
____Obi-Wan Kenobi 5.00
____Yoda...5.00

EPIII:ROTS. Sculpted slurpee cups.
____Yoda [CU10] 5.00

Applause
Classic trilogy character plastic sculpted mugs.
____C-3PO [CU01] 7.00
____Darth Vader [CU02]...........................7.00
____Stormtrooper [CU03] 7.00
____Wicket the Ewok [CU04]......................7.00

EPI character plastic sculpted mugs.
____Anakin Skywalker [CU05] 6.00
____C-3PO [CU06].................................6.00
____Jar Jar Binks [CU07]...........................7.00
____Queen Amidala [CU08] 7.00

Tumbler with no-spill travel lid and handle.
____Darth Maul [CU11] 12.00
____Jar Jar [CU12] 12.00

Burger King, Argentina
EPIII:ROTS. Colored cups with sculpted Darth Vader lid.
____Darth Vader, black [CU13] 20.00
____Darth Vader, red [CU14] 20.00

Burger King, Germany
EPIII:ROTS motion cups.
____#1 Anakin / Vader...........................15.00
____#2 Anakin / Yoda 15.00
____#3 Epic Duel 15.00

Burger King, Singapore
EPIII:ROTS.
____Saga characters [CU15]....................10.00

Cingular
____Celebration 3 [CU16] 5.00

Coca-Cola / 7-11
____Admiral Ackbar / Lando Calrissian and Nien Nunb [CU17] 7.00
____Admiral Ackbar, Lando, Luke and Droids / Han Solo in Carbonite [CU18] 8.00
____Bib Fortuna, Gamorrean Guard and Jabba / Max Rebo Band [CU19] 7.00

CU01

CU02

CU03

CU04

CU05

CU06

CU07

CU08

CU09

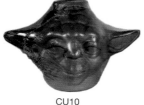
CU10

CU11

CU12

CU13

CU14

CU15

CU16

CU17 front / rear

CU18 front / rear

CU19 front / rear

CU20 front / rear

CU21 front / rear

CU22 front / rear

CU23 front / rear

CU24 front / rear

CU25 front / rear CU26 front / rear CU27 front / rear CU28 CU29 CU30 CU31 CU32 CU33

CU34 CU35 CU36 CU37 CU38 CU39 CU40 CU41 CU42 CU43

CU44 CU45 CU46 CU47 CU48 CU49 CU50 CU51 CU52 CU53

____Biker Scouts / Scout and Han Solo [CU20]..........7.00
____Chewbacca, Han, Leia / Droid [CU21]..................7.00
____Chewbacca, Han, Lando, Luke (skiff) / Ben Kenobi and Luke [CU22]..................7.00
____Darth Vader and Luke Duel / Darth Vader and Emperor [CU23]..................7.00
____Emperor's Throne Room / Emperor's Royal Guards [CU24]..................7.00
____Imperial Moff / Imperial Dignitaries [CU25] 8.00
____Ishi Tib, Jawas and Klaatu / Lando [CU26] 7.00
____Jabba Sail Barge / C-3PO, Ree-Yees and Yak Face [CU27]..................7.00
____Wicket / Ewok, Wicket and AT-ST 7.00

Coca-Cola / Frozen Coke

Majik Markets.

____1 Han Solo / Chewbacca..................10.00
____2 The Final Chase 10.00
____3 Tusken Raiders / Jawas 10.00
____4 Darth Vader 10.00
____5 R2-D2 / C-3PO 10.00
____6 Ben (Obi-Wan) Kenobi 10.00
____7 Luke Skywalker / Princess Leia Organa..........10.00
____8 The Light Sabers..................10.00

Seven Eleven.

____1 Han Solo / Chewbacca [CU28] 8.00
____2 The Final Chase [CU29]..................8.00
____3 Tusken Raiders / Jawas [CU30] 8.00
____4 Darth Vader [CU31] 8.00
____5 R2-D2 / C-3PO [CU32] 8.00
____6 Ben (Obi-Wan) Kenobi [CU33]..................8.00
____7 Luke Skywalker / Princess Leia Organa [CU34]..................8.00
____8 The Light Sabers [CU35] 8.00

Coca-Cola / Grubee's

____C-3PO / R2-D2 [CU36]..................5.00

Coca-Cola / Koolee

____1 Stormtrooper [CU37]..................12.00
____2 Chewbacca and Han Solo [CU38] 12.00
____3 Trash Compactor [CU39] 12.00
____5 Battle Above The Death Star [CU40] 12.00
____6 Luke in Falcon Gunwell..................12.00
____7 Mos Eisley [CU41]..................12.00
____8 Luke Skywalker [CU42]..................12.00
____9 Luke Training with Remote [CU43] 12.00
____10 Darth Vader, Leia and Tarkin [CU44]..................12.00
____11 Chewbacca, Han and Luke in Disguise [CU45]..................12.00
____12 C-3PO and R2-D2 [CU46] 12.00
____13 Princess Leia [CU47]..................12.00
____14 Tusken Raiders and Bantha [CU48] 12.00
____15 Jawas and R2-D2 [CU49] 12.00
____16 Tusken Raider Attacks Luke [CU50]..................12.00
____17 Darth Vader Questions Rebel Soldier [CU51]..................12.00

CU54 CU55 CU56 CU57 CU58 CU59 CU60 CU61 CU62 CU63 CU64

CU65 CU66 CU67 CU68 front / rear CU69 CU70 CU71 CU72 CU73

CU74 CU75 CU76 CU77 CU78 CU79 CU80 CU81 CU82 CU83 CU84 CU85

Dishes: Cups

CU86

CU87

CU88

CU89

CU90

CU91

CU92

CU93

CU94

CU95

CU96

CU97

CU98

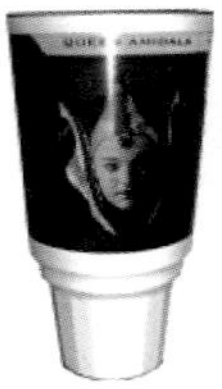
CU99

CU100

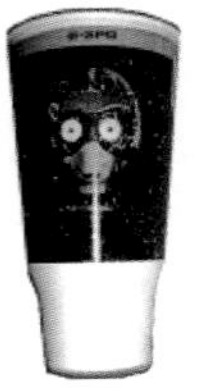
CU101

CU102

CU103

CU104

CU105

CU106

CU107

CU108

CU109

CU110

CU111

CU112

____19 Han Solo, Luke and Princess Leia [CU52] 12.00
____Ben and Darth Vader Duel 12.00
____Ben Kenobi 12.00
____Leia and Luke Swing to Safety [CU53] 12.00

Coca-Cola
____Ben Kenobi [CU54]..10.00
____Boba Fett [CU55] 10.00
____C-3PO and R2-D2 [CU56] 10.00
____Chewbacca [CU57] 10.00
____Darth Vader and Tarkin [CU58] 10.00
____Han Solo 10.00
____Luke Skywalker and Princess Leia [CU59] 10.00
____Tie Fighter vs. X-Wing Fighter [CU60] 10.00

Coca-Cola, Hong Kong
EPIII:ROTS. Clear colored cups with Darth Vader lid.
____Anakin Skywalker, red [CU61] 15.00
____Clone trooper, clear [CU62] 15.00
____Darth Vader, gray [CU63] 15.00
____Darth Vader, red [CU64] 15.00

Deka
____Empire Strikes Back 6oz. [CU65]........................12.00
____Empire Strikes Back 11oz. [CU66].......................10.00
____Empire Strikes Back 17oz. [CU67].......................12.00
____Return of the Jedi 6oz. 9.00
____Return of the Jedi 11oz. [CU68] 10.00
____Return of the Jedi 17oz. 12.00
____Star Wars 6oz. [CU69] 15.00
____Star Wars 11oz. [CU69] 10.00
____Star Wars 17oz. [CU69] 12.00

General Mills
____SW 11oz. Cheerios mail-in premium [CU70] 18.00

25th anniversary, mail-in premiums.
____Heroes, blue-rimmed [CU71] 5.00
____Villains, red-rimmed [CU72] 5.00

Hallmark
17oz. plastic cups.
____EPI Qui-Gon and Darth Maul [CU73] 3.00
____EPII Anakin and Jango [CU74] 3.00
____EPIII Darth Vader and Yoda [CU75] 3.00

Hungry Jacks
EPII:AOTC.
____Clone trooper [CU76] 7.00
____Darth Vader [CU77]..7.00
____Padme Amidala [CU78] 7.00
____Yoda [CU79] 7.00

EPIII:ROTS.
____Anakin Skywalker 8.00
____C-3PO 8.00
____General Grievous 8.00
____R2-D2 ....8.00

Jay Franco and Sons
____MosEspa Arena Podracing tumbler, features pit droids [CU80] 8.00

KFC
EPI: The Phantom Menace.
____Boss Nass..5.00
____Jar Jar Binks 5.00
____Jedi 5.00
____Queen Amidala [CU81] 5.00

KFC, Mexico
EPI: The Phantom Menace.
____Boss Nass [CU82]...6.00
____Caballeros Jedi [CU83] 6.00
____Jar Jar Binks [CU84]..6.00
____Reine Amidala [CU85]...6.00

Masterfoods USA
ROTS.
____Darth Vader sip cup with M&Ms inside 3.00

McDonalds, Australia
Coca Cola premium.
____Empire Strikes Back [CU86]................................25.00

Pepperidge Farms
____The Creatures [CU87]..12.00
____The Endor Forest [CU88] 12.00
____The Rebels [CU89] 12.00
____The Vehicles [CU90] 12.00
____The Villains [CU91] 12.00

Pepsi Cola
____Star Wars Cantina: Fao Schwarz, Las Vegas [CU92]...10.00

Darth Vader, AT-AT, Death Star SW:SE promotion.
____QT [CU93] 6.00
____Unbranded [CU94] 6.00

EPI:TPM. 44oz. fluted, ridged.
____Battle Droid [CU95]...4.00
____C-3PO [CU96]...4.00
____Obi-Wan Kenobi [CU97] 4.00
____Padme [CU98]...4.00
____Queen Amidala [CU99] 4.00
____Sebulba [CU100]..4.00

EPI:TPM. 44oz. tapered, smooth.
____C-3PO [CU101]...4.00
____Darth Sidious [CU102] 4.00
____Jar Jar Binks [CU103]...4.00
____Obi-Wan Kenobi [CU104] 4.00
____Queen Amidala [CU105] 4.00
____Sebulba [CU106]...4.00

Star Wars Special Edition.
____C-3PO [CU107] 10.00
____Darth Vader [CU108] 10.00
____R2-D2 [CU109]..10.00
____Stormtrooper [CU110] 10.00

Pepsi Cola, Mexico
EPI: The Phantom Menace.
____Queen Amidala [CU111] 5.00
____Qui-Gon vs. Darth Maul [CU112] 5.00

Pizza Hut
Star Wars special edition take-out cups with lid.
____"The Trilogy," 12oz. [CU113].....................................4.00
____Luke and Darth Vader on Bespin gantry, 16oz. [CU114] 4.00

Star Wars trilogy.
____C-3PO [CU115] 5.00
____Chewbacca [CU116]..5.00
____Darth Vader [CU117]...5.00
____R2-D2 [CU118] 5.00

Pizza Hut, Holland
____SW:SE take-out [CU119] 4.00

Spearmark Int.
____EPII Flip Top Flask [CU120] 5.00
____Star Wars classic sport tumbler[CU121] 12.00
____Vader and Stormtroopers / Luke [CU122] 5.00

Super Live Adventure
____Characters and Millennium Falcon / Indiana Jones [CU123]...15.00

CU113

CU114

CU115

CU116

CU117

CU118

CU119

CU120

CU121

CU122

CU123

CU124

CU125

CU126

CU127

CU128

CU129

CU130

CU131

CU132

CU133

CU134 front / rear

CU135

CU136

CU137

CU138

CU139

CU140

CU141

CU142

CU143

CU144

CU145

____R2-D2 cup with coin slot in top; use as bank when emptied [CU124] 15.00

Taco Bell
____Defeat the Dark Side character cup, any [CU125] 6.00

Episode I: The Phantom Menace.
____Darth Maul, large [CU126] 3.00
____Jar Jar Binks, medium [CU127] 3.00
____Obi-Wan Kenobi, large [CU128] 3.00
____Queen Amidala, medium [CU129] 3.00

Special Edition with lenticular scenes.
____A New Hope 7.00
____Empire Strikes Back [CU130] 7.00
____Return of the Jedi [CU131] 7.00
____Star Wars logo [CU132] 7.00

Star Wars Special Edition.
____C-3PO, medium 3.00
____Darth Vader, large 3.00
____R2-D2, small 3.00

Theater Promos
____Darth Vader/Luke Dual and Jabba's Throne Room, 20oz. [CU133] 7.00
____Kenner game piece attached ("Win SW Toys"), 32oz. 7.00
____SW and ESB art, 20oz. 7.00
____SW and ESB art, 32oz. [CU134] 9.00

Zak Designs
____Anakin Skywalker / Sebulba sport tumbler with lid [CU135] 7.00
____Anakin Skywalker Juice cup, blue, 8oz. [CU136] 7.00
____Darth Maul sport tumbler with lid [CU137] 8.00
____Darth Maul tumbler with no-spill travel lid [CU138] 11.00
____Jar Jar Binks tumbler with no-spill travel lid [CU139] 8.00
____Pod Race Juice cup, transparent blue, 8oz. [CU140] 5.00
____Podracer half-sculpted sports bottle [CU141] 8.00
____Podracer sport tumbler with lid [CU142] 7.00

EPIII:ROTS.
____Darth Vader covered with straw 8.00

Tumbler with no-spill travel lid.
____Darth Vader [CU143] 10.00
____Qui-Gon Jinn [CU144] 8.00
____Space Battle [CU145] 10.00

Dishes: Dish Sets

Deka
____3-piece children's set, Wicket [DID01] 35.00
____ROTJ: Baby's First Feeding Set 45.00
____ROTJ: Dinnerware set 35.00

Kelloggs, Korea
____R2-D2 breakfast droid, bagged [DID02] 35.00

Kelloggs, Malaysia
____R2-D2 breakfast droid, boxed 45.00

Sigma
____"The World of Star Wars Fantasy Childset" ceramic, boxed [DID03] 85.00

Spearmark Int.
____Classic Trilogy children's set, soft sided bag [DID04] 35.00

Zak Designs
3-piece sets: plate, bowl, tumbler.
____EPI:TPM, boxed [DID05] 12.00
____EPIII:ROTS, boxed [DID06] 15.00
____EPIII:ROTS, clear packed 12.00

Dishes: Egg Cups

Bonbon Buddies
____Ceramic double egg cup with milk chocolate eggs [EGC01] 14.00

Dishes: Glasses

____Episode I icons [GA01] 15.00
____Feel the Force [GA02] 7.00
____Star Wars carnival glass [GA03] 45.00

Glazed from Australia.
____Anakin Skywalker [GA04] 8.00

Glazed, from Holland.
____Artoo Detoo [GA05] 12.00
____C-3PO [GA06] 12.00
____Chewbacca [GA07] 12.00
____Darth Vader [GA08] 12.00
____Emperor's Royal Guard [GA09] 12.00
____Han Solo [GA10] 12.00
____Luke Skywalker [GA11] 12.00
____Obi-Wan Kenobi [GA12] 12.00
____Princess Leia [GA13] 12.00
____Stormtrooper [GA14] 12.00
____Yoda [GA15] 12.00

Amora
____Chewbacca and Ewok [GA16] 19.00
____Dath Vader and Stormtroopers [GA17] 19.00
____Vader and Luke Duel [GA18] 19.00
____Yoda and Luke [GA19] 19.00

Burger King
Star Wars.
____C-3PO and R2-D2 [GA20] 20.00
____Chewbacca [GA21] 20.00
____Darth Vader [GA22] 20.00
____Luke Skywalker [GA23] 20.00

Empire Strikes Back.
____C-3PO and R2-D2 [GA24] 15.00
____Darth Vader [GA25] 15.00
____Lando Calrissian [GA26] 15.00
____Luke Skywalker [GA27] 15.00

Thin decal, button-bottoms, exclusive to Ohio.
____C-3PO and R2-D2 [GA28] 25.00
____Darth Vader [GA29] 25.00
____Lando Calrissian [GA30] 25.00
____Luke Skywalker [GA31] 25.00

DID01

DID02 combined and separated

DID03

DID04

DID05

DID06

EGC01 closed & chocolate egg

GA01

GA02 front / rear

GA03

GA04 front / rear

GA05

GA06

GA07

GA08

Dishes: Glasses

GA09 GA10 GA11 GA12 GA13 GA14 GA15 GA16 GA17 GA18 GA19

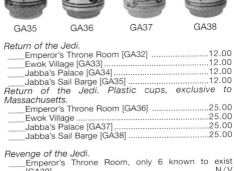

GA20 GA21 GA22 GA23 GA24 GA25 GA26 GA27 GA28 GA29 GA30 GA31 GA32 GA33 GA34

GA35 GA36 GA37 GA38

Return of the Jedi.
____Emperor's Throne Room [GA32] 12.00
____Ewok Village [GA33] 12.00
____Jabba's Palace [GA34] 12.00
____Jabba's Sail Barge [GA35] 12.00
Return of the Jedi. Plastic cups, exclusive to Massachusetts.
____Emperor's Throne Room [GA36] 25.00
____Ewok Village 25.00
____Jabba's Palace [GA37] 25.00
____Jabba's Sail Barge [GA38] 25.00

Revenge of the Jedi.
____Emperor's Throne Room, only 6 known to exist [GA39] ....N/V

Coca-Cola
1977 Prototype fast food premium glasses.
____Ben Kenobi [GA40] 330.00

Disney / MGM
____Tatooine shot glass, blue [GA41] 10.00
____Tatooine shot glass, clear [GA42] 10.00

Downpace Ltd.
EPI:TPM.
____Anakin Skywalker [GA43] 6.00
____Battle Droid [GA44] 6.00
____Jar Jar [GA45] 6.00
____Jedi Knight (Obi-Wan) [GA46] 6.00
____Pod Race 6.00
____Sith Lord (Darth Maul) 6.00

Hasbro
Includes action figure. Target exclusives.
Wave 1.
____A New Hope, Ben Kenobi [GA47] 10.00
____Attack of the Clones, Anakin Skywalker [GA48] 10.00
____Empire Strikes Back, Luke Skywalker snowspeeder pilot [GA49] 10.00
____Phantom Menace, Darth Maul [GA50] 10.00
____Return of the Jedi, Leia as Jabba's captive [GA51] 10.00
Wave 2, not officially released.
____A New Hope, Han Solo [GA52] 50.00
____Empire Strikes Back, Yoda [GA53] 50.00
____Return of the Jedi, Boba Fett 50.00
Wave 3.
____Revenge of the Sith, Clone Trooper [GA54].......10.00
____Revenge of the Sith, General Grievous [GA55] ..10.00
____Revenge of the Sith, Obi-Wan Kenobi [GA56]....10.00

Wave 4, Revenge of the Sith.
____A New Hope, Han Solo [GA57] 10.00
____Empire Strikes Back, Yoda [GA58] 10.00
____Return of the Jedi, Boba Fett [GA59] 10.00
Wave 5.
____A New Hope, Princess Leia 15.00
____Empire Strikes Back, Darth Vader 15.00
____Return of the Jedi, Stormtrooper.......................15.00

Pepsi Cola
____EPI: Anakin Skywalker [GA60] 8.00
____EPI: Queen Amidala [GA61] 8.00
____EPI: Qui-Gon Jinn [GA62] 8.00
____EPI: R2-D2 [GA63] 8.00
____TPM 2-pack: heroes and villains 40.00
____TPM heroes, clear etched glass [GA64] 16.00
____TPM villains, clear etched glass [GA65] 16.00

Pepsi Cola, Holland
____C-3PO Star Wars Trilogy, Holland [GA66] 13.00

Pepsi Cola, Hong Kong
____C-3PO [GA67] 16.00
____Darth Vader [GA68] 16.00
____R2-D2 [GA69] 16.00
____Stormtrooper [GA70] 16.00

Pepsi Cola, Mexico
____C-3PO 10.00
____Darth Vader 10.00
____R2-D2 ....10.00
____Stormtrooper 10.00

GA39 GA40 GA41 GA42 GA43 front and rear GA44 front and rear GA45 front and rear GA46 front and rear GA47

GA48 GA49 GA50 GA51 GA52 GA53

GA54 GA55 GA56 GA57 GA58 GA59

       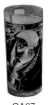  

| GA60 | GA61 | GA62 | GA63 | GA64 filled | GA65 filled | GA66 | GA67 | GA68 | GA69 | GA70 |

Pepsi Cola, Thailand

____C-3PO icon on blue background 18.00
____Darth Vader icon on yellow background 20.00
____R2-D2 icon on red background 20.00
____Stormtrooper icon on red background 22.00

Pizza Hut, Australia

____Darth Vader..65.00

Dishes: Glasses, Shot

Cards, Inc.

____6-pack collector set, tin storage box...................65.00
____Clone Trooper [E2W01] 15.00
____Darth Vader [E2W02]...15.00
____Darth Vader, lava [E2W03].................................15.00
____Epic Duel [E2W04]...15.00
____General Grievous [E2W05]..................................15.00
____Yoda [E2W06] 15.00

Dishes: Mugs

____C-3PO ceramic [MUM01] 9.00
____Darth Maul / Desert Duel [MUM02] 7.00
____Darth Vader ceramic [MUM03]...............................9.00
____Darth Vader ceramic, stars in eyes [MUM04]........8.00
____Darth Vader travel mug [MUM05] 20.00
____Darth Vader with lid 16.00
____Jabba the Hutt from SW:SE [MUM06] 5.00

| E2W01 | E2W02 | E2W03 | E2W04 | E2W05 | E2W06 |

____R2-D2 cermaic hand-painted [MUM07] 3.00
____Special Edition art [MUM08] 14.00

Episode I, Tasse.
____Darth Maul, Obi-Wan and Qui-Gon [MUM09] 8.00
____Naboo Fighter [MUM10].......................................8.00

Plastic thermal mugs, EPI:TPM.
____Anakin Skywalker [MUM11] 7.00
____Darth Maul [MUM12] 7.00
____Jar Jar Binks [MUM13] 7.00
____Queen Amidala [MUM14] 7.00

SW:SE glass tankards. Limited edition, numbered.
____C-3PO [MUM15]..12.00
____Yoda [MUM16] 12.00

Applause
Ceramic figural mugs, EPI.
____Darth Maul [MUM17] 17.00

____Jar Jar Binks [MUM18]..17.00
____R2-D2 [MUM19] 17.00
Classic trilogy.
____Bib Fortuna [MUM20]...18.00
____Boba Fett [MUM21] 20.00
____C-3PO [MUM22]...18.00
____Chewbacca [MUM23]...18.00
____Darth Vader [MUM24]..18.00
____Darth Vader, metalized [MUM25] 22.00
____Emperor Palpatine [MUM26] 18.00
____Gamorrean Guard [MUM27]..................................18.00
____Han Solo [MUM28]...18.00
____Luke Skywalker [MUM29] 18.00
____Obi-Wan Kenobi [MUM30] 18.00
____Princess Leia [MUM31] 18.00
____Stormtrooper [MUM32]...18.00
____Tusken Raider [MUM33].......................................20.00

Bonbon Buddies
____Darth Vader..14.00

MUM01 front / side   MUM02 side 1 / side 2   MUM03   MUM04   MUM05

MUM06   MUM07   MUM08 side 1 / side 2   MUM09   MUM10

MUM11 side 1 / side 2   MUM12 side 1 / side 2   MUM13 side 1 / side 2   MUM14 side 1 / side 2

MUM15   MUM16   MUM17   MUM18   MUM19   MUM20   MUM21   MUM22   MUM23

Dishes: Mugs

MUM24

MUM25

MUM26

MUM27

MUM28

MUM29

MUM30

MUM31

MUM32

MUM33

MUM34

MUM35

MUM36

California Originals
____ Darth Vader, 5.5" tall, black inside 45.00
____ Darth Vader, 5.5" tall, white inside 47.00

Ceramic, sculpted by Jim Rumph.
____ Ben Kenobi [MUM34] 115.00
____ Chewbacca [MUM35] 155.00
____ Darth Vader [MUM36] 115.00

Cards, Inc.
____ Darth Vader [MUM37] 14.00
____ Grievous [MUM38] 14.00
____ Vader, Sith [MUM39] 14.00
____ Yoda, Jedi [MUM40] 14.00
____ Yoda, Jedi Master [MUM41] 14.00

EPIII:ROTS dark mugs.
____ Anakin Skywalker [MUM42] 18.00
____ Darth Vader "Villain" [MUM43] 18.00
____ Darth Vader [MUM44] 18.00

____ Epic lightsaber duel [MUM45] 18.00
____ General Grievous [MUM46] 18.00
____ Palpatine "Evil" [MUM47] 18.00
____ Yoda "Justice" [MUM48] 18.00

EPIII:ROTS sculpted characters.
____ Clone Trooper [MUM49] 20.00
____ Coruscant Trooper 20.00
____ Darth Vader [MUM50] 20.00
____ General Grievous [MUM51] 20.00
____ Kashyyyk Trooper 20.00
____ Shock Trooper 20.00
____ Yoda [MUM52] 20.00

EPIII:ROTS white mugs with Star Wars logo.
____ Anakin Skywalker [MUM53] 18.00
____ Clone Trooper [MUM54] 18.00
____ Darth Vader [MUM55] 18.00
____ Obi-Wan Kenobi [MUM56] 18.00
____ Yoda [MUM57] 18.00

Thermal, image changes.
____ Clone Trooper 14.00
____ Darth Vader 14.00
____ General Grievous 14.00
____ R2-D2 .... 14.00
____ Stormtrooper 14.00
____ Yoda 14.00

Crystal Craft
____ Anakin Skywalker, podracer [MUM58] 7.00
____ Darth Maul [MUM59] 7.00
____ Jar Jar [MUM60] 7.00
____ Jedi vs. Sith [MUM61] 7.00
____ Obi-Wan Kenobi [MUM62] 7.00
____ Qui-Gon Jinn [MUM63] 7.00
____ Starfighters [MUM64] 10.00

Deka
SW 10oz.
____ Star Wars [MUM65] 15.00

ESB 10oz.
____ Boba Fett and Darth Vader [MUM66] 10.00
____ Chewbacca, C-3PO and R2-D2 [MUM67] 10.00
____ Han Solo, Princess Leia and Luke Skywalker [MUM68] 10.00
____ Yoda [MUM69] 10.00

ROTJ 10oz.
____ C-3PO, R2-D2 and Wicket / Princess Leia and Ewoks [MUM70] 8.00
____ Darth Vader, Emperor's Royal Guard, Luke Skywalker and Yoda [MUM71] 8.00
____ Wicket the Ewok [MUM72] 10.00

Disney / MGM
____ C-3PO and Star Tours logo 10.00
____ Galactic Empire [MUM73] 14.00
____ R2-D2 and Star Tours logo [MUM74] 10.00
____ Rebel Alliance [MUM75] 14.00
____ Star Tours logo, silver metallic finish [MUM76] 10.00
____ Star Tours logo, silver metallic finish, tankard [MUM77] 24.00
____ Yoda, Silent Knight, Jedi Knight [MUM78] 35.00

MUM37 side 1 / side 2

MUM38 side 1 / side 2

MUM39 side 1 / side 2

MUM40 side 1 / side 2

MUM41 side 1 / side 2

MUM42

MUM43

MUM44

MUM45

MUM46

MUM47

MUM48

MUM49

MUM50

MUM51

MUM52

MUM53

MUM54

MUM55

MUM56

MUM57

MUM58

MUM59

MUM60

MUM61

MUM62

MUM63

MUM64

Star Wars Weekends.
____2003 Mickey and Yoda.................................24.00
____2004 Mickey and Minnie, ANH [MUM79] 24.00
____2005 Darth Vader / Mickey 24.00
____2005 Logo 24.00

Downpace Ltd.
____Boba Fett [MUM80] 12.00
____C-3PO [MUM81]..8.00
____Darth Vader [MUM82]....................................12.00
____Luke Skywalker [MUM83] 10.00
____Princess Leia [MUM84] 10.00
____Stormtrooper [MUM85]....................................8.00

Galerie Chocolates
Character goblets.
____Chewbacca [MUM86]......................................20.00
____Darth Vader [MUM87]....................................20.00
____Yoda 20.00

Character mugs.
____Chewbacca 10.00
____Darth Vader 10.00
____R2-D2 ....10.00

Hamilton Collection
____Darth Vader and Luke Skywalker [MUM88].......12.00
____Han Solo [MUM89]..12.00
____Imperial Walkers [MUM90]..................................12.00
____Luke Skywalker and Yoda [MUM91] 12.00
____Millennium Falcon Cockpit [MUM92]................12.00
____Princess Leia [MUM93] 12.00
____R2-D2 and Wicket [MUM94] 12.00

____Space Battle Scene [MUM95] 12.00

Houze Magic Color Inc.
____Star Wars logo [MUM96] 35.00

Kiln Craft Potteries
____Return of the Jedi, colored line art [MUM97] 10.00

Kinnerton Confectionery
____Battle above Death Star [MUM98]......................12.00
____Battle above Death Star with chocolate Death Star [MUM99]..18.00
____Lightsaber Duel with chocolate Death Star [MUM100]..17.00

Long Island Distributing Co. Ltd.
____Darth Vader [MUM101] 7.00
____Imperial Insigna [MUM102]................................7.00
____Rebel Insigna [MUM103] 7.00
____See-Threepio [MUM104] 7.00

____Stormtrooper [MUM105]....................................7.00

Lucasfilm
____EPIII:ROTS glass tankard [MUM106].................20.00

M&M World
____Dark side character line up 14.00
____Jedi character line up..14.00

NECA
____Star Wars concept art with original logo, limited to 5,000 [MUM107]..25.00

EPII:AOTC ceramic figural mugs, limited to 5,000 each.
____Clone trooper [MUM108] 14.00
____Jango Fett [MUM109] 14.00

EPII:AOTC decal mugs, limited to 10,000 each.
____Heroes [MUM110]..7.00
____Villains [MUM111]..7.00

MUM65 side 1 / side 2

MUM66 side 1 / side 2

MUM67 side 1 / side 2

MUM68 side 1 / side 2

MUM69 side 1 / side 2

MUM70 side 1 / side 2

MUM71 side 1 / side 2

MUM72 side 1 / side 2

MUM73

MUM74

MUM75

MUM76

MUM77

MUM78

MUM79

MUM80

MUM81

MUM82

MUM83

MUM84

MUM85

MUM86

Dishes: Mugs

MUM87 MUM88 MUM89 MUM90 MUM91 MUM92 MUM93

MUM94 MUM95 MUM96 MUM97 MUM98 MUM99 MUM100

EPII:AOTC glass tankards, limited to 10,000 each.
____Droids [MUM112] 18.00
____Jedi [MUM113] 18.00
____Villains [MUM114].................................18.00

Rawcliffe
____Darth Vader manga art [MUM115] 14.00
____ROTS logo [MUM116] 10.00
____ROTS teaser art [MUM117] 10.00

15 oz. mugs, 2-sided.
____Galactic Heroes [MUM118] 18.00
____Princess Leia [MUM119] 18.00
____Yoda [MUM120] 18.00

Pewter logo on 12oz. mug with curved lip and base.
____20th Anniversary [MUM121]....................12.00
____Boba Fett's Helmet [MUM122]..................12.00
____Boba Fett with gun.............................12.00

____Darth Vader's lightsaber 12.00
____Darth Vader......................................12.00
____Darth Vader with clenched fist [MUM123]..........12.00
____Imperial emblem [MUM124]...................12.00
____Mandalorean emblem [MUM125] 12.00
____Obi-Wan Kenobi [MUM126].................12.00
____Princess Leia [MUM127] 12.00
____Rebel logo 12.00
____Star Wars Celebration II 25.00
____Star Wars logo [MUM128] 12.00
____The Magic of Myth [MUM129] 22.00
____Yoda [MUM130] 12.00

Sigma
____10th Anniversary [MUM131]....................15.00
____Star Wars with thermal ink 15.00

Cartoon-style art.
____Boba Fett and Chewbacca [MUM132] 17.00

____C-3PO and R2-D2 [MUM133] 17.00
____Darth Vader, Princess Leia, Stormtrooper [MUM134]..17.00
____Luke Skywalker and Yoda [MUM135] 17.00

Sculpted figural mugs, vintage.
____Biker Scout [MUM136]..........................35.00
____C-3PO [MUM137]...............................35.00
____Chewbacca [MUM138] 35.00
____Darth Vader [MUM139]........................35.00
____Gamorrean Guard [MUM140]..................35.00
____Han, Hoth [MUM141] 35.00
____Klaatu [MUM142] 35.00
____Lando, Skiff Guard [MUM143]................35.00
____Leia [MUM144] 35.00
____Luke, Pilot [MUM145]........................35.00
____Stormtrooper 35.00
____Wicket [MUM146]..............................35.00
____Yoda [MUM147].................................35.00

MUM101 MUM102 MUM103 MUM104 MUM105 MUM106 MUM107

MUM108 MUM109 MUM110 MUM111 MUM112 MUM113 MUM114 MUM115

MUM116 MUM117 MUM118 MUM119 MUM120 MUM121 MUM122

MUM123 MUM124 MUM125 MUM126 MUM127 MUM128

MUM129

MUM130

MUM131

MUM132 side 1 / side 2

MUM133 side 1 / side 2

MUM134 side 1 / side 2

MUM135 side 1 / side 2

MUM136

MUM137

MUM138

MUM139

MUM140

MUM141

MUM142

MUM143

MUM144

MUM145

MUM146

MUM147

MUM148

MUM149 side 1 / side 2

Skywalker Ranch
____Skywalker Ranch logo [MUM148] 12.00

Spearmark Int.
____Vader and Stormtroopers / classic art [MUM149] 8.00

starwars.com
In 2003 the official Star Wars website offered 13 themed art galleries with approximately 12 images in each gallery. Fans could order mugs from an online merchandiser with their choice of images. Only galleries are documented below.
____Bounty Hunters gallery, each 12.00
____Clone Wars gallery, each 12.00
____Creatures gallery, each 12.00
____Droids gallery, each 12.00
____Holiday Art gallery, each 12.00
____Jedi gallery, each 12.00
____Logos gallery, each 12.00

____Padme gallery, each...12.00
____Poster Art gallery, each......................................12.00
____Princess Leia gallery, each...................................12.00
____Rebels gallery, each...12.00
____Sith gallery, each 12.00
____Vehicles gallery, each 12.00

Dishes: Plates

Deka
Classic trilogy compartment plates.
____Empire Strikes Back [DIL01] 14.00
____Return of the Jedi [DIL02] 14.00
____Star Wars [DIL03] 14.00

Sigma
____The World of Star Wars Fantasy Childset [DIL04] 15.00

Spearmark Int.
____Star Wars classic art [DIL05] 8.00

Zak Designs
Pod Race plates featuring Anakin and Sebulba.
____Round [DIL06]..3.00
____Shaped [DIL07] 4.00

Dishes: Steins

Avon
____SW:SE Luke vs. Vader [MST01]..........................65.00

Dram Tree
Ceramic relief steins.
____Star Wars [MST02]...25.00
____Empire Strikes Back [MST03] 25.00
____Return of the Jedi [MST04] 25.00

DIL01

DIL02

DIL03

DIL04

DIL05

DIL06

DIL07

MST01 side 1 / front / side 2

MST02

MST03

MST04

MST05

MST06

MST07

Dishes: Steins

MST08 side 1 / side 2   MST09 side 1 / side 2   MST10 side 1 / side 2   SPN01 - SPN07

SPN08-SPN11   SPN12   SPN13   SPN14   SPN15   SPN16   SPN17   SPN18

SPN19   SPN20   SPN21   DSP01   DSP02   DSP03   DSP04-05   DSP06   DSP07   DSP08   DSP09

DSP10   DSP11   DSP12   DSP13   DSP14   DSP15

Hinged lid, topped with pewter figure.
    Boba Fett, limited to 3,000 [MST05] 85.00
    Darth Vader, limited to 1,977 [MST06] 115.00
    Yoda, limited to 3,000 [MST07] 85.00

Metallic Impressions
    Star Wars [MST08] 35.00
    Empire Strikes Back [MST09] 35.00
    Return of the Jedi [MST10] 35.00

Dishes: Utensils

Spoons, dated 1977 and numbered in series.
    #1 Luke Skywalker [SPN01] 7.00
    #2 Princess Leia Organa [SPN02] 7.00
    #3 Han Solo [SPN03] 7.00
    #4 Chewbacca the Wookiee [SPN04] 7.00
    #5 See Threepio [SPN05] 7.00
    #6 Artoo Detoo [SPN06] 7.00
    #7 Darth Vader [SPN07] 7.00

Birchcroft
Spoons, made of China. Limited to 500 pieces each.
    Clone Trooper [SPN08] 8.00
    Mace Windu [SPN09] 8.00
    Obi-Wan Kenobi [SPN10] 8.00
    Yoda [SPN11] 8.00

Kelloggs
Cereal premiums, plastic. Light-up saber spoons.
    Blue 3.00

DSQ01   DSQ02   DSQ03   DT01   DT02   DT03   DT04

    Green 3.00
    Red [SPN12] 3.00

Cereal premiums, plastic.
    Anakin Skywalker [SPN13] 6.00
    C-3PO [SPN14] 6.00
    Darth Maul [SPN15] 6.00
    Jar Jar Binks [SPN16] 6.00
    Obi-Wan Kenobi [SPN17] 6.00
    Queen Amidala [SPN18] 6.00

Kelloggs, Korea
Cereal premiums, plastic. Light-up saber spoons. Assembled in package
    Blue 5.00
    Green 5.00
    Red [SPN19] 5.00

Zak Designs
2-pack spoon and fork.
    EPI:TPM Podracer [SPN20] 6.00
    EPIII:ROTS Darth Vader [SPN21] 8.00

Dispensers: Candy

Cap Candy
    Jango Fett gum dispenser [DSP01] 6.00
    Naboo Fighter dispenser includes display stand and Skittles [DSP02] 8.00
    R2-D2 dispenser includes M and M's candies [DSP03] 8.00

Masterfoods USA
M&M Minis inside light-up saber.
    Blue [DSP04]...3.00
    Red [DSP05] 3.00

Toy & Pogo mini M&M dispensers, boxed. Asia exclusive packaging.
    C-3PO [DSP06]...8.00
    Death Star [DSP07]..8.00
    Storm Trooper [DSP08]..8.00
    Yoda [DSP09] 8.00

Toy & Pogo mini M&M dispensers.
    Anakin Skywalker [DSP10] 5.00
    C-3PO [DSP11]...5.00
    Death Star [DSP12]..5.00
    Obi-Wan [DSP13]...5.00
    Storm Trooper [DSP14]..5.00
    Yoda [DSP15] 5.00

Dispensers: Soap / Lotion

Heart Art Collection Ltd.
Japan.
    R2-D2 [DSQ01]...35.00

Jay Franco and Sons
    Darth Maul dispenser [DSQ02] 16.00
    Jar Jar Binks dispenser [DSQ03].......................14.00

Display Cases

Code 3 Collectibles
    For replica ships, plexiglass................................65.00

Master Replicas
    For Jedi mini-lightsabers, plexiglass 45.00
    For Sith mini-lightsabers, plexiglass 45.00

Pride Displays
Museum quality.
    Gold series, limited to 1,000 ....750.00
    Silver series 500.00

Dog Tags

Applause
    Darth Maul [DT01]...7.00
    Naboo Fighter [DT02] 7.00
    Obi-Wan Kenobi [DT03] 7.00
    Trade Federation Droid Fighter [DT04].................7.00

DH01 DH02 DH03 DH04 DH05 DH06 DRK01 DKS01 front / top HP01 HP02 HP03

E3E01 E2E01 SUE01 SUE02 SUE03 SUE04 SUE05 SUE06 SUE07

Doorknob Hangers

Antioch

____C-3PO [DH01]..5.00
____Darth Vader [DH02]..5.00
____Jedi Welcome / Do Not Disturb [DH03] 5.00
____Sith Lord Beware / Do Not Disturb [DH04] 5.00
____Yoda / Please Enter [DH05] 5.00

Scholastic

____Endor Rebel Heroes 1.00
____Jabba the Hutt 1.00
____Sheet of 4: Endor Heroes and Jabba [DH06]........4.00

Drawing Instruments

Helix

____C-3PO and R2-D2 illustration on tin containing drawing instruments..46.00

Drink Holders

Disney / MGM

____Jedi Training Acadamy coozy [DRK01] 8.00

Drink Shakers

Disney / MGM

____Mos Eisley Cantina [DKS01] 10.00

Earphones

Philips

____C-3PO [HP01]...26.00
____Darth Vader [HP02]..26.00
____Luke Skywalker [HP03] 26.00

Easter Egg Coloring Kits

Dudley Eggs

____Star Wars [E3E01] 5.00

Easter Eggs

Mello Smello

____Plastic, 60-count sticker sheet [E2E01] 5.00

Erasers

Death Star cardback.

____C-3PO [SUE01]..6.00
____Darth Vader [SUE02]..6.00
____R2-D2 [SUE03] 6.00

Sculpted busts.

____Artoo Detoo [SUE04] 4.00
____C-3PO [SUE05]..4.00
____Darth Vader [SUE06]..4.00
____Stormtrooper [SUE07] 4.00

Shaped erasers.

____C-3PO 4.00
____R2-D2, white 4.00

Butterfly Originals
Sculpted characters.

____Admiral Ackbar [SUE08] 7.00
____Baby Ewok [SUE09] 7.00
____Bib Fortuna [SUE10] 7.00
____Darth Vader [SUE11]..7.00
____Emperor's Royal Guard [SUE12] 7.00
____Gamorrean Guard [SUE13].....................................7.00
____Jabba the Hutt [SUE14] 7.00
____Max Rebo [SUE15] 7.00
____R2-D2 [SUE16] 7.00
____Wicket the Ewok [SUE17]..7.00
____Yoda [SUE18] 7.00
____3-pack: C-3PO, Darth Vader, Millennium Falcon, [SUE19]...15.00
____3-pack: C-3PO, Darth Vader, Millennium Falcon, glow-in-dark [SUE20]...9.00
____3-pack: Gamorrean Guard, Jabba the Hutt, Speederbike Trooper [SUE21] 18.00
____Emperor's Royal Guard flat rectangular with decal [SUE22]...10.00

Flomo

____Death Star II scene [SUE23] 2.00

Grand Toys
Erasers are part of larger school supply packages.

____Gold SW logo on black [SUE24] 1.00
____Queen Amidala emblem 2.00

Grosvenor

____White, in SW wrap [SUE25] 3.00

HC Ford
Die-cut.

____Admiral Ackbar [SUE26] 8.00
____Boba Fett [SUE27] 8.00
____C-3PO [SUE28]..8.00
____Chewbacca [SUE29]...8.00
____Darth Vader [SUE30]..8.00
____Gamorrean Guard [SUE31].....................................8.00
____Jabba the Hutt [SUE32] 8.00
____R2-D2 [SUE33] 8.00
____Wicket the ewok [SUE34]..8.00

Perfumed. Removable rectangular plastic case.
Return of the Jedi.

____C-3PO and R2-D2, apple [SUE35]........................6.00
____Chewbacca, orange [SUE36] 6.00
____Darth Vader, grape [SUE37] 6.00
____Ewok, strawberry [SUE38] 6.00
____Gamorrean Guard, mint [SUE39] 6.00
____Han Solo, lime [SUE40] 6.00

Star Wars.

____Han Solo [SUE41]...12.00
____Luke Skywalker [SUE42] 12.00
____Princess Leia [SUE43] 12.00

SUE08 SUE09 SUE10 SUE11 SUE12 SUE13 SUE14 SUE15 SUE16 SUE17 SUE18

SUE19 SUE20 SUE21 SUE22 SUE23 SUE24 SUE25 SUE26 SUE27 SUE28 SUE29 SUE30

Erasers

| SUE31 | SUE32 | SUE33 | SUE34 | SUE35 | SUE36 | SUE37 | SUE38 | SUE39 | SUE40 | SUE41 | SUE42 | SUE43 |

| SUE44 | SUE45 | SUE 45 variation | SUE45 variation | SUE45 variation | SUE46 | SUE47 |

| SUE48 | SUE49 | SUE50 | SUE51 | SUE52 | SUE53 | SUE54 | SUE55 |

          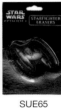 

| SUE56 | SUE57 | SUE58 | SUE59 | SUE60 | SUE61 | SUE62 | SUE63 | SUE64 | SUE65 | SUE66 |

Record erasers, ROTJ.
____Luke and Vader on Bespin gantry [SUE44] 8.00
____Poster art [SUE45] 8.00

Helix
Pear-shaped, line art characters above name.
____Artoo Detoo [SUE46] 5.00

____Chewbacca [SUE47]...............................5.00
____Darth Vader 5.00
____Han Solo [SUE48] 5.00
____Luke Skywalker [SUE49]..........................5.00
____Moff Tarkin 5.00
____Princess Leia [SUE50] 5.00
____See Threepio [SUE51]............................5.00

Impact, Inc.
2-packs. Flat erasers.
____Anakin Skywalker and Jar Jar Binks [SUE52] 4.00
____Darth Maul and Qui-Gon Jinn [SUE53] 4.00

3-packs. Sculpted figurines.
____Anakin, R2-D2, Jar Jar Binks [SUE54] 8.00
____Watto, Darth Maul, Sebulba [SUE55] 8.00

6-packs. Flat mini erasers.
____Anakin in Podracer [SUE56] 4.00
____Jedi vs. Sith [SUE57] 4.00
____Space Battle [SUE58] 4.00

____Anakin figurine [SUE59] 5.00
____Darth Maul figurine [SUE60] 6.00
____Lightsaber [SUE61]............................5.00
____Naboo Fighter [SUE62].........................2.50
____R2-D2 figurine [SUE63].........................5.00
____Sebulba figurine [SUE64] 6.00

| SUE67 | SUE68 | SUE69 | SUE70 | SUE71 | EWL01 |

| EWL02 | EWG01 | EWG02 | EWG03 |

| EWG04 | EWG05 | EWG06 | EWG07 |

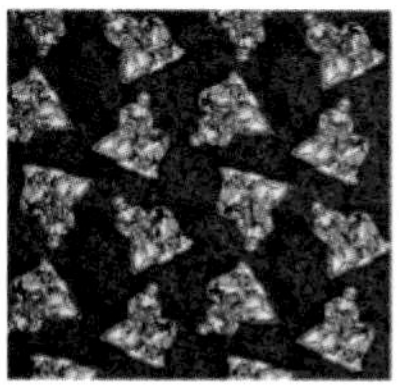
F2B01
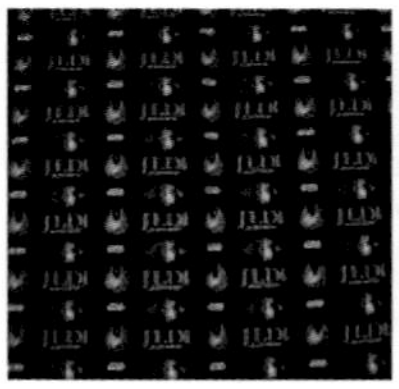
F2B02
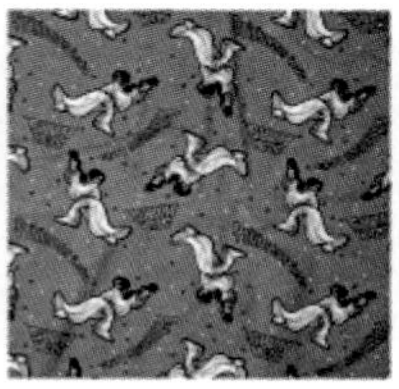
F2B03
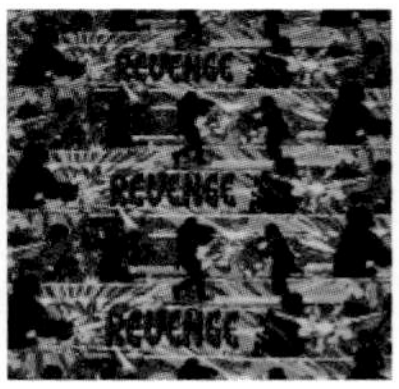
F2B04
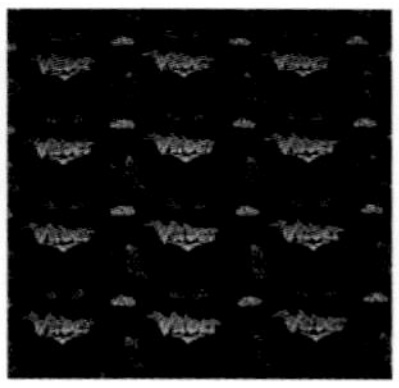
F2B05
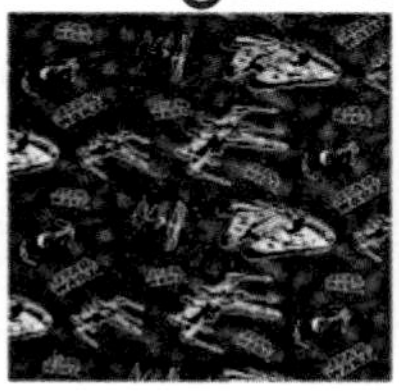
F2B06
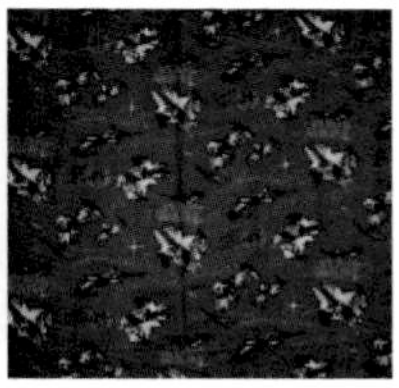
F2B07

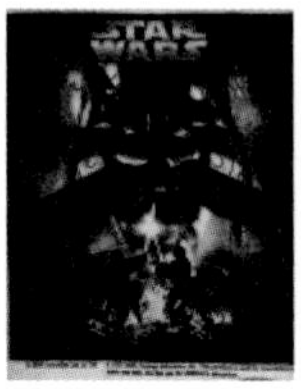
F2B08
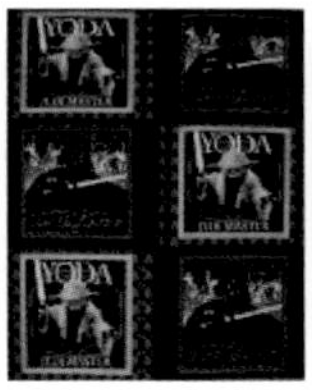
F2B09
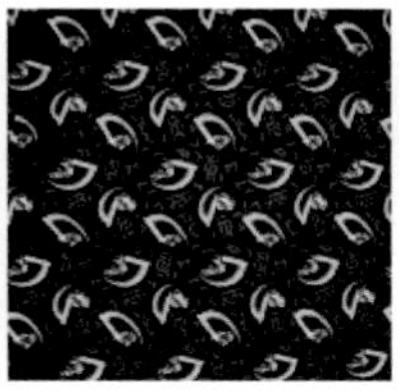
F2B10
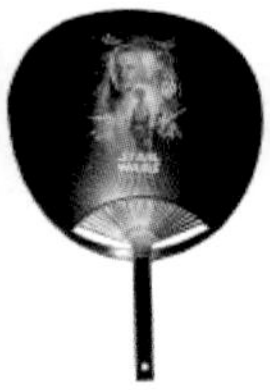
FAN01
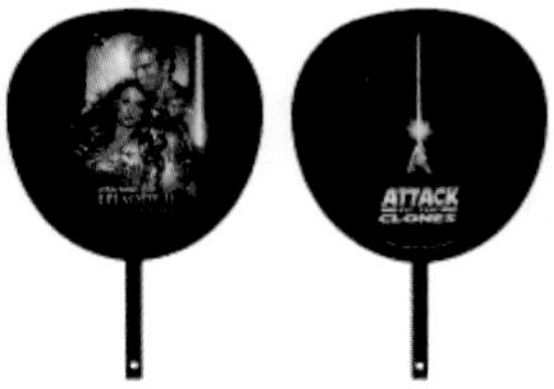
FAN02 front and rear
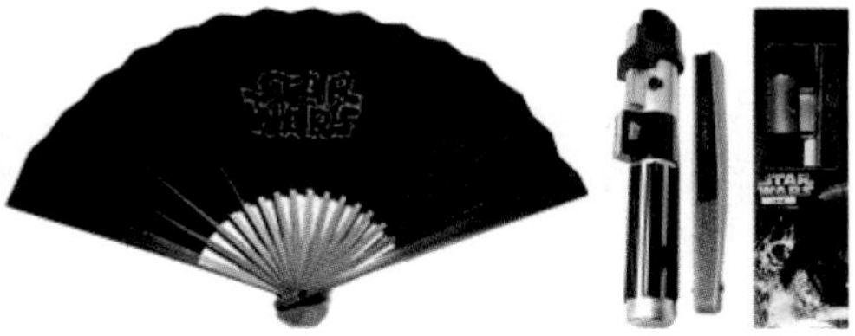
FAN03-06 opened (rear) / loose / boxed

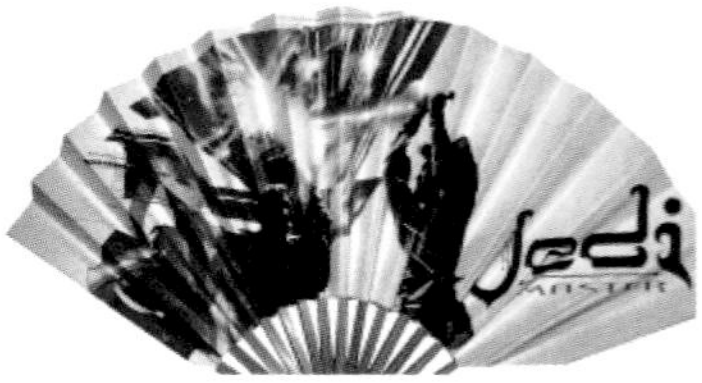
FAN03
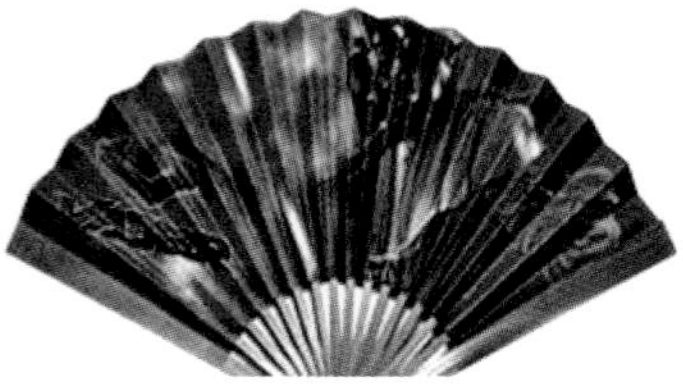
FAN04
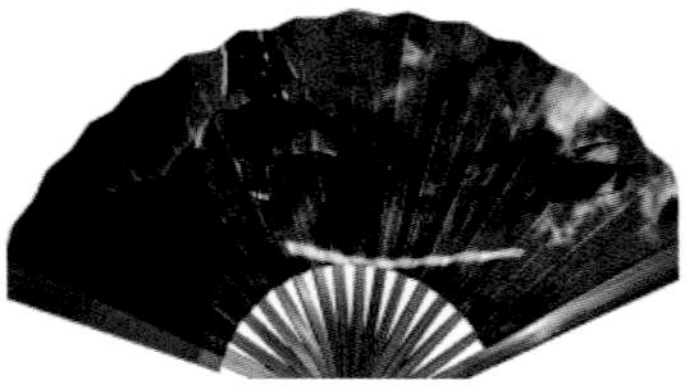
FAN05
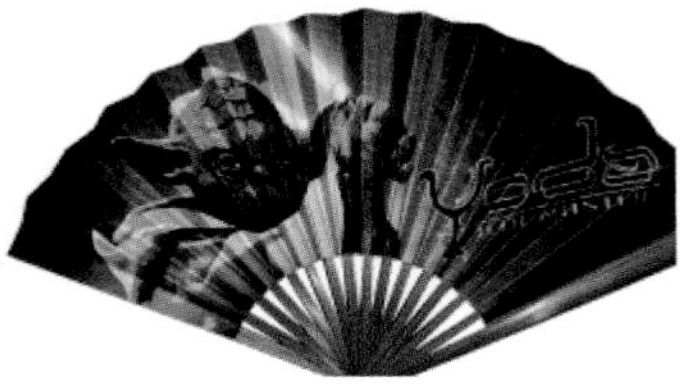
FAN06

____Trade Federation Droid Fighter [SUE65] 2.50
____Watto figurine [SUE66] 5.00

Merlin
____Darth Vader image [SUE67] 1.00
____R2-D2 image [SUE68]..2.00

Pyramid
____SW logo, 1"x1.75" [SUE69] 1.00

Q-Stat
____Obi-Wan eraser with Darth Maul pencil sharpener on card [SUE70]..7.00
____Obi-Wan Kenobi, shaped [SUE71].........................3.00

Takara
____R2-D2 ....60.00

Eyewear: Contact Lenses

LensQuest
____Imperial Logo [EWL01]..90.00
____Rebel Alliance [EWL02] 90.00

Eyewear: Sunglasses

I M T Accessories
____Anakin Skywalker, silver frames [EWG01] 6.00
____Chewbacca, green frames 6.00
____Chewbacca, orange frames [EWG02] 6.00
____Darth Vader (left), red frames [EWG03] 6.00
____Darth Vader (right), red frames 6.00
____Darth Vader, blue frames [EWG04]........................6.00
____General Grievous, orange frames..........................6.00
____Star Wars (C-3PO and R2-D2), black frames [EWG05]..6.00
____Star Wars (C-3PO and R2-D2), blue frames [EWG06]..6.00

Scholastic
____Jedi Apprentice...3.00

Fabrics

Springs Industries, Inc.
Textiles by the yard.
____C-3PO and R2-D2 [F2B01]..................................8.00
____Jedi justice pattern [F2B02] 8.00
____Princess Leia [F2B03] 10.00
____Revenge orange fleece [F2B04].........................14.00
____Revenge Vader pattern [F2B05] 8.00
____Starfighters pattern (classic trilogy) [F2B06] 8.00
____Starfighters pattern (EPIII) [F2B07].......................8.00
____Vader / Epic Duel wall panel [F2B08]..................15.00
____Yoda and Darth Vader panels [F2B09] 8.00
____Yoda pattern [F2B10] 8.00

Fan Club Materials

Fan Club
____Membership card 3.00
____New Member Kit 14.00

Paizo Publishing / Fan Club
2003 Membership Kit.
____2 letters, member card, 3 postcards, sticker sheet, mini-standee, patch 18.00

2004 Membership Kit.
____2 letters, member card, 2 posters, callender, book coupon, backdrop, original hand-painted Ewoks cartoon animation cell..35.00

Fans

Japan, limited edition.
____EPI: TPM, hand fan [FAN01] 14.00
____EPII: AOTC, hand fan [FAN02] 14.00

Baleno
____Clone Troopers 10.00
____Darth Vader and Clone Trooper 10.00

Tomy
Japan. Paper and babmoo fans in plastic lightsaber handles.
____Anakin and Obi-Wan (Jedi) [FAN03]...................25.00
____Darth Vader A [FAN04] 25.00
____Darth Vader B [FAN05] 25.00
____Yoda [FAN06] 25.00

Figurines: Ceramic

Sigma
____Bib Fortuna [CLF01] 28.00
____Boba Fett [CLF02] 55.00
____C-3PO and R2-D2 [CLF03] 45.00
____Darth Vader [CLF04]...45.00
____Emperor Palpatine [CLF05] 38.00
____Gamorrean Guard [CLF06].................................35.00
____Han Solo [CLF07]..40.00
____Klaatu [CLF08] 28.00
____Lando Calrissian [CLF09]....................................35.00
____Luke Skywalker [CLF10] 40.00
____Princess Leia Boushh Disguise [CLF11] 35.00
____Wicket the Ewok [CLF12]...................................40.00

Figurines: Porcelain

France. 1st series feves. Hand painted porcelain or ceramic figurines.
____A-Wing fighter [PF01] 7.00
____AT-AT [PF02] 7.00
____C-3PO [PF03] 10.00
____Darth Vader's Tie Fighter [PF04]...........................7.00
____Darth Vader [PF05]...10.00
____Imperial Star Destroyer [PF06] 7.00
____Millennium Falcon [PF07] 8.00
____R2-D2 [PF08] 10.00
____Sand Crawler [PF09]..7.00
____Slave I [PF10] 7.00
____Snowspeeder [PF11] 7.00
____Star Wars classic logo [PF12]................................8.00
____X-Wing Fighter [PF13]...7.00

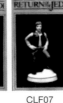

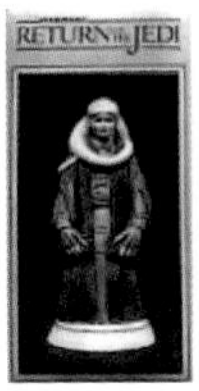
CLF01
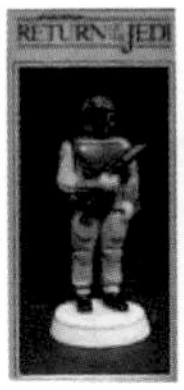
CLF02
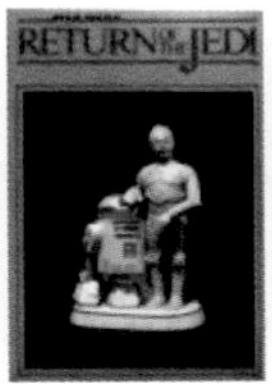
CLF03
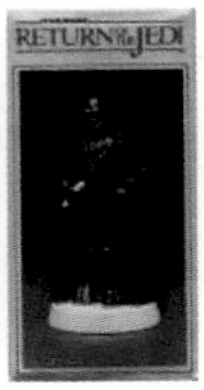
CLF04
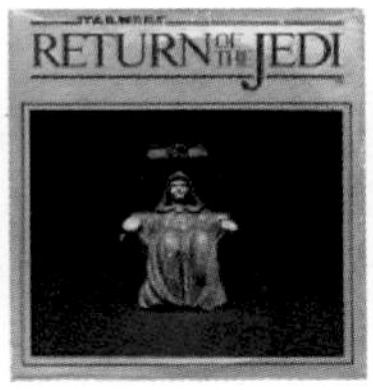
CLF05
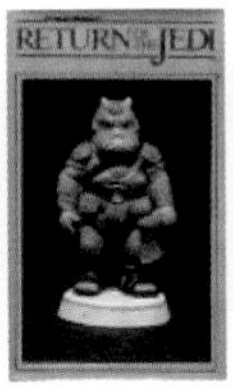
CLF06
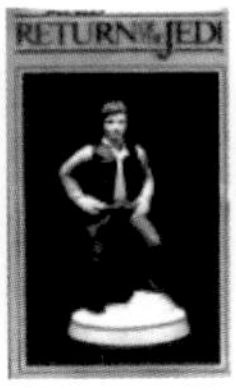
CLF07
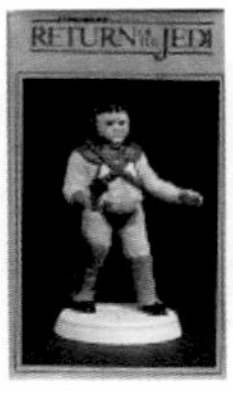
CLF08
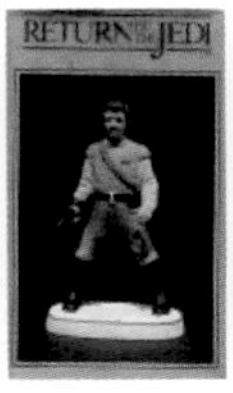
CLF09
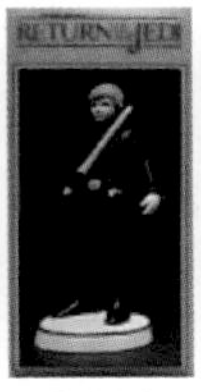
CLF10
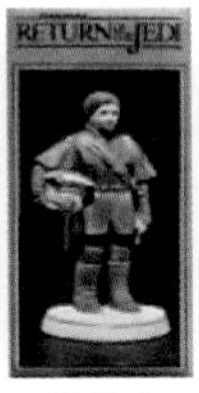
CLF11
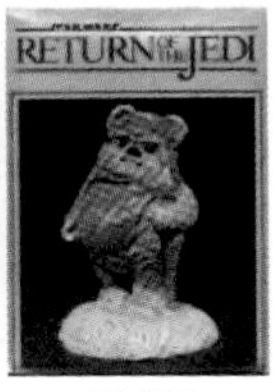
CLF12

Figurines: Porcelain

PF01   PF02   PF03   PF04   PF05   PF06   PF07

PF08   PF09   PF10   PF11   PF12   PF13

PF14   PF15   PF16   PF17   PF18   PF19   PF20   PF21   PF22   PF23

France. 2nd series feves. Hand-painted porcelain or ceramic figurines made to be put inside either an Epiphany or King cake.

____C-3PO [PF14] 5.00
____Chewbacca [PF15] 5.00
____Darth Maul [PF16]..5.00
____Darth Vader [PF17] 5.00
____Jango Fett [PF18] 5.00
____Queen Amidala [PF19].....................................5.00
____R2-D2 [PF20] 5.00
____Star Wars classic logo [PF21]............................5.00
____Stormtrooper [PF22] 5.00
____Yoda [PF23]..5.00

M&M World
Approx. 6" tall with removable base. Limited to 10,000 each.

____Boba Fett 45.00
____Darth Maul 45.00
____Darth Vader 45.00
____Luke Skywalker 45.00
____Princess Leia 45.00

Film Frames

20th Century Fox
____ANH 70mm, any frame.....................................20.00
____ESB 70mm, any frame 15.00
____Revenge of the Jedi, 70mm title frame 45.00
____ROTJ 70mm, any frame.....................................15.00

Rye by Post
Double film cell, framed.
____A New Hope 50.00
____Attack of the Clones 50.00
____Return of the Jedi..50.00
____The Empire Strikes Back 50.00
____The Phantom Menace 50.00

Duet film cell, framed.
____A New Hope & Attack of the Clones 70.00

Film cell and artwork. Signed and framed.
____Darth Vader Artwork and Film Cell, signed......195.00

Film cell duet, framed.
____The Empire Strikes Back & Return of the Jedi ..40.00

Film cell mini-montage, framed.
____A New Hope 85.00
____Attack of the Clones 85.00
____Return of the Jedi...85.00
____The Empire Strikes Back 85.00
____The Phantom Menace 85.00

Film cell trio, framed.
____A New Hope 98.00
____Attack of the Clones...98.00
____The Empire Strikes Back 98.00

Film cell, framed.
____A New Hope 45.00
____Attack of the Clones 45.00

____Return of the Jedi..45.00
____The Empire Strikes Back 45.00
____The Phantom Menace 45.00

Framed film strips from Star Wars, limited to 1,000. Each is unique.
____Star Wars, single strip 69.00
____Empire Strikes Back, double strip 69.00
____Empire Strikes Back, single strip......................69.00

Large film cell, framed, montage.
____A New Hope...195.00
____Attack of the Clones 195.00
____Return of the Jedi 195.00
____Star Wars Saga 195.00
____The Empire Strikes Back 195.00

Willitts Designs
Star Wars 70mm film frame in a 7.5"x2.75" acrylic holder with artwork or movie scenes.
____Ben Kenobi [3:263] 26.00
____C-3PO [FC01] 26.00
____Chewbacca [3:263] 26.00
____Creatures [3:263] 26.00
____Darth Vader [3:263] 26.00
____Galactic Empire 26.00
____Han Solo [3:263]..26.00
____Luke Skywalker [FC02].....................................26.00
____Princess Leia [3:263] 26.00
____R2-D2 [FC03] 26.00
____Rebel Alliance [3:263]......................................26.00
____Stormtroopers [FC04].......................................26.00

FC01

FC02

FC03

FC04

FC05

FC06

FC07

FC08   FC09

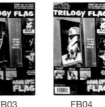

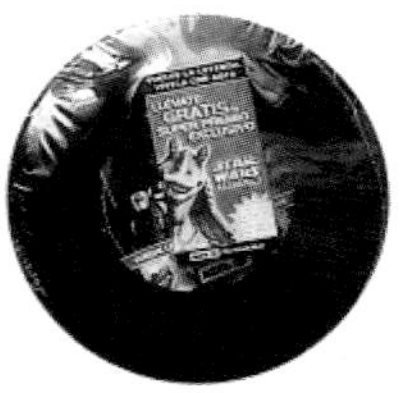
FPF01

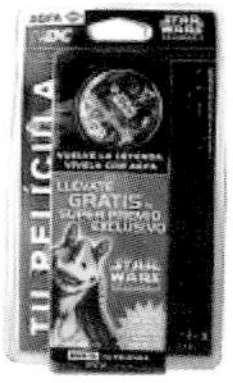
FPF02

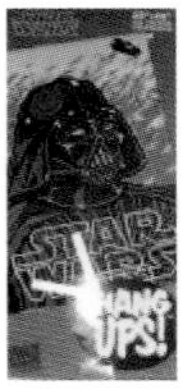
FB01

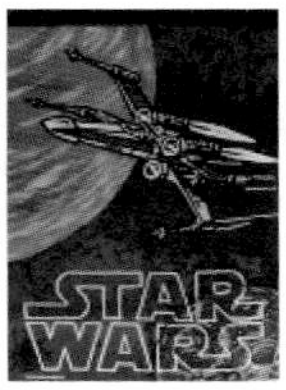

FB02 opened

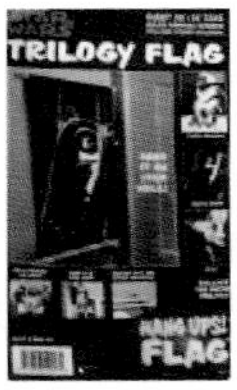

FB03

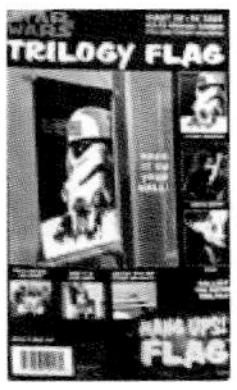

FB04

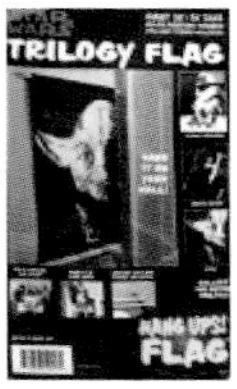

FB05

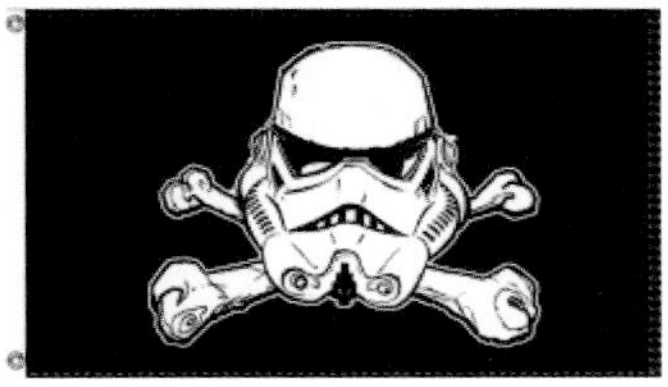
FB06

Empire Strikes Back 70mm film frame in a 7.5"x2.75" acrylic holder with artwork or movie scenes.
____Boba Fett, special edition 26.00
____Darth Vader [2:268] 26.00
____Han Solo and Princess Leia [FC05] 26.00
____Imperial Attack [FC06] 26.00
____Jedi Training [2:268] 26.00
____Lando Calrissian [2:268] 26.00
____Light Saber Duel, special edition [FC07] 75.00
____Luke 26.00
____Luke Skywalker on Cloud City 26.00
____Master Yoda [2:268] 26.00
____Millennium Falcon [2:268] 26.00
____Rebel Alliance 26.00
____Rebel Escape [2:268] 26.00

Return of the Jedi 70mm film frame in a 7.5"x2.75" acrylic holder with artwork or movie scenes.
____Aliens of Jabba's Palace [2:268] 26.00
____Darth Vader [FC08] 26.00
____Droids [2:268] 26.00
____Emperor Palpatine 26.00
____Ewoks 26.00
____Final Confrontation 26.00
____General Han Solo [FC09] 26.00
____Imperial Forces [2:268] 26.00
____Jabba the Hutt Special Edition 26.00
____Jedi [2:268] 26.00
____Jedi Emerges [2:268] 26.00
____Princess Leia [2:268] 26.00
____Rebellion [2:268] 26.00
____Turning Points [2:268] 26.00

Collector's Box Sets. Four frames included.
____Empire Strikes Back, first edition 125.00
____Empire Strikes Back, second edition 125.00
____Return of the Jedi 145.00

Film

Agfa
____3-pack with free frisbee [FPF01] 21.00
____3-pack with free yo-yo [FPF02] 18.00

Flags

Great Scott
____Darth Vader [FB01] 18.00
____X-wing fighter [FB02] 18.00

Star Wars trilogy art. 20"x36".
____Darth Vader [FB03] 18.00
____Stormtrooper [FB04] 18.00
____Yoda [FB05] 18.00

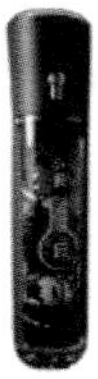
LG01

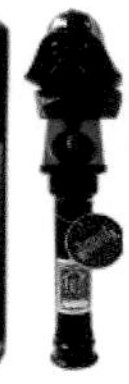
LG02

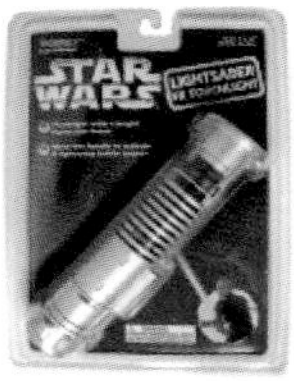

LG03

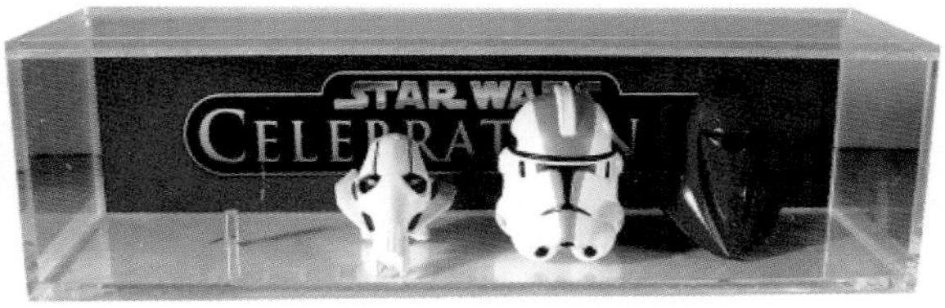

F1H01

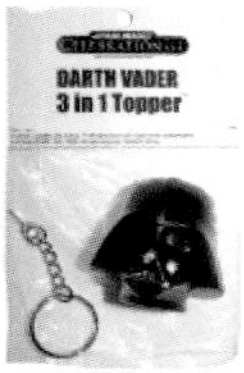

F1H02

Lucasfilm
____Stormtrooper skull and crossbones, 3'x5' 1-sided [FB06] 45.00

Flashlights

M&M World
____Mpire promotional [LG01] 30.00

Super Live Adventure
____Darth Vader with rotating head [LG02] 125.00

Tiger Electronics
____Lightsaber FX Torchlight [LG03] 15.00

Foam Heads

____3-pack Grievous, Clone, Royal Guard in acrylic case, Celebration 3 exclusive [F1H01] 25.00
____Clone Trooper, Celebration 2 .... 6.00
____Darth Vader, Celebration 3 premium with 4-day ticket, fan club exclusive [F1H02] 10.00

Folders

Thailand. Theater give-aways.
____C-3PO / R2-D2 [SUF01] 12.00
____Darth Vader / Anakin [SUF02] 12.00
____Jedi / Sith [SUF03] 12.00

Animations
EPIII:ROTS.
____Darth Vader helmet 2.00
____Darth Vader lightsaber down 2.00
____Darth Vader lightsaber up 2.00

Impact, Inc.
____Anakin Skywalker [SUF04] 2.00
____Darth Maul / Darth Sidious [SUF05] 2.00
____Jar Jar [SUF06] 2.00
____Jedi vs. Sith [SUF07] 3.00
____Pod Race [SUF08] 3.00
____Queen Amidala [SUF09] 2.00
____Qui-Gon Jinn [SUF10] 2.00
____R2-D2 / C-3PO [SUF11] 2.00
____Space Battle [SUF12] 3.00

Mead
____"Freeze You Rebel Scum" [SUF13] 3.00
____"May The Force Be With You" [SUF14] 3.00
____"May The Force Be With You" 4.00
____"Never Underestimate The Power Of The Dark Side" [SUF15] 3.00
____B-Wing Attack [SUF16] 4.00
____Bounty Hunters neon: IG-88, Greedo, Boba Fett [SUF17] 6.00
____C-3PO 4.00
____C-3PO R2-D2 neon [SUF18] 6.00
____C-3POs Phrases / C-3PO [SUF19] 3.00
____Darth Vader 4.00

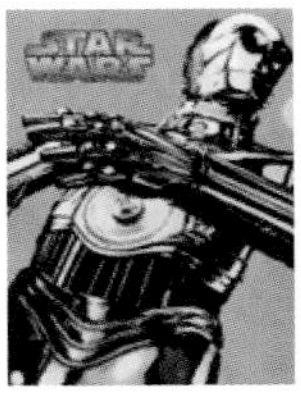
SUF01

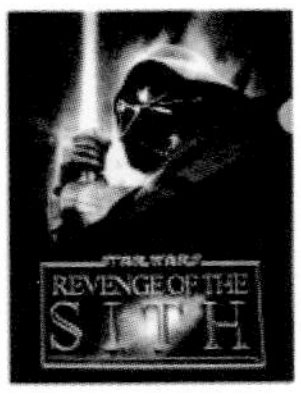

SUF02

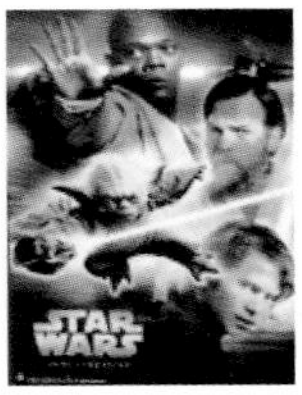
SUF03

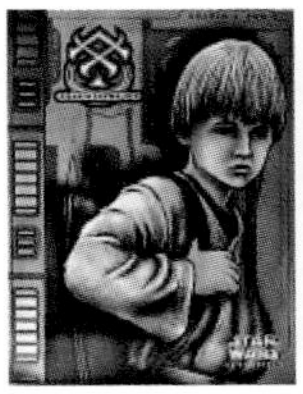
SUF04

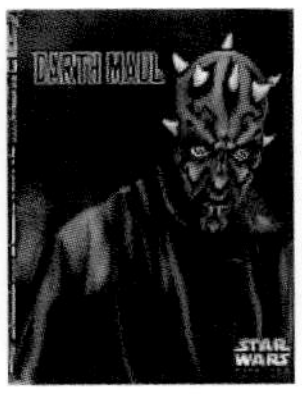

SUF05

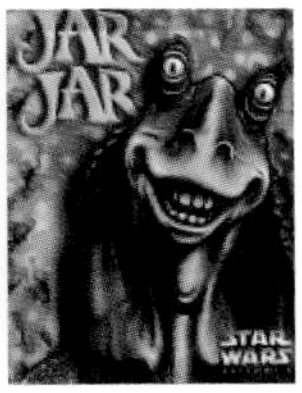

SUF06

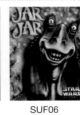

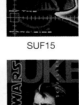

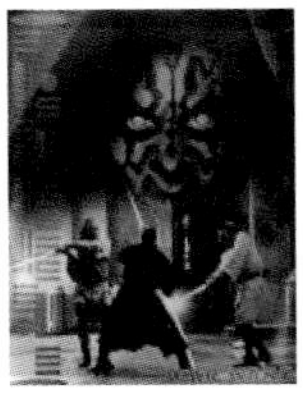
SUF07

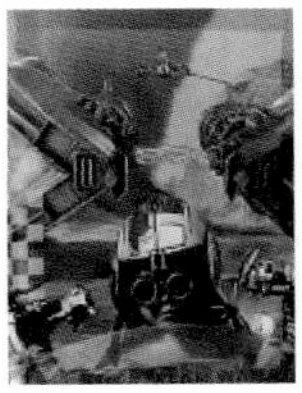
SUF08

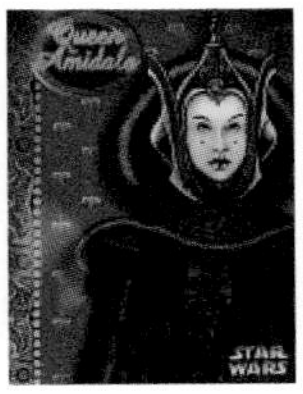
SUF09

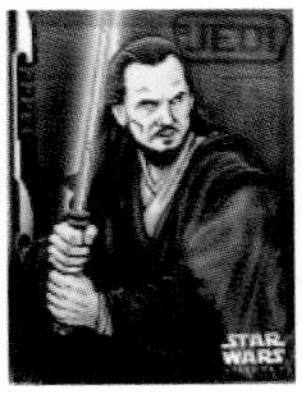
SUF10

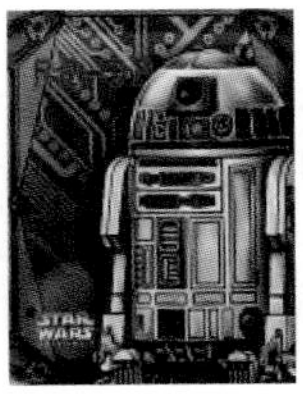
SUF11

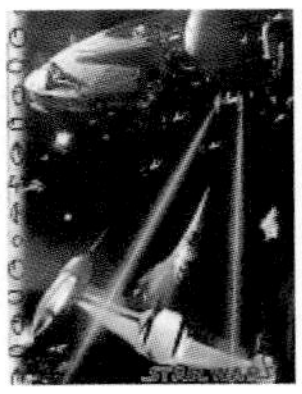
SUF12

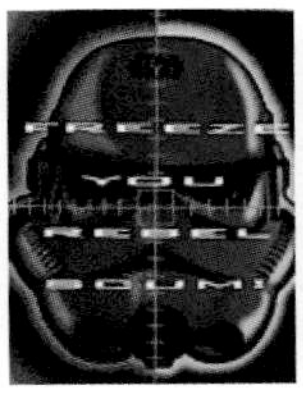
SUF13

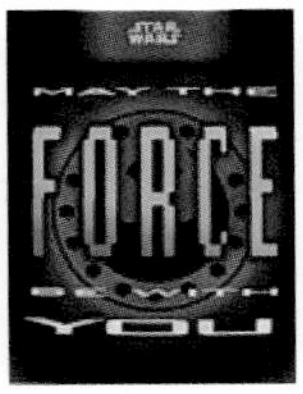

SUF14

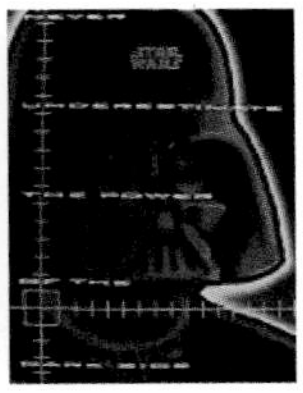
SUF15

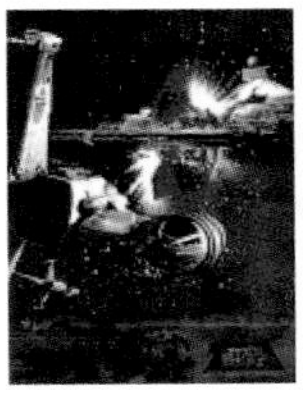
SUF16

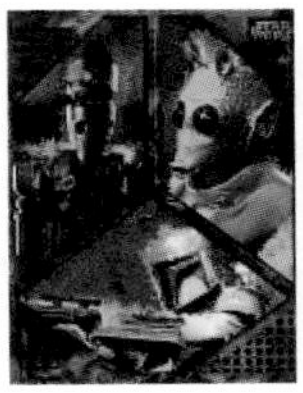
SUF17

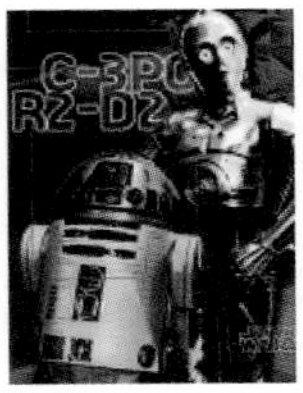

SUF18

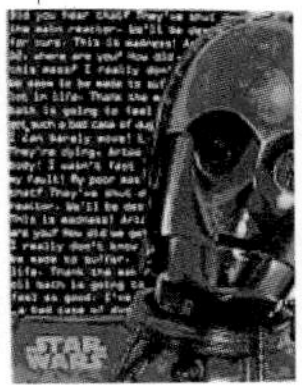
SUF19

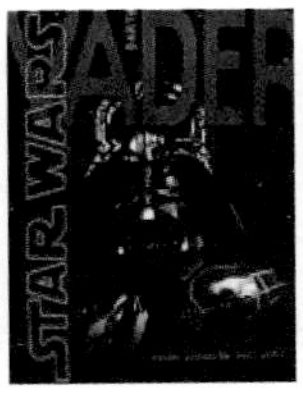

SUF20

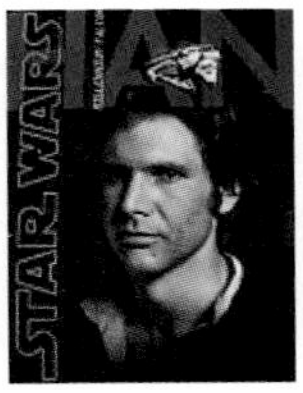

SUF21

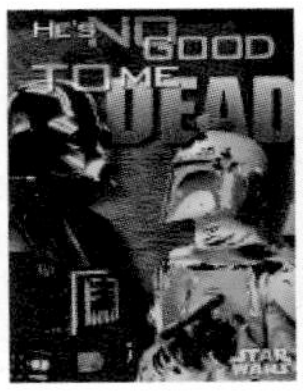
SUF22

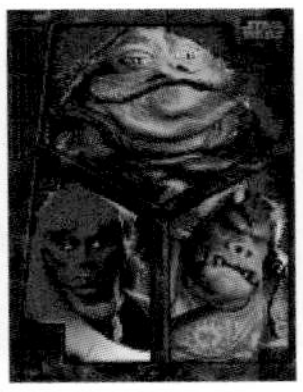
SUF23

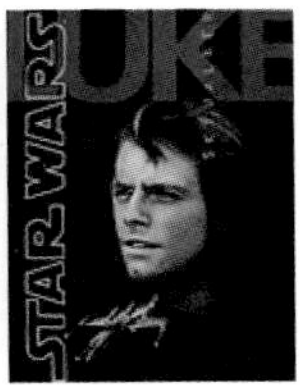

SUF24

Folders

SUF25 SUF26 SUF27 SUF28 SUF29 SUF30 SUF31 SUF32 SUF33

SUF34 SUF35 SUF36 SUF37 SUF38 SUF39 SUF40 SUF41 SUF42

SUF43 SUF44 SUF45 FF01 FF02 FF03 FF04 FF05

____Darth Vader, Dark Lord of the Sith [SUF20] 3.00
____Han / Millennium Falcon [SUF21].........................3.00
____Han Solo 4.00
____He's No Good To Me Dead neon, Boba Fett, Darth Vader [SUF22]...6.00
____Jabba's Palace neon: Jabba the Hutt, Bib Fortuna, Gamorrean guard [SUF23]..............................6.00
____Luke Skywalker [SUF24].................................3.00
____Opening Crawl / Stormtrooper / Tanavive IV [SUF25]...3.00
____Princess Leia's Plea / R2-D2 [SUF26] 3.00
____Princess Leia [SUF27].....................................3.00
____Princess Leia..4.00
____R2-D2 ....4.00
____Space Ships..4.00
____Starfighters [SUF28]...3.00
____Tatooine neon: bantha, tusken raider, jawa [SUF29]..6.00
____Title Crawl 4.00
____Yoda's speech / Yoda [SUF30].........................3.00
____Yoda 4.00

Vintage.
____Ben Kenobi / Stormtroopers [SUF31] 11.00
____C-3PO and R2-D2 [SUF32] 10.00
____Chewbacca, Han, and Luke [SUF33]................11.00
____Darth Vader and Stormtroopers........................10.00
____Leia and Luke [SUF34].....................................10.00
____X-Wing and Tie Figter [SUF35] 11.00

Pyramid
Episode II: Attack of the Clones.
____Anakin vs. Obi-Wan 2.00

IPF01

IPF02

____Sith Lords 2.00
____Villains 2.00

Stuart Hall
____B-Wing, and Tie Interceptor [SUF36] 8.00
____Bounty Hunters 11.00
____C-3PO and R2-D2 [SUF37] 8.00
____C-3PO, R2-D2, and Wicket the Ewok [SUF38] ...8.00
____Character collage [SUF39] 11.00
____Chewbacca 11.00
____Darth Vader..11.00
____Darth Vader and Stormtroopers [SUF40] 8.00
____Darth Vader, Emperor Palpatine, Luke Skywalker [SUF41]...8.00
____Jabba the Hutt and Salacious Crumb [SUF42] 8.00
____Luke on Dagobah [SUF43]..............................11.00
____Max Rebo Band [SUF44] 8.00
____Speeder Bikes [SUF45] 8.00
____Yoda on Dagobah [SUF46] 11.00

Freeze Frame Slides

Kenner
____8D8 ....2.00
____Admiral Ackbar 2.00
____AT-AT Driver 15.00
____Ben (Obi-Wan) Kenobi 2.00
____Biggs Darklighter 2.00
____Boba Fett (typographical error)..........................5.00
____C-3PO 2.00
____Captain Piett [FF01] 2.00
____Chewbacca as Boussh's Bounty (scene error) 5.00
____Darth Vader...2.00
____Darth Vader, Removable Helmet 3.00
____Death Star Droid 3.00
____Death Star Trooper [FF02] 6.00
____Emperor's Royal Guard......................................2.00
____Emperor Palpatine 2.00
____Endor Rebel Soldier [FF03]................................2.00
____EV-9D9 ....2.00
____Ewoks 3.00
____Gamorrean Guard 2.00
____Garindan (Long Snoot) 2.00
____Grand Moff Tarkin 2.00
____Han Solo 2.00

____Han Solo, Bespin 2.00
____Han Solo, Carbonite Block 2.00
____Han Solo, Endor 2.00
____Hoth Rebel Soldier 2.00
____Hoth Snowtrooper 2.00
____Ishi Tib 2.00
____Lak Sivrak 2.00
____Lando Calrissian, General 2.00
____Lando Calrissian, Skiff Disguise 2.00
____Lobot..2.00
____Luke Skywalker, Bespin 2.00
____Luke Skywalker, Blastshield Helmet 2.00
____Luke Skywalker, Ceremonial 2.00
____Luke Skywalker, Stormtrooper Disguise 2.00
____Malakili (Rancor Keeper)....................................2.00
____Mon Mothma 2.00
____Nien Nunb 2.00
____Orrimaarko (Prune Face)....................................2.00
____Pote Snitkin..4.00
____Princess Leia, Ewok Celebration [FF04]................2.00
____Princess Leia, Hoth 3.00
____Princess Leia, Jabba's Prisoner 3.00
____Princess Leia, New Likeness 3.00
____R2-D2, Death Star Trash Compactor [FF05] 3.00
____R2-D2, Imperial Trash Compactor 5.00
____Rebel Fleet Trooper 2.00
____Ree-Yees 6.00
____Saelt-Marae (Yak Face).....................................2.00
____Sandtrooper 20.00
____Stormtrooper..3.00
____Tie-Fighter Pilot..3.00
____Ugnaughts..2.00
____Weequay...75.00
____Zuckuss...2.00

Furniture: Inflatable

Baleno
Episode III children's chairs.
____Darth Vader [IPF01] 25.00
____Yoda [IPF02] 25.00

Idea Nuova
____Plush Inflatable Lounger [IPF03] 25.00

IPF03 IPF04 IPF05 IPF06 IPF07 IPF08 IPF09

BHD01

BHD02

BHD03

BHD04

FUC01

FUC02

FUC03

FUC04

FUC05

FUC06

FUC07

FUC08

FUC09

FUC10

FUC11

FUC12

FUC13

FUC14

FUC15

FUC16

FUC17

FUC18

Intex Recreation Corp.

____C-3PO Junior Chair 30"x22.5"x22" [IPF04]........10.00
____Darth Maul Chair 48"x42"x36" [IPF05] 20.00
____Jar Jar Chair 37"x32"x31.5" [IPF06] 15.00
____Queen Amidala Chair 38"x32"x31.5" [IPF07] 15.00
____R2-D2 Junior Chair 30.5"x23"x22.5" [IPF08] 10.00

Kellytoy

____Sith Lord inflatable chair [IPF09] 18.00

Furniture: Beds

Kidnap Furniture Ltd.
Headboards.
____R2-D2 and C-3PO [BHD01]..........................225.00
____Vader, Luke. Stormtrooper [BHD02] 275.00

Monkey Business
____Darth Vader, toddler [BHD03]............................65.00

Toy Quest
____Jedi Starfighter, inflatible [BHD04] 45.00

Furniture: Chairs

____Darth Vader, beanbag [FUC01] 10.00
____Wicket beanbag [FUC02] 45.00

EPIII:ROTS folding camp-style chairs.
____Clone [FUC03] 20.00
____Darth Vader [FUC04] 20.00
____Darth Vader eyes [FUC05] 20.00
____Darth Vader, childrens [FUC06] 20.00
____Epic duel, childrens [FUC07] 20.00
____Jedi [FUC08]..20.00

EPIII:ROTS folding saucer camp-style chairs.
____Darth Vader [FUC09] 20.00

EPIII:ROTS.
____Darth Vader, children's folding 15.00

American Toy and Furniture Co.
____Wicket the Ewok rocker [FUC10].......................80.00

Return of the Jedi. Blue wood with white logo.
____Banner back [FUC11]..15.00
____Full back [FUC12]..15.00

Character World Ltd.
____Anakin and Sebulba, beanbag [FUC13] 25.00

Martin Yaffe
EPI:TPM. Rocking chairs.
____Anakin Skywalker [FUC14]..................................60.00
____Queen Amidala 60.00

Pipsqueaks
EPI:TPM. Hardwood.
____Anakin [FUC15] 175.00
____Jar Jar [FUC16] 175.00
____Sebulba [FUC17] 175.00
____Watto [FUC18] 175.00

Slumber Trek
Australia.
____Darth Vader beanbag 15.00

Furniture: Clothes Racks

Adam Joseph Industries
____C-3PO and R2-D2 ....45.00
____Max Rebo Band 45.00

American Toy and Furniture Co.
____Luke and Darth Vader Dueling [FUR01].............95.00

Furniture: Desks

American Toy and Furniture Co.
____Ewoks 2-sided desk with benches 195.00
____Return of the Jedi desk and chair [FUD01]......145.00
____Wicket activity desk and bench [FUD02] 125.00

Born to Play
____Episode I desk and stool [FUD03] 94.00

Furniture: Nightstands

American Toy and Furniture Co.
____Return of the Jedi nightstand [FUN01] 145.00

Furniture: Stools

Monkey Business.
____Sith Lord 20.00

Furniture: Tables

EPIII:ROTS.
____Darth Vader card table, 2 chairs [FUT01] 75.00
____Darth Vader round table, 2 chairs [FUT02] 75.00

American Toy and Furniture Co.
____Ewoks pinic table...125.00
____Ewoks table with 2 chairs 135.00
____Return of the Jedi with 2 chairs [FUT03] 135.00

Pipsqueaks
____EPI: Podracer Table, hardwood [FUT04]..........175.00

FUR01

FUD01

FUD02

FUD03

FUN01

FUT01

FUT02

FUT03 tabletop

FUT04 tabletop

Furniture: Toy Storage

FUU01   FUU02 assembled and boxed   FUU03   FUU04   FUU05   FUU06

Furniture: Toy Storage

American Toy and Furniture Co.
____Ewoks toy chest [FUU01] 125.00
____R2-D2 toychest [FUU02] 95.00

Born to Play
____Episode I [FUU03] 96.00

Monkey Business
____9-Bin toy organizer, epic duel art [FUU04]..........35.00
____Darth Vader, EPIII [FUU05] 35.00

Worlds Apart
____Pop'n'Fun R2-D2 Pop-Tidey [FUU06] 54.00

Game Pieces: Promotional

New Zealand.
____Count Dooku [GM01] 2.00

Burger King
____Everybody Wins, scratch-off [GM02] 4.00

Burger King, UK
EPIII:ROTS Choose Your Destiny scratch-off cards.
____Anakin Skywalker [GM03].............................3.00
____Bail Organa [GM04] 3.00
____C-3PO [GM05] 3.00

GM01   GM02

____Chancellor Palpatine [GM06] 3.00
____Chewbacca [GM07] 3.00
____Clone Trooper [GM08] 3.00
____Count Dooku [GM09] 3.00
____Darth Sidious [GM10] 3.00
____Darth Vader [GM11] 3.00
____General Grievous [GM12] 3.00
____Mace Windu [GM13].................................3.00
____Obi-Wan Kenobi [GM14]............................3.00
____Padme Amidala [GM15] 3.00
____R2-D2 [GM16] 3.00
____Tarfful [GM17] 3.00
____Yoda [GM18] 3.00

Cheesestrings
12 diffferent Saga Secrets game pieces.
Game pieces, each
____Anakin Skywalker [GM19] 1.00
____Boba Fett [GM20] 1.00
____Darth Maul [GM21] 1.00
____Darth Vader [GM22] 1.00
____Luke and Leia [GM23] 1.00
____Luke and Yoda [GM24] 1.00
____Obi-Wan Kenobi [GM25]............................1.00
____Princess Leia [GM26] 1.00
____Qui-Gon Jinn [GM27] 1.00
____R2-D2 and C-3PO [GM28] 1.00
____Stormtroopers [GM29] 1.00
____Yoda [GM30] 1.00

Coca-Cola, Canada
Vinyl inserts under bottle caps.
____A Luke Skywalker [GM31] 2.00
____B Princess Leia..................................2.00
____C Ben (Obi-Wan) Kenobi [GM32] 2.00
____D Darth Vader [GM33] 2.00
____E Han Solo [GM34] 2.00
____F Chewbacca 2.00
____G C-3PO [GM35] 2.00
____H R2-D2 [GM36] 2.00

Frito Lay
"...Can't Resist" peel-to-win game pieces.
____Anakin / Helping [GM37].........................1.00
____Darth Maul / Pursuit [GM38]......................1.00

____Darth Sidious / Domination [GM39] 1.00
____Jar Jar / Appetite [GM40] 1.00
____Mace Windu / Inquiry [GM41].....................5.00
____Nute and Rune / Cowardice [GM42] 1.00
____Obi-Wan / Honor [GM43] 1.00
____Padme / Curiosity [GM44] 1.00
____Queen Amidala / Duty [GM45] 1.00
____Qui-Gon / Instincts [GM46].......................1.00
____R2-D2 / Bravery [GM47] 1.00
____Sebulba / Cheating [GM48] 1.00
____Watto / Chance [GM49] 1.00

Kelloggs, Australia
____Ewok Adventure Collect-a-Prize game piece, any
[GM50] 6.00

Picture Name Decoder Discs.
____#1: Princess Leia is cared for by Ewoks
[GM51] 18.00
____#2: Ewoks on the forest moon of Endor
[GM52] 16.00
____#3: Han Solo and C-3PO hatch a plan
[GM53] 16.00
____#4: Max Rebo plays keyboards [GM54] 16.00
____#5: Gamorrean Guard on Jabba's sail barge
[GM55] 16.00
____#6: Our heroes held captive on moon of Endor
[GM56] 16.00
____#7: C-3PO, and Logray the ewok [GM57]....16.00
____#8: Luke Skywalker rescues Princess Leia
[GM58] 16.00
____#9: Jabba the Hutt with Bib Fortuna [GM59] 16.00
____#10: Squidhead in Jabba the Hutt's palace
[GM60] 16.00
____#11: Darth Vader awaits the Emperor
[GM61] 16.00
____#12: Lando Calrissian and Nien Nunb
[GM62] 16.00
____#13: Chewbacca captures AT-ST Walker
[GM63] 16.00
____#14: Salacious Crumb [GM64]....................16.00
____#15: Luke Skywalker fights Gamorrean Guards
[GM65] 16.00
____#16: Jabba turns Leia into dancing girl
[GM66] 16.00

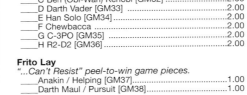

GM03   GM04   GM05   GM06   GM07

GM08   GM09   GM10   GM11   GM12

GM13   GM14   GM15   GM16   GM17

GM19 GM20 GM21 GM22 GM23 GM24 GM25 GM26 GM27 GM28 GM29 GM30

GM31 GM32 GM33 GM34 GM35 GM36

GM37 GM38 GM39 GM40 GM41 GM42 GM43 GM44

GM45 GM46 GM47 GM48 GM49 GM50

Pepsi Cola, UK
Bottle Labels.
____Find the Rebel Alliance to Win [GM67] 1.00

Star Wars Trilogy Trivia
Scratch Off: ANH
____Another name for Ben Kenobi is: [GM68] 5.00
____Luke's uncle is named: [GM69] 5.00
____Princess Leia claims she was on a diplomatic mission from: [GM70]...........5.00
____The Death Star's vulnerable point is: [GM71]........5.00

Scratch Off: ESB
____During their duel, Darth Vader cuts off Luke's: [GM72] 5.00
____In what substance is Han frozen? [GM73]...........5.00
____Who does Luke encounter in a cave during his Jedi training? [GM74]...........5.00
____Who eventually fixes the Falcon's hyperdrive motivator? [GM75]...........5.00

Scratch Off: ROTJ
____Leia kills Jabba the Hutt with her: [GM76]...........5.00
____The Ewoks live on the forest moon of: [GM77] 5.00
____Who falls in love with Princess Leia? [GM78] 5.00
____Who kills the Emperor? [GM79] 5.00

Taco Bell
Feel the Force peel-off game.
____1 Luke Skywalker [GM80]...........2.00
____2 Princess Leia [GM81]...........2.00
____3 Han Solo ($100,000 prize winner) ....N/V
____4 Obi-Wan Kenobi [GM82] 2.00
____5 Lando Calrissian [GM83] 2.00
____6 C-3PO [GM84]...........2.00
____7 Emperor Palpatine [GM85] 2.00
____8 Darth Vader ($10,000 prize winner) ....N/V
____9 Yoda ($1,000 prize winner) ....N/V
____10 Chewbacca [GM86]...........2.00
____11 R2-D2 [GM87]...........2.00
____12 – 20 (instant prize winner), each 10.00

____21 Nien Nunb (food winner) [GM88] 10.00
____22 Rancor monster (food winner) 10.00
____23 Salacious Crumb (food winner) [GM89] 10.00
____24 Tusken Raider (food winner) 10.00

Toys R Us
____Destroy The Death Star scratch off [GM90]..........4.00

Tricon Global Restaurants, Inc.
Defeat the Dark Side instant winners.
____$10,000 VISA shopping spree 50.00
____2 pc chicken meal/KFC; or combo meal/Taco Bell 4.00
____3 pc chicken snack/KFC; or nachos supreme/Taco Bell 4.00
____Apple Imac computer...........10.00
____Bread sticks/Pizza Hut; or regular nachos/Taco Bell 4.00
____Crispy strip/KFC; or original taco/Taco Bell 4.00
____Crispy Strip/KFC; or soft taco/Taco Bell 4.00

GM51 GM52

GM53 GM54 GM55 GM56 GM57 GM58 GM59

GM60 GM61 GM62 GM63 GM64 GM65 GM66

Game Pieces: Promotional

GM67

GM68   GM69   GM70   GM71   GM72   GM73   GM74

GM75   GM76   GM77   GM78   GM79   GM80-GM89   GM80   GM81   GM82   GM83   GM84

GM85   GM86   GM87   GM88   GM89   GM90   GM91 front and rear   GM92

GM93   GM94   GM95   GM96   GM97   GM98   GM99

GM100   GM101   GM102   GM103   GM104   GM105   GM106

___Darth Maul CD-player 7.00
___Indiv. side item/KFC; or regular nachos/Taco Bell 4.00
___Indiv. side item/KFC; Pepsi 2 liter or 2 dine-in beverages/Pizza Hut 4.00
___Individual dessert/KFC; or cinnamon twists/Taco Bell [GM91] 4.00
___Lincoln Navagator 55.00
___Lucas Learning SW:EPI PC/Mac game 7.00
___LucasArt Entertainment SW:EPI CD-Rom game 8.00
___Meade refracting telescope 9.00
___Medium 3 topping pizza/Pizza Hut; or 8 pc chicken meal/KFC 4.00
___Nintendo 64 with EPI Racer cartridge 7.00
___Official SW Fan Club membership 5.00
___Pepsi 2 liter or 2 dine-in beverages/Pizza Hut; or original taco/Taco Bell [GM92] 4.00
___Pepsi 2 liter or 2 dine-in beverages/Pizza Hut; or regular nachos/Taco Bell 4.00
___Seneca Sports wheeled sports pkg. 10.00
___Star Wars Speeder 75.00
___THX home entertainment system 12.00
___Trip for 2 around the world................................75.00

Defeat the Dark Side.
#1 – #3: $10,000 winner pink set.
___#01 Ric Olie [GM93] 0.50
___#02 Daultay Dofine, 50 produced 75.00
___#03 R2-D2 [GM94] 0.50
#4 – #5: $1,000 winner purple set.
___#04 Yoda, 1500 produced 60.00
___#05 Mace Windu [GM95] 0.50

#6 – #10: $1,000,000 winner orange set.
___#06 Sebulba [GM96]..0.50
___#07 Anakin Skywalker 0.50
___#08 Watto [GM97]...0.50
___#09 C-3PO [GM98] 0.50
___#10 Shmi Skywalker, 1 produced.......................N/V
#11 – #15: $1,000,000 winner green set.
___#11 Darth Maul [GM99]......................................0.50
___#12 Qui-Gon Jinn [GM100].................................0.50
___#13 Battle Droid, 1 produced ....N/V
___#14 Jar Jar Binks [GM101]..................................0.50
___#15 Boss Nass [GM102].....................................0.50
#16 – #20: $1,000,000 winner red set.
___#16 Queen Amidala [GM103] 0.50
___#17 Senator Palpatine [GM104]..........................0.50
___#18 Obi-Wan Kenobi [GM105]............................0.50
___#19 Darth Sidious [GM106]................................0.50
___#20 Chancellor Velorum, 1 produced..................N/V
___Unopened 2-pack 1.50
___Unopened pack of 50 ....25.00

Walkers
"Can You Resist?" Scratch off game. Episode I characters.
___Any character [GM107].......................................5.00

Games: Foosball
Sportcraft
___EPIII:ROTS foosball, Walmart exclusive [GFZ01]...75.00

Games: Pachinko
Star Wars Jedi Knights, handheld.
___Blue [PG01] 35.00
___Red [PG02] 35.00

GM107 samples   GFZ01   PG01   PG02   PG03

| G1C01 | NH01 | NH02 | NH03 | NH04 | NH05 | NH06 |

| NH07 | NH08 | NH09 | NH10 | NH11 | NH12 | NH13 |

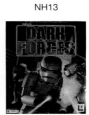

| NH14 | NH15 | NH16 | NH17 | NH18 | NH19 | NH20 | NH21 |

Sankyo Co., Ltd.
____Star Wars [PG03] 1,650.00

Games: Video Controllers

Intec
Console controllers.
____Darth Vader Jedi Hunter for PS2 ....35.00
____Darth Vader Jedi Hunter for XBOX 35.00
____PS2 2-pack Jedi and Sith glow [G1C01]...........45.00
____Yoda for PS2, Blockbuster exclusive..................50.00

Games: Video

____Empire Strikes Back for Commodore 64, cassette
[NH01]...32.00
____Star Wars for Namcot [NH02] 82.00

Broderbund
____Star Wars for PC [NH03] 45.00

Capcom USA
____Star Wars for Gameboy [NH04] 25.00
____The Empire Strikes Back for Gameboy 25.00

Domark
____Star Wars for Acorn and ZX Spectrum 48k / 128k
[NH05]..19.00

Eidos Interactive
____Lego Star Wars for Game Cube 35.00
____Lego Star Wars for PC 35.00
____Lego Star Wars for PS2 ....35.00
____Lego Star Wars for Xbox 35.00

Electronic Arts
____Episode I: The Phantom Menace........................10.00

Hasbro
____Millennium Falcon Cd-Rom Playset [NH06] 50.00
____Star Wars Monopoly for PC 15.00
____Star Wars Monopoly, deluxe edition for PC
[NH07]..25.00

J V C
____Star Wars for Nintendo 35.00
____Super Return of the Jedi for Super Nintendo
[NH08]...50.00
____Super Star Wars for Nintendo 45.00
____Super The Empire Strikes Back for Super Nintendo
[NH09]...45.00
____The Empire Strikes Back for Nintendo 20.00

Lucas Learning
____Anakin's Speedway, Build and Drive
[NH10]..12.00
____Droidworks, Science and Technology
[NH11]...12.00
____Early Leaning, Activity Center [NH12] 12.00
____Gungan Frontier, Ecology and Nature
[NH13]...12.00

____Gungan Frontier, EPI [NH14] 18.00
____Jabba's Game Galaxy, Math [NH15] 12.00
____Pit Droids, Logic and Reasoning [NH16]...........12.00
____Pit Droids: 300+ Puzzles to Drive You Nuts! for
Windows and MacIntosh [NH17].......................30.00
____Yoda's Challenge, Activity Center [NH18] 12.00

LucasArts
____3-Pack: Star Wars Racer, EPI Insider's Guide, The
Phantom Menace for PC [NH19] 40.00
____B-Wing for PC 35.00
____Battlefront for Macintosh 50.00
____Battlefront for PC 50.00
____Battlefront for PS2 ....50.00
____Battlefront for Xbox 50.00
____Dark Forces for Macintosh [NH20] 28.00
____Dark Forces for PC [NH21] 25.00
____Dark Forces for Playstation [NH22] 54.00
____Dark Forces II: Jedi Knight for PC [NH23]..........35.00
____Droidworks, EPI [NH24] 45.00
____Episode I Racer for Gameboy [NH25] 42.00
____Episode I Racer for Nintendo 64 [NH26] 35.00
____Flight of the Falcon, Gameboy Advance 45.00
____Imperial Pursuit for PC [NH27]..........................35.00
____Jar Jar's Adventure 12.00
____Jedi Knight: Mysteries of the Sith for PC
[NH28]..65.00
____Jedi Power Battles for Playstation [NH29]..........54.00
____Jedi Power Battles for Playstation, gold premium pkg.
[NH30]...66.00
____Knights of the Old Republic, Sith Lords
[NH31]..35.00

| NH22 | NH23 | NH24 | NH25 | NH26 | NH27 | NH28 |

| NH29 | NH30 | NH31 | NH32 | NH33 | NH34 | NH35 | NH36 |

Games: Video

NH37

NH38

NH39

NH40

NH41

NH42

NH43

NH44

NH45

NH46

NH47

NH48

NH49

NH50

NH51

___LucasArts Archives Vol. II: Star Wars Collection for PC [NH32]....................47.00
___LucasArts Xbox Experience [NH33]....................10.00
___Masters of Teras Kasi for Playstation [NH34]....29.00
___Mysteries of the Sith expanded missions for Dark Forces II....................14.00
___Obi-Wan for Xbox [NH35]....................65.00
___Racer Revenge for Playstation 2 [NH36]....................55.00
___Rebel Assault for PC....................25.00
___Rebel Assault for Sega....................20.00
___Rebel Assault II for Macintosh [NH37]....................39.00
___Rebel Assault II for PC....................35.00
___Rebel Assault II for Playstation [NH38]....................45.00
___Rebel Strike preview disc, GameCube [NH39]....................15.00
___Rebellion for PC [NH40]....................35.00
___Republic Commando for PC....................54.00
___Republic Commando for Xbox....................54.00
___Revenge of the Sith for PC....................50.00
___Rogue Leader for Xbox [NH41]....................65.00
___Rogue Squadron for Nintendo 64 [NH42]....................55.00
___Rogue Squadron for PC....................35.00
___Shadows of the Empire for Nintendo [NH43]....65.00
___Shadows of the Empire for PC [NH44]....................25.00
___Star Wars Episode III for PS2....................50.00
___Star Wars Episode III for Xbox....................50.00
___Star Wars Galaxies [NH45]....................50.00
___Star Wars Galaxies, deluxe....................80.00
___Starfighter for Playstation 2 [NH46]....................54.00
___Starfighter for Xbox....................65.00
___Super Bombad Racing for Playstation 2 [NH47]....................50.00
___Super Star Wars for Super Famicom [NH48]....65.00
___Super The Empire Strikes Back for Super Famicom [NH49]....................67.00
___SW Demolition for Playstation [NH50]....................54.00
___SW Demolition for Playstation, demo only [NH51]....................10.00
___Tie Fighter for PC [NH52]....................50.00
___X-Wing Flight School for PC....................28.00
___X-Wing vs. Tie Fighter for PC [NH53]....................35.00
___X-Wing vs. Tie Fighter, Balance of Power campaigns for PC [NH54]....................35.00
___Yoda Stories for Gameboy Color [NH55]....................26.00
___Yoda Stories for PC [NH56]....................15.00

Battlefront for PS2 limited edition action packs with Unleashed figure.

___Chewbacca [NH57]....................60.00
___Clone Trooper [NH58]....................60.00
___Luke pilot [NH59]....................60.00

United Kingdom.

___SW Demolition for Dreamcast [NH60]....................50.00

Lucasfilm Games

___Night Shift (parody) for Commodore 64....................45.00
___Night Shift (parody) for PC [NH61]....................34.00
___X-Wing collector's edition for PC [NH62]....................39.00
___X-Wing for PC [NH63]....................35.00

Mastertronic

___Droids, Adventures of R2-D2 and C-3PO, Commodore 64 cassette [NH64]....................15.00

Nintendo

___Nintendo 64 console with EPI PodRacer cartridge and strategy guide....................120.00
___Star Wars for Famicom....................55.00
___Super Return of the Jedi for Gameboy....................17.00

Parker Bros.

___Return of the Jedi: Death Star Battle, Atari 2600 [NH65]....................15.00
___Star Wars: Jedi Arena, Atari 2600 [NH66]....................15.00
___Star Wars: The Arcade Game, Atari 2600 [NH67]....................15.00
___Star Wars: The Arcade Game, Atari 5200 [NH68]....................17.00
___Star Wars: The Arcade Game, Colecovision [NH69]....................17.00
___Star Wars: The Empire Strikes Back, for Intellivision [NH70]....................15.00
___The Empire Strikes Back, Atari 2600 [NH71]......30.00

Parody Interactive

___Star Warped for PC [NH72]....................10.00
___Star Warped for PC, Special Edition [NH73]......12.00

Sega

___Racer for Dreamcast [NH74]....................25.00
___Star Wars: The Arcade Game for Sega....................20.00
___SW Chess for Sega, CD-ROM [NH75]....................17.00

Software Toolworks

___SW Chess software for IBM-compatible computers, CD-ROM....................21.00

NH52

NH53

NH54

NH55

NH56

NH57

NH58

NH59

NH60

NH61

NH62

NH63

NH64

NH65

NH66

NH67

NH68

NH69

NH70

NH71

NH72

NH73

NH74

| NH75 | NH76 | NH77 | NH78 | NH79 | NH80 | NH81 | NH82 |

| GTC01 | | GTC02 | | GTC03 | GTC04 | GTC05 | GTC06 | GTC07 |

| GTC08 | GTC09 | GTC10 | GTC11 | GTC12 | GTC13 | GTC14 | GTC15 | GTC16 | GTC17 |

____SW Chess software for IBM-compatible computers, floppy disks [NH76] 14.00

The Hit Squad
____Star Wars for the Amstrad 464/664/6128, cassette [NH77] 8.00

THQ
____The New Droid Army for Gameboy Advanced [NH78]...45.00

Totally Games
____X-Wing vs. TIE Fighter, The Acadamy [NH79]...25.00

Ubisoft
____Apprentice of the Force for GBA [NH80]............25.00

US Gold
____Star Wars for Sega Game Gear 25.00
____Star Wars for Sega Master system [NH81] 25.00
____X-Wing [NH82] 35.00

Zipdisk
____Star Wars 15.00

Gift Cards

Blockbuster Video
____Battlefront $15 [GTC01] 15.00
____Star Wars 7-Week Rental Card [GTC02] 10.00
____Yoda $10 [GTC03] 10.00

Books-a-Million
Episode III: Revenge of the Sith.
____C-3PO and R2-D2 [GTC04] 5.00
____Darth Vader [GTC05]...5.00
____Epic Duel [GTC06] 5.00
____Master Yoda [GTC07] 5.00

Borders, Inc.
____Anakin in podracer helmet, $25 gift card 7.00
____Darth Maul, $50 gift card 12.00

Episode III: Revenge of the Sith.
____Darth Vader [GTC08]...5.00

Burger King
____Episode III characters 8.00

Lenticular scenes from each movie.
____EP1: Darth Maul 5.00
____EP2: Yoda vs. Count Dooku 5.00
____EP3: Anakin Skywalker 5.00
____EP4: Luke Skywalker 5.00
____EP5: Boba Fett 5.00
____EP6: Jabba the Hutt 5.00

| GTC18 | GTC19 | GTC20 | GTC21 | GTC22 | GTC23 |

Hot Topic
____Movie poster art on C-3PO and R2-D2 hanger card [GTC09] 5.00

K-Mart
$50 cash cards, available monthly in 1999.
____Anakin in podracer helmet, May...........................8.00
____Darth Maul, September 8.00
____Jar Jar Binks, June 8.00
____Queen Amidala, August 8.00
____Qui-Gon Jinn, July [GTC10] 8.00

LucasArts
60 day pre-paid game cards.
____Boba Fett [GTC11] 4.00
____Darth Vader [GTC12] 4.00
____Human [GTC13] 4.00
____Mos Eisley [GTC14] 4.00
____Wookiee [GTC15] 4.00

Suncoast
____Anakin Skywalker 5.00
____Darth Maul [GTC16] 5.00

Target
____Darth Vader, lights up and breaths [GTC17] 5.00

Tower Records
____Anakin and Padme [GTC18]...................................5.00
____Jango [GTC19] 5.00
____Movie poster art [GTC20] 5.00
____Yoda [GTC21] 5.00

Toys R Us
____Battlefront $10 gift card [GTC22] 5.00
____Darth Vader [GTC23]..5.00

Walmart
____EPIII:ROTS video game, PlayStation2 ....3.00
____EPIII:ROTS video game, Xbox 3.00

Reflective; combine to make one image.
____Anakin Skywalker, C-3PO, and R2-D2 ....5.00
____Darth Vader 5.00
____General Grievous and Darth Sidious 5.00
____Obi-Wan Kenobi 5.00
____Tri Fighters and Jedi Starfighter 5.00
____Yoda and Clone Trooper.......................................5.00

Gift Certificates

Clarks
____Clarks gift certificate featuring Star Wars images to promote SW line of Clarks shoes [GC01] 14.00

Gift Tags

____10-pack, R2-D2 and Jar Jar Binks [PFF01] 5.00

Cleo
____30 Foil-Leaf Gift Tags, EPI [PFF02] 5.00

GC01 side 1

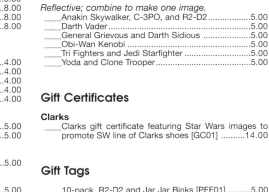

GC01 side 2

Gift Tags

| PFF01 front and rear | PFF02 | PFF03 | PFF04 | PFF05 | PFF06 | PFF07 |

| PFF08 | PFF09 | PFF10 | PFG01 | PFG02 | PFG03 | PFG04 |

| PFG05 | PFG06 | PFG07 | PFG08 | PFG09 | PFG10 | PFG11 | PFG12 |

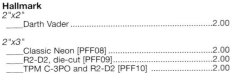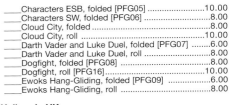

| PFG13 | PFG14 | PFG15 | PFG16 |

Drawing Board Greeting Cards, Inc.
____C-3PO and R2-D2, card art [PFF03] 5.00
____C-3PO and R2-D2, card photo 5.00
____C-3PO and R2-D2, 5-pack [PFF04]...................12.00
____Cloud City, card [PFF05].....................................6.00
____Darth Vader and Luke Duel, card 5.00
____Ewoks Hang-Gliding, tag 5.00
____Leia, Luke, and Han, card [PFF06].......................5.00
____R2-D2, stick-on decoration 9.00
____X-Wing Fighter, card [PFF07] 4.00
____Yoda, stick-on decoration...................................8.00

Hallmark
2"x2"
____Darth Vader 2.00

2"x3"
____Classic Neon [PFF08] 2.00
____R2-D2, die-cut [PFF09]......................................2.00
____TPM C-3PO and R2-D2 [PFF10] 2.00

Gift Wrap

Ambassador
____Star Wars Classic Trilogy, blue starfield background 15
sq ft roll [PFG13]...6.00

____Star Wars Classic Trilogy, neon action art 15 sq. ft.
roll 5.00
____Star Wars Classic Trilogy, starship battles on blue
technical background, folded [PFG01].................8.00
____TPM character art, 15 sq. ft. roll 4.00

Episode II: Attack of the Clones.
____Characters and vehicles against blue starfield, 15 sq ft
roll 5.00

Cleo
____Podracerr, red sparkled 8 sq. ft. roll...................7.00
____Space Battle, black sparkled 8 sq. ft. roll 7.00

Danilo Promotions Ltd.
____Darth Maul, 2 sheets, 2 tags [PFG02] 5.00

Drawing Board Greeting Cards, Inc.
____"Happy Birthday" with photos, folded [PFG03] 8.00
____"Happy Birthday" with photos, roll [PFG14] 10.00
____C-3PO, R2-D2, Darth Vader, and battle scene, 12 ft roll
[PFG15]...15.00
____C-3PO, R2-D2, Darth Vader, and battle scene, 16 ft
roll 25.00
____C-3PO, R2-D2, Darth Vader, and battle scene, 5 ft
roll 10.00
____C-3PO, R2-D2, Darth Vader, and battle scene, folded
[PFG04] 8.00

____Characters ESB, folded [PFG05] 10.00
____Characters SW, folded [PFG06] 8.00
____Cloud City, folded 8.00
____Cloud City, roll 10.00
____Darth Vader and Luke Duel, folded [PFG07] 6.00
____Darth Vader and Luke Duel, roll 8.00
____Dogfight, folded [PFG08] 8.00
____Dogfight, roll [PFG16].......................................10.00
____Ewoks Hang-Gliding, folded [PFG09] 6.00
____Ewoks Hang-Gliding, roll 8.00

Hallmark, UK
Episode II, folded.
____Characters [PFG10] 6.00
____Characters and Vehicles space theme, blue foil
[PFG11] 6.00

Marks and Spencer
2 Sheets, 2 tags.
____Episode I: The Phantom Menace [PFG12]............3.00

Glow in the Dark Decorations

Glow Zone
____Wall Plaque, Anakin Skywalker [HD01] 11.00
____Wall Plaque, Darth Maul [HD02]..........................9.00

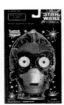

| HD01 | HD02 | HD03 | HD04 | HD05 | HD06 | HD07 | HD08 | HD09 |

| HD10 | HD11 | HD12 | HD13 | HD14 | HD15 | HD16 |

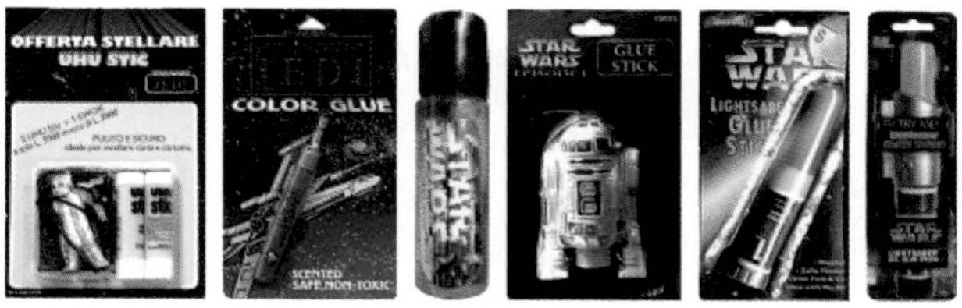

SUG01 SUG02 SUG03 SUG04 SUG05 SUG06

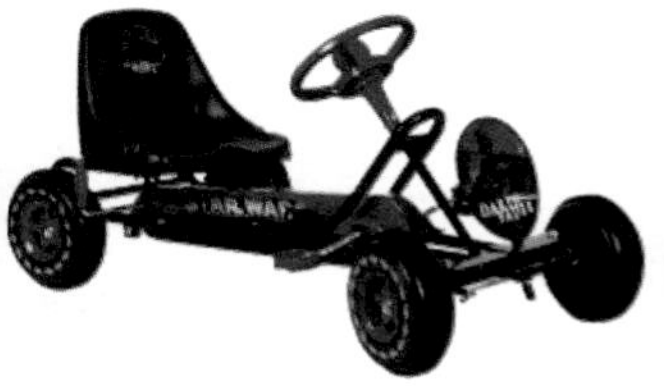

GMC01

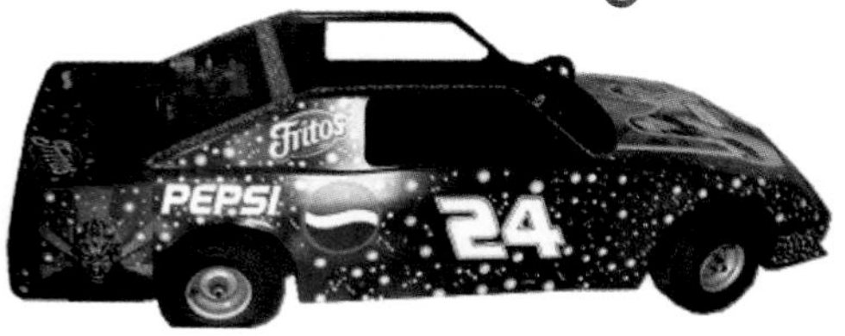

GMC02

8 Glow in the dark decorations.
____Luke, Millennium Falcon, Vader, TIE, X-Wing, R2-D2, C-3PO, Boba Fett [2:278] 7.00
____Qui-Gon Jinn, Jedi Logo, Obi-Wan Kenobi, Jar Jar Binks, Darth Maul, R2-D2, Battle Droid on Stap, Naboo Starfighter [HD03] 8.00

Illuminations
36-Piece Action Wall Scenes in plastic envelope.
____Droids [2:278] 6.00
____Jedi vs. Sith [2:278] 6.00
____Land Battle [2:278] 6.00
____Space Battle [2:278] 6.00

Box of 79 pieces.
____Battle Zone [2:278]....................................18.00
____Characters [HD04] 16.00

Box of approx. 40 pieces.
____Characters [2:278] 7.00
____Land Battle [2:278] 7.00
____Podrace [2:278]....................................7.00
____Space Battle [2:278] 7.00

Decals, character's head.
____C-3PO [HD05]....................................7.00
____Darth Maul [HD06] 7.00
____Jar Jar Binks [HD07]....................................7.00
____Obi-Wan Kenobi [HD08] 7.00

Decals, flat 10"x9.5" Action Wall Scenes.
____Droids [HD09]....................................12.00
____Gugan Adventure [HD10] 12.00
____Jedi vs. Sith [HD11] 12.00
____Podrace [HD12] 12.00
____Space Battle [HD13]....................................12.00
____Trade Federation Invasion [HD14] 12.00

Decals, flat 13"x10.5" Action Wall Scenes.
____Battle Droids [HD15] 12.00
____Jedi [HD16]....................................12.00

Glue

Beecham Italia S.p.A.
UHU glue stick with Kenner ewok figure.
____Logray [SUG01] 165.00
____Lumat....................................165.00
____Paploo 165.00
____Teebo [2:278] 165.00
____Warok....................................165.00

Butterfly Originals
____Color glue, ROTJ [SUG02] 8.00

Flomo
____SW logo on prismatic background [SUG03] 3.00

Impact, Inc.
____R2-D2 Gluestick [SUG04]....................................2.00

Rose Art Industries
____Lightsaber gluestick [SUG05]....................................7.00
____Lightsaber gluestick, ROTS [SUG06] 3.00

Gocarts

____Darth Vader [GMC01] 175.00
____Darth Vader gocart, 6v rechargable 175.00
____Darth Vader motorbike, 12v rechargable 275.00

Manco Productions
____Episode I, motorized [GMC02] 1,075.00

Goodie Bags

Look-o-Look
____Chupa Chup sucker, sticker, and Chewbacca head sucker holder [GB01] 6.00

Tapper Candies
EPI:TPM: Character mask, Darth Maul sticker, Smarties candy, Chupa-Chup lollipop, Jedi vs. Sith coin battle game.
____Anakin, lightsaber yo-yo [3:273]....................................5.00
____Anakin, slap band 5.00
____Darth Maul, lightsaber yo-yo [GB02] 5.00
____Darth Maul, slap band [3:273] 5.00

Episode II: Attack of the Clones.
____Activity card, sticker, party favor, and candy [GB03]....................................3.00

Greeting Cards

____Darth's newphew... Bruce Vader [GR01] 10.00
____Yoda delivering presents using the force, 10 cards with envelopes 19.00

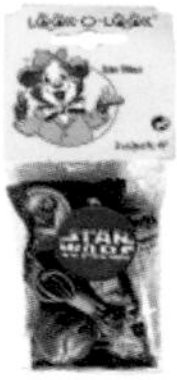

GB01

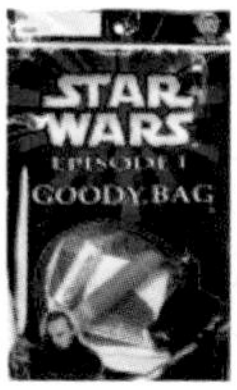

GB02

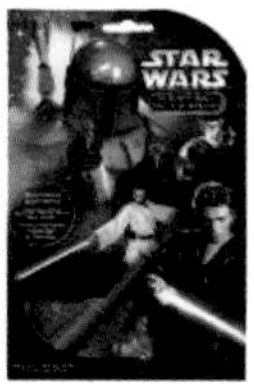

GB03

Episode II. Appoximately 8"x5"
____Heroes / Celebrate [GR02] 5.00
____Jango Fett / Happy Birthday [GR03] 5.00
____Obi-Wan Kenobi / Have a Great Day [GR04]........5.00
____Padme Amidala / Enjoy Your Birthday [GR05]......5.00

France, vintage. Tous ensemble pour le le meilleur et pour l'empire
____Classic book cover art [GR06] 5.00
____Heroes on Hoth [GR07] 5.00
____Leia / Jabba [GR08] 5.00
____Luke [GR09] 5.00
____Movie poster cover art [GR10] 5.00
____Novel cover art [GR11] 5.00
____R2-D2 / C-3PO [GR12]....................................5.00

France, vintage. Un anniversaire intergalactique
____Chewbacca [GR13]....................................5.00
____Darth Vader [GR14]....................................5.00

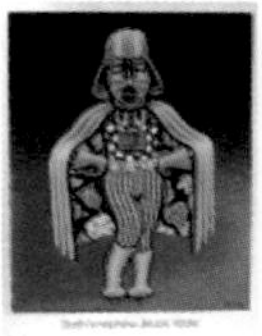

GR01

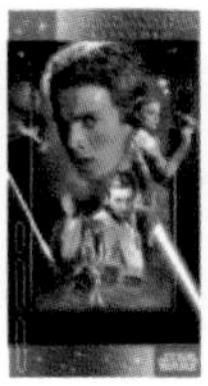

GR02

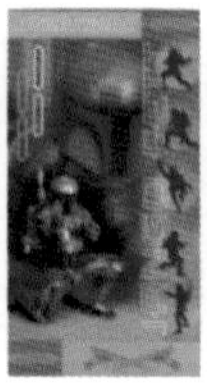

GR03

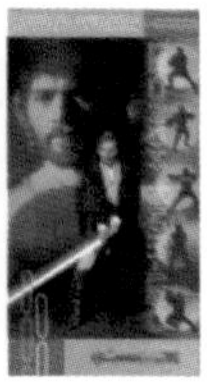

GR04

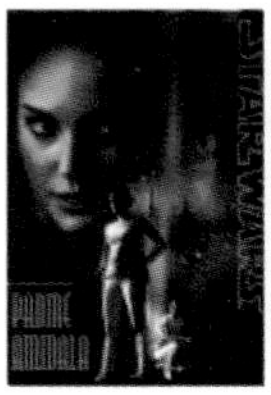

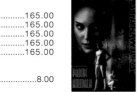

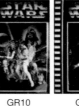

GR05

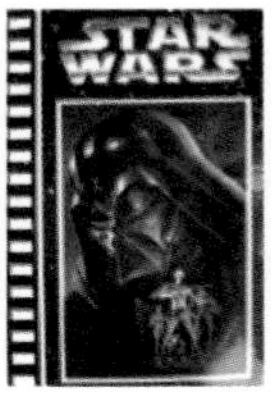

GR06

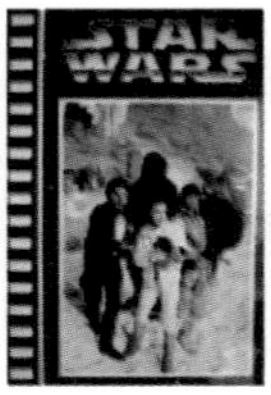

GR07

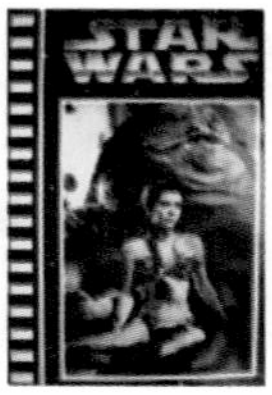

GR08

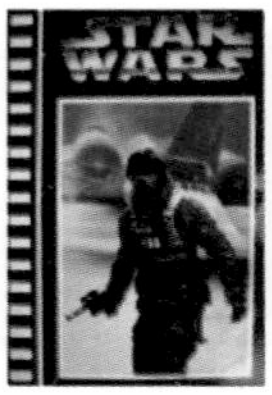

GR09

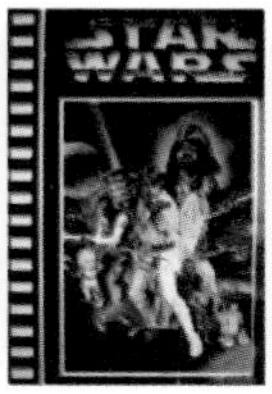

GR10

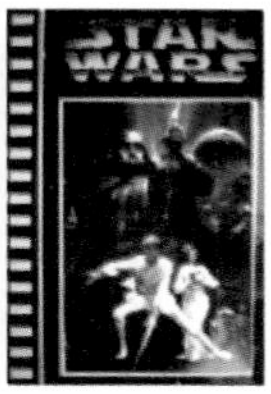

GR11

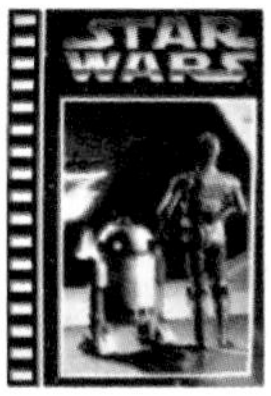

GR12

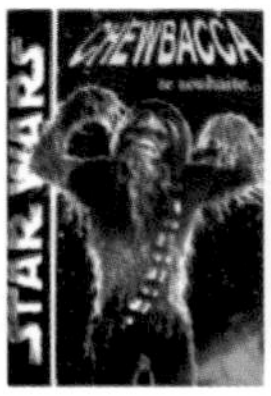

GR13

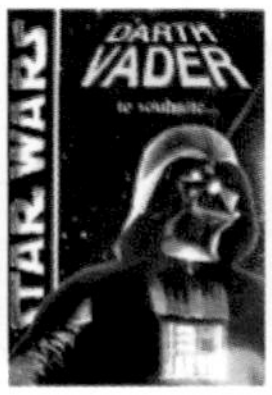

GR14

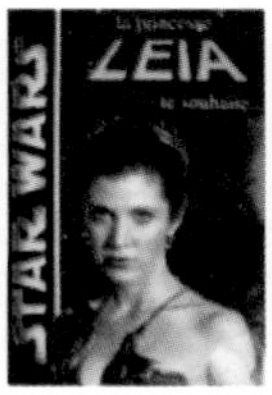

GR15

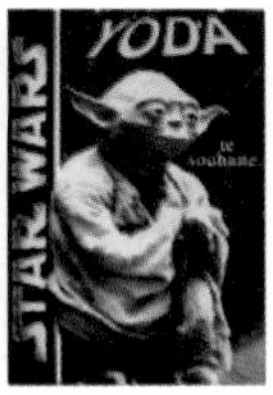

GR16

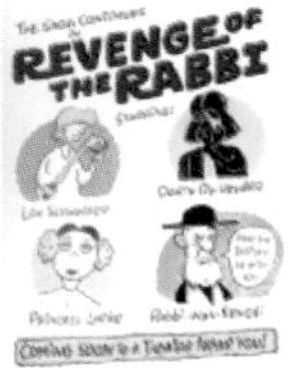

GR17

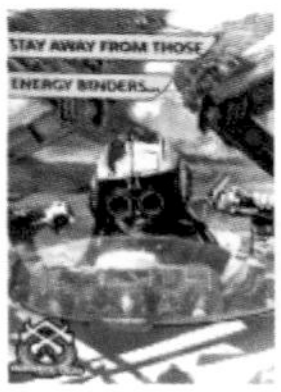

GR18

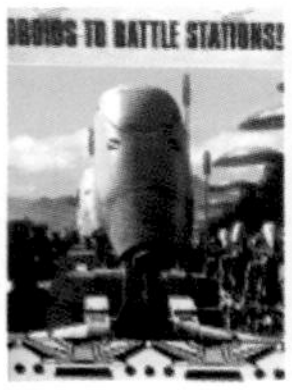

GR19

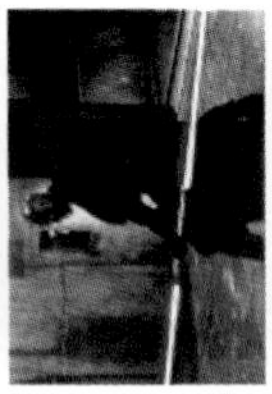

GR20

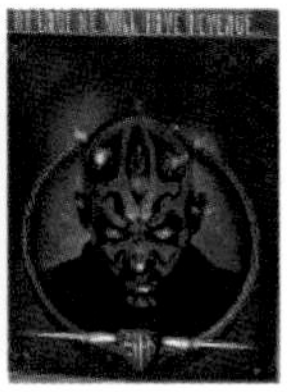

GR21

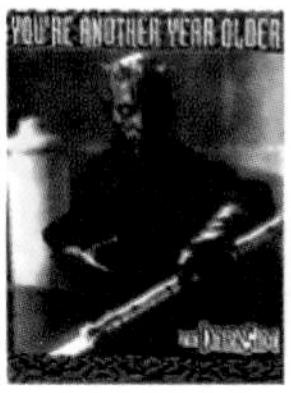

GR22

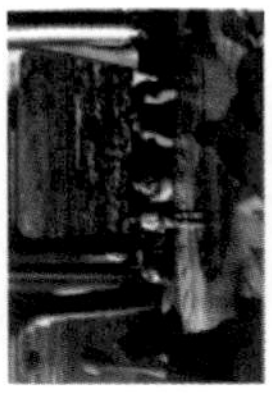

GR23

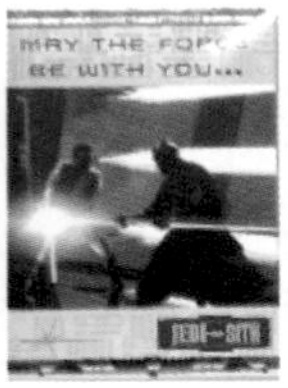

GR24

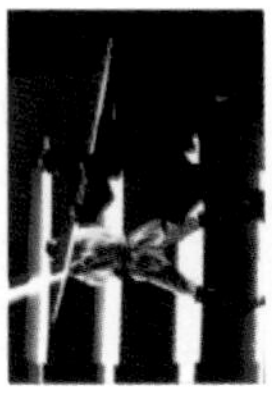

GR25

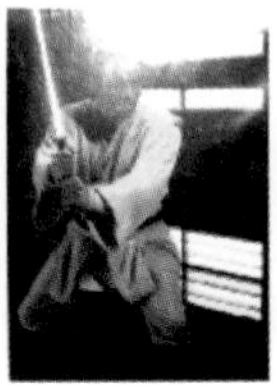

GR26

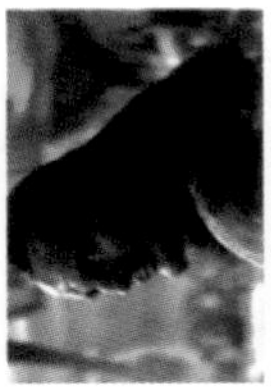

GR27

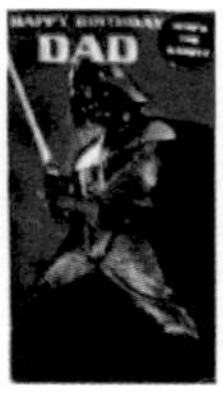

GR28

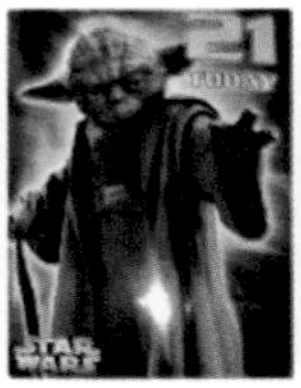

GR29

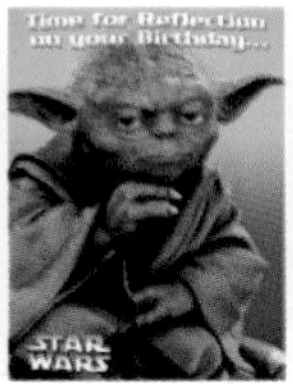

GR30

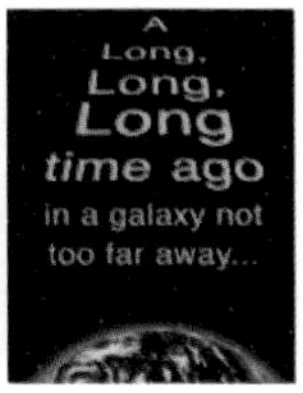

GR31

Greeting Cards

GR32　GR33　GR34　GR35　GR36　GR37　GR38　GR39　GR40

GR41　GR42　GR43　GR44　GR45　GR46　GR47　GR48　GR49　GR50

GR51　GR52　GR53　GR54　GR55　GR56　GR57　GR58　GR59　GR60

____Leia [GR15] 5.00
____Yoda [GR16] 5.00

98% Funny
____Revenge of the Rabbi [GR17] 10.00

Danilo Promotions Ltd.
____Anakin, "Stay away from those energy binders..." [GR18] 5.00
____Battle Droid, "Droids to Battle Stations!" [GR19] 5.00
____Darth Maul [GR20] 3.00
____Darth Maul, "At last we will have revenge..." [GR21] 4.00
____Darth Maul, "You're another year older..." [GR22] 4.00
____Jedi Council [GR23] 4.00
____Jedi vs. Sith, "May the Force be with you..." [GR24] 4.00
____Obi-Wan Kenobi, "May The Force Be With You On Your Birthday!", mini standee 8.00
____Obi-Wan vs. Darth Maul [GR25] 3.00
____Obi-Wan, padawan [GR26] 3.00
____Qui-Gon Jinn [GR27] 3.00
____Qui-Gon Jinn with glittered border, blank 6.00
____Qui-Gon Jinn, "You May Be Another Year Older..." / "But You Still Have Much To Learn." 5.00

UK.
____Darth Vader, "Happy Birthday Dad" / "May the Force be with you," includes "Who's the Daddy" button [GR28] 4.00

____Yoda, "21 Today" / "Happy Birthday — Be Mindful — Use The Force," talking card [GR29] 8.00
____Yoda, "Time for Reflection on your Birthday" / "Hope it's not too disturbing," mirror inside [GR30] 4.00

DCI Studios
Tomato Cards.
____A Long, long, long time ago in a galaxy not too far away ... you were born. Happy Birthday [GR31] ..4.00
____Far away in a galaxy, a long, long time ago ... You were born. [GR32] 6.00

Drawing Board Greeting Cards, Inc.
____C-3PO and R2-D2 floating away with balloons 7.00
____C-3PO and R2-D2, "For A Fine Boy," embossed 7.00
____C-3PO sitting and thinking, embossed 9.00
____C-3PO, R2-D2, Aliens, Gamorrean Guard, embossed 6.00
____Chewbacca, "Do Not Fear" 8.00
____Chewbacca, Han, Leia, R2-D2, C-3PO, Jabba the Hutt, Wicket 4.00
____Darth Vader with Drawn Lightsaber 7.00
____Darth Vader, "Space Bulletin for Grandson" 7.00
____Ewok and Princess Leia [GR33] 7.00
____Ewoks: Archery Range 7.00
____Ewoks: Baby Ewoks 8.00
____Ewoks: Ewok in Glider 7.00
____Ewoks: Fishing 7.00
____Ewoks: Nature Study 7.00
____Ewoks: Playing Music......................................7.00
____Ewoks: Princess Kneesaa and Baga 7.00

____Ewoks: Swimming 7.00
____Female Ewok, "For A Very Special Girl"..............6.00
____Han, Leia, and Luke [GR34] 6.00
____Hoojibs and R2-D2, embossed 7.00
____Leia and Luke on Speederbike [GR35] 7.00
____X-Wing Fighters, "Intergalactic Greetings" [GR36] 7.00
____X-Wing Fighters, "To An Out-Of-This-World Boy" [GR37] 8.00

Blue border design.
____C-3PO and Luke Skywalker in Ben's Hut, "They don't make 'em like you anymore!" [GR38]...................7.00
____C-3PO holding birthday cake, and R2-D2, "Have a Happy Birthday..." / "...it's the human thing to do" [GR39] 8.00
____C-3PO Lost on Tatooine, "Lost without you!" [GR40] 7.00
____C-3PO, "Feeling Kinda Rusty" / "How about a warm lubricant bath?" [GR41] 7.00
____C-3PO, "Sorry haven't written" / "...but I'm only human!" [GR42] 7.00
____Chewbacca, "Not feeling well?" / "May you soon have the strength of a Wookiee!" [GR43] 7.00
____Chewbacca, "You're Weird" / "...but wonderful!" [GR44] 7.00
____Darth Vader, "Don't Play Games With Me!!!" / "Write!!!" [GR45] 7.00
____Darth Vader, "Happy Birthday, Earthling!" [GR46] 7.00
____Luke Skywalker, "Hold it right there..." / "...and have a happy birthday" [GR47] 7.00

GR61　GR62　GR63　GR64　GR65　GR66　GR67　GR68　GR69　GR70　GR71　GR72　GR73

GR74　GR75　GR76　GR77　GR78　GR79　GR80　GR81　GR82　GR83

GR84 GR85 GR86 GR87 GR88 GR89 GR90 GR91 GR92 GR93

GR94 GR95 GR96 GR97 GR98 GR99 GR100 GR101 GR102 GR103

GR104 GR105 GR106 GR107 GR108 GR109 GR110 GR111 GR112 GR113

____Millennium Falcon, "Greetings from Tatooine" [GR48] 7.00
____Obi-Wan, "May the force be with you" [GR49]..10.00
____R2-D2 and C-3PO, "29 Again!?!?" / "It boggles the memory bank!" [GR50] 9.00
____R2-D2, "From Your Faithful Droid" / "Within the innards of me is a message..." [GR51].................7.00
____Space Dogfight, "Would have written sooner..." / "But I just haven't had a minute!" [GR52] 7.00
____Trash Compactor, "There's no escaping..." / "...another birthday" [GR53] 8.00

Friendship, die-cut.
____Darth Vader and Emperor's Royal Guards, "May The Force Be With You" [GR54] 6.00

Halloween.
____C-3PO with Mask, "Trick or Treat" [GR55] 8.00
____Chewbacca, Han, and Luke, "From The Alliance" / "Happy Halloween" [GR56] 8.00
____Darth Vader with bats 9.00
____Luke Skywalker, "For An Out-Of-This-World Son" / "May your deflector shields protect you this Halloween!" [GR57]...................................8.00
____Millennium Falcon, "For An Earthling Girl" / "All Hallows Eve greetings from Tatooine!" [GR58] 8.00
____Obi-Wan Kenobi, "Happy Halloween" / "...and May The Force Be With You!" [GR59] 7.00
____Obi-Wan Kenobi, "Happy Halloween" / "...and May The Force Be With You!" [GR60] 8.00

____Princess Leia, "For An Out Of This World Daughter" / "Intergalactic wishes for a Happy Halloween!" [GR61] 8.00
____Space Dogfight, "For An Earthling Boy," "Intergalactic Greetings for a Happy Halloween!" [GR62] 8.00

Happy Birthday, die-cut, large.
____Boba Fett, die-cut 12.00
____C-3PO holding cake, "From your friendly droid!" [GR63]..10.00
____Chewbacca [GR64] 10.00
____Darth Vader lightsaber drawn, "The Empire commands you to have a Happy Birthday!" [GR65]...10.00
____Han, Leia, and Luke, "Happy Birthday from the Alliance! [GR66] 10.00
____Luke on Tauntaun, "Wishing You the Happiest Birthday in the Galaxy" [GR67] 10.00
____Obi-Wan Kenobi, "Happy Birthday and May The Force Be With You" [GR68] 10.00
____R2-D2 and C-3PO [GR69] 10.00
____R2-D2, "Puh-Wheet! Puh-Wheet!" / "That's Droid talk for 'Hello, Earthling'" [GR70] 7.00
____Stormtrooper, "Have a Happy Birthday - Darth Vader Wants It That Way" [GR71] 11.00
____Yoda, "May You live to be 800!" [GR72]................9.00

Happy Birthday.
____C-3PO and Ewoks, "Hope you have a royal time. Happy Birthday" [GR73] 7.00
____C-3PO and R2-D2, "Happy Birthday" [GR74] 4.00
____C-3PO and R2-D2, "Have a Happy Birthday" 7.00

____C-3PO, "You're 12..." / "Hope it's the best day on Earth since your birth!" [GR75]...............................8.00
____Chewbacca, "Now that you're 7..." [GR76] 8.00
____Chewbacca, Han, and Leia, "Happy Birthday" [GR77]..8.00
____Darth Vader, 11th birthday [GR78] 8.00
____Darth Vader, fold-out game card, birthday............8.00
____Ewoks: Kenner Preschool Birthday Club Card 12.00
____Max Rebo Band, "Droopy, Si, Max, and I hope your birthday strikes a happy note!" [GR79] 7.00
____Obi-Wan Kenobi, "Honored one, now that you're 10..." [GR80]...7.00
____R2-D2 and Wicket, "Happy birthday to a wonderful friend!" [GR81] 7.00
____R2-D2, "Earthling, my calculations confirm that you are 9." [GR82] 8.00
____Stormtrooper, 8th birthday 7.00
____Wicket with Ewok Children, "Have a birthday filled with wonderful surprises!" [GR83] 7.00
____Yoda, "A Birthday Puzzle for You" [GR84] 8.00

Holidays.
____C-3PO and R2-D2, "Enjoy the Holidays" / "It's the human thing to do" [GR85] 10.00
____C-3PO and R2-D2, "For An Earthling Girl" / "In keeping with the ancient humanoid custom... Christmas Kisses to you!" [GR86] 7.00
____C-3PO and R2-D2, "Peace and Goodwill" 7.00
____C-3PO, "For An Out Of This World Grandson" / "From our galaxy ... to your galaxy... Happy Holidays" [GR87] 7.00

GR114 GR115 GR116 GR117 GR118 GR119 GR120 GR121 GR122 GR123

GR124 GR125 GR126 GR127 GR128 GR129 GR130 GR131 GR132 GR133

Greeting Cards

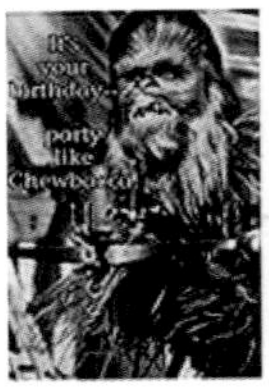

GR134

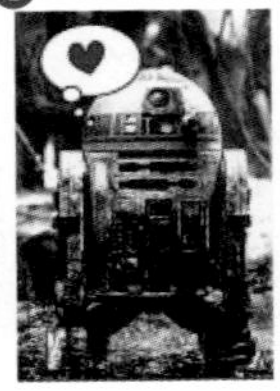

GR135

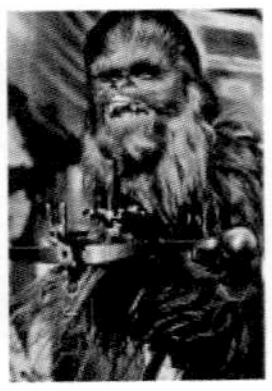

GR136

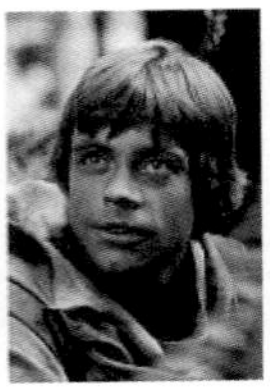

GR137

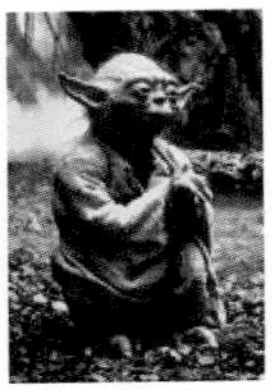

GR138

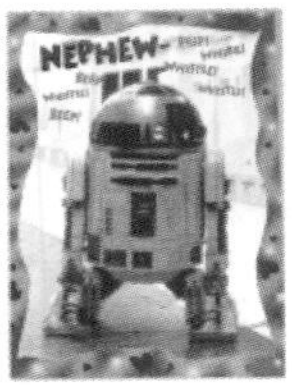

GR139

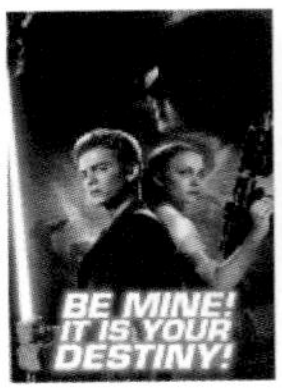

GR140

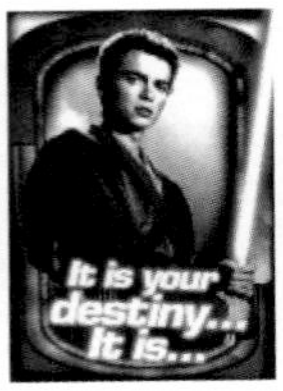

GR141

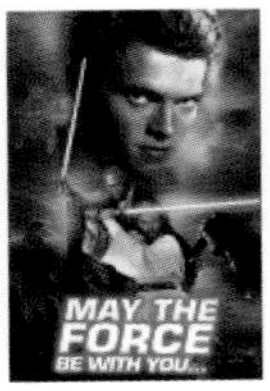

GR142

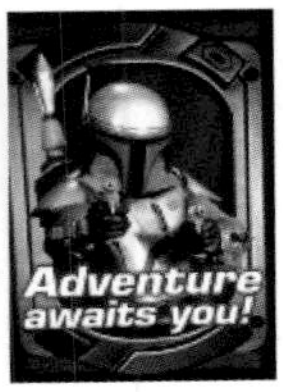

GR143

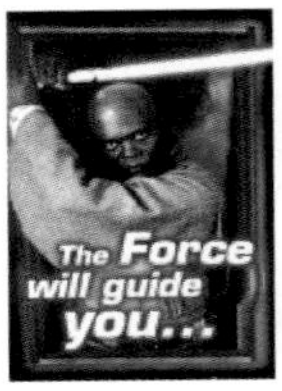

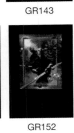

GR144

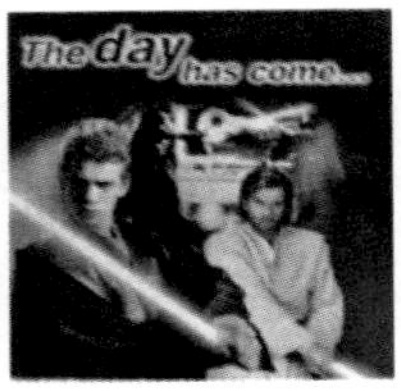

GR145

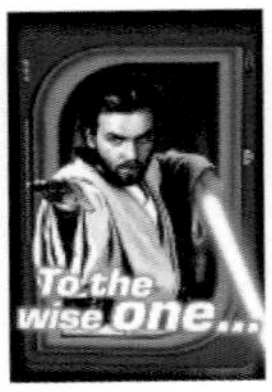

GR146

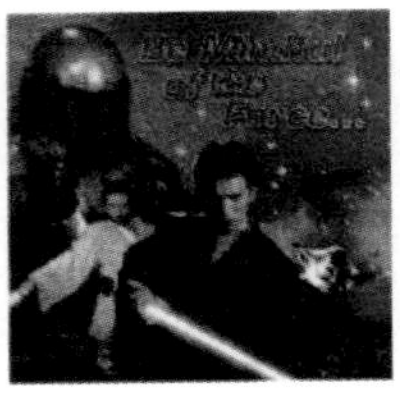

GR147

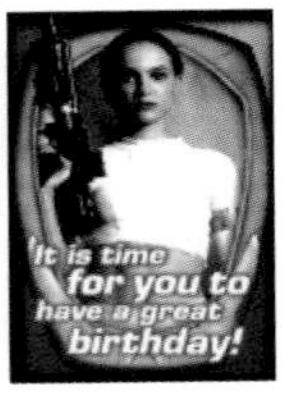

GR148

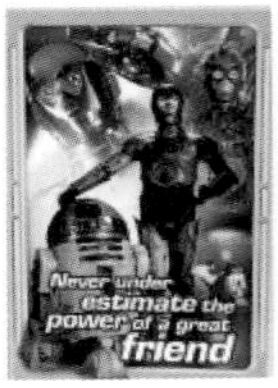

GR149

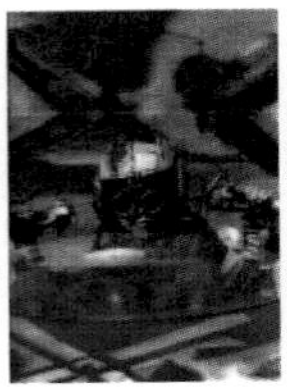

GR150

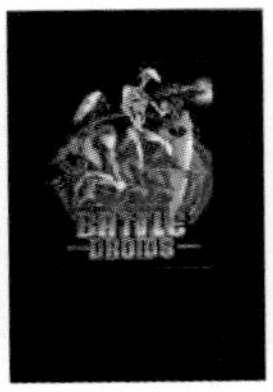

GR151

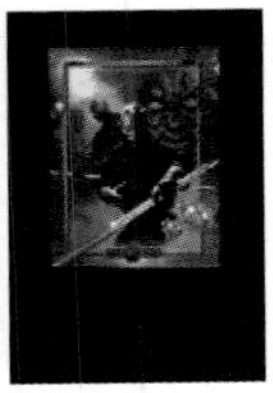

GR152

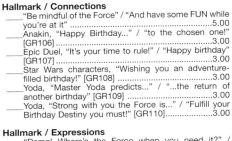

____Chewbacca, "Happy Holidays" / "To a favorite bipedal earthling!" [GR88] 8.00
____Princess Leia and R2-D2, "For An Out Of This World Granddaughter" / "The code is broken and the message is clear— Have a Merry Christmas and a Happy New Year" [GR89] 8.00
____R2-D2 with wreath 7.00

Valentines Day.
____C-3PO & R2-D2, "To Son On Valentines Day"......7.00
____C-3PO, "Valentine Greetings"...............................7.00
____R2-D2, "A Valentine Message for You" 7.00

Fan Club
____C-3PO, R2-D2, Santa, 1999 Christmas reproduction of Star Wars Christmas album cover [GR90] 2.00
____Jawas Christmas, 1999 reproduction of original card Lucas sent to employees [GR91] 2.00

Gamma International Ltd.
____Children's Mask Card, Darth Vader [GR92] 12.00

Character standee.
____C-3PO and R2-D2, Droid Duo [GR93] 4.00
____Darth Vader, "The Force is Strong with this one..." [GR94] 4.00
____TIE Fighter, "Happy Birthday" [GR95] 3.00

Classic trilogy cards with button included.
____"The Force is Strong With This One" Luke Skywalker [GR96] 9.00
____Darth Vader, "Join me..." [GR97] 9.00
____Han Leia and Luke / Support the Alliance. Happy Birthday [GR98] 9.00
____Han Solo, "I have a bad feeling about this......" [GR99] 9.00
____Millennium Falcon, "Punch it Chewie!" [GR100] 9.00
____Obi-Wan, "May the Force be with You" [GR101] 9.00
____Princess Leia, "Help me Obi-Wan Kenobi..." [GR102] 9.00
____Stormtroopers, "Happy Birthday" [GR103] 9.00
____X-Wing fighter [GR104] 11.00
____Yoda, "May the Force be with You" [GR105]........9.00

Hallmark / Connections
____"Be mindful of the Force" / "And have some FUN while you're at it" 5.00
____Anakin, "Happy Birthday..." / "to the chosen one!" [GR106] 3.00
____Epic Duel, "It's your time to rule!" / "Happy birthday" [GR107] 3.00
____Star Wars characters, "Wishing you an adventure-filled birthday!" [GR108] 3.00
____Yoda, "Master Yoda predicts..." / "...the return of another birthday" [GR109] 3.00
____Yoda, "Strong with you the Force is..." / "Fulfill your Birthday Destiny you must!" [GR110]....................3.00

Hallmark / Expressions
____"Damn! Where's the Force when you need it?" / "On your birthday may you not suffer the humiliation of saber-droop." [GR111] 8.00
____"Have a speed-chasing, podracing..." / "...wizard cool BLAST of a Birthday!" [GR112] 5.00
____"May The Force Be With You / Mighty Blasters / At Last We Will Have Revenge" / "Wishing you and Adventure-filled Birthday." [GR113] 4.00
____C-3PO, "Oh, dear — I can't bear to watch..." / "Hope you're FULLY operational soon." [GR114] 6.00
____C-3PO, "That's funny, the damage doesn't look as bad from out here." / "Happy 40th" [GR115]........3.00
____Darth Vader, "It is useless to resist. There is no escape. It is your destiny. It is..." / "Your Birthday! Hope it's happy!" [GR116] 5.00
____Darth Vader, "Valentine, there's a disturbance in the Force" / "Must be all these Valentine wishes coming your way" 5.00
____Leia, "Me? Forget Your Birthday?" / "I'd Just As Soon Kiss A Wookiee!" [GR117] 4.00
____Mace Windu and Obi-Wan, "Your task of obtaining a high school diploma is complete..." 3.00

Episode II: Attack of the Clones.
____Anakin, "You Have Completed Your Course of Knowledge... / A Graduate You Have Become." ..3.00
____Be Mindful of the Force ... And have some cake while you're at it. Happy Birthday! [GR118] 3.00
____Mace Windu and Obi-Wan, "Your Task of Obtaining A High School Diploma is Complete... " 3.00

Hallmark / Shoebox Greetings
____"Got It!" [GR119]....................................3.00
____"Hi!" [GR120]....................................3.00
____"I'm the luckiest girl in the galaxy" [GR121]..........3.00
____"I am ready." [GR122] 3.00
____"Intergalactic PMS hits Princess Leia" [GR123] 3.00
____"Like it?" [GR124] 3.00
____"Luke learns that true friends put up with a lot" [GR125] 3.00
____"Party" [GR126] 3.00
____"Think about a flowing cape. Seriously." [GR127] 3.00
____"True friends never let each other get cut in half by a lightsaber" [GR128]....................................3.00
____"Vader, get away from my office, now!" [GR129] 3.00
____"You want to know where your destiny lies, Luke?" [GR130] 3.00
____"You will regret this rash assault, Luke!" [GR131] 3.00
____"You! See a stylist!" [GR132] 3.00
____"Dang! There it goes again" [GR133] 3.00
____"It's your birthday... party like Chewbacca" [GR134] 3.00
____(Artoo-Detoo with a heart) [GR135] 3.00
____(Chewbacca) [GR136]....................................3.00
____(Luke Smiling) [GR137] 3.00
____(Yoda Standing) [GR138] 3.00

Hallmark
____Nephew - Happy Valentines Day to the nearest nephew in the galaxy! [GR139]............................6.00

Hallmark, Australia
____Anakin and Padme, "Be Mine! It is your destiny!" [GR140] 5.00
____Anakin, "It is your destiny! It is..." ... your birthday!" [GR141] 5.00
____Heroes, "May the Force be with You..." [GR142] 5.00
____Jango, "Adventure awaits you!" [GR143]..............5.00
____Mace Windu, "The Force will guide you" ... "to the most galactic party ever! Happy Birthday." [GR144] 5.00
____Obi-Wan and Anakin, "The day has come..." [GR145] 3.00
____Obi-Wan, "To the wise one..." [GR146] 5.00
____Obi-Wan, Anakin, and Jango, "Be mindful of the Force..." [GR147] 3.00
____Padme, "It is time for you to have a great birthday!" [GR148] 5.00
____R2-D2 and C-3PO, "Never underestimate the power of a great friend" [GR149]....................................7.00

3D image card attached to blank greeting card.
____Anakin Skywalker [GR150] 4.00
____Battle Droids [GR151]....................................4.00

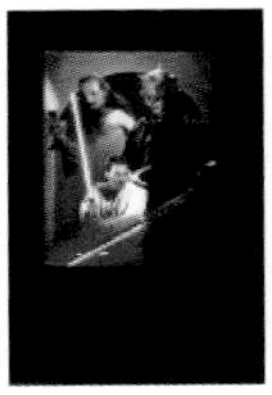

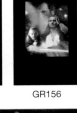

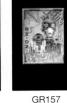

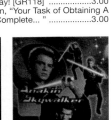

GR153

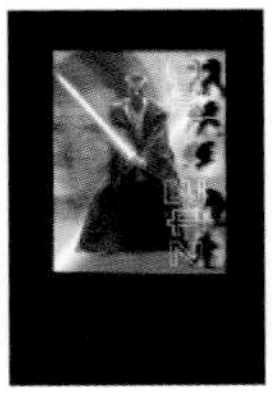

GR154

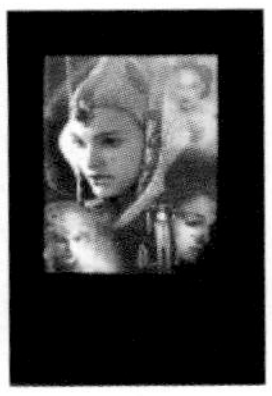

GR155

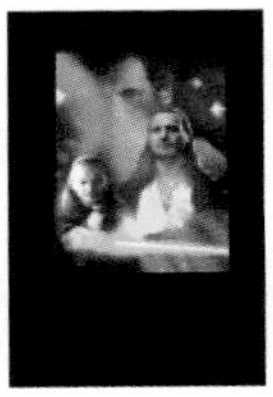

GR156

GR157

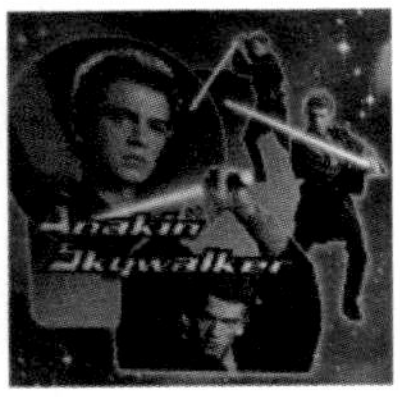

GR158

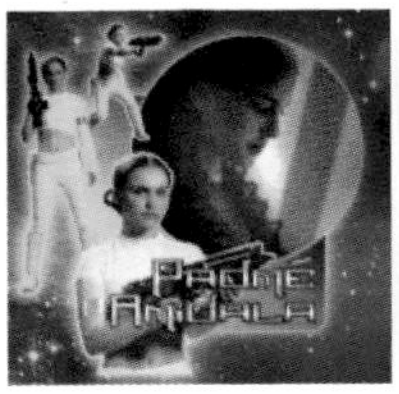

GR159

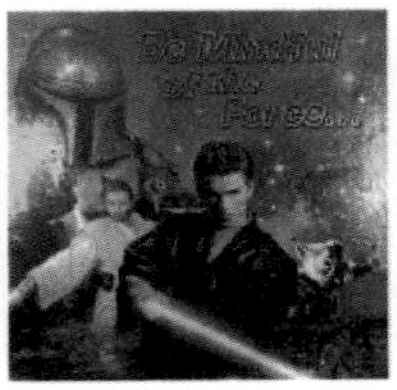

GR160

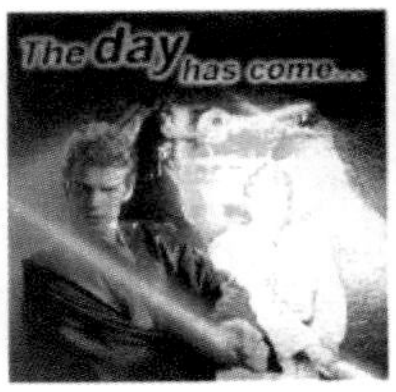

GR161

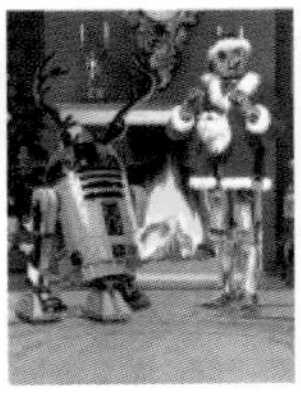

GR162

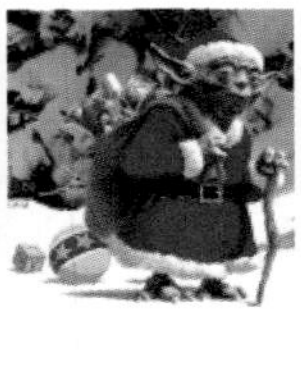

GR163

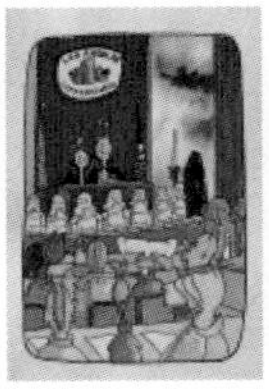

GR164

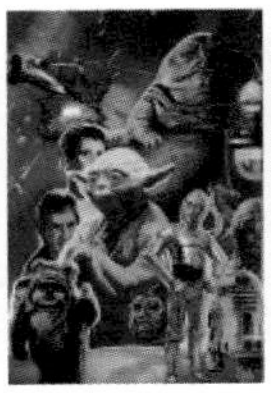

GR165

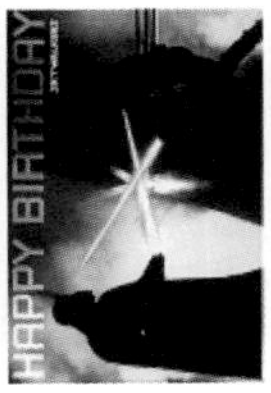

GR166

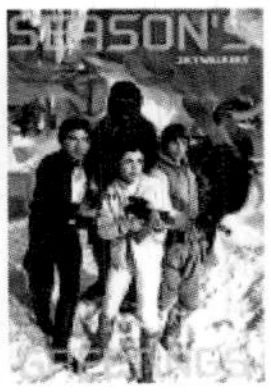

GR167

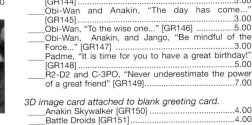

VAL01

VAL02

VAL03

VAL04

VAL05

VAL06

VAL07

VAL08

VAL09

VAL10

VAL11

VAL12

VAL13

VAL14

VAL15

VAL16

VAL17

VAL18

VAL19

____Darth Maul [GR152] 4.00
____Jedi vs. Sith [GR153] 4.00
____Obi-Wan Kenobi [GR154] 4.00
____Queen Amidala [GR155] 4.00
____Qui-Gon Jinn [GR156] 4.00
____R2-D2 / C-3PO [GR157] 4.00

6"x6".
____Anakin [GR158] 3.00
____Padme [GR159] 3.00

Holofoil covers.
____Be Mindful of the Force... [GR160] 3.00
____The Day has Come... [GR161] 3.00

Hallmark, UK
____Anakin Skywalker 8.00
____Be Mindful of the Force... ....8.00
____Birthday wishes from the dark side 8.00
____Padme Amidala 8.00
____The day has come... / to celebrate your birthday 8.00

Hasbro
Packaged with Holiday Edition action figures.
____2002 Santa C-3PO and Reindeer R2 [GR162] 3.00
____2003 Santa Yoda [GR163] 3.00
____2004 Jawas with gifts 5.00
____2005 Darth Vader building stormtrooper snowman 7.00

Lucas Companies
Private printing. Not for sale to the general public.
____1983 Ewok Santa, Lucasfilm 85.00
____1999 "Happy Holidays," Lucas Digital 25.00
____1999 Jawas catching toys from the sky, Lucas Learning 25.00
____1999 Podracer pilots caroling, Lucasfilm 25.00
____2000 "Happy Holidays," LucasArts 25.00
____2000 "May all of your dreams come true in the New Year," Lucasfilm 25.00
____2000 Christmas stars, Lucas Digital 25.00
____2001 "Seasons Greetings" / "From all your friends at Lucas Digital Ltd." 25.00
____2001 "Wishing you Peace..." / "From Our Worlds to Yours," Lucasfilm 25.00
____2001 Snow angel / "Wanna Play?," LucasArts ..25.00
____2002 Game figures on motorcycle / "Oh what fun it is to ride!!," LucasArts 25.00
____2002 Yoda "Exactly alike, no two are..." / "Beautiful all," Lucasfilm 25.00
____2002 Yoda with candle / "May the Magic of this Holiday Season light up your year," Lucas Digital 25.00
____2003 Yoda stellar horizon / "Envisioning unlimited possibilities for the New Year" 25.00
____2004 Snowflake representing different company divisions 25.00

Our Town
____Los Angeles City Council, "May The Force Be With You" [GR164] 5.00

Portal
____"May the Force Be With You on your Birthday" [GR165] 5.00

Skywalkers
____"Happy Birthday" / "From All Of Us In The Rebel Alliance" [GR166] 12.00
____"Seasons Greetings" / "From All Of Us In The Rebel Alliance" [GR167] 12.00

Greeting Cards: Valentines, Boxed

Drawing Board Greeting Cards, Inc.
Classroom valentines, packages of 32.
____C-3PO and R2-D2 [VAL01] 16.00
____EWOK [VAL02] 16.00
____Return of the Jedi [VAL03] 14.00
____Wicket the Ewok [VAL04] 16.00

Hallmark
Packages of 32.
____32 Metallic Valentines, EPI [VAL05] 5.00
____32 Valentines with 48 fun stickers, EPII [3:416] 4.00

Hallmark, Canada
Episode II: Attack of the Clones, packages of 32.
____32 Valentines with 48 fun stickers, French text and packaging [VAL06] 4.00

Paper Magic Group
Classic trilogy.
____30 Stand-Up Valentines; 10 different designs 8.00
____30 Valentines; 10 different designs [VAL07] 5.00
____32 Holofoil Valentines; 10 different designs and 48 "seals" [VAL08] 7.00
____40-Card Valentine Kit; 10 different designs, 48 "seals," 2 bookmarks, window cling [VAL09] 9.00
____Deluxe Valentine Kit: Window Cling, 3D Display, 40 Valentines, 45 Stickers [VAL10] 9.00
____Holographic Valentines: 30 stand-up Valentines with envelopes [VAL11] 7.00

Episode I: The Phantom Menace.
____28 Deluxe Fold and Seal cards with seals [VAL12] 9.00
____32 Fold and Seal cards with seals [VAL13] 7.00

Episode II: Attack of the Clones.
____30 Foil Valentines, Anakin box [VAL14] 4.00
____30 Foil Valentines, Anakin box, punch out hanger [VAL15] 4.00
____30 Foil Valentines, window box [VAL16] 5.00
____30 Foil Valentines, Yoda box [VAL17] 4.00
____32 Valentines with seals [3:416] 3.00
____32 Valentines with seals, punch out hanger [VAL18] 3.00

Episode III: Revenge of the Sith.
____34 Flashy Foil Valentines [VAL19] 3.00

Growth Charts

Random House
____Star Wars "Grow" chart [PEG01] 16.00

Guidemaps

Disney / MGM
Star Wars Weekends, 2000.
____May 19 – 21 [DGM01] 2.00

Star Wars Weekends, 2001.
____May 04 – 06 ....2.00
____May 11 – 13 ....2.00
____May 18 – 20 ....2.00
____May 25 – 27 ....2.00

DGM01

PEG01

GTP01

GTP02

Guitar Cases

Fernandes
____Star Wars logo, hard-sided [2:281] 270.00
____Star Wars logo, soft-sided 135.00

Guitar Picks

Fernandes
Unopened packages. Contain 1 random pick and 1 checklist card.
____2002 Classic Trilogy [GTP01] 8.00
____2003 EPII:AOTC [GTP02] 8.00

Classic Trilogy, 2002.
____01 Darth Vader [GTP03] 4.00
____02 Stormtrooper [GTP04] 4.00
____03 R2-D2 [GTP05] 4.00
____04 C-3PO [GTP06] 4.00
____05 Boba Fett [GTP07] 4.00
____06 Luke Skywalker [GTP08] 4.00
____07 Princess Leia [GTP09] 4.00
____08 Han Solo [GTP10] 4.00
____09 Yoda [GTP11] 4.00
____10 Chewbacca [GTP12] 4.00
____11 Jabba the Hutt [GTP13] 8.00
____12 Jawa [GTP14] 8.00
____13 Ewok [GTP15] 8.00
____14 Tusken Raider [GTP16] 8.00
____15 Tie Fighter Pilot [GTP17] 8.00
____16 Rebel Alliance [GTP18] 8.00
____17 Galactic Empire, holographic [GTP19] 24.00
____18 Darth Vader, holographic [GTP20] 24.00
____19 Stormtrooper, holographic [GTP21] 24.00
____20 Boba Fett, holographic [GTP22] 24.00
____Counter display box, empty 3.00

EPII:AOTC 2003.
____01 Anakin Skywalker [GTP23] 8.00
____02 Padme Amidala [GTP24] 8.00
____03 Obi-Wan Kenobi [GTP25] 8.00
____04 Yoda [GTP26] 8.00
____05 Mace Windu [GTP27] 8.00
____06 Clone Trooper [GTP28] 8.00
____07 Jango Fett [GTP29] 8.00
____08 Count Dooku [GTP30] 8.00
____09 Zam Wesell [GTP31] 8.00
____10 Super Battle Droid [GTP32] 8.00
____11 Count Dooku Icon [GTP33] 8.00
____12 R2-D2 [GTP34] 8.00
____13 C-3PO [GTP35] 8.00
____14 Clone Trooper [GTP36] 8.00
____15 Jedi Starfighter [GTP37] 8.00
____16 Anakin Skywalker / Darth Vader [GTP38] 8.00
____17 Jango Fett, hologram [GTP39] 24.00
____18 Anakin Skywalker, hologram [GTP40] 24.00

Guitar Picks

| GTP03 | GTP04 | GTP05 | GTP06 | GTP07 | GTP08 | GTP09 | GTP10 | GTP11 | GTP12 |

| GTP13 | GTP14 | GTP15 | GTP16 | GTP17 | GTP18 | GTP19 | GTP20 | GTP21 | GTP22 |

| GTP23 | GTP24 | GTP25 | GTP26 | GTP27 | GTP28 | GTP29 | GTP30 | GTP31 | GTP32 |

| GTP33 | GTP34 | GTP35 | GTP36 | GTP37 | GTP38 | GTP39 | GTP40 | GTP41 | GTP42 |

GT01

GT02

GT03

GT04

GT05

____19 Yoda, hologram 24.00
____20 Clone Trooper, hologram [GTP41] 24.00
____21 Secret, hologram (Jango Fett) [GTP42] 24.00
____22 Clone Trooper Red, hologram mail-away 28.00
____23 Clone Trooper Yellow, holo. mail-away 28.00
____Counter display box, empty 3.00

Guitar Straps

Fernandes
____Darth Vader [3:276] 35.00
____Star Wars logo [3:276] 35.00
____Vader and Stormtrooper [3:276] 35.00

Guitars

Fernandes
Nomad models.
____Boba Fett [GT01] 450.00

____Darth Vader 450.00
____Stormtrooper [GT02] 450.00

Nomad models. Series 2, limited to 75.
____Boba Fett 650.00

Retrorocket models, series 1, hard cases, limit 250.
____Darth Vader [GT03] 950.00
____Stormtrooper [GT04] 950.00

Retrorocket models, series 2, hard cases, limited to 75.
____Boba Fett [GT05] 1,200.00
____Yoda 1,200.00

Gum Holders

Bonbon Buddies
Gum Buddy.
____Vader above flames [GH01] 8.00
____Vader at right [GH02] 8.00
____Vader below flames [GH03] 8.00

Meiji
Xylish 3-pack of chewing gum stick packets.
____Anakin Skywalker, blue [GH04] 8.00
____Anakin Skywalker, green [2:281] 8.00
____Anakin Skywalker, red [3:276] 8.00
____C-3PO, blue [2:281] 8.00
____C-3PO, green [GH05] 8.00
____C-3PO, red [3:276] 8.00
____Clone Trooper, blue [2:281] 8.00
____Clone Trooper, green [2:281] 8.00
____Clone Trooper, red [GH06] 8.00
____Jango Fett, blue [GH07] 8.00
____Jango Fett, green [2:281] 8.00
____Jango Fett, red [3:276] 8.00
____R2-D2, blue [2:281] 8.00
____R2-D2, green [GH08] 8.00
____R2-D2, red [3:276] 8.00

Gumball Machines

Comic Images
____Darth Vader [G3M01] 35.00
____Yoda [G3M02] 35.00

Gym Sets

Gym Dandy
Scount Walker Command Towers.
____With 7 ft. slide 475.00

| GH01 | GH02 | GH03 | GH04 | GH05 | GH06 | GH07 | GH08 | G3M01 | G3M02 |

GY01 boxed   GY01 open   GEL01   HAR01 box and close-up

HRK01   HGH01   HGH02   HGH03   HGH04

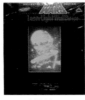

HGH05   HGH06   HG01   SKI01 box   SKI01 skate   SKI02 skate

____With Speederbike ride 525.00
____With Swingset and Speederbike ride 725.00
____Speederbike swing add-on [GY01] 185.00

Mitsubishi
Japan.
____Star Cars, C-3PO and R2-D2 [HRK01] 24.00

Fantasma
8"x10" matted.
____Darth Vader..35.00
____Space Battle [HG01] 35.00

Hair Gel

Avon, Mexico
____Anakin and Clones [GEL01] 8.00

Hairbrushes

Avon, Mexico
____Padme Amidala [HAR01] 12.00

Handbills

Imax
EPII:AOTC. Approximately 3.75"x8.75"
____Size Matters Not, November 1st 5.00

Major Cineplex
EPII:AOTC. Approximately 5.5"x8.5"
____Anakin Skywalker 5.00
____Count Dooku..5.00
____Geonosis..5.00
____Jango Fett..5.00
____Mace Windu 5.00
____Obi-Wan Kenobi 5.00
____Padme Amidala...5.00
____Zam Wesell..5.00

Handkerchiefs

Iwamota
____C-3PO and R2-D2, ESB movie credits 18.00
____Luke on Dagobah, ESB The Saga Continues 18.00

Marubeni
____Darth Vader, Bespin gantry 18.00
____R2-D2 and Wicket 18.00

Helmets, Sports

Dynacraft
____Darth Maul multisport, children's [HGH01] 17.00
____Queen Amidala multisport, children's [HGH02] ..17.00

M.V. Sports and Leisure Ltd.
____Darth Maul [HGH03]..35.00
____Death Star Attack [HGH04] 30.00
____Jar Jar Binks [HGH05] 31.00
____Sith Probe Droids [HGH06] 20.00

Holograms

3D Arts
2x2" in 3.75x2.75" acrylic stand.
____C-3PO and R2-D2 ....12.00
____Darth Vader...12.00
____Millennium Falcon 12.00
____X-Wing Fighter 12.00

4"x6" in matted frame.
____Darth Vader...30.00
____Millennium Falcon 30.00

A.H. Prismatic
____Millennium Falcon, 5"x7" matted......................23.00

Ice Skates

Brookfield Athletic
____Vader and Emperor's Royal Guards [SKI01] 50.00
____Wicket the Ewok [SKI02] 35.00

Inflatables

Burger King
EPIII:ROTS.
____Darth Vader 9'x12' [INT01] 575.00

Pepsi Cola
EPI:TPM inflatable display cans.
____Mountain Dew [INT02] 25.00
____Pepsi [INT03] 25.00
____Pepsi, gold Yoda [INT04] 50.00

EPIII:ROTS.
____Anakin Skywalker's Jedi Starfighter [INT05] 35.00

Instrument Knobs

Fernandes
English packaging.
____Boba Fett [GTK01] 15.00

INT01   INT02   INT03   INT04   INT05

GTK01   GTK02   GTK03   GTK04   GTK05   GTK06   GTK07   GTK08

Instrument Knobs

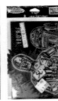

| PFI01 | PFI02 | PFI03 | PFI04 | PFI05 | PFI06 | PFI07 | PFI08 | PFI09 | PFI10 | PFI11 |

____C-3PO [GTK02] 15.00
____Darth Vader [GTK03] 15.00
____Stormtrooper [GTK04] 15.00

Japanese packaging.
____Boba Fett [GTK05] 15.00
____C-3PO [GTK06] 15.00
____Darth Vader [GTK07] 15.00
____Stormtrooper [GTK08] 15.00

Invitations

____C-3PO, R2-D2, Naboo Fighter: Invitaciones te Invito a mi Fiesta [PFI01] ......
____Darth Vader, "Attention! A Birthday Party," 8-pack [PFI02] 7.00

Drawing Board Greeting Cards, Inc.
8-packs.
____C-3PO and R2-D2 [2:282] 10.00
____C-3PO and R2-D2, postcards 8.00
____Cloud City [PFI03] 10.00
____Darth Vader and Luke Duel [PFI04] 10.00
____Ewoks Hang-Gliding 8.00
____Heroes and Villains 10.00
____R2-D2 [PFI05] 10.00

Party Express
8-packs.
____"Be Mindful of the Force..." [PFI06] 4.00
____Darth Vader, "Feel the Force..." [PFI07] 8.00
____Droids with Star Wars logo, neon [PFI08] 5.00
____Obi-Wan, Qui-Gon, "Nothing can stop us..." [PFI09] 4.00
____R2-D2 [PFI10] 8.00

Unique
8-packs.
____Qui-Gon vs. Maul art [PFI11] 4.00

Invitations: Event

DK Publishing
____1999 book release, talking 15.00

Lucasfilm
____2003 Nov 5, Presidio Club 175.00
____Celebration III Exhibitor Reception 5.00

Ipods and Accessories

Covers.
____Darth Vader for iPod 30.00

Apple Computer, Inc.
____EPIII:ROTS logo [A1P01] 300.00

XtremeMac
Covers.
____Darth Vader for iPod Nano 30.00
____Darth Vader for iPod Shuffle [A1P02] 25.00
____Yoda for iPod Shuffle [A1P03] 25.00

Iron-On Transfers

____Star Wars, Tie fighter and X-Wing in front of red planet 5.00

Ballantine
Dye transfers from Iron-On Transfer book.
____Artoo Detoo [2:283] 3.00
____C-3PO and Luke [2:283] 3.00
____C-3PO and R2-D2 / Star Wars [2:283] 3.00
____Chewbacca [2:283] 3.00
____Chewbacca and Han Solo [2:283] 3.00
____Darth Vader [2:283] 3.00
____Darth Vader / Space Battle [2:283] 3.00
____Han Solo [2:283] 3.00
____Jawas [2:283] 3.00
____Luke Skywalker [2:283] 3.00
____See Threepio [2:283] 3.00
____Star Wars Hildebrandt art [2:283] 3.00
____Star Wars McQuarrie concept art [2:283] 3.00
____Stormtroopers 3.00
____Tusken Raider [2:283] 3.00
____X-Wing fighters [2:283] 3.00

Factors, Etc.
____"Darth Vader Lives" 4.00
____"May The Force Be With You" 4.00
____Boba Fett 3.00
____C-3PO [2:283] 4.00
____C-3PO and R2-D2 [2:283] 4.00
____Chewbacca [2:283] 4.00
____Chewie [2:283] 4.00
____Darth Vadar Lives (misspelled) [2:283] 4.00
____Darth Vader helmet and ships [2:283] 4.00
____Darth Vader, glitter [2:283] 4.00
____Empire Strikes Back logo [2:283] 3.00
____Empire Strikes Back poster art 3.00
____Han Solo and Chewbacca [2:283] 4.00
____Jawa, glitter [2:283] 4.00
____Lando Calrissian 3.00
____Luke and Yoda 3.00
____Luke on Tauntaun 3.00
____Luke with X-Wing 3.00
____May the Force be with You [2:283] 4.00
____Millennium Falcon 3.00
____Princess Leia 4.00
____R2-D2 [2:283] 4.00
____Star Destoryer 3.00

____Star Wars Hildebrandt poster art [2:283] 4.00
____Star Was logo, glitter 4.00
____Tie Fighter 3.00
____X-Wing Fighter 3.00
____Yoda, glitter [2:283] 3.00

Flex-print
Australia.
____C-3PO 8.00
____Darth Vader 8.00
____Han Solo / Chewbacca 8.00
____R2-D2 ......8.00

Jewelry: Barrettes

Factors, Etc.
____C-3PO [JBA01] 14.00
____Darth Vader [JBA02] 14.00
____R2-D2 [JBA03] 14.00

Jewelry: Bracelets

Disney / MGM
____Star Tours admission band [3:150] 6.00

Walt Disney Weekends. Rubber bracelets.
____Imperial logo 10.00
____Rebel Alliance logo 10.00

Factors, Etc.
____C-3PO, gold finished head 14.00
____Darth Vader, black painted head 14.00
____R2-D2, unfinished metal 14.00
____Stormtrooper, white painted head 14.00
____X-Wing, unfinished metal 14.00

Jewelry: Bracelets, Charm

Factors, Etc.
____C-3PO, Chewbacca, R2-D2 ......35.00
____C-3PO, Darth Vader, R2-D2 [JCB01] 35.00
____Chewbacca, Stormtrooper, X-Wing [JCB02] 35.00

Jewelry: Cufflinks

Flip-up black boxes
____2-sets: Jedi / R2-D2 [CLK01] 35.00
____C-3PO and R2-D2, lenticular [CLK02] 16.00
____Darth Maul, lenticular [CLK03] 16.00
____Jar Jar Binks [CLK04] 14.00
____R2-D2 [CLK05] 24.00

| A1P01 | A1P02 | A1P03 | JBA01 | JBA02 | JBA03 | JCB01 |

| JCB02 | CLK01 | CLK02 | CLK03 | CLK04 | CLK05 | CLK06 | CLK07 |

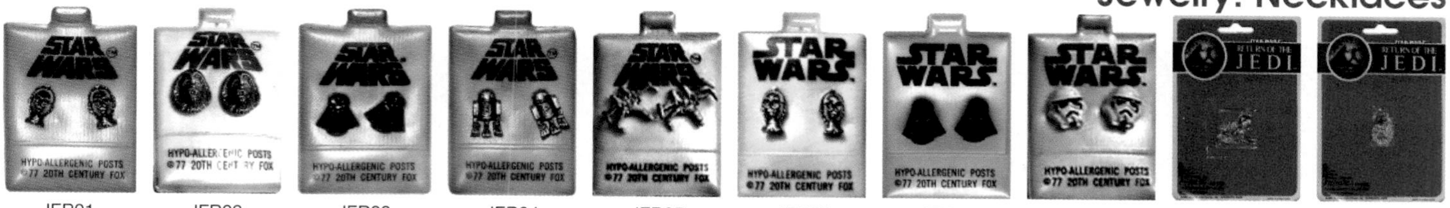

JER01 JER02 JER03 JER04 JER05 JER06 JER07 JER08 JNK01 JNK02

Flip-up red boxes
____Darth Maul [CLK06] 31.00
____R2-D2 [CLK07] 24.00

Jewelry: Earrings

Factors, Etc.
Clip-on.
____C-3PO 25.00
____Darth Vader 25.00
____R2-D2 ....25.00

Round trademark.
____C-3PO [JER01] 12.00
____Chewbacca [JER02] 35.00
____Darth Vader [JER03] 12.00
____R2-D2 [JER04] 12.00
____Stormtrooper 12.00
____X-Wing [JER05] 16.00

Small trademark.
____C-3PO [JER06] 12.00
____Chewbacca 35.00
____Darth Vader [JER07] 12.00
____R2-D2 ....12.00
____Stormtrooper [JER08] 12.00
____X-Wing 16.00

Jewelry: Necklaces

Adam Joseph Industries
Charms, gold colored blister packed to red cardbacks.
____C-3PO [JNK01] 15.00
____Emperor's Royal Guard [JNK02] 15.00
____Ewok [JNK03] 15.00
____R2-D2 [JNK04] 15.00
____Salacious Crumb [JNK05] 10.00

Charms, gold colored on black plastic hang cards.
____C-3PO [JNK06] 10.00
____Emperor's Royal Guard [JNK07] 10.00

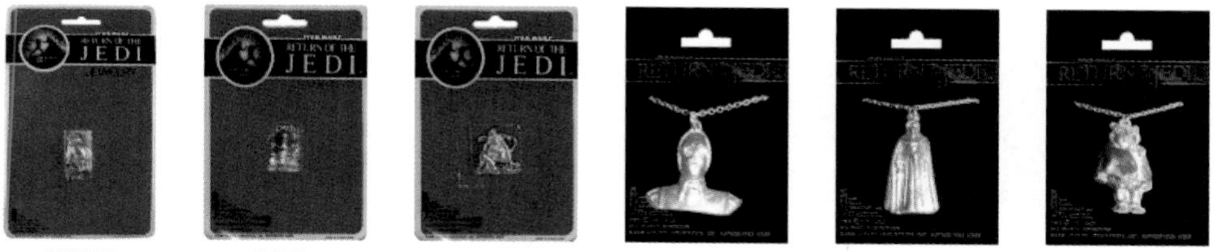

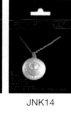

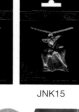

JNK03 JNK04 JNK05 JNK06 JNK07 JNK08

____Ewok [JNK08] 10.00
____May The Force Be With You [JNK09] 8.00
____R2-D2 [JNK10] 10.00
____Rebel Alliance logo [JNK11] 8.00
____Return of the Jedi logo [JNK12] 8.00
____Salacious Crumb [JNK13] 10.00
____X-Wing Fighter Pilot [JNK14] 8.00
____Yoda [JNK15] 10.00

Die-cast pendants, painted.
____Darth Vader [JNK16] 12.00
____R2-D2 [JNK17] 12.00
____Yoda [JNK18] 12.00

Creative Conventions
10th anniversary McQuarrie art.
____A New Hope 8.00
____Darth Vader in Flames 8.00
____Yoda 8.00

Factors, Etc.
C-3PO, brass colored, articulated.
____Bagged 12.00
____Boxed [JNK19] 45.00
____Carded [JNK20] 30.00
____Loose [JNK21] 12.00

Chewbacca, painted, articulated.
____Bagged 12.00
____Boxed [JNK22] 45.00
____Carded [JNK23] 30.00
____Loose 18.00

Darth Vader helmet, painted.
____Bagged 12.00
____Boxed [JNK24] 12.00
____Carded [JNK25] 30.00
____Loose 12.00

R2-D2, steel colored, articulated.
____Bagged 12.00
____Boxed [JNK26] 45.00
____Carded [JNK27] 30.00
____Loose 12.00

Stormtrooper helmet, painted.
____Bagged 12.00
____Boxed [JNK28] 45.00
____Carded [JNK29] 30.00
____Loose [JNK30] 12.00

X-Wing Fighter, steel colored.
____Bagged 20.00
____Boxed [JNK31] 45.00
____Carded [JNK32] 30.00
____Loose 12.00

Jap Industries
Sterling silver, sculpted.
____Han Solo in Carbonite 200.00

Noble Design
Lightsaber platinum platinum electroplate pendants with colored jade blades. 24" chain.
____Darth Vader 200.00

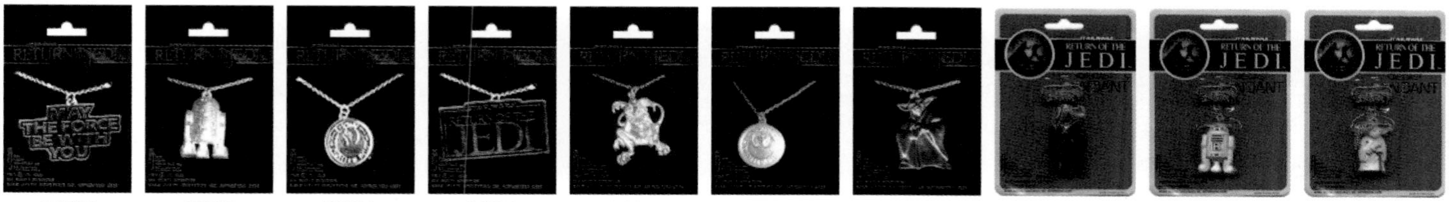

JNK09 JNK10 JNK11 JNK12 JNK13 JNK14 JNK15 JNK16 JNK17 JNK18

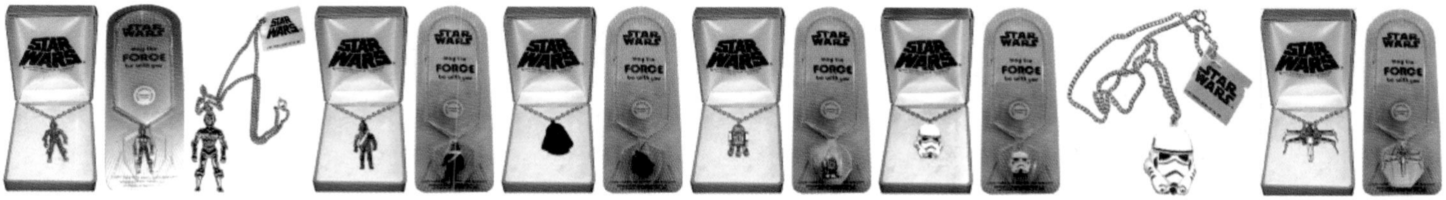

JNK19 JNK20 JNK21 JNK22 JNK23 JNK24 JNK25 JNK26 JNK27 JNK28 JNK29 JNK30 JNK31 JNK32

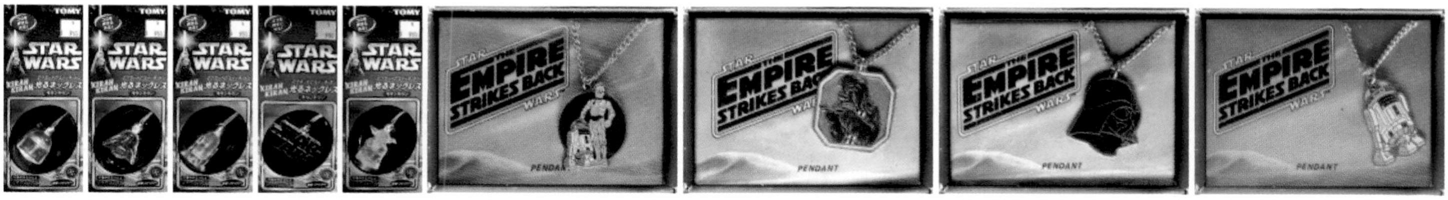

JNK33 JNK34 JNK35 JNK36 JNK37 JNK38 JNK39 JNK40 JNK41

Jewelry: Necklaces

JNR01   JNR02   JNR03 red   JNR03 blue   JNR04   JNR05   JNR06   JNR07

JNR08   JNR09   JNR10   JNR11   JNR12   JNR13   JNR14   JNR15   JNR16

JNR17   JNR18   JNR19   JNR20   JNR21   JNR22   JNR23   JNR24

____Luke Skywalker 200.00
____Mace Windu...200.00
____Yoda 200.00

Tomy
Light-Up necklaces.
____Boba Fett [JNK33] 15.00
____Darth Vader [JNK34]................................15.00
____R2-D2 [JNK35] 12.00
____Star Wars logo [JNK36] 12.00
____Yoda [JNK37] 12.00

Unlicensed
____C-3PO 1.25" enamel 11.00
____Millennium Falcon (small)...........................12.00
____R2-D2 .75" enamel 11.00
____Star Wars logo and stars 9.00
____Star Wars logo, trapazoid design.................8.00
____Tie Fighter (small) 17.00

Wallace Berrie and Co.
Pendants.
____C-3PO and R2-D2 [JNK38] 17.00
____Chewbacca [JNK39]................................17.00
____Darth Vader [JNK40]................................17.00
____R2-D2 [JNK41] 17.00

Jewelry: Rings

Fan made, sterling silver, sculpted.
____Darth Vader [JNR01].................................65.00

Gumball machine trinkets.
____Stormtrooper red or blue [JNR02] 3.00
____Tie Fighter red or blue [JNR03] 3.00

Decopac
Made as cupcake toppers.
____C-3PO [JNR04] 2.00
____Darth Vader [JNR05]..................................2.00
____R2-D2 [JNR06] 2.00

Factors, Etc.
____C-3PO, set 1 ....8.00
____Chewbacca, set 1 ....8.00
____Darth Vader, set 2 ....8.00
____R2-D2, set 1 ....8.00
____Set 1, 3 rings [JNR07] 30.00
____Set 2, 3 rings 30.00
____Stormtrooper, set 2 ....8.00
____X-Wing, set 2 ....8.00

Jap Industries
Imperial set.
____3-piece boxed set: Darth Vader, Boba Fett,
Stormtrooper, limited to 300 sets 800.00
____Boba Fett [JNR08]...................................250.00
____Darth Vader 250.00
____Stormtrooper 250.00

Rebel set.
____3-piece boxed set, limited to 300 sets 800.00
____C-3PO 250.00
____Chewbacca 250.00
____R2-D2 [JNR09]...250.00

Sterling silver, sculpted.
____Admiral Ackbar [JNR10] 175.00
____Bib Fortuna [JNR11] 175.00
____Biker Scout [JNR12] 175.00
____Bith [JNR13]..175.00
____Boba Fett [JNR14] 175.00
____C-3PO [JNR15] 175.00
____Chewbacca [JNR16] 175.00
____Darth Vader [JNR17] 175.00
____Gamorrean Guard [JNR18] 175.00
____Jabba the Hutt [JNR19] 175.00
____Jawa [JNR20]...350.00
____R2-D2 [JNR21]..175.00
____Rancor [JNR22]...175.00
____Stormtrooper [JNR23] 175.00
____Tusken Raider [JNR24] 175.00
____Wicket [JNR25] 175.00
____Yoda [JNR26]..175.00

EPI:TPM.
____C-3PO [JNR27] 175.00
____Darth Maul [JNR28] 175.00
____Jar Jar Binks [JNR29] 175.00
____Sebulba [JNR30].......................................175.00

Wallace Berrie and Co.
Adjustable rings in small, medium, and large sizes.
____"May The Force Be With You" [JNR31] 10.00
____C-3PO and R2-D2 [JNR32] 10.00
____Darth Vader [JNR33]..................................10.00
____R2-D2 [JNR34] 10.00
____X-Wing Fighter [JNR35] 10.00
____Yoda [JNR36] 10.00

JNR25   JNR26   JNR27   JNR28   JNR29   JNR30   JNR31

JNR32   JNR33   JNR34   JNR35   JNR36

KE01　KE02　KE03　KE04　KE05　KE06　KE07

KE08　KE09　KE10　KE11　KE12　KE13　KE14　KE15　KE16　KE17

KE18　KE19　KE20　KE21　KE22　KE23　KE24　KE25　KE26　KE27

Keychains

___Darth Tater [KE01]..8.00
___Darth Vader helmet, shaped plastic [KE02] 8.00
___Episode I logo, plastic [KE03]..............................4.00
___The Power of Myth [KE04] 14.00

Belgium, rubber.
___Vader 10.00
___Yoda 10.00

EPII:AOTC. Metal.
___Anakin / Vader, clip [KE05] 4.00
___Anakin and Padme, ring [KE06] 4.00
___Jango, clip [KE07] 4.00
___Obi-Wan, ring [KE08] 4.00
___Yoda and Mace Windu, ring [KE09] 4.00

Gold colored plastic.
___Darth Vader 8.00
___General Grievous 8.00
___Stormtrooper..8.00

Japan. Pet Bear, blister and cardback package.
___Darth Vader..15.00
___Stormtrooper 15.00
___Yoda 15.00

Japan. Pet Bear, color bear package.
___Boba Fett 15.00
___Darth Vader..15.00
___Stormtrooper 15.00

Japan.
___Blaster, Han Solo 5.00
___Lightsaber, Luke Skywalker (ANH) 5.00
___Lightsaber, Luke Skywalker (ROTJ).......................5.00
___Lightsaber, Obi-Wan (ANH)..................................5.00
___R2-D2 etched with padded case [KE10] 15.00

3D Arts
Square lasergram keychains.
___C-3PO and R2-D2 ....28.00
___Darth Vader...28.00
___X-wing Fighter 28.00
___Yoda 28.00

A.H. Prismatic
Hologram in 2" plastic square.
___AT-AT [KE11] 6.00
___C-3PO and R2-D2 [KE12]......................................6.00
___Darth Vader [KE13] 6.00
___Millennium Falcon...6.00
___X-Wing Fighter [KE14] 6.00
___X-Wing vs. TIE Fighter, SW logo [KE15]................6.00

Adam Joseph Industries
___Darth Vader [KE16] 9.00
___Millennium Falcon [KE17] 9.00
___Princess Kneesaa [KE18] 8.00
___R2-D2 [KE19] 9.00
___Wicket [KE20] 8.00
___Yoda [KE21]..9.00

Applause
___Jedi vs. Sith on blue oval 4.00

3D metal, articulated.
___Jar Jar Binks [KE22]..12.00
___Jar Jar Binks, carded [KE23]................................10.00
___Pit Droid [KE24] 14.00
___Pit Droid, carded [KE25]......................................10.00
___Watto [KE26]..12.00
___Watto, carded 10.00
___Watto, Pit Droid, Jar Jar, carded [KE27] 25.00

Flat vinyl.
___Boba Fett [KE28]..4.00
___Darth Maul [KE29]...4.00
___Darth Vader [KE30]..4.00
___Greedo [KE31]...4.00
___Jar Jar Binks [KE32]...4.00
___Stormtrooper [KE33]...4.00

PVC figures on cardbacks.
___Anakin Skywalker 8.00
___Darth Maul [KE34]...8.00
___Destroyer Droid 8.00
___Jar Jar Binks 8.00
___Obi-Wan Kenobi 8.00
___Pit Droid 8.00
___Queen Amidala 8.00
___Qui-Gon Jinn...8.00

PVC figures.
___Anakin Skywalker [KE35] 4.00
___Darth Maul [KE36]..4.00
___Destroyer Droid [KE37] 4.00
___Jar Jar Binks 4.00
___Obi-Wan Kenobi [KE38] 4.00

KE28　KE29　KE30　KE31　KE32　KE33　KE34　KE35　KE36　KE37

KE38　KE39　KE40　KE41　KE42　KE43　KE44　KE45　KE46

Keychains

KE47 KE48 KE49 KE50 KE51 KE52 KE53 KE54 KE55 KE56 KE57 KE58 KE59 KE60

KE61 KE62 KE63 KE64 KE65 KE66 KE67 KE68 KE69 KE70 KE71 KE72 KE73 KE74 KE75

KE76 KE77 KE78 KE79 KE80 KE81 KE82 KE83 KE84 KE85 KE86 KE87 KE88 KE89

____Pit Droid [KE39]...4.00
____Queen Amidala [KE40] 4.00
____Qui-Gon Jinn [KE41]..4.00

Avon
Gold colored; same style as Playco Toys. Brown boxes.
____Darth Vader...9.00
____Luke Skywalker...9.00
____Stormtrooper...9.00

Banpresto
Sculpted metal figures.
____C-3PO [KE42]..12.00
____Darth Vader [KE43]..12.00
____Millennium Falcon [KE44]..................................12.00
____R2-D2 [KE45]...12.00
____X-Wing fighter [KE46].......................................12.00

C and D Visionaries, Inc.
____Anakin collage [KE47].......................................3.00
____ANH Movie Poster [KE48] 3.00
____Boba Fett [KE49]..3.00
____Chewbacca and Han [KE50]..............................3.00
____Darth Vader's TIE fighter [KE51]........................3.00
____Darth Vader [KE52]...3.00
____Darth Vader flaming helmet [KE53]....................3.00
____Darth Vader on Bespin [KE54]............................3.00
____Darth Vader with Emperor [KE55].......................3.00
____Droids on Endor [KE56]......................................3.00
____Evil — Darth Vader [KE57] 3.00
____General Grievous, close-up [KE58].....................3.00
____General Grievous [KE59]....................................3.00
____Han in carbonite [KE60].....................................3.00
____Lightsaber fight [KE61] 3.00
____My other transport is the Millennium Falcon
    [KE62]..3.00
____Obi-Wan Kenobi [KE63]......................................3.00
____Princess Leia [KE64]...3.00
____Princess Leia captive [KE65] 3.00
____Princess Leia captive close-up [KE66]................3.00
____Return of the Jedi logo [KE67]............................3.00
____Sith / Darth Vader [KE68]...................................3.00
____Sith Lord [KE69]..3.00
____Star Wars logo [KE70].......................................3.00
____Who's Your Daddy? [KE71]..................................3.00
____Wicket [KE72] 3.00

____Yoda (concentrating) [KE73]...............................3.00
____Yoda and Luke [KE74] 3.00
____Yoda collage [KE75]..3.00
____Yoda sitting [KE76]..3.00
____Yoda standing [KE77]...3.00
____Yoda with lightsaber [KE78]...............................3.00
____Yoda, "Do... or do not." [KE79]...........................3.00

Cards, Inc.
Enamel.
____Darth Vader [KE80] 8.00
____Darth Vader eyes [KE81] 8.00
____Epic Duel [KE82]...8.00
____Jedi [KE83] 8.00
____Sith Lord [KE84] 8.00
____Yoda eyes [KE85] 8.00

Etched metal.
____Clone Trooper [KE86]...8.00
____Darth Vader [KE87] 8.00
____Grievous [KE88] 8.00
____Jedi [KE89] 8.00

Hedz, sculpted.
____Boba Fett 15.00
____C-3PO...15.00
____Chewbacca..15.00
____Clone Trooper..15.00
____Darth Maul...15.00
____Darth Vader..15.00
____Jango Fett..15.00
____R2-D2..15.00
____Stormtrooper...15.00
____Yoda..15.00

Manga style, die-cut rubber.
____Boba Fett 12.00
____Darth Vader..12.00
____Droids 12.00
____Han Solo and Chewbacca....................................12.00
____Luke and Leia...12.00
____Yoda vs. Darth Sidious..12.00

Cingular
____Star Wars Vader Viper, Celebration 3 exclusive
    [KE90] 5.00

Classico
3-D laser engraved glass cube keychains with illumina-tion.
____Darth Vader, illumiated red.................................24.00

Coca-Cola
____R2-D2 Co-bot miniature [KE91]...........................12.00

Creative Conventions
1.5"x2" white background.
____Darth Vader in Flames 8.00
____Luke Skywalker, "A New Hope" logo...................8.00
____Yoda in circle..8.00

Crystal Craft
____Bravo Squadron [KE92] 6.00
____Jedi [KE93] 7.00
____Naboo Royal Starship [KE94].............................7.00
____Podracing [KE95]..6.00
____Star Wars Episode I logo [KE96].........................7.00
____The Dark Side [KE97]...7.00

Disney / MGM
____Empire / Rebellion, spinning [KE98]...................12.00
____Jedi Training Acadamy [KE99] 8.00
____Triangular deisgn w/Star Tours logo [KE100] 8.00

Characters.
____Boba Fett [KE101]..8.00
____Stormtrooper [KE102]...8.00

Star Wars Weekends.
____2001 R2-D2 projecting hologram Mickey
    [KE103]..24.00
____2003 Logo spinner [KE104] 8.00
____2004 Mickey and Minnie poster art [KE105] 8.00
____2005 Darth Vader / Mickey.................................8.00
____2006 WDW logo 8.00

Downpace Ltd.
Classic trilogy characters.
____Boba Fett [KE106]..7.00
____Boba Fett with gun..7.00
____C-3PO [KE107]..7.00
____Darth Vader helmet [KE108]...............................7.00
____Darth Vader profile [KE109] 7.00

KE90 KE91 KE92 KE93 KE94 KE95 KE96 KE97 KE98 front / rear

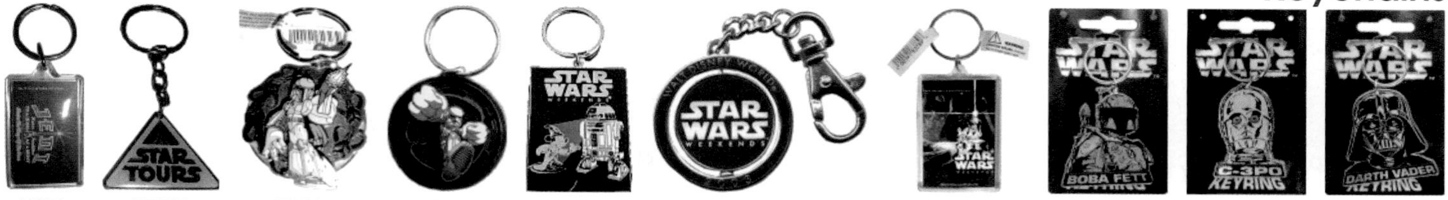

KE99 KE100 KE101 KE102 KE103 KE104 KE105 KE106 KE107 KE108

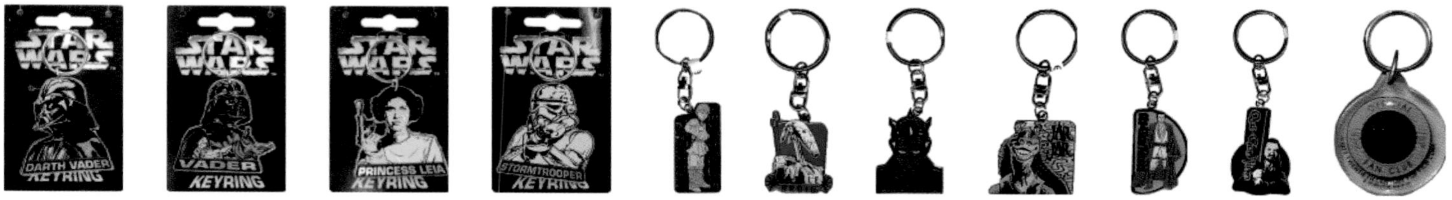

KE109 KE110 KE111 KE112 KE113 KE114 KE115 KE116 KE117 KE118 KE119

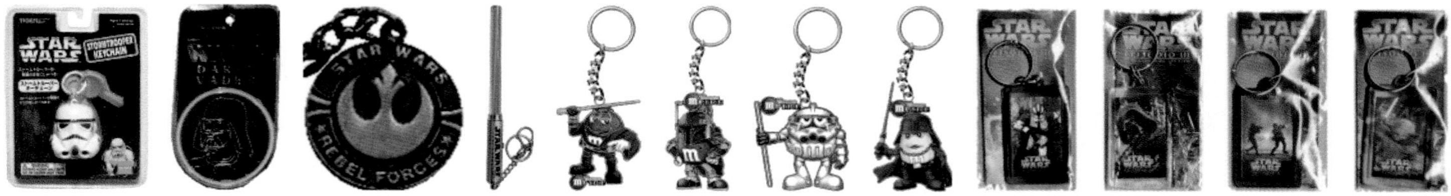

KE120 KE121 KE122 KE123 KE124 KE125 KE126 KE127 KE128 KE129 KE130 KE131

____Darth Vader reaching [KE110] 7.00
____Princess Leia [KE111] 7.00
____R2-D2 ....7.00
____Stormtrooper [KE112] 7.00
____Yoda 7.00

Episode I characters.
____Anakin Skywalker [KE113] 6.00
____Battle Droid [KE114] 6.00
____Darth Maul [KE115] 6.00
____Jar Jar Binks [KE116] 6.00
____Obi-Wan Kenobi [KE117] 6.00
____Qui-Gon Jinn [KE118] 6.00

Factors, Etc.
____C-3PO..12.00
____Chewbacca 12.00
____Darth Vader helmet, 1.25" painted black............12.00
____R2-D2 1" unpainted metal 12.00
____Stormtrooper helmet, 1" painted white 12.00
____X-wing Fighter, 2" unpainted 12.00

Fan Club
____10th Anniversary 1.5" square plastic 11.00
____Official Star Wars Fan Club, 1977 [KE119] 18.00

Hasbro
Galactic Heroes danglers.
____Boba Fett 5.00
____Han Solo 5.00
____Luke Skywalker...5.00
____Yoda 5.00

Hasbro, Japan
Plays one phrase or sound.
____Stormtrooper, US release w/sticker [KE120] 6.00

Hickock
Mexico.
____Admiral Ackbar..15.00
____Bib Fortuna..15.00
____C-3PO..15.00
____Chewbacca 15.00
____Darth Vader..15.00
____Emperor Palpatine 15.00
____Han Solo 15.00
____Lando Calrissian...15.00
____Luke Skywalker 15.00
____Princess Leia 15.00
____R2-D2 ....10.00
____Stormtrooper 15.00

Hollywood Pins
____"20-Years 1977-1997" 9.00
____"Power of the Dark Side" 6.00
____Darth Vader, mask [KE121].....................................7.00
____Darth Vader, mask (small) 5.00
____Darth Vader, portrait 5.00
____Millennium Falcon...6.00
____New Republic 5.00
____New Republic, antique finish 6.00
____R2-D2 ....7.00
____Rebel Forces..6.00
____Rebel Forces, antique finish [KE122] 6.00
____Yoda 5.00

LucasArts
____Lightsaber, blinks, Jedi Outcast Collector's Edition premium [KE123] 12.00

Lucasfilm
____Skywalker Ranch screwdriver keyring 15.00

M&M World
____M&M Anakin [KE124] 10.00
____M&M Boba Fett [KE125] 10.00
____M&M Clone Trooper [KE126] 10.00
____M&M Darth Vader [KE127] 10.00

Movistar
Argentina. Nokia 1100 set of 4 with tin.
____Clone Trooper [KE128] 8.00
____Darth Vader [KE129] 8.00
____Epic Duel [KE130] 8.00
____Yoda [KE131] 8.00

KE132 KE133 KE134 KE135 KE136

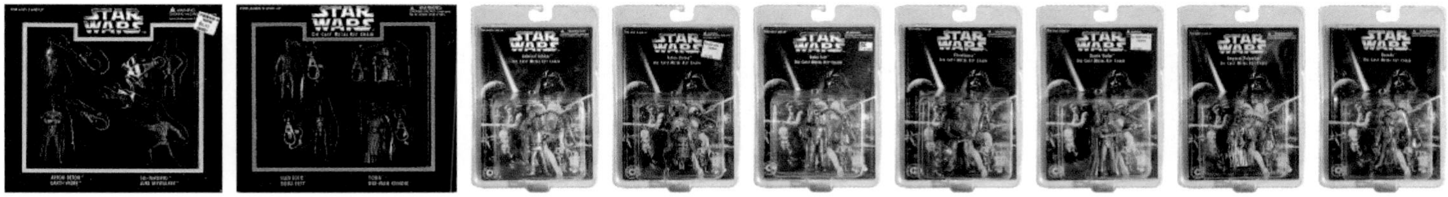

KE137 KE138 KE139 KE140 KE141 KE142 KE143 KE144 KE145

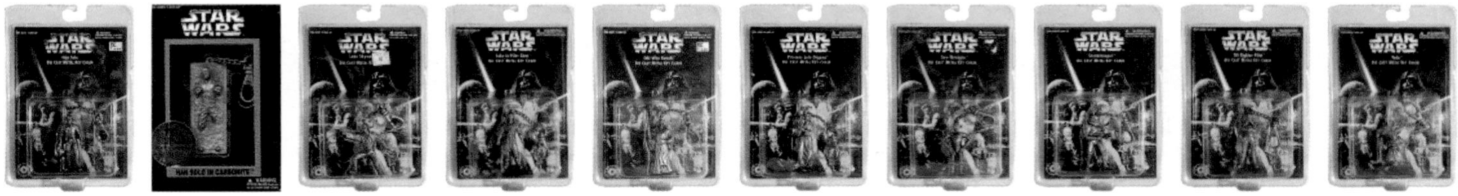

KE146 KE147 KE148 KE149 KE150 KE151 KE152 KE153 KE154 KE155

Keychains

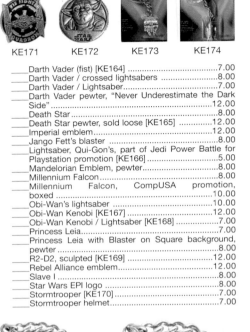

KE156   KE157   KE158   KE159   KE160   KE161   KE162   KE163

KE164   KE165   KE166   KE167   KE168   KE169   KE170   KE171   KE172   KE173   KE174

Pepsi Cola
____Star Wars Trilogy, presented to Taco Bell managers [KE132] 23.00

Pin USA
____Clone Trooper [KE133] 8.00
____Darth Vader [KE134] 8.00
____Sith [KE135] 8.00
____Vader helmet, flames [KE136]................8.00

Playco Toys
____4-Pack Artoo Detoo, Darth Vader, Luke Skywalker, See Threepio [KE137]...............................18.00
____4-Pack Boba Fett, Han Solo, Obi-Wan Kenobi, Yoda [KE138]...18.00
____Admiral Ackbar [KE139] 6.00
____Artoo-Detoo [KE140]............................5.00
____Boba Fett [KE141]...............................5.00
____Chewbacca [KE142] 6.00
____Darth Vader [KE143]............................5.00
____Emperor Palpatine [KE144].....................6.00
____Greedo [KE145]..................................6.00
____Han Solo [KE146]...............................5.00
____Han Solo in Carbonite, FAO Schwarz exclusive, numbered [KE147]...................................12.00
____Luke Skywalker [KE148]........................5.00
____Luke Skywalker in X-Wing Gear [KE149] 6.00

____Obi-Wan Kenobi [KE150] 5.00
____Princess Leia [KE151].........................6.00
____See Threepio [KE152] 5.00
____Stormtrooper [KE153] 6.00
____Tie Fighter Pilot [KE154] 6.00
____Yoda [KE155] 5.00

Playco Toys, Canada
Figures are gold painted and packaged in square window boxes.
____Artoo-Detoo [KE156] 6.00
____Darth Vader [KE157] 6.00
____Luke Skywalker [KE158] 6.00
____See Threepio [KE159] 6.00

Rawcliffe
____20 Year Anniversary brushed 8.00
____20 Year Anniversary enamelized [KE160]..............8.00
____Anakin's lightsaber 8.00
____Bantha skull 8.00
____Blaster Pistol, sculpted [KE161]...............12.00
____Blaster Rifle pewter, sculpted 12.00
____Boba Fett's Helmet [KE162] 7.00
____Boba Fett's helmet 8.00
____Boba Fett Blas Tech EE-3 Rifle [KE163].............7.00
____Boba Fett Icon 7.00
____Chewbacca's head 8.00

____Darth Vader (fist) [KE164] 7.00
____Darth Vader / crossed lightsabers 8.00
____Darth Vader / Lightsaber.......................7.00
____Darth Vader pewter, "Never Underestimate the Dark Side" 12.00
____Death Star 8.00
____Death Star pewter, sold loose [KE165] 12.00
____Imperial emblem................................12.00
____Jango Fett's blaster 8.00
____Lightsaber, Qui-Gon's, part of Jedi Power Battle for Playstation promotion [KE166] 5.00
____Mandelorian Emblem, pewter....................8.00
____Millennium Falcon..............................8.00
____Millennium Falcon, CompUSA promotion, boxed 10.00
____Obi-Wan's lightsaber 10.00
____Obi-Wan Kenobi [KE167] 12.00
____Obi-Wan Kenobi / Lightsaber [KE168] 7.00
____Princess Leia 7.00
____Princess Leia with Blaster on Square background, pewter 8.00
____R2-D2, sculpted [KE169] 12.00
____Rebel Alliance emblem..........................12.00
____Slave I 8.00
____Star Wars EPI logo 8.00
____Stormtrooper [KE170]...........................7.00
____Stormtrooper helmet............................7.00

KE175   KE176   KE177   KE178   KE179   KE180

KE181   KE182   KE183   KE184

KE185   KE186   KE187   KE188

KE189   KE190   KE191   KE192   KE193

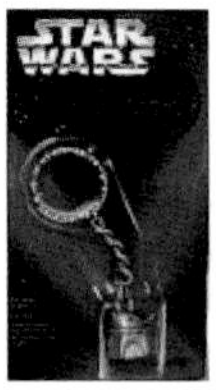
KE194
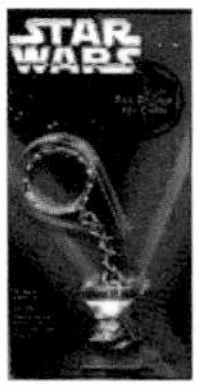
KE195

KE196

KE197

KE198

KE199

KE200

KE201

KE202

KE203

KE204

KE205

KE206

KE207

KE208

KE209

KE210

KE211

____Stormtrooper helmet....................8.00
____Stormtrooper rifle (E-11)....................8.00
____Tie Squadron [KE171]....................7.00
____Wookie Blaster....................8.00
____Yoda, "Try not. Do. Or do not. There is no try." [KE172]....................12.00
____Yoda, "Try not. Do. Or do not. There is no try." 8.00
____Yoda, standing on a rock....................8.00

Blue Rebel Alliance blister card.
____Millennium Falcon, blue Rebel Alliance blister card [KE173]....................7.00
____R2-D2 [KE174]....................7.00

Classic vehicles series.
____AT-AT [KE175]....................12.00
____AT-ST [KE176]....................12.00
____Sand Skiff [KE177]....................12.00
____Shuttle Tydirium [KE178]....................12.00
____Tie Fighter [KE179]....................12.00

EPI TPM.
____Anakin Skywalker emblem....................8.00
____Battle Droid blaster [KE181]....................12.00
____Darth Maul, "At last we will have revenge!"........10.00
____Gungan Sub....................8.00
____Jar Jar Binks....................10.00
____Pit Droid....................10.00
____Podracing....................7.00
____Queen Amidala's Gun [KE182]....................12.00
____Royal Starship....................10.00
____Trade Federation Starfighter badge....................8.00

EPII AOTC.
____Anakin Lightsaber [KE183]....................12.00
____Clone Trooper Helmet [KE180]....................12.00
____Jango Pistol [KE185]....................12.00
____Jedi Starfighter [KE186]....................12.00
____Slave 1 [KE187]....................12.00

Logo series.
____Celebration II [KE188]....................7.00
____Empire Strikes Back [KE189]....................12.00
____Episode I [KE190]....................12.00
____Magic of Myth....................15.00
____Return of the Jedi [KE191]....................12.00

____Shadows of the Empire [KE192]....................12.00
____Star Wars [KE193]....................12.00
____Star Wars Special Edition, painted [KE184]..........9.00

Red Galactic Empire blister card.
____Boba Fett helmet [KE194]....................7.00
____Darth Vader helmet [KE195]....................7.00
____Death Star [KE196]....................7.00

Showa Note
EPII:AOTC. Metal.
____Jango Fett [KE197]....................4.00
____R2-D2 [KE198]....................4.00

Stiefelmayer-Contento
3-D laser engraved glass cube keychains with illumination.
____AT-RT, illumiated red....................24.00
____C-3PO, illumiated blue....................24.00
____Clone Trooper, illumiated red....................24.00
____Emperor (lightning), illumiated blue....................24.00
____Emperor (lightsaber), illumiated red....................24.00
____Han Solo, illumiated blue....................24.00
____R2-D2, illumiated blue....................24.00
____Star Wars logo, illumiated red....................24.00
____Yoda, illumiated blue....................24.00

Takara
____R2-D2 inflatable [KE199]....................37.00

Japan.
____Star Wars viewer, 12 movie scenes [KE200]......35.00

The LEGO Group
EPIII:ROTS
____Chewbacca [KE201]....................8.00
____Darth Vader [KE202]....................8.00
____R2-D2 [KE203]....................8.00
____Yoda [KE204]....................8.00

Lego mini-figures.
____C-3PO....................12.00
____Darth Maul bagged [KE205]....................12.00
____Darth Vader bagged [KE206]....................12.00
____Darth Vader carded [KE207]....................12.00
____Luke, X-Wing pilot [KE208]....................12.00

____R2-D2 carded [KE209]....................12.00
____Snowtrooper....................12.00
____Stormtrooper [KE210]....................12.00
____Yoda carded [KE211]....................12.00

Tiger Electronics
____C-3PO, flashlight [KE212]....................7.00
____Death Star, records and plays back [KE213]........7.00
____Lightsaber, lights and makes sound, extends and retracts [KE214]....................7.00
____R2-D2, digial clock [KE215]....................7.00
____R2-D2, digial clock, plastic hangcard [KE216]......7.00

EPII:AOTC Force Link.
____Anakin Skywalker's Speeder....................12.00
____Jango Fett's Slave I....................12.00
____Obi-Wan Kenobi's Jedi Starfighter....................12.00
____Zam Wesell's Speeder....................12.00

Plays one phrase or sound.
____Boba Fett [KE217]....................7.00
____Chewbacca [KE218]....................6.00
____Darth Vader [KE219]....................6.00
____Jabba the Hutt....................6.00
____Luke Skywalker [KE220]....................6.00
____Millennium Falcon [KE221]....................6.00
____Star Destroyer [KE222]....................6.00
____Stormtrooper [KE223]....................6.00

Tomy
Miniature weapons with light-up features.
____Blaster, Han Solo....................8.00
____Lightsaber, Darth Vader....................8.00
____Lightsaber, Luke Skywalker ANH....................8.00
____Lightsaber, Luke Skywalker ROTJ....................8.00
____Lightsaber, Obi-Wan Kenobi....................8.00

UA Movie Theaters
Hong Kong.
____Qee, black [KE224]....................8.00
____Qee, white [KE225]....................8.00

Unlicensed
____6-Pack, any 6 hanging off header copied from Hasbro header, each [KE226]....................36.00
____Wicket [KE227]....................12.00

KE212

KE213

KE214

KE215

KE216

KE217

KE218

KE219

KE220

KE221

KE222

KE223
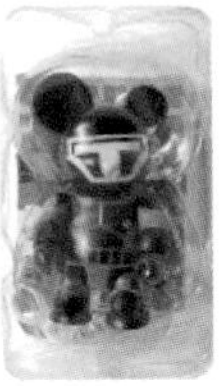
KE224

KE225

KE226

KE227 Set 1

KE227 Set 2

KE227 Set 3

KE228

Keychains

      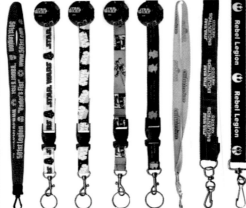

| KY01 | KY02 | KY03 | KY04 | LMS0 | LMS02 |

| LM01 | LM02 | LM03 | LM04 | LM05 | LLS01 | L1A01 L1A02 L1A03 L1A04 L1A05 L1A06 L1A07 L1A08 L1A09 |

Williams

____C-3PO, Star Wars Episode I Pinball [2:287] 14.00
____Darth Maul, Episode I Pin 2000 [2:287] 14.00
____R2-D2 [2:287] 7.00
____Trade Federation Driod Starfighter [2:287] 16.00
____Wrench, Official pinball pit droid [2:287] 12.00

Keys: Hotel

Celebration 3. Sponsored by Target.
____Darth Vader [KY01] 5.00
____Darth Vader with lightsaber down [KY02] 5.00
____Darth Vader with lightsaber up [KY03] 5.00
____Epic Duel [KY04] 5.00

Kites

General Mills
Star Wars mail-in premiums.
____Delta-wing flyer [2:287] 19.00
____Diamond flyer [3:281] 19.00

Palitoy
____X-Wing and Tie Fighter wing shaped 42.00

Spectra Star
____Darth Vader Parasail Kite 12.00
____Speeder Bike 50 ft dragon kite [KI01] 22.00
____Wacky Winder in Darth Vader pkg. 5.00

Box kites.
____Characters [KI07] 17.00
____ROTJ Characters [KI08] 17.00

Delta wing kites.
____Characters [KI09] 8.00
____Darth Vader..11.00
____Death Star Trench [KI02].....................................8.00

Diamond kites.
____Boba Fett 6.00

____Darth Vader..16.00
____Luke Skywalker vs Darth Vader 8.00
____Millennium Falcon 16.00

Figure kites.
____Darth Vader [KI10] 14.00
____Luke Skywalker [KI11] 14.00
____Wicket the Ewok [KI12] 12.00

Streamer Kites.
____Darth Vader [KI03] 8.00
____Darth Vader [KI13] 8.00
____Droids [KI04] 12.00
____Ewoks on Gliders [KI05].................................10.00

The Kite Factory
____Darth Vader figure kite [KI14] 12.00
____Luke vs. Vader art, delta wing [KI15] 12.00

Worlds Apart
____C-3PO and R2-D2 pocket kite [KI06] 12.00
____Jar Jar Binks delta wing [KI16].............................8.00
____Naboo Fighter stunt kite [2:287] 8.00
____ROTJ: Darth Vader [KI17]................................12.00

Lamp Shades

____Star Wars, B/W scenes [LMS01] 46.00

Hay Jax
____ROTJ characters on brown background 38.00

Scanlite
____ESB Kit-form with free poster [LMS02] 35.00

Lamps

____EPI Space battle, ceramic w/shade [LM01] 45.00

Character Lamps.
____R2-D2 [LM02] 75.00

France.
____Plasma (ball) lamp [LM03] 75.00

Wall lights.
____Darth Maul [LM04] 20.00

Idea Nuova
____EVA lamp [LM05] 20.00

Windmill Ceramics
____Chewbacca 25.00
____Darth Vader...15.00
____R2-D2 ....15.00

Lanyards

____Clip and Carry lanyard [L1A01].........................8.00

501st Legion
____www.501st.com [L1A02] 5.00

C and D Visionaries, Inc.
____Darth Vader [L1A03]..4.00
____Star Wars logo [L1A04].....................................4.00
____Yoda [L1A05]..4.00
____Yoda, "There is no Try" [L1A06] 4.00

Lucasfilm
____Celebration 2 fanclub exclusive.........................11.00
____Celebration 3 fanclub exclusive [L1A07] 5.00

Mexico Collector Convention 2004
____Star Wars Encuentros Mexico [L1A08]..................5.00

Rebel Legion
____Rebel Legion [L1A09] 5.00

Laser Light Spinner

Fantasma
____Star Wars logo and ships [LLS01] 10.00

| KI01 | KI02 | KI03 | KI04 | KI05 | KI06 | KI07 | KI08 | KI09 | KI10 | KI11 | KI12 | KI13 | KI14 | KI15 | KI16 | KI17 |

LL01 LL02 LL03 LL04

LCP01 LCP02 LCP03

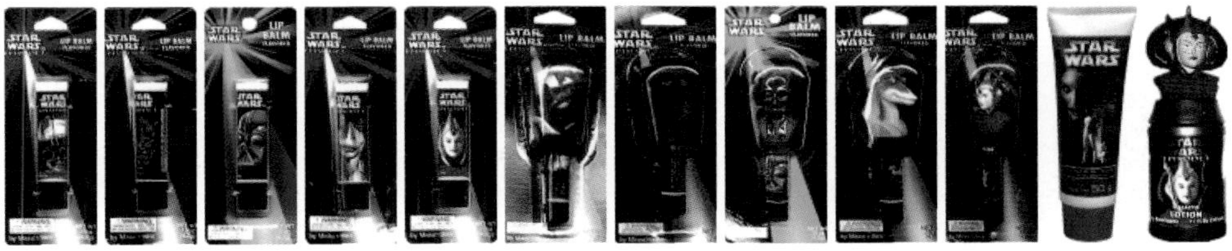

LPB01 LPB02 LPB03 LPB04 LPB05 LPB06 LPB07 LPB08 LPB09 LPB10 LOT01 LOT02

Laser Pointers

Japan.
____Lightsaber hilt design 65.00

Laundry Bags

Adam Joseph Industries
____C-3PO and R2-D2 [LL01] 25.00
____Darth Vader and Emperor's Royal Guards 25.00
____Princess Kneesaa and Wicket [LL02] 25.00
____Wicket the Ewok [LL03] 25.00
____Wicket the Ewok (and Bagga) [LL04] 25.00

License Plates

Disney / MGM
____Boba Fett [LCP01] 18.00
____Jedi Training Acadamy [LCP02] 18.00
____Stormtrooper [LCP03] 18.00

starwars.com
In 2003 the official Star Wars website offered 13 themed art galleries with approximately 12 images in each gallery. Fans could order vanity license plates from an online merchandiser with their choice of images.
____Bounty Hunters gallery, each 12.00
____Clone Wars gallery, each 12.00
____Creatures gallery, each 12.00
____Droids gallery, each 12.00
____Holiday Art gallery, each 12.00
____Jedi gallery, each 12.00
____Logos gallery, each 12.00
____Padme gallery, each 12.00
____Princess Leia gallery, each 12.00
____Rebels gallery, each 12.00
____Sith gallery, each 12.00
____Vehicles gallery, each 12.00

Lip Balm

Avon, Mexico
____EPII: Anakin and Padme label 7.00

Minnetonka
Picture of character on barrel.
____Anakin Skywalker [LPB01] 5.00
____Darth Maul [LPB02] 5.00
____Darth Vader [LPB03] 5.00
____Jar Jar Binks [LPB04] 5.00
____Queen Amidala [LPB05] 5.00
Sculpt of character on cap.
____Anakin Skywalker [LPB06] 7.00
____Darth Maul [LPB07] 7.00
____Darth Vader [LPB08] 7.00
____Jar Jar Binks [LPB09] 7.00
____Queen Amidala [LPB10] 7.00

Lotion

Avon, Mexico
____Queen Amidala hand cream [LOT01] 8.00

Minnetonka
____Queen Amidala [LOT02] 6.00

Lottery Scratch-Off Tickets

EPIII:ROTS. Australia.
____Anakin Skywalker [WIN01] 6.00
____C-3PO [WIN02] 6.00
____Chewbacca [WIN03] 6.00
____Clone Trooper 6.00
____Darth Vader [WIN04] 6.00
____Emperor 6.00
____General Grievous 6.00
____Obi-Wan Kenobi 6.00
____R2-D2 [WIN05] 6.00
____Yoda [WIN06] 6.00

EPIII:ROTS. Belgium.
____C-3PO [WIN07] 10.00
____Chewbacca 10.00
____Darth Vader [WIN08] 10.00
____Obi-Wan Kenobi [WIN09] 10.00
____Yoda [WIN10] 10.00

EPIII:ROTS. France.
____Anakin Skywalker 10.00
____Chewbacca 10.00
____Darth Vader 10.00
____General Grievous 10.00
____Han Solo 10.00
____Jango Fett 10.00
____Luke Skywalker 10.00
____Obi-Wan Kenobi 10.00
____Princess Leia 10.00
____Queen Amidala 10.00
____R2-D2 and C-3PO 10.00
____Yoda 10.00

EPIII:ROTS. U.K.
____Anakin [WIN11] 8.00
____C-3PO and R2-D2 [WIN12] 8.00
____Chewbacca [WIN13] 8.00
____Darth Maul [WIN14] 8.00
____Darth Sidious [WIN15] 8.00
____Darth Vader [WIN16] 8.00
____Han Solo [WIN17] 8.00
____Luke Skywalker [WIN18] 8.00
____Mace Windu [WIN19] 8.00
____Obi-Wan [WIN20] 8.00
____Queen Amidala [WIN21] 8.00
____Yoda [WIN22] 8.00

WIN01 WIN02 WIN03 WIN04 WIN05

WIN06 WIN07 WIN08 WIN09 WIN10 WIN11 WIN12 WIN13

WIN14 WIN15 WIN16 WIN17 WIN18 WIN19 WIN20 WIN21 WIN22

Lottery Scratch-Off Tickets

 WIN23
 WIN24
 WIN25
 WIN26
 WIN27
 WIN28
 WIN29

 WIN30
 WIN31
 WIN32
 WIN33
 WIN34
 WIN35
 WIN36

 WIN37
 WIN38
 WIN39
 WIN40
 WIN41
 WIN42
 WIN43

 WIN44
 WIN45
 WIN46
 WIN47
 WIN48
 WIN49
 WIN50

EPIII:ROTS. U.S. California.
____ ANH: C-3PO and R2-D2 [WIN23] 4.00
____ ANH: Heroes [WIN24] 4.00
____ AOTC: poster art [WIN25] 4.00
____ AOTC: Yoda [WIN26] 4.00
____ ESB: Falcon cockpit [WIN27] 4.00
____ ESB: Yoda, Lando, Vader, Boba Fett [WIN28] 4.00
____ ROTJ: Emperor and Darth Vader [WIN29] 4.00
____ ROTJ: Emperor, Luke, Vader, Yoda [WIN30] 4.00
____ ROTS: Epic Duel [WIN31] 4.00
____ ROTS: Vader art logo [WIN32] 4.00
____ TPM: Darth Maul [WIN33] 4.00
____ TPM: poster art [WIN34] 4.00

EPIII:ROTS. U.S. Montana.
____ Anakin Skywalker 4.00
____ C-3PO and R2-D2 .... 4.00
____ Chewbacca 4.00
____ Darth Sidious 4.00

____ Darth Vader 4.00
____ General Grievous 4.00
____ Obi-Wan Kenobi 4.00
____ Yoda 4.00

EPIII:ROTS.
____ Retailer exclusive card [WIN35] 25.00

EPIII:ROTS Mexico
____ Anakin and Padme [WIN36] 10.00
____ Anakin Skywalker podracing [WIN37] 10.00
____ Attack of the Clones movie poster art [WIN38] 10.00
____ C-3PO and R2-D2 [WIN39] 10.00
____ C-3PO, Jabba, Princess Leia [WIN40] 10.00
____ Chewbacca, Han, C-3PO, Princess Leia [WIN41] 10.00
____ Clone Troopers [WIN42] 10.00
____ Darth Maul [WIN43] 10.00

____ Darth Vader and Boba Fett [WIN44] 10.00
____ Darth Vader, Revenge of the Sith [WIN45] 10.00
____ Emperor, Luke, Darth Vader, Yoda [WIN46] 10.00
____ Han Solo [WIN47] 10.00
____ Han Solo, Princess Leia, Luke Skywalker [WIN48] 10.00
____ Hoth speeder snow battle with AT-ATs [WIN49] 10.00
____ Jedi Starfighters [WIN50] 10.00
____ Mace Windu and Obi-Wan Kenobi [WIN51] 10.00
____ Millennium Falcon flees Death Star II [WIN52] 10.00
____ Palpatine, Obi-Wan, Anakin, and R2-D2 [WIN53] 10.00
____ Queen Amidala [WIN54] 10.00
____ Stormtrooper [WIN55] 10.00
____ The Plantom Menace movie poster art [WIN56] 10.00
____ X-Wing Fighters [WIN57] 10.00
____ Yoda [WIN58] 10.00
____ Yoda, Lando Calrissian, Darth Vader, Boba Fett [WIN59] 10.00

Atlantic Lottery Corporation Inc.
EPIII:ROTS. Canada.
____ Darth Vader [WIN60] 8.00
____ Epic Duel [WIN61] 8.00
____ R2-D2 and C-3PO [WIN62] 8.00
____ Yoda [WIN63] 8.00

British Columbia Lottery Corp.
____ Anakin Skywalker 4.00

 WIN51
 WIN52
 WIN53
 WIN54

 WIN55
 WIN56
 WIN57
 WIN58
 WIN59
 WIN60
 WIN61
 WIN62
 WIN63

| WIN64 | WIN65 | WIN66 | WIN67 | WIN68 | WIN69 | WIN70 | WIN71 | WIN72 | WIN73 | WIN74 |

____Boba Fett 4.00
____C-3PO and R2-D2 ....4.00
____Chewbacca 4.00
____Darth Vader 4.00
____Emperor Palpatine 4.00
____Han Solo 4.00
____Luke Skywalker...................................4.00
____Obi-Wan Kenobi 4.00
____Princess Leia 4.00
____Queen Amidala 4.00
____Yoda 4.00

K-Mart
Promotional game ticket.
____Anakin Skywalker [WIN64] 4.00
____C-3PO [WIN65] 4.00
____Jango fett [WIN66] 4.00
____Obi-Wan Kenobi [WIN67] 4.00
____Padme Amidala [WIN68].......................4.00

La Francaise des Jeux
Instant lottery ticket.
____C-3PO [WIN69] 3.00
____Dark Maul [WIN70] 3.00
____Jar Jar Binks [WIN71] 3.00
____Mace Windu [WIN72] 3.00
____Obi-Wan Kenobi [WIN73] 3.00
____Qui-Gon Jinn [WIN74] 3.00
____R2-D2 [WIN75] 3.00
____Reine Amidala [WIN76] 3.00
____Yoda [WIN77] 3.00

Lunch Boxes

____Podrace, plastic with thermos [LX01] 20.00

EPI:TPM. Shaped, includes bottle.
____Anakin Skywalker [LX02] 18.00
____Darth Maul with sandwich case [LX03] 18.00

AZ Designz
Australia.
____Darth Maul [LX04] 8.00
____Jar Jar [LX05] 8.00

Big Dog
____The Empire Bites Back [LX06] 35.00

Calego International
EPI:TPM. Soft-sided bags.
____Queen Amidala [LX07] 17.00
____Starfighters [LX08] 8.00
____Starfighters, dome [LX09] 8.00

Canadian Thermos Products
____ANH: movie art, plastic blue [LX10]....................34.00
____ANH: movie art, plastic red 34.00
____Dogfight over Death Star [LX11] 34.00
____ESB: movie art, plastic [LX12] 34.00
____ROTJ: movie art, plastic [LX13] 34.00

Galerie Chocolates
____Darth Vader, shaped tin 8.00

Jollibee
____R2-D2 lunch accessory kit [LX14] 65.00

Kelloggs, Korea
____R2-D2 lunch accessory kit................................65.00

King Seeley-Thermos
____DROIDS: Plastic. Cartoon C-3PO and R2-D2 on lid. Thermos with cartoon droids [LX15] 45.00
____ESB: Metal. Dagobah Swamp and Hoth Battle. Thermos with Yoda [LX16] 85.00
____ESB: Metal. Millennium Falcon and Luke, R2-D2 and Yoda. Thermos with Yoda [LX17].......................55.00
____ESB: Plastic. Chewbacca, Han, Leia and Luke on lid. Thermos with Yoda. [LX18] 35.00
____ESB: Plastic. Logo with photo inserts. Thermos with Yoda. [LX19]......................................43.00
____EWOKS: plastic. Ewoks on lid. Thermos with Ewok [LX20] 32.00
____ROTJ: Metal. Jabba's Palace and Space Battle. Thermos with Ewok [LX21] 35.00
____ROTJ: Plastic. Luke and Jabba's Palace Creatures. Plain thermos [LX22] 41.00
____ROTJ: Plastic. R2-D2 and Wicket on lid. Thermos with Ewok [LX22] 32.00
____SW: Metal. Space Battle and Mos Eisley, no art on top, bottom, or sides 85.00

| WIN75 | WIN76 | WIN77 |

____SW: Metal. Space Battle and Mos Eisley. Thermos with C-3PO and R2-D2 [LX23]...........................63.00
____SW: Plastic. Darth Vader and stormtroopers on decal. [LX24] 45.00
____SW: Plastic. Darth Vader, C-3PO and R2-D2 on decal. C-3PO and R2-D2 thermos.[LX25] 57.00

Pyramid
Episode I: The Phantom Menace.
____Anakin Skywalker podracer [LX26] 12.00
____Darth Maul bust, includes bottle [LX27] 12.00
____Darth Maul full-body, includes bottle [LX28] 12.00
____Darth Maul, Style A [LX29] 6.00
____Darth Maul, Style B [LX30] 7.00
____Darth Maul, Style C [LX31] 7.00
____Jar Jar, style A [LX32] 6.00
____Jar Jar, style B [LX33] 7.00
____Jar Jar, style C 7.00
____Jedi vs. Sith, Style A [LX34] 6.00
____Jedi vs. Sith, Style B [LX35] 7.00
____Jedi vs. Sith, Style C 7.00
____Jedi, style A [LX36] 6.00
____Jedi, style B 7.00
____Jedi, style C 7.00
____Podracing, Style A [LX37] 6.00
____Podracing, Style B 7.00
____Podracing, Style C 7.00
____Podracing, style A [LX38] 6.00
____Podracing, style B..7.00
____Podracing, style C [LX39]..................................7.00
____Queen Amidala, style A 6.00
____Queen Amidala, style B [LX40]...........................7.00
____Queen Amidala, style C 7.00

| LX01 | LX02 | LX03 | LX04 | LX05 | LX06 |

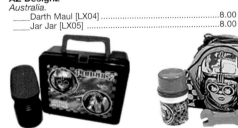    

| LX07 | LX08 | LX09 | LX10 | LX11 | LX12 |

| LX13 | LX14 assembled | LX14 open | LX15 | LX16 | LX17 |

Lunch Boxes

LX18

LX19

LX20

LX21

LX22

LX23

LX24

LX25

LX26

LX27

LX28

LX29

LX30

LX31

LX32

LX33

LX34

LX35

LX36

Episode II: Attack of the Clones. Soft-sided lunchboxes wiith thermos or sports waterbottle included.
____Anakin Skywalker [LX41] 12.00
____Clone Trooper [LX42] 14.00
____Heroes [LX43] 12.00
____Heroes with waterbottle attached [LX44] 14.00
____Jedi Training Acadamy [LX45] 12.00

Spearmark Int.
____EPII Cool Bag, sandwich box, sportsbottle 9.00

Plastic, classic art decal featuring Luke and Leia, Vader and Stormtrooper.
____Double thermos [LX46].....................................21.00
____Rectangular [LX47] 15.00

Thermos Co.
EPIII:ROTS.
____Darth Vader [LX48] 18.00
____Darth Vader dual compartment [LX49] 18.00

Hard plastic with graphic thermos.
____Jango Fett with Slave I thermos [LX50]...............15.00
____Jedi battles with duel thermos [LX51] 15.00
____R2-D2 and C-3PO sculpted front [LX52]............15.00
____Yoda [LX53] 15.00

Metal lunchboxes with plain white thermos.
____Episode II Heroes and Villains [LX54] 25.00
____Movie / Soundtrack poster art [LX55] 35.00

Zak Designs
EPIII:ROTS.
____Darth Vader hard plastic [LX56] 20.00
____Darth Vader sandwich carrier [LX57] 6.00
____Darth Vader soft vinyl [LX58] 18.00

LX37

LX38

LX39

LX40

LX41

LX42

LX43

LX44

LX45

LX46

LX47

LX48

LX49

LX50

LX51

LX52

LX53

LX54

LX55

LX56

LX57

LX58

| MAG01 | MAG02 |  HOX01 |  HOX02 |  HOX03 |  HOX04 |  HOX05 |  HOX06 | HOX07 |

| HOX08 |  HOX09 |  HOX10 | HOX11 | HOX12 | HOX13 | HOX14 | HOX15 | HOX16 | HOX17 |

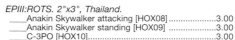 

| HOX18 | HOX19 | HOX20 |  HOX21 | HOX22 | HOX23 | HOX24 | HOX25 |

Magnetic Playsets

AT-A-Boy
____Mix 'N' Match Adventure Playset [MAG01] 10.00

Lucas Learning
____Droidworks [MAG02] 10.00

Rose Art Industries
____EPIII:ROTS 10.00

Magnets

1970s monster magnet series.
____Mono, Darth Vader likeness [HOX01] 4.00

3.5"x5" movie image inside border trim.
____Anakin Skywalker [HOX02] 2.00
____Darth Maul [HOX03] 2.00
____Jar Jar [HOX04] 2.00
____Naboo Space Battle [HOX05] 2.00
____Obi-Wan Kenobi [HOX06] 2.00
____Queen Amidala [HOX07] 2.00

Celebration 1.
____Anakin Skywalker 8.00

Celebration 3.
____Clone Trooper [HOX18] 8.00
____Darth Vader [HOX19] 8.00
____General Grievous [HOX20] 8.00
____Royal Guard [HOX21] 8.00

EPIII:ROTS. 2"x3", Thailand.
____Anakin Skywalker attacking [HOX08] 3.00
____Anakin Skywalker standing [HOX09] 3.00
____C-3PO [HOX10] 3.00
____Darth Sidious [HOX11] 3.00
____Darth Vader [HOX12] 3.00
____General Grievous [HOX13] 3.00
____Obi-Wan Kenobi [HOX14] 3.00
____Padme [HOX15] 3.00
____R2-D2 [HOX16] 3.00
____Yoda [HOX17] 3.00

Mpire, approx 2" round.
____Anakin 2.00
____C-3PO 2.00
____Chewbacca 2.00
____Clone Trooper 2.00
____Cound Dooku 2.00
____Darth Maul 2.00
____Darth Vader 2.00
____Emperor 2.00
____Han 2.00
____Luke 2.00
____Obi-Wan 2.00
____Princess Leia 2.00
____Queen Amidala 2.00

20th Century Fox, Thailand
EPII movie promotion, 1.75"x2.75".
____Anakin Skywalker [HOX22] 4.00
____Padme Amidala [HOX23] 4.00

A.H. Prismatic
____Darth Vader, hologram [HOX24] 7.00
____X-Wing Fighter in combat, hologram [HOX25]......7.00

Adam Joseph Industries
____Chewbacca [HOX26] 6.00
____Chewbacca, Darth Vader, R2-D2, and Yoda [HOX27] 12.00
____Wicket and Kneesaa [HOX28] 8.00

Applause
3D sculpted magnets.
____4-pack boxed: Naboo Fighter, Battle Droid on Stap, Jar Jar Binks, Watto [HOX29] 21.00
____Battle Droid [HOX30] 6.00
____Jar Jar Binks [HOX31] 6.00
____Naboo fighter [HOX32] 5.00
____Watto [HOX33] 6.00

Die-cut magnets with stamped detailing.
____AT-AT [HOX34]...4.00
____Millennium Falcon 4.00
____Snowspeeder [HOX35] 4.00
____Tie fighter [HOX36] 4.00
____X-Wing fighter [HOX37] 4.00

Episode I die-cut magnets with stamped detailing.
____Naboo starfighter [HOX38] 4.00
____Trade Federation Droid fighter [HOX39] 4.00

AT-A-Boy
____ANH Falcon cockpit 4.00
____B-wings in battle 4.00
____Ben holding lightsaber 4.00
____Ben Kenobi [2:290] 4.00
____Ben Kenobi portrait [2:290].....................................4.00
____Boba Fett in Cloud City corridor 4.00
____Bounty hunter line-up 4.00

        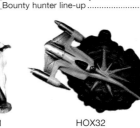  

| HOX26 |  HOX27 | HOX28 | HOX29 | HOX30 | HOX31 | HOX32 | HOX33 |

| HOX34 | HOX35 |  HOX36 | HOX37 | HOX38 |  HOX39 |

Magnets

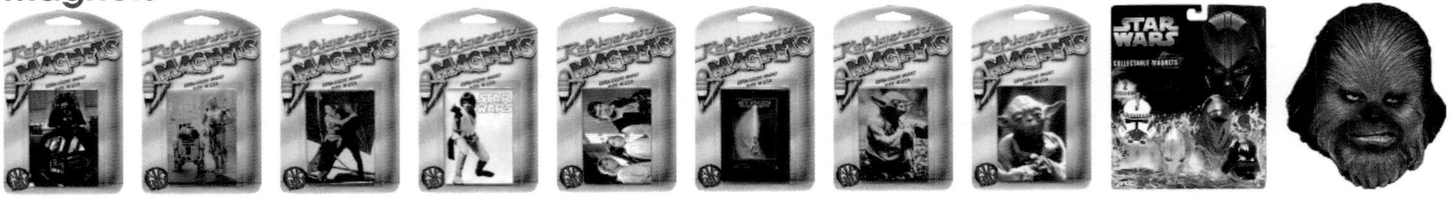

HOX40 HOX41 HOX42 HOX43 HOX44 HOX45 HOX46 HOX47 HOX48 HOX49

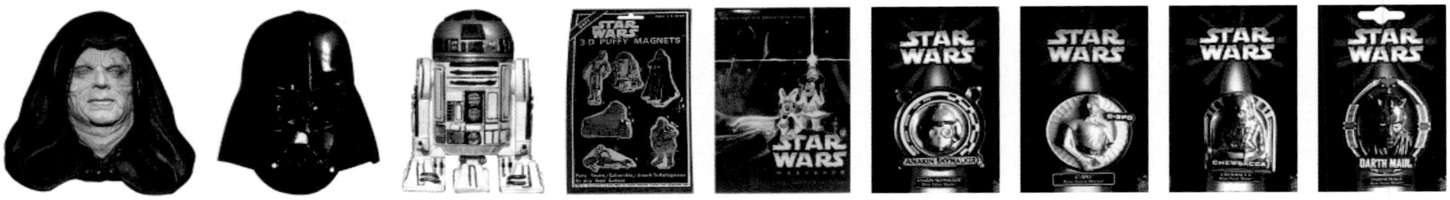

HOX50 HOX51 HOX52 HOX53 HOX54 HOX55 HOX56 HOX57 HOX58

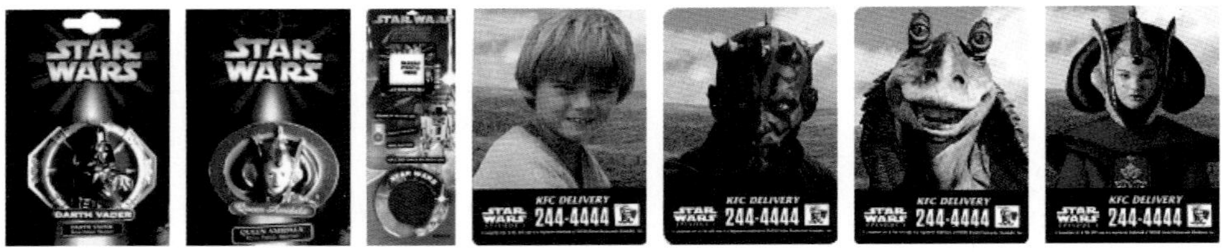

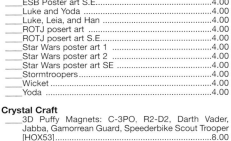

HOX59 HOX60 HOX61 HOX62 HOX63 HOX64 HOX65

____C-3PO portrait [2:290] 4.00
____Chewbacca, snow covered 4.00
____Darth Vader flanked by two stormtroopers 4.00
____Darth Vader portrait [2:290] 4.00
____Darth Vader portrait (shuttle ramp in background) [HOX40] 4.00
____Darth Vader reaches out on Cloud City gantry 4.00
____Darth Vader silhouetted in ESB freeze chamber ..4.00
____Darth Vader with beige background....................4.00
____Droids in Blockade Runner corridor [HOX41] 4.00
____Droids in Hoth base corridor 4.00
____Emperor Palpatine portrait 4.00
____ESB 'A' poster with credits [2:290]....................4.00
____ESB Luke in the tree....................4.00
____Falcon in flight [2:290] 4.00
____Han and Chewbacca blasting [2:290] 4.00
____Han and Leia kiss (ESB) 4.00
____Han blasting 4.00
____Han in gunner chair [2:290] 4.00
____Han on tauntaun 4.00
____Han portrait....................4.00
____Han Solo [2:290] 4.00
____Holochess aboard the Falcon 4.00
____Interior of Ben's house 4.00
____Leia consoles Luke [2:290]....................4.00
____Leia hand on hip, gun up 4.00
____Leia on Falcon 4.00
____Leia programming R2-D2 ....4.00
____Luke and Leia ROTJ swing [HOX42] 4.00
____Luke and X-wing in swamp 4.00
____Luke looking at the sunsets [2:290] 4.00
____Luke playing with T-16 [2:290] 4.00
____Luke portrait [HOX43] 4.00
____Luke sees charred relatives [2:290] 4.00
____Luke, Leia, and Han in Death Star [HOX44]..........4.00
____R2-D2 ....4.00
____ROTJ 'A' poster with credits [HOX45] 4.00
____Sandtrooper on dewback [2:290]....................4.00
____Stormtrooper in freeze chamber 4.00
____Stormtroopers blasting [2:290]....................4.00
____SW 'C' poster with credits 4.00
____TIE Interceptor 4.00
____TIE shooting Falcon amid asteroids....................4.00
____X-wing in flight 4.00
____X-wing shooting Vader's TIE Fighter 4.00
____Yoda [HOX46] 4.00
____Yoda (close-up) [HOX47] 4.00
____Yoda in his house 4.00
____Yoda on Luke's back [2:290] 4.00

Cards, Inc.
____4-pack Collectible Magnets: Shock Trooper, General Grievous, Royal Guard, Darth Vader [HOX48] 25.00
____C-3PO 5.00
____Chewbacca [HOX49] 5.00
____Clone Trooper 5.00
____Commander Cody 5.00
____Darth Sidious [HOX50] 5.00
____Darth Vader [HOX51] 5.00
____General Grievous 5.00
____R2-D2 [HOX52] 5.00

Classico
2"x3" rectangular.
____Boba Fett 4.00
____Darth Maul 4.00
____Darth Vader (ESB)....................4.00
____Darth Vader (ROTJ)....................4.00
____Droids in Blockade Runner corridor....................4.00
____ESB Poster art 1 ....4.00
____ESB Poster art 2 ....4.00
____ESB Poster art S.E....................4.00
____Luke and Yoda 4.00
____Luke, Leia, and Han 4.00
____ROTJ posert art 4.00
____ROTJ posert art S.E....................4.00
____Star Wars poster art 1 ....4.00
____Star Wars poster art 2 ....4.00
____Star Wars poster art SE 4.00
____Stormtroopers....................4.00
____Wicket 4.00
____Yoda 4.00

Crystal Craft
____3D Puffy Magnets: C-3PO, R2-D2, Darth Vader, Jabba, Gamorrean Guard, Speederbike Scout Trooper [HOX53]....................8.00

Disney / MGM
____Jedi Training Academy 6.00

Star Tours.
____C-3PO 4.00
____Logo 4.00
____R2-D2 ....4.00

Star Wars Weekends.
____2004 Mickey Mouse and Minnie Mouse poster art [HOX54]....................8.00
____2005 Darth Vader / Mickey....................8.00
____2006 Poster art 8.00

Galoob
____Magnetic base with 200 mini-Millennium Falcons, Toy Fair give-away 1997 ....24.00

Giftware International
Resin fridge magnets.
____Anakin Skywalker [HOX55]....................8.00
____C-3PO [HOX56] 12.00
____Chewbacca [HOX57] 12.00

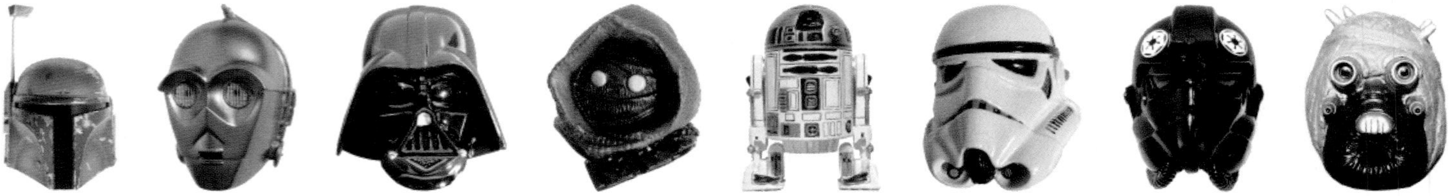

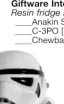

HOX66 HOX67 HOX68 HOX69 HOX70 HOX71 HOX72 HOX73

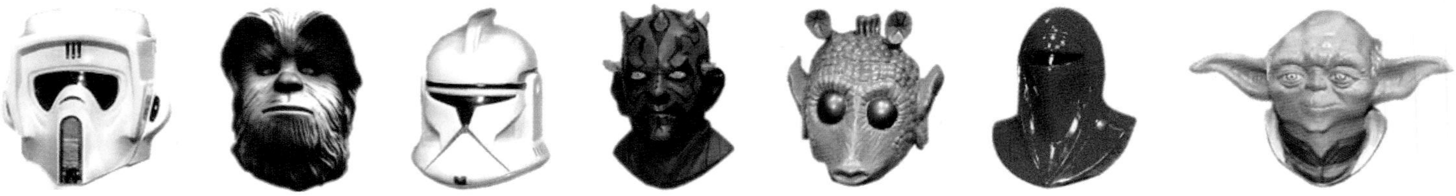

HOX74 HOX75 HOX76 HOX77 HOX78 HOX79 HOX80

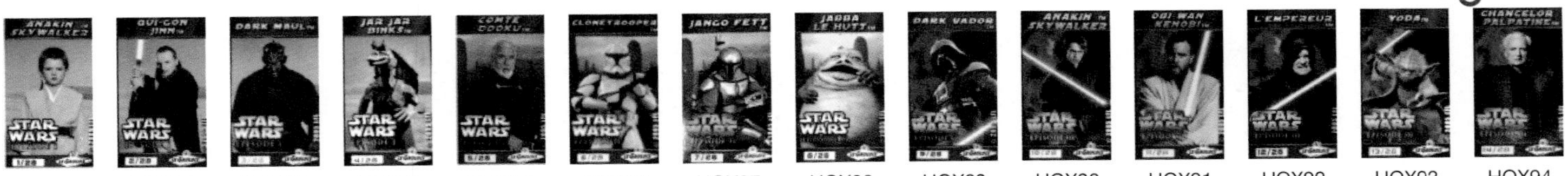

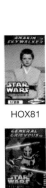

HOX81 HOX82 HOX83 HOX84 HOX85 HOX86 HOX87 HOX88 HOX89 HOX90 HOX91 HOX92 HOX93 HOX94

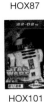

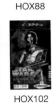

HOX95 HOX96 HOX97 HOX98 HOX99 HOX100 HOX101 HOX102 HOX103 HOX104 HOX105 HOX106 HOX107 HOX108

____Darth Maul [HOX58] 10.00
____Darth Vader [HOX59] 12.00
____Queen Amidala [HOX60] 10.00

Glow Zone
Refrigerator magnets.
____Darkside / Jedi sheet of 10 ......8.00
____Naboo Battle sheet of 7 ......8.00

Hot Topic
____Darth Vader 4.00
____Magnet Set [HOX61] 8.00

Movie poster art.
____ANH 4.00
____ESB 4.00

Howard Eldon
____A New Hope, triangular logo 8.00
____Return of the Jedi, Yoda in circle 8.00
____The Empire Strikes Back, Darth Vader in flames ..8.00

KFC
____Anakin Skywalker [HOX62] 5.00
____Darth Maul [HOX63] 5.00
____Jar Jar Binks [HOX64] 5.00
____Queen Amidala [HOX65] 5.00

Kotobukiya
Series 1.
____Boba Fett (mystery / chase piece) [HOX66] 25.00
____C-3PO [HOX67] 8.00
____Darth Vader [HOX68] 8.00
____Jawa [HOX69] 8.00
____R2-D2 [HOX70] 8.00
____Stormtrooper [HOX71] 8.00
____TIE Fighter Pilot [HOX72] 8.00
____Tusken Raider [HOX73] 8.00

Series 2.
____Biker Scout [HOX74] 8.00
____Boushh (mystery / chase piece) 8.00
____Chewbacca [HOX75] 8.00
____Clone Trooper [HOX76] 8.00
____Darth Maul [HOX77] 8.00
____Greedo [HOX78] 8.00
____Royal Guard [HOX79] 8.00
____Yoda [HOX80] 8.00

Series 3.
____(Mystery) 8.00
____Clone Trooper 8.00
____Commander Cody 8.00
____Gamorrean Guard 8.00
____General Grievous 8.00
____General Grievous Bodyguard 8.00
____Jango Fett 8.00
____The Emperor 8.00

Le Gaulois
____1 Anakin Skywalker [HOX81] 2.00
____2 Qui-Gon Jinn [HOX82] 2.00
____3 Darth Maul [HOX83] 2.00
____4 Jar Jar Binks [HOX84] 2.00
____5 Comte Dooku [HOX85] 2.00
____6 Clonetrooper [HOX86] 2.00
____7 Jango Fett [HOX87] 2.00
____8 Jabba le Hutt [HOX88] 2.00
____9 Dark Vador [HOX89] 2.00
____10 Anakin Skywalker [HOX90] 2.00
____11 Obi-Wan Kenobi [HOX91] 2.00
____12 L'Emereur [HOX92] 2.00
____13 Yoda [HOX93] 2.00
____14 Chancelor Palpatine [HOX94] 2.00
____15 General Grievous [HOX95] 2.00
____16 Cewbacca [HOX96] 2.00
____17 Tarfful [HOX97] 2.00
____18 Mace Windu [HOX98] 2.00
____19 Padme Amidala [HOX99] 2.00
____20 Bail Oragan [HOX100] 2.00
____21 R2-D2 [HOX101] 2.00
____22 C-3PO [HOX102] 2.00
____23 Luke Skywalker [HOX103] 2.00
____24 Obi-Wan Kenobi [HOX104] 2.00
____25 Princess Leia [HOX105] 2.00
____26 Yan Solo [HOX106] 2.00
____27 Lando Calrissian [HOX107] 2.00
____28 Boba Fett [HOX108] 2.00

Mega-Mags
Giant Magnets.
____Darth Vader [HOX109] 12.00
____Millennium Falcon [HOX110] 15.00

Pepsi Cola
Hologram magnets, gold background.
____Anakin Skywalker [HOX111] 8.00
____Battle Droid [HOX112] 8.00
____Boss Nass [HOX113] 8.00
____C-3PO [HOX114] 8.00
____Captain Tarpals [HOX115] 8.00
____Darth Maul [HOX116] 8.00
____Darth Vader [HOX117] 8.00
____Episode I Logo [HOX118] 8.00
____Jar Jar Binks [HOX119] 8.00
____Mace Windu [HOX120] 8.00
____Nute Gunray [HOX121] 8.00
____Queen Amidala [HOX122] 8.00
____R2-D2 [HOX123] 8.00
____Sebulba [HOX124] 8.00
____Watto [HOX125] 8.00
____Yoda [HOX126] 8.00

Hologram magnets, silver background.
____Anakin Skywalker 5.00

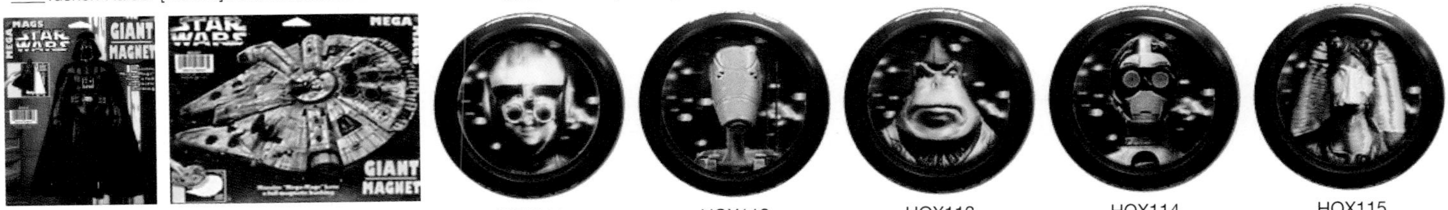

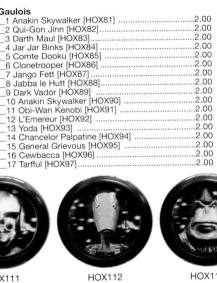

HOX109 HOX110 HOX111 HOX112 HOX113 HOX114 HOX115

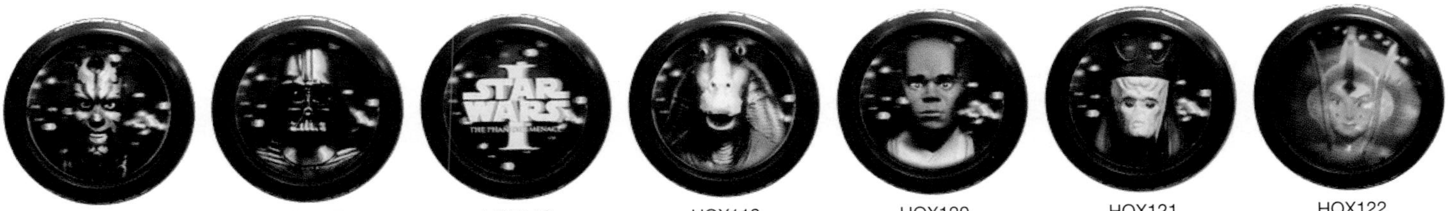

HOX116 HOX117 HOX118 HOX119 HOX120 HOX121 HOX122

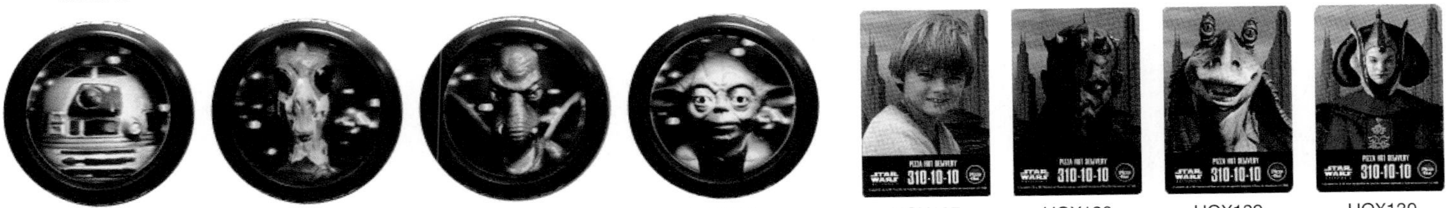

HOX123 HOX124 HOX125 HOX126 HOX127 HOX128 HOX129 HOX130

Magnets

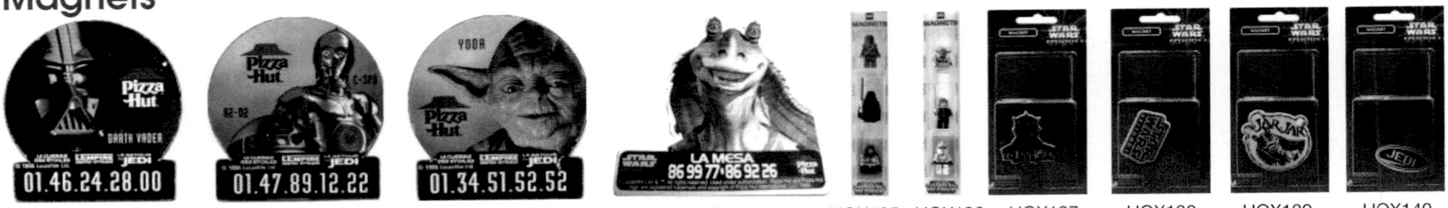

HOX131 HOX132 HOX133 HOX134 HOX135 HOX136 HOX137 HOX138 HOX139 HOX140

____Battle Droid 5.00
____Boss Nass 5.00
____C-3PO 5.00
____Captain Tarpals 5.00
____Darth Maul 5.00
____Darth Vader 5.00
____Episode I Logo 5.00
____Jar Jar Binks 5.00
____Mace Windu 5.00
____Nute Gunray 5.00
____Queen Amidala 5.00
____R2-D2 ....5.00
____Sebulba 5.00
____Watto 5.00
____Yoda 5.00

Pizza Hut
____Anakin Skywalker [HOX127] 3.00
____Darth Maul [HOX128] 3.00
____Jar Jar Binks [HOX129] 3.00
____Queen Amidala [HOX130] 3.00

Pizza Hut, France
____Darth Vader [HOX131] 8.00
____R2-D2 and C-3PO [HOX132] 8.00
____Yoda [HOX133] 8.00

Pizza Hut, Mexico
____Jar Jar Binks [HOX134] 6.00

Scholastic
____EPIII:ROTS cover art 5.00

The LEGO Group
3-packs.
____Chewbacca, Darth Vader, Obi-Wan [HOX135] ..25.00
____Yoda, Anakin, Clone [HOX136] 25.00

World Wide Licenses Ltd.
____Darth Maul - The Dark Side [HOX137] 6.00
____Episode I logo [HOX138] 6.00
____Jar Jar [HOX139] 6.00
____Jedi [HOX140] 6.00

Matchboxes

Hollywood Match Company
Classic trilogy characters.
____10-pack: characters 35.00
____C-3PO [MBC01] 3.00
____Chewbacca [MBC02] 3.00
____Darth Vader [MBC03] 3.00
____Han Solo [MBC04] 3.00
____Luke Skywalker [MBC05] 3.00
____Obi-Wan Kenobi [MBC06] 3.00
____Princess Leia [MBC07] 3.00
____R2-D2 [MBC08] 3.00
____Stormtroopers [MBC09] 3.00
____SW: movie poster art [MBC10] 3.00

Classic trilogy movie posters.
____10-pack: movie posters 35.00
____ANH international art [MBC11] 3.00
____ANH SE poster art [MBC12] 3.00
____ESB classic international art [MBC13] 3.00
____ESB international art [MBC14] 3.00
____ESB SE poster art [MBC15] 3.00
____ROTJ classic international art [MBC16] 3.00
____ROTJ international art [MBC17] 3.00
____ROTJ SE poster art [MBC18] 3.00
____SW classic international art [MBC19] 3.00
____SW:SE Trilogy Logo [MBC20] 3.00

Episode I characters.
____10-pack: EPI characters 35.00
____Anakin Skywalker [MBC21] 3.00
____C-3PO [MBC22] 3.00
____Darth Maul [MBC23] 3.00
____Jabba the Hutt [MBC24] 3.00
____Jar Jar Binks [MBC25] 3.00
____Obi-Wan Kenobi [MBC26] 3.00
____Queen Amidala [MBC27] 3.00
____Qui-Gon Jinn [MBC28] 3.00
____Sebulba [MBC29] 3.00
____Watto [MBC30] 3.00

Episode I description on blue swatch.
____10-pack EPI 35.00
____Anakin Skywalker [MBC31] 3.00
____Battle Droids [MBC32] 3.00
____Darth Maul [MBC33] 3.00
____EPI (aliens) [MBC34] 3.00
____EPI (podrace) [MBC35] 3.00
____Jar Jar Binks [MBC36] 3.00
____Obi-Wan Kenobi [MBC37] 3.00
____Queen Amidala [MBC38] 3.00
____Qui-Gon Jinn [MBC39] 3.00
____Yoda [MBC40] 3.00

Episode II characters.
____10-pack 35.00
____Anakin and Obi-Wan [MBC41] 3.00
____Anakin and Padme [MBC42] 3.00
____Anakin composite [MBC43] 3.00
____Anakin with lightsaber [MBC44] 3.00
____Mace Windu and Obi-Wan Kenobi [MBC45] 3.00
____Obi-Wan composite [MBC46] 3.00
____Obi-Wan, Padme, and Anakin [MBC47] 3.00
____Padme Amidala [MBC48] 3.00
____Padme and Anakin forbidden [MBC49] 3.00
____Padme composite [MBC50] 3.00

Episode II promotions.
____10-pack 35.00
____Anakin Skywalker [MBC51] 3.00
____Count Dooku [MBC52] 3.00
____Geonosian Warrior [MBC53] 3.00
____Jango Fett [MBC54] 3.00
____Jango Fett composit [MBC55] 3.00
____Mace Windu [MBC56] 3.00
____Movie Poster [MBC57] 3.00
____Obi-Wan Kenobi [MBC58] 3.00
____Padme Amidala [MBC59] 3.00
____Zam Wesell [MBC60] 3.00

Mats

____Change mat, California lottery [MT01] 8.00

MBC01 MBC02 MBC03 MBC04 MBC05 MBC06 MBC07 MBC08 MBC09 MBC10 MBC11 MBC12 MBC13 MBC14 MBC15

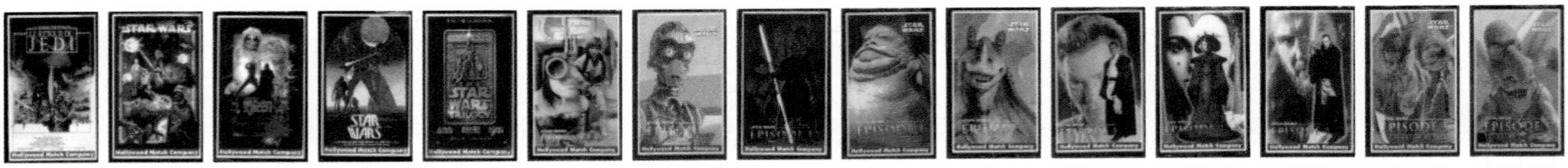

MBC16 MBC17 MBC18 MBC19 MBC20 MBC21 MBC22 MBC23 MBC24 MBC25 MBC26 MBC27 MBC28 MBC29 MBC30

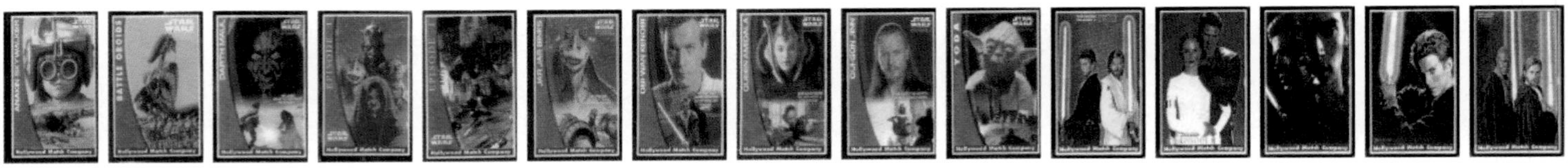

MBC31 MBC32 MBC33 MBC34 MBC35 MBC36 MBC37 MBC38 MBC39 MBC40 MBC41 MBC42 MBC43 MBC44 MBC45

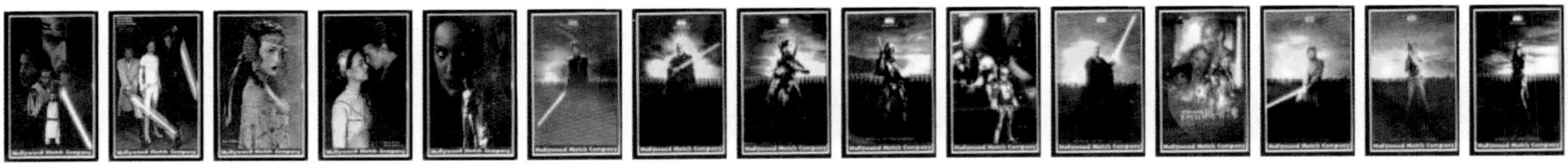

MBC46 MBC47 MBC48 MBC49 MBC50 MBC51 MBC52 MBC53 MBC54 MBC55 MBC56 MBC57 MBC58 MBC59 MBC60

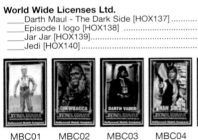

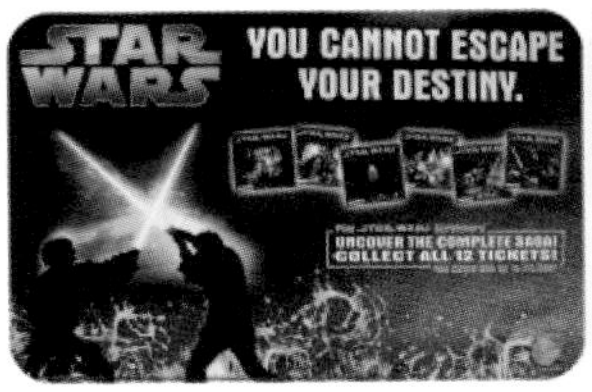
MT01

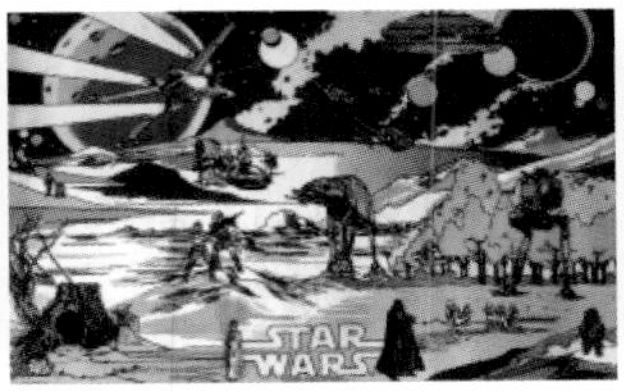
MT02

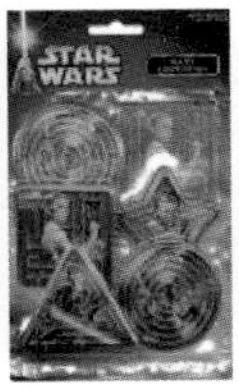
MZ01

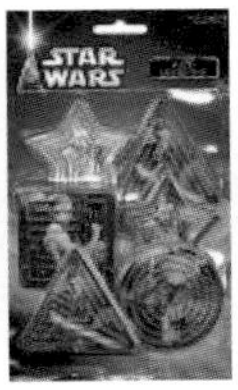
MZ02

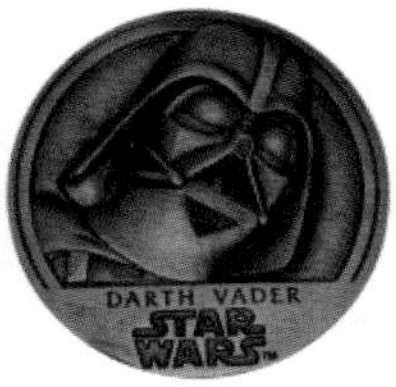
MDC01

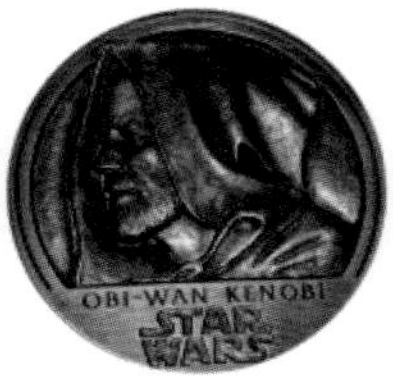
MDC02

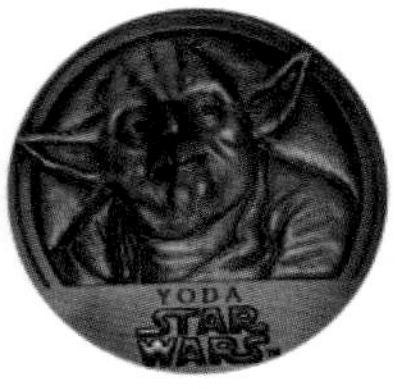
MDC03

Recticel Sutcliffe Ltd.
____Play mat, artwork from all 3 movies, 24.5"x39" [MT02] 135.00

Mazes: Party

Tapper Candies
6-pack party fun games.
____Anakin, Padme, Obi-Wan, Jango Fett [MZ01] 3.00
____Anakin, Padme, Obi-Wan, Jango Fett, alternate assortment [MZ02] 3.00

Medallions

Craft House
____C-3PO and R2-D2 / Darth Vader [MDC04] 12.00
____Han Solo / Princess Leia [MDC05] 12.00
____Luke Skywalker / Yoda [MDC06] 12.00

Noble Studios
4" pewter medallion.
____Darth Vader [MDC01] 65.00
____Obi-Wan Kenobi [MDC02] 65.00
____Yoda [MDC03] 65.00

Media: Audio – Cassettes

____An Hour of Superthemes [R2C01] 10.00
____Cinema Gala [R2C02]..10.00
____Galactic Funk by Mecco [R2C03] 10.00
____Return of the Jedi / Empire Strikes Back / Star Wars, Chromium Dioxide [R2C04] 10.00
____Return of the Jedi / Empire Strikes Back / Star Wars, full cover [R2C05]..10.00
____Return of the Jedi / Empire Strikes Back / Star Wars, white border [R2C06] 10.00
____Return of the Jedi / Empire Strikes Back / Star Wars, white border with text [R2C07] 10.00
____Return of the Jedi soundtrack, movie poster cover [R2C08]..10.00
____Return of the Jedi soundtrack, movie poster cover, red and black text on white bottom 1/3rd [R2C09]..10.00
____Return of the Jedi soundtrack, National Philharmonic Orchstra [R2C10] 10.00
____Return of the Jedi soundtrack, National Philharmonic Orchstra, saber cover [R2C11] 10.00
____Star Wars in High Fidelity [R2C12]......................10.00
____Star Wars, A Stereo Space Odyssey [R2C13]..10.00
____Star Wars, The original Motion Picture Soundtrack [R2C14]..10.00
____Star Wars, white banner above and below [R2C15]..10.00
____Story of Star Wars, white banner above and below [R2C16]..10.00
____The Empire Strikes Back, Luke / Hoth cover [R2C17]..10.00

German.
____Kreig der Sterne [R2C18] 10.00

Norway releases.
____Stjerne krigen [R2C19] 24.00

Seven Star Chrome Series.
____30 The Empire Strikes Back [R2C20] 10.00
____65 Return of the Jedi [R2C21] 10.00

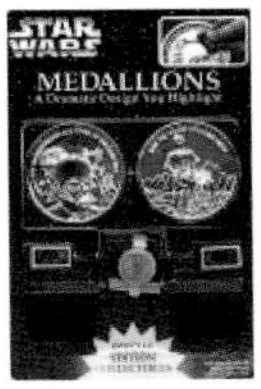
MDC04

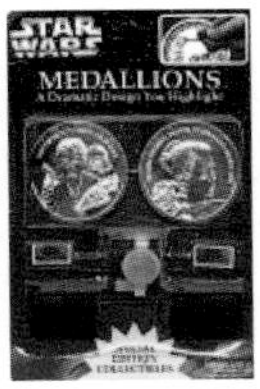
MDC05

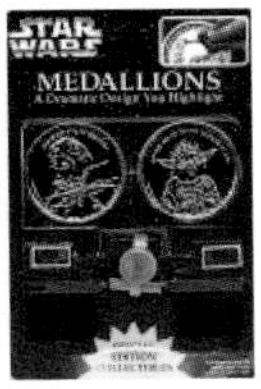
MDC06

20th Century Fox
____Star Wars Twin Pack, set of 2 [R2C22] 10.00
____Star Wars, Vader cover [R2C23] 10.00
____Story of Star Wars [R2C24] 11.00
____Story of Star Wars, Parts 1 and 2 [R2C25] 10.00

Buena Vista Records
Read-along stories.
____3-pack: SW, ESB, ROTJ Trilogy [R2C26]............12.00
____Adventures in ABC [R2C27]..................................10.00
____Adventures in Colors and Shapes 10.00
____Droid World [R2C28] 10.00
____Empire Strikes Back..10.00
____Ewoks Join the Fight 10.00
____Ewoks: The Battle for Endor [R2C29] 10.00
____Planet of the Hoojibs 10.00
____Rebel Mission to Ord Mantell 10.00
____Return of the Jedi [R2C30] 10.00
____Star Wars [R2C31] 10.00

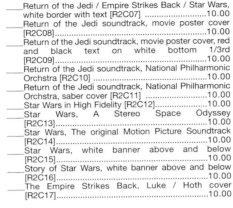

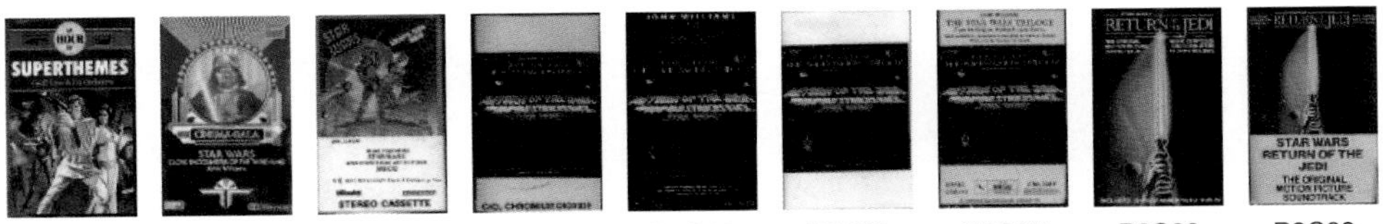
R2C01 R2C02 R2C03 R2C04 R2C05 R2C06 R2C07 R2C08 R2C09

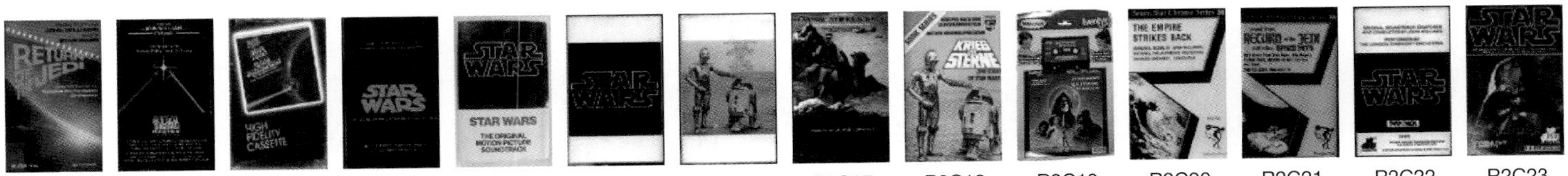
R2C10 R2C11 R2C12 R2C13 R2C14 R2C15 R2C16 R2C17 R2C18 R2C19 R2C20 R2C21 R2C22 R2C23

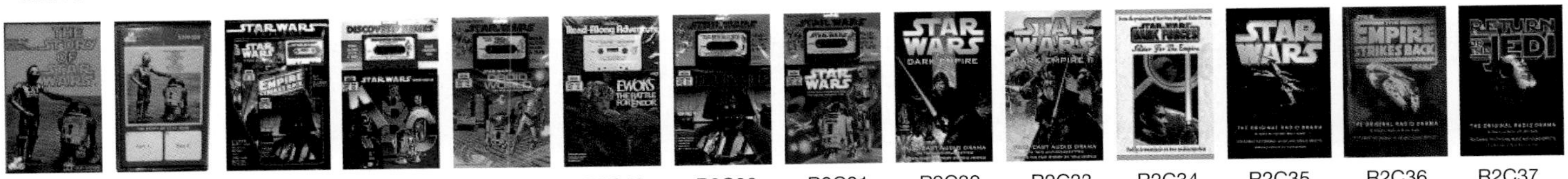
R2C24 R2C25 R2C26 R2C27 R2C28 R2C29 R2C30 R2C31 R2C32 R2C33 R2C34 R2C35 R2C36 R2C37

R2C38 R2C39 R2C40 R2C41 R2C42 R2C43 R2C44 R2C45 R2C46 R2C47 R2C48 R2C49 R2C50

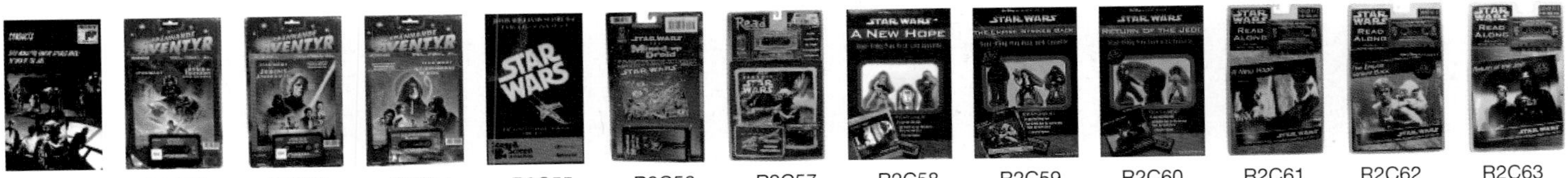
R2C51 R2C52 R2C53 R2C54 R2C55 R2C56 R2C57 R2C58 R2C59 R2C60 R2C61 R2C62 R2C63

Media: Audio – Cassettes

 R4C01
 R4C02
 R4C03
 R4C04
 R4C05
 R4C06
 R4C07

 R4C08
 R4C09
 R4C10
 R4C11
 R4C12
 R4C13
 R4C14

The Story of... Read-along stories.
____Star Wars 12.00
____Empire Strikes Back [3:224].................12.00
____Return of the Jedi................................12.00

German Releases
24 page book with read-along tape.
____Das Imperium Schlagt Zuruck 20.00
____Jedi Ritter 20.00

Highbridge Company
Full Cast Audio Drama, 2 cassettes.
____Dark Empire [R2C32] 18.00
____Dark Empire II [R2C33]........................18.00
____Dark Forces: Soldier for the Empire [R2C34] 18.00

Original Radio Drama as heard on National Public Radio, original music/effects.
____SW: 13 episodes, 6 cassettes [R2C35] 35.00
____ESB: 10 episodes, 5 cassettes [R2C36] 35.00
____ROTJ: 6 episodes, 3 cassettes [R2C37] 25.00
____Trilogy gift pack, 14 cassettes 85.00

Pickwick
____Sounds of Star Wars [R2C38] 10.00

Polygram Records
____Christmas in the Stars [R2C39] 26.00
____Star Wars Soundtrack [R2C40] 14.00
____The Adventures of Luke Skywalker, SW/ESB [R2C41]..10.00
____The Empire Strikes Back, Vader starfield cover [R2C42]...10.00

____The Empire Strikes Back, Vader starfield full cover [R2C43]..10.00

Rainbow
Read along cassettes.
____Star Wars [R2C44] 10.00

Rhino
Star Wars Episode I 24-page book and tape read-along with Micromachine vehicle pack-in.
____(No pack-in) [R2C45]...........................8.00
____Anakin's Podracer [R2C46] 11.00
____Flash Speeder [R2C47] 11.00
____Sith Infilterator [R2C48] 11.00

RSO Records
____Empire Strikes Back, music from [R2C49] 10.00

Skywalkers
____A Wind to Shake the Stars [R2C50]....................21.00

Sony Classical
____Star Wars Trilogy, John Williams and the Skywalker Symphony [R2C51] 10.00

Spelto
Sweden releases.
____Irymd-Imperiet Slar Tillbaka (ESB) [R2C52]........15.00
____Jedins Aterkomst (ROTJ) [R2C53] 15.00
____Stjarnornas Krig (SW) [R2C54].........................15.00

Stage and Screen Productions
____A Saga in Outter Space [R2C55] 10.00

TV Kids
____The Mixed Up Droid [R2C56].............................14.00

TW Kids
Read along with bonus toy included.
____Star Wars, five stickers 6.00
____Empire Strikes Back, snowspeeder Micromachine [R2C57]...8.00
____Return of the Jedi, Millennium Falcon Micromachine..8.00

Walt Disney Records
Read along cassettes with 3 Applause mini-pvc figures.
____A New Hope [R2C58]..14.00
____Empire Strikes Back [R2C59]............................14.00
____Return of the Jedi [R2C60] 14.00

Read along cassettes.
____A New Hope [R2C61]..6.00
____Empire Strikes Back [R2C62]............................6.00
____Return of the Jedi [R2C63]................................6.00

Media: Audio – CDs

____Battle of the Heroes from ROTS [R4C01] 17.00
____Duel of the Fates radio edit single [R4C02] 6.00
____Empire Strikes Back soundtrack, National Philharmonic Orchstra [R4C03] 10.00
____Figrin D'an and the Modal Nodes [R4C04] 12.00
____Max Reebo Band [R4C05] 12.00
____Space Themes 8.00

 R4C15
 R4C16
 R4C17
 R4C18
 R4C19
 R4C20
 R4C21

 R4C22
 R4C23
 R4C24
 R4C25
 R4C26
 R4C27
 R4C28

 R4C29
 R4C30
 R4C31
 R4C32
 R4C33
 R4C34
 R4C35

____Space Trax Commerative Edition by Starlight Orchestra, includes 3 St. Vincent postage stamps. [R4C06] 8.00
____Space Trax: The best of Science Fiction Movies and TV, 3 bonus collectible Star Wars stamps 25.00
____TPM Ultimate Edition 2 CD set [R4C07] 50.00

Alec Empire
____Generation Star Wars, music [R4C08] 15.00

Arista Records
____SW Trilogy: The Original Soundtrack Anthology 4 CD set 26.00

BCI Music
____A Tribute to the Music of Star Wars [R4C09] 7.00

Big Ear Music
____Music inspired by the Star Wars Saga by Hollywood Symphony Orchestra [R4C10] 8.00

BMG Entertainment
____Max Rebo Band: Jedi Rocks, selected from the Original Motion Picture Soundtrack ROTJ:SE 8.00

CBS Records
____John Williams, The Star Wars Trilogy 38.00

Delta
____Music of the Star Wars Saga by Bruno Bertone Orchestra [R4C11] 16.00

Fan Club, UK
____Galactic Uplink, November 2001 [R4C12] 8.00

Film Orchestra
____A Tribute to the Music of Star Wars [R4C13] 7.00

Force Records
____Soundtrack from Caravan of Courage and Ewok Adventure [R4C14] 8.00

Highbridge Company
____ESB: Original Radio Drama as heard on National Public Radio, original music/effects; 10 episodes, 5 CDs [R4C15] 55.00
____ROTJ: The Original Radio Drama; 3 hours, 3 CDs 35.00
____SW: Original Radio Drama as heard on National Public Radio, original music/effects; 13 episodes, 7 CDs 60.00
____Trilogy radio drama CD set; 29 episodes on 15 CDs [R4C16] 110.00
____Trilogy radio drama deluxe CD set; 15 CDs in a foil-stamped slipcase [R4C17]..............................160.00

K R B Music Company
____Music from the Star Wars Trilogy.....................10.00

Kid Rhino
____Junior Jedi Training Manual [R4C18] 23.00

Lake Shore Records
____Synthesized Star Wars [R4C19].......................10.00

Laserlight
____Music of the Star Wars Saga by Bruno Bertone Orchestra Vol. 1 and 2 [R4C20] 22.00

Mercury Records
____The Best of Meco 9.00

Oglio Entertainment Group
____Cocktails in the Cantina music [R4C21] 15.00

Polygram Records
____The Empire Strikes Back soundtrack 18.00

RCA Victor
____ANH SE Original Soundtrack Recording 24.00
____ANH SE Original Soundtrack Recording, deluxe edition packaging 28.00
____Cantina Band picture disc CD single.................18.00
____Darth Vader helmet shaped CD single................22.00
____ESB SE Original Soundtrack Recording 24.00
____ESB SE Original Soundtrack Recording, deluxe edition packaging [R4C22] 28.00
____Rebo Band picture disc CD single 18.00
____Return of the Jedi music [R4C23] 19.00
____ROTJ SE Original Soundtrack Recording 24.00
____ROTJ SE Original Soundtrack Recording, deluxe edition packaging 28.00

Rhino
____Christmas in the Stars [R4C24] 16.00

Star Wars Episode I 24-page book and read-along CD with bonus Micromachine.
____(No Micromachine) [R4C25] 12.00
____Anakin's Podracer MicroMachine 14.00
____Gungan Sub MicroMachine 15.00
____Sith Infiltrator MicroMachine 14.00

Sony Classical
____A New Hope special 2 CD set 22.00
____Empire Strikes Back special 2 CD set................22.00
____EPIII Revenge of the Sith with bonus DVD 30.00
____Return of the Jedi special 2 CD set.................22.00
____Star Wars Trilogy Collector's Edition Soundtracks 50.00
____The Star Wars Trilogy [R4C26] 15.00

EPII:AOTC movie soundtracks. Limited edition includes bonus track.
____Anakin and Padme cover [R4C27]......................18.00
____Jango Fett cover [R4C28] 18.00
____Yoda cover [R4C29] 18.00

Media: Audio – Records

EPII:AOTC movie soundtracks.
____Anakin and Padme cover [R4C30].......................14.00
____Jango Fett cover [R4C31] 14.00
____Movie poster art cover [R4C32].........................14.00
____Yoda cover [R4C33]...14.00

Sony Music Soundtrax
____The Phantom Menace Ultimate Edition 32.00
____The Phantom Menace with fold-out poster 6.00

Style Wars
____Style Wars, Free The Funk, parody cover [R4C34] 14.00

Varese Sarabande Records
____Shadows of the Empire 35.00

Wasabees
____Duel of the Fates dance remixes [R4C35] 5.00

Media: Audio – Records

____"What can you get a Wookiee for Christmas?," 45rpm [R1C01] 16.00
____Christmas in the Stars [R1C02] 65.00
____Empire Strikes Back soundtrack, National Philarmonic Orchstra [R1C03] 22.00
____Meco plays music from ESB [R1C04] 4.00
____Music from Star Wars performed by The Electric Moog Orchestra [R1C05] 5.00
____Star Sounds [R1C06] 10.00
____Star Wars and other Space Movie Themes by Geoff Love and his Orchestra [R1C07] 35.00
____Star Wars and other Space Themes by Geoff Love 25.00
____Star Wars Episode I Soundtrack [R1C08] 9.00
____Star Wars Theme / Cantina Band by Meco, 45rpm [R1C09]..15.00
____Star Wars, also a Space Odyssey by the London Philharmonic Orchestra [R1C10] 10.00
____Star Wars, London Philharmonic Orchestra [R1C11]..15.00
____Themes from the movies [R1C12] 10.00

20th Century Fox
Radio spots.
____1977 Star Wars, 30 seconds each, on 7" 33rpm l.p. [R1C13] 117.00

____Main Theme, 45rpm 12.00
____Main Theme, 45rpm Japanese release [R1C14]..23.00
____Star Wars soundtrack, 2 albums [R1C15] 18.00
____Story of Star Wars 14.00
____Story of Star Wars, picture disc album [R1C16]..21.00

R1C01   R1C02   R1C03   R1C04   R1C05   R1C06   R1C07

R1C08   R1C09   R1C10   R1C11   R1C12   R1C13   R1C14

R1C15   R1C16   R1C17   R1C18   R1C19   R1C20   R1C21

Media: Audio – Records

R1C22

R1C23

R1C24

R1C25

R1C26

R1C27

R1C28

20th Century Fox, Brazil
____Star Wars Soundtrack, 2 albums [R1C17]..........35.00

20th Century Fox, Mexico
Mexico.
____Star Wars Soundtrack, 2 albums [R1C18]..........18.00

20th Century Fox, Spain
____Star Wars Soundtrack, 2 albums [R1C19]..........35.00

Buena Vista Records
24 Page read alongs. Book and record.
____Star Wars [R1C20] 12.00
____Empire Strikes Back [R1C21].............................12.00
____Return of the Jedi [R1C22] 12.00

____Adventures in ABC 10.00
____Adventures in Colors and Shapes [R1C23] 10.00
____Droid World [R1C24] 10.00
____Ewoks Join the Fight [R1C25] 10.00
____Ewoks, The Battle for Endor [R1C26] 15.00
____La Guerre Des Etoiles [R1C27] 18.00
____Planet of the Hoojibs [R1C28] 10.00
____Rebel Mission to Ord Mantell [R1C29] 10.00

Albums, "The Story Of..."
____Empire Strikes Back 12.00
____Return of the Jedi [R1C30] 12.00
____ROTJ, picture disc (Ewok picture on record) [R1C31] 20.00
____Star Wars 12.00

Force Records
____Star Wars Ewoks (soundtracks) 35.00

Gamma
____La Guerra De las Galaxias, soundtrack [R1C32].............15.00

Kid Stuff
____Star Wars [R1C33] 5.00

London Records
____Star Wars and Close Encounters by Los Angeles Philharmonic Orchestra [R1C34] 12.00

Peter Pan
____Empire Strikes Back and other title themes [R1C35].............25.00
____Irwin Strikes Back, ESB parody [R1C36]............25.00

Philips
Japan.
____Star Wars / Clone Encounters themes [R1C37].............10.00

Pickwick
____Sounds of Star Wars [R1C38] 12.00

Polydor
Movie soundtracks.
____Empire Strikes Back [R1C39].............................45.00
____Return of the Jedi [R1C40] 45.00

RCA
____Music from John Williams' Close Encounters and Star Wars [R1C41] 5.00
____Star Wars and other Galactic Funk by Meco [R1C42].............18.00

Japan.
____Galactic Funk by Meco [R1C43] 18.00

RSO Records
____Empire Jazz [R1C44] 12.00
____Empire Strikes Back, music from [R1C45] 12.00
____ESB Medley by Meco [R1C46] 25.00
____The Adventures of Luke Skywalker, The Empire Strikes Back [R1C47]..............................35.00

Sony Classical
____Episode I soundtrack, 2 albums 34.00

Wonderland Records
____Theme from Star Wars [R1C48] 10.00

Media: Audio – Tapes, 8-Track

____Empire Strikes Back [R3C01].............................35.00

____Empire Strikes Back, Vader label [R3C02]............4.00
____Music from Star Wars by Electric Moog Orchestra [R3C03] 5.00
____Music From Star Wars, outline [R3C04] 4.00
____Patrick Gleeson's Star Wars [R3C05].......................4.00
____Return of the Jedi, gray [R3C06] 35.00
____Return of the Jedi, white [R3C07] 4.00
____ROTJ, ESB, SW [R3C08] 4.00
____Spaced Out Disco [R3C09] 4.00
____Star Wars / Close Encounters [R3C10] 4.00
____Star Wars / Close Encounters, dawn label [R3C11].............4.00
____Star Wars Ferrante and Teicher [R3C12] 4.00
____Star Wars Galactic Funk, black with full label [R3C13].............4.00
____Star Wars Galactic Funk, black with orange label [R3C14].............4.00
____Star Wars Galactic Funk, black with orange label, white text on case [R3C15] 4.00
____Star Wars Galactic Funk, white with full label [R3C16].............4.00
____Star Wars Galactic Funk, white with orange label [R3C17].............4.00
____Star Wars soundtrack, black nebula with track listings [R3C18].............14.00
____Star Wars soundtrack, black with track listings [R3C19].............4.00
____Star Wars soundtrack, blue [R3C20] 8.00
____Star Wars soundtrack, blue with track listings [R3C21].............4.00
____Star Wars soundtrack, gray [R3C22] 8.00
____Star Wars soundtrack, white with black label [R3C23].............4.00
____Star Wars soundtrack, white with pink label [R3C24].............4.00
____Star Wars The Planets [R3C25] 4.00
____Star Wars, black with black label, block [R3C26].............4.00
____Star Wars, black with black label, outline [R3C27].............4.00
____Star Wars, Vader label [R3C28] 4.00
____Story of Star Wars, blue [R3C29].......................12.00
____Story of Star Wars, blue with track listings [R3C30].............12.00
____Story of Star Wars, gray [R3C31] 8.00

R1C29

R1C30

R1C31 side 1

R1C31 side 2

R1C32

R1C33

R1C34

R1C35

R1C36

R1C37

R1C38

R1C39

R1C40

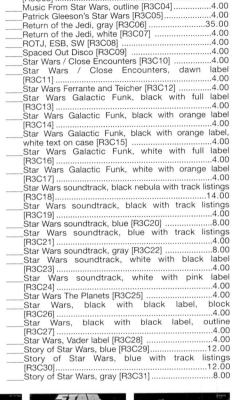
R1C41

R1C42

R1C43

R1C44

R1C45

R1C46

R1C47

R1C48

R3C01

R3C02

R3C03

R3C04

R3C05

R3C06

R3C07

R3C08

R3C09

R3C10

R3C11

R3C12

R3C13

R3C14

R3C15

R3C16

R3C17

R3C18

R3C19

R3C20

R3C21

R3C22

R3C23

R3C24

R3C25

R3C26

R3C27

R5C01 boxed

R5C0101 reel 1 and reel 2

R3C28

R3C29

R3C30

R3C31

R3C32

____Themes from Star Wars, New York New York, etc. [R3C32] 4.00

Media: Audio – Tapes, Reel-to-Reel

20th Century Fox
____Star Wars Soundtrack 65.00
____Star Wars Soundtrack and Story of Star Wars, boxed set [R5C01] 125.00
____Story of Star Wars 50.00

Memo Boards

Day Runner
Wipe-off board with 1999 paper calendar and pen.
____Darth Maul 8.00
____Jar Jar Binks 8.00
____R2-D2 [SUI01] 8.00
____Yoda [SUI02] 8.00

Icarus
Wipe clean memo board with marker.
____Chewbacca, Han Solo, Lando Calrissian 22.00
____Darth Vader and Stormtroopers.........................24.00
____Han Solo, Luke Skywalker, Princess Leia [SUI03] 22.00

Junior Achievment
____Message Center, limited to approx 500 ....135.00

Union
____10th anniversary, plastic with pocket for paper and pen, magnetic back 20.00

Memo Pads

Impact, Inc.
3"x5", 60 sheets.
____Anakin [SUM01] 2.00
____Darth Maul [SUM02] 2.00
____Jar Jar [SUM03] 2.00
____Obi-Wan [SUM04]...2.00

50 sheets, die-cut.
____Darth Maul [SUM05] 3.00
____Jar Jar [SUM06] 3.00
____Queen Amidala [SUM07] 3.00

Jollibee
____C-3PO paper dispenser 10.00

Pyramid
____Anakin Skywalker 2.00
____Mace Windu 2.00

Stuart Hall
____Aliens [SUM08] 6.00
____Boba Fett 8.00
____C-3PO and R2-D2 [SUM09] 8.00
____Darth Vader and Stormtroopers 8.00
____Luke Skywalker in Bepin fatigues 8.00

____Millennium Falcon Escaping a Star Destroyer 8.00
____Yoda 8.00

Milk Caps
Stanpac
____Darth Vader, "The Force Is With You" [2:305]...26.00

Mini-Movies

Interlace4D
Limited to 10,000.
____Attack on Battleship [MM01] 20.00
____Darth Maul [MM02]..20.00
____Explosion: Podracer Cockpit [MM03] 20.00

SUI01

SUI02

SUI03

SUM01

SUM02

SUM03

SUM04

SUM05

SUM06

SUM07

SUM08

SUM09

Mini-Movies

| MM01 | MM02 | MM03 | MM04 | MM05 | MM06 | MM07 | MM08 | HOM01 |

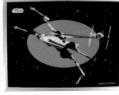

| HOM02 | HOM03 | HOM04 | HOM05 | HOM06 | HOM07 | HOM08 |

| HOM09 | HOM10 | HOM11 | HOM12 | HOM13 | HOM14 | MBL01 | MBL02 |

____Jedi vs. Battledroids [MM04] 20.00
____Podracer Crash [MM05] 20.00
____Podracer Through Arches [MM06] 20.00
____Qui-Gon vs. Battledroids [MM07] 20.00
____Space Battle [MM08] 24.00

Mirrors

____C-3PO and R2-D2, 8"x10" [HOM01] 25.00
____Darth Vader, The Empire Strikes Back, 12"x12" foil relfection [HOM02] 35.00
____Darth Vader, The Empire Strikes Back, 12"x12" glass painted 35.00
____Darth Vader, The Empire Strikes Back, 12"x12" glass reflection [HOM03] 35.00
____Luke (pilot), C-3PO, R2-D2 [HOM04].................35.00
____Luke, C-3PO, R2-D2 (art) [HOM05] 35.00
____Star Wars [HOM06] 35.00

| MR01 | MR02 | MR03 |

Cosalt Exporters Ltd.
____Death Star Battle [HOM07] 65.00

Factors, Etc.
3" round, mirrored back.
____Darth Vadar Lives (misspelled) [HOM08] 15.00

Lightline Industries
Silver frame 20"x30"
____C-3PO and R2-D2 [HOM09] 60.00
____Chewbacca and Han Solo [HOM10] 45.00
____Darth Vader [HOM11]......................................65.00
____Darth Vader vs. Obi-Wan Kenobi [HOM12] 75.00
____Dogfight [HOM13] 50.00

Sigma
____Darth Vader [HOM14]......................................35.00

Mobiles

Glow Zone
____Episode I glow-in-the-dark mobile, Naboo Fighter, Droid Fighter, Naboo, Trade Fed. Battleship [MBL01]...8.00

KFC
____TPM cup topper mobile, 2 pieces with slots for toppers 3.00

Circle danglers, Naboo fighter on back.
____Anakin Skywalker 4.00

____Boss Nass...4.00
____Jar Jar Binks...4.00
____Obi-Wan Kenobi 4.00
____Queen Amidala 4.00
____Qui-Gon Jinn...4.00

Pepsi Cola
____Mobile: X-Wings vs. Ties, Star Wars SE Trilogy [MBL02] 11.00

Model Rockets

Estes
____A-Wing starter set 45.00
____Darth Vader's Tie Fighter complete launch set, flies over 500 feet [MR01]...45.00
____Darth Vader's Tie Fighter, boxed [MR02] 35.00
____Death Star starter set 35.00
____Death Star, boxed [MR03] 25.00
____Millennium Falcon 18.00
____Naboo Fighter with R2-D2 launcher, flys up to 330 feet [MR04] 40.00
____Naboo Fighter, flies up to 330 feet [MR05] 9.00
____Naboo Royal Starship mini, flies up to 300 feet [MR06]...8.00
____Naboo Royal Starship, flies up to 300 feet [MR07]...45.00
____Proton Torpedo, boxed 35.00
____R2-D2 EPI Flying Model Rocket Starter Set, flies up to 100 feet [MR08]...16.00
____R2-D2 EPI, flies up to 100 feet [MR09] 9.00

| MR04 | MR05 | MR06 | MR07 | MR08 | MR09 | MR10 | MR11 | MR12 |

| MR13 | MR14 | MR15 | MR16 | MR17 | MR18 | MR19 |

MOM01

MOM02

MOM03

MOM04

MOM05

MOM06

MOM07

MOM08

MOM09

MOM10

MP01

MP02

MP03

____R2-D2, bagged...35.00
____R2-D2, bagged 15th Anniversary [MR10] 25.00
____R2-D2, boxed [MR11] 40.00
____R2-D2 with recovery parachute 30.00
____Red Squadron X-Wing Starfighter, prebuilt [MR12] 11.00
____Shuttle Tydirium 23.00
____Sith Infilterator, flys up to 200 feet [MR13] 45.00
____Star Destroyer 24.00
____Tie Fighter with recovery parachute 25.00
____Tie Fighter, bagged [MR14] 29.00
____Tie Fighter, bagged 15th Anniversary 25.00
____Trade Federation Battleship 40.00
____Trade Federation Droid Fighter 40.00
____Trade Federation Droid Fighter, flies up to 215 feet [MR15]...9.00
____X-Wing and Darth Vader's Tie Fighter starter set 65.00
____X-Wing Fighter North Coast Rocketry, 20"x18" with recovery parachute, deluxe 130.00
____X-Wing Fighter, bagged 26.00
____X-Wing Fighter, bagged 15th Anniversary 28.00
____X-Wing Fighter, boxed 40.00
____X-Wing starter set [MR16] 35.00
____X-Wing with recovery parachute 20.00
____X-Wing, boxed Maxi-Brute [MR17] 65.00
____X-Wing, mini, blister pkg. [MR18].......................9.00
____Y-Wing starter set [MR19] 45.00

Models: Metal

AMT/Ertl
____Naboo Fighter, 1:48 scale, pre-painted with stand [MOM01]..24.00

EPIII:ROTS. Diecast, screwdriver included.
____Anakin Skywalker's starfighter [MOM02] 45.00
____Obi-Wan Kenobi's starfighter [MOM03]..............45.00
____Separatist Droid Trifighter [MOM04] 40.00

Remco
Steel Tec.
____Millennium Falcon [MOM05] 50.00
____X-Wing Fighter [MOM06] 25.00

Tsukuda
____AT-AT and Snowspeeder [MOM07] 95.00
____AT-ST and Snowspeeder [MOM08] 95.00
____Millennium Falcon and Slave I [MOM09] 125.00
____Star Destroyer with Millennium Falcon and Rebel Transport [MOM10] 135.00
____Tie Fighter and X-Wing Fighter 120.00

Models: Paper

Ukraine.
____X-Wing 25.00

Milton Bradley
3D Creations.
____Chewbacca [MP01] 35.00
____Darth Vader [MP02] 35.00

Powerhouse Museum
Star Wars Magic of Myth.
____Metro Monorail, Sydney Australia [MP03] 12.00

Models: Plastic

Airfix
____AT-AT, ESB [MOP01]...29.00
____Luke's Snowspeeder, ESB [MOP02] 24.00
____Slave I, ESB [MOP03] 75.00

AMT/Ertl
____3-Piece Set: B-Wing, X-Wing, Tie Interceptor, ROTJ Snap-together [MOP04].......................................25.00
____A-Wing Fighter, ROTJ snap. [MOP05] 22.00
____AT-AT, ROTJ 20.00
____AT-AT, Snap-Fast...8.00
____AT-ST, Snap-Fast [MOP06]..................................8.00
____B-Wing Fighter, ROTJ ltd. ed. gold [MOP07] 36.00
____Battle on Ice Planet Hoth, ESB [MOP08] 15.00
____Cantina Action Scene [MOP09] 24.00
____Darth Vader's Tie Fighter, SW 12.00
____Darth Vader's Tie Fighter, SW flight display [MOP10] 22.00
____Darth Vader's Tie Fighter, SW flight display with free Shadows of the Empire comic [MOP11] 27.00
____Darth Vader's Tie Fighter, SW with paint [MOP12] 17.00
____Darth Vader, SW [MOP13] 12.00
____Death Star [MOP14] 28.00
____Encounter with Yoda on Dagobah, ESB [MOP15] 16.00
____Imperial Tie Fighters...14.00
____Jabba's Throne Room, ROTJ [MOP16] 15.00
____Luke Skywalker's Snowspeeder, ESB 16.00
____Millennium Falcon, ROTJ 18.00
____Millennium Falcon, ROTJ cutaway [MOP17]......35.00
____Rancor, Collector's Edition [MOP18] 65.00
____Rebel base, ESB 18.00
____Shuttle Tydirium, ROTJ [MOP19] 15.00
____Slave I, ESB [MOP20] 16.00
____Speeder Bike, ROTJ..20.00
____Star Destroyer, ESB [MOP21] 12.00
____Star Destroyer, ESB with fiber optic lights [MOP22] 75.00
____Tie Interceptor, ROTJ limited edition gold [MOP23] 45.00
____Tie Interceptor, ROTJ Snap-together.................16.00
____X-Wing Fighter, Electronic [MOP24] 24.00
____X-Wing Fighter, ROTJ.......................................12.00
____X-Wing Fighter, ROTJ flight display 20.00
____X-Wing Fighter, ROTJ limited edition gold [MOP25] 35.00
____X-Wing Fighter, ROTJ with paint 15.00
____X-Wing Fighter, Snap-together [MOP26]............12.00
____Xizor's Virago, SOTE [MOP27]...........................20.00

MOP01

MOP02

MOP03

MOP04

MOP05

MOP06

MOP07

MOP08

Models: Plastic

MOP09

MOP10

MOP11

MOP12

MOP13

MOP14

MOP15

MOP16

MOP17

MOP18

MOP19

MOP20

MOP21

MOP22

MOP23

2005 re-releases.
____ AT-AT Walker [MOP28] 14.00
____ AT-ST Walker [MOP29] 14.00
____ B-Wing Fighter 14.00
____ Darth Vader's TIE-Fighter 17.00
____ Death Star [MOP30] 25.00
____ Millennium Falcon [MOP31] 25.00
____ Naboo Starfighter 14.00
____ Slave I 17.00
____ Snowspeeder [MOP32] 14.00
____ Speeder Bike 17.00
____ Star Destroyer 25.00
____ TIE Interceptor 14.00
____ X-Wing 17.00
____ X-Wing snap together [MOP33] 14.00

EPIII:ROTS.
____ Corporate Alliance Droid 44.00
____ Jedi Starfighter 32.00

Episode I: The Phantom Menace.
____ Anakin's Podracer [MOP34] 12.00
____ Droid Fighters (3 in kit) [MOP35] 14.00
____ Gungan Sub [MOP36] 39.00
____ Landing Ship, Snapfast Mini [MOP37] 6.00
____ Large Transport, Snapfast Mini [MOP38] 5.00
____ Naboo Fighter [MOP39] 12.00
____ Republic Cruiser, Snapfast Mini [MOP40] 6.00
____ Sith Infilterator, Snapfast Mini [MOP41] 7.00
____ STAP [MOP42] 16.00
____ Trade Federation Battle Tank [MOP43] 18.00

Clipper
____ R2-D2 .... 35.00

Fine Molds
____ Jedi Starfighter [MOP44] 34.00
____ Millennium Falcon 165.00
____ Slave I [MOP45] 34.00

____ TIE Fighter [MOP46] 34.00
____ TIE Interceptor [MOP47] 34.00
____ X-Wing Fighter 34.00

Original Trilogy Collection style packaging.
____ TIE Fighter 35.00
____ TIE Interceptor 35.00
____ X-Wing Fighter [MOP48] 35.00
____ X-Wing Fighter, free brass C-3PO 40.00

Harbert
____ Caccia T.I.E. [MOP49] 25.00

Kenner, UK
____ R2-D2, SW [MOP50] 45.00

Lili Ledy
____ Darth Vader's Tie Fighter [MOP51] 75.00
____ Luke Skywalker's X-Wing Fighter [MOP52] 75.00

MOP24

MOP25

MOP26

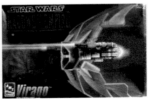

MOP27

MOP28

MOP29

MOP30

MOP31

MOP32

MOP33

MOP34

MOP35

MOP36

MOP37

MOP38

MOP39

MOP40

MOP41

MOP42	MOP43	MOP44	MOP45	MOP46

MOP47	MOP48	MOP49	MOP50	MOP51

MOP52	MOP53	MOP54	MOP55	MOP56

Meccano
____Z-6PO (C-3PO) [MOP53] 45.00

MPC
____A-Wing Fighter, ROTJ Snap-together [MOP54] 22.00
____AT-AT, ESB [MOP55]...................................35.00
____AT-ST, ROTJ [MOP56]................................35.00
____AT-ST, ROTJ commerative edition sticker [MOP57] 15.00
____B-Wing Fighter, ROTJ Snap-together [MOP58] 35.00
____Battle on Ice Planet Hoth, ESB [MOP59] 36.00
____C-3PO, ROTJ [MOP60] 15.00
____C-3PO, SW...48.00
____C-3PO, SW reduced box [MOP61] 35.00
____C-3PO, SW with ESB sticker [MOP62] 95.00
____Darth Vader's Tie Fighter, SW [MOP63].............45.00
____Darth Vader's Tie Fighter, SW reduced box [MOP64]...35.00

____Darth Vader's Tie Fighter, SW reduced box commera-tive edition sticker [MOP65]...............................25.00
____Darth Vader, SW with Glo-Light saber [MOP66]..55.00
____Darth Vader, SW with Glo-Light saber, commemora-tive edition [MOP67]......................................20.00
____Darth Vader, SW action model [MOP68] 75.00
____Encounter with Yoda on Dagobah, ESB [MOP69] 50.00
____Jabba the Hutt Throne Room, ROTJ [MOP70] 43.00
____Luke Skywalker's Snowspeeder, ESB [MOP71] 40.00
____Luke Skywalker's Snowspeeder, ESB commerative edition sticker [MOP72]..................30.00
____Luke Skywalker's X-Wing Fighter, SW [MOP73] 45.00
____Luke Skywalker's X-Wing Fighter, SW reduced box [MOP74] 35.00
____Millennium Falcon, ROTJ [MOP75] 65.00

____Millennium Falcon, ROTJ commerative edition sticker [MOP76] 45.00
____Millennium Falcon, SW with lights [MOP77] 125.00
____R2-D2, ROTJ [MOP78]..................................22.00
____R2-D2, SW [MOP79] 45.00
____R2-D2, SW reduced box [MOP80].....................35.00
____Rebel base, ESB [MOP81] 35.00
____Rebel base, ESB commerative edition sticker [MOP82] 24.00
____Shuttle Tydirium, ROTJ [MOP83] 38.00
____Slave I, ESB [MOP84] 75.00
____Speeder Bike, ROTJ [MOP85] 28.00
____Star Destroyer, ESB [MOP86] 35.00
____Tie Fighter, ROTJ 18.00
____Tie Interceptor, ROTJ Snap-together.................20.00
____Van, Darth Vader, SW Snap-together 50.00
____Van, Luke Skywalker, SW Snap-together [MOP87] 50.00
____Van, R2-D2, SW Snap-together [MOP88] 50.00
____X-Wing Fighter, ROTJ [MOP89] 20.00

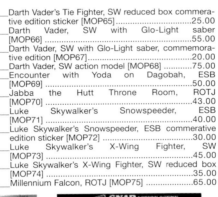

MOP57	MOP58	MOP59	MOP60	MOP61	MOP62

MOP63	MOP64	MOP65	MOP66	MOP67	MOP68

MOP69	MOP70	MOP71	MOP72	MOP73

Models: Plastic

MOP74

MOP75

MOP76

MOP77

MOP78

MOP79

MOP80

MOP81

MOP82

MOP83

MOP84

MOP85

MOP86

MOP87

MOP88

____X-Wing Fighter, ROTJ snap-tog [MOP90] 20.00
____Y-Wing Fighter, ROTJ [MOP91] 50.00

Mirr-a-Kits, ROTJ.
____AT-ST [MOP92] 16.00
____Shuttle Tydirium [MOP93] 16.00
____Speeder Bike [MOP94] 16.00
____Tie Interceptor 16.00
____X-Wing Fighter 16.00
____Y-Wing Fighter [MOP95] 16.00

Structor wind-ups, ROTJ.
____AT-AT [MOP96] 27.00
____AT-ST [MOP97] 27.00
____C-3PO [MOP98] 27.00

MPC/Ertl
____3-Piece Set: B-Wing, X-Wing, Tie Interceptor, ROTJ
Snap-together 36.00
____A-Wing Fighter, ROTJ snap-together 17.00

____AT-AT, ROTJ [MOP99] 20.00
____AT-ST, ROTJ 10.00
____Darth Vader's Tie Fighter, SW 15.00
____Darth Vader, SW 15.00
____Luke Skywalker's Snowspeeder, ESB 20.00
____Millennium Falcon, ROTJ 20.00
____Rebel base, ESB 15.00
____Shuttle Tydirium, ROTJ 17.00
____Speeder Bike, ROTJ 18.00
____Star Destroyer, ESB 15.00
____Tie Interceptor, ROTJ snap-together
[MOP100] 14.00
____X-Wing Fighter, ROTJ 12.00
____X-Wing Fighter, ROTJ snap-together
[MOP101] 12.00
____Y-Wing Fighter, ROTJ 35.00

Polydata
1/6 scale, pre-painted, limited to 9,000.
____Ben Kenobi [2:308]................................75.00

____Lando Calrissian [2:308]..........................75.00
____Luke Skywalker [2:308]............................75.00
____Princess Leia [2:308].............................75.00
____Tusken Raider [2:308].............................75.00

1/6 scale, pre-painted.
____Ben Kenobi [MOP102] 25.00
____Lando Calrissian [MOP103] 27.00
____Luke Skywalker [MOP104] 25.00
____Princess Leia [MOP105]............................25.00
____Tusken Raider [MOP106] 33.00

Scale Model Technologies
____Imperial Probe Droid 75.00

Takara
____C-3PO 75.00
____R2-D2 [MOP107] 75.00
____TIE Fighter [MOP108] 150.00
____X-Wing [MOP109] 150.00

MOP89

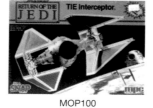
MOP90

MOP91

MOP92

MOP93

MOP94

MOP95

MOP96

MOP97

MOP98

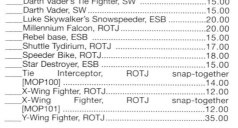
MOP99

MOP100

MOP101

MOP102   MOP103   MOP104   MOP105   MOP106   MOP107   MOP108   MOP109

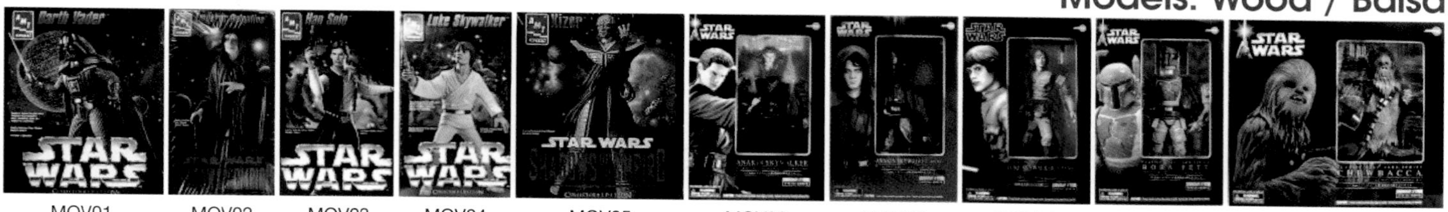

MOV01 MOV02 MOV03 MOV04 MOV05 MOV06 MOV07 MOV08 MOV09 MOV10

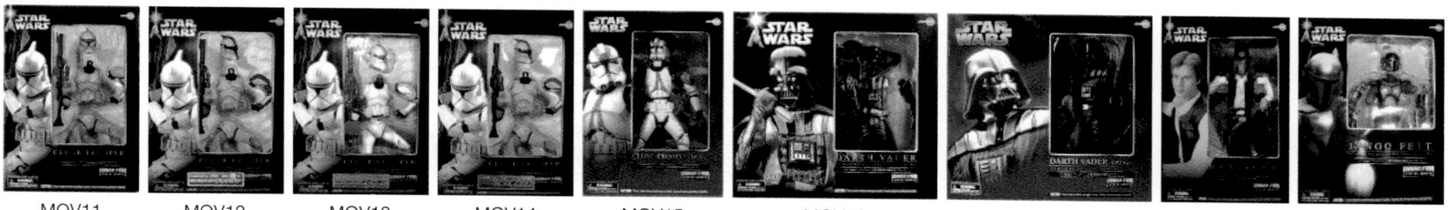

MOV11 MOV12 MOV13 MOV14 MOV15 MOV16 MOV17 MOV18 MOV19

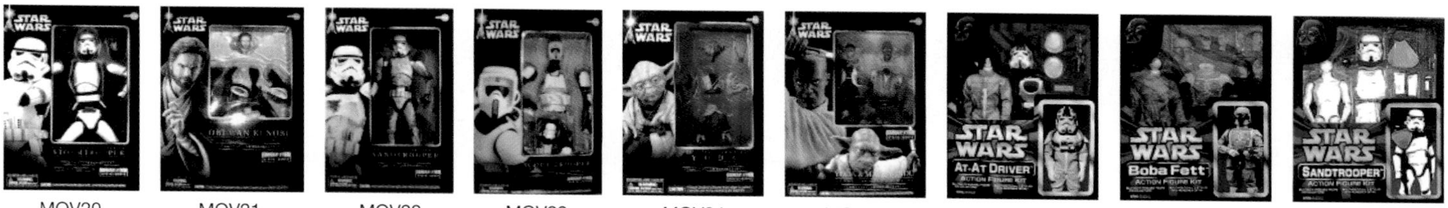

MOV20 MOV21 MOV22 MOV23 MOV24 MOV25 MOV26 MOV27 MOV28

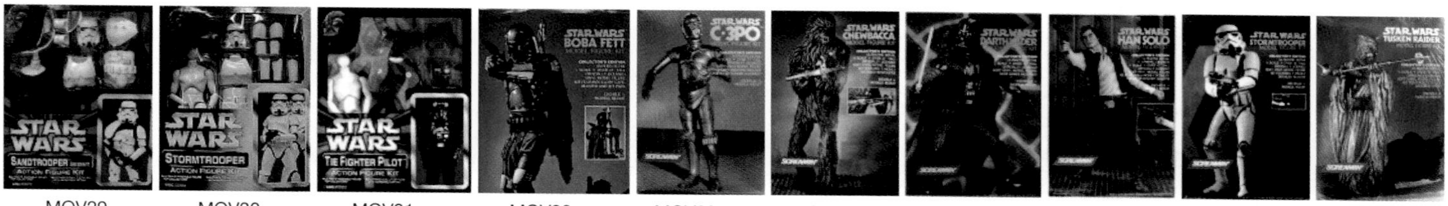

MOV29 MOV30 MOV31 MOV32 MOV33 MOV34 MOV35 MOV36 MOV37 MOV38

Models: Resin

Argonauts

____Darth Vader....................95.00
____Millennium Falcon....................95.00
____Star Destroyer....................95.00
____Stormtrooper....................95.00
____Tie Fighter [2:308]....................95.00
____Tie Interceptor....................95.00
____X-Wing Fighter....................95.00
____Y-Wing Fighter [2:308]....................95.00

Kaiyodo

1/15 scale.

____Boba Fett....................85.00
____Chewbacca....................55.00
____Darth Vader....................85.00
____Han Solo....................66.00
____Stormtrooper....................74.00
____Wicket Warrick....................85.00
____Yoda....................85.00

Tsukuda

____Wicket W. Warrick [2:308]....................45.00

Models: Vinyl

AMT/Ertl

____Darth Vader [MOV01]....................23.00
____Emperor Plapatine, SOTE [MOV02]....................34.00
____Han Solo [MOV03]....................23.00
____Luke Skywalker [MOV04]....................23.00
____Prince Xizor, SOTE [MOV05]....................20.00

Kaiyodo

1/6 scale.

____R2-D2....................50.00
____Stormtrooper....................45.00

Kotobukiya

____Anakin Skywalker [MOV06]....................125.00
____Anakin Skywalker, Mustafar [MOV07]....................100.00
____Bespin Luke [MOV08]....................150.00
____Boba Fett [MOV09]....................100.00
____Chewbacca [MOV10]....................100.00
____Clone Trooper [MOV11]....................100.00
____Clone Trooper Captain [MOV12]....................275.00
____Clone Trooper Commander [MOV13]....................125.00
____Clone Trooper Lieutenant, ltd to 1,000, Art of Star Wars exhibition [MOV14]....................425.00
____Clone Trooper 501st [MOV15]....................100.00
____Clone Trooper Shocktrooper, ltd. to 1,000....................150.00
____Commander Bly....................100.00
____Darth Maul....................125.00
____Darth Vader [MOV16]....................125.00
____Darth Vader, Mustafar [MOV17]....................100.00
____Han Solo [MOV18]....................100.00
____Jango Fett [MOV19]....................150.00
____Luke Stormtrooper [MOV20]....................100.00
____Obi-Wan Kenobi [MOV21]....................125.00
____Princess Leia....................100.00
____R2-D2 and C-3PO....................150.00
____Sandtrooper Corporal, StarWarsShop.com US exclusive, limited to 500....................175.00
____Sandtrooper Corporal, Toys R Us Japan exclusive, limited to 1,000 [MOV22]....................150.00
____Sandtrooper Sergeant, Hobbyshop Kotobukiya Japan exclusive, limited to 1,000....................150.00
____Sandtrooper Sergeant, StarWarsShop.com US exclusive, limited to 500....................175.00
____Scout Trooper [MOV23]....................150.00
____Shock Trooper, Toys R Us exclusive....................225.00
____Snowtrooper....................100.00
____Stormtrooper....................125.00
____Yoda [MOV24]....................50.00
____Yoda and Mace Windu [MOV25]....................175.00

Marmit

Action Figure Kits.

____AT-AT Driver [MOV26]....................70.00
____Boba Fett [MOV27]....................200.00
____Sandtrooper [MOV28]....................200.00
____Sandtrooper Sargeant [MOV29]....................150.00
____Stormtrooper [MOV30]....................200.00
____Tie Fighter Pilot [MOV31]....................135.00

Screamin' Products Inc

1/4 scale.

____Boba Fett [MOV32]....................75.00

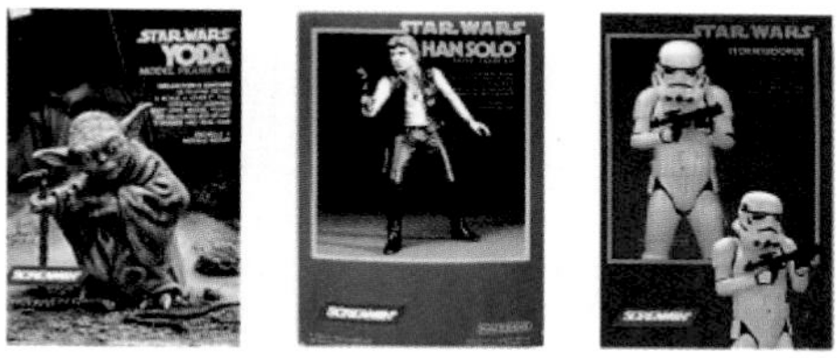

MOV39 MOV40 MOV41

____C-3PO [MOV33]....................55.00
____Chewbacca [MOV34]....................75.00
____Darth Vader [MOV35]....................55.00
____Han Solo [MOV36]....................65.00
____Luke Skywalker....................70.00
____Stormtrooper [MOV37]....................60.00
____Tusken Raider [MOV38]....................75.00
____Yoda [MOV39]....................75.00

1/6 scale.

____Boba Fett....................65.00
____C-3PO....................50.00
____Darth Vader....................50.00
____Han Solo [MOV40]....................50.00
____Princess Leia....................75.00
____R2-D2....................70.00
____Stormtrooper [MOV41]....................45.00

Models: Wood / Balsa

Estes

Balsa wood glider models.

____A-Wing Fighter [MOB01]....................6.00
____Star Destroyer [MOB02]....................3.00
____X-Wing Fighter [MOB03]....................3.00
____Y-Wing Fighter [MOB04]....................3.00

Catapult launching Episode I flying model kits. Balsa wood.

____Naboo fighter [MOB05]....................11.00
____Naboo Royal Starship [MOB06]....................11.00

Models: Wood / Balsa

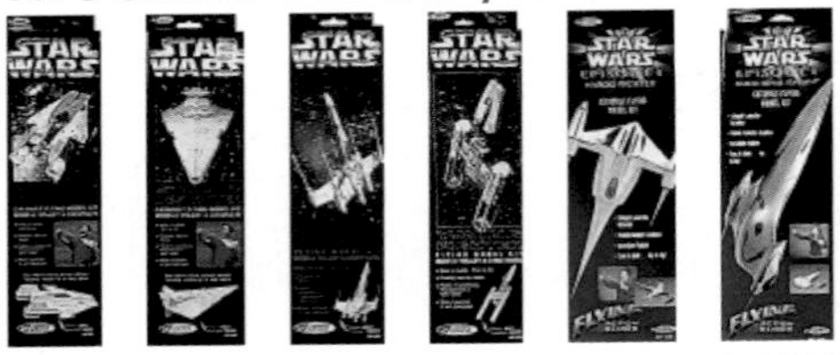

MOB01 MOB02 MOB03 MOB04 MOB05 MOB06

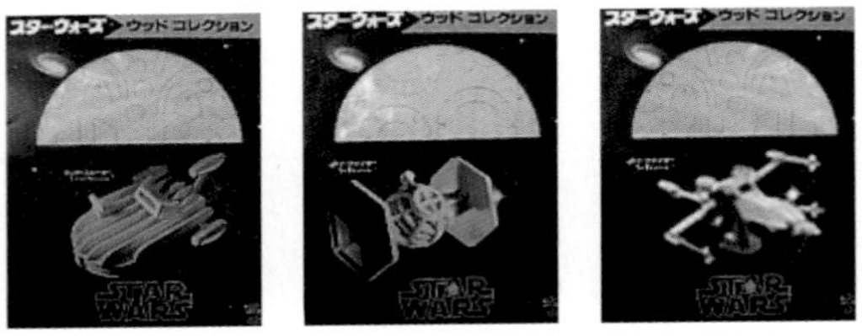

MOB07 MOB08 MOB09

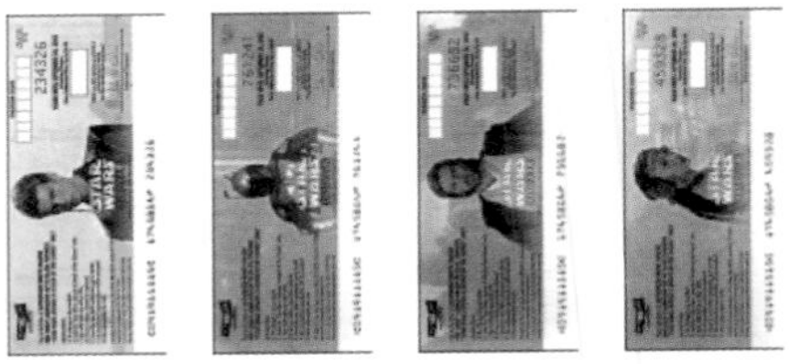

MVC01 MVC02 MVC03 MVC04

Takara

____Landspeeder [MOB07] 85.00
____R2-D2 ....85.00
____Tie Fighter [MOB08] 85.00
____X-Wing Fighter [MOB07] 85.00

Movie Cash Certificates

The Properties Group
Cereal premiums during EPII:AOTC.

____Anakin Skywalker [MVC01]..4.00
____Jango Fett [MVC02] 4.00
____Obi-Wan Kenobi [MVC03] 4.00
____Padme Amidala [MVC04] 4.00

Movies: DVDs

____A Galaxy Far Far Away [DVD01] 18.00
____Droids [DVD02]..15.00
____Ewoks [DVD03]..15.00
____Star Wars vs. Star Trek [DVD04] 12.00
____Starwoids [DVD05] 24.00
____Thumbwars: The Phantom Cuticle [DVD06] 10.00

20th Century Fox

____Caravan of Courage / The Battle for Endor........15.00
____Classic trilogy collection 60.00
____Classic trilogy collection widescreen..................75.00
____Clone Wars, vol. 1 [DVD07] 15.00
____Clone Wars, vol. 1 wholesale club packaging [DVD08]..15.00
____Clone Wars, vol. 2 ....15.00
____Clone Wars, vol. 2 wholesale club packaging....15.00
____EPI: Phantom Menace [DVD09] 25.00
____EPI: Phantom Menace widescreen [DVD10] 25.00
____EPI: Phantom Menace, limited edition, region 4 [DVD11]..45.00
____EPI: Phantom Menace, wholesale package [DVD12]..45.00
____EPII: Attack of the Clones [DVD13] 30.00
____EPII: Attack of the Clones, widescreen [DVD14]..25.00
____EPII: Attack of the Clones, widescreen wholesale [DVD15]..30.00
____EPIII: Revenge of the Sith [DVD16] 40.00
____EPIII: Revenge of the Sith widescreen [DVD17]..40.00
____R2-D2: Beneath the Dome [DVD18] 14.00
____Saga boxed set: 2002 EPI and EPII [DVD19] 40.00
____Star Wars Classic Trilogy full frame 3-disc set ..35.00
____Star Wars Classic Trilogy full frame 4-disc set ..50.00
____Star Wars Classic Trilogy wide screen...............50.00
____Star Wars Classic Trilogy wide screen 3-disc set..35.00

Classic trilogy DVD with bonus original theatrical version.

____Star Wars A New Hope 45.00
____The Empire Strikes Back 45.00
____Return of the Jedi..45.00

20th Century Fox, Canada

____Clone Wars, vol. 1 ....15.00

A&E

____Star Wars Empire of Dreams for Emmy consideration, not for resale [DVD20] 200.00

InterActual

____THX Ultimate Demo Disc [DVD21]......................65.00

Jim Henson Home Entertainment

____Muppet Show, Best of, includes Mark Hamill / Luke Skywalker [DVD22]..35.00

Magna
Turkey.

____Dunyayi Kurtaran Adam [DVD23].......................65.00

MMG

____Star Ballz, adult parody [DVD24] 15.00

Passport Video

____Stars of SW: Interviews with the Cast 16.00

The Sun / World News

____Heroes and Villains [DVD25] 15.00

Movies: Films

____La Guerre des Etoiles..45.00

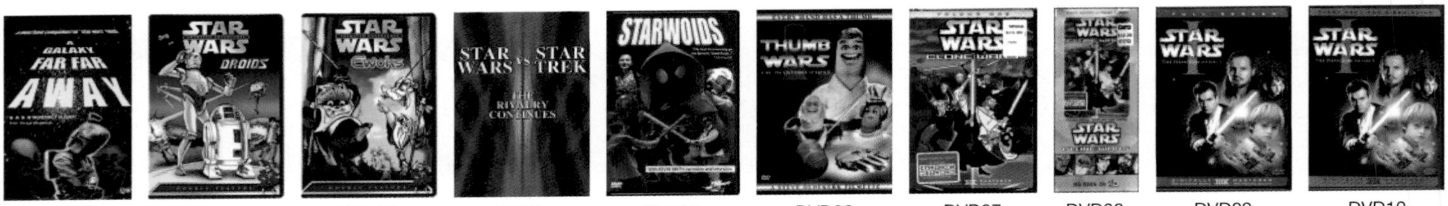

DVD01 DVD02 DVD03 DVD04 DVD05 DVD06 DVD07 DVD08 DVD09 DVD10

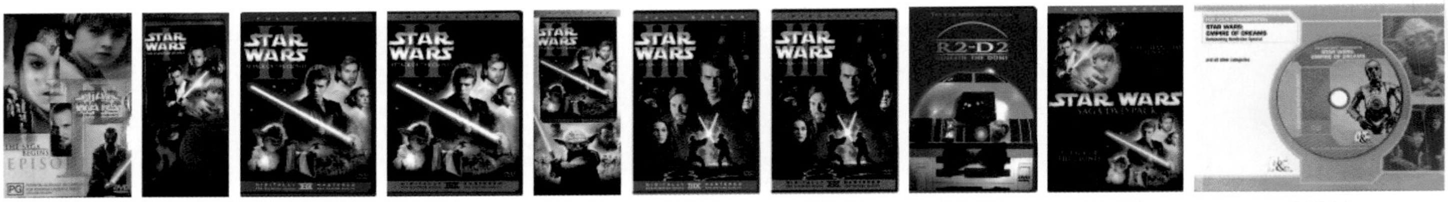

DVD11 DVD12 DVD13 DVD14 DVD15 DVD16 DVD17 DVD18 DVD19 DVD20

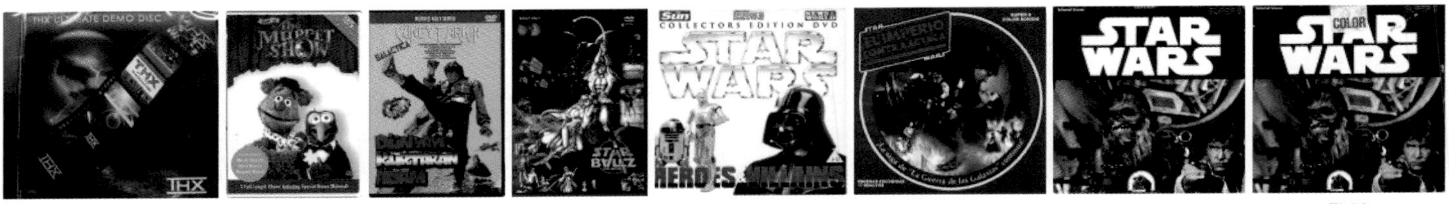

DVD21 DVD22 DVD23 DVD24 DVD25 FL01 FL02 FL03

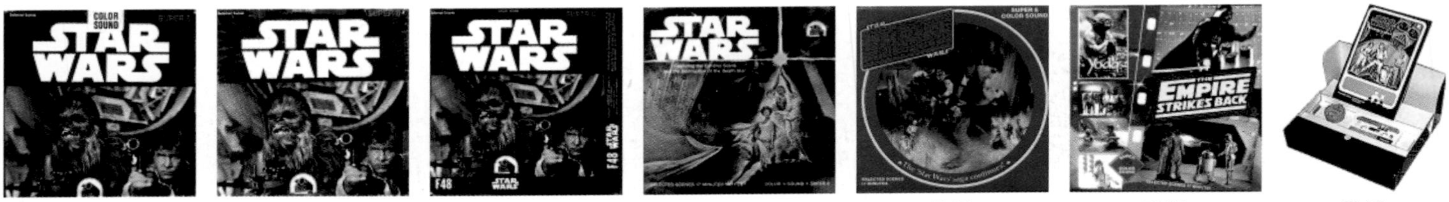

FL04 FL05 FL06 FL07 FL08 FL09 FL10

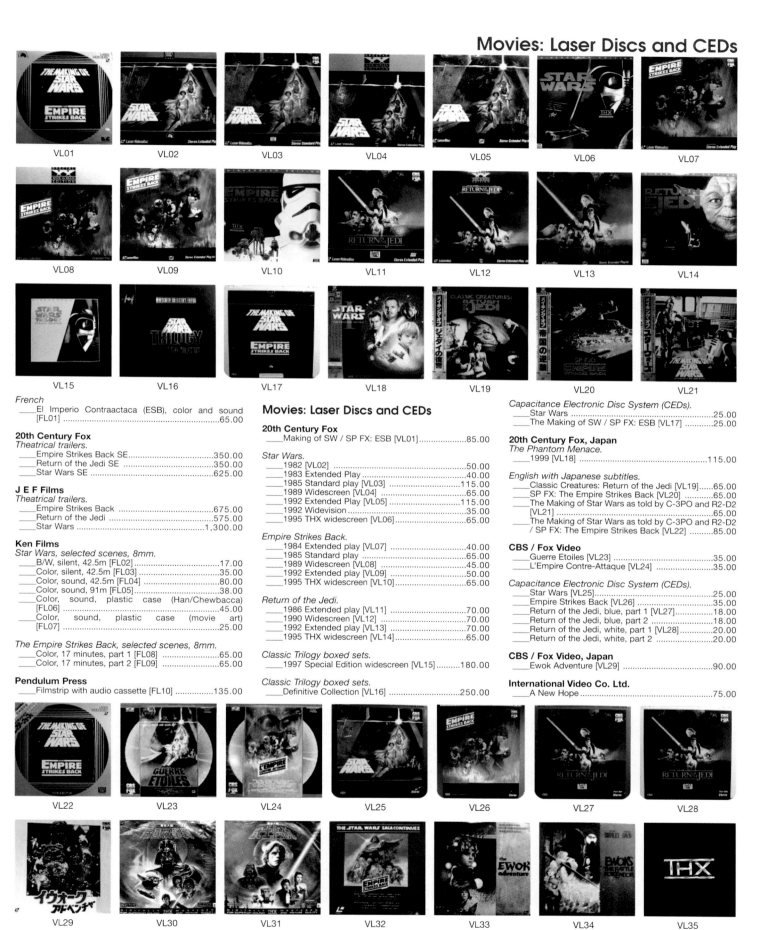

VL01   VL02   VL03   VL04   VL05   VL06   VL07

VL08   VL09   VL10   VL11   VL12   VL13   VL14

VL15   VL16   VL17   VL18   VL19   VL20   VL21

French
____El Imperio Contraactaca (ESB), color and sound [FL01] 65.00

20th Century Fox
Theatrical trailers.
____Empire Strikes Back SE....................................350.00
____Return of the Jedi SE 350.00
____Star Wars SE 625.00

J E F Films
Theatrical trailers.
____Empire Strikes Back 675.00
____Return of the Jedi 575.00
____Star Wars 1,300.00

Ken Films
Star Wars, selected scenes, 8mm.
____B/W, silent, 42.5m [FL02] 17.00
____Color, silent, 42.5m [FL03] 35.00
____Color, sound, 42.5m [FL04] 80.00
____Color, sound, 91m [FL05] 38.00
____Color, sound, plastic case (Han/Chewbacca) [FL06] 45.00
____Color, sound, plastic case (movie art) [FL07] 25.00

The Empire Strikes Back, selected scenes, 8mm.
____Color, 17 minutes, part 1 [FL08] 65.00
____Color, 17 minutes, part 2 [FL09] 65.00

Pendulum Press
____Filmstrip with audio cassette [FL10] 135.00

Movies: Laser Discs and CEDs

20th Century Fox
____Making of SW / SP FX: ESB [VL01]....................85.00

Star Wars.
____1982 [VL02] 50.00
____1983 Extended Play 40.00
____1985 Standard play [VL03] 115.00
____1989 Widescreen [VL04] 65.00
____1992 Extended Play [VL05] 115.00
____1992 Widevision 35.00
____1995 THX widescreen [VL06]....................65.00

Empire Strikes Back.
____1984 Extended play [VL07] 40.00
____1985 Standard play 65.00
____1989 Widescreen [VL08] 45.00
____1992 Extended play [VL09] 50.00
____1995 THX widescreen [VL10]....................65.00

Return of the Jedi.
____1986 Extended play [VL11] 70.00
____1990 Widescreen [VL12] 70.00
____1992 Extended play [VL13] 70.00
____1995 THX widescreen [VL14]....................65.00

Classic Trilogy boxed sets.
____1997 Special Edition widescreen [VL15]..........180.00

Classic Trilogy boxed sets.
____Definitive Collection [VL16] 250.00

Capacitance Electronic Disc System (CEDs).
____Star Wars 25.00
____The Making of SW / SP FX: ESB [VL17] 25.00

20th Century Fox, Japan
The Phantom Menace.
____1999 [VL18] 115.00

English with Japanese subtitles.
____Classic Creatures: Return of the Jedi [VL19]......65.00
____SP FX: The Empire Strikes Back [VL20] 65.00
____The Making of Star Wars as told by C-3PO and R2-D2 [VL21] 65.00
____The Making of Star Wars as told by C-3PO and R2-D2 / SP FX: The Empire Strikes Back [VL22] 85.00

CBS / Fox Video
____Guerre Etoiles [VL23] 35.00
____L'Empire Contre-Attaque [VL24] 35.00

Capacitance Electronic Disc System (CEDs).
____Star Wars [VL25]....................................25.00
____Empire Strikes Back [VL26] 35.00
____Return of the Jedi, blue, part 1 [VL27]..............18.00
____Return of the Jedi, blue, part 2 ....18.00
____Return of the Jedi, white, part 1 [VL28].............20.00
____Return of the Jedi, white, part 2 ....20.00

CBS / Fox Video, Japan
____Ewok Adventure [VL29] 90.00

International Video Co. Ltd.
____A New Hope....................................75.00

VL22   VL23   VL24   VL25   VL26   VL27   VL28

VL29   VL30   VL31   VL32   VL33   VL34   VL35

Movies: Laser Discs and CEDs

VDC01 VV01 VV02 VV03 VV04 VV05 VV06 VV07 VV08 VV09

VV10 VV11 VV12 VV13 VV14 VV15 VV16 VV17 VV18 VV19 VV20 VV21

VV22 VV23 VV24 VV25 VV26 VV27 VV28 VV29 VV30 VV31 VV32 VV33

____Empire Strikes Back [VL30] 75.00
____Return of the Jedi [VL31] 75.00

Lightning
____The Empire Strikes Back [VL32] 35.00

MGM / UA
Ewoks, live action.
____1990 The Ewok Adventure [VL33] 45.00
____1991 The Battle for Endor [VL34].......................45.00

Skywalker Sound
____THX WOW, includes scenes from classic trilogy [VL35] 75.00

Movies: Video Storage Cases

20th Century Fox
____SW:EPI plastic case with lenticular cover, TRU exclusive for pre-ordering video [VDC01] 8.00

Movies: Video Cassettes

20th Century Fox
____Bart Wars: Simpsons Strike Back [VV01] 27.00

The Phantom Menace.
____2000 [VV02] 20.00

____2000 Widescreen [VV03] 30.00
____2000 Widescreen Video Collector's Edition [VV04] 40.00

Attack of the Clones.
____2003 [VV05] 10.00
____2003 Widevision 18.00

Star Wars.
____1982 [VV06] 20.00
____1982 Beta 20.00
____1982 Video Rental Library [VV07] 20.00
____1982 Video Rental Library beta 20.00
____1983 [VV08] 20.00
____1983 Beta [VV09] 20.00
____1984 [VV10] 20.00
____1984 Beta 65.00
____1990 [VV11] 25.00
____1992 [VV12] 16.00
____1992 Special Letterbox Collector's Edition [VV13] 18.00
____1995 THX [VV14] 20.00
____1995 THX widescreen [VV15]...........................14.00
____1997 Special Edition [VV16].............................18.00
____1997 Special Edition widevision [VV17].............16.00
____2000 THX SE [VV18].......................................22.00
____2000 THX SE widevision [VV19] 20.00

The Empire Strikes Back.
____1984 [VV20] 28.00
____1984 Beta 12.00
____1990 [VV21] 25.00

____1992 ....25.00
____1992 Special Letterbox Collector's Edition [VV22] 35.00
____1995 THX [VV23] 16.00
____1995 THX widescreen [VV24]...........................25.00
____1997 Special Edition [VV25].............................18.00
____1997 Special Edition widescreen [VV26] 23.00
____2000 THX SE [VV27].......................................12.00
____2000 THX SE widescreen [VV28]......................15.00

Return of the Jedi.
____1986 [VV29] 15.00
____1986 Beta 12.00
____1990 ....16.00
____1992 [VV30] 18.00
____1992 Letterbox Collector's Edition [VV31] 20.00
____1995 THX [VV32] 23.00
____1995 THX widescreen [VV33]...........................23.00
____1997 Special Edition [VV34].............................20.00
____1997 Special Edition widescreen [VV35] 20.00
____2000 THX SE [VV36].......................................20.00
____2000 THX SE widescreen [VV37]......................20.00

Classic Trilogy Boxed Set.
____1990 [VV38] 65.00
____1992 [VV39] 115.00
____1995 THX [VV40] 65.00
____1995 THX widescreen [VV41]...........................85.00
____1997 Special Edition [VV42].............................135.00
____1997 Special Edition widevision [VV43] 65.00
____1997 Special Edition, L.E. Collector's Set [VV44] 95.00

VV34 VV35 VV36 VV37 VV38 VV39 VV40 VV41 VV42

VV43 VV44 VV45 VV46 VV47 VV48 VV49 VV50 VV51

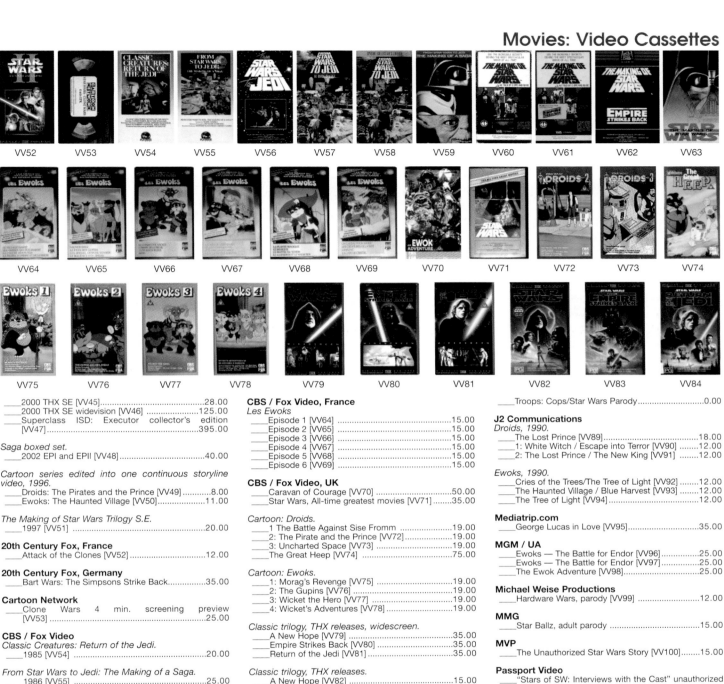

VV52	VV53	VV54	VV55	VV56	VV57	VV58	VV59	VV60	VV61	VV62	VV63
VV64	VV65	VV66	VV67	VV68	VV69	VV70	VV71	VV72	VV73	VV74	
VV75	VV76	VV77	VV78	VV79	VV80	VV81	VV82	VV83	VV84		

____2000 THX SE [VV45]...........................28.00
____2000 THX SE widevision [VV46].............125.00
____Superclass ISD: Executor collector's edition [VV47]..395.00

Saga boxed set.
____2002 EPI and EPII [VV48]....................40.00

Cartoon series edited into one continuous storyline video, 1996.
____Droids: The Pirates and the Prince [VV49]...........8.00
____Ewoks: The Haunted Village [VV50].................11.00

The Making of Star Wars Trilogy S.E.
____1997 [VV51] 20.00

20th Century Fox, France
____Attack of the Clones [VV52] 12.00

20th Century Fox, Germany
____Bart Wars: The Simpsons Strike Back................35.00

Cartoon Network
____Clone Wars 4 min. screening preview [VV53] 25.00

CBS / Fox Video
Classic Creatures: Return of the Jedi.
____1985 [VV54] 20.00

From Star Wars to Jedi: The Making of a Saga.
____1986 [VV55] 25.00
____1986 Beta 25.00
____1989 [VV56] 25.00
____1992 [VV57] 25.00
____1992 Special Collector's Edition [VV58]...............25.00
____1995 [VV59] 25.00

The Making of Star Wars.
____1979 [VV60] 35.00
____1980 [VV61] 25.00
____1980 Beta 12.00
____1982 SP FX: ESB 15.00
____1983 SP FX: ESB Beta [VV62] 20.00
____1995 Cereal mail-in premium [VV63] 20.00

CBS / Fox Video, France
Les Ewoks
____Episode 1 [VV64] 15.00
____Episode 2 [VV65] 15.00
____Episode 3 [VV66] 15.00
____Episode 4 [VV67] 15.00
____Episode 5 [VV68] 15.00
____Episode 6 [VV69] 15.00

CBS / Fox Video, UK
____Caravan of Courage [VV70] 50.00
____Star Wars, All-time greatest movies [VV71].......35.00

Cartoon: Droids.
____1 The Battle Against Sise Fromm 19.00
____2: The Pirate and the Prince [VV72]...............19.00
____3: Uncharted Space [VV73] 19.00
____The Great Heep [VV74] 75.00

Cartoon: Ewoks.
____1: Morag's Revenge [VV75] 19.00
____2: The Gupins [VV76] 19.00
____3: Wicket the Hero [VV77] 19.00
____4: Wicket's Adventures [VV78] 19.00

Classic trilogy, THX releases, widescreen.
____A New Hope [VV79]..............................35.00
____Empire Strikes Back [VV80] 35.00
____Return of the Jedi [VV81] 35.00

Classic trilogy, THX releases.
____A New Hope [VV82] 15.00
____Empire Strikes Back [VV83] 15.00
____Return of the Jedi [VV84] 15.00

Dairylea promotions.
____Droids: Tale of Roon Comets [VV85] 55.00
____Ewoks: Night of the Strangers [VV86] 55.00

Disney / MGM
____Star Tours, presskit edition [VV87]................65.00

Fan Made
____Millennium's End, Fandom Menace [VV88] 16.00
____Star Wars, The Dark Redemption 14.00

____Troops: Cops/Star Wars Parody......................0.00

J2 Communications
Droids, 1990.
____The Lost Prince [VV89]............................18.00
____1: White Witch / Escape into Terror [VV90] 12.00
____2: The Lost Prince / The New King [VV91] 12.00

Ewoks, 1990.
____Cries of the Trees/The Tree of Light [VV92] 12.00
____The Haunted Village / Blue Harvest [VV93] 12.00
____The Tree of Light [VV94] 12.00

Mediatrip.com
____George Lucas in Love [VV95]......................35.00

MGM / UA
____Ewoks — The Battle for Endor [VV96]...............25.00
____Ewoks — The Battle for Endor [VV97]...............25.00
____The Ewok Adventure [VV98]........................25.00

Michael Weise Productions
____Hardware Wars, parody [VV99] 12.00

MMG
____Star Ballz, adult parody 15.00

MVP
____The Unauthorized Star Wars Story [VV100].......15.00

Passport Video
____"Stars of SW: Interviews with the Cast" unauthorized video 16.00

VV85	VV86	VV87	VV88

VV89	VV90	VV91	VV92	VV93	VV94	VV95	VV96	VV97	VV98	VV99	VV100

Movies: Video Discs

VD01 VD02 VD03 CLM01 CLM02 CLM03 PFJ01 PFJ02

PFJ03 PFJ04 PFJ05 PFJ06 PFJ07 PFK01 PFK02

    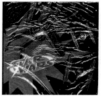 

PFK03 PFK04 PFK05 PFK06 PFK07 PFK08 PFK09

PFK10 PFK11 PFK12 PFK13 PFK14 PFK15 PFK16

Movies: Video Discs

Video Now
____The Story of Star Wars 3 disc set [VD01] 20.00

Videovan Entertainnment
____Episode I: The Phantom Menace [VD02]............49.00
____Trilogy Boxed Set with EP2 footage [VD03] 49.00

Music Boxes

Sigma
____Ion Turrent with C-3PO [CLM01].....................125.00
____Max Rebo Band [CLM02] 75.00
____Wicket and Princess Kneesaa [CLM03].............75.00

Name Badges

20th Century Fox
____Star Wars early style logo [PFJ01] 4.00

Disney / MGM
____Star Wars Weekends Cast Member [PFJ02] 15.00

Drawing Board Greeting Cards, Inc.
16-packs.
____Darth Vader [PFJ03]..16.00
____Star Wars logo [PFJ04] 16.00

KFC
Employee name badges, "Welcome to Naboo."
____Anakin Skywalker [PFJ05] 10.00
____Darth Maul 10.00
____Jar Jar Binks [PFJ06] 10.00
____Obi-Wan Kenobi [PFJ07] 10.00
____Queen Amidala..10.00

Starlog
____Starlog salutes Star Wars 5.00

Napkins

Deeko
____Star Wars [PFK01] 10.00

Drawing Board Greeting Cards, Inc.
____C-3PO and R2-D2, beverage...........................14.00
____C-3PO and R2-D2, dinner [PFK02] 14.00
____Cloud City, beverage 14.00
____Cloud City, dinner [PFK03]..............................14.00
____Darth Vader and Luke Duel, beverage...............14.00
____Darth Vader and Luke Duel, dinner [PFK04] 14.00
____Ewoks Hang-Gliding, beverage [PFK05] 10.00
____Ewoks Hang-Gliding, dinner [PFK06] 10.00

Party Express
Classic trilogy.
____Dogfight over Death Star, dinner [PFK07] 8.00
____Ships in neon colors, dinner [PFK08]..................5.00
____Star Wars Saga, beverage [PFK09] 5.00
____Star Wars Saga, dinner..5.00

Episode I: The Phantom Menace.
____Obi-Wan Kenobi, beverage [PFK10] 3.00
____Qui-Gon Jinn, dinner [PFK11].............................4.00

Episode II: Attack of the Clones.
____Anakin, Padme, Obi-Wan, dinner [PFK12] 3.00
____Jango, Obi-Wan and Anakin, beverage [PFK13] ..4.00

Episode III: Revenge of the Sith.
____Darth Vader, dinner [PFK14] 4.00
____Yoda, beverage [PFK15] 4.00

Quela
____Vader / Imperial logo [PFK16]..............................6.00

Nightlights

Adam Joseph Industries
____C-3PO disc-cut [HON01] 10.00
____C-3PO sculpted [HON02]....................................12.00
____Darth Vader sculpted [HON03] 12.00
____R2-D2 die-cut [HON04] 10.00
____Yoda die-cut [HON05] 10.00
____Yoda sculpted [HON06] 12.00

Ewoks.
____Princess Kneesaa sculpted [HON07]....................8.00
____Wicket sculpted [HON08] 8.00

Northlight, Ltd.
____R2-D2 [HON09] 75.00

HON01 HON02 HON03 HON04 HON05 HON06 HON07 HON08 HON09

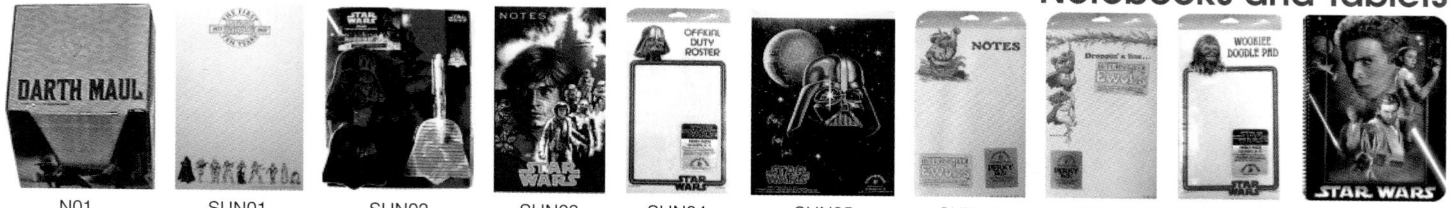

N01 SUN01 SUN02 SUN03 SUN04 SUN05 SUN06 SUN07 SUN08 SUN09

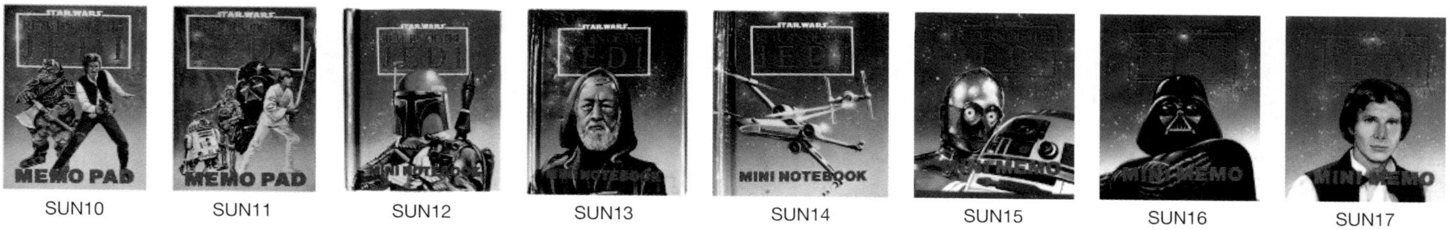

SUN10 SUN11 SUN12 SUN13 SUN14 SUN15 SUN16 SUN17

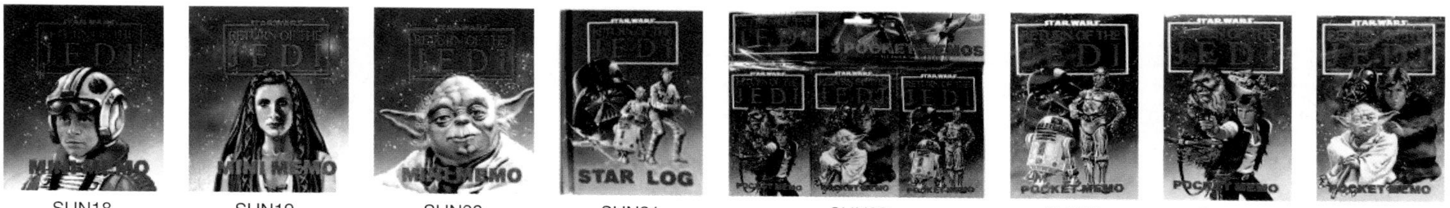

SUN18 SUN19 SUN20 SUN21 SUN22 SUN23 SUN24 SUN25

Note Cubes

Impact, Inc.
____Darth Maul [N01]..4.00

Notebooks and Tablets

____10th Anniversary notepads [SUN01] 8.00
____Collector tin set with light-up pen [SUN02]........10.00

Animations
____Darth Vader helmet 3.00

EPIII:ROTS. 80 sheets wide-ruled, spiral.
____Darth Vader art 4.00
____Darth Vader helmet 4.00
____Darth Vader lightsaber down 4.00
____Darth Vader lightsaber up......................................4.00

Antioch
____"Lost City of the Jedi" art [SUN03] 4.00

Drawing Board Greeting Cards, Inc.
____Darth Vader Official Duty Roster [SUN04] 7.00
____Darth Vader, Death Star, and Tie Fighters, 25 sheets [SUN05] 18.00
____Ewok with horn, "Notes" [SUN06] 7.00
____Ewoks notepad, "Droppin' a Line" [SUN07] 7.00
____Wookiee Doodle Pad [SUN08] 7.00

Grosvenor
Episode II: Attack of the Clones, spiral.
____Heroes, A4 [SUN09] 5.00

HC Ford
Memo pads.
____Gamorrean Guard / Han Solo [SUN10] 8.00
____R2-D2, C-3PO / Darth Vader / Luke Skywalker [SUN11]..8.00

Mini-Notebooks, hardcover.
____Boba Fett [SUN12] 5.00
____Obi-Wan Kenobi [SUN13].......................................5.00
____Space Battle [SUN14]..5.00

Mini memo pads.
____C-3PO and R2-D2 [SUN15] 4.00
____Darth Vader [SUN16] 4.00
____Han Solo [SUN17]...4.00
____Luke Skywalker [SUN18] 4.00
____Princess Leia [SUN19] 4.00
____Yoda [SUN20] 4.00

Notebooks, hardcover.
____Star Log [SUN21] 10.00

Pocket memo pads.
____3-pack: Droids, Han and Chewbacca, Luke and Yoda [SUN22] 15.00
____C-3PO and R2-D2 [SUN23] 6.00
____Han and Chewbacca [SUN24] 6.00
____Luke and Yoda [SUN25] 6.00

Impact, Inc.
50 sheets 8"x10.5" wide ruled, spiral.
____Anakin Skywalker [SUN26].....................................3.00
____Anakin Skywalker, Podracer [SUN27] 3.00
____Jar Jar 3.00
____Jedi vs. Sith [SUN28] 3.00
____Queen Amidala [SUN29].......................................3.00
____Qui-Gon Jinn [SUN30] 3.00
____R2-D2 / C-3PO 3.00
____Sith Lord [SUN31]..3.00
____Space Battle over Naboo [SUN32].........................3.00

90 sheets 6"x9". Rubber cover with character icon.
____Anakin Skywalker [SUN33].....................................4.00
____Darth Maul [SUN34] 4.00
____Jar Jar Binks [SUN35] 4.00
____Queen Amidala [SUN36]..4.00

180 sheets, 5"x7" wide ruled, spiral.
____Jedi vs. Sith [SUN37] 2.00

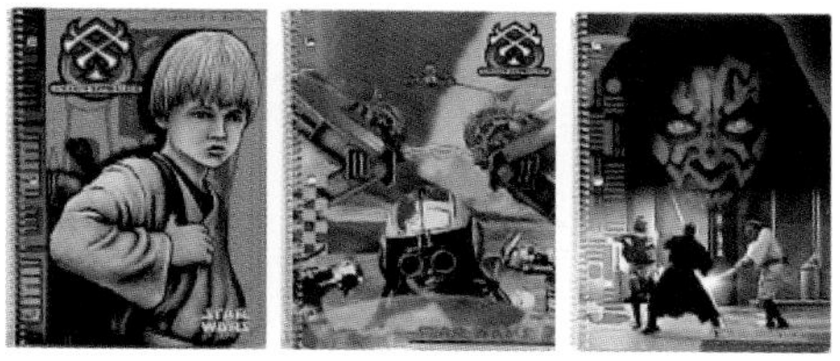

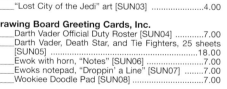

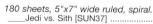

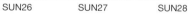

SUN26 SUN27 SUN28

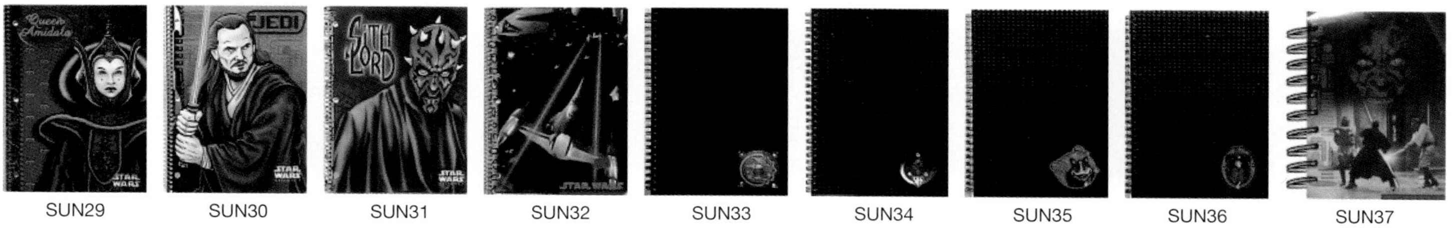

SUN29 SUN30 SUN31 SUN32 SUN33 SUN34 SUN35 SUN36 SUN37

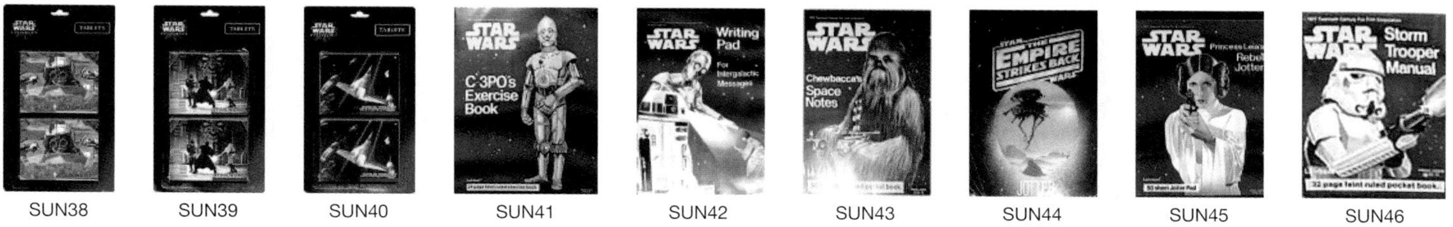

SUN38 SUN39 SUN40 SUN41 SUN42 SUN43 SUN44 SUN45 SUN46

Notebooks and Tablets

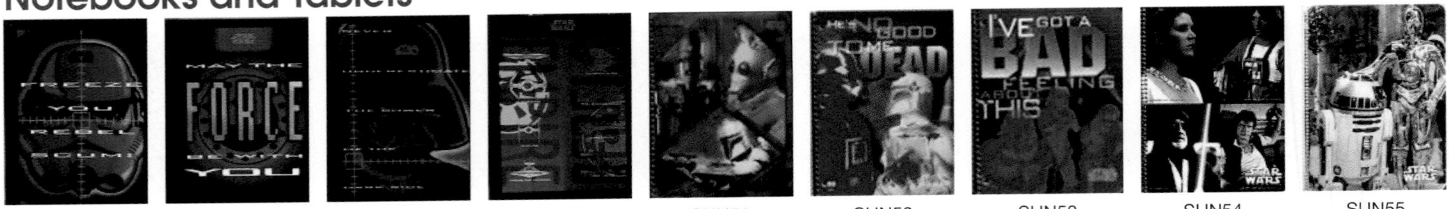

SUN47 SUN48 SUN49 SUN50 SUN51 SUN52 SUN53 SUN54 SUN55

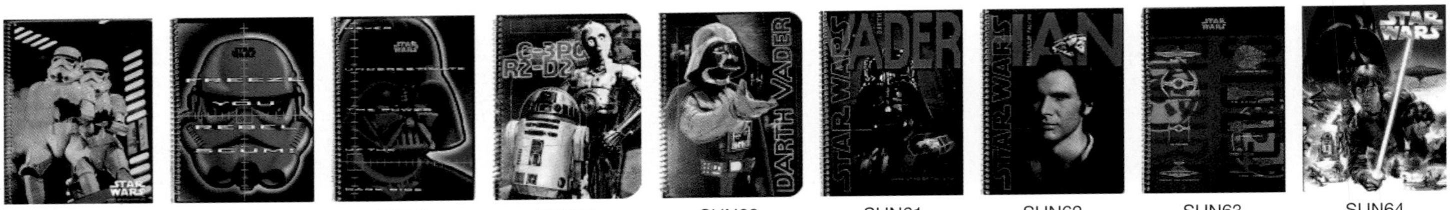

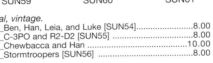

SUN56 SUN57 SUN58 SUN59 SUN60 SUN61 SUN62 SUN63 SUN64

Packages of 2.
____Anakin Skywalker Podracer [SUN38]....................4.00
____Jedi vs. Sith [SUN39]..4.00
____Space Battle [SUN40]..4.00

Letraset
____C-3PO's Exercise Book [SUN41]........................14.00
____C-3PO / R2-D2, Intergalactic Msgs [SUN42] 10.00
____Chewbacca's Space Notes [SUN43]..................10.00
____ESB jotter, probedroid cover [SUN44]................17.00
____Princess Leia's Rebel Jotter [SUN45] 10.00
____Stormtrooper Manual [SUN46]............................10.00

Magic World
50 page, graph paper.
____ARC-170s 6.00
____Darth Vader 6.00
____Jedi Starfighter, ground 6.00
____Jedi Starfighter, space 6.00

Mead
180 ruled sheets, 5.5"x3.5".
____"Freeze You Rebel Scum!" [SUN47].......................4.00
____"May The Force Be With You" [SUN48] 4.00
____"Never Underestimate The Power of the Dark Side" [SUN49]...4.00
____Star Wars Star Fighters [SUN50] 4.00

Neon colors, spiral.
____Bounty hunters [SUN51]...3.00
____He's no good to me DEAD [SUN52]........................3.00
____I've got a BAD feeling about this [SUN53]............3.00

Spiral, vintage.
____Ben, Han, Leia, and Luke [SUN54]........................8.00
____C-3PO and R2-D2 [SUN55] 8.00
____Chewbacca and Han 10.00
____Stormtroopers [SUN56] 8.00

Spiral.
____"Freeze You Rebel Scum" [SUN57] 3.00
____"May The Force Be With You" 3.00
____"Never Under Estimate The Power of the Dark Side" [SUN58]...3.00
____C-3PO / R2-D2 [SUN59]..8.00
____Darth Vader [SUN60] 8.00
____Darth Vader, Dark Lord of Sith [SUN61]................3.00
____Han and Millennium Falcon [SUN62] 3.00
____Starships [SUN63] 3.00
____Stormtroopers...3.00

Merlin
____ESB cover [SUN64]...3.00
____Luke / X-Wing starfighter [SUN65]........................5.00
____Vader / TIE fighter [SUN66] 5.00

Shaped
____Darth Vader [SUN67] 7.00
____Stormtrooper [SUN68] 7.00

Spiral.
____Boba Fett [SUN69] 5.00

Palitoy
____Bounty Hunter Capture Log [SUN70] 27.00

Pyramid
EPII:AOTC pocket notebooks.
____Anakin Skywalker [SUN71]..3.00
____Mace Windu [SUN72] 3.00

Episode II: Attack of the Clones, spiral.
____C-3PO / R2-D2 [SUN73]..4.00
____Heroes [SUN74] 4.00
____Jango Fett [SUN75] 4.00
____Villains [SUN76]..4.00

Q-Stat
____Obi-Wan Kenobi [SUN77] 2.00

Queen
____Star Wars. Shows sandtrooper, Luke/C-3PO, Han/Chewbacca [SUN78] 12.00

Scribe
Mexico. EPII:AOTC, spiral.
____C-3PO / R2-D2 [SUN79]..5.00
____Heroes [SUN80] 5.00
____Jango Fett [SUN81] 5.00
____Padme / Space [SUN82] 5.00
____Padme Amidala [SUN83] 5.00
____Zam Wesell [SUN84]..5.00

Mexico. ROTJ, spiral.
____AT-ST [SUN85] 12.00
____Lightsaber [SUN86] 12.00
____Millennium Falcon [SUN87] 12.00
____Princess Leia, Jabba's Prisoner [SUN88] 12.00
____Yoda [SUN89]...12.00

Stuart Hall
____C-3PO and R2-D2 ....10.00
____Doodle Pad: Max Rebo Band [SUN90] 6.00
____Millennium Falcon and Star Destroyer................10.00
____Pencil Tablet: R2-D2 and Wicket the Ewok [SUN91]...8.00
____Scribble Pad: C-3PO and R2-D2 outside Jabba's Palace [SUN92]..8.00

Learn to Letter and Write series.
____Boba Fett [SUN93] 12.00

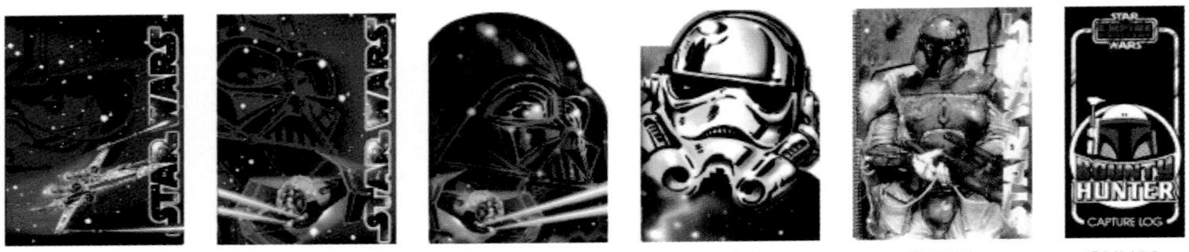

SUN65 SUN66 SUN67 SUN68 SUN69 SUN70

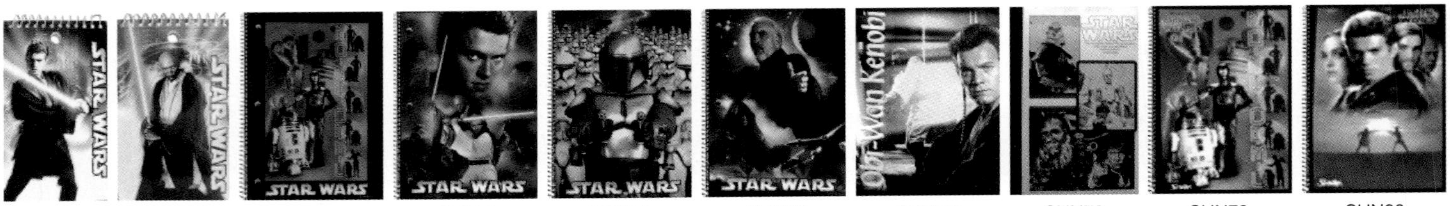

SUN71 SUN72 SUN73 SUN74 SUN75 SUN76 SUN77 SUN78 SUN79 SUN80

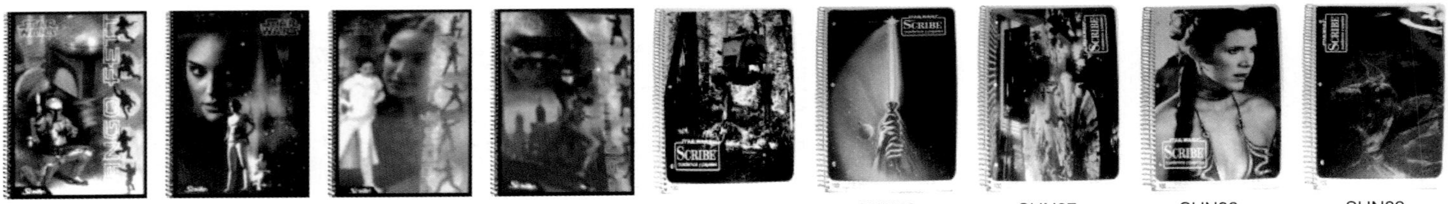

SUN81 SUN82 SUN83 SUN84 SUN85 SUN86 SUN87 SUN88 SUN89

| SUN90 | SUN91 | SUN92 | SUN93 | SUN94 |

| SUN95 | SUN96 | SUN97 | SUN98 | SUN99 | SUN100 | SUN101 |

| SUN102 | SUN103 | SUN104 | SUN105 | SUN106 | SUN107 | SUN108 | SUN109 | SUN110 |

____Darth Vader / Stormtroopers [SUN94] 12.00
____Ewok Hang-gliding [SUN95]...............................5.00
____Luke Skywalker [SUN96] 12.00
____Yoda 12.00

Pocket memo pads, 3"x5" vetical.
____Boba Fett 6.00
____C-3PO and R2-D2 ....6.00
____Character montage 6.00
____Darth Vader and Stormtroopers 6.00
____Luke Skywalker [SUN97] 6.00

Pocket memo pads.
____Biker Scouts 4.00
____C-3PO, R2-D2, and Wicket 4.00
____Darth Vader and Luke Skywalker 4.00
____Jabba the Hutt 4.00
____Max Rebo Band 4.00
____Space battle scene..4.00

Spiral.
____2-1B, Aliens, Bounty Hunters, Probot, Ugnaught
[SUN98]...8.00
____B-Wing and Tie Fighter [SUN99] 7.00
____Boba Fett [SUN100] 8.00
____C-3PO and R2-D2 ....8.00
____C-3PO, R2-D2 and Wicket [SUN101]...................5.00
____Chewbacca 9.00
____Darth Vader and Stormtroopers [SUN102]...........8.00
____Darth Vader on Bespin 9.00
____Darth Vader, Emperor Palpatine, Luke Skywalker
[SUN103]...7.00

____Darth Vader, Han, Lando, Leia, and Luke 9.00
____Han, Leia, and Luke on Hoth [SUN104]...............9.00
____Jabba and Salacious Crumb 8.00
____Leia and Luke on Bespin, Hoth snowtroopers
[SUN105]..9.00
____Luke and Stormtroopers on Bespin 8.00
____Luke on Dagobah 8.00
____Max Rebo Band [SUN106] 6.00
____Millennium Falcon and Star Destroyer
[SUN107]..10.00
____Princess Leia, Luke, Ben, Han [SUN108]..............9.00
____R2-D2 and Wicket the Ewok 8.00
____Speeder Bikers [SUN109]..................................6.00
____Vader Silhouette 9.00
____Yoda [SUN110] 9.00

Tokyo Queen
____Darth Vader / Rebel base [SUN111] 25.00
____Death Star battle / Droid [SUN112] 25.00
____Droids / Death Star corridor [SUN113] 25.00
____Escape Pod [SUN114]......................................25.00
____Luke / R2 / Death Star battle [SUN115] 25.00

Notecards

Drawing Board Greeting Cards, Inc.
____C-3PO and R2-D2, box of 10 with envelopes
[PPN01]..17.00
____C-3PO, Chewbacca, and Darth Vader, assorted box of
12 [PPN02] 18.00
____Ewoks, 4 assorted designs [PPN03]....................4.00
____Hildebrandt Art, box of 10 with envelopes
[PPN04]..18.00
____R2-D2 fold covers, box of 12 [PPN05] 23.00

Nutcrackers

Steinbach
____Darth Vader, limited to 2,000 [NTC01].............375.00
____Darth Vader, limited to 7,500 pieces
[NTC02] 250.00

Oil Lamps

Lamplight Farms Inc.
____Star Wars oil lamp, base shows drawings of Darth
Vader, R2-D2, C-3PO; originally shipped with fuel,
wick, and wax seal [OLM01] 85.00

Ornaments

Christopher Radko
Individually mouth-blown glass ornaments.
____C-3PO [CO01] 35.00
____C-3PO and R2-D2 [CO02]................................125.00
____Chewbacca [CO03] 35.00
____Darth Vader [CO04] 35.00
____Darth Vader on second Death Star [CO05]......100.00
____Darth Vader, lightsaber drawn [CO06]..............100.00
____Ewoks [CO07] 125.00
____Stormtrooper [CO08] 35.00
____Yoda [CO09] 40.00

Hallmark
1996
____AT-AT, Tie Fighter, X-Wing Fighter [CO10] 44.00
____Millennium Falcon [CO11] 47.00

1997
____C-3PO and R2-D2 [CO12] 27.00
____Darth Vader [CO13] 34.00
____Luke Skywalker, Bespin [CO14].........................36.00
____Yoda [CO15] 27.00

1998
____Boba Fett [CO16] 44.00
____Ewoks, set of 3 [CO17] 35.00
____Princess Leia [CO18] 24.00
____Star Wars Lunchbox [CO19] 24.00
____X-Wing Fighter [CO20] 26.00

1999
____Chewbacca [CO21] 16.00
____Darth Vader's Tie Fighter [CO22] 25.00

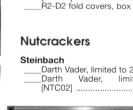

| SUN111 | SUN112 | SUN113 | SUN114 |

| SUN115 | PPN01 | PPN02 | PPN03 | PPN04 | PPN05 | NTC01 | NTC02 | OLM01 |

Ornaments

CO01 CO02 CO03 CO04 CO05 CO06 CO07 CO08 CO09

CO10 CO11 CO12 CO13 CO14 CO15 CO16 CO17 CO18

CO19 CO20 CO21 CO22 CO23 CO24 CO25 CO26

____Han Solo [CO23] 18.00
____Max Rebo Band, set of 3 [CO24].......................14.00
____Naboo Fighter [CO25] 20.00
____Queen Amidala [CO26] 15.00

2000
____Darth Maul [CO27]...14.00
____Gungan Sub [CO28].......................................10.00
____Jedi Council [CO29].......................................14.00
____Obi-Wan Kenobi [CO30]..................................14.00
____Qui-Gon Jinn [CO31].......................................10.00
____Stormtrooper [CO32]......................................15.00

2001
____Anakin Skywalker [CO33].................................15.00
____Battle of Naboo, set of 3 [CO34].....................15.00
____Empire Strikes Back Lunchbox [CO35]..............15.00
____Jar Jar Binks [CO36]......................................15.00
____Naboo Royal Starship [CO37]..........................20.00
____R2-D2 (Classic series #5) [CO38].....................15.00

2002
____Darth Vader, Final Duel [CO39] 24.00
____Death Star II [CO40]......................................24.00
____Jango Fett [CO41]..24.00
____Luke Skywalker, Final Duel [CO42]....................24.00
____Obi-Wan Kenobi [CO43]..................................24.00
____Slave I [CO44] 24.00

2003
____C-3PO (Classic series #7) [CO45] 20.00
____Clone Troopers [CO46]...................................15.00
____Padme Amidala [CO47]....................................15.00
____TIE Fighter [CO48]...25.00
____Yoda, Jedi Master [CO49]...............................15.00

2004
____Anakin Skywalker [CO50]................................15.00
____Chewbacca and C-3PO [CO51]........................15.00
____Star Destroyer and Blockade Runner [CO52] 30.00
____Star Wars: A New Hope poster [CO53] 20.00

2005
____Clone Trooper Lieutenant [CO54] 15.00
____Darth Vader Bespin gantry [CO55]....................19.00
____Jedi Starfighter [CO56]...................................28.00
____Princess Leia captive [CO57]............................15.00
____TIE Advanced & Millennium Falcon [CO58]........15.00

2006
____Anakin Skywalker and Obi-Wan Kenobi
[CO59]...28.00
____Asajj Ventress, Anakin Skywalker, and Yoda Clone
Wars miniatures [CO60].............................15.00
____Imperial AT-AT and Rebel Snowspeeder
[CO61]...28.00
____Luke Skywalker and Yoda [CO62] 15.00

Kurt S. Adler, Inc.
2-piece holiday ornament sets. 2005.
____Boba Fett / EPIV [CO63] 10.00
____C-3PO / EPI:TPM [CO64]................................10.00

CO27 CO28 CO29 CO30 CO31 CO32 CO33 CO34 CO35 CO36

CO37 CO38 CO39 CO40 CO41 CO42 CO43 CO44 CO45

CO46 CO47 CO48 CO49 CO50 CO51 CO52 CO53 CO54

CO55 CO56 CO57 CO58 CO59 CO60 CO61 CO62

CO63 CO64 CO65 CO66 CO67 CO68 CO69 CO70 CO71

CO72 CO73 CO74 CO75 CO76 CO77 CO78 CO79 CO80 CO81 CO82

____Darth Vader / EPIII:ROTS [CO65]........................10.00
____Yoda / EPII:AOTC [CO66]....................................10.00

Ceramic holiday ornaments. 2005.
____Boba Fett [CO67] 15.00
____C-3PO [CO68] 15.00
____Chewbacca [CO69] 15.00
____Darth Vader [CO70] 15.00
____R2-D2 [CO71]..15.00
____Yoda [CO72] 15.00

Ceramic holiday ornaments. 2006.
____Boba Fett [CO73] 15.00
____C-3PO [CO74] 15.00
____Chewbacca [CO75] 15.00
____Darth Vader [CO76] 15.00
____Emperor Palpatine [CO77] 15.00
____Luke Skywalker, X-Wing Pilot [CO78] 15.00
____Princess Leia [CO79] 15.00
____Queen Amidala [CO80] 15.00

____Stormtrooper [CO81] 15.00
____Yoda [CO82] 15.00

Hand crafted glass holiday ornaments. 4" helmets. 2005.
____Boba Fett [CO83] 20.00
____C-3PO [CO84] 20.00
____Darth Vader [CO85] 20.00

Hand crafted glass holiday ornaments. 5". 2005.
____Boba Fett [CO86] 25.00
____C-3PO and R2-D2 [CO87] 20.00
____Darth Vader [CO88] 25.00
____Star Wars logo [CO89] 20.00
____Yoda [CO90] 20.00

Hand crafted glass holiday ornaments. 5". 2006.
____C-3PO and R2-D2 [CO91] 15.00
____Darth Vader [CO92] 15.00
____Yoda [CO93] 15.00

Holiday ornament gift set in tin storage box. One full-figure plus two heads. 2005.
____Darth Vader / Yoda and C-3PO [CO94] 15.00
____Yoda / Darth Vader and Boba Fett [CO95] 15.00

Holiday ornament gift set. One full-figure plus two heads. 2005.
____Darth Vader / Yoda and C-3PO [CO96] 15.00
____Yoda / Darth Vader and Boba Fett [CO97] 15.00

M&M full sculpted resin ornaments. Two figures in diorama scene. 2005.
____Droids [CO98]...15.00
____Emperor and Vader [CO99] 15.00
____Luke vs. Vader [CO100] 15.00
____Movie Poster pose [CO101]..................................15.00

M&M Mpire characters. Sold boxed. 2005.
____Bobba Fett (misspelling) [CO102] 15.00
____C-3PO [CO103] 15.00

CO83 CO84 CO85 CO86 CO87 CO88 CO89 CO90 CO91 CO92 CO93

CO94 CO95 CO96 CO97 CO98 CO99 CO100 CO101

CO102 CO103 CO104 CO105 CO106 CO107 CO108 CO109

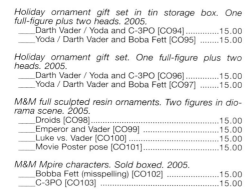

Ornaments

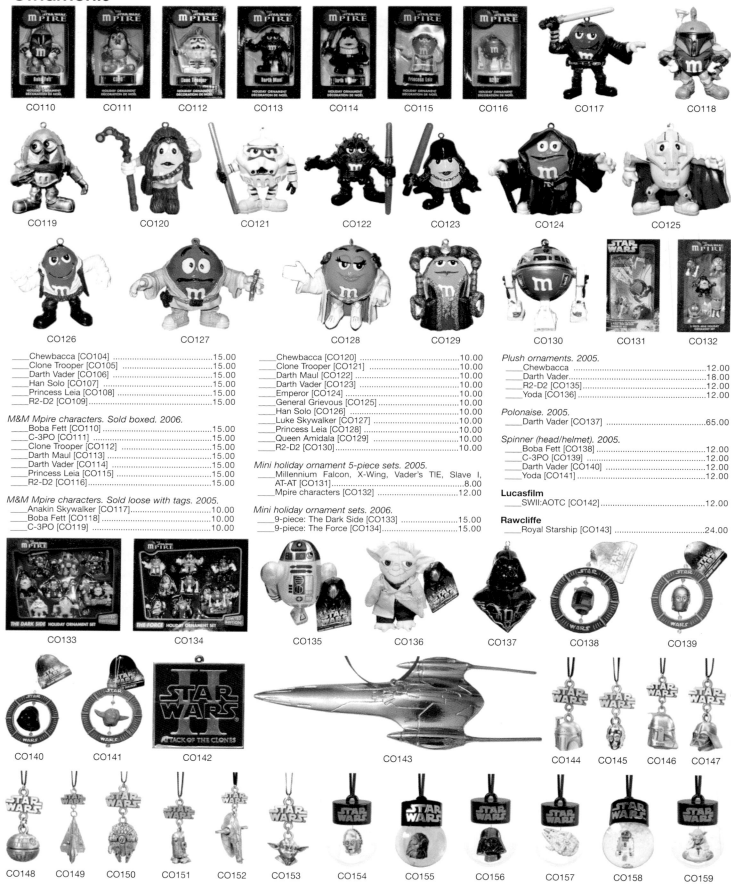

CO110   CO111   CO112   CO113   CO114   CO115   CO116   CO117   CO118

CO119   CO120   CO121   CO122   CO123   CO124   CO125

CO126   CO127   CO128   CO129   CO130   CO131   CO132

___Chewbacca [CO104]	15.00
___Clone Trooper [CO105]	15.00
___Darth Vader [CO106]	15.00
___Han Solo [CO107]	15.00
___Princess Leia [CO108]	15.00
___R2-D2 [CO109]	15.00

M&M Mpire characters. Sold boxed. 2006.
___Boba Fett [CO110]	15.00
___C-3PO [CO111]	15.00
___Clone Trooper [CO112]	15.00
___Darth Maul [CO113]	15.00
___Darth Vader [CO114]	15.00
___Princess Leia [CO115]	15.00
___R2-D2 [CO116]	15.00

M&M Mpire characters. Sold loose with tags. 2005.
___Anakin Skywalker [CO117]	10.00
___Boba Fett [CO118]	10.00
___C-3PO [CO119]	10.00

___Chewbacca [CO120]	10.00
___Clone Trooper [CO121]	10.00
___Darth Maul [CO122]	10.00
___Darth Vader [CO123]	10.00
___Emperor [CO124]	10.00
___General Grievous [CO125]	10.00
___Han Solo [CO126]	10.00
___Luke Skywalker [CO127]	10.00
___Princess Leia [CO128]	10.00
___Queen Amidala [CO129]	10.00
___R2-D2 [CO130]	10.00

Mini holiday ornament 5-piece sets. 2005.
___Millennium Falcon, X-Wing, Vader's TIE, Slave I, AT-AT [CO131]	8.00
___Mpire characters [CO132]	12.00

Mini holiday ornament sets. 2006.
___9-piece: The Dark Side [CO133]	15.00
___9-piece: The Force [CO134]	15.00

Plush ornaments. 2005.
___Chewbacca	12.00
___Darth Vader	18.00
___R2-D2 [CO135]	12.00
___Yoda [CO136]	12.00

Polonaise. 2005.
___Darth Vader [CO137]	65.00

Spinner (head/helmet). 2005.
___Boba Fett [CO138]	12.00
___C-3PO [CO139]	12.00
___Darth Vader [CO140]	12.00
___Yoda [CO141]	12.00

Lucasfilm
___SWII:AOTC [CO142]	12.00

Rawcliffe
___Royal Starship [CO143]	24.00

CO133   CO134   CO135   CO136   CO137   CO138   CO139

CO140   CO141   CO142   CO143   CO144   CO145   CO146   CO147

CO148   CO149   CO150   CO151   CO152   CO153   CO154   CO155   CO156   CO157   CO158   CO159

CO160 CO161 CO162 CO163 CO164 CO165 CO166

PAB01 - PAB28 package fronts PAB01 PAB02 PAB03 PAB04 PAB05 PAB06 PAB07 PAB08

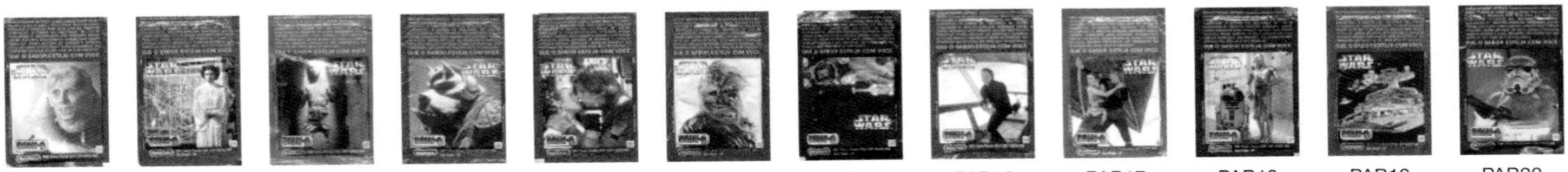

PAB09 PAB10 PAB11 PAB12 PAB13 PAB14 PAB15 PAB16 PAB17 PAB18 PAB19 PAB20

PAB21 PAB22 PAB23 PAB24 PAB25 PAB26 PAB27 PAB28 PAB29 PAB30 PAB31 PAB32

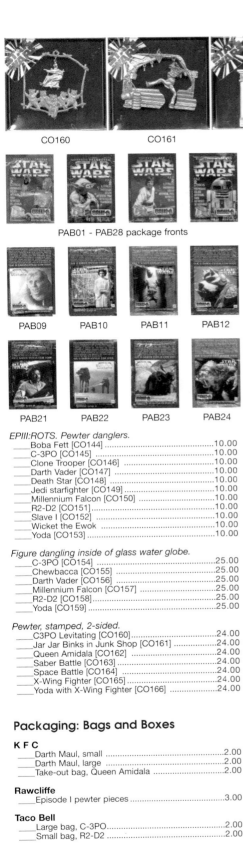

EPIII:ROTS. Pewter danglers.
____Boba Fett [CO144] 10.00
____C-3PO [CO145] 10.00
____Clone Trooper [CO146] 10.00
____Darth Vader [CO147] 10.00
____Death Star [CO148] 10.00
____Jedi starfighter [CO149] 10.00
____Millennium Falcon [CO150] 10.00
____R2-D2 [CO151] 10.00
____Slave I [CO152] 10.00
____Wicket the Ewok 10.00
____Yoda [CO153] 10.00

Figure dangling inside of glass water globe.
____C-3PO [CO154] 25.00
____Chewbacca [CO155] 25.00
____Darth Vader [CO156] 25.00
____Millennium Falcon [CO157] 25.00
____R2-D2 [CO158] 25.00
____Yoda [CO159] 25.00

Pewter, stamped, 2-sided.
____C3PO Levitating [CO160] 24.00
____Jar Jar Binks in Junk Shop [CO161] 24.00
____Queen Amidala [CO162] 24.00
____Saber Battle [CO163] 24.00
____Space Battle [CO164] 24.00
____X-Wing Fighter [CO165] 24.00
____Yoda with X-Wing Fighter [CO166] 24.00

Packaging: Bags and Boxes

K F C
____Darth Maul, small 2.00
____Darth Maul, large 2.00
____Take-out bag, Queen Amidala 2.00

Rawcliffe
____Episode I pewter pieces 3.00

Taco Bell
____Large bag, C-3PO 2.00
____Small bag, R2-D2 ....2.00

Packaging: Beverage

2005 300ml cone topped cans, color.
____Anakin Skywalker 8.00
____Queen Amidala 8.00
____R2-D2 and C-3PO 8.00
____Yoda 8.00

2005 350ml cans, color.
____Chancellor Palpatine 5.00
____Darth Vader 5.00
____General Grievous 5.00
____Han Solo and Chewbacca 5.00
____Obi-Wan Kenobi 5.00
____Princess Leia 5.00
____Stormtrooper 5.00

BelaVista
Brazil. Brin-o powdered drink mix with Star Wars scenes. 60 different scenes in set.
Packages, each
____X-Wing above Dagobah, laranja [PAB01] 3.00
____Han attacks on Cloud City, laranja [PAB02] 3.00
____Yoda trains Luke, framboesa [PAB03] 3.00
____C-3PO on Tatooine, laranja [PAB04] 3.00
____Luke in Dagobah cave, framboesa [PAB05] 3.00
____Vader confronts Leia, uva [PAB06] 3.00
____ROTJ poster lightsaber, morango [PAB07] 3.00
____Luke in Ben's hut, laranja [PAB08] 3.00
____Bib Fortuna, morango [PAB09] 3.00
____Leia during Yavin battle, framboesa [PAB10] 3.00
____Han Solo in carbonite, laranja [PAB11] 3.00
____Gamorrean Guard, framboesa [PAB12] 3.00
____Han and Leia, "The Kiss," morango [PAB13] 3.00
____Chewbacca on Hoth, framboesa [PAB14] 3.00
____X-Wings coming around Yavin, uva [PAB15] 3.00
____Luke on sail barge, morango [PAB16] 3.00
____Luke and Leia flee sail barge, laranja [PAB17] 3.00
____Droids on blockade runner, uva [PAB18] 3.00
____Falcon evades Star Destroyer, framboesa [PAB19] 3.00
____Stormtrooper on Cloud City, uva [PAB20] 3.00
____Lando in Falcon cockpit, uva [PAB21] 3.00
____AT-ATs attacking, uva [PAB22] 3.00
____Tusken on Bantha, morango [PAB23] 3.00
____Rancor, laranja [PAB24] 3.00
____Death Star chasm, uva [PAB25] 3.00
____Medical frigate, laranja [PAB26] 3.00
____ROTJ poster art, morango [PAB27] 3.00
____X-wing leaving Dagobah, laranja [PAB28] 3.00

Coca-Cola, Hong Kong
Episode III: Revenge of the Sith cans.
____Boxed collector's set of six, limited to 310 ....75.00
____Coca-Cola, Anakin 5.00
____Coca-Cola, Darth Vader 5.00
____Coca-Cola, R2-D2 and C-3PO 5.00
____Sprite, Clone Trooper 5.00
____Sprite, Obi-Wan Kenobi 5.00
____Vanilla Coke, Yoda 5.00

Coca Cola, Macau
Episode III: Revenge of the Sith cans.
____Anakin Skywalker [PAB29] 20.00
____C-3PO and R2-D2 [PAB30] 20.00
____Darth Vader [PAB31] 20.00

Fan Club
____EPI Anakin's Destiny in acrylic case, Fan Club exclusive 50.00
____EPI Soda Pop storage case, two door front, Naboo fighter handles, Fan Club exclusive 35.00

Hi-C
____Hi-C can label with droids pictured. T-shirt and cap offer [2:317] 7.00
____Hi-C cans with droids pictured. T-shirt and cap offer [2:317] 25.00

Nestlé
____Nestl'e's Quik can with pendant offer on label 20.00

Pepsi Cola
Episode I: Production samples. Tests using classic trilogy characters.
____Moutain Dew, C-3PO color 250.00
____Pepsi One, Han Solo 175.00
____Pepsi, Luke Skywalker [PAB32] 175.00

PAB33 PAB34 PAB35 PAB36

Episode I: Production samples. Tests using EPI characters.
____4-pack, color box [2:317] 250.00
____Anakin Skywalker [PAB33] 40.00
____Chancellor Valorum [PAB34] 40.00
____Obi-Wan Kenobi [PAB35] 40.00
____Padme Naberrie [PAB36] 40.00

Episode I: The Phantom Menace. 1 liter bottles.
____Diet Pepsi, Queen Amidala 4.00
____Mountain Dew, Darth Maul 4.00
____Pepsi One, EPI C-3PO 4.00
____Pepsi, Anakin Skywalker 4.00
____Storm, Battle Droid 4.00

Packaging: Beverage

Episode I: The Phantom Menace. 2 liter bottles.
____Diet Pepsi, Queen Amidala..................................4.00
____Mountain Dew, Darth Maul................................4.00
____Pepsi One, C-3PO...4.00
____Pepsi, Anakin Skywalker 4.00
____Storm, Battle Droid..4.00

PAB37   PAB38

Episode I: The Phantom Menace. 12oz. cans.
12-packs.
____Diet Pepsi, Queen Amidala [PAB37]....................4.00
____Mountain Dew, Darth Maul [2:317]...................4.00
____Pepsi One, C-3PO [2:317] 4.00
____Pepsi, Anakin Skywalker [2:318] 4.00
____Storm, Jar Jar Binks 4.00

24-packs.
____Diet Pepsi, Padme 4.00
____Mountain Dew, Darth Maul [2:317]...................4.00
____Pepsi One, C-3PO [2:317] 4.00
____Pepsi, Anakin Skywalker [2:318] 4.00
____Storm, Jar Jar Binks [2:318] 4.00

Episode I: The Phantom Menace. 12oz. cans. NY.
____#01 Pepsi, Anakin Skywalker [PAB38] 1.00
____#02 Pepsi, Sebulba...1.00
____#03 Pepsi, Qui-Gon Jinn 1.00
____#04 Pepsi, Watto..1.00
____#05 Pepsi, Jabba the Hutt 1.00
____#06 Pepsi, Senator Palpatine 1.00
____#07 Pepsi, R2-D2 ....1.00
____#08 Pepsi, Darth Sidious 1.00
____#09 Mountain Dew, Darth Maul 1.00
____#10 Mountain Dew, Jar Jar 1.00
____#11 Mountain Dew, Mace Windu 1.00
____#12 Mountain Dew, Obi-Wan Kenobi...................1.00
____#13 Mountain Dew, Captain Panaka 1.00
____#14 Mountain Dew, Rune Haako 1.00
____#15 Mountain Dew, Ric Olie 1.00
____#16 Mountain Dew, Destroyer Droid 1.00
____#17 Diet Pepsi, Queen Amidala 1.00
____#18 Diet Pepsi, Padme...1.00
____#19 Diet Pepsi, Shmi Skywalker 1.00
____#20 Diet Pepsi, Battle Droid 1.00
____#21 Pepsi One, Chancellor Valorum 1.00
____#22 Pepsi One, C-3PO..1.00
____#23 Pepsi One, Nute Gunray 1.00
____#24 Pepsi One, Boss Nass.....................................1.00

PAB39   PAB40   PAB41   PAB42   PAB43   PAB44

PAB45   PAB46   PAB47   PAB48   PAB49   PAB50

PAB51   PAB52   PAB53   PAB54   PAB55   PAB56

PAB57   PAB58   PAB59   PAB60   PAB61   PAB62

Episode I: The Phantom Menace. 12oz. cans.
____#1 Pepsi, Anakin Skywalker [PAB39] 1.00
____#2 Pepsi, Sebulba [PAB40]...................................1.00
____#3 Pepsi, Qui-Gon Jinn [PAB41] 1.00
____#4 Pepsi, Watto [PAB42].....................................1.00
____#5 Pepsi, Jabba the Hutt [PAB43] 1.00
____#6 Pepsi, Senator Palpatine [PAB44] 1.00
____#7 Pepsi, R2-D2 [PAB45].....................................1.00
____#8 Pepsi, Darth Sidious [PAB46] 1.00
____#9 Mountain Dew, Darth Maul [PAB47] 1.00
____#10 Mountain Dew, Jar Jar [PAB48].....................1.00
____#11 Mountain Dew, Mace Windu [PAB49] 1.00
____#12 Mountain Dew, Obi-Wan Kenobi [PAB50]......1.00
____#13 Mountain Dew, Captain Panaka [PAB51] 1.00
____#14 Mountain Dew, Rune Haako [PAB52]..............1.00
____#15 Mountain Dew, Ric Olie [PAB53] 1.00
____#16 Mountain Dew, Destroyer Droid [PAB54] 1.00
____#17 Diet Pepsi, Queen Amidala [PAB55] 1.00
____#18 Diet Pepsi, Padme [PAB56]...........................1.00
____#19 Diet Pepsi, Shmi Skywalker [PAB57]..............1.00
____#20 Diet Pepsi, Battle Droid [PAB58] 1.00
____#21 Pepsi One, Chancellor Valorum [PAB59].........1.00
____#22 Pepsi One, C-3PO [PAB60] 1.00
____#23 Pepsi One, Nute Gunray [PAB61] 1.00
____#24 Pepsi One, Boss Nass [PAB62] 1.00

PAB63   PAB64   PAB65   PAB66   PAB67   PAB68

____Mountain Dew, "Gold Yoda" [PAB63] 90.00
____Pepsi One, "Gold Yoda" [PAB64].......................35.00
____Pepsi, "Destiny" [PAB65]..................................125.00
____Pepsi, "Gold Yoda" [PAB66]..............................35.00
____Storm, Jar Jar Binks [PAB67]...............................3.00
____Storm, Qui-Gon Jinn [PAB68]...............................3.00

PAB69   PAB70   PAB71   PAB72

Episode I: The Phantom Menace. 16oz. bottles. Lipton Tea; natural and flavors.
____Natural, Obi-Wan Kenobi [PAB69] 4.00
____Natural Lemon, Obi-Wan Kenobi [PAB70] 4.00
____Raspberry, Obi-Wan Kenobi [PAB71]...................4.00
____Raspberry, Watto 4.00
____Sweetened w/Lemon, Obi-Wan Kenobi.................4.00
____Sweetened, Watto [PAB72]..................................4.00

PAB73   PAB74   PAB75   PAB76   PAB77   PAB78

PAB79   PAB80   PAB81   PAB82   PAB83

Episode I: The Phantom Menace. 20oz. bottles.
____Diet Mountain Dew, Padme [PAB73] 4.00
____Diet Pepsi, Queen Amidala [PAB74].....................4.00
____Lipton Tea, Brisk Lemon, Obi-Wan Kenobi 4.00
____Lipton Tea, Brisk, Obi-Wan Kenobi [PAB75] 4.00
____Lipton Tea, Sweetened, Watto [PAB76] 4.00
____Mountain Dew, Darth Maul [PAB77].....................4.00
____Mug Root Beer, Sebulba [PAB78].........................4.00
____Orange Slice, Jar Jar Binks [PAB79] 4.00
____Pepsi One, C-3PO [PAB80]...................................4.00
____Pepsi, Anakin Skywalker [PAB81].........................4.00
____Storm, Battle Droid [PAB82] 4.00
____Wild Cherry Pepsi, Capt. Panaka [PAB83]............4.00

PAB84

Episode III: Revenge of the Sith. 2 liter bottles.
____Caffine free diet Pepsi, R2-D2 and C-3PO 3.00
____Diet Mountain Dew, clone trooper 3.00
____Diet Pepsi, Chewbacca..3.00
____Mountain Dew, General Grievous [PAB84]...........3.00
____Pepsi, Darth Vader 3.00

PAB85   PAB86   PAB87

PAB88   PAB89   PAB90

PAB91   PAB92

Episode III: Revenge of the Sith. 12oz. cans.
12-packs.
____Caffine free diet Pepsi, Yoda [PAB85] 3.00
____Diet Mountain Dew, Yoda [PAB86] 3.00
____Diet Pepsi, Yoda [PAB87] 3.00
____Mountain Dew, Yoda [PAB88]...............................3.00
____Pepsi, Yoda [PAB89] 3.00
____Sierra Mist, Yoda...3.00

24-packs.
____Diet Pepsi, Yoda [PAB90] 3.00
____Mountain Dew, Yoda [PAB91]...............................3.00
____Sierra Mist, Yoda [PAB92]...................................3.00

Star Wars Special Edition. 1 liter bottles.
____Pepsi, Darth Vader 2.00

PAB93   PAB94   PAB95   PAB96

Star Wars Special Edition. 2 liter bottles.
____Caffine Free Diet, Stormtrooper [PAB93] 4.00
____Caffine Free Pepsi, Darth Vader 2.00
____Diet Mountain Dew, AT-AT 4.00
____Diet Pepsi, Stormtrooper [PAB94] 4.00
____Mountain Dew, Millennium Falcon [PAB95] 4.00
____Pepsi, Darth Vader [PAB96] 1.00
____Pepsi, Stormtrooper 2.00

Star Wars Special Edition. 3 liter bottles.
____Diet Pepsi, Stormtrooper 4.00
____Pepsi, Darth Vader 2.00

Star Wars Special Edition. 12oz. cans.
12-packs.
____Caffine Free Diet Pepsi, Stormtrooper 4.00
____Diet Mountain Dew, Speederbikes [2:318]............4.00
____Diet Pepsi, Stormtrooper [2:318] 4.00
____Mountain Dew, Luke...4.00
____Mountain Dew, X-Wings [2:318] 4.00
____Pepsi, Darth Vader 2.00
____Pepsi, Stormtrooper 2.00
____Pepsi, Yoda...2.00

24-packs.
____Caffine Free Diet Pepsi, Stormtrooper [2:318] 4.00
____Caffine Free Pepsi, Darth Vader 2.00
____Diet Pepsi, Stormtrooper 4.00
____Mountain Dew, X-Wings [2:318] 4.00
____Pepsi, C-3PO [2:318] 2.00
____Pepsi, Darth Vader [2:318] 2.00
____Pepsi, Yoda [2:318]...2.00

PAB97   PAB98   PAB99   PAB100

PAB101   PAB102   PAB103   PAB104

____Diet Pepsi, "Gold Yoda" [PAB97] 35.00
____Diet Pepsi, R2-D2 [PAB98] 2.00
____Diet Pepsi, Stormtrooper [PAB99] 2.00
____Pepsi, Darth Vader [PAB100] 2.00
____Pepsi, SW:SE logo [PAB101] 2.00
____Pepsi, Vader's Tie fighter, production sample [PAB102] 340.00
____Pepsi, Vader's Tie fighter, production sample Death Star background [PAB103] 340.00
____Winner - Gold Yoda Redemption Can – factory sealed empty [PAB104] 65.00

PAB106   PAB107

Star Wars Special Edition. 20oz. bottles.
____Caffine Free Diet Pepsi, Stormtrooper 4.00
____Caffine Free Pepsi, Darth Vader 2.00
____Diet Pepsi, Stormtrooper [PAB106] 4.00
____Pepsi, Darth Vader [PAB107] 1.00

PAB108 PAB109 PAB110 PAB111 PAB112 PAB113

Pepsi Cola, Argentina
Episode I: The Phantom Menace 325ml cans.
____Anakin Skywalker [PAB108] 5.00
____Darth Maul [PAB109] 5.00
____Jar Jar Binks [PAB110] 5.00
____Obi-Wan Kenobi [PAB111] 5.00
____Queen Amidala [PAB112] 5.00
____Qui-Gon Jinn [PAB113]..........................5.00

PAB122 PAB123 PAB124 PAB125 PAB126

Pepsi Cola, Austria
____Anakin Skywalker, Pepsi [PAB122].................5.00
____Jar Jar Binks, Pepsi Max [PAB123] 5.00
____Queen Amidala, Diet Pepsi [PAB124]..............5.00
____Qui-Gon Jinn, Pepsi [PAB125] 5.00
____Yoda, 7-Up [PAB126] 5.00

PAB114   PAB115   PAB116   PAB117

PAB118   PAB119   PAB120   PAB121

Pepsi Cola, Australia
____Anakin Skywalker, Pepsi [PAB114].......................4.00
____C-3PO, 7-Up [PAB115].....................................4.00
____Darth Maul, Pepsi [PAB116] 4.00
____Jar Jar Binks, Pepsi Max [PAB117] 4.00
____Obi-Wan Kenobi, Pepsi [PAB118] 4.00
____Queen Amidala, Diet Pepsi [PAB119]...................4.00
____Qui-Gon Jinn, Pepsi [PAB120] 4.00
____Watto, Mountain Dew [PAB121] 4.00

PAB127   PAB128   PAB129   PAB130

PAB131   PAB132   PAB133   PAB134

Pepsi Cola, Brazil
____Anakin Skywalker, Pepsi [PAB127]...................5.00
____Darth Maul, Pepsi [PAB128] 5.00
____Jar Jar Binks, Pepsi [PAB129] 5.00
____Obi-Wan Kenobi, Pepsi [PAB130] 5.00
____Qui-Gon Jinn, Pepsi [PAB131] 5.00
____Rainha Amidala, Diet Pepsi [PAB132] 5.00
____Rainha Amidala, Pepsi [PAB133] 5.00
____Yoda, 7-Up [PAB134] 5.00

PAB135 PAB136 PAB137 PAB138 PAB139 PAB140

PAB141 PAB142 PAB143 PAB144 PAB145 PAB146

Pepsi Cola, Canada
____#1 Anakin Skywalker, Pepsi [PAB135] 1.00
____#2 Sebulba, Pepsi [PAB136].............................1.00
____#3 Qui-Gon Jinn, Pepsi [PAB137] 1.00
____#4 Watto, Pepsi [PAB138].................................1.00
____#5 Jabba, Pepsi [PAB139] 1.00
____#6 Senator Palpatine, Pepsi [PAB140] 1.00
____#7 R2-D2, Pepsi [PAB141] 1.00
____#8 Darth Sidious, Pepsi [PAB142] 1.00
____#9 Darth Maul, Mountain Dew [PAB143] 1.00
____#10 Jar Jar Binks, Mountain Dew [PAB144] 1.00
____#11 Mace Windu, Mountain Dew [PAB145] 1.00
____#12 Obi-Wan Kenobi, Mt. Dew [PAB146].............1.00
____#13 Queen Amidala, Diet Pepsi [PAB147] 1.00
____#14 Padme, Diet Pepsi [PAB148].......................1.00

PAB147   PAB148   PAB149   PAB150

PAB151   PAB152   PAB153   PAB154

____#15 Shmi Skywalker, Diet Pepsi [PAB149]............1.00
____#16 Battle Droid, Diet Pepsi [PAB150] 1.00
____#17 Chancellor Valorum, 7-Up [PAB151] 1.00
____#18 C-3PO, 7-Up [PAB152] 1.00
____#19 Nute Gunray, 7-Up [PAB153]........................1.00
____#20 Boss Nass, 7-Up [PAB154] 1.00

PAB155   PAB156   PAB157

Pepsi Cola, France
Episode I: The Phantom Menace 330ml cans.
____Anakin Skywalker [PAB155] 5.00
____Darth Maul [PAB156] 5.00
____Queen Amidala [PAB157] 5.00

PAB158   PAB159   PAB160   PAB161

PAB162 PAB163 PAB164 PAB165 PAB166

PAB167   PAB168   PAB169

Pepsi Cola, Germany
Episode I: The Phantom Menace 1.5l bottles.
____Anakin Skywalker, Pepsi [PAB158]......................3.00

Episode I: The Phantom Menace 1l bottles.
____Darth Maul, Pepsi [PAB159] 3.00
____Qui-Gon Jinn, Pepsi [PAB160] 3.00

Episode I: The Phantom Menace 2l bottles.
____Anakin Skywalker, Pepsi [PAB161]......................5.00

Episode I: The Phantom Menace 330ml cans.
____Jar Jar Binks, Pepsi Boom [PAB162] 4.00
____Qui-Gon Jinn, Pepsi [PAB163] 4.00
____Rainha Amidala, Pepsi Light [PAB164]...............4.00
____Watto, Mirando [PAB165] 4.00
____Yoda, 7-Up [PAB166] 4.00

Episode I: The Phantom Menace 500ml cans.
____Darth Maul, Pepsi [PAB167] 5.00
____R2-D2, Pepsi Max [PAB168]............................5.00

Star Wars Special Edition cans.
____Darth Vader [PAB169] 8.00

Packaging: Beverage

PAB170   PAB171   PAB172   PAB173

PAB174   PAB175   PAB176   PAB177   PAB178

Pepsi Cola, Greece
Episode I: The Phantom Menace cans.
```
____Anakin Skywalker [PAB170] ...................8.00
____C-3PO [PAB171] ...................................8.00
____Jar Jar Binks [PAB172] .........................8.00
____Obi-Wan Kenobi [PAB173] .....................8.00
____Queen Amidala [PAB174] ......................8.00
____Qui-Gon Jinn [PAB175] .........................8.00
____R2-D2 [PAB176] ..................................8.00
____Watto [PAB177] ...................................8.00
____Yoda [PAB178] ....................................8.00
```

PAB179 PAB180 PAB181 PAB182 PAB183 PAB184

PAB185   PAB186   PAB187   PAB188   PAB189

Pepsi Cola, Holland
Episode I: The Phantom Menace cans.
```
____Anakin Skywalker, Pepsi [PAB179].......................3.00
____Jar Jar Binks, Pepsi Max [PAB180] .....................3.00
____Qui-Gon Jinn, Pepsi [PAB181] ............................3.00
____R2-D2, Pepsi Max [PAB182]................................3.00
____Watto, Sisi [PAB183].........................................3.00
____Yoda, 7-Up [PAB184].........................................3.00
```

Star Wars Special Edition cans.
```
____7-Up [PAB185] ....................................8.00
____Pepsi [PAB186] ..................................8.00
____Pepsi Max [PAB187] ...........................8.00
____Slice, prizes [PAB188]........................8.00
____Slice, tickets [PAB189] .......................8.00
```

PAB190   PAB191   PAB192   PAB193   PAB194

PAB195   PAB196   PAB197

Pepsi Cola, Italy
Episode I: The Phantom Menace 330ml cans.
```
____Anakin Skywalker, Pepsi [PAB190] ...................4 . 0 0
____C-3PO, 7-Up [PAB191] ....................................4 . 0 0
____Darth Maul, Pepsi [PAB192].............................4 . 0 0
____Qui-Gon Jinn, Pepsi [PAB193].........................4 . 0 0
____R2-D2, Pepsi Max [PAB194] ............................4 . 0 0
```

Star Wars Special Edition cans.
```
____Darth Vader [PAB195] .........................8.00
____Millennium Falcon [PAB196]................8.00
____Stormtrooper [PAB197].......................8.00
```

PAB198 PAB200 PAB202 PAB204 PAB206 PAB208

PAB199 PAB201 PAB203 PAB205 PAB207 PAB209

Pepsi Cola, Japan
```
____Darth Maul, full-body top [PAB198] ...................7.00
____Darth Maul, full-body bottom [PAB199] ..............4.00
____Nute Gunray, full-body top [PAB200] ................7.00
____Nute Gunray, full-body bottom [PAB201]............4.00
____Obi-Wan Kenobi, full-body bottom [PAB202] ......4.00
____Obi-Wan Kenodi, full-body top [PAB203] ...........4.00
____Queen Amidala, full-body top [PAB204] ............7.00
____Queen Amidala, full-body bottom [PAB205] .......4.00
____R2-D2, full-body top [PAB206] ........................7.00
____R2-D2, full-body bottom [PAB207].....................4.00
____Watto, full-body top [PAB208] .........................7.00
____Watto, full-body bottom [PAB209] ....................4.00
```

2005 350ml cans, color.
```
____Luke Skywalker.....................................5.00
```

PAB210   PAB211   PAB212   PAB213

EPII:AOTC cans.
```
____Anakin Skywalker [PAB210] ................................7.00
____Clone troopers [PAB211] ...................................7.00
____Jango Fett [PAB212] ..........................................7.00
____Jedi [PAB213] ...................................................7.00
```

PAB214   PAB215   PAB216   PAB217

PAB218   PAB219   PAB220   PAB221   PAB222

PAB223 PAB224 PAB225 PAB226 PAB227 PAB228

Episode I: The Phantom Menace 350ml cans.
```
____Anakin Skywalker [PAB214] ................................6.00
____C-3PO, gold rim [PAB215] ..................................6.00
____C-3PO, gold rim, celebration 2000 [PAB216]........7.00
____Darth Maul [PAB217] .........................................6.00
____Jar Jar Binks [PAB218] ......................................6.00
____Obi-Wan Kenobi [PAB219] .................................6.00
```

```
____Queen Amidala [PAB220] ....................................6.00
____R2-D2 [PAB221] ................................................6.00
____R2-D2, gold rim [PAB222] ..................................6.00
```

Episode I: The Phantom Menace 500ml cans.
```
____Anakin Skywalker [PAB223] ................................6.00
____C-3PO, gold rim [PAB224] ..................................6.00
____C-3PO, gold rim, celebration 2000 [PAB225]........7.00
____Darth Maul [PAB226] .........................................6.00
____Queen Amidala [PAB227] ...................................6.00
____R2-D2, gold rim [PAB228] ..................................6.00
```

PAB229   PAB230   PAB231   PAB232

Pepsi Cola, Korea
Episode I: The Phantom Menace 250ml cans.
```
____Darth Maul [PAB229] .........................................4.00
____Jar Jar Binks [PAB230] ......................................4.00
____Queen Amidala [PAB231] ...................................4.00
____Qui-Gon Jinn [PAB232]........................................4.00
```

PAB233   PAB234   PAB235   PAB236

Pepsi Cola, Malaysia
Episode I: The Phantom Menace 325ml cans.
```
____Anakin Skywalker [PAB233] ................................4.00
____Darth Maul [PAB234] .........................................4.00
____Jar Jar Binks [PAB235] ......................................4.00
____Queen Amidala [PAB236] ...................................4.00
```

PAB237   PAB238   PAB239   PAB240   PAB241

PAB242 PAB243 PAB244 PAB245 PAB246 PAB247

Pepsi Cola, Mexico
Episode I: The Phantom Menace 355ml cans.
```
____Anakin Skywalker [PAB237] ................................3.00
____Darth Maul [PAB238] .........................................3.00
____Jar Jar Binks [PAB239] ......................................3.00
____Queen Amidala [PAB240] ...................................3.00
```

Star Wars Special Edition bottles.
```
____Darth Vader, Pepsi 1/2 liter [PAB241] ..................8.00
```

Star Wars Special Edition cans.
```
____Darth Vader, Pepsi [PAB242] ..............................8.00
____Millennium Falcon, 7-Up [PAB243]......................8.00
____Stormtrooper, KAS [PAB244]...............................8.00
____Stormtrooper, Orange [PAB245] ..........................8.00
____Stormtrooper, Pepsi Light [PAB246]......................8.00
____Stormtrooper, Pepsi Max [PAB247] ......................8.00
```

PAB248 PAB249 PAB250 PAB251 PAB252 PAB253

Pepsi Cola, New Zealand
```
____Anakin Skywalker, Pepsi [PAB248]......................4.00
```

____Jar Jar Binks, Pepsi Max [PAB249] 4.00
____Queen Amidala, Diet Pepsi [PAB250].................4.00
____Sebulba, Miranda [PAB251] 4.00
____Watto, Mountain Dew [PAB252] 4.00
____Yoda, 7-Up [PAB253] 4.00

PAB267   PAB268   PAB269   PAB270

PAB294 PAB295 PAB296 PAB297 PAB298 PAB299

PAB254

Pepsi Cola, Poland
Star Wars Special Edition cans.
____Darth Vader, Pepsi [PAB254] 12.00

PAB271   PAB272   PAB273   PAB274

PAB300   PAB301   PAB302   PAB303   PAB304

____#5 Darth Maul, Kas Limon [PAB271] 6.00
____#6 Obi-Wan Kenobi, Kas Narania [PAB272]..........6.00
____#7 Yoda, 7-Up [PAB273].................................6.00
____#8 Jar Jar Binks, Pepsi Boom [PAB274] 6.00

PAB255   PAB256   PAB257   PAB258

Pepsi Cola, Portugal
____Anakin Skywalker, Pepsi [PAB255].....................4.00
____C3-PO, 7-Up [PAB256] 4.00
____Qui-Gon Jinn, Pepsi [PAB257] 4.00
____Yoda, 7-Up [PAB258] 4.00

PAB275   PAB276   PAB277   PAB278   PAB279

PAB305   PAB306   PAB307   PAB308   PAB309

Pepsi Cola, UK
Episode I: The Phantom Menace 150ml cans.
____Anakin Skywalker, Pepsi [PAB294].....................3.00
____Jar Jar Binks, Pepsi Max [PAB295] 3.00
____Obi-Wan Kenobi, Diet Pepsi [PAB296].................3.00
____Queen Amidala, Diet Pepsi [PAB297] 3.00
____Qui-Gon Jinn, Pepsi [PAB298] 3.00
____R2-D2, Pepsi Max [PAB299]..............................3.00

PAB259   PAB260

Pepsi Cola, Puerto Rico
Star Wars Special Edition cans.
____R2-D2 [PAB259] 8.00
____Stormtrooper [PAB260].................................8.00

PAB280   PAB281   PAB282   PAB283   PAB284

Star Wars Special Edition cans.
____Darth Vader, Pepsi (large helmet) [PAB275] 8.00
____Darth Vader, Pepsi (small helmet) [PAB276]..........8.00
____Millennium Falcon, Pepsi [PAB277] 8.00
____Stormtrooper, Pepsi (large helmet) [PAB278]........8.00
____Stormtrooper, Pepsi (small helmet) [PAB279] 8.00
____Stormtrooper, Pepsi Free [PAB280] 8.00
____Stormtrooper, Pepsi Light (large flash)
     [PAB281] 8.00
____Stormtrooper, Pepsi Light (large helmet)
     [PAB282] 8.00
____Stormtrooper, Pepsi Light (small flash)
     [PAB283] 8.00
____Stormtrooper, Pepsi Light (small helmet)
     [PAB284] 8.00

Episode I: The Phantom Menace cans.
____Anakin Skywalker, Pepsi [PAB300].....................4.00
____C3-PO, 7-Up [PAB301].....................................4.00
____C3-PO, 7-Up Lite [PAB302] 4.00
____Jar Jar Binks, Pepsi Max [PAB303] 4.00
____Obi-Wan Kenobi, Diet Pepsi [PAB304].................4.00
____Queen Amidala, Diet Pepsi [PAB305]..................4.00
____Qui-Gon Jinn, Pepsi [PAB306] 4.00
____R2-D2, Pepsi Max [PAB307]..............................4.00
____Yoda, 7-Up [PAB308] 4.00
____Yoda, 7-Up Lite [PAB309]................................4.00

PAB261   PAB262   PAB263   PAB264   PAB265

Pepsi Cola, Singapore
____Anakin Skywalker Podrace [PAB261] 64.00
____Darth Maul [PAB262] 5.00
____Jar Jar Binks [PAB263] 5.00
____Qui-Gon Jinn [PAB264]...................................5.00

Star Wars Special Edition cans.
____Darth Vader, Pepsi 8.00
____Millennium Falcon, 7-Up [PAB265]......................8.00

PAB285   PAB286   PAB287   PAB288

Pepsi Cola, Thailand
Star Wars Special Edition cans.
____Darth Vader, Pepsi [PAB285] 12.00
____Millennium Falcon, Orange Slice [PAB286] 12.00
____Millennium Falcon, Strawberry Slice [PAB287] ..12.00
____Stormtrooper, Pepsi [PAB288] 12.00

PAB310   PAB311   PAB312   PAB313

Star Wars Special Edition bottles.
____Pepsi Max 1.5l 2.00

Star Wars Special Edition cans.
____Darth Vader, Pepsi [PAB310] 4.00
____Millennium Falcon, 7-Up [PAB311].....................4.00
____Stormtrooper, Diet Pepsi [PAB312] 4.00
____Stormtrooper, Pepsi [PAB313]..........................4.00

PAB266

Pepsi Cola, South Africa
Star Wars Special Edition cans.
____Darth Vader, Pepsi [PAB266] 12.00

Pepsi Cola, Spain
____#1 Anakin Skywalker, Pepsi [PAB267] 6.00
____#2 Qui-Gon Jinn, Pepsi [PAB268] 6.00
____#3 Reina Amidala, Diet Pepsi [PAB269] 6.00
____#4 R2-D2, Pepsi Max [PAB270] 6.00

PAB289   PAB290   PAB291   PAB292   PAB293

Pepsi Cola, Turkey
Episode I: The Phantom Menace 350ml cans.
____Anakin Skywalker [PAB289] 4.00
____C-3PO [PAB290]..4.00
____Darth Maul [PAB291] 4.00
____Jar Jar Binks [PAB292] 4.00
____Kralice Amidala [PAB293] 4.00

Red Bull, Thailand
____Anakin Skywalker 5.00
____Anakin Skywalker (lightsaber high)......................5.00
____Anakin Skywalker (lightsaber low) 5.00
____Clone Commander 5.00
____Clone Trooper 5.00
____Clone Trooper (running) 5.00
____Darth Sidious 5.00
____Darth Vader 5.00
____Darth Vader (facing left) 5.00
____Darth Vader (facing right) 5.00
____General Grievous' mask 5.00
____General Grievous (2 lightsabers) 5.00
____General Grievous (walking)...............................5.00
____Grievous' Bodyguard 5.00
____Jedi Starfighter and ARC-170s 5.00
____Jedi Starfighter under attack 5.00
____Jedi Starfighters 5.00
____Obi-Wan (starship coridor) 5.00
____Obi-Wan Kenobi 5.00
____Obi-Wan vs. Anakin 5.00
____R2-D2 and C-3PO 5.00
____Tri-Fighters 5.00
____Yoda (leaping) 5.00
____Yoda (lightsaber high) 5.00
____Yoda (lightsaber left) 5.00

Packaging: Candy

PAC01

PAC02

PAC03

PAC04

PAC05

PAC06

PAC07

PAC08

PAC09

PAC10

PAC11

PAC12

PAC13

PAC14

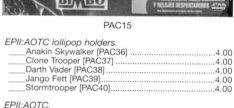
PAC15

Packaging: Candy

____TV 20-pack Episodio I [PAC01] 25.00

Gummy style candy from Spain.
____8-pack with Jar Jar header 20.00
____Anakin [PAC02] 4.00
____Darth Maul [PAC03] 4.00
____Jar Jar [PAC04] 4.00
____R2-D2 [PAC05] 4.00

Bazooka Bubblegum
____Darth Vader counter display [PAC06] 26.00

Bimbo
Bimbo Cao 3-pack, free sticker inside.
____Anakin Skywalker [PAC07] 6.00
____Battle Droid, 4-pack [PAC08] 8.00
____Darth Maul [PAC09] 6.00
____Darth Maul, 4-pack [PAC10] 8.00
____Queen Amidala [PAC11] 6.00

Bimbo Cao Tubo, free sticker inside.
____Queen Amidala [PAC12] 5.00
____Qui-Gon Jinn [PAC13] 5.00

Mi Merienda, free sticker inside.
____Darth Maul [PAC14] 5.00
____Queen Amidala [PAC15] 5.00

Cadbury
____EPI 8-pk w/masks on back [PAC16] 6.00

____EPI Choc. egg and 2 choc. bars [PAC17] 8.00
____EPI Textured milk chocolate bar [PAC18].............2.00

EPI 6 textured milk chocolate bars in cardboard lightsaber tube.
____Blue [PAC19] 15.00
____Green [PAC20] 15.00
____Red, double [PAC21] 20.00

Treat size crunchies in plastic character container.
____Darth Maul [PAC22] 8.00
____R2-D2 [PAC23] 10.00

Candy Max
Mexico. Duncan gum wrappers.
____Anakin Skywalker [PAC24] 1.00
____Darth Maul [PAC25] 1.00
____Jar Jar Binks [PAC26] 1.00
____Queen Amidala [PAC27] 1.00

Cap Candy
EPI:TPM Battle Pops with pushbutton battle action.
____Darth Maul [PAC28] 2.00
____Obi-Wan Kenobi [PAC29] 2.00
____Qui-Gon Jinn [PAC30] 2.00

____Darth Maul Light Saber [PAC31] 2.00
____Jar Jar Binks Monster Mouth candy [PAC32] 4.00
____Obi-Wan Kenobi Lightsaber [PAC33] 2.00

EPI:TPM Spin Pops with motorized dueling action.
____Darth Maul[PAC34] 3.00
____Qui-Gon Jinn [PAC35].......................................3.00

EPII:AOTC lollipop holders.
____Anakin Skywalker [PAC36] 4.00
____Clone Trooper [PAC37] 4.00
____Darth Vader [PAC38] 4.00
____Jango Fett [PAC39] 4.00
____Stormtrooper [PAC40].......................................4.00

EPII:AOTC.
____Count Dooku Lightsaber Candy [PAC41]..............5.00
____R2-D2 Galaxy Dipper [PAC42] 3.00

EPIII:ROTS lollipop holders.
____Chewbacca [PAC43] 3.00
____Darth Vader [PAC44] 3.00
____Yoda [PAC45] 3.00

EPIII:ROTS Spliquid in light-up sabers.
____Blue [PAC46] 3.00
____Red [PAC47] 3.00

EPIII:ROTS Spin pops with motorized action.
____Chewbacca [PAC48] 6.00
____Darth Vader [PAC49] 6.00

Film Action Container filled with Tart n'Tinys.
____Anakin Skywalker [PAC50] 2.00
____Darth Sidious [PAC51] 2.00
____Jar Jar Binks [PAC52] 2.00
____Queen Amidala [PAC53] 2.00
____R2-D2 [PAC54] 2.00

Chupa Chups
____Laser-pop, light-up [PAC55] 4.00

PAC16

PAC17

PAC18 wrapped and each chocolate pattern produced

PAC22

PAC23

PAC24

PAC25

PAC26

PAC27

PAC28   PAC29   PAC30

PAC19 - PAC21

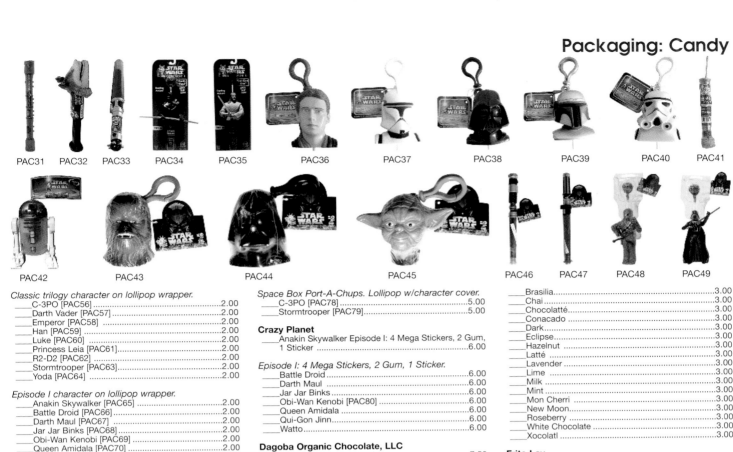

PAC31 PAC32 PAC33 PAC34 PAC35 PAC36 PAC37 PAC38 PAC39 PAC40 PAC41

PAC42 PAC43 PAC44 PAC45 PAC46 PAC47 PAC48 PAC49

Classic trilogy character on lollipop wrapper.
____C-3PO [PAC56] 2.00
____Darth Vader [PAC57] 2.00
____Emperor [PAC58] 2.00
____Han [PAC59] 2.00
____Luke [PAC60] 2.00
____Princess Leia [PAC61] 2.00
____R2-D2 [PAC62] 2.00
____Stormtrooper [PAC63] 2.00
____Yoda [PAC64] 2.00

Episode I character on lollipop wrapper.
____Anakin Skywalker [PAC65] 2.00
____Battle Droid [PAC66] 2.00
____Darth Maul [PAC67] 2.00
____Jar Jar Binks [PAC68] 2.00
____Obi-Wan Kenobi [PAC69] 2.00
____Queen Amidala [PAC70] 2.00
____Qui-Gon Jinn [PAC71] 2.00
____Watto [PAC72] 2.00

Episode I tin canisters, originally contained 8 fantasy ball lollipops.
____Anakin Skywalker [PAC73] 5.00
____Jedi Heroes [PAC74] 5.00
____Queen Amidala [PAC75] 5.00
____Sith Villains [PAC76] 5.00

Pop Machines.
____C-3PO and Stormtrooper 5.00
____Darth Vader [PAC77] 5.00
____Darth Vader and Luke 5.00
____Han and Chewbacca 5.00

Space Box Port-A-Chups. Lollipop w/character cover.
____C-3PO [PAC78] 5.00
____Stormtrooper [PAC79] 5.00

Crazy Planet
____Anakin Skywalker Episode I: 4 Mega Stickers, 2 Gum, 1 Sticker 6.00

Episode I: 4 Mega Stickers, 2 Gum, 1 Sticker.
____Battle Droid 6.00
____Darth Maul 6.00
____Jar Jar Binks 6.00
____Obi-Wan Kenobi [PAC80] 6.00
____Queen Amidala 6.00
____Qui-Gon Jinn 6.00
____Watto 6.00

Dagoba Organic Chocolate, LLC
____Cacao powder 8oz. canister 7.50
____Choco drops 8oz. pouch 7.15
____Chocolate syrup 64 oz. ....N/V
____Hot chocolate 8oz. canister 7.50
____Prime materia 1 lbs. packet 15.00

Boxed sets.
____Gift Box: 12 bars, Hot Chocolate, Cacao Powder 55.00
____Sampler: 4 Bars, Choco Drops, Hot Chocolate, Cacao Powder 35.00

Chocolate bars, 2oz.
____12-bar gift box 36.00
____4-bar gift pack 12.00

____Brasilia...3.00
____Chai...3.00
____Chocolatté...3.00
____Conacado..3.00
____Dark...3.00
____Eclipse...3.00
____Hazelnut..3.00
____Latté..3.00
____Lavender...3.00
____Lime...3.00
____Milk..3.00
____Mint...3.00
____Mon Cherri..3.00
____New Moon...3.00
____Roseberry..3.00
____White Chocolate....................................3.00
____Xocolatl...3.00

Frito Lay
____Cracker Jack tin, oversized replica of Pepsi can #1, Anakin Skywalker, TRU exclusive [PAC81]...........8.00

Harmony Foods
____Darth Vader jelly tin [PAC82].................6.00
____The droids jelly tin [PAC83]...................6.00

Hersheys
ESB Photo on 6-pack of candy.
____Kit Kat (Luke on Tauntaun) [PAC84]....................16.00
____Milk Chocolate (C-3PO & R2-D2) [PAC85] 16.00
____Milk Chocolate with Almonds (Chewbacca) [PAC86]..16.00
____Mr. Goodbar (Darth Vader) [PAC87]....................16.00

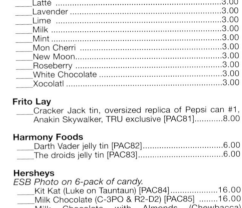

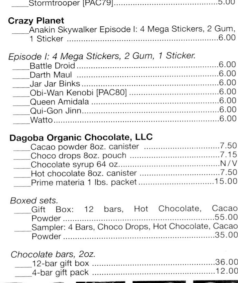

PAC50 PAC51 PAC52 PAC53 PAC54 PAC55 PAC56 PAC57 PAC58 PAC59 PAC60 PAC61 PAC62

PAC63 PAC64 PAC65 PAC66 PAC67 PAC68 PAC69 PAC70 PAC71 PAC72 PAC73 PAC74 PAC75 PAC76

PAC77 PAC78 PAC79 PAC80 PAC81 PAC82 PAC83 PAC84 PAC85 PAC86 PAC87

PAC88

PAC89

PAC90

PAC91

PAC92

PAC93

PAC94

PAC95

PAC96

PAC97

PAC98

PAC99

PAC100

PAC101

PAC102

PAC103

PAC104

PAC105

PAC106

PAC107

PAC108

PAC109

PAC110

PAC111

PAC112

PAC113 PAC114 PAC115

____Reese's Crunchy Peanut Butter Cups (Darth Vader) [PAC88]....16.00
____Reese's Peanut Butter Cups (Boba Fett) [PAC89]....16.00
____Rollo (Luke on Tauntaun) [PAC90]....16.00
____Whatchamacallit (Darth Vader) [PAC91]....16.00

Hollywood Chewing Gum
____Blanchur [PAC92]....1.00
____Green Fresh [PAC93]....1.00
____Ice Fresh [PAC94]....1.00
____Parfum [PAC95]....1.00
____Power Mint [PAC96]....1.00

Kinnerton Confectionery
____Box of 9 Chocolate Shapes [PAC97]....14.00
____Darth Vader milk chocolate lollipop, foiled [PAC98]....5.00
____R2-D2 shaped tin [PAC99]....9.00

Fruit flavoured shaped jellies in cardboard EPI character package.
____Darth Maul [PAC100]....4.00
____Jar Jar Binks [PAC101]....4.00

Hexagon tin containers.
____Anakin Skywalker in podracer gear [PAC102]....14.00
____Darth Maul [PAC103]....14.00

Hollow chocolate eggs with Star Wars jelly shapes.
____Cut-out bookmark on box [PAC104]....17.00
____folded container [PAC105]....5.00

Jelly shapes in folded cardboard container with collectible badge premium.
____R2-D2 [PAC106]....5.00
____Stormtrooper [PAC107]....7.00

Jelly shapes in tin with decorative character bust.
____Anakin [PAC108]....5.00
____Darth Maul [PAC109]....5.00
____Darth Vader [PAC110]....5.00
____Jar Jar Binks [PAC111]....5.00
____R2-D2 [PAC112]....5.00

Masterfoods USA
3 Musketeers with glow-in the dark wrappers.
____11.00 oz (contains individual packets.)....2.00
____"What is Anakin's secret?"....0.50
____"What is Chancellor Palpatine's secret?"....0.50
____"Who's home planet is Kashyyyk?"....0.50
____"Who is a Sith Lord?"....0.50
____"Who is R2-D2's master?"....0.50
____"Who was Anakin's Jedi mentor?"....0.50
____"Who was Count Dooku's Jedi mentor?"....0.50

Lucas Crazy Hair.
____Darth Vader....4.00
____R2D-Goo [PAC113]....4.00
____Wookiee Kiss [PAC114]....4.00

M-azing crunchy with glow-in the dark wrappers.
____11.10 oz (contains individual packets.)....2.00
____"What is Anakin's secret?"....0.50
____"Who is a Sith Lord?"....0.50
____"Who is R2-D2's master?"....0.50
____"Who was Anakin's Jedi mentor?"....0.50

M-azing peanut butter with glow-in the dark wrappers.
____11.10 oz (contains individual packets.)....2.00
____"Who is a Sith Lord?"....0.50
____"Who is R2-D2's master?"....0.50
____"Who was Anakin's Jedi mentor?"....0.50

M&M Minis.
____0.53oz. green tube....2.00
____1.08oz. black tube [PAC115]....3.00
____1.94oz. black tube....3.00
____1.94oz. gold tube....3.00
____1.94oz. green tube....3.00

M&M Peanut with glow-in the dark wrappers.
____11.23 oz (contains individual packets.)....2.00
____"What is Anakin's secret?"....0.50
____"Who's home planet is Kashyyyk?"....0.50
____"Who is a Sith Lord?"....0.50
____"Who is R2-D2's master?"....0.50
____"Who was Anakin's Jedi mentor?"....0.50
____"Who was Count Dooku's Jedi mentor?"....0.50

M&M Plain with glow-in the dark wrappers.
____11.17 oz (contains individual packets.)....2.00
____"What is Anakin's secret?"....0.50
____"Who's home planet is Kashyyyk?"....0.50
____"Who is a Sith Lord?"....0.50
____"Who is R2-D2's master?"....0.50
____"Who was Anakin's Jedi mentor?"....0.50
____"Who was Count Dooku's Jedi mentor?"....0.50

M&Ms collectible packaging.
1 – 6: Jedi Mix, 3.14oz.
____1: Anakin Skywalker....0.25
____2: C-3PO and R2-D2....0.25
____3: Obi-Wan Kenobi....0.25
____4: Han Solo....0.25
____5: Queen Amidala....0.25
____6: Mace Windu....0.25
7 – 12: peanut Jedi mix, 3.27oz.
____7: Anakin Skywalker....0.25
____8: C-3PO and R2-D2....0.25
____9: Obi-Wan Kenobi....0.25
____10: Luke Skywalker....0.25
____11: Chewbacca....0.25
____12: Princess Leia....0.25

PAC116

PAC117

PAC118

PAC119

PAC120

PAC121

PAC122

PAC123

PAC124

PAC125

PAC126

PAC127

PAC128

13 – 18: Darth mix, 3.14oz.
____13: Darth Vader 0.25
____14: Darth Sidious 0.25
____15: General Grievous 0.25
____16: Darth Maul 0.25
____17: Boba Fett 0.25
____18: Clone Trooper 0.25
19 – 24: peanut Darth mix, 3.27oz.
____19: Darth Vader 0.25
____20: Darth Sidious 0.25
____21: General Grievous 0.25
____22: Darth Maul 0.25
____23: Boba Fett 0.25
____24: Count Dooku....0.25
25 – 28: Jedi mix, 14oz.
____25: Princess Leia [PAC116] 0.25
____26: Obi-Wan Kenobi [PAC117] 2.00
____27: C-3PO [PAC118]....2.00
____28: Luke Skywalker [PAC119]....2.00
29 – 32: peanut Jedi mix, 14oz.
____29: Queen Amidala 0.25
____30: Chewbacca....0.25
____31: Han Solo 0.25
____32: Anakin Skywalker 0.25
33 – 36: dark chocolate Darth mix, 14oz.
____33: Clone Trooper [PAC120] 2.00
____34: Darth Maul [PAC121] 2.00
____35: Darth Vader [PAC122]....2.00
____36: Darth Tyrannus [PAC123] 2.00
37 – 40: peanut dark chocolate Darth mix, 14oz.
____37: Darth Vader....0.25
____38: Darth Tyrannus 0.25
____39: General Grievous 0.25
____40: Boba Fett [PAC124] 2.00
41 – 44: Jedi mix, 21.3oz.
____41: Princess Leia 0.25
____42: Obi-Wan Kenobi 0.25
____43: C-3PO....0.25
____44: Luke Skywalker....0.25
45 – 48: peanut Jedi mix, 21.3oz.
____45: Queen Amidala 0.25
____46: Chewbacca....0.25
____47: Han Solo 0.25
____48: Anakin Skywalker 0.25
49 – 52: dark chocolate Darth mix, 21.3oz.
____49: Clone Trooper 0.25
____50: Darth Maul 0.25
____51: Darth Vader....0.25
____52: Darth Tyrannus 0.25
53 – 56: peanut dark chocolate Darth mix, 21.3oz.
____53: Darth Vader....0.25
____54: Darth Tyrannus 0.25
____55: General Grievous 0.25
____56: Boba Fett 0.25
57 – 60: Jedi mix, 5.3oz.
____57: Princess Leia [PAC125] 0.25
____58: Obi-Wan Kenobi [PAC126] 0.25
____59: C-3PO [PAC127]....0.25
____60: Luke Skywalker [PAC128]....0.25
61 – 64: peanut Jedi mix, 5.3oz.
____61: Queen Amidala 0.25
____62: Chewbacca....0.25
____63: Han Solo 0.25
____64: Anakin Skywalker 0.25
65 – 68: dark chocolate Darth mix, 5.3oz.
____65: Clone Trooper 0.25
____66: Darth Maul 0.25
____67: Darth Vader....0.25
____68: Darth Tyrannus 0.25
69 – 72: peanut dark chocolate Darth mix, 5.3oz.
____69: Darth Vader....0.25
____70: Darth Tyrannus 0.25
____71: General Grievous 0.25
____72: Boba Fett 0.25

____Dark chocolate 52.0 oz. [PAC129] 6.00

Milky Way with glow-in the dark wrappers.
____11.24 oz (contains individual packets.) 2.00
____"What is Anakin's secret?" 0.50
____"Who is R2-D2's master?" 0.50
____"Who loses the battle on Mustafar?" 0.50
____"Whose home planet is Dagobah?" 0.50

Skittles collectible packaging.
1 – 4: original flavors, 2.17oz.
____1: Anakin Skywalker [PAC130] 0.25
____2: Obi-Wan Kenobi [PAC131] 0.25
____3: Darth Vader [PAC132]....0.25
____4: General Grevious [PAC133] 0.25
5 – 8: tropical flavors, 2.17oz.
____5: Darth Maul [PAC134] 0.25
____6: Darth Sidious [PAC135] 0.25
____7: Jabba the Hutt [PAC136] 0.25
____8: Queen Amidala [PAC137] 0.25
9 – 12: wild berry flavors, 2.17oz.
____9: Chewbacca [PAC138]....0.25
____10: Yoda [PAC139] 0.25
____11: Boba Fett [PAC140] 0.25
____12: C-3PO and R2-D2 [PAC141] 0.25
13 – 16: sour flavors, 1.8oz.
____13: Han Solo [PAC142]....0.25
____14: Princess Leia [PAC143] 0.25
____15: Luke Skywalker [PAC144]....0.25
____16: Darth Vader [PAC145]....0.25
17 – 20: original flavors, 4oz.
____17: Anakin Skywalker [PAC146] 0.25
____18: Obi-Wan Kenobi [PAC147] 0.25

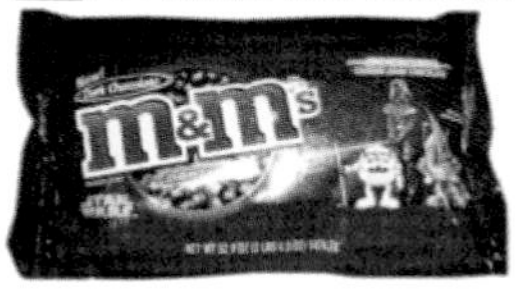

PAC129

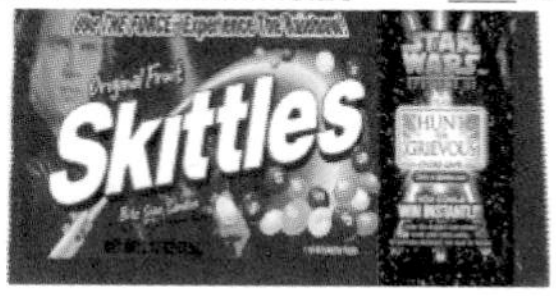

PAC130

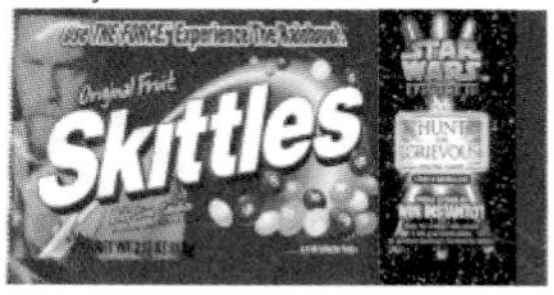

PAC131

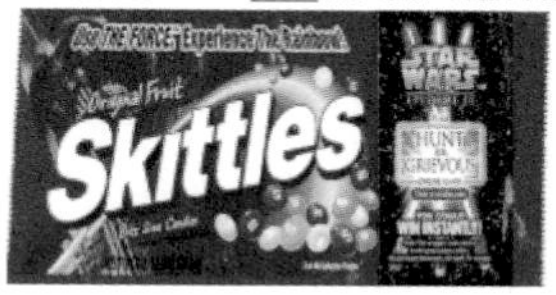

PAC132

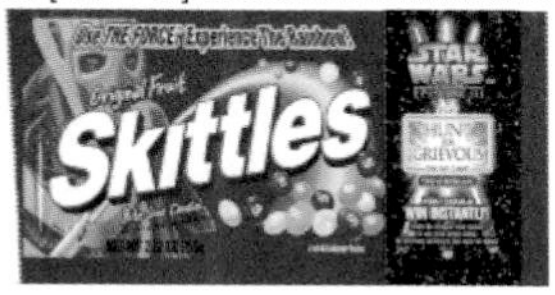

PAC133

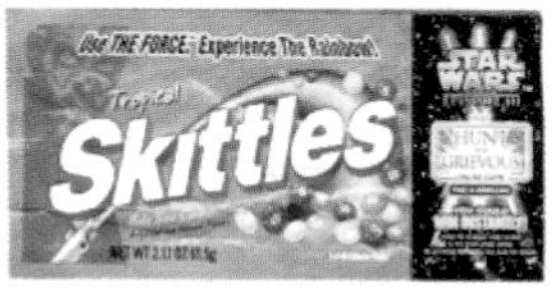

PAC134

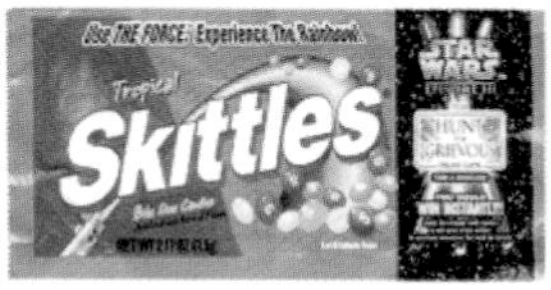

PAC135

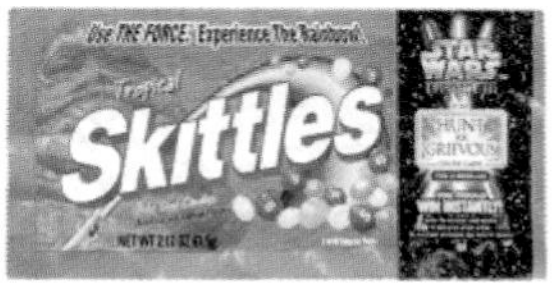

PAC136

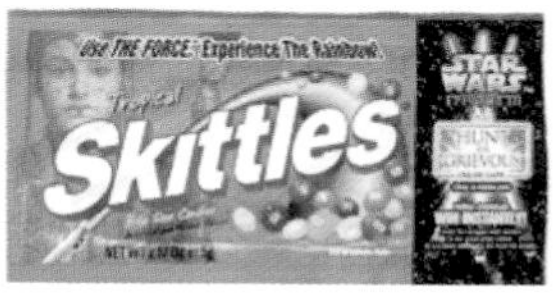

PAC137

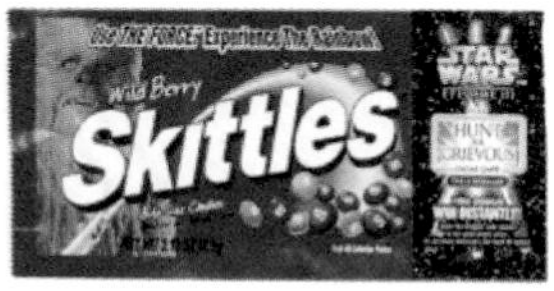

PAC138

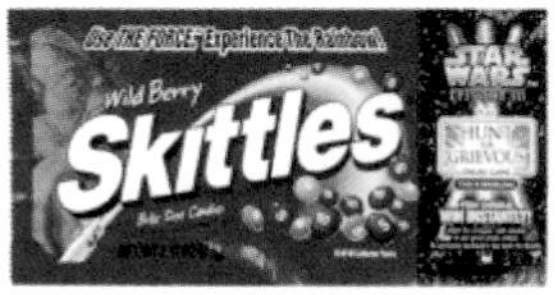

PAC139

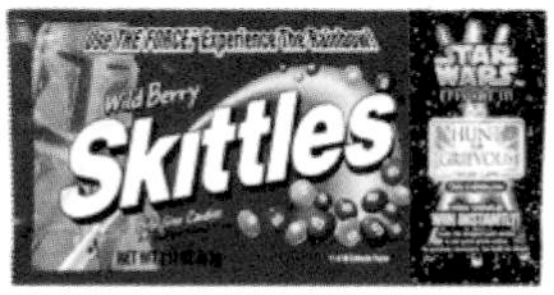

PAC140

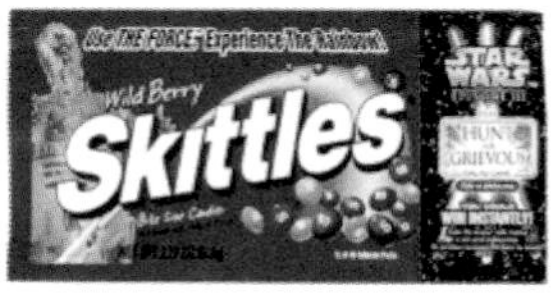

PAC141

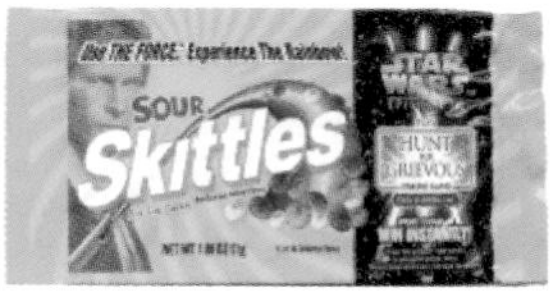

PAC142

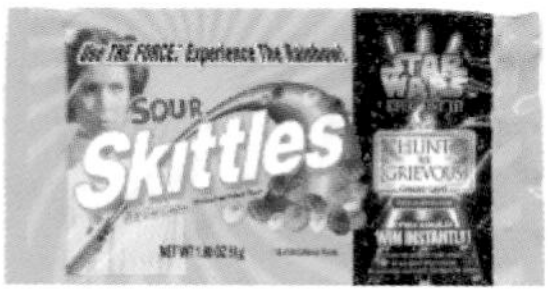

PAC143

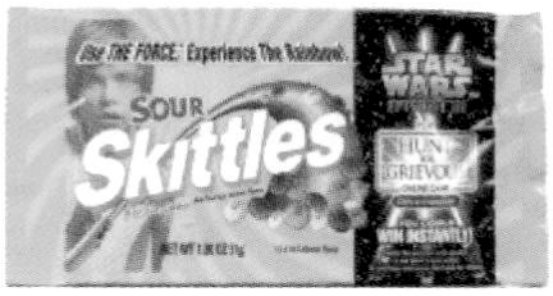

PAC144

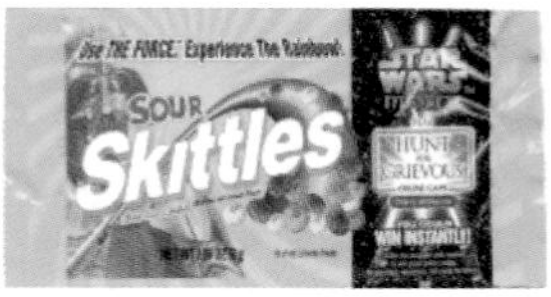

PAC145

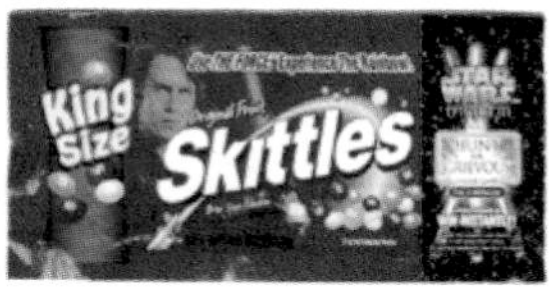

PAC146

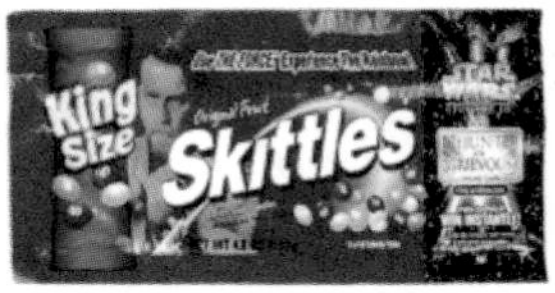

PAC147

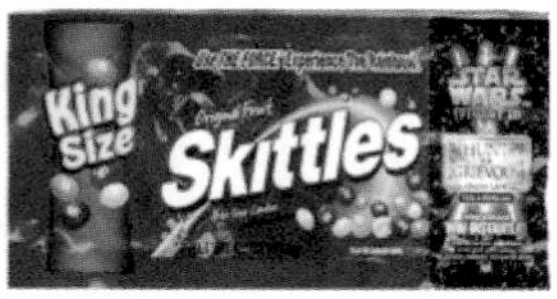

PAC148

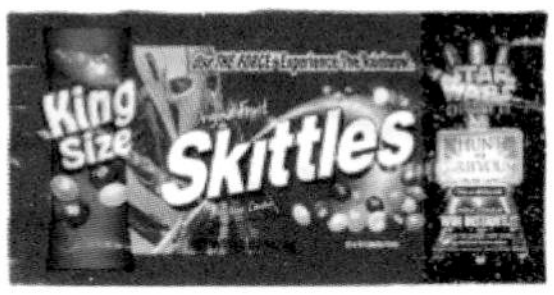

PAC149

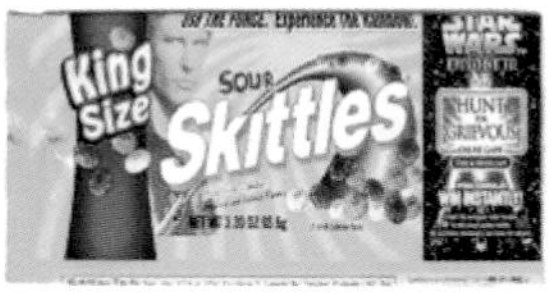

PAC150

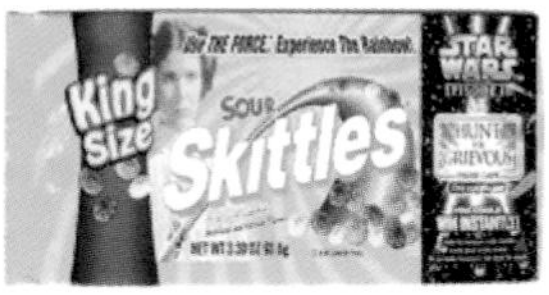

PAC151

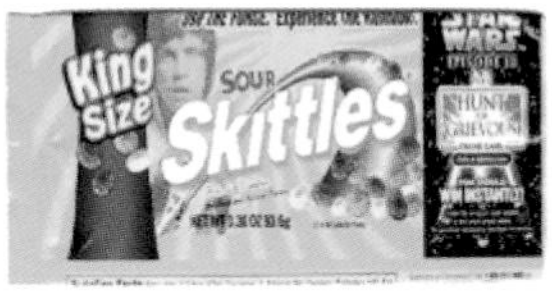

PAC152

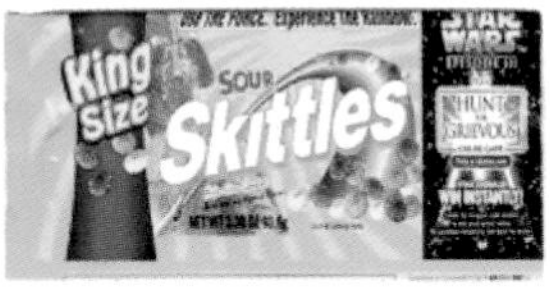

PAC153

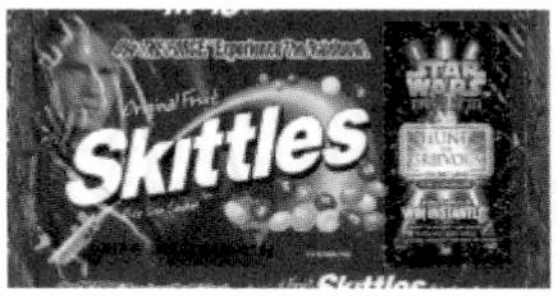

PAC154

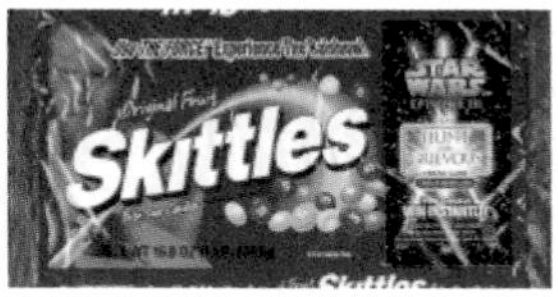

PAC155

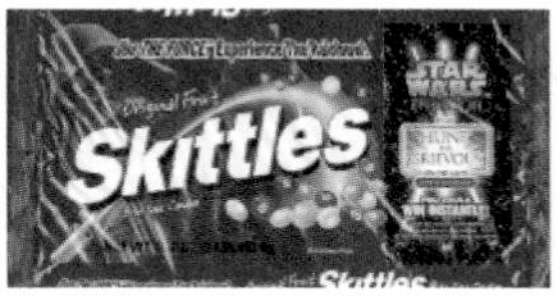

PAC156

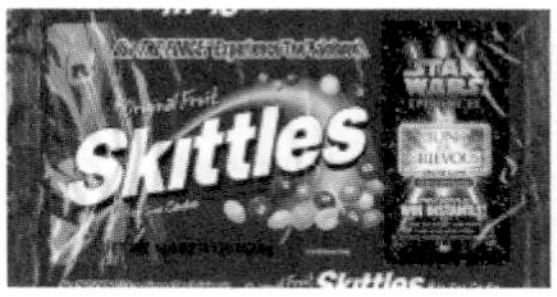

PAC157

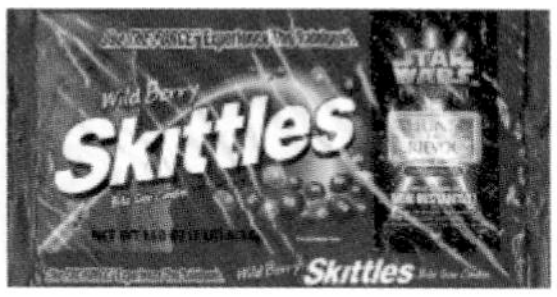

PAC158

Packaging: Candy

PAC159

PAC160

PAC161

PAC162

PAC163

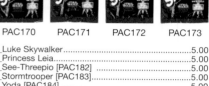

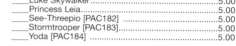

PAC164

PAC165

PAC166

PAC167

PAC168

PAC169

PAC170

PAC171

PAC172

PAC173

PAC174

PAC175

PAC176

PAC177

____19: Darth Vader [PAC148]..0.25
____20: General Grevious [PAC149] 0.25

<u>*21 – 24: sour flavors, 3.3oz.*</u>

____21: Han Solo [PAC150]..0.25
____22: Princess Leia [PAC151] 0.25
____23: Luke Skywalker [PAC152]..............................0.25
____24: Darth Vader [PAC153].....................................0.25

<u>*25 – 28: original flavors, 16oz.*</u>

____25: Anakin Skywalker [PAC154] 1.00
____26: Obi-Wan Kenobi [PAC155] 1.00
____27: Darth Vader [PAC156]......................................1.00
____28: General Grevious [PAC157] 1.00

<u>*29 – 32: wild berry flavors, 16oz.*</u>

____29: Chewbacca [PAC158].......................................1.00
____30: Yoda [PAC159] 1.00
____31: Boba Fett [PAC160] 1.00
____32: C-3PO and R2-D2 [PAC161] 1.00

<u>*33 – 36: sour flavors, 13.3oz.*</u>

____33: Han Solo [PAC162]..0.25
____34: Princess Leia [PAC163] 0.25
____35: Luke Skywalker [PAC164]...............................0.25
____36: Darth Vader [PAC165]......................................0.25

<u>*37 – 40: original flavors, 6.75oz.*</u>

____37: Anakin Skywalker [PAC166] 0.25
____38: Obi-Wan Kenobi [PAC167] 0.25
____39: Darth Vader [PAC168]......................................0.25
____40: General Grevious [PAC169] 0.25

<u>*41 – 44: wild berry flavors, 6.75oz.*</u>

____41: Chewbacca [PAC170].......................................0.25
____42: Yoda [PAC171] 0.25
____43: Boba Fett [PAC172] 0.25
____44: C-3PO and R2-D2 [PAC173] 0.25

<u>*45 – 48: sour flavors, 5.35oz.*</u>

____45: Han Solo [PAC174] 2.00
____46: Princess Leia [PAC175] 2.00
____47: Luke Skywalker [PAC176]...............................2.00
____48: Darth Vader [PAC177]......................................2.00

Skittles with glow-in the dark wrappers.

____13.30 oz (contains individual packets.) 2.00
____"What is Anakin's secret?" 0.50
____"Who's home planet is Kashyyyk?" 0.50
____"Who is a Sith Lord?" 0.50
____"Who is R2-D2's master?" 0.50
____"Who was Anakin's Jedi mentor?" 0.50
____"Who was Count Dooku's Jedi mentor?" 0.50

Snickers with glow-in the dark wrappers.

____11.18 oz (contains individual packets.) 2.00
____"What is Anakin's secret?" 0.50
____"Who's home planet is Kashyyyk?" 0.50
____"Who is a Sith Lord?" 0.50
____"Who is R2-D2's master?" 0.50
____"Who loses the battle on Mustafar?" 0.50
____"Who was Count Dooku's Jedi mentor?" 0.50
____"Whose home planet is Dagobah?" 0.50

Starburst with glow-in the dark wrappers.

____13.30 oz (contains individual packets.) 2.00
____"What is Anakin's secret?" 0.50
____"Who is a Sith Lord?" 0.50
____"Who is R2-D2's master?" 0.50

Twix with glow-in the dark wrappers.

____11.24 oz (contains individual packets.) 2.00
____"Who is a Sith Lord?" 0.50
____"Who is R2-D2's master?" 0.50
____"Who was Anakin's Jedi mentor?" 0.50

Valentines Day box.

____Darth Vader / Anakin Skywalker, "I Am Your..." / "Valentine"..6.00

Meiji

____Star Wars movie candy [PAC178] 32.00
____The Phantom Menace, with bonus trading card [PAC179]..11.00

Nestlé

____Nesquik chocolate [PAC180] 4.00
____Nestlés chocolate candybar wrapper with pendant offer 12.00

Pepsico Snacks

Pegalactico.

____Artoo-Detoo 5.00
____Chewbacca 5.00
____Darth Vader [PAC181] 5.00
____Ewok 5.00
____Han Solo 5.00
____Luke Skywalker...5.00
____Princess Leia..5.00
____See-Threepio [PAC182] 5.00
____Stormtrooper [PAC183]...5.00
____Yoda [PAC184] 5.00

Pez Candy, Inc.

____Pez Display Box 14.00

Ricolino

Candy Max.

____Anakin Skywalker [PAC185] 2.00
____Darth Maul [PAC186] 2.00
____Jar Jar Binks [PAC187]..2.00
____Queen Amidala [PAC188] 2.00

Rowntree

____Fruit Lolly 4-pack, Star Wars tatoos in box [PAC189] 9.00

Sellos

____Candy-filled rubber stamper [PAC190].................2.00

Sonrics

____Bombiux Death Star shaped candy holders, from Star Wars Special Edition [PAC191].............................3.00

Fantasy Ball wrappers. Classic trilogy character on lollipop wrapper.

____C-3PO 2.00
____Darth Vader 2.00
____Emperor 2.00
____Han 2.00
____Luke 2.00
____Princess Leia..2.00
____R2-D2 ....2.00
____Stormtrooper..2.00
____Yoda 2.00

Landia. Star Wars Special Edition. Opened box makes playscenes. 2 boxes per scene.

____Death Star #1 ....3.00
____Death Star #2 ....3.00
____Sarlaac #1 ....3.00
____Sarlaac #2 ....3.00
____Tatooine #1 ....3.00
____Tatooine #2 ....3.00

Tambola

____Chocolate egg wrapper, X-Wing fighter [PAC192] 1.00

Topps

Boxes, empty: sculpted candy dispensers.

____ESB I [1:270] 3.00
____ESB II 3.00
____ROTJ 2.00

Boxes, empty: wax packs.

____SW series 1 ....20.00
____SW series 2 ....18.00
____SW series 3 [3:314] 18.00
____SW series 4 ....18.00

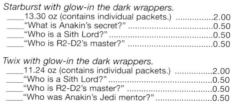

PAC178

PAC179

PAC180

PAC181

PAC182

PAC183

PAC184

PAC185

PAC186

PAC187

PAC188

PAC189

PAC190

PAC191

PAC192

PAC193 PAC194 PAC195 PAC196 PAC197 PAC198 PAC199 PAC200 PAC201

PAC202 PAC203 PAC204 PAC205 PAC206 PAC207 PAC208

____SW series 5 [3:314] 18.00
____ESB series 1 ....4.00
____ESB series 2 [3:314] 4.00
____ESB series 3 [3:314] 4.00
____ROTJ series 1 ....4.00
____ROTJ series 2 ....4.00

Candy dispensers, sculpted.
<u>*ESB Series 1.*</u>
____Boba Fett [PAC193] 2.00
____C-3PO [PAC194] 2.00
____Chewbacca [PAC195] 2.00
____Darth Vader [PAC196] 2.00
____Stormtrooper [PAC197] 2.00
<u>*ESB series 2.*</u>
____2-1B [PAC198] 2.00
____Bossk [PAC199] 2.00
____Tauntaun [PAC200] 2.00
____Yoda [PAC201] 2.00
<u>*ROTJ series 1.*</u>
____Admiral Ackbar [PAC202] 2.00
____Baby Ewok [PAC203] 2.00
____Darth Vader [PAC204] 2.00
____Ewok [PAC205] 2.00
____Jabba the Hutt [PAC206] 2.00
____Sy Snootles [PAC207] 2.00

Candy dispensers, sculpted with exclusive trading card.
____4-pack on header card [PAC208] 18.00
____C-3PO [2:323} 3.00
____Chewbacca [2:323} 3.00
____Darth Vader [2:323} 3.00
____Yoda [2:323} 3.00

Wax packs, sealed.
____SW series 1 [3:314] 12.00
____SW series 2 [3:314] 7.00
____SW series 3 [3:314] 7.00
____SW series 4 [3:314] 7.00
____SW series 5 [3:314] 5.00
____ESB series 1 [3:314] 3.00
____ESB series 2 [3:314] 3.00
____ESB series 3 [3:314] 3.00
____ROTJ series 1 [3:314] 3.00
____ROTJ series 2 [3:314] 3.00

Wax pack wrappers.
____SW series 1 [3:314] 5.00
____SW series 2 [3:314] 5.00
____SW series 3 [3:314] 4.00
____SW series 4 [3:314] 4.00
____SW series 5 [3:314] 4.00
____ESB series 1 [3:314] 2.00
____ESB series 2 [3:314] 2.00
____ESB series 3 [3:314] 2.00
____ROTJ series 1: Darth Vader [3:314] 2.00
____ROTJ series 1: Jabba the Hutt [3:314] 2.00
____ROTJ series 1: Luke Skywalker [3:314] 2.00
____ROTJ series 1: Wicket the Ewok [3:314] 2.00
____ROTJ series 2: Baby Ewok [3:314] 2.00
____ROTJ series 2: C-3PO [3:314] 2.00
____ROTJ series 2: Lando as Skiff Guard [3:314] 2.00
____ROTJ series 2: Princess Leia [3:314] 2.00

Packaging: Cards

Beckett Associates
____Trading Card Game 3 Star Wars Packs (random) 5.00

Decipher
Jedi Knights CCG.
<u>*Base set 11 card boosters.*</u>
____Darth Vader, 1st day [TR01] 7.00
____Darth Vader [TR02] 4.00
____Darth Vader, 1st day, wrapper only 2.00
____Darth Vader, wrapper only 1.00

<u>*Masters of the Force, 11 card booster.*</u>
____Palpatine, 1st day [TR03] 4.00
____Palpatine [TR04] 7.00
____Palpatine, 1st day, wrapper only 2.00
____Palpatine, wrapper only 1.00
<u>*Premiere limited edition starter decks.*</u>
____The Alliance, 1st day 18.00
____The Alliance [TR05] 15.00
____The Alliance, 1st day, box only....................5.00
____The Alliance, box only....................3.00
____The Empire, 1st day [TR06] 15.00
____The Empire [TR07] 18.00
____The Empire, 1st day, box only 5.00
____The Empire, box only 3.00
<u>*Scum and Villany, 11 card boosters.*</u>
____Boba Fett, 1st day 7.00
____Boba Fett [TR08]....................4.00
____Boba Fett, 1st day, wrapper only 2.00
____Boba Fett, wrapper only 1.00

Star Wars CCG.
____A New Hope, 5 card expansion 3.00
____Dagobah, 9 card expansion, limited [TR09] 3.00
____Hoth, 15 card expansion, limited [TR10] 3.00
____Premiere 60 card starter set [TR11] 15.00
<u>*Premiere Enhanced, 15 card booster, unlimited.*</u>
____Booster pack, sealed 4.00
____Retail display box 5.00
<u>*Premiere Enhanced, 15 card booster, unlimited with character premium card.*</u>
____Boba Fett [TR12] 16.00
____Darth Vader [TR13] 16.00
____Han Solo 16.00

TR01 TR02 TR03 TR04 TR05 TR06 TR07

TR08 TR09 TR10 TR11 TR12 TR13 TR14 TR15 TR16 TR17 TR18 TR19

TR20 TR21 TR22 TR23 TR24 TR25 TR26 TR27 TR28 TR29 TR30

Packaging: Cards

PAD01

PAD02

PAD03

PAD04

PAD05

PAD06

PAD07

PAD08

PAD09

PAD10

PAD11

PAD12

PAD13

PAD14

PAD15

PAD16

PAD17

PAD18

PAD19

PAD20

____Leia Organa 16.00
____Luke Skywalker [TR14]..16.00
____Obi-Wan Kenobi [TR15] 16.00

Rogues and Scoundrels
____Boba Fett, 11 card booster [TR16]........................4.00
____Han Solo, 11 card booster [TR17] 4.00

Young Jedi CCG.
Battle of Naboo.
____11 card booster [TR18]...4.00
____Two customized starter decks [TR19] 10.00

Duel of Fates.
____11 card booster [TR20]...4.00
____Two 30 card customized starter decks 10.00

Menace of Darth Maul.
____11 card booster [TR21]...4.00
____Two customized starter decks [TR22] 10.00

Premiere Enhanced, four booster packs with premium card.
____Darth Maul [TR23] 16.00
____Mace Windu 16.00
____Queen Amidala..16.00
____Qui-Gon Jinn 16.00
____Sebulba 16.00
____Trade Federation Tank 16.00

The Jedi Council.
____11 card booster [TR24]...4.00
____Two customized starter decks [TR25] 10.00

Topps
____Clone Wars, 7 trading cards [TR26] 4.00
____Star Wars Galaxy retail display box 5.00
____Star Wars Galaxy 2 retail display box 5.00
____Star Wars Galaxy 3 retail display box 5.00

Topps, Ireland
____ESB Initial Stickers plus bubblegum wrapper [2:324] 4.00

Topps, UK
Episode II: Attack of the Clones, wrapper only.
____Count Dooku [TR27] 0.50
____Jango Fett [TR28] 0.50
____Obi-Wan Kenobi [TR29] 0.50
____Padme Amidala [TR30] 0.50

Packaging: Cereal

General Mills
EPII Cereal boxes, empty.
____Cheerios, collectible cup and bowl offer [PAD01] 4.00
____Cheerios, free toy car offer [PAD02] 4.00
____Chex Corn, temporary tatoos and clone crunch recipe [PAD03] 6.00
____Chex Rice, temporary tatoos and clone crunch recipe [PAD04] 6.00
____Cinnamon Toast Crunch, lightsaber light-up pen inside [PAD05]...4.00
____Cinnamon Toast Crunch, Movie Cash inside [PAD06] 4.00
____Cocoa Puffs, lightsaber light-up pen inside [PAD07] 4.00
____Cookie Crisp, collectible cup and bowl offer [PAD08] 4.00
____Episode II cereal 2-pack [PAD09]..........................6.00
____Episode II Cereal, Collector's Edition #1 [PAD10] 4.00
____Episode II Cereal, Collector's Edition #2 [PAD11] 4.00
____Golden Grahams, free toy car offer [PAD12] 4.00
____Golden Grahams, Movie Cash inside [PAD13]......4.00
____Honey Nut Cheerios, free toy car offer [PAD14] 4.00
____Honey Nut Cheerios, lightsaber light-up pen inside [PAD15] 4.00
____Honey Nut Cheerios, lightsaber light-up pen inside, 2-pack [PAD16] 4.00
____Honey Nut Chex, collectible cup and bowl offer [PAD17] 4.00
____Honey Nut Chex, free toy car offer [PAD18] 4.00
____Lucky Charms, Movie Cash inside [PAD19]..........4.00
____Reeses Puffs, lightsaber light-up pen inside [PAD20] 4.00
____Trix, Movie Cash inside [PAD21]...........................4.00

Vintage cereal boxes, empty.
____Any box, Star Wars Collector Cards [PAD22]..40.00
____Any box, Star Wars Mini-Poster [PAD23]............32.00
____Any box, Star Wars Stick-Ons [PAD24] 46.00
____Cheerios with 16oz. Tumbler mail-in offer [PAD25]...25.00
____Cheerios with promotion/toy rebate 45.00
____Lucky Charms with mobiles offer [PAD26] 45.00

Kelloggs
Cereal boxes, empty.
____Any with SOTE cut-out cards on back [PAD27]..18.00
____Fruitloops for Han Solo figure mail-in [PAD28]..16.00
____Raisin Bran, videos: Experience the Force [PAD29]..12.00
____Raisin Bran, videos: Save up to $7.00...............12.00

EPI Cereal boxes with free poster on back, empty.
____Choco Krispies, Anakin's podracer [PAD30] 10.00
____Choco Krispies, Sebulba 10.00
____Honey Loops, Padme 10.00
____Honey Loops, Queen Amidala [PAD31] 10.00
____Miel Pops, Jar Jar [PAD32] 10.00
____Miel Pops, Jar Jar on Kaadu 10.00
____Rice Krispies, R2-D2 repairing podracer [PAD33]..10.00
____Rice Krispies, R2-D2 repairing royal star-ship 10.00
____Smacks, Darth Maul Naboo [PAD34].................10.00
____Smacks, Darth Maul Tatooine 10.00

EPI Cereal boxes, empty.
____Chocos with free mini-statue [PAD35] 7.00

EPIII cereal boxes, empty.
____8-pack 8.56oz. [PAD36] 5.00
____Apple Jacks 15oz, Jedi mind game [PAD37]........4.00
____Corn Flakes, 18oz, Anakin Skywalker, EPIII information [PAD38] 4.00
____Corn Flakes, 18oz, C-3PO and R2-D2, EPIII information [PAD39] 4.00
____Corn Flakes, 24oz, Anakin Skywalker, EPIII information [PAD40] 4.00
____Corn Flakes, 24oz, C-3PO and R2-D2, EPIII information 4.00
____Corn Pops 15oz, Jedi mind game [PAD41] 4.00

PAD21

PAD22

PAD23

PAD24

PAD25

PAD26

PAD27

PAD28

PAD29

PAD30

PAD31

PAD32

PAD33

PAD34

PAD35

PAD36

PAD37

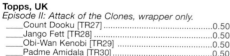

PAD38 PAD39 PAD40 PAD41 PAD42 PAD43 PAD44 PAD45 PAD46 PAD47 PAD48

PAD49 PAD50 PAD51 PAD52 PAD53 PAD54 PAD55 PAD56 front and rear PAD57

____Corn Pops 19.5oz, with free SaberSpoon [PAD42] 4.00
____Crispix 12oz, R2-D2 snack bowl offer [PAD43] 4.00
____Frosted Flakes 20oz, with free SaberSpoon [PAD44] 4.00
____Frosted Mini-Wheats 24.3oz, free DVD offer [PAD45] 4.00
____Frosted Mini-Wheats big bite 20.4oz, free DVD offer [PAD46] 4.00
____Frosted Mini-Wheats maple and brown sugar, 16.5oz, free DVD offer [PAD47] 4.00
____Fruit Loops 15oz, with free SaberSpoon 4.00
____Fruit Loops 18oz, with free SaberSpoon 4.00
____Honey Smacks 17.6oz, with free SaberSpoon [PAD48] 4.00
____Raisin Bran Crunch 18.2oz, Jedi mind game [PAD49] 4.00
____Smorz 10.5oz, Jedi mind game [PAD50] 4.00
____Star Wars 11.8oz, Darth Vader box [PAD51] 8.00
____Star Wars 11.8oz, Darth Vader box, $1.00 off coupon [PAD52] 8.00
____Star Wars 11.8oz, Yoda box [PAD53] 8.00
____Star Wars 11.8oz, Yoda box, $1.00 off coupon [PAD54] 8.00

Vintage cereal boxes, empty.
____Any box with video tape mail-in [PAD55] 12.00
____Any with ROTJ Decoder Game Piece inside....11.00
____Apple Jacks, for comic book mail-in 10.00
____C-3PO's, rebel-rocket premium [PAD56] 25.00
____C-3PO's, Stick'R cards premium [PAD57] 30.00

C-3PO's with cut-out character mask on back panel.
____C-3PO mask [PAD58] 35.00
____C-3PO mask and 25 cent coupon [PAD59] 35.00
____Darth Vader mask [PAD60] 35.00
____Darth Vader mask and 25 cent coupon 35.00
____Luke Skywalker mask [PAD61] 35.00
____Luke Skywalker mask and 25 cent coupon 35.00
____Stormtrooper mask [PAD62] 35.00
____Stormtrooper mask and 25 cent coupon 35.00

Kelloggs, Australia
EPIII cereal boxes, empty. Jedi mind game.
____Coco Pops 4.00
____Frosties 4.00
____Fruit Loops 4.00
____Mini-Wheats [PAD63] 4.00
____Rice Bubbles....4.00
____Sultana Bran 4.00

Kelloggs, Canada
Cereal box with Star Wars "magic eye" back, empty.
____Corn Pops [PAD64] 8.00
____Frosted Mini-Wheats [PAD65] 8.00
____Mini-Wheats [PAD66] 8.00

Cereal box with Star Wars SE Trilogy hologram, empty.
____Corn Flakes, Empire Strikes Back [PAD70] 7.00
____Corn Pops, Return of the Jedi [PAD71] 7.00
____Frosted Flakes, Star Wars [PAD72] 7.00

EPII Cereal boxes, empty.
____Episode II cereal [PAD73] 24.00
____Episode II cereal 2-pack with Clone trooper mask [PAD74] 24.00

EPII Cereal boxes, empty. Rubik's Cube premium.
____Corn Pops [PAD75] 6.00
Frosted Flakes [PAD76] 6.00
____Fruit Loops [PAD77] 6.00
____Raisin Bran [PAD78] 6.00
____Rice Krispies [PAD79] 6.00

Kelloggs, France
EPI Cereal boxes, empty.
____Choco Krispies with free mini bust [PAD80] 5.00
____Crackles [PAD81] 8.00
____Frosties with free mini bust [PAD82] 5.00
____Miel Pops with free breakfast spoon [PAD83] 5.00
____Smacks with free breakfast spoon [PAD84] 8.00

Kelloggs, Germany
EPI Cereal boxes, empty.
____Chocos with free crystal scene [PAD85] 8.00
____Frosties with free crystal scene [PAD86] 8.00
____Fruit Loops with free mini-statue [PAD87] 8.00
____Smacks with free mini-statue [PAD88] 8.00

EPII Cereal boxes, empty.
____Smacks, mini-statue scene viewer premium 8.00

Kelloggs, Greece
EPI Cereal boxes, empty.
____Honey Pops with free mini-statue premium [PAD89] 14.00

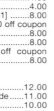

PAD58 front and rear PAD59 PAD60 PAD61 PAD62 PAD63 PAD64 PAD65 PAD66

PAD70 PAD71 PAD72 PAD73 PAD74 PAD75 PAD76 PAD77 PAD78 PAD79

PAD80 PAD81 PAD82 PAD83 PAD84 PAD85 PAD86 PAD87 PAD88 PAD89

Packaging: Cereal

| PAD90 | PAD91 | PAD92 | PAD93 | PAD94 | PAD95 | PAD96 | PAD97 | PAD98 | PAD99 |

| PAD100 | PAD101 | PAD102 | PAD103 | PAD104 | PAD105 | PAD106 | PAD107 |

| PAD108 | PAD109 | PAD110 | PAD111 | PAD112 | PAD113 | PAD114 |

Kelloggs, Italy
EPI Cereal boxes, empty.
____Chocos [PAD90] 7.00
____Frosties [PAD91] 7.00

Kelloggs, Mexico
Cereal boxes, empty.
____EPIII:ROTS 10.00
____Honey Nut, videos: Making of SW $5.99 ....10.00

Kelloggs, Sweden
EPI Cereal boxes, empty.
____Choco Krispies with free mini-statue [PAD92] 8.00
____Smacks [PAD93] 7.00

Kelloggs, Thailand
EPIII cereal boxes, empty.
____Chocos Chex, with 2 free gyros [PAD94] 10.00
____Coacoa Frosties, with 2 free gyros [PAD95] 10.00
____Cocoa Krispies, with 2 free gyros [PAD96] 10.00
____Corn Flakes, with 2 free gyros [PAD97] 10.00
____Frosties, with 2 free gyros [PAD98] 10.00
____Fruit Loops, with 2 free gyros [PAD99] 10.00

Kelloggs, UK
EPI cereal boxes, empty.
____8-pack, variery [PAD100] 12.00

Nestlé
Cereal boxes, empty.
____Estrellitas with free coin [PAD101] 12.00
____Nesquik [PAD102]...12.00

Nestlé, Argentina
EPII Cereal boxes, empty.
____Nesquik 210g [PAD103] 15.00

Nestlé, Czechoslovakia
EPII Cereal boxes, empty. Lenticular card premium.
____Chocapic [PAD104] 28.00
____Nesquick [PAD105]..10.00

Nestlé, Mexico
EPII Cereal boxes, empty.
____Cheerios 375g [PAD106] 15.00
____Chocapic 550g [PAD107] 15.00
____Crunch 580g [PAD108] 15.00
____La Lechera Flakes 440g [PAD109] 15.00
____La Lechera Flakes 630g 15.00
____Nesquick 380g 15.00
____Nesquik 560g [PAD110] 15.00
____Nesquik 750g [PAD111] 15.00
____Trix 340g [PAD112] 15.00
____Trix 480g [PAD113] 15.00
____Zucosos 660g [PAD114]....................................15.00

Packaging: Cheese

Dairylea
____Cheese spread [3:318] 20.00

Animated character on cheese wedge paper wrapper.
____Baga [3:318] 10.00

____C-3PO [3:318]..10.00
____Chirpa [3:318] 10.00
____Kneesaa [3:318] 10.00
____Latara [3:318] 10.00
____Logray [3:318] 10.00
____Malani [3:318] 10.00
____R2-D2 [3:318] 10.00
____Shodu [3:318] 10.00
____Teebo [3:318] 10.00
____Wicket [3:318] 10.00
____Winda [3:318] 10.00

Packaging: Cleaners

Dixon
____EPI:TPM Dixon Blue Energy with Active Perls [3:318]...15.00

Pine-Sol
____Pine-Sol bottle with Star Wars Label.................25.00

Packaging: Cookies

Burtons
____Star Wars Biscuits [PAG01] 14.00

Individual wrappers.
____C-3PO [PAG02] 2.00
____Darth Vader [PAG03]..2.00
____Luke Skywalker [PAG04]......................................2.00
____Princess Leia [PAG05] 2.00
____R2-D2 [PAG06] 2.00
____Yoda [PAG07] 2.00

Cadbury
____Biscuits, EPI [PAG08] 4.00

Gamesa
Arcoiris.
____R2-D2 [PAG09] 5.00

| PAG01 | PAG02 | PAG03 | PAG04 | PAG05 | PAG06 | PAG07 | PAG08 |

 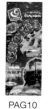   

| PAG09 | PAG10 | PAG11 | PAG12 | PAG13 | PAG14 | PAG15 | PAG16 |

| PAG17 | PAG18 | PAG19 | PAG20 | PAG21 | PAG22 |

| PAG23 | PAG24 | PAG25 | PAG26 |

| PAG27 | PAG28 | PAG29 |

Chocolate Chokis.
____EPI: Anakin [PAG10] 4.00
____EPI: Jar Jar [PAG11] 4.00
____EPI: Padme [PAG12] 4.00
____Luke Skywalker [PAG13]..5.00

Emperador.
____C-3PO 75g [PAG14] 4.00
____Darth Vader 75g [PAG15] 4.00
____Darth Vader 825g [PAG16] 6.00

Flups.
____Darth Maul [PAG17] 6.00
____Obi-Wan [PAG18] 6.00

Merengue.
____Luke Skywalker [PAG19]......................................4.00

Piruetas.
____R2-D2 [PAG20] 4.00

Keebler
Cookie jar mail-in premium.
____Chips Deluxe chocolate lovers 15oz. [PAG21]......3.00

____Chips Deluxe original 18oz. [PAG22] 3.00
____ELFudge double stuffed 12oz. [PAG23] 3.00
____ELFudge original 15oz. [PAG24]..........................3.00
____Fudge Shoppe deluxe grahams 12.5oz.
[PAG25]..3.00
____Fudge Shoppe grasshopper 10oz. [PAG26]..........3.00
____Fudge Shoppe Lava stripes 11.5oz. [PAG27] 3.00
____Fudge sticks 8.5oz. [PAG28] 3.00
____Grahams cinnamon crisp 14oz. [PAG29] 3.00

Nabisco
Individual cookie packets featuring original artwork.
____Anakin in Pod Race Helmet 4.00
____C-3PO and R2-D2 [PAG30] 4.00
____Darth Maul on Sith Speeder [PAG31]....................4.00
____Jedi vs. Jedi [PAG32] 4.00
____Obi-Wan with Maul Background [PAG33] 4.00
____Trade Federation Battleship [PAG34] 4.00

Pepperidge Farms
Vintage cookie boxes featuring mail-in cup offer.
____Rebel Alliance I, vanilla [PAG35] 22.00
____Rebel Alliance II, peanut butter [PAG36] 22.00
____The Imperial Forces, chocolate [PAG37] 22.00

Packaging: Facial Tissue

Puffs
____Bespin [PAT01] 16.00
____Dagobah [PAT02] 16.00
____Hoth [PAT03]..16.00

Zewa
Belgium. Softis.
____Anakin Skywalker [PAT04] 12.00
____C-3PO [PAT05] 12.00
____Chewbacca [PAT06] 12.00
____Luke Skywalker [PAT07] 12.00
____Qui-Gon Jinn [PAT08]...12.00
____Yoda [PAT09] 12.00

Packaging: Food Wrappers

Burger King
EPIII:ROTS. Choose you Destiny game.
____Fry wrapper, king size [PAF01] 2.00

| PAG30 | PAG31 | PAG32 | PAG33 | PAG34 | PAG35 | PAG36 | PAG37 |

| PAT01 | PAT02 | PAT03 | PAT04 | PAT05 |

| PAT06 | PAT07 | PAT08 | PAT09 |

Packaging: Food Wrappers

PAF01

PAF02

PAF03

PAF04

PAF05

PAF06

PAF08

PAF09

PAF10

PAF11

PAF12

PAF13

PAF14

PAF15

PAF16

____Fry wrapper, large [PAF02] 2.00
____Fry wrapper, medium [PAF03] 2.00
____Fry wrapper, small..2.00
____Paper bag [PAF04] 3.00

ConAgra Foods
Chef Boyardee canned pasta. Clone Wars promotion. Beef Ravioli. Count Dooku and Battle Droids. 15oz.
 ____6-pack [PAF05] 6.00
 ____8-pack [PAF06] 8.00
 ____Anakin Skywalker 1.25
 ____Asajj Ventress 1.25
 ____Count Dooku [PAF08] 1.25
 ____Obi-Wan Kenobi 1.25
 ____Yoda 1.25
Beefaroni. Mace Windu and Battle Droids. 15oz.
 ____Anakin Skywalker 1.25
 ____Count Dooku [PAF09] 1.25
 ____Mace Windu 1.25
 ____Obi-Wan Kenobi 1.25
 ____Yoda 1.25
Mini Beef Rav. C-3PO, R2-D2, Battle Droids. 15oz.
 ____Asajj Ventress 1.25
 ____Count Dooku 1.25
 ____Mace Windu [PAF10] 1.25
 ____Obi-Wan Kenobi 1.25
 ____Yoda 1.25
Overstuffed Beef Ravioli. Obi-Wan Kenobi and Durge. 15oz.
 ____Anakin Skywalker 1.25
 ____Obi-Wan Kenobi [PAF11] 1.25
 ____Yoda 1.25

Spaghetti and Meatballs. Anakin Skywalker and Asajj Ventress. 15oz.
 ____Asajj Ventress 1.25
 ____Mace Windu 1.25
 ____Obi-Wan Kenobi [PAF12] 1.25

Chef Boyardee pasta. Clone Wars promotion. Boxed deep dish meals.
 ____Cheese Lover's Lasagna. Padme Amidala, Yoda, and Count Dooku [PAF13] 4.00
 ____Cheese Pizza Kit. Anakin Skywalker and Asajj Ventress [PAF14] 4.00
 ____Cheesy Burger Macaroni. Durge and Obi-Wan Kenobi [PAF15] 4.00
 ____Pepperoni and Sausage Rotini. Mace Windu and Battle Droids [PAF16] 4.00

Frigo
 ____La Guerra de las Galaxias [PAF17].................7.00
 ____La Guerra de las Galaxias, individual wrappers [PAF18] 1.00

Heinz
Star Wars pasta shapes in tomato sauce.
 ____Darth Maul hologram, 400g [PAF19] 7.00
 ____Darth Maul, 400g [PAF20]..........................5.00
 ____Jar Jar Binks, 205g [3:319]..........................5.00
 ____Starfighters hologram, 205g [PAF21] 7.00

Kelloggs
 ____Rice Krispies Treats, 8-pack, EPIII cookie jar offer [PAF22] 5.00

Cereal and milk bars 6-pack, EPIII cookie jar offer.
 ____Cocoa Krispies [PAF23] 5.00
 ____Froot Loops [PAF24]....................................5.00
 ____Frosted Flakes [PAF25]................................5.00

Mail-in plate premium.
 ____Eggo cinnamon toast 10 sets of 4 [PAF26] 5.00
 ____Eggo French toaster sticks 32 sticks [PAF27] 5.00
 ____Eggo homestyle 16-pack [PAF28] 5.00
 ____Eggo minis 10 sets of 4 [PAF29] 5.00
 ____Eggo waf-fulls strawberry 6-pack [PAF30]............5.00
 ____Eggo waffles chocolate chip 10-pk. [PAF31] 5.00

Pop-tarts 12-pack, "Listen for Vader Music."
 ____Brown Sugar Cinnamon [PAF32] 5.00
 ____Chocolate chip [PAF33] 5.00
 ____Frosted blueberry [PAF34] 5.00
 ____Frosted cherry [PAF35] 5.00
 ____Frosted Chocolate Fudge [PAF36] 5.00
 ____Frosted strawberry [PAF37] 5.00
 ____S'mores [PAF38] 5.00
 ____Strawberry [PAF39] 5.00
 ____Wild Berry [PAF40] 5.00

Pop-tarts 12-pack.
 ____Star Wars lava berry [PAF41] 8.00

Kelloggs, UK
Cereal and milk bars. EPIII sticker dispenser offer.
 ____Coco Pops [PAF42]..5.00
 ____Frosties [PAF43] 5.00
 ____Rice Krispies [PAF44] 5.00

PAF17

PAF18

PAF19

PAF20

PAF21

PAF22

PAF23

PAF24

PAF25

PAF26

PAF27

PAF28

PAF29

PAF30

PAF31

PAF32

PAF33

PAF34

PAF35

PAF36

PAF37

PAF38

PAF39

PAF40

PAF41

PAF42

PAF43

PAF44

PAF45

PAF46

PAF47

PAF48

PAF49

PAF50

PAF51

PAF52

KFC
Paper barrels, Episode I.

____Battle above Naboo, large [PAF45] 4.00
____Battle above Naboo, medium [PAF46]..................3.00
____Defenders of Naboo, large [PAF47] 4.00
____Defenders of Naboo, medium [PAF48]..................3.00
____Ground assault, large [PAF49] 4.00
____Ground assault, medium [PAF50]............................3.00
____Invasion of Theed, large [PAF51] 4.00
____Invasion of Theed, medium [PAF52].......................3.00
____Star Wars Special Edition, medium [PAF53] 5.00

KFC, Australia
Jar Jar Binks kids' meal food boxes.

____Fries box [PAF54] 3.00
____Nugget box [PAF55] 3.00

La vache qui rit
____Contains one Episode 1 trading card....................5.00

Masterfoods USA
Kudos 10 packs.

____EPI, variety [PAF56]...5.00
____EPII, variety [PAF57]..5.00
____EPIII, M&Ms Darth Vader, Obi-Wan, Anakin with Anakin card on back [PAF58] 5.00
____EPIII, M&Ms Darth Vader, Obi-Wan, Anakin with Obi-Wan card on back [PAF59] 5.00
____EPIII, M&Ms Yoda, Chewbacca, Obi-Wan [PAF60] 5.00
____EPIV, Snickers [PAF61] 5.00
____EPV 5.00
____EPVI, Peanut butter [PAF62].................................5.00

Meiji
____Seasoning packets [PAF63] 11.00

Nagatanien
____Curry, contains individual packets [PAF64] 23.00

____Anakin Skywalker – salmon [PAF65] 3.00
____Battle Droid – salmon [PAF66] 4.00
____C-3PO - salmon [PAF67] 3.00
____Darth Maul – okaka [PAF68]..................................4.00
____Darth Maul – salmon [PAF69].................................3.00
____Darth Sidious – salmon [PAF70]............................3.00
____Obi-Wan Kenobi – okaka [PAF71] 3.00
____Obi-Wan Kenobi – salmon [PAF72] 3.00
____Queen Amidala – okaka [PAF73] 3.00
____Queen Amidala (Senate) – salmon [PAF74] 3.00
____Qui-Gon Jinn – okaka [PAF75] 3.00
____R2-D2 – salmon [PAF76]..3.00
____Sebulba – salmon [PAF77].....................................3.00
____Shmi Skywalker – salmon [PAF78].......................3.00
____Yoda – okaka [PAF79]..4.00

Large packets.

____Contains food plus one Episode I sticker [PAF80] 6.00

PAF53

PAF54

PAF55

PAF56

PAF57

PAF58 rear

PAF59 rear

PAF60

PAF61

PAF62

PAF63

PAF64

PAF65

PAF66

PAF67

PAF68

PAF69

PAF70

PAF71

PAF72

PAF73

PAF74

PAF75

PAF76

PAF77

PAF78

PAF79

PAF80

Packaging: Food Wrappers

| PAF81 | PAF82 | PAF83 | PAF84 | PAF85 | PAF86 | PAF87 | PAF88 |

| PAF89 | PAF90 | PAF91 | PAF92 | PAF93 | PAF94 | PAF95 |

| PAF96 | PAF97 | PAF98 | PAF99 | PAF100 | PAF101 | PAF102 |

| PAF103 | PAF104 | PAF105 | PAF106 | PAF107 | PAF108 | PAF109 | PAF110 | PAF111 |

Nestlé
____Nesquik chocolate milk powder [PAF81] 8.00

Nestlé, Philippines
____2-pack Wonder Cup Trilogy Treats 7.00

Parmalat Food, Inc.
Cheestrings, EPII Connector Card inside.
____Cheddar flavor [PAF82]............................3.00
____Pizza flavor [PAF83] 3.00

Pizza Hut
____Anakin Skywalker [PAF84] 7.00
____Darth Maul [PAF85]...............................9.00
____Jar Jar Binks [PAF86] 9.00
____Nute Gunray, New Yorker size [PAF87] 15.00
____Queen Amidala [PAF88] 9.00
____R2-D2, personal size [PAF89] 12.00

EPI:TPM. Large – collect all 4 to make mural.
____Darth Maul [PAF90] 12.00
____Darth Sidious [PAF91] 12.00
____Obi-Wan Kenobi [PAF92] 12.00
____Qui-Gon Jinn [PAF93].............................12.00

EPI:TPM. Medium – collect all 4 to make mural.
____Anakin Skywalker [PAF94] 12.00
____C-3PO [PAF95].....................................12.00
____Jar Jar Binks [PAF96]............................12.00
____Queen Amidala [PAF97].........................12.00

SW:SE pizza boxes.
____C-3PO and Millennium Falcon [PAF98] 3.00
____Darth Vader and Star Destroyer [PAF99] 5.00
____R2-D2 and X-Wing Fighter [PAF100] 4.00
____Stormtrooper [PAF101] 4.00

Pizza Hut, Australia
EPI:TPM pizza boxes.
____Anakin Skywalker [PAF102] 9.00
____Jar Jar Binks [PAF103] 9.00
____Queen Amidala [PAF104] 9.00

SW:SE pizza boxes.
____Bespin Duel [PAF105].............................12.00
____Bespin Duel, personal size [PAF106] 15.00

Taco Bell
Carry-out food bags, EPI.
____Darth Maul 2.00
____Jar Jar Binks [PAF107] 2.00
____Kid's meal, advertises toys [PAF108] 3.00

Carry-out food bags.
____C-3PO [PAF109] 2.00
____Darth Vader [PAF110] 2.00
____R2-D2 [PAF111] 2.00

Wonder Bread
____Wonder Bread wrapper with Star Wars trading card premium 35.00

Packaging: Fruit Snacks

Betty Crocker
Empty boxes. Backpack tag premium.
____Fruit By The Foot, Anakin Skywalker [DDS01]......6.00
____Fruit By The Foot, Mace Windu [DDS02] 6.00
____Fruit By The Foot, Obi-Wan Kenobi [DDS03]........6.00
____Fruit By The Foot, Yoda [DDS04] 6.00
____Fruit Roll-Ups, Anakin Skywalker [DDS05]............6.00
____Fruit Roll-Ups, Mace Windu [DDS06]................6.00
____Fruit Roll-Ups, Obi-Wan Kenobi [DDS07] 6.00
____Fruit Roll-Ups, Yoda [DDS08] 6.00

Empty boxes.
____Jedi Berry Blast, six .75oz. Rolls with Magic Motion Sticker premium [DDS09] 1.00

Empty wrappers.
____Anakin Skywalker [DDS10] 1.00
____Barriss Offee [DDS11].............................1.00
____Luke Skywalker [DDS12] 1.00
____Luminara Unduli [DDS13] 1.00
____Mace Windu [DDS14] 1.00
____Obi-Wan Kenobi [DDS15] 1.00
____Stass Allie [DDS16] 3.00
____Yoda [DDS17] 1.00

Fruit strip backing. Jedi trivia / Jedi facts.
____Jango Fett's Gun 1.00

| DDS01 | DDS02 | DDS03 | DDS04 | DDS05 | DDS06 | DDS07 | DDS08 | DDS09 |

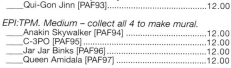

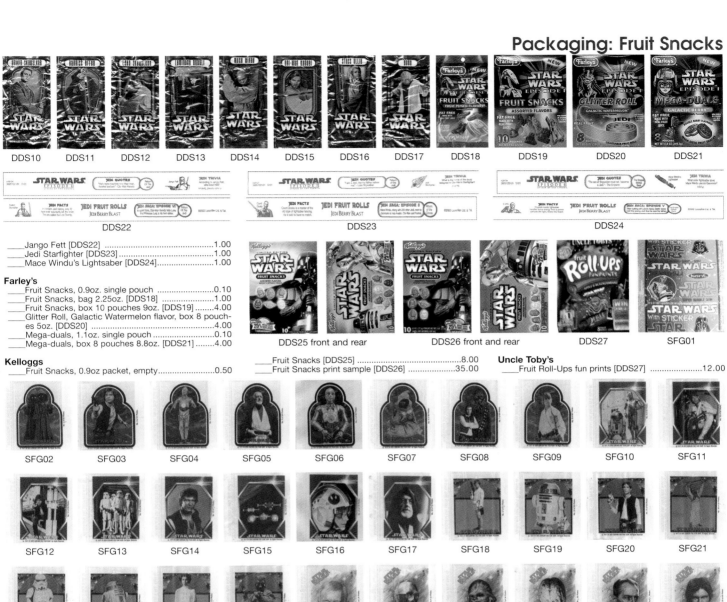

DDS10 DDS11 DDS12 DDS13 DDS14 DDS15 DDS16 DDS17 DDS18 DDS19 DDS20 DDS21

DDS22

DDS23

DDS24

____Jango Fett [DDS22] 1.00
____Jedi Starfighter [DDS23] 1.00
____Mace Windu's Lightsaber [DDS24]......................1.00

Farley's
____Fruit Snacks, 0.9oz. single pouch 0.10
____Fruit Snacks, bag 2.25oz. [DDS18] 1.00
____Fruit Snacks, box 10 pouches 9oz. [DDS19] 4.00
____Glitter Roll, Galactic Watermelon flavor, box 8 pouch-
  es 5oz. [DDS20] 4.00
____Mega-duals, 1.1oz. single pouch 0.10
____Mega-duals, box 8 pouches 8.8oz. [DDS21] 4.00

Kelloggs
____Fruit Snacks, 0.9oz packet, empty.......................0.50

DDS25 front and rear   DDS26 front and rear   DDS27   SFG01

____Fruit Snacks [DDS25] 8.00
____Fruit Snacks print sample [DDS26] 35.00

Uncle Toby's
____Fruit Roll-Ups fun prints [DDS27] 12.00

SFG02 SFG03 SFG04 SFG05 SFG06 SFG07 SFG08 SFG09 SFG10 SFG11

SFG12 SFG13 SFG14 SFG15 SFG16 SFG17 SFG18 SFG19 SFG20 SFG21

SFG22 SFG23 SFG24 SFG25 SFG26 SFG27 SFG28 SFG29 SFG30 SFG31

SFG32 SFG33 SFG34 SFG35 SFG36 SFG37 SFG38 SFG39 SFG40 SFG41

SFG42 SFG43 SFG44 SFG45 SFG46 SFG47 SFG48 SFG49 SFG50 SFG51

SFG52 SFG53 SFG54 SFG55 SFG56 SFG57 SFG58 SFG59 SFG60 SFG61 SFG62

Packaging: Gum

| PAJ01 | PAJ02 | PAK01 | PAK02 | PAK03 | PAK04 | PAK05 | PAK06 | PAK07 |

| PAK08 | PAK09 |

Packaging: Gum

Kent
Turkey.
____Super bubble gum [SFG01] 2.00

Topps
____1) Jawas [SFG02] 5.00
____2) Han Solo aiming blaster [SFG03] 5.00
____3) C-3PO full body [SFG04] 5.00
____4) Ben Kenobi [SFG05] 5.00
____5) C-3PO above the knees [SFG06] 5.00
____6) Jawa sitting [SFG07] 5.00
____7) Han and Chewbacca [SFG08] 5.00
____8) Luke [SFG09] 5.00
____9) R2-D2 and C-3PO [SFG10] 5.00
____10) Luke in gunner chair [SFG11] 5.00
____11) Han on Falcon ramp [SFG12] 5.00
____12) Stormtroopers [SFG13] 5.00
____13) Han on Falcon's ramp [SFG14] 5.00
____14) X-wings and Y-wing [SFG15] 5.00
____15) Luke in X-wing helmet [SFG16] 5.00
____16) Ben with lightsaber [SFG17] 5.00
____17) Luke holding gun [SFG18] 5.00
____18) R2-D2 [SFG19] 5.00
____19) Han [SFG20] 5.00
____20) Tusken Raider [SFG21] 5.00
____21) Stormtrooper [SFG22] 5.00
____22) R2-D2 [SFG23] 5.00
____23) Princess Leia [SFG24] 5.00
____24) Tusken pointing gaffi stick [SFG25] ...5.00
____25) Ben Kenobi [SFG26] 5.00
____26) C-3PO, dirty, shoulders up [SFG27]...5.00
____27) Chewbacca headshot [SFG28] 5.00
____28) Alien (not seen in movie) [SFG29] 6.00
____29) Grand Moff Tarkin [SFG30] 5.00
____30) Han with collar open [SFG31] 5.00
____31) Darth Vader airbrush portrait [SFG32] ...5.00
____32) Luke in X-wing, no helmet [SFG33] ...5.00
____33) Tusken Raider headshot [SFG34]......5.00
____34) Sandtrooper [SFG35] 5.00
____35) Stormtrooper [SFG36] 5.00
____36) Leia in Yavin war room [SFG37] 5.00
____37) Cantina band member [SFG38] 5.00

____38) Luke as stormtrooper, no helmet [SFG39] 5.00
____39) C-3PO [SFG40] 5.00
____40) Luke [SFG41] 5.00
____41) Millennium Falcon [SFG42] 5.00
____42) Han shooting [SFG43] 5.00
____43) Tarkin, face only [SFG44] 5.00
____44) Luke in X-Wing gear [SFG45] 5.00
____45) Luke [SFG46] 5.00
____46) R2-D2 and C-3PO [SFG47] 5.00
____47) C-3PO [SFG48] 5.00
____48) Escape pod rear view [SFG49]........5.00
____49) Leia and Luke after Death Star escape
[SFG50] 5.00
____50) Luke and Leia [SFG51] 5.00
____51) Chewbacca and Han [SFG52] 5.00
____52) Ben and Luke [SFG53] 5.00
____53) Stormtroopers [SFG54]................5.00
____54) Luke (X-Wing gear) and Leia [SFG55] ...5.00
____55) Uncle Owen and Luke [SFG56] 5.00
____56) Luke and C-3PO [SFG57] 5.00
____Unopened box [SFG58] 230.00
____Unopened pkg., Han Solo [SFG59] 5.00
____Unopened pkg., Darth Vader [SFG60] ...5.00
____Unopened pkg., Luke Skywalker [SFG61] ...5.00
____Unopened pkg., Princess Leia [SFG62] ...5.00

Packaging: Ice Cream

Blue Bunny
____Darth Vader frozen confection with gumball
eyes box 5.00
____Darth Vader frozen confection with gumball
eyes wrapper 3.00
____Star Wars bomb pop individual wrapper ...3.00
____Star Wars bomb pop package 5.00

Campina Ijsfabbrieken
____ROTJ promotion on wrapper... premium stickers were
ESB! [2:327] 6.00

Lyons Maid
Ice Lolly wrappers, Star Wars.
____Artoo-Detoo R2-D2 ....5.00
____Chewbacca 5.00
____Darth Vader 5.00
____See-Threepio C-3PO 5.00
____Stormtroopers 5.00
____Tusken Raiders 5.00

Ice Lolly wrappers, Empire Strikes Back.
____Boba Fett 5.00
____Darth Vader 5.00
____Lando Calrissian 5.00
____Princess Leia Organa 5.00
____Tauntaun 5.00
____Yoda 5.00

Masterfoods USA
____M&M's ice cream cones 6-pack [PAJ02] 5.00
____M&M's ice cream sandwiches [PAJ01]...............5.00

Pauls
____ROTJ with Jedi Jelly [2:327] 25.00
____SW Popsicles 10-pack.....................42.00

Peters
____ROTJ with Jedi Jelly [2:327] 25.00

Wells
____Battle Droid Ice wrapper [2:327].........3.00

Packaging: Kids' Meals

Burger Chef
Funmeal trays.
____C-3PO puppet [PAK01] 30.00
____Darth Vader card game [PAK02] 30.00
____Flight game with spinner [PAK03] 30.00
____Punch-out Landspeeder [PAK04] 30.00
____R2-D2 puppet [PAK05] 30.00
____Tie Fighter [PAK06].........................30.00
____X-wing fighter [PAK07] 30.00

Burger King
EPIII:ROTS.
____Anakin Skywalker 8.00
____Darth Vader 8.00
____General Grievous 8.00
____Yoda 8.00

Burger King, Argentina
EPIII:ROTS.
____Darth Vader / Yoda 10.00

KFC, Australia
Cardboard full-color boxes.
____SW:SE 4.00
____SW:SE, toy inside [PAK08] 5.00
____SW:TPM [PAK09] 3.00
____SW:TPM, toy inside 5.00

KFC, Mexico
Cardboard full-color boxes.
____SW:TPM [3:321] 7.00
____SW:TPM, bucket style 9.00

Taco Bell
Fun Meal boxes.
____Star Wars 4.00
____Empire Strikes Back 4.00
____Return of the Jedi [3:321] 4.00

Packaging: Paper Cups

Dixie / Northern Inc.
Star Wars.
____Chewbacca and Han Solo [PAP01] 30.00
____Darth Vader [PAP02] 30.00
____Death Star Battle [PAP03] 30.00
____Droids [PAP04] 25.00
____Luke Skywalker 30.00
____Obi-Wan Kenobi 30.00
____Princess Leia [PAP05] 30.00
____Stormtrooper [PAP06] 30.00

| PAP01 | PAP02 | PAP03 | PAP04 | PAP05 | PAP06 | PAP07 | PAP08 | PAP09 |

| PAP10 | PAP11 | PAP12 | PAP13 | PAP14 | PAP15 | PAP16 | PAP17 | PAP18 | PAP19 | PAP20 | PAP21 | PAP22 | PAP23 |

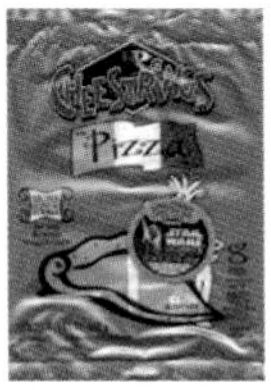
PAS01
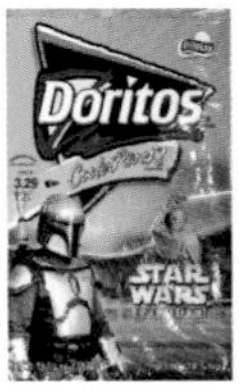
PAS02
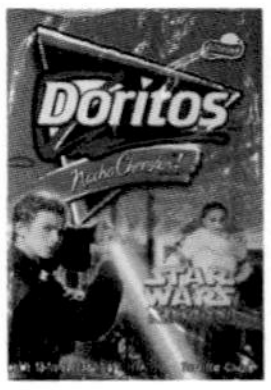
PAS03
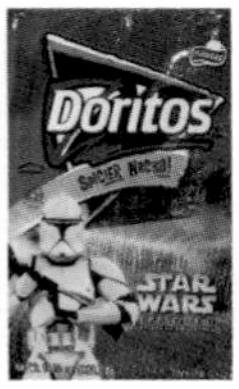
PAS04
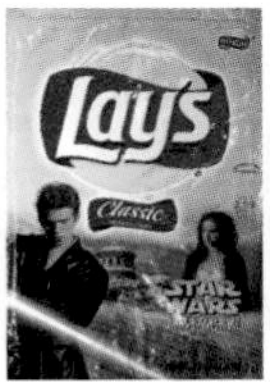
PAS05
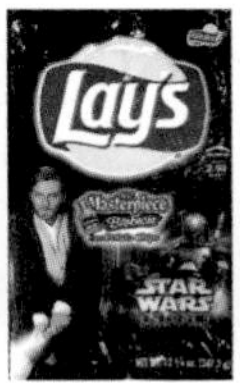
PAS06
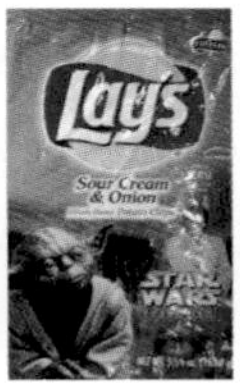
PAS07
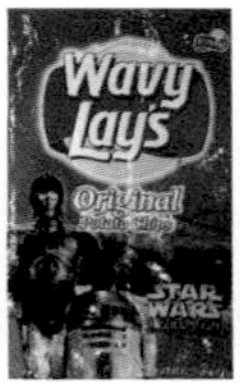
PAS08
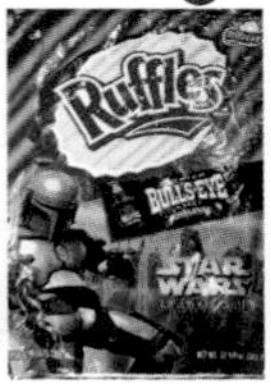
PAS09
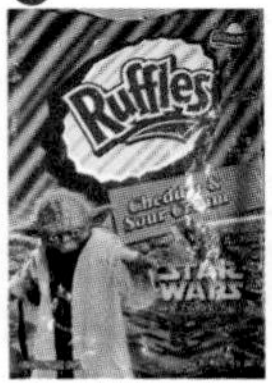
PAS10
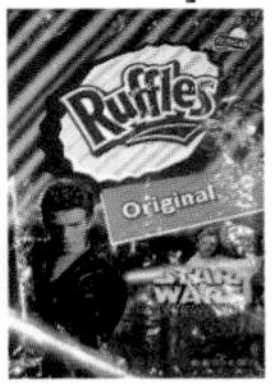
PAS11
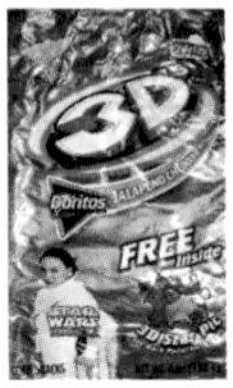
PAS12
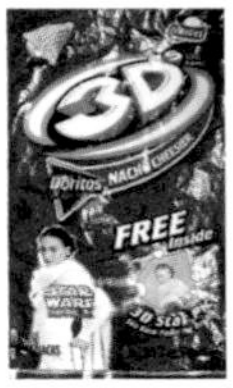
PAS13
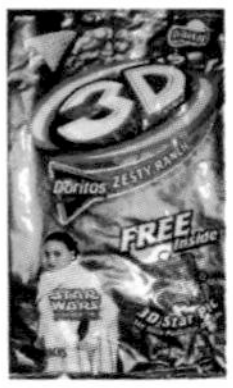
PAS14
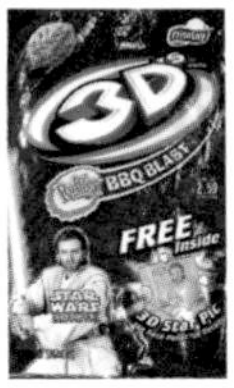
PAS15
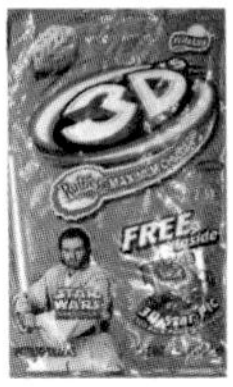
PAS16
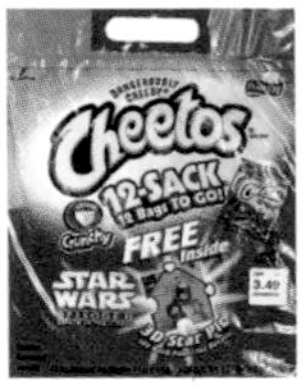
PAS17
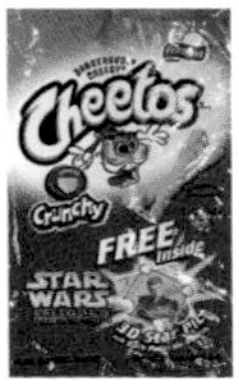
PAS18
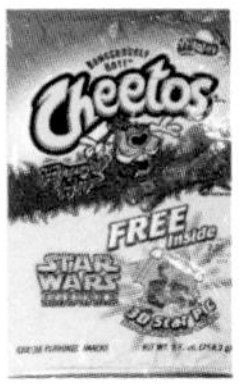
PAS19
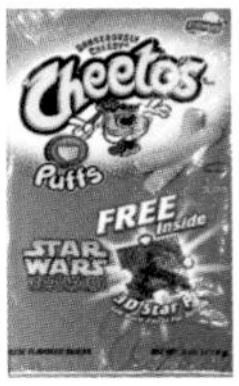
PAS20

Empire Strikes Back. $1.00 cash refund offer.
____AT-AT and Snowspeeder [PAP07] 25.00
____Darth Vader..25.00
____Luke on Tauntaun...25.00
____Millennium Falcon 25.00
____Star Destroyer 25.00
____Twin-pod Cloud Car...25.00
____X-Wing in Swamp [PAP08]...................................25.00
____Yoda [PAP09] 25.00

Empire Strikes Back.
____AT-AT and Snowspeeder 25.00
____Darth Vader [PAP10]..25.00
____Luke on Tauntaun [PAP11] 25.00
____Millennium Falcon [PAP12]...................................25.00
____Star Destroyer [PAP13]...25.00
____Twin-pod Cloud Car [PAP14] 25.00
____X-Wing in Swamp..25.00
____Yoda [PAP15] 25.00

Return of the Jedi.
____B-Wing, Luke Skywalker and Yoda, red logo [PAP16] 20.00
____Darth Vader, Emperor, Emperor's Royal Guard [PAP17] 15.00
____Ewoks [PAP18] 20.00
____Jabba the Hutt and Princess Leia [PAP19] 20.00

Star Wars Saga.
____C-3PO and R2-D2 [PAP20] 25.00
____Darth Vader [PAP21]...25.00
____Han Solo, Leia and Stormtroopers [PAP22] 20.00
____Luke Skywalker and Yoda [PAP23] 20.00

Packaging: Shoes

Buster Brown and Co.
Shoeboxes.
____Episode II [3:321] 7.00
____Episode II with free sunglasses [3:321] 12.00
____Episode III toddler..5.00
____Episode III youth 5.00
____Episode III, Saga design 7.00

Kid Nation
____Episode I shoebox [3:321] 7.00

Stride Rite
____Shoe Bag for Clarks shoes [3:321] 12.00

Shoeboxes.
____ROTJ images [3:321] 24.00
____SW MTFBWY 20.00
____X-wings [3:321]..18.00

Packaging: Snack Chips

____CheeStrings, Pizza, EPII [PAS01] 5.00

Frito Lay
Cheetos with 3D motion card inside.
____13.5oz. 3.00
____15.5oz. 3.00
Doritos Cooler Ranch w/3D motion card inside.
____14.5oz. 3.00
Doritos Nacho Cheesier 3Ds with game card inside.
____10oz. 3.00
____2.5oz. 3.00
____6oz. 3.00
Doritos Nacho Cheesier R2-D2 cartoon with game card inside.
____14.5oz. 3.00
____25oz. 3.00
____3.5oz. 3.00
Doritos Nacho Cheesier with 3D motion card inside.
____14.5oz. 3.00
Doritos Nacho Cheesier with motion disc inside.
____2.125oz. 3.00
____3.5oz. 3.00
Doritos Pizza Cravers with 3D motion card inside.
____14.5oz. 3.00
Doritos Pizza Cravers with motion disc inside.
____2.125oz. 3.00
____3.5oz. 3.00
Doritos Smokey Red BBQ Qui-Gon Jinn cartoon.
____14.5oz. with game card inside 3.00
____3.5oz. 2.00
Doritos Taco Supreme with 3D motion card inside.
____14.5oz. 3.00
Doritos Taco Supreme with motion disc inside.
____2.125oz. 3.00
____3.5oz. 3.00

EPII:AOTC with character pictures on package.
____Doritos Cooler Ranch 13.5oz., Mace Windu and Jango [PAS02] 2.00
____Doritos Nacho Cheese 13.5oz., Anakin and Padme [PAS03] 2.00
____Doritos Spicier Nacho 13.5oz., Clone Trooper [PAS04] 2.00
____Lays Classic 12.25oz., Anakin and Padme [PAS05] 2.00
____Lays Classic 5.5oz., Anakin and Padme 2.00
____Lays KC Masterpiece Barbecue 12.25oz., Obi-Wan and Jango [PAS06] 2.00
____Lays Sour Cream and Onion 12.25oz., Yoda and Obi-Wan [PAS07] 2.00
____Lays Sour Cream and Onion 5.5oz., Yoda and Obi-Wan 2.00
____Lays Wavy 12.25oz., C-3PO and R2-D2 [PAS08] 2.00
____Ruffles BBQ Blast 7oz., Jango Fett [PAS09] 2.00
____Ruffles Cheddar Sour Cream 7oz., Yoda [PAS10] 2.00
____Ruffles Original 12.25oz., Anakin and Obi-Wan [PAS11] 2.00

EPII:AOTC. 3D Star Pic Premiums in package.
____3D's Doritos Jalipino Cheddar 7oz [PAS12]..........2.00
____3D's Doritos Nacho Cheesier 7oz [PAS13]............2.00
____3D's Doritos Zesty Ranch 7oz [PAS14] 2.00
____3D's Ruffles BBQ Blast 7oz. [PAS15] 2.00
____3D's Ruffles Maximum Cheddar 7oz. [PAS16]......2.00
____3D's Ruffles Supreme Sour Cream 7oz.................2.00
____Cheetos Crunchy 12-pack [PAS17] 2.00
____Cheetos Crunchy 9.5oz. [PAS18] 2.00
____Cheetos Flamin' Hot 9.5oz. [PAS19] 2.00
____Cheetos Puffs 11oz. [PAS20] 2.00
____Cheetos Puffs 12-pack [PAS21] 2.00
____Cheetos X's and O's 2.00
____Cracker Jack [PAS22] 2.00
____Doritos Cooler Ranch 12-pack [PAS23] 2.00

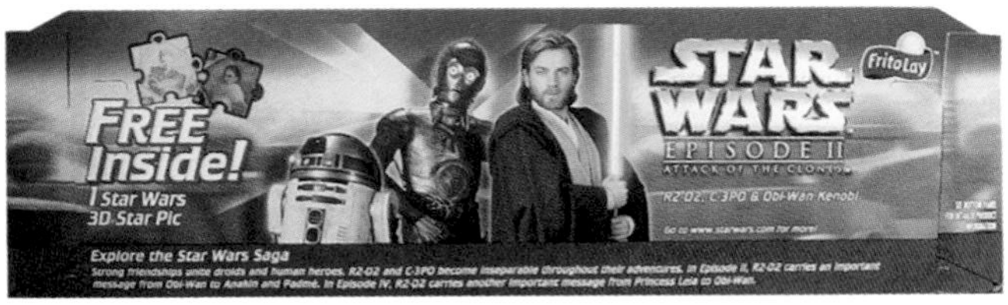

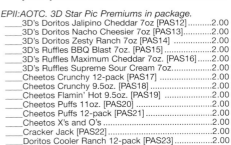

PAS21
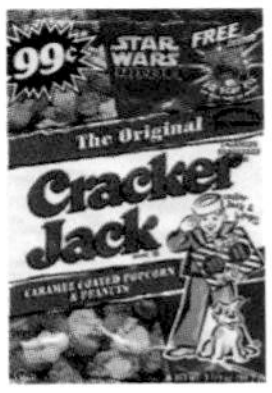
PAS22
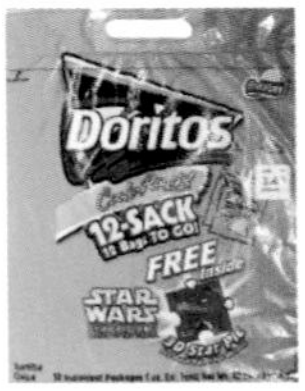
PAS23
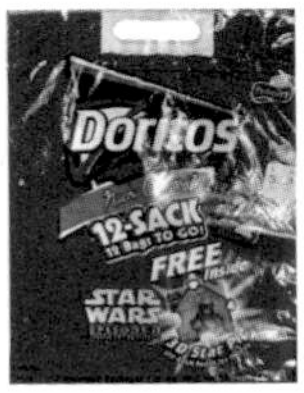
PAS24
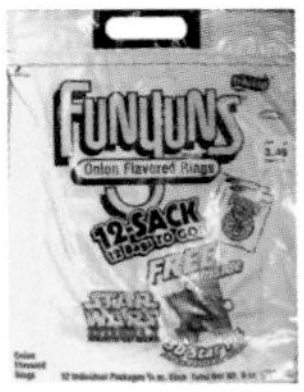
PAS25
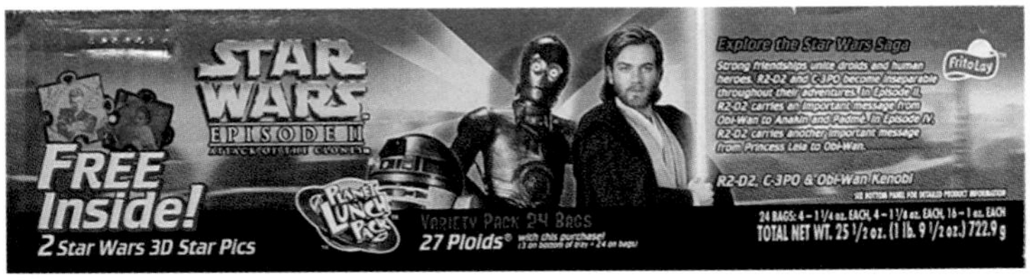

PAS26
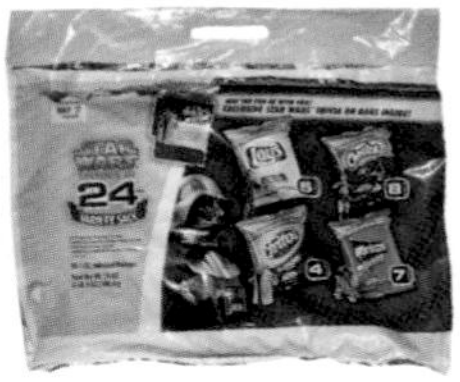
PAS27
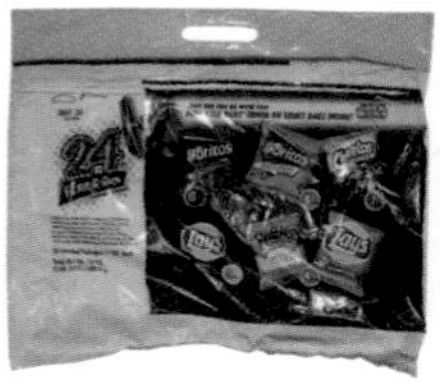
PAS28
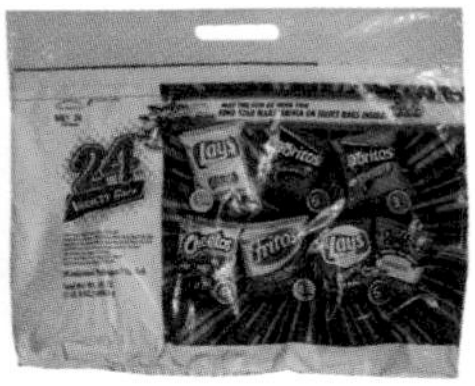
PAS29

Packaging: Snack Chips

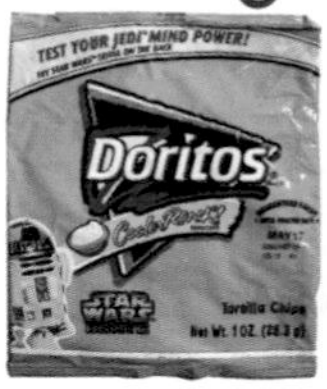

PAS30

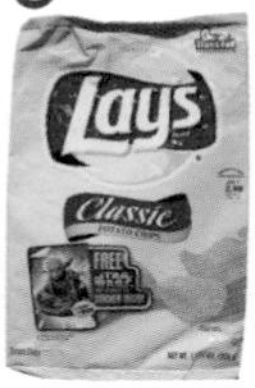

PAS31

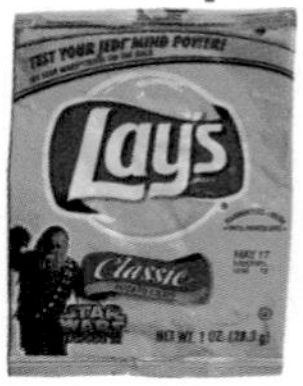

PAS32

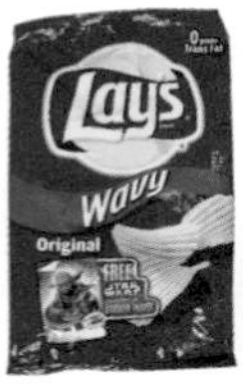

PAS33

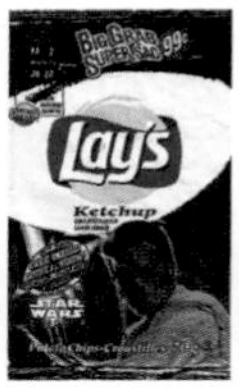

PAS34

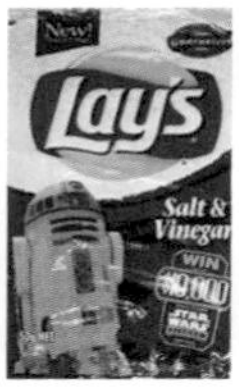

PAS35

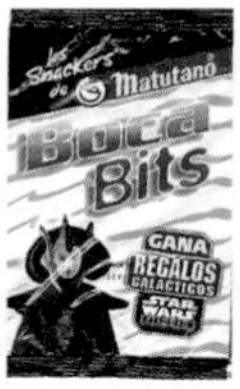

PAS36

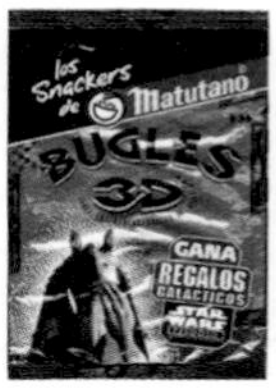

PAS37

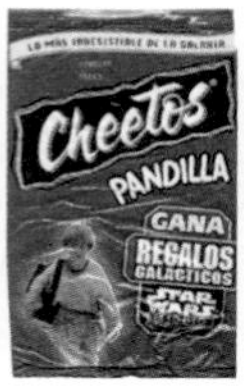

PAS38

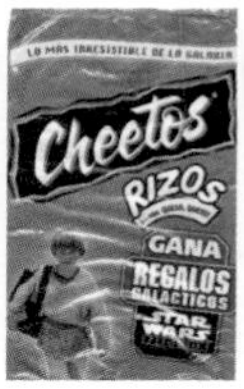

PAS39

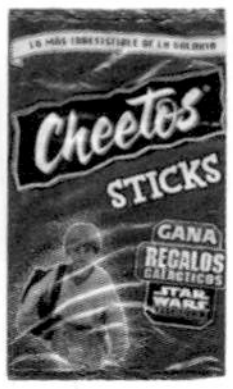

PAS40

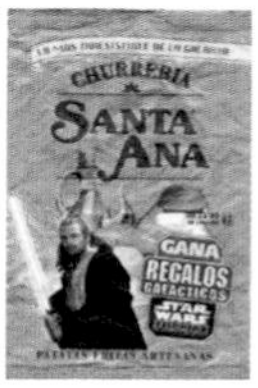

PAS41

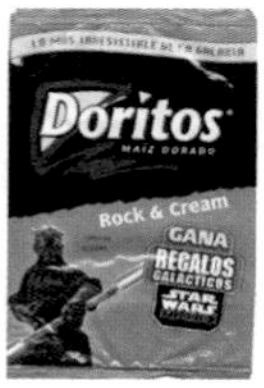

PAS42

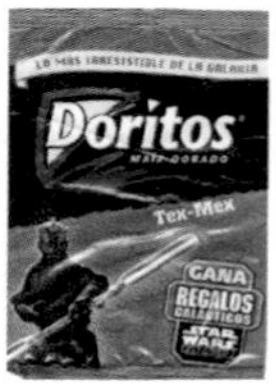

PAS43

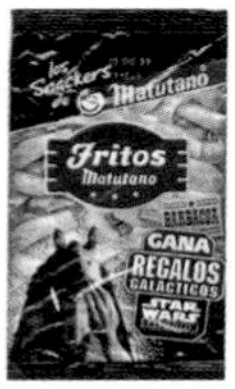

PAS44

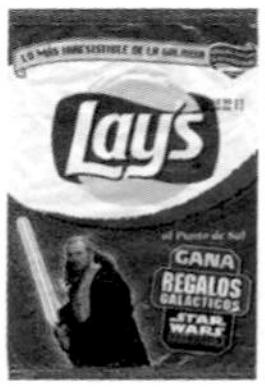

PAS45

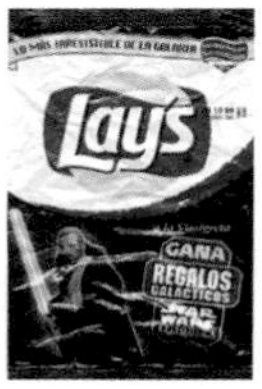

PAS46

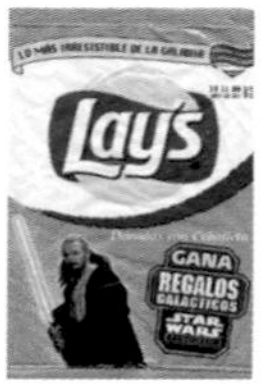

PAS47

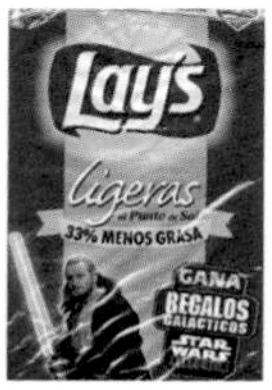

PAS48

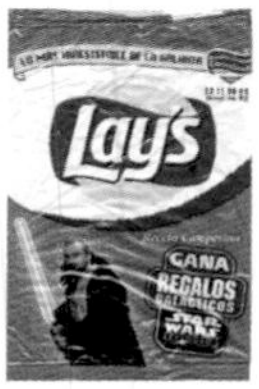

PAS49

____Doritos Nacho Cheesier 12-pack [PAS24] 2.00
____Funyuns 12-pack [PAS25] 2.00
____Lays Planet Lunch 24-pack box with two premiums [PAS26] 4.00

EPIII:ROTS with character pictures on package.
24 pack assortment packs.
____Darth Vader graphic [PAS27] 5.00
____TIE fighter graphic [PAS28]....................................5.00
____X-wing fighter graphic [PAS29]..............................5.00

Cheetos.
____Crunchy 1oz., C-3PO 2.00
____Crunchy 1oz., General Grievous 2.00
____Crunchy 1oz., Wicket 2.00
____Twisted 2 5/8 oz., Darth Vader and Yoda................2.00
____Twisted 9.5oz., Darth Vader and Yoda................10.00

Doritos.
____Cooler ranch 1oz., Han Solo 2.00
____Cooler ranch 1oz., Princess Leia 2.00
____Cooler ranch 1oz., R2-D2 [PAS30] 2.00

Fritos.
____Original 1oz., Luke 2.00
____Original 1oz., Obi-Wan 2.00
____Original 1oz., Yoda 2.00

Lays.
____Classic 11.5oz., sticker premium [PAS31] 3.00
____Classic 1oz., Anakin Skywalker (young)................2.00
____Classic 1oz., Chewbacca [PAS32] 2.00
____Classic 1oz., Padme..2.00
____Wavy 11.5oz., sticker premium [PAS33]................3.00

Lays Classic Potato Chips Anakin Skywalker photo.
____3oz. 2.00
____5.5oz. 2.00
____5.5oz. with game card inside 3.00
____7.5oz. 2.00
____12.25oz. 2.00
____13.25oz. with game card inside 3.00

Lays Classic Potato Chips Qui-Gon Jinn photo.
____21.5oz. with poster offer..5.00

Lays Ketchup Flavored Potato Chips w/ EPI card offer.
____70g [PAS34] 2.00

Lays Pizza Flavored Potato Chips with Obi-Wan Kenobi action figure offer.
____1.75oz. 4.00
____3.25oz. 4.00
____6oz. 4.00
____9oz. 4.00
____14oz. 4.00

Lays Potato Chips with Obi-Wan Kenobi action figure offer.
____1.75oz. 4.00
____3.25oz. 4.00
____6oz. 4.00
____9oz. 4.00
____14oz. 4.00

Lays Salt and Vinegar Potato Chips, Jar Jar Binks photo.
____5.5oz. with game card inside 3.00
____7.5oz. 2.00
____13.5oz. with game card inside 3.00

Lays Salt and Vinegar Potato Chips, R2-D2 photo.
____50g with game card inside [PAS35] 3.00

Lays Sour Cream and Onion Potato Chips, Queen Amidala photo.
____3oz. 2.00
____5.50z. with game card inside 3.00
____7.5oz. 2.00
____13.5oz. with game card inside 3.00

Lays Toasted Onion and Cheese Potato Chips, Obi-Wan Kenobi photo.
____3oz. 2.00
____5.5oz. with game card inside 3.00
____13.5oz.with game card inside................................3.00

Multi-pack boxes with adventure game printed inside box with cut-out game pieces on insert card.
____A New Hope 8.00
____Empire Strikes Back 8.00
____Return of the Jedi 8.00

Matutano Snack Ventures

Boca Bits.
____15g with Jar Jar toy offer on back 4.00
____27g with Queen Amidala photo [PAS36] 3.00
____50g with Queen Amidala photo 3.00

Bugles 3-D's.
____36g with Jar Jar photo [PAS37] 3.00
____65g with Jar Jar photo 3.00
____85g with Jar Jar photo 3.00

Cheetos. Anakin Skywalker photo packages.
____Pandilla, 14g with Jar Jar toy offer on back 4.00
____Pandilla, 31g [PAS38] 3.00
____Pandilla, 75g 3.00
____Pelotazos, 22g with Jar Jar toy offer on back 4.00
____Rizos, 14g with Jar Jar toy offer on back 4.00
____Rizos, 27g [PAS39] 3.00
____Rizos, 57g 3.00
____Sticks, 18g with Jar Jar toy offer on back 4.00
____Sticks, 36g [PAS40] 3.00
____Sticks, 70g 3.00

Churreria Santa Ana. Qui-Gon Jinn photo packages.
____41g [PAS41] 3.00
____120g 3.00
____170g 3.00

Doritos. Darth Maul photo packages.
____Rock and Cream, 110g..3.00
____Rock and Cream, 80g [PAS42]................................3.00
____Tex-Mex, 110g 3.00
____Tex-Mex, 30g [PAS43] 3.00
____Tex-Mex, 44g 3.00
____Tex-Mex, 80g 3.00

Fritos. Jar Jar Binks photo packages.
____Matutano Barbacoa, 130g 3.00
____Matutano Barbacoa, 50g [PAS44] 3.00
____Matutano Barbacoa, 95g 3.00
____Matutano Ketchup, 25g with Jar Jar toy offer 4.00

Lays. Qui-Gon Jinn photo packages.
____125g 3.00
____170g 3.00
____ 30g 3.00
____ 44g 3.00
____A la Vinagreta [PAS46] 3.00
____A la Vinagreta, 160g 3.00
____Doradas con Cebolleta, 110g [PAS47]....................3.00

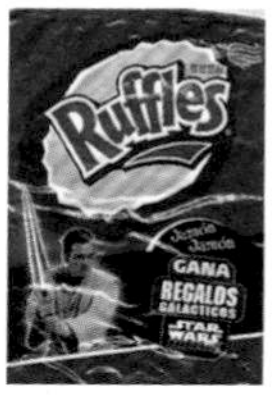

PAS50

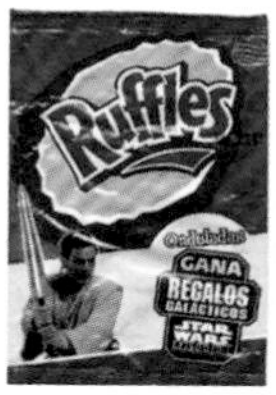

PAS51

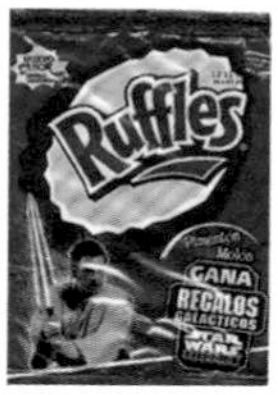

PAS52

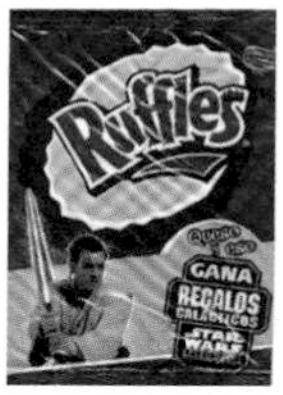

PAS53

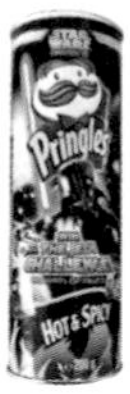

PAS54

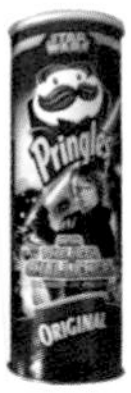

PAS55

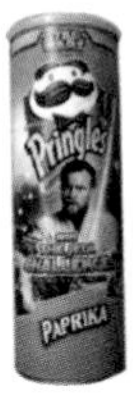

PAS56

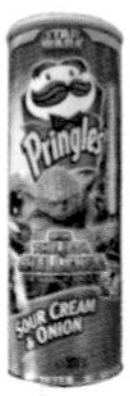

PAS57

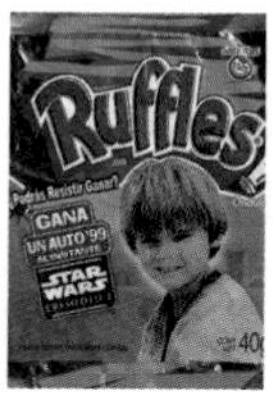

PAS58

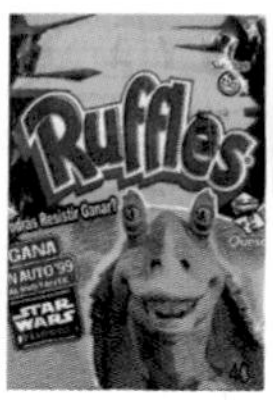

PAS59

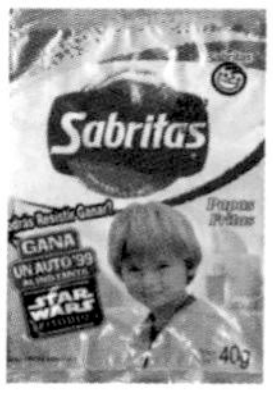

PAS60

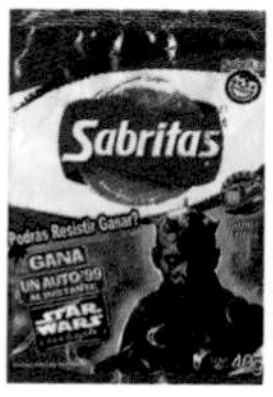

PAS61

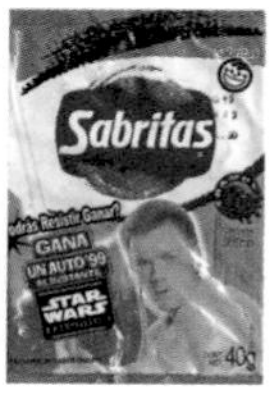

PAS62

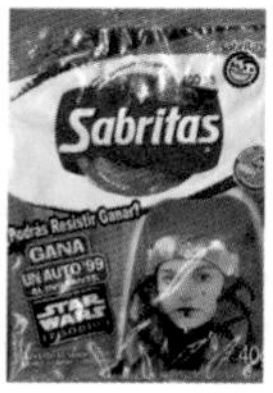

PAS63

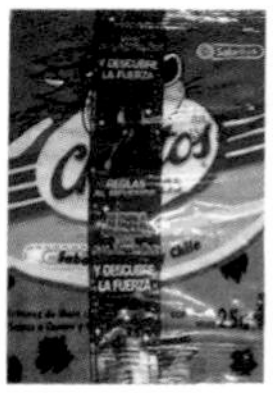
PAS64

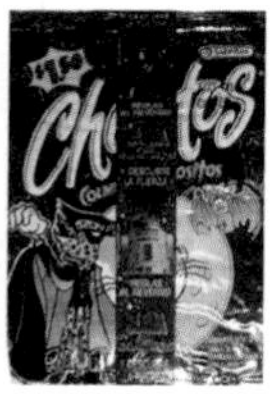
PAS65

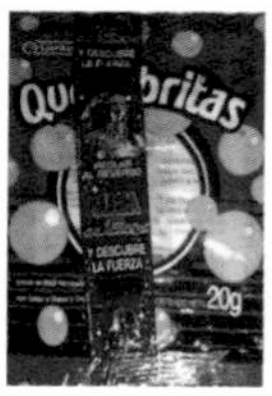
PAS66

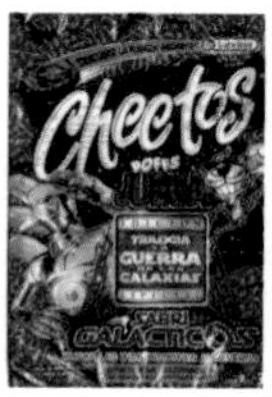

PAS67

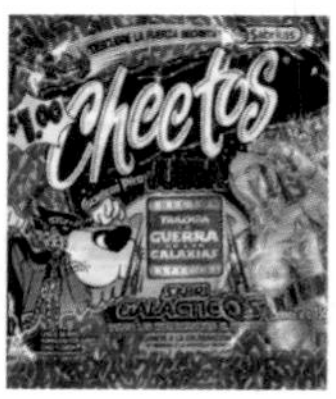

PAS68

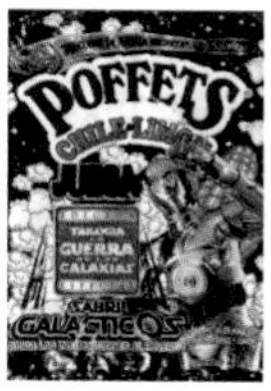

PAS69

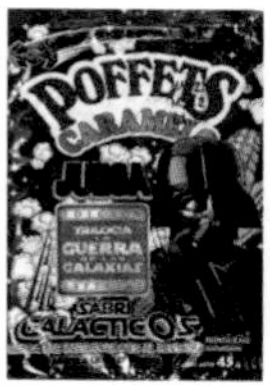

PAS70

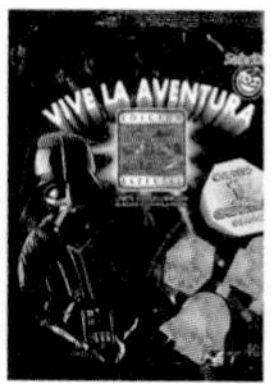

PAS71

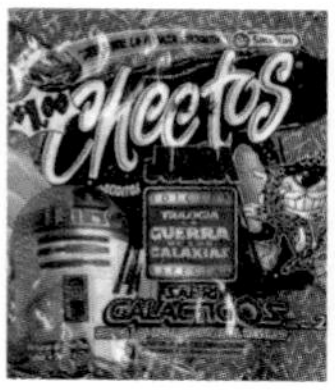

PAS72

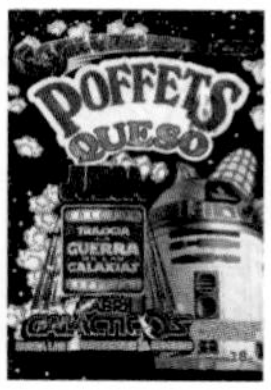

PAS73

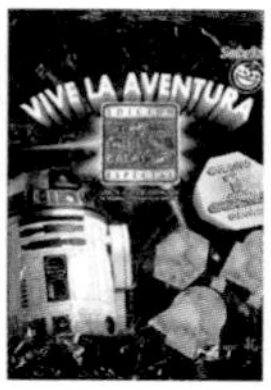

PAS74

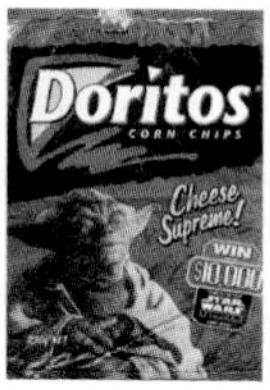

PAS75

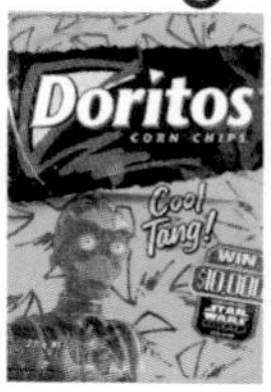

PAS76

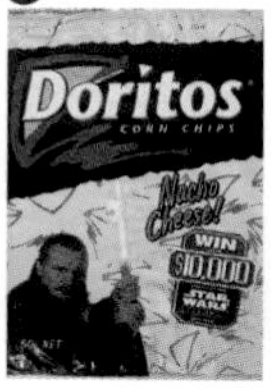

PAS77

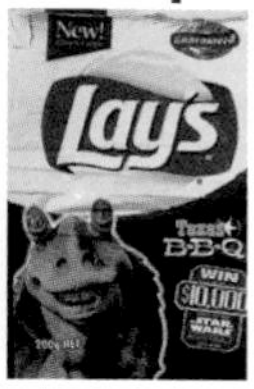

PAS78

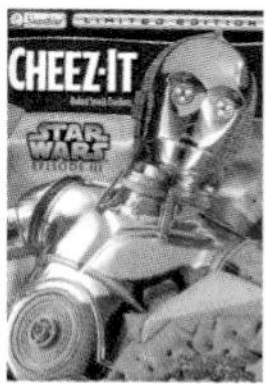

PAS79

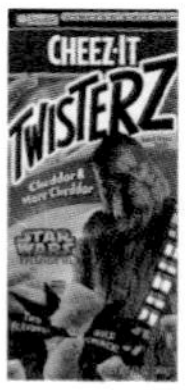

PAS80

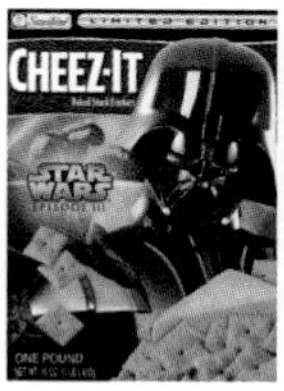

PAS81

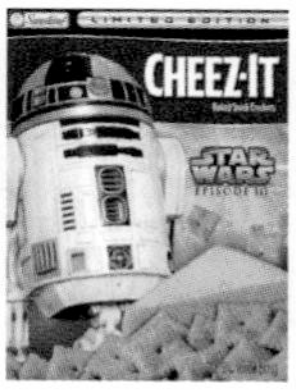

PAS82

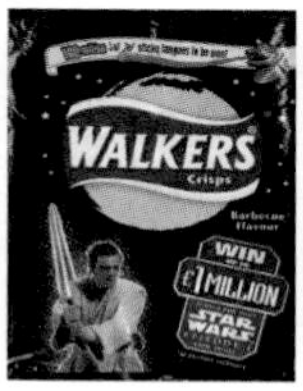

PAS83

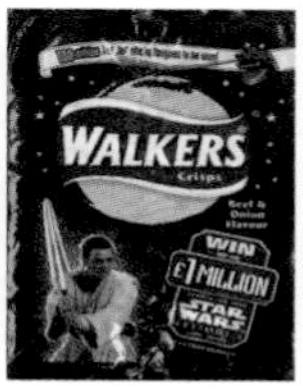

PAS84

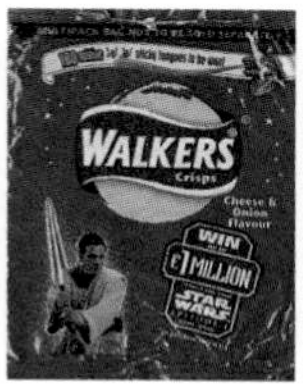

PAS85

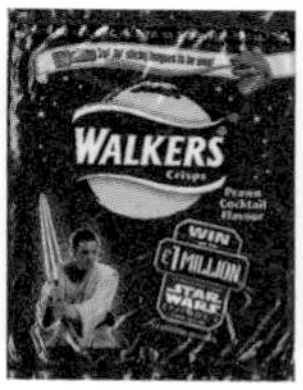

PAS86

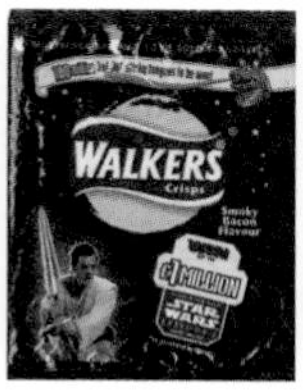

PAS87

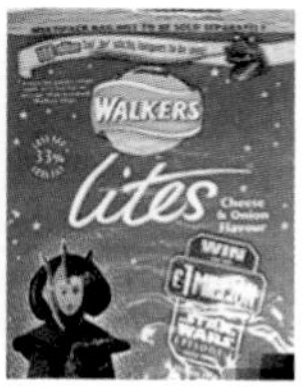

PAS88

____Doradas con Cebolleta, 160g 3.00
____Doradas con Cebolleta, 44g 3.00
____Ligeras 33% Menos Grasa, 140g 3.00
____Ligeras 33% Menos Grasa, 30g [PAS48] 3.00
____Ligeras 33% Menos Grasa, 44g 3.00
____Receta Campesina, 110g [PAS49] 3.00
____Receta Campesina, 160g 3.00

Ruffles. Obi-Wan Kenobi photo packages.

____Alioli ole, 110g 3.00
____Alioli ole, 160g 3.00
____Alioli ole, 44g 3.00
____Jamon Jamon, 110g 3.00
____Jamon Jamon, 30g 3.00
____Jamon Jamon, 44g [PAS50] 3.00
____Onduladas, 125g 3.00
____Onduladas, 170g 3.00
____Onduladas, 44g [PAS51] 3.00
____Pimenton Molon, 110g 3.00
____Pimenton Molon, 160g 3.00
____Pimenton Molon, 44g [PAS52] 3.00
____Queso y eso, 110g 3.00
____Queso y eso, 160g 3.00
____Queso y eso, 44g 3.00

Proctor and Gamble

EPIII:ROTS. Pringles, 200g canisters

____Hot and Spicy [PAS54] 8.00
____Original [PAS55] 8.00
____Paprika [PAS56] 8.00
____Sour Cream and Onion [PAS57] 8.00

Sabritas

Episode I: The Phantom Menace.

____Ruffles, Anakin [PAS58] 2.00
____Ruffles, Jar Jar [PAS59] 2.00
____Sabritas, Anakin [PAS60] 2.00
____Sabritas, Darth Maul [PAS61] 2.00
____Sabritas, Obi-Wan [PAS62] 2.00
____Sabritas, Queen Amidala [PAS63] 2.00

Star Wars Special Edition / Feel the Force.

____Cheetos [PAS64] 4.00
____Cheetos, colmulos pico [PAS65] 4.00
____Quesosabritas [PAS66] 4.00

Star Wars Special Edition.

____C-3PO, Cheetos [PAS67] 3.00
____C-3PO, Cheetos colmulos pico [PAS68] 4.00
____C-3PO, Poffets chile-limon [PAS69] 3.00
____Darth Vader, Poffets caramelo [PAS70] 3.00
____Darth Vader, Vive La Aventura [PAS71] 4.00
____R2-D2, Cheetos torciditos [PAS72] 3.00
____R2-D2, Poffets queso [PAS73] 3.00
____R2-D2, Vive La Aventura [PAS74] 4.00

Smith's Snackfood

Episode I: The Phantom Menace.

Doritos Corn Chips, Cheese Supreme with Yoda packaging.

____230g [PAS75] 3.00
____50g 3.00

Doritos Corn Chips, Cool Tang with C-3PO packaging.

____230g [PAS76] 3.00
____50g 3.00

Doritos Corn Chips, Nacho Cheese with Qui-Gon packaging.

____230g 3.00
____50g [PAS77] 3.00

Doritos Corn Chips, Original with Queen Amidala packaging.

____230g 3.00

Lays multi-packs.

____12pk. Flavour Mix, C-3PO pkg. 3.00
____12pk. Original, Anakin pkg. 3.00
____12pk. Texas BBQ, Jar Jar pkg. 3.00
____18pk. Flavour Mix, Yoda pkg. 3.00

Lays, Cheddar Cheese and Onion with Amidala packaging.

____100g 3.00
____200g 3.00
____50g 3.00

Lays, Original with Anakin packaging.

____100g 3.00
____50g 3.00

Lays, Roast Chicken with Obi-Wan packaging.

____100g 3.00
____250g 3.00
____50g 3.00

Lays, Salt and Vinegar with R2-D2 packaging.

____250g 3.00
____550g 3.00

Lays, Texas BBQ with Jar Jar packaging.

____100g 3.00
____200g [PAS78] 3.00
____50g 3.00

Sunshine Biscuits L.L.C.

EPIII:ROTS. Cheez-It Crackers.

____C-3PO 16oz. [PAS79] 5.00
____Chewbacca Twisterz 13oz. [PAS80] 8.00
____Darth Vader 16oz. [PAS81] 5.00
____R2-D2 10oz. [PAS82] 5.00

Walkers

Episode I: The Phantom Menace.

Crisps, Obi-Wan Kenobi packaging.

____Barbecue [PAS83] 2.00
____Beef and onion [PAS84] 2.00
____Cheese and onion 2.00
____Cheese and onion, multipack [PAS85] 2.00
____Prawn cocktail, multipack [PAS86] 2.00
____Smoky Bacon, multipack [PAS87] 2.00

Lites, Queen Amidala packaging.

____Cheese and onion [PAS88] 2.00
____Salted [PAS89] 2.00

Monster Munch, Jar Jar packaging.

____Pickled Onion [PAS90] 3.00

Sundog popcorn, Jar Jar packaging.

____ [PAS91] 2.00

Star Wars Special Edition.

Crisps, C-3PO packaging.

____06-pack cheese and onion [PAS92] 4.00
____06-pack mixed flavors [PAS93] 4.00
____10-pack mixed flavors [PAS94] 4.00
____Beef and onion [PAS95] 3.00
____Cheese and onion [PAS96] 3.00
____Cream cheese and chive [PAS97] 3.00
____Roast chicken [PAS98] 3.00
____Salt and vinegar [PAS99] 3.00
____Salted [PAS100] 3.00
____Smokey bacon [PAS101] 3.00

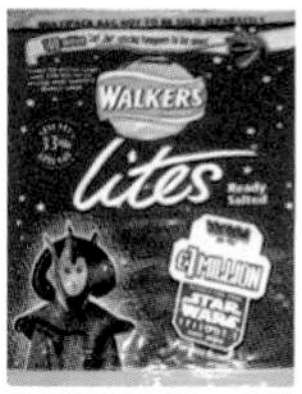

PAS89

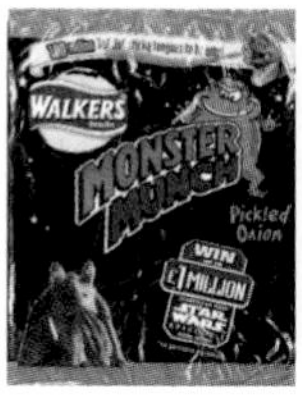

PAS90

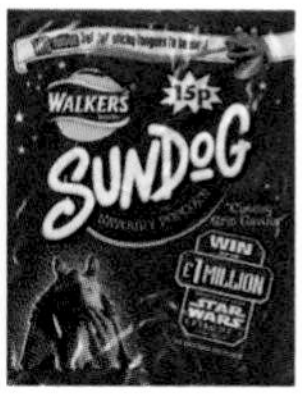

PAS91

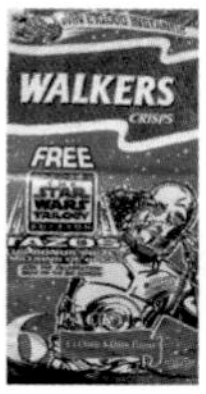

PAS92

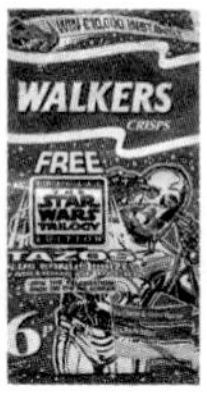

PAS93

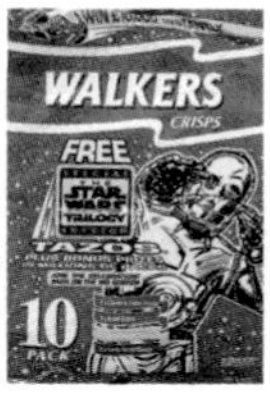

PAS94

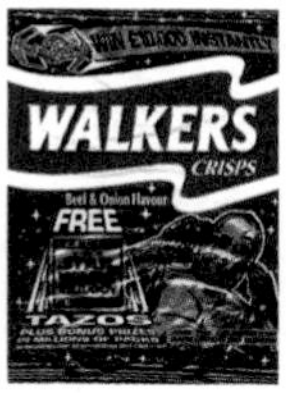

PAS95

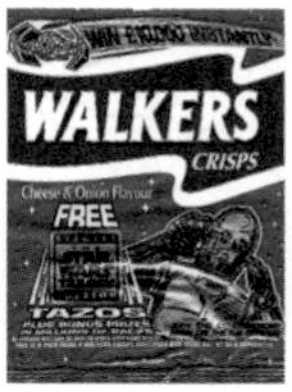

PAS96

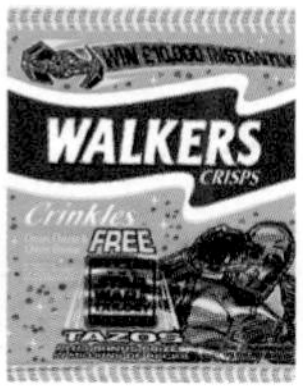

PAS97

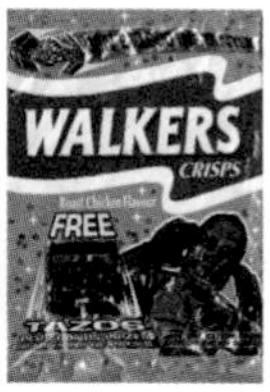

PAS98

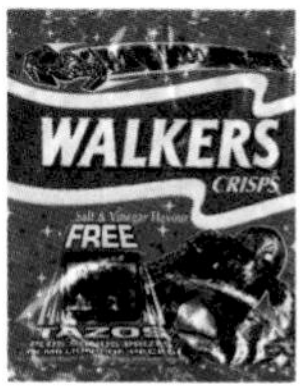

PAS99

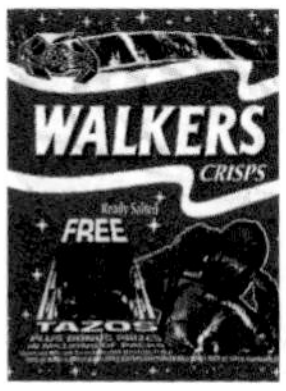

PAS100

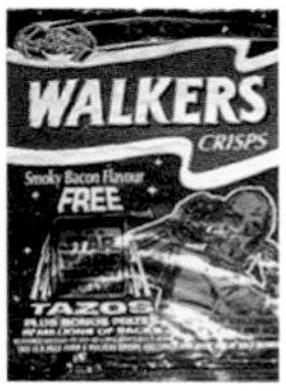

PAS101

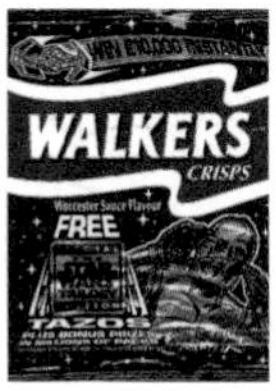

PAS102

PAS103

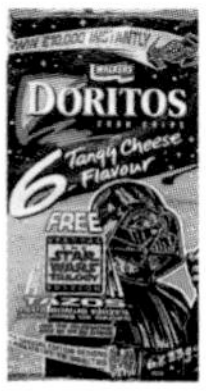

PAS104

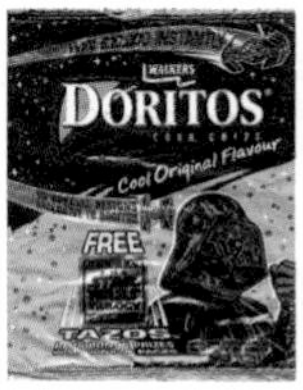

PAS105

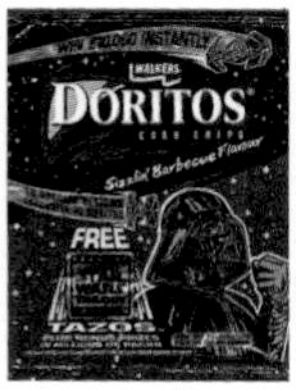

PAS106

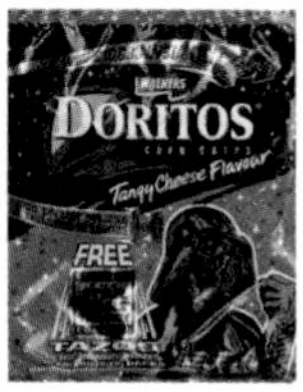

PAS107

Packaging: Snack Chips

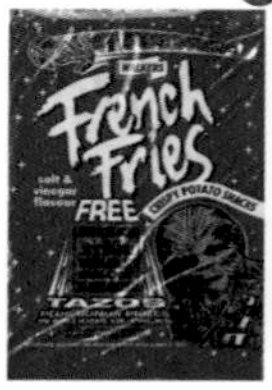
PAS108

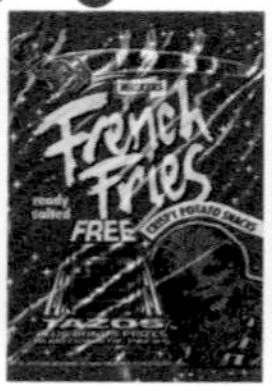
PAS109

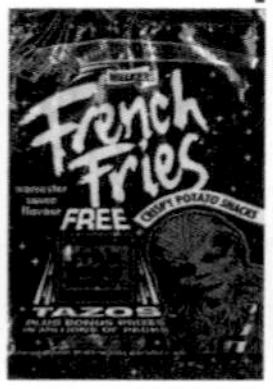
PAS110

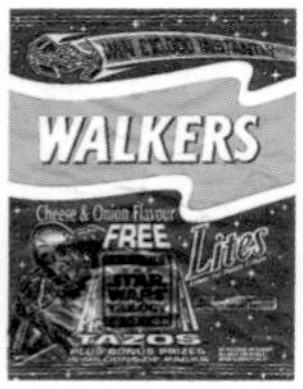
PAS111

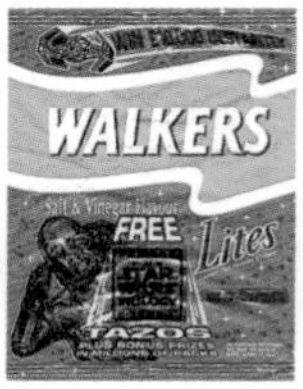
PAS112

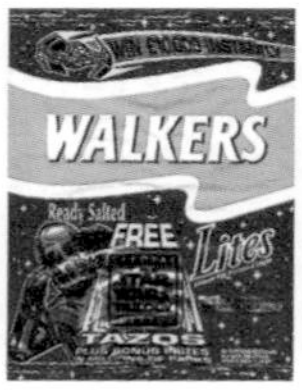
PAS113

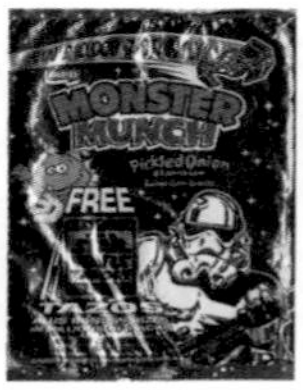
PAS114

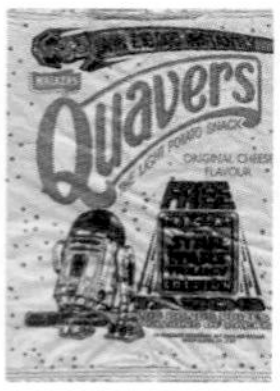
PAS115

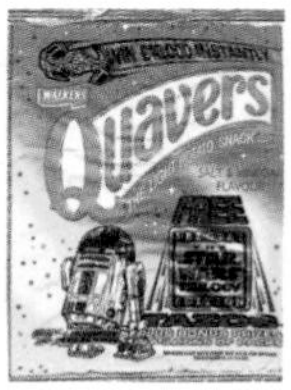
PAS116

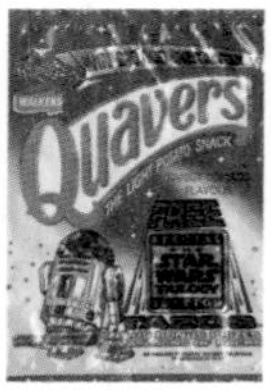
PAS117

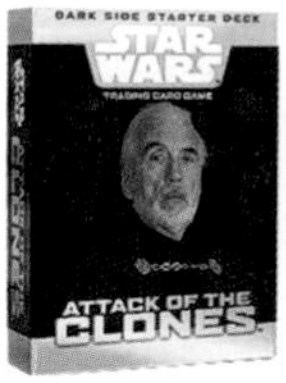
TGP01

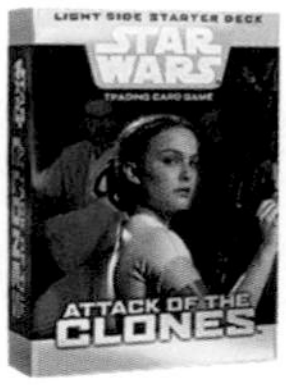
TGP02

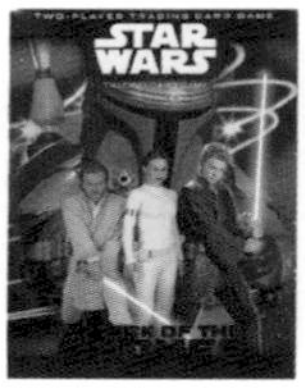
TGP03

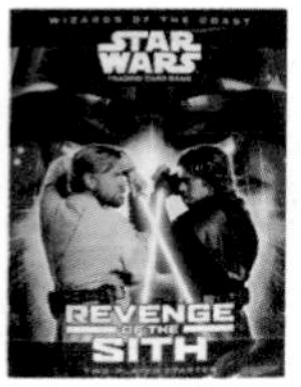
TGP04

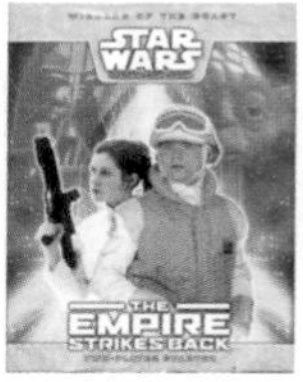
TGP05

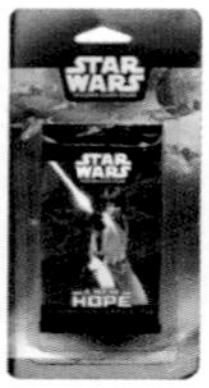
TGP06

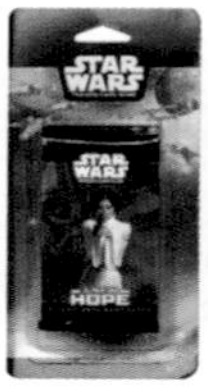
TGP07

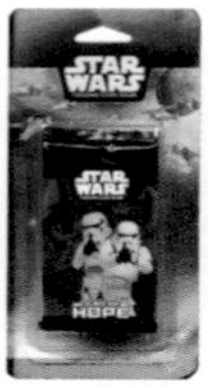
TGP08

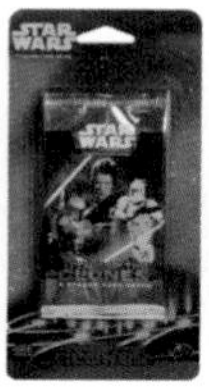
TGP09

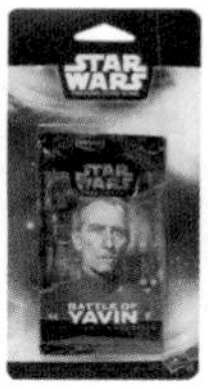
TGP10

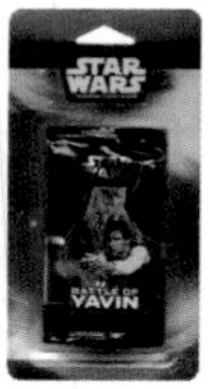
TGP11

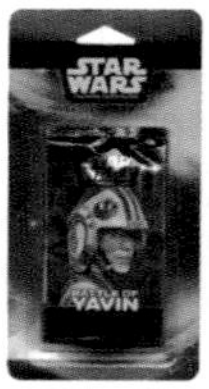
TGP12

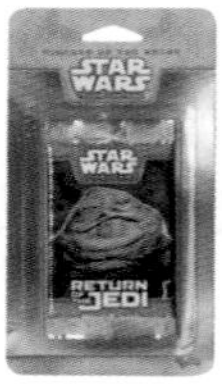
TGP13

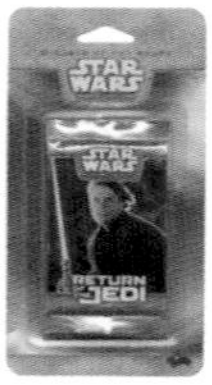
TGP14

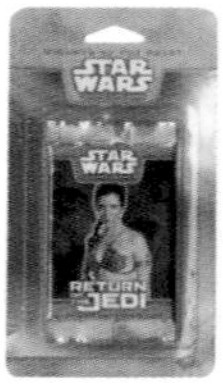
TGP15

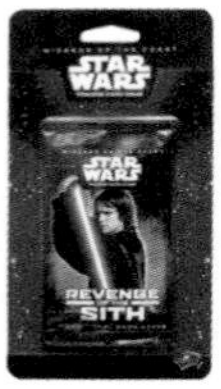
TGP16

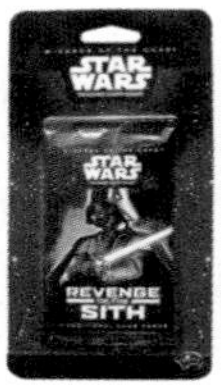
TGP17

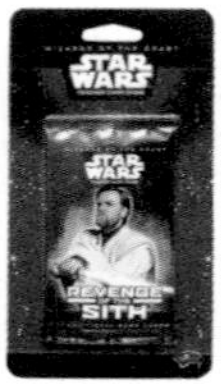
TGP18

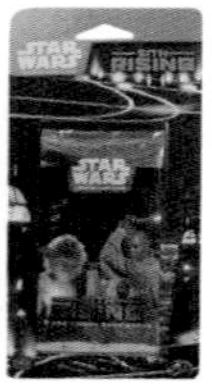
TGP19

____Worchester sauce [PAS102] 3.00

Doritos, Darth Vader packaging.
____06-pack mixed flavors [PAS103] 4.00
____06-pack tangy cheese [PAS104] 4.00
____Original [PAS105] 3.00
____Sizzlin' barbeque [PAS106]....................................3.00
____Tangy cheese [PAS107] 3.00

French Fries, Chewbacca packaging.
____Salt and vinegar [PAS108] 3.00
____Salted [PAS109] 3.00
____Worcester sauce [PAS110] 3.00

Lites, C-3PO packaging.
____Cheese and onion [PAS111]..................................3.00
____Salt and vinegar [PAS112] 3.00
____Salted [PAS113] 3.00

Monster Munch, Stormtrooper packaging.
____Pickled Onion [PAS114] 3.00

Quavers, R2-D2 packaging.
____Cheese [PAS115] 3.00
____Salt and vinegar [PAS116] 3.00
____Tangy tomato [PAS117] 3.00

Packaging: TCG

Wizards of the Coast
2-Player Trading Card Game.
____Advanced Starter Deck, dark side [TGP01]........10.00
____Advanced Starter Deck, light side [TGP02]........10.00
____Attack of the Clones [TGP03] 25.00
____Revenge of the Sith [TGP04] 25.00
____The Empire Strikes Back [TGP05] 25.00

A New Hope. 11 additional game cards.
____Luke Skywalker [TGP06]..3.00
____Princess Leia [TGP07] 3.00
____Stormtroopers [TGP08]..3.00

Attack of the Clones. Packets of 5 random cards.
____1 packet of 5 random cards [TGP09]....................4.00
____2 packets of 5 random cards 8.00

Battle of Yavin. 11 additional game cards.
____Grand Moff Tarkin [TGP10]....................................3.00
____Han and Chewbacca [TGP11] 3.00
____Luke Skywalker, pilot [TGP12] 3.00

Return of the Jedi. 11 additional game cards.
____Jabba the Hutt [TGP13] 4.00
____Luke Skywalker [TGP14]..4.00
____Princess Leia [TGP15] 4.00

Revenge of the Sith. 11 additional game cards.
____Anakin Skywalker [TGP16] 3.00
____Darth Vader [TGP17]...3.00
____Obi-Wan Kenobi [TGP18] 3.00

Sith Rising. 11 additional game cards.
____Count Dooku..3.00
____Darth Maul 3.00
____Yoda 3.00

Sith Rising.Packets of 5 random cards.
____2 packets of 5 random cards [TGP19] 5.00

Packaging: Yogurt

Dairylea
Plastic cups with printed characters.
____Admiral Ackbar, pineapple 8.00
____Chewbacca, fudge 8.00
____Darth Vader, black cherry 8.00
____Ewoks, bananna 8.00
____Jabba the Hutt, peach melba..................................8.00
____Luke Skywalker, rapsberry 8.00
____Princess Leia, strawberry 8.00
____Yoda, gooseberry 8.00

Yoplait
24ct. box of glow in the dark lightsaber tube packaging.
____Strawberry splash and berry blue blast [PAY01] 2.00

8-pack box featuring glow in the dark lightsaber tubes.
____Burstin' melon berry and cool cotton candy [PAY02] 2.00
____Red raspberry and paradise punch [PAY03] 2.00
____Rootbeer float and banana split [PAY04] 2.00
____Strawberry kiwi kick and chill out cherry 2.00
____Strawberry splash and berry blue blast 2.00
____Watermelon meltdown and strawberry banana burst [PAY05] 2.00

Glow in the dark lightsaber tubes.
____Anakin Skywalker, cool cotton candy [PAY06] 1.00
____Barriss Offee, burstin' melon berry [PAY07]..........1.00
____Count Dooku, strawberry splash [PAY08] 1.00
____Darth Maul, chill out cherry [PAY09].......................1.00
____Darth Vader, strawberry splash [PAY10]................1.00
____Ki-Adi Mundi, burstin' melon berry [PAY11]..........1.00
____Kit Fisto, bananna split [PAY12] 1.00
____Luke Skywalker, berry blue blast [PAY13] 1.00
____Luminara Unduli, watermelon meltdown [PAY14] 1.00
____Mace Windu, red raspberry [PAY15] 1.00
____Obi-Wan Kenobi (EPII), strawberry banana burst [PAY16] 1.00
____Obi-Wan Kenobi (EPIV), rootbeer float [PAY17] 1.00
____Plo Koon, berry blue blast [PAY18] 1.00
____Qui Gon Jinn, strawberry kiwi kick [PAY19] 1.00
____Shaak Ti, cool cotton candy [PAY20] 1.00
____Stass Allie, paradise punch [PAY21].......................1.00
____Yoda, Banana Split [PAY22] 1.00

Pads: Sports

Episode I glove, knee and elbow pad set.
____Knee and elbow pads in plastic Darth Maul case [SFT01] 16.00

Dynacraft
Episode I glove, knee and elbow pad sets.
____Darth Maul [SFT02] 16.00
____Queen Amidala [SFT03] 16.00

M.V. Sports and Leisure Ltd.
Episode I glove, knee and elbow pad set.
____Darth Maul knee and elbow pads [SFT04] 14.00

Seneca Sports Inc.
Protective gear backpack with knee pads, elbow pads, wrist guards, water bottle.
____Imperial Assault [SFT05] 14.00
____R2-D2 [SFT06] 16.00

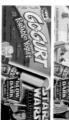

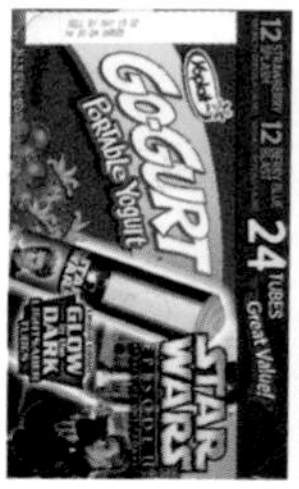
PAY01

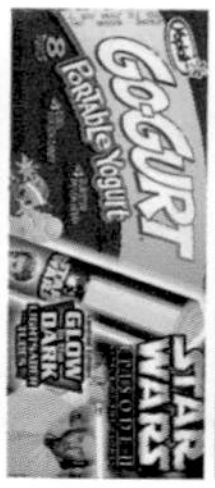
PAY02

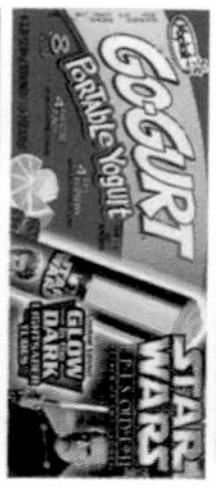
PAY03

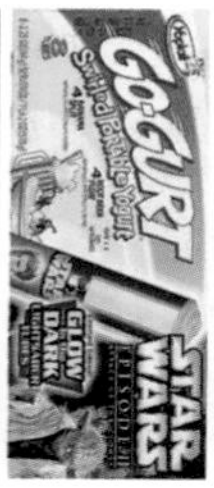
PAY04

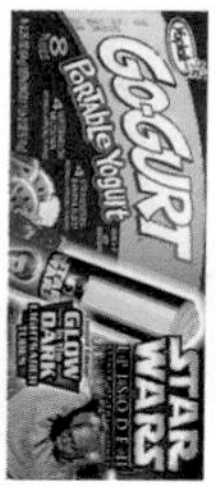
PAY05

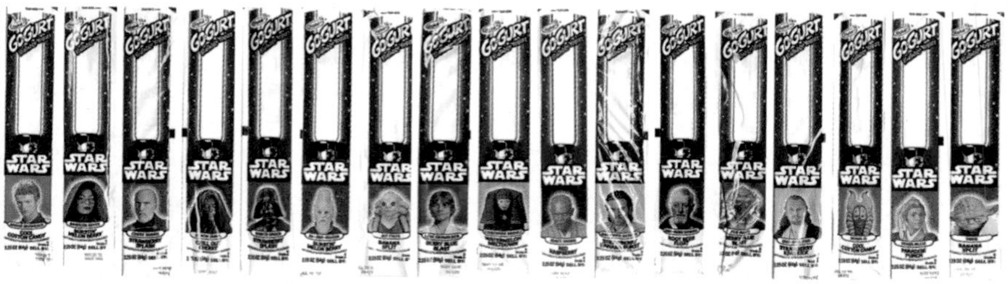
PAY06 through PAY22 — individual wrapper tubes

SFT01	SFT02	SFT03	SFT04	SFT05	SFT06	TRP01	PCL01

MDP01	SUJ01	SUJ02	SUJ03	SUJ04	SUJ05

SUJ06	SUJ07	SUJ08	PRT01

Pails: Trick or Treat

Rubies
____Darth Vader [TRP01] 8.00

Paint

Testers
____Detail paints for vinyl kits [MDP01].........................6.00

Paper Clips

Flomo
____Star Wars, spring operated [PCL01].......................2.00

Paper Reinforcements

Butterfly Originals
____48-pack, ROTJ foil [SUJ01] 7.00

Individual reinforcement stickers. Distributed in gumball machine capsules. 1.5"x1.5" square.
____C-3PO [SUJ02] 3.00
____Darth's TIE Fighter 3.00
____Darth Vader [SUJ03] 3.00
____Galactic Emperor 3.00
____Han Solo [SUJ04] 3.00
____Jabba the Hutt [SUJ05] 3.00
____Luke Skywalker..3.00
____Millennium Falcon...3.00
____R2-D2 [SUJ06] 3.00
____Salacious Crumb [SUJ07].....................................3.00
____Shuttle Tyderium 3.00
____TIE Fighter [SUJ08]..3.00

Paper Toweling

Zewa
____Episode III with free yoda plush [PRT01].............35.00

Paperweights

____10th Anniv., spring hinge, magnet back 24.00

3D Arts
____Darth Vader..15.00
____Yoda 15.00

Fossil, Inc.
____25th anniversary, incl. with watch [3:326] 25.00

Party Bags

Drawing Board Greeting Cards, Inc.
Bags are valued in original 8-packs.
____Darth Vader and Luke duel [PFA01] 8.00
____Ewoks [PFA02] 8.00

Hunter Leisure
____EPIII:Vader / Jedi [PFA03]......................................5.00

Party Express
____EPIII:ROTS Darth Vader treat boxes [PFA04].......3.00

Bags are valued in original 8-packs.
____Classic. Millennium Falcon flees Death Star [PFA05]...3.00
____Classic. Neon [PFA06] 5.00
____EPI:TPM. Darth Maul with Jedi vs. Sith scene in background [PFA07]..3.00
____EPII:AOTC. Jango and Jedi [PFA08] 3.00
____Star Wars Saga [PFA09] 3.00

Quela
____Darth Vader neon, 8-pack [PFA10].......................8.00

Unique
____EPI: Jedi vs. Sith [PFA11] 6.00

Party Banners

Drawing Board Greeting Cards, Inc.
____ESB Birthday [PFC01] 12.00

Party Express
Celebration, Happy Birthday.
____EPI:TPM [PFC02] 4.00
____EPII:AOTC [PFC03]...4.00
____EPIII:ROTS [PFC04] 4.00
____Star Wars Saga [PFC05]..6.00

Unique
____Jedi vs. Sith [PFC06] 6.00

Party Blowouts

Drawing Board Greeting Cards, Inc.
4-packs.
____ESB: Darth Vader [PFD01] 6.00
____Ewoks 6.00
____ROTJ: Darth Vader [PFD02] 6.00

Hunter Leisure
____Jedi [PFD03] 6.00

Party Express
____Classic trilogy. X-Wing vs. Tie fighter [PFD04]......3.00
____EPI:TPM. Jedi and Sith silhouettes [PFD05] 3.00

PFA01	PFA02	PFA03	PFA04	PFA05	PFA06	PFA07

PFA08	PFA09	PFA10	PFA11	PFC01	PFC02	PFC03	PFC04	PFC05	PFC06

Party Blowouts

| PFD01 | PFD02 | PFD03 | PFD04 | PFD05 | PFD06 | PFD07 | PFD08 | PFD09 |

| PD01 | PD02 | PD03 | PD04 | NF01 | NF02 | PFH01 | PFH02 |

| PFH03 | PFH04 | PFH05 | PFH06 | PFH07 | PPP01 | PPP02 | PPP03 |

____EPII:AOTC. Jedi silhouettes [PFD06] 3.00
____EPIII:ROTS. Darth Vader [PFD07].....................3.00
____Saga: X-Wing, Tie Fighter and Millennium Falcon [PFD08] 3.00

Unique
EPI:TPM.
____Darth Maul vs. Jedi [PFD09]....................6.00

Party Decorations

Party Express
Crepe paper streamers with character silouettes.
____Jedi and Sith [PD01]................................3.00
____Jedi Duel [PD02] 3.00

Wall hangings, set of 3.
____Classic trilogy starships [PD03] 9.00
____Jedi vs. Sith [PD04] 7.00

Party Games

Party Express
____Space Battle [NF01] 7.00

Unique
____Star Wars lightsaber game [NF02].....................10.00

Party Hats

Drawing Board Greeting Cards, Inc.
____Star Wars punch-out, 8-pack [PFH01] 17.00

Vintage. 8-pack of cone hats.
____Cloud City...10.00
____Darth Vader and Luke Duel 10.00
____Ewoks Hang-Gliding [PFH02].............................8.00

Party Express
8-pack of cone hats.
____Battle above Death Star [PFH03] 4.00
____Droids with Star Wars logo, neon [PFH04]............5.00
____EPI:TPM. Jar Jar Binks [PFH05]..........................3.00
____EPII:AOTC. Jedi Duel [PFH06] 5.00
____Star Wars Saga [PFH07]..................................7.00

Passports

____Passport to universe, Star Wars SE [PPP01]......18.00

Ballantine
____Star Wars Intergalactic Passport [PPP2] 24.00

Pepsi Cola
____Anakin [3:326] 3.00
____Qui-Gon Jinn [3:326]................................3.00
____Watto [PPP03].......................................3.00

Patches

____Corellia, Millennium Falcon [PT01].....................25.00
____ESB logo, large [PT02] 20.00
____Star Wars Special Edition [PT03] 25.00

Celebration 3 logo.
____Cloth [PT04] 10.00
____Rubber [PT05] 10.00

Celebration III, 3 part.
____DC Metro Area Star Wars Collecting Club 20.00
____Ohio Star Wars Collectors Club 20.00
____Pennsylvania Star Wars Collecting Society........20.00
____Protoype, uncut with metallic thread, limited to 10 ....75.00

Celebration III, POTF style logo.
____DC Metro Area Star Wars Collecting Club, black border 15.00
____DC Metro Area Star Wars Collecting Club, gold border 15.00

Japan.
____Anakin 10.00
____Clone Trooper (helmet) 10.00
____Darth Vader..10.00
____Darth Vader (flaming helmet) 10.00
____Darth Vader (helmet) [PT06] 10.00
____Darth Vader (imperial cog) 10.00
____Darth Vader (sunrise) 10.00
____Darth Vader oval......................................10.00
____Darth Vader shield 10.00
____Grievous [PT07] 10.00
____Jedi [PT08] 10.00
____Jedi Starfighter 10.00
____ROTS logo 10.00
____Sith [PT09] 10.00
____Sith Lord 10.00
____Star Wars logo [PT10] 10.00
____Vader 10.00
____Yoda [PT11] 10.00

20th Century Fox
____EPIII:ROTS DVD release promotional 12.00

Boy Scouts of America
____1997 Fall Fellowship [PT12] 25.00

| PT01 | PT02 | PT03 | PT04 | PT05 | PT06 | PT07 | PT08 |

| PT09 | PT10 | PT11 | PT12 | PT13 | PT14 | PT15 | PT16 |

PT17 · PT18 · PT19 · PT20 · PT21 · PT22 · PT23 · PT24

PT25 · PT26 · PT27 · PT28 · PT33 · PT34 · PT38 · PT39

____1997 Olde Mill Star Wars Adventure [PT13] 25.00
____1998 GFRC Day Camp [PT14]............................10.00
____Cub Scout Winter Event [PT15] 35.00

Catalina Council.
____1978 D2 Roundup [PT16].....................................35.00

Catawba Lodge 459 NOAC.
____1994 [PT17] 40.00

Central Okanagan.
____1998 Cuboree Camp Dunlop [PT18] 35.00

Chicago.
____1982 Camporall [PT19] 5.00

Chickasaw.
____1978 Cub Day Camp [PT20] 25.00

Eastern Okla Council.
____1978 Scout Regatta [PT21] 35.00

Eluwak.
____1997 Eluwak Strikes Back Camporee [PT22] 20.00

FCC Powahay District.
____1995 Spring Camporee [PT23]............................35.00

Fort A.P. Hill National Jamboree.
____2001 Sith Park Empire Council, red border [PT24] 20.00
____2001 Sith Park Empire Council, silver mylar border [PT25] 20.00

Grand River Cubs.
____1978 Canadian Star War-EE [PT26]....................25.00

Great Salt Lake Coucil.
____Jedi Training Camp [PT27] 25.00

Illiniwek.
____1978 Webelos Camporee [PT28] 35.00

Jamboree Staff.
____2001 blue border [PT29] 20.00
____2001 pink border [PT30]....................................20.00
____2001 white border [PT31]...................................20.00
____2001 yellow border [PT32] 20.00

Kiowa District.
____1981 Camporee [PT33] 35.00

Lake Huron Area Coucil.
____1982 Day Camp [PT34] 30.00

Los Angeles Area Council NOAC.
____2000 3-part set, black border [PT35].................50.00
____2000 3-part set, light blue border [PT36]...........50.00
____2000 3-part set, silver mylar border [PT37]......150.00

Los Angeles Area Council Pow Wow.
____1997 Red border, staff [PT38] 50.00
____1997 Yellow border, participant [PT39] 50.00

Marin Council.
____1997 Yoda brown border [PT40]........................85.00
____1997 Yoda gold mylar border [PT41]................250.00
____1997 Yoda green border [PT42] 55.00
____1997 Yoda yellow border [PT43] 40.00

Marin National Jamboree.
____1993 [PT44] 60.00
____2001 Black border, Fund Raiser [PT45] 40.00

____2001 Gold mylar border, Donor [PT46] 125.00
____2001 Green border, Jamboree Trader [PT47]...35.00
____2001 Red border, Special Recognition [PT48]...150.00
____2001 Silver mylar border, Troop Leadership [PT49]...250.00

Menawa.
____1999 Camporee, ghost issue [PT50] 10.00

Mid-America Council.
____1978 Scout-O-Rama [PT51]................................35.00

Middle Tennesse Council.
____Join the Force [PT52] 20.00

Occoneechee Council.
____2005 Sea Scout Ship inner Obi-Wan and Anakin 7.00
____2005 Sea Scout Ship outter Anakin...................10.00
____2005 Sea Scout Ship outter C-3PO and R2-D2 ....10.00
____2005 Sea Scout Ship outter Darth Vader 10.00
____2005 Sea Scout Ship outter Obi-Wan 10.00
____2005 Sea Scout Ship outter Yoda 10.00
____2005 Sea Scout Ship outter Yoda / Force..........10.00

Pioneer Valley Council.
____1997 Cub Day Camp [PT53] 10.00

Ridgewood / Glen Rock Council.
____1997 Jamboree [PT54].......................................55.00

Shelter Rock.
____1994 [PT55] 15.00

PT29 · PT30 · PT31 · PT32

PT35 · PT36 · PT37 · PT40 · PT41

PT42 · PT43

PT44 · PT45 · PT46 · PT47 · PT48 · PT49

Patches

PT50

PT51

PT52

PT53

PT54

PT55

PT60

PT56

PT57

PT58

PT59

PT61

PT62

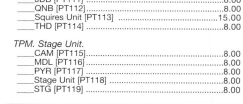
PT63

PT64

Tah Heetch Lodge NOAC.
____2000 silver mylar border, regular [PT56] 75.00
____2000 yellow border, contingent [PT57] 175.00
____2002 silver mylar border, regular [PT58] 75.00
____2002 yellow border, Contingent 150.00
____2004 [PT59] 60.00

Tecumseh District.
____1977 Star Wars Camporee [PT60] 15.00

Valley Trails District.
____1981 Space O Ree [PT61] 15.00

West Scarborough.
____1999 Katimavih [PT62] 20.00

Western Star.
____Spring Camporee [PT63] 15.00

Yosemite Area Council.
____1978 Cub Day Camp [PT64] 35.00

Cast and Crew
____A New Hope, no TM [PT65] ....N/V
____Blue Harvest, silk-screened hat patch [PT67] ......N/V

____Blue Harvest, embroidered hat patch [PT66] 575.00
____ESB, Vader in Flames [PT68] 50.00
____ILM [PT69] 25.00
____ILM VFX 02, Attack Gunship [PT70] 65.00
____Norwegian Unit / Star Wars set of 2 [PT71] 150.00
____Norwegian Unit Cast and Crew Patch Set, formerly in the collection of Producer, Gary Kurtz ....N/V
____Revenge hat patch [PT72] 65.00
____Skywalker Ranch [PT73] 30.00
____Star Wars, early lettering style [PT74] 125.00
____The Star Wars [PT75] ....N/V
____Yoda Revenge, 5"x3" [PT76] 150.00
____Yoda, Revenge screenwriter [PT77] 100.00

ILM VFX Crew 99.
____Battle Droid Tank [PT78] 15.00
____Boss Nass [PT79] 15.00
____Darth Maul [PT80] 15.00
____Jar Jar [PT81] 15.00
____Naboo Fighter [PT82] 15.00
____Pod Racer [PT83] 15.00
____Queen Amidala [PT84] 15.00
____SWI [PT85] 15.00
____Watto [PT86] 15.00

TPM. Animation Unit.
____Animation Unit [PT87] 15.00
____BNS [PT88] 8.00
____DRD [PT89] 8.00
____JJB [PT90] 8.00
____WTO [PT91] 8.00

TPM. Knoll Unit.
____CLP [PT92] 8.00

____FBB [PT93] 8.00
____Knoll Unit [PT94] 15.00
____PRS [PT95] 8.00
____SPB [PT96] 8.00

TPM. Muren Unit.
____GGB [PT97] 8.00
____Muren Unit [PT98] 15.00
____NSP [PT99] 8.00
____OGB [PT100] 8.00
____UWS [PT101] 8.00

TPM. Production Unit.
____ACT [PT102] 8.00
____ART [PT103] 8.00
____CGS [PT104] 8.00
____EDL [PT105] 8.00
____PRO [PT106] 8.00
____Production Unit [PT107] 15.00
____SCN [PT108] 8.00
____TEC [PT109] 8.00

TPM. Squires Unit.
____GSR [PT110] 8.00
____JDB [PT111] 8.00
____QNB [PT112] 8.00
____Squires Unit [PT113] 15.00
____THD [PT114] 8.00

TPM. Stage Unit.
____CAM [PT115] 8.00
____MDL [PT116] 8.00
____PYR [PT117] 8.00
____Stage Unit [PT118] 8.00
____STG [PT119] 8.00

PT65

PT68

PT69

PT66

PT67

PT70

PT71 1 of 2

PT71 2 of 2

PT72

PT73

PT74

PT75

PT76

PT77

PT78

PT79

PT80

PT81

PT82

PT83

PT84

PT85

PT86

PT87

PT88   PT89   PT90   PT91

PT94

PT92   PT93   PT95   PT96

PT97

PT98   PT99   PT100   PT101

PT107

PT102   PT103   PT104   PT105

Code 3 Collectibles

Insignia patches Included with replica vehicle.

____501st / TIE Fighter 20.00
____Clone Trooper / Republic Gunship 20.00
____Imperial / AT-ST 20.00
____Mandalorian / Slave I 20.00
____Rebel / Millennium Falcon 20.00
____Rebel / X-Wing Fighter 20.00
____Skywalker Ranch firetruck [PT120] 50.00

Data East

____Star Wars Pinball [PT121] 70.00

Dixie / Northern Inc.

____4th Place Prize, Darth Vader Appearance sweepstakes [PT122] 65.00

Emergency Services

____Rochester, NY Fire Department [PT123] 25.00
____Skywalker Ranch [PT124] 125.00
____Ventura, CA Police Department [PT125] 80.00

Factors, Etc.

____Brotherhood of Jedi Knights 3" original [PT126] 25.00

____Brotherhood of Jedi Knights 3.5" second issue [PT127] 20.00
____Darth Vadar Lives (misspelled) [PT128] 10.00
____Darth Vader, clenched fist [PT129].....................10.00
____May the Force be with You [PT130]....................10.00
____Rebel Forces, green accents [PT131] 25.00
____Rebel Forces, tan accents [PT132] 25.00
____Star Wars 3.5" original [PT133] 10.00
____Star Wars 4" [PT134] 10.00
____Star Wars Pyramid Logo [PT135].......................20.00
____Star Wars Pyramid Logo w/o TM [PT136]..........25.00

Fan Club

____A New Hope [PT137] 10.00
____ESB 10th Anniversary [PT138]...........................40.00
____ESB First 10 Years [PT139] 50.00
____ESB logo, red outline [PT140] 5.00
____ESB logo, white outline [PT141]...............................5.00
____Official Fan Club [PT142] 15.00
____Official Fan Club, 2nd issue [PT143] 8.00
____Return logo [PT144] 5.00
____Revenge logo [PT145] 10.00
____Vader in Flames [PT146] 8.00
____Yoda / Return [PT147] 15.00
____Yoda / Revenge [PT148]...............................20.00

PT106   PT108   PT109

Fan Made

____Alpha Base [PT149] ....N/V
____B-Wing [PT150] 35.00
____Blue Harvest [PT151] 15.00
____Clone "il" [PT152] 7.00
____Clone Insignia [PT153] 6.00
____Darth (name tag) [PT154] 12.00
____Darth Maul Estrogen Brigade 2 [PT155]................N/V
____David Holsinger [PT156] 8.00
____Dewback Squadron [PT157] 12.00
____Dewback Squadron [PT158] 12.00
____Dewback Squadron (brown) [PT159] 12.00
____Drug Wars [PT160] 10.00
____ESB Silver Mylar [PT161] 25.00

PT113

PT110   PT111   PT112   PT114

PT118

PT115   PT116   PT117   PT119

PT120   PT121   PT122   PT123   PT124   PT125   PT126   PT127   PT128

Patches

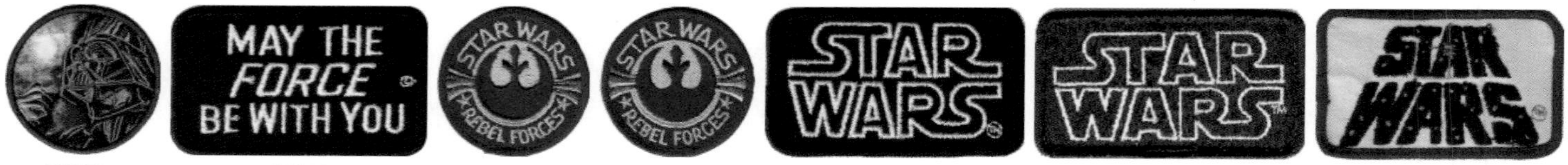

PT129 PT130 PT131 PT132 PT133 PT134 PT135

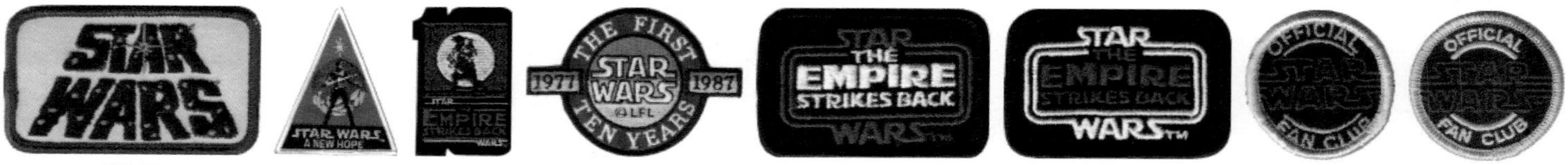

PT136 PT137 PT138 PT139 PT140 PT141 PT142 PT143

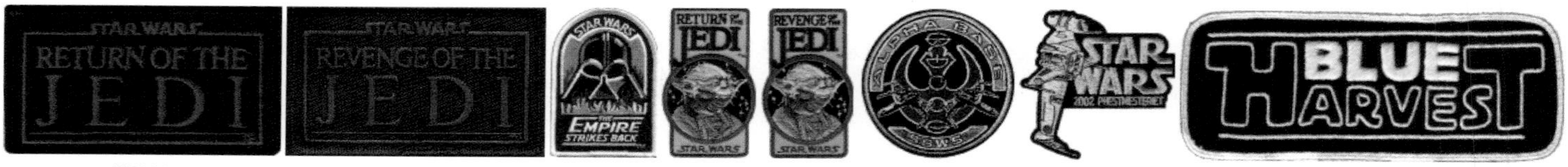

PT144 PT145 PT146 PT147 PT148 PT149 PT150 PT151

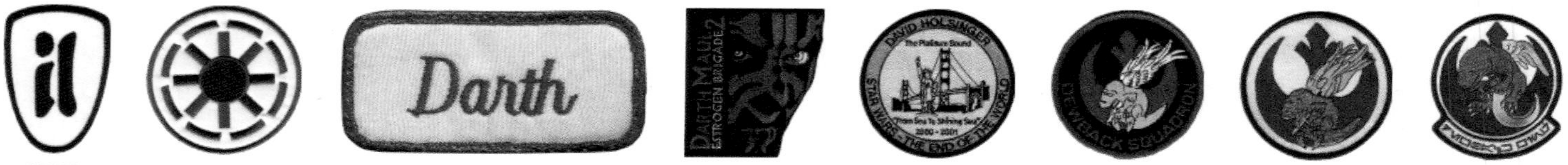

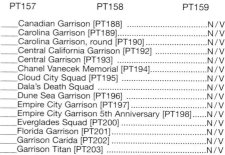

PT152 PT153 PT154 PT155 PT156 PT157 PT158 PT159

____Imperial Navy (black/red) [PT162]........................6.00
____Imperial Navy (red/black) [PT163]........................6.00
____Imperial Navy (white/red) [PT164]........................6.00
____Jedi Five 1601 ....10.00
____M.A.C.H. X-wing [PT165] 40.00
____Maskin Gefle [PT166] 20.00
____May The Force Be With You [PT167]..................20.00
____Rogue Squadron fighter burt, blue [PT168]........10.00
____Rogue Squadron fighter burt, white [PT169]......10.00
____Rogue Squadron patches [PT170]......................10.00
____Star Wars Team Spirit [PT171] 25.00
____Star Wars: Han, Luke, Leia....................................8.00
____Starship Fan Federation [PT172] 30.00
____StarWars-Force.com [PT173] 7.00
____The Force [PT174] 15.00
____Vader [PT175] 8.00
____Wraith Squadron [PT176].....................................10.00
____www.liningup.net [PT177] 35.00
____X-Wing Snoopy [PT178] ....N/V

501st Legion.

____501st Legion [PT179] ....N/V
____501st Legion, version 2 [PT180]............................N/V
____69th Dewback Cavalry [PT181] ....N/V
____Alpine Garrison [PT182] ....N/V
____Alpine Garrison, 2nd issue [PT183] ....N/V
____Australia-New Zealand Garrison [PT184]..............N/V
____Belgian Garrison [PT185] ....N/V
____Bloodfin Garrison [PT186] ....N/V
____Brazilian Garrison [PT187] ....N/V
____Canadian Garrison [PT188] ....N/V
____Carolina Garrison [PT189].......................................N/V
____Carolina Garrison, round [PT190]...........................N/V
____Central California Garrison [PT192] ....N/V
____Central Garrison [PT193] ....N/V
____Chanel Vanecek Memorial [PT194].........................N/V
____Cloud City Squad [PT195] ....N/V
____Dala's Death Squad ....N/V
____Dune Sea Garrison [PT196] ....N/V
____Empire City Garrison [PT197] ....N/V
____Empire City Garrison 5th Anniversary [PT198]......N/V
____Everglades Squad [PT200] ....N/V
____Florida Garrison [PT201]...N/V
____Garrison Carida [PT202] ....N/V
____Garrison Titan [PT203] ....N/V

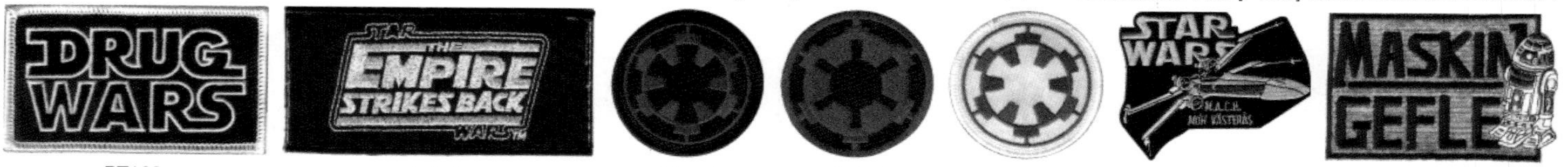

PT160 PT161 PT162 PT163 PT164 PT165 PT166

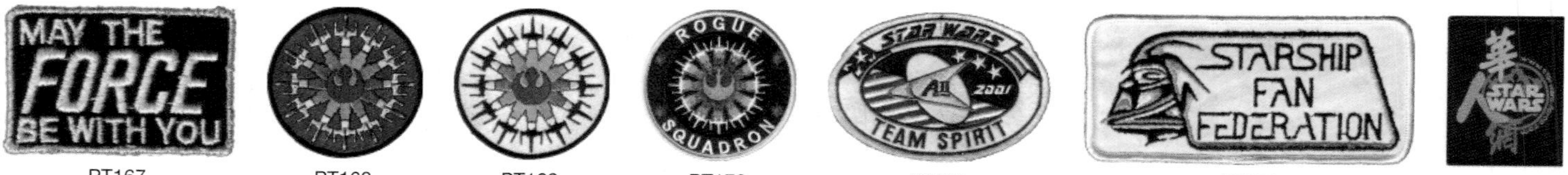

PT167 PT168 PT169 PT170 PT171 PT172 PT173

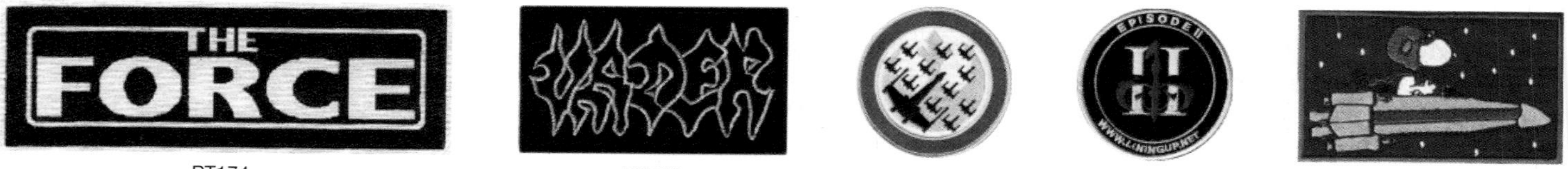

PT174 PT175 PT176 PT177 PT178

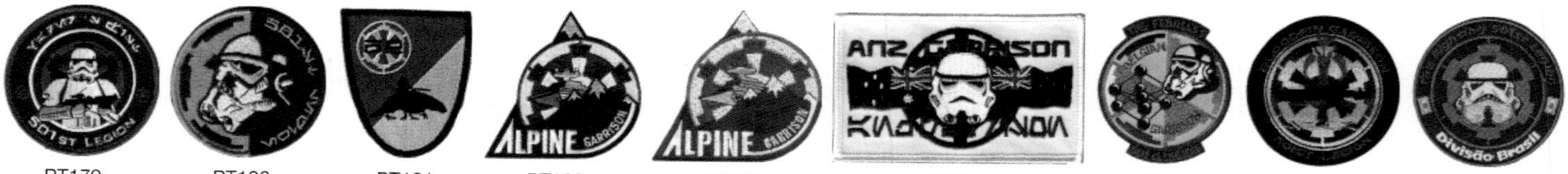

PT179 PT180 PT181 PT182 PT183 PT184 PT185 PT186 PT187

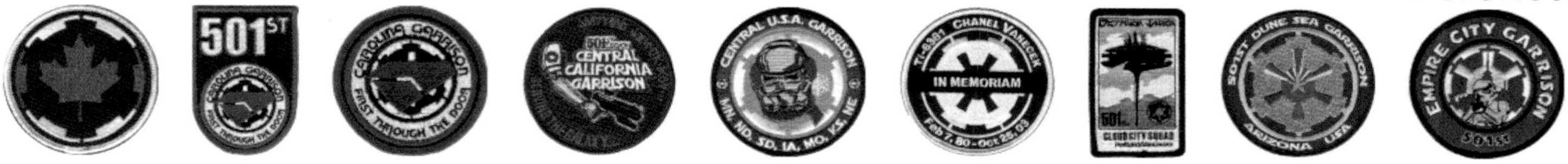

PT188 PT189 PT190 PT192 PT193 PT194 PT195 PT196 PT197

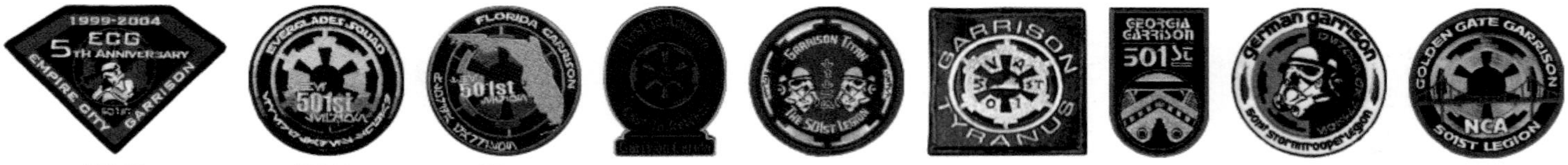

PT198 PT200 PT201 PT202 PT203 PT204 PT205 PT206 PT207

PT208 PT209 PT210 PT211 PT212 PT213 PT214 PT215 PT216

____Garrison Tyranus [PT204] .... N/V
____Georgia Garrison [PT205] .... N/V
____German Garrison [PT206] .... N/V
____Goldengate [PT207] .... N/V
____Italian Garrison [PT208] .... N/V
____Japanese Garrison [PT209] .... N/V
____Jolly Rogers Squadron Bomber [PT210] .... N/V
____Jolly Rogers Squadron Fighter [PT211] .... N/V
____Jolly Rogers Squadron Pilots [PT212] .... N/V
____Midwest Garrison [PT213] .... N/V
____Mos Eisley Police [PT214] .... N/V
____Mountain Garrison [PT215] .... N/V
____Neon City Garrison [PT216] .... N/V
____New England 02 [PT217] .... N/V
____New England Garrison [PT218] .... N/V
____New England Garrison [PT219] .... N/V
____New England Garrison Imperial Academy [PT220] .... N/V
____Nordic Garrison .... N/V
____North Carolina Squad, So. Garrison [PT221] .... N/V
____Ohio Garrison [PT222] .... N/V
____Omega Wing [PT223] .... N/V
____Pacific Outpost [PT224] .... N/V
____Path Finders [PT225] .... N/V
____Phantom Squadron [PT226] .... N/V
____Pikes Peak Squad [PT227] .... N/V
____Pouldre Valley Squad .... N/V
____Southern California Garrison-original [PT228] .... N/V
____Southern California 2nd version [PT229] .... N/V
____Southern Outpost [PT230] .... N/V
____Sovereign Protectors [PT231] .... N/V
____Star Garrison - original .... N/V
____Star Garrison - second version [PT232] .... N/V
____Star Garrison [PT233] .... N/V
____Swiss Garrison [PT234] .... N/V
____Tampa Bay Squadron [PT235] .... N/V
____Tampa Bay Squad - second version [PT236] .... N/V
____Tampa Garrison [PT237] .... N/V
____Terror Australis [PT238] .... N/V
____TK-118's Groupies [PT239] .... N/V
____Trooper Groupies [PT240] .... N/V
____United Kingdom [PT241] .... N/V
____Venezuelan Garrison .... N/V
____Virginia Squad .... N/V

Boba Fett insignia.
____2" reversed [PT242] 6.00
____3" [PT243] 6.00
____4" 6.00
____Rectangular [PT244] 6.00

Imperial insignia.
____[PT245] .... N/V
____8" felt [PT246] 10.00
____Red [PT247] 7.00
____Variation 1 [PT248] 7.00
____Variation 2 [PT249] 7.00
____Variation 3 [PT250] 7.00
____Variation 4 [PT251] 7.00
____Variation 5 [PT252] 7.00

Letter patches.
____C-3PO [PT253] 3.00
____R2-D2 [PT254] 3.00

Mandalorian insignia.
____Red on gray [PT255] 7.00
____Red on white [PT256] 7.00

Rebel insignia.
____Blue with yellow border [PT257] 7.00
____Hexagon [PT258] 10.00
____Red on blue, white stars, blue border [PT259] 7.00
____Red on white, red border [PT260] 7.00
____Red shaped [PT261] 7.00
____Red with yellow border [PT262] 7.00

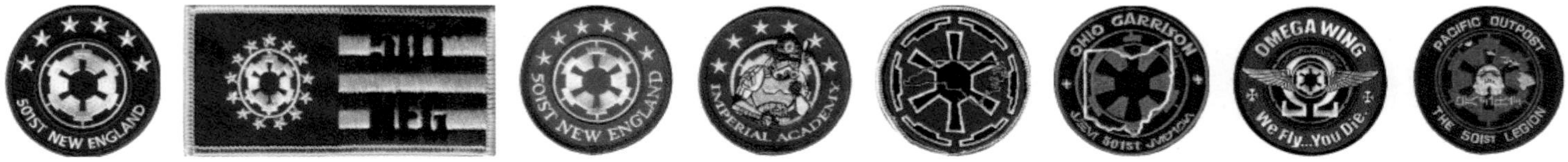

PT217 PT218 PT219 PT220 PT221 PT222 PT223 PT224

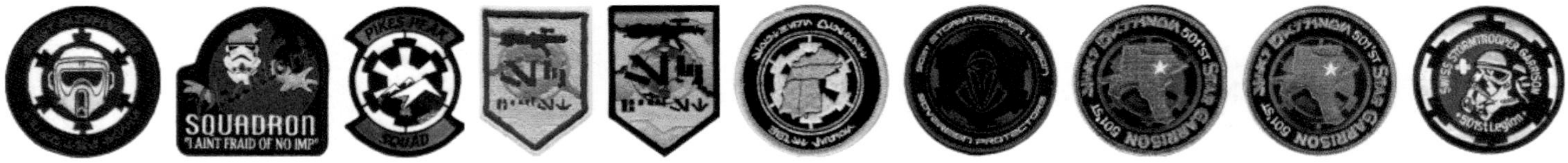

PT225 PT226 PT227 PT228 PT229 PT230 PT231 PT232 PT233 PT234

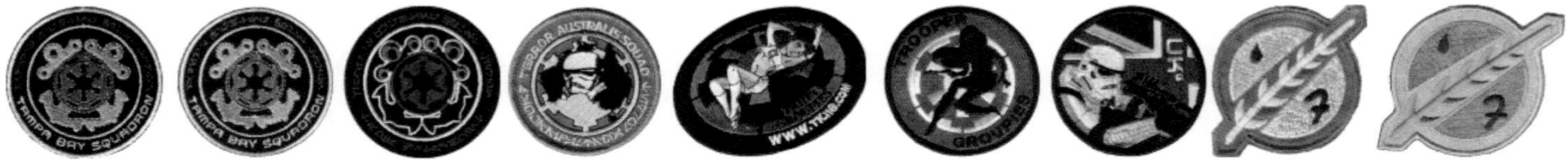

PT235 PT236 PT237 PT238 PT239 PT240 PT241 PT242 PT243

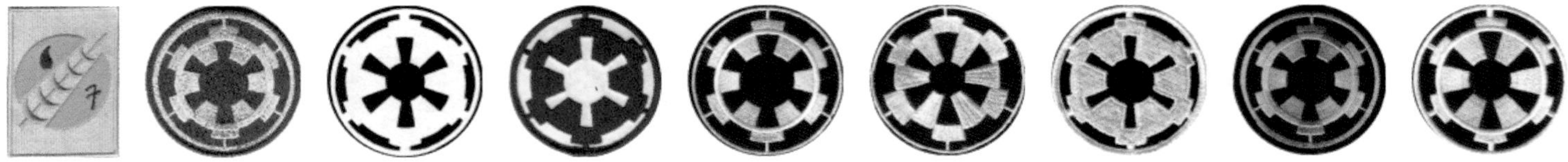

PT244 PT245 PT246 PT247 PT248 PT249 PT250 PT251 PT252

Patches

PT253 - PT254 PT255 PT256 PT257 PT258 PT259 PT260 PT261 PT262

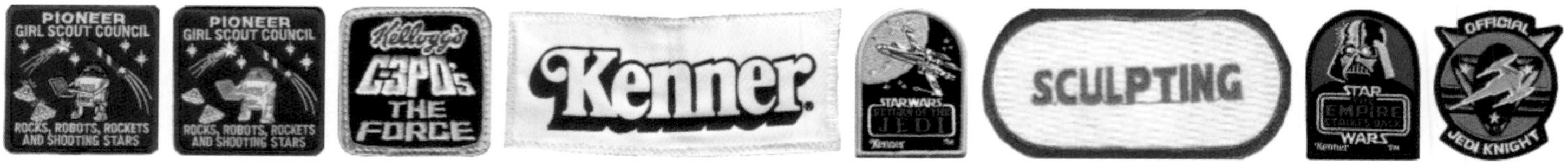

PT263 PT264 PT265 PT266 PT267 PT268 PT269 PT270

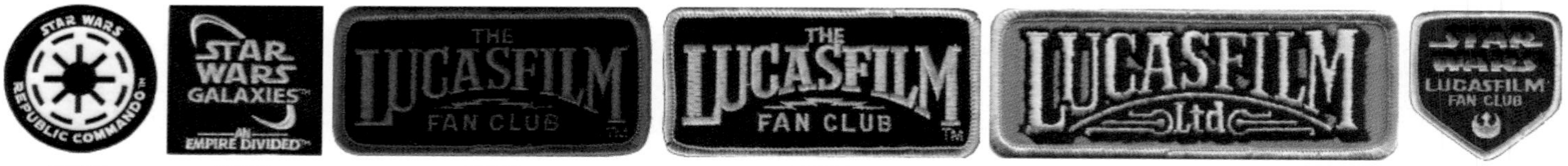

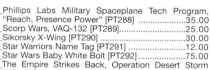

PT271 PT272 PT273 PT274 PT275 PT276

Rebel Legion.
____Kessel Base 15.00

Girl Scouts USA
Pioneer Girl Scout Coucil.
____Blue detail [PT263] 20.00
____Pink detail [PT264] 20.00

Kelloggs
____C-3PO's "The Force" cap, premium [PT265] 50.00

Kenner
____Hat patch [PT266]..N/V
____ROTJ, internal [PT267]......................................125.00
____Sculpting smock patch [PT268] ....N/V
____Star Wars / ESB sweepstakes 3rd prize [PT269] 25.00

Kid Rhino
____Official Jedi Knight [PT270] 5.00

LucasArts
____Republic Commando [PT271] 5.00
____Star Wars Galaxies [PT272] 10.00

Lucasfilm Fan Club
____Logo, red on black [PT273] 5.00
____Logo, silver on black [PT274] 5.00
____Lucasfilm, Ltd. [PT275] 10.00
____Star Wars [PT276]..5.00

Media Play
____Darth Vader, ROTS soundtrack [PT277] 10.00

Mexico City Convention
____Logo, hat patch [PT278]......................................35.00

Military
____1709 Air Refueling Wing [PT279] 15.00
____AVDET 67 USCGC Glacier [PT280] 75.00
____Aviano Italy 95 [PT281] 25.00
____Darth Vader F-4 Phanton [PT282] 25.00
____Darth Vader Life Support [PT283] 25.00
____Fabulous Flying Fiends, CT (Cope Thunder) 91-3 [PT284] 20.00
____May the Force Be with You, black, helmet bag patch [PT285] 25.00
____Phantom Menace, Feel The Force [PT286] 10.00
____Phillips Labs Military Spaceplane Tech Program, "Global Engagement" [PT287] 35.00
____Phillips Labs Military Spaceplane Tech Program, "Reach, Presence Power" [PT288] 35.00
____Scorp Wars, VAQ-132 [PT289]...........................25.00
____Sikorsky X-Wing [PT290] 30.00
____Star Warriors Name Tag [PT291] 12.00
____Star Wars Baby White Bolt [PT292]...................75.00
____The Empire Strikes Back, Operation Desert Storm [PT293] 10.00
____The Empire Strikes Back, Operation Desert Storm, no date, larger size [PT294]......................................20.00
____The Phantom NFO [PT295] 25.00
____USS George Washington[PT296]........................25.00
____VF-33 Starfighters [PT297]................................75.00
____Yoda Buckeye [PT298].......................................30.00
____Yoda Name Tag [PT299].....................................35.00

Star Warriors, VAQ 209.
____3.5" cut edge [PT300] 10.00
____3.75" cut edge [PT301] 10.00
____4" merrowed edge [PT302] 10.00
____4.25" merrowed edge, subdued [PT303]...........20.00
____5" cut edge [PT304] 10.00
____5.25" bullion [PT305] 50.00
____Detached tab [PT306] 10.00
____Round [PT307] 25.00

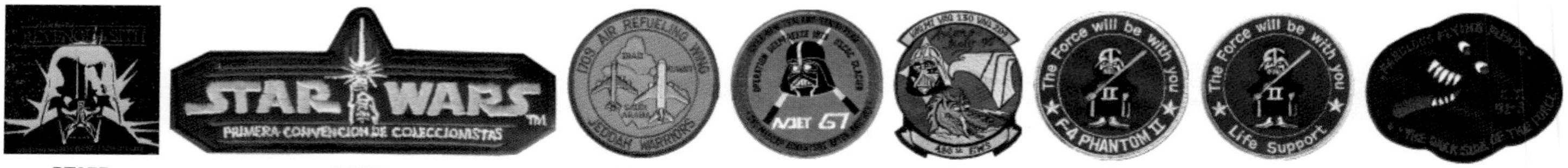

PT277 PT278 PT279 PT280 PT281 PT282 PT283 PT284

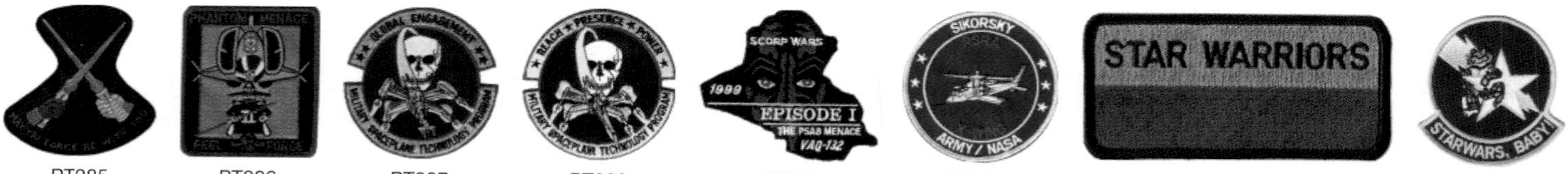

PT285 PT286 PT287 PT288 PT289 PT290 PT291 PT292

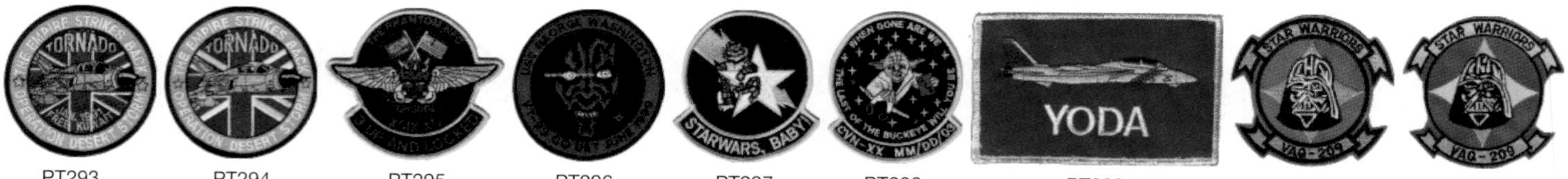

PT293 PT294 PT295 PT296 PT297 PT298 PT299 PT300 PT301

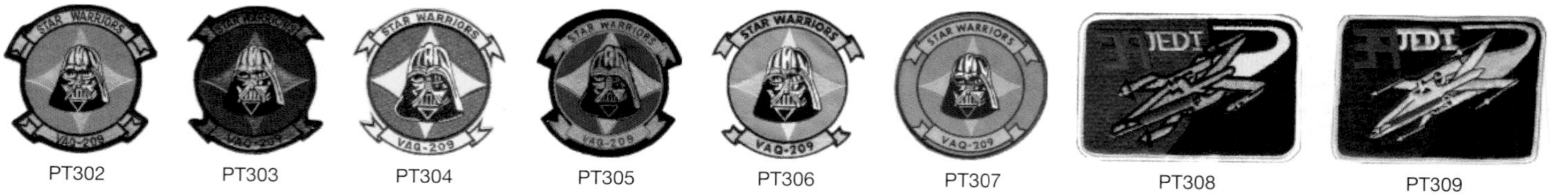

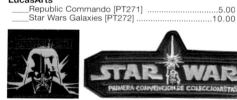

PT302 PT303 PT304 PT305 PT306 PT307 PT308 PT309

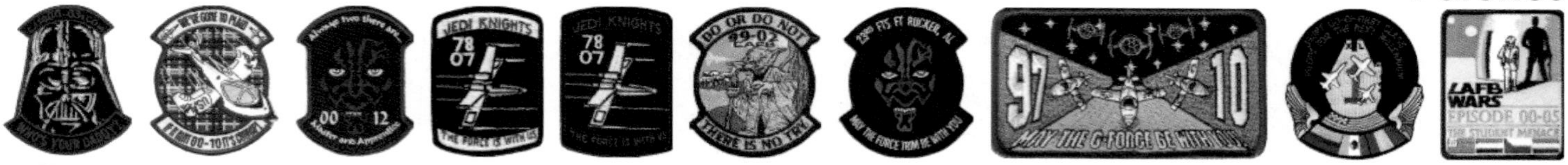

PT310 PT311 PT312 PT313 PT314 PT315 PT316 PT317 PT318 PT319

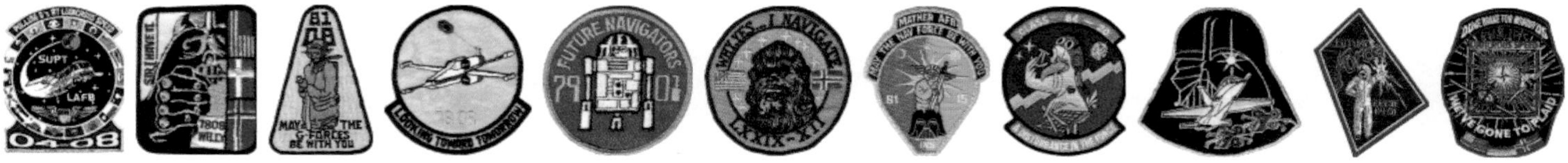

PT320 PT321 PT322 PT323 PT324 PT325 PT326 PT327 PT328 PT329 PT330

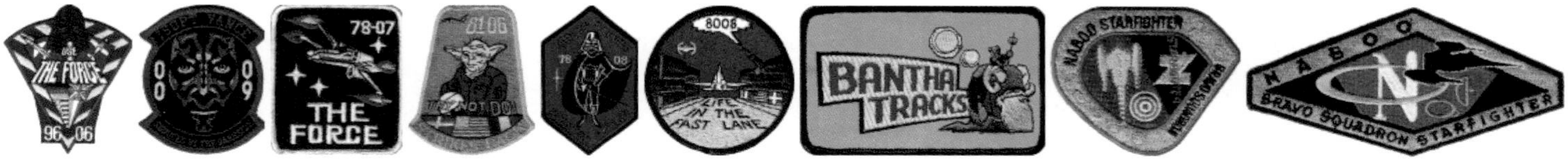

PT331 PT332 PT333 PT334 PT335 PT336 PT337 PT338 PT339

USAF Academy 39th Squadron
____Gray [PT308]..40.00
____White [PT309]..55.00

USAF Classes.
____Columbus AFB 00-03 [PT310]..............................75.00
____Columbus AFB 00-10 [PT311]..............................35.00
____Columbus AFB 00-12 [PT312]..............................50.00
____Columbus AFB 78-07 [PT313]..............................60.00
____Columbus AFB 78-07 2nd version [PT314]........60.00
____Columbus AFB 99-02 [PT315]..............................50.00
____Ft. Rucker (US Army) 02-01 [PT316] 25.00
____Hondo AFB 97-10 [PT317]...................................50.00
____Laughlin AFB 00-01 [PT318] 50.00
____Laughlin AFB 00-05 [PT319] 50.00
____Laughlin AFB 04-08 [PT320] 20.00
____Laughlin AFB 78-08 [PT321] 60.00
____Laughlin AFB 81-08 [PT322] 75.00
____Mather AFB 78-09 [PT323] 60.00
____Mather AFB 79-01 [PT324] 60.00
____Mather AFB 79-12 [PT325] 65.00
____Mather AFB 81-15 [PT326] 50.00
____Mather AFB 84-20 [PT327] 20.00
____Reese AFB 78-07 [PT328] 60.00
____Reese AFB 84-01 [PT329] 25.00
____Sheppard AFB 00-05 [PT330] 35.00
____Sheppard AFB 96-06 [PT331] 50.00
____Vance AFB 00-09 [PT332] 50.00
____Vance AFB 78-07 [PT333] 75.00
____Vance AFB 81-06 [PT334] 75.00
____Williams AFB 78-08 [PT335] 85.00
____Williams AFB 80-08 [PT336] 50.00

Paizo Publishing / Fan Club
2003.
____Bantha Tracks [PT337] 12.00

Pepsi
____Bravo Squadron [PT338] 10.00
____Bravo Squadron, diamond [PT339] 10.00
____Naboo Starfighter [PT340] 10.00

Leather jacket patches, promotional.
____Naboo Bravo Squadron [PT341] 75.00
____Trade Federation Starfighter [PT342]...................75.00

RebelScum.com
____Rebelscum, Celebration 3 [PT343] 20.00

Sales Corp. of America
Scarf and hat patches.
____C-3PO [PT344]..10.00
____Chewbacca [PT345]...10.00
____Darth Vader [PT346]..15.00
____Darth Vader [PT347]..15.00
____Ewok [PT348] 5.00
____Gamorrean Guard [PT349]......................................15.00
____R2-D2 [PT350] 15.00

Scholastic
____May The Force Be With You iron-on [PT351]........8.00

Star Tours
____Endor Express, shoulder patch [PT352] 100.00
____Eurodisney Land - Rex [PT353]...........................40.00
____Galactic Empire [PT354]..12.00
____Logo [PT355] 25.00
____Logo on blue triangle [PT356] 35.00
____Logo on gray triangle [PT357] 100.00
____Logo on white triangle [PT358] 40.00
____Rebel Alliance [PT359] 12.00
____Tour Director [PT360] 25.00

Thinking Cap
____ESB hat patch [PT361]...15.00
____Yoda Hat Patch [PT362]..35.00

Unlicensed
____25th Anniversary [PT363] 10.00
____Clone Army [PT364] 5.00
____Clone Training [PT365] 8.00
____Corellia [PT366] 10.00
____Darth Vader Lives [PT367] 10.00
____May The Force Be With You [PT368]...................10.00

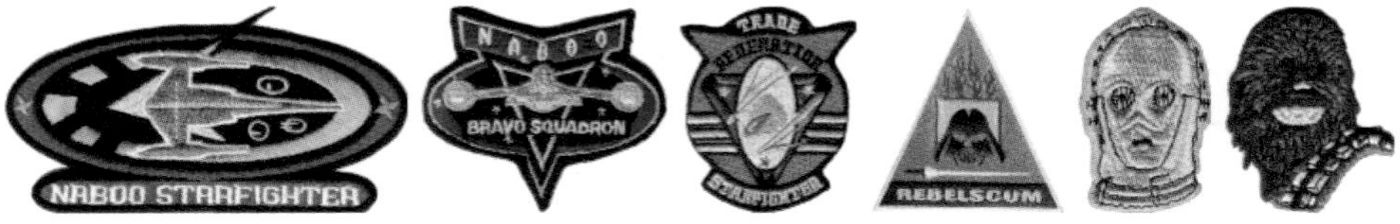

PT340 PT341 PT342 PT343 PT344 PT345

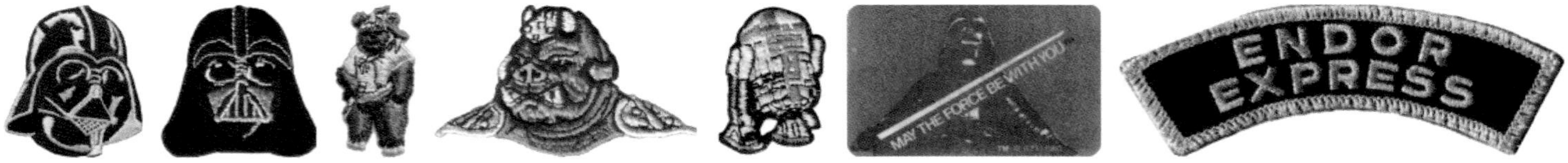

PT346 PT347 PT348 PT349 PT350 PT351 PT352

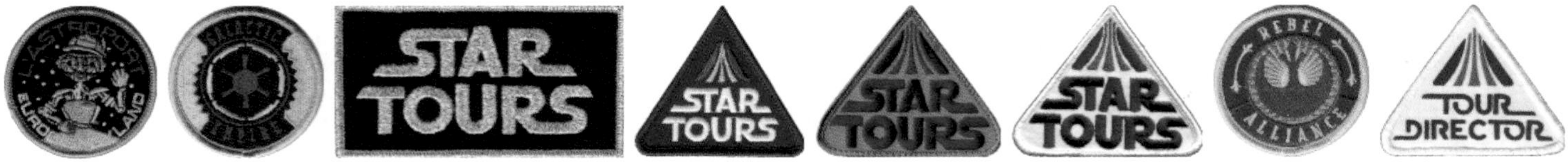

PT353 PT354 PT355 PT356 PT357 PT358 PT359 PT360

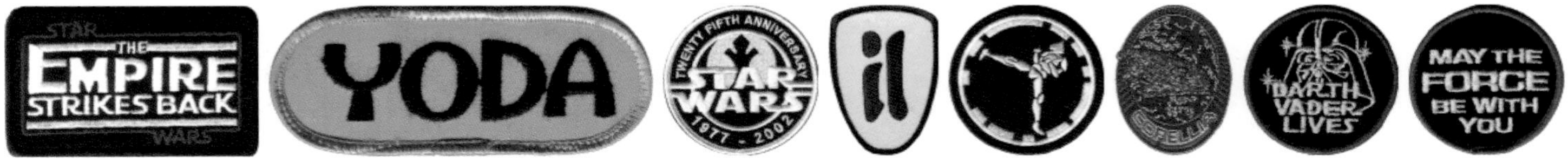

PT361 PT362 PT363 PT364 PT365 PT366 PT367 PT368

Patches

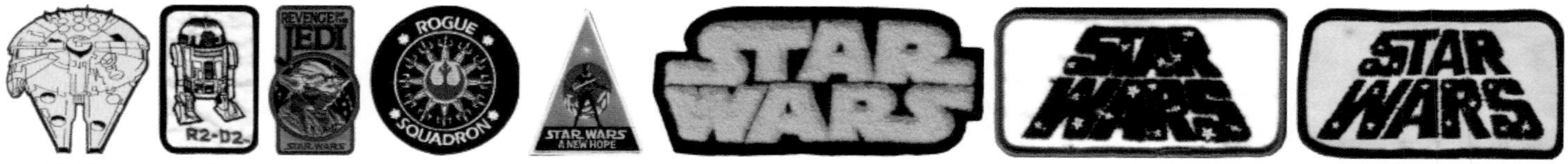

PT369 PT370 PT371 PT372 PT373 PT374 PT375 PT376

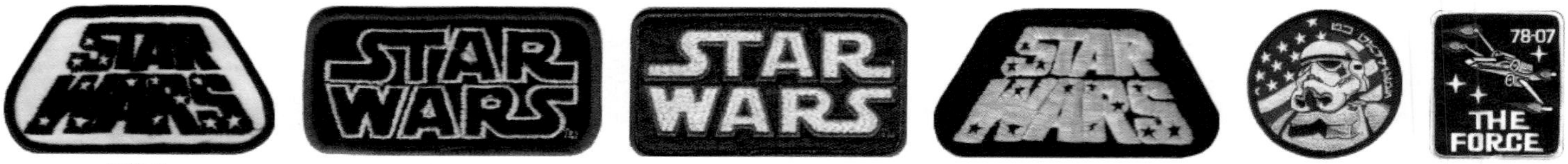

PT377 PT378 PT379 PT380 PT381 PT382

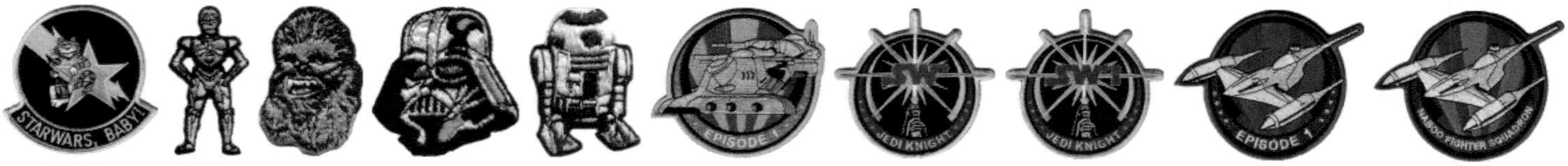

PT383 PT384 PT385 PT386 PT387 PT388 PT389 PT390 PT391 PT392

PT393 PT394 PT395 PT396 PT397 PT398 PT399 PT400 PT401 PT402 PT403 PT404

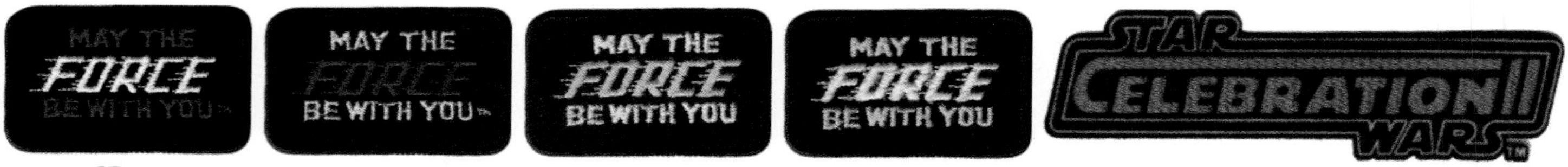

PT405 PT406 PT407 PT408 PT409

____Millennium Falcon, yellow [PT369]....................10.00
____R2-D2, bordered [PT370]....................15.00
____Revenge of the Jedi – reproduction [PT371]......10.00
____Rogue Squadron [PT372]....................10.00
____Star Wars A New Hope – reproduction, no TM [PT373]....................10.00
____Star Wars Chenille [PT374]....................35.00
____Star Wars oval....................6.00
____Star Wars, black on white with gold stars in lettering, red border [PT375]....................15.00
____Star Wars, black on white with stars in lettering, black border [PT376]....................10.00
____Star Wars, black on white with white stars in lettering, black border, angled edges [PT377]....................10.00
____Star Wars, gold on black, blue border [PT378] ..15.00
____Star Wars, silver on black with red outline around lettering, black border [PT379]....................30.00
____Star Wars, white on black with black stars in lettering, black border, angled edges [PT380]....................10.00
____Stormtrooper patriot [PT381]....................15.00
____Vance AFB 78-07 repro. USAF [PT382]....................12.00
____VF-33 Starfighters repro. [PT383]....................10.00

Color, figural.
____C-3PO [PT384]....................5.00
____Chewbacca [PT385]....................5.00
____Darth Vader [PT386]....................5.00
____R2-D2 [PT387]....................5.00

Episode I.
____Battle Tank, Episode I [PT388]....................8.00
____Battle Tank, Star Wars....................8.00
____Jedi Knight, SW [PT389]....................8.00
____Jedi Knight, SWI [PT390]....................8.00
____Naboo Fighter Episode I [PT391]....................8.00
____Naboo Fighter Squadron [PT392]....................8.00
____Pod Racer [PT393]....................8.00

Joy Patch. Space Robot, yellow android on red background, yellow border.
____Space Robot [PT394]....................15.00

Joy Patch. Space Robot, yellow droid on blue background, yellow trim.
____Blue dome, blue eye, multi-details [PT395]........15.00
____Blue dome, green eye [PT396]....................15.00
____Blue dome, red eye [PT397]....................15.00
____Blue dome, red eye, multi-details [PT398]..........15.00
____Green dome, blue eye [PT399]....................15.00
____Green dome, red eye [PT400]....................15.00
____Red dome, blue eye [PT401]....................15.00
____Red dome, green eye [PT402]....................15.00

Joy Patch.
____Space Wars [PT403]....................15.00
____Starship, X-Wing [PT404]....................15.00

May the Force Be With You. (Motion blur effect)
____Red and white lettering [PT405]....................12.00
____White and red lettering [PT406]....................12.00
____White and yellow lettering [PT407]....................12.00
____Yellow and white lettering [PT408]....................12.00

Wizards of the Coast
____Star Wars Celebration II [PT409]....................10.00

Patterns

Butterick
____Darth Vader (5186) [APA01]....................14.00
____Luke and Leia (5175) [APA02]....................14.00

McCall's
____Ewok Costume [APA03]....................18.00
____Five Patterns, ESB [APA04]....................35.00
____Night Wear, ROTJ [APA05]....................12.00
____Robes and Cloaks [APA06]....................4.00
____Shirt, ROTJ....................12.00

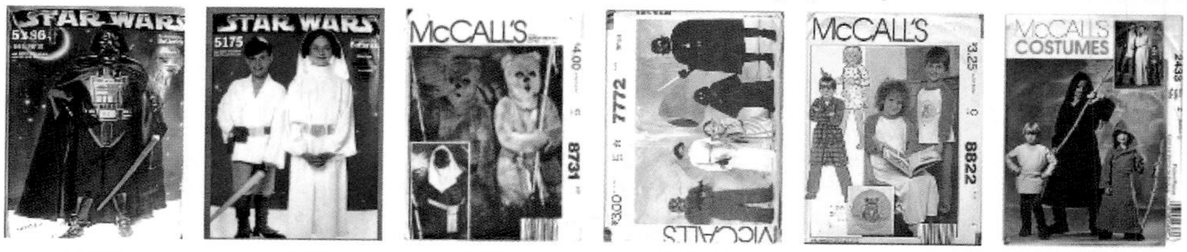

APA01 APA02 APA03 APA04 APA05 APA06

Simplicity Pattern Co.
____0577 Padme and Leia....................12.00
____0579 Anakin, Utapu administrator, Obi-Wan......12.00

Pencil Cases / Boxes

____Darth Maul tin [SUK01]....................5.00
____Darth Maul tin, shaped [SUK02]....................7.00
____Jedi vs. Sith, zippered [SUK03]....................4.00
____Queen Amidala tin [SUK04]....................5.00
____Queen Amidala, zippered [SUK05]....................6.00

A.H. Prismatic
____Holographic sticker on metal box [SUK06]..........8.00

Animations
____Sith Lord....................4.00

Butterfly Originals
____Vader and Luke duel [SUK07]....................5.00

Creata Promotions
____C-3PO and R2-D2 [SUK08]....................9.00

Flomo
____Vader / Star Destroyer / DSII, prism [SUK09]......6.00

Frankel N Roth
Bags of Character, Return of the Jedi zip pouches.
____Luke in Jabba's Palace [SUK10]....................15.00
____Rebel Hanger [SUK11]....................15.00

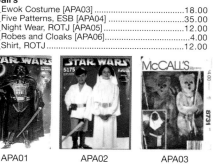

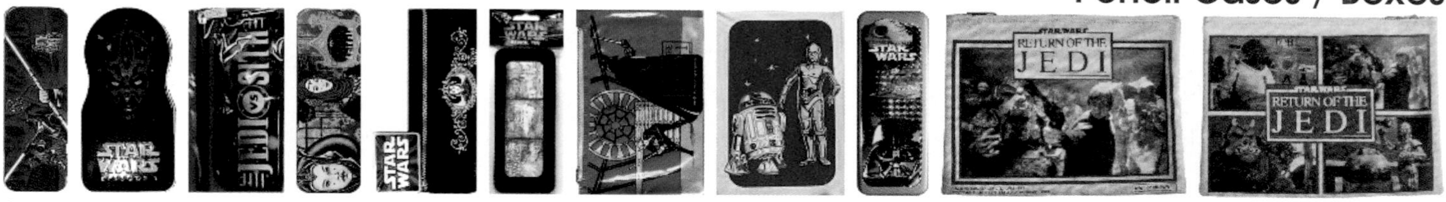

SUK01 SUK02 SUK03 SUK04 SUK05 SUK06 SUK07 SUK08 SUK09 SUK10 side 1 SUK10 side 2

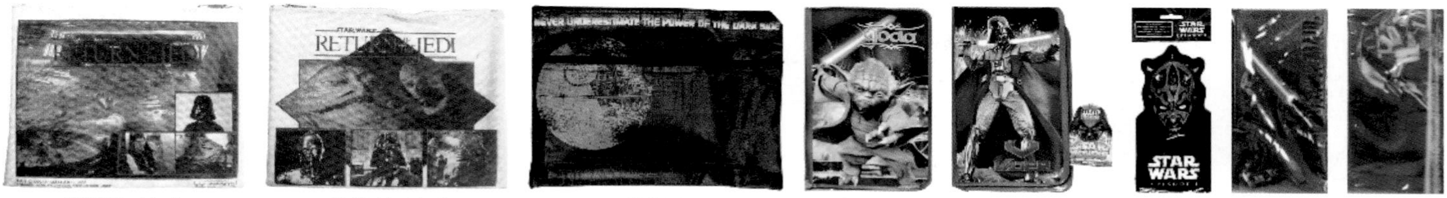

SUK11 side 1 SUK 11 side 2 SUK12 SUK13 SUK14 SUK15 SUK16 SUK17

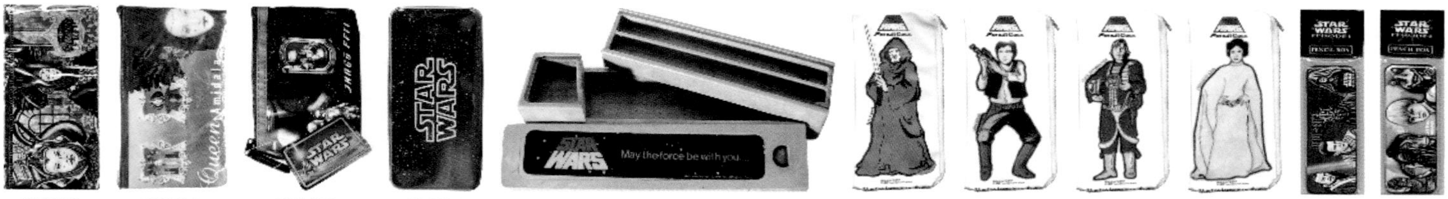

SUK18 SUK19 SUK20 SUK21 SUK22 SUK23 SUK24 SUK25 SUK26 SUK27 SUK28

Funtastic Pty. Ltd.
Double pouch, zippered, 9"x12".
____C-3PO / R2-D2, "May the Force be with You" 8.00
____Darth Vader, "Never Underestimate The Power Of The Dark Side" [SUK12] 8.00

Galerie Chocolates
Electronic game cases with M&Ms inside.
____Darth Vader / Epic Duel [SUK13] 5.00
____Yoda / R2-D2 and C-3PO [SUK14] 5.00

Grand Toys
____Darth Maul character shaped, zippered [SUK15] 8.00

Zippered pencil bags.
____Darth Maul [SUK16] 3.00
____Destroyer Droid [SUK17] 3.00
____Queen Amidala, art [SUK18] 3.00
____Queen Amidala, photos [SUK19] 3.00

Grosvenor
____Jango Fett, zippered [SUK20] 6.00
____SW logo on black starfield, tin [SUK21] 4.00

HC Ford
____Darth Vader, spaceships, and ROTJ logo, zippered plastic 12.00

Helix
____"May The Force be With You" [SUK22] 45.00

Zippered, plastic.
____Ben Kenobi [SUK23] 16.00
____C-3PO 16.00
____Darth Vader 16.00
____Han Solo [SUK24] 16.00
____Luke Skywalker [SUK25] 16.00
____Princess Leia [SUK26] 16.00
____R2-D2 ....16.00
____Stormtrooper 16.00

Impact, Inc.
____"Jedi vs. Sith," tin box [SUK27] 4.00
____"Tatooine," tin box [SUK28] 4.00
____Anakin Skywalker Podracing [SUK29] 4.00
____Darth Maul with lightsaber tin [SUK30] 8.00
____Darth Maul, zippered [SUK31] 4.00
____Jar Jar Transformable Pencil Case: sharpener, glue, eraser, ruler, tape, paper clips [SUK32] 12.00
____Pod racer pencil pouch 6.00

Magic World
____General Grievous / Yoda 10.00

Mead
Zipper pouches with reinfornced binder holes.
____Darth Vader, black [SUK33] 5.00
____Darth Vader, blue [SUK34] 5.00
____Darth Vader, patch [SUK35] 5.00
____Star Wars patch, blueprint design [SUK36] 5.00
____Yoda, patch [SUK37] 5.00

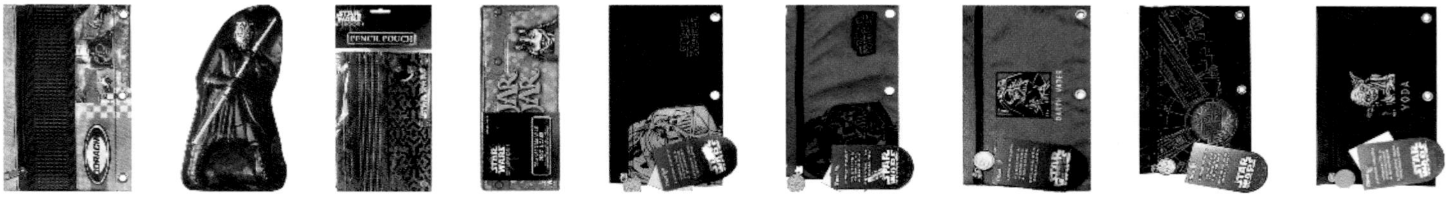

SUK29 SUK30 SUK31 SUK32 SUK33 SUK34 SUK35 SUK36 SUK37

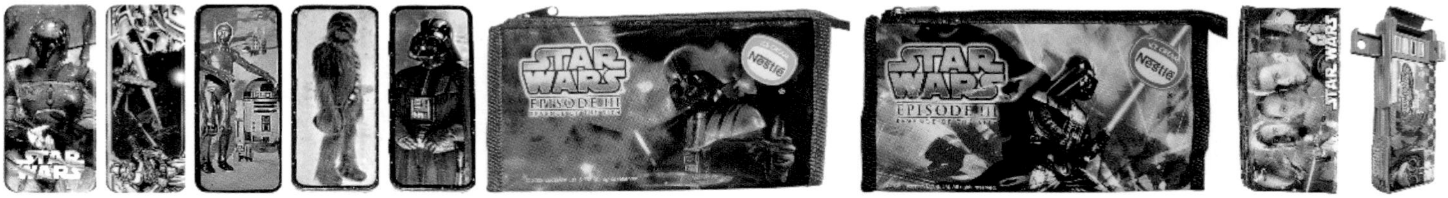

SUK38 SUK39 SUK40 SUK41 SUK42 SUK43 SUK44 SUK45 SUK46

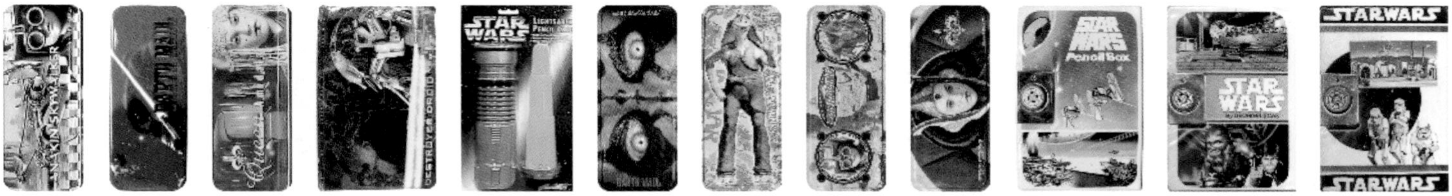

SUK47 SUK48 SUK49 SUK50 SUK51 SUK52 SUK53 SUK54 SUK55 SUK56 SUK57 SUK58

Pencil Cases / Boxes

| SUL01 | SUP01 | SUP02 | SUP03 | SUP04 | SUP05 | SUP06 | SUP07 |

      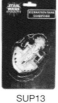  

| SUP08 | SUP09 | SUP10 | SUP11 | SUP12 | SUP13 | SUP14 | SUP15 | SUP16 |

| SUP17 | SUP18 | SUP19 |

Merlin
____Boba Fett, tin [SUK38] 10.00
____Stormtroopers / dogfight, tin [SUK39] 12.00

Metal Box Ltd.
Tin boxes.
____C-3PO [SUK40] 12.00
____Chewbacca [SUK41] 12.00
____Darth Vader [SUK42] 12.00
____R2-D2 [SUK43] 12.00
____Yoda [SUK44] 12.00

Nestlé, Philippines
EPIII:ROTS.
____Darth Vader [SUK43] 10.00
____Darth Vader attacking [SUK44] 10.00

Pyramid
Zippered pencil bags.
____Episode II heroes [SUK45] 3.00

Q-Stat
____EPI Podracing, mechanical compartments [SUK46] 8.00

Pencil tins.
____Anakin Skywalker [SUK47] 5.00
____Darth Maul [SUK48] 5.00
____Queen Amidala [SUK49] 5.00

Zippered pencil bags.
____Destroyer Droid [SUK50] 3.00

Rose Art Industries
____Lightsaber pencil case [SUK51] 6.00

Sunburst Merchandising
Episode I, tin.
____Darth Maul [SUK52] 5.00
____Jar Jar Binks [SUK53] 5.00
____Podracing [SUK54] 5.00
____Queen Amidala [SUK55] 5.00

YAM
Combination lock.
____Death Star / Rebel Base [SUK56] 15.00
____Han & Chewbacca / Falcon [SUK57] 15.00
____Stormtroopers / Tatooine [SUK58] 15.00

Pencil Cups

HC Ford
____Artwork of characters, 4" high metal 16.00

Sigma
____Yoda [SUL01] 65.00

Pencil Sharpeners

Keychains.
____R2-D2 and C-3PO 5.00
____Yoda 5.00

Animations
____Darth Vader 0.50

Butterfly Originals
____Darth Vader, sculpted [SUP01] 8.00
____Wicket the Ewok sharpener with deal and die-cut eraser in blister pack [SUP02] 12.00

Figural characters.
____R2-D2 [SUP03] 8.00
____Yoda [SUP04] 8.00

Flomo
____Star Wars, round prism [SUP05] 3.00

Grand Toys
____Queen Amidala emblem, round [SUP06] 2.00
____Queen Amidala, round [SUP07] 2.00

Grosvenor
____Star Wars logo, round [SUP08] 2.00

HC Ford
Line drawing on dome shaped sharpener.
____C-3PO and R2-D2 ....17.00
____Darth Vader and Stormtrooper [SUP09] 17.00
____Han Solo and Chewbacca 17.00
____Luke and Leia 17.00

Oval shaped sharpener with image.
____Darth Vader and X-Wing fighter [SUP10]............10.00

Helix
____Death Star shaped [SUP11] 85.00

Impact, Inc.
____Destroyer Droid sharpener/eraser [SUP12] 6.00
____Federation Tank sculpted [SUP13] 4.00

Jollibee
____Obi-Wan Kenobi 10.00

Merlin
____Darth Vader, round [SUP14] 4.00

Pyramid
____Jango Fett, round [SUP15] 2.00
____R2-D2, figural [SUP16] 4.00
____Yoda, figural [SUP17] 6.00

Q-Stat
____Darth Maul, round [SUP18]........................2.00

Rose Art Industries
____Millennium Falcon sculpted [SUP19] 6.00

Pencil Toppers

Butterfly Originals
____C-3PO [PNT01].................................4.00
____Darth Vader [PNT02]............................4.00
____Emperor's Royal Guard [PNT03] 4.00
____Wicket [PNT04]................................4.00

HC Ford
____Admiral Ackbar [PNT05] 5.00
____Bib Fortuna [PNT06] 5.00
____Chewbacca [PNT07].............................5.00

| PNT01 | PNT02 | PNT03 | PNT04 | PNT05 | PNT06 | PNT07 | PNT08 |

| PNT09 | PNT10 | PNT11 | PNT12 | PNT13 | PNT14 | PNT15 | PNT16 | PNT17 | PNT18 | PNT19 | PNT20 | PNT21 |

    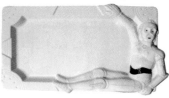

PNT22   PNT23   PNT24   PNT25   PNT26   PNT27   SUQ01

___Darth Vader, short 5.00
___Darth Vader, tall [PNT08].........................5.00
___Gamorrean Guard [PNT09].......................5.00
___Han Solo [PNT10] 5.00
___Imperial Guard [PNT11] 5.00
___Luke Skywalker [PNT12].........................5.00
___R2-D2 [PNT13] 5.00
___Wicket [PNT14] 5.00
___Yoda [PNT15] 5.00

Kelloggs, Singapore
Cereal premiums, EPII:AOTC.
___Anakin [PNT16] 5.00
___C-3PO [PNT17] 5.00
___Clone Trooper [PNT18] 5.00
___Darth Vader [PNT19] 5.00
___Jango Fett [PNT20] 5.00
___R2-D2 [PNT21] 5.00
___Yoda 5.00

Nestlé, Philippines
EPIII:ROTS. Wonder Cup premiums.
___Anakin Skywalker 5.00
___C-3PO 5.00
___Clone Trooper 5.00
___Darth Vader 5.00
___Obi-Wan Kenobi 5.00
___Yoda 5.00

EPIII:ROTS. Wonder Cup premiums. Gold chase figures.
___Anakin Skywalker 8.00
___C-3PO 8.00
___Clone Trooper 8.00
___Darth Vader 8.00
___Obi-Wan Kenobi 8.00
___Yoda 8.00

Vending Supply
Look-alikes. From vending machiens. Multiple colors.
___Darth Vader [PNT22] 5.00
___Greedo [PNT23] 5.00
___R2-D2 [PNT24] 5.00
___R5-D4 [PNT25] 5.00
___Robot [PNT26] 5.00
___Stormtrooper [PNT27]............................5.00

Pencil Trays

Sigma
___C-3PO [SUQ01] 20.00

Pencils

___Colored pencils with R2-D2 top [SUU01] 17.00

Animations
___ROTS 8 pencils and sharpener, Vader theme 4.00
___Pencil, Darth Vader 0.25

Butterfly Originals
4-packs. Darth Vader header card with ROTJ logo.
___C-3PO [SUU02].....................................6.00
___Darth Vader [SUU03] 6.00
___ROTJ logo [SUU04] 5.00

Character-topped ROTJ pencils.
___C-3PO [SUU05]....................................6.00
___Darth Vader [SUU06] 6.00
___Emperor's Royal Guard [SUU07] 6.00
___Wicket the Ewok [SUU08] 6.00

Pop-a-Point. "May The Force Be With You."
___2-pack [SUU09] 8.00
___6-pack, colored [SUU10] 15.00

Disney / MGM
___Star Tours, reflective [SUU11].....................4.00

Fan Club
___Empire Strikes Back logo and Character Strip
[SUU12]...5.00
___Star Wars logo and Character strip 5.00

Fantasma
Foil backgrounds.
___Star Wars logo and line art [SUU13] 3.00
___Star Wars logo and line art, fringe topped
[SUU14]...4.00

Flomo
Classic trilogy starship silhouettes with SW logo.
___Blue [SUU15] 3.00
___Gray [SUU16] 3.00
___Red [SUU17] 3.00

Funtastic Pty. Ltd.
___C-3PO / R2-D2 [SUU18]...........................2.00
___C-3PO / R2-D2 3-pack [SUU19] 5.00

Grand Toys
Episode I pencil with character topper.
___2-pack with lightsaber handle toppers [SUU20] ..4.00
___Anakin Skywalker [SUU21]........................3.00
___Darth Maul [SUU22] 3.00
___Jar Jar Binks [SUU23] 3.00

Grosvenor
___10-pack, droid, logo, presharpened [SUU24] 4.00

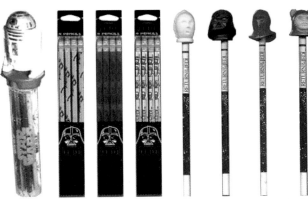   

SUU01   SUU02   SUU03   SUU04   SUU05   SUU06   SUU07   SUU08   SUU09   SUU10   SUU11 - SUU18

      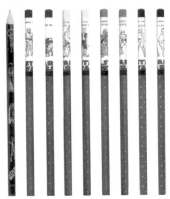 

SUU19   SUU20   SUU21   SUU22   SUU23   SUU24   SUU25   SUU26-SUU29 front and rear   SUU30

Pencils

| SUU31-SUU36 | SUU37 | SUU38 | SUU39 | SUU40 | SUU41 | SUU42 | SUU43 | SUU44-45 |

| SUU46 | SUU47 | SUU48 | SUU49 | USD01 | USD02 | USD03 | USD04 |

PEN01

PEN02

PEN03

____C-3PO, Lando, R2-D2, Boba Fett, logo, gold on black
[SUU25]...2.00

HC Ford
____C-3PO and R2-D2 [SUU26] 6.00
____Chewbacca and Han Solo [SUU27].............6.00
____Darth Vader and Stormtroopers [SUU28]..............6.00
____Darth Vader and X-Wing Fighter 4.00
____Luke Skywalker and Princess Leia [SUU29] 6.00

Helix
____"May The Force Be With You" 2.00
____Stormtrooper packaging, 10 colored pencils........8.00

Character-topped pencils.
____C-3PO 3.00
____Darth Vader 3.00
____R2-D2 ....3.00
____Stormtrooper..3.00

Hunter Leisure, Ltd.
____6-pack, ROTS 8.00

Magic World
____6 pack, colored 10.00

Mead
____4-pack [SUU30] 3.00
____C-3PO, Chewbacca, R2-D2 [SUU31]....................0.50
____Darth Vader, Luke, Leia [SUU32] 0.50
____Darth Vader, Stormtrooper, Boba Fett
[SUU33]...0.50
____Luke, Leia, Han [SUU34] 0.50

Merlin
____Star Wars Darth Vader [SUU35] 4.00
____Star Wars TIE fighters [SUU36] 4.00
____X-Wings and Alliance logo [SUU37].....................4.00

Pentech
Episode I character pencils.
____2-pack with Anakin and Amidala pencil toppers
[SUU38]...4.00
____2-pack with Darth Maul and Jar Jar pencil toppers
[SUU39]...4.00
____2-pack with lightsaber pencil sharpener
[SUU40]...5.00
____8-pack [SUU41] 6.00

Pyramid
____10-pack, pens and pencils, AOTC [SUU42]..........6.00

____6-pack, AOTC characters [SUU43] 7.00
____SW logo and starfield, gold on black [SUU44] 2.00

Q-Stat
*Colored pencils. Black barrel with gold Star Wars logo.
Part of the Jar Jar Binks art kit.*
____Any of 6 colors, ea. [SUU45] 0.25

*Pencil sets. 2 pencils, pencil pouch, sharpener, and
eraser.*
____Jedi vs. Sith 6.00
____Pod Race 6.00

Rose Art Industries
EPIII:ROTS. Mechanical.
____4-pack [SUU46] 6.00

EPIII:ROTS. Pencils with toppers.
____2-pack "E-Racer" toppers 3.00
____3-pack 3.00

EPIII:ROTS.
____4-pack, 1 of each design 4.00
____8-pack, 2 of each design 8.00
____Clone Troopers 1.00
____General Grievous 1.00
____Star Wars 1.00
____Vader 1.00

Foil.
____3-pack [SUU47] 5.00
____6-pack [SUU48] 5.00

Star Wars Kids
____StarWarsKids.com [SUU49] 3.00

Pennants

____10th Anniversary [PEN01] 28.00

Ice Capades
Ice Capades and Ewoks.
____Wicket [PEN02] 35.00

Mexico Collector Convention 2003
____POTF style logo, felt...15.00

Star Tours
____C-3PO, R2-D2, and Rex [PEN03] 25.00

Pennies: Elongated
Star Wars.
____C-3PO / R2-D2 [USD01] 15.00
____Chewbacca [USD02] 15.00
____Creatures / Stormtrooper / Tusken Raiders / Jawas
[USD03] 15.00
____Lord Darth Vader [USD04] 15.00

Disney / MGM
Star Tours.
____Mickey / Starspeeder 3000 ....10.00

Pens and Markers

Butterfly Originals
____C-3PO card with markers; 1 black and 1 blue
[SUV01]...11.00
____Darth Vader (black or blue) [SUV02]....................8.00
____Darth Vader helmet on clip [SUV03] 6.00
____ROTJ with logo and Characters, blue ink, 2-pack
[SUV04]...7.00

Chupa Chups
Sculpted character pens with concealed lollipops.
____Darth Vader [SUV05]...8.00
____Stormtrooper [SUV06] 8.00

Comic Images
Bobble pens.
____Darth Vader [SUV07]..5.00
____Yoda [SUV08] 5.00

Disney / MGM
____Set of 3: Star Tours logo, C-3PO, R2-D2
[SUV09]...15.00

Fan Club
____Floaty Pen, Star Wars Insider renewal premium
[SUV10]..25.00

Fan Club, UK
Black-ink revealing logo and character.
____C-3PO [SUV11] 35.00
____Darth Vader [SUV12] 35.00
____R2-D2 [SUV13] 35.00

Fantasma
____Star Wars logo and line art on foil background, ball
point 4.00

Fisher
____Rebel Fighter pen, black rubberized grip, "Star Wars"
on clip, and Rebel emblem on end [SUV14] 20.00
____Titanium space pen, "Star Wars" and "May The Force
Be With You" imprinted on barrel 45.00
____Titanium space pen, "Star Wars" and "May The Force
Be With You" imprinted on barrel, Dave Prowse auto-
graphed, limited edition of 200 [SUV15] 70.00

| SUV01 | SUV02 | SUV03 | SUV04 | SUV05 | SUV06 | SUV07 | SUV08 |

| SUV09 | SUV10 | SUV11 | SUV12 | SUV13 | SUV14 | SUV15 | SUV16 |

Funtastic Pty. Ltd.
____SW logo on technical background. Included in art kits. Valued each. [SUV16] 1.00

General Mills
Episode II lightsaber light-up pens. Cereal premiums.
____Anakin Skywalker, blue blade [SUV17].................8.00
____Count Dooku, red blade [SUV18] 5.00
____Darth Vader, red blade [SUV19] 5.00
____Luke Skywalker, green blade [SUV20] 5.00
____Mace Windu, purple blade [SUV21] 5.00

Grosvenor
Star Wars Saga, package of 3.
____C-3PO, R2-D2 and logo on each [SUV22]............7.00

Helix
Colored felt tips, boxed set.
____Set of five [SUV23] 25.00
____Set of ten 36.00

Jollibee
____Darth Vader with light-up lightsaber 10.00

Mead
____8-pack, each color has own character illustration on barrel [SUV24]...7.00

____C-3PO "They've Shut Down The Main Reactor..." [SUV25] 3.00
____Darth Vader "I Find Your Lack of Faith Distrubing" [SUV26] 3.00
____Princess Leia and R2-D2 "Help Me Obi-Wan Kenobi..." [SUV27] 3.00
____Stormtroopers "Freeze You Rebel Scum" [SUV28] 3.00

Merlin
Printed pen barrels and caps.
____X-Wing Squadron Incom T-65 [SUV29] 2.00

Penline
Characters printed on pen barrels and caps.
____Darth Vader [SUV30]..5.00
____Han Solo [SUV31]...5.00
____Luke Skywalker [SUV32]..5.00
____R2-D2 [SUV33] 5.00

Pentech
____3-pack of ballpoint pens, sculpted as lightsabers, EPI [SUV34] 5.00
____6-pack of character ballpoint pens, EPI [SUV35] 4.00
____Darth Maul ballpoint, includes collectors tin [SUV36]...15.00

6-packs. Each barrel has own illustrated character.
____Darth Maul [SUV37] 8.00
____Jar Jar Binks [SUV38]..8.00

Q-Stat
Colored barrel with gold Star Wars logo.
____Any of 6 colors, ea. [SUV39].................................0.25

Episode I: The Phantom Menace.
____Blue barrel pen with lightsaber handle [SUV40] 4.00

Rose Art Industries
____Set of 3, Vader in Flames [SUV41] 3.00
____Super Stamper Washable Markers [SUV42] 7.00

EPIII:ROTS.
____2-pack Anakin and Darth Vader 7.00

Star Wars washable markers
____Set of 5, thin [SUV43] 3.00
____Set of 8, character [SUV44] 8.00

Star Wars Celebration II
Glowing pens.
____Blue [SUV45] 20.00
____Red [SUV46]...20.00

| SUV17 | SUV18 | SUV19 | SUV20 | SUV21 | SUV22 | SUV23 |

Pens and Markers

SUV24

SUV25

SUV26

SUV27

SUV28

SUV29

SUV30

SUV31

SUV32

SUV33

SUV34

SUV35

SUV36

SUV37

SUV38

Super Live Adventure
____3-pen set: Indiana Jones, Star Wars, and SLA [SUV47]..16.00

SUV39

SUV40

SUV41

The CDM Company
Clip pens.
____Darth Vader..12.00

POD Pens.
____Star Wars, Comic Con exclusive, limited to 2,500 [SUV48]..45.00

Writing System Connect and Build Pens. EPII:ROTS
____Chewbacca [SUV49]......................................15.00
____Darth Vader [SUV50] 15.00
____R2-D2 [SUV51]..15.00
____Yoda [SUV52]..15.00

Writing System Connect and Build Pens.
____Anakin Skywalker [SUV53].................................19.00
____C-3PO [SUV54] 19.00
____Chewbacca [SUV55] 19.00
____Clone Trooper [SUV56]....................................19.00
____Darth Maul [SUV57] 19.00
____Darth Vader [SUV58] 19.00
____Jango Fett [SUV59] 19.00
____Luke Skywalker [SUV60]...................................19.00
____Obi-Wan Kenobi [SUV61]..................................19.00
____Paploo [SUV62] 19.00
____R2-D2 [SUV63]..19.00
____Stormtrooper [SUV64] 19.00

____Tusken Raider [SUV65]....................................19.00
____Yoda [SUV66] 25.00

Tiger Electronics
____Lightsaber, 4 Sound FX, 12 second record/playback, voice changer [SUV67].......................................12.00

Electronic character pens speak phrase. Record-and-playback function.
____C-3PO [2:341]..8.00
____Darth Vader [SUV69]......................................8.00
____X-Wing Pilot 8.00
____X-Wing Pilot, cardboard header card [SUV70]......8.00

Pewter
____Luke Skywalker on light-up stand [PEW01] 45.00
____Princess Leia and Luke statue, classic logo pose 450.00
____Qui-Gon figurine and lightsaber keychain, Jedi Power Battle for Playstation promotion 16.00

SW:SE logo, 3"x3.5".
____1996 Star Wars Summit, ltd to 750 [PEW02] 75.00
____1997, limited to 40,000 ....35.00

SUV42

SUV43

SUV44

SUV45

SUV46

SUV47

SUV48

| SUV49 | SUV50 | SUV51 | SUV52 | SUV53 | SUV54 | SUV55 | SUV56 | SUV57 | SUV58 |

| SUV59 | SUV60 | SUV61 | SUV62 | SUV63 | SUV64 | SUV65 | SUV66 |

Black Falcon
____Darth Vader pendant from art portfolio 45.00

Danbury Mint
Collectible chess pieces.
____AT-ST, rook [PEW03] 38.00
____Boba Fett, bishop [PEW04] 38.00
____C-3PO, rook [PEW05] 38.00
____Chewbacca, knight [PEW06] 38.00
____Darth Vader, bishop [PEW07] 38.00
____Death Star, queen [PEW08] 38.00
____Emperor, king [PEW09] 38.00
____Ewok with spear, pawn [PEW10] 38.00
____Han, bishop [PEW11] 38.00
____Imperial Probot, rook [PEW12].............38.00
____Leia, knight [PEW13] 38.00
____Luke, bishop [PEW14] 38.00
____Millennium Falcon, queen [PEW15] 38.00
____Obi-Wan and Yoda, king [PEW16] 38.00
____R2-D2, rook [PEW17] 38.00
____Speeder Bike Trooper, knight [PEW18] 38.00
____Stormtrooper, pawn [PEW19] 38.00
____Tusken Raider on Bantha, knight [PEW20] 38.00

Franklin Mint
Collector's edition for Star Wars 20th anniversary.
____AT-AT [PEW21].....................................300.00
____Millennium Falcon, 7"x5" with black plastic base [PEW22] 300.00

Collector's edition in pewter and gold for Star Wars 15th anniversary.
____AT-AT [PEW23].....................................260.00
____Millennium Falcon, 7"x5" with black plastic base [PEW24] 260.00

Heritage / Star Trek Galore
____Bantha with two Sand People riders [PEW25] ..25.00
____Bantha, no riders or saddle [PEW26]...............15.00
____C-3PO [PEW27] 10.00
____Chewbacca [PEW28] 10.00
____Darth Vader [PEW29] 10.00
____Han Solo (STG only)..............................15.00
____Jawa [PEW29] 10.00
____Luke Skywalker [PEW30] 10.00
____Obi-Wan Kenobi [PEW31] 10.00
____Princess Leia [PEW32] 10.00
____R2-D2 [PEW33] 10.00
____Sand Person, standing [PEW34] 10.00
____Snitch (Grindan) [PEW35]......................10.00
____Stormtrooper [PEW36] 10.00

| SUV67 | SUV68 | SUV69 |

Rawcliffe
____A-Wing Fighter [PEW37] 40.00
____Admiral Ackbar [PEW38] 20.00
____Anakin Skywalker [PEW39] 24.00
____Anakin Skywalker (Boxed with Hasbro's Deluxe Monopoly CD Game) [PEW40]....................12.00
____B-Wing Fighter [PEW41] 45.00
____Battle Droid [PEW42] 25.00
____Bib Fortuna [PEW43] 20.00
____Boba Fett [PEW44]...24.00
____C-3PO [PEW45] 20.00
____Chewbacca [PEW46] 22.00
____Darth Maul [PEW47]..36.00
____Darth Vader's Tie Fighter, deluxe limited to 15,000 [PEW48] 125.00
____Darth Vader [PEW49] 34.00
____Death Star II, limited to 4,500 [PEW50] 86.00
____Droopy McCool [PEW51] 19.00
____Emperor [PEW52]..20.00
____Federation Droid Starfighter [PEW53] 48.00
____Federation Large Transport [PEW54]..................62.00
____Federation Tank [PEW55].....................................62.00
____Gamorrean Guard [PEW56] 20.00
____Han Solo [PEW57]...20.00
____Imperial Star Destroyer [PEW58] 75.00
____Jabba and Leia, limited to 2,005 [PEW59] 200.00
____Jabba the Hutt [PEW60].......................................48.00
____Jar Jar Binks [PEW61]...29.00

____Lando Calrissian [PEW62] 20.00
____Luke Skywalker [PEW63] 22.00
____Max Rebo [PEW64] 29.00
____Millennium Falcon [PEW65] 50.00
____Millennium Falcon, deluxe limited to 15,000 [PEW66] 110.00
____Naboo Starfighter [PEW67] 48.00
____Naboo Starfighter, deluxe limited to 1,000 [PEW68] 200.00
____Nute Gunray [PEW69] 29.00
____Obi-Wan Kenobi [PEW70] 23.00
____Obi-Wan Kenobi (TPM) [PEW71] 29.00
____Outrider [PEW72] 35.00
____Princess Leia [PEW73] 20.00
____Princess Leia as Jabba's prisoner [PEW74] 18.00
____Princess Leia as Jabba's prisoner promotion (round base) [PEW75]..15.00
____Queen Amidala [PEW76] 25.00
____Qui-Gon Jinn [PEW77] 29.00
____R2-D2 [PEW78] 22.00
____Royal Starship [PEW79] 48.00
____Sail Barge [PEW80] 45.00
____Shuttle Tydirium [PEW81]......................................50.00
____Slave I [PEW82] 40.00
____Snowspeeder [PEW83] 35.00
____Speeder Bike [PEW84] 48.00
____Stormtrooper [PEW85] 23.00
____Stormtrooper Dark Forces promo [PEW86]........14.00

Pewter

____Sy Snootles [PEW87] 19.00
____Tie Bomber [PEW88] 40.00
____Tie Fighter [PEW89] 42.00
____Tie Interceptor, dlx. ltd to 7,500 [PEW90] 125.00
____Watto [PEW91] 29.00
____Wicket [PEW92] 20.00
____X-wing Fighter [PEW93] 45.00
____X-wing Fighter, dlx. ltd. to 15,000 [PEW94]........95.00
____Y-Wing Fighter [PEW95] 50.00
____Yoda [PEW96]......................................20.00

EPIII:ROTS. Scenes.

____Epic Duel [PEW97]................................125.00
____Yoda vs. Sidious [PEW98] 125.00

EPIII:ROTS.

____Anakin Skywalker [PEW99] 30.00
____Clone Trooper [PEW100] 30.00
____General Grievous' Guard [PEW101]................30.00
____General Grievous [PEW102]......................30.00
____Obi-Wan Kenobi [PEW103] 30.00

Episode II vehicles.

____Anakin's Speeder [PEW104] 35.00
____Jedi Starfighter [PEW105] 35.00
____Jedi Starfighter, limited to 900 [PEW106] 200.00
____Republic Gunship [PEW107] 40.00
____Zam's Speeder [PEW108] 40.00

Episode II: Attack of the Clones.

____Anakin Skywalker [PEW109] 18.00
____Clone Trooper [PEW110] 18.00
____Count Dooku [PEW111] 18.00
____Jango Fett [PEW112] 18.00
____Mace Windu [PEW113] 18.00
____Obi-Wan [PEW114] 18.00
____Padme Amidala [PEW115] 18.00
____Super Battle Droid [PEW116] 18.00
____Yoda [PEW117]...................................15.00
____Zam Wesell [PEW118] 18.00

Show West March 5, 1996.

____X-Wing Fighter dlx, ltd. to 4,500 [PEW119] 375.00

PEW01 PEW02 PEW03 PEW04 PEW05 PEW06 PEW07 PEW08 PEW09 PEW10 PEW11 PEW12 PEW13 PEW14 PEW15

PEW16 PEW17 PEW18 PEW19 PEW20 PEW21 PEW22 PEW23 PEW24

PEW25 PEW26 PEW27 PEW28 PEW29 PEW30 PEW31 PEW32 PEW33 PEW34

PEW35 PEW36 PEW37 PEW38 PEW39 PEW40 PEW41 PEW42 PEW43 PEW44 PEW45 PEW46

PEW47 PEW48 PEW49 PEW50 PEW51 PEW52 PEW53 PEW54 PEW55

PEW56 PEW57 PEW58 PEW59 PEW60 PEW61 PEW62 PEW63

PEW64 PEW65 PEW66 PEW67 PEW68 PEW69 PEW70 PEW71 PEW72

PEW73 PEW74 PEW75 PEW76 PEW77 PEW78 PEW79 PEW80 PEW81 PEW82

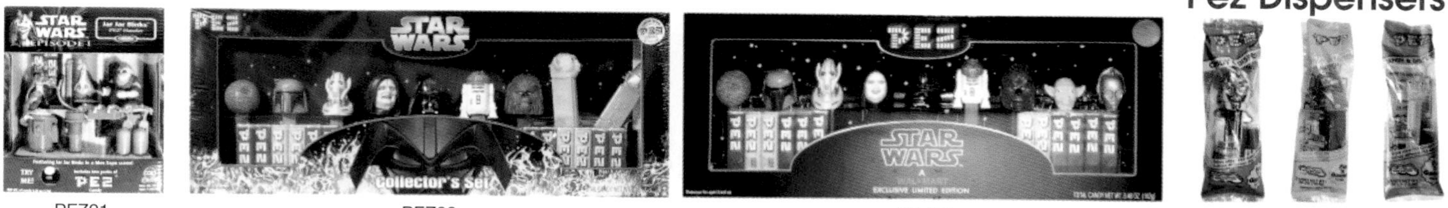

PEZ01 PEZ02 PEZ03 PEZ04 PEZ05 PEZ06

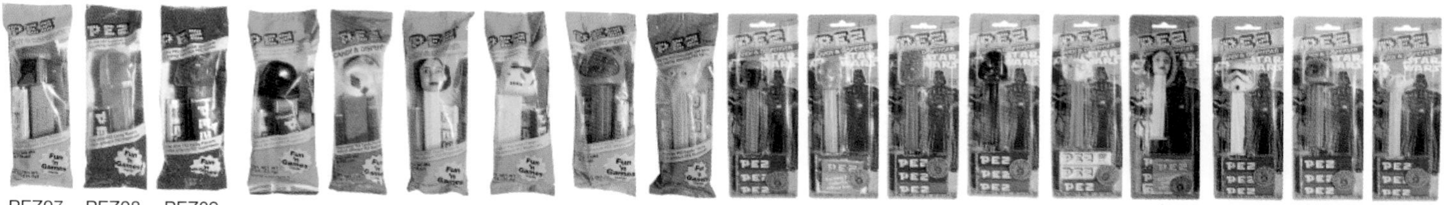

PEZ07 PEZ08 PEZ09 PEZ10 PEZ11 PEZ12 PEZ13 PEZ14 PEZ15 PEZ16 PEZ17 PEZ18 PEZ19 PEZ20 PEZ21 PEZ22 PEZ23 PEZ24

Skywalker Ranch November 3 and 4, 1994.
____X-Wing Fighter deluxe, "Taking the Galaxy by Force" 375.00

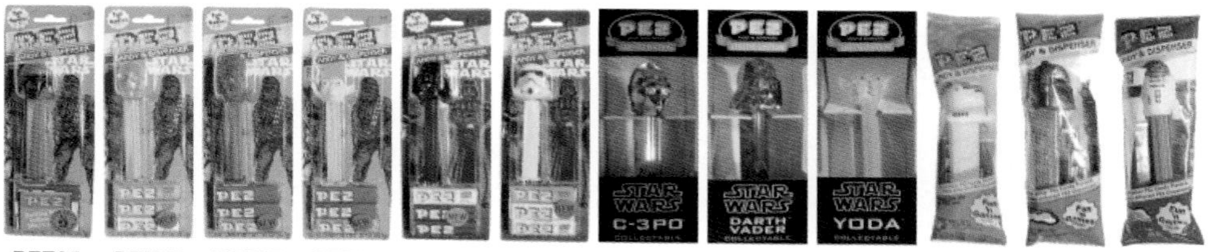

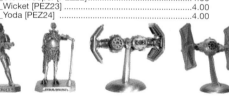

PEZ25 PEZ26 PEZ27 PEZ28 PEZ29 PEZ30 PEZ31 PEZ32 PEZ33 PEZ34 PEZ35 PEZ36

Pez Dispensers

Cap Candy
____Jar Jar Binks PEZ Handler, battery operated [PEZ01] 10.00

Pez Candy, Inc.
____Star Wars Collector's Box, limited to 250,000 (numbered) [PEZ02] 16.00
____Star Wars Collector's Box, limited to 250,000 (numbered) with exclusive glow-in-the-dark Emperor figure, Walmart exclusive [PEZ03] 18.00

Classic Interacive series.
____C-3PO, golden [PEZ04] 16.00
____Darth Vader, crystal [PEZ05] 12.00
____Yoda, crystal [PEZ06] 12.00

Classic trilogy, bagged, any color package (red, green, and blue).
____Boba Fett [PEZ07] 2.00
____C-3PO [PEZ08] 2.00
____Chewbacca [PEZ09] 2.00
____Darth Vader [PEZ10] 2.00
____Luke in X-Wing Gear [PEZ11] 2.00
____Princess Leia [PEZ12] 2.00
____Stormtrooper [PEZ13] 2.00
____Wicket [PEZ14] 2.00
____Yoda [PEZ15] 2.00

Classic trilogy. Blue cardback with Darth Vader and Stormtrooper.
____Boba Fett [PEZ16] 4.00
____C-3PO [PEZ17] 4.00
____Chewbacca [PEZ18] 4.00
____Darth Vader [PEZ19] 4.00
____Luke in X-Wing Gear [PEZ20] 4.00
____Princess Leia [PEZ21] 4.00
____Stormtrooper [PEZ22] 4.00
____Wicket [PEZ23] 4.00
____Yoda [PEZ24] 4.00

Classic trilogy. Green cardback with C-3PO, Chewbacca, and Yoda.
____Boba Fett [PEZ25] 5.00
____C-3PO [PEZ26] 5.00
____Chewbacca [PEZ27] 5.00
____Yoda [PEZ28] 5.00

Classic trilogy. Purple cardback with Darth Vader and Stormtrooper.
____Darth Vader [PEZ29] 5.00
____Stormtrooper [PEZ30] 5.00

Collector Series, limited to 10,000 each. Boxed with display stand.
____C-3PO, golden [PEZ31] 25.00
____Darth Vader, crystal [PEZ32] 25.00
____Yoda, crystal [PEZ33] 25.00

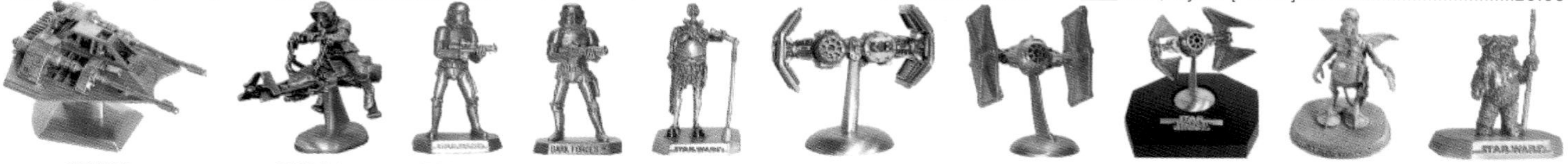

PEW83 PEW84 PEW85 PEW86 PEW87 PEW88 PEW89 PEW90 PEW91 PEW92

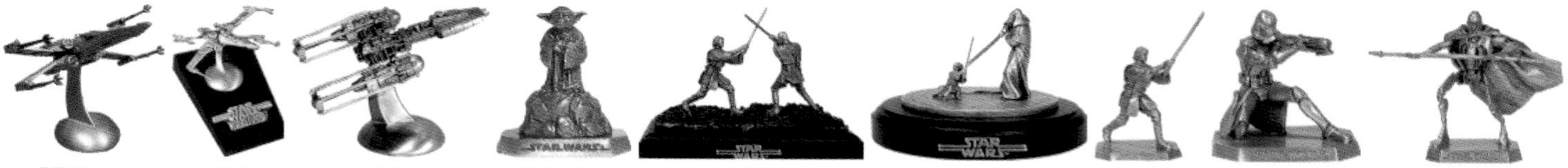

PEW93 PEW94 PEW95 PEW96 PEW97 PEW98 PEW99 PEW100 PEW101

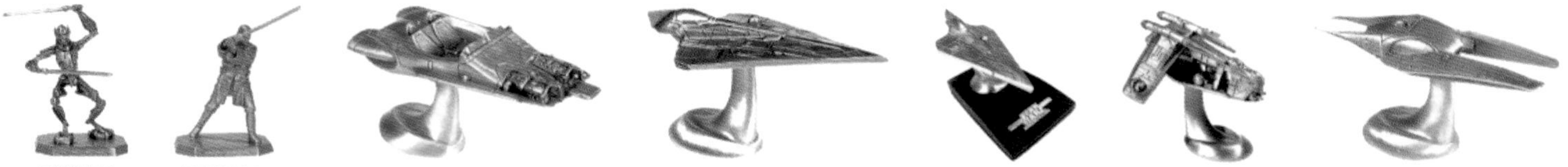

PEW102 PEW103 PEW104 PEW105 PEW106 PEW107 PEW108

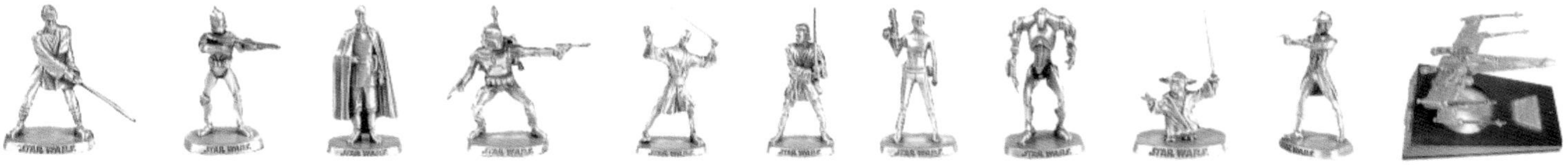

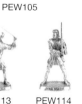

PEW109 PEW110 PEW111 PEW112 PEW113 PEW114 PEW115 PEW116 PEW117 PEW118 PEW119

Pez Dispensers

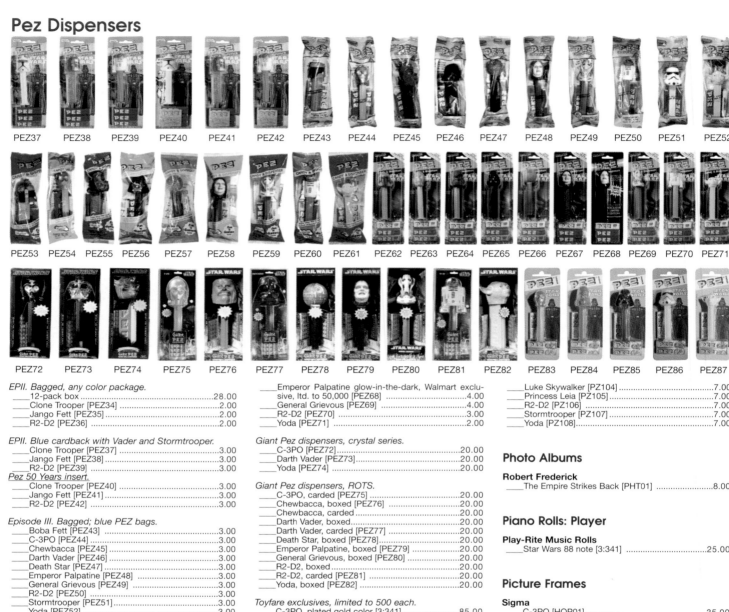

PEZ37 PEZ38 PEZ39 PEZ40 PEZ41 PEZ42 PEZ43 PEZ44 PEZ45 PEZ46 PEZ47 PEZ48 PEZ49 PEZ50 PEZ51 PEZ52

PEZ53 PEZ54 PEZ55 PEZ56 PEZ57 PEZ58 PEZ59 PEZ60 PEZ61 PEZ62 PEZ63 PEZ64 PEZ65 PEZ66 PEZ67 PEZ68 PEZ69 PEZ70 PEZ71

PEZ72 PEZ73 PEZ74 PEZ75 PEZ76 PEZ77 PEZ78 PEZ79 PEZ80 PEZ81 PEZ82 PEZ83 PEZ84 PEZ85 PEZ86 PEZ87

EPII. Bagged, any color package.
____12-pack box 28.00
____Clone Trooper [PEZ34] 2.00
____Jango Fett [PEZ35] 2.00
____R2-D2 [PEZ36] 2.00

EPII. Blue cardback with Vader and Stormtrooper.
____Clone Trooper [PEZ37] 3.00
____Jango Fett [PEZ38] 3.00
____R2-D2 [PEZ39] 3.00
Pez 50 Years insert.
____Clone Trooper [PEZ40] 3.00
____Jango Fett [PEZ41] 3.00
____R2-D2 [PEZ42] 3.00

Episode III. Bagged; blue PEZ bags.
____Boba Fett [PEZ43] 3.00
____C-3PO [PEZ44] 3.00
____Chewbacca [PEZ45] 3.00
____Darth Vader [PEZ46] 3.00
____Death Star [PEZ47] 3.00
____Emperor Palpatine [PEZ48] 3.00
____General Grievous [PEZ49] 3.00
____R2-D2 [PEZ50] 3.00
____Stormtrooper [PEZ51] 3.00
____Yoda [PEZ52] 3.00

Episode III: Bagged; red, blue, or green bags.
____Boba Fett [PEZ53] 2.00
____C-3PO [PEZ54] 2.00
____Chewbacca [PEZ55] 2.00
____Darth Vader [PEZ56] 2.00
____Death Star [PEZ57] 5.00
____Emperor Palpatine [PEZ58] 5.00
____General Grievous [PEZ59] 5.00
____R2-D2 [PEZ60] 5.00
____Yoda [PEZ61] 2.00

Episode III: Carded.
____Boba Fett [PEZ62] 2.00
____C-3PO [PEZ63] 2.00
____Chewbacca [PEZ64] 3.00
____Darth Vader [PEZ65] 2.00
____Death Star [PEZ66] 3.00
____Emperor Palpatine [PEZ67] 3.00

____Emperor Palpatine glow-in-the-dark, Walmart exclu-
sive, ltd. to 50,000 [PEZ68] 4.00
____General Grievous [PEZ69] 4.00
____R2-D2 [PEZ70] 3.00
____Yoda [PEZ71] 2.00

Giant Pez dispensers, crystal series.
____C-3PO [PEZ72] 20.00
____Darth Vader [PEZ73] 20.00
____Yoda [PEZ74] 20.00

Giant Pez dispensers, ROTS.
____C-3PO, carded [PEZ75] 20.00
____Chewbacca, boxed [PEZ76] 20.00
____Chewbacca, carded 20.00
____Darth Vader, boxed 20.00
____Darth Vader, carded [PEZ77] 20.00
____Death Star, boxed [PEZ78] 20.00
____Emperor Palpatine, boxed [PEZ79] 20.00
____General Grievous, boxed [PEZ80] 20.00
____R2-D2, boxed 20.00
____R2-D2, carded [PEZ81] 20.00
____Yoda, boxed [PEZ82] 20.00

Toyfare exclusives, limited to 500 each.
____C-3PO, plated gold color [3:341] 85.00
____Darth Vader, plated chrome color [3:341] 85.00

Pez Candy, Inc., UK
Classic trilogy. Blue cardback with Darth Vader.
____C-3PO [PEZ83] 4.00
____Chewbacca [PEZ84] 4.00
____Darth Vader [PEZ85] 4.00
____Stormtrooper [PEZ86] 4.00
____Yoda [PEZ87] 4.00

Pez Refills

Pez Candy, Inc.
Pez refill with classic trilogy character sticker.
____C-3PO [PZ101] 7.00
____Darth Vader [PZ102] 7.00
____Han Solo [PZ103] 7.00

____Luke Skywalker [PZ104] 7.00
____Princess Leia [PZ105] 7.00
____R2-D2 [PZ106] 7.00
____Stormtrooper [PZ107] 7.00
____Yoda [PZ108] 7.00

Photo Albums

Robert Frederick
____The Empire Strikes Back [PHT01] 8.00

Piano Rolls: Player

Play-Rite Music Rolls
____Star Wars 88 note [3:341] 25.00

Picture Frames

Sigma
____C-3PO [HOP01] 35.00
____Darth Vader [HOP02] 25.00
____R2-D2 [3:341] 30.00

Pinatas

Hallmark
____Darth Vader ribbon [P2N01] 15.00

Pins

____C-3PO / R2-D2, blue with logo [PI01] 5.00
____Darth Vader look-alike [PI02] 5.00
____Episode I logo, elipse [PI03] 4.00
____Star Wars Episode I logo [PI04] 6.00
____The Power of Myth [PI05] 8.00

          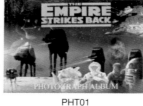  

PZ101 PZ102 PZ103 PZ104 PZ105 PZ106 PZ107 PZ108 PHT01 HOP01 HOP02 P2N01

PI01 PI02 PI03 PI04 PI05 PI06 PI07 PI08

PI09 PI10 PI11 PI12 PI13 PI14 PI15 PI16 PI17 PI18

PI19 PI20 PI21 PI22 PI23 PI24 PI25 PI26 PI27 PI28

Art of Star Wars, Kyoto Museum, Japan, sets of 3.

____Clone Trooper, Jedi Acadamy, Jango [PI06]	18.00
____Darth Vader, R2-D2, Stormtrooper [PI07]	18.00
____Millennium Falcon, X-Wing, Death Star II [PI08]	18.00

3D Arts
Square lasergram.

____C-3PO and R2-D2	6.00
____Darth Vader	6.00
____Millennium Falcon	6.00
____X-Wing Fighter	6.00

501st Legion

____Japanese Garrison [PI29]	10.00

Activa Consumer Promotions Corp.
Canada. Winnipeg Free Press.

____Anakin Skywalker [PI09]	5.00
____Bail Organa [PI10]	5.00
____Boba Fett [PI11]	5.00
____C-3PO [PI12]	5.00
____Chewbacca [PI13]	5.00
____Count Dooku [PI14]	5.00
____Darth Maul [PI15]	5.00
____Darth Sidious [PI16]	5.00
____Darth Vader [PI17]	5.00
____General Grievous [PI18]	5.00
____Han Solo [PI19]	5.00
____Jabba the Hutt [PI20]	5.00
____Luke Skywalker [PI21]	5.00
____Mace Windu [PI22]	5.00
____Obi-Wan Kenobi [PI23]	5.00
____Padme Amidala [PI24]	5.00
____Princess Leia [PI25]	5.00
____R2-D2 [PI26]	5.00
____Stormtrooper [PI27]	5.00
____Yoda [PI28]	5.00

Adam Joseph Industries
Brass colored, sculpted, blister packed to red cardbacks.

____C-3PO [PI30]	25.00
____Emperor's Royal Guard [PI31]	25.00

Brass, sculpted.

____"May The Force Be With You" [PI32]	8.00
____C-3PO [PI33]	8.00
____Emperor's Royal Guard [PI34]	8.00
____R2-D2 [PI35]	8.00
____Return of the Jedi logo [PI36]	8.00
____Salacious Crumb [PI37]	8.00
____Star Wars logo [PI38]	8.00
____The Force [PI39]	8.00
____Wicket the Ewok [PI40]	8.00
____X-Wing Pilot [PI41]	8.00
____Yoda [PI42]	8.00

Plastic, sculpted.

____Princess Kneesaa [3:342]	3.00
____Wicket the Ewok [2:345]	3.00

Applause

____Anakin Skywalker [PI45]	3.00
____Battle Droid [PI46]	4.00
____C-3PO [PI47]	3.00

____Darth Maul [PI48]	3.00
____Darth Sidious	8.00
____Episode I:TPM Logo [PI49]	5.00
____Jar Jar Binks [PI50]	3.00
____Naboo Starfighter [PI51]	3.00
____Obi-Wan Kenobi [PI52]	3.00
____Queen Amidala [PI53]	3.00
____Qui-Gon Jinn [PI54]	3.00
____R2-D2 [PI55]	4.00
____Trade Federation Droid Fighter [PI56]	3.00

Framed Collections.

____Dark Side: Darth Maul, Darth Sidious, Battle Droid, Droid Starship, EPI Logo [PI57]	35.00

Atari
Black and silver, promotional.

____C-3PO	23.00
____Darth Vader	23.00
____R2-D2	23.00

PI29 PI30 PI31

PI32 PI33 PI34 PI35 PI36 PI37 PI38 PI39 PI40 PI41 PI42

PI45 PI46 PI47 PI48 PI49 PI50 PI51 PI52 PI53 PI54 PI55 PI56

Pins

PI57

PI58

PI59

PI60

PI61

PI62

PI63

PI64

PI65

PI66

PI67

PI68

PI69   PI70

PI71

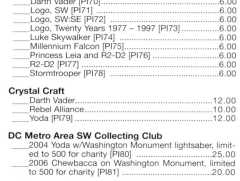

PI72

PI73   PI74   PI75

C2 Ventures
____SWCII VIP [PI58] 130.00

Cards, Inc.
Enamel.
____General Grievous [PI59] 10.00
____Jedi [PI60] 10.00
____Lightsaber [PI61] 10.00
____Sith [PI62] 10.00

Etched metal.
____Clone Trooper [PI63]...10.00
____Darth Vader [PI64] 10.00
____General Grievous [PI65] 10.00
____Jedi emblem [PI66] 10.00
____Lightsaber [PI67] 10.00
____Republic emblem [PI68] 10.00

Castoline
____Chewbacca [PI69]..6.00

____Darth Vader [PI70]...6.00
____Logo, SW [PI71]...6.00
____Logo, SW:SE [PI72] 6.00
____Logo, Twenty Years 1977 – 1997 [PI73] 6.00
____Luke Skywalker [PI74]...6.00
____Millennium Falcon [PI75].......................................6.00
____Princess Leia and R2-D2 [PI76] 6.00
____R2-D2 [PI77]..6.00
____Stormtrooper [PI78] 6.00

Crystal Craft
____Darth Vader...12.00
____Rebel Alliance...10.00
____Yoda [PI79]...12.00

DC Metro Area SW Collecting Club
____2004 Yoda w/Washington Monument lightsaber, limit-
    ed to 500 for charity [PI80] 25.00
____2006 Chewbacca on Washington Monument, limited
    to 500 for charity [PI81] 20.00

Disney / MGM
____C-3PO / Disneyland 35 year anniversary
    [PI82]..18.00
____Chewbacca [PI83]..8.00
____Darth Vader [PI84]...8.00
____Jedi Starfighter, EPII opening night premium
    [PI85]..35.00
____R2-D2 [PI86]...6.00
____Stormtrooper [PI94] 12.00
____Yoda, Silent Knight, Jedi Knight [PI95] 18.00

Star Tours.
____15th Anniversary [PI87] 14.00
____1987 ....15.00
____Logo [PI88]..14.00
____Paris logo [PI89]..18.00
____Tatooine Express [PI90]...9.00
____The Leader In Galactic Sightseeing [PI91]............9.00
____Star Tours (hidden Mickey) [PI92] 18.00
____Star Tours press and preview [PI93] 35.00

PI76

PI77

PI78

PI79

PI80

PI81

PI82

PI83

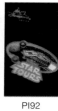

PI84

PI85

PI86

PI87

PI88

PI89

PI90

PI91

PI92

PI93

PI94

PI95

PI96   PI97   PI98   PI99   PI100   PI101   PI102   PI103

PI104   PI105   PI106   PI107   PI108   PI109   PI110   PI111   PI112

PI113   PI114   PI115   PI116   PI117   PI118   PI119   PI120   PI121   PI122   PI123

May 2000, dangler pin limited to 3,000.
___Anakin [PI96] 18.00
___Boba Fett [PI97] 26.00
___Chewbacca [PI98] 18.00
___Chewbacca, signed by designer [PI99] 18.00
___Darth Vader [PI100] 18.00
___Princess Leia [PI101] 18.00
___R2-D2 [PI102] 18.00

May 2000, limited to 7,500.
___Mickey head with laser light [PI103] 11.00

May 2001, limited to 2001.
___Darth Vader's Tie Fighter [PI104] 24.00
___Han Solo [PI105] 24.00
___Luke Skywalker [PI106] 24.00
___Millennium Falcon [PI107] 24.00
___Naboo Fighter [PI108] 24.00
___Obi-Wan Kenobi [PI109]....................18.00
___R2-D2 projecting hologram Mickey [PI110]........30.00
___X-Wing Fighter [PI111] 24.00
___Yoda [PI112] 18.00

May 2001.
___Commemorative set, framed and signed by artists,
    limited to 50 ....335.00

May 2002, limited to 2002.
___Anakin Skywalker [PI113]...............................15.00
___Boba Fett [PI114] 15.00
___C-3PO [PI115] 15.00
___Clone Trooper [PI116].........................15.00
___Count Dooku [PI117] 15.00

___Darth Maul [PI118].............................15.00
___Darth Vader's Tie Fighter [PI119] 15.00
___Darth Vader [PI120].............................15.00
___Death Star [PI121] 15.00
___Han Solo [PI122] 15.00
___Jango Fett [PI123]...............................15.00
___Jedi Starfighter [PI124].......................15.00
___Kamino Duel, light up ltd. to 3,500 [PI125] 15.00
___Luke Skywalker [PI126] 15.00
___Millennium Falcon [PI127] 15.00
___Naboo Starfighter [PI128] 15.00
___Padme Amidala [PI129] 15.00
___Princess Leia [PI130] 15.00
___R2-D2 [PI131] 15.00
___R2-D2 and C-3PO, light up limited to 2,500
    [PI132]...15.00
___Slave I [PI133]..................................15.00
___Space Battle, light up [PI134] 15.00
___Stormtrooper [PI135]..........................15.00
___Super Battle Droid [PI136] 15.00

___Super Battle Droid attacking [PI137] 15.00
___Tie Fighter [PI138] 15.00
___X-Wing Fighter [PI139] 15.00
___Yoda [PI140]....................................15.00
___Zam Wesell's Speeder [PI141] 15.00

May 2003, limited to 2000. Spinner pins.
___Anakin Skywalker [PI142] 16.00
___Artoo Detoo [PI143] 16.00
___C-3PO [PI144] 16.00
___Clone Trooper [PI145].......................16.00
___Count Dooku [PI146] 16.00
___Jango Fett [PI147] 16.00
___Mace Windu [PI148] 16.00
___Obi-Wan Kenobi [PI149]....................16.00
___Padme Amidala [PI150] 16.00
___Yoda [PI151] 16.00

May 2003, limited to 250.
___Framed set of 15 [PI152] 250.00

PI124   PI125   PI126   PI127   PI128   PI129   PI130

PI131   PI132   PI133   PI134   PI135   PI136   PI137   PI138   PI139   PI140   PI141

PI142   PI143   PI144   PI145   PI146   PI147   PI148   PI149   PI150   PI151   PI152

Pins

PI153   PI154   PI155   PI156   PI157   PI158   PI159   PI160   PI161

PI162   PI163   PI164   PI165   PI166   PI167   PI168   PI169   PI170   PI171   PI172

Disney Weekends May 2003, limited to 3,500.
____Anakin and Padme [PI153] 14.00
____Clone Troopers [PI154] 14.00
____Count Dooku and Obi-Wan [PI155] 14.00
____Count Dooku and Yoda [PI156] 14.00

Disney Weekends May 2003, limited to 500.
____Villains, set of 5 pewter, wood box [PI157] 110.00

Disney Weekends May 2003, limited to 7,000.
____Mickey and Yoda [PI158] 18.00

Disney Weekends May 2003.
____Build-a-pin, any style [PI159] 18.00

Disney Weekends May 2004.
____Droids, boxed set of 6, limited to 750 [PI160] ...175.00
____Framed set of 11, limited to 250 [PI161] 250.00
____Jedi Mickey, 3" limited to 500 [PI162] 35.00

Limited to 1,000.
____Anakin Skywalker padawan [PI163] 12.00
____Anakin Skywalker pod racer [PI164] 12.00
____Darth Maul [PI165] 12.00
____Darth Vader [PI166] 12.00
____Emperor Palpatine [PI167] 12.00
____Luke and Yoda [PI168] 12.00
____Luke vs. Darth Vader [PI169] 12.00
____Mickey and Minnie / movie poster [PI170] 18.00
____Obi-Wan vs. Darth Vader [PI171] 12.00
____Yoda, EPII [PI172] 12.00

Disney Weekends May 2005.
____Chewbacca and Tarfful [PI173] 15.00
____Clone Troopers [PI174] 15.00
____Darth Vader and Darth Sidious [PI175] 15.00
____EPIII:ROTS Opening Day 2005 [PI176] 35.00
____Grievous vs. Obi-Wan [PI177] 15.00
____Logo 15.00
____Logo, jumbo [PI178] 15.00

____Mace Windu vs. Darth Sidious [PI179] 15.00
____Obi-Wan and Boga [PI180] 15.00
____Obi-Wan vs. Anakin [PI181] 15.00
____Set of 3 Anakin's Transformation pins, boxed [PI182] ...35.00
____Set of 4 Sith Lord pins, boxed 75.00
____Set of 5 WDW logo pins, boxed, limited to 500 [PI183] ...165.00
____Set of 9 pins framed, ltd. to 100 [PI184] 250.00
____Yoda vs. Darth Sidious [PI185] 15.00

Disney Weekends May 2006.
____Defend-ears of the Kingdom, ltd. to 1,000, only avail. with purchase of hand painted cel [PI186] 90.00
____Jumbo logo pin, ltd to 750 [PI187] 150.00
____Set of 8 boxed, Hero/Villain with lightsaber, limited to 500 ...250.00
____Set of 9 framed, all eight saga scene pins plus Yoda vs. Vader, ltd to 100 [PI188] 250.00
____Yoda vs. Vader logo [PI189] 35.00

PI173   PI174   PI175   PI176   PI177   PI178   PI179   PI180

PI181   PI182   PI183   PI184

PI185   PI186   PI187   PI188   PI189   PI190

PI191   PI192   PI193   PI194   PI195   PI196   PI197

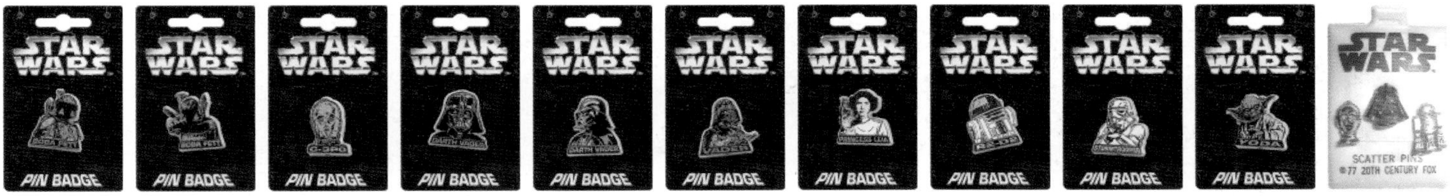

PI198 PI199 PI200 PI201 PI202 PI203 PI204 PI205 PI206 PI207 PI208

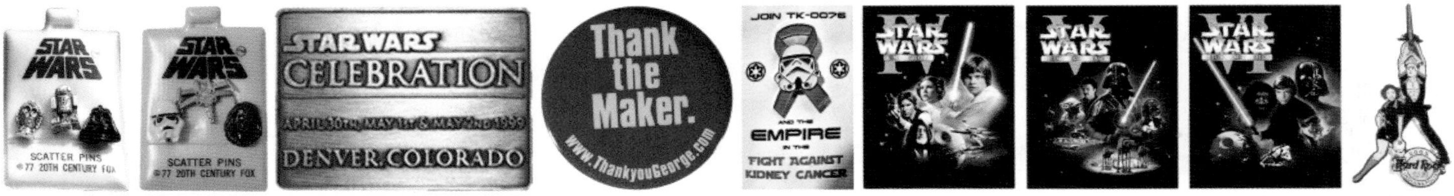

PI209 PI210 PI211 PI212 PI213 PI214 PI215 PI216 PI217

Saga scenes.

____Darth Vader Confronts Luke [PI190] 15.00
____Darth Vader Destroys Emperor [PI191] 15.00
____Han Solo fights Stormtroopers [PI192] 15.00
____Jabba the Hutt and Leia [PI193] 15.00
____Obi-Wan Detains Jango Fett [PI194] 15.00
____Qui-Gon Jinn vs. Darth Maul [PI195] 15.00
____R2-D2 and C-3PO [PI196] 15.00
____Yoda Confronts Darth Sidious [PI197] 15.00

Downpace Ltd.
Character pin badges.

____Boba Fett [PI198] 7.00
____Boba Fett with gun [PI199]....................................7.00
____C-3PO [PI200]..7.00
____Darth Vader helmet [PI201]....................................7.00
____Darth Vader profile [PI202] 7.00
____Darth Vader reaching [PI203] 7.00
____Princess Leia [PI204] 7.00
____R2-D2 [PI205] 7.00
____Stormtrooper [PI206] 7.00
____Yoda [PI207] 7.00

Factors, Etc.
Scatter pins.

____Darth Vader, C-3PO, R2-D2 [PI208]....................25.00
____Darth Vader, C-3PO, R2-D2, revised logo [PI209]..20.00
____Stormtrooper, X-Wing, Chewbacca [PI210]........35.00

Fan Club

____Star Wars Celebration, Denver Colorado brass [PI211]..18.00

Fan Made

____"Thank the Maker" www.ThankYouGeorge.com [PI212] 8.00
____TK-0076 fight against kidney cancer [PI213]......10.00

Fox Studios
DVD classic trilogy promotion.

____A New Hope [PI214] 5.00
____Empire Strikes Back [PI215] 5.00
____Return of the Jedi [PI216].......................................5.00

Hard Rock Cafe

____2005 Luke and Leia, Indianapolis, limited to 300 [PI217] 175.00

Hasbro
Power of the Jedi 2001 Tour.

____Amanaman [PI218] 18.00
____Boba Fett [PI219] 18.00
____Ellors Madak [PI220] 18.00

Hollywood Pins

____"Freeze You Rebel Scum!" [PI221] 6.00
____"May The Force Be With You" [PI222] 5.00
____"Taking the Galaxy", SW Summit exclusive 65.00
____Admiral Ackbar [PI223] 7.00
____AT-AT [PI224]..8.00
____Ben Kenobi [PI225] 8.00
____Black Sun logo [PI226] 4.00
____Boba Fett [PI227] 10.00
____Boba Fett Insignia (Round) 7.00
____Boba Fett, "He's No Good To Me Dead" [PI228] 6.00

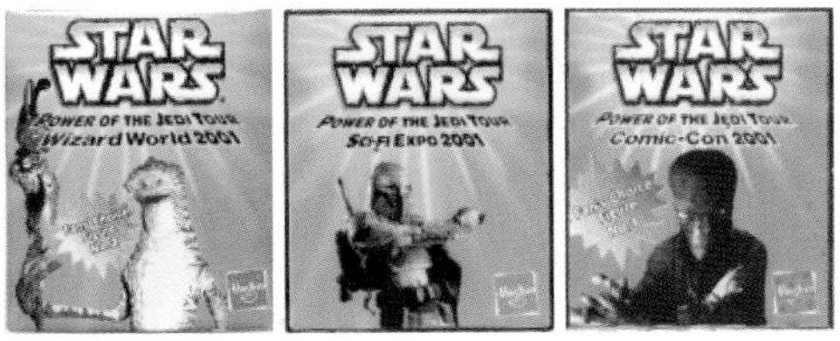

PI218 PI219 PI220

____C-3PO [PI229]...8.00
____C-3PO, "We're Doomed..." [PI230] 7.00
____Chewbacca [PI231] 12.00
____Darth Vader [PI232] 12.00
____Darth Vader helmet 4.00
____Darth Vader helmet, sculpted [PI233]...................6.00
____Darth Vader, "Power of the Dark Side..." [PI234] 7.00
____Emperor's Royal Guard...6.00
____Emperor [PI235] 10.00
____Far Star 3.00
____Gamorrean Guard [PI236]..6.00
____Imperial Emblem 6.00
____Jabba the Hutt [PI237] 6.00
____Jabba the Hutt 6.00
____Lando Calrissian [PI238]..8.00
____Lightsabers crossed over Star Wars logo 8.00
____Luke on Tauntaun [PI239]....................................12.00
____Max Rebo Band [PI240]..12.00
____Millennium Falcon [PI241].......................................8.00

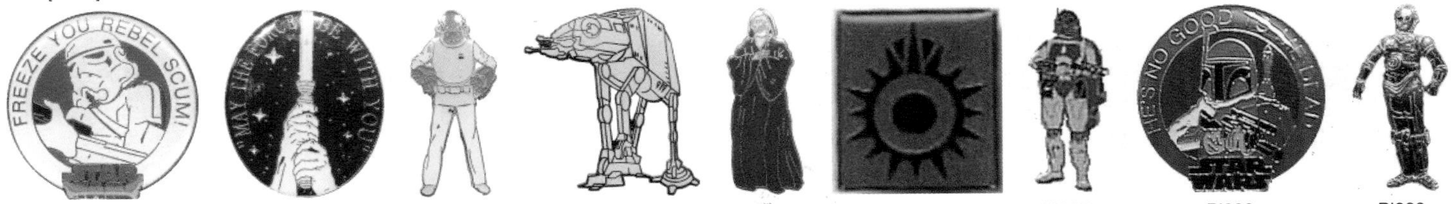

PI221 PI222 PI223 PI224 PI225 PI226 PI227 PI228 PI229

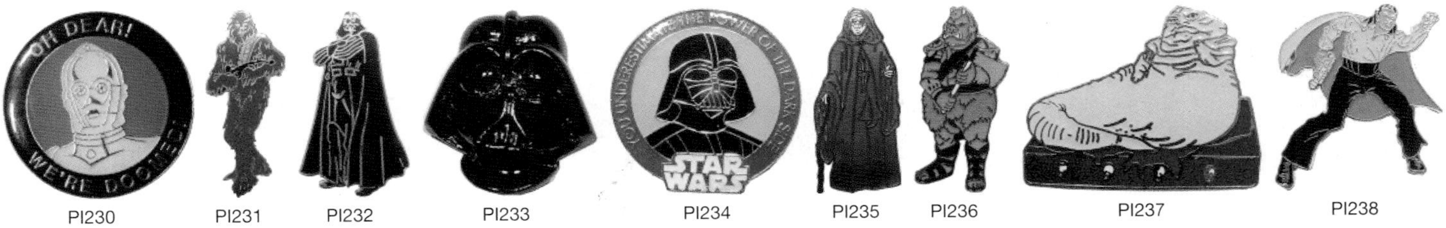

PI230 PI231 PI232 PI233 PI234 PI235 PI236 PI237 PI238

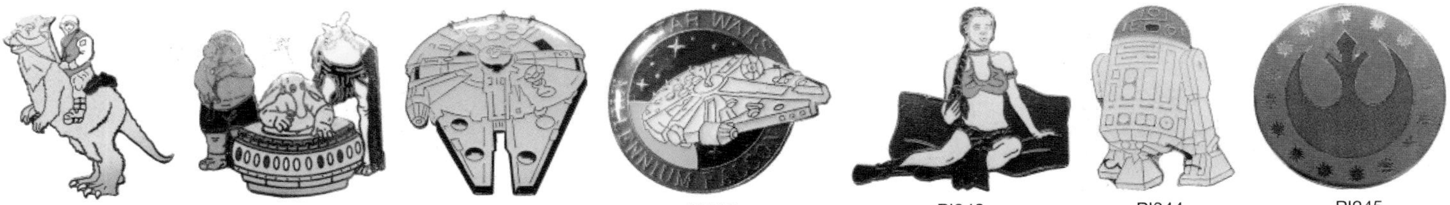

PI239 PI240 PI241 PI242 PI243 PI244 PI245

Pins

PI246   PI247   PI248   PI249   PI250   PI251   PI252

PI253   PI254   PI255   PI256   PI257   PI258

PI259   PI260   PI261   PI262   PI263

KFC
Episode I: The Phantom Menace.
____Queen Amidala, employee pin [PI263] 6.00

Little League Baseball
Division 1 umpire.
____Darth Vader, "Come over to the blue side," blue..10.00
____Darth Vader, "Come over to the blue side," cyan 10.00
____Darth Vader, "Come over to the blue side," purple 10.00
____Darth Vader, "Come over to the blue side," red..10.00
____Darth Vader, "Come over to the blue side," white 10.00

South Carolina Division 1.
____C-3PO [PI264] 18.00
____Luke Skywalker [PI265] 25.00
____Princess Leia [PI266] 25.00

Lucas Arts
____Star Wars Galaxies, limited to 3,000 [PI267] 10.00

Lucasfilm
____Framed set of 16, artwork from CIII badges, limited to 275 [PI268] 150.00

M&M World
____Mpire..30.00
____Mpire Dark Side 30.00
____Mpire Jedi 30.00

Characters, flat painted brass.
____Anakin Skywalker 10.00
____Darth Vader..10.00
____The Emperor..10.00

Characters, sculpted.
____Anakin Skywalker [PI269]....................18.00
____Boba Fett [PI270] 18.00
____C-3PO and R2-D2 [PI271] 18.00
____Chewbacca and Han Solo [PI272]......18.00
____Darth Maul [PI273] 18.00
____Darth Vader [PI274] 18.00

____Millennium Falcon, round [PI242] 9.00
____Princess Leia [PI243] 8.00
____R2-D2 [PI244] 8.00
____Rebel Alliance logo, large [PI245] 5.00
____Rebel Alliance logo, large gold [PI246] 7.00
____Rebel Alliance logo, mini 6.00
____Rebel Alliance logo, small...........................6.00
____Rebel Alliance logo, small gold 5.00
____Rebel Alliance logo, small red 5.00
____Rebel Forces 5.00
____Return of the Jedi [PI247] 15.00
____Slave I 9.00
____Star Wars [PI248] 15.00
____Star Wars 20th Anniversary [PI249] 8.00
____Star Wars Trilogy Special Edition, antique finish [PI250] 6.00
____Stormtrooper [PI251] 10.00
____The Empire Strikes Back [PI252] 15.00
____Tie Fighter [PI253]......................................9.00
____TIE Fighter Squadron [PI254].............15.00

____Tie Fighter, round [PI255] 8.00
____Wicket the Ewok [PI256]..........................8.00
____X-Wing Fighter [PI257] 6.00
____X-Wing Fighter, round [PI258].................8.00
____X-Wing Fighter, sculpted [PI259] 6.00
____Yoda [PI260] 8.00
____Yoda, "Try Not..." 7.00

Howard Eldon
10th anniversary, enameled.
____C-3PO 7.00
____Darth Vader 7.00
____Empire Strikes Back logo 8.00
____R2-D2 ....7.00
____Return of the Jedi logo 8.00
____Star Wars logo [PI261] 8.00

Jedicon
Germany.
____1997 Jedi Con [PI262] 12.00

PI264   PI265   PI266   PI267   PI268

PI269   PI270   PI271   PI272   PI273   PI274   PI275

PI276   PI277   PI278   PI279   PI280   PI281   PI282

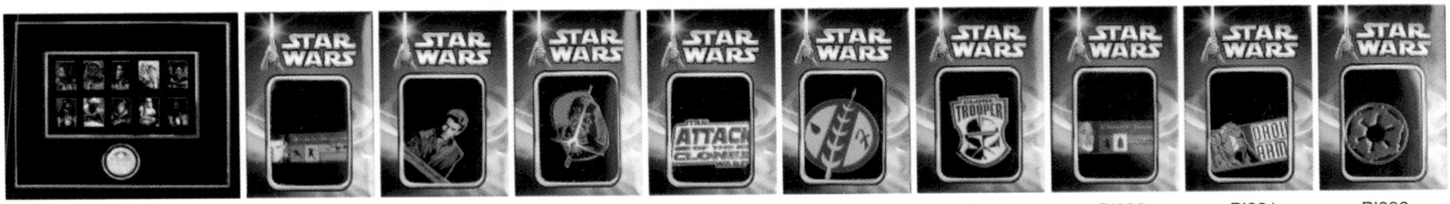

PI283 PI284 PI285 PI286 PI287 PI288 PI289 PI290 PI291 PI292

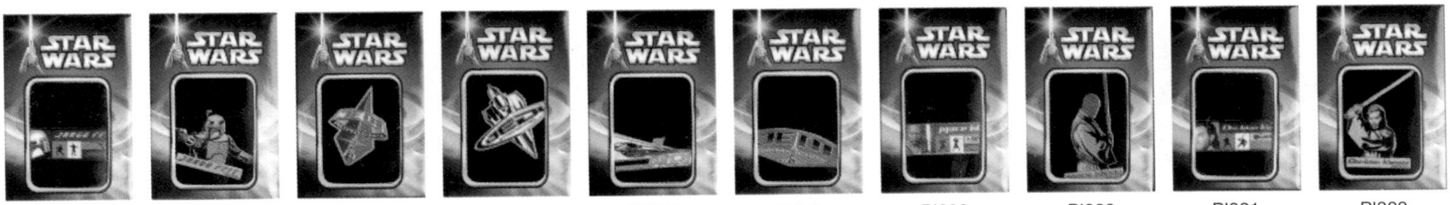

PI293 PI294 PI295 PI296 PI297 PI298 PI299 PI300 PI301 PI302

____General Grievous [PI275] 18.00
____Luke Skywalker [PI276] 18.00
____Obi-Wan Kenobi [PI277]..18.00
____Princess Leia [PI278] 18.00
____Stormtrooper [PI279] 18.00
____The Emperor [PI280] 18.00

McDonalds
____May The Fries Be With You [PI281] 26.00

Pin USA
10-pin framed sets.
____Attack of the Clones, limited to 2,002 [PI282] 115.00
____Silver Anniversary, limited to 1,977 [PI283] 110.00

____Anakin Skywalker Portrait [PI284] 8.00
____Anakin Skywalker Torso [PI285] 8.00
____Anakin/Vader Logo [PI286] 8.00
____Attack of the Clones Logo [PI287] 8.00
____Boba Fett Logo [PI288]..8.00
____Clone Trooper Logo [PI289] 8.00
____Count Dooku Portrait [PI290] 8.00
____Droid Army Logo [PI291] 8.00
____Imperial Logo [PI292] 8.00
____Jango Fett Portrait [PI293] 8.00
____Jango Fett Torso [PI294]..8.00
____Jedi Academy Logo [PI295] 8.00
____Jedi Starfighter 3 Logo [PI296]................................8.00
____Jedi Starfighter Logo [PI297] 8.00
____Jedi Training Academy Logo [PI298] 8.00
____Mace Windu Portrait [PI299].....................................8.00

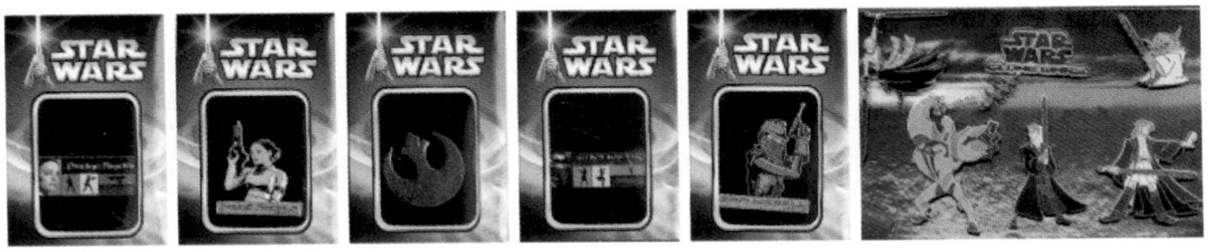

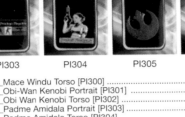

PI303 PI304 PI305 PI306 PI307 PI308

____Mace Windu Torso [PI300] 8.00
____Obi-Wan Kenobi Portrait [PI301] 8.00
____Obi Wan Kenobi Torso [PI302] 8.00
____Padme Amidala Portrait [PI303] 8.00
____Padme Amidala Torso [PI304] 8.00
____Rebel Logo [PI305] 8.00
____Zam Wessell Portrait [PI306] 8.00
____Zam Wessell Torso [PI307] 8.00

Clone Wars.
____Boxed set of 6 [PI308] 75.00

Celebration III souvenir.
____Celebration 3 logo [PI309] 25.00

EPIII:ROTS.
____"HERO" [PI310]..8.00
____Anakin Skywalker [PI311] 8.00
____Boba Fett [PI312] 8.00
____C-3PO and R2-D2 [PI313] 8.00

____Chewbacca [PI314]...8.00
____Clone Trooper [PI315] 8.00
____Clone Trooper helmet [PI316] 8.00
____Darth Vader [PI317]...8.00
____Darth Vader helmet [PI318].......................................8.00
____General Grievous [PI319] 8.00
____General Grievous helmet [PI320] 8.00
____Han Solo [PI322]..8.00
____Jedi Starfighter Creed [PI323] 8.00
____Jedi starship on shield [PI324] 8.00
____Jedi wings on shield [PI325].......................................8.00
____Jedi, round, blue and gold [PI326] 8.00
____Jedi, round, blue and silver [PI327] 8.00
____Lightsaber raised [PI328] 8.00
____Luke Skywalker [PI329] 8.00
____Princess Leia [PI330] 8.00
____Sith [PI331] 8.00
____Vader's helmet / flames [PI332] 8.00
____Vader helmet between flames [PI333] 8.00
____Yoda [PI334] 8.00

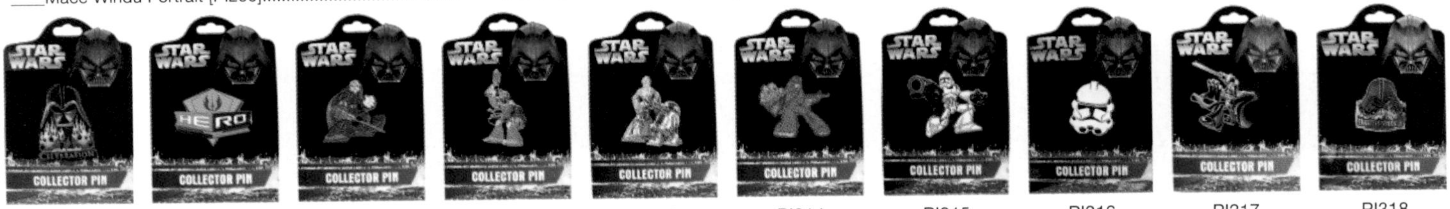

PI309 PI310 PI311 PI312 PI313 PI314 PI315 PI316 PI317 PI318

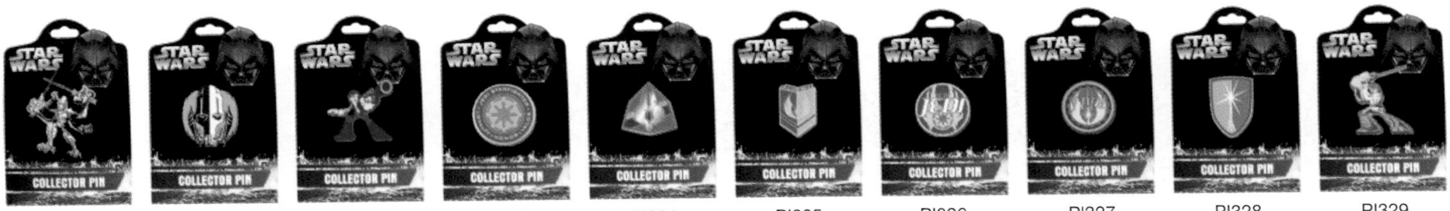

PI319 PI320 PI322 PI323 PI324 PI325 PI326 PI327 PI328 PI329

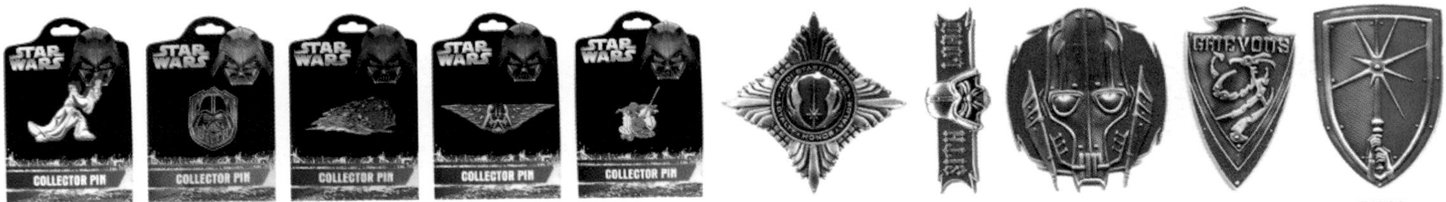

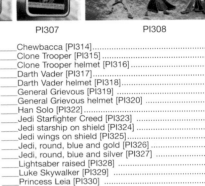

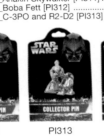

PI330 PI331 PI332 PI333 PI334 PI335 PI336 PI337 PI338 PI339

Pins

PI340   PI341   PI342

PI343

PI344   PI345

PI346   PI347   PI348   PI349   PI350   PI351   PI352   PI353   PI354   PI355

PI356   PI357   PI358   PI359   PI360

PI361   PI362

3" silver cast metal with enamel inlay.
____"Jedi Starfighter," "Loyalty, honor, valor" [PI335].....................................40.00
____"Sith Lord" [PI336] 40.00
____General Grevious [PI337] 40.00
____Grevious [PI338] 40.00
____Lightsaber raised [PI339] 40.00

5 pin framed sets with art.
____Darth Vader [PI340] 110.00
____Yoda [PI341] 110.00

Set of 3 to celebrate Classic Trilogy DVD release.
____A New Hope..10.00
____Empire Strikes Back................................10.00
____Return of the Jedi....................................10.00

RebelScum.com
____RebelScum.com blue 8.00
____RebelScum.com red [PI342]....................8.00
____Star Wars is Forever, Celebration 3 [PI343]........10.00

Scholastic
____Yoda, "Read, You Will." [PI344] 8.00

Skywalker Ranch
____"Taking the Galaxy by Force," November 3 and 4, 1994 [PI345]..............................77.00

Sunburst Merchandising
____Bravo Squadron [PI346] 8.00
____Episode I logo [PI347]..............................8.00

____The Dark Side [PI348]..............................8.00
____Trade Federation Starfighter [PI349]......................8.00

SWChicks.com
____"Fight for the Cure of breast cancer" [PI350] 25.00

Takara
____C-3PO [PI351] 20.00
____R2-D2 [PI352]..20.00
____X-Wing Starfighter [PI353] 25.00

Wallace Berrie and Co.
Medals.
____Boba Fett [PI354] 11.00
____Chewbacca [PI355] 11.00
____Darth Vader with ESB logo [PI356] 11.00
____Millennium Falcon Pilot [PI357]............11.00
____X-Wing Fighter Pilot [PI358]..................11.00
____Yoda, May The Force Be With You [PI359] 11.00

Wizards of the Coast
____Star Wars Celebration II [PI360]....................18.00
____Star Wars Celebration II, pewter [PI361] 10.00
____Star Wars Trading Card Game [PI362] 5.00

Pins: Lapel

Factors, Etc.
____C-3PO, set 1 [JLP01] 6.00
____Chewbacca, set 2 ....6.00

____Darth Vader, set 1 [JLP02] 6.00
____R2-D2, set 1 [JLP03] 6.00
____Stormtrooper, set 2 [JLP04] 6.00
____X-Wing, set 2 ....6.00

Pitchers

Theater concession promotions. 50oz. Pitchers with movie artwork.
____Return of the Jedi [DIP01] 17.00
____Star Wars / Empire Strikes Back [DIP02]............14.00

Deka
90oz. with lid.
____Empire Strikes Back.................................22.00
____Return of the Jedi [DIP03] 22.00
____Star Wars [DIP04].....................................22.00

Place Cards

Drawing Board Greeting Cards, Inc.
____C-3PO and R2-D2, 8-pack [PFM01] 9.00

Placemats

Barcel
____Vader and General Grievous on wheelbike [PFN01]..............................20.00
____Vader and General Grievous, lava [PFN02] 20.00
____Vader, General Grievous, Commander Cody [PFN03]..............................20.00

Burger King
____ESB glasses, promotional [PFN04] 7.00
____Everybody Wins game, ESB promotional [PFN05] 8.00
____Play the Choose Your Destiny Game [PFN06]......3.00

Dixie
Empire Strikes Back.
____AT-ATs 7.00
____Galaxy scene [PFN07] 7.00
____Luke and Darth Vader [PFN08]..................7.00
____Yoda and Luke [PFN09] 7.00

Drawing Board Greeting Cards, Inc.
____Maze, 8-pack [PFN10] 26.00

Habib's Restaurant
Brazil. EPII:AOTC Character memory games.
____Action [PFN11] 6.00
____Art [PFN12] 6.00
____Close-ups [PFN13] 6.00

JLP01   JLP02   JLP03   JLP04   DIP01   DIP02   DIP03   DIP04   PFM01

PFN01

PFN02

PFN03

PFN04

PFN05

PFN06

PFN07

PFN08

PFN09

PFN10

PFN11

PFN12

PFN13

PFN14

PFN15

PFN16

PFN17

PFN18

PFN19

PFN20

Icarus

____Darth Vader, Luke, Imperial Guards, and Speeder Bikes...25.00
____Jabba the Hutt, Princess Leia, Lando Calrissina, and Wicket.................................25.00

ROTJ logo, 9"x11".
____Bounty Hunters [PFN14] 25.00
____C-3PO and R2-D2 [PFN15] 25.00
____Ewoks [PFN16]..................................25.00
____Luke on Tauntaun [PFN17]................25.00

Star Wars logo, 9"x11".
____Chewbacca, Han, and Lando [PFN18] 25.00
____Darth Vader and Stormtroopers [PFN19]..........25.00
____Yoda [PFN20] 25.00

Pizza Hut
____Don't Leave Coruscant Without Them [PFN21] 2.00

____Jedi Trivia / Jedi Wisdom [PFN22] 2.00
____Kids Pack advertisement [PFN23] 4.00

Sigma
____ESB, 4-pack [PFN24] 65.00

Plate Racks

Hamilton Collection
____15th Anniversary, hangs on wall [PLR01] 43.00

Plates: Collector

Cards, Inc.
4" mini plates with display stand.
____Darth Vader [PL01]...15.00

____General Grievous [PL02] 15.00
____Jedi Duel [PL03] 15.00
____Lord Vader [PL04]...15.00
____The Droids [PL05]..15.00
____Yoda [PL06] 15.00

8", limited to 3,000.
Series I.
____Darth Vader [PL07] 65.00
____Luke Skywalker [PL08] 65.00
____R2-D2 [PL09] 65.00
____Stormtrooper [PL10]..65.00
Series II.
____Anakin Skywalker [PL11] 65.00
____Clone Trooper [PL12] 65.00
____General Grievous [PL13] 65.00
____Obi-Wan Kenobi [PL14].......................................65.00
Series III.
____Boba Fett [PL15] 65.00
____C-3PO [PL16] 65.00
____Han Solo [PL17] 65.00
____Lando Calrissian [PL18] 65.00
Series IV.
____Battle Droids [PL19] 65.00
____Darth Maul [PL20] 65.00
____Padme Amidala [PL21]...65.00
____Qui-Gon Jinn [PL22] 65.00
Series V.
____Heroes and Villains [PL23] 65.00
____Jedi [PL24] 65.00
____Sith [PL25] 65.00
____The Duel [PL26] 65.00

PFN21

PFN22

PFN23

PFN24 1 of 4

PFN24 2 of 4

PFN24 3 of 4

PFN24 4 of 4

PLR01

Plates: Collector

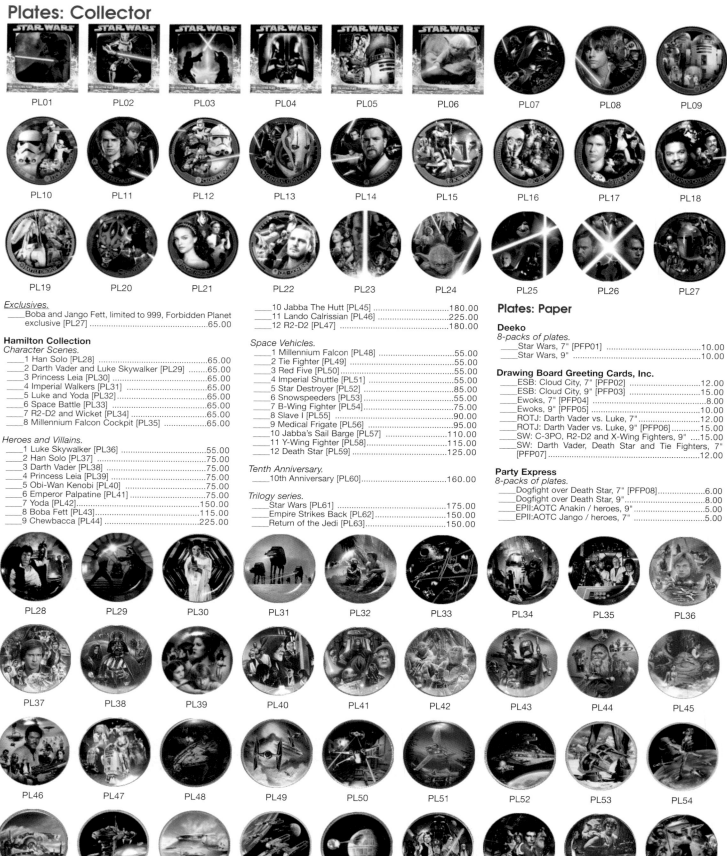

PL01 PL02 PL03 PL04 PL05 PL06 PL07 PL08 PL09

PL10 PL11 PL12 PL13 PL14 PL15 PL16 PL17 PL18

PL19 PL20 PL21 PL22 PL23 PL24 PL25 PL26 PL27

Exclusives.
____Boba and Jango Fett, limited to 999, Forbidden Planet
exclusive [PL27] 65.00

Hamilton Collection
Character Scenes.
____1 Han Solo [PL28] 65.00
____2 Darth Vader and Luke Skywalker [PL29] 65.00
____3 Princess Leia [PL30] 65.00
____4 Imperial Walkers [PL31] 65.00
____5 Luke and Yoda [PL32] 65.00
____6 Space Battle [PL33] 65.00
____7 R2-D2 and Wicket [PL34] 65.00
____8 Millennium Falcon Cockpit [PL35] 65.00

Heroes and Villains.
____1 Luke Skywalker [PL36] 55.00
____2 Han Solo [PL37] 75.00
____3 Darth Vader [PL38] 75.00
____4 Princess Leia [PL39] 75.00
____5 Obi-Wan Kenobi [PL40] 75.00
____6 Emperor Palpatine [PL41] 75.00
____7 Yoda [PL42] 150.00
____8 Boba Fett [PL43].......................................115.00
____9 Chewbacca [PL44] 225.00

____10 Jabba The Hutt [PL45] 180.00
____11 Lando Calrissian [PL46] 225.00
____12 R2-D2 [PL47] 180.00

Space Vehicles.
____1 Millennium Falcon [PL48] 55.00
____2 Tie Fighter [PL49] 55.00
____3 Red Five [PL50] 55.00
____4 Imperial Shuttle [PL51] 55.00
____5 Star Destroyer [PL52] 85.00
____6 Snowspeeders [PL53] 55.00
____7 B-Wing Fighter [PL54]..................................75.00
____8 Slave I [PL55] 90.00
____9 Medical Frigate [PL56] 95.00
____10 Jabba's Sail Barge [PL57] 110.00
____11 Y-Wing Fighter [PL58]...............................115.00
____12 Death Star [PL59] 125.00

Tenth Anniversary.
____10th Anniversary [PL60]................................160.00

Trilogy series.
____Star Wars [PL61] 175.00
____Empire Strikes Back [PL62] 150.00
____Return of the Jedi [PL63]...............................150.00

Plates: Paper

Deeko
8-packs of plates.
____Star Wars, 7" [PFP01] 10.00
____Star Wars, 9" 10.00

Drawing Board Greeting Cards, Inc.
____ESB: Cloud City, 7" [PFP02] 12.00
____ESB: Cloud City, 9" [PFP03] 15.00
____Ewoks, 7" [PFP04] 8.00
____Ewoks, 9" [PFP05] 10.00
____ROTJ: Darth Vader vs. Luke, 7" 12.00
____ROTJ: Darth Vader vs. Luke, 9" [PFP06]............15.00
____SW: C-3PO, R2-D2 and X-Wing Fighters, 9" 15.00
____SW: Darth Vader, Death Star and Tie Fighters, 7"
[PFP07]...12.00

Party Express
8-packs of plates.
____Dogfight over Death Star, 7" [PFP08]..................6.00
____Dogfight over Death Star, 9" 8.00
____EPII:AOTC Anakin / heroes, 9" 5.00
____EPII:AOTC Jango / heroes, 7" 5.00

PL28 PL29 PL30 PL31 PL32 PL33 PL34 PL35 PL36

PL37 PL38 PL39 PL40 PL41 PL42 PL43 PL44 PL45

PL46 PL47 PL48 PL49 PL50 PL51 PL52 PL53 PL54

PL55 PL56 PL57 PL58 PL59 PL60 PL61 PL62 PL63

PFP01 PFP02 PFP03 PFP04 PFP05 PFP06 PFP07 PFP08 PFP09

PFP10 PFP11 PFP12 PFP13 PFP14 PYH01 PYH02 PYH03

____EPIII:ROTS Darth Vader / Yoda, 9" [PFP09] 5.00
____EPIII:ROTS Darth Vader, 7" [PFP10] 4.00
____Obi-Wan Kenobi, 7" [PFP11] 5.00
____Qui-Gon Jinn, 9" [PFP12] 5.00
____Star Wars Saga, 7" 6.00
____Star Wars Saga, 9" [PFP13] 6.00

Unique
8-packs of plates.
____Darth Maul vs. Jedi [PFP14] 6.00

Play Houses

____Magic Pop Up tent [PYH01].............................35.00

ERO Industries
____EPI:TPM 40"x30"x44" [PYH02] 25.00

Worlds Apart
____Pop-Out Play Tunnel, space scenes [3:347] 37.00
____Pop-Up Naboo Fighter [PYH03] 54.00

Playing Cards

____EPI perforated sheets with gum bits [CP01] 15.00
____EPIII:ROTS [CP02] 6.00
____Star Wars Classic Trilogy [CP03] 6.00
____Star Wars Prelude [CP04] 6.00

Russian. Deck of 36 cards (4 suits, 6-A).
____EPII:AOTC [CP05]...12.00
____EPIII:ROTS [CP06] 12.00

Character Games, Ltd.
____Attack of the Clones [CP07] 6.00
____Classic Star Wars [CP08] 8.00

Character
____Revenge of the Sith [CP09] 8.00

Disney / MGM
____Rebel Alliance / Galatic Empire, plastic storage tray
[CP10]..10.00

Fan Made
Fighting 501st.
____Imperial Logo ....N/V

Glow Zone
____Glow-in-the-Dark [CP11] 18.00

International Playing Card Company
Printed in English and French.
____2 decks in collector's tin [CP12] 17.00
____Heros deck [CP13] 6.00
____Villains deck [CP14] 6.00

Pog Slammers

Canada Games
Available in 8 colors: red, yellow, blue, green, purple, bronze, silver, gold.
____1 Star Wars [TZB01] 3.00
____2 Empire Strikes Back [TZB02] 3.00
____3 Return of the Jedi [TZB03] 3.00
____4 Luke [TZB04] 3.00
____5 Leia [TZB05]..3.00
____6 Han [TZB06]...3.00
____7 Darth Vader [TZB07] 3.00
____8 Jabba the Hutt [TZB08] 3.00

Topps
Available in black, gold, and silver.
____Ben Kenobi [3:348] 3.00
____Boba Fett [2:351] 4.00

____Darth Vader [2:351] 4.00
____Emperor Palpatine [2:351] 3.00
____Han Solo [2:351] 3.00
____Luke Skywalker [2:351] 3.00
____Princess Leia [TZB09] 4.00
____Stormtrooper [2:351] 3.00

Pogs

Sheets of 6 using unlicensed art.
____Darkness 3.00
____Heroes [1:293] 3.00

Canada Games
Set of 70, numbered 9 – 78. Numbers 1 – 8 are pog slammers. (Images in 2nd edition, page 351. Checklist in 3rd edition, page 348.)
____Pogs 9 – 78, each..1.00

Kent
Turkey. "Floppies" distributed in gum. Set of 40, numbered. (Images and checklist in 3rd ed., pg. 349.)
____Floppies pogs 1 – 40, each 1.00

Nagatanien
2.5" round. Set of 20, numbered. (Images in 2nd edition, page 352. Checklist in 3rd edition, page 350.)
____Pogs 1 – 20, each...1.20

Schmidt
Set of 70, numbered. (Images in 3rd edition, page 349. Checklist in 3rd edition, page 350.)
____Pogs 1 – 70, each...1.80

Tomy
Advertising – In Store Now!!
____Clone Trooper [3:350] 5.00
____Yoda [3:350] 5.00

CP01

CP02 CP03 CP04 CP05 CP06 CP07

CP08 CP09 CP10 CP11 CP12 CP13 CP14

TZB01 TZB02 TZB03 TZB04 TZB05 TZB06 TZB07 TZB08 TZB09

Pogs

IPT01 IPT02 IPT03 IPT04 IPT05 IPT06

IPT07 IPT08 IPT09 IPT10 SWP01 SWP02

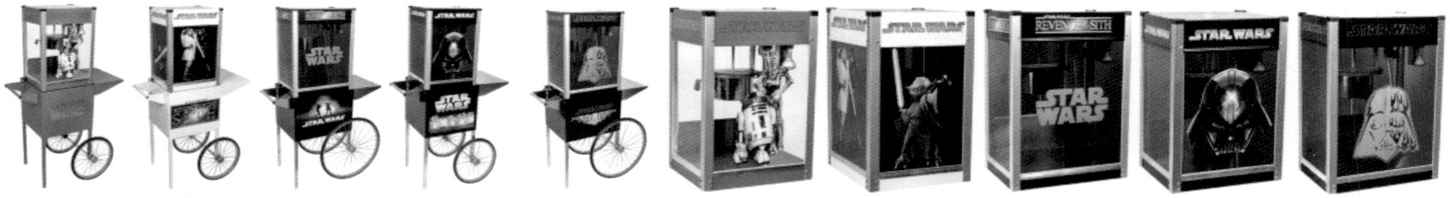

P1C01 P1C02 P1C03 P1C04 P1C05 P1C06 P1C07 P1C08 P1C09 P1C10

Topps
Set of 70 numbered and 2 "00" promo pogs. (Images in 2nd ed., pg. 353. Checklist in 3rd ed., pg. 350.)
____Pogs 1 – 70, each 1.80
____Pog 00 – A, C-3PO and R2-D2 ....6.00
____Pog 00 – B, Darth Vader 6.00

Set of 10 galaxy art, foil, numbered pogs. (Images in 2nd ed., pg. 353. Checklist in 3rd ed., pg. 350.)
____Pogs 1 – 10, each 1.00

Pool Toys

Frito Lay
____Yoda, "May the Fun be with you" [IPT01] 25.00

Episode I game card prizes.
____Pod Racer [IPT02] 130.00
____Sith Macrobinoculars 75.00

Intex Recreation Corp.
____Anakin's Pod Racer Lounge [IPT03] 20.00
____Gungan Sub Ride-In [IPT04] 9.00
____Jar Jar 2 Person Ride-In [IPT05] 14.00
____Landspeeder Boat Lounge [IPT06] 20.00
____Millennium Falcon Island/River Raft [IPT07] 20.00
____Naboo Starfighter Ride-In 12.00
____Naboo Starfighter Ride-On [IPT08] 14.00
____Trade Federation Droid Starfighter Ride-In 12.00
____Trade Federation Droid Starfighter Ride-On [IPT09] 14.00

Sport Fun, Inc.
____Space Battle Waterslide [IPT10] 15.00

Pools

Intex Recreation Corp.
Children's pools.
____Jar Jar's World Aquarium Pool 25.00
____Pod Racing Snapset Pool [SWP01] 25.00
____Trade Federation Droid Control Ship Spray Pool [SWP02] 25.00

Popcorn Poppers

Snappy Popcorn
Popcorn poppers with cart.
____Droids 4oz. [P1C01] 1,200.00
____Jedi 4oz. [P1C02] 1,200.00
____ROTS 6oz. [P1C03] 1,400.00
____Vader 4oz. [P1C04] 1,200.00
____Vader 6oz. [P1C05] 1,400.00

Popcorn poppers.
____Droids 4oz. 16"x14"x24" [P1C06] 650.00
____Jedi 4oz. 16"x14"x24" [P1C07] 650.00
____ROTS 6oz. 20"x14"x26" [P1C08] 850.00
____Vader 4oz. 16"x14"x24" [P1C09] 650.00
____Vader 6oz. 20"x14"x26" [P1C10] 650.00

Postcards

____R2-D2 and C-3PO aboard rebel blockage runner [PSC01] 3.00
____The First Ten Years, Star Wars [PSC02] 6.00

Art of Star Wars, Kyoto Museum 2003.
____C-3PO and R2-D2 [PSC03] 7.00
____Clone Trooper [PSC04] 7.00
____Darth Vader's mask for Anakin Skywalker's reveal [PSC05] 7.00
____Jango Fett [PSC06] 7.00
____The Art of Star Wars [PSC07] 7.00

20th Century Fox
____A New Hope [PSC08] 4.00
____Empire Strikes Back [PSC09] 4.00
____Return of the Jedi [PSC10] 4.00
____SW:SE logo [PSC11] 4.00
____The Phantom Menace promotional [PSC12] 4.00

3D Arts
Lasergrams.
____C-3PO and R2-D2 ....3.00
____Darth Vader [PSC13] 3.00
____Millennium Falcon [PSC14] 3.00
____X-Wing Fighter [PSC15] 3.00

A.H. Prismatic
____Darth Vader holographic foil image 6.00
____Millennium Falcon and Tie Fighters holographic foil image 6.00
____Millennium Falcon in Astroid Field holographic foil image 6.00

ArtCard
EPII:AOTC promotional cards. Given out at theaters before the movie release.
____Anakin Skywalker [PSC16] 3.00
____Count Dooku [PSC17] 3.00
____Geonosian [PSC18] 3.00

PSC01 PSC02 PSC03 PSC04 PSC05 PSC06 PSC07 PSC08 PSC09 PSC10 PSC11 PSC12 PSC13 PSC14

PSC15 PSC16 PSC17 PSC18 PSC19 PSC20 PSC21 PSC22 PSC23 PSC24 PSC25 PSC26 PSC27 PSC28

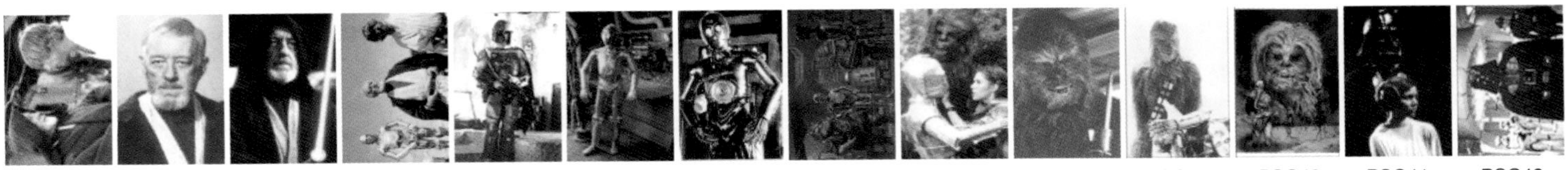

PSC29 PSC30 PSC31 PSC32 PSC33 PSC34 PSC35 PSC36 PSC37 PSC38 PSC39 PSC40 PSC41 PSC42

PSC43 PSC44 PSC45 PSC46 PSC47 PSC48 PSC49 PSC50 PSC51 PSC52 PSC53 PSC54 PSC55 PSC56

____Jango Fett [PSC19]........3.00
____Mace Windu [PSC20]........3.00
____Obi-Wan Kenobi........3.00
____Padme Amidala [PSC21]........3.00
____Yoda........3.00
____Zam Wesell [PSC22]........3.00

Boomerang Media Cards
Clone Wars. Toonami.
____Anakin Skywalker [PSC23]........3.00
____Clone Trooper [PSC24]........3.00
____General Grievous [PSC25]........3.00
____Yoda [PSC26]........3.00

Classico
____A-Wing fighter [PSC27]........2.00
____ASP Droid, SW:SE [PSC28]........2.00
____Ben and Luke [PSC29]........2.00
____Ben Kenobi [PSC30]........2.00
____Ben with lightsaber [PSC31]........3.00
____Ben, Luke, and C-3PO view Mos Eisley [PSC32]........3.00
____Boba Fett portrait [PSC33]........2.00
____C-3PO aboard Millennium Falcon [PSC34]........3.00
____C-3PO above oil bath [PSC35]........2.00
____C-3PO and R2-D2 face EV-99 [PSC36]........2.00
____C-3PO, Chewie, and Leia in forest [PSC37]........2.00
____Chewbacca [PSC38]........2.00
____Chewbacca and C-3PO in parts [PSC39]........2.00
____Chewbacca ESB, art [PSC40]........5.00
____Darth Vader and Princess Leia [PSC41]........3.00
____Darth Vader and troops in Cloud City [PSC42]........2.00
____Darth Vader on Cloud City [PSC43]........3.00
____Darth Vader on the Blockade Runner........2.00
____Darth Vader pointing [PSC44]........3.00
____Darth Vader silhouette in carbon chamber [PSC45]........2.00
____Dewback, SW:SE........2.00
____Droids on the Blockade Runner [PSC46]........2.00
____Emperor extreme close-up [PSC47]........2.00
____Emperor on ramp, pointing [PSC48]........2.00
____ESB art [PSC49]........5.00
____ESB Japanese movie poster artwork (Lando and Falcon prominent)........2.00
____ESB:SE poster........2.00
____Falcon blasting out of Mos Eisley, SW:SE [PSC50]........2.00
____Han and Jabba, SW:SE [PSC51]........2.00
____Han and Leia kiss (ESB) [PSC52]........2.00
____Han and Leia kiss (ROTJ) [PSC53]........3.00
____Han in Rebel base [PSC54]........3.00
____Han portrait [PSC55]........2.00
____Han Solo on Endor [PSC56]........3.00
____Jabba the Hutt [PSC57]........2.00
____Jabba the Hutt close-up from SW:SE [PSC58]........3.00
____Jabba the Hutt from SW:SE [PSC59]........2.00
____Jawas blasting [PSC60]........2.00
____Lando extreme close-up [PSC61]........2.00
____Leia as Jabba prisoner [PSC62]........2.00
____Luke and Han in the trash compactor [PSC63]........3.00
____Luke and Leia on barge [PSC64]........2.00
____Luke and Vader duel [PSC65]........3.00
____Luke boards X-Wing on Yavin 4 [PSC66]........3.00
____Luke carrying Yoda [PSC67]........2.00
____Luke in Falcon's gunwell [PSC68]........3.00
____Luke in front of moisture vaparator [PSC69]........3.00
____Luke in stormtrooper disguise [PSC70]........3.00
____Luke in the tree on Dagobah [PSC71]........2.00
____Luke on taun taun [PSC72]........3.00
____Luke shooting [PSC73]........2.00
____Luke slicing Fett's gun [PSC74]........2.00
____Luke standing (promo) [PSC75]........3.00
____Luke under Cloud City [PSC76]........3.00
____Luke, Leia, and Han in Death Star [PSC77]........2.00
____Princess Leia in ceremonial gown [PSC78]........2.00
____R2-D2 in canyon [PSC79]........2.00
____Ronto in Mos Eisley [PSC80]........3.00
____ROTJ 'B' movie poster........2.00
____ROTJ:SE poster........2.00
____Sandcrawler, SW:SE [PSC81]........2.00
____Sandtrooper, SW:SE [PSC82]........2.00
____Sandtroopers and dewback [PSC83]........3.00
____Stormtroopers [PSC84]........2.00
____Stormtroopers blasting [PSC85]........2.00
____SW 'A' movie poster........2.00
____SW:SE poster........2.00
____Swoop scares Ronto in Mos Eisley [PSC86]........3.00
____Tie fighters in Death Star trench [PSC87]........3.00
____Tusken Raider [PSC88]........2.00
____Vader in Hoth rebel base [PSC89]........3.00
____Wicket [PSC90]........2.00
____X-wing fleet [PSC91]........3.00
____X-wing fleet, SW:SE [PSC92]........3.00
____X-wing launch, SW:SE [PSC93]........2.00
____X-wings approach Death Star [PSC94]........3.00
____X-Wings in Death Star trench [PSC95]........2.00
____Yoda [PSC96]........3.00
____Yoda in his house [PSC97]........2.00
____Yoda, art [PSC98]........5.00

Clone Wars.
____Asajj Ventress, Anakin, Yoda [PSC99]........3.00
____Asajj Ventress, Durge, Count Dooku [PSC100]........3.00
____Clone Troopers [PSC101]........3.00
____Mace Windu, Obi-Wan, Anakin, Yoda [PSC102]........3.00
____Obi-Wan vs. Durge [PSC103]........3.00
____Yoda, Obi-Wan, Anakin, Mace Windu, Clones [PSC104]........3.00

EPII:AOTC.
____"Anakin Skywalker"........2.00
____"Jango Fett"........2.00
____"Mace Windu"........2.00
____"Zam Wesell"........2.00
____Anakin Skywalker........2.00
____Anakin Skywalker and Obi-Wan Kenobi........2.00
____Anakin Skywalker and Padme Amidala........2.00
____Bounty Hunters........2.00
____C-3PO and R2-D2........2.00
____Connections........2.00
____Count Dooku........2.00
____Episode II movie poster........2.00
____Jango Fett........2.00
____Mace Windu........2.00
____Obi-Wan Kenobi........2.00
____Padme Amidala........2.00
____The Sith........2.00
____Zam Wesell........2.00

EPIII:ROTS.
____Anakin Skywalker........3.00
____Anakin Skywalker (angry)........3.00
____Anakin Skywalker (art)........3.00
____Anakin Skywalker and Padme Amidala........3.00
____Chancellor Palpatine........3.00

PSC57 PSC58 PSC59 PSC60 PSC61 PSC62 PSC63 PSC64 PSC65 PSC66 PSC67 PSC68 PSC69 PSC70

PSC71 PSC72 PSC73 PSC74 PSC75 PSC76 PSC77 PSC78 PSC79 PSC80 PSC81 PSC82 PSC83 PSC84

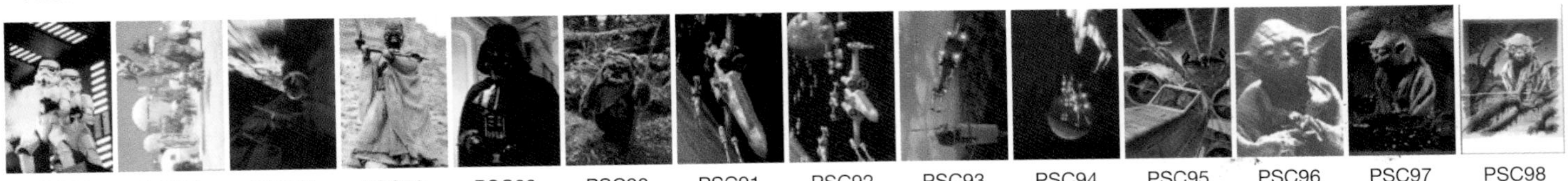

PSC85 PSC86 PSC87 PSC88 PSC89 PSC90 PSC91 PSC92 PSC93 PSC94 PSC95 PSC96 PSC97 PSC98

Postcards

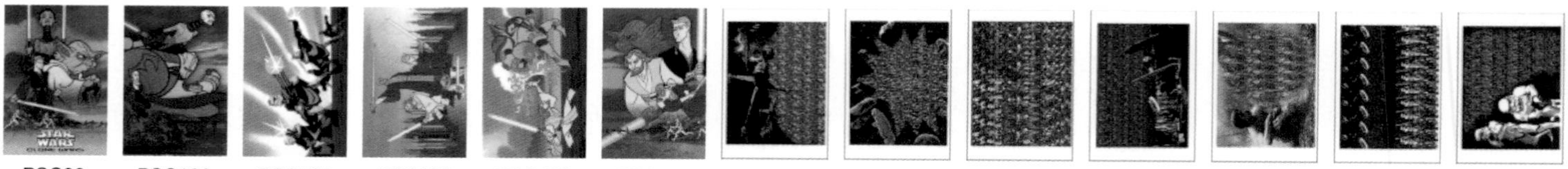

PSC99 PSC100 PSC101 PSC102 PSC103 PSC104 PSC105 PSC106 PSC107 PSC108 PSC109 PSC110 PSC111

PSC112 PSC113 PSC114 PSC115 PSC116 PSC117 PSC118 PSC119 PSC120 PSC121 PSC122 PSC123 PSC124 PSC125

____Chewbacca 3.00
____Clone Trooper 3.00
____Darth Sidious 3.00
____Darth Vader 3.00
____Darth Vader (with lightsaber) 3.00
____Darth Vader and Jedi Duel 3.00
____General Grievous' Guard 3.00
____General Grievous 3.00
____General Grievous (art) 3.00
____General Grievous (with lightsabers) 3.00
____Holographic Yoda 3.00
____Obi-Wan Kenobi (blue) 3.00
____Obi-Wan Kenobi (brown) 3.00
____Obi-Wan Kenobi (smiling) 3.00
____Obi-Wan Kenobi (surrounded) 3.00
____Padme Amidala 3.00
____Padme Amidala in Senate 3.00
____Revenge of the Sith one sheet 3.00
____Revenge of the Sith teaser poster 3.00
____Wookies 3.00
____Yoda (art) 3.00
____Yoda (standing) 3.00
____Yoda (with lightsaber) 3.00
____Yoda in Palpatine's Office 3.00

Episode I: The Phantom Menace.
____Anakin Skywalker, Naboo Pilot 2.00
____Anakin Skywalker, Podracer 2.00
____Anakin Skywalker, Tatooine 2.00
____Darth Maul, Naboo Hanger 2.00
____Darth Maul, Tatooine close-up 2.00
____Darth Maul, Tatooine day 2.00
____Darth Maul, Tatooine night 2.00
____Jar Jar Binks, peeking 2.00
____Jar Jar Binks, surprised 2.00
____Mace Windu 2.00
____Movie poster version A 2.00
____Movie poster version B 2.00
____Obi-Wan Kenobi, Droid Control Ship 2.00
____Obi-Wan Kenobi, Naboo Power Complex 2.00
____Queen Amidala 2.00
____Queen Amidala, Naboo Hanger 2.00
____Qui-Gon and Obi-Wan, Droid Control Ship 2.00
____Qui-Gon Jinn, art 2.00
____Qui-Gon Jinn, Droid Control Ship 2.00
____Qui-Gon Jinn, Naboo Hanger 2.00
____R2-D2 ....2.00
____Yoda 2.00

Magic eye.
____B-Wing Attack [PSC105] 4.00
____Battle in the Astroids [PSC106] 4.00
____Heroes collage [PSC107] 4.00
____Hoth Astroid Field [PSC108] 4.00
____Luke on Dagobah [PSC109] 4.00
____Starships, Stormtroopers, Droids [PSC110] 4.00
____Stormtroopers [PSC111] 4.00

Comic-Con International
2003, San Diego.
____1 of 4 Boba Fett [PSC112] 3.00
____2 of 4 Yoda [PSC113] 3.00
____3 of 4 Asajj Ventress [PSC114] 3.00
____4 of 4 Clone Troopers [PSC115] 3.00

Disney / MGM
____Bespin [PSC116] 4.00
____C-3PO and R2-D2 Star Tours, 8"x10" 3.00
____Endor [PSC117] 4.00
____Han Solo Star Tours, 8"x10" 3.00
____Luke Skywalker Star Tours, 8"x10" 3.00
____Star Tours, 4"x6" 2.00
____Stormtroopers Star Tours, 8"x10" 3.00
____Tatooine [PSC118] 4.00
____The Ultimate Adventure, Star Tours [PSC119] 4.00

Drawing Board Greeting Cards, Inc.
____20-pack, Greetings Eathlings 38.00
____Greetings Earthling [PSC120] 6.00

Empire Strikes Back, rounded corners.
____AT-AT's attack on Hoth [PSC121] 8.00
____Luke and Han on Hoth [PSC122] 8.00
____Luke and Vader on Bespin gantry [PSC123] 8.00
____R2-D2 repairs C-3PO [PSC124] 8.00

Fan Club, UK
____Collector's set of 9 postcards, Maul cover 25.00

Fan Made
StarWarsCards.net. Limited edition.
____2004/2005 sketch by Dale Smith III 1.00

StarWarsCards.net. Limited to 250.
____2003 1 of 3 – Leia and R2 ....1.00
____2003 2 of 3 – Luke and Yoda 1.00
____2003 3 of 3 – Jabba's throne room 1.00

Filmwert Berlin
Christmas theme.
____C-3PO and R2-D2 in Santa's workshop 6.00
____C-3PO and R2-D2 shopping 6.00
____Santa C-3PO and reindeer R2-D2 ....6.00
____Santa Yoda 6.00

I T V Digital
____Obi-Wan sock monkey [PSC125] 5.00

Icons Authentic Replicas
____Advertisement for replica weapons [PSC126] 4.00

Living Waters Publications
Unique Tracts – Pro-Christian message with scripture references on the back of cards with Episode I scenes.
____Darth Maul 4.00
____Jedi vs. Sith 4.00
____Obi-Wan Kenobi 4.00
____Queen Amidala 4.00

LucasArts
____Dark Forces II promotional [PSC127] 4.00
____Dark Forces promotional [PSC128] 4.00
____X-Wing vs. Tie Fighter [PSC129] 4.00

M&M World
EPIII:ROTS.
____"Aren't you a little round for a stormtrooper?" [PSC130] 5.00
____"Born to be dark" [PSC131] 5.00
____"Dare to go to the Dark Side" [PSC132] 5.00
____"I've got a bad feeling about this!" [PSC133] 5.00

Odeon
____EPII:AOTC "Book Now" movie premiere [PSC134] 5.00

Oral-B
Dental check-up reminders.
____C-3PO and R2-D2 [PSC135] 6.00
____Chewbacca, Han, Leia, Luke, C-3PO [PSC136] 6.00
____Ewoks 6.00
____Jabba the Hutt and Bib Fortuna [PSC137] 6.00
____Luke and Darth Vader [PSC138] 6.00

Paizo Publishing / Fan Club
____Greetings from lovely Geonosis [PSC139] 4.00
____Hello from Corsucant [PSC140] 4.00
____Rides the waves, beautiful Kamino [PSC141] 4.00

Pop-Shots
____Birthday Greetings from Mos Eisley [PSC142] 8.00
____C-3PO and Ewoks, Happy Birthday, They Think You're Some Sort of God [PSC143] 7.00
____C-3PO and R2-D2, We've Been Through A Lot Together [PSC144] 7.00
____C-3PO and R2-D2, You Artoo Older Then Me, Happy Birthday [PSC145] 7.00
____Falcon Cockpit, It Seems Like A Millennium Since Your Last Birthday 7.00
____Leia and Han, Help Me Obi-Wan Kenobi, I Think I'm Falling In Love [PSC146] 7.00
____The Duel, You Have Learned Much, Young One, Happy Birthday [PSC147] 7.00
____Yoda, When 900 Years Old You Reach..., Happy Birthday [PSC148] 8.00

PSC126 PSC127 PSC128 PSC129 PSC130 PSC131 PSC132 PSC133 PSC134 PSC135 PSC136 PSC137 PSC138

PSC139 PSC140 PSC141 PSC142 PSC143 PSC144 PSC145 PSC146 PSC147 PSC148

PSC149

PSC150

PSC151

PSC152

PSC153

PSC154

PSC155

PSC156

PSC157

PSC158

PSC159

PSC160

PSC161

ScopeCard
EPII:AOTC promotional cards. Designed to be mailed.
____8 set, sealed in envelope 25.00
____Anakin Skywalker 3.00
____Count Dooku...3.00
____Geonosian...3.00
____Jango Fett..3.00
____Mace Windu 3.00
____Obi-Wan Kenobi 3.00
____Padme Amidala..3.00
____Zam Wesell 3.00

Sony Ericsson
EPIII:ROTS.
____Anakin Skywalker 5.00
____Emperor Palpatine 5.00
____General Grievous 5.00
____Obi-Wan Kenobi 5.00
____Yoda 5.00

Starpics Co. Ltd.
EPIII:ROTS charactures.
____Anakin Skywalker 4.00
____Boba Fett 4.00
____C-3PO and R2-D2 ....4.00
____Chewbacca...4.00
____Clone Trooper 4.00
____Darth Maul 4.00
____Darth Vader with lightsaber drawn 4.00
____Darth Vader, lightsaber and balled fist 4.00
____Darth Vader, Force push w/lightsaber drawn.........4.00
____Emperor Palpatine 4.00
____General Grievous, 2 lightsabers 4.00
____General Grievous, 4 lightsabers 4.00
____Han Solo 4.00
____Luke and Leia 4.00
____Luke Skywalker..4.00
____Luke Skywalker, X-Wing pilot 4.00
____Mace Windu 4.00
____Obi-Wan Kenobi 4.00
____Padme Amidala..4.00
____Princess Leia...4.00
____Princess Leia as Jabba's captive 4.00
____Stormtrooper..4.00
____Tarfful...4.00
____Wicket 4.00
____Yoda, Force push 4.00
____Yoda, Force push 4.00
____Yoda, lightsaber drawn 4.00

EPIII:ROTS. Art on white background with logo.
____Anakin Skywalker 4.00
____Darth Vader 4.00
____General Grievous 4.00
____Obi-Wan Kenobi 4.00
____Yoda 4.00

EPIII:ROTS.
____Anakin and Obi-Wan clash under an image of Palpatine 4.00
____Anakin and Obi-Wan clash under the vision of Darth Vader 4.00
____Anakin collage...4.00
____Anakin in front of flame pattern 4.00
____Anakin parrying in front of Vader image.................4.00
____Anakin Skywalker, "Jedi" 4.00
____ARC-170s, "Victory!" 4.00
____Clone Trooper 4.00
____Clone Trooper collage...4.00
____Clone trooper in front of flame background...........4.00
____Darth Vader 4.00
____Darth Vader 1/2 mask..4.00
____Darth Vader driving lightsaber into planet surface 4.00
____Darth Vader facing right with background of destruction 4.00
____Darth Vader facing right, looking left 4.00
____Darth Vader helmet glowing red 4.00
____Darth Vader illuminated red, red mist.....................4.00
____Darth Vader looking left with lightsaber ready to strike 4.00
____Darth Vader metal flames 4.00
____Darth Vader red and blue over logo 4.00
____Darth Vader right hand up, lightsaber angled down 4.00
____Darth Vader right profile with lightsaber at salute...4.00
____Darth Vader slashing left with lightsaber 4.00
____Darth Vader stalking 4.00
____Darth Vader sunset 4.00
____Darth Vader upright, white background 4.00
____Darth Vader, "Vader"...4.00
____Darth Vader, epic duel image in helmet 4.00
____Darth Vader, red mist facing forward 4.00
____Darth Vader, red mist facing left 4.00
____Darth Vader, view from below.................................4.00
____Epic Duel..4.00
____Epic Duel in Vader cut-out image...........................4.00
____Epic Duel on white 4.00
____General Grievous bust with lightsaber 4.00
____General Grievous charging from flames.................4.00
____General Grievous in front of Grievous image.........4.00
____General Grievous with 2 lightsabers 4.00
____General Grievous with 2 lightsabers in front of flame pattern..4.00
____General Grievous, "Grievous"..................................4.00
____General Grievous, "Revenge of the Sith"...............4.00
____Jedi Starfighters, "Honor!" 4.00
____Jedi Starfighters, "Justice!" 4.00
____Obi-Wan Kenobi 4.00
____Star Wars EPIII Vader logo 4.00
____Vader and Emperor..4.00
____Vader collage 4.00
____Yoda 4.00
____Yoda blocking with lightsaber (far) 4.00
____Yoda blocking with lightsaber (near) 4.00
____Yoda collage 4.00

Suncoast
____Celebration II, May 3-5, 2002 ....3.00

The LEGO Group
____Anakin / Darth Vader [PSC149] 3.00
____AT-TE [PSC150]...3.00
____Cloud Car [PSC151] 3.00
____Cloud City [PSC152]..3.00
____EPI Speeder Chase [PSC153] 3.00
____Jango Fett's Slave I vs. Obi-Wan's Jedi Starfighter [PSC154] 3.00
____Jango Fett [PSC155]...3.00
____Just Imagine... Speeder Bikes [PSC156] 2.00
____Just Imagine... X-Wing Fighter [PSC157]...............2.00
____Republic Gunship [PSC158]....................................3.00
____Super Battle Droid [PSC159] 3.00
____Use The Force, shows Darth Vader [PSC160] 3.00

Topps
____B-Wing / Slave 1 Vehicles promo [PSC161] 5.00

TrooperClerks.com
____Trooper Clerks..5.00

Posters

____"All I needed to know about life I learned from Star Wars" [2:357] 35.00
____American one-sheet poster checklist revised, 27"x40" rolled [X01] 16.00
____American one-sheet poster checklist, 27"x40" rolled [2:357]...95.00
____Are Your Children Fully Immunized?, 14"x22 [X02] 85.00
____Battle Above Death Star II [2:357] 20.00
____Boba Fett [2:357] 20.00
____C-3PO and R2-D2, red background, 18.5"x23" [2:357]..12.00
____Chewbacca, Hoth, 12"x17" [2:357] 25.00
____Empire Strikes Back radio broadcast, 27"x40"...50.00
____Empire Strikes Back radio broadcast, 27"x40" reprint [X03] 16.00
____Empire Strikes Back, 24"x36" Collector's Edition, similar to style "A" [2:357] 10.00
____Empire Strikes Back, 24"x36", similar to advance style [3:354]...10.00
____EPIII DVD: Own it on DVD November 1..............15.00
____ESB 25th anniversary..45.00

X01

X02

X03

X04

X05

X06

X07

X08

X09

X10

X11

X12

X13

X14

X15

X16

X17

Posters

| X18 | X19 | X20 | X21 | X22 | X23 | X24 | X25 |

____Heir to the Empire, 28"x22" [2:357] 20.00
____Star Wars in Concert, 27"x40" [X04] 50.00
____Star Wars in Concert, 27"x40" reprint 16.00
____Star Wars, concept poster [3:354] 415.00
____Star Wars, concept, reprint, 27"x40" 16.00

17x22.
____A Long Time Ago In A Galaxy Far, Far Away 10.00

EPII: Japan
____DVD release 25.00

Italy.
____Han Solo / Boba Fett [2:357] 55.00

Japan.
____22"x39" [X05] 24.00

Mexico, EPII:AOTC.
____Anakin's Destiny [X06] 10.00
____Clone Trooper [X07] 15.00
____Droideka [X08] 17.00

Mexico. EPI:TPM.
____Anakin podracer [X09] 15.00
____Darth Maul [X10] 15.00
____Obi-Wan Kenobi [X11] 15.00

20th Century Fox
____EPII:AOTC. Theatrical release 45.00
____EPII:AOTC. Theatrical teaser 30.00
____MTFBWY: One Year Old Today 350.00
____SW:SE Join the Celebration [2:357].................65.00
____THX Video Poster, 27"x40" [3:354] 50.00

EPI:TPM advertising.
____One businessman, One gambler, Watto [X12] 145.00
____One hero, One destiny, Anakin [X13].............145.00
____One love, One quest, Queen Amidala [X14] 165.00
____One mind, One mission, Battle Droid [X15] 165.00

Episode III: Revenge of the Sith.
____Darth Vader, "Who's Your Daddy" 11"x17" Father's Day promo [X16] 10.00
____Theater 2-sided [X17]......................................45.00
____Theater advance...45.00

20th Century Fox, Canada
____EPI:TPM On Video April 4, 27"x40" [X18] 20.00

20th Century Fox, Iceland
____EPII:AOTC. Theatrical release 75.00

20th Century Fox, Thailand
Episode II: Attack of the Clones.
____Heroes, theater [2:357] 125.00
____Villains, theater [2:357].................................125.00

At-A Glance
____Anakin 6.00
____Darth Maul 6.00
____Jar Jar 6.00
____Jedi Battle 6.00
____Pod Race 6.00
____Queen Amidala 6.00
____Space Battle 6.00

Burger King
ESB Poster, 18"x24".
____Bespin [X19] 14.00
____Dagobah [X20] 14.00
____Hoth [X21] 14.00

C and D Visionaries, Inc.
____Darth Vader, epic duel 12.00
____Darth Vader, Sith 12.00

Classic trilogy.
____Heroes 12.00
____Villains...12.00

CBS / Fox Video
____Star Wars Trilogy, 25"x38" [2:357] 85.00

Celebration I
____Star Wars Celebration 5.00

Coca-Cola
Distributed in 1977 through fast food restaurants.
____Chewbacca [X22] 16.00
____Darth Vader [X23] 16.00
____Luke Skywalker [X24] 16.00
____R2-D2 and C-3PO [X25].....................................16.00

Code 3 Collectibles
3D mini-posters.
____Empire Strikes Back, Celebration 3 exclusive 120.00
____Return of the Jedi, 10th Anniversary 35.00
____Revenge of the Sith, Darth Vader 35.00

3D posters.
____A New Hope style D..80.00
____A New Hope, limited to 3,000 pieces 80.00
____Empire Strikes Back...80.00
____Return of the Jedi...80.00
____Revenge of the Jedi...80.00
____Revenge of the Sith, Best Buy exclusive...........80.00

Dark Horse Comics
____EPII: AOTC, 2-sided with Lucas Books 5.00
____Graphic Novel Chronology, 2-sided 5.00
____Star Wars Timeline (color) 5.00
____Vader's Quest 4-page pull-out 5.00

Decipher
CCG posters.
____Cloud City, "as you wish," 25.5"x33.5" 5.00
____Darth Vader, "You have only begun to discover your power," 22"x28" 5.00
____Jabba's Palace, "Soon you will learn to appreciate me," 25.5"x33.5" 5.00
____Star Wars Special Edition LE 9 card expansion set, 10.5"x33" 10.00

Disney / MGM
Star Wars Weekends.
____2003 Mickey and Yoda...25.00
____2005 Darth Vader / Mickey 25.00

Dixie / Northern Inc.
____Storycard poster, mail-in premium [X26] 35.00

Duncan Heinz
Mail-in poster premiums.
____C-3PO and R2-D2 [X27]......................................15.00
____Darth Vader [X28] 15.00
____Han and Leia [X29]...15.00
____Luke Skywalker [X30]...15.00

Encuentros
____2004 Encuentros [3:354] 65.00

Esso
Co-produced with Pepsi.
____Anakin Skywalker [X31] 5.00
____Darth Maul [X32] 5.00

Co-produced with Walkers.
____Jar Jar Binks [X33] 5.00
____Obi-Wan Kenobi [X34] 5.00

| X26 | X27 | X28 | X29 | X30 | X31 | X32 | X33 |

| X34 | X35 | X36 | X37 | X38 |

X39   X40   X41   X42   X43   X44

X45   X46   X47   X48   X49   X50   X51

Fan Club
____Star Wars Celebration [X35] 25.00

Fox Video
____27x40 DVD Art, Vader 25.00

Freegels
Brazil.
____Poster to attach set of 50 cards [X36] 20.00

Frito Lay
11"x17" Find the Hero Inside, Publix exclusives.
____Dark Destiny 5.00
____Fett Family 5.00
____Jedi Justice 5.00
____Skywalker Saga 5.00

Hasbro
____2002 Figure Collection, Celebration II exclusive [X37] 20.00
____Clone Wars, action figures [X38] 7.00
____Clones on battlefield, exclusive poster from Entertainment Earth 4-figure set 5.00
____Jedi and Heores, Wizardcon 2002 exclusive [X39] 15.00
____OTC Classic Scene with action figures, 2004 Comic-Con exclusive [X40] 15.00
____Revenge of the Sith – 56 action figures 15.00

Hasbro, Australia
____2002 Figure Collection, Toys R Us exclusive [X41] 35.00

Hi-C
____ROTJ, 2-sided mail-in premium 25.00

Highbridge Audio
____Star Wars NPR broadcast, "Now Available on Cassette and Compact Discs" [2:357] 22.00

ILM
____Yoda and the Hulk [X42] 45.00

Kelloggs, Singapore
EPIII:ROTS. 15"x20".
____Anakin Skywalker [X43] 15.00
____C-3PO and R2-D2 [X44] 15.00
____Clone Trooper [X45] 15.00
____Darth Vader [X46] 15.00
____Emperor Palpatine [X47] 15.00
____General Grievous [X48] 15.00
____Mace Windu [X49] 15.00
____Obi-Wan Kenobi [X50] 15.00
____Yoda [X51] 15.00

Kenner
Planetary maps.
____Death Star 11.00
____Endor 8.00
____Tatooine 8.00

Lucasfilm
____Clone Wars 20.00
____Clone Wars season 1 [X52] 20.00
____Clone Wars season 2 [X53] 20.00
____Clone Wars volume II [X54] 20.00
____Primera Star Wars Convencion 25.00
____Size Matters Not, IMAX replica [X55] 45.00

M&M World
____The Dark Side of Chocolate [X56] 20.00

Mello Smello
12"x18" lenticular. Classic trilogy.
____Heroes [X57] 20.00
____Villains [X58] 20.00

12"x18" lenticular.
____Anakin Skywalker / Darth Vader [X59] 20.00
____Darth Vader [X60] 20.00
____Darth Vader [X61] 20.00
____Darth Vader and Palpatine [X62] 20.00
____General Grievous [X63] 20.00
____Jedi Master Yoda [X64] 20.00

8"x10" lenticular.
____Darth Vader 15.00
____General Grievous 15.00
____Han Solo 15.00
____Jedi Master Yoda 15.00
____Jedi Starfighters 15.00
____Luke Skywalker 15.00
____R2-D2 ....15.00
____R2D2 and C3PO 15.00

Revenge of the Sith DVD release promotions
____Anakin and Obi-Wan, 8"x10" 15.00
____Boba Fett, 8"x10" 20.00
____Clone Troopers, 8"x10" 15.00
____Darth Vader, 8"x10" 15.00
____Jedi Knights, 12"x18" 25.00

Revenge of the Sith lenticular 3D.
____General Grievous [X65] 25.00
____Master Yoda [X66] 25.00
____R2-D2 [X67] 25.00
____Starfighters [X68] 25.00

X52   X53   X54   X55   X56   X57   X59

X60   X61   X62   X63   X64

Posters

X65

X66

X67

X68

X69

Mexico Collector Convention 2003
____2003 July 12 and 13, rolled 85.00

N.S.W. Building Society Ltd.
____Ewoks poster to collector stickers for SW savings
 account...18.00
____ROTJ poster to collector stickers for SW savings
 account...13.00

Orquesta Pops De Mexico
____2004 Julio Star Wars en Concierto [3:354] 95.00

Paizo Publishing / Fan Club
____ROTJ 20th Anniversary, folded [X69] 25.00

Pepsi Cola
Special Edition promo, distributed through Pizza Hut.
____Star Wars 8.00
____Empire Strikes Back 8.00
____Return of the Jedi 8.00

Photomosaics
____Darth Vader 35.00
____Jedi Master Yoda 35.00

Proctor and Gamble
Mail-in poster premiums.
____Droids [X70] 15.00
____Heroes Battle [X71] 15.00
____Lightsaber Duel [X72] 15.00

Rolling Thunder Graphics
____Darth Vader, signed by Dave Dorman 65.00

Sales Corp. of America
11"x14" sold flat.
____Battle 8.00
____Darth [X73] 8.00
____Emperor 8.00
____Ewoks 8.00
____Jabba 8.00
____Jedi Cast 8.00
____Jedi Poster 8.00
____Lightsaber 8.00
____Saber Duel 8.00
____Speeder 8.00

Scholastic
____Anakin, "The Force runs strong in those who read"
 EPI...3.00

*EPII Adventures, 14"x17". Included with monthly mag-
azines.*
____Anakin Skywalker 1.00
____Arena Battle 1.00
____Boba Fett (young) 1.00
____Clone Army 1.00
____Count Dooku..1.00
____Dexter Jettster 1.00
____Jango Fett 1.00
____Kamino 1.00
____Mace Windu 1.00
____Obi-Wan Kenobi 1.00
____Padme Amidala 1.00
____Yoda 1.00

SciPubTech
Cutaway posters, 36"x24".
____AT-AT and snowspeeder [X74] 20.00
____AT-AT and snowspeeder, deluxe 40.00
____Millennium Falcon [X75] 20.00
____Millennium Falcon, deluxe 40.00
____X-Wing Fighter [X76] 20.00
____X-Wing Fighter, deluxe 40.00

Skywalkers
____The Empire Strikes Back [X77] 32.00
____Your pictorial guide to the major characters
 [X78] 25.00

Smithsonian Institute
____SW: The Magic of Myth, Oct. 1997 – Oct. 1998
 [X79] 24.00

Sony Classical
____EPII:AOTC. Soundtrack release [X80] 30.00

Star Wars Insider
____136 Vintage Action Figures with common
 variations 22.00
____Galaxy Poster Map...15.00

Sunshine Biscuits L.L.C.
____Darth Vader, mail-in premium.............................10.00

Taco Bell
EPI:TPM premiums, 17"x22".
____No. 1 Anakin Skywalker 10.00
____No. 2 Qui-Gon Jinn 10.00
____No. 3 Watto 10.00
____No. 4 Darth Maul [X81].....................................10.00

The LEGO Group
17"x22".
____X-Wing and Falcon flee the Death Star 5.00

2-sided, 19"x24".
____Astroid Ambush / Clone Troopers 5.00
____Republic Gunship / Republic Gunship 5.00
____Speeder Chase / Republic Gunships 5.00
____Tusken Attack / Arena Droids...............................5.00

Theatrical
Star Wars first advance.
____27"x41" folded...350.00
____27"x41" rolled [2:358] 400.00

Star Wars advance, style "B."
____27"x41" folded [2:358]..200.00
____27"x41" rolled [2:358] 350.00

Star Wars style "A."
____14"x36" [2:358] 125.00
____27"x41" folded [2:358] 300.00
____27"x41" rolled [2:358] 395.00
____28"x22" folded 300.00
____28"x22" rolled [2:358] 395.00
____30"x41" 775.00
____40"x60" rolled 700.00
____41"x81" folded [2:358] 750.00
____81"x81" [2:358] 525.00
____Reprint 27"x40" 16.00
____Reprint, 38"x27" 25.00

Star Wars style "C."
____27"x41" folded [2:358]..350.00
____27"x41" rolled [2:358] 450.00
____Reprint, 26.5"x40" 16.00

Star Wars style "D."
____27"x41" folded [2:358]..400.00
____27"x41" rolled [2:358] 450.00
____30"x41" 795.00
____40"x60" 775.00
____Reprint, 27"x40" 16.00

Star Wars "Happy Birthday."
____27"x41" rolled [3:355] 2,000.00

Star Wars reissue 1979.
____27"x41" folded 140.00
____27"x41" rolled [2:358] 185.00

X70

X71

X72

X73

X77

X78

X79

X74

X75

X76

X80

| X81 | X82 | X83 | X84 | X85 | X86 | X87 |

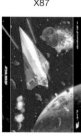

| X88 | X89 | X90 | X91 | X92 | X93 | X94 |

Star Wars reissue 1981.
____14"x36" 75.00
____27"x41" folded [2:358] 200.00
____27"x41" rolled [2:358] 250.00
____28"x22" folded 100.00
____28"x22" rolled [2:358] 140.00
____30"x41" 75.00
____40"x60" 100.00

Star Wars reissue 1982.
____14"x36" 75.00
____27"x41" folded [2:358] 200.00
____27"x41" rolled [2:358] 225.00
____28"x22" folded 140.00
____28"x22" rolled [2:358] 180.00
____30"x41" 165.00
____40"x60" 325.00

Star Wars 10th Anniversary.
____27"x41" mylar [2:358] 150.00
____27"x41" rolled, Struzan [2:358] 300.00

Empire Strikes Back advance, style "A."
____27"x41" folded [2:358] 450.00
____27"x41" rolled [2:358] 500.00
____41"x81" folded [2:358] 2,000.00
____Reprint 27"x40" rolled 16.00

Empire Strikes Back, style "A."
____14"x36" [2:358] 175.00
____27"x41" folded [2:358] 400.00
____27"x41" rolled [2:358] 465.00
____28"x22" folded 450.00
____28"x22" rolled 525.00
____30"x41" 485.00
____40"x60" 875.00
____Reprint 27"x40" 16.00

Empire Strikes Back, style "B."
____14"x36" [2:358] 100.00
____27"x41" folded [2:358] 125.00
____27"x41" rolled [2:358] 155.00
____28"x22" folded 100.00
____28"x22" rolled 125.00
____30"x41" 175.00
____40"x60" 175.00
____Reprint 27"x40" 16.00

Empire Strikes Back, style "C."
____27"x41" folded 90.00
____27"x41" rolled 100.00
____Reprint 27"x40" [2:358] 16.00

Empire Strikes Back, style "D."
____27"x41" rolled [2:358] 100.00
____Reprint 27"x40" 16.00

Empire Strikes Back re-release 1981.
____14"x36" [2:358] 75.00
____27"x41" folded [2:358] 75.00
____27"x41" rolled [2:358] 100.00
____28"x22" folded 75.00
____28"x22" rolled 100.00
____30"x41" 100.00
____40"x60" 450.00

Empire Strikes Back re-release 1982.
____14"x36" [2:358] 75.00
____27"x41" folded [2:358] 70.00
____27"x41" rolled [2:358] 75.00
____28"x22" folded 75.00
____28"x22" rolled 100.00
____30"x41" 80.00
____40"x60" 100.00

Empire Strikes Back 10th anniversary.
____27"x41" art [2:358] 125.00
____27"x41" gold mylar [2:359] 350.00
____27"x41" silver mylar [2:359] 300.00

Revenge of the Jedi first advance.
____27"x41" folded 550.00
____27"x41" rolled 775.00

Revenge of the Jedi first advance, second version.
____27"x41" folded 375.00
____27"x41" rolled [2:359] 525.00

Return of the Jedi, style "A."
____14"x36" [2:359] 125.00
____27"x41" folded [2:359] 125.00
____27"x41" rolled [2:359] 175.00
____28"x22" folded 100.00
____28"x22" rolled 150.00
____30"x41" 125.00
____40"x60" 325.00
____Reprint 27"x40" 16.00

Return of the Jedi, style "B."
____14"x36" [2:359] 125.00
____27"x41" folded [2:359] 125.00
____27"x41" rolled [2:359] 195.00
____28"x22" folded 100.00
____28"x22" rolled 150.00
____30"x41" 125.00
____40"x60" 425.00
____Reprint 27"x40" 16.00

Return of the Jedi re-release 1985.
____14"x36" [2:359] 60.00
____27"x41" folded [2:359] 50.00
____27"x41" rolled [2:359] 75.00
____28"x22" folded 100.00
____28"x22" rolled 160.00
____30"x41" 75.00
____40"x60" 150.00

Return of the Jedi 10th anniversary advance.
____27"x41" rolled 240.00
____Reprint 27"x40" [3:355] 16.00

Return of the Jedi 10th anniversary.
____27"x41" rolled [2:359] 100.00

Caravan of Courage, style "A."
____27"x41" folded 50.00
____27"x41" rolled [2:359] 85.00

Caravan of Courage, style "B."
____27"x41" folded 50.00
____27"x41" rolled [3:355] 85.00

Star Wars Special Edition.
____Advance, 24"x36" soundtrack [2:359] 20.00
____Advance, 27"x40" (ROTJ March 14) [2:359] 40.00
____Advance, 27"x40" (ROTJ March 7) [2:359] 50.00
____Empire Strikes Back 27"x40" [2:359] 50.00
____Empire Strikes Back, 40"x30" rolled, double-sided 30.00
____Reprint Return of the Jedi, 27"x40" [2:359] 16.00
____Reprint Star Wars, 27"x40" [2:359] 16.00
____Return of the Jedi 27"x40" [2:359] 40.00
____Return of the Jedi 27"x40", double-sided [2:359] 65.00
____Return of the Jedi, 27"x40", double-sided (ROTJ March 14) [2:359] 40.00
____Return of the Jedi, 27"x40", single-sided (ROTJ March 7) [2:359] 50.00
____Return of the Jedi, 40"x30" rolled, double-sided [2:359] 30.00
____Star Wars, 27"x40" [2:359] 50.00
____Star Wars, 27"x40", double-sided 65.00
____Star Wars, 40"x30" rolled, double-sided 40.00

The Phantom Menace, advance.
____27"x40", rolled [3:355] 40.00
____27"x40", rolled, double-sided [2:359] 120.00

The Phantom Menace.
____27"x40", rolled [2:359] 20.00

Attack of the Clones, advance.
____108"x60" [2:359] 340.00
____27"x40", rolled [2:359] 50.00
____27"x40", rolled, double-sided [2:359] 100.00

Attack of the Clones.
____27"x40", rolled [2:359] 40.00
____27"x40", rolled, double-sided [3:355] 60.00

Theatrical, Foreign
Argentina.
____Star Wars style "C," 29"x43" [2:359] 150.00

Australia.
____3 In One Programme [2:359] 375.00
____3 In One Programme, 13"x30" [2:359] 150.00
____3 In One Programme, 27"x39" reprint 14.00
____Star Wars style "C," 13"x30" [2:359] 175.00

Belgian.
____Star Wars style "A," 14"x22" [2:359] 150.00

French.
____Star Wars similar to style "A," 47"x63" folded [2:359] 300.00
____Empire Strikes Back similar to style "B," 47"x63" folded [2:359] 225.00

German.
____EPI:TPM 23"x32" [2:359] 40.00
____Kampf um Endor (Ewoks: The Battle for Endor), 23"x33" [2:359] 35.00

Indian.
____Empire Strikes Back, 27"x41", character frames across top [2:359] 100.00

Posters

Italy.
____Star Wars style "A," 13"x27" [2:359] 100.00
____Star Wars style "A," 55"x79" [2:359] 300.00
____Star Wars, 39"x55" [3:355] 250.00
____Star Wars, 40"x28" [3:355] 175.00
____ESB style "B," 13"x27" [2:359] 80.00
____ESB, style "B," 39"x55" [2:359] 250.00

Japan, 20"x29".
____Star Wars [2:360] 350.00
____Star Wars advance [2:360] 300.00
____Star Wars advance 1982 [2:360] 275.00
____Star Wars style "A," 1982 [2:360] 250.00
____Return of the Jedi, style "A" [2:360] 50.00
____Return of the Jedi, style "B" [3:355] 50.00

Poland.
____Star Wars, 27"x39" [2:360] 750.00

Spanish. 27"x40", double-sided.
____EPI:TPM [2:360] 20.00
____EPI:TPM advance [2:360] 95.00

Topps
____18"x22" Star Wars Galaxy Deluxe Trading Cards from Topps on Sale Here 20.00
____25 Years, 12"x18" [X82] 15.00
____Attack of the Clones movie cards 12.00
____ESB Press Sheet, mail-in premium 45.00

EPII:AOTC.
____Move cards poster, tri-folded, 2-sides 5.00

Trends International Corp.
____George Lucas Episode II Selects, SWCII exclusive [2:360] 25.00

EPI:TPM, 24"x36".
____Advance design [2:360] 10.00
____EPI:TPM [2:360] 10.00
____Heroes 10.00
____Heroes, foil [2:360] 30.00
____Jar Jar [X83] 10.00
____Jedi vs. Sith [X84] 10.00
____Queen Amidala [X85] 8.00
____Queen Amidala 2, foil [X86] 20.00
____Space Battle, foil [X87] 20.00
____Villains [X88] 10.00
____Villains, foil 30.00

EPII:AOTC, 22"x34".
____Anakin 2570 [X89] 9.00
____Darkside 2585 [X90] 9.00
____Jango Fett 2590 [X91] 9.00
____Jedi Knight 2580 [X92] 9.00
____Padme 2575 [X93] 9.00
____Space Battle 2595 [X94] 9.00

XM01   XM02   XM03

Episode II: Attack of the Clones.
____Star Wars One Sheet 2560, 25"x35" [2:360] 16.00

Vanity Fair
____February 1999 Cover, 23.5c [2:360] 35.00

Williams
____Don't Panic – You've Got Flippers [2:360] 24.00

Wizards of the Coast
____ESB TCG promo, 25"x22" 5.00

Posters: Mini

Blockbuster Video, Mexico
Episode II DVD pre-order premium.
____Anakin and Padme [XM01] 3.00
____Blockbuster envelope to store 3 mini-posters [XM02] 2.00
____Jango Fett [XM03] 3.00
____Yoda [XM04] 3.00

General Mills
Cereal premiums.
____Mini poster with scene to color on rear 15.00

Nabisco, Australia
Wheeties premiums.
____An Imperial Stormtrooper [XM06] 15.00
____An X-Wing Fighter [XM07] 15.00
____Ben Kenobi [XM08] 15.00
____Han and Chewbacca [XM09] 15.00
____Imperial Stormtroopers [XM10] 15.00
____Luke Skywalker [XM11] 15.00
____Luke Skywalker and his Uncle [XM12] 15.00
____On Board the Millennium Falcon [XM13] 15.00
____Tuscan Raiders [XM14] 15.00

The LEGO Group
Mini Building Sets.
____Snowspeeders attacking AT-STs, 10.5"x17" 4.00

Topps
Empire Strikes Back widevision mini-posters.
____1 Advance one-sheet 5.00
____2 Domestic one-sheet 5.00
____3 Style B 5.00
____4 Australian one-sheet 5.00
____5 German one-sheet 5.00
____6 Radio Show 5.00

Return of the Jedi widevision mini-posters.
____1 Advance one-sheet 5.00
____2 One-sheet style B 5.00
____3 Re-release one-sheet [XM05] 5.00
____4 Japanese 5.00
____5 Japanese 5.00
____6 Polish 5.00

Press Kits

20th Century Fox
____1977 catalog of new releases [2:361] 25.00
____ESB:SE Cd-rom multi-media presskit [2:361] 55.00
____ROTJ:SE, incl. booklet and 14 slides 35.00
____Star Wars Pressbook [2:361] 85.00
____SW:SE Cd-rom multi-media presskit 53.00

Programs
____10th Anniversary program 10.00
____Celebration 25.00
____Celebration revised program listing 10.00
____Dallas Comiccon 2005 ....5.00
____EPIII:ROTS [PRG01] 25.00

Japan.
____Star Wars [PRG02] 35.00

20th Century Fox
____Dreams for this Gerneation and the Next – 1996 Show West [PRG03] 30.00

Dallas Comic Con
____2003 Aayla Secura cover [PRG04] 5.00
____2003 April: Dallas Comicon, Dave Dorman cover [PRG05] 10.00

Dragon Con
____Dragon Con '99 with Darth Maul cover 8.00

Encuntros
____2004 [PRG06] 20.00

Fan Club
____SW Celebration II vendors program [PRG07] 18.00

George Fenmore Associates
____Return of the Jedi, Official Collectors Edition [PRG08] 22.00
____Star Wars, first edition smooth cover [PRG09] 45.00
____Star Wars, second edition textured cover 24.00
____The Empire Strikes Back [PRG10] 45.00

Mexico Collector Convention
____1999 [PRG11] 35.00
____2003 July 12 and 13 ....35.00

Orquesta Pops De Mexico
____2004 Julio [PRG12] 5.00

Philharmonic Orchestra of Indianapolis
____25th Anniversary Concert 2.00

San Diego Museum of Art
____Star Wars The Magic of Myth: September 25, 1999 – January 2, 2000 [PRG13] 4.00

starwars.com
____Celebration III program guide 5.00

Super Live Adventure
____Super Live Adventure, Japan [PRG14] 20.00

Washington Museums
____Star Wars The Magic of Myth, commerative edition [PRG15] 10.00

Wizards of the Coast
____Celebration II on-site program schedule 5.00
____Star Wars Celebration II [PRG16] 12.00

Yerba Buena Gardens
____The Art of Star Wars: Dec 27, 1994 – March 12, 1995 [PRG17] 4.00

XM04   XM05   XM06   XM07   XM08   XM09

XM10   XM11   XM12   XM13   XM14

 PRG01
 PRG02
 PRG03
 PRG04
 PRG05
 PRG06
 PRG07
 PRG08

 PRG09
 PRG10
 PRG11
 PRG12
 PRG13
 PRG14
 PRG15
 PRG16
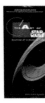 PRG17

Publications

20th Anniversary Poster Magazine
____Star Wars Heroes [2:362] 6.00
____Star Wars Villains 6.00

20th Century Fox
____Empire Strikes Back pressbook [2:362]..............74.00

321 Contact
____1980 March/April, "Amazing Movies! Could They Really Happen?" [PB01] 8.00

Adastra
____Issue 11, ESB cover [PB02] 6.00

Amazing Heroes
____#13"Star Wars in Comics" cover 6.00

American Cinematographer
____1977 July Star Wars cover [2:362].......................85.00
____1980 June ESB cover [PB03]............................45.00
____ROTJ, R2-D2 and C-3PO on cover [PB04] 35.00

American Film
____1977 April "George Lucas in Outer Space" [PB05] 12.00
____1983 June Return of the Jedi special effects articles [PB06] 7.00

Arena
____2002 issue 123, Hayden Christensen interview [2:362] 5.00

ATS Tracts
____The True Force religious tract [PB07] 4.00

Bananas
____No. 63, 1983, Scenes we won't see in Star Wars III [PB08] 12.00

Bantha Tracks
____Issues 1-35 ea. (1977-87).............................6.00
____Issue 34, includes soundtrack record 14.00

Best of Starlog
____Vol. 1: Luke from ESB on cover, assorted articles [PB09] 7.00
____Vol. 2: Yoda on cover, assorted articles [PB10] 7.00
____Vol. 4: Jabba on cover, assorted articles [PB11] 7.00
____Vol. 5: Luke and Darth Vader duel on cover, assorted articles..7.00
____Vol. 6: Empire Strikes Back articles [PB12] 7.00

Burger King
____Adventures vol. 16, no. 5 (Star Wars toys)............3.00

Calgary Herald
____Comic Book Vol. 2, No. 23, April 8, 1979 [3:358]..10.00

Chicago Tribune
____1980 May 4 Headline "Empire Strikes Back" 12.00

Cinefantastique
____20th Anniversary, SW:SE [2:362] 9.00
____Vol. 10, No. 2 Review of Empire Strikes Back [2:362] 8.00
____Vol. 12, No. 5 / Vol 12, No. 6 (Double Issue) "The Revenge of the Jedi" 23.00
____Vol. 13, No. 4 Jedi Plot Revealed 10.00
____Vol. 6, No. 4 / Vol. 7, No. 1 (Double Issue) "Making Star Wars" [PB13] 35.00

Cinefex
____No. 02, August 1980, special effects articles 65.00
____No. 03, Empire Strikes Back cover [2:362] 57.00
____No. 13, Return of the Jedi film production 35.00
____No. 65, ILM 20th anniversary, Millennium Falcon cover..20.00
____No. 74, Jar Jar Binks cover 18.00

Cinema, Germany
____2002 May, 25 years of Star Wars [2:362] 5.00

Cinema, Hungary
____2002 May, 25 years of Star Wars [2:362] 5.00

Cinemacabre
____No. 6, Summer 1984, Luke Skywalker on Sailbarge Deck [2:362] 5.00

Cinescape
____1996 February, "Star Wars Forever" [2:362]..........4.00

Collecting Toys
____1995 August, "Star Wars breaks loose!" [2:362] 3.00
____1997 February, "Star Wars Forever" [2:362]..........3.00

Collector's Universe
____The Definitive Star Wars Secondary Market Price Guide [PB14]...5.00

Collectors Compendium
____Return of the Jedi 9.00
____Star Wars [3:358] 9.00
____Star Wars and Empire Strikes Back [PB15] 9.00

Comic Collector's Magazine
____No. 139, October 1977, Star Wars interviews, behind the scenes and comic art 8.00

Comics Interview
____1994 No. 130 Spotlight on Star Wars 4.00

Comics Journal
____No. 2, Empire Strikes Back issue 8.00
____No. 37, Star Wars comics and movie issue [PB16] 8.00

Comics Scene
____Darth Vader on cover and article on ROTJ comic 11.00

Commodore User's Magazine
____No. 3, Star Wars cover, SW games issue 4.00

Computer Graphics World
____2002 June, Yoda cover [PB17] 5.00

Cracked Magazine
____"Phantom Menace Exposed" [2:362] 5.00

 PB01
 PB02
 PB03
 PB04
 PB05
 PB06
 PB07
 PB08
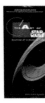 PB09

 PB10
 PB11
 PB12
 PB13
 PB14
 PB15
 PB16
 PB17
 PB18

Publications

PB19

PB20

PB21

PB22

PB23

PB24

PB25

PB26

PB27

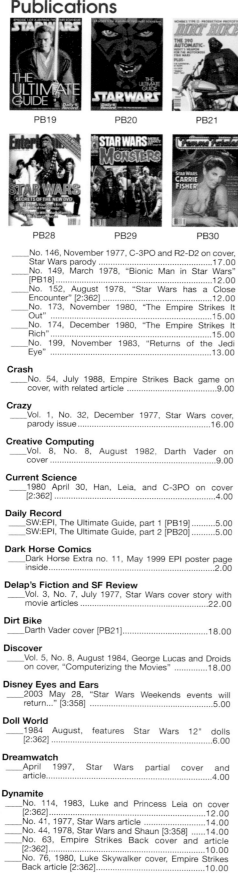
PB28

PB29

PB30

PB31

PB32

PB33

PB34

PB35

PB36

____No. 146, November 1977, C-3PO and R2-D2 on cover, Star Wars parody 17.00

____No. 149, March 1978, "Bionic Man in Star Wars" [PB18] 12.00

____No. 152, August 1978, "Star Wars has a Close Encounter" [2:362] 12.00

____No. 173, November 1980, "The Empire Strikes It Out" 15.00

____No. 174, December 1980, "The Empire Strikes It Rich" 15.00

____No. 199, November 1983, "Returns of the Jedi Eye" 13.00

Crash
____No. 54, July 1988, Empire Strikes Back game on cover, with related article 9.00

Crazy
____Vol. 1, No. 32, December 1977, Star Wars cover, parody issue 16.00

Creative Computing
____Vol. 8, No. 8, August 1982, Darth Vader on cover 9.00

Current Science
____1980 April 30, Han, Leia, and C-3PO on cover [2:362] 4.00

Daily Record
____SW:EPI, The Ultimate Guide, part 1 [PB19] 5.00
____SW:EPI, The Ultimate Guide, part 2 [PB20] 5.00

Dark Horse Comics
____Dark Horse Extra no. 11, May 1999 EPI poster page inside 2.00

Delap's Fiction and SF Review
____Vol. 3, No. 7, July 1977, Star Wars cover story with movie articles 22.00

Dirt Bike
____Darth Vader cover [PB21].................................18.00

Discover
____Vol. 5, No. 8, August 1984, George Lucas and Droids on cover, "Computerizing the Movies" 18.00

Disney Eyes and Ears
____2003 May 28, "Star Wars Weekends events will return..." [3:358] 5.00

Doll World
____1984 August, features Star Wars 12" dolls [2:362] 6.00

Dreamwatch
____April 1997, Star Wars partial cover and article...4.00

Dynamite
____No. 114, 1983, Luke and Princess Leia on cover [2:362]..12.00

____No. 41, 1977, Star Wars article 14.00

____No. 44, 1978, Star Wars and Shaun [3:358] 14.00

____No. 63, Empire Strikes Back cover and article [2:362]..12.00

____No. 76, 1980, Luke Skywalker cover, Empire Strikes Back article [2:362]..10.00

Electric Company
____1977 December, "Star Wars!" [3:358] 10.00

____1980 July, Darth Vader Cover, "Will The Bad Guys Win?" [PB22]..8.00

____1983 April / May, Yoda cover, Star Wars articles 7.00

____1984 November, "The Ewoks – Star Wars' Furry Heroes" [PB23] 7.00

Electronic Gaming Monthly
____Featuring: "Super Star Wars" [2:363] 3.00

Empire Strikes Back
____ESB Official Collector's Edition 8.00
____ESB Poster Album 16.00

Empire
2002 April 26. Episode II, Lucas Strikes Back.
____Anakin Skywalker cover [PB24] 5.00
____Count Dooku cover [PB25] 5.00
____Padme Amidala cover [PB26]..............................5.00
____Windu and Kenobi cover [PB27] 5.00

Enterprise Spotlight
____No. 4, Star Wars special 3.00

Entertainment Weekly
____1997 January 10, Luke Skywalker cover, SE articles 7.00

____1999 June 11, Inside the New Star Wars [2:363] 6.00

____1999 May 21, Inside Star Wars [2:363] 6.00

____2002 April 26, Summer Movie Preview, Star Wars AOTC article 4.00

____2004 September 24, Star Wars secret of the new DVD [PB28] 4.00

Epic Illustrated
____1980 October, "Special Preview: Revenge of the Jedi" [2:363] 12.00

Esquire
____2002 June, God Save The Queen 6.00

Family Circle
____1980 August 5, "The Empire Strikes Back" [2:363] 4.00

Famous Monsters
____Movie Aliens: Darth Vader cover, reprinted articles from "Famous Monsters" 12.00

____No. 137, Star Wars special issue 24.00

____No. 138, R2-D2 cover, articles............................12.00

____No. 139, Star Wars cover, articles [PB29] 20.00

____No. 140, Star Wars articles [2:363] 10.00

____No. 142, Darth Vader cover [2:363] 7.00

____No. 145, Empire Strikes Back article [2:363]......13.00

____No. 146, Star Wars Article [2:363] 7.00

____No. 147, Star Wars cover, articles [2:363] 7.00

____No. 148, Darth Vader cover [2:363] 12.00

____No. 153, David Prowse interview.........................7.00

____No. 156, Empire Strikes Back cover, articles 12.00

____No. 165, Empire Strikes Back special issue 20.00

____No. 166, Empire Strikes Back cover 12.00

____No. 167, Empire Strikes Back cover 12.00

____No. 174, Star Wars cover 12.00

____No. 177, Yoda cover...12.00

____No. 190, Empire Strikes Back cover 12.00

Fangoria
____1980 No. 6, "C-3PO from the Inside" [2:363] 9.00

Fantascene
____No. 3, 1977, "The Star Wars" 16.00

Fantastic Films
____Vol. 1, No. 1, April 1978, articles and interviews 12.00

____Vol. 1, No. 4, August 1978, The Weapons of Star Wars [2:363] 12.00

____Vol. 1, No. 8, April 1979, "Star Wars Strikes Back" 10.00

____Vol. 2, No. 2, June 1979, "One Last Time Down The Death Trench" 8.00

____Vol. 3, No. 2, July 1980, interviews Larry Kasdan and Dennis Muren (effects photographer) [2:363]........8.00

____Vol. 3, No. 3, September 1980, Chewbacca cover, Gary Kurtz interview [2:363]......................................10.00

____Vol. 3, No. 4, October 1980, Yoda cover, articles [2:363] 8.00

____Vol. 3, No. 5, December 1980, Clone wars explained [3:358] 16.00

____Vol. 3, No. 7, February 1981, articles [2:363]........8.00

____Vol. 3, No. 8, April 1981, articles [2:363] 8.00

____Vol. 3, No. 9, June 1981, cover of characters on radio, "Star Wars Comes To Radio"............................14.00

____Vol. 4, No. 1, August 1981, articles 8.00

____Vol. 4, No. 4, April 1982, "From Star Wars to Empire to Revenge of the Jedi" 10.00

____Vol. 5, No. 2, "Revenge of the Jedi"....................9.00

____Vol. 5, No. 3, Return of the Jedi cover and articles [2:363] 8.00

____Vol. 5, No. 4, Return of the Jedi cover and articles...8.00

____Vol. 5, No. 5, Return of the Jedi cover and articles...8.00

Fantasy Film Preview
____1977, Star Wars special effects 5.00

Fantasy Modeling
____No. 6, Star Wars miniature models 4.00

Femme Fatales
____1999 Vol. 8 No. 1, Star Wars Carrie Fisher [PB30] 9.00

Film Csillag
____2002 April, Anakin and Obi-Wan cover [2:363] 6.00

Film Review
____1978 February, "Loaded with SW facts and pictures" [3:358] 7.00

____1980 August, "Carrie Fisher and Mark Hamill Talk About Their Roles in Empire" 8.00

____1980 July, "More Photos from the Empire Strikes Back" 5.00

____1980 June, "Star Wars Rage Again Against the Empire" 5.00

____1983 July, "Star Wars – The Final Force Filled Phase"...6.00

Film, Poland
____2002 May, Mace Windu cover [PB31] 5.00

Films and Filming
____1977 August, Star Wars preview [2:363] 11.00

____1978 February, Mark Hamill Interview [2:363] 11.00

Finescale Modeler
____No. 43, Summer 1983, Jedi diorama cover 5.00

Flicks
____1997 April Vol. 10, exclusive SW merchandise pull-out 4.00

Fortune
____1980 October 6, "The Empire Pays Off" 9.00

Future Life
____1980 August, "The Making of Empire – Star Wars Returns" [2:363] 6.00

Future
____No. 1, April 1978, Star Wars advertising posters [2:363]...16.00
____No. 19, Empire Strikes Back preview....................8.00
____No. 20, Empire Strikes Back cover and article 8.00

Gamester
____Giant pull-out game of Star Wars [PB32] 16.00

Gateways
____No. 6, Star Wars role-playing game 6.00

High Drive Publications, Inc.
____SW Generation fanzine 1992 #1, black-and-white photocopied issue 5.00
____SW Generation fanzine 1992, #2, black-and-white photocopied issue 5.00
____SW Generation fanzine 1997 #1 Vol. 2 "quarterly" with a color glossy cover [PB33] 4.00

Hollywood Studio Magazine
____Vol. 12, No. 5, June 1978, articles 6.00

Home Viewer Marquee
____1984 The Empire Strikes Back on Video [2:363] 3.00

Hot Dog
____No. 17, 1983, Star Wars action figures article 7.00
____No. 22, 1983, "The Magic of Luke Skywalker" [3:358] 7.00

House of Hammer
____No. 13, article 4.00
____No. 16, articles and poster 8.00

Jack and Jill
____Carrie Fisher, Princess Leia in The Empire Strikes Back [3:358] 6.00
____Yoda, the Jedi Master in The Empire Strikes Back [2:364] 6.00

Kino
____2002 May, Obi-Wan Kenobi cover [2:364] 5.00

Kitbuilders
____Issue 2, Spring 1997, "Customizing Kaiyodo's Boba Fett" [PB34] 22.00

Kuifje
____Vol. 38, No. 5, Return of the Jedi articles 6.00

L'ecran Fantastique
____No. 13, ESB articles 12.00
____No. 31, ROTJ cover and articles 12.00
____No. 33, ESB cover / special effects articles 12.00
____No. 37, ROTJ cover and articles 12.00
____No. 38, ROTJ cover and articles 12.00
____No. 86, 10th Anniversary article 7.00

LA Life
____1996 June 10, "May The Force Continue" [2:364] 4.00

LA Times
____1977 June 14, George Lucas on Opening Night 24.00

Ladies Home Journal
____1983 September, "Jedimania: Why We Love Those Star Warriors" 9.00

Lego Magazine
____2002 May – June, EPII cover [2:364] 3.00
____2004 January, All New Classics [3:358] 3.00

Lego Mania
____1999 March – April: cover and SW articles [2:364]...3.00
____1999 May – June: cover and SW articles 3.00
____2000 March – April: cover and SW articles.........3.00

Life
____1977: The Year In Pictures [2:364] 21.00
____Vol. 4, No. 1, January 1981, Yoda cover 26.00
____Vol. 6, No. 6, June 1983, "Father of the Jedi" [2:364]..12.00

Look-In
____1980 May 20, ESB [PB35] 10.00

Lucas Books
____Star Wars Collectible Bonus Magazine 3.00

LucasArts
____Knights of the Old Republic [3:359] 5.00

Lucasfilm Fan Club
____Any issue with non-Star Wars cover 5.00
____Any issue with Star Wars cover [PB36] 8.00

Mad Magazine
____1978 January No. 196, "Star Bores" [2:364] 16.00
____1979 December No. 203, "The Mad Star Wars Musical" [2:364] 18.00
____1979 March No. 197, "A 'Mad' Look at Star Wars" 15.00
____1981 January No. 220, "The Empire Strikes Out" [2:364] 13.00
____1982 April No. 230, "The Star Wars Log – Mad's version of George Lucas' presonal log" 10.00
____1983 October No. 242, "Star Bores – Rehash of the Jedi" 10.00
____1983 Summer, Mad Supersepcial 11.00
____1996 Star Wars Spectacular [2:364]......................6.00
____1999 September, The Phantom Menace [3:359] 4.00
____Star Wars Macarena [2:364] 6.00

Mad Movies
____1980 No. 20, Empire Strikes Back cover...........10.00

Marvel Super Special
____No. 16, The Empire Strikes Back [PB37]............16.00
____No. 27, Return of the Jedi [PB38] 16.00

Maxximo Evento
____No. 4, El Ataque De Los Clones [PB39] 20.00

Media Spotlight
____1977 October, "Incredible Star Wars" [PB40] 18.00

Mediascene Preview
____Vol. 1, No. 22, November 1976, Star Wars cover and feature news [2:364]...........................35.00

____Vol. 2, No. 11, "Darth Vader returns with a new ally, Boba Fett"...8.00
____Vol. 2, No. 4, August 1980, interview with Mark Hamill 12.00
____Vol. 3, No. 2, interview with Brian Johnson (special effects) 5.00

Metropolis
____2002 July 12, Anakin cover [PB41] 4.00

Midnight Marquee
____No. 29, Yoda cover, Empire Strikes Back review 7.00

Military Modeler
____Vol. 7, No. 11, Millennium Falcon cover...............6.00

Modesto Bee
____1977 June 5, Star Wars 7.00

Monsters
____No. 38, R2-D2 cover 5.00

Movie Aliens Illustrated
____1979 Darth Vader on cover [2:364]........................3.00

Movie Monsters
____Vol. 1, No. 3, Fall 1981, Darth Vader and Bounty Hunters cover 8.00

Movie News
____1977 Sept / Oct., "Star Wars" The Smash Hit of the Year! [2:364] 16.00

Muppet Magazine
____Vol. 1, No. 3, Summer 1983, Muppets dressed as Star Wars characters on cover 14.00

National Enquirer
____1983 June 21, cover shows Shuttle Tydirium, story 5.00

New Times
____1978 June 24, "Why America loves the 'Star Wars' heroes" [PB42] 10.00

New Voyager
____No. 4, Summer 1983, Return of the Jedi articles...5.00

New Yorker
____1997 January 6, George Lucas interview and Star Wars articles 6.00

News 31
____2002 May 9-22, EPII charity preview screening mini-poster inside 12.00

Newsweek
____1977 Special Issue: Pictures of '77 [2:364] 18.00
____Vol. 89, No. 22, May 30, 1977, "Fun In Space"..32.00

Nickelodeon
____1997 March, Star Wars Strikes Back [2:364] 6.50

Night and Day
____2002 April 28, EPII Special Collector's Issue......25.00

NY Times
____1980 December 20, Saga beyond Star Wars 4.00

PB37 PB38 PB39 PB40 PB41 PB42 PB43 PB44 PB45

PB46 PB47 PB48 PB49 PB50 PB51 PB52 PB53 PB54

Publications

Official Souvenir Magazine
____Episode I: The Phantom Menace [3:359] 7.00

OKE
____2002 May, Anakin and Amidala cover [2:364] 5.00

On Location
____Revenge of the Jedi, In Yuma [PB43] 55.00

Orbit and SF Terra Presenteren
____Return of the Jedi special issue 8.00

Orbit
____No. 13, Winter 1981, Empire Strikes Back cover and articles...8.00

Origina
____1999 Julio, Darth Maul cover [2:364] 6.00

Owl
____1982 November, Robots [PB44]............................8.00

Parade
____Issue 324, November 1977, "Elvis – and other Pop tragedies" [2:365] 4.00

Paris Match
____Queen Amidala on cover [2:365] 2.00

People
____1977 July 18, article [2:365] 10.00
____1977, Vol. 8, No. 26, R2-D2 cover, article 14.00
____1978 August 14, Carrie Fisher and Darth Vader on cover, article [PB45] 14.00
____1980 June 9, Yoda cover, article 14.00
____1980, July 7, 1980, Empire Strikes Back on cover and article 14.00
____1981 August 31, Vol. 16, No. 9, Mark Hamill and Yoda cover, Hamill interview [2:365] 12.00
____1983 June 20, Vol. 19, No. 24, Darth Vader cover, article 8.00
____1983 June 6, Carrie Fisher cover, article [2:365]..14.00
____1997 February 3, 20th Anniversary article, focusing on actors 7.00

Photoplay
____1978 February, Star Wars cover [2:365]................6.00
____1978 January, Star Wars cover [2:365] 6.00
____1980 June, Empire Strikes Back cover 8.00

Pizzazz
____No. 1, C-3PO and R2-D2 on cover [PB46] 9.00
____No. 2, Mr. Spock, Alien, Darth Vader on cover [2:365] 9.00

Playboy
____1983 July, "Carrie Fisher answers 20 questions" [2:365]..17.00
____2005, June, "Star Wars Collector's Issue" [PB47] 20.00

Popular Mechanics
____The machines of Star Wars Episode I [PB48] 5.00

Portal
____2002 May, Padme cover [PB49]............................5.00

Posters Monthly
Star Wars (A New Hope)
____No. 1, "May The Force Be With You" [3:360]........8.00
____No. 2, "Darth Vader Lives!" [2:365]........................8.00
____No. 3, "Han Solo – Rogue Spacer" [2:365] 8.00
____No. 4, "Soldiers of the Empire" [2:365] 8.00
____No. 5, "The Threepio File" [2:365] 8.00
____No. 6, "The Spaceships of Star Wars" [2:365]......8.00
____No. 7, "The Droids of Star Wars" [2:365] 8.00
____No. 8, "Ben Kenobi, Man or Legend?" [2:365] 8.00
____No. 9, "Special Issue" [2:365]................................8.00
____No. 10, "The Return of Evil" [2:365] 8.00
____No. 11, "The Men Behind The Masks" [2:365]......8.00
____No. 12, "The Cantina Aliens" [2:365] 8.00
____No. 13, "The Model Squad" [2:365] 8.00
____No. 14, "War in Space – Fact and Fiction" [2:365] 8.00
____No. 15 "Empire Latest"...8.00
____No. 16..12.00
____No. 17, "Escape Through Hyperspace" [2:365]...16.00
____No. 18, "The Empire Gets Closer" [2:365]..........16.00
Empire Strikes Back
____No. 1, "Back In Action!" [3:360] 5.00
____No. 2, "The Dark Lord" [2:365]..............................5.00
____No. 3, "The Mysteries of Yoda" [2:365] 5.00
____No. 4, "AT-AT Attack" [2:365] 5.00
____No. 5, "Han Solo – Hero and Scoundral" (Hoth cover) [2:365] 5.00
____No. 5, "Han Solo – Hero and Scoundral" (Stormtrooper cover) [2:365] 35.00
Return of the Jedi
____No. 1, "At Last The Waiting Is Over!" [3:360]........6.00
____No. 2, "Inside Jabba the Hutt's Court" [2:365] 6.00
____No. 3, "A Close-Up Look At Transport and Weapons" [2:365] 6.00
____No. 4, "In Depth Look At The Space Battle" [2:365] 6.00

Premiere
____1997 February, 20th Anniversary article................3.00
____2002 May, Anakin and Amidala cover [2:365] 5.00

Preview
____1977 September, "Star Wars" [3:360] 4.00

Prevue
____1983 Vol. 2, No. 2, Luke and Leia on Desert Skiff Cover [2:365]..4.00

Questar
____No. 1, 1978, "The Triumph of Star Wars" [PB50] 12.00
____No. 8, August 1980, "The Making of an Empire: Star Wars Returns" 12.00

Radio Times
1999 July 3-9.
____Darth Maul cover [2:365] 2.00
____Obi-Wan Kenobi cover [2:365] 2.00
____Queen Amidala cover [2:365] 2.00
____Qui-Gon Jinn cover [2:365]..................................2.00

Read
____1977 May 11, "A Few Friendly Faces Welcome You to a Weird World" [3:360] 17.00

Reel Fantasy
____No. 1, Star Wars articles [PB51]............................8.00

Republic Scene
____1981 George Lucas standing behind Star Destroyer model [2:366] 14.00

Request
____2002 May / June, Hayden Christiansen gives in to the Dark Side [PB52]..4.00

Return of the Jedi Poster Book
____No. 1 Death Star battle..7.00
____No. 2 Wicket 7.00
____No. 3 Rancor / Han Solo 7.00
____No. 4 Darth Vader / Space Battle..........................8.00

Review
____Vol. 2, No. 12, Luke and Leia cover, interview with Richard Marquand 9.00
____Vol. 2, No. 14, Interview with Billy Dee Williams 10.00

Rolling Stone
____1977 August 25, The Force Behind George Lucas [2:366]..15.00
____1980 August 12, The Empire Strikes Back 15.00
____1980 July 24, "Slaves to the Empire" [2:366] 17.00
____1999 June 24, Free Inside 18"x22" Star Wars poster [2:366]..12.00
____No. 400/401, Darth Vader, Princess Leia on Beach, interviews with George Lucas and Carrie Fisher 25.00

Scholastic Action
____1977 October 8, Luke in Landspeeder on cover [2:366]..11.00

Sci-Fi Entertainment
____1997 February, Star Wars cover [2:366]................6.00
____1998 February, George Lucas Speaks [2:366]......7.00

Sci-Fi Universe
____1994 July, The Next Star Wars Trilogy cover story 9.00
____1995 November, Star Wars Lives cover................6.00

Science and Fantasy
____1977 Winter, Interviews with actors and article on music [PB53]..3.00

Science Fiction Age
____1997 March, "Star Wars Special Issue" [PB54] 5.00

Science Fiction, Horror and Fantasy
____Vol. 1, No. 1, Fall 1997, Star Wars collector edition [2:366] 6.00
____Vol. 1, No. 2, "Mark Hamill reveals the problems in making Star Wars'" [3:360]....................................8.00

Scintillation
____No. 13, June 1977, "George Lucas brings the excitement back" [2:366] 9.00

Screen Superstar
____No. 8, 1977, Star Wars articles [PB55] 10.00

Seventeen
____1983 March 19, interviews on location 6.00

SFTV
____No. 7, Star Wars costumes article 8.00

SFX
____1997 June 1, 4 Stunning FX Shots from Star Wars Trilogy Special Edition [2:366] 7.00
____1997 March, "Discover how Lucasfilm recreated the myth" [2:366]...7.00

Sick
____No. 2, The Empire Strikes Oil [PB56]..................18.00

Sky
____2000 March, "All four hits together on British television" [2:366] 8.00

Space Review
____2002 May, Star Wars Episode II [2:366] 5.00

Space Wars
____1977 October, Star Wars articles [PB57] 10.00
____1978 June, Star Wars vs. Close Encounters comparison article [2:366]..10.00

Star Blaster
____Vol. 1, No. 2, Vader cover, droids article 8.00

Star Encounters
____Vol. 1, No. 1, April 1978, Making of Star Wars article [PB58] 7.00

Star Force
____1981 April, "Star Wars III Preview" [2:366]............9.00
____1981 October, Revenge of the Jedi article 10.00
____Vol. 1, No. 1, "Star Wars II: The Empire Fights Back Again!" [2:366]..6.00
____Vol. 2, No. 3, Darth Vader, Lando, and ESB scenes on cover, Return of the Jedi article 8.00

Star Quest Comix
____Star Wars revisited [2:366] 4.00

Star Warp
____1978 April, includes posters [3:361]......................7.00
____1978 June [3:361] 4.00

Star Wars Adventures
____#01 2002 October, Anakin Skywalker poster........2.00
____#02 2002 December, Obi-Wan Kenobi poster......2.00
____#03 2003 January, Yoda poster [3:361] 2.00
____#04 2003 February, Count Dooku poster..............2.00
____#05 2003 March, C-3PO, The Droid That's Seen it All [PB59] 2.00
____#06 2003 April, Nute Gunray, Jango Fett poster 2.00
____#07 2003 May, Padme, young Boba Fett poster [3:361] 2.00
____#08 2003 June, The Skywalker Family, Padme Amidala poster 2.00
____#09 2003 July, Samuel L. Jackson the Amazing Mace, Mace Windu poster [3:361] 2.00
____#10 2003 August, Vehicles of Star Wars, Kamino poster [3:361] 2.00
____#11 2003 September, Beasts and Creatures, Dexter Jettster poster [3:361]..2.00
____#12 2003 October, Explore the Star Wars Galaxy, Clone Army poster [3:361] 2.00
____#13 2003 November, World of Star Wars, Arena Battle poster [3:361] 2.00

Star Wars Galaxy Collector Magazine
____No. 1: Double sided poster 21"x16" George Lucas '98 Artwork and "Struzan: By The Book" [2:366] 8.00
____No. 2: [2:366] 8.00
____No. 3: 8.00
____No. 4: Double sided poster 21"x16" "One Year Old Today" and "Suitable for Framing" [2:366]............8.00
____No. 5: double sided poster 21"x14" Slave Leia and "Coming to your Galaxy this summer"..................8.00
____No. 6: 8.00
____No. 7: 8.00
____No. 8: Double sided poster 21"x16" and Applause Products for EP1 TPM 1999.................................8.00

Star Wars Galaxy Magazine
____Issue 1 ....15.00

_____Issues 2 – 4, each 12.00
_____Issues 5 – 8, each 10.00
_____Issues 9 – 13, each 7.00

Star Wars Gamer
_____Issue 1 ....6.00
_____Issues 2 – 10, each 4.00

Star Wars Insider
Lucasfilm Fan Club.
_____Issues 1 – 22, each 5.00
Star Wars Insider.
_____Issues 23 – present [PB60], each 3.00

Star Wars Kids
Scholastic. Classic Trilogy. (Checklist in 3rd edition, page 362. Images in 3rd edition, page 361.)
_____#00 Preview issue, Luke Skywalker [2:366] 2.00
_____Issues #1 – 11, each 3.00

Scholastic. Prequel Saga. (Checklist in 3rd edition, page 362.)
_____Issues #1 – 14 [PB61], each 3.00

Star Wars Newspaper
_____1977 Single issue [2:366] 14.00

Star Wars Spectacular
_____Tribute magazine to Star Wars [2:366]................12.00

Star Wars The Official Magazine
_____#1 1998 April/May, Vader cover [2:366] 5.00
_____#2 1998 June/July, Leia cover [2:366] 5.00
_____#3 1998 August/September, C-3PO cover [2:366] 5.00

Star Wars: Making of the World's Greatest Movie
_____1977 Behind the scenes articles 17.00

Starblazer
_____1986 December, Darth Vader cover 6.00

Starburst
_____1987 Winter Special, Star Tours and 10th Annivesary articles 12.00
_____1993 Classic Sci-Fi Special, Star Wars cover 10.00
_____1996 Outer Space Special, Star Wars Special Edition article 8.00
_____1997 March, Revival of Star Wars 5.00
_____No. 1, Star Wars cover 18.00
_____No. 2, "3PO Unmasked" article 15.00
_____No. 3, Star Wars article 12.00
_____No. 8, Empire Strikes Back article 12.00
_____No. 22, Empire Strikes Back article 10.00
_____No. 23, Empire Strikes Back articles and poster 10.00
_____No. 24, Star Wars interviews 8.00
_____No. 25, Empire interviews 8.00
_____No. 26, Empire Strikes Back special effects article 10.00
_____No. 43, Star Wars article 8.00
_____No. 58, Return of the Jedi articles 10.00
_____No. 59, Return of the Jedi articles 10.00
_____No. 60, C-3PO article 8.00
_____No. 61, Carrie Fisher interview 10.00
_____No. 93, Return of the Jedi Video article 5.00
_____No. 208, Snowtrooper cover 8.00
_____No. 223, Darth Vader cover, George Lucas interview 10.00
_____No. 225, Present and future of Star Wars article ..8.00

Starfix
_____1980, Return of the Jedi issue 8.00

Starlog
_____No. 7, X-Wing and Tie fighter on cover [2:366] 34.00
_____No. 8, Star Wars (Sept. 1977) [2:367] 26.00
_____No. 14, Star Wars Matte Painter [3:362] 7.00
_____No. 16, "Invisible Visions of Star Wars" article 8.00
_____No. 17, Effects and Ralph McQuarrie articles 9.00
_____No. 18, "Star Wars" sequel [2:367]......................7.00
_____No. 19, Cantina creatures on cover, Star Wars Holiday Special article [PB62]...15.00

_____No. 24, Science Fiction Spectacular [2:367] 8.00
_____No. 31, Empire Strikes Back cover, review 12.00
_____No. 35, Darth Vader cover [2:367] 9.00
_____No. 36, Boba Fett and Darth Vader cover 10.00
_____No. 37, Millennium Falcon cover 8.00
_____No. 40, Luke and Yoda cover [2:367].....................8.00
_____No. 41, Luke and Yoda cover, Mark Hamill interview 9.00
_____No. 48, Luke and Yoda cover [2:367].....................8.00
_____No. 50, Boba Fett cover [2:367].......................10.00
_____No. 51, Luke Skywalker cover 8.00
_____No. 56, Darth Vader cover 8.00
_____No. 65, Luke Skywalker cover 8.00
_____No. 69, Return of the Jedi cast cover [2:367] 9.00
_____No. 71, Han, Leia and Luke cover, ROTJ articles and interviews 12.00
_____No. 72, Mark Hamill interview 8.00
_____No. 74, Return of the Jedi creatures article 9.00
_____No. 76, Return of the Jedi preview article 9.00
_____No. 80, Return of the Jedi special effects cover and article [2:367]...8.00
_____No. 82, Return of the Jedi special effects article and interview with Emperor [2:367]...........................10.00
_____No. 84, Frank Oz discusses Yoda article 9.00
_____No. 86, Return of the Jedi special effects article 8.00
_____No. 90, Ewok Adventure article 9.00
_____No. 93, Return of the Jedi speeder bike special effects article [2:367] 7.00
_____No. 94, Return of the Jedi special effects article [2:367] 7.00
_____No. 96, Peter Cushing interview 16.00
_____No. 99, C-3PO cover 8.00
_____No. 100, George Lucas interview.......................10.00
_____No. 101, Ewoks live action TV movie [2:367]...11.00
_____No. 104, Chewbacca cover, Peter Mayhew interview [2:367] 9.00
_____No. 115, Star Tours articles 7.00
_____No. 118, George Lucas / Star Tours cover [PB63] 7.00
_____No. 120, 10th Annveriary cover [2:367] 12.00
_____No. 127, George Lucas interview 7.00
_____No. 237, George Lucas explains why he did SW:SE [2:367] 7.00
_____No. 274, Defining Yodaisms [2:367] 7.00
_____Starlog Scrap Book Vol. 1 [2:367] 18.00

Stripschrift
_____No. 142, December 1980, Empire Strikes Back cover, Ralph McQuarrie article 12.00

Sunday Mirror
_____EPI:TPM part 1 [2:367] 5.00
_____EPI:TPM part 2 [2:367] 5.00

Sunday Times
_____The New Star Wars [2:367]...........................5.00

The Big Issue
_____1999 March, "George Lucas" on the Movie of the Year [3:362] 4.00

Tiger Beat Star
_____1977 October, "Star Wars Interview" [2:367] 9.00

Time Magazine
_____1977 May 30, "Years Best Movie: Star Wars" [2:367]...26.00
_____1980 May 19, "The Empire Strikes Back" [2:367]...14.00

_____1983 May 23, "Star Wars III: The Return of the Jedi" [2:367] 14.00
_____1997 February 10, The Return of Star Wars cover [2:367] 8.00
_____1999 April 26, "The Complete Guide to The Phantom Menace" [2:367] 4.00
_____2002 April 29, "Yoda Strikes Back," an exclusive guide to Episode II [PB64] 6.00

Title
_____2002 August, R2-D2 cover, international collectibles / SWCII coverage [3:362] 25.00

Today's Collector
_____1999, Vol. 7 No. 6, "Collecting Star Wars" [2:367] 5.00

Topps
_____20th Anniversary Commerative Magazine, collector version: gold foil logo [2:367]...........................15.00
_____20th Anniversary Commerative Magazine, collector version: gold foil logo, bagged with trading cards [2:367] 19.00
_____20th Anniversary Commerative Magazine, newsstand version: flat ink logo [2:367] 8.00
_____20th Anniversary Commerative Magazine, special collectors version: blue foil logo, bagged with trading cards [2:367] 45.00

Total Film
_____Star Wars, '70s Haircuts, '90s action! [2:367] 3.00

Tribute
_____Classic Trilogy [3:362]...........................5.00

True – UFOs and Outer Space Quarterly
_____No. 19, Fall 1980, AT-ATs on cover, "The Empire Strikes Back...But Not Out!"...........................4.00

Tudorka
_____2002 May, Star Wars II Resz [2:368] 5.00

TV Guide
1999 June 12 – 18.
_____1 of 4 Jar Jar Binks [2:368]...........................3.00
_____2 of 4 Jabba the Hutt [2:368] 3.00
_____3 of 4 ....3.00
_____4 of 4 Boss Nass [2:368] 3.00

1999 May 15 – 21. Combined covers create one picture.
_____1 of 4 Anakin Skywalker [2:368]...........................3.00
_____2 of 4 Qui-Gon Jinn [2:368] 3.00
_____3 of 4 Obi-Wan Kenobi [2:368] 3.00
_____4 of 4 Queen Amidala [2:368] 3.00

2002 May 11 – 17. Lenticular cards adhered to cover.
_____Anakin Skywalker and Obi-Wan / Darth Vader and Ben Kenobi 5.00
_____Anakin Skywalker and Padme Amidala 5.00
_____Anakin Skywalker on Geonosis 5.00

2005 May 1 – 7. Lenticular cards adhered to cover.
_____Anakin and Darth Vader 5.00
_____Padme and Leia [PB65] 5.00
_____The Emperor 5.00
_____The Final Battle 5.00
_____The Wookiees [PB66] 5.00

TV This Week
_____1978 November 12, Washington Star TV Listing with article on 1978 SW Holiday Special...................9.00

PB55 PB56 PB57 PB58 PB59 PB60

PB61 PB62 PB63 PB64 PB65 PB66 PB67 PB68 PB69

Publications

TV Times
____Vancouver, 8-26-77 Star Wars cover [PB67] 25.00

US
____Vol. 4, No. 7, July 22, 1980, "The Good Guys of Star Wars" [2:368] 10.00
____Vol. 8, No. 13, June 20, 1983, Return of the Jedi cover and articles [2:368] 8.00

Vanity Fair
____1999 February, "The Force Is Back At Last!" with Bonus Foldout [2:368] 7.00
____2003 March, "From Real Wars to Star Wars" [3:362] 7.00
____2005, February, "Star Wars Spectacular!" [PB68] 7.00

Variety
____1997 February 3, "Star Wars in Outer Space" 7.00

Video Gaming Illustrated
____1983 February "SW Spectacular" [2:368] 5.00

Vogue
____Natalie Portman – Star Wars Queen 5.00

VOX
____Anakin and Obi-Wan cover [2:368].....................5.00

Weird Worlds
____No. 06, Darth Vader and other monsterous movie meanies [PB69] 6.00

Who Weekly
____2000 Sept. 30, "The new Darth Vader unmasked and on-set secrets revealed" [2:368] 12.00

World Publishers
UK Souvenir Annuals.
____1998 [2:368] 17.00
____2000 [2:368] 12.00

WOW
____1978 Issue 21, Luke and droids on cover [2:368] 4.00

PRC01

PRC02

PRC03

Punch-Out Activities

Frito Lay
Build-a-droids.
____C-3PO [PRC01]..4.00
____R2-D2 [PRC02]..4.00

General Mills
Punch-out spaceships, cereal premiums.
____Landspeeder [PRC03]..11.00
____Millennium Falcon [PRC04] 11.00
____Tie Fighter [PRC05] 11.00
____X-Wing Fighter [PRC06]......................................11.00

Paizo Publishing / Fan Club
____Fan Club 2003 membership mini-standee [PRC07]...5.00

Puppets

Applause
____Jar Jar Binks, latex [YE01] 20.00
____Yoda, latex [YE02] 20.00

Disney / MGM
____Ewok, green hood [YE03]....................................26.00

Kenner
____Yoda hand puppet [YE04] 65.00

Palitoy
____Yoda hand puppet 65.00

Regal
____Chewbacca hand puppet 850.00

Puppets: Paper

Frigo
Food premiums.
____Boba Fett [2:369] 4.00
____C-3PO [2:369] 4.00
____Caza Imperial (Tie Fighter) [2:369] 4.00
____Chewbacca [2:369] 4.00
____Emperador (Emperor) [2:369] 4.00
____Estrella de la Muerte (Death Star) [2:369].............4.00
____Ewock [2:369] 4.00
____Halcon Milenario (Millennium Falcon) [2:369].........4.00
____Han Solo [2:369] 4.00
____Jabba [2:369] 4.00
____Lord Vader [2:369] 4.00
____Luke [2:369] 4.00
____Obi-Wan [2:369] 4.00

____Princess Leia [2:369]...4.00
____R2-D2 [2:369] 4.00
____Soldado Imperial (Stormtrooper) [2:369] 4.00
____X-Wing [2:369] 4.00
____Yoda [2:369] 4.00

Purses / Carry Bags

Accessory Network
____ANH art / Darth Vader reversible 35.00
____Darth Vader [PC01]...35.00
____Darth Vader / Revenge [PC02]............................35.00

Adam Joseph Industries
____Ewoks 10.00
____Princess Kneesa, shaped [PC03]........................35.00
____Princess Kneesaa and Wicket 12.00
____Wicket the Ewok 10.00
____Wicket the Ewok, shaped 12.00

Giftware International
____Chewbacca [PC04] 17.00
____Darth Vader [PC05]...17.00
____Jar Jar Binks [PC06] 14.00
____R2-D2 [PC07] 17.00

Kathrine Baumann Design
____Queen Amidala miniaudiere, limited to 75 [PC08]..475.00

Push Pins

Rose Art Industries
____Star Wars set of 12 [PP01] 7.00

Radios and Cassette Players

Kenner
____Luke Skywalker AM headset radio [HM01]......525.00
____R2-D2 radio [HM02]...225.00

Micro Games of America
____C-3PO AM/FM Radio..30.00
____Darth Vader AM/FM Radio 18.00
____Millennium Falcon cassette player.......................34.00

Takara
____R2-D2, "Drink Coca-Cola" [HM04] 325.00

Tiger Electronics
____R2-D2 Data Droid [HM05] 35.00
____R2-D2, flat with belt clip 24.00

PRC04

PRC05

PRC06

PRC07

YE01

YE02

YE03

YE04

PC01

PC02

PC03

PC04

PC05

PC06

PC07

PC08

PP01

HM01

HM02

HM03

HM04 boxed and open

HM05

HM06

Remote Controls

Kash 'N' Gold
____Lightsaber Universal Remote Control with sound effects [RMC01] 35.00

Telemania
____Darth Maul's Sith Infiltrator universal remote [RMC02] 40.00

RMC01

RMC02

Replicas

Code 3 Collectibles
____AT-ST vehicle [REP01] 400.00
____Darth Vader's TIE Fighter Signature Series, limited to 500......................................500.00
____Darth Vader's TIE Fighter, limited to 5,000 ......365.00
____Millennium Falcon 300.00
____Republic Gunship [REP02] 315.00
____Skywalker Ranch Engine 1589 with replica patch, limited to 7,500....................................300.00
____Slave I, limited to 5,000 [REP03]......................300.00
____Slave I, limited to 500 signature series 500.00
____X-Wing fighter, Red Five, limited to 1,000 signature series 500.00
____X-Wing fighter, Red Five, limited to 5,000 [REP04] 300.00

Don Post
Life size, cast from original props.
____Boba Fett [3:369] 6,000.00
____See Threepio....................................15,000.00
____Stormtrooper, limited to 500 pieces [3:369] 4,500.00

Icons Authentic Replicas
Replicas in plexiglass display cases.
____Lightsaber, Darth Vader's, limited to 10,000 [REP05]..................................350.00
____Lightsaber, Luke Skywalker's, limited to 10,000 ....350.00
____Lightsaber, Obi-Wan Kenobi's, limited to 10,000 ....350.00
____Tie Fighter, limited to 1,977 ....1,500.00
____X-Wing Fighter, limited to 1,977 [REP06] 1,950.00

Illusive Originals
Life-sized.
____Han Solo in Carbonite prop replica, limited to 2,500 [3:369] 2,800.00

Master Replicas
____AT-AT vehicle [REP07] 400.00
____Boba Fett's Blaster, limited edition 580.00
____Boba Fett's Blaster, signature edition 680.00
____Darth Vader helmet, 1:1 using original studio molds 1,000.00
____Darth Vader helmet, 1:1 using original studio molds, signature edition (Hayden Christensen) limited to 500 ....1,600.00
____Emperor's cane, limited to 1,500 [REP08] 225.00

____Han Solo's Blaster 650.00
____Jango Fett blaster set, limited to 1,500 [REP09] 475.00
____Jedi Training Remote, limited to 2,500 [REP10] 250.00
____Lightsaber, Anakin Skywalker FX edition 130.00
____Lightsaber, Anakin Skywalker LE 360.00
____Lightsaber, Anakin Skywalker ROTS...................500.00
____Lightsaber, Count Dooku, limited to 3,500 pieces [REP11] 300.00
____Lightsaber, Darth Maul's, limited to 2,500........450.00
____Lightsaber, Darth Maul's, signature series, limited to 1,000 ....560.00
____Lightsaber, Darth Maul battle damaged 350.00
____Lightsaber, Darth Maul FX edition, dual 250.00
____Lightsaber, Darth Maul FX edition, single 175.00
____Lightsaber, Darth Vader's Empire Strikes Back Limited to 2000 ....350.00
____Lightsaber, Darth Vader's FX edition 130.00
____Lightsaber, Darth Vader's, limited to 7,500 [REP12] 350.00
____Lightsaber, Darth Vader's, signature series, limited to 1,000 ....1,200.00
____Lightsaber, Luke Skywalker's FX edition..........130.00
____Lightsaber, Luke Skywalker's, limited to 3,500 [REP13] 350.00
____Lightsaber, Mace Windu's FX edition 130.00
____Lightsaber, Mace Windu's, limited to 1,750 ......450.00
____Lightsaber, Obi-Wan Kenobi's, limited to 3,500 [REP14] 350.00
____Lightsaber, Obi-Wan Kenobi's, weathered [REP15] 500.00
____Lightsaber, Yoda's [REP16] 300.00
____Lightsaber, Yoda's EPIII ROTS limited edition 250.00
____Medal of Yavin 200.00
____Princess Leia blaster 400.00
____Rebel blaster 400.00
____Stormtrooper blaster 400.00
____Thermal Detonator, "as built by" edition, limited to 750......................................265.00
____Thermal Detonator, limited to 1,000 [REP17] 225.00
____Thermal Detonator, signature edition, limited to 750 ....335.00

Collector's Society memberhship kit.
____Card, Darth Maul .45 saber, Darth Vader patch, report [REP18]..45.00

Lightsabers .45 scale.
____Anakin Skywalker, black chrome, StarWarsShop.com exclusive [REP19]................................65.00

____Anakin Skywalker, ROTS 45.00
____Count Dooku..45.00
____Count Dooku, 18k gold, 250 produced............150.00
____Darth Maul 45.00
____Darth Sidious, Best Buy exclusive [REP20]..65.00
____Darth Sidious, chrome Eurpean exclusive, limited to 5,000..75.00
____Darth Vader..45.00
____Luke Skywalker [REP21] 45.00
____Luke Skywalker, ROTJ, limited to 1,500, eBay exclusive 65.00
____Mace Windu [REP22] 45.00
____Mace Windu, 18k gold, 250 produced 175.00
____Obi-Wan Kenobi [REP23]..............................45.00
____Obi-Wan Kenobi 18k gold, 150 produced, Celebration 3 exclusive 375.00
____Obi-Wan Kenobi ANH, as first built, 18k gold, Collector Society exclusive 125.00
____Obi-Wan Kenobi ANH, weathered, limited to 500, Wal-mart exclusive 45.00
____Obi-Wan Kenobi prequel, as first built, 18k gold, 250 produced, 2004 convention exclusive 175.00
____Obi-Wan Kenobi prequel, as first built, 2004 convention exclusive [REP24] 45.00
____Obi-Wan Kenobi, Celebration 3 exclusive [REP25]..45.00
____Yoda, black chrome, 2005 Comic-con exclusive [REP26]..65.00
____Yoda, chrome Eurpean exclusive, limited to 5,000 ....75.00

.45 scle lightsaber plexiglass display cases.
____Jedi Collection 45.00
____Sith Collection 45.00
____Star Wars 35.00

Vehicles. Studeo scale.
____Millennium Falcon......................................N/V
____Y-Wing Studio 1,575.00

Rubies
____Darth Vader life size display figure 4,500.00

Shepperton Design Studios
____Stormtrooper ANH Stunt Helmets from original molds 850.00

Tomy
Lightsabers.
____Darth Vader 325.00
____Luke Skywalker 325.00

REP01

REP02

REP03

REP04

REP05

REP06

REP07

REP08

REP09

REP10

REP11

REP12

REP13

REP14

REP15

REP16

REP17

REP18

REP19

REP20

REP21

REP22

REP23

REP24

REP25

REP26

Role Playing Game

RPG01 RPG02 RPG03 RPG04 RPG05 RPG06 RPG07 RPG08 RPG09 RPG10 RPG11 RPG12 RPG13 RPG14

RPG15 RPG16 RPG17 RPG18 RPG19 RPG20 RPG21 RPG22 RPG23 RPG24 RPG25 RPG26

Role Playing Game

TSR Hobbies
____ Gamemaster Screen [RPG01] 10.00

West End Games
Adventure journals. Star Wars element pictured on cover.
____ 1 B-Wing [RPG02] 17.00
____ 2 Rancor [RPG03] 14.00
____ 3 Stormtrooper [RPG04] 15.00
____ 4 Royal Guard [RPG05] 12.00
____ 5 2-1B [RPG06] 12.00
____ 6 Millennium Falcon [RPG07] 12.00
____ 7 X-Wing and TIE Fighter [RPG08] 12.00
____ 8 Santa Yoda [RPG09] 12.00
____ 9 Bounty hunters [RPG10] 12.00
____ 10 Hoth battle [RPG11] 12.00
____ 11 Speederbike [RPG12] 12.00
____ 12 Mos Eisley [RPG13] 12.00
____ 13 Star Destroyer [RPG14] 12.00
____ 14 Y-Wing [RPG15] 15.00
____ 15 Luke in X-Wing gear [RPG16] 15.00

Adventure supplements.
____ Battle for the Golden Sun [RPG17] 12.00
____ Black Ice 12.00
____ Black Sands of Socorro [RPG18] 14.00
____ Classic Adventures [RPG19] 16.00
____ Classic Adventures II [RPG20] 15.00
____ Classic Adventures III [RPG21] 16.00
____ Classic Adventures IV [RPG22] 15.00
____ Crisis on Cloud City 12.00
____ Darkstryder Campaign [RPG23] 14.00
____ Darkstryder Campaign: Endgame [RPG24] 17.00
____ Darkstryder Supplement: Kathol Rift 18.00
____ Death in the Undercity 12.00
____ Domain of Evil 12.00
____ Flashpoint: Brak Sector 13.00
____ Goroth [RPG25] 12.00
____ Graveyard of Alderaan 12.00
____ Imperial Double-Cross [RPG26] 18.00
____ Instant Adventures [RPG27] 14.00
____ Isis Coordinates 12.00

____ Live Action Adventures [RPG28] 20.00
____ Mission to Lianna 12.00
____ No Disintegrations 20.00
____ Otherspace [RPG29] 12.00
____ Otherspace II: Invasion [RPG30] 12.00
____ Planet of the Mists 12.00
____ Riders of the Maelstrom [RPG31] 12.00
____ Scavenger Hunt [RPG32] 12.00
____ Secrets of the Sisar Run [RPG33] 14.00
____ Starfall 12.00
____ Strike Force: Shantipole [RPG34] 12.00
____ Supernova [RPG35] 13.00
____ Tapanu Sector [RPG36] 18.00
____ Tatooine Manhunt [RPG37] 12.00
____ The Abduction 14.00
____ The Game Chambers of Questal [RPG38] 12.00
____ The Politics of Contraband [RPG39] 12.00
____ Twin Stars of Kira 13.00

Background books.
____ Cracken's Rebel Field Guide [RPG40] 18.00
____ Cracken's Rebel Operatives [RPG41] 18.00
____ Creatures of the Galaxy [RPG42] 18.00
____ Death Star Technical Companion [RPG43] 18.00
____ Droids [RPG44] 16.00
____ Galladinium's Fantastic Technology 18.00
____ Hideouts and Strongholds [RPG45] 18.00
____ Operation: Elrod [RPG46] 12.00
____ Pirates and Privateers 18.00
____ Planets of the Galaxy Vol. I [RPG47] 18.00
____ Planets of the Galaxy Vol. II [RPG48] 18.00
____ Planets of the Galaxy Vol. III [RPG49] 18.00
____ Platt's Starport Guide 25.00
____ Shadows of the Empire Planets Guide [RPG50] 18.00
____ Star Wars Planet Collection 25.00
____ Wanted by Cracken 18.00
____ Wretched Hives of Scum and Villainy [RPG51] 17.00

Galaxy guides.
____ 1 A New Hope [RPG52] 14.00
____ 2 Yavin and Bespin [RPG53] 14.00
____ 3 The Empire Strikes Back, either cover [RPG54] 14.00

____ 4 Alien Races 14.00
____ 5 Return of the Jedi [RPG55] 14.00
____ 6 Tramp Freighters [RPG56] 14.00
____ 7 Mos Eisley 14.00
____ 8 Scouts [RPG57] 14.00
____ 9 Fragments from the Rim 14.00
____ 10 Bounty Hunters 14.00
____ 11 Criminal Organizations 14.00
____ 12 Aliens 14.00

Gamemaster equipment.
____ Gamemasters Handbook, 2nd ed. [RPG58] 24.00
____ Gamemasters Kit [RPG59] 18.00
____ Gamemasters Screen [RPG60]..................8.00
____ Gamemasters Screen handbook 24.00
____ Gamemasters Screen, 2nd edition [RPG61] 8.00

Rule books.
____ Introductory game rulebook [RPG62] 24.00
____ Star Wars: The Role Playing Game primary, 2nd edition [RPG63] 20.00
____ Star Wars: The Role Playing Game, companion 18.00
____ Star Wars: The Role Playing Game, primary [RPG64] 22.00

Sourcebooks.
____ Classic Campaigns [RPG65] 14.00
____ Dark Empire [RPG66] 17.00
____ Dark Force Rising [RPG67] 17.00
____ Han Solo and the Corporate Sector [RPG68] 17.00
____ Heir to the Empire [RPG69] 17.00
____ Imperial [RPG70] 17.00
____ Last Command [RPG71] 17.00
____ Movie Trilogy 17.00
____ Rebel Alliance, either cover [RPG72]........17.00
____ Shadows of the Empire 25.00
____ Star Wars, either cover [RPG73] 17.00
____ The Truce at Bakura [RPG74] 15.00

West End Games, Brazil
Adventure supplements.
____ Batalla por el Sol Dorado [RPG75] 15.00

RPG27 RPG28 RPG29 RPG30 RPG31 RPG32 RPG33 RPG34 RPG35 RPG36 RPG37 RPG38

RPG39 RPG40 RPG41 RPG42 RPG43 RPG44 RPG45 RPG46 RPG47 RPG48 RPG49 RPG50 RPG51

RPG52 RPG53 RPG54 RPG54 RPG55 RPG56 RPG57 RPG58 RPG59 RPG60 RPG61 RPG62 RPG63

RPG64 | RPG65 | RPG66 | RPG67 | RPG68 | RPG69 | RPG70 | RPG71 | RPG72 | RPG72 | RPG73

RPG73 | RPG74 | RPG75 | RPG76 | RPG77 | RPG78 | RPG79 | RPG80 | RPG81 | RPG82 | RPG83 | RPG84

RPG85 | RPG86 | RPG87 | RPG88 | RPG89 | RPG90 | RPG91 | RPG92 | RPG93 | RPG94 | RPG95

RPG96 | RPG97 | RPG98 | RPG99 | RPG100 | RPG101 | RPG102 | RPG103 | RPG104 | RPG105 | RPG106 | RPG107

Role Playing Miniatures

RPM01 RPM02 RPM03 RPM04 RPM05 RPM06 RPM07 RPM08 RPM09 RPM10

RPM11 RPM12 RPM13 RPM14 RPM15 RPM16 RPM17 RPM18 RPM19 RPM20

RPM21 RPM22 RPM23 RPM24 RPM25 RPM26 RPM27 RPM28 RPM29 RPM30 RPM31 RPM32 RPM33 RPM34

RPM35 RPM36 RPM37

____Clone Commander Gree #23 (R) 8.00
____Corran Horn #52 (R) 8.00
____Coruscant Guard #46 (C) 0.50
____Crab Droid #39 (U) 4.00
____Dark Jedi #7 (U) 1.00
____Dark Jedi Master #8 (U) 1.00
____Dark Side Enforcer #9 (U) 1.00
____Dark Trooper Phase I #47 (C) 0.50
____Dark Trooper Phase II #48 (U) 1.00
____Darth Bane #10 (V) 23.00
____Darth Malak #11 (V) 20.00
____Darth Maul, Champion of the Sith #40 (R) 16.00
____Darth Nihilus #12 (V) 24.00
____Darth Sidious, Dark Lord of the Sith #41 (R) 12.00
____Darth Vader, Champion of the Sith #49 (V) 20.00
____Depa Billaba #24 (R) 9.00
____Even Piell #25 (R) 8.00
____Exar Kun #13 (V) 24.00
____General Windu #26 (R) 12.00

RPM38 RPM39 RPM40

____Gundark #56 (U) 0.50
____HK-47 #57 (V) 20.00
____Hoth Trooper with ATGAR Cannon #43 (R) 14.00
____Jacen Solo #53 (V) 16.00
____Jaina Solo #54 (V) 21.00
____Jedi Consular #2 (U) 1.00
____Jedi Guardian #3 (U) 1.00
____Jedi Padawan #27 (U) 0.50
____Jedi Sentinel #4 (U) 1.00
____Jedi Weapon Master #28 (U) 2.00
____Kashyyyk Trooper #29 (C) 0.50
____Luke Skywalker, Young Jedi #44 (V) 18.00
____Mas Amedda #30 (R) 8.00
____Massassi Sith Mutant #14 (U) 0.50
____Octuptarra Droid #42 (R) 9.00
____Old Republic Commander #5 (U) 1.00
____Old Republic Soldier #6 (C) 0.50
____Queen Amidala #31 (R) 10.00
____Qui-Gon Jinn, Jedi Master #32 (R) 9.00
____R5 Astromech Droid #58 (C) 0.50
____Republic Commando – Boss #33 (U) 0.50
____Republic Commando – Fixer #34 (C) 0.50
____Republic Commando – Scorch #35 (C) 0.50
____Republic Commando – Sev #36 (C) 0.50
____Saleucami Trooper #37 (C) 0.50
____Sandtrooper 50 (C) 0.50
____Sith Assault Droid #15 (U) 2.00
____Sith Trooper #16 (C) 0.50
____Sith Trooper #17 (C) 0.50
____Sith Trooper Commander #18 (U) 1.50
____Snowtrooper with E-Web Blaster #51 (R) 12.00
____Ugnaught Demolitionist #59 (C) 0.50
____Ulic Qel-Droma #19 (V) 16.00
____Utapau Trooper #38 (C) 0.50
____Varactyl Wrangler #60 (C) 0.50
____Yoda of Dagobah #45 (V) 18.00

Miniatures Game. Clone Strike Game.

____Booster Pack: Clone Trooper graphic [RPM45] 12.00
____Booster Pack: Mace Windu graphic [RPM46] 12.00
____Booster Pack: Super Battle Droid graphic [RPM47] 12.00
____Starter Set [RPM48] 20.00

Miniatures Game. Clone Strike miniatures.

____Aayla Secura (VR) 20.00
____Aerial Clone Trooper Captain (R) 17.00
____Agen Kolar (R) 6.00
____Anakin Skywalker (VR) 20.00
____Aqualish Spy (C) 0.50
____ARC Trooper (UC) 5.00
____Asajj Ventress (R) 16.00
____Aurra Sing (VR) 54.00
____Battle Droid (C) 0.50
____Battle Droid Officer (UC) 2.00
____Battle Droid on STAP (R) 10.00
____Captain Typho (R) 10.00
____Clone Trooper (C) 0.50
____Clone Trooper Commander (UC) 2.00
____Clone Trooper Grenadier (C) 0.50
____Clone Trooper Sergeant (C) 0.50
____Count Dooku (VR) 26.00
____Dark Side Acolyte (UC) 7.00
____Darth Maul (VR) 44.00
____Darth Sidious (VR) 26.00
____Destroyer Droid (R) 24.00
____Devaronian Bounty Hunter (C) 0.50
____Durge (R) 14.00
____Dwarf Spider Droid (R) 12.00
____General Grievous (VR) 18.00
____General Kenobi (R) 8.00
____Geonosian Drone (C) 0.50
____Geonosian Overseer (UC) 1.00
____Geonosian Picador on Orray (R) 16.00
____Geonosian Soldier (UC) 1.00
____Gran Raider (C) 0.50
____Gungan Cavalry on Kaadu (R) 7.00
____Gungan Infantry (C) 0.50
____Ishi Tib Scout (UC) 1.00
____Jango Fett (R) 14.00
____Jedi Guardian (UC) 1.00
____Ki-Adi-Mundi (R) 15.00
____Kit Fisto (R) 14.00
____Klatooinian Enforcer (C) 0.50
____Luminara Unduli (R) 12.00
____Mace Windu (VR) 27.00
____Naboo Soldier (UC) 1.00
____Nikto Soldier (C) 0.50
____Padme Amidala (VR) 22.00

RPM41 RPM42 RPM43 RPM44 RPM45 RPM46 RPM47 RPM48 RPM49 RPM50 RPM51 RPM52

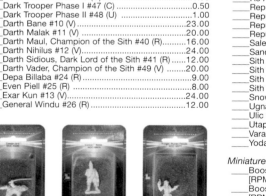

____Plo Koon (R) 12.00
____Quarren Raider (UC) 1.00
____Qui-Gon Jinn (VR) 24.00
____Quinlan Vos (VR)..26.00
____Rodian Mercenary (UC) 1.00
____Saesee Tiin (R) 15.00
____Security Battle Droid (C).......................................0.50
____Super Battle Droid (UC) 1.00
____Weequay Mercenary (C) 0.50
____Wookiee Commando (UC) 1.00
____Yoda (VR) 27.00
____Zam Wesell (R) 15.00

Miniatures Game. Rebel Storm Game.
____Booster Pack: Boba Fett graphic 12.00
____Booster Pack: Han Solo graphic 12.00
____Booster Pack: Stormtrooper graphic..................12.00
____Starter Set 20.00

Miniatures Game. Rebel Storm miniatures promotional pieces.
____Elite Stormtrooper (P), Comic Con 2004 exclusive..15.00
____MonCalimari Officer (P), Origins exclusive.........15.00

Miniatures Game. Rebel Storm miniatures.
____4-LOM (R) 8.00
____Bespin Guard (C) 0.50
____Boba Fett (VR) 35.00
____Bossk (R)...5.00
____Bothan Spy (U) 1.00
____C-3P0 (R) 6.00
____Chewbacca (R) 6.00
____Commando on Speeder Bike (VR).......................18.00
____Darth Vader, Dark Jedi (R) 8.00
____Darth Vader, Sith Lord (VR) 13.00
____Dengar (R) 6.00
____Duros Mercenary (U)..1.00
____Elite Hoth Trooper (U) 1.00
____Elite Rebel Trooper (C) 0.50
____Elite Snowtrooper (U) 1.00
____Elite Stormtrooper (U) 1.00
____Emperor Palpatine (VR) 20.00
____Ewok (C) 0.50
____Gamorrean Guard (U) 1.00
____General Veers (R) 5.00
____Grand Moff Tarkin (R) 5.00
____Greedo (R)...5.00
____Han Solo (R) 11.00
____Heavy Stormtrooper (U) 1.00
____Hoth Trooper (C) 0.50
____IG-88 (R) 7.00
____Imperial Officer (U) 1.00
____Ithorian Scout (U) 1.00
____Jabba the Hutt (VR) 18.00
____Jawa (C) 0.50
____Lando Calrissian (R) 8.00
____Luke Skywalker, Jedi Knight (VR) 16.00
____Luke Skywalker, Rebel (R) 18.00
____Mara Jade, Emperor's Hand (R).............................12.00
____Mon Calamari Mercenary (C) 0.50
____Obi-Wan Kenobi (VR) 19.00
____Princess Leia, Captive (VR) 12.00
____Princess Leia, Senator (R) 7.00
____Probe Droid (VR)..18.00
____Quarren Assassin (U) 1.00
____R2-D2 (R) 12.00
____Rebel Commando (U) 1.00
____Rebel Officer (U) 1.00
____Rebel Pilot (C)..0.50
____Rebel Trooper (C) 0.50
____Rebel Trooper (C) 0.50
____Royal Guard (U) 1.00
____Sandtrooper on Dewback (VR) 20.00
____Scout Trooper (U) 1.00
____Scout Trooper on Speeder Bike (VR)....................20.00
____Snowtrooper (C) 0.50
____Stormtrooper (C) 0.50
____Stormtrooper (C) 0.50
____Stormtrooper (C) 0.50
____Stormtrooper Officer (U) 1.00
____Tusken Raider (C) 0.50
____Tusken Raider (P) 5.00
____Twi'lek Bodyguard (U)...1.00
____Twi'lek Scoundrel (C) 0.50
____Wampa (VR) 20.00
____Wookiee Soldier (C) 0.50
____Wookiee Soldier (P)...5.00

Miniatures Game. Revenge of the Sith Game.
____Booster Pack: Anakin Skywalker [RPM49] 10.00
____Booster Pack: Darth Sidious [RPM50]................10.00
____Booster Pack: Yoda [RPM51].................................10.00
____Starter Set [RPM52] 20.00

Miniatures Game. Revenge of the Sith miniatures.
____Agen Kolar, Jedi Master #1 (R).............................8.00
____Alderaan Trooper #2 (U) 1.00
____Anakin Skywalker, Jedi Knight #3 (R) 12.00
____Anakin Skywalker, Sith Apprentice #56 (VR) 25.00
____AT-RT #4 (VR) 22.00
____Bail Organa #5 (VR) 9.00
____Battle Droid #25 (C) 0.50
____Battle Droid #26 (C) 0.50
____Boba Fett, Young Mercenary #42 (R) 8.00
____Bodyguard Droid #27 (U) 1.00
____Bodyguard Droid #28 (U) 1.00
____Captain Antilles #6 (R) 5.00
____Chagrian Mercenary Commander #43 (U) 1.00
____Chewbacca of Kashyyyk #7 (VR)........................12.00
____Clone Trooper #8 (C)...0.50
____Clone Trooper #9 (C)...0.50
____Clone Trooper Commander #10 (U) 1.00
____Clone Trooper Gunner #11 (C) 0.50
____Dark Side Adept #57 (U)..1.00
____Darth Tyranus #29 (R)...12.00
____Darth Vader #58 (VR) 20.00
____Destroyer Droid #30 (R) 14.00
____Devaronian Soldier #44 (C)......................................0.50
____Emperor Palpatine, Sith Lord #59 (VR) 28.00
____General Grievous, Jedi Hunter #31 (VR) 28.00
____General Grievous, Supreme Commander #32 (R)...6.00
____Gotal Fringer #45 (U) 1.00
____Grievous's Wheel Bike #33 (VR)..........................17.00
____Human Mercenary #46 (U) 1.00
____Iktotchi Tech Specialist #47 (U) 1.00
____Jedi Knight #12 (U) 1.00
____Mace Windu, Jedi Master #13 (VR) 22.00
____Medical Droid #48 (R) 7.00
____Mon Mothma #14 (VR) 9.00
____Muun Guard #34 (U) 1.00
____Nautolan Soldier #49 (C)..0.50
____Neimoidian Soldier #36 (U) 1.00
____Neimoidian Soldier #35 (U).......................................1.00
____Obi-Wan Kenobi #15 (R) 10.00
____Polis Massa Medic #16 (C)..0.50
____R2-D2, Astromech Droid #17 (VR)........................18.00
____Royal Guard #60 (U) 1.00
____San Hill #37 (R)..4.00
____Senate Guard #18 (U) 1.00
____Separatist Commando #38 (C)..................................0.50
____Shaak Ti #19 (R)...12.00
____Sly Moore #50 (R) 5.00
____Stass Allie #20 (R)...8.00
____Super Battle Droid #39 (C) 0.50
____Super Battle Droid #40 (C) 0.50
____Tarfful #21 (R) 5.00
____Tion Medon #51 (R) 7.00
____Utapaun Soldier #52 (C) 0.50
____Utapaun Soldier #53 (C) 0.50
____Wat Tambor #41 (R) 5.00
____Wookiee Berserker #22 (C)......................................0.50
____Wookiee Scout #23 (U) 1.00
____Yoda, Jedi Master #24 (R) 20.00
____Yuzzem #54 (C)..0.50
____Zabrak Fringer #55 (C) 0.50

Miniatures Game. Star Wars: Universe.
____Abyssin Black Sun Thug #12 (C) 0.50
____Acklay #13 (Huge U) 12.00
____Admiral Ackbar #43 (VR) 12.00
____ASP-7 #14 (U)...4.00
____AT-ST #33 (HUGE R) 14.00
____B'omarr Monk #15 (R) 7.00
____Baron Fel #34 (VR) 10.00
____Battle Droid #6 (U) 1.00
____Bith Rebel #44 (C)..0.50
____Chewbacca, Rebel Hero #45 (R) 10.00
____Clone Trooper #1 (C)...0.50
____Clone Trooper on BARC Speeder #2 (HUGE R) 14.00
____Dark Side Marauder #35 (U)....................................6.00
____Dark Trooper Phase III #36 (U) 4.00
____Darth Maul on Sith Speeder #7 (VR) 19.00
____Darth Vader, Jedi Hunter #37 (R) 20.00
____Dash Rendar #16 (R) 8.00
____Dr. Evazan #17 (VR) 8.00
____Dresselian Commando #46 (C)..................................0.50
____Elite Clone Trooper #3 (U)..1.00
____Flash Speeder #4 (U) 8.00
____Gonk Power Droid #18 (C) 2.00
____Grand Admiral Thrawn #38 (VR) 24.00
____Guri #19 (R)...1.00
____Hailfire Droid #8 (HUGE U).....................................12.00
____Han Solo, Rebel Hero #47 (R) 11.00
____Kaminoan Ascetic #20 (C) 0.50
____Kyle Katarn #52 (VR) 12.00
____Lando Calrissian, Hero of Tanaab #21 (R) 6.00
____Lobot #22 (R) 7.00
____Luke Skywalker, Jedi Master #53 (VR)..................25.00
____Luke Skywalker on Tauntaun #48 (R)...................12.00
____New Republic Commander #54 (C) 0.50
____New Republic Trooper #55 (C) 0.50
____Nexu #23 (U) 4.00
____Nien Nunb #49 (R) 6.00
____Nightsister Sith Witch #39 (U) 5.00
____Noghri #40 (U)...6.00
____Nom Anor #57 (R)...9.00
____Nute Gunray #9 (R)...6.00
____Obi-Wan Kenobi on Boga #5 (HUGE VR) 23.00
____Ponda Baba #24 (R) 6.00
____Prince Xizor #25 (VR) 16.00
____Princess Leia, Rebel Hero #50 (R).........................12.00
____Rancor #26 (HUGE VR) 31.00
____Reek #27 (HUGE U) 12.00
____Rodian Black Sun Vigo #28 (U) 2.00
____Shistavanen Pilot #29 (U) 1.00
____Stormtrooper #41 (C) 0.50
____Stormtrooper Commander #42 (U)...........................1.00
____Super Battle Droid #10 (C) 0.50
____Super Battle Droid Commander #11 (U) 4.00
____Tusken Raider on Bantha #30 (HUGE U) 9.00
____Vornskr #31 (C) 0.50
____Warmaster Tsavong Lah #58 (VR) 14.00
____Wedge Antilles #51 (R) 8.00
____X-1 Viper Droid #32 (HUGE U) 8.00
____Young Jedi Knight #56 (C) 0.50
____Yuuzhan Vong Subaltern #59 (U) 2.00
____Yuuzhan Vong Warrior #60 (C) 0.50

Miniatures Game.
____AT-AT Imperial Walker Colossal Pack 65.00

Scenario Packs.
____Attack on Endor. Includes an AT-ST, 3 stormtroopers, 4 maps, abbreviated scenario book 50.00
____Rancor Attack! 35.00

Starship Battles game.
____Huge booster 15.00
____Starter Set 40.00

Rugs

____C-3PO and R2-D2 area rug [RU01] 19.00
____Podracing, 26"x43" [RU02] 12.00

Skywalker Ranch
____Skywalker Ranch [3:371] 125.00

Rulers

____ROTJ, box of 12 ....144.00

Butterfly Originals
____6" with ROTJ logo and battle scenes 8.00
____12" with ROTJ logo and characters on glossy label [SUR01] 10.00
____12" with SW logo and ROTJ vehicles and characters...12.00

Flomo
____18cm Hoth scene, lenticular [SUR02] 5.00

Grand Toys
____Battle Droids [SUR03]...3.00
____Darth Maul [SUR04] 3.00
____Queen Amidala, art [SUR05]..................................3.00
____Queen Amidala, jewelry [SUR06] 3.00

Grosvenor
____6" Clone Trooper [SUR07] 3.00

HC Ford
____6" Return of the Jedi [SUR08] 7.00

Helix
____12" with stormtroopers pressed on back [SUR09] 18.00

Impact, Inc.
EPI: The Phantom Menace.
____12" Stencil [SUR10] 5.00

RU01

RU02

Rulers

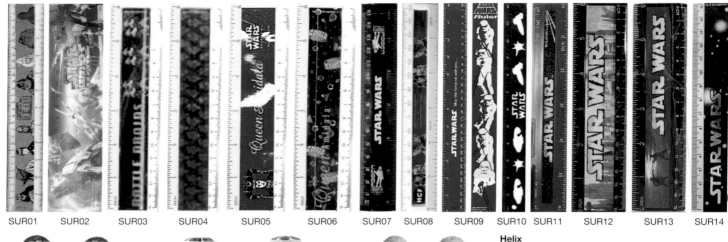

SUR01 SUR02 SUR03 SUR04 SUR05 SUR06 SUR07 SUR08 SUR09 SUR10 SUR11 SUR12 SUR13 SUR14

HOY01　　　　HOY02　　　　HOY03

Jollibee
____Yoda tape measure 15.00

Merlin
____Darth Vader, TIE fighter..3.00
____SW logo on red ruler [SUR11] 3.00

Pyramid
EPII: Attack of the Clones.
____6" Corsucant [SUR12] 2.00
____6" Duel [SUR13] 2.00

Q-Stat
____Star Wars logo in space [SUR14]..........................3.00

Salt Shakers

Japan, 1998.
____Yoda salt and pepper shakers, green feet, different
eye paint then Sigma [HOY01] 145.00

Sigma
____R2-D2 and R5-D4 [HOY02] 225.00
____Yoda stamped Sigma on bottom [HOY03] 245.00

School Boxes

Impact, Inc.
____"Jedi vs. Sith" [SBX01] 4.00

____Jar Jar Binks, sculpted [SBX02]............................9.00
____Watto, Sebulba, Anakin, and Jar Jar [SBX03] 4.00

School Kits

Animations
____EPIII:ROTS: 2 folders, notebook, 3 pencils, eraser,
sherpener, ruler, notepad 15.00

Butterfly Originals
____ROTJ School Kit with Ruler, Pencil, Pencil Bag,
Sharpener and Eraser [SUS01] 14.00

Flomo
____Clip, eraser, scissors, sharpener, 2 pencils, prism
sticker [SUS02]...15.00
____Prismatic pencil box, 2 pencils, 18cm ruler, glue, clip,
eraser, and sharpener [SUS03] 18.00
____Prismatic pencil box, 2 pencils, clip, eraser, and
sharpener [SUS04] 15.00

Grand Toys
Zippered pouch, ruler, sharpener, eraser.
____Darth Maul [SUS05] 7.00
____Destroyer Droid [SUS06] 7.00
____Queen Amidala art [SUS07] 7.00
____Queen Amidala photo[SUS08] 7.00

Grosvenor
____School stationary set: pencil case, sharpener, eraser,
pencil, ruler [SUS09]...8.00

Helix
____Chewbacca and Han padded front, assorted school
supplies, large [SUS10] 47.00
____Pencil box, pencils, eraser and sharpener 34.00
____Star Destroyer padded front, assorted school sup-
plies, small [SUS11] 36.00

Hunter Leisure, Ltd.
____Fun Pack, EPIII:ROTS: color-your-own puzzle, scrib-
bler, sticker book, sticker sheet, crayons
[SUS12]..15.00

Impact, Inc.
____Carry-Along School Set, carry case, pencil pouch, 2
pencils, memo pad,.pencil sharpener, eraser, glue
stick, 12" ruler [SUS13] 8.00
____Study Kit, "Jedi vs. Sith" eraser, ruler, pencil sharpen-
er, vinyl zippered case [SUS14] 9.00
____Study Kit, "Tatooine" eraser, ruler, pencil sharpener,
vinyl zippered pencil case [SUS15] 9.00
____Value Pack, "Anakin's Pod" portfolio, theme book,
memo pad, pencil, zippered pencil case, sharpener,
eraser, ruler...14.00
____Value Pack, "Jedi vs. Sith" portfolio, theme book,
memo pad, pencil, zippered pencil case, sharpener,
eraser, ruler...14.00
____Zip Pouch, "Jedi vs. Sith" theme book, memo pad,
ruler, pencil, sharpener, and sticker sheet 6.00
____Zip Pouch, "Tatooine" theme book, memo pad, ruler,
pencil, sharpener, and sticker sheet......................6.00

Merlin
____Darth Vader value pack, 2 pencils, eraser, sharpener,
ruler [SUS16] 12.00
____Generic, pencil, R2 image eraser, 6" ruler,
sharpener 7.00
____Star Wars, pencil, R2 image eraser, 6" ruler,
sharpener [SUS17] 10.00

N.S.W. Building Society Ltd.
____Gift pack for opening savings account, same contants
as SUS01 ....35.00

Pyramid
____Study kit, 4 pieces: pencil pouch, eraser, sharpener,
Coruscant ruler [SUS18]...5.00

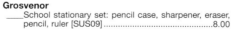

SBX01　　　　SBX02　　　　SBX03　　　SUS01　　　SUS02　　　SUS03　　　SUS04

SUS05　　　SUS06　　　SUS07　　　SUS08　　　SUS09　　　　SUS10　　　　SUS11　　SUS12　　　SUS13

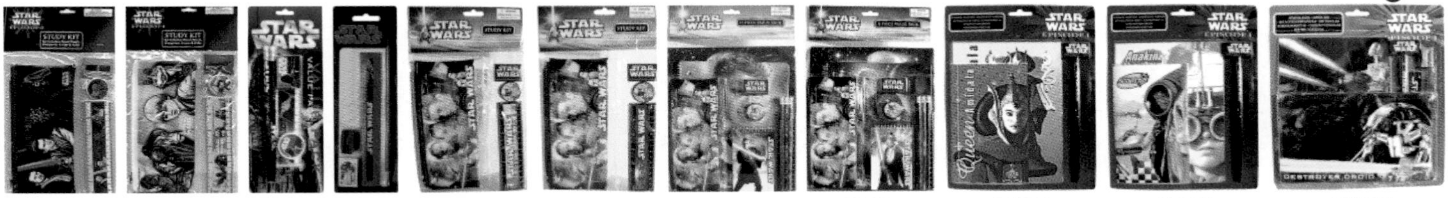

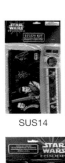

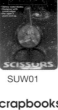

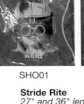

SUS14 SUS15 SUS16 SUS17 SUS18 SUS19 SUS20 SUS21 SUS22 SUS23 SUS24

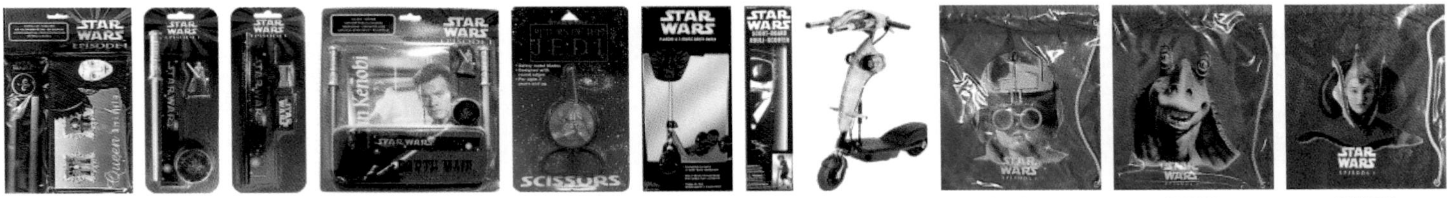

SUS25 SUS26 SUS27 SUS28 SUW01 SCT01 SCT02 SCT03 SHO01 SHO02 SHO03

____Study kit, 4 pieces: pencil pouch, eraser, sharpener, Kamino ruler [SUS19] 5.00

Value packs, 11 pieces. Character themes.
____Anakin Skywalker [SUS20]....................12.00
____Count Dooku [SUS21] 12.00

Q-Stat
____Bumper Pack, "Obi-Wan Kenobi" Unlined writing pad, lined notepad, crayons, pencil, eraser....................12.00
____Bumper Pack, "Queen Amidala" Unlined writing pad, lined notepad, pencil, eraser [SUS22] 7.00
____Fun Pack, Queen Amidala address book, Anakin writing pad, pencil, eraser 6.00
____Fun Pack, Sebulba address book, Anakin writing pad, pencil, eraser [SUS23] 6.00
____School Pack, Trade Federation Droids, pencil, eraser, sharpener, battle droid tablet, destroyer droid pencil pouch [SUS24] 11.00
____School Set, "Queen Amidala" writing pad, ruler, pencil sharpener, eraser [SUS25] 8.00
____School Set, lightsaber pencil, ruler, Obi-Wan eraser, Darth Maul sharpener [SUS26]....................7.00
____School Set, pencil, ruler, eraser, sharpener [SUS27] 5.00
____Tin Set, "Obi-Wan Kenobi" lined notepad, die-cut eraser, Darth Maul pencil sharpener, tin, Star Wars ruler, 2 lightsaber pens [SUS28] 14.00

Scissors

Butterfly Originals
____ROTJ safety scissors [SUW01] 12.00

Scooters

Sport Fun, Inc.
____Darth Vader 3 wheel scooter [SCT01] 40.00
____Darth Vader scootboard [SCT02]....................25.00

Zap World
____Stap Scooter, motorized [SCT03] 950.00

Scrapbooks

Letraset
____Collage of character photos [SCB01] 28.00

Shades: Automobile

Mpire characters.
____Boba Fett [C1S01] 15.00
____Count Dooku [C1S02] 15.00
____Darth Vader [C1S03]....................15.00
____General Grievous [C1S04] 15.00

Sheet Music

____Anakin's Theme, easy piano [MBS01] 5.00
____Ewok Celebration [MBS02]....................5.00
____Star Wars Main Theme, easy piano [MBS03] 5.00

Fox Fanfare Music
____Cantina Band Dan Coates Easy Piano Solo 5.00
____ESB Han Solo and the Princess....................5.00
____ESB Medley 5.00
____SW (Main Title) Dan Coates Piano Solo....................5.00
____SW (Main Title) Original Piano Solo [MBS04]........5.00

Schaum
____Star Wars (Main Title) [MBS05]....................7.00

Shoe Lace Tags

____Stamped Metal with Logo [2:383] 16.00

Shoe Laces

C and D Visionaries, Inc.
____Star Wars, glow-in the-dark [PES01] 5.00

Stride Rite
27" and 36" lengths.
____Ewoks and ROTJ logo with Ewoks [PES02] 7.00
____Return of the Jedi Logo [PES03] 5.00
____Star Wars Logo, Darth Vader helmet [PES04] 7.00
____Star Wars Logo with Droids [PES05] 8.00
____Star Wars Logo, Spaceships [PES06] 8.00

Shoebags

____Anakin Skywalker [SHO01] 11.00
____Jar Jar Binks [SHO02] 11.00
____Queen Amidala [SHO03] 11.00

Shower Curtains

Jay Franco and Sons
____TPM: Space Battle, vinyl [SC01] 12.00

Signs

Hot Topic
____"My other transport..." car sign [SGN01] 5.00

Norben
____Anakin Skywalker Podracer [SGN02]....................4.00
____Jedi vs. Sith [SGN03] 4.00

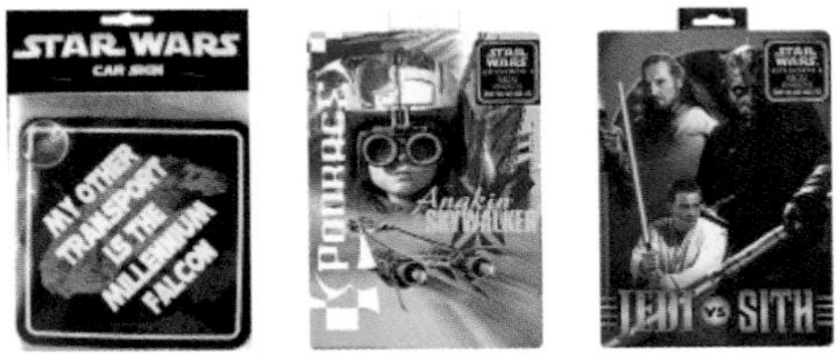

SGN01 SGN02 SGN03

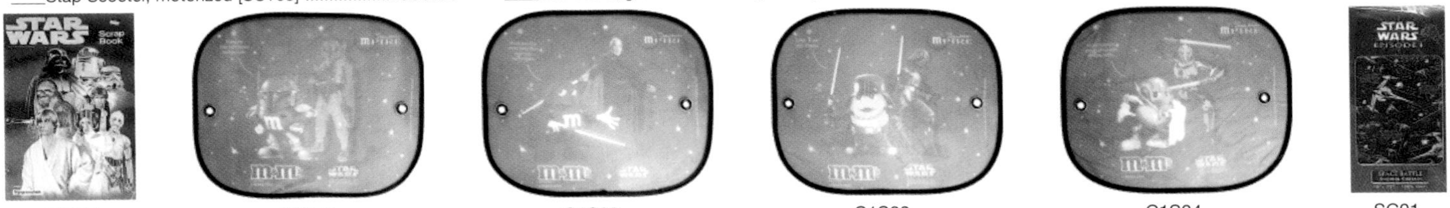

SCB01 C1S01 C1S02 C1S03 C1S04 SC01

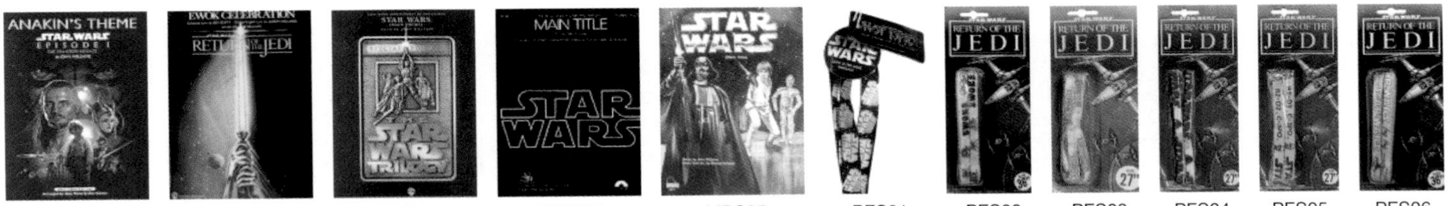

MBS01 MBS02 MBS03 MBS04 MBS05 PES01 PES02 PES03 PES04 PES05 PES06

Signs

| SGN04 | SGN05 | SGN06 | SKB01 | SKB02 | SKB03 | SKB04 | SKB05 | SKB06 | SKB07 | SKB08 | WS01 | SNT01 |

| SKR01 | SKR02 | SKR03 | SKR04 | SKR05 | SKR06 | SKR07 |

| CSB01 | CSB02 | CSB03 | CSB04 | CSB05 | CSB06 | CSB07 | CSB08 | CSB09 | CSB10 | CSB11 |

| CSB12 | CSB13 | CSB14 | CSB15 |

Tin Signs International
Movie poster artwork, 15"x24" tin.
____Empire Strikes Back [SGN04] 20.00
____Star Wars [SGN05] 18.00

Unique
____Party Door Sign, 27"x60", Darth Maul, "The Party's Here!" [SGN06] 5.00

Skateboards

____Star Wars [SKB01] 15.00

EPIII:ROTS.
____Darth Vader [SKB02] 25.00
____Darth Vader small 10.00
____Millennium Falcon (poster art) 25.00

| SG01 | SG02 | SG03 |

Brookfield Athletic
____Darth Vader and Luke Skywalker Duel 45.00

M.V. Sports and Leisure Ltd.
____Darth Maul 25.00
____Jar Jar Binks [SKB03] 25.00

Plan B
____Boba Fett 43.00
____Darth Vader 43.00
____Yoda 43.00

Seneca Sports Inc.
____C-3PO and R2-D2 [SKB04] 14.00
____Darth Maul, double-sided decal [SKB05] 19.00
____Darth Vader [SKB06] 24.00
____Death Star trench battle (McQuarrie art) 24.00
____Yoda (McQuarrie art) [SKB07] 24.00

Sport Fun, Inc.
____Anakin Skywalker / Clone Trooper [SKB08] 30.00
____Jango Fett / Slave I [SKB09] 30.00

Skates: Roller / In-line

____Anakin Skywalker, podracer [SKR01] 23.00

Brookfield Athletic
____Darth Vader and Royal Guards [SKR02] 85.00
____Wicket the Ewok [SKR03] 68.00

Seneca Sports Inc.
____Darth Maul, gray with red accents [SKR04] 18.00
____Imperial Runner Quad Skates [SKR05] 24.00
____R2-D2 [SKR06] 18.00
____Rogue Squadron [SKR07] 23.00

Slap Bands

Tapper Candies
____Jedi and Sith, 4-pack [WS01] 4.00

Sleeping Bags

____Royal Guard, Stormtrooper, Vader [CSB01] 25.00

EPIII:ROTS.
____Darth Vader [CSB02] 15.00
____Darth Vader w/backpack [CSB03] 25.00
____Epic duel [CSB04] 15.00
____Epic duel under Vader's helmet [CSB05] 15.00
____Heroes and Villains [CSB06] 15.00

Bibb Co.
____ESB: Boba Fett (J.C. Penney) 40.00
____ESB: Lord Vader's Chamber 35.00
____ESB: Spectre [CSB07] 35.00
____ESB: Yoda [CSB08] 45.00
____ROTJ: Jabba the Hutt, Ewoks, etc. 35.00
____ROTJ: logos from all 3 films 25.00
____ROTJ: Star Wars Adventure [CSB09] 40.00
____ROTJ: Star Wars Saga [CSB10] 35.00
____SW: Galaxy [CSB11] 35.00

ERO Industries
____Anakin Skywalker, podracer [CSB12] 22.00
____Luke and Darth Vader [CSB13] 20.00
____R2-D2 with metallic accents [CSB14] 45.00
____Space Battle, TPM [CSB15] 22.00

SlumberTrek
____Darth Vader 15.00

Snow Tubes

Intex Recreation Corp.
____Darth Maul [SNT01] 16.00

Snowglobes

Department 56
____Snowspeeder vs. AT-AT on Hoth [SG01] 65.00

| SG04 | SG05 | SG06 | SG07 | SG08 | SG09 | SG10 |

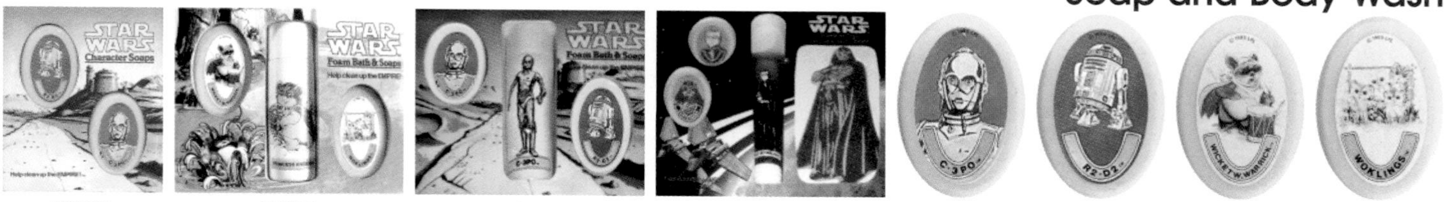

TOS01 TOS02 TOS03 TOS04 TOS05 TOS06 TOS07 TOS08

Kurt S. Adler, Inc.
____Santa Yoda, musical [SG02] 35.00

NECA
____Astroid Battle, limited to 5,000 [SG03] 55.00

Rawcliffe
Snow globes.
____Yoda vs. Darth Sidious [SG04]...........................50.00
____Hoth Battle [SG05] 40.00

Water globes.
____Anakin vs. Obi-Wan duel [SG06] 60.00
____C-3PO and R2-D2 [SG07] 15.00
____Darth Vader [SG08] 15.00
____Movie poster style "A" artwork [SG09] 100.00
____Yoda [SG10] 15.00

Soap and Body Wash

Addis
2-packs. Character soaps.
____Baby Ewoks and Wicket 20.00
____C-3PO and R2-D2 [TOS01] 20.00
____Darth Vader and Luke Skywalker.........................20.00

3-packs. Foam bath and soaps.
____Baby Ewoks and Wicket [TOS02] 25.00
____C-3PO and R2-D2 [TOS03] 25.00
____Darth Vader and Luke Skywalker.........................25.00

4-packs. Shower gel, sponge, and soaps.
____Baby Ewoks and Wicket 30.00
____C-3PO and R2-D2 ....30.00
____Darth Vader and Luke Skywalker [TOS04] 30.00

Individual bars.
____C-3PO [TOS05] 10.00
____Darth Vader...10.00
____Luke Skywalker 10.00
____R2-D2 [TOS06] 10.00
____Wicket W. Warrick [TOS07] 10.00
____Woklings [TOS08]...10.00

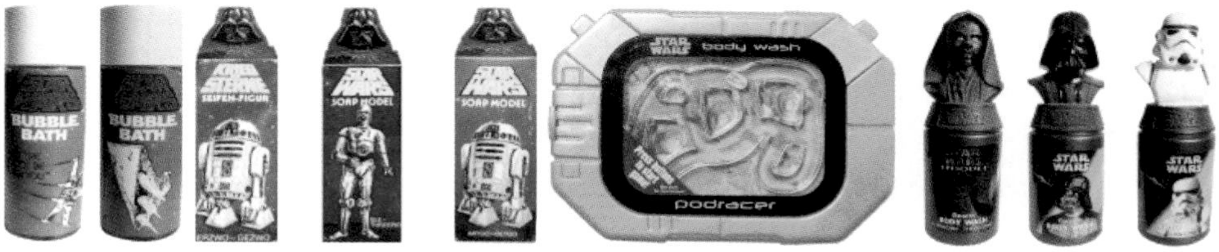

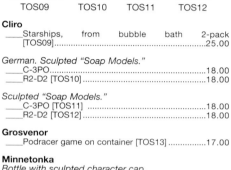

TOS09 TOS10 TOS11 TOS12 TOS13 TOS14 TOS15 TOS16

Cliro
____Starships, from bubble bath 2-pack [TOS09]..25.00

German. Sculpted "Soap Models."
____C-3PO..18.00
____R2-D2 [TOS10] 18.00

Sculpted "Soap Models."
____C-3PO [TOS11] 18.00
____R2-D2 [TOS12] 18.00

Grosvenor
____Podracer game on container [TOS13] 17.00

Minnetonka
Bottle with sculpted character cap.
____Darth Maul [TOS14] 6.00
____Darth Vader [TOS15]..6.00
____Stormtrooper [TOS16] 6.00

Galactic Glycerine Soap, 3.5oz. Gift Inside: character figure.
____Anakin Skywalker 5.00
____C-3PO [TOS17]...5.00
____Chewbacca [TOS18]..5.00
____Darth Maul [TOS19] 5.00
____Darth Vader [TOS20]...5.00
____Jar Jar Binks [TOS21]...5.00
____Queen Amidala [TOS22] 5.00
____R2-D2 [TOS23] 5.00
____Yoda [TOS24] 5.00

Minnetonka, Canada
Galactic Glycerine Soap, 3.5oz., bi-language.
____Anakin Skywalker [TOS25] 5.00
____C-3PO 5.00
____Chewbacca 5.00
____Darth Maul [TOS26] 5.00
____Darth Vader 5.00
____Jar Jar Binks 5.00
____Queen Amidala 5.00
____R2-D2 ....5.00
____Yoda 5.00

Omni Cosmetics
4-packs. 1oz. bars, sculpted character images.
____R2-D2, C-3PO, Vader, Lando [TOS27] 18.00
____Leia, Luke, Yoda, and Chewbacca [TOS28] 18.00

4oz. bars, sculpted characters, tri-logo packaging.
____Luke Skywalker [TOS29]...8.00
____Princess Leia [TOS30] 8.00

4oz. bars, sculpted character images.
____C-3PO [TOS31]..6.00
____Darth Vader [TOS32]..6.00
____Gamorrean Guard [TOS33].......................................6.00
____Luke Skywalker [TOS34]..6.00
____Princess Leia [TOS35] 6.00
____Wicket the Ewok [TOS36]...6.00
____Yoda [TOS37] 6.00

Style International
____Anakin Skywalker [TOS38].....................................10.00

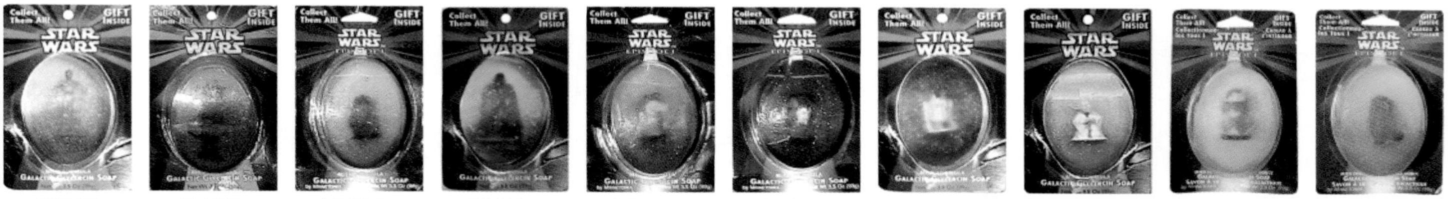

TOS17 TOS18 TOS19 TOS20 TOS21 TOS22 TOS23 TOS24 TOS25 TOS26

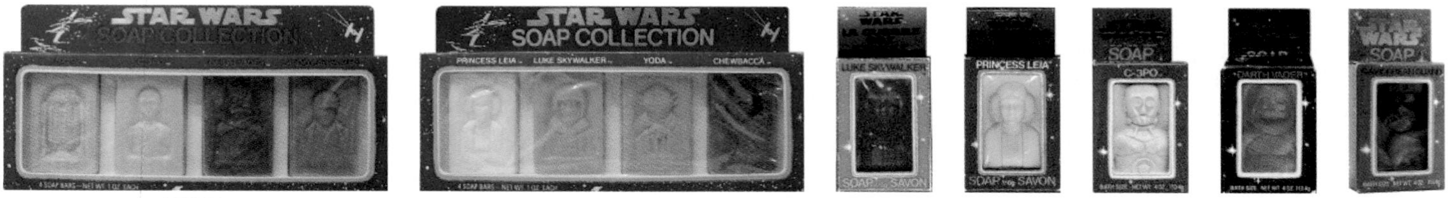

TOS27 TOS28 TOS29 TOS30 TOS31 TOS32 TOS33

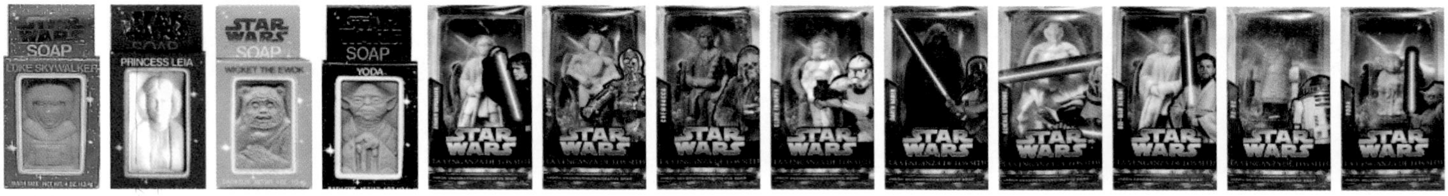

TOS34 TOS35 TOS36 TOS37 TOS38 TOS39 TOS40 TOS41 TOS42 TOS43 TOS44 TOS45 TOS46

Soap and Body Wash

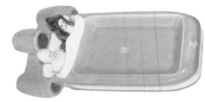

HOQ01 HOQ02 HOQ03

TOB01 TOB02 TOB03 TOB04 TOB05 TOB06 TOB07 TOB08 TOB09 TOB10 TOB11 TOB12 TOB13 TOB14

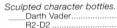

TOB15 TOB16 TOB17 TOB18 TOB19 TOB20 TOB21 TOB22 TOB23 TOB24 TOB25 TOB26 TOB27 TOB28

____C-3PO [TOS39] 10.00
____Chewbacca [TOS40] 10.00
____Clone Trooper [TOS41].....................................10.00
____Darth Vader [TOS42] 10.00
____General Grievous [TOS43] 10.00
____Obi-Wan [TOS44] 10.00
____R2-D2 [TOS45]...10.00
____Yoda [TOS46] 10.00

Soap Dishes

Jay Franco and Sons
____Anakin seated in podracer [HOQ01] 16.00
____Star Wars decal, starfighters [HOQ02] 6.00

Sigma
____Landspeeder soap dish [HOQ03] 45.00

Soap: Bubble Bath

Addis
____Ben Kenobi...32.00
____C-3PO [TOB01] 32.00
____Chewbacca [TOB02] 32.00
____Darth Vader [TOB03] 32.00
____Han Solo [TOB04] 32.00
____Luke Skywalker [TOB05] 32.00
____Princess Leia 32.00
____Wicket the Ewok [TOB06] 32.00

Foam Bath
____Princess Kneesa [TOB07] 10.00

Cliro
Bubble bath in character labeled cans.
____2-pack Imperial Cruiser with foam shampoo
        [TOB08]...65.00
____C-3PO...25.00
____Darth Vader [TOB09]...25.00
____R2-D2 [TOB10]...25.00

Sculpted character bottles.
____Darth Vader 25.00
____R2-D2 ....25.00

Cosrich Group, Inc.
Sculpted character cap.
____R2-D2 ....8.00
____Yoda 8.00

Grosvenor
____Darth Vader [TOB11] 16.00
____Galactic Bath Foam [TOB12] 16.00
____Gungan Bongo [TOB13]......................................12.00
____Jango Fett [TOB14] 16.00
____R2-D2, non-electronic [TOB15] 10.00

Minnetonka
____Darth Vader with foil label [TOB16] 3.00
____Gungan Sub with Tub Fizzers [TOB17] 6.00
____Jar Jar Binks sculpted character cap
        [TOB18]..5.00
____Jar Jar Binks with foil label [TOB19] 3.00
____Yoda sculpted character cap [TOB20] 5.00

Omni Cosmetics
____Battle Scene "refuling station" 8.00
____Chewbacca figural bottle [TOB21]......................12.00
____Darth Vader figural bottle [TOB22]......................12.00
____Jabba the Hutt figural bottle [TOB23] 12.00
____Luke Skywalker [TOB24] 18.00
____Princess Leia figural bottle [TOB25] 12.00
____R2-D2 [TOB26]...18.00
____Wicket the Ewok figural bottle [TOB27]..............12.00
____Yoda figural bottle [TOB28] 12.00

Soap: Shampoo

Cliro
____Starships, can [TOP01] 25.00

Consumer Products
____ESB Foam Bath and Shampoo set [TOP02] 35.00

Grosvenor
____Darth Maul figural bottle [TOP03] 12.00
____R2-D2 shower foam, electronic [TOP04]............12.00

Minnetonka
____Anakin Skywalker bottle with sculpted character cap
        [TOP05]...6.00
____Anakin Skywalker galactic shampoo [TOP06] 6.00
____C-3PO bottle with sculpted character cap
        [TOP07]...6.00

Omni Cosmetics
____Battle Scene "refuling station" [TOP08] 8.00
____Luke Skywalker, 2oz. From travel kit [TOP09] 3.00

Figural bottles inside Sears mailer packaging.
____Darth Vader..85.00
____Jabba the Hutt 40.00
____Luke Skywalker 70.00
____R2-D2 ....75.00
____Wicket the Ewok 50.00
____Yoda 75.00

Figural bottles.
____Darth Vader..14.00
____Jabba the Hutt 14.00
____Luke Skywalker 14.00
____R2-D2 ....14.00
____Wicket the Ewok 14.00
____Yoda 14.00

Sponges

Addis
____Darth Vader pictured on one side 17.00

Sprinklers

Sport Fun, Inc.
____Vader Force sprinkler [SPR01]............................10.00

TOP01 TOP02 TOP03 TOP04 TOP05 TOP06 TOP07 TOP08 TOP09 SPR01

CLS01   CLS02   CLS03   CLS04   CLS05   CLS06

R01   R02   R03   R04   R05   R06   R07   R08   R09   R10

R11   R12   R13   R14   R15   R16   R17   R18

R19   R20   R21   R22   R23   R24   R25

Stamp Collecting Kits

H.E. Harris and Company
SW Postage Stamp Collecting Kit: album, 24 SW "stamps," 35 real stamps, 300 hinges, and magnifier.
____Bagged [CLS01]...30.00
____Boxed [CLS02]..35.00

6 SW seals, 10 genuine stamps, 300 hinges.
____Cantina Scenes [CLS03] 45.00
____Death Star 45.00
____Escape from Death Star [CLS04].......................45.00
____Heroes 45.00
____Space Ships [CLS05] 45.00
____Tatooine Residents [CLS06]...............................45.00

Stampers

Adam Joseph Industries
____Admiral Ackbar [R01] 6.00
____Biker Scout [R02]...6.00
____C-3PO [R03] 6.00
____Chewbacca [R04] 6.00
____Darth Vader [R05] 6.00
____Emperor's Royal Guard [R06] 6.00
____Gamorrean Guard [R07] 6.00
____Millennium Falcon [R08] 6.00
____Tie Fighter [R09] 6.00
____Wicket [R10] 6.00
____X-Wing Pilot [R11]...6.00
____Yoda [R12]...6.00

3 in 1.
____Princess Kneesaa [R13] 8.00
____Wicket [R14] 8.00

All Night Media Inc.
____Set of six, clear plastic case with color artwork of stamps 24.00

Disney / MGM
____Star Tours Stamp Set [R15] 20.00

Pyramid
____R2-D2 [R16] 5.00
____Yoda [R17]...5.00

Rose Art Industries
____Sticker and Stamper Studio, over 175 pieces in vinyl carry case [R18] 19.00

____4 Piece gift set: R2-D2, C-3PO, Darth Vader, Stormtrooper [R19] 18.00
____C-3PO [R20] 4.00
____Darth Vader [R21] 4.00
____R2-D2 [R21] 4.00
____Stormtrooper [R23] 4.00
____Yoda [R24] 6.00

EPIII:ROTS. 2-pack of roller stampers.
____Clone Trooper and C-3PO & R2-D2 ....6.00
____Yoda and Darth Vader [R25] 6.00

Stamps: Postage

EPII sheet of 1 stamp 25,00. Limited to 2,000.
____Naboo Fighter [3:382] 15.00
____STAP [3:382] 15.00

EPII sheet of 9 stamps 5,00 each. Limited to 2,000.
____Blue [3:382] 15.00
____Brown [3:382] 15.00
____Light blue [3:382] 15.00

Tatarstan.
____5.00 Empire Strikes Back 3.00
____5.00 Phantom Menace 3.00
____5.00 Return of the Jedi 3.00
____5.00 Star Wars 3.00
____Sheet of 12 classic movies...................................5.00

Australia Post
____25th Anniversary stamp kit, souvenir stamp sheet, booklet of 10 postcards 35.00
____25th Anniversary stamp sheet [PS01] 20.00
____Episode II stamp sheet [PS02].............................20.00
____Episode III stamp sheet [PS03] 20.00

Chechenia
____9-sheet Episode I plus classic trilogy [2:387].......6.00

Republique Centrafricaine
____3-sheet 600f Star Wars [2:387] 12.00

Republique Du Mali
____9-sheet 180f Return of the Jedi [2:387] 8.00
____9-sheet 310f Star Wars [2:387]............................8.00
____9-sheet 320f Empire Strikes Back [2:387] 8.00

Republique Togolaise
____1-sheet 2000f Star Wars stamp [2:387]...............11.00
____9-sheet 190f Return of the Jedi [2:387] 8.00
____9-sheet 350f Empire Strikes Back [2:387] 8.00

SSCA
____Darth Vader Stamp Wallet, gold [2:387].............50.00

PS01   PS02   PS03   PS04   PS05

Stamps: Postage

ST01   ST02   ST03   ST04   ST05   ST06   ST07   ST08   ST09

ST10   ST11   ST12   ST13   ST14   ST15   ST16   ST17   ST18   ST19   ST20

ST21   ST22   ST23   ST24   ST25   ST26   ST27   ST28   ST29   ST30   ST31   ST32

____Darth Vader Stamp Wallet, silver [2:387] 40.00
____First Day Cover Collection $1 .00 stamp on 3 different
    envelope designes with covers 20.00
____Stamp Collection folder with sheet of nine
    $1.00 stamps, and sheet of three triangular $2.00
    stamps 25.00
____Stormtrooper Stamp Wallet, gold [2:387] 50.00
____Stormtrooper Stamp Wallet, silver [2:387]..........40.00
____Yoda Stamp Wallet, gold [2:387] 50.00
____Yoda Stamp Wallet, silver [2:387] 40.00

Walsall Security Printers
*3-sheet souvenir $2 triangular self-adhesive foil stamps;
3 designs: 1995 video artwork, St. Vincent and
Grenadines.*
____.999 pure silver stamps 15.00
____23 carat gold foil stamps 22.00
____Foil stamps [PS04] 5.00

____6-sheet 35-cent horizontal stamps 3.00

*9-sheet $1 vertical self-adhesive foil stamps; 3 designs:
1995 video artwork, St. Vincent and Grenadines.*
____.999 pure silver foil stamps [PS05] 15.00
____23 carat gold foil stamps 24.00
____Foil stamps 7.00

Standees
____Anakin Skywalker, Mpire – tabletop 5.00
____Darth Vader, Mpire – tabletop..............................5.00
____The Emperor, Mpire – tabletop 5.00

20th Century Fox
____First Time on DVD, Sept 21 [ST01] 95.00

EPI:TPM. Pre-order standees.
____Approx. 5' [ST02] 32.00
____Countertop [ST03] 8.00

Advanced Graphics
Classic trilogy.
____Admiral Ackbar [ST04] 25.00
____Ben Kenobi [ST05] 25.00
____Boba Fett [ST06] 28.00
____C-3PO [ST07] 25.00
____Chewbacca [ST08] 25.00
____Darth Vader with Lightsaber [ST09] 25.00
____Darth Vader without Lightsaber 25.00
____Emperor's Royal Guard [ST10]............................25.00
____Emperor Palpatine 25.00
____Han Solo [ST11] 25.00
____Han Solo, Stormtrooper Disguise [ST12].............25.00
____Jawa [ST13] 35.00
____Luke Skywalker [ST14] 25.00
____Princess Leia [ST15]...25.00
____Princess Leia, Jabba's Prisoner [ST16] 25.00
____R2-D2 [ST17] 25.00
____Stormtrooper [ST18] 25.00
____Tusken Raider [ST19] 27.00
____Yoda [ST20] 25.00

Episode I: The Phantom Menace.
____Anakin Skywalker [ST21] 26.00
____Battle Droid [ST22] 29.00
____C-3PO [ST23] 26.00
____Darth Maul, Jedi Duel [ST24] 26.00
____Darth Maul, Tatooine [ST25]...............................26.00
____Jar Jar Binks [ST26] 26.00
____Obi-Wan Kenobi [ST27] 26.00
____OOM-9 [ST28] 26.00
____Padme Amidala [ST29].......................................26.00
____Queen Amidala [ST30] 26.00
____Qui-Gon Jinn [ST31]...26.00
____Watto [ST32]..26.00

ST33   ST34   ST35   ST36   ST37   ST38   ST39   ST40

ST41   ST42   ST43   ST44   ST45   ST46   ST47   ST48   ST49   ST50

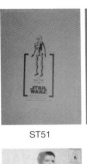
ST51

ST52

ST53

ST54

ST55

ST56

ST57

ST58

ST59

ST60

ST61

ST62

ST63

ST64

ST65

ST66

ST67

ST68

ST69

ST70

ST71

ST72

ST73

ST74

ST75

ST76

ST77

ST78

ST79

Episode II: Attack of the Clones.
____ Anakin Skywalker, 6'2" [ST33] 25.00
____ Clone Trooper, 6'1" [ST34] 25.00
____ Jango Fett 6'1" [ST35] 25.00
____ Mace Windu 6'3" [ST36] 25.00
____ Obi-Wan Kenobi 5'11" [ST37] 25.00
____ Padme Amidala 5'6" [ST38] 25.00
____ Yoda [ST39] 25.00
____ Zam Wesell 5'7" [ST40] 25.00

Episode III: Revenge of the Sith.
____ Anakin Skywalker [ST41] 30.00
____ Chewbacca [ST42] 30.00
____ Clone Trooper [ST43] 30.00
____ Clone Trooper, yellow [ST44] 30.00
____ Darth Sidious [ST45] 30.00
____ General Grievous [ST46] 30.00
____ Obi-Wan Kenobi [ST47] 30.00
____ R2-D2 and C-3PO [ST48] 30.00
____ Yoda [ST49] 30.00

Bantam Books
____ C-3PO and Jawas [ST50] 45.00

Cardboard Cut-Out Co. Ltd.
Desk Top Cut-Outs.
____ Anakin Skywalker 5.00
____ Chewbacca 5.00
____ Darth Vader 5.00
____ Storm Trooper 5.00

DK Publishing
EPI:TPM. 3D paper engineered.
____ Battle Droid [ST51] 95.00
____ Destroyer Droid [ST52] 140.00
____ Pit Droid [ST53] 115.00
____ R2-D2 [ST54] 120.00

Factors, Etc.
____ Boba Fett 40.00
____ C-3PO..34.00
____ Chewbacca 34.00
____ Darth Vader 34.00
____ R2-D2 ....34.00

Frito Lay
Episode I: The Phantom Menace.
____ Queen Amidala, "You Could Win..." [ST55] 34.00
____ Qui-Gon Jinn, "Collect all 12..." [ST56] 34.00

Kelloggs
____ Standee promotes C-3PO cereal [ST57] 65.00

Movie Cards
Jaycé Carterie.
____ Darth Vader [ST58] 5.00
____ Luke Skywalker [ST59] 5.00
____ Princess Leia [ST60] 5.00
____ R2-D2 [ST61] 5.00
____ Yoda [ST62] 5.00

Pepsi Cola
Episode I: The Phantom Menace.
____ Boss Nass, Pepsi [ST63] 27.00
____ Darth Maul, Mountain Dew [ST64] 27.00
____ Jar Jar Binks, Mountain Dew [ST65] 27.00
____ Mace Windu, Pepsi [ST66]...................................27.00
____ Obi-Wan Kenobi, Mountain Dew [ST67] 27.00
____ Queen Amidala, Pepsi [ST68] 27.00
____ Qui-Gon Jinn, Pepsi [ST69] 27.00
____ Watto, Pepsi [ST70] 24.00

Pizza Hut
____ Darth Vader 6' with lightsaber standee promoting Pepsi during SWSE 18.00

Random House
____ Darth Vader [ST71]...115.00

Sales Corp. of America
____ C-3PO and R2-D2 ....20.00
____ Darth Vader and Emperor's Royal Guard 20.00
____ Wicket the Ewok 15.00

The Empeiros Group
EPI:TPM. Desktop, approximately 12" tall.
____ Darth Maul [ST72] 3.00
____ Darth Sidious [ST73] 3.00
____ Jar Jar Binks [ST74] 3.00
____ Obi-Wan Kenobi [ST75] 3.00
____ Queen Amidala [ST76] 3.00
____ Sebulba [ST77] 3.00
____ Watto [ST78] 3.00

Wizards of the Coast
____ SW Roleplaying Game [ST79] 75.00

Stationery

Drawing Board Greeting Cards, Inc.
____ SW Lap Pack Folder with Droids on Paper, Plain Envelopes; 10 sheets, 10 envelopes 29.00
____ SW R2-D2 Die-cut Paper; 18 sheets, 12 envelopes, boxed [SUX01] 20.00
____ SW Stationery with X-Wing on Paper, Battle Envelope; 18 sheets, 12 env, boxed [SUX02]......................25.00

HC Ford
____ Fancy Stationery set [SUX03] 35.00
____ Stationery – Pencil Top Gift Set: random pencil, eraser, mini memo, 2 toppers [SUX04]......................35.00

SUX01

SUX02

SUX03

SUX04

SUX05

SUX06

SUX07

SUX08

Stationery

FH01   FH02   FH03   FH04   FH05   FH06   FH07   FH08   FH09

FH10   FH11   FH12   FH13   FH14   FH15   FH16   FH17

FH18   FH19   FH20   FH22   FH21

Letraset

____Envelopes, 12-pack, illustrated in front corner, and on rear [SUX05] 12.00

Mead

____Boba Fett, C-3PO, Darth Vader, Stormtroopers, and Yoda, 16 envelopes, 15 sheets [SUX06] 8.00

____Darth Vader, 16 envelopes, 15 sheets [SUX07] 7.00

____X-Wings, 16 envelopes, 15 sheets [SUX08]..........7.00

Star Wars Corporation

____Corporate envelope with original logo [3:383]..45.00

Statues and Busts

Life-sized characters.

____Watto 510.00

____Yoda, some given away to promote EPI video release at Blockbuster [FH01] 510.00

Yoda, life-sized by Lawrence A Noble.

____Artist Proof, limited to 6 ....65,000.00

____Regular edition, limited to 25 [FH02] 15,000.00

Applause

____Bounty Hunters, limited to 5,000 [FH03]..........135.00

____Clash of the Jedi diorama [FH04] 42.00

____Darth Maul [FH05] 28.00

____Darth Maul jedi duel, limited to 20,000 Suncoast exclusive [FH06] 25.00

____Darth Vader in Meditation Chamber, FAO Schwarz exclusive, limited to 5,000 [FH07] 75.00

____Duel of Fates [FH08] 46.00

____Emperor, Darth Vader, Prince Xizor, limited to 5,000 [FH09]..70.00

____Han Solo Release from Carbonite, built-in light, limited to 2,500 [FH10]..145.00

____Jabba the Hutt with Slave Leia, limited to 5,000 [FH11] 70.00

____Leia's Rescue statuette, Luke, Leia, Han, Chewbacca, limited to 5,000 [FH12].....................................45.00

____Luke in bacta tank, limited to 1,500 [FH13] 170.00

____Obi-Wan Kenobi [FH14] 25.00

____Queen Amidala [FH15] 25.00

____Qui-Gon Jinn [FH16] 25.00

____Qui-Gon Jinn and Obi-Wan Kenobi, lights up [FH17]..125.00

____Rancor statueette, limited to 5,000 [FH18] 45.00

____Sandtrooper and Dewback, limited to 5,000 [FH19]..70.00

____Wampa Attack, limited to 3,000 [FH20]..............75.00

Bespin duel characters on light-up bases.

____Darth Vader [FH21] 100.00

____Luke Skywalker [FH22] 100.00

Attakus

____Boba Fett Japan edition, limited to 200 ....300.00

____Darth Maul Japan edition, limited to 200 ....300.00

____Wicket the Ewok, limited to 1,500...................350.00

Series 1.

Limited edition statuettes. 1,500 produced of each.

____Boba Fett [FH23] 1,200.00

____Darth Maul [FH24] 450.00

____Han Solo in Carbonite [FH25] 260.00

____Princess Leia [FH26] 345.00

____R2-D2 [FH27]...215.00

____Yoda [FH28] 300.00

FH23   FH24   FH25   FH26   FH27   FH28   FH29   FH30   FH31

FH32   FH33   FH34   FH35   FH36   FH37   FH38   FH39

FH40   FH41   FH42   FH43   FH44   FH45   FH46   FH47   FH48

FH49   FH50   FH51   FH52   FH53   FH54   FH55   FH56   FH57   FH58

FH59   FH60   FH61   FH62 1 of 3   FH62 2 of 3   FH63   FH64   FH65

Series 2.
Limited edition statuettes. 1,500 produced of each.
____C-3PO [FH29] 365.00
____Darth Vader [FH30] 365.00
____Emperor's Royal Guard [FH31] 365.00
____Emperor Palpatine [FH32] 445.00
____Luke Skywalker X-Wing pilot [FH33] ...300.00
____Stormtrooper [FH34] 365.00
Limited edition statuettes. 750 produced of each.
____Jabba the Hutt [FH35] 950.00
____Jabba the Hutt and Princess Leia [FH36] 1,450.00

Series 3.
Limited edition statuettes. 1,500 produced of each.
____Chewbacca [FH37] 500.00
____Clone Trooper [FH38] 300.00
____Darth Vader II 900.00
____Han Solo [FH39]..................................390.00
____Jango Fett [FH40] 400.00
____Jawa [FH41]..300.00
____Obi-Wan Kenobi [FH42].....................390.00
____Padme Amidala [FH43] 350.00
Limited edition statuettes. 750 produced of each.
____Salacious Crumb and Jabba's pipe [FH44].....390.00
____Salacious Crumb [FH45].....................250.00

Series 4.
Limited edition statuettes. 1,500 produced of each.
____General Grievous 580.00
____TIE Fighter Pilot 400.00
____Tusken Raider 390.00
____Wicket W. Warrick 280.00
____Yoda, EPII..300.00

Special edition.
Limited edition statuettes. 250 produced of each.
____Yoda, bronze, Fan Club excl. [FH46]............1,150.00

Bowen Designs Inc.
Bronze statues on granite bases. Limited to 100 pieces.
____Darth Vader 14.5" tall [FH47] 3,000.00

Bronze statues on granite bases. Limited to 50 pieces.
____Boba Fett 13.5" tall [FH48] 3,400.00
____Chewbacca 19.5" tall [FH49] 3,000.00
____The Rancor 15" tall [FH50] 3,000.00

Cinemacast
____Darth Vader, limited to 10,000 [FH51] 250.00
____Luke and Leia, movie poster pose [FH52] 195.00
____Luke and Leia, pewter [FH53] 250.00

Code 3 Collectibles
3D movie poster art.
____Star Wars 80.00
____10 year anniversary, Star Wars 80.00
____Empire Strikes Back...80.00
____Empire Strikes Back Celebration 3 exclusive [FH54].........................100.00
____Return of the Jedi...80.00

Compulsion Gallery
____Boba Fett, 27.5" tall, 25 lbs. [FH55] 750.00
____C-3PO, 27" tall, 25 lbs. [FH56] 700.00
____Darth Vader, 32" tall, 40 lbs. [FH57] 750.00
____R2-D2, 19" tall, 30 lbs. [FH58]........................700.00

Disney / MGM
____Boba Fett metal 3D [FH59] 85.00

Don Post
____Boba Fett life-size replica 3,800.00

Fan Club
____Darth Vader ceramic, ltd. to 1,500 [FH60] 65.00

Franklin Mint
____"Duel of the Jedi" on custom base with glass dome [FH61] 85.00

Gentle Giant Studios
Bust-Ups, 2" – 3" in height.
____3-pack Stormtroopers 20.00
____Blackhole Stormtrooper chase bust [FH62] 15.00
____Chewbacca translucent, included with Crimson Empire trade paperback [FH63]..........................25.00
____Clonetrooper, blue, Toyfair 2004 exclusive [FH64]...35.00
____Spirit of the Rebellion, clear set of 4, summer convention exclusives, ltd. to 5,000 [3:385] 45.00
____Spirit of the Rebellion, glow-in-the-dark set of 4, summer convention excl., ltd. to 500 [3:385] 75.00
____Stormtrooper Army Builder set 15.00

Boxed Set 1: Clones.
____4-pack, clean 25.00
____4-pack, dirty 30.00
____Clone Trooper, clean, gun.............................8.00
____Clone Trooper, clean, rifle............................8.00
____Clone Trooper, dirty, gun..............................8.00
____Clone Trooper, dirty, rifle.............................8.00
____Commander Gree, clean, gun.......................12.00
____Commander Gree, clean, rifle.......................12.00
____Commander Gree, dirty, gun 12.00
____Commander Gree, dirty, rifle.............12.00
____Coruscant Trooper, clean, gun 8.00
____Coruscant Trooper, clean, rifle......................8.00
____Coruscant Trooper, dirty, gun 8.00
____Coruscant Trooper, dirty, rifle.......................8.00
____Tactical Ops 501st Trooper, clean, gun 8.00
____Tactical Ops 501st Trooper, clean, rifle.........8.00
____Tactical Ops 501st Trooper, dirty, gun 8.00
____Tactical Ops 501st Trooper, dirty, rifle 8.00
____Utapau Trooper, clean, gun 8.00
____Utapau Trooper, clean, rifle...........................8.00
____Utapau Trooper, dirty, gun 8.00
____Utapau Trooper, dirty, rifle.............................8.00

Boxed Set 2: Bounty Hunters.
____4-LOM 8.00
____7-pack 35.00
____Boba Fett 8.00
____Bossk 8.00
____Darth Vader 8.00
____Dengar..8.00
____IG-88 ....8.00
____Zuckuss 8.00

Boxed Set 3: Mos Eisley Cantina Band.
____5-Pack 25.00
____Figrin D'an...8.00
____Ickabel..8.00
____Nalan...8.00
____Tech...8.00
____Tedn 8.00

Convention exclusive.
____Darth Vader standing in flames [FH65] 35.00

Exclusives.
____Jango Fett silver, SanDiego ComicCon 2005 exclusive [FH66] 15.00

Series 1.
____Yoda clear, limited to 5,000 [FH67] 10.00

FH66   FH67   FH68   FH69   FH70   FH71   FH72   FH73

FH74   FH75   FH76   FH77   FH78   FH79   FH80

Statues and Busts

FH81 FH82 FH83 FH84 FH85 FH86 FH87 FH88

FH89 FH90 FH91 FH92 FH93 FH94 FH95 FH96 FH97

FH98 FH99 FH100 FH101 FH102 FH103 FH104

Series 1: Heroes.
____C-3PO...8.00
____Chewbacca....................................8.00
____Han Solo.......................................8.00
____Luke Skywalker.............................8.00
____Princess Leia, blaster up 15.00
____Princess Leia, pointing blaster......8.00
____Yoda..8.00
Series 2.1: Sith holograph. Action Figure Xpress exclusives.
____Darth Maul 15.00
____Darth Vader..................................15.00
Series 2.2: Sith holograph. Dark Horse Comics: Crimson Empire trade paperback exclusive.
____Darth Sidious 10.00
Series 2: Sith.
____Count Dooku / Darth Tyrannus [FH68]...............12.00
____Darth Maul closed mouth...............12.00
____Darth Maul evil smile 8.00
____Darth Sidious / Emperor Palpatine.......................8.00
____Darth Vader closed fist [FH69].......12.00
____Darth Vader open hand [FH70].........8.00
____Imperial Royal Guard 8.00
____Imperial Stormtrooper both hands on blaster 8.00
____Imperial Stormtrooper One hand on blaster [FH71].........8.00
____Imperial Stormtrooper with heavy blaster rifle 8.00
____Stormtrooper, long rifle 8.00
Series 3: Bounty Hunters.
____4-LOM [FH72].................................12.00
____Boba Fett [FH73]...............................8.00
____Boba Fett silver [FH74].....................20.00
____Bossk [FH75].....................................8.00

____Dengar [FH76]....................................8.00
____Jango Fett [FH77]...............................8.00
____Zuckuss [FH78]...................................8.00
Series 4: ROTS.
____Clone Trooper with Pistol [FH79]....8.00
____Clone Trooper with rifle [FH80]........8.00
____Darth Sidious [FH81].........................8.00
____Darth Vader (Anakin) [FH82]............8.00
____General Grievous [FH83] 8.00
____Obi-Wan [FH84]..................................8.00
____Yoda [FH85] 8.00
Series 5: Hoth.
____AT-AT Driver [FH86].........................8.00
____AT-AT Driver, transparent blue 20.00
____Darth Vader [FH87]............................8.00
____Darth Vader, transparent blue 20.00
____Han Solo [FH88]..................................8.00
____Han Solo, transparent blue 20.00
____Luke Skywalker [FH89].......................8.00
____Luke Skywalker, transparent blue 20.00
____Snowtrooper [FH90] 8.00
____Snowtrooper, transparent blue.........10.00
____Wampa [FH91] 8.00
____Wampa, transparent blue 20.00
Series 6: MosEisley.
____Bith [FH92] 8.00
____Greedo [FH93].....................................8.00
____Han Solo [FH94]..................................8.00
____Obi-Wan Kenobi [FH95]......................8.00
____Obi-Wan Kenobi spirit 25.00
____Ponda Baba [FH96] 8.00
____Snaggletooth, blue 32.00
____Snaggletooth, red [FH97] 8.00

Series 7: Clone Wars (animated).
____Anakin Skywalker [FH98] 8.00
____ARC Trooper [FH99] 8.00
____General Grievous [FH100]..................8.00
____Obi-Wan Kenobi [FH101] 8.00
____Padme Amidala [FH102]......................8.00
____Yoda [FH103] 8.00

Maqette, Clone Wars, animated style.
____Anakin Skywalker, limited to 3,000 ....100.00
____ARC Trooper, limited to 2,500 [FH104] 100.00
____ARC Trooper, unpainted chin (mass released error)..................100.00
____Asajj Ventress, limited to 2,500 [FH105] 160.00
____Barriss Offee and Luminara Unduli, limited to 3,000 [FH106]..................100.00
____General Grievous, limited to 3,500 ....100.00
____Obi-Wan Kenobi, limited to 2,500 [FH107] 100.00
____Padme, limited to 1,000 [FH108]......................640.00
____Republic Commandos, colored, limited to 400 ....675.00
____Republic Commandos, limited to 400.............550.00
____Yoda, limited to 7,500 [FH109].........................80.00

Maquette, animated style.
____Boba Fett 135.00
____Darth Vader 135.00
____Princess Leia 135.00

Mini-busts, approximately 6" tall. Holiday VIP exclusives, each limited to 200.
____2004 Sandtrooper chromed [FH110]............1,375.00
____2005 Salicious Crumb with Santa hat 1,200.00

FH105 FH106 FH107 FH108 FH109 FH110 FH111 FH112

FH113 FH114 FH115 FH116 FH117 FH118 FH119 FH120 FH121

FH122   FH123   FH124   FH125   FH126   FH127   FH128   FH129   FH130   FH131

FH132   FH133   FH134   FH135   FH136   FH137   FH138   FH139   FH140   FH141

Mini-busts, approximately 6" tall.

____Anakin Skywalker, limited to 2,500 [FH111] 65.00
____Biker Scout, limited to 7,500 ....75.00
____Blackhole Stormtrooper, Blister Event Japan exclusive, limited to 1,000 ....425.00
____Boba Fett, limited to 7,500 [FH112] 325.00
____Bossk, limited 5,000 [FH113] 65.00
____C-3PO (EPII), Art of Star Wars exclusive, limited to 2,500 ....175.00
____C-3PO chome, MBNA customer exclusive, limited to 2,500 [FH114] 245.00
____C-3PO gold plated, MBNA customer exclusive, limited to 8,000 ....65.00
____C-3PO, limited to 8,000 [FH115] 60.00
____Chewbacca 65.00
____Clone Trooper (blue), San Diego Comic-Con International and WizardWorld Chicago convention exclusive, limited to 1,000 [FH116] 450.00
____Clone Trooper (green), limited to 2,500 ....180.00
____Clone Trooper (ROTS) 65.00
____Clone Trooper 501st Special Ops 65.00
____Clone Trooper Captain (red), limited to 7,500 [FH117] 85.00
____Clone Trooper Commander (yellow), limited to 7,500 [FH118] 85.00
____Clone Trooper Pilot, Wizard World LA exclusive, limited to 2,500 [FH119] 225.00
____Clone Trooper Utapau 65.00
____Clone Trooper, limited to 7,500 [FH120] 65.00
____Count Dooku, limited to 2,500 [FH121] 65.00
____Darth Vader ROTS, limited to 20,000 ....90.00
____Darth Vader smoked, MBNA customer exclusive, limited to 4,000 [FH122] 160.00
____Darth Vader, limited to 3,500 [FH123] 200.00
____Emperor Palpatine, limited to 4,500 ....65.00
____Gamorrean Guard, limited to 4,000 [FH124] 65.00
____General Grievous 65.00
____Grand Moff Tarkin, limited to 6,000 [FH125] 65.00
____Greedo, limited to 7,500 [FH126] 65.00
____Han Solo 65.00
____Han Solo, stormtrooper disguise [FH127] 50.00
____IG-88, limited to 5,000 [FH128] 50.00
____Jango Fett chromed, MBNA customer exclusive, limited to 5,000 [FH129] 225.00
____Jango Fett, limited to 2,500 [FH130] 65.00
____Jano Fett chromed, 2005 Comic-con excl. 135.00

____Lando Calrissian in Skiff Guard Disguise, limited to 4,000 ....65.00
____Luke Skywalker, conventions exclusive, limited to 3,500 [FH131] 175.00
____Luke Skywalker, X-Wing pilot, limited to 7,500 [FH132] 35.00
____Mace Windu, limited to 2,500 [FH133] 65.00
____Obi-Wan Kenobi, limited to 2,500 [FH134] 65.00
____Padme Amidala, limited to 2,500 [FH135] 65.00
____Plo Koon 65.00
____Princess Leia as Boushh, limited to 5,000 [FH136]...50.00
____Qui-Gon Jinn 65.00
____Salacious Crumb (with C-3PO head), limited to 2,500 ....135.00
____Sandtrooper Corporal, Celebration 3 exclusive, limited to 2,500 ....245.00
____Sandtrooper Sergeant (white pauldron), limited to 15,000...50.00
____Sandtrooper Squad Leader (orange pauldron), limited to 15,000 [FH137]....................................35.00
____Stormtrooper chromed [FH138] 150.00
____Stormtrooper, limited to 10,000 [FH139].........100.00
____Yoda ESB, limited to 15,000 ....65.00
____Yoda with lightsaber, limited to 2,500 [FH140]...350.00
____Zam Wesell, limited to 2,500 [FH141] 65.00

Statues.

____Boba Fett, limited to 6,500 ....200.00
____C-3PO, limited to 3,000 ....185.00
____Chewbacca, limited to 3,000, collector club exclusive [FH142]....................................180.00
____Darth Maul, international edition, limited to 2000 ....175.00
____Darth Maul, U.S. edition, limited to 3000 ....175.00
____Darth Vader chrome, Blister Event Japan exclusive, limited to 2,500 ....450.00
____Darth Vader, 14", limited to 7,500 ....285.00
____Darth Vader, 15" chome with light-up lightsaber, limited to 2,500.......................................450.00
____Luke and Tauntaun, limited to 4,000 ....185.00
____Obi-Wan Kenobi, Clone Wars 300.00
____Rancor 280.00
____Sandtrooper and Dewback, ltd to 1,500..........280.00

____Scout Trooper on Speeder Bike, limited to 5,000 ....200.00
____Yoda (Clone Wars), approx 2' 575.00

Gentle Giant Studios, Japan
Bust-Ups, 2" – 3" in height.
Series 3: Bounty Hunters.
____4-LOM...8.00
____Boba Fett...8.00
____Boba Fett silver..8.00
____Bossk 8.00
____Dengar...8.00
____Jango Fett..8.00
____Zuckuss..8.00

Illusive Originals
____Admiral Ackbar, bust maquette, limited to 10,000 [FH143]...95.00
____Boba Fett bust maquette, limited to 10,000 [FH144]...180.00
____Chewbacca maquette, limited to 7,500 [FH145]...125.00
____Darth Vader Reveals Anakin Skywalker maquette, limited to 9,500 [FH146]...........................850.00
____Jabba the Hutt maquette, limited to 5,000 [FH147]...275.00
____Rancor maquette, limited to 9,500 [FH148] 540.00
____Yoda maquette, limited to 9,500 [FH149] 775.00

Kilian Enterprises
____Yoda, ESB 10th anniversary, limited to 50 [3:385]..775.00

Legends in 3-Dimensions
____Gamorrean Guard, 14" tall, limited to 3,000 [FH150]...155.00

Nine inch tall busts, limited edition with certificate of authenticity.
____Boba Fett, 5000 produced [FH151]..................160.00
____Cantina Band Member, 2500 produced [FH152]..125.00
____Emperor Palpatine, 2500 produced [FH153] 65.00
____Greedo, 2500 produced [FH154] 65.00
____Tusken Raider, 2500 produced [FH155] 170.00

FH142   FH143   FH144   FH145   FH146   FH147

FH148   FH149   FH150   FH151   FH152   FH153   FH154   FH155

Statues and Busts

FH156

FH157

FH158

FH159

FH160

FH161

FH162

FH163

FH164

FH165

Lucasfilm
____Chewbacca, 2005 gift...N/V

Master Replicas
____C-3PO 149.00

Pepsi Cola
____Ewok, limited to 3,500.....................................735.00

Life-sized character statues.
____Anakin Skywalker...2,300.00
____Darth Maul [FH156] 2,300.00
____Jar Jar Binks [FH157] 2,300.00
____Watto [FH158] 875.00
____Yoda [FH159] 1,400.00

Pepsi, Japan
Sound Big Cap sets.
____1: Luke Skywalker and Darth Vader....................45.00
____2: Han Solo and Chewbacca 45.00
____3: Princess Leia and Stormtrooper 45.00
____4: C-3PO and R2-D2 ....45.00
____5: Anakin Skywalker and Queen Amidala 45.00
____6: Yoda and Emperor Palpatine 45.00
____7: Obi-Wan Kenobi and General Grievous 45.00

Reds, Inc.
____Darth Vader 3', pre-painted [FH160] 830.00

Royal Tara
____Luke Skywalker, limited to 1000 pieces, autographed C.O.A. [FH161]...350.00
____Obi-Wan Kenobi with Bohemian crystal lightsaber, limited to 1000 pieces [FH162] 500.00

Rubies
____Clone Trooper helmet with base, limited to 7,500 [FH163]..1,200.00
____Darth Vader helmet with base, limited to 5,000 ....1,200.00
____Jango Fett helmet with base, limited to 5,000 ....1,200.00
____Yoda bust, limited to 5,000 [FH164] 200.00
____Yoda, EPII lifesized [FH165]..............................750.00

Sideshow Collectibles
1/4 scale.
____Ben Obi-Wan Kenobi with exclusive Jedi Training Remote, limited to 1,250 #71411 ....290.00
____Ben Obi-Wan Kenobi with exclusive Jedi Training Remote, limited to 2,250 #7141 ....175.00
____Boba Fett, ltd to 1,250 #71511 ....250.00
____Darth Vader with exclusive Mouse Droid, limited to 2,000 #71171 ....350.00
____Darth Vader, limited to 2,500 #7117................425.00
____General Grievous with exclusive Fabric Cape and clasp, limited to 1,500 #71261 ....500.00
____General Grievous, limited to 2,500 #7126 ......475.00
____Han Solo with exclusive Yavin Medal of Honor, limited to 250 #71181..300.00
____Han Solo, limited to 2,500 #7118...................230.00
____Luke Skywalker, 2005 Comic-Con Exclusive for pick-up, ltd to 500 #71161 ....155.00
____Luke Skywalker, 2005 Comic-Con Exclusive Non-Attendee, ltd to 500 #71161SC...............135.00
____Luke Skywalker, ltd to 2,500 #7116 ....225.00
____Princess Leia with exclusive Stormtrooper Blaster, ltd to 1,000 #71191 ....325.00
____Princess Leia, ltd to 1,250 #7119 ....200.00

Tomy
Approximately 6cm tall. Miniature dioramas. Series 1.
____AT-AT [3:386] 5.00
____Darth Vader / Stormtroopers [3:386] 5.00
____Millennium Falcon [3:386].....................................5.00
____R2-D2 and C-3PO [3:386] 5.00
____X-Wing [3:386] 5.00

Approximately 6cm tall. Miniature dioramas. Series 2.
____Boba Fett with carbonite Han [3:386] 5.00
____Darth Maul vs. Qui-Gon Jinn [3:386] 5.00
____Han Solo and Chewbacca [3:386] 5.00
____Luke Skywalker on sailbarge [3:386] 5.00
____Yoda on Dagobah [3:386] 5.00

Approximately 6cm tall. Miniature dioramas. Series 3.
____Anakin on Speeder Bike [3:386] 5.00
____Gunship over AT-TE [3:386] 5.00
____Jedi Starfighter [3:386] 5.00
____Slave I [3:386] 5.00
____Yoda [3:386] 5.00

Stencils

Takara
____C-3PO [SSC01]...8.00
____Darth Vader's Tie Fighter 8.00
____Death Star [SSC02]..8.00
____Landspeeder [SSC03]...8.00
____Millennium Falcon [SSC04].......................................8.00
____R2-D2 ....8.00
____Star Destroyer 8.00
____Tie Fighter 8.00
____X-Wing 8.00
____Y-Wing..8.00

Stickers

____7 characters, 2 X-Wings, puffy [SV01] 6.00
____Bib Fortuna, Jabba the Hutt, Lando as Guard, Gamorrean, Leia as Boushh [SV02] 8.00
____C-3PO and Imperial Crusier look-alikes [SV03] 4.00
____Let's See It In THX, 2" round, Star Wars Celebration '99, promotional [SV04] 1.00
____May the Floss be with You [SV05] 1.00
____Revenge of the Sith Original Motion Picture Soundtrack, cloth 5.00

Classic trilogy scenes.
____JSL-01A Chewbacca, Vader/logo, Slave I, A-wing, Yoda, logo, Boba Fett [SV06] 3.00
____JSL-01B Luke, TIE interceptor, Jawa, C-3PO, Wicket, planet, Millennium Falcon, Jabba [SV07]..............3.00
____JSL-01C Admiral Ackbar, Chewbacca, Rancor, logo, Star Destroyer, Han, Darth Vader [SV08] 4.00

France.
____EPI, C179B, sheet of 5 [SV09] 4.00
____EPI, C179C, sheet of 6 [SV10] 4.00
____EPI, C180A, sheet of 8 [SV11] 4.00
____EPI, C180B, sheet of 8 [SV12] 4.00
____EPI, C180C, sheet of 9 [SV13] 4.00
____EPI, C181A, sheet of 11 [SV14] 4.00
____EPI, C181B, sheet of 11 [SV15] 4.00
____EPI, C181C, sheet of 8 [SV16] 4.00

Hungarian. Classic trilogy and EPI characters. Unnumbered set of 19. (Images and checklist in 3rd edition, page 387.)
____Stickers [SV17], each 3.00
____Set of 19...45.00

Japan.
____9-sheet: C-3PO, Darth Vader, Sand People, 5 non-Star Wars ships, X-Wing Fighter [SV18] 12.00
____Box of 48 ....94.00

ROTJ, 4 per sheet.
____B-Wing Attack, Max Rebo Band, Emperor vs. Luke, Endor Forest [SV19] 8.00
____Rancor, Speederbike Chase, AT-ST Attack, Imperial Shuttle [SV20] 8.00
____Rebel Fleet, Jabba's Palace, DS II Reactor, Escape from Jabba's Sail Barge [SV21] 8.00

3D Arts
6"x6" holographic stickers.
____C-3PO and R2-D2 ....4.00
____Darth Vader..4.00
____Millennium Falcon...4.00
____X-Wing Fighter 4.00

501st Legion
____501st New England (Garrison), 3" round 2.00

A.H. Prismatic
Holographic.
____9 Stickers; Uncut Sheet 24.00
____AT-AT [SV22] 2.00
____B-Wing [SV23]..2.00

SSC01

SSC02

SSC03

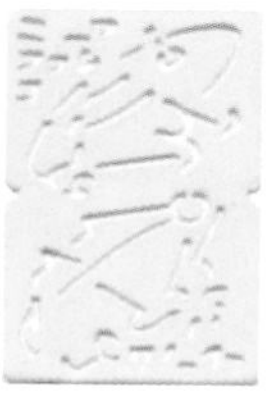
SSC04

SV01

SV02

SV03

SV04

SV05

SV06

SV07

SV08

SV09

SV10

SV11

SV12

SV13

SV14

SV15

SV16

SV17 sample

SV18

SV19

SV20

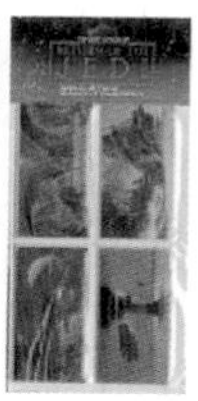
SV21

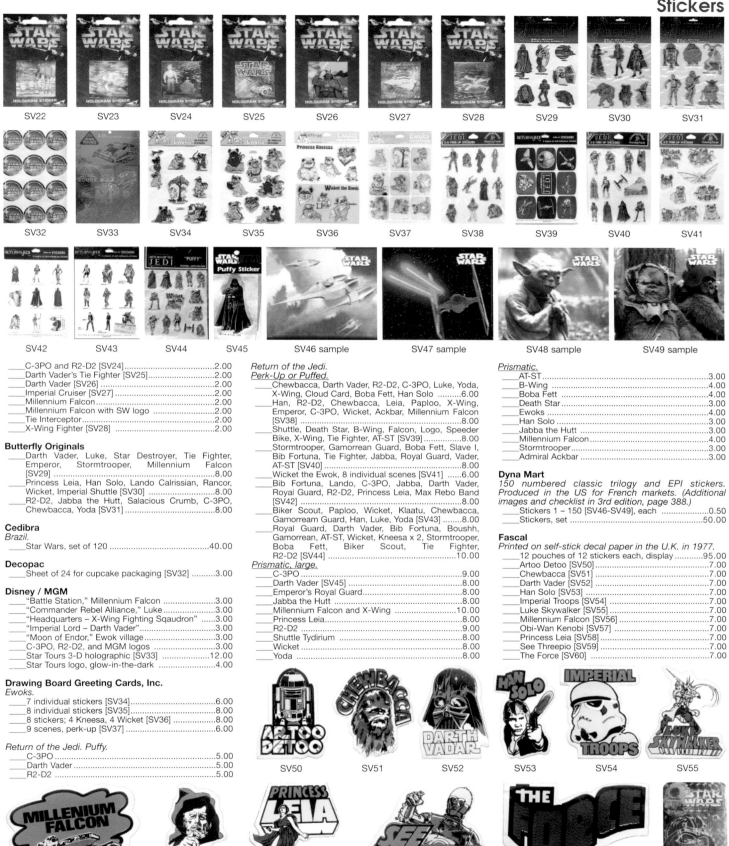

SV22 SV23 SV24 SV25 SV26 SV27 SV28 SV29 SV30 SV31

SV32 SV33 SV34 SV35 SV36 SV37 SV38 SV39 SV40 SV41

SV42 SV43 SV44 SV45 SV46 sample SV47 sample SV48 sample SV49 sample

____C-3PO and R2-D2 [SV24].....................................2.00
____Darth Vader's Tie Fighter [SV25]..........................2.00
____Darth Vader [SV26] 2.00
____Imperial Cruiser [SV27] 2.00
____Millennium Falcon 2.00
____Millennium Falcon with SW logo 2.00
____Tie Interceptor 2.00
____X-Wing Fighter [SV28] 2.00

Butterfly Originals
____Darth Vader, Luke, Star Destroyer, Tie Fighter, Emperor, Stormtrooper, Millennium Falcon [SV29] 8.00
____Princess Leia, Han Solo, Lando Calrissian, Rancor, Wicket, Imperial Shuttle [SV30] 8.00
____R2-D2, Jabba the Hutt, Salacious Crumb, C-3PO, Chewbacca, Yoda [SV31] 8.00

Cedibra
Brazil.
____Star Wars, set of 120 ....40.00

Decopac
____Sheet of 24 for cupcake packaging [SV32] 3.00

Disney / MGM
____"Battle Station," Millennium Falcon 3.00
____"Commander Rebel Alliance," Luke 3.00
____"Headquarters – X-Wing Fighting Sqaudron" 3.00
____"Imperial Lord – Darth Vader" 3.00
____"Moon of Endor," Ewok village 3.00
____C-3PO, R2-D2, and MGM logos 3.00
____Star Tours 3-D holographic [SV33] 12.00
____Star Tours logo, glow-in-the-dark 4.00

Drawing Board Greeting Cards, Inc.
Ewoks.
____7 individual stickers [SV34]..................................6.00
____8 individual stickers [SV35]..................................8.00
____8 stickers; 4 Kneesa, 4 Wicket [SV36] 8.00
____9 scenes, perk-up [SV37] 6.00

Return of the Jedi. Puffy.
____C-3PO 5.00
____Darth Vader 5.00
____R2-D2 ....5.00

Return of the Jedi.
Perk-Up or Puffed.
____Chewbacca, Darth Vader, R2-D2, C-3PO, Luke, Yoda, X-Wing, Cloud Card, Boba Fett, Han Solo 6.00
____Han, R2-D2, Chewbacca, Leia, Paploo, X-Wing, Emperor, C-3PO, Wicket, Ackbar, Millennium Falcon [SV38] 8.00
____Shuttle, Death Star, B-Wing, Falcon, Logo, Speeder Bike, X-Wing, Tie Fighter, AT-ST [SV39] 8.00
____Stormtrooper, Gamorrean Guard, Boba Fett, Slave I, Bib Fortuna, Tie Fighter, Jabba, Royal Guard, Vader, AT-ST [SV40] 8.00
____Wicket the Ewok, 8 individual scenes [SV41] 6.00
____Bib Fortuna, Lando, C-3PO, Jabba, Darth Vader, Royal Guard, R2-D2, Princess Leia, Max Rebo Band [SV42] 8.00
____Biker Scout, Paploo, Wicket, Klaatu, Chewbacca, Gamorream Guard, Han, Luke, Yoda [SV43] 8.00
____Royal Guard, Darth Vader, Bib Fortuna, Boushh, Gamorrean, AT-ST, Wicket, Kneesa x 2, Stormtrooper, Boba Fett, Biker Scout, Tie Fighter, R2-D2 [SV44] 10.00

Prismatic, large.
____C-3PO 9.00
____Darth Vader [SV45] 8.00
____Emperor's Royal Guard.......................................8.00
____Jabba the Hutt 8.00
____Millennium Falcon and X-Wing 10.00
____Princess Leia 8.00
____R2-D2 ....9.00
____Shuttle Tydirium 8.00
____Wicket 8.00
____Yoda 8.00

Prismatic.
____AT-ST 3.00
____B-Wing 4.00
____Boba Fett 4.00
____Death Star 3.00
____Ewoks 4.00
____Han Solo 3.00
____Jabba the Hutt 3.00
____Millennium Falcon 4.00
____Stormtrooper 3.00
____Admiral Ackbar 3.00

Dyna Mart
150 numbered classic trilogy and EPI stickers. Produced in the US for French markets. (Additional images and checklist in 3rd edition, page 388.)
____Stickers 1 – 150 [SV46-SV49], each 0.50
____Stickers, set 50.00

Fascal
Printed on self-stick decal paper in the U.K. in 1977.
____12 pouches of 12 stickers each, display 95.00
____Artoo Detoo [SV50]...7.00
____Chewbacca [SV51] 7.00
____Darth Vader [SV52] 7.00
____Han Solo [SV53] 7.00
____Imperial Troops [SV54] 7.00
____Luke Skywalker [SV55] 7.00
____Millennium Falcon [SV56] 7.00
____Obi-Wan Kenobi [SV57] 7.00
____Princess Leia [SV58] 7.00
____See Threepio [SV59] 7.00
____The Force [SV60] 7.00

SV50 SV51 SV52 SV53 SV54 SV55

SV56 SV57 SV58 SV59 SV60 SV61

289

Stickers

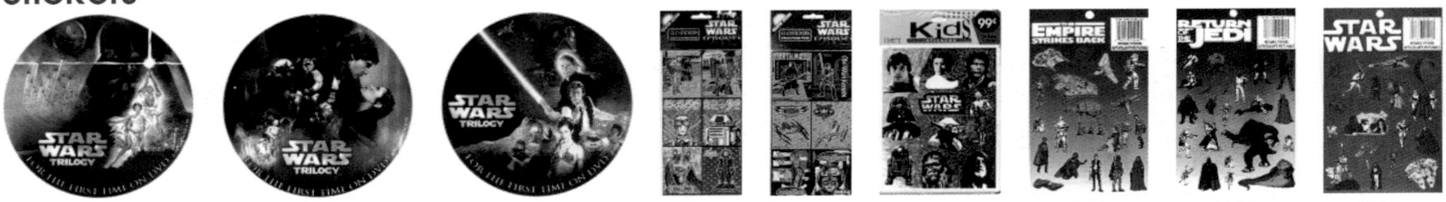

SV62 SV63 SV64 SV65 SV66 SV67 SV68 SV69 SV70

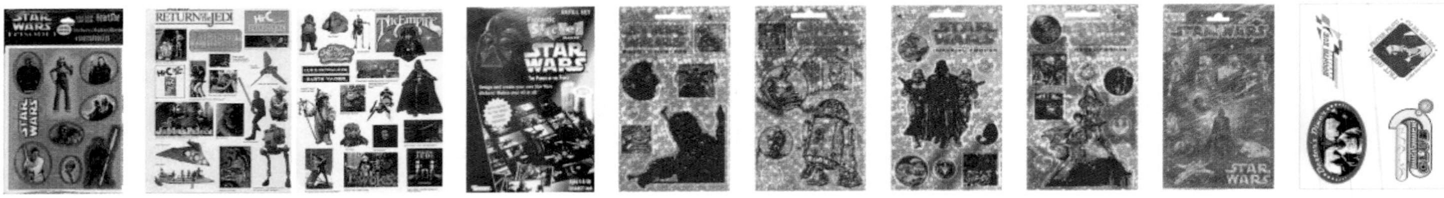

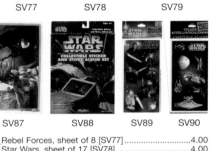

SV71 SV72 SV73 SV74 SV75 SV76 SV77 SV78 SV79

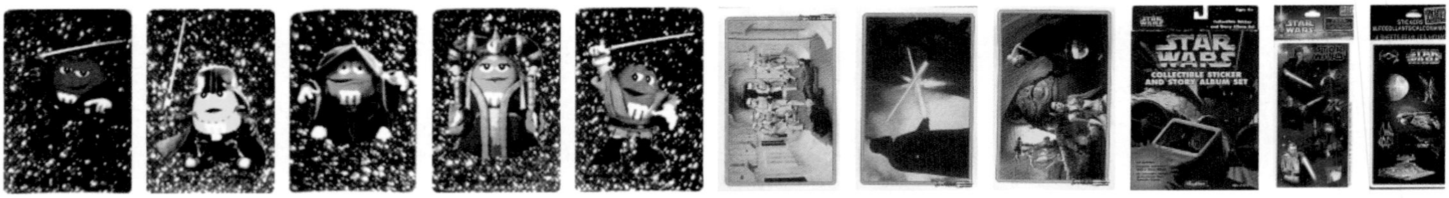

SV80 SV81 SV82 SV83 SV84 SV85 SV86 SV87 SV88 SV89 SV90

Flomo
____Vader / Death Star II, prismatic [SV61]..................3.00

Fox Studios
DVD classic trilogy promotional. Walmart exclusives.
____A New Hope [SV62] 2.00
____Empire Strikes Back [SV63] 2.00
____Return of the Jedi [SV64] 2.00

Glow Zone
Six Episode I Glo Stickers.
____Anakin, Qui-Gon, C-3PO, R2-D2, Jar Jar, Queen Amidala [SV65] 6.00
____Darth Maul, Obi-Wan, Trade Federation Fighter, Naboo Fighter, Sebulba, Anakin [SV66] 6.00

Hallmark
____Kids Stickers, 4 sheets [SV67] 3.00

Classic trilogy series.
____Empire Strikes Back [SV68] 4.00
____Return of the Jedi [SV69] 4.00
____Star Wars [SV70]..4.00

Heartline
Episode I: The Phantom Menace.
____8 stickers, 4 sheets...4.00
____9 stickers, 4 sheets [SV71] 4.00

Hi-C
____ROTJ double sticker sheet, folded. Hi-C premium [SV72] 7.00

Kenner
____Fantastic Sticker Maker Star Wars refill kit, forty photos and machine tape refill [SV73] 12.00

M&M World
Mpire characters with prism backgounds.
____A New Hope [SV80] 2.00
____A New Hope [SV81] 2.00
____A New Hope [SV82] 2.00
____A New Hope [SV83] 2.00
____A New Hope [SV84] 2.00

MAUCCI S.A.
Argentina.
____Sheet of 10: Darth Vader 5.00
____Sheet of 13: C-3POx4, Jawasx2, Max Rebo band, Gammorrean Guard, R2-D2, Cantina band, Rancor...5.00
____Sheet of 13: Yoda, R2-D2, Jawasx2, Ben, Luke, Han, Chewbacca, Boba Fett, Stormtrooper, Biker scout, Tarkin, Princess Leia..5.00
____Sheet of 18 concept art 5.00
____Sheet of 23, movie scenes......................................5.00
____Sheet of 23: characters 5.00
____Sheet of 23: movie scenes......................................5.00
____Sheet of 6: Boba Fett, Darth Vader, Biker Scout, Snowtrooper, Stormtrooper, Emperor 5.00
____Sheet of 7, vehicles art...5.00

Merlin Publishing Internat'l Ltd.
____Bounty Hunters, sheet of 6 [SV74].........................4.00
____Droids, sheet of 7 [SV75] 4.00
____Imperial Forces, sheet of 8 [SV76] 4.00
____Rebel Forces, sheet of 8 [SV77]..............................4.00
____Star Wars, sheet of 17 [SV78] 4.00

Paizo Publishing / Fan Club
____Sheet of 4: Dexter's Diner, Boonta Eve Classic, Outlander Club, Corellian Spice Freighters Guild [SV79] 3.00

Panini / Skybox
66 numbered stickers. Some combine to create complete image. (Images in 2nd edition, page 392. Checklist in 3rd edition, page 389.)
____Stickers 1 – 29: ANH [SV85], each.........................0.25
____Stickers 30 – 55: ESB [SV86], each 0.25
____Stickers 56 – 66: ROTJ [SV87, each].....................0.25
____66 stickers with album [SV88] 18.00

Panini / Topps
____ROTJ 180 stickers with album...........................27.00

Panini
156 numbered stickers with some images requiring 2 and 3 stickers to complete, plus A – X and S1 – S36. (Checklist in 3rd edition, page 389.)
____Stickers 1 – 156, each 0.65
____Stickers 1 – 156, set 45.00
____Stickers A – X, each 0.75
____Stickers A – X, set 15.00
____Stickers S1 – S36, each 0.45
____Stickers S1 – S36, set 15.00

Paper Magic Group
____Stick-R-Treats, AOTC, bag of 18 ....6.00

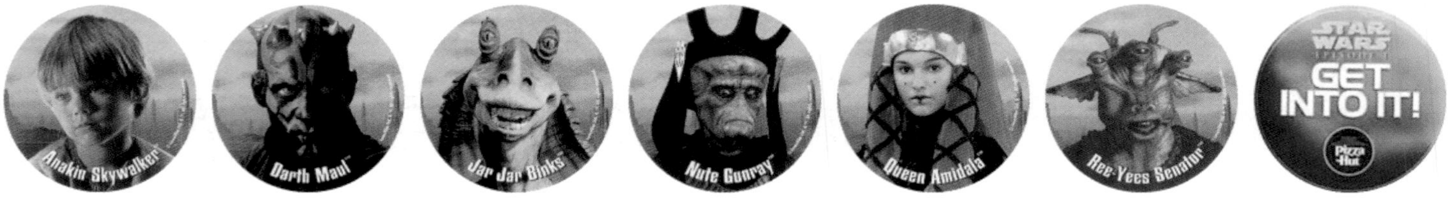

SV91 SV92 SV93 SV94 SV95 SV96 SV97

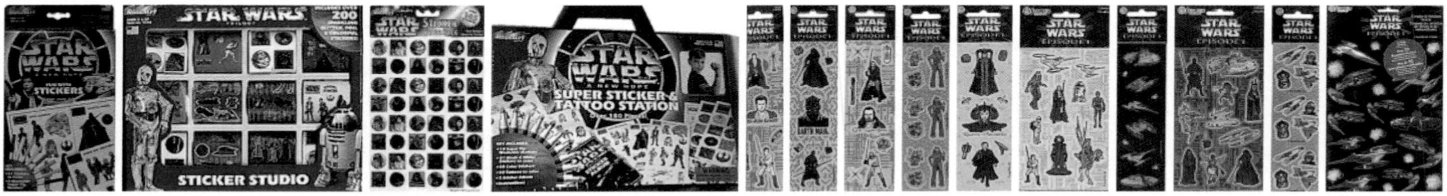

SV98 SV99 SV100 SV101 SV102 SV103 SV104 SV105 SV106 SV107 SV108 SV109 SV110 SV111

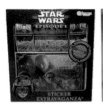

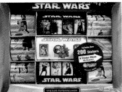

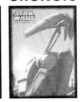

SV112 SV113 SV114 SV115 SV116 SV117 SV118 SV119 SV120 SV121 SV122

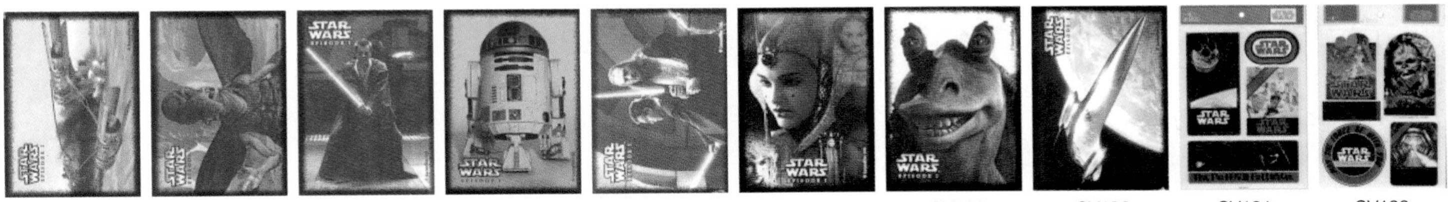

SV123 SV124 SV125 SV126 SV127 SV128 SV129 SV130 SV131 SV132

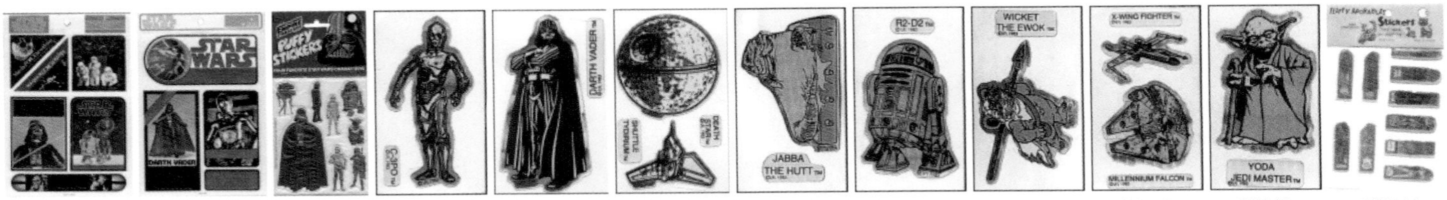

SV133 SV134 SV135 SV136 SV137 SV138 SV139 SV140 SV141 SV142 SV143 SV144

Party Express
____EPII:AOTC. [SV89] 3.00
____EPIII:ROTS. 3.00
____Logo, (2) Tie Interceptors, (2) X-Wings, Millennium Falcon, Death Star, and Imperial Cruiser [SV90] 3.00

Pizza Hut
Episode I character stickers, 2" round.
____Anakin Skywalker [SV91] 1.50
____Darth Maul [SV92] 1.50
____Jar Jar Binks [SV93] 1.50
____Nute Gunray [SV94] 1.50
____Queen Amidala [SV95] 1.50
____Ree Yees Senator [SV96] 1.50

Episode I Promotion, Germany
____SW:EPI "Get Into It!," blue, green, orange, or red [SV97] 1.50

Rose Art Industries
____Fun With Stickers [SV98] 7.00
____Sticker Studio, over 200 stickers [SV99] 7.00
____Sticker Value Pack, 145 stickers [SV100] 5.00
____Super Sticker and Tattoo Station with case, black case [SV101] 11.00
____Super Sticker and Tattoo Station with case, purple case 17.00

EPIII:ROTS.
____Fun with tattoos and stickers 6.00

Sandylion
____6-stickers, Obi-Wan Kenobi [SV102] 4.00
____7-stickers, Darth Maul [SV103] 4.00
____8-stickers, Qui-Gon Jinn [SV104] 4.00
____9-stickers, Jar Jar Binks [SV105] 4.00
____9-stickers, Queen Amidala [SV106] 4.00
____10-stickers, Heroes, 2 sheets [SV107] 8.00
____10-stickers, Space Battle [SV108] 4.00
____11-stickers, Villains, 2 sheets [SV109] 8.00
____12-stickers, Pod racing [SV110] 4.00
____21-stickers, Create-A-Scene [SV111] 5.00
____EPI Sticker Extravaganza [SV112] 4.00
____EPII Sticker Extravaganza w/album [SV113] 6.00

Collector series stickers. 3 in each pack.
____#1 "Space Battle": Starfighter Attack, Royal Starship, Naboo Starfighter [SV114] 3.00
____#2 "Ground Battle": Jar Jar Binks, Battle Droid, Fambaa [SV115] 3.00
____#3 "Podrace": Anakin Skywalker, Sebulba, Podrace Explosion [SV116] 3.00
____#4 "Jedi": Qui-Gon Jinn, Obi-Wan Kenobi, Jedi vs. Sith [SV117] 3.00
____#5 "Villains": Darth Sidious, Darth Maul, Nute Gunray [SV118] 3.00
____#6 "Droids": R2-D2, Destroyer Droid, C-3PO 3.00

EPI vendpack stickers.
____1 Naboo Space Battle [SV119] 2.00
____2 Darth Maul [SV120] 2.00
____3 Anakin Skywalker (Podracer) [SV121] 2.00
____4 Battle Droid [SV122] 2.00
____5 Anakin's Podracer [SV123] 2.00
____6 Watto [SV124] 2.00
____7 Obi-Wan Kenobi [SV125] 2.00
____8 R2-D2 [SV126] 2.00
____9 Qui-Gon Jinn and Obi-Wan Kenobi [SV127] 2.00
____10 Queen Amidala [SV128] 2.00
____11 Jar Jar Binks [SV129] 2.00
____12 Amidala's Royal Starship [SV130] 2.00

Smart
____Darth Vader for prepaid cellphone service, 1.5"x3" lenticular 2.00
____Darth Vader for prepaid cellphone service, 4" round 3.00

Star Wars Insider
____"See You At Star Wars Celebration..." 3"x5" 2.00

Tokyo Queen
Japan.
____Escape pod, MTFBWY, Luke and C-3PO, TIE fighter [SV131] 26.00
____Hildebrandt art, Chewbacca, MTFBWY, stormtrooper [SV132] 26.00
____MTFBWYx2, stormtroopers, Vader, droids, Han and Chewbacca [SV133] 26.00
____X-Wing / Deathstar, Vader, C-3PO [SV134] 24.00

Topps
____ESB [SV135] 7.00

Topps, Canada
____Galactic Empire, sheet of 10 ....3.00
____Rebel Alliance, sheet of 10 ....3.00

Vending Supply
Die-cut stickers with prism background.
____C-3PO [SV136] 6.00
____Darth Vader [SV137] 6.00
____Death Star and Shuttle Tydirium [SV138] 6.00
____Jabba the Hutt [SV139] 6.00
____Princess Leia 6.00
____R2-D2 [SV140] 6.00
____Royal Guard 6.00
____Wicket the Ewok [SV141] 6.00
____X-Wing Fighter / Millennium Falcon [SV142] 6.00
____Yoda Jedi Master [SV143] 6.00

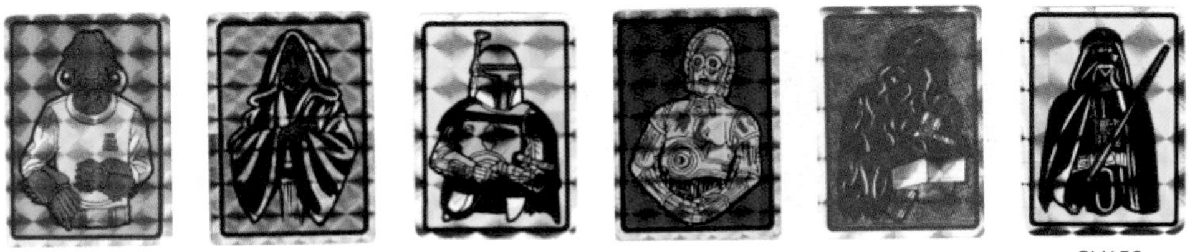

SV145 SV146 SV147 SV148 SV149 SV150

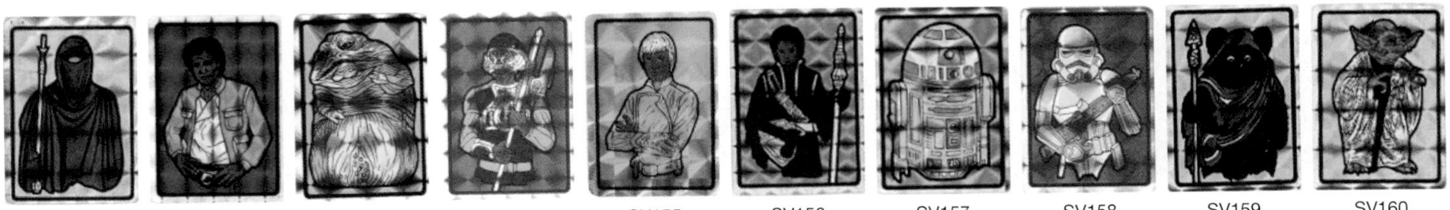

SV151 SV152 SV153 SV154 SV155 SV156 SV157 SV158 SV159 SV160

Stickers

SEJ01

SEJ02

SEJ03

SEJ04

SEJ05 SEJ06 SEJ07 SEJ08 SEJ09

SEJ10

SEJ11

SEJ12

SEJ13

SEJ14

Fluffy Adorable.
____ROTJ puffed, bookmark art [SV144] 4.00

ROTJ stickers with reflective background.
____Admiral Ackbar [SV145] 15.00
____Ben Kenobi [SV146] 4.00
____Boba Fett [SV147]..4.00
____C-3PO [SV148] 4.00
____Chewbacca [SV149] 4.00
____Darth Vader [SV150] 4.00
____Emperor's Royal Guard [SV151].............................10.00
____Han Solo [SV152] 4.00
____Jabba the Hutt [SV153] 10.00
____Lando as Skiff Guard [SV154] 4.00
____Luke Skywalker [SV155] 4.00
____Princess Leia as Boushh [SV156] 35.00
____R2-D2 [SV157] 4.00
____Stormtrooper [SV158] 10.00
____Wicket [SV159] 4.00
____Yoda [SV160]...4.00

Stickers: ANH

Panini
256 numbered stickers. Some images requiring 2 and 3 stickers to complete. (Checklist in 3rd ed., pg. 391.)
____Stickers 1 – 256, each 0.15
____Stickers 1 – 256, set 46.00

Stickers: AOTC

Daily Star
____Sheet 1, 8 round stickers [SEJ01] 4.00
____Sheet 2, 9 round stickers [SEJ02] 4.00

Hallmark, UK
____Anakin, Jango, Obi-Wan, Dooku, Zam, Mace, Padme, C-3PO, and R2-D2 ....6.00

____Dooku, logo, Yoda, Slave I, Mace, Anakin, Padme, Jango, Jedi Starfighter, Obi-Wan 6.00
____Padme, EPII Heroes, EPI Characters, Anakin 6.00
____Padme, Obi-Wan, Jango, Anakin, Mace, C-3PO 6.00

Heartline
____Anakin, logo, Yoda, Dooku, Slave I, Jango, Obi-Wan, Jedi Starfighter, 4 sheets of 8 [SEJ03] 2.00
____Anakin, logo, Yoda, Dooku, Slave I, Jango, Obi-Wan, Jedi Starfighter, Padme, Mace, space x 2, 4 sheets of 12 ....3.00
____Jango Fett, 2 sheets of 1 [SEJ04] 3.00

Merlin Publishing Internat'l Ltd.
____Unopened package of six stickers.....................5.00

Merlin, Italy
Stickers depicting LEGO mini figures, L1-L8, each.
____L1 Zam Wesell 4.00
____L2 Anakin Skywalker 4.00
____L3 Count Dooku 4.00
____L4 Yoda 4.00
____L5 Jango Fett 4.00
____L6 Boba Fett 4.00
____L7 Obi-Wan Kenobi 4.00
____L8 Clone Trooper 4.00

Sandylion
____Heroes and Villains, 2 sheets of 17 [SEJ05]..........5.00

Foil background.
____Heroes, 1 sheet of 9 [SEJ06] 2.00

STP01

STP02 sample

STP03

STP04

STP05

STP06

STP07

STP08

STP09

STP10

STP11

STP12

STP25

STP26

STP13

STP14

STP15

STP16

STP17

STP18

STP27

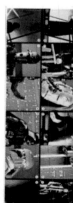
STP28

STP19

STP20

STP21

STP22

STP23

STP24

STP29

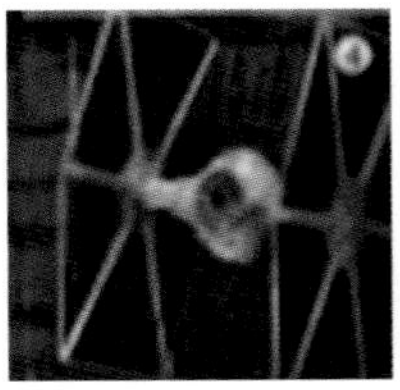
STP30 sample

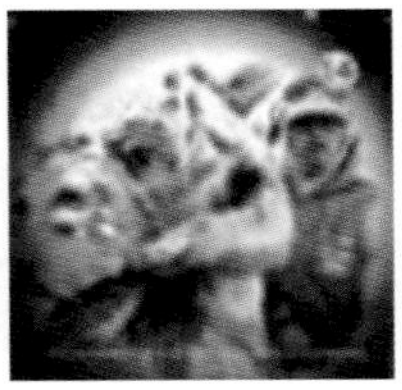
STP31 sample

STP32 sample

STP33

STP34

STP35

____Jedi, 1 sheet of 10 [SEJ07] 2.00
____Vehicles, 1 sheet of 8 [SEJ08] 2.00
____Villains, 1 sheet of 10 [SEJ09] 2.00

SmileMakers series, 2"x2" square.
____Anakin Skywalker [SEJ10] 1.00
____Count Dooku [SEJ11] 1.00
____Jango Fett [SEJ12] 1.00
____Obi-Wan Kenobi [SEJ13] 1.00
____Padme Amidala [SEJ14] 1.00

STP36

STP37

STP38

STP39

STP40

STP41

Stickers: Parody

Garbage Pail Kids
____Ashcan Andy [3:393] 2.00

Stickers: Premiums

20th Century Fox, Thailand
____EPII:AOTC sheet of 8 [STP01] 8.00

ARI
Turkey. 42 numbered rectangular stickers distributed inside gum packets. (Additional images and checklist in 3rd edition, page 393.)
____Stickers 1 – 42 [STP02], each 2.00
____Stickers 1 – 42, set 100.00

Betty Crocker
Magic Motion sticker cards.
____EPI: Qui-Gon vs. Darth Maul [STP03] 2.00
____EPII: Obi-Wan vs. Count Dooku [STP04] 2.00
____EPII: Obi-Wan vs. Jango Fett 2.00
____EPIV: Obi-Wan vs. Darth Vader [2:395] 2.00
____EPV: Luke Skywalker vs. Darth Vader 2.00
____EPVI: Luke vs. Darth Vader [2:395] 2.00

Bimbo
Set of 20 numbered stickers.
____1 Anakin Skywalker [STP05] 1.50
____2 Obi-Wan Kenobi [STP06] 1.50
____3 Obi-Wan vs. Anakin [STP07] 1.50
____4 Darth Vader [STP08] 1.50
____5 Darth Sidious [STP09] 1.50
____6 General Grievous [STP10] 1.50
____7 Yoda [STP11] 1.50
____8 Anakin Skywalker [STP12] 1.50
____9 Darth Sidious [STP13] 1.50
____10 General Grievous [STP14] 1.50
____11 Mace Windu [STP15] 1.50
____12 Obi-Wan Kenobi [STP16] 1.50
____13 Darth Vader [STP17] 1.50
____14 Yoda [STP18] 1.50
____15 Mace Windu [STP19] 1.50
____16 R2-D2 [STP20] 1.50
____17 Anakin Skywalker [STP21] 1.50
____18 C-3PO [STP22] 1.50
____19 Yoda [STP23] 1.50
____20 Darth Vader [STP24] 1.50

Break
Australia.
____Ewok stickers and poster, mail-in premium 45.00

Burger King
ESB Super Scenes. Sheets of 12 stickers each.
____Sheet A [STP25] 6.00
____Sheet B [STP26] 6.00
____Sheet C [STP27] 6.00
____Sheet D [STP28] 6.00

Campina Ijsfabbrieken
____C-3PO and R2-D2 .... 11.00
____Darth Vader 11.00
____Darth Vader and Death Star Gunner [STP29] 11.00
____Luke and Yoda 11.00
____Star Destroyer 11.00
____Stormtrooper 11.00

Chupa Chups
Set of 24 numbered stickers distributed in candy lollipops. (Checklist in 3rd edition, page 393.)
____Stickers 1 – 24, each 1.75
____Stickers 1 – 24, set 18.00

Costa
Argentina. 40 square numbered stickers distributed inside food products.
____Stickers 1 – 13 ANH [STP30], each 0.50
____Stickers 14 – 27 ESB [STP31], each 0.50
____Stickers 28 – 40 ROTJ [STP32], each 0.50
____Stickers 1 – 40, set 25.00

Dark Horse Comics
____Star Wars Starfighter Crossbones 1.00

Doggis
Argentina. Set of 4 distributed in Hot Dog packages. (Images in 3rd edition, page 394.)
____Anakin [STP33] 2.00
____Count Dooku 2.00
____Mace Windu 2.00
____Obi-Wan Kenobi 2.00

Frito Lay
EPIII:ROTS. Sticker game pieces.
____Chewbacca 1.00
____Darth Vader 1.00
____Mace Windu [STP34] 1.00
____Obi-Wan Kenobi 1.00
____Padme 1.00
____R2-D2 .... 1.00
____Yoda 1.00

Fundy Star
Hungary. Distributed inside candy bars. Set of 12, unnumbered. (Images and checklist in 3rd edition, page 394.)
____Jar Jar Binks 3.00
____Naboo Starfighters 3.00
____Obi-Wan Kenobi 3.00
____Queen Amidala 3.00
____Space Battle 3.00
____Watto 3.00

General Mills
Stick-on scenes. 4 mini-sets: characters, creatures, robots, scenes.
Characters.
____Ben (Obi-Wan) Kenobi [3:394] 6.00
____Han Solo [3:394] 6.00
____Luke Skywalker [STP36] 6.00
____Princess Leia Organa [3:394] 6.00
Creatures.
____Chewbacca [STP37] 6.00
____Darth Vader [3:394] 6.00
____Jawa [3:394] 6.00
____Stormtroopers [3:394] 6.00
Robots.
____Artoo-Detoo (R2-D2) [3:394] 6.00
____C-3PO and R2-D2 [STP38] 6.00
____Luke repairs C-3PO [3:394] 6.00
____See-Threepio (C-3PO) [3:394] 6.00
Scenes.
____Attack on Darth Vader's Ship [STP39] 6.00
____Ben cuts off the tractor beam [3:394] 6.00
____Cockpit of the Millennium Falcon [3:394] 6.00
____Han Solo, Princess Leia and Luke [3:394] 6.00

General Mills, Canada
Stick-on scenes. 2 mini-sets: characters and creatures.
Characters.
____Ben (Obi-Wan) Kenobi [3:394] 6.00
____Han Solo [3:394] 6.00
____Luke Skywalker [STP40] 6.00
____Princess Leia Organa [3:394] 6.00
Creatures.
____Chewbacca [STP41] 6.00
____Darth Vader [3:394] 6.00
____Jawa [3:394] 6.00
____Stormtroopers [3:394] 6.00

Harpers, New Zealand
Dog Chow. Set of 12.
____1 C-3PO, Chewbacca, Leia [STP42] 75.00
____2 Darth Vader [STP43] 75.00
____3 Luke and Gamorrean guards [STP44] 75.00
____4 Salacious Crumb [STP45] 75.00
____5 Gamorrean Guard [STP46] 75.00
____6 Darth Vader, Luke Skywalker [STP47] 75.00
____7 Wicket [STP48] 75.00
____8 Han Solo [STP49] 75.00
____9 Jabba the Hutt [STP50] 75.00
____10 Luke Skywalker [STP51] 75.00
____11 Stormtroopers [STP52] 75.00
____12 B-Wing Fighters [STP53] 75.00

Hollywood Chewing Gum
France. Set of 20 unnumbered stickers distributed in gum packets.
____Stickers 1 – 20, each 1.00
____Stickers 1 – 20, set 12.00

STP42

STP43

STP44

STP45

STP46

STP47

STP48

STP49

STP50

STP51

STP52

STP53

Stickers: Premiums

STP54 sample

STP55 sample

STP56 sample

STP57 sample

STP58 sample

STP59

STP60 sample

STP61 sample

STP62 spl.

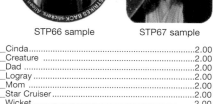

STP63

STP64

STP65

STP66 sample

STP67 sample

Kelloggs

Set of 10 numbered stickers. Stickers are adhered to trading cards for backing. (Images and checklist in 3rd edition, page 395.)

____Stickers 1 – 10 [ST54], each 7.00
____Stickers 1 – 10, set 45.00

Kelloggs, Canada

Stick'R Cards. Set of 10 numbered stickers. Card premiums continue numbering as 11 – 20. (Images and checklist in 3rd edition, page 395.)

____Stickers 1 – 10 [ST55], each 7.00
____Stickers 1 – 10, set 45.00

Kelloggs, New Zealand

Return of the Jedi sticker game pieces.

____Admiral Ackbar [3:395] 5.00
____Bib Fortuna [3:395] 5.00
____Chewbacca [3:395] 5.00
____Darth Vader [3:395] 5.00
____Ewoks [3:395] 5.00
____Han Solo [3:395] 5.00
____Jabba the Hutt [STP56] 5.00
____Luke Skywalker [3:395] 5.00
____Max Rebo [3:395] 5.00
____Princess Leia [3:395] 5.00
____See Threepio [3:395] 5.00
____Yoda [3:395] 5.00

Kent

Turkey. Rectangular artwork stickers distributed inside gum packets. 112 numbered stickers. (Additional images and checklist in 3rd edition, page 395.)

____Stickers 1 – 112 [STP57], each 1.00
____Stickers 1 – 112, set 85.00

MGM / UA

____Ewoks – The Battle for Endor sheet of six 14.00

N.S.W. Building Society Ltd.

Stickers designed to be added to promotional Ewoks poster.

____Baak 2.00
____Boy 2.00
____Cave 2.00
____Cinda 2.00
____Creature 2.00
____Dad 2.00
____Logray 2.00
____Mom 2.00
____Star Cruiser 2.00
____Wicket 2.00

Stickers designed to be added to promotional ROTJ poster.

____Bib Fortuna 2.00
____Gamorrean Guard 2.00
____Han 2.00
____Jabba 2.00
____Lando 2.00
____Luke 2.00
____Princess Leia 2.00
____Salacious Crumb 2.00
____Wicket 2.00
____X-Wing fighter 2.00

Nagatanien

20 numbered stickers. (Images in 2nd edition, page 395. Checklist in 3rd edition, page 396.)

____Stickers 1 – 20 [STP58], each 1.25
____Stickers 1 – 20, set 12.00

Nintendo Power Magazine

____Rogue Squadron [STP59] 2.00

Pepsi Cola

____Jedi vs. Sith 1.00

Pez Candy, Inc.

U.K. Stickers were distributed through Pez refill packs.

____C-3PO [3:396] 2.00
____Darth Vader [2:396] 2.00
____Han Solo [2:396] 2.00
____Luke Skywalker [2:396] 2.00
____Princess Leia [STP60] 2.00
____R2-D2 [2:396] 2.00
____Stormtrooper [2:396] 2.00
____Yoda [2:396] 2.00

Russian

37 numbered stickers. (Images and checklist in 3rd edition, page 397.)

____Stickers 1 – 37 [STP61], each 3.40
____Stickers 1 – 37, set 100.00

Schick

TPM stickers.

____Anakin Skywalker [3:397] 4.00
____Darth Maul [2:396] 4.00
____Jar Jar Binks [STP62] 4.00
____Obi-Wan Kenobi [2:396] 4.00
____Qui-Gon Jinn [2:396] 4.00

Tip-Top, New Zealand

Jedi Jelly.

____C-3PO surrounded by Ewoks [3:397] 8.00
____Warock [STP63] 8.00
____Wicket [3:397] 8.00
____Wicket, R2, and C-3PO [3:397] 8.00

R2-D2 Space Ice.

____Death Star [3:397] 3.00
____Han and Chewie [3:397] 3.00
____Han in Gunwell [STP64] 3.00
____Luke vs. Vader Painting [3:397] 3.00
____Millennium Falcon in Docking Bay [3:397] 3.00
____Pilots in Hangar [3:397] 3.00
____Princess Leia and R2 [3:397] 3.00
____Purchase of the Droids [3:397] 3.00
____Sandcrawler [3:397] 3.00
____These Aren't the Droids You're Looking For [3:397] 3.00
____TIE Pilot [3:397] 3.00
____Tusken Raiders [3:397] 3.00
____Vader on the Rebel Ship [3:397] 3.00
____X-Wing Battle in Trench [3:397] 3.00
____X-Wing in Trench [3:397] 3.00

Twinkies premiums.

____Chewbacca [3:397] 5.00
____Darth Vader [3:397] 5.00
____Luke Skywalker [3:397] 5.00
____Princess Leia [3:397] 5.00
____See Threepio [3:397] 5.00
____Yoda [STP65] 5.00

UFO

____C-3PO [3:397] 5.00
____Chewbacca [2:396] 5.00
____Princess Leia [STP66] 5.00
____Yoda [2:396] 5.00

Walkers

Square stickers are 1.5"x1.5".

____Anakin Skywalker [2:396] 1.00
____Darth Maul [2:396] 1.00
____Jar Jar Binks [2:396] 1.00
____Jar Jar Binks (pose) [2:396] 1.00
____Obi-Wan Kenobi [2:396] 1.00
____Queen Amidala [2:396] 1.00
____Qui-Gon Jinn [STP67] 1.00

Stickers: ROTJ

Germany.

____Sheet of 8: Logray, Leia, Yoda, Chief Chirpa, Han, X-Wing, lightsaber, Luke and Vader duel 15.00
____Sheet of 8: Vader, Yoda, Royal Guard, Endor Heroes, Star Barrle, Heroes, Star Destroyer, Ewoks [OSA01] 15.00

C and D Visionaries, Inc.

____R2-D2 and C-3PO 2.00

Fun Products

Color plastic stickers are 4.5".

____3-Pack, random 20.00
____6-Pack, random 40.00
____Admiral Ackbar [OSA02] 6.00
____Baby Ewoks [OSA03] 6.00
____C-3PO [OSA04] 6.00
____Chewbacca [OSA05] 6.00

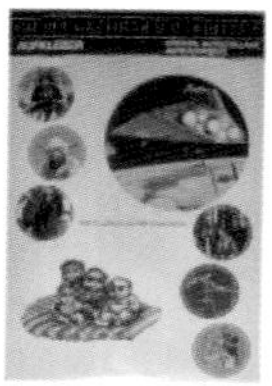
OSA01

OSA02

OSA03

OSA04

OSA05

OSA06

OSA07

OSA08

OSA09

OSA10

OSA11

OSA12

OSA13

OSA14

A1S01

A1S02

A1S03

A1S04

A1S05

A1S06

A1S07

A1S08

A1S09

A1S10

A1S11

A1S12

A1S13

A1S14

A1S15

A1S16

A1S17

A1S18

A1S19

A1S20

A1S21

A1S22

A1S23

A1S24

A1S25

A1S26

A1S27

A1S28

A1S29

A1S30

A1S31

A1S32

A1S33

____Darth Vader [OSA06]............................6.00
____Gamorrean Guard [OSA07]....................6.00
____Jabba the Hutt / Salacious Crumb [OSA08] 6.00
____Klaatu [OSA09] 6.00
____Paploo [OSA10] 6.00
____R2-D2 [OSA11] 6.00
____Shuttle Tydirium [OSA12] 6.00
____Yoda the Jedi Master [OSA13] 6.00

Color puffed plastic stickers are 4.5".
____Admiral Ackbar 6.00
____Baby Ewoks [OSA14] 6.00
____C-3PO 6.00
____Chewbacca 6.00
____Darth Vader 6.00
____Gamorrean Guard 6.00
____Jabba the Hutt 6.00
____Klaatu 6.00
____Paploo 6.00
____R2-D2 ....6.00
____Shuttle Tydirium 6.00
____Yoda 6.00

Salo
Same as US Topps set.
____180 stickers 75.00

Topps
180 numbered stickers. Some scenes require multiple stickers to complete. (Checklist in 3rd ed., pg. 397.)
____Stickers 1 – 180, each 0.10
____Stickers 1 – 180, set 25.00

Ultra-Figus
240 numbered El Regreso del Jedi stickers.
____Stickers 1 – 240, each 0.25
____Stickers 1 – 240, set 55.00

Stickers: ROTS

C and D Visionaries, Inc.
____Chewbacca [A1S01] 2.00
____Clone Trooper [A1S02] 2.00
____Darth Vader Sith Lord [A1S03] 2.00
____Yoda, round [A1S04] 2.00

Round.
____Anakin vs. Obi-Wan [A1S05] 2.00
____C-3PO and R2-D2 [A1S06].................2.00
____Darth Vader [A1S07] 2.00
____Darth Vader (close-up) [A1S08] 2.00
____General Grievous [A1S09] 2.00
____Yoda [A1S10] 1.00

Sheets of 10.
____Darth Vader, Anakin, Darth Vader, Clones, epic duel, Anakin, Yoda, Darth Vader, Jedi, Darth Vader 3.00

____Epic duel, Darth Vader, epic duel, Jedi, Vader in flames, Jedi, 4 small 3.00
____Jabba, Death Star duel, X-wing, ceremony, Obi-Wan, Luke, Han Solo, Princess Leia, logo, Death Star escape [A1S11].....................................3.00

Sheets of 8.
____Han Solo, droids, Obi-Wan, Death Star duel, C-3PO on Tatooine, Princess Leia, X-Wings, R5-D4 [A1S12] 3.00

Fun Stuff
Sheets of 9.
____Obi-Wan, Yoda, Darth Vader, Boba Fett, Chewbacca, C-3PO and R2-D2, General Grievous, Clone Trooper, Anakin [A1S13]...................................10.00

Heart
Japan.
____Clone Trooper, General Grievous, Yoda [A1S14] 7.00
____Darth Vader [A1S15] 7.00
____Darth Vader, Sith [A1S16] 7.00
____Darth Vader, Vader [A1S17] 7.00
____Yoda Jedi Master [A1S18] 7.00
____Yoda, Sith Lord, Darth Vader [A1S19] 7.00

Mello Smello
____60-count sheet [A1S20] 4.00
____Stickers for Trick-or-treaters, 24 boxes bagged ..5.00

Glittered stickers.
____3-pack 5.00
____501st Shock Trooper [A1S21] 5.00
____501st Shock Trooper, "First In, Last Standing" [A1S22] 0.75
____Anakin Skywalker [A1S23] 0.75
____Chewbacca [A1S24] 0.75
____Darth Vader [A1S25] 0.75
____Darth Vader (helmet) [A1S26] 0.75
____Epic Duel [A1S27] 0.75
____General Grievous [A1S28] 0.75
____Jedi Starfighters [A1S29] 0.75
____Revenge of the Sith [A1S30] 0.75
____The Emperor, "Power" [A1S31] 0.75
____Yoda [A1S32] 0.75

Unlicensed
____Sheet of 14 with glitter backgrounds [A1S33] 5.00

Stickers: TPM

Comic-style drawings.
____CF372-1 R2-D2/C-3PO, Darth Maul, Queen Amidala, Rebellion logo, Obi-Wan, Qui-Gon [SEI01] 7.00
____CF372-2 C-3PO, R2-D2/Luke, Yoda, Qui-Gon, Obi-Wan, Queen Amidala [SEI02] 7.00
____CF372-3 Obi-Wan, Queen Amidala, Imperial logo, Qui-Gon vs. Maul, R2-D2, Jabba [SEI03] 7.00

Sheet of 7.
____Maul/battleship/logo, Padme/Obi-Wan, Rodarian, Anakin/logo, Gungan Sub, C-3PO [SEI04]...........3.00

Swiss. Sheets of 9.
____Jar Jar, R2-D2, Battleship, Amidala/logo, TC-14, Maul, Royal Starship, Yoda, Watto [SEI05] 6.00
____Sebulba, Maul, Sith Infilterator, Anakin/logo, R2-D2, Nute Gunray, Droid, Blaster, Qui-Gon [SEI06] 6.00

Caltex
South Africa. Set of 8, unnumbered.
____Anakin Skywalker [SEI07] 5.00
____C-3PO [3:398] 5.00
____Darth Maul [3:398] 5.00
____Jar Jar Binks [3:398]............................5.00
____Obi-Wan Kenobi [3:398] 5.00
____Queen Amidala [3:398] 5.00
____Qui-Gon Jinn [3:398] 5.00
____R2-D2 [3:398] 5.00

Crazy Planet
Mega stickers. Set of 32, numbered. (Additional images and checklist in 3rd edition, page 399.)
____Stickers 1 – 32 [SEI08], each 2.00
____Stickers 1 – 32, set............................24.00

Mini stickers. Set of 24, numbered. (Images and checklist in 3rd edition, page 399.)
____Stickers 1 – 24 [SEI09], each 1.25
____Stickers 1 – 24, set............................18.00

Stickers: TPM

SEI01　SEI02　SEI03　SEI04　SEI05　SEI06　SEI07 sample　SEI08 sample　SEI09 sample　SEI10 sample　SEI11 sample

    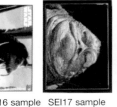 

SEI12 sample　SEI13 sample　SEI14 sample　SEI15 sample　SEI16 sample　SEI17 sample　SEI18 sample

Duncan
36 stickers, numbered. (Images and checklist in 3rd edition, page 399.)
____Stickers 1 – 36 [SEI10], each 2.00
____Stickers 1 – 36, set..........................25.00

Linden
Chile. Set of 40, numbered. (Images in 3rd edition, page 400. Checklist in 3rd edition, page 399.)
____Stickers 1 – 40 [SEI11], each 0.50
____Stickers 1 – 40, set..........................20.00

Meiji
Japan. Set of 24 numbered stickers distributed inside boxes of chocolate. (Images and checklist in 3rd edition page 400.)
____Stickers 1 – 24 [SEI12], each 1.00
____Stickers 1 – 24, set..........................20.00

Merlin Publishing Internat'l Ltd.
244 numbered stickers. (Checklist in 3rd ed., pg. 400.)
____Stickers 1 – 244, each 0.20
____Stickers 1 – 244, set 45.00

Merlin, Italy
Italy. Printed for Hasbro 1999 catalog. Numbered H1 – H15. (Images and checklist in 3rd ed., pg. 401.)
____Stickers H1 – H15 [SEI13], each 4.00

Pepsi Cola
____Heroes [3:401]....................................1.00
____Jedi vs. Sith [3:401] 1.00
____Qui-Gon, Jar Jar, Maul, Amidala [SEI14] 1.00
____Sebulba, Anakin / Podracer [3:401] 1.00

Ricolino
26 numbered stickers. (Images in 2nd edition, page 398. Checklist in 3rd edition page 401.)
____Stickers 1 – 26 [SEI15], each 0.50
____Stickers 1 – 26, set..........................25.00

Sabritas
39 stickers, numbered. (Images in 2nd edition, page 399. Checklist in 3rd edition page 402.)
____Stickers 1 – 39 [SEI16], each 0.50
____Stickers 1 – 39, set..........................30.00

Salo
176 numbered stickers, plus foil stickers numbered A-W. Public service / PSA stickers randomly inserted. (Images in 2nd edition, page 400. Checklist in 3rd edition, page 402.)
____Public Service stickers, each 1.00
____Stickers 1 – 176 [SEI17], each 0.15
____Stickers 1 – 176, set 35.00
____Stickers A – W [SEI18], each 1.00
____Stickers A – W, set 25.00

Stockings: Holiday

Kurt S. Adler, Inc.
Characture art.
____Darth Vader [C1C01] 20.00
____Yoda [C1C02]....................................20.00

Cuffed with art.
____Darth Vader, Sith [C1C03] 10.00
____Vader (helmet) [C1C04] 10.00
____Yoda, Jedi [C1C05] 10.00

Plush.
____Darth Vader [C1C06] 15.00
____Yoda [C1C07] 15.00

Straws

Applause
Sold loose with tag.
____Jar Jar Binks Sipper [SSS01] 5.00
____Pit Droid Sipper [SSS02] 5.00
____R2-D2 Sipper [SSS03] 5.00
____Watto Sipper [SSS04].........................5.00

Applause, UK
Sold on cards.
____Jar Jar Binks Sipper [SSS05] 6.00
____Pit Droid Sipper 6.00
____R2-D2 Sipper 6.00
____Watto Sipper [SSS06]..........................6.00

Zak Designs
EPI:TPM. Packaged in plastic bags.
____Anakin Skywalker [SSS07] 6.00
____Darth Maul [SSS08] 6.00
____Jar Jar Binks [SSS09].........................6.00
____Queen Amidala [SSS10] 6.00

EPIII:ROTS. Boxed.
____Darth Vader [SSS11]..........................6.00

String Dispensers

Sigma
____R2-D2 with scissors [SUY01] 175.00

Subway Tickets

SMRT
Classic trilogy.
____EPIV Star Wars style A [2:402] 7.00
____EPIV Star Wars style B [2:402] 7.00
____EPV Empire Strikes Back style A [2:402] 7.00
____EPV Empire Strikes Back style B [2:402] 7.00
____EPVI Return of the Jedi [2:402] 7.00
____Folder for EPIV tickets [2:402] 8.00

Episode I.
____Heroes [SWT01] 5.00
____Queen Amidala [SWT02]......................5.00
____Sith Lord, Darth Maul [SWT03]...............5.00
____Villains [SWT04] 5.00

Suitcases

Adam Joseph Industries
____Darth Vader and Royal Guards [LS01]................75.00
____Kneesaa and Wicket, 17"x10.25" 45.00
____Kneesaa and Wicket, 18"x11.5" [LS02]..............45.00

Premier Luggage
____Heroes and villains, ESB 2-sided [LS03] 55.00

Pyramid
Pilot style carry-ons.
____Anakin / Podracing 15.00
____Jedi 15.00
____Podracing with Anakin and Sebulba [LS04] 16.00
____Sith [LS05].......................................15.00

Wheeled carry-ons with pull-up handles.
____Boba Fett 27.00
____Darth Vader......................................27.00
____Luke Skywalker..................................27.00
____Stormtrooper [LS06]............................27.00

Super Packs

Antioch
Classic trilogy.
____Memo board with pen, 2 wallet cards, 1 tasseled bookmark, 1 die-cut bookmark, 1 doorknob hanger [SPP01]..11.00

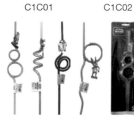 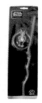      

C1C01　C1C02　C1C03　C1C04　C1C05　C1C06　C1C07

 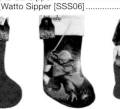  

SSS01-SSS04　SSS05　SSS06　SSS07 - SSS10　SSS11　SUY01　SWT01　SWT02　SWT03　SWT04

LS01

LS02

LS03

LS04

LS05

LS06

SPP01

SPP02

SPP03

HOS01

HOS02

HOS03

HOS04

TC01

TC02

TC03

TC04

TC05

TC06

TC07

TC08

TC09

TC10

TC11

SUT01

SUT02

Episode I: The Phantom Menace.
____Memo board with pen, 2 wallet cards, 1 tasseled bookmark, 1 die-cut bookmark [SPP02] 11.00
____Memo board with pen, journal, doorknob hanger, 1 tasseled bookmark, 3 wallet cards [SPP03]...24.00

Switch Plates and Covers

Hot Topic
____ANH movie poster art [HOS01] 8.00

Kenner
Switcheroos.
____C-3PO [HOS02] 65.00
____Darth Vader [HOS03] 75.00
____R2-D2 [HOS04]...75.00

Table Covers

Deeko
____Space Battle, sold in pkg. of 3 [TC01]................21.00

Drawing Board Greeting Cards, Inc.
____C-3PO, R2-D2, and Star Wars logo [TC02]........18.00
____Cloud City and Characters [TC03].....................16.00
____Darth Vader and Luke Dueling [TC04] 12.00
____Ewoks flying Gliders, 54"x96" [TC05] 10.00

Party Express
____Classic trilogy spaceships [TC06] 8.00
____EPI:TPM. Tech design with silouettes [TC07] 5.00
____EPII:AOTC. Jedi duel [TC08] 5.00
____EPIII:ROTS. 5.00
____Star Wars Saga [TC09] 7.00

Quela
____Darth Vader neon [TC10] 8.00

Unique
____Jedi vs. Sith, drawn [TC11] 6.00

Tape Dispensers

Butterfly Originals
____Darth Vader [SUT01]...8.00

Sigma
____C-3PO, ceramic [SUT02] 85.00

Tattoos

____Darth Vader Comic-Con 2004 excl. [TTO01] 3.00

Australia. EPIII:ROTS.
____Tattstack. Tattoos, tin, applicator [TTO02]..........20.00

Big Dog
____Dog Wars, sheet of 5 [TTO07] 3.00

General Mills
EPII:AOTC cereal premium.
____Anakin / Zam Wesell [TTO03].................................2.00
____Obi-Wan / Jango Fett [TTO04].................................2.00
____Padme / Battle Droid [TTO05] 2.00
____Yoda / Count Dooku [TTO06] 2.00

Lyons Maid
Ice cream premiums. Strips of 3, unused.
____Admiral Ackbar, Darth Vader, Bib Fortuna [3:405] 5.00
____Chewbacca, Gamorrean Guard, R2-D2 [3:405] 2.00
____Greedo, Stormtrooper, Han [3:405] 5.00
____Jabba the Hutt, Obi-Wan, Princess Leia [3:405] 5.00
____Wicket, Emperor, Luke [3:405] 5.00
____Yoda, Boba Fett, C-3PO [3:405].............................5.00

Ice cream premiums.
____Admiral Ackbar 2.00
____Bib Fortuna 2.00
____Boba Fett 2.00
____C-3PO 2.00
____Chewbacca 2.00
____Darth Vader 2.00
____Emperor 2.00
____Gamorrean Guard 2.00
____Greedo 2.00
____Han Solo 2.00
____Jabba the Hutt [3:405] 2.00
____Luke Skywalker 2.00
____Obi-Wan Kenobi 2.00
____Princess Leia 2.00
____R2-D2 ....2.00
____Stormtrooper...2.00
____Wicket 2.00
____Yoda 2.00

Mello Smello
Classic trilogy.
____Boba Fett, Darth Vader, C-3PO, Chewbacca, Landspeeder, Millennium Falcon, Vader, Leia, Darth Vader, Star Wars, X-Wing [TTO08] 5.00
____Darth Vader, R2-D2, Jawa, Luke, TIE fighter, Chewbacca, Vader's TIE, X-Wing, Vader, Han Solo, C-3PO, Princess Leia, Obi-Wan, Millennium Falcon, Star Wars [TTO09] 5.00
____TIE, Jawa, X-wings, Leia, Vader's TIE, Droids, Obi-Wan 3.00
____X-Wing, Tusken Raider, Chewbacca and Han, Han Solo, R2-D2, landspeeder 3.00

ROTS.
____Darth Vader, Vader, Grievous, Jedi emblem, duel, Vader's helmet, Jedi, ARC-170, Vader, Jedi, Grievous, Grievous [TTO10]...5.00
____Darth Vader, Vader, Jedi, Hero, Vader, helmet, Yoda, Jedi emblem, Sith, Sith Lord [TTO11] 5.00
____Shield, Jedi Starfighter, Darth Vader, Sith, General Grievous, lightsaber battle, ARC-170, Jedi 3.00
____Sith Lord 3.00
____Vader in flames, Anakin's Jedi Starfighter, Jedi symbol, Jedi, Sith, Republic, Sith Lord........................3.00

Norben
Skin Transfers, reusable.
____Anakin and Sebulba [TTO12] 4.00
____Jedi vs. Sith [TTO13] 4.00

TTO01

TTO02

TTO03

TTO04

TTO05

TTO06

Tattoos

TTO07

TTO08

TTO09

TTO10

TTO11

TTO12

TTO13

TTO14

TTO15

TTO16

Party Express
____5-pack...5.00

Pepsi
EPI:TPM.
____Darth Maul / "Sith Lord" 3.00
____Queen Amidala / "Queen Amidala" 3.00
____Qui-Gon Jinn / Naboo Fighter 3.00

Rose Art Industries
____Fun with Tattoos [TTO14] 9.00

Tapper Candies
____EPI:TPM, pkg. of 16 [TTO15] 4.00
____EPII:AOTC, pkg. of 6 [TTO16]................4.00

Tazos

Australia. 80 Tazos numbered from 81 – 160 plus three special "Connect-a-Tazo" starship cards. (Images in 2nd ed., pg. 494. Checklist in 3rd ed., pg. 405.)
____81 – 100 lenticular motion scenes, each 0.75
____101 – 130 octagon shaped, each.........................0.75
____131 – 140 3D images, each 0.75
____141 – 160 holographic foil, each 0.75
____Shuttle (Connect-a-Tazo) 3.00
____TIE Fighter (Connect-a-Tazo) 3.00
____X-Wing (Connect-a-Tazo) 3.00

China. 40 numbered Tazos. 15 holographic foil Tazos numbered variously throughout the set. (Checklist in 3rd edition, page 406.)
____Holofoil, each 2.25
____Regular, each 1.00

Mexico. 50 numbered Tazos plus 1 bonus Tazo. (Images in 2nd ed., pg. 405. Checklist in 3rd ed., pg. 406.)
____1 – 50, each 0.75
____Bonus: Darth Vader.........................2.00

Poland. 50 numbered Tazos. (Checklist in 3rd edition, page 406.)
____1 – 50, each 0.75

HOT01

HOZ01

HOZ02

UK. 50 numbered Tazos. (Checklist in 3rd ed., pg. 406.)
____1 – 50, each 0.75

Teapots

Sigma
____Luke on Tauntaun teapot [HOT01] 345.00

Totally Teapots
____Darth Vader, limited to 100 ....500.00

Telephones

American Telecommunications
____Darth Vader Speakerphone [HOZ01] 95.00

Sound Trax
____Darth Vader [HOZ02] 124.00
____R2-D2 [HOZ03]..............................65.00

Telemania
____R2-D2, Episode I Box [HOZ04] 65.00

Tiger Electronics
Compact phones.
____Darth Maul [HOZ05] 17.00
____Queen Amidala [HOZ06] 17.00

Tents

Monkey Business
____Darth Vader [T3T01] 15.00
____Epic duel [T3T02] 15.00

Thank You Cards

____C-3PO: "Thanks," 8-pack.........................4.00

Drawing Board Greeting Cards, Inc.
____R2-D2 Thank You Cards, 8-pack [TN01] 12.00

Heartline
____Darth Vader, Thank You 5.00
____Yoda, Thank You, I Do! 5.00

Party Express
"Thanks!" 8-packs.
____AOTC heroes [TN02].........................4.00
____Darth Vader [TN03].........................4.00
____Jar Jar Binks [TN04] 4.00

Thermos

____Darth Vader.........................10.00
____Darth Vader pop-up thermos [THM01] 47.00
____Darth Vader thermos jar 15.00

King Seeley – Thermos
____Empire Strikes Back: Darth Vader [THM02]........14.00
____Empire Strikes Back: Yoda [THM03] 8.00
____Ewoks: Princess Kneesa [THM04].....................11.00
____Return of the Jedi: Wicket [THM05].........8.00
____Star Wars: R2-D2 and C-3PO [THM06] 8.00

Thermos Co.
____Geonosis Duel.........................5.00
____Slave I [THM07].........................5.00

Zak Designs
____Anakin and Sebulba with cup lid [THM10] 10.00

Sip N' Snack Canteens.
____Anakin and Sebulba [THM08] 7.00
____Anakin and Sebulba, podrace cup [THM09] 11.00
____Anakin Skywalker [THM11]..................................7.00

Thimbles

Birchcroft
China thimbles, hand painted collection 1.
____C-3PO [SEW01] 5.00
____Chewbacca [SEW02] 5.00
____Darth Vader [SEW03] 5.00
____General Jan Dodonna [SEW04] 5.00
____Grand Moff Tarkin [SEW05] 5.00
____Han Solo [SEW06] 5.00
____Leia Organa [SEW07] 5.00
____Luke Skywalker [SEW08] 5.00
____R2-D2 [SEW09] 5.00
____Yoda [SEW10] 5.00

China thimbles, hand painted collection 2.
____Darth Maul [SEW11] 5.00
____Darth Sidious [SEW12] 5.00
____Exar Kun [SEW13].........................5.00
____Freedon Nadd [SEW14] 5.00
____Naga Sadow [SEW15] 5.00
____Obi-Wan Kenobi [SEW16].........................5.00
____Palpatine [SEW17] 5.00
____Senate Statue [SEW18] 5.00
____Too-Onebee [SEW19] 5.00
____Ulic Qel-Droma [SEW20] 5.00
____Wicket [SEW21] 5.00

China thimbles, hand painted collection 3.
____Anakin Skywalker [SEW22]................................8.00

HOZ03

HOZ04

HOZ05

HOZ06

TN01

TN02

TN03

TN04

THM01

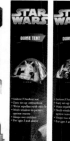

THM02

THM03 blue

THM03 red

THM04

THM05

THM06

THM07

THM08

THM09

THM10

THM11

T3T01

T3T02

| SEW01 | SEW02 | SEW03 | SEW04 | SEW05 | SEW06 | SEW07 | SEW08 | SEW09 | SEW10 |

| SEW11 | SEW12 | SEW13 | SEW14 | SEW15 | SEW16 | SEW17 | SEW18 | SEW19 | SEW20 |

| SEW21 | SEW22 | SEW23 | SEW24 | SEW25 | SEW26 | SEW27 | SEW28 | SEW29 | SEW30 |

| SEW31 | SEW32 | SEW33 | SEW34 | SEW35 | SEW36 | SEW37 | SEW38 | SEW39 | SEW40 |

____Clone Trooper [SEW23] 8.00
____Count Dooku [SEW24] 8.00
____Jango Fett [SEW25] 8.00
____Mace Windu [SEW26]...8.00
____Obi-Wan Kenobi [SEW27]......................................8.00
____Yoda [SEW28] 8.00
____Zam Wesell [SEW29]...8.00

China thimbles, hand painted collection 4.
____Ben Kenobi [SEW30] 8.00
____Chewbacca [SEW31] 8.00
____Darth Vader [SEW32] 8.00
____Grand Moff Tarkin [SEW33] 8.00
____Han Solo [SEW34] 8.00
____Lando Calrissian [SEW35] 8.00
____Luke Skywalker [SEW36] 8.00
____MonMothma [SEW37]..8.00
____Princess Leia [SEW38] 8.00
____Yoda [SEW39] 8.00

China thimbles, hand painted.
____A New Hope movie poster art [SEW40] 8.00

Tickets

____Celebration at Celbration III, Admit 1 [TKT01] 5.00

20th Century Fox
____1985, The Star Wars Trilogy, one performance only
[TKT02] 10.00
____IMAX opening day, EPII [TKT03] 10.00

Charity Preview Passes.
____Episode I 18.00
____Episode II 18.00

Disney / MGM
____Star Tours, cast premiere [TKT04] 3.00

Hasbro
____2004 Trivial Pursuit DVD Edition tryout, Comicon
exclusive [TKT05] 10.00

Lucasfilm
____1997 SW:SE Commerative.................................50.00
____1999 EPI Potters Field [TKT06] 25.00
____1999 EPI Royal Film Performance...................100.00

Philharmonic Orchestra of Indianapolis
____25th Anniversary Concert [TKT07].....................10.00
____25th Anniversary Concert reservation card, color-
coded for section seating [2:408].........................4.00

Tissue Covers

Jay Franco and Sons
____Space Battle scenes, 2 sided [TIS01] 11.00

Toothbrush Holders

____Toothbrush and light-up beaker [HOW01]..........18.00

Grosvenor
____Darth Maul, electronic [HOW02] 38.00
____Droid Fighter and Naboo Fighter [HOW03] 32.00
____Jar Jar Binks, 3D [HOW04] 16.00

Jay Franco and Sons
____Anakin / Sebulba 2-sided sculpt [HOW05] 8.00

Sigma
____Snowspeeder toothbrush holder [HOW06] 75.00

Toothbrushes

Avon, Mexico
____Anakin Skywalker [TOT01] 7.00
____C-3PO [TOT02] 7.00
____Padme Amidala 7.00
____R2-D2 [TOT03] 7.00

| TKT01 | TKT02 | TKT03 | TKT04 |

| TKT05 | TKT06 | TKT07 | TIS01 | HOW01 | HOW02 | HOW03 | HOW04 | HOW05 side 1 and side 2 | HOW06 |

Toothbrushes

| TOT01 | TOT02 | TOT03 | TOT04 | TOT05 | TOT06 | TOT07 | TOT08 | TOT09 | TOT10 | TOT11 | TOT12 |

| TOT13 | TOT14 | TOT15 | TOT16 | TOT17 | TOT18 | TOT19 | TOT20 | TOT21 | TOT22 | TOT23 | TOT24 | TOT25 | TOT26 | TOT27 | TOT28 | TOT29 | TOT30 | TOT31 | TOT32 | TOT33 |

Colgate
Classic trilogy.
____Darth Vader [TOT04] 4.00
____Droids on Tatooine [TOT05] 4.00
____Luke Skywalker, Pilot [TOT06] 4.00
____Luke Skywalker, Pilot (Space Battle) [TOT07] 6.00
____Princess Leia [TOT08]..........................4.00
____Princess Leia (Rebel Insignia) [TOT09]..................6.00

EPI: The Phantom Menace toothbrush with sculpted EPI character toothbrush holder and toothpaste.
____Darth Maul / Darth Maul [TOT10].....................12.00
____Jar Jar Binks (Naboo) / Jar Jar [TOT11] 12.00
____Queen Amidala / Amidala [TOT12] 12.00

EPI: The Phantom Menace toothbrush with sculpted EPI character toothbrush holder.
____Anakin Skywalker / Anakin [TOT13] 7.00
____Anakin Skywalker / R2-D2 [TOT14] 7.00
____Jar Jar Binks (Naboo) / Jar Jar [TOT15]...............7.00

____Jar Jar Binks (Naboo) / R2-D2 [TOT16] 7.00
____Obi-Wan (Jedi vs. Sith) / Darth Maul [TOT17] 7.00
____Obi-Wan (Jedi vs. Sith) / R2-D2 [TOT18] 7.00
____Queen Amidala (Coruscant) / Amidala [TOT19] 7.00
____Queen Amidala (Coruscant) / R2-D2 [TOT20] 7.00
____"Jedi vs. Sith" / Darth Maul [TOT21] 4.00

EPI: The Phantom Menace.
____Anakin Skywalker [TOT22] 4.00
____C-3PO [TOT23] 4.00
____Darth Maul [TOT24] 4.00
____Jar Jar Binks (Naboo) [TOT25] 4.00
____Jar Jar Binks (Tatooine) [TOT26] 4.00
____Obi-Wan (Jedi vs. Sith) [TOT27]..........................4.00
____Queen Amidala (Coruscant) [TOT28] 4.00
____Queen Amidala (Travel Gown) [TOT29] 4.00

Sculpted character handle.
____Anakin Skywalker as podracer pilot [TOT30] 5.00
____Darth Vader [TOT31] 6.00

____Jar Jar Binks [TOT32] 5.00
____Yoda [TOT33] 8.00

Colgate, Singapore
EPI: The Phantom Menace.
____Anakin Skywalker [TOT34] 5.00
____Jar Jar Binks (Naboo) [TOT35] 5.00
____Jedi vs. Sith [TOT36] 5.00
____Queen Amidala (Coruscant) [TOT37] 5.00

Grosvenor
____Jango Fett, figural [TOT38] 12.00
____Lightsaber, handle blinks red [TOT39] 6.00

Kenner
Battery operated.
____Star Wars [TOT40] 85.00
____Empire Strikes Back...75.00
____Return of the Jedi...85.00
____Wicket the Ewok [TOT41]...................................55.00

| TOT34 | TOT35 | TOT36 | TOT37 | TOT38 | TOT39 | TOT40 | TOT41 | TOT42 | TOT43 |

| TOT44 | TOT45 | TOT46 | TOT47 | TOT48 | TOT49 | TOT50 | TOT51 | TOT52 | TOT53 | TOT54 | TOT55 | TOT56 |

| TTP01 | TTP02 | TTP03 | TTP04 | TTP05 | TTP06 | TTP07 | TTP08 | TTP09 | TTP10 |

Oral-B

    C-3PO and R2-D2 ....5.00
    Chewbacca and Han Solo [TOT42] 5.00
    Darth Vader 5.00
    Ewoks 5.00
    Luke Skywalker 5.00
    Princess Leia [TOT43].....................................5.00

Shrink wrapped without packaging cardback.
    C-3PO and R2-D2 [TOT44] 3.00
    Chewbacca and Han Solo [TOT45] 3.00
    Darth Vader [TOT46].......................................3.00
    Ewoks [TOT47] 3.00
    Jedi Masters (premium) [TOT48] 11.00
    Luke Skywalker [TOT49] 3.00
    Princess Leia [TOT50].....................................3.00

Canada. **Shrink wrapped without packaging card-back. English and French text.**
    C-3PO and R2-D2 [TOT51] 5.00
    Chewbacca and Han Solo [TOT52] 5.00
    Darth Vader [TOT53].......................................5.00
    Ewoks [TOT54] 5.00
    Luke Skywalker [TOT55]...................................5.00
    Princess Leia [TOT56].....................................5.00

Toothpaste

Colgate
Galactic Bubblemint flavor.
    Anakin Skywalker [TTP01] 6.00

    Darth Vader and Death Star [TTP02] 6.00
    Droids on Tatooine [TTP03] 6.00
    Jar Jar Binks [TTP04]......................................6.00
    Jedi vs. Sith [TTP05].......................................6.00

Tartar Control with free teen/adult toothbrush.
    C-3PO (TPM) [TTP06]..8.00
    Darth Maul [TTP07]...8.00
    Darth Vader [TTP08] 8.00
    Princess Leia [TTP09] 8.00
    Queen Amidala [TTP10] 8.00

Totes: Record and Tape

Buena Vista Records
    Return of the Jedi cassette tote [PER01] 20.00
    Star Wars / Empire Strikes Back record tote for 45 RPMs [PER02] 15.00

Towels: Bath

Bibb Co.
    Boba Fett with Darth Vader and C-3PO, Cloud City, R2-D2 and Yoda..10.00
    Darth Vader, Chewbacca, Han, Leia, Luke, R2-D2 and C-3PO [2:410]...10.00
    Darth Vader, Leia, Luke, R2-D2 and C-3PO..10.00
    R2-D2 ....10.00

Bath towel and wash mitt set.
    ROTJ [CTB01] 50.00

Franco Manufacturing Company
    Darth Vader, hooded 20.00

Towels: Beach

    C-3PO and R2-D2 [CTL01] 15.00
    Darth Vader [CTL02].......................................15.00

Austria. EPIII:ROTS.
    Darth Vader / Epic Duel [CTL03] 20.00

Classic trilogy. 30"x60".
    C-3PO and R2-D2 [CTL04] 18.00
    Darth Vader [CTL05].......................................18.00
    Return of the Jedi classic poster art [CTL06] 18.00

EPI:TPM. 30"x60"
    Anakin Skywalker, Podrace [CTL07] 20.00
    Darth Maul [CTL08] 18.00
    Jar Jar Binks [CTL09].....................................18.00
    Naboo Space Battle [CTL10] 18.00
    Queen Amidala, Celebration [CTL11] 20.00

EPII:AOTC. 30"x60"
    "Heroes," Anakin, Mace, Yoda, Obi-Wan, Padme [CTL12] 18.00
    "Laser Fight," Anakin and Obi-Wan ... Vader vs. Kenobi [CTL13]...35.00

| PER01 | PER02 | CTB01 front and rear | CTL01 | CTL02 | CTL03 | CTL04 | CTL05 | CTL06 |

Towels: Beach

CTL07 CTL08 CTL09 CTL10 CTL11 CTL12 CTL13 CTL14 CTL15 CTL16 CTL17 CTL18 CTL19

CTL23 CTL24 CTL25 CTL26 CTL27 CTL28 CTL29 CTL30 CTL31 CTH01 CTH02 CTH03

CTH04 CTH05 CWC01 CWC02 CWC03 CWC04 CWC05 CWC06

____"Villains," Palpatine, Maul, Dooku, Vader 18.00
____Jedi Starfighter [CTL14].....................................35.00

EPIII:ROTS towel sacks 30"x60".
____Darth Vader / Sith Lord [CTL15]..........................15.00
____Jedi [CTL16]..15.00

EPIII:ROTS.
____Darth Vader [CTL17]..15.00
____Darth Vader silouette art [CTL18] 5.00

Japan.
____Boba Fett [CTL19]...35.00
____Darth Vader [CTL20]..35.00
____R2-D2 [CTL21] 35.00
____Yoda [CTL22] 35.00

Bibb Co.
____Boba Fett, Cloud City, Darth Vader, R2-D2 and
C-3PO, snowspeeders, Yoda.............................20.00
____Boba Fett, Darth Vader, Chewbacca, Han, Leia, Luke,
R2-D2 and C-3PO [CTL23]...............................20.00
____Boba Fett, Darth Vader, Leia, Luke, R2-D2 ....20.00
____C-3PO, Chewbacca, Darth Vader, Han, Leia, Luke,
and R2-D2 [CTL24]..15.00
____C-3PO, R2-D2, and planets [CTL25] 25.00
____Chewbacca with planets 35.00
____Darth Vader with planets 30.00
____Darth Vader, Death Star, Jawas, and Storm-
troopers 20.00
____Darth Vader, Tie Fighters, logo..........................18.00
____Main heros circled by Ewoks, ships, Jabba's palace,
and Darth Vader 16.00
____Max Rebo Band, R2-D2 and Wicket, Jabba the
Hutt...25.00
____ROTJ art, Luke and Darth Vader Duel in front of Darth
Vader silouette [CTL26] 45.00
____Wicket the Ewok 15.00
____Yoda with Dagobah tree....................................30.00

Jay Franco and Sons
____Anakin Skywalker, Podrace [CTL27] 12.00
____Boba Fett [CTL28] 18.00

____Droids on black background, white reverse 18.00
____Droids on white background, white reverse 18.00
____Princess Leia [CTL29] 18.00
____Queen Amidala, Coruscant [CTL30] 12.00
____Stormtrooper "Freeze you rebel scum" 18.00
____TPM movie poster art [CTL31].........................12.00
____Vader helmet, space battle 18.00
____Vader on black background, white reverse 18.00

Towels: Hand

3-piece washcloth and hand towel, EPI:TPM
____Anakin Skywalker [CTH01]...............................17.00

Bibb Co.
____Boba Fett, Darth Vader, speeders [CTH02] 8.00
____C-3PO and R2-D2 ....8.00
____C-3PO, Leia, Luke, R2-D2 ....8.00
____Darth Vader and Dogfight..................................8.00
____R2-D2 [CTH03] 8.00

Westpoint Stevens
2-piece washcloth and hand towel, EPI:TPM
____Anakin Skywalker 14.00
____Jar Jar Binks 14.00
____Queen Amidala..14.00
____Starfighters [CTH04]...14.00
____Starships [CTH05] 11.00

Towels: Wash Cloths

Bibb Co.
____Boba Fett and Darth Vader................................8.00
____C-3PO and R2-D2 [CWC01]................................8.00
____Darth Vader 8.00
____Hoth (Ice planet) [CWC02] 8.00
____R2-D2 ....8.00
____X-wing fighter 8.00
____Yoda [CWC03]..8.00

Tex U.K.
____Darth Maul [CWC04]...4.00
____Jar Jar Binks [CWC05] 4.00
____Queen Amidala [CWC06] 4.00

Toys: 12" Creatures – 1995 – 1999 (POTF2)

Hasbro
____Captain Tarpals and Kaadu, Target exclusive
[V1A01]..65.00
____Dewback and Sandtrooper, Toys R Us exclusive
[V1A02]...95.00

Kenner
____Han Solo and Tauntaun, Toys R Us exclusive
[V1A03] 65.00

Toys: 12" Creatures – 2002 – 2004 (Saga)

Hasbro
Star Wars Saga, classic trilogy.
____Luke Skywalker and Tauntaun, Toys R Us exclusive
[V2A01] 75.00

Toys: 12" Dolls

Hot Toys
____George Lucas, limited to 500 [AAV01]...............85.00

Medicom
____Darth Vader 250.00
____Darth Vader with burned face, limited to 1,000 Japan
exclusive 275.00
____Luke Skywalker, Jedi Knight 250.00
____Stormtrooper 225.00

V1A01   V1A02   V1A03   V2A01   AAV01   AAV02

A1V01

A1V02

A1V03

A1V04

A1V05

A1V06

A1V07

A1V08

A1V09

A1V10

A1V11

A1V12

A1V13

Robert Tonner
____Queen Amidala Trunk Set, FAO Schwarz exclusive, ltd. to 200 [AAV02] 1,975.00

Toys: 12" Dolls – 1978 – 1986 (Vintage)

Kenner
____Ben Kenobi [A1V01].....................................495.00
____Boba Fett, ESB [A1V02]...........................1,100.00
____Boba Fett, SW [A1V03] 1,100.00
____C-3PO [A1V04]..295.00
____Chewbacca [A1V05] 200.00
____Darth Vader [A1V06] 550.00
____Han Solo [A1V07]..650.00
____IG-88 [A1V08]..1,500.00
____Jawa [A1V09]...310.00
____Luke Skywalker [A1V10] 425.00
____Princess Leia Organa [A1V11].....................260.00
____R2-D2 [A1V12]..295.00
____Stormtrooper [A1V13] 425.00

Kenner, Australia
____Chewbacca, ESB [2:10].............................1,750.00
____Darth Vader, ESB 1,750.00

Lili Ledy
____Darth Vader 2,250.00
____Han Solo [2:10] 980.00
____Jawa [2:10]..950.00
____Luke Skywalker [2:10] 2,200.00
____Princess Leia [2:10] 1,050.00
____R2-D2 [2:10]..1,000.00
____Tusken Raider [2:10] 2,070.00

Meccano
____Boba Fett, ESB 770.00
____Chewbacca, ESB..415.00
____Jawa, SW [3:06]..555.00
____Princess Leia, SW 590.00
____Stormtrooper, SW 545.00

Takara
____Princess Leia Organa......................................655.00

Toltoys
____Boba Fett, SW 675.00

Toys: 12" Dolls – 1995 – 2000 (POTF2)

Hasbro
____Chewbacca, molded fur [A2V01] 15.00
____Han Solo with magnetic detonators [A2V02]..30.00
____Luke Skywalker with Dianoga tentacle [A2V03]..20.00
____Obi-Wan Kenobi, glow in the dark lightsaber [A2V04] 20.00
____Ponda Baba, removable arm [A2V05] 20.00
____Princess Leia with chain [A2V06].......................25.00

Kenner
2-packs.
____Death Star Gunner and Grand Moff Tarkin, FAO Schwarz exclusive, ltd. to 15,000 [A2V07]..65.00
____Emperor Palpatine and Emperor's Royal Guard, Target exclusive [A2V08] 50.00

____Han Solo and Luke Skywalker in Stormtrooper Disguises, KB Toys exclusive, limited to 20,000 [A2V09] 60.00
____Han Solo in Carbonite, Target exclusive [A2V10] 35.00
____Luke and Bib Fortuna with gloves, FAO Schwarz exclusive [A2V11]...85.00
____Luke and Bib Fortuna without gloves, FAO Schwarz exclusive [A2V12]..85.00
____Luke and Wampa, Target exclusive [A2V13] 45.00
____Princess Leia as Jabba's Prisoner and Bartender R2-D2, FAO Schwarz exclusive. [A2V14] 65.00
____Wedge Antilles and Biggs Darklighter, FAO Schwarz exclusive [A2V15] 75.00

3-packs.
____Luke Skywalker, Princess Leia as Boushh, Han Solo in Bespin Outfit, KB Toys exclusive [A2V16] 60.00

4-packs.
____Luke Skywalker (Hoth), Han Solo (Hoth), Snowtrooper, AT-AT Driver, JC Penney exclusive [A2V17]........50.00

6" series.
____Jawa [A2V18] 15.00
____R2-D2 [A2V19] 25.00
____R5-D4 [A2V20] 25.00
____Wicket, Walmart exclusive [A2V21] 25.00
____Yoda [A2V22] 40.00

Flap boxes.
____Admiral Ackbar [A2V23] 20.00
____AT-AT Driver, Service Merch. excl. [A2V24] 30.00
____Boba Fett [A2V25]...40.00
____C-3PO [A2V26]..35.00

A2V01

A2V02

A2V03

A2V04

A2V05

A2V06

A2V07

A2V08

A2V09

A2V10

A2V11

A2V12

A2V13

A2V14

A2V15

A2V16   A2V17   A2V18   A2V19   A2V20

A2V21   A2V22   A2V23   A2V24   A2V25   A2V26   A2V27   A2V28   A2V29

A2V30   A2V31   A2V32   A2V33   A2V34   A2V35   A2V36   A2V37   A2V38   A2V39   A2V40

Cantina Band Members, Walmart exclusives.

____Doikk N'ats [A2V27]	35.00
____Figrin D'an [A2V28]	35.00
____Ickabel [A2V29]	35.00
____Nalan [A2V30]	35.00
____Tech [A2V31]	35.00
____Tedn [A2V32]	35.00
____Chewbacca [A2V33]	45.00
____Darth Vader, dark blue card, black lightsaber [A2V34]	30.00
____Darth Vader, light blue card, black and silver lightsaber	20.00
____Darth Vader, light blue card, black and silver lightsaber, black and gold foil logo	20.00
____Darth Vader, lt. blue card, black lightsaber	20.00
____Greedo, J.C. Penney exclusive. [A2V35]	25.00
____Han Solo, dark blue card, unpainted pouch [A2V36]	30.00

____Han Solo, light blue card, painted pouch	20.00
____Han Solo, light blue card, painted pouch, black and gold foil logo	20.00
____Han Solo, light blue card, unpainted pouch	20.00
____Lando Calrissian [A2V37]	20.00
____Luke Skywalker Bespin Fatigues [A2V38]	20.00
____Luke Skywalker X-Wing Pilot [A2V39]	25.00
____Luke Skywalker, dark blue card, binoculars on belt, black lightsaber [A2V40]	30.00
____Luke Skywalker, dark blue card, binoculars on card, black lightsaber	20.00
____Luke Skywalker, light blue card, black and silver lightsaber	20.00
____Luke Skywalker, light blue card, black and silver lightsaber, black and gold foil logo	20.00
____Luke Skywalker, lightt blue card, black lightsaber	20.00
____Obi Wan Kenobi, dark blue card, silver belt buckle, black lightsaber [A2V41]	25.00

____Obi Wan Kenobi, light blue card, gold belt buckle, black and silver lightsaber	20.00
____Obi Wan Kenobi, lt. blue card, gold belt buckle, black & silver lightsaber, black and gold foil logo	45.00
____Obi Wan Kenobi, light blue card, silver belt buckle, black and silver lightsaber	20.00
____Obi Wan Kenobi, light blue card, silver belt buckle, black lightsaber	20.00
____Princess Leia [A2V42]	25.00
____Sandtrooper, Diamond exclusive. [A2V43]	35.00
____Stormtrooper [A2V44]	30.00
____Tie Fighter Pilot [A2V45]	35.00
____Tusken Raider with Blaster, printed warning [A2V46]	25.00
____Tusken Raider with Blaster, warning sticker	25.00
____Tusken Raider with Gaderffii Stick, printed warning	30.00
____Tusken Raider, with Gaderffii Stick, warning sticker	30.00

A2V41   A2V42   A2V43   A2V44   A2V45   A2V46   A2V47   A2V48   A2V49   A2V50   A2V51

A2V52   A2V53   A2V54   A2V55   A2V56   A2V57   A2V58   A2V59   A2V60   A2V61

| A2V62 | A2V63 | A2V64 | A2V65 | A2V66 | A2V67 | A2V68 | A6V01 | A6V02 |

| A6V03 | A6V04 | A6V05 | A7V01 | A7V02 | A7V03 | A7V04Z |

Window boxes.

____AT-AT Driver [A2V47] 25.00
____Barquin D'an [A2V48] 15.00
____Chewbacca Boushh's Bounty [A2V49] 25.00
____Emperor Palpatine [A2V50] 15.00
____Emperor Palpatine fully poseable [A2V51]..........15.00
____Grand Moff Tarkin [A2V52] 20.00
____Greedo [A2V53] 20.00
____Han Solo Hoth Gear [A2V54] 20.00
____Luke Skywalker Ceremonial [A2V55] 15.00
____Luke Skywalker Hoth Gear [A2V56]...................20.00
____Luke Skywalker Jedi [A2V57]...............................20.00
____Luke Skywalker Jedi with glow-in-dark lightsaber
[A2V58] 20.00
____Princess Leia in Hoth Gear, Service Merchandise
exclusive [A2V59] 20.00
____Sandtrooper with Imperial Droid [A2V60] 30.00
____Snowtrooper, blue highlights 200.00
____Snowtrooper, gray highlights [A2V61] 20.00

Kenner, Canada
Bi-language packaging.
____Han Solo, Quickdraw Action 70.00
____Luke Skywalker, Swinging Lightsaber Action
[A2V62] 35.00

Kenner, UK
____Boba Fett 35.00
____Dark Vador [A2V63] 32.00
____Han Solo [A2V64] 45.00
____Han Solo, Quickdraw Action [A2V65] 70.00
____Luke Skywalker [A2V66] 45.00
____Luke Skywalker, Swinging Lightsaber Action
[A2V67] 45.00
____Obi-Wan Kenobi [A2V68] 32.00

Toys: 12" Dolls –
1999 – 2000 Portrait Edition

Hasbro
____#1 Princess Leia Ceremonial Gown [A6V01] 20.00
____#2 Queen Amidala black gown [A6V02] 25.00
____#3 Queen Amidala red gown [A6V03] 25.00
____Queen Amidala and Qui-Gon Jinn [A6V04] 80.00
____Queen Amidala Return to Naboo [A6V05] 25.00

Toys: Action Figure 12" Dolls –
1999 – 2000 Queen Amidala Fashion

Hasbro
____Beautiful Braids Padme [A7V01] 12.00
____Hidden Majesty [A7V02].....................................12.00
____Royal Elegance [A7V03] 12.00
____Ultimate Hair [A7V04] 12.00

Toys: Action Figure 12" Dolls –
1999 – 2001 (TPM)

Hasbro
6" series.
____Anakin Skywalker [A3V01] 15.00
____Pit Droids [A3V02] 15.00
____R2-A6 [A3V03] 15.00

2-Packs.
____Chancellor Valorum / Senate Guard [A3V04]......65.00

Frame boxes.
____Battle Droid [A3V05]..20.00
____Darth Maul [A3V06]...35.00
____Jar Jar Binks [A3V07]...20.00
____Obi-Wan Kenobi [A3V08] 20.00
____Qui-Gon Jinn [A3V09]..20.00
____Qui-Gon Jinn error on back of box 35.00
____Watto [A3V10]..15.00

Window boxes.
____Anakin Skywalker, podracer [A3V11] 50.00
____Battle Droid Commander [A3V12] 30.00
____Boss Nass [A3V13]..40.00
____Mace Windu [A3V14]...35.00
____Qui-Gon Jinn, Tatooine gray poncho.................50.00
____Qui-Gon Jinn, Tatooine tan poncho [A3V15] 25.00
____Sebulba [A3V16]..30.00

Hasbro, UK
Multi-language packaging.
____Battle Droid [A3V17]..20.00
____Watto [A3V18]...15.00

Toys: Action Figure 12" Dolls –
2001 – 2002 (POTJ)

Hasbro
____4-LOM with concussion rifle [A4V01] 40.00
____Bossk with blaster rifle [A4V02] 35.00

| A3V01 | A3V02 | A3V03 | A3V04 | A3V05 | A3V06 | A3V07 |

| A3V08 | A3V09 | A3V10 | A3V11 | A3V12 | A3V13 | A3V14 | A3V15 | A3V16 | A3V17 | A3V18 |

Toys: Action Figure 12" Dolls – 2001 – 2002

| A4V01 | A4V02 | A4V03 | A4V04 | A4V05 | A4V06 | A4V07 | A4V08 | A4V09 |

| A5V01 | A5V02 | A5V03 | A5V04 | A5V05 | A5V06 | A5V07 | A5V08 | A5V09 | A5V10 |

| A5V11 | A5V12 | A5V13 | A5V14 | A5V15 | A5V16 | A5V17 | A5V18 | A5V19 | A5V20 | A5V21 |

____Death Star Droid [A4V03].....................................25.00
____Death Star Trooper [A4V04] 20.00
____Han Solo, stormtrooper disguise [A4V05] 30.00
____IG-88 [A4V06] 40.00
____Luke Skywalker, 100th figure [A4V07] 50.00

2-Packs.
____Luke Skywalker and Yoda [A4V08] 45.00
____Sith Lords, Vader and Maul [A4V09] 60.00

Toys: Action Figure 12" Dolls –
2002 – 2004 (Saga)

Hasbro
Blue packaging, deluxe.
____Jango Fett [A5V01]..70.00
____Princess Leia in Boushh Disguise [A5V02] 30.00

Blue packaging.
____Anakin Skywalker [A5V03] 25.00
____Anakin Skywalker, Battle [A5V04] 30.00
____AT-ST Driver [A5V05] 30.00
____Clone Commander (yellow), KB Toys exclusive
[A5V06] 30.00
____Clone Trooper [A5V07] 30.00
____Clone Trooper (red), KB Toys exclusive
[A5V08] 30.00
____Count Dooku [A5V09]...30.00
____Dengar [A5V10] 30.00
____Gamorrean Guard [A5V11] 30.00
____Genosian Warrior [A5V12] 25.00
____Han Solo [A5V13] 20.00
____Imperial Officer [A5V14] 25.00
____Ki-Adi Mundi [A5V15] 40.00
____Lando Calrissian Skiff Guard, helmet down
[A5V16] 30.00
____Lando Calrissian Skiff Guard, helmet forward
[A5V17] 30.00

____Mace Windu, TRU exclusive [A5V18] 30.00
____Obi-Wan Kenobi [A5V19] 20.00
____Padme Amidala [A5V20] 40.00
____Plo Koon, Fan Club exclusive [A5V21] 165.00
____Super Battle Droid [A5V22] 20.00
____Zam Wesell [A5V23] 15.00
____Zuckuss [A5V24] 30.00

Gold bar packaging.
____Biker Scout [A5V25]...60.00
____Ewoks 2-pack [A5V26]...40.00
____Garindan [A5V27]...20.00
____Jawas 2-pack [A5V28]..25.00
____Luke Skywalker, Jedi [A5V29] 20.00
____Obi-Wan Kenobi, aged [A5V30] 25.00
____Yoda [A5V31] 30.00

Toys: Action Figure 12" Dolls –
2004 (Original Trilogy Collection)

Hasbro
No sticker on corner of box.
____Boba Fett, blue jumpsuit 60.00
____Boba Fett, gray jumpsuit 40.00
____Chewbacca, KB Toys exclusive [A8V01] 35.00
____Luke Skywalker [A8V02] 25.00
____Stormtrooper [A8V03]...40.00

Star Wars sticker on corner of box.
____Boba Fett [A8V04] 70.00
____Luke Skywalker [A8V05]......................................35.00
____Stormtrooper 50.00

| A5V22 | A5V23 | A5V24 | A5V25 | A5V26 | A5V27 | A5V28 |

| A5V29 | A5V30 | A5V31 | A8V01 | A8V02 | A8V03 | A8V04 | A8V05 |

A9V01

A9V02

A9V03

A9V04

A9V05

A9V06

A9V07

B101

B102

B103

B104

B105

B106

A1A01

A1A02

A1A03

A1A04

A2A01

Toys: Action Figure 12" Dolls – 2005 (ROTS)

Hasbro
```
____Anakin Skywalker, Ultimate Villain [A9V01] ........60.00
____Bariss Offee [A9V02] ...........................20.00
____Chewbacca, KB Toys exclusive [A9V03] ...........39.00
____Clone Trooper [A9V04] ..........................30.00
____General Grievous [A9V05] .......................30.00
____Shaak Ti [A9V06] ...............................25.00
____The Emperor [A9V07] ............................20.00
```

Toys: Action Figure 12" Dolls – 2005 – 2007

Sideshow Collectibles
Heroes of the Rebellion.
```
____Han Solo, Bespin [B101] ........................100.00
```

Lords of the Sith.
```
____Darth Maul .....................................95.00
____Darth Vader (Anakin) Sith Apprentice, San Diego
     Comic-Con exclusive, limited to 6,000 ..........325.00
____Sith Probe Droid expansion pack ................45.00
```

Order of the Jedi.
```
____Anakin Skywalker [B102] .........................80.00
____Anakin  Skywalker  (ROTS)  with  exclusive
     hologram .......................................175.00
____Kit Fisto [B103] ................................100.00
____Kit Fisto with exclusibe battle droid head......150.00
____Luke Skywalker, Jedi [B104] .....................90.00
____Luke Skywalker, Jedi with excl. blaster.........150.00
____Mace Windu [B105] ...............................95.00
____Obi-Wan Kenobi (ROTS) ...........................100.00
____Obi-Wan  Kenobi  (ROTS)  with  exclusive  General
     Grievous blaster [B106] ........................175.00
____Plo Koon .......................................150.00
```

Toys: Action Figure 12" Dolls – Electronic, 1995 – 1999 (POTF2)

Kenner
```
____Boba Fett, KB Toys exclusive [A1A01] ...........75.00
____Darth Vader [A1A02].............................40.00
```

A2A02

A2A03

A2A04

A2A05

A3A01

A3A02

2-pack.
```
____C-3PO and R2-D2 [A1A03] ........................50.00
____Obi Wan vs. Darth Vader, J.C. Penney exclusive
     [A1A04] .......................................35.00
```

Toys: Action Figure 12" Dolls – Electronic, 1999 – 2000 (TPM)

Hasbro
```
____C-3PO [A2A01]...................................40.00
____Darth Maul [A2A02] .............................20.00
____Jar Jar Binks [A2A03]...........................20.00
____Qui-Gon Jinn [A2A04] ...........................20.00
____TC-14, KB Toys exclusive [A2A05] ...............30.00
```

Toys: Action Figure 12" Dolls – Electronic, 2002 (AOTC)

Hasbro
Electronic Battling.
```
____Jango Fett [A3A01]..............................30.00
____Obi-Wan Kenobi [A3A02] .........................25.00
```

Toys: Action Figure 12" Vehicles – 1995 – 1999 (POTF2)

Hasbro
```
____Speeder Bike with Scout Trooper [A1A01] ........160.00
```

Toys: Action Figure 12" Vehicles – 1999 – 2000 (TPM)

Hasbro
```
____Darth Maul with Sith Speeder [A2A01] ...........90.00
```

Toys: Action Figure 12" Vehicles – 2001 – 2002 (POTJ)

Hasbro
```
____Speeder Bike with Luke Skywalker [A3A01] .......45.00
```

Toys: Action Figure 12" Vehicles – 2002 – 2004 (Saga)

Hasbro
```
____Princess Leia on Speeder Bike [A4A01] ..........45.00
```

Toys: Action Figure Accessories – 1978 – 1986 (Vintage)

Kenner
```
____Ewok Assault Catapult, ROTJ [A1C01] ............40.00
____Ewok Combat Glider, ROTJ [A1C02]................40.00
____Radar Laser Cannon, ESB [A1C03].................20.00
____Radar Laser Cannon, ROTJ [A1C04]................15.00
```

A1A01

A2A01

A3A01

A4A01

Toys: Action Figure Accessories – 1978 – 1986

A1C01

A1C02

A1C03

A1C04

A1C05

A1C06

A1C07

A1C08

A1C09

A2C01

A3C01

A3C02

____Survival Kit, mail-in promotion [A1C05] 20.00
____Tri-Pod Laser Cannon, ESB [A1C06] 20.00
____Tri-Pod Laser Cannon, ROTJ [A1C07] 15.00
____Vehicle Maint. Energizer, ESB [A1C08] 20.00
____Vehicle Maint. Energizer, ROTJ [A1C09] 15.00

Lili Ledy
____Ewok Assault Catapult 90.00
____Ewok Combat Glider 160.00

Toys: Action Figure Accessories – 1995 – 1999 (POTF2)

Kenner
Freeze-frame accessories.
____Binocular viewer, 2 exclusive slides [1:6] 25.00
____Storage folder [A2C01].......................................15.00

Toys: Action Figure Accessories – 1999 – 2001 (TPM)

Hasbro
____Flash Cannon [A3C01] 15.00
____Gungan Assault Cannon with Jar Jar Binks [A3C02] 15.00
____Gungan Catapult [A3C03] 15.00

Accessory packs.
____Hyperdrive Repair Kit [A3C04] 30.00
____Naboo Accessory Set [A3C05] 6.00
____Podracer Fuel Station [A3C06] 25.00
____Rappel Line Attack [A3C07]................................12.00
____Sith Accessory Set [A3C08] 6.00
____Tatooine Disguise Set [A3C09]............................25.00
____Tatooine Accessory Set [A3C10]..........................6.00
____Underwater Accessory Set [A3C11].....................6.00

Battle Bags.
____Sea Creatures: Angel Fish, Trigger, Soe, Opee Sea Killer [A3C12] 5.00
____Sea Creatures: Faa, Colo Claw Fish, Grouper, Sando Aqua Monster [A3C13] 5.00
____Swamp Creatures: Mott, Ikopi, Kaadu, Falumpaset [A3C14] 5.00
____Swamp Creatures: Nuna, Shaak, Pikobis, Fambaa [A3C15] 5.00

____CommTech Chip, model 2, any [1:6] 65.00

CommTech chip readers.
____.0000 with logo sticker.....................................20.00
____.0000 without logo sticker 20.00
____.0100 with logo sticker.....................................20.00
____.0100 without logo sticker [A3C16] 20.00

Hasbro, Canada
____Gungan Assault Cannon [A3C17] 15.00

Tri-language packaging.
____CommTech chip reader [A3C18] 20.00

Hasbro, Spain
____CommTalk chip reader [A3C19] 20.00

Hasbro, UK
____Gungan Assault Cannon 15.00

Accessory packs. Tri-language packaging.
____Naboo 8.00
____Sith 8.00
____Tatooine 8.00
____Underwater 8.00

A3C03

A3C04   A3C05   A3C06   A3C07

A3C08   A3C09   A3C10   A3C11   A3C12   A3C13   A3C14   A3C15

A3C16   A3C17   A3C18   A3C19

A4C01

A4C02

A4C03

A4C04

A4C05

A1D01

A1D02

A1D03

A1D04

A1D05

A1D06

A2D01

A2D02

A2D03

Toys: Action Figure Accessories – 2002 – 2004 (Saga)

Hasbro

____Ewok with Attack Glider [A4C01].......................20.00

Single figure with movie accessories.
____Arena Conflict, AOTC [A4C02]...........................15.00
____Death Star, ANH [A4C03].................................15.00
____Endor Victory, ROTJ [A4C04]...........................15.00
____Hoth Survival, ESB [A4C05].............................15.00

Hasbro, UK
Single figure with movie accessories.
____Arena Conflict, AOTC....................................15.00
____Death Star, ANH...15.00
____Endor Victory, ROTJ......................................15.00
____Hoth Survival, ESB..15.00

Toys: Action Figure Creatures – 1978 – 1986 (Vintage)

Kenner

____Hoth Wampa, ESB, box shows Luke in Hoth gear [A1D01]..85.00
____Patrol Dewback, SW [A1D02]............................85.00
____Patrol Dewback, Collector Series [A1D03] 100.00
____Rancor Monster, ROTJ [A1D04]........................85.00
____Tauntaun, open belly, ESB [A1D05]...................80.00
____Tauntaun, solid belly, ESB [A1D06] 75.00
____Wampa, ESB, box shows Rebel Commander [1:208]..100.00

Kenner, Canada

____Patrol Dewback, ESB [2:12] 250.00
____Patrol Dewback, ESB includes Stormtrooper figure [2:12] 500.00

____Patrol Dewback, ESB includes Stormtrooper figure blacked out 400.00
____Patrol Dewback, ESB includes Stormtrooper figure orange sticker 900.00

Lili Ledy
____Rancor Monster, ROTJ 185.00

Meccano
____Hoth Wampa, ROTJ......................................90.00

Palitoy
____Hoth Wampa, ROTJ.......................................75.00
____Rancor Monster, ROTJ 185.00
____Tauntaun open belly, ESB 135.00

Toys: Action Figure Creatures – 1995 – 1999 (POTF2)

Kenner

____Bantha / Tusken Raider .00 [A2D01] 48.00
____Dewback / Sandtrooper .00...............................45.00
____Dewback / Sandtrooper .01 [A2D02] 20.00
____Jabba / Han Solo .00 ....60.00
____Jabba / Han Solo .01 ....20.00
____Jabba / Han Solo .02 [A2D04] 15.00
____Rancor / Luke .00 [A2D03].................................65.00
____Ronto / Jawa .00 [A2D05].................................15.00
____Tauntaun / Han Solo .00 [A2D06]......................90.00
____Tauntaun / Luke .00 [A2D07]...........................20.00
____Wampa / Luke .00 [A2D08] 50.00

A2D04

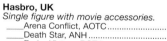

A2D05

A2D06

A2D07

A2D08

Toys: Action Figure Creatures – 1995 – 1999

A2D09

A2D10

A2D11

A3D01

A3D02

A3D03

A3D04

A3D05

A3D06

A3D07

Kenner, Italy
____Jabba / Han Solo [A2D09] 40.00
Kenner, UK
____Jabba / Han Solo [A2D10] 40.00
____Ronto / Jawa .00 [A2D11] 45.00

Toys: Action Figure Creatures –
1999 – 2001 (TPM)

Hasbro
____Ammo Wagon w/Falumpaset [A3D01]................50.00
____Eopie and Qui-Gon Jinn [A3D02] 130.00
____Fambaa, FAO Schwarz exclusive [A3D03] 125.00
____Jabba Glob [A3D04] 10.00
____Jabba the Hutt with Announcer [A3D05]...........30.00
____Kaadu and Jar Jar Binks [A3D06] 15.00
____Opee and Qui-Gon Jinn [A3D07] 10.00

Hasbro, UK
____Ammo Wagon w/Falumpaset [A3D08]................35.00
____Jabba the Hutt with Announcer [A3D08]...........20.00
____Opee and Qui-Gon Jinn 20.00

Toys: Action Figure Creatures –
2002 – 2004 (AOTC)

Hasbro
____Acklay .0000 [A4D01] 35.00
____Acklay .0100 [A4D02] 35.00
____Nexu with snapping jaws [A4D03] 15.00
____Nexu with snapping jaws, new pose
[A4D04] 12.00
____Reek [A4D05] 15.00

Hasbro, Canada
Tri-language packaging.
____Acklay [A4D06] 35.00
____Nexu [A4D07] 8.00
____Reek [A4D08] 25.00

A3D08

A3D09

A4D01

A4D02

A4D03

A4D04

A4D05

A4D06

A4D07

A4D08

A5D01   A5D02   A5D03   A6D01   AVA201

AVA202   A1F01   A1F02

Toys: Action Figure Creatures –
2002 – 2004 (Saga)

Hasbro
Saga gold-bar, blister card packaging.
____Jabba's Palace Court Denizens [A5D01] 20.00
____Jabba the Hutt [A5D02] 15.00
____Wampa with Hoth cave [A5D03] 20.00

Toys: Action Figure Creatures –
2005 (ROTS)

Hasbro
____Boga with Obi-Wan Kenobi [A6D01] 25.00

Toys: Action Figure Display Stands

Kenner
Vintage.
____Display Arena, mailer pkg................................145.00
____Display Stand, ESB 360.00
____Display Stand, mailer pkg. [1:215] 300.00
____Display Stand, SW [AVA202] 350.00

Pride Displays
Limited to 3,000 pieces, mail-order only.
____A New Hope, limited to 3,000 [AVA201] 55.00

A1F03   A1F04   A1F05

Toys: Action Figure Playsets –
1978 – 1986 (Vintage)

Kenner
Star Wars packaging.
____Cantina Adventure Set, Sears exclusive [A1F01]..700.00
____Creature Cantina [A1F03] 250.00
____Death Star Space Station [A1F02] 500.00
____Droid Factory [A1F04] 125.00
____Land of the Jawas [A1F05] 160.00

Empire Strikes Back packaging.
____Cloud City, Sears exclusive [A1F06] 420.00
____Dagobah, Luke with backpack [A1F07] 120.00
____Dagobah, Vader and Luke battle [A1F08] 150.00
____Dagobah, Backpack sticker [A1F09]................135.00

____Darth Vader's Star Destroyer [A1F11] 145.00
____Hoth Ice Planet [A1F12]...................................225.00
____Imperial Attack Base [A1F13] 125.00
____Rebel Command Center [A1F10] 245.00
____Turret and Probot [A1F15] 145.00

Return of the Jedi packaging.
____Ewok Village [A1F14] 300.00
____Jabba the Hutt [A1F16]......................................65.00
____Jabba the Hutt, Sears box [A1F17] 75.00
____Jabba the Hutt Dungeon with 8D8, Sears exclusive [A1F18]..125.00
____Jabba the Hutt Dungeon with Amanaman [A1F19]..300.00

Kenner, Canada
Star Wars packaging.
____Death Star [3:14] 230.00
____Land of the Jawas, incl. one figure [2:13] 1,000.00

A1F06   A1F07   A1F08   A1F09   A1F10

A1F11   A1F12   A1F13   A1F14

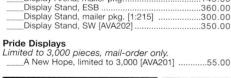

Toys: Action Figure Playsets – 1978 – 1986

A1F15

A1F16

A1F17

A1F18

A1F19

A1F20

A1F21

A1F22

A1F23

A2F01

A2F02

A2F03

Empire Strikes Back packaging.
_____Hoth Ice Planet, 3 free mini-figures offer......1,500.00
_____Hoth Ice Planet, includes Imperial Snow
     Stormtrooper [2:13] 1,500.00
_____Turret and Probot...195.00

Return of the Jedi packaging.
_____Jabba the Hutt 85.00

Lili Ledy
Return of the Jedi packaging.
_____Jabba the Hutt..155.00

Meccano
Return of the Jedi packaging.
_____Ewok Village...135.00

Palitoy
Star Wars packaging.
_____Cantina [A1F20] 450.00

_____Cantina, 4 free mini-figures offer, sales samples
     only 900.00
_____Death Star [A1F21]...1,350.00
_____Droid Factory [A1F22] 430.00
_____Land of the Jawas [A1F23] 675.00

Empire Strikes Back packaging.
_____Darth Vader's Star Destroyer 165.00
_____Turret and Probot...160.00

Return of the Jedi.
Tri-logo packaging.
_____Endor Attack [2:14] 150.00
_____Ewok Combat [2:14] 150.00
_____Ewok Village [2:14]..135.00
_____Hoth Rescue [2:14] 200.00

Toltoys
Star Wars packaging.
_____Death Star 585.00

Toys: Action Figure Playsets –
1995 – 1999 (POTF2)

Hasbro
_____Jabba's Palace Pop-Up [A2F01] 20.00

Kenner
_____Cantina at Mos Eisley [A2F02]............................25.00
_____Death Star Escape [A2F03] 20.00
_____Detention Block Rescue [A2F04] 20.00
_____Endor Attack [A2F05]..35.00
_____Hoth Battle [A2F06]..40.00
_____Mos Eisley Pop-Up Cantina [A2F07] 20.00

Kenner, UK
_____Death Star Escape, green pkg. [A2F08] 35.00
_____Death Star Escape, red pkg. [A2F09] 20.00
_____Detention Block Rescue, grn. pkg. [A2F10] 35.00
_____Detention Block Rescue, red pkg. [A2F11] 20.00

A2F04

A2F05

A2F06

A2F07

A2F08

A2F09

A2F10

A2F11

A3F01

A3F02

A4F01

A5F01

A6F01

Toys: Action Figure Playsets –
1999 – 2001 (TPM)

Hasbro
____Theed Generator Complex with Battle Droid
[A3F01] 25.00
____Theed Hanger, motorized with Qui-Gon Jinn and fall-
apart Battle Droid [A3F02] 35.00

Toys: Action Figure Playsets –
2001 – 2002 (POTJ)

Hasbro
____Carbon Freezing Chamber with exclusive Bespin
Security Guard [A4F01] 50.00

Toys: Action Figure Playsets –
2002 – 2004 (Saga)

Hasbro
____Arena Battle [A5F01] 50.00

Toys: Action Figure Playsets –
2005 (ROTS)

Hasbro
____Mustafar Final Battle [A6F02].............................35.00
____Mustafar Final Battle with four bonus clone troopers,
Sam's Club exclusive [A6F01] 60.00

Toys: Action Figure Storage Cases –
1978 – 1986 (Vintage)

Kenner
____C-3PO, metallic finish, ROTJ [A1G01]................35.00
____Chewbacca Bandolier, ROTJ [A1G02]................20.00
____Darth Vader [A1G03] 40.00

A6F02

A1G01

A1G02

____Darth Vader $1.00 rebate sticker 65.00
____Darth Vader 3 free figs [2:14]............................600.00
____Laser Rifle, ROTJ [A1G04] 40.00
____Vinyl ESB logo / SW scenes [A1G05] 100.00
____Vinyl ESB logo / Yoda [A1G06] 60.00
____Vinyl ESB Yoda / Wampa [A1G07].....................80.00
____Vinyl ROTJ [A1G08] 135.00
____Vinyl SW [A1G09] 45.00

Kenner, UK
____Star Wars [A1G10] 35.00

Toys: Action Figure Storage Cases –
1995 – 1999 (POTF2)

Just Toys
____Darth Vader, for Bend-ems figures 20.00

Kenner
____C-3PO, talking [A2G01] 35.00
____Collector's Case [A2G02] 65.00

Millennium Falcon case with bonus action figure.
____Imperial Scan Technician [A2G03] 30.00
____Imperial Scan Technician, Mexico Sticker Covers
UPC 30.00
____Wedge, 1st helmet 35.00
____Wedge, corrected helmet [A2G04].....................25.00

Toys: Action Figure Storage Cases –
1999 – 2001 (TPM)

Hasbro
____R2-D2 with exclusive rolling Destroyer Droid figure
[A3G01]..20.00

A1G03

A1G04

A1G05

A1G06

A1G07

A1G08

A1G09

A1G10

A2G01

A2G02

A2G03

A2G04

Toys: Action Figure Storage Cases – 2004

A3G01

A4G01

A4G02

A4J01

A4J02

A4J03

A4J04

Toys: Action Figure Storage Cases – 2004 (Original Trilogy Collection)

Hasbro
2 bonus figures included.
____C-3PO with Chewbacca and Han Solo figures, Walmart exclusive [A4G01] 50.00
____Darth Vader with Boba Fett and Stormtrooper, Walmart exclusive [A4G02] 60.00

Toys: Action Figure Storage Cases – 2005 (ROTS)

Hasbro
2 bonus figures included.
____Darth Vader with Anakin Skywalker and Clonetrooper, Walmart exclusive [A4J01] 50.00
____Darth Vader with Darth Vader and Obi-Wan Kenobi, K-Mart exclusive 25.00

Clear clamshell.
____5-pack, Target exclusive [A4J02] 12.00
____5-pack, Target exclusive recalled [A4J03] 15.00
____Celebration 3 for Darth Vader excl. [A4J04]..........5.00

Toys: Action Figure Vehicles – 1978 – 1986 (Vintage)

Glasslite
____ATL Interceptor [A1H01] 450.00
____Side Gunner [A1H02] 315.00
____Tie Fighter [A1H03] 500.00
____Tie Interceptor [A1H04] 675.00
____X-Wing Fighter [A1H05] 425.00

Kenner
____AT-AT All Terrain Attack Transport ESB [A1H06] 450.00
____AT-AT All Terrain Attack Transport ESB, $1.00 off sticker [A1H07] 560.00
____AT-AT All Terrain Attack Transport ROTJ [A1H08] 375.00
____AT-ST Scout Walker ESB [A1H09] 85.00
____AT-ST Scout Walker ROTJ Endor [A1H10] 65.00
____AT-ST Scout Walker ROTJ Hoth [A1H11] 225.00
____B-Wing Fighter ROTJ [A1H12] 250.00
____Darth Vader TIE Fighter SW [A1H13] 175.00
____Darth Vader TIE Fighter SW Collector Series [A1H14] 100.00
____Ewok Battle Wagon POTF [A1H15] 325.00
____Imperial Cruiser ESB [A1H16] 125.00
____Imperial Shuttle ROTJ [A1H17] 450.00

____Imperial Sniper POTF [A1H18] 125.00
____Imperial Troop Transport SW [A1H19] 175.00
____Imperial Troop Transport ESB [A1H20] 150.00
____Landspeeder Company store sticker 205.00
____Landspeeder SW [A1H21] 75.00
____Landspeeder SW with Special Offer 475.00
____Landspeeder SW Collector Series [A1H22].......45.00
____Landspeeder, Sonic SW [A1H23] 620.00
____Millennium Falcon SW [A1H24] 450.00
____Millennium Falcon ESB [A1H25] 400.00
____Millennium Falcon ROTJ [A1H26] 250.00
____One-Man Sand Skimmer POTF [A1H27] 85.00
____Rebel Armored Snowspeeder ESB blue background [A1H28] 225.00
____Rebel Armored Snowspeeder ESB pink background [A1H29] 130.00
____Rebel Transport ESB blue background [A1H30] 190.00
____Rebel Transport ESB yellow background [A1H31] 175.00
____Sandcrawler, radio controlled SW [A1H32]......665.00
____Security Scout POTF [A1H33] 95.00
____Slave I ESB [A1H34] 200.00
____Slave I ESB, action play setting...................1,220.00
____Speeder Bike ROTJ [A1H35] 35.00
____Tatooine Skiff POTF [A1H35] 485.00
____TIE Fighter SW [A1H37] 140.00
____TIE Fighter SW with free figs 950.00
____TIE Fighter ESB [A1H38] 195.00

A1H01

A1H02

A1H03

A1H04

A1H05

A1H06

A1H07

A1H08

A1H09

A1H10

A1H11

A1H12

A1H13

A1H14

A1H15

A1H16

A1H17

A1H18

A1H19

A1H20

A1H21

A1H22

| A1H23 | A1H24 | A1H25 | A1H26 | A1H27 | A1H28 |

| A1H29 | A1H30 | A1H31 |

____TIE Fighter with Battle Damage [A1H39]..........145.00
____TIE Interceptor ROTJ [A1H40]..........................195.00
____Twin-Pod Cloud Car ESB [A1H41] 135.00
____X-Wing Fighter SW [A1H42]............................175.00
____X-Wing Fighter ESB Dagobah box [A1H43] 495.00
____X-Wing Fighter ESB red box [A1H44] 250.00
____X-Wing Fighter with Battle Damage ESB [A1H45] 275.00
____X-Wing Fighter with Battle Damage ROTJ [A1H46]..165.00
____Y-Wing Fighter ROTJ [A1H47]..........................175.00

Droids packaging.
____A-Wing Fighter [A1H48]....................................450.00
____ATL Interceptor [A1H49] 175.00
____Side Gunner [A1H50] 100.00

Mini-rigs.
____AST-5 Armored Sentinel Transport ROTJ [A1H51]...25.00
____CAP-2 Captivator ESB [A1H52]..........................35.00
____CAP-2 Captivator ROTJ [A1H53]........................25.00
____Desert Sail Skiff ROTJ [A1H54]..........................55.00
____Endor Forest Ranger ROTJ [A1H55] 75.00
____INT-4 Interceptor ESB [A1H56] 30.00
____INT-4 Interceptor ROTJ [A1H57].........................45.00
____ISP-6 Imperial Shuttle Pod ROTJ [A1H58] 25.00
____MLC-3 Mobile Laser Cannon ESB [A1H59] 35.00
____MLC-3 Mobile Laser Cannon ESB incl. Rebel Commander...600.00
____MLC-3 Mobile Laser Cannon ROTJ [A1H60] 25.00
____MTV-7 Multi-Terrain Vehicle ESB [A1H61] 35.00

____MTV-7 Multi-Terrain Vehicle ESB incl. AT-AT Driver 600.00
____MTV-7 Multi-Terrain Vehicle ROTJ [A1H62]........25.00
____PDT-8 Personnel Deployment Transport ESB [A1H63]..30.00
____PDT-8 Personnel Deployment Transport ROTJ..20.00

Kenner, Canada
____AT-ST Scout Walker incl. action figure 750.00
____B-Wing Fighter ROTJ 185.00
____Darth Vader's TIE Fighter SW 140.00
____Rebel Armored Snowspeeder ESB incl. mini-action figure 1,500.00
____Sandcrawler, radio control ESB [A1H64].........750.00
____Slave I ESB incl. mini-action figure 1,500.00
____Twin-Pod Cloud Car ESB incl. mini-action figure 1,250.00

Lili Ledy
____AT-ST ROTJ 145.00
____B-Wing Fighter ROTJ 355.00
____Darth Vader's TIE Fighter ROTJ 225.00
____Imperial Shuttle ROTJ 750.00
____Millennium Falcon ROTJ 575.00
____Rebel Snowspeeder ROTJ 185.00
____Speederbike ROTJ 135.00
____Y-Wing Fighter ROTJ 290.00

Mini-rigs.
____CAP-2 Captivator ROTJ 100.00
____CLM-3 Cannon Laser Mobile ROTJ 100.00

____INT-4 Interceptor ROTJ 100.00

Meccano
____Landspeeder 350.00

Palitoy
____AT-AT All Terrain Attack Transport ESB 375.00
____AT-ST Scout Walker ROTJ 95.00
____Darth Vader's TIE SW 215.00
____Imperial Shuttle ROTJ 650.00
____Imperial Troop Transport SW 165.00
____Landspeeder 150.00
____Millennium Falcon ESB 260.00
____Rebel Armored Snowspeeder ESB 185.00
____Rebel Snowspeeder ROTJ 185.00
____Slave I ESB 225.00
____Slave I ROTJ 265.00
____Speeder Bike ROTJ 50.00
____TIE Fighter SW 270.00
____X-Wing Fighter SW 235.00
____X-Wing Fighter with Battle Damage ESB [A1H45]290.00

Mini-rigs.
____AST-5 Armoured Sentinel Transport ROTJ 25.00
____CAP-2 Captivator ESB 25.00
____CAP-2 Captivator ROTJ 25.00
____Desert Sail Skiff ROTJ tri-logo 75.00
____Endor Forest Ranger ROTJ tri-logo 75.00
____Imperial Sniper ROTJ tri-logo 175.00
____MTV-7 Multi-Terrain Vehicle ESB 25.00
____One-Man Sand Skimmer ROTJ tri-logo 75.00
____Security Scout ROTJ tri-logo 200.00

| A1H32 | A1H33 | A1H34 | A1H35 |

| A1H36 | A1H37 | A1H38 | A1H39 | A1H40 | A1H41 |

| A1H42 | A1H43 | A1H44 | A1H45 | A1H46 | A1H47 |

Toys: Action Figure Vehicles – 1995 – 1999

A1H48 A1H49 A1H50 A1H51 A1H52 A1H53

A1H54 A1H55 A1H56 A1H57 A1H58

A1H59 A1H60 A1H61 A1H62 A1H63

A1H64

____Tatooine Skiff tan, Target exclusive [A2H01]...50.00
____Y-Wing Fighter with Y-Wing Pilot, Target exclusive [A2H02]..95.00

Kenner
____A-Wing Fighter with A-Wing Fighter Pilot .00 [A2H03]...35.00
____Airspeeder with Airspeeder Pilot .00 [A2H04] 20.00
____Boba Fett's Slave I .00, purple box [A2H05] 50.00
____Boba Fett's Slave I .01, green box [A2H06].........60.00
____Cloud Car w/Cloud Car Pilot [A2H07] 18.00
____Cruisemissile Trooper .00 [A2H08]....................25.00
____Darth Vader's Tie Fighter .00 [A2H09] 40.00
____Dash Rendar's Outrider .00, purple box [A2H10]..48.00
____Dash Rendar's Outrider .01, green box [A2H11]..65.00
____Imperial AT-AT with AT-AT Commander and AT-AT Driver .00 [A2H12] 135.00
____Imperial AT-AT with AT-AT Commander and AT-AT Driver .01 ....135.00
____Imperial AT-ST .00 [A2H13].............................75.00
____Imperial Speeder Bike with Biker Scout .00 [A2H14]..25.00
____Landspeeder .00 [A2H15]................................16.00
____Luke's T-16 Skyhopper .00 [A2H16] 25.00
____Millennium Falcon .00 [A2H17] 80.00
____Rebel Snowspeeder .00 [A2H18]......................60.00
____Speeder Bike with Biker Scout .00, EU.............15.00
____Speeder Bike with Endor Leia .00 [A2H19].........25.00
____Speeder Bike with Endor Leia .01 ....15.00
____Speeder Bike with Endor Leia .02 ....15.00
____Speeder Bike with Endor Luke .00 no glove on box photo [A2H20] 20.00
____Speeder Bike with Endor Luke .00 no glove on box photo or figure 135.00
____Speeder Bike with Endor Luke .01 [A2H21] 18.00
____Swoop with Swoop Rider .00 [A2H22] 15.00
____Tie Fighter .00 [A2H23] 50.00

Toys: Action Figure Vehicles – 1995 – 1999 (POTF2)

Hasbro
____Tatooine Skiff green, Target exclusive................80.00

A2H01

A2H02

A2H03

A2H04

A2H05 A2H06 A2H07 A2H08 A2H09 A2H10 A2H11

A2H12 A2H13 A2H14 A2H15 A2H16

A2H17

A2H18   A2H19   A2H20 detail   A2H21 detail   A2H21   A2H22

A2H23   A2H24   A2H25   A2H26   A2H27   A2H28

A2H29   A2H30   A2H31   A2H32   A2H33   A2H34

____X-Wing Fighter .00, red box [A2H24]..................35.00
____X-Wing Fighter .01, green box [A2H25].............90.00
____X-Wing Fighter, Power FX [A2H26] 80.00

Kenner, Canada
____Speeder Bike with Biker Pilot (Leia without poncho) [A2H27].............................16.00

Kenner, Italy
____Luke e il T-16 Skyhopper [A2H28] 40.00
____Rebel Snowspeeder [A2H29].............................45.00

Kenner, UK
____A-Wing Fighter with A-Wing Fighter Pilot [A2H30]..23.00
____Darth Vader's Tie Fighter [A2H31] 23.00
____Imperial AT-ST [A2H32] 69.00
____Landspeeder [A2H33] 19.00
____Luke's T-16 Skyhopper [A2H34] 22.00
____Millennium Falcon [A2H35] 88.00

____Rebel Snowspeeder [A2H36]..............................62.00
____Speeder Bike w/Bike Pilot [A2H37] 18.00
____Speeder Bike w/Biker Scout [A2H38] 27.00
____Speeder Bike w/Endor Leia [A2H39] 23.00
____Speeder Bike w/Endor Luke [A2H40] 23.00
____Tie Fighter [A2H41]...36.00
____Tie Fighter with free Stormtrooper figure [A2H42]..85.00
____X-Wing Fighter [A2H43] 42.00
____X-Wing Fighter with free Luke Skywalker figure [A2H44]..85.00

Toys: Action Figure Vehicles – 1999 – 2001 (TPM)

Hasbro
____Anakin's Podracer with Anakin [A3H01] 20.00

____Armored Scout Tank with Battle Droid .0000, droid in window on box [A3H02]....................................25.00
____Armored Scout Tank with Battle Droid .0100 [A3H03]...15.00
____Flash Speeder [A3H04] 15.00
____Gungan Scout Sub with Obi-Wan Kenobi [A3H05]...25.00
____Naboo Fighter .01 'Launching Proton Torpedo', old logo [A3H06]...48.00
____Naboo Fighter .0200 'Launching Proton Torpedo With Real Sounds', old logo [A3H07].........................35.00
____Naboo Fighter .0300 'With Real Movie Lights and Sounds', new logo [A3H08] 20.00
____Naboo Royal Starship [A3H09] 175.00
____Sebulba's Pod Racer with Sebulba [A3H10] 20.00
____Sith Attack Speeder with Darth Maul [A3H11] ..25.00
____Sith Speeder with Darth Maul [A3H12] 10.00
____Stap and Battledroid [A3H13].............................20.00
____Trade Fed. Droid Fighters [A3H14] 20.00
____Trade Federation Tank [A3H15] 65.00

A2H35   A2H36   A2H37   A2H38   A2H38

A2H39   A2H40   A2H41   A2H42   A2H43   A2H44

A3H01   A3H02   A3H03   A3H04   A3H05

Toys: Action Figure Vehicles – 1999 – 2001

A3H06

A3H07

A3H08

A3H09

A3H10

A3H11

A3H12

A3H13

A3H14

A3H15

A3H16

A3H17

A3H18

A3H19

A3H20

A3H21

A3H22   A3H23

A3H24   A3H25

A3H26   A3H27   A3H28

Hasbro, Canada
____Armored Scout Tank with Battle Droid [A3H16] 10.00
____Sith Speeder with Darth Maul [A3H17] 17.00
____STAP and Battledroid [A3H18] 24.00

Hasbro, Italy
____Armored Scout Tank with Battle Droid [A3H19] 16.00

Hasbro, UK
____Anakin's Pod Racer with Anakin Skywalker [A3H20] 25.00
____Armored Scout Tank with Battle Droid [A3H21] 16.00
____Naboo Fighter [A3H22] 18.00
____Sebulba's Pod Racer with Sebulba [A3H23] 25.00
____Sith Speeder with Darth Maul [A3H24] 10.00
____Stap and Battledroid [A3H25] 24.00
____Trade Federation Droid Fighters [A3H26] 16.00

Kenner
____STAP and Battledroid, sneak preview box, beige support rod [A3H27] 20.00
____STAP and Battledroid, sneak preview box, white support rod 20.00

Kenner, UK
____STAP and Battledroid, sneak preview box [A3H28] 11.00

Toys: Action Figure Vehicles – 2001 – 2002 (POTJ)

Hasbro
____AT-ST, Speederbike, Paploo [A4H01] 100.00
____B-Wing Fighter with Unique Rebel Pilot [A4H02] 100.00

____Luke Skywalker's Snowspeeder [A4H03] 70.00
____Tie Bomber with Unique Imperial Pilot [A4H04] 65.00
____Tie Interceptor with Unique Imperial Pilot [A4H05] 95.00

Toys: Action Figure Vehicles – 2002 – 2004 (Saga)

Hasbro
Classic trilogy.
____A-Wing Fighter with Pilot [A5H01] 35.00
____Imperial Shuttle, FAO Schwarz exclusive [A5H02] 225.00
____Imperial TIE Fighter, KB Toys excl. [A5H03] 50.00
____Landspeeder, includes Luke Skywalker figure, TRU exclusive [A5H04] 30.00

A4H01

A4H02

A4H03

A4H04

A4H05   A5H01   A5H02   A5H03   A5H04

A5H05

A5H06

A5H07

A5H08

A5H09

A5H10

A5H11

A5H12

A5H13

A5H14

A5H15

A5H16

_____ Luke Skywalker's X-Wing Fighter, with R2-D2 figure,
TRU exclusive [A5H05]..60.00
_____ Red Leader's X-Wing Fighter [A5H06]...............60.00
_____ Tie Bomber with Imperial Pilot [A5H07].............50.00

Prequel trilogy.
_____ Anakin Skywalker's Speeder [A5H08] 16.00
_____ Anakin Skywalker's Swoop [A5H09] 25.00
_____ Darth Tyrannus's Speeder Bike [A5H10] 25.00
_____ Jango Fett's Slave I [A5H11] 50.00
_____ Jedi Starfighter [A5H12]................................30.00
_____ Jedi Starfighter w/Obi-Wan, window box 40.00
_____ Republic Gunship [A5H13].............................85.00
_____ Zam Wesell's Speeder [A5H14] 16.00

Hasbro, Canada
Prequel trilogy, tri-language packaging.
_____ Anakin Skywalker's Speeder [A5H15] 20.00
_____ Jango Fett's Slave I [A5H17] 35.00
_____ Jedi Starfighter [A5H16] 30.00
_____ Republic Gunship [A5H18] 50.00
_____ Zam Wesell's Speeder [A5H19] 20.00

A5H17

A5H18

A5H19

_____ 2-pack, TIE Fighter and X-Wing Fighter, warning
sticker [A7H02]...150.00
_____ Darth Vader's Fighter [A7H03]..........................70.00
_____ Millennium Falcon [A7H04] 55.00
_____ Millennium Falcon with 6 figures, Sam's Club
exclusive. [A7H05] 75.00

_____ Sandcrawler with RA-7 and 2 Jawas, Diamond
exclusive [A7H06]...70.00
_____ Slave I, Target exclusive [A7H07].......................85.00
_____ TIE Fighter [A7H08] 60.00
_____ X-Wing Fighter [A7H09] 50.00
_____ Y-Wing Fighter [A7H10] 100.00

Toys: Action Figure Vehicles –
2003 – 2005 (Clone Wars)

Hasbro
_____ AAT Armored Assault Tank [A6H01]....................75.00
_____ Anakin Skywalker's Jedi Starfighter [A6H02]......90.00
_____ Geonosian Starfighter [A6H03] 60.00
_____ Hailfire Droid [A6H04]....................................90.00
_____ Jedi Starfighter [A6H05] 70.00
_____ Republic Gun Ship [A6H06].............................100.00

Toys: Action Figure Vehicles – 2004 –
2005 (Original Trilogy Collection)

Hasbro
_____ 2-pack, TIE Fighter and X-Wing Fighter, printed warning, some assembly required [A7H01] 150.00

A6H01

A6H02

A6H03

A6H04

A6H05

A6H06

A7H01

A7H02

A7H03

A7H04

Toys: Action Figure Vehicles – 2005 – 2006

A7H05

A7H06

A7H07

A7H08

A7H09

A7H10

Toys: Action Figure Vehicles –
2005 – 2006 (ROTS)

Hasbro

____Anakin's Jedi Starfighter 30.00

____Anakin's Jedi Starfighter, with Anakin Skywalker [A8H01]...85.00
____Anakin's Jedi Starfighter, preview [A8H02] 45.00
____ARC-170 Fighter [A8H03] 75.00
____ARC-170 Fighter with bonus 3 Clone Pilots and R2 droid, Sam's Club exclusive [A8H04] 100.00
____AT-RT with AT-RT Driver [A8H05] 25.00
____AT-RT with AT-RT Driver and bonus clone trooper [A8H06] 50.00
____Barc Speeder with Barc Trooper [A8H07] 25.00
____Barc Speeder with Barc Trooper and bonus wookiee warrior [A8H08] 50.00
____Droid Tri-Fighter [A8H09] 30.00
____Grievous' Wheelbike [A8H10] 30.00
____Obi-Wan Kenobi's Jedi Starfighter [A8H11].......30.00
____Obi-Wan Kenobi's Jedi Starfighter with Obi-Wan Kenobi [A8H12] 50.00
____Plo Koon's Jedi Starfighter [A8H13] 60.00
____Republic Gunship [A8H14] 85.00
____Wookiee Flyer w/Wookiee Warrior [A8H15] 25.00

Hasbro, Canada
Tri-language packaging.
____Anakin's Jedi Starfighter 20.00
____Anakin's Jedi Starfighter, sneak preview 20.00
____AT-RT with AT-RT Driver 20.00
____Barc Speeder with Barc Trooper 20.00
____Droid Tri-Fighter 20.00
____Grievous' Wheelbike 20.00
____Obi-Wan Kenobi's Jedi Starfighter....................20.00
____Republic Gunship...35.00
____Wookiee Flyer w/Wookiee Warrior [A8H16] 25.00

Toys: Action Figure Vehicles –
2005 – 2006 (The Saga Collection)

Hasbro
____Anakin's Jedi Starfighter [A9H01] 25.00

A8H01

A8H02

A8H03

A8H04

A8H05

A8H06

A8H07

A8H08

A8H09

A8H10

A8H11

A8H12

A8H13

A8H14

A8H15

A8H16

A9H01

A9H02

A9H03

A9H04

A9H05

A9H06

A9H07

A9H08

A9H09

A9H10   A9H11   A9H12   A9H13   A9H14   A9H15

AVA01   AVA02   AVA03   AVA04   AVA05   AVA06

AVA07   AVA08   AVA09   P3U01

____ Darth Vader's Sith Starfighter 35.00
____ Darth Vader's TIE Fighter, caution sticker on box [A9H02] 35.00
____ Darth Vader's TIE Fighter, printed warning on box [A9H03] 25.00
____ Droid Tri-Fighter [A9H04] 35.00
____ Endor AT-AT [A9H05] 90.00
____ Grievous' Wheelbike [A9H06] 30.00
____ Hailfire Droid 40.00
____ Imperial Shuttle 65.00
____ Kit Fisto's Jedi Starfighter [A9H07] 35.00
____ Luke Skywalker's Dagobah X-Wing [A9H08] 45.00
____ Mace Windu's Jedi Starfighter [A9H09] 30.00
____ Millennium Falcon, TRU exclusive [A9H10] 55.00
____ Obi-Wan's Jedi Starfighter [A9H11] 30.00
____ Republic Gunship, Clone Wars [A9H12] 100.00
____ Rogue Two Snowspeeder [A9H13] 45.00
____ TIE Fighter with pilot [A9H14] 80.00
____ TIE Fighter, exclusive paint deco and (Battle of Yavin) pilot 50.00
____ TIE Fighter, exclusive paint deco and (POTF2) pilot [A9H15] 50.00
____ Trade Federation AAT 40.00

Toys: Action Figure Vehicles – 2006 – 2007 (30th Anniversary)

Hasbro
____ AAT [AVA01] 35.00
____ Darth Vader's Sith Starfighter [AVA02] 35.00
____ Hailfire Droid [AVA03] 40.00
____ Mace Windu's Jedi Starfighter [AVA04] 35.00
____ Obi-Wan Kenobi's Jedi Starfighter [AVA05] 30.00
____ SaeSee Tiin's Jedi Starfighter [AVA06] 35.00
____ Sith Infiltrator [AVA07] 50.00
____ TIE Fighter [AVA08] 40.00
____ V-Wing Starfighter [AVA09] 45.00

Toys: Action Figure Vehicles – Mini

Hasbro
____ Naboo Fighter, 8 mini-figures [P3U01] 75.00
____ Naboo Fighter, Anakin figure [3:23] 25.00

Toys: Action Figures – 1977 (Earlybird)

Kenner
____ Mailer with certificate [2:317] 335.00
____ Mailer with figures w/packaging [1:265] 420.00

Toys: Action Figures – 1978 – 1986 (Vintage)

Clipper
Netherland. Star Wars.
____ Artoo-Detoo 425.00
____ Ben Kenobi [2:55] 360.00
____ Chewbacca [2:55] 340.00
____ Darth Vader 850.00
____ Death Squad Commander [3:45] 320.00
____ Han Solo [2:55] 590.00
____ Jawa 290.00
____ Luke Skywalker [2:55] 540.00
____ Princess Leia Organa [2:55] 480.00
____ Sand People 390.00
____ See-Threepio 350.00
____ Stormtrooper [2:55] 360.00

Empire Strikes Back.
____ 4-LOM 400.00
____ AT-AT Commander 90.00
____ Ben Kenobi 125.00
____ Bespin Security Guard [2:55] 135.00
____ Dengar 95.00
____ Hammerhead 120.00
____ Rebel Commander 140.00
____ Rebel Soldier 75.00
____ Rebel Soldier 75.00
____ Walrusman [3:45] 160.00
____ Zuckuss 125.00

Return of the Jedi.
____ Biker Scout 85.00
____ Chief Chirpa 65.00
____ Darth Vader 85.00
____ Luke Skywalker (Jedi Knight) 95.00
____ Lumat 0.00
____ Ree Yees 65.00

Csillagok Haboruja
____ Biker Scout [2:55] 325.00

____ Boba Fett [2:55] 1,500.00
____ C-3PO [2:55] 325.00
____ Chewbacca [2:55] 325.00
____ Darth Vader [2:55] 450.00
____ Han Solo [2:55] 325.00
____ Luke Skywalker [2:55] 350.00
____ Princess Leia [2:55] 325.00
____ Snowtrooper [3:45] 325.00
____ Wicket [2:55] 235.00

Glasslite
Star Wars O Poder Da Forca.
____ C-3PO [3:45] 300.00
____ Chewbacca [2:55] 300.00
____ Darth Vader [2:55] 400.00
____ Guerreiro Imperial 600.00
____ Han Solo [2:55] 275.00
____ Luke Skywalker [2:55] 300.00
____ Princess Leia [2:55] 350.00
____ R2-D2 [2:55] 155.00

Harbert
Star Wars.
____ Ben (Obi-Wan) Kenobi [3:45] 450.00
____ C1P8 (R2-D2) [AV01] 250.00
____ Capo Jawa (Jawa) [AV02] 250.00
____ Chewbacca [AV03] 395.00
____ Comandante Squadra (Death Squad Commander) [AV04] 250.00
____ D3B0 (C-3PO) [AV05] 435.00
____ Death Star Droid 230.00
____ Greedo 295.00
____ Hammerhead 270.00
____ Lord Darth Fener (Darth Vader) [AV06] 300.00
____ Luke Skywalker [AV07] 345.00
____ Luke Skywalker X-Wing Pilot 250.00
____ Power Droid 200.00
____ Principessa Leila Organa [AV08] 345.00
____ R5-D4 .... 235.00
____ Sabbipode (Sandpeople) [AV09] 245.00
____ Snaggletooth 200.00
____ Stormtrooper 225.00
____ Walrusman 260.00

AV01   AV02   AV03   AV04   AV05   AV06   AV07   AV08   AV09

Toys: Action Figures – 1978 – 1986

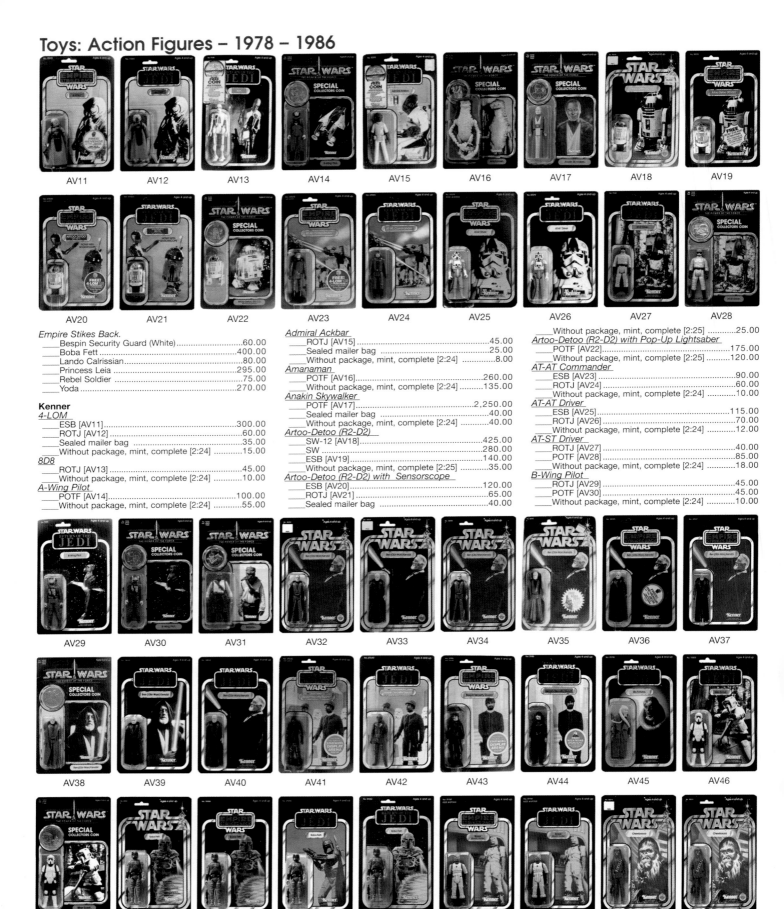

AV11   AV12   AV13   AV14   AV15   AV16   AV17   AV18   AV19

AV20   AV21   AV22   AV23   AV24   AV25   AV26   AV27   AV28

Empire Stikes Back.
____Bespin Security Guard (White)...........................60.00
____Boba Fett 400.00
____Lando Calrissian..80.00
____Princess Leia 295.00
____Rebel Soldier 75.00
____Yoda..270.00

Kenner
4-LOM
____ESB [AV11]...300.00
____ROTJ [AV12]..60.00
____Sealed mailer bag 35.00
____Without package, mint, complete [2:24] 15.00
8D8
____ROTJ [AV13]..45.00
____Without package, mint, complete [2:24] 10.00
A-Wing Pilot
____POTF [AV14]...100.00
____Without package, mint, complete [2:24] 55.00

Admiral Ackbar
____ROTJ [AV15]..45.00
____Sealed mailer bag 25.00
____Without package, mint, complete [2:24] 8.00
Amanaman
____POTF [AV16]...260.00
____Without package, mint, complete [2:24] 135.00
Anakin Skywalker
____POTF [AV17]..2,250.00
____Sealed mailer bag 40.00
____Without package, mint, complete [2:24] 40.00
Artoo-Detoo (R2-D2)
____SW-12 [AV18]...425.00
____SW 280.00
____ESB [AV19]...140.00
____Without package, mint, complete [2:25] 35.00
Artoo-Detoo (R2-D2) with Sensorscope
____ESB [AV20]...120.00
____ROTJ [AV21]..65.00
____Sealed mailer bag 40.00

____Without package, mint, complete [2:25] 25.00
Artoo-Detoo (R2-D2) with Pop-Up Lightsaber
____POTF [AV22]...175.00
____Without package, mint, complete [2:25] 120.00
AT-AT Commander
____ESB [AV23]...90.00
____ROTJ [AV24]..60.00
____Without package, mint, complete [2:24] 10.00
AT-AT Driver
____ESB [AV25]...115.00
____ROTJ [AV26]..70.00
____Without package, mint, complete [2:24] 12.00
AT-ST Driver
____ROTJ [AV27]..40.00
____POTF [AV28]..85.00
____Without package, mint, complete [2:24] 18.00
B-Wing Pilot
____ROTJ [AV29]..45.00
____POTF [AV30]..45.00
____Without package, mint, complete [2:24] 10.00

AV29   AV30   AV31   AV32   AV33   AV34   AV35   AV36   AV37

AV38   AV39   AV40   AV41   AV42   AV43   AV44   AV45   AV46

AV47   AV48   AV49   AV50   AV51   AV52   AV53   AV54   AV55

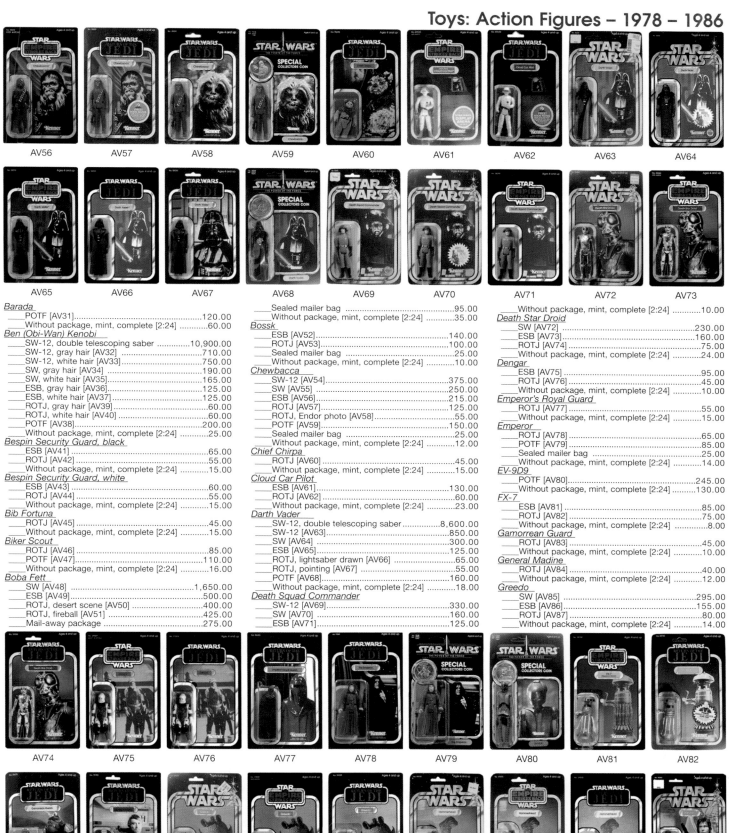

AV56   AV57   AV58   AV59   AV60   AV61   AV62   AV63   AV64

AV65   AV66   AV67   AV68   AV69   AV70   AV71   AV72   AV73

Barada
____POTF [AV31]...120.00
____Without package, mint, complete [2:24] 60.00

Ben (Obi-Wan) Kenobi
____SW-12, double telescoping saber 10,900.00
____SW-12, gray hair [AV32]................................710.00
____SW-12, white hair [AV33]................................750.00
____SW, gray hair [AV34] 190.00
____SW, white hair [AV35].................................165.00
____ESB, gray hair [AV36].................................125.00
____ESB, white hair [AV37].................................125.00
____ROTJ, gray hair [AV39] 60.00
____ROTJ, white hair [AV40] 60.00
____POTF [AV38]...200.00
____Without package, mint, complete [2:24] 25.00

Bespin Security Guard, black
____ESB [AV41]..65.00
____ROTJ [AV42]..55.00
____Without package, mint, complete [2:24] 15.00

Bespin Security Guard, white
____ESB [AV43] 60.00
____ROTJ [AV44] 55.00
____Without package, mint, complete [2:24] 15.00

Bib Fortuna
____ROTJ [AV45]..45.00
____Without package, mint, complete [2:24] 15.00

Biker Scout
____ROTJ [AV46]..85.00
____POTF [AV47]...110.00
____Without package, mint, complete [2:24] 16.00

Boba Fett
____SW [AV48] 1,650.00
____ESB [AV49]..500.00
____ROTJ, desert scene [AV50] 400.00
____ROTJ, fireball [AV51]...................................425.00
____Mail-away package 275.00

____Sealed mailer bag 95.00
____Without package, mint, complete [2:24] 35.00

Bossk
____ESB [AV52]...140.00
____ROTJ [AV53]..100.00
____Sealed mailer bag 25.00
____Without package, mint, complete [2:24] 10.00

Chewbacca
____SW-12 [AV54]..375.00
____SW [AV55] 250.00
____ESB [AV56]...215.00
____ROTJ [AV57]..125.00
____ROTJ, Endor photo [AV58] 55.00
____POTF [AV59]...150.00
____Sealed mailer bag 25.00
____Without package, mint, complete [2:24] 12.00

Chief Chirpa
____ROTJ [AV60]...45.00
____Without package, mint, complete [2:24] 15.00

Cloud Car Pilot
____ESB [AV61]...130.00
____ROTJ [AV62]...60.00
____Without package, mint, complete [2:24] 23.00

Darth Vader
____SW-12, double telescoping saber 8,600.00
____SW-12 [AV63]...850.00
____SW [AV64] 300.00
____ESB [AV65]...125.00
____ROTJ, lightsaber drawn [AV66] 65.00
____ROTJ, pointing [AV67] 55.00
____POTF [AV68]...160.00
____Without package, mint, complete [2:24] 18.00

Death Squad Commander
____SW-12 [AV69]...330.00
____SW [AV70] 160.00
____ESB [AV71]...125.00

____Without package, mint, complete [2:24] 10.00

Death Star Droid
____SW [AV72]..230.00
____ESB [AV73]...160.00
____ROTJ [AV74]...75.00
____Without package, mint, complete [2:24] 24.00

Dengar
____ESB [AV75]..95.00
____ROTJ [AV76]...45.00
____Without package, mint, complete [2:24] 10.00

Emperor's Royal Guard
____ROTJ [AV77]...55.00
____Without package, mint, complete [2:24] 15.00

Emperor
____ROTJ [AV78]...65.00
____POTF [AV79]...85.00
____Sealed mailer bag 25.00
____Without package, mint, complete [2:24] 14.00

EV-9D9
____POTF [AV80]...245.00
____Without package, mint, complete [2:24] 130.00

FX-7
____ESB [AV81]..85.00
____ROTJ [AV82]...75.00
____Without package, mint, complete [2:24] 8.00

Gamorrean Guard
____ROTJ [AV83]...45.00
____Without package, mint, complete [2:24] 10.00

General Madine
____ROTJ [AV84]...40.00
____Without package, mint, complete [2:24] 12.00

Greedo
____SW [AV85]..295.00
____ESB [AV86]...155.00
____ROTJ [AV87]...80.00
____Without package, mint, complete [2:24] 14.00

AV74   AV75   AV76   AV77   AV78   AV79   AV80   AV81   AV82

AV83   AV84   AV85   AV86   AV87   AV88   AV89   AV90   AV91

| AV92 | AV93 | AV94 | AV95 | AV96 | AV97 | AV98 | AV99 | AV100 |

| AV101 | AV102 | AV103 | AV104 | AV105 | AV106 | AV107 | AV108 | AV109 |

Hammerhead
____ SW [AV88] 270.00
____ ESB [AV89] 120.00
____ ROTJ [AV90] 75.00
____ Sealed mailer bag 16.00
____ Without package, mint, complete [2:24] 10.00

Han Solo
____ SW-12, large head [AV91] 1,000.00
____ SW-12, small head [AV92] 775.00
____ SW, large head 650.00
____ SW, small head [AV93]................................540.00
____ ESB, large head 245.00
____ ESB, small head [AV94] 300.00
____ ROTJ, Death Star scene [AV95] 165.00
____ ROTJ, Mos Eisley scene [AV96] 185.00
____ Without package, mint, complete [2:24] 25.00

Han Solo Bespin
____ ESB [AV97]..145.00
____ Bespin ROTJ [AV98] 75.00
____ Without package, mint, complete [2:24] 18.00

Han Solo Hoth Battle Gear
____ ESB [AV99] 95.00
____ ROTJ [AV100] 75.00
____ Without package, mint, complete [2:24] 15.00

Han Solo in Carbonite Chamber
____ POTF [AV101]...275.00
____ Without package, mint, complete [2:24] 125.00

Han Solo Trench Coat
____ ROTJ [AV102] 50.00
____ POTF [AV103]...500.00
____ Without package, mint, complete [2:24] 22.00

IG-88
____ ESB [AV104]..190.00
____ ROTJ [AV105] 80.00
____ Without package, mint, complete [2:24] 10.00

Imperial Commander
____ ESB [AV106]..85.00
____ ROTJ [AV107] 50.00
____ Sealed mailer bag 15.00
____ Without package, mint, complete [2:24] 10.00

Imperial Dignitary
____ POTF [AV108]...155.00
____ Without package, mint, complete [2:24] 90.00

Imperial Gunner
____ POTF [AV109]...165.00
____ Without package, mint, complete [2:25] 85.00

Imperial Stormtrooper in Hoth Weather Gear
____ ESB [AV110]..145.00
____ ROTJ [AV111]..60.00
____ Without package, mint, complete [2:25] 18.00

Imperial Tie Fighter Pilot
____ ESB [AV112]..130.00
____ ROTJ [AV113] 90.00
____ Without package, mint, complete [2:25] 16.00

Jawa
____ SW-12, cloth cape [AV114] 290.00
____ SW-12, plastic cape [AV115]......................3,500.00
____ SW [AV116] 200.00
____ ESB [AV117]..125.00
____ ROTJ [AV118] 50.00

| AV110 | AV111 | AV112 | AV113 | AV114 | AV115 | AV116 | AV117 | AV118 |

| AV119 | AV120 | AV121 | AV122 | AV123 | AV124 | AV125 | AV126 | AV127 |

| AV128 | AV129 | AV130 | AV131 | AV132 | AV133 | AV134 | AV135 | AV136 |

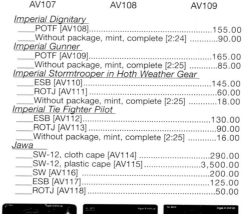

AV137

AV138

AV139

AV140

AV141

AV142

AV143

AV144

AV145

AV146

AV147

AV148

AV149

AV150

AV151

AV152

AV153

AV154

____POTF [AV119]....................140.00
____Without package, mint, complete [2:25] 17.00

Klaatu
____ROTJ, palace outfit [AV120]....................50.00
____ROTJ, skiff outfit [AV121]....................50.00
____Without package, mint, complete [2:25] 10.00

Lando Calrissian
____ESB [AV122]....................80.00
____ESB, no teeth [AV123]....................80.00
____ROTJ [AV124]....................45.00
____Without package, mint, complete [2:25] 14.00

Lando Calrissian General
____POTF [AV125]....................145.00
____Without package, mint, complete [2:25] 95.00

Lando Calrissian Skiff Outfit
____ROTJ [AV126]....................45.00
____Without package, mint, complete [2:25] 14.00

Leia Organa Bespin Gown
____ESB, front view, crew neck [AV127]....................185.00
____ESB, front view, turtle neck [AV128]....................190.00
____ESB, profile, crew neck....................200.00
____ESB, profile, turtle neck [AV129]....................195.00
____ROTJ, crew neck [AV130]....................125.00
____ROTJ, turtle neck [AV131]....................145.00
____Without package, mint, complete [2:25] 25.00

Lobot
____ESB [AV132]....................65.00
____ROTJ [AV133]....................45.00
____Without package, mint, complete [2:25] 10.00

Logray
____ROTJ [AV134]....................60.00
____Without package, mint, complete [2:25] 18.00

Luke Skywalker
____SW-12, double telescoping saber....................4,800.00
____SW-12 [AV135]....................850.00
____SW [AV136]....................235.00
____ESB, blonde hair [AV137]....................250.00
____ESB, brown hair [AV138]....................285.00
____ROTJ, blonde hair, Gunwell [AV139]....................180.00
____ROTJ, blonde hair, Tatooine [AV140]....................240.00
____ROTJ, brown hair [AV141]....................290.00
____Without package, mint, complete [2:25] 40.00

Luke Skywalker Battle Poncho
____POTF [AV142]....................170.00
____Without package, mint, complete [2:25] 85.00

Luke Skywalker Bespin Fatigues
ESB, looking, blonde hair [AV143]....................140.00
____ESB, looking, brown hair [AV144]....................200.00
____ESB, walking, blonde hair [AV145]....................245.00
____ESB, walking, brown hair [AV146]....................245.00
____ROTJ, blonde hair [AV147]....................145.00
____ROTJ, brown hair [AV148]....................95.00
____Without package, mint, complete [2:25] 20.00

Luke Skywalker Hoth Battle Gear
____ESB [AV149]....................125.00
____ROTJ [AV150]....................80.00
____Without package, mint, complete [2:25] 18.00

Luke Skywalker Jedi
____ROTJ, blue lightsaber [AV151]....................175.00
____ROTJ, green lightsaber [AV152]....................95.00
____POTF [AV153]....................270.00
____Without package, mint, complete [2:25] 40.00

Stormtrooper Disguise
____POTF [AV154]....................365.00
____Without package, mint, complete [2:25] 165.00

Luke Skywalker X-Wing Pilot
____SW [AV155]....................250.00
____ESB [AV156]....................150.00
____ROTJ [AV158]....................65.00
____POTF [AV157]....................165.00
____Without package, mint, complete [2:25] 15.00

Lumat
____ROTJ [AV159]....................60.00
____POTF [AV160]....................75.00
____Without package, mint, complete [2:25] 55.00

Nien Nunb
____ROTJ [AV161]....................70.00
____Sealed mailer bag....................30.00
____Without package, mint, complete [2:25] 10.00

Nikto
____ROTJ [AV162]....................40.00
____Without package, mint, complete [2:25] 20.00

Paploo
____ROTJ [AV163]....................55.00
____POTF [AV164]....................80.00
____Without package, mint, complete [2:25] 34.00

Power Droid
____SW [AV165]....................200.00
____ESB [AV166]....................130.00
____ROTJ [AV167]....................50.00
____Without package, mint, complete [2:25] 14.00

Princess Leia Organa
____SW-12 [AV168]....................675.00
____SW [AV169]....................240.00
____ESB [AV170]....................295.00
____ROTJ [AV171]....................390.00
____Without package, mint, complete [2:25] 50.00

Princess Leia Combat Poncho
____ROTJ [AV172]....................50.00
____POTF [AV173]....................115.00
____Without package, mint, complete [2:25] 35.00

Princess Leia Hoth
____ESB [AV174]....................160.00
____ROTJ [AV175]....................95.00
____Without package, mint, complete [2:25] 28.00

AV155

AV156

AV157

AV158

AV159

AV160

AV161

AV162

AV163

AV164

AV165

AV166

AV167

AV168

AV169

AV170

AV171

AV172A

Toys: Action Figures – 1978 – 1986

AV173 AV174 AV175 AV176 AV177 AV178 AV179 AV180 AV181

AV182 AV183 AV184 AV185 AV186 AV187 AV188 AV189 AV190

Princess Leia Organa Boushh Disguise
____ ROTJ [AV176] 60.00
____ Sealed mailer bag 35.00
____ Without package, mint, complete [2:25] 20.00

Pruneface
____ ROTJ [AV177] 40.00
____ Sealed mailer bag 20.00
____ Without package, mint, complete [2:25] 14.00

R5-D4
____ SW [AV178] 235.00
____ ESB [AV179] 120.00
____ ROTJ (Arfive-Defour) [AV180]........................60.00
____ Without package, mint, complete [2:25] 18.00

Rancor Keeper
____ ROTJ [AV181] 40.00
____ Without package, mint, complete [2:25] 12.00

Rebel Commander
____ ESB [AV182] 140.00
____ ROTJ [AV183] 50.00
____ Without package, mint, complete [2:25] 9.00

Rebel Commando
____ ROTJ [AV184] 50.00
____ Without package, mint, complete [2:25] 10.00

Rebel Soldier
____ ESB [AV185] 75.00
____ ROTJ [AV186] 40.00
____ Sealed mailer bag 12.00
____ Without package, mint, complete [2:25] 11.00

Ree-Yees
____ ROTJ [AV187] 40.00
____ Without package, mint, complete [2:25] 10.00

Romba
____ POTF [AV188] 100.00
____ Without package, mint, complete [2:25] 55.00

Sandpeople
____ SW-12 [AV189]...390.00
____ SW [AV190] 170.00
____ ESB [AV191] 120.00
____ ROTJ (Tusken Raider) [AV192] 80.00
____ Without package, mint, complete [2:25] 24.00

See-Threepio (C-3PO)
____ SW-12 [AV193]...350.00
____ SW [AV194] 230.00
____ ESB [AV195] 200.00
____ Without package, mint, complete [2:25] 25.00

See-Threepio (C-3PO) with Removable Limbs
____ ESB [AV196] 100.00
____ ROTJ [AV197] 75.00
____ POTF [AV198] 120.00
____ Sealed mailer bag 14.00
____ Without package, mint, complete [2:25] 10.00

Snaggletooth
____ SW [AV199] 200.00
____ ESB [AV200] 160.00
____ ROTJ [AV201] 65.00
____ W/o package, mint, complete (blue) [2:26] 180.00
____ W/o package, mint, complete (red) [2:26] 12.00

Squidhead
____ ROTJ [AV202] 45.00
____ Without package, mint, complete [2:26] 15.00

AV191 AV192 AV193 AV194 AV195 AV196 AV197 AV198 AV199

AV200 AV201 AV202 AV203 AV204 AV205 AV206 AV207 AV208

AV209 AV210 AV211 AV212 AV213 AV214 AV215 AV216 AV217

AV218

AV219

AV220

AV221

AV222

AV223

AV224

AV225

AV226

Star Destroyer Commander
- ____ESB [AV203] 125.00
- ____ROTJ [AV204] 80.00
- ____Without package, mint, complete [2:24] 10.00

Stormtrooper
- ____SW-12 [AV205] 425.00
- ____SW [AV206] 225.00
- ____ESB [AV207] 125.00
- ____ROTJ [AV208] 65.00
- ____POTF [AV209] 260.00
- ____Without package, mint, complete [2:26] 18.00

Teebo
- ____ROTJ [AV210] 50.00
- ____POTF [AV211] 200.00
- ____Without package, mint, complete [2:26] 15.00

Too-Onebee (2-1B)
- ____ESB [AV212] 95.00
- ____ROTJ [AV213] 50.00
- ____Without package, mint, complete [2:24] 10.00

Ugnaught
- ____ESB [AV214] 80.00
- ____ROTJ [AV215] 45.00
- ____Without package, mint, complete [2:26] 10.00

Walrusman
- ____SW [AV216] 280.00
- ____ESB [AV217] 135.00
- ____ROTJ [AV218] 65.00
- ____Without package, mint, complete [2:26] 9.00

Warok
- ____POTF [AV219] 125.00
- ____Without package, mint, complete [2:26] 78.00

Weequay
- ____ROTJ [AV220] 40.00
- ____Without package, mint, complete [2:26] 10.00

Wicket Warrick
- ____ROTJ [AV221] 50.00
- ____POTF [AV222] 200.00
- ____Without package, mint, complete [2:26] 26.00

Yak Face
- ____POTF, weapon included [AV223] 2,190.00
- ____POTF, weapon not included 1,995.00
- ____Without package, mint, complete [2:26] 225.00

Yoda
- ____ESB, brown snake [AV224] 350.00
- ____ESB, orange snake [AV225] 275.00
- ____ROTJ [AV226] 175.00
- ____POTF [AV227] 585.00
- ____Without package, mint, complete [2:26] 25.00

Zuckuss
- ____ESB [AV228] 125.00
- ____ROTJ [AV229] 60.00
- ____Without package, mint, complete [2:26] 12.00

Kenner, Australia
- ____AT-AT Driver POTF [AV230] 1,350.00
- ____Gamorrean Guard POTF [AV231] 675.00
- ____Nikto POTF [AV232] 650.00

Kenner, Canada

Star Wars 12 back with Guerre Des Etoiles on front.
- ____Ben (Obi-Wan) Kenobi [AV234] 575.00
- ____C-3PO [AV235] 510.00
- ____Darth Vader [AV236] 680.00
- ____Jawa [AV237] 510.00
- ____R2-D2 [AV238] 550.00
- ____Stormtrooper [AV239] 590.00

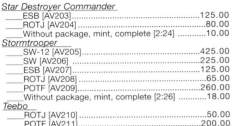

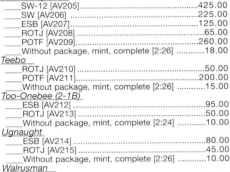

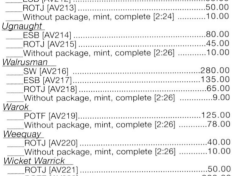

AV227

AV228

AV229

AV230

AV231

AV232

Star Wars.
- ____Luke Skywalker [AV233] 575.00

Empire Strikes Back.
- ____2-1B 82.00
- ____AT-AT Driver 79.00
- ____Ben (Obi-Wan) Kenobi 55.00
- ____Bespin Guard white 66.00
- ____Boba Fett 315.00
- ____Bossk 135.00
- ____C-3PO 92.00
- ____Chewbacca 110.00
- ____Darth Vader 98.00
- ____Death Squad Commander 110.00
- ____Death Star Droid 145.00
- ____Dengar 71.00
- ____FX-7 .... 65.00
- ____Greedo 125.00
- ____Hammerhead 135.00
- ____Han Solo Bespin 149.00
- ____Han Solo Hoth 114.00
- ____Han Solo large head 245.00
- ____IG-88 .... 154.00
- ____Imperial Commander [AV240] 64.00
- ____Imperial Stormtrooper in Hoth Weather Gear 88.00
- ____Jawa 110.00
- ____Lando Calrissian, no teeth 66.00
- ____Lobot 54.00
- ____Luke Skywalker Bespin Fatigues 160.00
- ____Luke Skywalker X-Wing Pilot 133.00
- ____Luke Skywalker, blonde 185.00
- ____Power Droid 115.00
- ____Princess Leia 165.00
- ____Princess Leia Bespin 170.00
- ____Princess Leia Hoth 160.00
- ____R2-D2 .... 85.00
- ____R5-D4 .... 160.00
- ____Rebel Commander 71.00
- ____Rebel Soldier 77.00
- ____Sand People 99.00
- ____Snaggletooth 136.00
- ____Stormtrooper 95.00
- ____Ugnaught 46.00
- ____Walrusman 135.00
- ____Yoda 135.00

Empire Strikes Back, Sears Canada exclusive.
- ____Dengar [3:50] .... N/V
- ____General Veers [2:61] .... N/V
- ____Han Solo (Cloud City Outfit) [2:61] .... N/V
- ____Lobot (Lando's Aid) [2:61] .... N/V
- ____Luke Skywalker (Hoth Outfit) [2:61] .... N/V
- ____R2-D2 with Parascope [2:61] .... N/V
- ____Ugnaught [2:61] .... N/V

Return of the Jedi.
- ____C-3PO, ROTJ sticker covers ESB logo 245.00
- ____Luke Skywalker, Jedi Knight Outfit 95.00
- ____Princess Leia Organa in Combat Poncho 85.00

Kenner, Germany

Empire Strikes Back.
- ____Ben (Obi-Wan) Kenobi 215.00
- ____Han Solo [2:61] 205.00
- ____Han Solo, Bespin outfit 220.00
- ____Leia Organa, Bespin gown 205.00
- ____Leia Organa, Hoth outfit 195.00
- ____Power Droid 75.00
- ____Princess Leia Organa 225.00
- ____Rebel Commander [2:61] 135.00
- ____Stormtrooper [2:61] 215.00
- ____Yoda [2:61] 275.00

Return of the Jedi.
- ____Boba Fett 825.00
- ____Luke Skywalker 410.00
- ____Luke Skywalker, brown hair [2:61] 325.00

Lili Ledy

Return of the Jedi.
- ____8D8 .... 125.00
- ____Admiral Ackbar [AV241] 195.00
- ____Artoo Detoo 332.00
- ____AT-ST Driver [AV242] 150.00
- ____B-Wing Pilot [AV243] 135.00
- ____Ben (Obi-Wan) Kenobi 125.00
- ____Bib Fortuna 185.00
- ____Biker Scout [AV244] 175.00
- ____Boba Fett [AV245] 415.00
- ____C-3PO Removable Limbs [AV246] 195.00
- ____Chewbacca [AV247] 230.00
- ____Chief Chirpa 125.00
- ____Cloud Car Pilot 130.00
- ____Darth Vader 125.00
- ____Emperador [AV248] 125.00
- ____Emperor's Royal Guard [AV249] 180.00
- ____Gamorrean Guard 125.00
- ____General Madine 285.00
- ____Han Solo, Bespin [AV250] 135.00

AV233

AV234

AV235

AV236

AV237

AV238

AV239

AV240

Toys: Action Figures – 1978 – 1986

AV241 AV241 back AV242 AV243 AV244 AV245 AV246 AV247 AV248

AV249 AV250 AV251 AV252 AV253 AV254 AV255 AV256 AV257

AV258 AV259 AV260 AV261 AV262 AV263 AV264 AV265 AV266

____Han Solo, Endor [AV251] 125.00
____Imperial Commander [AV252] 125.00
____Imperial Tie-Fighter Pilot [AV253] 255.00
____Jawa, cloth cape [AV254] 255.00
____Klaatu Skiff Guard [AV255] 125.00
____Klaatu, palace outfit [AV256] 189.00
____Lando Calrissian [AV257] 140.00
____Lando Calrissian, Skiff Guard 170.00
____Leia Organa, Bespin 215.00
____Logray 160.00
____Luke Skywalker, Bespin 125.00
____Luke Skywalker, Jedi 125.00
____Lumat [AV258] 155.00
____Nien Numb 165.00
____Nikto [AV259] 125.00
____Paploo [AV260] 125.00
____Princess Leia Organa 125.00
____Princess Leia Organa Disfraz de Boushh [AV261] 520.00
____Princess Leia Organa, Endor [AV262] 125.00
____Prune Face [AV263] 125.00
____Rancor Keeper 125.00
____Rebel Commander...125.00
____Ree Yees 184.00
____See Threepio [AV264] 155.00
____Squid Head 150.00
____Star Destroyer Commander................................175.00
____Stormtrooper 125.00
____Teebo [AV265] 125.00
____Weequay 130.00
____Wicket W. Warrick 125.00
____Yoda 125.00
____Zuckuss [AV266] 215.00

Meccano
La Guerre Des Etoiles.
____Ben Kenobi [3:51] 265.00
____Chewbacca [3:51] 695.00
____Cispeo (Z-6PO) [3:51] 525.00
____Dark Vador [3:51] 750.00
____Death Squad Commander [2:62] 272.00
____Death Star Droid [2:62] 370.00
____Dedeu (D2-R2) [3:51] 395.00
____Greedo [3:51] 475.00
____Hammerhead [2:62] 335.00
____Jawa [3:51] 85.00
____L'nomme des Sables (Sandpeople) [3:51].......395.00
____Luc (Luke Skywalker) [3:51] 625.00
____Power Droid [3:51] 350.00
____Princess Leia [3:51] 395.00
____Snaggle Tooth [3:51] 495.00

____Soldat Imperial (Stormtrooper) 375.00
____Walrusman [3:51] 550.00

L'Empire Contre-Attaque.
____Conducteur AT-AT 325.00
____FX-7 ....85.00
____Garde Bespin [2:62] 275.00
____Hoth Stormtrooper.......................................145.00
____IG-88 ....190.00
____Imperial Commander 85.00
____Lando Calrissian 80.00
____Rebel Soldier 75.00
____Ugnaught 80.00
____Yoda, brown snake [3:51] 750.00

La Guerre Des Etoiles.
____Han Solo 345.00
____Luke Skywalker X-Wing Pilot 250.00
____R5-D4 ....235.00

Le Retour Du Jedi.
____AT-AT Driver 70.00
____Biker Scout 85.00
____Boba Fett [3:51] 895.00
____IG-88 [2:62] 125.00
____Logray [3:51] 145.00
____Luc (Tenue Bespin) 95.00
____Yan (Han) Solo 165.00
____Yoda 175.00
____Z6PO [2:62] 95.00

Palitoy
Star Wars.
____Ben (Obi-Wan) Kenobi 795.00
____C-3PO [3:51] 435.00
____Chewbacca 500.00
____Darth Vader 580.00
____Death Squad Commander 185.00
____Death Star Droid 260.00
____Greedo 325.00
____Hammerhead 400.00
____Han Solo 560.00
____Jawa 360.00
____Luke Skywalker X-Wing Pilot 430.00
____Power Droid 400.00
____R2-D2 ....215.00
____Sand People 285.00
____Snaggletooth 350.00
____Stormtrooper 475.00
____Walrusman 400.00

Empire Strikes Back.
____4-LOM 350.00
____AT-AT Commander 85.00
____AT-AT Driver 85.00
____Bespin Guard, black 95.00
____Bespin Guard, white.....................................95.00
____Imperial Commander 175.00
____Imperial Tie Fighter Pilot 110.00
____Luke Skywalker Hoth 155.00
____Ugnaught [2:62] 270.00

Return of the Jedi.
____Boba Fett 250.00
____Darth Vader 95.00
____General Madine [3:51] 125.00
____Han Solo Bespin 75.00
____Rebel Soldier 75.00
____Stormtrooper 100.00

Return of the Jedi multi-language packaging.
____Admiral Ackbar 125.00
____Bespin Guard, black 125.00
____Bespin Guard, white 195.00
____Bib Fortuna 50.00
____Biker Scout [2:62] 115.00
____Bossk 70.00
____Cloud Car Pilot [2:62].................................1,200.00
____Greedo [2:62] 165.00
____Klaatu, palace outfit [3:51] 50.00
____Logray 75.00
____Princess Leia Boushh disguise [2:62] 85.00
____Rebel Commando 70.00
____Ree Yees 75.00
____Snaggletooth 125.00
____Squidhead 60.00

Return of the Jedi tri-logo packaging.
____2-1B [AV267] 110.00
____4-LOM 45.00
____8D8 [AV268] 165.00
____A-Wing Pilot [AV269] 165.00
____Admiral Ackbar [AV270] 75.00
____Amanaman [AV271] 175.00
____Anakin Skywalker [AV272] 145.00
____Artoo-Detoo (R2-D2) Pop-Up Lightsaber [AV273]............................200.00
____Artoo-Detoo (R2-D2) with Sensorscope [AV274]..............................125.00
____AT-AT Commander [AV275] 125.00
____AT-AT Driver [AV276] 105.00
____AT-ST Driver [AV277] 85.00

AV267 AV268 AV269 AV270 AV271 AV272 AV273 AV274 AV275

AV276 AV277 AV278 AV279 AV280 AV281 AV282 AV283 AV284

___B-Wing Pilot [AV278] 85.00	___FX-7 [AV294]...85.00	___Lando Calrissian General [AV311]....................135.00
___Barada [AV279] 135.00	___Gamorrean Guard [AV295]..................160.00	___Lando Calrissian Skiff Outfit [AV312]...........100.00
___Ben (Obi-Wan) Kenobi [AV280] 200.00	___General Madine [AV296] 2,750.00	___Lando Calrissian, no teeth...............................150.00
___Bespin Security Guard, white 32.00	___Hammerhead 60.00	___Lobot [AV313] 125.00
___Bib Fortuna [AV281] 135.00	___Han Solo [AV297].......................125.00	___Logray [AV314]..65.00
___Biker Scout [AV282] 85.00	___Han Solo Bespin [AV298] 135.00	___Luke Skywalker Battle Poncho [AV315] 175.00
___Boba Fett [AV283] 635.00	___Han Solo Hoth Battle Gear [AV299]....110.00	___Luke Skywalker Bespin Fatigues, blonde
___Boba Fett, loose; sky blue instead of gray 170.00	___Han Solo in Carbonite [AV300] 225.00	hair 365.00
___Boba Fett; sky blue instead of gray 1,275.00	___Han Solo Trench Coat [AV301] 135.00	___Luke Skywalker Bespin Fatigues, brown hair
___Bossk [AV284] 71.00	___IG-88 [AV302]..............................235.00	[AV316] 135.00
___Boushh [AV285] 149.00	___Imperial Commander [AV303]...........125.00	___Luke Skywalker Hoth Battle Gear 34.00
___Chewbacca [AV286]........................165.00	___Imperial Dignitary [AV304]...............150.00	___Luke Skywalker Imperial Stormtrooper Outfit
___Chief Chirpa [AV287] 100.00	___Imperial Gunner [AV305] 195.00	[AV317] 425.00
___Darth Vader [AV288] 125.00	___Imperial Stormtrooper in Hoth Battle Gear	___Luke Skywalker Jedi Knight Outfit [AV318].....130.00
___Death Squad Commander 64.00	[AV306]...195.00	___Luke Skywalker X-Wing Pilot [AV319].............200.00
___Death Star Droid [AV289] 110.00	___Imperial Tie Fighter Pilot [AV307] 115.00	___Luke Skywalker, blonde hair [AV320] 300.00
___Dengar [AV290] 125.00	___Jawa, cloth cape 350.00	___Luke Skywalker, brown hair [AV321] 300.00
___Emperor's Royal Guard [AV291]............80.00	___Klaatu, Palace Outfit [AV308]............45.00	___Lumat [AV322] 125.00
___Emperor [AV292] 135.00	___Klaatu, Skiff Outfit [AV309] 215.00	___Nien Nunb [AV323]...150.00
___EV-9D9 [AV293] 130.00	___Lando Calrissian [AV310] 95.00	___Nikto [AV324] 75.00

AV285 AV286 AV287 AV288 AV289 AV290 AV291 AV292 AV293

AV294 AV295 AV296 AV297 AV298 AV299 AV300 AV301 AV302

AV303 AV304 AV305 AV306 AV307 AV308 AV309 AV310 AV311

Toys: Action Figures – 1978 – 1986

AV312 AV313 AV314 AV315 AV316 AV317 AV318 AV319 AV320

AV321 AV322 AV323 AV324 AV325 AV326 AV327 AV328 AV329

____Paploo [AV325] 150.00
____Power Droid 60.00
____Princess Leia Combat Poncho [AV326].............38.00
____Princess Leia Organa [AV327] 200.00
____Princess Leia Organa Bespin Gown [AV328] 90.00
____Princess Leia Organa Hoth Outfit [AV329] 155.00
____Pruneface [AV330] 65.00
____R5-D4 [AV331] 150.00
____Rancor Keeper [AV332] 75.00
____Rebel Commander [AV333] 75.00
____Rebel Commando [AV334] 235.00
____Rebel Soldier [AV335] 100.00
____Ree-Yees [AV336]...75.00
____Romba [AV337]...125.00
____See-Threepio (C-3PO) with Removable Limbs
[AV338]...135.00
____Squidhead [AV339]...95.00
____Stormtrooper [AV340] 280.00
____Teebo [AV341]..95.00
____Tusken Raider [AV342]....................................115.00

____Ugnaught [AV343] 90.00
____Walrusman 84.00
____Warok [AV344] 135.00
____Weequay [AV345]..135.00
____Wicket Warrick [AV346] 95.00
____Yak Face [AV347] 485.00
____Yoda, brown snake [AV348] 75.00
____Yoda, orange snake [AV349] 545.00
____Zuckuss [AV350] 150.00

PBP
Spain. El Imperio Contra ataca.
____Ben Kenobi 125.00
____C-3PO 200.00
____Darth Vader 125.00
____Lando Calrissian 110.00
____Luke Skywalker 230.00
____Luke Skywalker Bespin Outfit 140.00
____R2-D2 ....160.00
____Ugnaught 80.00

El Retorno Del Jedi.
____Admirante Ackbar...65.00
____Artoo Detoo with Sensorscope, original card
graphic 250.00
____B-wing Pilot 75.00
____Chewbacca 125.00
____Darth Vader 195.00
____Emperor's Royal Guard 175.00
____General Madine 55.00
____Hoth Stormtrooper...145.00
____Jefe Chirpa 130.00
____Logray 75.00
____Luke Skywalker Hoth Battle Gear 125.00
____Ree-Yees 75.00

____See Threepio, original card graphic 245.00
____Snaggletooth 85.00
____Weequay 175.00
____Yoda 95.00
____Zuckuss 125.00

Popy
____S 1 Boba Fett [AV351] 1,000.00
____S 2 Darth Vader [AV352] 400.00
____S 3 R2-D2 [AV353]...200.00
____S 4 C-3PO [AV354] 175.00
____S 5 Luke Skywalker, Bespin [AV355]...............275.00
____S 6 Han Solo, Hoth [AV356] 200.00
____S 7 Chewbacca [AV357] 185.00
____S 8 Luke Skywalker [AV358] 375.00
____S 9 Han Solo [AV359] 350.00
____S10 Imperial Snowtrooper [AV360] 400.00
____S11 Death Star Droid [AV361] 225.00
____S12 Rebel Soldier [AV362].............................175.00
____S13 Luke Skywalker, X-Wing Pilot [AV363]......200.00
____S14 R5-D4 [AV364]..300.00
____S15 Stormtrooper [AV365]..............................400.00

Takara
Star Wars.
____Artoo-Detoo 525.00
____Ben (Obi-Wan) Kenobi [3:53]..........................450.00
____Chewbacca 450.00
____Darth Vader 550.00
____Han Solo 700.00
____Luke Skywalker 600.00
____Princess Leia 600.00
____Sandpeople 750.00
____See-Threepio 445.00
____Stormtrooper 450.00

AV330 AV331 AV332

AV333 AV334 AV335 AV336 AV337 AV338 AV339 AV340 AV341

AV342 AV343 AV344 AV345 AV346 AV347 AV348 AV349 AV350

| AV351 | AV352 | AV353 | AV354 | AV355 | AV356 | AV357 | AV358 | AV359 | AV360 | AV361 | AV362 |

| AV366 | AV367 | AV368 | AV369 | AV370 | AV371 | AV372 | AV363 | AV364 | AV365 |

Top Toys
Argentina, ROTJ packaging.
____Chewbacca [AV366]........................325.00
____Darth Vader [AV367].......................150.00
____Logray [AV368].............................225.00
____Luke Skywalker, Jedi [AV369] 270.00
____Osito Ewok [AV370] 185.00
____Stormtrooper [AV371] 150.00
____Yoda [AV372] 325.00

Toys: Action Figures –
1978 – 1986 (Vintage) Multi-Packs

ROTJ 4-pack, German and French text.
____AT-AT Commander, C-3PO (removable limbs), Stormtrooper, Emperor's Royal Guard 400.00
____Bib Fortuna, Ben Kenobi. Emperor, IG-88 ......400.00

ROTJ 4-pack, Italian / English text.
____Darth Vader, Princess Leia Organa (Hoth Outfit), Paploo, Imperial Commander 350.00
____Lumat, Emperor, Cloud Car Pilot, Teebo..........350.00
____Rebel Commander, Lando, Lobot, Biker Scout 375.00
____Squid Head, Emperor's Royal Guard, B-Wing Pilot, AT-ST Driver 350.00

Kenner
____Sy Snootles and the Max Rebo Band [AVM01] 150.00

2-Pack.
____ROTJ, 2 random figures without weapons [AVM02] 145.00

3-Packs, Empire Strikes Back.
____Bespin Alliance: Bespin Security Guard, Lando, Luke 560.00
____Bespin Set 2: C-3PO, Ugnaught, Cloud Car Pilot 485.00
____Bespin Set: Han Solo Bespin Outfit, Ugnaught, Lobot 575.00
____Hoth Rebels: Han, Rebel Commander, FX-7 ..550.00
____Imperial Forces: Bossk, Stormtrooper, IG-88 ....625.00
____Imperial Set: Imperial Commander, Dengar, AT-AT Driver 1,600.00
____Imperial Set: Zuckuss, AT-AT Driver, Tie Fighter Pilot 530.00
____Rebel Set 2: Princess Leia Hoth Outfit, R2-D2 Sensorscope, Luke Skywalker Hoth Outfit 660.00
____Rebel Set: 2-1B, Princess Leia Hoth Outfit, Rebel Commander 530.00

3-Packs, Star Wars.
____Android Set: C-3PO, R2-D2, Chewbacca........350.00
____Creature Set: Hammerhead, Walrus Man, Greedo 1,500.00
____Droid Set: R5-D4, Death Star Droid, Power Droid 1,250.00
____Hero Set 1: Han Solo, Princess Leia Organa, Ben Kenobi 300.00
____Hero Set 2: Luke X-Wing Pilot, Ben Kenobi, Han Solo 480.00
____Villain Set 2: Sand People, Boba Fett, Snaggletooth 3,000.00
____Villain Set: Stormtrooper, Darth Vader, Death Squad Commander 800.00

6-Packs.
____AT-AT Driver, Darth Vader, IG-88, Rebel Soldier, Hoth Stormtrooper, Yoda [AVM03] 765.00
____C-3PO, Darth Vader, Han Solo Hoth Outfit, R2-D2 Sensorscope, Rebel Soldier, Hoth Stormtrooper [AVM04] 670.00

White catalog mailer boxes.
____10-pack 39312: Yoda, FX7, Luke Skywalker Bespin Fatigues, Leia Organa Bespin Gown, Lando, Security Guard, Rebel Soldier, Han Solo Hoth Outfit, Imperial Stormtrooper, IG88 ....435.00
____3-pack 48-62374: Emperor's Royal Guard, Darth Vader, Boba Fett 275.00
____3-pack 49-59033: Admiral Ackbar, General Madine, Rebel Commando [2:54] 150.00
____3-pack 49-59041: Gamorrean Guard, Squid Head, Bib Fortuna [AVM05] 150.00
____3-pack 71740: Darth Vader, The Emperor, Emperor's Royal Guard [2:54] 150.00
____4-pack 38841: C-3PO, R2-D2, Yoda, Luke Skywalker X-Wing Pilot 225.00
____4-pack 38934: R2D2, Yoda, Luke Skywalker Bespin Fatigues, FX7 ....225.00
____4-pack 39550: Greedo, (blue) Snaggletooth, Hammerhead, Walrusman 650.00
____4-pack 48-62355: Darth Vader, Boba Fett, Luke Skywalker Bespin Fatigues, Yoda 300.00
____4-pack 69712: Han Solo Hoth Outfit, Luke Skywalker X-Wing Pilot, Lando......................165.00
____7-pack 71660: The Emperor, Klaatu Skiff Guard, Nikto, 8D8, Rancor Keeper, AT-ST Driver, Emperor's Royal Guard 360.00
____7-pack 71670: B-Wing Pilot, Princess Leia Organa in Combat Poncho, Wicket W. Warrick, Han Solo in Trench Coat, Prune Face, Teebo, Paploo 360.00
____8-pack 49-59228: AT-AT Commander, Luke Hoth, R2D2 Sensorscope, Zuckuss, Cloud Car Pilot, Tie Pilot, Bespin Security Guard (Black), C3PO Removable Limbs 385.00
____8-pack 49-59231: IG88, Bespin Security Guard (Black), Luke Skywalker X-Wing Pilot, Cloud Car Pilot, Stormtrooper, Greedo, Ben Kenobi, R2-D2..385.00
____9-pack 49-59035: Luke Skywalker Bespin Fatigues, Leia Organa Bespin Gown, Lando, Security Guard, Rebel Soldier, Han Solo Hoth Outfit, Imperial Stormtrooper, FX7, IG88 ....445.00

Kenner, Canada
3-Packs, blingual packaging.
____Creature Set: Hammerhead, Walrusman, Greedo 1,075.00
____Droid Set: R5-D4, Death Star Droid, Power Droid..1,075.00
____Villain Set: Tusken Raider, Boba Fett, Snaggletooth 1,075.00

3-Packs. Empire Strikes Back, Sears exlusives.
____Imperial Tie Fighter Pilot, Rebel Soldier, Zuckuss 1,850.00
____R5-D4, R2-D2, Death Star Droid [2:54]........1,850.00

| AVM01 | AVM02 |

| AVM03 | AVM04 | AVM05 | AVM06 |

Toys: Action Figures – 1978 – 1986 Multi-Packs

AVS101

AVS102

AVS103

AVS104

AVS105

AVS106

AVS107

AVS108

AVS109

AVS110

AVS111

AVS112

AVS113

AVS114

AVS115

AVS116

AVS117

AVS118

AVS119

AVS120

AVS121

AVS122

AVS123

AVS124

AVS125

4-Packs. Include 3 standard carded figures, and one Sears exclusive figure shrink wrapped to card.

____AT-AT Driver, Dengar, Han Hoth, exclusive R2-D2 with pop-up saber ....N/V
____Bossk, Luke, Leia, exclusive General Veers..........N/V
____R2-D2, Leia Bespin, C-3PO, exclusive Han Bespin ....N/V
____Stormtrooper, IG-88, Leia Hoth, exclusive Luke Hoth ....N/V

7-Packs. Include 6 standard carded figures, and one Sears exclusive figure shrink wrapped to card.

____Bespin Guard (white), Han (large head), Lando (no teeth), Luke (blonde), IG-88, Boba Fett, exclusive Lobot ....N/V
____Death Star Droid, Power Droid, C-3PO, R2-D2, FX-7, R5-D4, exclusive Dengar ....N/V
____Luke Bespin, Hoth Stormtrooper, Darth Vader, Leai Bespin, Hoth Rebel Soldier, Bossk, exclusive Han Bespin ....N/V
____Luke X-Wing, Death Squad Commander, Han Hoth, Leia, Darth Vader, Stormtrooper, exclusive Tusk from Ugnaught ....N/V
____Luke, Greedo, Snaggletooth, Walrusman, Jawa, Hammerhead, exclusive Ben Kenobi ....N/V

Kenner, UK
____Ewok Combat Complete Playpack: 2 Ewoks, 2 Stormtroopers, Catapult, tri-logo 375.00
____Sy Snootles and Max Rebo Band [AVM06] 178.00

Parker Bros.
____2-Pack, plus accessory [1:45] 685.00
____2-Pack, plus vehicle [1:45] 790.00

____3-Pack of figures [2:54] 1,000.00
____4-Pack of figures [2:54] 575.00

Toys: Action Figures –
1985 – 1986 (Vintage Droids)

Glasslite
____C-3PO [AVS101] 300.00
____Jord Dusat [AVS102] 250.00
____Kea Moll [AVS103] 250.00
____Kez-Iban [AVS104] 250.00
____R2-D2 [AVS105] 250.00
____Thall Jorban [AVS106] 475.00
____Vlix [AVS107] 6,500.00
____Vlix, loose 4,300.00

Kenner
____A-Wing Pilot [AVS108] 250.00
____Boba Fett [AVS109] 1,775.00
____C-3PO [AVS110] [3:26] 200.00
____Without package, mint, complete 150.00
____Jann Tosh [AVS111] 65.00
____Without package, mint, complete 40.00
____Jord Dusat [AVS112] 75.00
____Without package, mint, complete 30.00
____Kea Moll [AVS113] 80.00
____Without package, mint, complete 50.00
____Kez-Iban [AVS114] 75.00
____Without package, mint, complete 40.00
____R2-D2 [AVS115] 150.00
____Without package, mint, complete [3:26] 150.00

____Sise Fromm [AVS116] 275.00
____Without package, mint, complete 200.00
____Thall Joben [AVS117] 80.00
____Without package, mint, complete 50.00
____Tig Fromm [AVS118] 165.00
____Without package, mint, complete 110.00
____Uncle Gundy [AVS119].....................................80.00
____Without package, mint, complete 45.00

Kenner, Canada
____A-Wing Pilot 150.00
____Boba Fett 1,085.00
____C-3PO...95.00
____Jann Tosh [AVS120] 65.00
____Jord Dusat [AVS121] 65.00
____Kea Moll [AVS122] 65.00
____Kez-Iban [AVS123] 65.00
____R2-D2 [AVS124] 250.00
____Sise Fromm 175.00
____Thall Joben 75.00
____Tig Fromm 165.00
____Uncle Gundy [AVS125].....................................55.00

Toys: Action Figures –
1985 – 1986 (Vintage Ewoks)

Kenner
____Dulok Scout [AVS201] 65.00
____Without package, mint, complete 30.00
____Dulok Shaman [AVS202] 65.00
____Without package, mint, complete 40.00
____King Gorneesh [AVS203] 65.00
____Without package, mint, complete 40.00
____Logray [AVS204]...65.00
____Without package, mint, complete 50.00
____Urgah Lady Gorneesh [AVS205] 65.00
____Without package, mint, complete 40.00
____Wicket [AVS206]...100.00
____Without package, mint, complete 75.00

Kenner, Canada
____Dulok Scout [2:65] 40.00
____Dulok Shaman 40.00
____King Gorneesh [2:65] 45.00
____Lady Ugrah Gorneesh [3:54] 45.00
____Logray..40.00
____Wicket..50.00

AVS201

AVS202

AVS203

AVS204

AVS205

AVS206

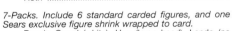

P3B01 P3B01 detail P3B02 detail P3B03 P3B04 P3B05 P3B06 P3B07

P3B08 P3B10 P3B09 detail P3B10 detail P3B12 P3B11 detail P3B12 detail P3B13 P3B14

P3B15 P3B15 detail P3B16 detail P3B17 P3B18 P3B19 P3B20 P3B21 P3B22

Toys: Action Figures –
1995 – 1999 (POTF2 1995 – 1996)

Kenner
Red card with image.
Ben Kenobi with lightsaber and removable cloak
____.00, long saber; close-up photo; brown belt 35.00
____.00, long saber; close-up photo; gold belt 35.00
____.00, short saber / long tray 1,750.00
____.01, long saber [P3B01] 35.00
____.01, short saber, holo 30.00
____.01, short saber; brown belt [P3B02].................15.00
____.01, short saber; gold belt 15.00
____Without package, mint, complete [3:27] 5.00
Boba Fett with sawed-off blaster rifle and jet pack
____.00, half hand circles; "Empire," on bio card......55.00
____.01, full hand circles [P3B03] 15.00
____.01, half hand circles; "Empire." on bio card......50.00
____.01, no chest emblem 550.00
____.01, no circle on one hand................................350.00
____.01, no circles or chest emblem 995.00
____.01, no shoulder emblem 500.00
____Without package, mint, complete [3:27] 10.00
C-3PO with realistic metalized body
____.00 [P3B04] 8.00
____Without package, mint, complete [3:27] 5.00
Chewbacca with bowcaster and heavy blaster rifle
____.00 [P3B05] 8.00
____Without package, mint, complete [3:27] 6.00
Darth Vader with lightsaber and removable cape
____.00, long saber [P3B06] 15.00
____.00, short saber 10.00
____.00, short saber / long tray................................45.00

____.00, tiny saber..10.00
____Without package, mint, complete [3:27] 5.00
Death Star Gunner w/radiation suit and blaster pistol
____.00, col. 1 [P3B07] 10.00
____Without package, mint, complete [3:27] 7.00
Greedo with Rodarian blaster rifle
____.00, col. 1 [P3B08] 10.00
____Without package, mint, complete [3:28] 4.00
Han Solo in carbonite
____.00 with carbonite freezing chamber [P3B09] 8.00
____.01 in carbonite block [P3B10] 6.00
____Without package, mint, complete [3:28] 4.00
Han Solo in Hoth gear w/blaster pistol & assault rifle
____.00, closed right hand [P3B11].............................8.00
____.00, open right hand [P3B12] 8.00
____Without package, mint, complete [3:28] 5.00
Han Solo with heavy assault rifle and blaster
____.00 [P3B13] 6.00
____Without package, mint, complete [3:28] 2.00

Jawas with glowing eyes and ionization blasters
____.00, col. 2 [P3B14] 18.00
____Without package, mint, complete [3:29] 10.00
Jedi Knight Luke w/lightsaber and removable cloak
____.00, black vest [P3B15] 12.00
____.00, tan vest [P3B16] 25.00
____Without package, mint, complete [3:29] 10.00
Lando Calrissian with heavy rifle and blaster pistol
____.00 [P3B17] 8.00
____Without package, mint, complete [3:29] 3.00
Luke Skywalker in Dagobah fatigues with lightsaber and blaster pistol
____.00, long saber 8.00
____.00, short saber [P3B18]......................................8.00
____.00, short saber / long tray..................................8.00
____00, short saber, new bubble, wholesale club ESB 3-pack 8.00
____.00, tiny saber 8.00
____Without package, mint, complete [3:29] 6.00

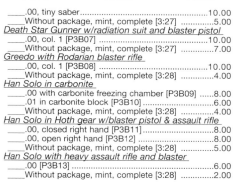     

P3B24 P3B23 detail P3B24 detail P3B25 P3B26 detail P3B27 detail

P3B27 P3B28 P3B29 P3B30 P3B30 detail P3B31 detail P3B32 P3B33

Toys: Action Figures – 1995 – 1999

P3B34

P3B35

P3B36

P3B37

P3B38

Luke Skywalker in Stormtrooper disguise with Imperial issue blaster
____.00, col. 2, OC photo [P3B19] 15.00
____Without package, mint, complete [3:29] 7.00
Luke Skywalker in X-wing fighter pilot gear with lightsaber and blaster pistol
____.00, long saber [P3B20] 8.00
____.01, long saber 8.00
____.01, short saber....................8.00
____.01, short saber / long tray....................15.00
____Without package, mint, complete [3:30] 6.00
Luke Skywalker with grappling hook blaster and lightsaber
____.00, long saber 15.00
____.00, short saber [P3B21]....................8.00
____.00, short saber / long tray 700.00
____Without package, mint, complete 6.00
Momaw Nadon "Hammerhead" with double-barreled blaster rifle
____.00, col. 2 [P3B22] 12.00
____Without package, mint, complete [3:30] 6.00
Princess Leia Organa w/laser pistol and assault rifle
____.00, 2 bands on belt [P3B23] 8.00
____.00, 3 bands on belt [P3B24] 8.00
____Without package, mint, complete [3:30] 3.00
R2-D2 with light-pipe eye port and retractable leg
____.00 [P3B25]....................10.00
____Without package, mint, complete [3:31] 6.00
R5-D4 with concealed missile launcher
____.00, col. 2, no warning [P3B26] 10.00
____.00, col. 2, warning sticker [P3B27]....................10.00
____Without package, mint, complete [3:31] 5.00
Stormtrooper with blaster rifle and heavy infantry cannon
____ .00, holo....................10.00
____.00, photo [P3B28] 10.00
____Without package, mint, complete [3:31] 6.00
Tatooine Stormtrooper with concussion grenade cannon
____.00, col. 1 [P3B29] 15.00
____Without package, mint, complete [3:31] 5.00
Tie Fighter Pilot with Imperial blaster pistol and rifle
____.00, warning sticker [P3B30] 10.00
____.01, warning is printed 10.00
____.02 [P3B31]....................10.00
____Without package, mint, complete [3:32] 5.00
Tusken Raider with gaderffi stick battle club
____.00, col. 2 ....10.00
____.00, col. 2, left hand closed [P3B32] 10.00
____Without package, mint, complete [3:32] 4.00
Yoda with Jedi trainer backpack and gimer stick
____.00, holo 20.00
____.00, photo 10.00
____.01 [P3B33]....................10.00
____Without package, mint, complete [3:32] 8.00

Kenner, Canada
Red card with image.
____Ben Kenobi [3:60]....................18.00
____Boba Fett [3:60] 18.00
____C-3PO square card [P3B34] 20.00
____Chewbacca square card [3:60] 20.00
____Darth Vader square card [3:60] 20.00
____Han Solo in Carbonite [3:60] 12.00
____Han Solo in Hoth Gear....................14.00
____Han Solo square card [3:60] 20.00
____Lando Calrissian [3:60] 9.00
____Luke Skywalker in Dagobah Fatigues [3:60]....................14.00
____Luke Skywalker in X-wing Gear [3:60]....................15.00
____Luke Skywalker Jedi Knight THX insert....................20.00
____Luke Skywalker square card 20.00
____Princess Leia Organa square card [3:60]....................20.00
____R2-D2 square card [3:60]....................20.00
____Stormtrooper square card [3:60] 20.00
____Tie Fighter Pilot new bubble 18.00
____Tie Fighter Pilot old bubble [3:60] 14.00
____Yoda [P3B35] 18.00

Kenner, Italy
Red card with image.
____Ben Kenobi Long saber [P3B36] 56.00
____Ben Kenobi Short saber [3:63]....................16.00
____Boba Fett [3:63] 21.00
____C1-P8 (R2-D2) [3:63] 20.00
____Chewbacca [3:63] 19.00
____D-3BO (C-3PO) [3:63] 14.00
____Darth Vader long saber [3:63] 37.00
____Darth Vader short saber....................18.00
____Han Solo [3:63]....................18.00
____Han Solo in Hoth Gear....................16.00
____Luke Skywalker [3:63] 14.00
____Luke Skywalker in Dagobah Fatigues [3:63]....................16.00
____Luke Skywalker in X-wing Gear [3:63]....................16.00
____Princess Leia Organa 19.00
____Stormtrooper [3:63] 24.00
____Tie Fighter Pilot [3:63] 13.00
____Yoda [3:63] 16.00

Kenner, Japan
Red U.S. card with image. Japanese sticker on back.
____Han Solo in Hoth Gear....................14.00
____Lando Calrissian....................12.00

Kenner, UK
Red card with image.
____Boba Fett new bubble [3:63] 22.00
____Boba Fett new bubble, sticker on barcode....................23.00
____Boba Fett old bubble 23.00
____Boba Fett THX insert 24.00
____C-3PO new bubble 14.00
____C-3PO old bubble [3:63] 14.00
____C-3PO THX insert [3:63]....................22.00
____Chewbacca new bubble 14.00
____Chewbacca old bubble [3:63] 14.00
____Chewbacca THX insert [3:63] 24.00
____Darth Vader new bubble, short saber 14.00
____Darth Vader new bubble, short saber with sticker on barcode 16.00
____Darth Vader old bubble, long saber....................18.00
____Darth Vader old bubble, short saber 14.00
____Darth Vader THX insert, long saber [3:64]....................20.00
____Han Solo [3:64]....................14.00
____Han Solo THX insert [3:64]....................20.00
____Han Solo in Hoth Gear [3:64]....................12.00
____Lando Calrissian [3:64]....................12.00
____Lando Calrissian THX insert....................23.00
____Luke Skywalker in Dagobah Fatigues short saber [3:64]....................15.00
____Luke Skywalker in X-wing Fighter Pilot Gear new bubble, short saber 14.00
____Luke Skywalker in X-wing Fighter Pilot Gear old bubble, long saber 18.00
____Luke Skywalker in X-wing Fighter Pilot Gear old bubble, short saber 14.00
____Luke Skywalker in X-wing Fighter Pilot Gear THX insert, long saber 24.00
____Luke Skywalker in X-wing Fighter Pilot Gear THX insert, short saber [3:64] 24.00
____Luke Skywalker Long saber....................18.00
____Luke Skywalker Short saber [P3B37] 14.00
____Luke Skywalker THX, long saber [3:64]....................24.00
____Obi-Wan Kenobi long saber [3:64]....................18.00
____Obi-Wan Kenobi short saber [3:64] 14.00
____Obi-Wan Kenobi THX insert [3:64]....................24.00
____Princess Leia Organa new bubble, 2 belt rings 14.00
____Princess Leia Organa old bubble [3:64]....................16.00
____Princess Leia Organa THX insert [P3B38] 23.00
____R2-D2 [3:64] 14.00
____R2-D2 THX insert 22.00
____Stormtrooper [3:64] 15.00
____Stormtrooper THX insert [3:64] 28.00
____Tie Fighter Pilot [3:64] 12.00
____Yoda new bubble 14.00
____Yoda old bubble [3:64] 15.00

Toys: Action Figures – 1995 – 1999 (POTF2 1996) SOTE

Kenner
Purple card with image, Shadows of the Empire.
Chewbacca in bounty hunter disguise
____.00 [P3C01] 8.00
____Without package, mint, complete [3:31] 5.00
Dash Rendar with heavy blaster pack
____.00 [P3C02]....................15.00
____Without package, mint, complete [3:31] 10.00
Leia in Boushh disguise
____.00 [P3C03]....................10.00
____.00, col. 1 ....300.00
____Without package, mint, complete [3:31] 5.00
Luke Skywalker in Imperial disguise
____.00 [P3C04]....................12.00
____Without package, mint, complete [3:31] 10.00
Prince Xizor with energy blade shields
____.00 [P3C05]....................12.00
____Without package, mint, complete [3:31] 5.00

Kenner, Canada
Purple card with foil image, Shadows of the Empire.
____Chewbacca in bounty hunter disguise [3:62]....................14.00
____Dash Rendar [3:62]....................19.00
____Luke Skywalker in Imperial Disguise [3:62] 21.00
____Prince Xizor [3:62]....................9.00
____Princess Leia in Boushh Disguise [P3C06] 12.00

Kenner, Italy
Orange card with foil image, Shadows of the Empire. Limited to 5,000.
____Chewbacca in bounty hunter disguise [P3C07]....................16.00
____Dash Rendar [3:62]....................21.00
____Luke Skywalker in Imperial Disguise 17.00
____Prince Xizor [3:62] 11.00

Kenner, UK
Orange card with foil image, Shadows of the Empire. Limited to 5,000.
____Chewbacca in bounty hunter disguise [3:62]....................30.00
____Dash Rendar [3:62]....................30.00
____Luke Skywalker in Imperial Dusguise [P3C08]....................33.00
____Prince Xizor [3:62] 29.00

P3C01

P3C02

P3C03

P3C04

P3C05

P3C06

P3C07

P3C08

P3D01

P3D02

P3D03

P3D04

P3D05

P3D06

P3D07

P3D08

P3D09

P3D10

P3D11

P3D12

P3D13

P3D13 detail

P3D14 detail

P3D15

P3D16

P3D17

P3D18

P3D19

P3D20

P3D21

P3D22

P3D23

P3D24

P3D25

P3D26

Toys: Action Figures – 1995 – 1999 (POTF2 1997)

Kenner

Green card with image.

2-1B Medic Droid with medical diagnostic computer
____.00, holo, col. 2 [P3D01] 8.00
____.00, photo, col. 2..8.00
____.01, holo, col. 2, new bubble 8.00
____.01, holo, col. 2, old bubble 8.00
____Without package, mint, complete [3:26] 6.00

4-LOM with blaster pistol and blaster rifle
____.00, holo, col. 2 [P3D02].......................................10.00
____Without package, mint, complete [3:26] 8.00

Admiral Ackbar with comlink wrist blaster
____.00, holo, col. 2 [P3D03] 8.00
____Without package, mint, complete [3:26] 4.00

ASP-7 Droid with spaceport supply rods
____.00, holo, col. 2 [3:56] 8.00
____.00, photo, col. 2 [P3D04]..8.00
____Without package, mint, complete [3:26] 4.00

AT-ST Driver with blaster rifle and pistol
____.00, holo, col. 2 [P3D05].......................................10.00
____.00, photo, col. 2 ....10.00
____.02, holo, col. 3, new bubble 8.00
____.02, holo, col. 3, old bubble 8.00
____Without package, mint, complete [3:27] 4.00

Ben (Obi-Wan) Kenobi with lightsaber and removable cloak
____.02, holo, col. 1, short saber, new bubble [P3D06] 8.00
____.02, holo, col. 1, short saber, old bubble 8.00
____.02, photo, col. 1 short saber, new bubble 8.00
____Without package, mint, complete [3:27] 5.00

Bespin Han Solo with heavy assault rifle and blaster
____.00, holo, col. 1 [P3D07].......................................10.00
____.00, photo, col. 1 ....10.00
____Without package, mint, complete [3:28] 3.00

Bib Fortuna with hold-out blaster
____.00, holo, col. 1..10.00
____.01, holo, col. 2, new bubble [3:56] 10.00
____.01, holo, col. 2, old bubble 10.00
____.01, photo, col. 2, new bubble [P3D08] 10.00
____Without package, mint, complete [3:27] 6.00

Boba Fett with sawed-off blaster rifle and jet pack
____.02, holo, col. 1..25.00
____.03, holo, col. 3..20.00
____.03, photo, col. 3 [P3D09] 20.00
____Without package, mint, complete [3:27] 10.00

Bossk with blaster rifle and pistol
____.00, holo, col. 2, new bubble 7.00
____.00, holo, col. 2, old bubble [P3D10] 7.00
____.00, photo, col. 2..7.00
____.01, holo, col. 2, new bubble 7.00
____.01, holo, col. 2, old bubble 7.00
____Without package, mint, complete [3:27] 5.00

C-3PO with realistic metalized body
____.01, holo, col. 1, new bubble 12.00
____.01, holo, col. 1, old bubble [P3D11] 12.00
____Without package, mint, complete [3:27] 5.00

Chewbacca with bowcaster and heavy blaster rifle
____.01, holo, col. 1, new bubble 10.00
____.01, holo, col. 1, old bubble 10.00
____.01, photo, col. 1, new bubble [P3D12]................10.00
____Without package, mint, complete [3:27] 6.00

Darth Vader with lightsaber and removable cape
____.01, holo, col. 1...10.00
____.02, holo, col. 3, new bubble [P3D13] 10.00
____.02, holo, col. 3, old bubble 10.00
____.02, holo, col. 3, SOTE 2-pack [P3D14] 125.00
____.02, photo, col. 3, new bubble...............................10.00
____Without package, mint, complete [3:27] 5.00

Death Star Gunner with blaster and assault rifle
____.01, holo, col. 1 [P3D15]...10.00
____.01, photo, col. 1 [3:56] 10.00
____.02, holo, col. 3, new bubble 10.00
____.02, holo, col. 3, old bubble 10.00
____Without package, mint, complete [3:27] 7.00

Dengar with blaster rifle
____.00, holo, col. 2 [P3D16]...12.00
____Without package, mint, complete [3:27] 6.00

Emperor's Royal Guard with force pike
____.00, holo, col. 3 [P3D17]...10.00
____.00, photo, col. 3 ....10.00
____Without package, mint, complete [3:27] 4.00

Emperor Palpatine with walking stick
____.00, holo, col. 1 ....9.00
____.01, holo, col. 3, new bubble [P3D18] 9.00
____.01, holo, col. 3, old bubble 9.00
____.01, photo, col. 3, new bubble [3:56] 9.00
____Without package, mint, complete [3:27] 3.00

EV-9D9 with datapad
____.00, holo, col. 2 [P3D19] 8.00
____Without package, mint, complete [3:28] 6.00

Gamorrean Guard with vibro axe
____.00, holo, col. 2 [P3D20]..12.00
____Without package, mint, complete [3:28] 10.00

Garindan (Long Snoot) with hold-out pistol
____.00, holo, col. 3 [P3D21] 6.00
____.00, photo, col. 3 [3:56]...6.00
____Without package, mint, complete [3:28] 4.00

Grand Moff Tarkin w/Imperial blaster rifle and pistol
____.00, holo, col. 2...15.00
____.01, holo, col. 3 [P3D22] 9.00
____.01, photo, col. 3 [3:57]...9.00
____Without package, mint, complete [3:28] 5.00

Greedo with blaster pistol
____.01, holo, col. 1 [P3D23] 8.00
____.01, photo, col. 1...8.00
____Without package, mint, complete [3:28] 4.00

Han Solo in carbonite with carbonite block
____.02, holo, col. 2, new bubble [P3D24] 10.00
____.02, holo, col. 2, old bubble 10.00
____.03, holo, col. 1..10.00
____.03, photo, col. 1 ....10.00
____Without package, mint, complete [3:28] 4.00

Han Solo in Endor gear with blaster pistol
____.00, holo, col. 1, new bubble [P3D25] 8.00
____.00, holo, col. 1, old bubble 8.00
____.00, photo, col. 1, new bubble 8.00
____.00, photo, col. 1, new bubble, brown pants [3:57] 8.00
____Without package, mint, complete [3:28] 5.00

Han Solo with heavy assault rifle and blaster
____.01, holo, col. 1, new bubble [P3D26] 6.00
____.01, holo, col. 1, old bubble 6.00
____.01, photo, col. 1, new bubble 6.00
____Without package, mint, complete [3:28] 2.00

Hoth Rebel Soldier with survival backpack and blaster rifle
____.00, holo, col. 2 [P3D27] 8.00
____.00, photo, col. 2...8.00
____.01, holo, col. 1, new bubble 8.00
____.01, holo, col. 1, old bubble 8.00
____Without package, mint, complete [3:28] 4.00

Jawas with glowing eyes and blaster pistols
____.01, holo, col. 2 [P3D28]..10.00
____.01, photo, col. 2 ....10.00
____.02, holo, col. 2, new bubble 10.00
____.02, holo, col. 2, old bubble 10.00
____Without package, mint, complete [3:29] 10.00

Lando Calrissian as skiff guard with skiff guard force pike
____.00, holo, col. 1, new bubble, gold circle 8.00
____.00, holo, col. 1, old bubble, gold circle [P3D29] 8.00
____.00, holo, col. 1, silver circle.....................................8.00
____Without package, mint, complete [3:29] 4.00

Lando Calrissian with heavy rifle and blaster pistol
____.01, holo, col. 1, ESB 3-pack [P3D30] 40.00
____Without package, mint, complete [3:29] 3.00

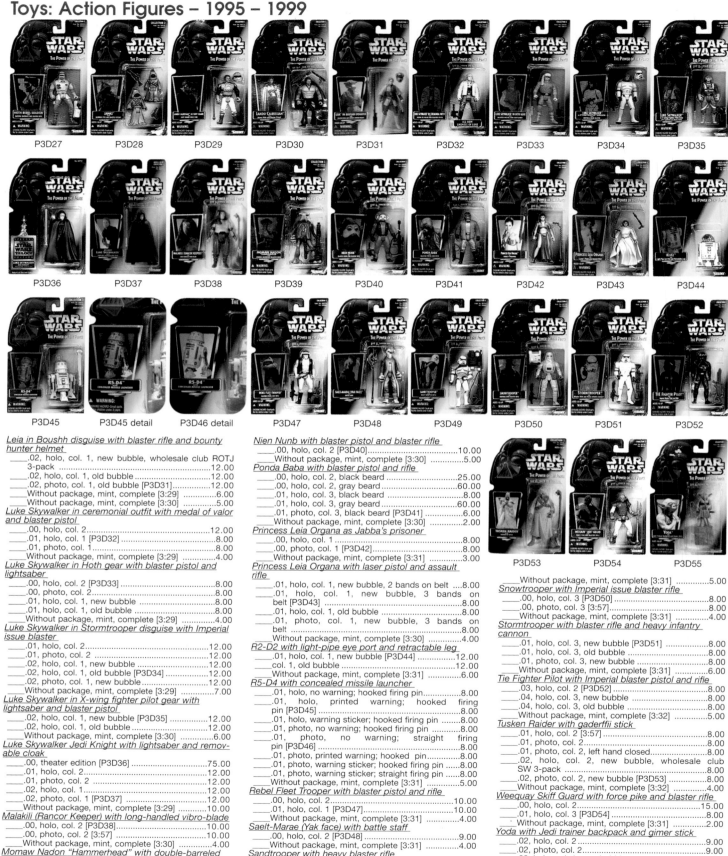

P3D27	P3D28	P3D29	P3D30	P3D31	P3D32	P3D33	P3D34	P3D35
P3D36	P3D37	P3D38	P3D39	P3D40	P3D41	P3D42	P3D43	P3D44
P3D45	P3D45 detail	P3D46 detail	P3D47	P3D48	P3D49	P3D50	P3D51	P3D52

P3D53	P3D54	P3D55

Leia in Boushh disguise with blaster rifle and bounty hunter helmet
____.02, holo, col. 1, new bubble, wholesale club ROTJ 3-pack 12.00
____.02, holo, col. 1, old bubble 12.00
____.02, photo, col. 1, old bubble [P3D31]........12.00
____Without package, mint, complete [3:29] 6.00
____Without package, mint, complete [3:30] 5.00
Luke Skywalker in ceremonial outfit with medal of valor and blaster pistol
____.00, holo, col. 2 ....12.00
____.01, holo, col. 1 [P3D32] 8.00
____.01, photo, col. 1 ....8.00
____Without package, mint, complete [3:29] 4.00
Luke Skywalker in Hoth gear with blaster pistol and lightsaber
____.00, holo, col. 2 [P3D33] 8.00
____.00, photo, col. 2 ....8.00
____.01, holo, col. 1, new bubble 8.00
____.01, holo, col. 1, old bubble 8.00
____Without package, mint, complete [3:29] 4.00
Luke Skywalker in Stormtrooper disguise with Imperial issue blaster
____.01, holo, col. 2 ....12.00
____.01, photo, col. 2 ....12.00
____.02, holo, col. 1, new bubble 12.00
____.02, holo, col. 1, old bubble [P3D34] 12.00
____.02, photo, col. 1, new bubble 12.00
____Without package, mint, complete [3:29] 7.00
Luke Skywalker in X-wing fighter pilot gear with lightsaber and blaster pistol
____.02, holo, col. 1, new bubble [P3D35] 12.00
____.02, holo, col. 1, old bubble 12.00
____Without package, mint, complete [3:30] 6.00
Luke Skywalker Jedi Knight with lightsaber and removable cloak
____.00, theater edition [P3D36] 75.00
____.01, holo, col. 2 ....12.00
____.01, photo, col. 2 ....12.00
____.02, holo, col. 1 ....12.00
____.02, photo, col. 1 [P3D37] 12.00
____Without package, mint, complete [3:29] 10.00
Malakili (Rancor Keeper) with long-handled vibro-blade
____.00, holo, col. 2 [P3D38] 10.00
____.00, photo, col. 2 [3:57] 10.00
____Without package, mint, complete [3:30] 4.00
Momaw Nadon "Hammerhead" with double-barreled blaster rifle
____.01, holo, col. 2 [P3D39] 10.00
____.01, photo, col. 2 ....10.00
____Without package, mint, complete [3:30] 5.00

Nien Nunb with blaster pistol and blaster rifle
____.00, holo, col. 2 [P3D40] 10.00
____Without package, mint, complete [3:30] 5.00
Ponda Baba with blaster pistol and rifle
____.00, holo, col. 2, black beard 25.00
____.00, holo, col. 2, gray beard 60.00
____.01, holo, col. 3, black beard 8.00
____.01, holo, col. 3, gray beard 60.00
____.01, photo, col. 3, black beard [P3D41] 6.00
____Without package, mint, complete [3:30] 2.00
Princess Leia Organa as Jabba's prisoner
____.00, holo, col. 1 ....8.00
____.00, photo, col. 1 [P3D42] 8.00
____Without package, mint, complete [3:31] 3.00
Princess Leia Organa with laser pistol and assault rifle
____.01, holo, col. 1, new bubble, 2 bands on belt 8.00
____.01, holo, col. 1, new bubble, 3 bands on belt [P3D43] 8.00
____.01, holo, col. 1, old bubble 8.00
____.01, photo, col. 1, new bubble, 3 bands on belt 8.00
____Without package, mint, complete [3:30] 4.00
R2-D2 with light-pipe eye port and retractable leg
____.01, holo, col. 1, new bubble [P3D44] 12.00
____col. 1, old bubble 12.00
____Without package, mint, complete [3:31] 6.00
R5-D4 with concealed missile launcher
____.01, holo, no warning; hooked firing pin 8.00
____.01, holo, printed warning; hooked firing pin [P3D45] 8.00
____.01, holo, warning sticker; hooked firing pin 8.00
____.01, photo, no warning; hooked firing pin 8.00
____.01, photo, no warning; straight firing pin [P3D46] 8.00
____.01, photo, printed warning; hooked pin 8.00
____.01, photo, warning sticker; hooked firing pin 8.00
____.01, photo, warning sticker; straight firing pin 8.00
____Without package, mint, complete [3:31] 5.00
Rebel Fleet Trooper with blaster pistol and rifle
____.00, holo, col. 2 ....10.00
____.01, holo, col. 1 [P3D47] 10.00
____Without package, mint, complete [3:31] 4.00
Saelt-Marae (Yak face) with battle staff
____.00, holo, col. 2 [P3D48] 9.00
____Without package, mint, complete [3:31] 4.00
Sandtrooper with heavy blaster rifle
____.01, holo, col. 1 ....8.00
____.01, photo, col. 1 ....8.00
____.02, holo, col. 3, new bubble [P3D49] 8.00
____.02, holo, col. 3, old bubble 8.00

____Without package, mint, complete [3:31] 5.00
Snowtrooper with Imperial issue blaster rifle
____.00, holo, col. 3 [P3D50] 8.00
____.00, photo, col. 3 [3:57] 8.00
____Without package, mint, complete [3:31] 4.00
Stormtrooper with blaster rifle and heavy infantry cannon
____.01, holo, col. 3, new bubble [P3D51] 8.00
____.01, holo, col. 3, old bubble 8.00
____.01, photo, col. 3, new bubble 8.00
____Without package, mint, complete [3:31] 6.00
Tie Fighter Pilot with Imperial blaster pistol and rifle
____.03, holo, col. 2 [P3D52] 8.00
____.04, holo, col. 3, new bubble 8.00
____.04, holo, col. 3, old bubble 8.00
____Without package, mint, complete [3:32] 5.00
Tusken Raider with gaderffii stick
____.01, holo, col. 2 [3:57] 8.00
____.01, photo, col. 2 ....8.00
____.01, photo, col. 2, left hand closed 8.00
____.02, holo, col. 2, new bubble, wholesale club SW 3-pack 8.00
____.02, photo, col. 2, new bubble [P3D53] 8.00
____Without package, mint, complete [3:32] 4.00
Weequay Skiff Guard with force pike and blaster rifle
____.00, holo, col. 2 ....15.00
____.01, holo, col. 3 [P3D54] 8.00
____Without package, mint, complete [3:31] 2.00
Yoda with Jedi trainer backpack and gimer stick
____.02, holo, col. 2 ....9.00
____.02, photo, col. 2 ....9.00
____.03, holo, col. 1, new bubble 9.00
____.03, holo, col. 1, old bubble [3:57] 9.00
____.03, photo, col. 1, new bubble [P3D55] 9.00
____Without package, mint, complete [3:32] 8.00

Estrela
Brazil. Green card with foil image.

____2-1B [P3D56] 8.00
____4-LOM 10.00
____Admiral Ackbar 8.00
____ASP-7 Doid 8.00
____AT-ST Driver 10.00
____Bossk 8.00
____Darth Vader 12.00
____Death Star Gunner 10.00
____Dengar 15.00
____Emperor's Royal Guard 10.00
____Emperor Palpatine 8.00
____EV-9D9 .... 6.00
____Gamorrean Guard 10.00
____Garindan 6.00
____Grand Moff Tarkin 10.00
____Greedo 8.00
____Han Solo in Bespin gear 8.00
____Han Solo in Endor Gear 8.00
____Hoth Rebel Soldier 6.00
____Jawas 12.00
____Lando Calrissian in Skiff Disguise 8.00
____Luke Skywalker in Hoth Gear 8.00
____Luke Skywalker in Stormtrooper Disguise 15.00
____Luke Skywalker Jedi Knight 12.00
____Malakili 10.00
____Momaw Nadon 8.00
____Nien Nunb 6.00
____Ponda Baba 8.00
____Princess Leia as Jabba's Prisoner 10.00
____R5-D4 .... 10.00
____Rebel Fleet Trooper 10.00
____Saelt-Marae 8.00
____Sandtrooper 8.00
____Snowtrooper 8.00
____Stormtrooper 9.00
____Tie Fighter Pilot 10.00
____Tusken Raider 8.00
____Weequay 10.00

Kenner, Canada
Green card with foil image.

____2-1B [3:61] 12.00
____4-LOM [3:61] 16.00
____Admiral Ackbar [3:61] 10.00
____ASP-7 Doid [3:61] 11.00
____AT-ST Driver [3:61] 11.00
____Bib Fortuna [3:61] 16.00
____Bossk [3:61] 14.00
____Darth Vader [3:61] 11.00
____Death Star Gunner [3:61] 12.00
____Dengar [3:61] 16.00
____Emperor's Royal Guard [3:61] 18.00
____Emperor Palpatine [3:61] 8.00
____EV-9D9 [3:61] 12.00
____Gamorrean Guard [3:61] 9.00
____Garindan [3:61] 7.00
____Grand Moff Tarkin [3:61] 8.00
____Greedo [3:61] 10.00
____Han Solo in Bespin gear [3:61] 7.00
____Han Solo in Endor Gear [3:61] 10.00
____Hoth Rebel Soldier [3:61] 8.00
____Jawas [P3D57] 15.00
____Lando Calrissian in Skiff Disguise [3:61] 9.00
____Luke Skywalker in Hoth Gear 10.00
____Luke Skywalker in Stormtrooper Disguise 10.00
____Luke Skywalker Jedi Knight 9.00
____Malakili 10.00
____Momaw Nadon [3:61] 14.00
____Nien Nunb [3:61] 9.00
____Ponda Baba [3:61] 9.00
____Princess Leia as Jabba's Prisoner [3:61] 10.00
____R5-D4 [3:61] 9.00
____Rebel Fleet Trooper 11.00
____Saelt-Marae [3:61] 10.00
____Sandtrooper [3:61] 16.00
____Snowtrooper [3:61] 8.00
____Stormtrooper [3:61] 12.00
____Tie Fighter Pilot 12.00
____Tusken Raider [3:62] 14.00
____Weequay [3:62] 8.00

P3D56

P3D57

P3D58

P3D59 rear

P3D60

P3D61

Kenner, Italy
Green card with photo image.

____Bossk 16.00
____Death Star Gunner 14.00
____Emperor Palpatine [3:63] 9.00
____Greedo [3:63] 12.00
____Han Solo in Carbonite 10.00
____Han Solo in Endor Gear 12.00
____Luke Skywalker in Hoth Gear 23.00
____Ponda Baba [3:63] 10.00
____Princess Leia in Boushh Disguise 20.00
____Sandtrooper [P3D58] 10.00
____Tusken Raider [3:63] 14.00

Kenner, Japan
Green U.S. card with image, Japanese sticker on back.

____ASP-7 Droid with spaceport supply rods .00, photo, col. 2 .... 12.00
____Bib Fortuna with hold-out blaster .01, photo, col. 2, new bubble 15.00
____C-3PO with Realistic Metalized Body .01, photo, col. 1, green tinted plastic [3:63] 17.00
____Grand Moff Tarkin with Imperial issue blaster rifle and pistol .01, photo, col. 3, no "Never Before Offered" sticker 25.00
____Greedo with blaster pistol .01, photo, col. 1 .... 14.00
____Malakili (Rancor Keeper) with long-handled vibro-blade .00, photo, col. 2 .... 15.00
____Momaw Nadon "Hammerhead" with double-barreled blaster rifle .01, photo, col. 2 .... 12.00
____Tusken Raider with gaderffii stick .02, photo, col. 2, new bubble [P3D59] 15.00
____Yoda with Jedi trainer backpack and gimer stick .03, photo, col. 1, new bubble 15.00

Kenner, UK
Green card with photo image, with tri-logo.

____Bossk new bubble 8.00
____Bossk old bubble [3:64] 9.00
____Death Star Gunner [3:64] 12.00
____Emperor Palpatine new bubble 12.00
____Emperor Palpatine new bubble, sticker on barcode 12.00
____Emperor Palpatine old bubble [3:64] 12.00
____Greedo [3:64] 12.00
____Han Solo in Carbonite new bubble 12.00
____Han Solo in Carbonite old bubble [3:64] 12.00
____Han Solo in Endor Gear new bubble, blue pants 12.00
____Han Solo in Endor Gear new bubble, brown pants 17.00
____Han Solo in Endor Gear old bubble, blue pants [3:64] 12.00
____Hoth Rebel Soldier 12.00
____Lando Calrissian in Skiff Disguise [3:64] 10.00
____Luke Skywalker in Hoth Gear new bubble, short saber 12.00
____Luke Skywalker in Hoth Gear old bubble, short saber 12.00
____Luke Skywalker in Stormtrooper Disguise 14.00
____Luke Skywalker Jedi Knight new bubble, short saber 15.00
____Luke Skywalker Jedi Knight old bubble, short saber [3:64] 13.00
____Ponda Baba [3:64] 13.00
____Princess Leia as Jabba's Prisoner [P3D60] 19.00
____Princess Leia in Boushh Disguise [3:64] 14.00
____Rebel Fleet Trooper [3:64] 10.00
____Sandtrooper new bubble 12.00
____Sandtrooper new bubble, sticker on barcode 12.00
____Sandtrooper old bubble [3:64] 12.00
____Tusken Raider [3:64] 12.00

Green card with photo image, without tri-logo.

____4-LOM 17.00
____Admiral Ackbar [3:64] 14.00
____Bib Fortuna 11.00
____Emperor's Royal Guard 13.00
____Endor Rebel Soldier [3:64] 10.00
____Ewok 2-pack (Wicket/Logray) [3:64] 18.00
____Gamorrean Guard 12.00
____Grand Moff Tarkin 12.00
____Han Solo in Bespin Gear [3:64] 12.00
____Jawas 17.00
____Luke Skywalker in Bespin Gear [3:64] 34.00
____Momaw Nadon (Hammerhead) 12.00
____Snowtrooper [P3D61] 12.00
____Weequay Skiff Guard [3:64] 22.00

Toys: Action Figures – 1995 – 1999 (POTF2 1998)

Kenner
Green card with Freeze Frame Action Slide.

8D8 with droid branding device
____.00, col. 2 [P3E01] 8.00
____Without package, mint, complete [3:26] 5.00

Admiral Ackbar with comlink wrist blaster
____.01, col. 2 [P3E02] 8.00
____Without package, mint, complete [3:26] 4.00

AT-AT Driver with Imperial issue blaster
____.00, col. 3, Fan Club exclusive [P3E03] 15.00
____Without package, mint, complete [3:26] 10.00

AT-ST Driver with blaster rifle and pistol
____.03, col. 3 [P3E04] 50.00
____Without package, mint, complete [3:27] 4.00

Bespin Han Solo with assault rifle and blaster pistol
____.01, col. 1 [P3E05] 8.00
____.02, col. 1 .... 8.00
____Without package, mint, complete [3:27] .... -.00

Bespin Luke Skywalker w/lightsaber & blaster pistol
____.00, col. 1 [P3E06] 8.00
____.01, col. 1 .... 8.00
____Without package, mint, complete [3:27] 3.00

P3E01

P3E02

P3E03

P3E04

P3E05

P3E06

P3E07

P3E08

P3E09

P3E10

P3E11

P3E12

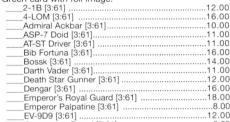

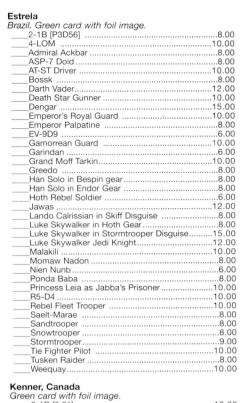

P3E13 P3E14 P3E15 P3E16 P3E17 P3E18 P3E19 P3E20 P3E21

Biggs Darklighter with blaster pistol
_____.00, col. 2 [P3E07] 12.00
_____Without package, mint, complete [3:27] 8.00
Boba Fett with sawed-off blaster rifle and jet pack
_____.04, col. 3, "Imprisioned" on slide [P3E08] 50.00
_____Without package, mint, complete [3:27] 10.00
C-3PO with realistic metalized body and cargo net
_____.00, col. 1 [P3E09] 8.00
_____Without package, mint, complete [3:27] 6.00
Captain Piett with blaster rifle
_____...and pistol .00, col. 3 [P3E10] 20.00
_____...and baton .00, col. 3 ....45.00
_____Without package, mint, complete [3:27] 16.00
Chewbacca as Boushh's Bounty with bowcaster
_____.00, col. 1 [P3E11]................................8.00
_____Without package, mint, complete [3:27] 5.00
Darth Vader with lightsaber and removable cape
_____.03, col. 3 [P3E12] 12.00
_____Without package, mint, complete [3:27] 5.00
Darth Vader with removable helmet and lightsaber
_____.00, col. 3 [P3E13] 20.00
_____Without package, mint, complete [3:27] 12.00
Death Star Droid with Mouse Droid
_____.00, col. 2, Fan Club exclusive [P3E14] 10.00
_____Without package, mint, complete [3:27] 8.00
Death Star Trooper with blaster rifle
_____.00, col. 3 [P3E15] 15.00
_____Without package, mint, complete [3:27] 10.00
Emperor's Royal Guard with force pike
_____.01, col. 3 [P3E16] 15.00
_____Without package, mint, complete [3:28] 4.00
Emperor Palpatine with walking stick
_____.02, col. 3 [P3E17] 8.00
_____Without package, mint, complete [3:28] 3.00
Endor Rebel Soldier with survival backpack and blaster rifle
_____.00, col. 1 [P3E18]................................8.00
_____.01, col. 1 ....8.00
_____Without package, mint, complete [3:28] 3.00
EV-9D9 with datapad
_____.01, col. 2 [P3E19] 8.00
_____Without package, mint, complete [3:28] 6.00
Ewoks: Wicket and Logray
_____.00, col. 2 [P3E20] 15.00
_____Without package, mint, complete [3:28] 12.00
Gamorrean Guard with vibro axe
_____.01, col. 2 [P3E21] 15.00
_____Without package, mint, complete [3:28] 10.00
Garindan with hold-out pistol
_____.01, col. 3 [P3E22] 25.00
_____Without package, mint, complete [3:28] 4.00

Grand Moff Tarkin with Imperial blaster rifle and pistol
_____.02, col. 3 [P3E23] 12.00
_____Without package, mint, complete [3:28] 5.00
Han Solo in carbonite with carbonite block
_____.04, col. 1 [P3E24] 6.00
_____.05, col. 1 ....6.00
_____Without package, mint, complete [3:28] 4.00
Han Solo in Endor gear with blaster pistol
_____.01, col. 1 ....8.00
_____.02, col. 1 [P3E25] 8.00
_____Without package, mint, complete [3:28] 5.00
Han Solo with blaster pistol
_____.02, col. 1 [P3E26] 6.00
_____Without package, mint, complete [3:28] 2.00
Hoth Rebel Soldier with survival backpack and blaster rifle
_____.02, col. 1 ....8.00
_____.03, col. 1 [P3E27] 8.00
_____Without package, mint, complete [3:28] 4.00
Ishi Tib with blaster rifle
_____.00, col. 3 [P3E28] 25.00
_____Without package, mint, complete [3:29] 20.00
Lak Sivrak with blaster pistol and vibro blade
_____.00, col. 2 ....10.00
_____.01, col. 2 [P3E29] 10.00
_____Without package, mint, complete [3:29] 6.00
Lando Calrissian as skiff guard with force pike
_____.01, col. 1 ....6.00
_____.02, col. 1 [P3E30] 6.00
_____Without package, mint, complete [3:29] 4.00
Lando Calrissian in General's gear with blaster pistol
_____.00, col. 1, 1 sticker on bubble..................8.00
_____.00, col. 1, 2 stickers on bubble [P3E31] 8.00
_____.01, col. 1, 1 sticker on bubble..................8.00
_____.01, col. 1, 2 stickers on bubble.................8.00
_____Without package, mint, complete [3:29] 3.00
Lobot with blaster pistol and transmitter
_____.00, col. 1 [P3E32] 10.00
_____Without package, mint, complete [3:29] 8.00
Luke Skywalker in cerimonial outfit with blaster pistol
_____.01, col. 1 [P3E33]................................8.00
_____Without package, mint, complete [3:29] 4.00
Luke Skywalker in Stormtrooper disguise with Imperial blaster
_____.03, col. 1 [P3E34] 10.00
_____.04, col. 1 ....10.00
_____Without package, mint, complete [3:29] 7.00
Luke Skywalker with blast shield and lightsaber
_____.00, col. 1 [P3E35] 10.00
_____Without package, mint, complete [3:29] 3.00

Malakili (Rancor Keeper) w/long-handled vibro-blade
_____.01, col. 2 [P3E36] 10.00
_____Without package, mint, complete [3:30] 5.00
Mon Mothma with baton
_____.00, col. 1 [P3E37] 10.00
_____Without package, mint, complete [3:30] 8.00
Nien Nunb with blaster pistol and rifle
_____.01, col. 2 [P3E38] 12.00
_____Without package, mint, complete [3:30] 7.00
Obi-Wan (Ben) Kenobi with lightsaber
_____.03, col. 1, short saber [P3E39] 8.00
_____.04, col. 1, short saber 8.00
_____Without package, mint, complete [3:27] 5.00
Orrimaarko (Prune Face) with blaster rifle
_____.00, col. 1 [P3E40] 8.00
_____Without package, mint, complete [3:30] 5.00
Pote Snitkin with force pike and blaster pistol
_____.00, col. 3, Fan Club exclusive [P3E41] 25.00
_____Without package, mint, complete [3:30] 8.00
Princess Leia Organa as Jabba's prisoner
_____.01, col. 1 [P3E42]................................8.00
_____.02, col. 1 ....8.00
_____Without package, mint, complete [3:31] 3.00
Princess Leia Organa in Ewok celebration outfit
_____.00, col. 1 ....8.00
_____.01, col. 1 [P3E43]................................8.00
_____Without package, mint, complete [3:30] 2.00
Princess Leia Organa in Hoth gear with blaster pistol
_____.00, col. 3, Fan Club exclusive [P3E44] 25.00
_____Without package, mint, complete [3:31] 7.00
Princess Leia Organa with blaster rifle and long-barreled pistol
_____.00, col. 1 [P3E45]................................8.00
_____Without package, mint, complete [3:31] 3.00
R2-D2 with accessories
_____.00, col. 1, "Death Star Trash Compactor" on FF slide [P3E46] 8.00
_____.00, col. 1, "Imperial Trash Compactor" on FF slide 50.00
_____Without package, mint, complete [3:31] 5.00
Rebel Fleet Trooper with blaster pistol and rifle
_____.01, col. 1, .01 sticker 10.00
_____.01, col. 1, .01 sticker, FF error [P3E47]...............10.00
_____.02, col. 1 ....10.00
_____Without package, mint, complete [3:31] 3.00
Ree-Yees with blaster pistols
_____.00, col. 3 [P3E48] 25.00
_____Without package, mint, complete [3:31] 5.00
Saelt-Marae (Yak face) with battle staff
_____.01, col. 2 [P3E49] 10.00
_____Without package, mint, complete [3:31] 4.00

P3E22 P3E23 P3E24 P3E25 P3E26 P3E27 P3E28 P3E29 P3E30

P3E31 P3E32 P3E33 P3E34 P3E35 P3E36 P3E37 P3E38 P3E39

| P3E40 | P3E41 | P3E42 | P3E43 | P3E44 | P3E45 | P3E46 | P3E47 | P3E48 |

| P3E49 | P3E50 | P3E51 | P3E52 | P3E53 | P3E54 | P3E55 | P3E56 | P3E57 |

| P3F01 | P3F02 | P3F03 | P3F04 | P3F05 | P3F06 | P3F07 | P3F08 | P3F09 |

Sandtrooper with concussion grenade cannon
____.03, col. 3 [P3E50] 175.00
____Without package, mint, complete [3:31] 5.00

Snowtrooper with Imperial blaster rifle
____.01, col. 3 [P3E51] 20.00
____Without package, mint, complete [3:31] 4.00

Stormtrooper with blaster rifle and heavy infantry cannon
____.02, col. 3 [P3E52] 12.00
____Without package, mint, complete [3:31] 6.00

Tie Fighter Pilot with Imperial blaster pistol and rifle
____.05, col. 3 [P3E53] 50.00
____Without package, mint, complete [3:32] 5.00

Ugnaughts with tool-kit
____.00, col. 2 [P3E54] 10.00
____Without package, mint, complete [3:32] 8.00

Weequay Skiff Guard with force pike and blaster rifle
____.02, col. 3 [P3E55] 425.00
____Without package, mint, complete [3:32] 2.00

Zuckuss with heavy assault blaster rifle
____.00, col. 3 [P3E56] 25.00
____Without package, mint, complete [3:32] 16.00

Kenner, Canada
Green card with Freeze Frame Action Slide.
____8D8 [3:62]..12.00
____Admiral Ackbar [3:62]..............................15.00
____AT-ST Driver [3:62] 58.00
____Ben (Obi-Wan) Kenobi [3:62] 15.00
____Bespin Han Solo [3:62] 15.00
____Biggs Darklighter [3:62] 20.00
____Boba Fett [3:62] 29.00
____C-3PO / Removable Limbs [3:62] 12.00
____Chewbacca as Boushh's Bounty [3:62]..........15.00

____Darth Vader [3:62]..................................15.00
____Emperor's Royal Guard [3:62] 26.00
____Emperor Palpatine [3:62] 15.00
____Endor Rebel Soldier [3:62] 8.00
____EV-9D9 [3:62] 15.00
____Ewok 2-Pack (Wicket/Logray) [3:62] 22.00
____Gamorrean Guard [3:62] 17.00
____Garindan [3:62] 15.00
____Grand Moff Tarkin [3:62] 15.00
____Han Solo [3:62] 15.00
____Han Solo in Endor Gear [3:62] 15.00
____Hoth Rebel Soldier [3:62] 15.00
____Lak Sivrak [3:62]....................................18.00
____Lando Calrissian as General [3:62].............9.00
____Lando Calrissian as skiff guard [3:62] 15.00
____Lobot [3:62]...10.00
____Luke Skywalker in Bespin Gear [3:62]........11.00
____Luke Skywalker in Cerimonial Attire [3:62]....14.00
____Luke Skywalker with Blastshield Helmet [3:62].................................14.00
____Malakili [3:62] 15.00
____MonMothma [3:62] 14.00
____Nien Nunb [3:62] 15.00
____Orrimaarko (Prune Face) [3:62] 15.00
____Princess Leia as Jabba's Prisoner [3:62]......15.00
____Princess Leia, Ewok celebration dress [3:62] 9.00
____Princess Leia Organa new likeness [3:62] 16.00
____R2-D2 with accessories [3:62] 14.00
____Rebel Fleet Trooper [3:62] 15.00
____Saelt-Marae (Yak Face) [3:62] 15.00
____Snowtrooper [3:63] 10.00
____Stormtrooper [3:63] 15.00
____Tie Fighter Pilot [3:63] 55.00
____Ugnaughts (2-pack) [3:63] 12.00
____Weequay [P3E57] 45.00

Toys: Action Figures –
1995 – 1999 (POTF2 1998) EU

Kenner
Green card with fold-out 3D playscene. Expanded Universe.
____Clone Emperor Palpatine .02, col. 2 [P3F01]......25.00
____Without package, mint, complete [3:28] 18.00
____Dark Trooper .01, col. 2 [P3F02] 45.00
____Without package, mint, complete [3:27] 35.00
____Grand Admiral Thrawn .02, col. 2 [P3F03] 20.00
____Without package, mint, complete [3:28] 15.00
____Imperial Sentinal .01, col. 2 [P3F04] 20.00
____Without package, mint, complete [3:28] 15.00
____Kyle Katarn .02, col. 2 [P3F05] 25.00
____Without package, mint, complete [3:29] 10.00
____Luke Skywalker .01, col. 2 [P3F06] 20.00
____Without package, mint, complete [3:30] 20.00

| P3G01 | P3G02 | P3G03 |

| P3G04 | P3G05 | P3G06 | P3G07 | P3G08 | P3G09 | P3G10 | P3G11 | P3G12 |

P3H01

P3H02

P3H03

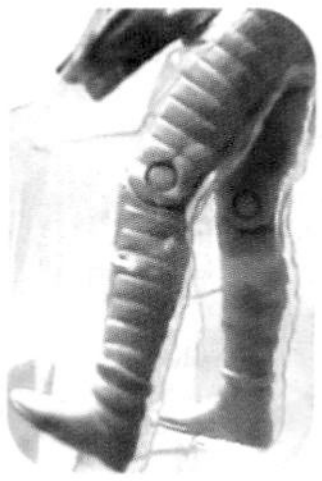
P3H03 detail

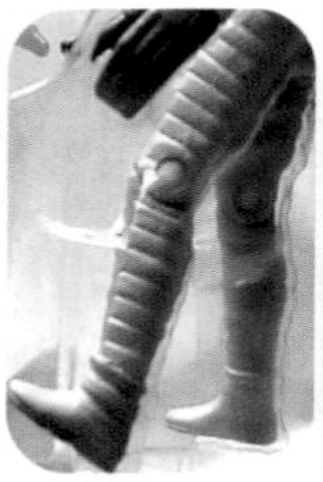
P3H04 detail

P3H05

P3H06

P3H07

P3H08

P3H09

P3H09 detail

P3H10 detail

P3H11

P3H12

CG01

CG02

CG03

CG04

____Mara Jade .03, col. 2 [P3F07] 30.00
____Without package, mint, complete [3:30] 16.00
____Princess Leia .03, col. 2 [P3F08] 30.00
____Without package, mint, complete [3:31] 25.00
____Spacetrooper .03, col. 2 [P3F09] 30.00
____Without package, mint, complete [3:30] 25.00

Toys: Action Figures – 1995 – 1999 (POTF2 1999)

Hasbro

Green card with FlashBack photo.

Anakin Skywalker with lightsaber

____.00 [P3G01]...15.00
____Without package, mint, complete [3:26] 8.00

Aunt Beru with service droid

____.00 [P3G02]...15.00
____Without package, mint, complete [3:27] 15.00

C-3PO with removable arm

____.00 [P3G03]...10.00
____Without package, mint, complete [3:27] 6.00

Kenner

Green card with FlashBack photo.

Ben (Obi-Wan) Kenobi with lightsaber

____.00 [P3G04]...10.00
____Without package, mint, complete [3:27] 7.00

Chewbacca with bowcaster rifle

____.00 [P3G05]...10.00
____Without package, mint, complete [3:27] 6.00

Darth Vader with lightsaber

____.00 [P3G06]...10.00
____Without package, mint, complete [3:27] 8.00

Emperor Palpatine with Force lightning

____.00 [P3G07]...15.00
____Without package, mint, complete [3:28] 12.00

Luke Skywalker with blaster rifle and electrobinoculars

____.00 [P3G08]...10.00
____Without package, mint, complete [3:30] 4.00

Princess Leia in ceremonial dress with medal of honor

____.00, Queen Amidala w/o make-up on FB 2,000.00
____.01 Padme flashback [P3G09] 10.00
____.01, Queen Amidala w/o make-up on FB 550.00
____Without package, mint, complete [3:30] 4.00

R2-D2 with launching lightsaber

____.00, lightsaber on left [P3G10] 10.00
____.00, lightsaber on right [P3G11] 50.00
____.01, lightsaber on left 10.00
____Without package, mint, complete [3:31] 8.00

Yoda with cane and boiling pot

____.00 [P3G12]...12.00
____Without package, mint, complete [3:32] 6.00

Kenner, Canada

Green card with FlashBack photo.

____Anakin Skywalker with Lightsaber [3:63] 14.00
____Aunt Beru with Service Droid [3:63]....................17.00
____Ben (Obi-Wan) Kenobi w/Lightsaber [3:63] 10.00
____C-3PO with Removable Arm [3:63] 11.00
____Chewbacca with Bowcaster Rifle [3:63] 11.00
____Darth Vader with Lightsaber [3:63] 16.00
____Emperor Palpatine w/Force Lightning [3:63] 16.00
____Luke Skywalker with blaster rifle and electro-binoculars [3:63] 8.00
____Princess Leia in Ceremonial Dress.......................8.00
____R2-D2 with Launching Lightsaber [3:63] 10.00
____Yoda with Cane and Boiling Pot [3:63] 16.00

Toys: Action Figures – 1995 – 1999 (POTF2 2000)

Hasbro

Green card with CommTech chip.

Admiral Motti with Imperial blaster

____.0000 [P3H01]..25.00
____Without package, mint, complete [3:26] 14.00

Darth Vader with Imperial interrigation droid

____.0000, foil chip 10.00
____.0000, white chip [P3H02] 10.00
____Without package, mint, complete [3:27] 5.00

Greedo with blaster

____.0000, foil chip [P3H03] 10.00
____.0000, white chip 10.00
____.0000, yellow joint pins [P3H04]...........................10.00
____Without package, mint, complete 5.00

Han Solo with blaster pistol and holder

____.0000, foil chip [P3H05] 8.00
____.0000, white chip 8.00
____Without package, mint, complete [3:28] 2.00

Jawa and "Gonk" droid

____.0000, foil chip [P3H06] 10.00
____.0000, no pegholes in feet 55.00
____.0000, peghole only in one foot 50.00
____.0000, white chip 10.00
____Without package, mint, complete [3:29] 8.00

Luke Skywalker with T16 Skyhopper model

____.0000, foil chip [P3H07] 8.00
____.0000, white chip 8.00
____Without package, mint, complete 3.00

Princess Leia with sporting blaster

____.0000 [P3H08]..25.00
____Without package, mint, complete [3:31] 20.00

R2-D2 with holographic Princess Leia

____.0000, half-moon foot pegs [P3H09] 25.00
____.0000, round foot pegs [P3H10] 100.00
____Without package, mint, complete [3:26] 16.00

Stormtrooper with blaster rifle rack

____.0000, foil chip [P3H11] 12.00
____.0000, white chip 12.00
____Without package, mint, complete [3:31] 8.00

Wuher with droid detector unit

____.0000...18.00
____.0100, white chip [P3H12] 20.00
____Without package, mint, complete [3:32] 18.00

Hasbro, Canada

Green card with CommTech chip.

____Admiral Motti with Imperial blaster 32.00
____Darth Vader with Interrigation Droid 18.00
____Greedo with blaster 9.00
____Han Solo with blaster pistol and holder................8.00
____Jawa and "Gonk" droid 8.00
____Luke Skywalker with T16 Skyhopper model 8.00
____Princess Leia with sporting blaster 28.00
____R2-D2 with holographic Princess Leia 45.00
____Stormtrooper with blaster rifle rack 18.00

Hasbro, UK

Green card with CommTech chip, tri-language package. Paper insert in figure bubble.

____Greedo 10.00
____Han Solo...10.00
____Jawa and Gonk 10.00
____Luke Skywalker 10.00

Toys: Action Figures – 1995 – 1999 (POTF2) Complete Galaxy

Kenner

____Dagobah with Yoda [CG01] 20.00
____Death Star with Darth Vader [CG02] 20.00
____Endor with Ewok [CG03] 20.00
____Tatooine with Luke Skywalker [CG04] 25.00

Toys: Action Figures – 1995 – 1999 (POTF2) Deluxe

Kenner

____Boba Fett with Wing-Blast Rocketpack .00 ......12.00
____Boba Fett with Wing-Blast Rocketpack .01 [P2S101] 12.00
____Crowd Control Stormtrooper .00 ....10.00
____Crowd Control Stormtrooper .01 [P2S102] 10.00
____Han Solo with Smuggler Flight Pack .00 [P2S103] 10.00
____Hoth Rebel Soldier with Radar Laser Gun .00 [P2S104] 10.00
____Imperial Probe Droid .00 orange back [P2S105] 30.00
____Imperial Probe Droid .01 ....10.00
____Imperial Probe Droid .02 [P2S106] 10.00
____Luke Skywalker with Desert Sport Skiff .00 [P2S107] 10.00
____Snowtrooper with E-Web Heavy Repeating Blaster .00 [P2S108] 10.00

Kenner, Canada

____Boba Fett [P2S109] 14.00
____Crowd Control Stormtrooper [P2S110] 14.00
____Han Solo [3:66]..9.00
____Hoth Rebel Soldier [3:66] 9.00
____Imperial Probe Droid [3:66] 16.00
____Luke Skywalker [3:66] 20.00
____Snowtrooper [3:66] 9.00

Kenner, Italy

____Boba Fett [3:66] 15.00
____Hoth Rebel Soldier [3:66]....................................15.00
____Snowtrooper [3:66]...15.00

Kenner, UK

____Han Solo [P2S11] 9.00
____Hoth Rebel Soldier 9.00
____Luke Skywalker [3:66] 24.00
____Snowtrooper 9.00

P2S101

P2S102

P2S103

P2S104

P2S105

P2S105 rear

P2S106 rear

Toys: Action Figures –
1995 – 1999 (POTF2) Electronic FX

Kenner

____Ben Kenobi .00 [P2S201]	8.00
____Darth Vader .00 [P2S202]	10.00
____Darth Vader .00 signed by David Prowse	40.00
____Emperor Palpatine .00 [P2S203]	10.00
____Emperor Palpatine .01	10.00
____Luke Skywalker .00 [P2S204]	8.00
____R2-D2 .00	8.00
____R2-D2 .01	8.00
____R2-D2 .02 [P2S205]	8.00

Kenner, Italy

____R2-D2 [3:66]	12.00

Kenner, UK

____Ben (Obi-Wan) Kenobi [3:66]	12.00
____Darth Vader [3:66]	12.00
____Luke Skywalker	12.00
____R2-D2 [3:66]	16.00

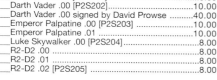

P2S107

P2S108

P2S109

P2S110

P2S111

Kenner, Canada

____Han Solo [3:66]	14.00
____Luke Skywalker [3:66]	14.00

Kenner, Italy

____Darth Vader [P2S304]	19.00

Toys: Action Figures –
1995 – 1999 (POTF2) Max Rebo Band

Kenner

2-packs, Walmart exclusive.

____Barquin D'an / Droopy McCool .00	35.00
____Barquin D'an / Droopy McCool .01 [P22M01]	35.00
____Joh Yowza / Sy Snootles .00 [P22M02]	35.00
____Max Rebo / Bodonawieedo .00 [P22M03]	25.00

Toys: Action Figures – 1995 – 1999
(POTF2) Millennium Minted Coins

Kenner

____Bespin Han Solo .00 [P2S401]	10.00
____Bespin Han Solo, words behind coin [P2S402]	25.00
____C-3PO .00 [P2S403]	12.00
____Chewbacca .00 [P2S404]	12.00
____Chewbacca, words behind coin	25.00
____Emperor Palpatine .00 [P2S405]	12.00
____Endor Leia .00	25.00
____Endor Leia .01 [P2S406]	15.00
____Endor Luke .00 [P2S407]	25.00
____Endor Luke .01	15.00
____Snowtrooper .00 [P2S408]	12.00
____Snowtrooper, words behind coin [P2S409]	25.00

Toys: Action Figures –
1995 – 1999 (POTF2) Gunner Stations

Kenner

____Darth Vader [P2S301]	15.00
____Han Solo [P2S302]	10.00
____Luke Skywalker [P2S303]	10.00

P2S201

P2S202

P2S203

P2S204

P2S205

P2S301

P2S302

P2S303

P2S304

P2S201

P22M01

P22M02

P22M03

P2S401

P2S402

P2S403

P2S404

P2S405

P2S406

P2S407

P2S408

P2S409

Toys: Action Figures – 1995 – 1999

| P2M01 | P2M02 | P2M03 | P2M04 | P2M05 |

| P2M06 | P2M07 | P2M08 | P2M09 | P2M10 |

Toys: Action Figures –

1995 – 1999 (POTF2) Multi-Packs

Hasbro
Cinema Scenes. Three figures action-posed in a movie scene box. Includes a display base.
____Cantina Aliens [P2M01] 15.00
____Jabba's Skiff Guards [P2M02] 12.00
____Jedi Spirits [P2M03] 25.00
____Rebel Pilots [P2M04] 25.00

Hasbro, Canada
Cinema Scenes. Three figures action-posed in a movie scene box. Includes a display base.
____Jedi Spirits [3:67] 10.00

Kenner
____4-pack classic [P2M06] 50.00

2-Packs, Fan Club exclusives.
____Kabe and Muftak .00 [P2M07]............................15.00
____Oola and Salacious Crumb .00 [P2M05] 25.00

3-Packs, 1997 Hong Kong commerative.
____Heroes [P2M09] 50.00
____Villains [P2M08] 75.00

Cinema Scenes. Three figures action-posed in a movie scene box. Includes a display base.
____Cantina Showdown .00 [P2M10] 12.00

____Cantina Showdown .01 ....12.00
____Death Star Escape .00 [P2M11].........................30.00
____Death Star Escape .01 ....30.00
____Final Jedi Duel .00 [P2M12] 25.00
____Final Jedi Duel .01 ....25.00
____Jabba's Dancers .00 [P2M13] 12.00
____Mynock Hunt .00 [P2M14] 35.00
____Purchase of the Droids .00 [P2M15] 16.00
____Purchase of the Droids .01 ....15.00

Collectors Packs. Three individual figures inside one display package.
____ANH: Stormtrooper Luke, Tusken Raider, Ben Kenobi [P2M16] 30.00
____ESB: Dagobah Luke, Lando Calrissian, Tie Fighter Pilot [P2M17] 75.00
____ROTJ: Jedi Luke, AT-ST Driver, Leia as Boushh [P2M18] 30.00
____Han Solo, Chewbacca, Lando Calrissian [P2M19] 35.00
____Luke Skywalker, Ben Kenobi, Darth Vader [P2M20] 35.00
____R2-D2, C-3PO, Stormtrooper [P2M21] 35.00

Kenner, Canada
Cinema Scenes. Three figures action-posed in a movie scene box. Includes a display base. Tri-logo packaging.
____Mynock Hunt [2:27] 65.00

Kenner, Japan
____10-Pack: Mos Eisley pop-up Cantina with ten carded action figures [P2M22].......................................220.00

Toys: Action Figures –

1995 – 1999 (POTF2) Princess Collection

Kenner
Princess Leia and one other character figure.
____Han Solo .00 [P22P01].......................................35.00
____Han Solo .01 ....10.00
____Luke Skywalker .00 [P22P02] 25.00
____Luke Skywalker .01 ....10.00
____R2-D2 .00 [P22P03]...25.00
____R2-D2 .01 ....10.00
____Wicket the Ewok .00 [P22P04]...........................25.00
____Wicket the Ewok .01 ....10.00

Toys: Action Figures –

1995 – 1999 (POTF2) SOTE 2-Packs

Kenner
____Boba Fett vs. IG-88 .00 [P22S01] 25.00
____Prince Xizor vs. Darth Vader .00 [P22S02] 20.00

Kenner, UK
Tri-language package.
____Boba Fett vs. IG-88 [3:68] 34.00
____Prince Xizor vs. Darth Vader [P22S03]................24.00

| P2M11 | P2M12 | P2M13 | P2M14 |

| P2M15 | P2M16 | P2M17 | P2M18 |

| P2M19 | P2M20 | P2M21 | P2M22 |

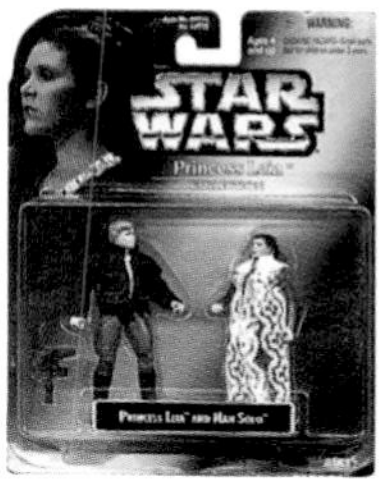

P22P01

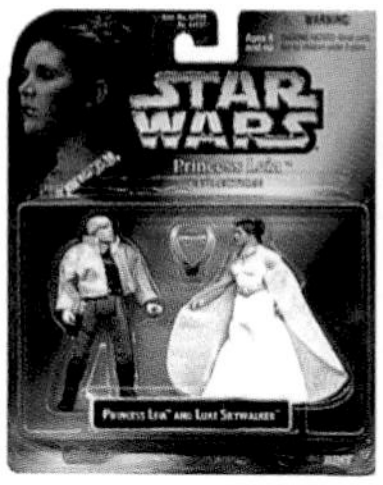

P22P02

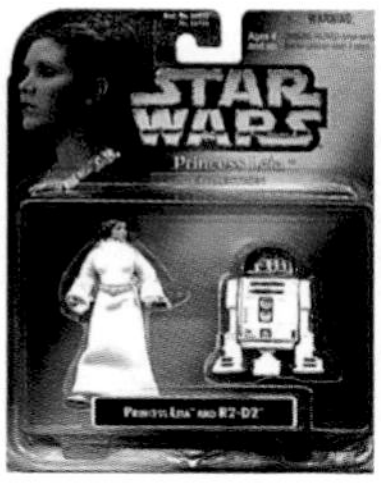

P22P03

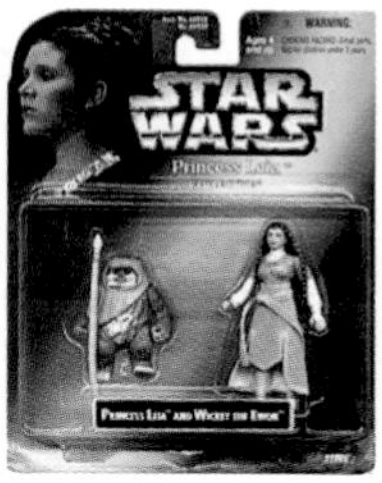

P22P04

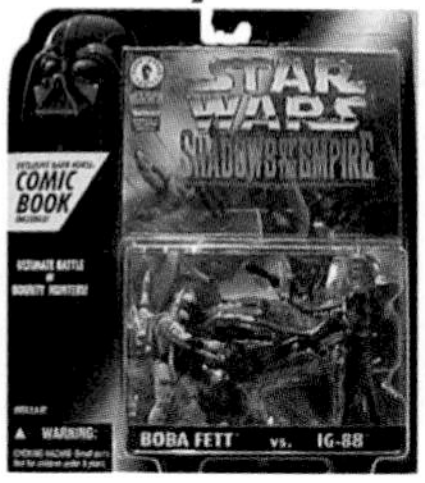

P22S01

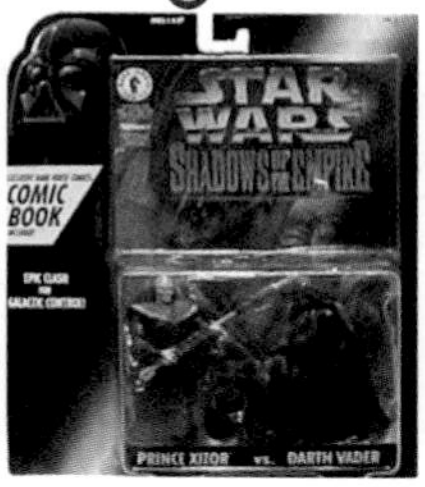

P22S02

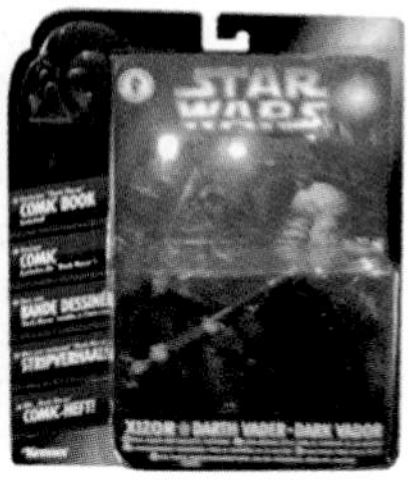

P22S03

Toys: Action Figures – 1999 – 2001 (EPI:TPM)

Hasbro

Adi Gallia with lightsaber
____.0000, col. 3 [P301] 8.00
____Without package, mint, complete 5.00

Anakin Skywalker Naboo Pilot with flight simulator
____.0000, col.1 [P302] 7.00
____Without package, mint, complete 2.00

Anakin Skywalker Naboo with comlink unit
____.0000 col. 1 [P303] 8.00
____.0100 .... 8.00
____Without package, mint, complete 5.00

Anakin Skywalker Tatooine with backpack and grease gun
____.00, col. 1, blue backpack [P304] 10.00
____.00, col. 1, brown backpack 10.00
____.0100, col. 1 .... 7.00
____Without package, mint, complete 2.00

Battle Droid with blaster rifle (Clean)
____.00, col. 1 [P305] 10.00
____.0100, col. 1 .... 10.00
____.0200, col. 1 .... 8.00
____Without package, mint, complete 5.00

Battle Droid with blaster rifle (Dirty)
____.00, col. 1 [P306] 8.00
____.0100, col. 1 .... 8.00
____.0200, col. 1 .... 8.00
____Without package, mint, complete 4.00

Battle Droid with blaster rifle (Shot)
____.00, col. 1 [P307] 8.00
____.0100, col. 1 .... 8.00
____.0200, col. 1 .... 8.00
____Without package, mint, complete 4.00

Battle Droid with blaster rifle (Sliced)
____.00, col. 1 [P308] 8.00
____.0100, col. 1 .... 8.00
____.0200, col. 1 .... 8.00
____Without package, mint, complete 4.00

Boss Nass with Gungan staff
____.0000, col. 3 [P309] 8.00
____.0100, col. 3 .... 6.00
____Without package, mint, complete [3:33] 2.00

C-3PO
____.00, col. 2 [P310] 9.00
____.0100, col. 2 .... 8.00
____Without package, mint, complete 2.00

Captain Panaka with blaster rifle and pistol
____.0000, col. 2 [P311] 12.00
____.0000, col. 2, sticker corrects CommTech 12.00
____.0100, col. 2, CommTech corrected 12.00
____Without package, mint, complete 6.00

Captain Tarpals with electropole
____.00, col. 3 .... 10.00
____.0100, col. 3 [P312] 10.00
____Without package, mint, complete [3:33] 5.00

Chancellor Valorum with ceremonial staff
____.00, col. 3 .... 10.00
____.0000, col. 3, printed warning [P313] 10.00
____.0000, col. 3, sticker covers printed warning 10.00
____.0100, col. 3 .... 9.00
____.0200, col. 3 .... 9.00
____Without package, mint, complete 4.00

Darth Maul Jedi Duel with double-bladed lightsaber
____.00, col. 1, new sculpt 10.00
____.00, col. 1, original sculpt [P314] 10.00
____.0000, col. 1 .... 10.00
____.0000, col. 1, black vest 200.00
____.0000, col. 1, white chip 10.00
____.0100, col. 1 .... 10.00
____Without package, mint, complete 4.00

Darth Maul Sith Lord, lightsaber w/removable blade
____.0000, col. 1 [P315] 10.00
____Without package, mint, complete 3.00

Darth Maul Tatooine with cloak and lightsaber
____.0000, col. 1 [P316] 10.00
____.0100, col. 1 .... 10.00
____.0100, col. 1, white chip 10.00
____Without package, mint, complete [3:33] 2.00

Darth Sidious
____.00, col. 2 [P317] 9.00
____.0100, col. 2 .... 9.00
____Without package, mint, complete [3:33] 6.00

Darth Sidious holograph
____.0000, col. 2 [P318] 30.00
____Without package, mint, complete 20.00

Destroyer Droid
____.0000, col. 2 [P319] 7.00
____Without package, mint, complete 5.00

Destroyer Droid battle damaged
____.0000, col. 1 [P320] 14.00
____Without package, mint, complete 7.00

Gasgano with Pit Droid
____.0100, col. 3 [P321] 6.00
____.0200, col. 3 .... 6.00
____Without package, mint, complete 3.00

Jar Jar Binks Naboo swamp with fish
____.0000, col. 1 [P322] 20.00
____Without package, mint, complete 15.00

Jar Jar Binks with Gungan battle staff
____.00, col. 1 [P323] 8.00
____.0100, col. 1 .... 6.00

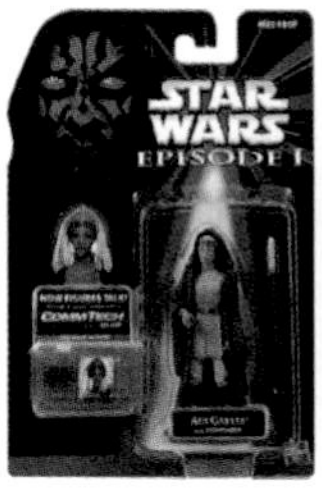

P301

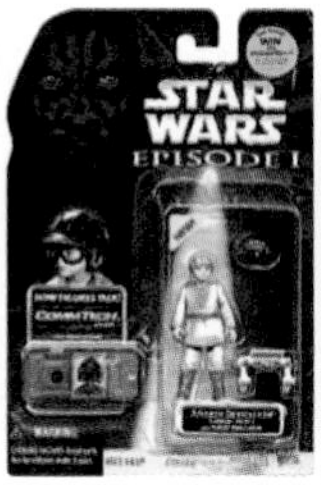

P302

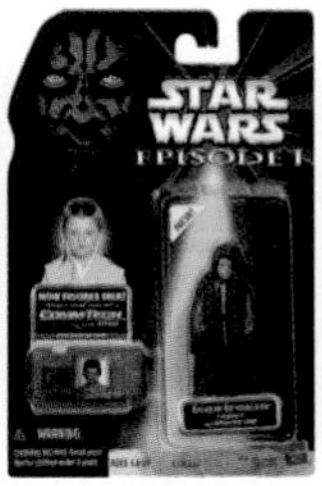

P303

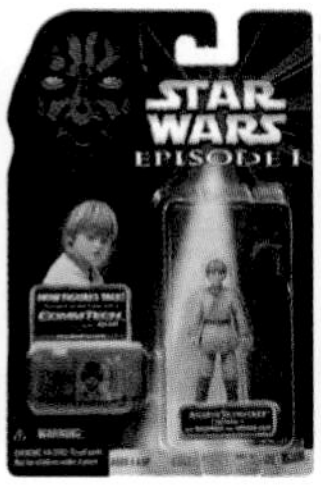

P304

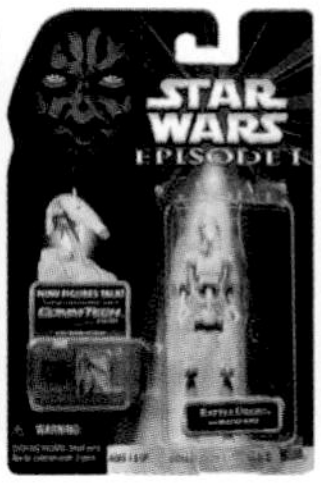

P305

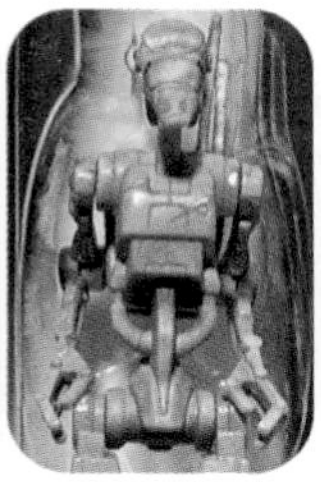
P306 detail

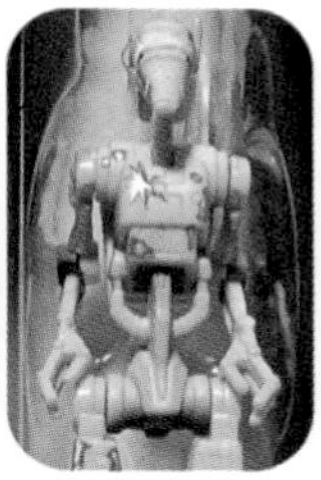
P307 detail

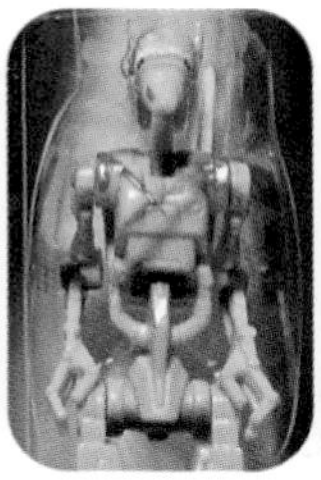
P308 detail

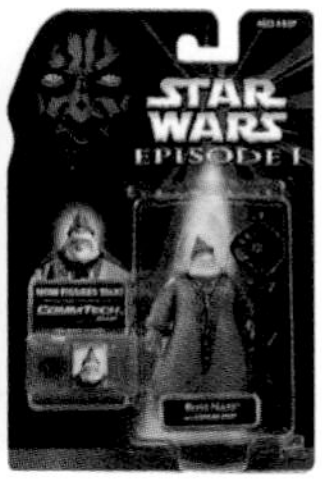

P309

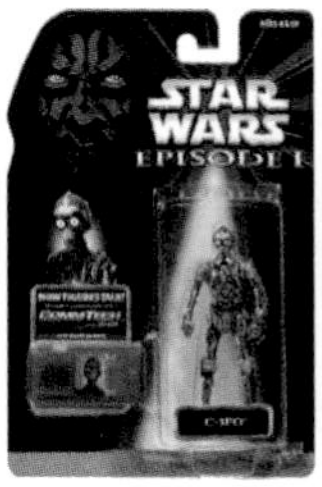

P310

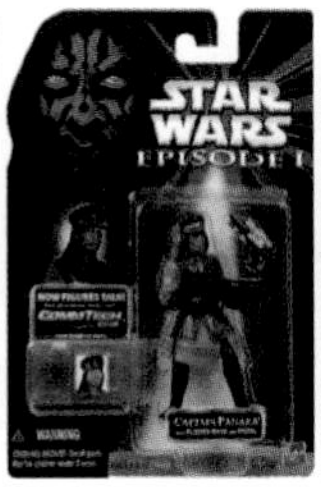

P311

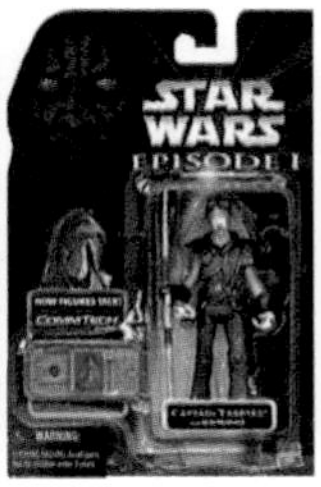

P312

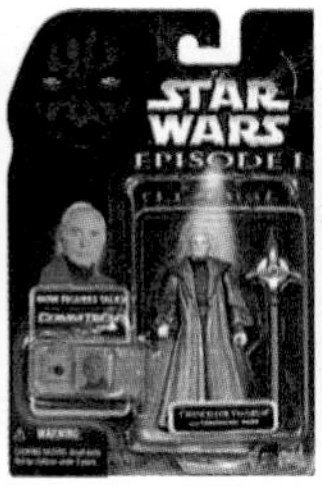

P313

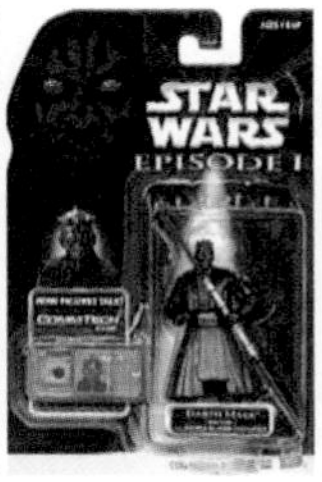

P314

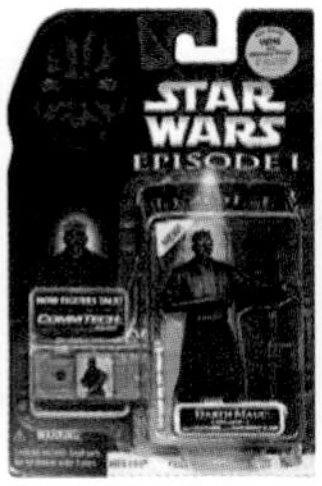

P315

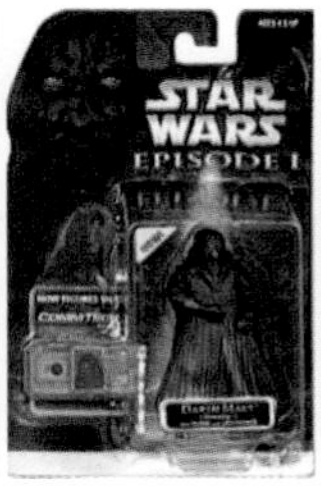

P316

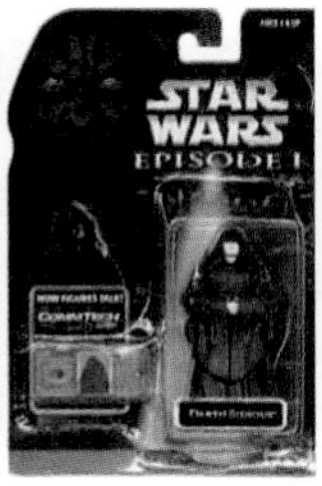

P317

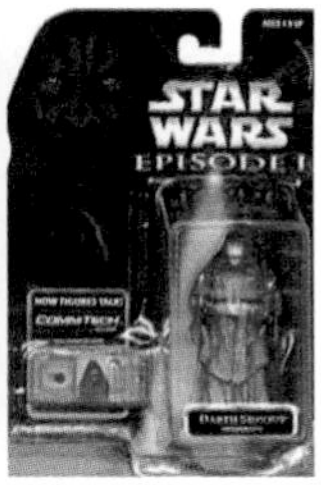

P318

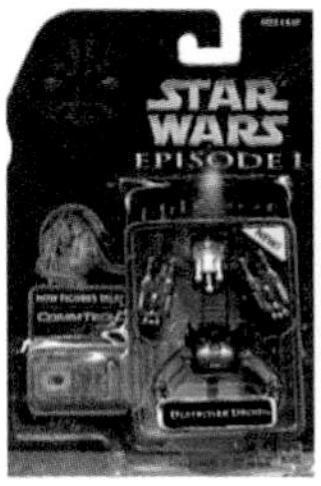

P319

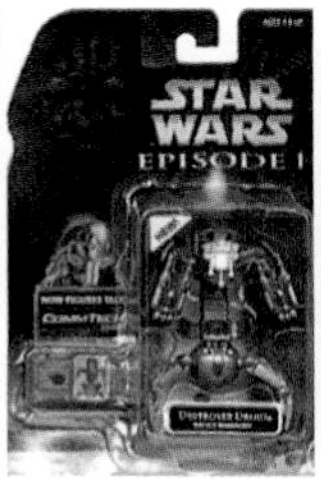

P320

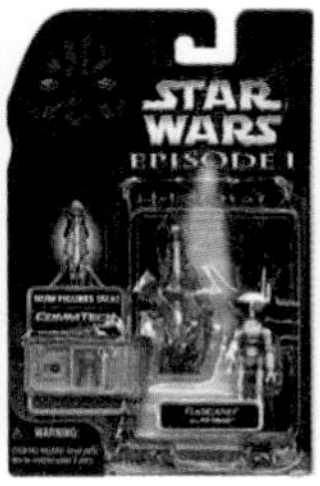

P321

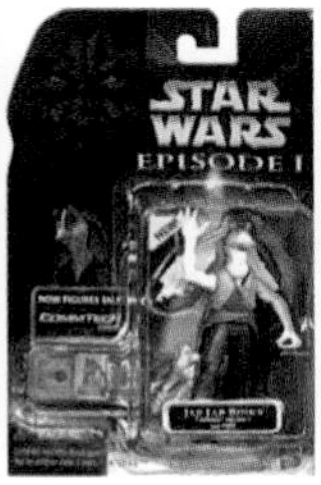

P322

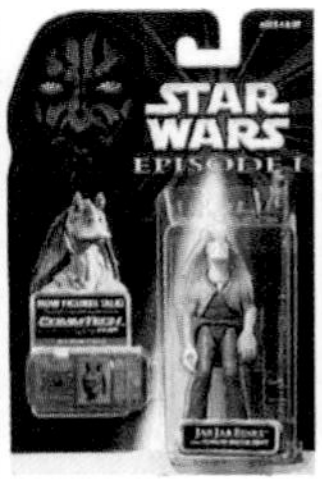

P323

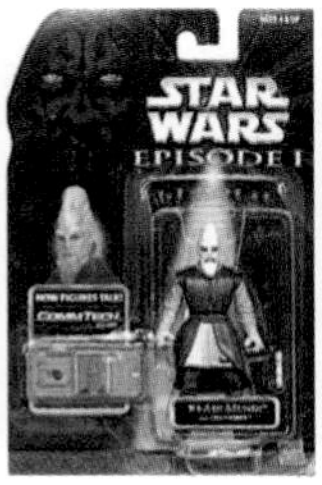

P324

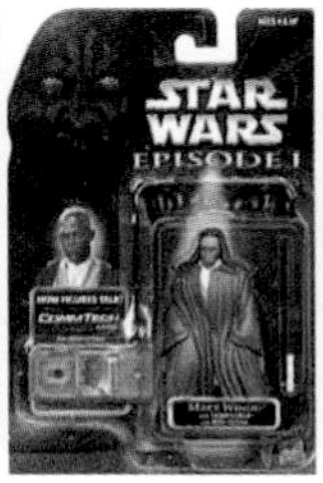

P325

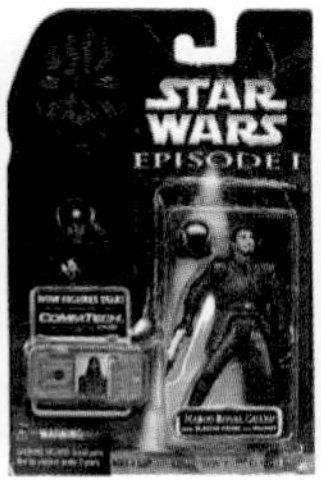

P326

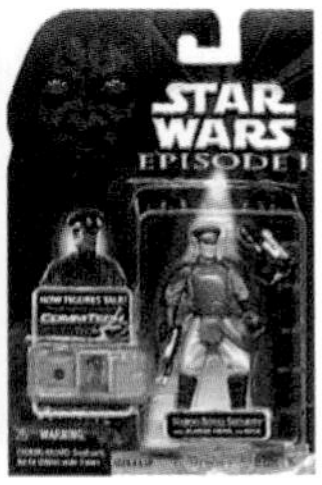

P327

Toys: Action Figures – 1999 – 2001

____.0200, col. 1 ....6.00
____Without package, mint, complete 3.00

Ki-Adi-Mundi with lightsaber
____.0000, col. 3 [P324] 8.00
____.0100, col. 3 ....6.00
____Without package, mint, complete [3:33] 4.00

Mace Windu with lightsaber and Jedi cloak
____.0000, col. 3 [P325] 8.00
____.0100, col. 3 ....8.00
____.0100, col. 3, white chip 8.00
____Without package, mint, complete 4.00

Naboo Royal Guard with laser pistol and helmet
____.0000, col. 2 [P326] 25.00
____Without package, mint, complete [3:33] ..18.00

Naboo Royal Security with blaster pistol and rifle
____.0000, col. 2 [P327] 10.00
____Without package, mint, complete [3:33] 8.00

Nute Gunray
____.0000, col. 2 [P328] 10.00
____Without package, mint, complete 4.00

Obi-Wan Kenobi Jedi Duel with lightsaber
____.00, col. 1 ....8.00
____.0100, col. 1 [P329] 8.00
____Without package, mint, complete 2.00

Obi-Wan Kenobi Jedi Knight
____.0000, col. 1 ....8.00
____Without package, mint, complete 3.00

Obi-Wan Kenobi Naboo with lightsaber and handle
____.0000, col. 1 ....8.00
____.0100, col. 1 [P330] 8.00
____Without package, mint, complete 3.00

Ody Mandrell with Otoga 222 pit droid
____.0000, col. 3 ....8.00
____.0100, col. 3 [P331] 8.00
____.0100, col. 3, white chip 8.00
____Without package, mint, complete 2.00

OOM-9 with blaster and binoculars
____.0000, col. 3 [P332] 8.00
____.0000, col. 3, binoculars mounted in bubble 28.00
____.0000, col. 3, white chip 8.00
____Without package, mint, complete 3.00

Padme Naberrie with pod race view screen
____.00, col. 1 [P333] 8.00
____.0100, col. 1 ....8.00
____Without package, mint, complete 4.00

Pit Droids (2-pack)
____.0000, col. 2 [P334] 20.00
____Without package, mint, complete 15.00

Queen Amidala Battle with ascension gun
____.0100, col. 2 [P335] 45.00

____Without package, mint, complete 30.00

Queen Amidala Coruscant
____.0100, col. 1 [P336] 10.00
____Without package, mint, complete [3:33] 5.00

Queen Amidala Naboo with blaster pistols
____.00, col. 1 [P337] 8.00
____.0100, col. 1 ....8.00
____Without package, mint, complete 4.00

Qui-Gon Jinn Jedi Duel with lightsaber
____.00, col. 1 [P338] 6.00
____.0100, col. 1 ....6.00
____Without package, mint, complete 2.00

Qui-Gon Jinn Jedi Master with lightsaber and comlink
____.0000, col. 1 [P339] 8.00
____Without package, mint, complete [3:33] 4.00

Qui-Gon Jinn Naboo with lightsaber and handle
____.0100, col. 1 [P340] 6.00
____Without package, mint, complete [3:33] 3.00

R2-B1 Astromech Droid with power harness
____.0000, col. 3 [P341] 40.00
____.0100, col. 3 ....35.00
____Without package, mint, complete 25.00

R2-D2 with booster rockets
____.0000, col. 2 ....8.00
____.0000, col. 2, small bubble [P342] 14.00
____Without package, mint, complete 4.00

Ric Olie with helmet and Naboo blaster
____.00, col. 2 [P343] 7.00
____.0100, col. 2 ....7.00
____.0100, col. 2, closed hand 7.00
____Without package, mint, complete [3:33] 2.00

Rune Haako
____.0000, col. 2 [P344] 9.00
____Without package, mint, complete [3:33] 4.00

Senator Palpatine with Senate cam droid
____.00, col. 2 [P345] 6.00
____.0100, col. 2 ....6.00
____Without package, mint, complete 3.00

Sio Bibble with blaster pistol
____.0000, col. 2 [P346] 30.00
____Without package, mint, complete [3:33] ..15.00

TC-14 protocol droid with serving tray
____.0000, col. 3 [P347] 45.00
____.0100, col. 3 ....40.00
____Without package, mint, complete [3:33] ..28.00

Watto with datapad
____.00, col. 2 [P348] 8.00
____.0100, col. 2 ....8.00
____Without package, mint, complete 3.00

Yoda with Jedi Council chair
____.0000, col. 2 [P349] 32.00
____.0000, col. 2, missing EPI logo [P350] 9.00
____Without package, mint, complete 4.00

Hasbro, Canada
Tri-language cards.
____Anakin Skywalker Naboo [3:70] 7.00
____Anakin Skywalker Tatooine [3:70] 7.00
____Battle Droid (Clean) [3:70] 7.00
____Battle Droid (Dirty) [P351] 12.00
____Battle Droid (Shot) [3:70] 7.00
____Battle Droid (Sliced) [3:70] 12.00
____Boss Nass [3:70] 7.00
____C-3PO [3:70] 6.00
____Captain Tarpals [3:70] 8.00
____Chancellor Valorum [3:70] 12.00
____Darth Maul Jedi Duel [3:70] 8.00
____Darth Maul Tatooine [3:70] 9.00
____Darth Sidious [3:70] 9.00
____Destroyer Droid [3:70] 14.00
____Gasgano and Pit Droid [3:70] 7.00
____Jar Jar Binks [3:70] 9.00
____Ki-Adi-Mundi [3:70] 8.00
____Mace Windu [3:70] 8.00
____Nute Gunray [3:70] 7.00
____Obi-Wan Kenobi Jedi Duel [3:70] 8.00
____Obi-Wan Kenobi Naboo [3:70] 7.00
____Ody Mandrell with Otoga 222 Pit Droid [3:70] 8.00
____OOM-9 [3:70] 15.00
____Padme Naberrie [3:70] 6.00
____Queen Amidala Coruscant [3:70] 11.00
____Queen Amidala Naboo [3:70] 9.00
____Qui-Gon Jinn Jedi Duel [3:70] 6.00
____Qui-Gon Jinn Naboo [3:70] 9.00
____R2-D2 [3:70] 6.00
____Ric Olie [3:70] 6.00
____Rune Haako [3:71] 6.00
____Senator Palpatine [3:71] 9.00
____Watto [3:71] 9.00
____Yoda [3:71] 7.00

Hasbro, UK
____Adi Gallia..8.00
____Anakin Skywalker..9.00
____Anakin Skywalker Naboo................................9.00
____Anakin Skywalker Naboo pilot [3:71] 9.00
____Battle Droid (Clean) 9.00
____Battle Droid (Dirty)..9.00
____Battle Droid (Shot) 9.00

P328 P329 P330 P331 P332 P333 P334 P335 P336

P337 P338 P339 P340 P341 P342 P343 P344 P345

P346 P347 P348 P349 P350 P351 P352 P353

| P3J01 | P3J02 | P3J03 | P3J04 | P3J05 | P3J06 | P3J07 | P3J08 |

____Battle Droid (Sliced) 9.00
____Boss Nass..9.00
____C-3PO...8.00
____Captain Tarpals 10.00
____Chancellor Valorum 11.00
____Dark Sidious holograph [3:71] 14.00
____Darth Maul [3:71] 9.00
____Darth Maul Sith Lord [3:71] 10.00
____Darth Maul Tatooine [3:71] 9.00
____Darth Sidious [3:71] 9.00
____Destroyer Droid [3:71] 9.00
____Gasgano and Pit Droid 9.00
____Jar Jar Binks [3:71] 8.00
____Jar Jar Binks Naboo Swamp 25.00
____Ki-Adi-Mundi..8.00
____Naboo Royal Guard [3:71] 13.00
____Nute Gunray 7.00
____Obi-Wan Kenobi [3:71] 9.00
____Obi-Wan Kenobi Jedi Knight 9.00
____Obi-Wan Kenobi Naboo 9.00
____OOM-9 ....9.00
____Padme Naberrie [3:71] 9.00
____Pit Droids [3:71] 16.00
____Queen Amidala [3:71] 10.00
____Queen Amidala Coruscant [3:71].........................10.00
____Qui-Gon Jinn [3:71] 9.00
____Qui-Gon Jinn Jedi Master 9.00
____Qui-Gon Jinn Naboo [P352] 9.00
____R2-D2 ....10.00
____Ric Olie [3:71] 9.00
____Rune Haako 10.00
____Senator Palpatine [3:71] 9.00
____Sio Bibble [3:71] 17.00
____Watto [3:71] 8.00
____Yoda with Jedi Council Chair [3:71] 9.00

Kenner
____Mace Windu, mail-away premium [P353] 15.00

Toys: Action Figures –
1999 – 2001 (EPI:TPM) 2" Scale

Hasbro
____Anakin Skywalker [P3J01] 15.00
____Battle Droid [P3J02] 15.00
____Darth Maul [P3J03].......................................15.00
____Jar Jar Binks [P3J04] 15.00
____Obi-Wan Kenobi [P3J05] 15.00

| P3L01 | P3L02 | P3L03 |

____Padme Naberrie [P3J06] 15.00
____Queen Amidala [P3J07] 15.00
____Qui-Gon Jinn [P3J08].....................................15.00

Toys: Action Figures –
1999 – 2001 (EPI:TPM) 2-Packs

Hasbro
____Any 2 Figures, only dist. through wholesale clubs [P3L01] 22.00
____CommTech plus any figure, only dist. through wholesale clubs [P3L02] 25.00
____The Final Lightsaber Duel [P3L03] 15.00

Hasbro, Canada
Tri-language packaging.
____The Final Lightsaber Duel 25.00

Toys: Action Figures –
1999 – 2001 (EPI:TPM) Bonus 2-Packs

Hasbro
Phantom Menace figure with bonus Pit Droid. Three colors of Pit Droid available.
Brown pit droid with:
____Anakin Skywalker [P3T01] 25.00
____Darth Maul [P3T02] 25.00
____Darth Sidious hologram [P3T03] 65.00
____Naboo Royal Guard [P3T04] 65.00
____Obi-Wan Kenobi [P3T05] 25.00
Cream pit droid with:
____Anakin Skywalker [P3T06] 25.00
____Darth Maul [P3T07] 25.00
____Darth Sidious hologram [P3T08] 65.00
____Naboo Royal Guard [P3T09] 65.00
____Obi-Wan Kenobi [P3T10] 25.00

| P3T01 | P3T02 | P3T03 | P3T04 | P3T05 | P3T06 |

| P3T07 | P3T08 | P3T09 | P3T10 | P3T11 | P3T12 | P3T13 | P3T14 | P3T15 |

| P3T16 | P3T17 | P3T18 | P3T19 | P3T20 | P3T21 | P3T22 | P3T23 | P3T24 |

Toys: Action Figures – 1999 – 2001

| P3T25 | P3T26 | P3T27 | P3T28 | P3T29 | P3T30 | P3T31 | P3T32 | P3T33 |

| P3T34 | P3T35 | P3T36 | P3T37 | P3T38 | P3T39 | P3T40 | P3T41 | P3T42 |

Tan pit droid with:
_____Anakin Skywalker [P3T11] 25.00
_____Darth Maul [P3T12] 25.00
_____Darth Sidious hologram [P3T13] 65.00
_____Naboo Royal Guard [P3T14] 65.00
_____Obi-Wan Kenobi [P3T15] 25.00

Phantom Menace figure with unpainted bonus Battle Droid.
_____Anakin Skywalker [P3T16] 20.00
_____Anakin Skywalker Naboo [P3T17] 25.00
_____Battle Droid (Clean) [3:72] 25.00
_____Battle Droid (Dirty) [P3T18] 25.00
_____Battle Droid (Shot) [P3T19] 25.00
_____Battle Droid (Sliced) [P3T20] 25.00
_____C-3PO [P3T21] 30.00
_____Capt. Panaka [P3T22] 25.00
_____Darth Maul Jedi Duel [P3T23] 25.00
_____Darth Maul Jedi Duel, resculpted face 25.00
_____Darth Maul Tatooine Battle Droid [P3T24] 25.00
_____Darth Sidious [P3T25] 25.00
_____Destroyer Droid [P3T26] 25.00
_____Jar Jar Binks [P3T27] 25.00
_____Naboo Royal Security [P3T28] 25.00
_____Nute Gunray [P3T29] 25.00
_____Obi-Wan Kenobi Jedi Duel [P3T30] 25.00
_____Obi-Wan Kenobi Naboo [P3T31] 20.00
_____Padme Newberrie [P3T32] 20.00
_____Queen Amidala [P3T33] 20.00
_____Queen Amidala Coruscant [P3T34] 25.00
_____Qui-Gon Jinn Jedi Duel [P3T35] 25.00
_____Qui-Gon Jinn Naboo [P3T36] 20.00
_____R2-D2 [P3T37] 25.00
_____Ric Olie [P3T38] 25.00
_____Rune Haako [P3T39] 25.00
_____Senator Palpatine [P3T40] 30.00
_____Watto [P3T41] 30.00
_____Yoda [P3T42] 25.00

Toys: Action Figures –
1999 – 2001 (EPI:TPM) Cinema Scenes

Hasbro
_____Mos Espa Encounter [P3M01] 15.00
_____Mos Espa Encounter, white chip 15.00
_____Tatooine Showdown [P3M02] 15.00
_____Tatooine Showdown, white chip 15.00
_____Watto's Box [P3M03] 35.00

Toys: Action Figures –
1999 – 2001 (EPI:TPM) Deluxe

Hasbro
_____Darth Maul [P3Z01] 12.00
_____Obi-Wan Kenobi [P3Z02] 12.00
_____Qui-Gon Jinn [P3Z03]..12.00

Hasbro, UK
_____Darth Maul [3:73] 12.00
_____Obi-Wan Kenobi 12.00
_____Qui-Gon Jinn 12.00

Toys: Action Figures –
1999 – 2001 (EPI:TPM) Light-Up

Hasbro
Holograph figures with holoprojector.
_____Darth Maul [P3401] 15.00
_____Qui-Gon Jinn [P3402]..15.00

Toys: Action Figures –
1999 – 2001 (EPI:TPM) Trophy

Hasbro
_____Darth Maul with Sith Infiltrator [P3901] 12.00

Toys: Action Figures –
2001 – 2002 (POTJ)

Hasbro
Boba Fett, 300th figure
_____.0100 [PJ01] 35.00
_____.0200 [PJ02] 30.00
_____Without package, mint, complete 25.00

EPII:AOTC sneak preview figures.
_____Clone Trooper [PJ03] 12.00
_____Without package, mint, complete 10.00
_____Jango Fett [PJ04] 8.00
_____Without package, mint, complete 6.00
_____R3-T7 [PJ05] 8.00
_____Without package, mint, complete 4.00
_____Zam Wesell [PJ06] 6.00
_____Without package, mint, complete 4.00

Green cards with Force Files.
Anakin Skywalker Mechanic
_____.0000, col. 1, force file 0000 [PJ07] 8.00
_____.0100, col. 1, force file 0100 ....6.00
_____Without package, mint, complete 3.00

| P3M01 | P3M02 | P3M03 | PJ01 | PJ02 | PJ03 |

| P3Z01 | P3Z02 | P3Z03 | P3401 | P3402 | P3901 | PJ04 | PJ05 | PJ06 |

PJ07 PJ08 PJ09 PJ10 PJ11 PJ12 PJ13 PJ14 PJ15

PJ16 PJ17 PJ18 PJ19 PJ20 PJ21 PJ22 PJ23 PJ24

Aurra Sing Bounty Hunter
____.0300, col. 1 [PJ08] 12.00
____.0400, col. 1 ....12.00
____Without package, mint, complete 8.00
Battle Droid Boomer Damage
____.0100, col. 1 [PJ09] 10.00
____.0300, col. 1 ....10.00
____.0400, col. 1 ....8.00
____Without package, mint, complete 5.00
Battle Droid Security
____.0000, col. 2 [PJ10] 12.00
____.0100, col. 2 ....12.00
____.0400, col. 2 ....12.00
____Without package, mint, complete 7.00
Ben (Obi-Wan) Kenobi Jedi Knight
____.0100, col. 1 [PJ11] 10.00
____Without package, mint, complete 6.00
Bespin Guard Cloud City Security
____.0400, col. 2 [PJ12] 10.00
____Without package, mint, complete 4.00
Boss Nass Gungan Sacred Place
____.0000, col. 2 [PJ13] 10.00
____.0100, col. 2 ....10.00
____Without package, mint, complete 5.00
Chewbacca Dejarik Champion
____.0000, col. 2, force file 0000 [PJ14] 10.00
____.0000, col. 2, force file 0100 ....10.00
____.0100, col. 2, force file 0100 ....100.00
____Without package, mint, complete 7.00
Chewbacca Millennium Falcon Mechanic
____.0300, col. 1 [PJ15] 10.00
____.0400, col. 1 ....10.00
____Without package, mint, complete 3.00
Coruscant Guard
____.0000, col. 2, force file 0000 [PJ16] 12.00

____.0100, col. 2, force file 0100 ....12.00
____.0300, col. 2, force file 0100 ....12.00
____.0400, col. 2, force file 0100 ....12.00
____Without package, mint, complete 8.00
Darth Maul Final Duel
____.0000, col. 1 [PJ17] 10.00
____.0000, col. 1, sticker on front [PJ18] 10.00
____.0100, col. 1, sticker on front 10.00
____Without package, mint, complete 2.00
Darth Maul Sith Apprentice
____.0000, col. 1 ....12.00
____.0300, col. 1 [PJ19] 12.00
____.0400, col. 1 ....12.00
____Without package, mint, complete 10.00
Darth Vader Dagobah
____.0100, col. 1 [PJ20] 10.00
____.0400, col. 1 ....10.00
____Without package, mint, complete 8.00
Darth Vader Emperors Wrath
____.0400, col. 1 [PJ21] 12.00
____Without package, mint, complete 6.00
Ellorrs Madak
____.0400, col. 2 [PJ22] 10.00
____Without package, mint, complete 3.00
Fode and Beed Podrace Announcer
____.0100, col. 2 [PJ23] 10.00
____.0400, col. 2 ....10.00
____Without package, mint, complete 5.00
Gungan Warrior
____.0000, col. 2 [PJ24] 10.00
____.0100, col. 2 ....10.00
____.0400, col. 2 ....10.00
____Without package, mint, complete 7.00
Han Solo Bespin Capture
____.0100, col. 1 [PJ25] 10.00

____.0300, col. 1 ....10.00
____.0400, col. 1 ....10.00
____Without package, mint, complete 3.00
Han Solo Death Star Escape
____.0400, col. 1 [PJ26] 8.00
____Without package, mint, complete 3.00
IG-88 Bounty Hunter
____.0100, col. 2, open right claw [PJ27] 10.00
____.0300, col. 2, closed right claw [PJ28] 10.00
____Without package, mint, complete 8.00
Jar Jar Binks Tatooine
____.0300, col. 2 ....8.00
____.0400, col. 2 [PJ29] 8.00
____Without package, mint, complete 6.00
Jek Porkins
____.0000, col. 2 [PJ30] 12.00
____.0100, col. 2 ....12.00
____.0300, col. 2 ....12.00
____Without package, mint, complete 4.00
K-3PO Echo Base Protocol Droid
____.0100, col. 2 [PJ31] 10.00
____.0300, col. 2 ....10.00
____.0400, col. 2 ....10.00
____Without package, mint, complete 5.00
Ketwol
____.0400, col. 2 [PJ32] 8.00
____Without package, mint, complete 2.00
Lando Calrissian Bespin Escape
____.0300, col. 2 ....10.00
____.0400, col. 2 [PJ33] 10.00
____Without package, mint, complete 8.00
Leia Organa Bespin Escape
____.0300, col. 1 [PJ34] 10.00
____.0400, col. 1 ....10.00
____Without package, mint, complete 6.00

PJ25 PJ26 PJ27 PJ27 detail PJ28 detail PJ29 PJ30 PJ31 PJ32

PJ33 PJ34 PJ35 PJ36 PJ37 PJ38 PJ39 PJ40 PJ41

Toys: Action Figures – 2001 – 2002

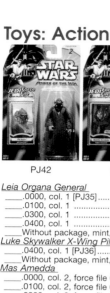

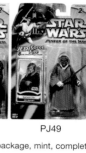

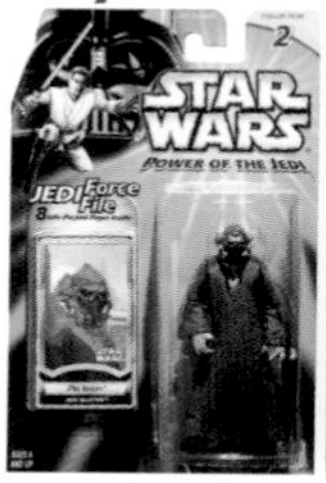
PJ42

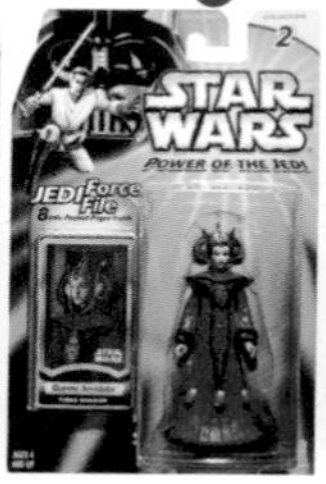
PJ43

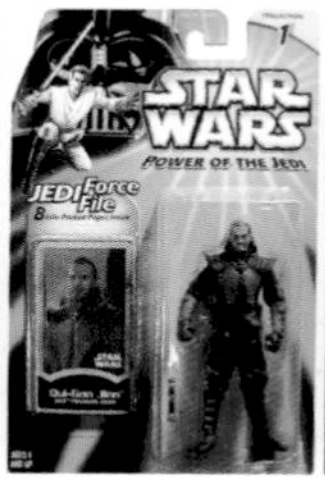
PJ44

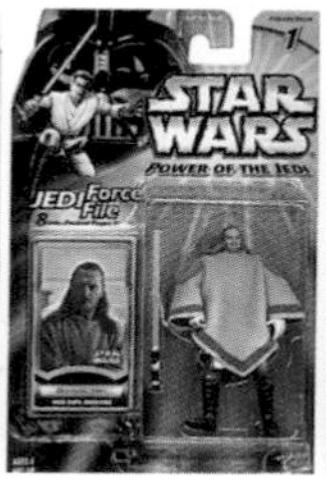
PJ45

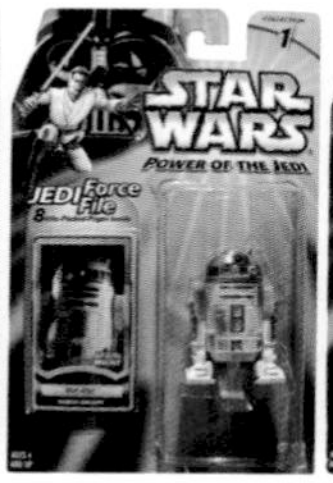
PJ46

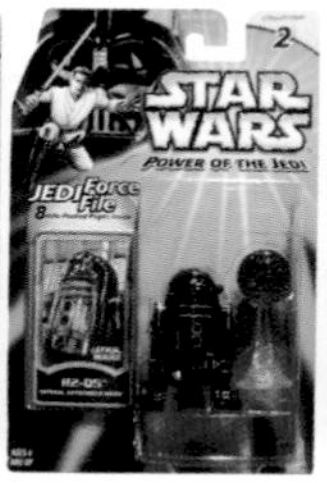
PJ47

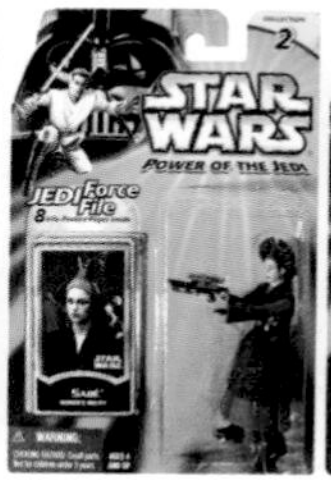
PJ48

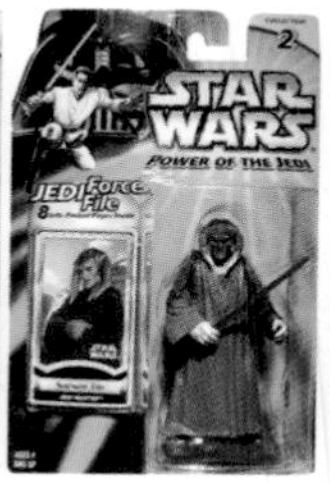
PJ49

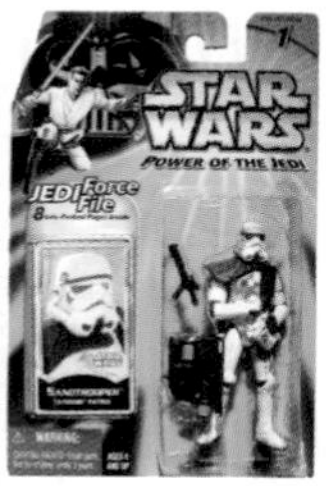
PJ50

Leia Organa General
____.0000, col. 1 [PJ35] 8.00
____.0100, col. 1 ..... 8.00
____.0300, col. 1 ..... 8.00
____.0400, col. 1 ..... 8.00
____Without package, mint, complete 6.00

Luke Skywalker X-Wing Pilot
____.0400, col. 1 [PJ36] 8.00
____Without package, mint, complete 6.00

Mas Amedda
____.0000, col. 2, force file 0100 [PJ37] 12.00
____.0100, col. 2, force file 0100 ..... 12.00
____.0300, col. 2, force file 0100 ..... 12.00
____.0400, col. 2, force file 0100 ..... 12.00
____Without package, mint, complete 4.00

Mon Calamari Officer
____.0100, col. 2 [PJ38] 12.00
____.0300, col. 2 ..... 12.00
____.0400, col. 2 ..... 10.00
____Without package, mint, complete 6.00

Obi-Wan Kenobi Cold Weather Gear
____.0300, col. 1 ..... 12.00
____.0400, col. 1 [PJ39] 12.00
____Without package, mint, complete 6.00

Obi-Wan Kenobi Jedi
____.0000, col. 1, force file 0100 [PJ40] 8.00
____.0100, col. 1, force file 0100 ..... 8.00
____Without package, mint, complete 5.00

Obi-Wan Kenobi Jedi Training Gear
____.0300, col. 2 ..... 8.00
____.0400, col. 2 [PJ41] 10.00
____Without package, mint, complete 8.00

Plo Koon Jedi Master
____.0100, col. 2 [PJ42] 12.00
____.0300, col. 2 ..... 12.00
____.0400, col. 2 ..... 12.00
____Without package, mint, complete 6.00

Queen Amidala Theed Invasion
____.0100, col. 2 [PJ43] 12.00
____.0300, col. 2 ..... 12.00
____.0400, col. 2 ..... 12.00
____Without package, mint, complete 8.00

Qui-Gon Jinn Jedi Training Gear
____.0400, col. 1 [PJ44] 10.00
____Without package, mint, complete 8.00

Qui-Gon Jinn Mos Espa Disguise
____.0000, col. 1, force file 0100 [PJ45] 8.00
____.0100, col. 1, force file 0100 ..... 8.00
____.0400, col. 1, force file 0100 ..... 10.00
____Without package, mint, complete 3.00

R2-D2 Naboo Escape
____.0000, col. 1 [PJ46] 10.00
____.0100, col. 1 ..... 10.00
____Without package, mint, complete 4.00

R2-Q5 Imperal Astromech Droid
____.0300, col. 2, "Imperial" misspelled 15.00
____.0400, col. 2, "Imperial" misspelled [PJ47] 15.00
____Without package, mint, complete 12.00

Sabe Queen's Decoy
____.0400, col. 2 [PJ48] 8.00
____Without package, mint, complete 6.00

Saesee Tiin Jedi Master
____.0100, col. 2 [PJ49] 10.00
____.0300, col. 2 ..... 10.00
____.0400, col. 2 ..... 10.00
____Without package, mint, complete 5.00

Sandtrooper Tatooine Patrol
____.0300, col. 1 ..... 15.00
____.0400, col. 1 [PJ50] 15.00
____Without package, mint, complete 10.00

Scout Trooper Imperial Patrol
____.0100, col. 1 [PJ51] 25.00
____.0300, col. 1 ..... 25.00
____.0400, col. 1, dirty w/blaster damage [PJ52] 12.00
____Without package, mint, complete 10.00

Sebulba Boonta Eve Challenge
____.0000, col. 2 ..... 12.00
____.0100, col. 2 [PJ53] 10.00
____.0400, col. 2 ..... 10.00
____Without package, mint, complete 8.00

Shmi Skywalker
____.0400, col. 2 [PJ54] 12.00
____Without package, mint, complete 6.00

Tessek
____.0300, col. 2 ..... 10.00
____.0400, col. 2 [PJ55] 10.00
____Without package, mint, complete 5.00

Tusken Raider Desert Sniper
____.0000, col. 2 [PJ56] 12.00
____.0100, col. 2 ..... 10.00
____.0300, col. 2 ..... 10.00
____.0400, col. 2 ..... 10.00
____Without package, mint, complete 6.00

Green cards without Force Files.

Boshek
____0700, col. 2 [PJ57] 15.00
____Without package, mint, complete 10.00

Eeth Koth
____0500, col. 2 [PJ58] 12.00
____Without package, mint, complete 6.00

FX-7
____Medical Droid 0000, col. 2 [PJ59] 10.00
____Without package, mint, complete 6.00

Imperial Officer
____0300, col. 2 [PJ60] 12.00
____Without package, mint, complete 8.00

Queen Amidala Royal Decoy
____0100, col. 2 [PJ61] 8.00
____Without package, mint, complete 5.00

R4-M9 and mouse droid
____0800, col. 2 [PJ62] 12.00
____Without package, mint, complete 9.00

Rebel Trooper – Tantive IV Defender
____0200, col. 2 [PJ63] 10.00
____Without package, mint, complete 5.00

Teebo
____0600, col. 2 [PJ64] 10.00
____Without package, mint, complete 6.00

Zutton (Snaggletooth)
____0400, col. 2, brown head [PJ65] 15.00
____0400, col. 2, pink head [PJ66] 15.00
____Without package, mint, complete 4.00

Hasbro, Canada

EPII:AOTC. Sneak preview figures. Tri-language.
____Clone Trooper [3:76] 15.00
____Jango Fett [3:76] 17.00
____R3-T7 [3:76] 15.00
____Zam Wesell [3:76] 12.00

Tri-language packaging with force file.
____Anakin Skywalker Mechanic 9.00
____Aurra Sing Bounty Hunter [3:75] 9.00
____Battle Droid Boomer Damage [3:75] 9.00
____Bespin Guard [3:75] 9.00
____Chewbacca Millennium Falcon Mechanic [3:75] 9.00
____Darth Maul Sith Apprentice [3:75] 9.00
____Darth Vader Dagobah, secret Luke sticker [3:75] 35.00
____Darth Vader Emperors Wrath [3:75] 9.00
____Ellors Madak [3:75] 9.00
____Han Solo Bespin Capture 9.00
____Han Solo Death Star Escape [3:75] 9.00
____IG-88 [3:75] 9.00
____Jar Jar Binks Tatooine 7.00
____K-3PO [3:75] 9.00
____Ketwol [3:75] 9.00
____Lando Calrissian Bespin Escape [3:75] 9.00

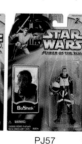

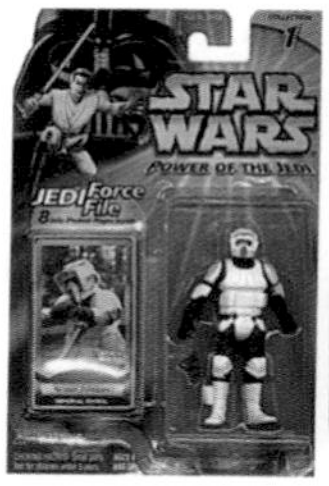
PJ51

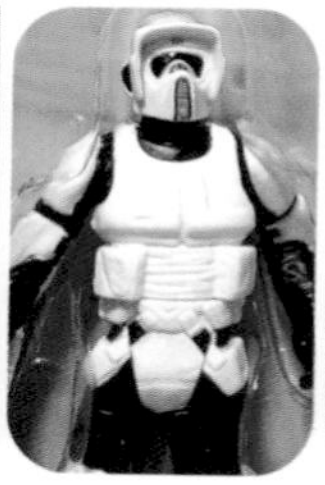
PJ51 detail

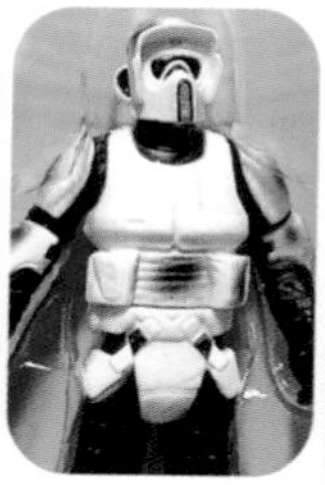
PJ52 detail

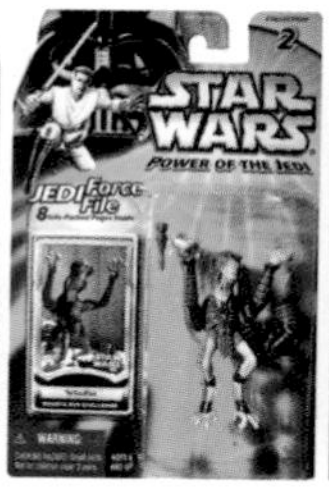
PJ53

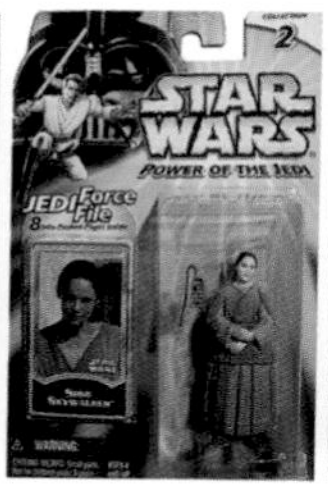
PJ54

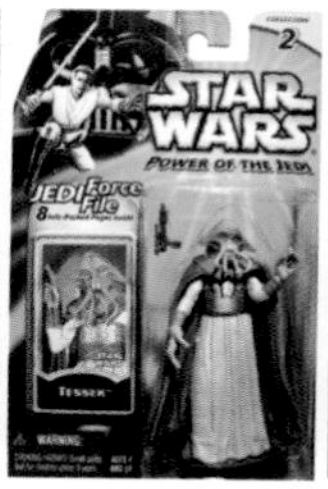
PJ55

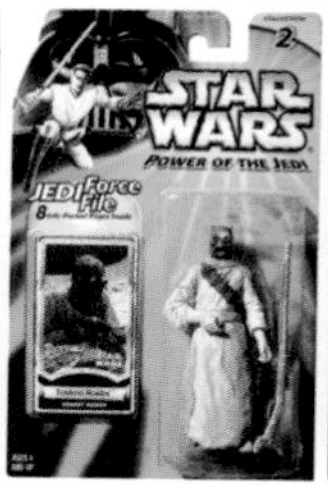
PJ56

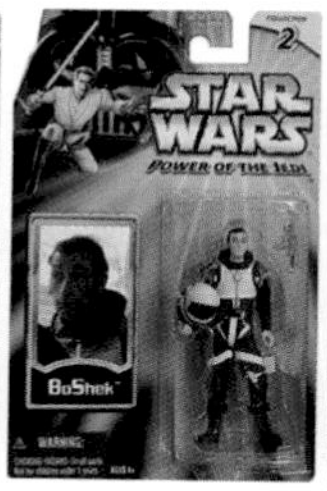
PJ57

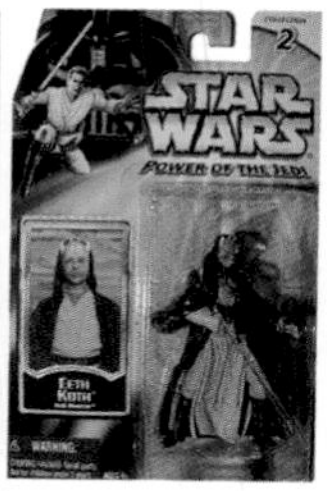
PJ58

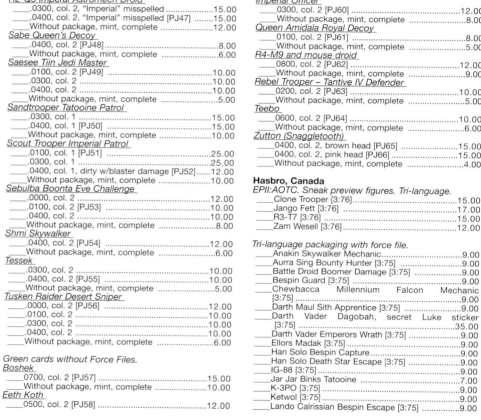

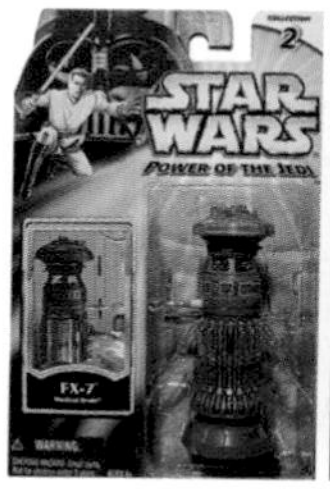
PJ59

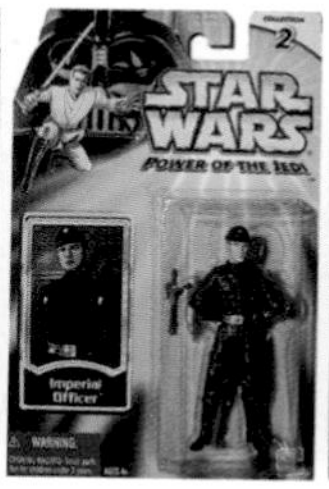
PJ60

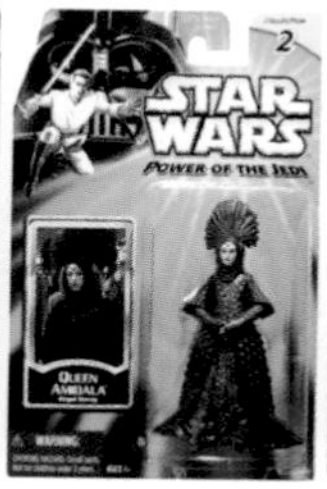
PJ61

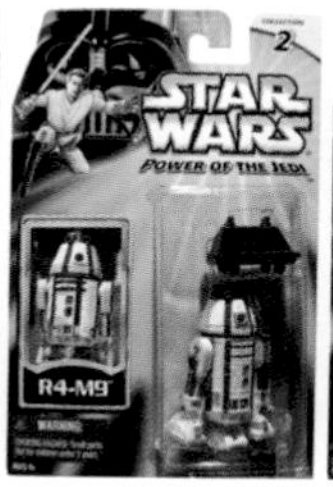
PJ62

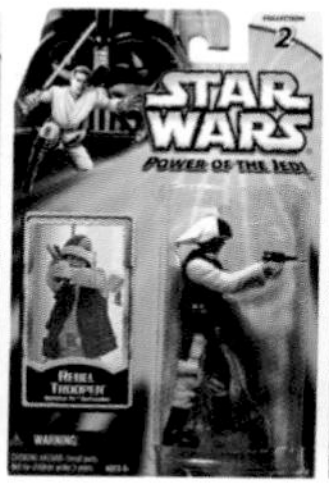
PJ63

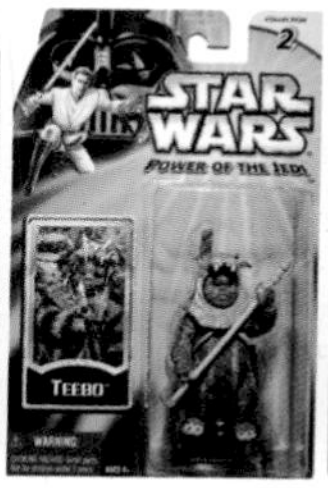
PJ64

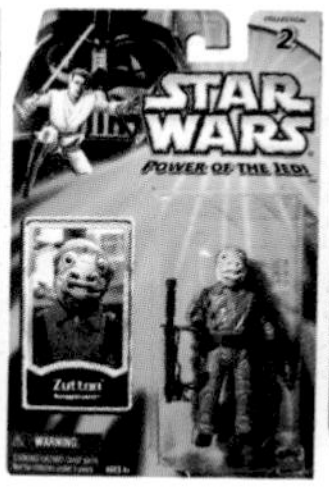
PJ65

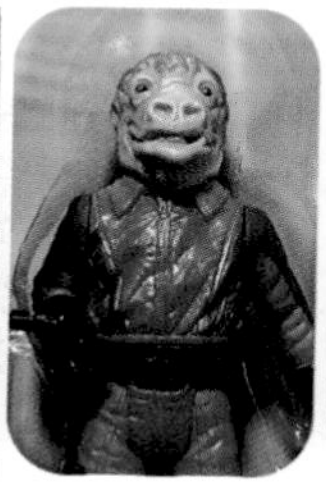
PJ65 detail

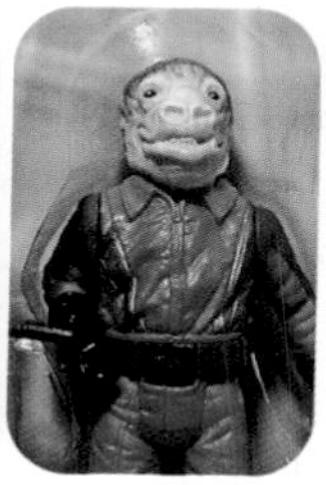
PJ66 detail

PJ201

SSD01

SSD02

SSD03

SSD04

SSD05

____Leia Organa Bespin Escape [3:75] 9.00
____Luke Skywalker X-Wing Pilot [3:75] 9.00
____Mon Calamari Officer 9.00
____Obi-Wan Kenobi Cold Weather Gear [3:75] 9.00
____Obi-Wan Kenobi Jedi Knight 9.00
____Obi-Wan Kenobi Jedi Training Gear [3:75] 9.00
____Plo Koon [3:75] 9.00
____Queen Amidala Theed Invasion [3:75] 9.00
____Qui-Gon Jinn Jedi Training Gear [3:75] 9.00
____R2-Q5 Imperial Astromech [3:75] 9.00
____Sabe Queen's Decoy [3:75] 7.00
____Saesee Tinn [3:76] 9.00
____Sandtrooper Tatooine Patrol [3:75] 9.00
____Scout Trooper Imperial Patrol [3:75] 9.00
____Scout Trooper, blaster damage [3:75] 9.00
____Shmi Skywalker [3:76] 9.00
____Tessek [3:76] 9.00

Tri-language packaging.
____Boba Fett, 300th figure [3:75] 35.00

Hasbro, UK
Classic trilogy characters. Bi-language with force file.
____Ben (Obi-Wan) Kenobi Jedi Knight [3:76] 9.00
____Darth Vader Dagobah [3:76] 9.00

EPI:TPM characters. Bi-language with force file.
____Darth Maul [3:76] 7.00
____Obi-Wan Kenobi [3:76] 7.00
____Qui-Gon Jinn [3:76] 7.00

Tomy
____Darth Vader Emperors Wrath, 100th figure
[3:76] 35.00

Toys: Action Figures –
2001 – 2002 (POTJ) 2-Packs

Hasbro
____Masters of the Dark Side [PJ201] 40.00

Toys: Action Figures –
2001 – 2002 (POTJ) Deluxe

Hasbro
Amanaman with Salacious Crumb
____0300 [SSD01] 20.00
____0600 ....12.00
Darth Maul with Sith attack droid
____0100 [SSD02] 20.00
____0500 ....20.00
Luke Skywalker in Echo Base bacta tank
____0000 [SSD03] 15.00
____0400 ....15.00
Princess Leia with sail barge cannon
____0200 [SSD04] 10.00

Hasbro, Canada
____Darth Maul [SSD05] 15.00
____Luke Skywalker [3:76] 15.00

PJF01

PJF02

PJF03

PJM01

Toys: Action Figures –
2001 – 2002 (POTJ) Mega

Hasbro
____Darth Maul [PJF01] 15.00
____Destroyer Droid [PJF02] 20.00
____Obi-Wan Kenobi [PJF03] 15.00

Toys: Action Figures –
2001 – 2002 (POTJ) Multi-Packs

Hasbro
____4-pack 846480640, Internet e-tailer offer
[PJM01] 25.00

Hasbro, Mexico
____4-pack, Spanish packaging [PJM02] 75.00

Toys: Action Figures –
2001 – 2002 Silver Anniversary 2-Packs

Hasbro
____"Death Star Escape" [PSS01] 18.00
____"Final Duel" [PSS03] 20.00
____"Swing to Freedom" [PSS02] 15.00

Hasbro, Canada
Tri-language.
____"Death Star Escape" [3:77] 18.00
____"Final Duel" [3:77] 18.00
____"Swing to Freedom" [PSS04] 18.00

Toys: Action Figures –
2002 – 2004 (Saga 2002)

Hasbro
Blue cards. 1st release with background insert.
Anakin Skywalker, Outland Peasant Disguise (02/01)
____Collection 1 [P4A01] 8.00

Battle Droid, Arena Battle (02/11)
____col. 2, white [P4A02] 10.00
Boba Fett, Kamino Escape (02/07)
____Collection 2 [P4A03] 8.00
Boba Fett, Kamino Escape (02/07)
____Collection 2, no number on insert card 8.00
C-3PO, Protocol Droid (02/04)
____Collection 1 [P4A04] 8.00
Captain Typho, Padme's Head of Security (02/09)
____Collection 2 [P4A05] 8.00
____Collection 2, no number on insert card 8.00
Dexter Jettster, Coruscant Informant (02/16)
____Collection 2, blue tape over 'pipe' [P4A06] 8.00
____Collection 2, lists pipe accessory 8.00
Genosian Warrior (02/15)
____Collection 2 [P4A07] 8.00
Jango Fett, Kamino Escape (02/13)
____Collection 1 [P4A08] 8.00
Kit Fisto, Jedi Master (02/05)
____Collection 1, With Force Action [P4A09] 10.00
Obi-Wan Kenobi, Coruscant chase (02/03)
____Collection 1 [P4A10] 8.00
Padme Amidala, Arena Escape (02/02)
____Collection 1, mole on left cheek, tape on gun
[P4A11] 8.00
____Collection 1, no mole, no tape on gun 8.00
Plo Koon, Arena Battle (02/12)
____Collection 2 [P4A12] 12.00
R2-D2, Coruscant sentry (02/14)
____Collection 1 [P4A13] 12.00
Shaak Ti, Jedi Master (02/10)
____Collection 2 [P4A14] 8.00
Super Battle Droid (02/06)
____Collection 1, battle damage sticker, dull figure
finish 12.00
____Collection 1, battle damage sticker, glossy figure fin-
ish [P4A15] 12.00
____Collection 1, no correction sticker over blast apart
legs image [P4A16] 12.00
Tusken Raider, Female with Tusken child (02/08)
____Collection 2 [P4A17] 12.00

Blue cards. Swirl pattern on background.
Anakin Skywalker, Hanger Duel (02/22)
____Col. 1, Dueling Lightsaber Action [P4A18] 10.00
____Col. 1, Dueling Lightsaber Action, missing "TM" next
to "Lightsabers" 10.00
____Col. 1, Secret Battle Feature, missing "TM" next to
"Lightsabers" 10.00

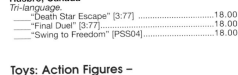
PJM02

PSS01

PSS02

PSS03

PSS04

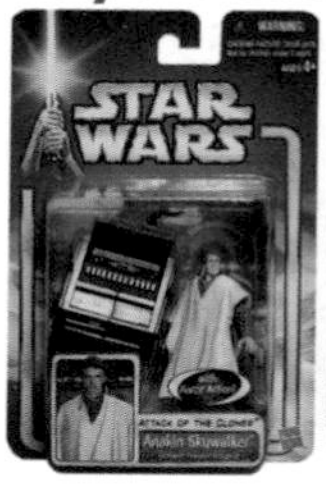
P4A01

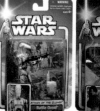

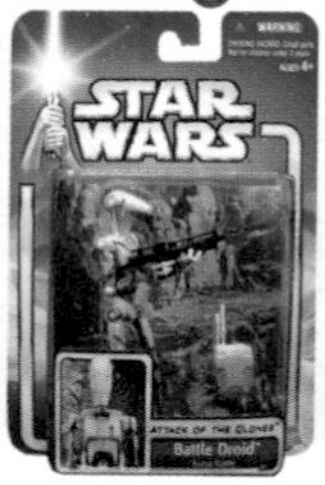
P4A02

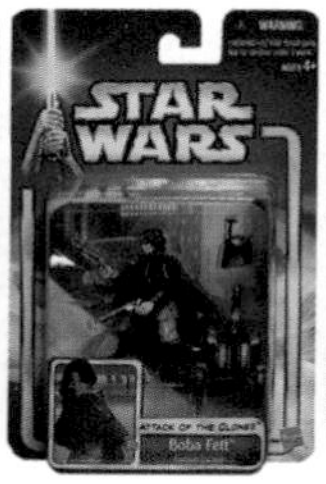
P4A03

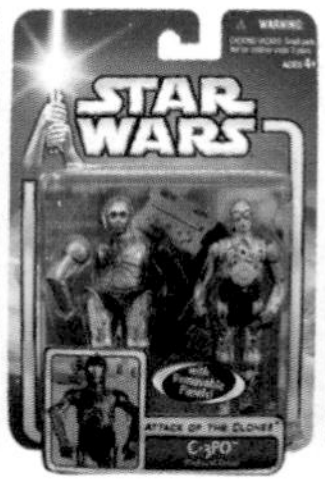
P4A04

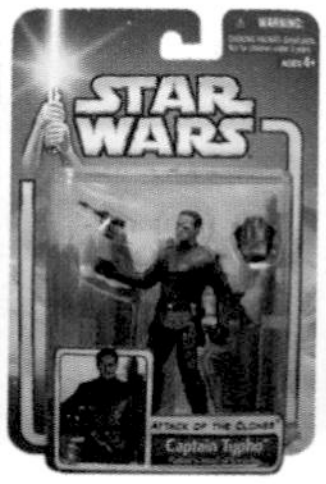
P4A05

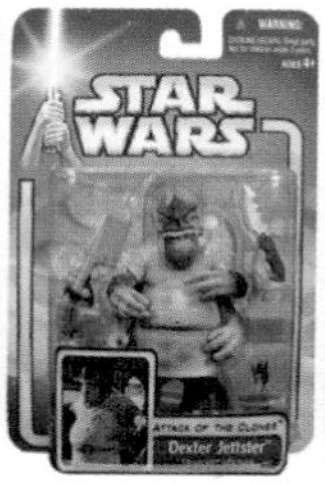
P4A06

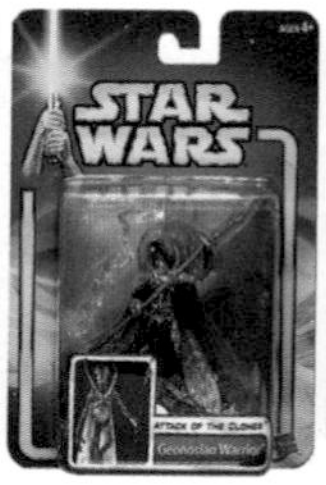
P4A07

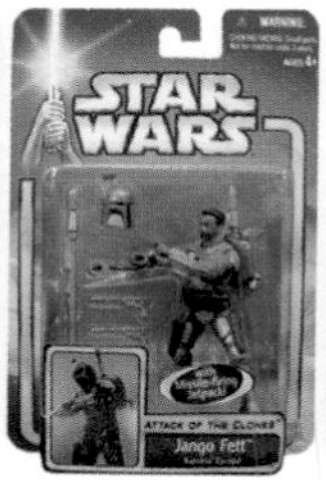
P4A08

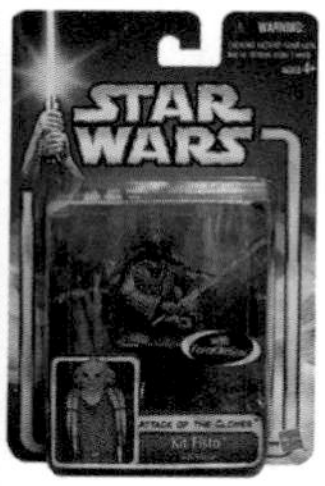
P4A09

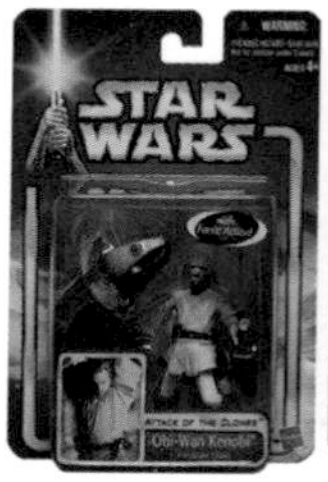
P4A10

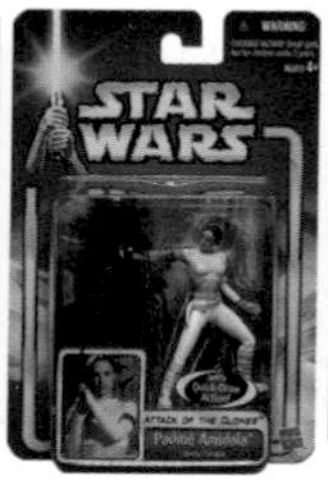
P4A11

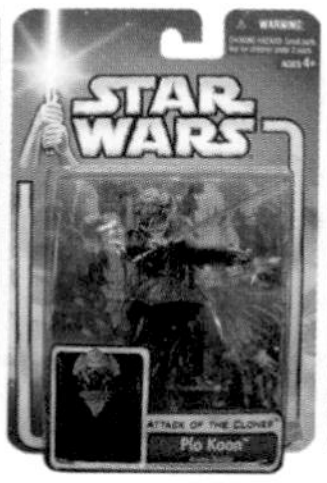
P4A12

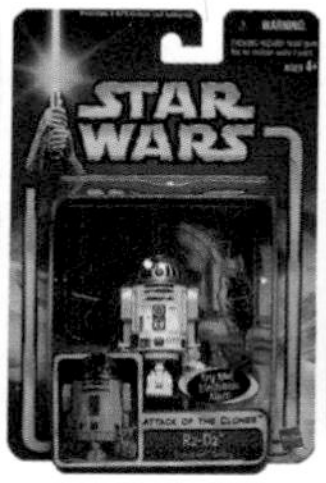
P4A13

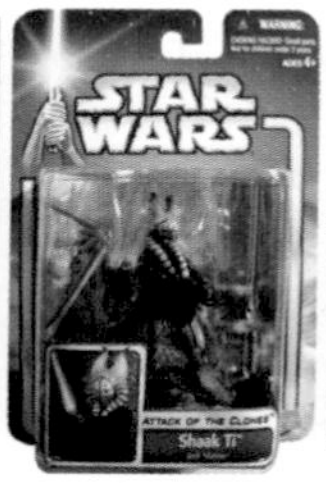
P4A14

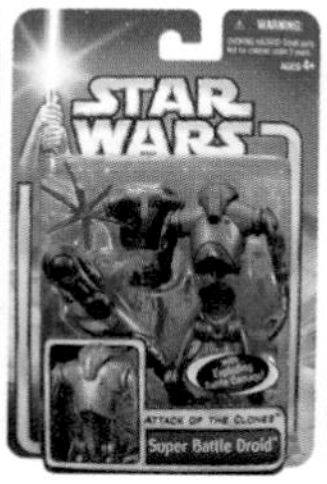
P4A15

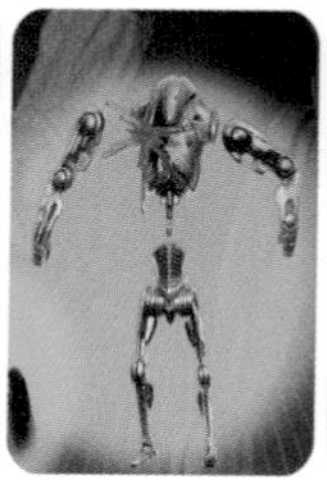
P4A15 rear detail

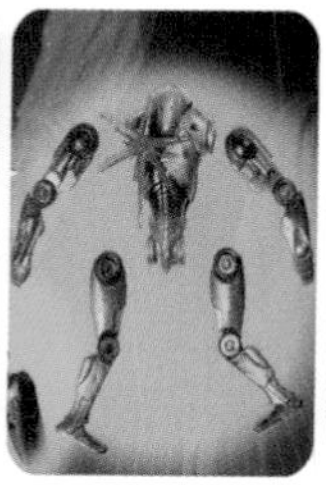
P4A16 rear detail

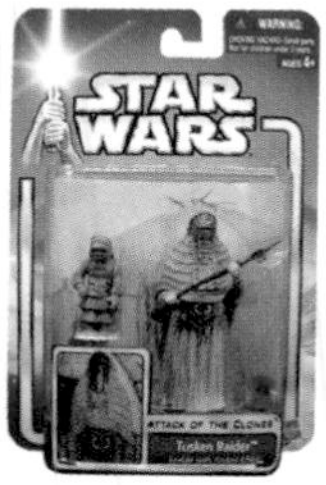
P4A17

____Col. 1, Secret Battle Feature [P4A19] 10.00
____Col. 1, Secret Battle Feature, tape over lightsaber 10.00
____Without package, mint, complete 2.00

Anakin Skywalker, Outland Peasant Disguise (02/01)
____Col.1 [P4A20] 7.00
____Col. 1, gun tray has a circular end 7.00
____Without package, mint, complete 2.00

Anakin Skywalker, Tatooine Attack (02/43)
____Col. 1, rifle held by bubble tab [P4A21] 8.00
____Col. 1, rifle held by tape 8.00
____Without package, mint, complete 3.00

Battle Droid, Arena Battle (02/11)
____Col. 2, beige [P4A22] 10.00
____Col. 2, red [P4A23] 15.00
____Without package, mint, complete 8.00

Boba Fett, Kamino Escape (02/07)
____Col. 2 [P4A24] 10.00
____Without package, mint, complete 5.00

C-3PO, Protocol Droid (02/04)
____Col. 1 [P4A25] 6.00
____Without package, mint, complete 3.00

Captain Typho, Padme's Head of Security (02/09)
____Col. 2 [P4A26] 6.00
____Without package, mint, complete 3.00

Chewbacca, Cloud City Capture (02/38)
____Col. 1 [P4A27] 8.00
____Without package, mint, complete 2.00

Clone Trooper (02/17)
____Col. 1, curved bubble, no tab over cannon........15.00
____Col. 1, curved bubble, tab over cannon 15.00
____Col. 1, red dots missing from package photo [P4A28] 15.00
____Col. 1, bubble over right arm [P4A29] 15.00
____Without package, mint, complete 8.00

Clone Trooper, Republic Gunship Pilot (02/49)
____Col. 1 [P4A30] 20.00
____Without package, mint, complete 16.00

Count Dooku, Dark Lord (02/27)
____Col. 1 [P4A33] 10.00
____Without package, mint, complete 7.00

Darth Maul, Sith Training (02/42)
____Col. 1, .3300 kneeling text [P4A31] 15.00
____Col. 1, .6000 corrected text [P4A32] 15.00
____Without package, mint, complete 8.00

Darth Vader, Bespin Duel (02/30)
____Col. 1 [P4A34] 10.00
____Without package, mint, complete 5.00

Destroyer Droid, Geonosis Battle (02/48)
____Col. 1 [P4A35] 10.00
____Without package, mint, complete 7.00

Dexter Jettster, Coruscant Informant (02/16)
____Col. 2, blue tape over "pipe" [P4A36] 8.00
____Col. 2, pipe accessory listed [P4A37] 8.00
____Col. 2, pipe accessory removed............................8.00
____Without package, mint, complete 2.00

Djas Puhr (02/40)
____Col. 2 [P4A38] 8.00
____Without package, mint, complete 2.00

Eeth Koth, Jedi Master (02/56)
____Col. 2 [P4A39] 20.00
____Without package, mint, complete 12.00

Endor Rebel Soldier (02/33)
____Col. 2, gun strap loose in bubble [P4A40]..........10.00
____Col. 2, gun strap under bubble 10.00
____Without package, mint, complete 3.00

Endor Rebel Soldier without beard (02/33)
____Col. 2, gun strap loose in bubble [P4A41]..........12.00
____Col. 2, gun strap under bubble 12.00
____Without package, mint, complete 6.00

Ephant Mon, Jabba's Head of Security (02/45)
____Col. 2, bubble around left hand [P4A42] 25.00
____Col. 2, bubble shaped under left hand 25.00
____Without package, mint, complete 18.00

Genosian Warrior (02/15)
____Col. 2 [P4A43] 10.00
____Without package, mint, complete 5.00

Han Solo, Endor Raid (02/37)
____Col. 1, gray action lever, right arm tray goes to top of bubble [P4A44] 8.00
____Col. 1, gray action lever, tray tapers off 8.00
____Col. 1, white action lever [P4A45] 8.00
____Without package, mint, complete 4.00

Imperial Officer (02/55)
____Col. 2, blond hair [P4A46] 20.00
____Col. 2, brown hair [P4A47] 20.00
____Without package, mint, complete 16.00

Jango Fett, Final Battle (02/31)
____Col. 1, accessory angled downward [P4A48] 8.00
____Col. 1, accessory angled upward [P4A49]............8.00
____Without package, mint, complete 5.00

Jango Fett, Kamino Escape (02/13)
____Col. 1, gray armor [P4A50]..................................12.00
____Col. 1, silver armor 12.00
____Without package, mint, complete 5.00

Jango Fett, Slave I Pilot (02/47)
____Col. 1 [P4A51] 8.00
____Without package, mint, complete 4.00

Jar Jar Binks, Gungan Senator (02/24)
____Col. 2, bubble ends at right hand [P4A52] 8.00
____Col. 2, bubble extends to right wrist 8.00
____Without package, mint, complete 2.00

Ki-Adi-Mundi, Jedi Master (02/44)
____Col. 2 [P4A53] 8.00
____Without package, mint, complete 5.00

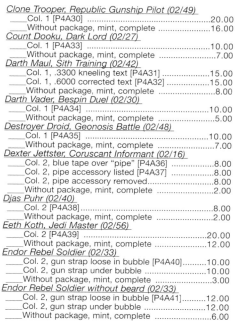

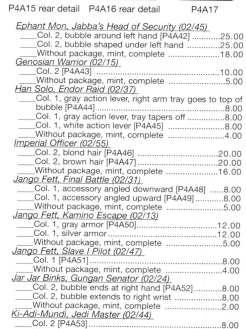

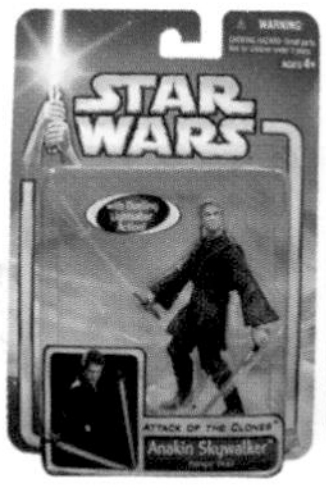
P4A18

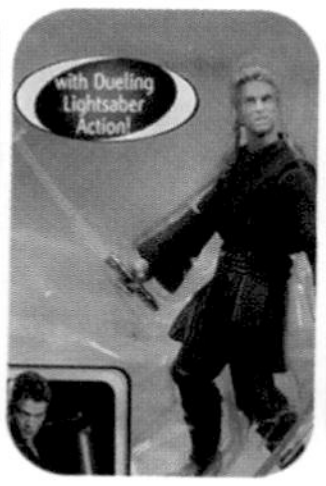

P4A18 detail

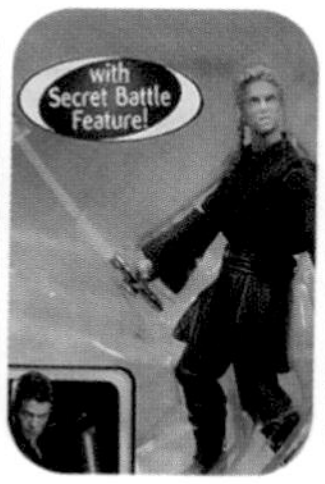

P4A19 detail

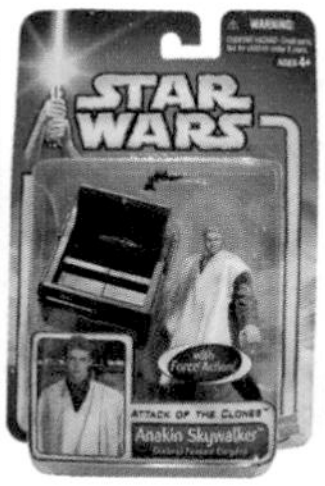
P4A20

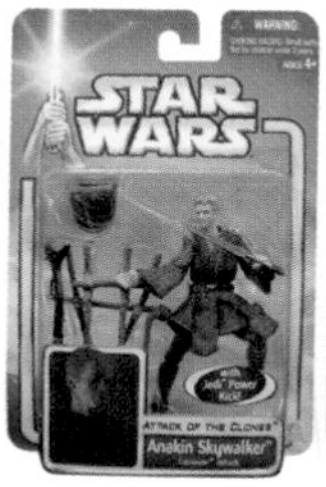
P4A21

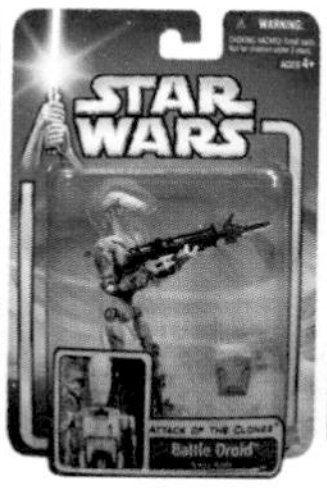
P4A22

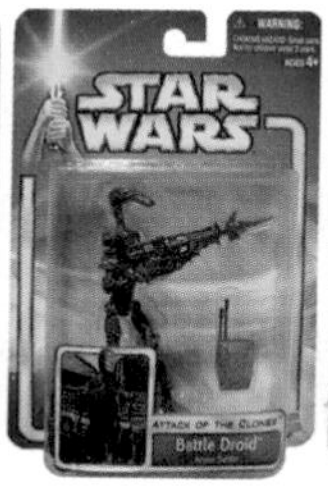
P4A23

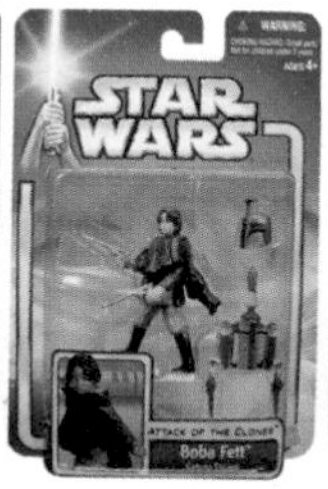
P4A24

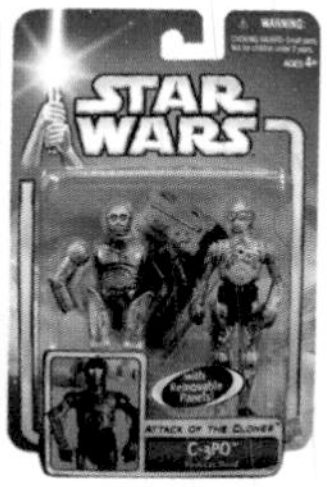
P4A25

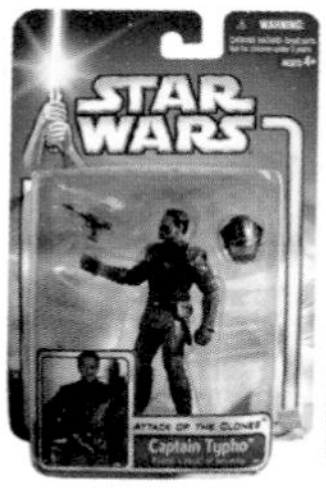
P4A26

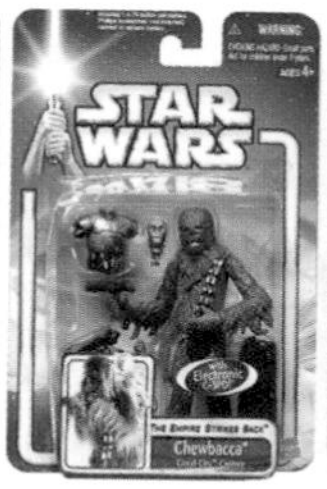
P4A27

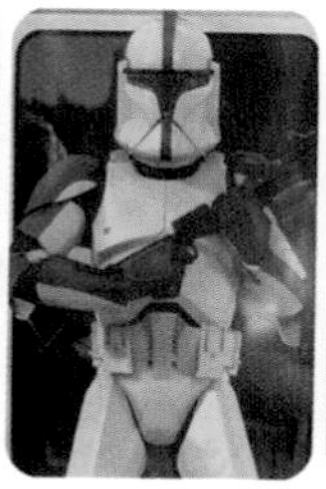
P4A28 detail

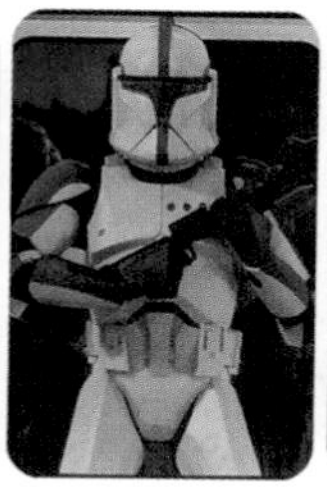
P4A29 detail

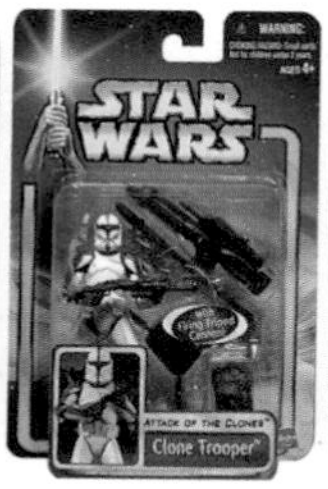
P4A29

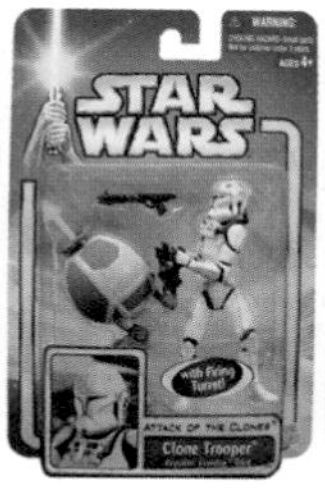
P4A30

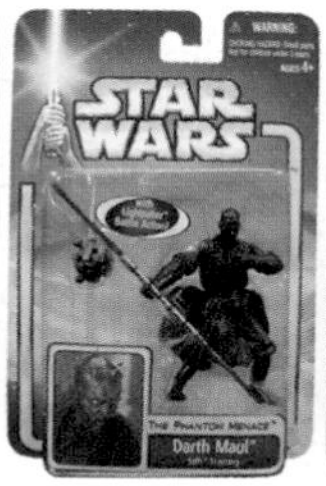
P4A31

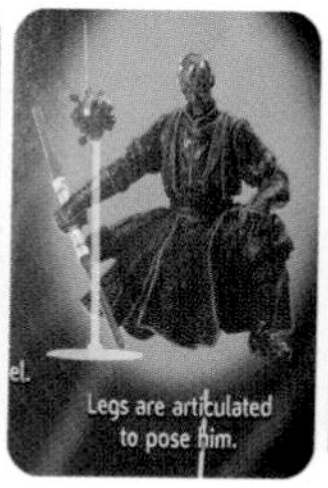

P4A31 rear detail

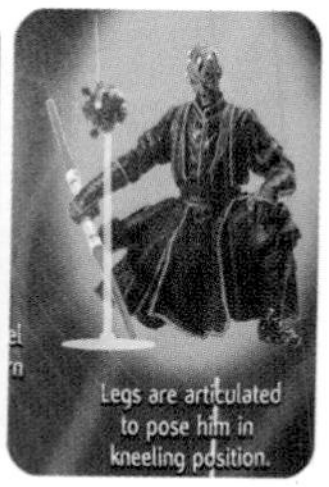

P4A32 rear detail

P4A33

P4A34

P4A35

P4A36

P4A36 detail

P4A37 detail

P4A38

P4A39

P4A40

P4A40 detail

P4A41

P4A41 detail

P4A42

P4A43

P4A44

P4A44 detail

P4A45 detail

Kit Fisto, Jedi Master (02/05)
____Col. 1, With Force Action....................................12.00
____Col. 1, With Slashing Lightsaber Action [P4A54]..12.00
____Without package, mint, complete 8.00
Lott Dod, Neimodian Senator (02/51)
____Col. 2 [P4A55]..8.00
____Without package, mint, complete 4.00
Luke Skywalker, Bespin Duel (02/29)
____Col. 1, bloody hand, magnetic [P4A56].............30.00
____Col. 1, bloody hand, magnetic, no tape on hand 30.00
____Col. 1, no blood, magnetic 10.00
____Col. 1, no blood, pegged [P4A57] 10.00
____Without package, mint, complete 4.00
Luminara Unduli, Jedi Master (02/26)
____Col. 2, "Removable Cloak" listed [P4A58] 8.00
____Col. 2, 1 blue tape over "Removable" [P4A59] 8.00
____Col. 2, 1 blue tape over "Removable Cloak" 8.00
____Col. 2, 2 blue tapes over "Removable Cloak" 8.00
____Without package, mint, complete 6.00
Mace Windu, Genosian Rescue (02/28)
____Col. 1 [P4A60]..8.00
____Without package, mint, complete 6.00
Massiff (02/34)
____Col. 2, bubble covers left front leg........................8.00
____Col. 2, bubble exposes area over left front leg [P4A61] 8.00
____Without package, mint, complete 6.00
Nikto, Jedi Knight (02/21)
____Col. 2 [P4A62] 15.00
____Without package, mint, complete 9.00
Obi-Wan Kenobi Jedi Starfighter Pilot (02/36)
____Col. 1 [P4A63]..8.00
____Without package, mint, complete 4.00

Obi-Wan Kenobi, Coruscant Chase (02/03)
____Col. 1 [P4A64]..6.00
____Without package, mint, complete 2.00
Orn Free Ta (02/35)
____Col. 2, bubble tabs, horns are unsecured [P4A65] 8.00
____Col. 2, bubble wings, horns are rubberbanded 8.00
____Without package, mint, complete 2.00
Padme Amidala, Arena Escape (02/02)
____Col. 1, mole on left cheek 10.00
____Col. 1, no mole, gun in bubble [P4A66].............10.00
____Col. 1, no mole, gun barrel in tray 10.00
____Without package, mint, complete 3.00
Padme Amidala, Corsucant Attack (02/41)
____Col. 1 [P4A67] 15.00
____Col. 1, original text on back...............................15.00
____Col. 1, text correction sticker on back 15.00
____Without package, mint, complete 6.00
Plo Koon, Arena Battle (02/12)
____Col. 2 [P4A68]..7.00
____Without package, mint, complete 6.00
Qui-Gon Jinn (02/32)
____Col. 2 [P4A69] 10.00
____Without package, mint, complete 5.00
R2-D2, Coruscant Sentry (02/14)
____Col. 1, round shoulder pegs [P4A70]..................12.00
____Col. 1, star design shoulder pegs [P4A71] 10.00
____Without package, mint, complete 5.00
Rebel Trooper, Tantive IV Defender (02/54)
____Col. 2, black hair [P4A72]...................................15.00
____Col. 2, brown hair [P4A73] 15.00
____Without package, mint, complete 12.00
Royal Guard, Coruscant Security (02/19)
____Col. 2, force pike extends into bubble tray [P4A74] 12.00

____Col. 2, force pike stays in main bubble 12.00
____Without package, mint, complete 6.00
Saesee Tiin, Jedi Master (02/20)
____Col. 2 [P4A75] 10.00
____Without package, mint, complete 8.00
Shaak Ti, Jedi Master (02/10)
____Col. 2 [P4A76] 12.00
____Without package, mint, complete 8.00
Super Battle Droid (02/06)
____Col. 1, battle damage sticker, dull figure finish [P4A77] 10.00
____Col. 1, battle damage sticker, glossy figure finish 10.00
____Col. 1, corrected cardback, dull figure finish 10.00
____Without package, mint, complete 6.00
Supreme Chancellor Palpatine (02/39)
____Col. 2 [P4A78]..8.00
____Col. 2, rubberbanded around neck 8.00
____Without package, mint, complete 3.00
Taun We, Kamino Cloner (02/25)
____Col. 2 [P4A79] 12.00
____Without package, mint, complete 6.00
Teebo (02/57)
____Col. 2 [P4A80] 25.00
____Without package, mint, complete 16.00
Teemto Pagalies, Pod Racer (02/46)
____Col. 1 [P4A81]..8.00
____Without package, mint, complete 3.00
Tusken Raider with Massiff (02/52)
____Col. 2 [P4A82] 10.00
____Without package, mint, complete 6.00
Tusken Raider, Female with Tusken child (02/08)
____Col. 2 [P4A83] 10.00
____Without package, mint, complete 5.00

P4A46

P4A47

P4A48

P4A49

P4A50

P4A51

P4A52

P4A53

P4A54

P4A55

P4A56

P4A56 detail

P4A57 detail

P4A58

P4A58 detail

P4A59

P4A60

P4A61

P4A62

P4A63

P4A64

P4A65

P4A66

P4A67

P4A68

P4A69

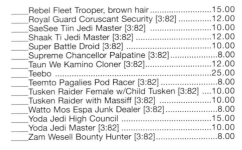

P4A70

P4A70 detail

P4A71 detail

P4A72

P4A72 detail

P4A73 detail

<u>*Watto, Mos Espa Junk Dealer (02/50)*</u>
____Col. 2 [P4A84]..8.00
____Without package, mint, complete 3.00
<u>*Yoda, Jedi High Council (02/53)*</u>
____Col. 1 [P4A85] 15.00
____Col. 1, tab extends over head 15.00
____Without package, mint, complete 5.00
<u>*Yoda, Jedi Master (02/23)*</u>
____Col. 1, missing "TM" next to lightsaber [P4A86]..10.00
____Col. 1, no tab over head 10.00
____Col. 1, tab extends over head 10.00
____Without package, mint, complete 4.00
<u>*Zam Wesell (02/18)*</u>
____Col. 1, Face Reveal Mask [P4A87] 10.00
____Col. 1, Face Reveal Mask, bubble angled above mask [P4A88] 8.00
____Col. 1, Face Reveal Mask, spoiler picture on back of card [P4A89] 8.00
____Col. 1, Quick Draw Action [P4A90] 8.00
____Without package, mint, complete 3.00

Hasbro, Canada
Blue cards. Swirl pattern on background. Tri-language.
____Anakin Skywalker Hangar Duel [3:81] 10.00
____Anakin Skywalker Outland Peasant Disguise [3:81] 7.00
____Anakin Skywalker Tatooine Attack [3:81] 8.00
____Battle Droid Arena Battle [3:81] 10.00
____Boba Fett Kamino Escape [3:81] 10.00
____C-3PO Protocol Droid [3:81]..................................6.00
____Captain Typho [3:81]...6.00
____Chewbacca Cloud City Capture [3:81].................8.00
____Clone Trooper [3:82]...15.00
____Clone Trooper Republic Gunship Pilot [3:82] 20.00
____Count Dooku Dark Lord [3:82]...........................10.00
____Darth Maul Sith Training [3:82]..........................15.00
____Darth Vader Bespin Duel [3:81] 10.00
____Destroyer Droid Arena Battle [3:82] 10.00
____Dexter Jettster Coruscant Informant [3:82] 8.00
____Djas Puhr Allien Bounty Hunter [3:81] 8.00
____Eeth Koth Jedi Master 20.00
____Endor Rebel Soldier [3:81]...................................10.00
____Endor Rebel Soldier without Beard [3:81] 10.00
____Ephant Mon Jabba's Head of Security 25.00
____Geonosian Warrior [3:82] 10.00
____Han Solo Endor Raid [3:81] 8.00
____Imperial Officer 1st sculpt 20.00
____Imperial Officer 2nd sculpt..................................20.00
____Jango Fett Final Battle [3:82]................................8.00
____Jango Fett Kamino Escape [3:82] 12.00
____Jango Fett Slave I Pilot [3:82]..............................8.00
____Jar Jar Binks Gungan Senator [3:82] 8.00
____Ki-Adi-Mundi Jedi Master [3:82]...........................8.00
____Kit Fisto Jedi Master [3:82] 12.00
____Lott Dod Neimoidian Senator [3:82].....................8.00
____Luke Skywalker Bespin Duel [3:81] 10.00
____Luminara Unduli Jedi Master [3:82] 8.00
____Mace Windu Geonosian Rescue [3:82] 8.00
____Massiff [3:82]...8.00
____Nikto Jedi Master [3:82].......................................15.00
____Obi-Wan Kenobi Coruscant Chase [3:82] 6.00
____Obi-Wan Kenobi Jedi Starfighter Pilot [3:82] 8.00
____Orn Free Ta [3:82] 8.00
____Padme Amidala Arena Escape [3:82] 10.00
____Padme Amidala Coruscant Attack [3:82]............15.00
____Plo Koon Arena Battle [3:82] 7.00
____Qui- Gon Jinn Jedi Master [3:82]........................10.00
____R2-D2 Coruscant Sentry [3:82] 10.00
____Rebel Fleet Trooper, black hair 15.00
____Rebel Fleet Trooper, brown hair..........................15.00
____Royal Guard Coruscant Security [3:82] 12.00
____SaeSee Tiin Jedi Master [3:82] 10.00
____Shaak Ti Jedi Master [3:82] 12.00
____Super Battle Droid [3:82] 10.00
____Supreme Chancellor Palpatine [3:82]....................8.00
____Taun We Kamino Cloner [3:82]...........................12.00
____Teebo 25.00
____Teemto Pagalies Pod Racer [3:82] 8.00
____Tusken Raider Female w/Child Tusken [3:82] 10.00
____Tusken Raider with Massiff [3:82] 10.00
____Watto Mos Espa Junk Dealer [3:82]......................8.00
____Yoda Jedi High Council 15.00
____Yoda Jedi Master [3:82] 10.00
____Zam Wesell Bounty Hunter [3:82]..........................8.00

Toys: Action Figures – 2002 – 2004 (Saga 2003)

Hasbro
Blue cards. Starburst pattern on background.
<u>*Aayla Secura (03/11)*</u>
____Col. 2, long belt strap [P4B01]...........................12.00
____Col. 2, short belt strap 12.00
____Without package, mint, complete [3:39] 8.00
<u>*Anakin Skywalker, Secret Ceremony (03/07)*</u>
____Col. 1 [P4B02] 10.00
____Without package, mint, complete [3:39] 8.00
<u>*Ashla and Jempa (03/16)*</u>
____Col. 2, rounded UPC correction sticker 8.00
____Col. 2, square UPC correction sticker 8.00
____Col. 2, UPC 0-76930-84970-5 [P4B03] 8.00
____Col. 2, wrong UPC 0-76930-84970-3 ....8.00
____Without package, mint, complete [3:39] 6.00
<u>*Bariss Offee (03/12)*</u>
____Col. 2 [P4B04] 12.00
____Without package, mint, complete [3:39] 6.00
<u>*Boba Fett, Pit of Carkoon (03/08)*</u>
____Col. 1, blue [P4B05] 18.00
____Col. 1, green [P4B06]..18.00
____Without package, mint, complete [3:36] 8.00
<u>*Chewbacca, Mynock Hunt (03/14)*</u>
____Col. 1 [P4B07] 10.00
____Without package, mint, complete [3:36] 5.00
<u>*Darth Tyrannus, Geonosian Escape (03/03)*</u>
____Col. 1 [P4B08] 15.00
____Without package, mint, complete [3:40] 12.00

P4A74

P4A75

P4A76

P4A77

P4A78

P4A79

P4A80

P4A81

P4A82

P4A83

P4A84

P4A85

P4A86

P4A87

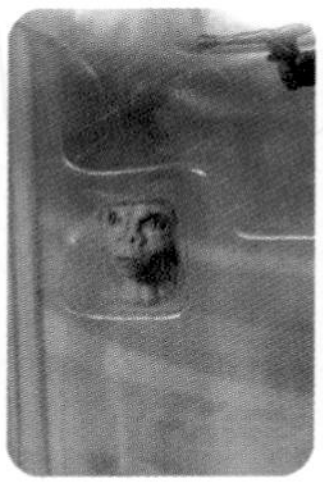
P4A87 detail

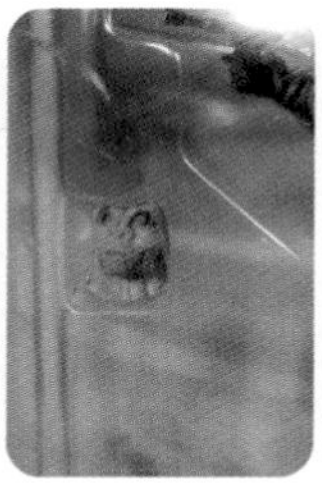
P4A88 detail

P4A89 rear detail

P4A90 rear detail

P4B01

P4B02

P4B03

P4B04

P4B05

P4B05 detail

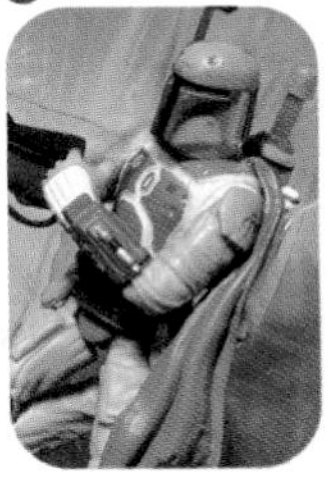
P4B06 detail

P4B07

P4B08

P4B09

P4B09 detail

P4B10 detail

P4B11

P4B12

P4B13

P4B14

P4B15

Han Solo, Hoth Rescue (03/13)
____Col. 1, blue coat, black-and-silver lightsaber handle [P4B09] 10.00
____Col. 1, blue coat, silver lightsaber handle [P4B10] 10.00
____Without package, mint, complete [3:37] 8.00
Lama Su and Clone Youth (03/10)
____Col. 2 [P4B11] 20.00
____Without package, mint, complete [3:41] 14.00
Mace Windu, Arena Confrontation (03/02)
____Col. 1 [P4B12] 20.00
____Without package, mint, complete [3:41] 8.00
Obi-Wan, Acklay Battle (03/01)
____Col. 1 [P4B13] 15.00
____Without package, mint, complete [3:41] 9.00
Padme Amidala, Droid Factory Chase (03/04)
____Col. 2 [P4B14] 20.00
____Without package, mint, complete [3:42] 8.00
R2-D2, Droid Factory Flight (03/09)
____Col. 1, long boosters [P4B15] 10.00
____Col. 1, short boosters 10.00
____Without package, mint, complete [3:42] 5.00
SP-4 and JN-66 (03/05)
____Col. 2, SP-4 has long codpiece [P4B16] 12.00
____Col. 2, SP-4 has short codpiece 12.00
____Without package, mint, complete [3:40] 8.00
Tusken Raider, Tatooine Camp Ambush (03/06)
____Col. 2 [P4B17] 18.00
____Col. 2, rubberbanded right arm 18.00
____Without package, mint, complete [3:42] 14.00
Yoda and Chian, Padawan Training (03/15)
____Col. 2, correct UPC 0-76930-84969-9 ....8.00
____Col. 2, no. 15, wrong UPC 0-76390-84969-7, long cane tray [P4B18] 8.00
____Col. 2, rounded UPC correction sticker, cane tray shortened 8.00
____Col. 2, square UPC correction sticker 8.00
____Without package, mint, complete 6.00

Hasbro, Canada
Blue cards. Starburst pattern on background. Tri-language.
____Anakin Skywalker Secret Ceremony 10.00
____Boba Fett The Pitt of Carcoon 18.00
____Chewbacca Mynock Hunt 10.00
____Han Solo Hoth Rescue..10.00
____Mace Windu Arena Confrontation 20.00
____Obi-Wan Kenobi Ackley Battle............................15.00
____R2-D2 Droid Factory Flight 10.00
____Yoda Jedi Master 12.00

Toys: Action Figures – 2002 – 2004 (Saga 2004)

Hasbro
Gold bar on blue card. 2003 – 2004 transition figures.
Aayla Secura
____(03/11) [P4C01]..10.00
____Without package, mint, complete [3:39] 8.00
Achk Med-Beq, Coruscant Outlander Club
____(03/37), col. 2 [P4C02] 10.00
____Without package, mint, complete [3:39] 8.00
Anakin Skywalker, Secret Ceremony
____(03/07), no col. [P4C03] 8.00
____Without package, mint, complete [3:39] 8.00
Ashla and Jempa
____(03/16), no col. [P4C04] 8.00
____Without package, mint, complete [3:39] 6.00
Ayy Vida, Outlander Nightclub Patron
____(03/38), col. 2, no rubberbands in bubble [P4C05]..10.00
____(03/38), col. 2, rubberband secures arms in bubble..10.00
____Without package, mint, complete [3:39] 8.00
Bail Organa, Alderaan Senator
____(03/33), col. 2 [P4C06] 10.00
____Without package, mint, complete [3:39] 8.00
Bariss Offee
____(03/12), no col. [P4C07] 12.00
____Without package, mint, complete [3:39] 6.00
Boba Fett, Pit of Carkoon
____(03/08), green [P4C08] 17.00
____Without package, mint, complete [3:36] 8.00
C-3PO, Tatooine Ambush
____(03/21), col. 1 [P4C09] 20.00
____Without package, mint, complete [3:36] 18.00
Coleman Trebor
____(03/24), col. 2 [P4C10] 25.00
____Without package, mint, complete [3:40] 14.00
Darth Maul, Theed Hangar Duel
____(03/25), col. 2 [P4C11] 10.00
____(03/25), col. 2, insert says no. 23........................10.00
____Without package, mint, complete [3:40] 3.00
Darth Vader, Death Star Clash
____(03/32), col. 2 [P4C12] 15.00
____Without package, mint, complete [3:36] 10.00
Darth Vader, Throne Room Duel
____(03/18), col. 1 [P4C13] 20.00
____(03/18), no col. [P4C14] 20.00

P4B16

P4B17

P4B18

____Without package, mint, complete [3:36] 15.00
Elan Sleazebaggano, Outlander Nightclub Encounter
____(03/40), col. 2, with ears [P4C15]........................15.00
____(03/40), col. 2, without ears [P4C16] 15.00
____Without package, mint, complete 12.00
Han Solo, Flight to Alderaan
____(03/27), col. 2 [P4C17] 8.00
____(03/27), col. 2, insert says no. 25 ....8.00
____Without package, mint, complete [3:37] 2.00
Han Solo, Hoth Rescue
____(03/13), no col., brown coat [P4C18] 15.00
____Without package, mint, complete [3:37] 8.00
Imperial Dignitary Janus Greejatus
____(03/35), col. 2 [P4C19] 12.00
____Without package, mint, complete [3:37] 10.00
Imperial Dignitary Kren Blista-Vanee
____(03/41), col. 2 [P4C20] 10.00
____Without package, mint, complete [3:38] 8.00

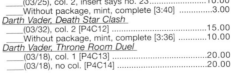

P4C01

P4C02

P4C03

P4C04

P4C05

P4C06

P4C07

P4C08

P4C09

P4C10

P4C11

P4C12

P4C13   P4C14   P4C15   P4C15 detail   P4C16 detail   P4C17   P4C18   P4C19   P4C20

P4C21   P4C22   P4C23   P4C24   P4C25   P4C26   P4C27   P4C28   P4C29

Jango Fett, Kamino Escape
____(03/20), col. 1, no arrow on back of card 12.00
____(03/20), col. 1, yellow arrow printed on back of card [P4C21].....................................12.00
____(03/20), col. 1, yellow arrow sticker on back of card.....................................12.00
____Without package, mint, complete [3:40] 5.00
Lt. Dannl Faytonni, Corsucant Outlander Club
____(03/29), col. 2, pink cup [P4C22] 15.00
____Without package, mint, complete [3:41] 13.00
Luke Skywalker, Tatooine Encounter
____(03/31), col. 2, clear base [P4C23].....................10.00
____Without package, mint, complete [3:38] 8.00
Luke Skywalker, Throne Room Duel
____(03/17), col. 1, left hand gloved [P4C24] 30.00
____(03/17), col. 1, right hand gloved [P4C25] 15.00
____(03/17), no col., right hand gloved 15.00
____Without package, mint, complete [3:38] 9.00
Obi-Wan Kenobi, Outlander Nightclub Encounter
____(03/39), col. 2 [P4C26] 10.00
____Without package, mint, complete [3:41] 8.00
Padme Amidala, Lars' Homestead
____(03/36), col. 2 [P4C27] 20.00
____Without package, mint, complete [3:41] 12.00
Padme Amidala, Secret Ceremony
____(03/22), col. 2 [P4C28] 20.00
____(03/22), col. 2, rubberband around left arm........20.00
____Without package, mint, complete [3:41] 12.00
Princess Leia Organa, Imperial Captive
____(03/26), col. 2 [P4C29] 10.00
____(03/26), col. 2, bubble tab around right hip 10.00
____Without package, mint, complete 2.00
Snowtrooper, Battle of Hoth
____(03/19), col. 1 ....15.00
____(03/19), no col. [P4C30] 15.00

____Without package, mint, complete [3:38] 10.00
Stormtrooper, concept
____(03/34), col. 2, fans' choice no. 4 [P4C31] 50.00
____Without package, mint, complete [3:39] 40.00
The Emperor, Throne Room
____(03/30), col. 2 [P4C32].....................................25.00
____Without package, mint, complete [3:39] 20.00
WA-7, Dexter's Diner
____(03/28), col. 2 [P4C33] 12.00
____Without package, mint, complete [3:42] 10.00
Wat Tambor
____(03/23), col. 2 [P4C34] 18.00
____Without package, mint, complete [3:42] 14.00
Yoda and Chian, Padawan Lightsaber Training
____(03/15), no col. [P4C35] 8.00
____Without package, mint, complete [3:49] 6.00

Gold bar on blue card. Hall of Fame assortment.
Anakin Skywalker, Geonosis Hanger Duel
____Age warning printed on front [P4C36] 8.00
____Age warning sticker on front [P4C37] 8.00
____Without package, mint, complete [3:39] 2.00
C-3PO, Death Star Rescue
____Clear base [P4C38] 12.00
____Dark base [P4C39] 12.00
____Without package, mint, complete [3:36] 10.00
Chewbacca, Escape from Hoth
____[P4C40] 8.00
____Without package, mint, complete [3:36] 5.00
Darth Maul, Theed Hanger Duel
____Clear base [P4C41] 10.00
____Dark base 10.00
____Without package, mint, complete [3:40] 3.00
Darth Vader, Death Star Clash
____Clear base [P4C42] 10.00

____Dark base 10.00
____Without package, mint, complete [3:36] 10.00
Han Solo, Flight to Alderaan
____Clear base [P4C43] 10.00
____Dark base [P4C44] 10.00
____Without package, mint, complete [3:37] 2.00
Luke Skywalker, Tatooine Encounter
____Clear base [P4C45] 10.00
____Dark base [P4C46] 10.00
____Without package, mint, complete [3:38] 8.00
Obi-Wan Kenobi, Corsucant Chase
____[P4C47]..10.00
____Without package, mint, complete [3:41] 2.00
Princess Leia Organa, Death Star Captive
____Clear base [P4C48] 10.00
____Dark base [P4C49] 10.00
____Without package, mint, complete 2.00
R2-D2, Tatooine Mission
____Clear base [P4C50] 10.00
____Dark base [P4C51] 10.00
____Without package, mint, complete [3:38] 5.00
Stormtrooper, Death Star Chase
____[P4C52]...20.00
____Without package, mint, complete 14.00
Yoda, Battle of Geonosis
____[P4C53]...10.00
____Without package, mint, complete [3:42] 5.00

Gold bar on blue cardback.
Admiral Ozzel, Executor Assault
____(04/16) [P4C54]...12.00
____Without package, mint, complete [3:36] 10.00
Bossk, Executor Meeting
____(04/18) [P4C55]...12.00
____Without package, mint, complete [3:36] 8.00

P4C30   P4C31   P4C32   P4C33   P4C34   P4C35   P4C36   P4C37 detail   P4C38

P4C39   P4C40   P4C41   P4C42   P4C43   P4C44   P4C45   P4C46   P4C47

 P4C48
 P4C49
 P4C50
 P4C51
 P4C52
 P4C53
 P4C54
 P4C55
 P4C56

 P4C57
 P4C58
 P4C59
 P4C60
 P4C61
 P4C62
 P4C63
 P4C64
 P4C65

 P4C66
 P4C67
 P4C68
 P4C69
 P4C70
 P4C71
 P4C72
 P4C73
 P4C74

Captain Antilles
___(04/15) [P4C56]...15.00
___Without package, mint, complete [3:36] 12.00

Dengar, Executor Meeting
___(04/17) [P4C57]...10.00
___Without package, mint, complete [3:37] 7.00

Dutch Vander (Gold Leader)
___(04/13) [P4C58]...15.00
___Without package, mint, complete [3:37] 12.00

General Jan Dodonna
___(04/12) [P4C59]...10.00
___Without package, mint, complete [3:37] 8.00

General Madine
___(04/20) [P4C60]...25.00
___Without package, mint, complete [3:37] 21.00

Han Solo, Endor Strike
___(04/19) [P4C61]...15.00
___Without package, mint, complete [3:37] 12.00

Hoth Trooper, Hoth Evacuation
___(04/01) [P4C62]...8.00
___Without package, mint, complete [3:37] 4.00

J'Quille
___(04/09) [P4C63]...15.00
___Without package, mint, complete [3:37] 13.00

Lando Calrissian, Death Star Attack
___(04/21) [P4C64]...20.00
___Without package, mint, complete [3:38] 16.00

Lando Calrissian, skiff guard disguise
___(04/07) [P4C65]...7.00
___Without package, mint, complete [3:38] 2.00

Luke Skywalker, Holographic
___(04/11) [P4C66]...12.00
___Without package, mint, complete [3:38] 8.00

Luke Skywalker, Hoth Attack
___(04/03) [P4C67]...8.00

___Without package, mint, complete [3:38] 5.00

Luke Skywalker, Jabba's Palace
___(04/04) [P4C68]...18.00
___Without package, mint, complete [3:38] 14.00

R-3PO, Hoth Evacuation
___(04/02) [P4C69]...10.00
___Without package, mint, complete 8.00

R1-G4
___(04/06) [P4C70]...15.00
___Without package, mint, complete [3:38] 10.00

R2-D2, Jabba's Sail Barge
___(04/05) [P4C71]...8.00
___Without package, mint, complete [3:38] 6.00

Rappertunie
___(04/08) [P4C72]...10.00
___Without package, mint, complete [3:38] 6.00

Tanus Spijek
___(04/10) [P4C73]...12.00
___Without package, mint, complete [3:39] 10.00

TIE Fighter Pilot
___(04/14) [P4C74]...12.00
___Without package, mint, complete [3:39] 8.00

Hasbro, Canada
Gold bar on blue card. Tri-language.
___Admiral Ozzel [3:82] 12.00
___Bossk [3:82] 12.00
___C-3PO, Death Star Rescue [3:82]...................12.00
___Captain Antilles [3:82] 15.00
___Chewbacca, Escape from Hoth [3:83] 8.00
___Darth Maul [3:83]...10.00
___Darth Vader, Death Star Clash [3:83] 10.00
___Dengar [3:83]...10.00
___Dutch Vander, Gold Leader [3:83] 15.00
___General Jan Dodonna [3:83] 10.00

___General Madine [3:83] 25.00
___Han Solo, Endor Strike [3:83]...........................15.00
___Han Solo, Flight to Alderaan [3:83] 2.00
___Hoth Trooper [3:83]...8.00
___J'Quille [3:83]..15.00
___Lando Calrissian, Death Star Attack [3:83] 20.00
___Lando Calrissian, Jabba's Sail Barge [3:83].........7.00
___Luke Skywalker, Holographic [3:83]...................12.00
___Luke Skywalker, Hoth Attack [3:83] 8.00
___Luke Skywalker, Jabba's Palace [3:83] 18.00
___Luke Skywalker, Tatooine Encounter [3:83] 10.00
___Obi-Wan Kenobi Coruscant Chase [3:83] 10.00
___Princess Leia Organa [3:83] 10.00
___R2-D2, Jabba's Sail Barge [3:83] 8.00
___R2-D2, Tatooine Mission [3:83] 10.00
___Rappertunie [3:83] 10.00
___Stormtrooper [3:83]...20.00
___Tanus Spijec [3:83]...12.00
___TIE Fighter Pilot [3:83] 12.00
___Yoda, Battle of Geonosis [3:83] 10.00

Toys: Action Figures –
2002 – 2004 (Saga) Deluxe / Ultra

Hasbro
___Anakin Skywalker with Force-Flipping Attack!
[AFD01] 8.00
___Anakin Skywalker with Lightsaber Slashing Action
[AFD02]...7.00
___C-3PO with Droid Factory Assembly Line
[AFD03]...12.00
___Clone Trooper with Speeder Bike [AFD04] 20.00

 AFD01
 AFD02
 AFD03
 AFD04
 AFD05
 AFD06
 AFD07

Toys: Action Figures – 2002 – 2004

AFD08   AFD09   AFD10   AFD11   AFD12   AFD13   AFD14

AFD15   AFD16   AFD17   AFD18   AFD19   AFD20   AFD21

AFD22   AFD23   AFD24   AFD25   AFD26

____Obi-Wan Kenobi, Kamino Confrontation [AFD26] 16.00

Hasbro, Canada

____Anakin Skywalker, Force-Flipping [3:84] 10.00
____Anakin Skywalker, Lightsaber Attack [3:84] 15.00
____C-3PO, Droid Factory [3:84] 15.00
____Clone Trooper with Speeder Bike [3:84] 10.00
____Darth Tyranus, Force-Flipping [3:84] 10.00
____Flying Geonosian with Attack Pod [3:84]............14.00
____Jango Fett, Electronic Jetpack [3:85] 15.00
____Mace Windu, Blast-Apart Battle Droid [3:85] 15.00
____Obi-Wan Kenobi, Force Flipping [3:85] 10.00
____Yoda with Force Powers [3:85] 15.00

____Darth Tyranus with Force-Flipping Attack! [AFD05] 7.00
____Flying Geonosian with Attack Pod [AFD06]........15.00
____Jango Fett with Electronic Jetpack and Snap-On Armor! [AFD07] 8.00
____Jango Fett with Electronic Jetpack and Snap-On Armor!, no pegholes in feet 35.00
____Jango Fett, Kamino Showdown [AFD08]............12.00
____Mace Windu with Blast-Apart (red) Battle Droid, red droid on header card [AFD09] 15.00
____Mace Windu with Blast-Apart (white) Battle Droid, red droid on header card [AFD10] 40.00
____Mace Windu with Blast-Apart (white) Battle Droid, white droid on header card [AFD11] 10.00
____Mace Windu with Blast-Apart (white) Battle Droid, white droid on header card, no pegholes in feet 25.00
____Obi-Wan Kenobi with Force-Flipping Attack! [AFD12] 6.00

____Obi-Wan Kenobi, Kamino Showdown [AFD13] 12.00
____Spider Droid [AFD14] 20.00
____Super Battle Droid Builder [AFD15] 15.00
____Yoda with Force Powers [AFD16] 12.00

Patrons with Cantina Bar Sections. Wal-mart exclusives.
____Dr. Evazan [AFD17] 125.00
____Greedo [AFD18] 20.00
____Kitik Keed'kak [AFD19] 75.00
____Momaw Nadon [AFD20] 15.00
____Ponda Baba [AFD21] 15.00
____Wuher [AFD22] 125.00

Ultra.
____C-3PO with escape pod [AFD23] 20.00
____General Reikein with Yavin tactical screen [AFD24] 15.00
____Jango Fett, Kamino Confrontation [AFD25]........12.00

Toys: Action Figures – 2002 – 2004 (Saga) Multi-Packs

Hasbro

____4-pack, random figures, age warning sticker, KB Toys exclusive [ASM01] 20.00
____4-pack, random figures, KB Toys exclusive [ASM02] 20.00
____Imperial Forces, Toys R Us excl. [ASM03]..........40.00
____Jedi Warriors, Toys R Us exclusive [ASM04]......30.00
____Skirmish at at Carkoon, Toys R Us exclusive [ASM05] 40.00
____The Battle of Hoth, Tauntaun's horn broken [ASM06] 45.00
____The Battle of Hoth, Tauntaun's horn not broken [ASM07] 45.00

ASM01   ASM02   ASM03   ASM04   ASM05   ASM06

ASM07 detail   ASM08   ASM09   ASM10   ASM11

ASM12

ASM13

ASM14

ASM15

____Ultimate Bounty, Bossk has shoulder emblems, Toys R Us exclusive [ASM08].....................................30.00
____Ultimate Bounty, Bossk missing shoulder emblems, Toys R Us exclusive 55.00

Death Star Trash Compactor Scene 2-packs, Wal-mart exclusives.
____#1 Luke Skywalker and Han Solo [ASM09]........45.00
____#2 Princess Leia and Chewbacca [ASM10] 45.00

EPII 2-packs. Clear plastic case with barcode stickers covering Hasbro barcodes, and round Bonus sticker. KMart exclusive.
____Anakin Duel / Anakin Peasant 14.00
____Anakin Skywalker / Obi-Wan Kenobi.................14.00
____Clone Trooper / Anakin Skywalker.....................14.00
____Jango Fett / Yoda [ASM11].................................14.00
____Obi-Wan Kenobi / Jango Fett 14.00
____Yoda / Clone Trooper 14.00

EPII 2-packs. Clear plastic case with barcode stickers covering Hasbro barcodes. BJ's Wholesale Club exclusive.
____Clone Trooper / Anakin Skywalker – Hangar Duel 18.00
____Jango Fett – Kamino Escape / C-3PO................18.00
____Mace Windu / Jango Fett – Final Battle 18.00
____Obi-Wan Kenobi – Super Battle Droid...............18.00
____Obi-Wan Kenobi / Zam Wesell..........................18.00
____Padme Amidala / Anakin Skywalker – Outland Peasant Disguise 18.00
____Padme Amidala / Kit Fisto 18.00
____R2-D2 / C-3PO...18.00
____Yoda / Count Dooku...18.00

Screen Scenes, 3-packs of figures posed.
____Geonosis War Room 1 [ASM12] 20.00
____Geonosis War Room 2 [ASM13] 20.00
____Jedi Council 1 [ASM14] 20.00
____Jedi Council 2 [ASM15] 20.00

Toys: Action Figures –
2003 – 2005 (Clone Wars)

Hasbro
Anakin Skywalker
____(03/42), glossy painted glove [ACW01] 10.00
____(03/42), matte painted glove 10.00
____Without package, mint, complete [3:43] 5.00
ARC Trooper
____(03/43), blue [ACW02] 25.00
____(03/43), red [ACW03] 60.00

____Without package, mint, complete [3:43] 18.00
Asajj Ventress
____(03/47) [ACW04]..30.00
____Without package, mint, complete [3:43] 24.00
Clone Trooper
____(03/50), kneeling [ACW05] 40.00
____(03/50), standing [ACW06] 40.00
____Without package, mint, complete [3:43] 28.00
Durge
____(03/46) [ACW07]..30.00
____Without package, mint, complete [3:43] 20.00
Kit Fisto
____(03/49) [ACW08]..30.00
____Without package, mint, complete [3:43] 22.00
Mace Windu
____(03/48) [ACW09]..20.00
____Without package, mint, complete [3:43] 14.00
Obi-Wan Kenobi
____(03/45) [ACW10]..10.00
____Without package, mint, complete [3:43] 5.00

ACW01

ACW02

ACW03

ACW04

ACW05

ACW06

ACW07

ACW08

ACW09

ACW10

ACW11

ACW12

ACW12 detail

ACW13

ACW14

ACW15

ACW16

ACW17

ACW18

ACW19

ACW20

ACW21

ACW22

ACW23

ACW24

ACW25

ACW26

ACW27

ACW28

ACW29

ACW30

ACW31

ACW32

Toys: Action Figures – 2003 – 2005

CVP01

CVP02

CVP03

CVP04

Saesee Tiin
____(03/51) [ACW11] 25.00
____Without package, mint, complete [3:43] 18.00
Yoda
____(03/44) [ACW12] 10.00
____(03/44), top of saber handle unpainted 10.00
____Without package, mint, complete [3:43] 6.0 0

Animation-style figures, Target exclusives.
Anakin Skywalker
____[ACW13] 12.00
____Without package, mint, complete [3:43] 8.00
Anakin Skywalker, duel
____[ACW14] 10.00
____Without package, mint, complete [3:43] 8.00
ARC Trooper
____[ACW15] 25.00
____Without package, mint, complete [3:43] 18.00
Asajj Ventress
____[ACW16] 15.00
____Season 3 package [ACW17] 15.00
____Without package, mint, complete [3:43] 12.00
Clone Trooper , blue
____Season 3 package [ACW18] 30.00
____Without package, mint, complete [3:43] 20.00
Clone Trooper, red
____Season 3 package [ACW19] 30.00
____Without package, mint, complete [3:43] 20.00
Clone Trooper, white
____[ACW20] 20.00
____Without package, mint, complete [3:43] 15.00
Clone Trooper, yellow
____Season 3 package [ACW21] 30.00
____Without package, mint, complete [3:43] 22.00
Count Dooku
____[ACW22] 10.00
____Season 3 package [ACW23] 10.00
____Without package, mint, complete [3:43] 6.00
Durge
____[ACW24] 10.00
____Season 3 package [ACW25] 10.00
____Without package, mint, complete [3:43] 8.00
General Grievous
____Season 3 package [ACW26] 25.00
____Without package, mint, complete [3:43] 18.00
Mace Windu
____[ACW27] 12.00
____Season 3 package [ACW28] 12.00
____Without package, mint, complete [3:43] 8.00
Obi-Wan Kenobi
____[ACW29] 12.00

____Season 3 package [ACW30] 12.00
____Without package, mint, complete [3:43] 8.00
Yoda
____[ACW31] 25.00
____Season 3 package [ACW32] 25.00
____Without package, mint, complete [3:43] 20.00

Hasbro, Canada
Animation-style figures, tri-language packaging.
____Anakin Skywalker 12.00
____ARC Trooper 25.00
____Clone Trooper, blue 30.00
____Clone Trooper, red 30.00
____Clone Trooper, yellow 30.00
____General Grevious 25.00

Toys: Action Figures –
2003 – 2005 (Clone Wars) Deluxe

Hasbro
Army of the Republic.
____Clone Trooper with Speeder Bike [CVP01] 20.00

Separatist Forces.
____Destroyer Droid Battle Launcher [CVP02] 12.00
____Durge with Swoop Bike [CVP03] 20.00
____Spider Droid [CVP04] 15.00

Toys: Action Figures –
2003 – 2005 (Clone Wars) Multi-Packs

Hasbro
2-pks. Clone Wars figure with bonus Clone Trooper.
____Anakin Skywalker / Clone Trooper Lieutenant
    [ACD01] 30.00
____Arc Trooper / Clone Trooper [ACD02] 30.00
____Arc Trooper, unpainted right shoulder / Clone
    Trooper 30.00
____Yoda / Clone Trooper Commander [ACD03] 25.00

3-packs.
____Clone Trooper Army [ACD04]...........................40.00
____Clone Trooper Army, blue [ACD05] 50.00
____Clone Trooper Army, green [ACD06] 40.00
____Clone Trooper Army, red [ACD07] 45.00
____Clone Trooper Army, yellow [ACD08].................45.00

____Droid Army [ACD11].......................................20.00
____Jedi Army [ACD09]...30.00
____Jedi Army, clone trooper side panel [ACD10] 45.00

4-packs. Super articulated clones with limited edition poster. Entertainment Earth exclusives.
____Blue, green, red, yellow 30.00
____Blue, green, red, yellow all battle damaged 40.00
____White x 4 ....25.00
____White x 4 all battle damaged 25.00

Toys: Action Figures – 2004 – 2005
(Original Trilogy Collection)

Hasbro
Bib Fortuna
____(OTC31) [AT01] 15.00
____Without package, mint, complete 9.00
Boba Fett
____(OTC14) [AT02] 25.00
____Without package, mint, complete 8.00
Bossk
____(OTC28) [AT03] 10.00
____Without package, mint, complete 8.00
C-3PO
____(OTC13) [AT04] 15.00
____Without package, mint, complete 10.00
Chewbacca
____(OTC08) [AT05] 15.00
____Without package, mint, complete 5.00
Cloud Car Pilot, Bespin
____(OTC19) [AT06] 8.00
____Without package, mint, complete 6.00
Darth Vader (Death Star)
____(OTC34) [AT07] 25.00
____Without package, mint, complete 10.00
Darth Vader (Hoth)
____(OTC29) [AT08] 25.00
____Without package, mint, complete 18.00
Darth Vader
____(OTC10) [AT09] 25.00
____Without package, mint, complete 10.00
Emperor, Executor Transmission
____ShopStarWars.com exclusive [AT10] 28.00
____Without package, mint, complete 18.00
Gamorrean Guard
____(OTC30) [AT11] 15.00
____Without package, mint, complete 9.00
General Madine
____(OTC36) [AT12] 21.00
____Without package, mint, complete 21.00
Greedo
____(OTC22) [AT13] 20.00
____Without package, mint, complete 15.00
Han Solo (AT-ST Driver)
____(OTC35) [AT14] 25.00
____Without package, mint, complete 12.00
Han Solo
____(OTC07) [AT15] 15.00
____Without package, mint, complete 2.00
IG-88
____(OTC27) [AT16] 15.00
____Without package, mint, complete 8.00

ACD01

ACD02

ACD03

ACD04

ACD05

ACD06

ACD07

ACD08

ACD09

ACD10

ACD11

AT01 AT02 AT03 AT04 AT05 AT06 AT07 AT08 AT09

AT10 AT11 AT12 AT13 AT14 AT15 AT16 AT17 AT18

AT19 AT20 AT21

Imperial Trooper
____(OTC38) [AT17] 20.00
____Without package, mint, complete 14.00
Jawas
____(OTC24) [AT18] 25.00
____Without package, mint, complete 18.00
Lando Calrissian (General)
____(OTC37) [AT19] 15.00
____Without package, mint, complete 9.00
Lando Calrissian (Skiff Guard)
____(OTC32) [AT20] 10.00
____Without package, mint, complete 7.00
Lobot, Bespin
____(OTC20) [AT21] 8.00
____Without package, mint, complete 7.00
Luke Skywalker (Bespin Gear)
____(OTC26) [AT22] 12.00
____Without package, mint, complete 9.00
Luke Skywalker, Dagobah
____(OTC01) [AT23] 12.00
____Handstand packaging 25.00
Luke Skywalker, Jedi
____(OTC06) [AT24] 15.00
____Without package, mint, complete 10.00
Luke Skywalker, X-Wing pilot
____(OTC05) [AT25] 16.00
____Without package, mint, complete 10.00
Obi-Wan Kenobi
____(OTC15) [AT26] 15.00
____Without package, mint, complete 9.00
Obi-Wan Kenobi Spirit, Dagobah
____(OTC03) [AT27] 15.00
____Without package, mint, complete 7.00
Princess Leia
____(OTC09) [AT28] 20.00
____Without package, mint, complete 15.00

Princess Leia (Slave Outfit)
____(OTC33) [AT29] 12.00
____Without package, mint, complete 9.00
Princess Leia, Bespin
____(OTC18) [AT30] 12.00
____Without package, mint, complete 9.00
R2-D2
____(OTC12) [AT31] 15.00
____Without package, mint, complete 8.00
R2-D2, Dagobah
____(OTC04) [AT32] 15.00
____Without package, mint, complete 10.00
Scout Trooper
____(OTC11) [AT33] 20.00
____Without package, mint, complete 10.00
Snowtrooper
____(OTC25) [AT34] 20.00
____Without package, mint, complete 10.00
Stormtrooper
____(OTC16) [AT35] 25.00
____Without package, mint, complete 10.00
TIE Fighter Pilot
____(OTC21) [AT36] 20.00
____Without package, mint, complete 8.00
Tusken Raider
____(OTC23) [AT37] 15.00
____Without package, mint, complete 10.00
Wedge Antilles
____Shop.StarWars.com exclusive 15.00
____Without package, mint, complete 8.00
Wicket
____(OTC17) [AT38] 20.00
____Without package, mint, complete 18.00
Yoda, Dagobah
____(OTC02) [AT39] 10.00
____Without package, mint, complete 5.00

Hasbro, Canada
Black cardback with starbust pattern and no printed scene behing the figure.
____Bib Fortuna..............................15.00
____Boba Fett [3:88] 25.00
____Bossk [3:88] 10.00
____C-3PO [3:88]...........................15.00
____Chewbacca [3:88] 15.00
____Cloud Car Pilot, Bespin [3:88] 8.00
____Darth Vader [3:88].....................25.00
____Gamorrean Guard 15.00
____General Madine 20.00
____Greedo [3:88] 20.00
____Han Solo [3:88]........................15.00
____Han Solo (AT-ST Driver) 25.00
____IG-88 [3:88]............................15.00
____Imperial Trooper 20.00
____Jawas [3:88] 25.00
____Lando Calrissian (General) 12.00
____Lando Calrissian (Skiff Guard) 10.00

AT22 AT23 AT24 AT25 AT26 AT27 AT28 AT29 AT30

AT31 AT32 AT33 AT34 AT35 AT36 AT37 AT38 AT39

Toys: Action Figures – 2004 – 2005

AOP01

AOP02

AOP02 rear

AOP03

AOP04

AOP05

AOP06

AOP07

____Lobot, Bespin [3:88] 8.00
____Luke Skywalker, Dagobah [3:88] 12.00
____Luke Skywalker, Jedi Knight [3:88] 15.00
____Luke Skywalker, X-Wing pilot [3:88] 16.00
____Luke Skywlker, Bespin [3:88] 12.00
____Obi-Wan Kenobi [3:88]......................................15.00
____Princess Leia [3:88] 20.00
____Princess Leia (Slave Outfit) 12.00
____Princess Leia, Bespin [3:88]...............................12.00
____R2-D2 [3:88] 15.00
____R2-D2, Dagobah [3:88] 15.00
____Scout Trooper [3:88]..20.00
____Snowtrooper [3:88]..20.00
____Spirit Obi-Wan [3:88] 15.00
____Stormtrooper [3:88] 25.00
____TIE Fighter Pilot [3:88] 20.00
____Tusken Raider [3:88]..15.00
____Wicket [3:88] 20.00
____Yoda [3:88] 10.00

AOP08

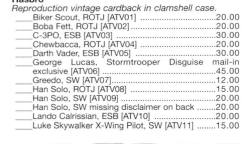

AOP09

Toys: Action Figures –
2004 – 2005 (Original Trilogy Collection)
Multi-Packs

Hasbro

____Bounty Hunter 7-pack, Diamond Comics exclusive
[AOP01] 35.00
____Endor Ambush [AOP02]....................................40.00
____Naboo Final Combat [AOP03] 20.00

Screen Scenes, 3-packs of figures posed.
____Jedi Council 1 [AOP04] 35.00
____Jedi Council 2 [AOP05] 35.00
____Jedi Council 3 [AOP06] 35.00
____Jedi Council 4 [AOP07] 35.00
____Mos Eisley Cantina 1 [AOP08] 40.00
____Mos Eisley Cantina 2 [AOP09] 40.00

Toys: Action Figures – 2004 – 2006
(Modern Vintage Packaging)

Hasbro
Reproduction vintage cardback in clamshell case.
____Biker Scout, ROTJ [ATV01] 20.00
____Boba Fett, ROTJ [ATV02]..................................20.00
____C-3PO, ESB [ATV03]...30.00
____Chewbacca, ROTJ [ATV04] 20.00
____Darth Vader, ESB [ATV05] 30.00
____George Lucas, Stormtrooper Disguise mail-in
exclusive [ATV06] 45.00
____Greedo, SW [ATV07]..12.00
____Han Solo, ROTJ [ATV08] 15.00
____Han Solo, SW [ATV09] 20.00
____Han Solo, SW missing disclaimer on back 20.00
____Lando Calrissian, ESB [ATV10] 20.00
____Luke Skywalker X-Wing Pilot, SW [ATV11] 15.00

ATV01

ATV02

ATV03

ATV04   ATV05   ATV06   ATV07   ATV08   ATV09   ATV10   ATV11   ATV12

ATV13   ATV14   ATV15   ATV16   ATV17   ATV18   ATV19   ATV20 rear   ATV21

A9T01

A9T02

A9T03

A9T04

A9T05

A9T06

A9T07

A9T08

A9T09

A9T10

A9T11

A9T12

A9T13

____Luke Skywalker, SW [ATV12] 20.00
____Obi-Wan Kenobi, SW [ATV13] 10.00
____Obi-Wan Kenobi, SW missing disclaimer on back 10.00
____Princess Leia, SW 20.00
____Princess Leia, SW missing disclaimer on back [ATV14] 20.00
____R2-D2, ROTJ [ATV15].......................................15.00
____Sand People, SW [ATV16] 12.00
____Stormtrooper, ROTJ [ATV17] 20.00
____Yoda, ESB [ATV18] 15.00

Hasbro, Canada
____Biker Scout, ROTJ [ATV19] 25.00
____Greedo, SW 25.00
____Han Solo, ROTJ 25.00
____Luke Skywalker X-Wing Pilot, SW 25.00
____Sand People, SW..25.00

Hasbro, Japan
____C-3PO, ESB [ATV20] 12.00

Hasbro, UK
____Darth Vader, ESB Woolworths exclusive [ATV21] 35.00

Toys: Action Figures – 2005 – 2007 (Saga2) Battle Packs

Hasbro
____Assault on Hoth, TRU exclusive [A9T01]...........45.00
____Battle Above the Sarlacc [A9T02] 20.00
____Battle of Felucia 20.00
____Capture of Tantive IV 20.00
____Clone Attack on Coruscant, Target exclusive [A9T03] 50.00
____Imperial Throne Room, Kmart excl. [A9T04] 55.00
____Jedi Temple Assault, Kmart excl. [A9T05] 55.00
____Jedi Training on Dagobah 20.00
____Jedi vs. Darth Sidious [A9T06]...........................20.00
____Jedi vs. Sepratists [A9T07].................................20.00
____Jedi vs. Sith [A9T08]...25.00
____Mace Windu's Attack Battalion [A9T09] 20.00
____Rebel vs. Empire [A9T10]...................................25.00
____Sith Lord Attack [A9T11] 20.00
____Skirmish in the Senate, Target exclusive [A9T12] 25.00
____The Hunt for General Grievous, TRU exclusive [A9T13] 40.00

Toys: Action Figures – 2005 (Saga)

Hasbro
Chewbacca, Hoth Escape
____[AT101] 12.00
____Without package, mint, complete [3:36] 5.00
Dannik Jerriko, Cantina Encounter
____[AT102] 15.00
____Without package, mint, complete 9.00
Darth Vader, Death Star Hangar
____[AT103] 20.00
____Without package, mint, complete [3:36] 10.00
Feltipern Trevagg, Cantina Encounter
____[AT104] 14.00
____Without package, mint, complete 10.00
Han Solo, Mos Eisley Escape
____[3:37] 10.00
____Without package, mint, complete 2.00
Luke Skywalker, Dagobah Training
____[AT105] 15.00
____Without package, mint, complete 10.00
Myo, Cantina Encounter
____[AT106] 12.00
____Without package, mint, complete 9.00
Pablo Jill, Geonosis Arena
____[AT107] 24.00
____Without package, mint, complete 15.00
Queen Amidala, Celebration
____[AT108] 18.00
____Without package, mint, complete 10.00
Rabe, Queen's Chambers
____[AT109] 18.00
____Without package, mint, complete 10.00
Sandtrooper, Tatooine Search
____[AT110] 45.00
____Without package, mint, complete 16.00
Scout Trooper, Endor Raid
____[AT111] 25.00
____Without package, mint, complete 18.00
Sly Moore, Corsucant Senate
____[AT112] 18.00
____Without package, mint, complete 9.00
Stormtrooper, Death Star Attack
____[AT113] 25.00
____Without package, mint, complete 10.00
Yarua, Corsucant Senate
____[AT114] 17.00
____Without package, mint, complete 8.00
Yoda, Dagobah Training
____[AT115] 16.00
____Without package, mint, complete 5.00

AT101

AT102

AT103

AT104

AT105

AT106

AT107

AT108

AT109

AT110

AT111

AT112

AT113

AT114

AT115

Toys: Action Figures – 2005

A6T01

ATD01

ATD02

ATD03

ATD04

AT301

AT302

AT303

AT304

AT305

AT306

AT307

AT308

AT309

AT310

AT311

Hasbro, Canada
____Pablo Jill, Genosis Arena 7.00
____Rabe, Queens Chambers 7.00
____Sly Moore, Corsucant Senate 7.00
____Yarua, Corsucant Senate 7.00

Toys: Action Figures – 2005 (Earlybird)

Hasbro
____Mailer with certificate, ltd to 50,000 [A6T01]......45.00
____Mailer with certificate, extended offer 45.00
____Mailer with figures and packaging......................50.00

Toys: Action Figures – 2005 (Episode III Preview)

Hasbro
General Grievous
____[ATD01] 15.00
____Without package, mint, complete 9.00
R4-G9
____[ATD02] 15.00
____Without package, mint, complete 8.00
Tion Medon
____[ATD03] 15.00
____Without package, mint, complete 6.00
Wookiee Warrior
____[ATD04] 8.00
____Without package, mint, complete 6.00

Toys: Action Figures – 2005 (Episode III)

Hasbro
Aayla Secura, Hologram
____(#67) [AT301]..15.00
____Without package, mint, complete 11.00
Aayla Secura, Jedi Knight
____(#32) [AT302]..6.00
____Without package, mint, complete 5.00
Agen Kolar, Jedi Master
____(#20) [AT303]..6.00
____Without package, mint, complete 4.00
Anakin Skywalker, battle damage
____(#50) [AT304]..9.00
____Without package, mint, complete 7.00
Anakin Skywalker, Lightsaber Attack!
____(#2) With red lightsaber [AT305] 6.00
____(#2) With red Sith lightsaber [AT306] 9.00
____(#2) With red transparent Sith lightsaber 10.00
____Without package, mint, complete 4.00
Anakin Skywalker, Slashing Attack
____(#28) [AT307]..6.00
____(#28) With yellow eyes [AT308] 25.00
____Without package, mint, complete 5.00
Ask Aak
____(#46) [AT309]..12.00
____Without package, mint, complete 9.00
AT-RT Driver
____(#54) Brown and white mask [AT310]....................8.00
____(#54) Brown mask [AT311] 8.00
____Without package, mint, complete 6.00

AT-TE Tank Gunner, Clone Army
____(#38) [AT312] 8.00
____Without package, mint, complete 6.00
Bail Organa, Republic Senator
____(#15) [AT313] 5.00
____Without package, mint, complete 2.00
Battle Droid, Separatist Army
____(#17) [AT314] 8.00
____Without package, mint, complete 7.00
C-3PO, Protocol Droid
____(#18) [AT315] 8.00
____Without package, mint, complete 6.00
Captain Antilles
____(#51) [AT316] 9.00
____Without package, mint, complete 6.00
Cat Miin, Separatist
____(#62) [AT317] 9.00
____Without package, mint, complete 7.00
Chancellor Palpatine, Supreme Chancellor
____(#14) [AT318] 6.00
____Without package, mint, complete 3.00
Chewbacca, Wookiee Rage
____(#5) [AT319] 6.00
____Without package, mint, complete 3.00
Clone Commander, green highlights
____(#33) [AT320] 9.00
____Without package, mint, complete 8.00
Clone Commander, red highlights
____(#33) [AT321] 8.00
____Without package, mint, complete 7.00
Clone Pilot
____(#34) Black armor (#34) [AT322] 20.00
____(#34) White armor (#34) [AT323]........................15.00
____Without package, mint, complete 12.00

AT312

AT313

AT314

AT315

AT316

AT317

AT318

AT319

AT320

AT321

AT322

AT323

AT324

AT325

AT326

AT327

AT328

AT329

AT330

AT331

AT332

AT333

AT334

AT335

AT336

AT337

AT338

AT339

AT340

AT341

AT342

AT343

AT344

AT345

AT346

AT347

Clone Trooper super articulated
____(#41) [AT324] 8.00
____Without package, mint, complete 7.00

Clone trooper, Quick-Draw Attack
____(#6) [AT325] 8.00
____(#6) Red and white armor (#6) [AT326] 9.00
____Without package, mint, complete 5.00

Clone Trooper, Target exclusive with display case
____[AT327] 35.00
____Without package, mint, complete 26.00

Commander Bacara
____(#49) [AT328] 12.00
____Without package, mint, complete 10.00

Commander Bly, Battle Gear
____(#57) White shoulder joints (#57) 14.00
____(#57) Yellow shoulder joints (#57) [AT329] 14.00
____(#57) With battle damaged armor (#57) 14.00
____Without package, mint, complete 12.00

Commander Gree, Battle Gear
____(#59) [AT330] 18.00
____Without package, mint, complete 14.00

Count Dooku
____(#13) [AT331] 6.00
____Without package, mint, complete 5.00

Darth Vader Duel at Mustafar, Lava Reflection, Target exclusive
____[AT332] 30.00
____Without package, mint, complete 25.00

Darth Vader lava reflection, Target exclusive
____[AT333] 90.00
____Without package, mint, complete 35.00

Darth Vader, Lightsaber Attack!
____(#11) [AT334] 6.00
____Without package, mint, complete 4.00

Destroyer Droid
____(#44) [AT335] 8.00
____Without package, mint, complete 7.00

Emperor Palpatine, Firing Force Lightning
____(#12) [AT336] 6.00
____Without package, mint, complete 2.00

Emperor, Holographic, Toys R Us exclusive, in-store premium
____[AT337] 25.00
____Without package, mint, complete 14.00

General Grievous
____(#36) [AT338] 8.00
____Without package, mint, complete 8.00

General Grievous, Four Lightsabers Attack!
____(#9) [AT339] 8.00
____Without package, mint, complete 6.00

Grievous' Bodyguard silver, Battle Attack!
____(#60) [AT340] 15.00
____Without package, mint, complete 8.00

Grievous' Bodyguard, Battle Attack!
____(#8) [AT341] 8.00
____Without package, mint, complete 6.00

Ki-Adi Mundi, Jedi Master
____(#29) [AT342] 6.00
____Without package, mint, complete 5.00

Kit Fisto, Jedi Master
____(#22) [AT343] 8.00
____Without package, mint, complete 5.00

Luminara Unduli, Jedi Master
____(#31) [AT344] 8.00
____Without package, mint, complete 5.00

Mace Windu, Force Combat
____(#10) [AT345] 8.00
____Without package, mint, complete 5.00

Mas Amedda, Republic Senator
____(#40) [AT346] 6.00
____Without package, mint, complete 2.00

Meena Tills
____(#47) [AT347] 16.00
____Without package, mint, complete 12.00

Mon Mothma, Republic Senator
____(#24) [AT348] 6.00
____Without package, mint, complete 2.00

Mustafar Sentry
____(#56) [AT349] 8.00
____Without package, mint, complete 6.00

Neimoidian Commander, Separatist Bodyguard
____(#63) [AT350] 8.00
____Without package, mint, complete 6.00

Neimoidian Warrior
____(#42) [AT351] 8.00
____Without package, mint, complete 5.00

Obi-Wan Kenobi Duel at Mustafar, Lava Reflection, Target exclusive
____[AT352] 30.00
____Without package, mint, complete 25.00

Obi-Wan Kenobi, Jedi Kick!
____(#27) [AT353] 6.00
____Without package, mint, complete 4.00

Obi-Wan Kenobi, pilot gear
____(#56) [AT354] 8.00
____Without package, mint, complete 5.00

Obi-Wan Kenobi, Slashing Attack
____(#1) [AT355] 6.00
____Without package, mint, complete 4.00

Padme, Republic Senator
____(#19) [AT356] 8.00
____Without package, mint, complete 3.00

AT348

AT349

AT350

AT351

AT352

AT353

AT354

AT355

AT356

AT357

AT358

AT359

AT360

AT361

AT362

AT363

AT364

AT365

Toys: Action Figures – 2005

AT366 AT367 AT368 AT369 AT370 AT371 AT372 AT373 AT374

AT375 AT376 AT377 AT378 AT379 AT380 AT381 AT382 AT383

Palpatine
____ (#35) Blue lightsaber [AT357] 35.00
____ (#35) Red lightsaber (#35) [AT358] 8.00
____ Without package, mint, complete 4.00

Passel Argente, Separatist Leader
____ (#61) [AT359] 8.00
____ Without package, mint, complete 6.00

Plo Koon, Hologram
____ (#66) [AT360] 9.00
____ Without package, mint, complete 8.00

Plo Koon, Jedi Master
____ (#16) [AT361] 6.00
____ Without package, mint, complete 4.00

Polis Massan, Medic
____ (#39) [AT362] 6.00
____ Without package, mint, complete 2.00

R2-D2
____ (#48) [AT363] 8.00
____ Without package, mint, complete 4.00

R2-D2, Droid Attack
____ (#7) [AT364] 6.00
____ Without package, mint, complete 5.00

R4-P17
____ (#64) Package number 64 [AT365] 8.00
____ (#64), Package number 68 ....8.00
____ (#64), package numbered as 68 and stickered as number 64 ....8.00
____ Without package, mint, complete 7.00

Royal Guard, Senate Security
____ (#23) Blue [AT366] 8.00
____ (#23) Red [AT367] 10.00
____ Without package, mint, complete 8.00

Saesee Tiin, Jedi Master
____ (#30) [AT368] 6.00
____ Without package, mint, complete 5.00

Shaak-Ti, Jedi Master
____ (#21) [AT369] 6.00
____ Without package, mint, complete 3.00

Super Battle Droid, Firing Arm Blaster!
____ (#4) [AT370] 8.00
____ Without package, mint, complete 5.00

Tactical Ops Trooper
____ (#65) [AT371] 18.00
____ Without package, mint, complete 10.00

Tarfful, Firing Bowcaster
____ (#25) [AT372] 8.00
____ Without package, mint, complete 4.00

Tarkin, Govenor
____ (#45) [AT373] 16.00
____ Without package, mint, complete 11.00

Utapaun Warrior
____ (#53) [AT374] 8.00
____ Without package, mint, complete 5.00

Utapu Shadow Trooper, Target exclusive with display case
____ With display case 35.00
____ Without package, mint, complete 20.00

A4T01 A4T02 A4T03 A4T04 A4T05 A4T06

A4T07 A4T08 A4T09 A4T10 A4T11 A4T12

A4T13 A4T14 A4T15 A4T16 A4T17 A4T18

A5T01

A5T02

A5T03

A7T01

A7T02

A7T03

A7T04

A8T01

A8T02

____General Grievous, Secret Lightsaber Attack!
[A4T11] 15.00
____Obi-Wan Kenobi and Super Battle Droid, Force Jump
Attack [A4T12] 8.00
____Obi-Wan Kenobi and Super Battle Droid, Force Jump
Attack, Super Battle Droid's leg is packed separate
[A4T13] 8.00
____Spider Droid [A4T14] 15.00
____Stass Allie with BARC Speed [A4T15]..........15.00
____Vulture Droid (green cockpit) [A4T16] 15.00
____Vulture Droid (red cockpit) [A4T17] 15.00
____Yoda with Can Cell [A4T18] 12.00

Vader's Medical Droid, Chopper Droid
____(#37) [AT375] 6.00
____Without package, mint, complete 2.00
Wookiee Commando, Kashyyyk Battle Bash
____(#58) [AT376] 8.00
____Without package, mint, complete 4.00
Wookiee Heavy Gunner
____(#64) Wrong number.......................................10.00
____(#68) [AT377] 8.00
____(#68) Corrected with sticker 10.00
____Without package, mint, complete 4.00
Wookiee Warrior
____(#43) Brown [AT378] 8.00
____(#43) Wookiee Warrior tan [AT379] 8.00
____Without package, mint, complete 5.00
Yoda, Firing Cannon
____(#3) [AT380] 6.00
____Without package, mint, complete 3.00
Yoda, Holographic, Toys R Us exclusive
____[AT381] 30.00
____Without package, mint, complete 19.00
Yoda, Spinning Attack
____(#26) [AT382] 6.00
____Without package, mint, complete 4.00

Zett Jukassa
____(#52) [AT383] 8.00
____Without package, mint, complete 6.00

Toys: Action Figures –
2005 (Episode III) Action Assortment

Hasbro
____Anakin Skywalker, Changes to Darth Vader
[A4T01] 15.00
____Anakin Skywalker, Changes to Darth Vader,
accessories are packed visibly in bubble
[A4T02] 15.00
____Clone Trooper with jet pack [A4T03] 15.00
____Clone Troopers, 3-pack [A4T04] 20.00
____Clone Troopers, 3-pack blue [A4T05] 30.00
____Clone Troopers, 3-pack green [A4T06] 30.00
____Clone Troopers, 3-pack red [A4T07] 15.00
____Crab Droid [A4T08]...15.00
____Darth Vader with operating table [A4T09] 15.00
____Emperor Palpatine / Darth Sidious [A4T10].......10.00

Toys: Action Figures –
2005 (Episode III) Battle Arena

Hasbro
Lever controlled action figure battle action.
____Anakin Skywalker vs. Count Dooku [A5T01] 12.00
____Bodyguard vs Obi-Wan [A5T02] 12.00
____Sidious vs. Mace [A5T03] 12.00

Toys: Action Figures –
2005 (Episode III) Evolutions

Hasbro
____Anakin to Darth Vader [A7T01]..........................25.00
____Clone Trooper (yellow) to Stormtrooper, "Rebulic"
error [A7T02]...35.00
____Clone Trooper (yellow) to Stormtrooper, "Republic"
corrected 30.00
____Clone Trooper to Stormtrooper [A7T03] 30.00
____Sith Lords [A7T04] 30.00

A3S01

A3S02

A3S03

A3S04

A3S05 detail

A3S06 detail

A3S06

A3S07 detail

A3S08 detail

A3S08

A3S09

A3S10

A3S11

A3S11 detail

A3S12 detail

A3S13

A3S14

A3S15

Toys: Action Figures – 2005

 A3S16
 A3S17
 A3S18
 A3S19
 A3S20
 A3S21
 A3S22
 A3S23
 A3S24

 A3S25
 A3S26
 A3S27
 A3S28
 A3S29
 A3S30
 A3S31
 A3S32
 A3S34

 A3S33 detail
 A3S34 detail
 A3S35 detail
 A3S36
 A3S37
 A3S38
 A3S39
 A3S40
 A3S41

Toys: Action Figures –
2005 (Episode III) Multi-packs

Hasbro
____9-piece Collector Pack with silver Darth Vader, KB Toys exclusive [A8T01] 50.00

Mega Buy 2-packs. Exclusive to Toy R Us and BJ's Wholesale Clubs.
____Agen Kolar / Mon Mothma 10.00
____Ask Aak / Polis Massan 10.00
____Bail Organa / AT-TE Tank Gunner [A8T02] 10.00
____Bail Organa / Mon Mothma 10.00
____Ki-Adi-Mundi / Luminara Unduli 10.00
____Mas Amedda / Agen Kolar 10.00
____Meena Tillis / Bail Organa 10.00
____Meena Tillis / Mon Mothma 10.00
____Mon Mothma / Count Dooku 10.00

____Mon Mothma / Luminara Undulli 10.00
____Polis Massan / Vader's Medical Droid 10.00
____R2-D2 / Emperor Palpatine 10.00
____Saesee Tiin / Plo Koon 10.00
____Shaak Ti / Agen Kolar 10.00
____Tarkin / Mon Mothma 10.00

Toys: Action Figures –
2006 (Saga Collection)

Hasbro
____Anakin Skywalker, ROTS (#25) [A3S01] 8.00
____AT-AT Driver (#09) [A3S02] 10.00
____Aurra Sing, Walmart exclusive (#70).....................8.00
____Barada (#04) [A3S03] 8.00
____Battle Droids 2-pack (#62) 8.00
____Bib Fortuna (#03) [A3S04]....................................6.00

____Boba Fett, jets in front (#06) [A3S05].................12.00
____Boba Fett, jets in back (#06) [A3S06] 14.00
____C-3PO, Battle of Endor, painted joints (#42) [A3S07] 8.00
____C-3PO, Battle of Endor, unpainted joints (#42) [A3S08] 8.00
____C-3PO, Battle of Geonosis (#17) [A3S09] 6.00
____C-3PO, Battle of Geonosis, battle droid head (#17) [A3S10] 6.00
____Chewbacca, Cloud City Escape (#54) 6.00
____Chewbacca, large shoulder ring connector (#05) [A3S11] 6.00
____Chewbacca, small shoulder ring connector (#05) [A3S12] 6.00
____Chief Chirpa (#39) [A3S13].................................12.00
____Clone Commander Appo (#64)................................8.00
____Clone Commander Cody (#24) [A3S14] 14.00
____Clone Commander Cody hologram (#56) 8.00
____Clone Trooper 442nd Siege Battalion (#57) 6.00
____Clone Trooper combat engineer (#69) 8.00

 A3S42
 A3S43
 A3S44
 A3S45
 A3S46
 A3S47
 A3S48
 A3S49
 A3S50

 A3S51
 A3S52
 A3S53
 A3S54
 A3S55
 A3S56
 A3S57
 A3S58
 A3S59

A3S60

A3S61

A3S62

A3S63

A3S64 detail

A3S65 detail

A3S66 detail

A3S66

A3S67

A3S68

A3S69

A3S70

A3S71

A3S72

A3S73

A3S74

A3S75

A3S76

A3S77

A3S78

A3S79

A3S80

A3S81

A3S82

A3S83

A3S84

A3S85

A3S86

A3S87

A3S88

A3S89

A3S90

A3S91

____Clone Trooper Fifth Fleet Security (#59)...............6.00
____Clone Trooper Sergeant (#60)..........................6.00
____Clone Trooper, ROTS (#26) [A3S15]....................10.00
____Darth Maul hologram (#48) [A3S16] 6.00
____Darth Maul Sith Training (#53) 6.00
____Darth Vader, Bespin (#38) [A3S17] 8.00
____Darth Vader, Emperor's Wrath (#45) 6.00
____Darth Vader, Hoth, lightsaber down (#13) [A3S18]........6.00
____Darth Vader, Hoth (#13) [A3S19]........................6.00
____Death Star Gunner (#41) [A3S20]......................10.00
____Dud Bolt and Mars Guo (#51) [A3S21]...................8.00
____Elite Corps Clone Trooper (#65) 8.00
____Emperor Palpatine (#43) [A3S22]......................10.00
____Firespeeder pilot (#22) [A3S23]........................6.00
____Foul Moudama (#29) [A3S24]..........................8.00
____Garindan (#34) [A3S25]..............................6.00
____General Grievous (#30) [A3S26].......................8.00
____General Grievous, Demise [A3S27] 25.00
____General Rieekan (#12) [A3S28]........................6.00

____General Veers (#07) [A3S29]..........................6.00
____Graga The Grorgmonger (#52) [A3S30] 8.00
____Han Solo (#35) [A3S31]..............................6.00
____Han Solo carbonite (#02) [A3S32] 6.00
____Hem Dazon, blue & clear glass (#33) [A3S33] 8.00
____Hem Dazon, blue & white glass (#33) [A3S34]......8.00
____Hem Dazon, clear glass (#33) [A3S35]................8.00
____Holographic Obi-Wan Kenobi (#63) 6.00
____Jango Fett (#20) [A3S36]............................6.00
____Kabe and Nabrun Leids, Walmart exclusive (#72)........8.00
____Ki-Adi-Mundy holographic (#27) [A3S37]..............8.00
____Kit Fisto (#55) 8.00
____Kitik Keed'kak, Walmart exclusive (#71) 8.00
____Labria, Walmart exclusive (#73).....................8.00
____Luke Skywalker (#36) [A3S38] 6.00
____Luke Skywalker, Endor (#44) [A3S39]..................6.00
____Lushros Dofine (#23) [A3S40] 6.00
____Major Bren Derlin (#08) [A3S41] 5.00
____Moff Jerjerrod (#40) [A3S42]..........................8.00

____Momaw Nadon, blue and clear glass (#31) 8.00
____Momaw Nadon, blue and white glass (#31) [A3S43]........8.00
____Momaw Nadon, clear glass (#31)......................8.00
____Naboo Soldier (#50) [A3S44] 8.00
____Obi-Wan Kenobi, Naboo (#47) [A3S45] 6.00
____Obi-Wan Kenobi, ROTS (#28) [A3S46]................6.00
____Padme Amidala (#68) 8.00
____Poggle the Lesser (#18) [A3S47] 5.00
____Power Droid (#14) [A3S48] 6.00
____Princess Leia Boushh Disguise (#01) [A3S49] 6.00
____R2-D2 (#10) [A3S50]................................6.00
____R4-M6, Walmart exclusive (#74)......................8.00
____R5-J2 (#58) 6.00
____R4-K5 (#67) 8.00
____R5-D4 (#32) [A3S51]..............................10.00
____Rebel Trooper, black (#46) [A3S52]...................8.00
____Rebel Trooper, white (#46) [A3S53]...................8.00

A3S92

A3S93

A3S94

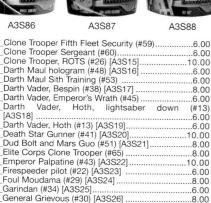

A3S95

A3S96

A3S97

A3S98

A3S99

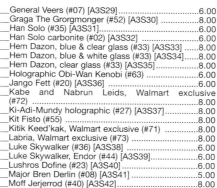

A3S100

A3S101

A3S102 sample

Toys: Action Figures – 2006

A3T01

____Rep Been (#49) [A3S54] 6.00
____Sandtrooper (#37) [A3S55] 10.00
____Scorch, Republic Commando (#21) [A3S56] 28.00
____Shadow Stormtrooper, Shop.StarWars.com exclusive
[A3S57]...15.00
____Snowtrooper (#11) [A3S58] 6.00
____Sora Bulq (#15) [A3S59] 6.00
____Sun Fac (#16) [A3S60] 6.00
____Super Battle Droid (#61) [A3S62]............6.00
____Yarael Poof (#66) [A3S60].......................8.00
____Yoda (#19) [A3S61] 6.00

Greatest Battles Collection.
____501st Legion Trooper [A3S62] 12.00
____AT-TE Tank Gunner [A3S63] 9.00
____C-3PO, corridor base, brown [A3S64] 7.00
____C-3PO, corridor base, gray [A3S65] 7.00
____C-3PO, lava base [A3S66] 20.00
____Clone Commander [A3S67] 9.00
____Count Dooku [A3S68].............................8.00
____Emperor Palpatine [A3S69] 10.00
____Kit Fisto [A3S70] 8.00
____Obi-Wan Kenobi [A3S71] 8.00
____Padme [A3S72] 6.00
____R2-D2 [A3S73] 7.00
____R4-G9 [A3S74] 8.00
____Royal Guard [A3S75] 9.00
____Shocktrooper [A3S76] 10.00
____Wookiee Warrior [A3S77] 6.00

Heroes and Villains Collection.
____Anakin Skywalker [A3S78] 8.00
____Chewbacca [A3S79] 7.00
____Clone Pilot [A3S80] 15.00
____Clone Trooper [A3S81] 15.00
____Commander Bacara [A3S82] 15.00
____Darth Vader [A3S83] 12.00
____Destroyer Droid [A3S84].......................10.00
____General Grievous [A3S85] 10.00
____Mace Windu [A3S86].................................8.00

A3T02

____Obi-Wan Kenobi [A3S87] 8.00
____R2-D2 [A3S88] 8.00
____Yoda [A3S89] 8.00

Separation of the Twins.
____Infant Leia Organa with Bail Organa [A3S90] 25.00
____Infant Luke Skywalker with Obi-Wan Kenobi
[A3S91]...25.00

Ultimate Galactic Hunt. Foil logo and base with silver - colored "holographic" figure.
____Anakin Skywalker [A3S92] 18.00
____AT-AT Driver [A3S93] 18.00
____Boba Fett [A3S94] 25.00
____Clone Commander Cody [A3S95] 25.00
____Darth Vader [A3S96] 25.00
____General Grievous [A3S97] 25.00
____Han Solo (Carbonite) [A3S98] 18.00
____Obi-Wan Kenobi [A3S99] 18.00
____Scorch (Republic Commando) [A3S100] 36.00
____Snowtrooper [A3S101] 16.00

Hasbro, Canada
Black background, tri-language.
____Any, each [A3S102]................................8.00

Hasbro, UK
____General Grievous, Demise of Grievous 25.00

Toys: Action Figures – 2006 – 2007
(Saga Collection Multi-packs)

Hasbro
____Death Star Briefing Room [A3T01]......................45.00

Hasbro, UK
____Episode III Gift Pack [A3T02] 65.00

Toys: Action Figures – 2007 (30th anniversary)

Hasbro
Anniversary cardback with character graphic and collector coin.
____Airborne Trooper [A4S01]..........................8.00
____Biggs Darklighter Academy Outfit 8.00
____Biggs Darklighter, Rebel Pilot [A4S02]..8.00
____Boba Fett animated 8.00
____C-3PO with Salacious Crumb 8.00
____CZ-3 ....8.00
____Darth Vader..8.00
____Death Star Trooper [A4S03]....................8.00
____Elis Helrot 8.00
____Galactic Marine [A4S04]..........................8.00
____Han Solo [A4S05]......................................8.00
____Hermi Odle 8.00
____Jawa and LIN Droid 8.00
____Luke Skywalker 8.00
____Luke Skywalker, ceremony outfit [A4S06] 8.00
____Luke Skywalker, Jedi 8.00
____M'iiyoom O'nith 8.00
____Mace Windu [A4S07]..................................8.00
____Mustafar Lava Miner [A4S08]...................8.00
____Obi-Wan Kenobi [A4S09]...........................8.00
____R2-D2 [A4S10]..8.00
____Rebel Honor Guard [A4S11] 8.00
____Stormtrooper, removable helmet 8.00
____Super Battle Droid [A4S12] 8.00
____Umpass-Stay 8.00

McQuarrie Concept Series. Anniversary cardback with character graphic and collector coin.
____Boba Fett [A4S13] 25.00
____Chewbacca 25.00
____Darth Vader..25.00
____Stormtrooper [A4S14].............................25.00

Toys: Action Figures – 2007 (30th anniversary) Multi-packs

Hasbro
Collector's tin sets.
____Episode 1: Darth Maul, Obi-Wan Kenobi, Qui-Gon
Jinn, R2-R9 [A5S01]................................30.00

A4S01   A4S02   A4S03   A4S04   A4S05   A4S06   A4S07   A4S08

A4S09   A4S10   A4S11   A5S12   A4S13   A4S14

Canada has an exclusive tri-language card style for their 30th anniversary figures.

This unique cardback features concept Darth Vader art behind each of the individual characters art used on the cardbacks for the international releases.

Canadian Sample

A5S01   A5S02   A5S03   A5S04

C3P01

C3P02

C3P03

C3P04

C3P05

C3P06

C3P07

C3P08

C3P09

C3P10

C3P11

C3P12

C3P13

C3P14

C3P15

C3P16

____Episode 2: Clone Trooper, Anakin Skywalker, Jango Fett, Count Dooku [A5S02] 30.00
____Episode 3: Mace Windu, Yoda, Anakin Skywalker, AT-RT Driver [A5S03] 30.00
____Episode 4: Sandtrooper, Princess Leia, Darth Vader, C-3PO [A5S04] 30.00
____Episode 5: Snowtrooper, Luke Skywalker, Han Solo, Chewbacca [A5S05].....................................30.00
____Episode 6: Scout Trooper, Darth Vader, Princess Leia, Rebel Commando [A5S06] 30.00
____Exclusive edition: Figrin D'an and the Modal Nodes, Walmart exclusive [A5S07]...............................35.00

Order 66 2-packs.
____Anakin Skywalker and Airborne Trooper 14.00
____Commander Neyo with Speeder Bike 14.00
____Darth Vader and Commander Bow 14.00
____Emperor and Shock Trooper 14.00
____Mace Windu and Galactic Marine 14.00
____Obi-Wan Kenobi and Clone Trooper 14.00
____Saleucami Trooper with Speeder Bike................14.00
____Yoda and Kashyyyk Trooper 14.00

Toys: Action Figures –
DVD Commerative Multi-packs

Hasbro
Clone Wars.
____I: Jedi Forces: Obi-Wan, Anakin, ARC Trooper [C3P01]...50.00
____I: Sith Attack Pack: Asajj Ventress, General Grievous, Durge [C3P02] 50.00
____II: Anakin Skywalker, Saesee Tiin, Clone Trooper [C3P03]..50.00
____II: Clone Commander Cody, Obi-Wan Kenobi, General Grievous [C3P04].......................................50.00

Classic Trilogy, The Saga Collection.
____A New Hope [C3P05]......................................35.00
____Empire Strikes Back [C3P06]............................35.00
____Return of the Jedi [C3P07]...............................35.00

Classic Trilogy.
____A New Hope [C3P08]......................................35.00
____Empire Strikes Back [C3P09]............................35.00
____Return of the Jedi [C3P10]...............................35.00

EPIII:ROTS.
____Anakin Skywalker, Mace Windu, Obi-Wan Kenobi [C3P11]..25.00
____Clone Troopers [C3P12]...................................25.00
____Emperor Palpatine, Darth Vader, Count Dooku [C3P13]..25.00

Hasbro, Canada
Classic Trilogy. Bi-language packaging.
____A New Hope [C3P14].....................................35.00
____Empire Strikes Back [C3P15]............................35.00
____Return of the Jedi [C3P16]...............................35.00

Toys: Action Figures – Exclusives

Big Alley
Custom figures to promote celebrity signings.
____Merceedes Ngoh, Aug 19, 2000 ....50.00
____Peter Mayhew, July 1, 2000..............................50.00
____Ray Park, Oct 7, 2000.....................................50.00

Disney / MGM
Disney exclusives. Droids from Star Tours.
____3T-RNE [AFE01] 25.00
____G-3 5LE [AFE02]..25.00
____MSE-1T [AFE03]...25.00

Hasbro
1998 Strategic Partners Meeting.
____Battle Droid on STAP, sneak preview 125.00

Astromech droid 5-pack.
____Series I: R3-T6, R3-T2, R2-C4, R4-A22, R2-Q2, Entertainment Earth exclusive [AFE04] 35.00
____Series II: R3-Y2, R2-M5, R2-A6, R4-E1, R2-X2, Entertainment Earth exclusive [AFE05] 35.00

ComicCon exclusives.
____2005 Princess Leia, Holographic [AFE06] 20.00
____2006 501st Stormtrooper [AFE07] 45.00

Commerative.
____500th Darth Vader [AFE08]................................15.00

Disney exclusives. Droids from Star Tours.
____3T-RNE 20.00
____3T-RNE on Saga card, not officially released [AFE09] 20.00

____DL-X2 [AFE10] 10.00
____G2-4T [AFE11] 10.00
____G2-9T [AFE12]...15.00
____G3-5LE 20.00
____G3-5LE on Saga card, not officially released [AFE13] 20.00
____MSE-IT 20.00
____MSE-IT on Saga card, not officially released [AFE14] 20.00
____R3-D3 [AFE15]...20.00
____R4-M9 [AFE16]...15.00
____R5-D2 [AFE17]...25.00
____RX-24 REX [AFE18]..20.00
____SK-Z38, pointed beak 20.00
____SK-Z38, rounded beak [AFE19].........................20.00
____WEG-1618 [AFE20]...15.00

Disney exclusives. Star Tours 2-packs.
____Jedi Mickey and Yoda with a blue lightsaber [AFE21] 50.00
____Jedi Mickey and Yoda with a green lightsaber [AFE22] 40.00

Game pack-ins.
____Biker Scout [AFE23]...35.00
____Biker Scout, "Not for resale" [AFE24] 25.00
____Biker Scout, sticker covers "Not for Resale"......50.00

AFE01

AFE02

AFE03

AFE04

AFE05

AFE06

AFE07

Toys: Action Figures – Exclusives

AFE08

AFE09

AFE10

AFE11

AFE12

AFE13

AFE14

AFE15

AFE16

AFE17

AFE18

AFE19

AFE20

AFE21

AFE22

AFE23

AFE24

AFE25

Holiday Edition.
____2002 C-3PO and R2-D2, Wal-mart [AFE27] 45.00
____2003 Yoda, Fan Club [AFE28] 25.00
____2004 Jawas, Entertainment Earth [AFE29] 20.00
____2005 Darth Vader, Fan Club [AFE30] 15.00

OTC figures. Cardback is invitation to DVD event.
____Darth Vader...75.00
____Han Solo..75.00
____Luke Skywalker, X-Wing Pilot 75.00
____Princess Leia 75.00

Shop.StarWars.com
____Covert Ops Clone Trooper [AFE31] 35.00
____Lucas Collector's Set [AFE32] 45.00

Silver colored figures.
____2002 Darth Vader, Toy Fair NYC [AFE33] 135.00
____2002 R2-D2 25th anniversary, Toys R Us exclusive
[AFE34] 30.00

____2003 Boba Fett, conventions [AFE35] 25.00
____2003 Boba Fett, MexiCon pkg [3:89]..................20.00
____2003 Clone Trooper, Toys R Us Exclusive
[AFE36] 25.00
____2004 Darth Vader, Toys R Us Exclusive
[AFE37] 25.00
____2004 Sandtrooper, conventions [AFE38] 25.00

Star Wars Reunion.
____Anakin Skywalker, Mai 2005 [AFE39]..................45.00

Toy fare.
____2005 Anakin / Darth Vader [AFE40]..................350.00

Japan Tour
____Aurra Sing...45.00
____Boba Fett 45.00
____Greedo 45.00
____Mas Amedda 45.00
____Rune Haako 45.00

Germany. Jedi-Con.
____2001 C-3PO, limited to 2,000 [AFE25] 55.00
____2004 Clone trooper / Super Battle Droid 2-pack,
limited to 2,500 [AFE26] 85.00

AFE26

AFE27

AFE28

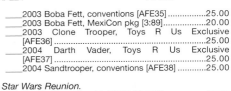
AFE29

AFE30

AFE31

AFE32

AFE33

AFE34

AFE35

AFE36

AFE37

AFE38

AFE39

AFE40

AFE41

AFE42

AFE43

AFE44

BAH01

BAH02

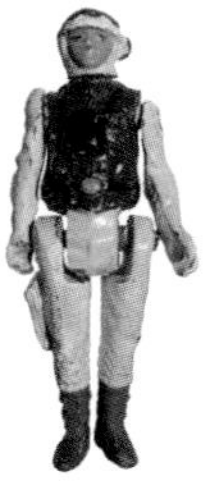

BAH03

Mexico City Convention

2002, June 28 – 30. 2-packs.

____Han Solo and Chewbacca [AFE41]..................190.00
____Obi-Wan Kenobi and Darth Vader [AFE42]......190.00

2004. 2-pack.

____Luke Skywalker Encounters Yoda [3:90] 70.00

Philidelphia Toy Expo

____Bib Fortuna..65.00
____Boba Fett 75.00
____Chewbacca 75.00
____R2-D2 ....75.00

Red Mercury

Custom figures to promote celebrity signings.

____David Prowse, April 28, 2000.............................80.00
____Jerome Blake, April 28, 2000..............................65.00
____Peter Mayhew, June 30, 2000 ....80.00

Star Wars Celebrations

____2002 Jorg Sacul [AFE43] 85.00
____2005 Darth Vader, electronic [AFE44] 60.00

Toys: Action Figures – Special Offer

Hasbro

Troop Builder Sets. 4-packs or "army builder" figures.

____Endor Rebel Soldiers 20.00
____Rebel Trooper [3:90]..25.00
____Sandtroopers 20.00
____Stormtroopers [3:90] 45.00

Kenner

____B'Omarr Monk [1:26] 15.00
____Ben Kenobi spirit [1:26] 10.00
____Cantina Band Member [1:26]...............................15.00
____Han Solo in stormtrooper disguise [1:26] 20.00

Kenner, UK

____Obi-Wan Kenobi spirit, ltd. to 40,000 [3:90] 40.00

Toys: Action Figures – Unlicensed, 1977 – 1986 (Vintage)

____3-pack, "Space Figures," 3 licensed figures in generic package [2:66] 275.00
____Darth Vader, approx. 6" tall with flashing lightsaber [2:66]...17.00
____Stormtrooper on Star Wars hanger card 41.00

2-Pack on ROTJ hanger card, figures are approximately 4" in height.

____C-3PO and Darth Vader 48.00
____C-3PO and R2-D2 ....51.00
____Chewbacca and Darth Vader..............................45.00
____Darth Vader and Darth Vader..............................50.00

Mexico. Modern bootleg of vintage figures.

____Admiral Ackbar [3:91]..12.00
____Bib Fortuna [3:91]..12.00
____Bossk [3:91] 12.00
____Chewbacca [3:91] 12.00
____Emperor's Royal Guard [3:91] 12.00
____Emperor [3:91] 12.00
____Gamorrean Guard [3:91] 25.00
____Greedo [BAH01] 12.00
____Imperial TIE Pilot [3:91] 12.00
____Klaatu (Palace) [3:91] 12.00
____Klaatu (Skiff) [3:91] 12.00
____Logray [3:91]..12.00
____Luke Skywalker 25.00
____Princess Leia 25.00
____R5-D4 ....25.00
____See-Threepio [3:91] 15.00
____Ugnaught [3:91] 12.00
____Weequay [3:91]...12.00
____Yoda 25.00

Mexico.

____Chewbacca [BAH02] 35.00
____Gamorrean Guard [3:91] 35.00

ModelTrem

Brazil lead figures. Aventura Na Galaxia, cardboard box packaging.

____2-1B ....N/V
____Ben Kenobi, lead lightsaber [3:433] ....N/V
____Ben Kenobi, plastic lightsaber blue [3:433] ....N/V
____Ben Kenobi, plastic lightsaber yellow [3:433] ......N/V
____Bespin Guard ....N/V
____Bib Fortuna ....N/V
____Biker Scout ....N/V
____Bossk ....N/V
____Chewbacca ....N/V
____Cloud Car Pilot ....N/V
____Darth Vader, lead lightsaber ....N/V
____Darth Vader, plastic lightsaber ....N/V
____Death Squad Commander ....N/V
____Emperor Palpatine ....N/V
____Gamorrean Guard ....N/V
____Han Solo ....N/V
____Han Solo, Hoth ....N/V
____Hoth Soldier ....N/V
____IG-88 ....N/V
____Imperial TIE Figher Pilot ....N/V
____Lando Calrissian ....N/V
____Lobot ....N/V
____Luke Skywalker, Hoth [BAH03].................................N/V
____Luke Skywalker, Jedi ....N/V
____Luke Skywalker, lead lightsaber yellow ....N/V
____Luke Skywalker, plastic lightsaber blue ....N/V
____Luke Skywalker, X-Wing Pilot..................................N/V
____Princess Leia..N/V
____Princess Leia, Hoth..N/V
____Sand People ....N/V
____See-Threepio ....N/V
____Snaggletooth..N/V
____Snowtrooper ....N/V
____Stormtrooper..N/V
____Wicket ....N/V
____Yoda ....N/V

Uzay

____AT Driver [2:66] 300.00
____Blue Stars [2:66] 950.00
____C-3PO, alone on card [2:66] 300.00
____C-3PO, card shows 2nd droid 414.00
____Chewbacca, close-up card 750.00
____Chewbacca, vegitation card [2:66] 425.00
____Darth Vader [2:66] 735.00
____Death Star Droid 650.00
____Emperor's Royal Guard, with cloak......................475.00
____Emperor's Royal Guard, w/o cloak [2:66] 475.00
____Head Man ....N/V
____Imperial Gunner [2:66] 800.00
____Imperial Stormtrooper (snowtrooper) 1,150.00
____MLC-3 Mini Rig 325.00
____MTV-7 Mini Rig 325.00
____R5-D4...650.00
____Stormtrooper [2:66] 310.00
____TIE Pilot 325.00

Toys: Action Figures: Unlicensed 1995 – 1999 (POTF2)

____AT-AT Driver on "Plastic Toys" header card [1:23] 125.00
____Speederbike with Luke Skywalker in Endor Gear, blister carded with illustration on back [BAG01] 25.00
____Stormtrooper, 10" hollow plastic with blaster [1:23]...25.00

____Darth Vader and Stormtrooper, each driving a Sport Skiff...12.00
____Luke Skywalker and Sport Skiff [3:92]................10.00
____Stormtrooper driving an alien sled......................17.00

2-Pack on POTF2 hanger card. Star Wars characters with alien ship.

____C-3PO and Darth Vader 24.00
____C-3PO and R2-D2 ....30.00
____C-3PO and Stormtrooper......................................24.00
____C-3PO and Yoda 28.00
____Darth Vader and Dagobah Luke 14.00
____Darth Vader and R2-D2 [BAG02] 30.00

Two figures on card; One is oversized.

____Ben Kenobi and Boba Fett [3:92] 20.00
____Darth Vader and IG-88 ....25.00

Bagged on a Landspeeder header card.

____Darth Vader and C-3PO driving a Landspeeder 18.00
____Two Sport Skiffs 11.00

Characters come in red, black, white. Figures are approximately 2" in height. Sold loose.

____C-3PO [1:23] 5.00
____Darth Vader [1:23] 3.00
____Luke Skywalker [1:23]..3.00

Deluxe Han Solo card.

____Deluxe Han [2:40] 5.00
____Deluxe Luke [3:92] 5.00
____Deluxe Stormtrooper [2:40] 5.00
____Speeder Bike and Scout [2:40] 16.00
____Swoop Bike and Rider [2:40] 5.00

Deluxe Stormtrooper card.

____Deluxe Han 5.00
____Deluxe Luke 5.00
____Swoop Bike Rider 14.00

La Guerra De Las Galaxias.

____Darth Vader and Stormtrooper.............................15.00
____Darth Vader and Stormtrooper with a Sport Skiff...21.00

POTF2 AT-ST Driver oversized card, figures approximately 5" in height.

____AT-ST Driver [3:92] 8.00
____Hoth Luke [2:41] 8.00
____Hoth Rebel Soldier [2:41] 8.00
____Imperial Gunner [2:41] 9.00

BAG01

BAG02

BAG03

BAG04

BAG05

BAG06

BAG07

BAG08

BAG09

BAG10

Toys: Action Figures – Unlicensed, 1995 – 1999

BAF01

BAF02

BAF03

BAF04

BAF05

BAF06

BAF07

BAF08

BAF09

BAF10

POTF2 C-3PO card.
____Chewbacca 5.00
____Darth Vader 5.00
____Dash Rendar 5.00
____Han Solo 5.00
____Han Solo in Hoth Gear 5.00
____Obi-Wan Kenobi 5.00
____Princess Leia [BAG03] 5.00
____R2-D2 ..... 11.00
____Stormtrooper 5.00
____Tie Fighter Pilot 5.00
____Yoda 5.00

POTF2 Chewbacca card, figures approximately 6".
____Bespin Luke [3:92] 11.00
____Lando as Skiff Guard [2:41] 9.00

POTF2 Chewbacca card. Random figures cast from unlicensed vintage molds.
____3-packs, any characters [3:92] 45.00

POTF2 Darth Vader card.
____2 Stormtroopers, PVC figures [2:41] 15.00

POTF2 Endor Han card.
____C-3PO [BAG04] 5.00
____R2-D2 [2:41] 6.00
____Yoda [2:41] 6.00

POTF2 Luke Dagobah card.
____Boba Fett 15.00
____C-3PO 5.00
____Chewbacca 5.00
____Darth Vader 5.00
____Han Hoth 5.00
____Han Solo 5.00
____Lando 5.00
____Luke Dagobah 5.00
____Luke Skywalker 7.00
____Luke X-Wing Pilot 6.00
____R2-D2 ..... 5.00
____Yoda [3:92] 7.00

POTF2 Luke in Stormtrooper Disguise card.
____2-1B 5.00
____AT-ST Driver 5.00
____Ben Kenobi [3:92] 5.00
____Bossk 5.00
____C-3PO [3:92] 5.00
____Darth Vader [2:41] 5.00
____Darth Vader bendy 12.00
____Death Star Gunner 12.00
____Greedo [3:92] 6.00
____Han Solo bendy [2:41] 12.00
____Hoth Rebel Soldier 5.00
____Imperial Gunner 6.00
____Jawas 5.00
____Leia Boushh 5.00
____Luke Hoth 5.00
____Luke Skywalker [3:92] 5.00
____Luke Stormtrooper 5.00
____Princess Leia [3:92] 5.00
____R5-D4 ..... 7.00
____Sandtrooper 5.00
____Stormtrooper [BAG05] 5.00
____Tusken Raider 5.00

POTF2 Luke Jedi card.
____C-3PO [3:92] 5.00
____Chewbacca [2:41] 5.00
____Chewbacca / Snoova [3:92] 5.00
____Han Solo, brown belt 5.00
____Han Solo, silver belt 5.00
____Leia / Boushh [BAG06] 5.00
____Luke in Imperial Guard Disguise 9.00
____Luke Skywalker 7.00
____Obi-Wan Kenobi [2:41] 5.00
____Princess Leia, red belt [3:92] 5.00
____Princess Leia, white belt 5.00
____R2-D2 [3:92] 6.00
____Stormtrooper 5.00
____Tie Pilot [2:41] 5.00
____Yoda [3:92] 5.00

POTF2 Luke Jedi oversized card, figures approximately 5" in height.
____Chewbacca / Snoova 8.00
____Darth Vader 8.00
____Dash Rendar 8.00
____Han Carbonite 8.00
____Han Hoth 8.00
____Lando 8.00
____Luke Jedi 8.00
____Momaw Nadon 8.00
____Tie Fighter Pilot 8.00
____Yoda 8.00

POTF2 Luke Skywalker card.
____Ben Kenobi [2:42] 5.00
____Boba Fett [3:93] 15.00
____C-3PO [2:42] 5.00
____Chewbacca 5.00
____Darth Vader [3:93] 5.00
____Han Hoth [2:42] 5.00
____Han Solo [2:42] 5.00
____Luke Skywalker [BAG07] 7.00
____Luke X-Wing Pilot [3:93] 6.00
____R2-D2 [2:42] 5.00
____Stormtrooper, on Star Hero card [3:93] 10.00
____Yoda [2:42] 5.00

POTF2 Sandtrooper oversized card, figures are approximately 5" in height.
____Luke Sandtrooper [3:93] 8.00
____Stormtrooper [2:42] 8.00

Spirit figures from Japan.
____Anakin Skywalker [1:26] 65.00
____Ben Kenobi [1:26] 50.00
____Yoda [1:26] 85.00

Star Warrs
____X-Wing similar to Galoob Micromachine with 2 micro-pilots and 2" figures: Luke, C-3PO and Vader 27.00

Thunderforce figures, approximately 11" in height.
____Darth Vader [3:93] 35.00
____Stormtrooper [3:93] 18.00

Galaxy Empire
Figures are approximately 6" in height.
____Boba Fett [2:40] 12.00
____Chewbacca [2:40] 9.00
____Chewbacca / Snoova [2:40] 6.00
____Darth Vader [BAG08] 9.00
____Han Solo [2:40] 9.00
____Luke Jedi [2:40] 9.00
____Stormtrooper [3:92] 9.00

Galaxy Heroes
____Darth Vader mask with Vader figure 4.00

Industrial Argentina
____Darth Vader 18.00

Space Power Warrior
Darth Vader character figures, approximately 8".
____Black armor [3:93] 26.00
____Black armor, Lost in Space Robot on package [3:93] 28.00
____White armor 19.00

Star Warrio
SOTE card, AT-ST Driver.
____Ben Kenobi [2:40] 5.00
____C-3PO [2:40] 5.00
____Chewbacca [3:93] 5.00
____Darth Vader [2:40] 5.00
____Han Solo [2:40] 5.00
____Luke in Imperial Disguise [3:93] 5.00
____Luke Skywalker [2:40] 5.00
____Princess Leia [2:40] 5.00
____Princess Leia / Boushh [3:93] 5.00
____R2-D2 [BAG09] 5.00
____Stormtrooper [2:40] 5.00
____Yoda [2:40] 7.00

SOTE card, Stormtrooper.
____Biker Scout 34.00
____Deluxe Han 8.00
____Deluxe Luke 8.00
____Han Solo in Carbonite 14.00
____Luke [3:93] 10.00
____Luke Jedi 10.00
____Stormtrooper 12.00
____Swoop Rider 10.00
____Tie Fighter Pilot 5.00

Vs 2-Pack
2-pack, figures approximately 5" in height.
____Boba Fett vs. Luke in Imperial Guard Disguise [3:93] 32.00
____Dash Rendar vs. Carbonite Han 16.00
____Imperial Guard Luke vs. Boba Fett 16.00
____Lando vs. Momaw Nadon [3:93] 19.00
____Leia / Boushh vs. Hoth Han [3:93] 16.00
____Prince Xizor vs. Jedi Luke [BAG10] 16.00

Toys: Action Figures – Unlicensed, 1999 – 2001 (EPI:TPM)

Anakin Skywalker card with fake CommTech chip.
____Darth Maul [BAF01] 9.00

C-3PO card with fake CommTech chip.
____C-3PO [3:94] 7.00
____Darth Sidious [3:94] 7.00
____Ric Olie [3:94] 7.00
____Senator Palpatine [3:94] 7.00
____Watto [BAF02] 7.00

Correct card with fake CommTech chip.
____Anakin Skywalker 7.00
____Darth Maul 7.00
____Jar Jar Binks 7.00
____Obi-Wan Kenobi 7.00
____Padme (Darth Maul card) 7.00
____Queen Amidala 7.00
____Qui-Gon Jinn 7.00

Darth Maul card with fake CommTech chip.
____Darth Maul [BAF03] 6.00

Darth Maul card with full-card bubble, figures are approximately 8" in height.
____Anakin Skywalker [3:94] 8.00
____Darth Maul [3:94] 12.00
____Jar Jar Binks [BAF04] 9.00
____Obi-Wan Kenobi [3:94] 8.00
____Qui-Gon Jinn [3:94] 8.00

Darth Maul card, figures are approximately 6" in height.
____Anakin Skywalker [3:94] 8.00
____C-3PO [3:94] 8.00
____Darth Maul [3:94] 12.00

AFX01

AFX02

AFX03

AFX04

AFX05

AFX06

____Obi-Wan Kenobi [3:94] 8.00
____Queen Amidala [3:94] 8.00
____Qui-Gon Jinn [BAF05]...8.00

Darth Maul Space Wars card.
2-packs.
____Darth Maul and Ric Olie [3:94] 20.00
____Darth Sidious and C-3PO [2:53] 20.00
____Senator Palpatine and Mace Windu [BAF06] 20.00
4-packs.
____Qui-Gon, Watto, Padme, Chancellor Velorum [3:94] 30.00
5-packs.
____Mace Windu, Ric Ollie, Pit Droid, Gasgano, Ki-Adi-Mundi [BAF07] 35.00

Figures are bagged with header card.
____Darth Maul 8.00
____Yoda 9.00

Queen Amidala card.
____Anakin Skywalker [3:94] 7.00
____Battle Droid (gold) [BAF08] 20.00
____Boss Nass 9.00
____C-3PO 7.00
____Chancellor Valorum...7.00
____Darth Maul [3:94] 9.00
____Darth Sidious 7.00
____Gasgano and Pit Droid.....................................10.00
____Jar Jar Binks [3:94] 7.00
____Ki-Adi-Mundy 7.00
____Mace Windu 7.00
____Obi-Wan Kenobi [BAF09] 7.00
____Padme [3:94] 7.00
____Queen Amidala [3:94] 7.00
____Qui-Gon Jinn [3:94] 7.00
____Ric Olie 7.00
____Senator Palpatine 7.00
____Watto 7.00

TPM card with classic trilogy art.
____Darth Sidious [BAF10] 15.00

Toys: Action Figures – Unlicensed 2002 – 2004 (Saga)

____Clone Trooper [AFX01] 15.00
____Jango Fett [AFX02]..15.00
____Obi-Wan Kenobi 15.00

2-packs.
____Jango Fett and Count Dooku 45.00
____Jango Fett and Obi-Wan Kenobi [AFX03] 45.00

3-packs.
____Count Dooku, Jango Fett, Anakin Skywalker 45.00
____Count Dooku, Jango Fett, Obi-Wan Kenobi [AFX04] 45.00

5-packs.
____Obi-Wan, Anakin, Mace Windu, Jango Fett, Count Dooku, carded horizontal [AFX05] 45.00
____Obi-Wan, Anakin, Mace Windu, Jango Fett, Count Dooku, carded vertical 45.00

6-packs.
____Clone Trooper, Han, Jango, Yoda, Vader, Obi-Wan [AFX06] 65.00

10-packs.
____Clonetroopers: 5 marching, 5 firing bagged 55.00

Toys: Action Figures – Unlicensed, 2005 (Episode III)

____Darth Vader similar to Jedi Force 15.00

Force Battler look-alikes.
____Darth Vader...20.00
____General Grievous 20.00

Toys: Action Fleet Classic Duels

Galoob
____Millennium Falcon vs. Tie Interceptor, Toys R Us exclusive [MMG01]..36.00
____X-Wing Fighter vs. Tie Fighter pewter colored, Zaap exclusive limited to 4,800 [MMG02] 200.00
____X-Wing Fighter vs. Tie Fighter, Toys R Us exclusive [MMG03]..36.00

Toys: Action Fleet Flight Controllers

Galoob
____Imperial, Darth Vader's TIE Fighter [MMM01] 15.00
____Imperial, Darth Vader's TIE Fighter with bonus X-Wing fighter targets [MMM02] 215.00
____Imperial, TIE Interceptor [MMM03] 30.00
____Rebel, X-Wing Fighter [MMM04] 15.00
____Rebel, X-Wing Fighter with bonus Tie fighter targets [MMM05] 215.00
____Rebel, Y-Wing Fighter [MMM06] 30.00

Toys: Action Fleet Playsets

Galoob
Classic trilogy, gold logo.
____Ice Planet Hoth [MNP01] 25.00
____The Death Star [MNP02] 25.00
____Yavin Rebel Base [MNP03] 25.00

Classic trilogy, silver logo.
____Ice Planet Hoth..34.00
____The Death Star 34.00

Episode I: The Phantom Menace.
____Naboo Hangar, Final Combat [MNP04] 18.00

MMG01

MMG02

MMG03

MMM01

MMM02

MMM03

MNP01

MNP02

MMM04

MMM05

MMM06

MNP03

MNP04

Toys: Action Fleet Series Alpha

MMR01 MMR02 MMR03 MMR04 MMR05 MMR06 MMR07 MMR08 MMR09

MMR10 MMR11 MMR12 MMR13

Toys: Action Fleet Series Alpha

Galoob
    ___B-Wing Fighter [MMR01] 10.00
    ___Imperial AT-AT [MMR02]..............................17.00
    ___Imperial Shuttle [MMR04].............................17.00
    ___Snowspeeder [MMR05]................................17.00
    ___Twin-Pod Cloud Car [MMR07]........................20.00
    ___X-Wing Starfighter [MMR08] 17.00
    ___Y-Wing Fighter [MMR09] 20.00

Includes Topps trading card.
    ___Imperial AT-AT [MMR03] 25.00
    ___Imperial Shuttle [3:95] 25.00
    ___Snowspeeder [MMR06] 25.00
    ___X-Wing Starfighter 25.00
    ___X-Wing Starfighter, white parts 38.00

Hasbro
    ___Naboo Fighter [MMR10] 125.00
    ___Royal Starship [MMR11] 100.00
    ___Sith Infiltrator [MMR12] 135.00
    ___Trade Federation Droid Fighter [MMR13] 80.00

Toys: Action Fleet Vehicles

Galoob / Gigi, Italy
    ___Rancor 35.00
    ___Sandcrawler 35.00
    ___Slave I..35.00

Galoob
Episode I: The Phantom Menace.
    ___Anakin's Pod Racer [MMA01] 10.00

    ___Fambaa with remote control power cord
    [MMA02]...15.00
    ___Flash Speeder [MMA03]...............................20.00
    ___Gungan Sub [MMA04]................................30.00
    ___Mars Guo's Pod Racer [MMA05] 25.00
    ___Naboo Fighter [MMA06]..............................15.00
    ___Republic Cruiser [MMA07]............................12.00
    ___Sebulba's Pod Racer [MMA08] 10.00
    ___Trade Federation Droid Fighter [MMA09] 10.00
    ___Trade Federation Landing Ship [MMA10] 30.00
    ___Trade Federation MTT [MMA11] 10.00
    ___Trade Federation Tank with remote control power cord
    [MMA12] 25.00

Release 1: Silver logo, limited edition sticker.
2-packs.
    ___Luke's Landspeeder / AT-ST, KB Toys exclusive
    [MMA13] 35.00

MMA01 MMA02 MMA03 MMA04 MMA05

MMA06 MMA07 MMA08 MMA09 MMA10

MMA11 MMA12 MMA13 MMA14 MMA15

MMA16 MMA17 MMA18 MMA19 MMA20 MMA21

MMA22

MMA23

MMA24

MMA25

MMA26

MMA27

MMA28

MMA29

MMA30

MMA31

MMA32

MMA33

MMA34

MMA35

MMA36

MMA37

MMA38

MMA39

___A-Wing Starfighter with C-3PO and Rebel Pilot...30.00
___Darth Vader's Tie Fighter with Darth Vader and Imperial Pilot...29.00
___Imperial AT-AT with Imperial Driver and Stormtrooper (note: actually includes Driver and Snowtrooper.) 29.00
___Imperial Shuttle Tydirium with Han Solo and Chewbacca 30.00
___Luke's X-Wing Starfighter with Luke Skywalker and R2-D2 ....25.00
___Rebel Snowspeeder with Luke Skywalker and Rebel Gunner 27.00

Release 2: Silver logo.
___2-Pack: Luke's Landspeeder / AT-ST, KB Toys exclusive...25.00
___A-Wing Starfighter with C-3PO and Rebel Pilot...20.00

___Darth Vader's Tie Fighter with Darth Vader and Imperial Pilot (battle damage, large) 19.00
___Darth Vader's Tie Fighter with Darth Vader and Imperial Pilot (no battle damage, small) 25.00
___Imperial AT-AT with Imperial Driver and Snowtrooper 24.00
___Imperial Shuttle Tydirium with Han Solo and Chewbacca 26.00
___Luke's X-Wing Starfighter with Luke Skywalker and R2-D2 ....19.00
___Rebel Snowspeeder with Luke Skywalker and Rebel Gunner 25.00

Release 3: Silver logo, box marked "Display Stand Included."
___A-Wing Starfighter with C-3PO and Rebel Pilot (battle damage) 18.00
___A-Wing Starfighter with C-3PO and Rebel Pilot (battle damage, old hinge) 20.00

___A-Wing Starfighter with C-3PO and Rebel Pilot (no battle damage) 24.00
___Darth Vader's Tie Fighter with Darth Vader and Imperial Pilot (battle damage, small) 24.00
___Darth Vader's Tie Fighter with Darth Vader and Imperial Pilot (no battle damage, large) 19.00
___Darth Vader's Tie Fighter with Darth Vader and Imperial Pilot (no battle damage, small) 17.00
___Imperial AT-AT with Imperial Driver and Snowtrooper (battle damage) 19.00
___Imperial AT-AT with Imperial Driver and Snowtrooper (no battle damage) 22.00
___Imperial Shuttle Tydirium with Han Solo and Chewbacca (battle damage) 24.00
___Imperial Shuttle Tydirium with Han Solo and Chewbacca (battle damage, old hinge) 20.00
___Imperial Shuttle Tydirium with Han Solo and Chewbacca (no battle damage) 26.00

MMA40

MMA41

MMA42

MMA43

MMA44

MMA45

MMA46

MMA47

MMA48

MMA49

MMA50

MMA51

MMA52

MMA53

MMA54

Toys: Action Fleet Vehicles

MMA55

MMA56

MMA57

MMA58

MMA59

MMA60

MMA61

MMA62

MMA63

MMA64

____Jawa Sandrawler with Jawa and Scavenger Droid 45.00
____Luke's X-Wing Starfighter with Luke Skywalker and R2-D2 (battle damage) 15.00
____Luke's X-Wing Starfighter with Luke Skywalker and R2-D2 (no battle damage) 24.00
____Rebel Snowspeeder with Luke Skywalker and Rebel Gunner (battle damage) 16.00
____Rebel Snowspeeder with Luke Skywalker and Rebel Gunner (no battle damage) 22.00
____Slave I with Boba Fett and Han Solo.................17.00
____Tie Interceptor with 2 Imperial Pilots 26.00
____Tie Interceptor with 2 Imperial Pilots (dark blue) 18.00
____Y-Wing Starfighter with Gold Leader and R2 Unit 14.00
____Y-Wing Starfighter with Rebel Pilot and R2 Unit 17.00

Release 4: Gold logo.
____A-Wing Starfighter with C-3PO and Rebel Pilot (battle damage) [MMA14] 18.00
____A-Wing with Mon Mothma and Pilot, green [MMA15] 30.00
____A-Wing with Mon Mothma and Pilot, green missing emblem..25.00
____AT-AT, remote control 2-button, full window box, KB Toys exclusive [MMA16]...................15.00
____AT-AT, remote control 2-button, KB Toys exclusive [MMA17]..15.00
____B-Wing Starfighter with Rebel Pilot and Admiral Ackbar [MMA18] 18.00
____Bespin Cloud Car with Cloud Car Pilot and Lobot [MMA19] 12.00
____Darth Vader's Tie Fighter with Darth Vader and Imperial Pilot (battle damage, small) [MMA20]..17.00
____E-Wing Starfighter with Rebel Pilot and R7 Droid [MMA21]..150.00
____Imperial AT-AT with Imperial Driver and Snowtrooper (battle damage) [MMA22]................17.00
____Imperial Landing Craft with Sandtrooper and Imperial Officer 50.00
____Imperial Shuttle Tydirium with Han Solo and Chewbacca [MMA23]....................................18.00

____Incom T-16 Skyhopper wiith Biggs Darklighter and Luke Skywalker [MMA24]....................25.00
____Jabba's Sail Barge with Saelt-Marae (Yak Face) and R2-D2 [MMA25]....................................60.00
____Jawa Sandrawler with Jawa and Scavenger Droid [MMA26] 30.00
____Luke's X-Wing Starfighter with Luke Skywalker and R2-D2 [MMA27] 12.00
____Millennium Falcon with Han Solo and Chewbacca 45.00
____Rancor with Gamorrean Guard and Luke Skywalker [MMA28] 30.00
____Rebel Blockade Runner with Princess Leia and Rebel Trooper [MMA29] 30.00
____Rebel Snowspeeder (Rogue Two colors) with Rebel Pilots and Rebel Gunner (battle damage) 18.00
____Rebel Snowspeeder with Luke Skywalker and Rebel Gunner (battle damage) [MMA30] 12.00
____Slave I with Boba Fett and Han Solo [MMA31] 15.00
____Tie Bomber with Imperial Pilot and Imperial Naval Trooper [MMA32] 15.00
____Tie Defender with Imperial TIE Pilot and Moff Jerjerrod [MMA33].....................................150.00
____Tie Fighter with Imperial Pilot and Grand Moff Tarkin [MMA34]..15.00
____Tie Interceptor with 2 Imperial Pilots [MMA35]..18.00
____Virago with Prince Xizor and Guri [MMA36] 48.00
____X-Wing with Jek Porkins and R2-Unit [MMA37]..18.00
____X-Wing with Wedge Antillies and R2 Unit 18.00
____Y-Wing Starfighter with Blue Leader and R2 Unit [MMA38] 15.00
____Y-Wing Starfighter with Gold Leader and R2 Unit 12.00
____Y-Wing Starfighter with Rebel Pilot and R2 Unit [MMA39]...15.00

White box.
____AT-AT, remote control 3-button, JCPenney exclusive 95.00
____Darth Vader's Tie Fighter, Avon exclusive 14.00
____Luke's X-Wing from Dagobah Swamp, Toyfare exclusive 20.00

____Luke's X-Wing Starfighter, Avon exclusive 14.00

Galoob, Canada
Episode I: The Phantom Menace.
____Republic Cruiser [MMA40] 12.00
____Sebulba's Podracer [MMA41] 16.00
____Trade Federation MTT [MMA42] 12.00

Gold logo, Main Event Toys, bi-language package.
____Imperial Landing Craft with Sandtrooper and Imperial Officer [MMA43] 55.00
____Millennium Falcon with Han Solo and Chewbacca [MMA44]...70.00
____Rebel Snowspeeder with Rebel Pilots and Rebel Gunner [MMA45] 55.00

Galoob, UK
Episode I: The Phantom Menace.
____Naboo Fighter [MMA46] 18.00
____Republic Cruiser [MMA47] 12.00
____Sebulba's Podracer [MMA48] 16.00
____Trade Federation MTT [MMA49] 12.00

Hasbro
Episode I: The Phantom Menace.
____Royal Starship [MMA50] 95.00
____Sith Infiltrator [MMA51] 95.00
____Trade Federation Droid Control Ship [MMA52] 95.00
____Trade Federation Tank [MMA53] 75.00

Star Wars Saga, classic trilogy.
____AT-AT [MMA54]..30.00
____Luke Skywalker's Snowspeeder [MMA55]..........30.00
____Millennium Falcon [MMA56] 20.00
____TIE Advanced x1 [MMA57] 15.00
____X-Wing Fighter [MMA58] 15.00

Star Wars Saga, prequel trilogy.
____AT-TE [MMA59] 20.00
____Jango Fett's Slave I [MMA60] 20.00
____Naboo N-1 Fighter [MMA61] 15.00
____Republic Assault Ship [MMA62] 40.00
____Republic Gunship [MMA63] 40.00
____Solar Sailor [MMA64] 20.00

Titanium Ultra series.
____ARC-170 [MMA65] 25.00
____AT-AT [MMA66] 25.00
____Darth Vader's TIE Advanced X1 [MMA67] 25.00
____Droid Tri-Fighter [MMA68].............................25.00
____Millennium Falcon [MMA69].............................25.00
____Repuiblic gunship [MMA70].............................25.00
____Slave I, Boba Fett [MMA71].............................20.00
____Snowspeeder [MMA72]...................................20.00
____X-Wing fighter [MMA73]..................................25.00

MMA65

MMA66

MMA67

MMA68

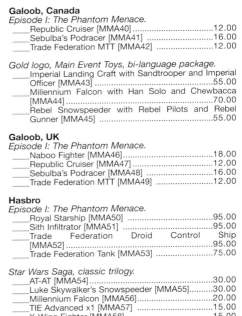

MMA69

MMA70

MMA71

MMA72

MMA73

MMD01

MMD02

MMD03

MMD04

MMD05

MMD06

MMD07

MMD08

MMD09

MMD10

MMD11

MMD12

MMD13

Toys: Action Masters

Kenner
____C-3PO [MMD01] 9.00
____C-3PO, Gold, mail-in exclusive 22.00
____Darth Vader [MMD02].......................................12.00
____Luke Skywalker [MMD03]....................................8.00
____R2-D2 [MMD04] 10.00
____Stormtrooper [MMD05] 10.00

4-Packs.
____C-3PO, Princess Leia, R2-D2, Obi-Wan Kenobi [MMD06]...30.00
____C-3PO, Princess Leia, R2-D2, Obi-Wan Kenobi; POTF style pkg. [MMD08] 33.00

6-Packs.
____Boba Fett, Han, Chewbacca, Darth Vader, Luke, Stormtrooper [MMD07] 36.00
____Boba Fett, Han, Chewbacca, Darth Vader, Luke, Stormtrooper; POTF style pkg. [MMD09] 45.00

Kenner, UK
____4-pack: C-3PO, Princess Leia, R2-D2, Obi-Wan Kenobi [MMD10]...33.00
____6-pack: Boba Fett, Han, Chewbacca, Darth Vader, Luke, Stormtrooper [MMD11] 45.00
____Darth Vader [MMD12] 7.00
____R2-D2 [MMD13] 7.00

Toys: Action Value Pack

Spectra Star
____Star Wars kite, frisbee, and yo-yo [AVQ01] 17.00

Toys: Balancing Toys

Galoob
____Balance of Power [BTY01] 19.00

Toys: Balls

Mondo
Italy.
____Episode I, 8" inflated [SBB01] 18.00

Tapper Candies
____Super Bounce balls, 4-pack [SBB02]....................4.00

Toys: Baseballs

Disney / MGM
____Star Tours, silver and black [BSB01] 19.00

Toys: Beach Balls
____20th anniversary with net [BHB01] 45.00

Target
____Darth Vader, gold and black [BHB02] 15.00

Toys: Binoculars

Tiger Electronics
____Darth Maul with listening device [BIN01]............28.00

Toys: Bop Bags

Baleno
Episode III.
____Darth Vader [YB01]..35.00
____Yoda [YB02] 35.00

Character
____Darth Vader with sound FX [YB03] 35.00

Clipper
____Darth Vader 230.00

Intex Recreation Corp.
____Darth Maul [YB04] 12.00

Kenner
____Chewbacca [YB05] 185.00
____Darth Vader [YB06] 125.00
____Jawa [YB07]..225.00
____R2-D2 [YB08]..125.00

AVQ01

BTY01

SBB01

SBB02

BSB01

BHB01

BHB02

BIN01

YB01

YB02 rear

YB03 front and rear

YB04

YB05

YB06

YB07

YB08

Toys: Building Block Toys and Figures

LO01

LO02

LO03

LO04

LO05

LO06

LO07

LO08

LO09

LO10

LO11

LO12

LO13

LO14

LO15

LO16

LO17

LO18

LO19

LO20

LO21

LO22

LO23

LO24

LO25

LO26

LO27

LO28

Toys: Building Block Toys and Figures

Lego / Pepsi / Lays / Target
____Guess and Win R2-D2, Target promotion 75.00
____Guess and Win Yoda, Target promotion 75.00

Lego / Walmart
____Clone Building Event clone trooper box, 93 with helmets, 52 without helmets [LO01] 330.00

The LEGO Group
____A-Wing Fighter (6207) [LO02]............................45.00
____A-Wing Fighter (7134) [LO03]............................44.00

____Anakin's Podracer (7131) [LO04] 35.00
____AT-AT (4483) [LO05] 135.00
____AT-ST (7657) 25.00
____AT-TE (4482) [LO06] 70.00
____B-Wing at Rebel Control Center (7180) [LO07] 55.00
____B-wing fighter (6208) [LO08] 45.00
____Battle Droid Carrier (7126) [LO09] 24.00
____Boba Fett's Slave I (6209) [LO10] 45.00
____Bounty Hunter Pursuit (7133) [LO11] 30.00
____Clone Troopers Battle Pack (7655) 15.00
____Cloud City (10123) [LO12] 200.00
____Darth Maul (10018) [LO13] 175.00
____Desert Skiff (7104) [LO14] 12.00

____Droid Escape (7106) [LO15]..............................14.00
____Droid Fighter (7111) [LO16] 14.00
____Droids Battle Pack (7654) 15.00
____Episode III Collector's Set (65771) [LO17].........75.00
____Ewok Attack (7139) [LO18].................................16.00
____Final Duel I (7200) [LO19].................................10.00
____Final Duel II (7201) [LO20].................................25.00
____Flash Speeder (7124) [LO21] 18.00
____General Grievous' Starfighter (7656) 25.00
____Geonosian Fighter (4478) [LO22]........................20.00
____Gungan Patrol (7115) [LO23] 15.00
____Gungan Sub (7161) [LO24] 45.00
____Gungan Sub (7161) and Naboo Swamp (7121)
Value Pack, Toys R Us exclusive 65.00

LO29

LO30

LO31

LO32

LO33

LO34

LO35

LO36

LO37

LO38

LO39

LO40

LO41

LO42

LO43

LO44

LO45

LO46

LO47

LO48

LO49

LO50

LO51

LO52

LO53

LO54

LO55

LO56

LO57

LO58 · LO59 · LO60 · LO61 · LO62 · LO63 · LO64 · LO65

LO66 · LO67 · LO68 · LO69 · LO70 · LO71

____Hailfire Droid (4481) [LO25] 50.00
____Imperial AT-ST (7127) [LO26] 16.00
____Imperial Inspection (7264) [LO27] 50.00
____Imperial Landing Craft (7659) [LO28].............65.00
____Imperial Shuttle (7166) [LO28] 42.00
____Imperial Star Destroyer (6211) [LO29].............100.00
____Jabba's Message (4475) [LO30]........................20.00
____Jabba's Palace (4480) [LO31] 30.00
____Jabba's Prize (4476) [LO32] 20.00
____Jabba's Sail Barge (6210) [LO33]......................75.00
____Jango Fett's Slave I (7153) [LO34] 50.00
____Jango Fett's Slave I (7153) bonus cargo case included (65153) [LO35]................................50.00
____Jedi Defense (7203) [LO36] 10.00
____Jedi Defense II (7204) [LO37] 10.00
____Jedi Duel (7103) [LO38] 10.00
____Jedi Starfighter (7143) [LO39] 18.00
____Landspeeder (7110) [LO40] 12.00
____Lightsaber Duel (7101) [LO41] 17.00
____Millennium Falcon (4504) [LO42] 50.00
____Millennium Falcon (4504), OTC packaging [LO43] 50.00
____Millennium Falcon (7190) [LO44] 125.00
____Mos Eisley Cantina (4501) [LO45] 30.00
____Mos Eisley Cantina (4501), OTC packaging [LO46] 30.00
____Mos Espa Podrace (7171) [LO47] 85.00
____Naboo Fighter (7141) [LO48] 30.00
____Naboo Swamp (7121) [LO49] 15.00
____Podrace Brick (7159) [LO50] 24.00
____Rebel Blockade Runner (10019) [LO51] 175.00
____Rebel Snowspeeder (4500) [LO52] 50.00
____Rebel Snowspeeder (4500), OTC packaging [LO53] 50.00

____Republic Gunship (7163) [LO54] 39.00
____Sandcrawler (10144) [LO55]...............................75.00
____Sith Infiltrator (7151) [LO56] 30.00
____Slave I (7144) [LO57] 40.00
____Snow Speeder (7130) [LO58] 40.00
____Speeder Bikes (7128) [LO59] 12.00
____T-16 Skyhopper (4477) [LO60] 15.00
____Tie Bomber (4479) [LO61] 40.00
____Tie Fighter (7146) [LO62] 24.00
____TIE Fighter (7263), OTC packaging [LO63] 20.00
____Tie Fighter and Y-wing (7150) [LO64] 65.00
____TIE interceptor (6206) [LO65] 25.00
____Trade Federation AAT (7155) [LO66] 20.00
____Trade Federation MTT (7184) [LO67] 25.00
____Tusken Raider Encounter (7113) [LO68] 10.00
____Twin-Pod Cloud Car (7119) [LO69] 12.00
____Ultimate Space Battle (7283) [LO70] 75.00
____V-wingfighter (6205) [LO71] 45.00
____Watto's Junk Yard (7186) [LO72] 35.00
____X-Wing Dagobah scene (4502) [LO73] 50.00
____X-Wing Dagobah scene (4502), OTC [LO74]......50.00
____X-Wing Fighter (7140) [LO75] 42.00
____Y-Wing Fighter (7658) 50.00

EPIII:ROTS.
____ARC-170 Fighter (7259) [LO76] 40.00
____Clone Scout Walker (7250) [LO77]......................10.00
____Clone Turbo Tank (7261) [LO78] 90.00
____Darth Transformation (7251) [LO79] 7.00
____Droid Tri-Fighter (7252) [LO80] 15.00
____General Grievous Chase (7255) [LO81] 20.00
____Jedi Starfighter and Vulture Droid (7256) [LO82] 20.00
____Mini ARC-170 (6967) [LO83] 15.00

____Mini Jedi Starfighter (6966) [LO84] 15.00
____Ultimate Lightsaber Duel (7257) [LO85] 30.00
____Wookiee Attack (7258) [LO86] 30.00
____Wookiee Catamaran (7260) [LO87] 50.00

Mindstorm developer kits.
____Darkside Developer [LO88] 95.00
____Droid Developer [LO89] 95.00

Mini Building Sets. Japan. Distributed by Kabaya.
____1 X-Wing Fighter [LO90].....................................15.00
____2 Slave I [LO91] 15.00
____3 TIE Interceptor [LO92] 15.00

Mini Building Sets.
____Anakin and Sebulba's Podracers (4485) [LO93] 10.00
____AT-AT (4489) [LO94] 10.00
____AT-ST and Snowspeeder (4486) [LO95].............10.00
____AT-TE (4495) [LO96] 10.00
____Imperial Shuttle (4494) [LO97] 10.00
____Jedi Starfighter and Slave I (4487) [LO98]..........10.00
____Millennium Falcon (4488) [LO99] 25.00
____MTT (4491) [LO100] 10.00
____Republic Gunship (4490) [LO101] 10.00
____Sith Infiltrator (4493) [LO102] 10.00
____Star Destroyer (4492) [LO103] 10.00
____TIE Advanced and X-Wing Fighter (4484) [LO104] 10.00
____Tie Fighter (3219), Lego Club exclusive [LO105] 25.00
____Tie Fighter (3219), Lego Club exclusive with club mailer packaging [LO106] 45.00
____TIE Interceptor (6965) [LO107] 10.00

LO72 · LO73 · LO74 · LO75 · LO76 · LO77 · LO78

LO79 · LO80 · LO81 · LO82 · LO83 · LO84 · LO85 · LO86

LO87 · LO88 · LO89 · LO90 · LO91 · LO92 · LO93 · LO94

LO95 · LO96 · LO97 · LO98 · LO99 · LO100 · LO101 · LO102 · LO103 · LO104

Toys: Building Block Toys and Figures

| LO105 | LO106 | LO107 | LO108 | LO109 | LO110 | LO111 | LO112 | LO113 |

| LO114 | LO115 | LO116 | LO117 | LO118 | LO119 | LO120 | LO121 | LO122 | LO123 |

| LO124 | LO125 | LO126 | LO127 | LO128 | LO129 |

Prebuilt statues.
____Darth Vader, FAO Schwarz exclusive 9,500.00

Promotional bricks.
____7251 Darth Vader Transformation, 2005 VIP Gala Feb 19 [LO108]....................................75.00
____Embossed with SW logo and April 20-May 1 2005 [LO109]....................................35.00
____Embossed with SW logo and TPM Lego characters; distributed at the SW Celebration in Denver CO, limited to 7,000 [LO110]....................28.00

Technics.
____Battle Droid (8001) [LO111] 30.00
____C-3PO (8007) [LO112] 50.00
____Darth Vader (8010) [LO113] 55.00
____Destroyer Droid (8002) [LO114] 50.00
____Jango Fett (8011) [LO115] 30.00
____Pit Droid (8000) [LO116]........................45.00
____R2-D2 (8009) [LO117] 20.00
____Stormtrooper (8008) [LO118] 50.00
____Super Battle Droid (8012) [LO119]..............35.00

Ultimate Collector series.
____AT-ST (10174) [LO120]..........................135.00
____Death Star II (10143) [LO121] 175.00
____Imperial Star Destroyer (10030) [LO122]........285.00
____Naboo Starfighter (10026) [LO123] 50.00
____Rebel Snowspeeder (10129) [LO124] 125.00
____TIE Collection (10131), OTC packaging [LO125]....................................95.00
____Tie Interceptor (7181) [LO126].................135.00
____X-Wing (7191) [LO127] 135.00
____Y-Wing Attack Starfighter (10134), OTC packaging [LO128]....................................135.00
____Yoda (7194) [LO129]............................95.00

Toys: Clip-Alongs

Craft Master
____Compass with crayon, R2-D2 [VCL01] 12.00
____Crayon holder, Darth Vader [VCL02] 12.00
____Wicket magnifying glass [VCL03] 16.00

Toys: Collector Fleet Toys

Kenner
Authentically styled with lights, sounds, and stand.
____Imperial Star Destroyer [YC01] 95.00
____Rebel Blockade Runner [YC02] 75.00
____Super Star Destroyer [YC03]..........................290.00

Toys: Crystals

Kelloggs
Cereal premiums.
____Blue – Naboo space battle [KP01] 5.00
____Box of 6, promotional 45.00
____Green – Gungan army [KP02]............................5.00
____Orange – Podrace [KP03]...............................5.00
____Purple – Jedi vs. Sith [KP04] 5.00
____Red – Jedi [KP05] 5.00
____Yellow – Battle droids [KP06] 5.00

| VCL01 | VCL02 | VCL03 | FT01 | FT02 | FT03 | FT04 | FT05 |

| YC01 | YC02 | YC03 |

 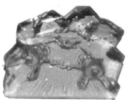   

| KP01 | KP02 | KP03 | KP04 | KP05 | KP06 |

TYD01   TYD02   TYD03   TYD04   TYD05

TYD06   TYD07   TYD08   TYD09   TYD10   TYD11

Toys: Decision Making Toys

Hasbro
____Ask The Force [FT01] 12.00
____Ask Yoda, 24 phrases [FT02] 24.00

Original Trilogy Collection.
____Ask Yoda, 24 phrases [FT03] 20.00

Revenge of the Sith.
____Call Upon Yoda [FT04] 25.00

Kenner
____Yoda the Jedi Master magic answer [FT05] 85.00

Toys: Diecast Toys

Clipper
____Land Speeder 50.00
____Tie Fighter 50.00
____X-Wing Fighter 50.00

Disney / MGM
____Parade Vehicle [TYD01] 12.00
____Starspeeder 3000 [TYD02]..................................35.00

Harbert
____Caccia Ala-X 160.00
____Caccia T.I.E. 145.00
____Hovercraft Scooter 185.00

Kenner
Boxed.
____Imperial Cruiser SW [TYD03] 185.00
____Imperial Cruiser SW with background [TYD04] ...600.00
____Imperial Cruiser ESB 165.00

____Millennium Falcon SW [TYD05] 150.00
____Millennium Falcon SW with background [TYD06] ...600.00
____Millennium Falcon ESB [TYD07] 165.00
____Tiebomber ESB [TYD08] 750.00
____Y-Wing Fighter SW [TYD09] 200.00
____Y-Wing Fighter SW with background [TYD10] ...600.00
____Y-Wing Fighter ESB [TYD11].............................185.00

Carded.
____Darth Vader Tie Fighter SW [TYD12] 55.00
____Darth Vader Tie Fighter ESB 55.00
____Darth Vader Tie Fighter catalog-order box 115.00
____Land Speeder SW [TYD13] 85.00
____Land Speeder ESB..85.00
____Land Speeder Catalog-order box 115.00
____Slave I ESB [TYD14] 125.00
____Snowspeeder ESB [TYD15]...............................125.00
____Tie Fighter SW 65.00
____Tie Fighter SW with price box [TYD16] 215.00
____Tie Fighter ESB 55.00
____Tie Fighter catalog-order box 115.00
____Twin-Pod Cloud Car ESB [TYD17].......................95.00
____X-Wing Fighter SW [TYD18] 75.00
____X-Wing Fighter ESB 75.00

Palitoy
____Imperial Cruiser 185.00
____Millennium Falcon 165.00

Star Force
Battery operated "Bump and Go."
____Millennium Falcon [TYD19] 35.00

Diecast vehicles featuring "pull-back" action.
____A-Wing Fighter [TYD20] 8.00
____Millennium Falcon [TYD21].................................8.00
____MonCal Cruiser [TYD22] 8.00
____X-Wing Fighter [TYD23] 8.00

Takara
____X-Wing Fighter [TYD24]....................................195.00

Carded vehicles, similar to Kenner's line.
____Landspeeder 95.00
____Tie Fighter 95.00
____X-Wing Fighter 95.00

Diecast characters, approximately 10".
____C-3PO [TYD25] 250.00
____Darth Vader [TYD26] 275.00

Space Alloy Zetca.
____C-3PO [TYD27] 175.00
____Landspeeder 175.00
____R2-D2 [TYD28] 175.00
____Tie Fighter [TYD29] 175.00
____X-Wing Fighter [TYD30]....................................175.00

Toltoys
Carded vehicles, similar to Kenner's line.
____Land Speeder...95.00
____Tie Fighter 100.00
____X-Wing Fighter 114.00

TYD12   TYD13   TYD14

TYD15   TYD16   TYD17   TYD18   TYD19   TYD20   TYD21   TYD22

TYD23   TYD24   TYD25   TYD26   TYD27   TYD28   TYD29   TYD30

Toys: Dolls – Collector

DC01 - DC03 TES01 TES02 TES03 TES04 TES05 TES06 TES07 TES08 TES09

TES10 TES11 TES12 TES13 TES14 TES15 TES16 TES17 TES18

TES19 TES20 TES21 TES22 TES23 TES24 TES25 TES26 TES27 TES28

TES29 TES30 TES31

Toys: Dolls – Collector

Madame Alexander
____Han Solo [DC01] 175.00
____Luke Skywalker [DC02] 175.00
____Princess Leia [DC03] 175.00

Toys: Dolls – Nesting

Hot Toys
____C-3PO...50.00
____Darth Vader..50.00
____General Grievous 50.00
____Obi-Wan Kenobi...50.00
____Sith 50.00
____Wookies 50.00

Toys: Electronic Toys

Gemmy Industries
Dashboard drivers.
____C-3PO [TES01]...10.00
____Darth Vader [TES02]..10.00
____Yoda [TES03] 10.00

Hasbro
"Deformed" palm talkers.
____Boba Fett [TES04] 20.00
____C-3PO [TES05]...15.00
____Chewbacca [TES06]..15.00
____Darth Vader [TES07]...15.00
____R2-D2 [TES08] 12.00
____Stormtrooper [TES09] 15.00

EPIII:ROTS "deformed" palm talkers.
____Boba Fett [TES10] 25.00
____C-3PO [TES11]...25.00
____Chewbacca [TES12]...25.00
____Darth Maul [TES13] 25.00
____Darth Vader [TES14]...25.00
____R2-D2 [TES15] 25.00
____Stormtrooper 25.00
____Yoda [TES16] 25.00

Force Link starships.
____Anakin Skywalker's Speeder [TES17] 15.00
____Jango Fett's Slave I [TES18] 15.00
____Obi-Wan Kenobi's Jedi Starfighter [TES19]........15.00
____Zam Wesell's Speeder [TES20] 15.00

Tiger Electronics
____Interactive Yoda [TES21] 39.00

Tomy
Classic trilogy "deformed" palm talkers.
____Boba Fett [TES22] 35.00
____C-3PO [TES23]..35.00
____Chewbacca [TES24]...35.00
____Darth Vader [TES25]..35.00
____Stormtrooper [TES26] 35.00

EPI:TPM "deformed" palm talkers.
____Battle Droid [TES27]...45.00
____Darth Maul [TES28] 45.00
____Jar Jar Binks [TES29]..45.00
____R2-D2 [TES30] 45.00
____Yoda [TES31] 45.00

Toys: Figure Makers

Kenner
____Droids figure maker kit [FMG01] 6.00
____Jedi figure maker kit [FMG02] 6.00
____Millennium Falcon figure maker kit [FMG03]......10.00
____Slave I figure maker kit [FMG04] 15.00
____Space Creatures figure maker kit [FMG05] 6.00

Toys: Figures – Attacktix

Hasbro
____Exclusive Battle Pack: 6 figures plus Republic gunship [FTX01] 35.00

Booster packs.
____Series 1 [FTX02] 9.00
____Series 2 [FTX03] 9.00
____Series 3, Han Solo vs. Stormtrooper [FTX04] 9.00
____Series 3, Luke vs. Tusken Raider [FTX05] 9.00
____Series 3, Obi-Wan vs. Darth Vader [FTX06] 9.00

FMG01 FMG02 FMG03 FMG04 FMG05

FTX01 FTX02 FTX03 FTX04 FTX05 FTX06 FTX07 FTX08 FTX09 FTX10

FTX11	FTX12	FTX13	FTX14	FTX15

Series 1. Battle Masters.
___AT-RT, no. 37 [FTX07].........................10.00
___Boga, no. 36 [FTX08] 16.00

Series 1.
___Agen Kolar, Jedi, no. 23 ....2.00
___Anakin Skywalker, Jedi, no. 26.........................2.00
___Bail Organa, Republic, no. 8.........................6.00
___Battle Droid, Droid Army, no.1 ....3.00
___Chewbacca, Wookiee, 22.........................8.00
___Clone Commander, Sepratist, no. 34, Starter 3.00
___Clone Lieutenant, Sepratist, no. 12 ....3.00
___Clone Sergeant, Republic, no. 35, Battle Case exclusive 4.00
___Clone Trooper, Republic, no. 4 ....2.00
___Clone Trooper, Sepratist, no. 5.........................3.00
___Commander Gree, Republic, no. 21 ....10.00
___Commaner Bly, Republic, no. 15 ....5.00
___Count Dooku, Sith, no. 11 ....8.00
___Darth Vader (Mustafar), Sith, no. 32, Starter 3.00
___Darth Vader, Sith, no. 16.........................6.00
___Emperor, Sith, no. 24 ....8.00
___General Grievous, Droid Army, no. 28.........................15.00
___Grevious Bodyguard, Droid Army, no. 13 ....7.00
___Ki Adi Mundi, Jedi, no. 18 ....6.00
___Mace Windu, Jedi, no. 19.........................7.00
___Neimodian Guard, Sepratist, no. 14.........................2.00
___Nute Gunray, Sepratist, no. 14.........................5.00
___Obi-Wan Kenobi, Jedi, no. 27.........................8.00
___Obi Wan Kenobi (Mustafar Duel), no. 31, SS........3.00
___Padme Amidala, Republic, no. 6 ....2.00
___Palpatine, Sepratist, no. 17.........................12.00
___Plo Koon, Jedi, no. 7 ....7.00
___Shaak Ti, Jedi, no. 20 ....12.00
___Super Battle Droid, Droid Army, no. 2 ....3.00
___Tarfful, Wookiee, no. 29 ....12.00
___V-Wing Pilot, Sepratist, no. 10 ....2.00
___Wookiee Commando, Republic, no. 33, Starter ..3.00
___Wookiee Commando, Wookiee, no. 9 ....5.00
___Wookiee Scout, Wookiee, no. 3 ....2.00
___Yoda, Jedi, no. 30 ....24.00

Promo baggie packaging.
___Clone Lieutenant [FTX09] 5.00
___Clone Trooper 5.00
___Commander Bly 5.00
___Count Dooku.........................8.00
___Neimoidian Guard 5.00
___Padme Amidala 5.00
___Plo Koon 8.00
___Super Battle Droid 5.00
___V-Wing Pilot 5.00
___Wookiee Commando 5.00
___Wookiee Scout 5.00
___Wookiee Scout 5.00

Series 2, Battle Masters.
___Republic Gunship, no. 31 [FTX10].........................18.00

Series 2, common.
___ARC Pilot, no. 5 ....3.00
___Clone Trooper, no. 3 ....3.00
___Grievous Bodyguard, no. 6.........................3.00
___Jedi Knight, no. 1 ....3.00
___Scout Trooper, no. 4 ....3.00
___Utapau Warrior, no. 2 ....3.00

Series 2, rare.
___Battle Droid Commander, no. 12 ....3.00

___Bossk, no. 13 ....3.00
___Clone Captain, no. 9 ....3.00
___Clone Commander, no. 8 ....3.00
___Jango Fett, no. 15.........................3.00
___Mace Windu, no. 16 ....3.00
___Neimoidian Captain, no. 10 ....3.00
___Princess Leia, no. 14 ....3.00
___Royal Guard, no. 7 ....3.00
___Wookiee Captian, no. 11 ....3.00

Series 2, super rare.
___Boba Fett, no. 30 ....3.00
___Chewbacca, no. 23 ....3.00
___Darth Maul, no. 26 ....3.00
___Darth Sidious, no. 25 ....3.00
___Darth Vader, no. 17 ....3.00
___Destroyer Droid, no. 19 ....3.00
___General Grievous, no. 24 ....3.00
___Han Solo, no. 28 ....3.00
___Kit Fisto, no. 27 ....3.00
___Luke Skywalker, no. 29 ....3.00
___Medic Droid, no. 20 ....3.00
___Obi-Wan Kenobi, no. 18 ....3.00
___R2-D2, no. 21 ....3.00
___Tion Medon, no. 22 ....3.00

Series 3, Battle Masters.
___Jabba the Hutt, no. 31 [FTX11].........................18.00

Series 3, common.
___Rebel Trooper 2.00
___Stormtrooper 2.00
___TIE Pilot 2.00
___Tusken Raider 2.00
___X-wing Pilot 2.00

Series 3, rare.
___Bossk 3.00
___Captain Antilles 3.00
___Chewbacca 3.00
___Death Star Gunner 3.00
___Greedo 3.00
___Imperial Officer 3.00
___Jawa 3.00
___Princess Leia 3.00
___Sandtrooper 3.00
___Tusken Sniper 3.00

Series 3, super rare.
___Biggs Darklighter 9.00
___Boba Fett 15.00
___C-3PO 16.00
___Darth Vader.........................10.00

FTX16	FTX17

___Hammerhead 12.00
___Han Solo 9.00
___Han Solo as Stormtrooper 15.00
___Heavy Stormtrooper 12.00
___Jawa Warlord 10.00
___Luke as Stormtrooper 10.00
___Luke Skywalker 8.00
___Obi-Wan Kenobi 16.00
___R2-Q5 ....14.00
___Tusken Warlord 8.00
___Wedge 7.00

Starter sets.
___Series 1 with starter CD [FTX12] 25.00
___Series 2 [FTX13] 15.00
___Series 3 [FTX14] 15.00
___Series 3, bonus extra battle figure [FTX15] 12.00
___Star Wars vs. Transformers [FTX16] 35.00

Storage case.
___With exclusive Clone Sergeant [FTX17]..............20.00

Toys: Figures – Bend-Ems

Just Toys
4-piece gift sets.
___Admiral Ackbar, Bib Fortuna, Boba Fett, Wicket, brass collectors coin, with bonus trading cards [TYB01] 35.00
___C-3PO, Darth Vader, R2-D2, Stormtrooper [TYB02].........................25.00
___C-3PO, Darth Vader, R2-D2, Stormtrooper, with bonus trading card [TYB03].........................25.00
___C-3PO, Han, Leia, Obi-Wan, with bonus trading card [TYB04].........................25.00
___Chewbacca, Stormtrooper, Wicket, Yoda 25.00

TYB01	TYB02	TYB03

TYB04	TYB05	TYB06	TYB07

Toys: Figures – Bend-Ems

TYB08 TYB09 TYB10 TYB11 TYB12 TYB13 TYB14 TYB15 TYB16

TYB17 TYB18 TYB19 TYB20 TYB21 TYB22 TYB23 TYB24 TYB25

____Chewbacca, Stormtrooper, Wicket, Yoda, with bonus trading card [TYB05] 25.00
____Darth Vader, Emperor, Luke Skywalker, R2-D2, with bonus trading card [TYB06] 25.00

8-piece gift sets.
____Darth Vader, Luke, C-3PO, Emperor, Stormtrooper, R2-D2, Leia, Wicket 35.00
____Darth Vader, Luke, C-3PO, R2-D2, Obi-Wan, Stormtrooper, Leia, Wicket 35.00
____Darth Vader, Luke, C-3PO, Yoda, Stormtrooper, R2-D2, Leia, Wicket 35.00

10-piece gift set.
____Ackbar, Bib Fortuna, Chewbacca, Darth Vader, Royal Guard, Han, Leia, Luke, R2-D2, Stormtrooper, brass collector coin, bonus trading cards [TYB07] 45.00

Admiral Ackbar
____20 back, Lando card [TYB08].......................8.00
____20 back, Mon Cal card, square bubble [TYB09] 10.00
____20 back, trench card, square bubble..................10.00

Bib Fortuna
____20 back, Bib card, square bubble [TYB10] 10.00

Boba Fett
____20 back, Luke / Leia card, square bubble [TYB11] 50.00

C-3PO
____8 back...10.00
____8 back, C-3PO card [TYB12] 7.00
____8 back, C-3PO card, micro-name, age warning on card corner 15.00
____8 back, C-3PO card, micro-name, age warning under bubble [TYB13]......................................15.00

____12 back, C-3PO card, square bubble [TYB14] 9.00
Chewbacca
____8 back 12.00
____8 back, Chewbacca card [TYB15] 8.00
____8 back, Chewbacca card, micro-name, age warning on card corner [TYB16] 10.00
____8 back, Chewbacca card, micro-name, age warning under bubble 10.00
____12 back, galaxy card, square bubble [TYB17] 10.00

Emperor's Royal Guard
____20 back, ERG card [TYB18].......................14.00
____20 back, Luke / Leia card, square bubble..........17.00

Gamorrean Guard
____20 back, Gamorrean card, square bubble [TYB19]..15.00

Han Solo
____8 back, Han card [TYB20] 10.00
____8 back, Han card with transitional "trading card" sticker [TYB21] 25.00
____12 back, galaxy card 18.00
____12 back, Gamorrean card 18.00
____12 back, Han card, square bubble [TYB22] 24.00
____20 back, Chewbacca card, large head [TYB23] 22.00
____20 back, DSII card, square bubble, large head [TYB24] 22.00

Lando Calrissian
____20 back, DSII card, square bubble [TYB25] 14.00

Lord Darth Vader
____8 back [TYB26]......................................11.00
____8 back, Vader card [TYB27] 11.00
____8 back, Vader card, micro-name [TYB28] 13.00
____8 back, Vader card, micro-name, age warning in corner 13.00

____12 back, Vader card, square bubble [TYB29] 14.00

Luke Skywalker X-Wing Pilot
____20 back, pilot card, square bubble [TYB30] 18.00

Luke Skywalker
____8 back [TYB31].......................................11.00
____8 back, Luke card 7.00
____8 back, Luke card, micro-name [TYB32]............12.00
____8 back, Luke card, micro-name, age warning in corner 12.00
____12 back, Luke card [TYB33].......................6.00

Obi-Wan Kenobi
____8 back [TYB34].......................................15.00
____8 back, Obi-Wan card [TYB35].......................9.00
____12 back, Obi-Wan card, square bubble..............16.00

Princess Leia
____8 back [TYB36].......................................17.00
____8 back, Leia card [TYB37] 12.00
____8 back, Leia card, micro-name [TYB38] 14.00
____12 back, galaxy card, square bubble 12.00
____20 back, galaxy card, square [TYB39] 14.00
____20 back, trench battle card, square bubble 14.00

R2-D2
____8 back [TYB40].......................................11.00
____8 back, R2-D2 card 6.00
____12 back, R2-D2 card [TYB41] 5.00
____20 back, galaxy card, sq. bubble [TYB42]........12.00

Stormtrooper
____8 back [TYB43].......................................9.00
____8 back, Stormtrooper card [TYB44]....................11.00
____8 back, Stormtrooper card, micro-name [TYB45]..12.00
____20 back, Bib card, square bubble [TYB46] 14.00

The Emperor
____12 back, emperor card 9.00

TYB26 TYB27 TYB28 TYB29 TYB30 TYB31 TYB32 TYB33 TYB34

TYB35 TYB36 TYB37 TYB38 TYB39 TYB40 TYB41 TYB42 TYB43

TYB44

TYB45

TYB46

TYB47

TYB48

TYB49

TYB50

TYB51

TYB52

TYB53

TYB54

TYB55

____12 back, galaxy card, sq. bubble [TYB47].........17.00
____12 back, trench battle card [TYB48] 9.00
____12 back, trench battle card, square bubble 10.00

Tusken Raider
____20 back, galaxy card, sq. bubble [TYB49].........15.00
____20 back, pilot card [TYB50] 13.00
____20 back, tusken card 15.00

Wicket the Ewok,
____12 back, galaxy card [TYB51] 35.00
____20 back, Ewok card, square bubble [TYB52] 24.00

Yoda the Jedi Master
____8 back...11.00
____8 back, Yoda card [TYB53].....................................9.00
____8 back, Yoda card, micro-name [TYB54]...........12.00
____20 back, DSII card, square bubble 12.00

Foreign cardback. No bendems logo, or trading card callout. International age symbol.
____Han Solo, 12 back, Galaxy card, square bubble [TYB55]...24.00

Toys: Figures – Epic Force

Hasbro
____Darth Maul [ZPF01] 15.00
____Obi-Wan Kenobi [ZPF02] 45.00
____Qui-Gon Jinn [ZPF03] 15.00

Kenner
____3-Pack: Ben Kenobi, Chewbacca, Han Solo, FAO Schwarz exclusive 120.00
____Ben Kenobi, FAO Schwarz excl. [ZPF04] 20.00
____Boba Fett [ZPF05] 20.00
____C-3PO [ZPF06] 12.00
____Chewbacca, FAO Schwarz excl. [ZPF07] 35.00
____Darth Vader [ZPF08] 20.00
____Han Solo, FAO Schwarz exclusive [ZPF09].......40.00
____Luke Skywalker, Bespin fatigues [ZPF10] 12.00
____Princess Leia [ZPF11] 12.00
____Stormtrooper [ZPF12] 20.00

Toys: Figures – Force Battlers

Hasbro
Approx. 7" scale.
____Anakin Skywalker, Lightsaber attack! [F1A01] 10.00
____Chewbacca, Boulder-launching backpack [F1A02] 10.00
____Chewbacca, Water firing blaster! [F1A03] 10.00
____Clone Trooper, Quick-draw blasting action! [F1A04] 15.00
____Darth Vader #2 [F1A05] 15.00

____Darth Vader, Slashing attack! [F1A06] 10.00
____Emperor Palpatine [F1A07] 10.00
____General Grievous, Balliastic buzz-disc [F1A08] 10.00
____General Grievous, Multiple lightsaber attack! [F1A09] 10.00
____Han Solo [F1A10] 10.00
____Jango Fett, Clamping claw [F1A11] 15.00
____Luke Skywalker [F1A12]......................................10.00
____Mace Windu, Firing Jedi gauntlet! [F1A13] 10.00
____Obi-Wan Kenobi, Lightsaber attack! [F1A14] 10.00
____Obi-Wan Kenobi, Slashing lightsaber attack [F1A15] 10.00
____Yoda [F1A16] 10.00

Hasbro, Canada
Approx. 7" scale, tri-language package.
____Anakin Skywalker, Lightsaber attack! 10.00
____Darth Vader, Slashing attack! 10.00
____General Grievous, Four-arm attack!....................10.00
____Obi-Wan Kenobi, Quick-draw attack! 10.00

Toys: Figures – Galactic Heroes

Hasbro
____Scout Trooper, San Diego Comic-Con exclusive [P1A01] 10.00

10-packs.
____EPII: Battle of Geonosis [P1A02] 25.00
____EPIII: Jedi Vs. Sith [P1A03] 25.00
____EPIV: Death Star Escape [P1A04] 25.00
____EPV: Vader's Bounty Hunters [P1A05]................25.00

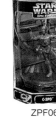

ZPF01   ZPF02   ZPF03   ZPF04   ZPF05   ZPF06   ZPF07   ZPF08   ZPF09

ZPF10   ZPF11   ZPF12   F1A01   F1A02   F1A03   F1A04   F1A05   F1A06   F1A07

F1A08   F1A09   F1A10   F1A11   F1A12   F1A13   F1A14   F1A15   F1A16

Toys: Figures – Galactic Heroes

P1A01

P1A02

P1A03

P1A04

P1A05

P1A06

P1A07

P1A08

P1A09

P1A10

P1A11

P1A12

P1A13

P1A14

P1A15

P1A16

P1A17

P1A18

P1A19

P1A20

P1A21

P1A22

P1A23

P1A24

2-packs, A New Hope, blue logo.
____C-3PO and Chewbacca [P1A06] 6.00
____Greedo and Han Solo [P1A07] 6.00
____Luke Skywalker and Han Solo in Stormtrooper
     disguises 6.00
____Luke Skywalker and Han Solo in Stormtrooper
     disguises, unpainted helmet brows [P1A08] 6.00
____Luke Skywalker and R2-D2 [P1A09] 6.00
____Obi-Wan Kenobi and Darth Vader [P1A10] 6.00
____Princess Leia and Han Solo [P1A11] 6.00
____Sandtrooper and Obi-Wan 6.00
____Sandtrooper and Obi-Wan, trooper has unpainted
     helmet brow [P1A12] 6.00
____Stormtroopers [P1A13] 6.00

____TIE Pilot and Wedge [P1A14] 6.00
____Tusken Raider and Jawa [P1A15].........................6.00

2-packs, A New Hope, red logo.
____C-3PO and Chewbacca [P1A16 ....6.00
____Luke Skywalker and R2-D2 [P1A17] 6.00
____Obi-Wan Kenobi and Darth Vader [P1A18] 6.00
____Princess Leia and Han Solo [P1A19] 6.00
____Tusken Raider and Jawa [P1A20].........................8.00

2-packs, Attack of the Clones, blue logo.
____Obi-Wan Kenobi and Jango Fett [P1A21] 6.00
____Padme Amidala and Anakin Skywalker [P1A22] ..6.00
____Yoda and Clone Trooper [P1A23] 6.00

2-packs, Bounty Hunters, blue logo.
____4-LOM and Bossk [P1A24] 10.00
____Bobba Fett and Dengar [P1A25] 12.00
____Bobba Fett and Dengar, insert shows characters
     reversed [P1A26] 6.00
____IG-88 and Zuckuss [P1A27] 6.00

2-packs, Bounty Hunters, red logo.
____4-LOM and Bossk [P1A28]..................................8.00
____Bobba Fett and Dengar [P1A29] 6.00

2-packs, Empire Strikes Back, white logo.
____Chewbacca   and   Disassembled   C-3PO
     [P1A30] 6.00

P1A25

P1A26

P1A27

P1A28

P1A29

P1A30

P1A31

P1A32

P1A33

P1A34

P1A35

P1A36

P1A37

P1A38

P1A39

P1A40

P1A41

P1A42

P1A43

P1A44

P1A45

P1A46

P1A47

P1A48

P1A49

P1A50

P1A51

P1A52

Toys: Figures – Jedi Force

P1A53　　P1A54　　P1A55　　P1A56　　P1A57　　P1A58

P1A59　　P1A60　　P1A61　　P1A62

____Luke Skywalker and Lando Calrissian [P1A31] 6.00
____Princess Leia and Darth Vader [P1A32] 6.00
____Rebel Trooper and Snow Trooper [P1A33]............6.00

2-packs, Phantom Menace, blue logo.
____Obi-Wan Kenobi and Darth Maul [P1A34] 6.00

2-packs, Return of the Jedi, blue logo.
____Jedi Luke Skywalker and Gamorrean Guard [P1A35] 12.00
____Lando Calrissian Skiff Guard and Nikto [P1A36] 6.00

2-packs, Return of the Jedi, red logo.
____Jedi Luke Skywalker and Gamorrean Guard [P1A37] 6.00

2-packs, Revenge of the Sith, blue logo.
____Battle Droid and Clone Trooper [P1A38] 8.00
____Emperor Palpatine and Shock Trooper [P1A39] 6.00

2-packs, Revenge of the Sith, red logo.
____Anakin Skywalker and Darth Tyrannus [P1A40] 6.00
____Chewbacca and Clone Trooper [P1A41] 6.00
____Dark Side Anakin and Clone Trooper [P1A42] 6.00
____Darth Sidious and Yoda [P1A43] 6.00
____Darth Vader and Holographic Emperor [P1A44] 8.00
____Mace Windu and Kit Fisto [P1A45] 6.00
____Obi-Wan Kenobi and Clone Trooper [P1A46] 8.00
____Obi-Wan Kenobi and General Grievous [P1A47] 6.00
____R2-D2 and Super Battle Droid [P1A48] 6.00
____Yoda and Kashyyyk Trooper [P1A49] 8.00

2-packs, vehicle with figure.
____Speederbike with Luke Skywalker [P1A50] 8.00
____Speederbike with Scout Trooper [P1A51] 8.00

2-packs.
____Luke Skywalker (Hoth) and Han Solo (Hoth) [P1A52] 10.00

Vehicles.
____2-in-1 Landspeeder Desert Crawler [P1A53]......15.00
____2-in-1 X-Wing Racer [P1A54]...............................15.00
____Millennium Falcon [P1A55]...................................10.00
____X-Wing [P1A56] 10.00

Playskool
____Arena Adventure [P1A57] 35.00
____Duel with Darth Maul [P1A58] 35.00
____Fast Through the Forest 0100 original Luke text [P1A59] 65.00
____Fast Through the Forest 0100 sticker correcting Luke text 65.00
____Fast Through the Forest 0500 corrected Luke text 65.00
____Millennium Falcon Adventure [P1A60] 75.00
____The Stompin' Wampa [P1A61]............................65.00
____X-Wing Adventure [P1A62] 35.00

Toys: Figures – Jedi Force

Hasbro
____Anakin Skywalker with Jedi Pod [P2A01] 12.00
____Anakin Skywalker w/Rescue Glider [P2A02] 10.00
____C-3PO and R2-D2 [P2A03] 10.00
____C-3PO and R2-D2 with hook on card 10.00
____Chewbacca with Wookiee Action Tool [P2A04] 10.00
____Chewbacca with Wookiee Scout Flyer sticker corrects asst number [P2A05] 10.00

____Darth Vader with Imperial Claw Droid, clear lightsaber [P2A06] 10.00
____Darth Vader with Imperial Claw Droid, red lightsaber no hook on card [P2A07] 25.00
____Darth Vader with Imperial Claw Droid, red lightsaber with hooked card [P2A08] 10.00
____Han Solo with Jet Bike [P2A09] 10.00
____Luke Skywalker hoverboard [P2A10] 10.00
____Luke Skywalker with Jedi Jet Pack [P2A11] 10.00
____Mace Windu w/Jedi grappling hook [P2A12] 10.00
____Yoda with Swamp Stomper [P2A13] 10.00

Creatures.
____Obi-Wan Kenobi with Boga [P2A14] 70.00

Vehicles.
____Luke Skywalker with Speederbike yellow flightsuit [P2A15] 25.00
____Luke Skywalker with Speederbike clear lightsaber [P2A16] 20.00
____Luke Skywalker with Speederbike green lightsaber [P2A17] 20.00
____X-Wing Fighter [P2A18] 40.00
____X-Wing Fighter, eBay exclusive [P2A19] 50.00

First 50, Hasbro COA, eBay exclusives.
____Chewbacca 75.00
____Darth Vader 75.00
____Luke Skywalker 75.00
____Luke Skywalker with Speederbike.....................45.00
____R2-D2 and C-3PO 75.00
____X-Wing Fighter...100.00

P2A01　P2A02　P2A03　P2A04　P2A05　P2A06　P2A07　P2A08　P2A09

P2A10　P2A11　P2A12　P2A13　P2A14　P2A15

P2A16　　P2A17　　P2A18　　P2A19

Toys: Figures – Kubrick

P1B01

P1B02

P1B03

P1B04

P1B05

P1B06

P1B07

P1B08

P1B09

Toys: Figures – Kubrick

Tomy

400% scale, boxed.

____Boba Fett [P1B01] 225.00
____Boba Fett ESB [P1B02] 275.00
____Han Solo in stromtrooper disguise, limited to 2,000 [P1B03] 150.00
____Imperial Bearbrick, includes 100% [P1B04] 150.00
____Luke Skywalker in stromtrooper disguise, limited to 2,000 ....150.00

Boxed set 1

____Speekerbike with Luke and Leia [P1B05] 135.00

Boxed set 2

____5-Pack: Spirit of Obi-Wan, Han Solo (Bespin), Paploo, R5-D4, R2 Imperial Droid. Toys R Us Japan exclusive [P1B07]...95.00

Boxed set 3

____4-Pack: Droopy McCool, Sy Snoodles, Max Rebo, Doda Bodonawieedo. Limited to 2005 pieces. [P1B06] 150.00

Boxed set 4

____5-Pack: Luke Skywalker (Ceremonial outfit), K-3PO, R5-A1, Ten Nunb, and Romba. Toys R Us Japan exclusive [P1B08]...85.00

Series 0

____Early Bird Kit with 4 figures [P1B09] 250.00

Series 1

____4-LOM [P1B10]..15.00
____Boba Fett [P1B11] 10.00
____Boba Fett / secret variation 125.00
____Bossk [P1B12] 10.00
____Dengar [P1B13] 15.00
____IG-88 [P1B14]..10.00
____Zuckuss [P1B15] 15.00

Series 2

____Cantina Band member 10.00
____Cantina Band member, alt. Instrument [P1B16]...10.00
____Greedo [P1B17] 25.00
____Han Solo [P1B18]...10.00
____Indiana Jones (Han Solo box) 175.00
____Obi-Wan Kenobi [P1B19]...................................25.00
____Sandtrooper, orange pauldron [P1B20] 10.00
____Sandtrooper, white pauldron 45.00
____Tusken Raider [P1B21]...25.00

Series 3

____AT-AT Driver [P1B22] 10.00
____Han Solo in Carbonite [P1B23] 10.00
____Han Solo released from Carbonite 45.00
____Jawa [P1B24] 10.00
____Lando Calrissian [P1B25].....................................10.00
____See Threepio [P1B26] 10.00
____Wicket [P1B27]..10.00

Series 4

____Darth Vader with removable helmet....................10.00
____DarthVader [P1B28] 10.00
____Emperor [P1B29] 10.00
____Han Solo, Hoth [P1B30].......................................10.00
____Luke Skywalker, Bespin [P1B31] 10.00
____Nien Numb [P1B32] 10.00
____Stormtrooper [P1B33] 10.00
____Stormtrooper / Han 100.00
____Stormtrooper / Luke 100.00

Series 5

____Admiral Ackbar [P1B34]..10.00
____Death Star Gunner [P1B35] 10.00
____Luke Skywalker, Jedi [P1B36] 10.00
____Princess Leia, captive [P1B37] 10.00
____Snaggletooth [P1B38] 10.00
____Yoda [P1B39] 10.00

Series 6

____Death Star Trooper...10.00
____Luke Skywalker, X-Wing Pilot 10.00
____R4-M9..10.00
____RA-7 (Death Star Droid) 10.00

P1B10

P1B11

P1B12

P1B13

P1B14 P1B15 P1B16 P1B17 P1B18 P1B19 P1B20 P1B21 P1B22 P1B23 P1B24 P1B25

P1B26 P1B27 P1B28 P1B29 P1B30 P1B31 P1B32 P1B33 P1B34 P1B35 P1B36 P1B37

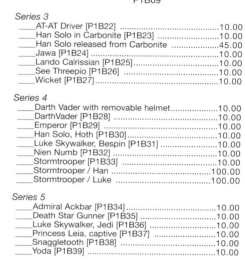

P1B38 P1B39 P1B40 P1B41 P1B42 P1B43 P1B44 P1B45 P1B46 P1B47

TYF01　TYF02　TYF03　TYF04　TYF05　TYF06　TYF07　TYF08　TYF09　TYF10

TYF11　TYF12　TYF13　TYF14　TYF15　TYF16　TYF17　TYF18　TYF19　TYF20

____Rebel Fleet Trooper 10.00
____TIE Fighter Pilot 10.00

Series 7
____Biker Trooper 10.00
____Emperor's Royal Guard 10.00
____Gamorrean Guard 10.00
____Lando Calrissian as Skiff Guard.......................10.00
____Leia Boushh Disguise 10.00
____Spirit of Anakin Skywalker 10.00

Special event, carded.
____Artoo Detoo, Wonder Festival '04 [P1B40] 150.00
____Boba Fett animated, Wonder Festival 2004 [P1B41] 200.00
____Boba Fett, Mediacom Toy Expo '03 [P1B42] ..550.00
____Commander Jorg Sacul, Medicom Toy Expo '06 [P1B43] 350.00
____Darth Vader, Medicom Toy Expo '05 [P1B44] 325.00
____Luke Skywalker [P1B45] 150.00
____Princess Leia hologram, World Characters Convention 19, limited to 500 [P1B46] 100.00
____Sandtrooper, Medicon Toy Expo 2004 at Parco, Tokyo Japan [P1B47] 350.00

Toys: Figures – Mini

Characture style, 2" tall. Glossy painted ceramic.
____Anakin Skywalker [TYF01] 3.00

____Battle Droid [TYF02] 3.00
____Boss Nass [TYF03] 3.00
____Darth Maul [TYF04] 3.00
____Darth Sidious [TYF05] 3.00
____Darth Vader [TYF06] 3.00
____Jabba the Hutt [TYF07] 3.00
____Jar Jar Binks [TYF08] 3.00
____Qui-Gon Jinn [TYF09] 3.00
____Yoda [TYF10] 3.00

Characture style, 2" tall. Glow-in-the-dark features.
____Anakin Skywalker [TYF11] 3.00
____Battle Droid [TYF12] 3.00
____Boss Nass [TYF13] 3.00
____Darth Maul [TYF14] 3.00
____Darth Sidious [TYF15]...3.00
____Darth Vader [TYF16] 3.00
____Jabba the Hutt [TYF17] 3.00
____Jar Jar Binks [TYF18] 3.00
____Qui-Gon Jinn [TYF19] 3.00
____Yoda [TYF20] 3.00

Characture style, 2" tall.
____Anakin Skywalker 3.00
____Battle Droid 3.00
____Boss Nass 3.00
____Darth Maul 3.00
____Darth Sidious 3.00
____Darth Vader 3.00
____Jabba the Hutt 3.00
____Jar Jar Binks 3.00
____Qui-Gon Jinn..3.00
____Yoda 3.00

EPI:TPM. Approximately 3" tall, round textured base, with removable weapons.
____Anakin Skywalker with backpack and grease gun [TYF21] 5.00
____Battle Droid with blaster [TYF22] 5.00
____Darth Maul with attached lightsaber [TYF23]........5.00
____Jar Jar Binks with Gungan staff [TYF24] 5.00
____Obi-Wan with blue lightsaber [TYF25] 5.00
____Padme with podrace viewscreen [TYF26] 5.00
____Queen Amidala with long pistol [TYF27] 5.00
____Qui-Gon Jinn with green lightsaber and Naboo pistol [TYF28] 5.00

EPI:TPM. Approximately 3" tall.
____Darth Maul 3.00

Applause
____4-Pack: Anakin Skywalker, Destroyer Droid, Jar Jar Binks, Queen Amidala [2:266] 12.00
____4-Pack: Darth Maul, Obi-Wan Kenobi, Qui-Gon Jinn, battle droid ground commander [2:266] 12.00
____5-Pack [2:266] 16.00
____5-Pack with bonus 6th figure, Blockbuster exclusive [2:266] 23.00
____6-Pack with display base [2:266] 26.00
____7-Pack, with exclusive Boba Fett [2:266] 24.00
____Admiral Ackbar [TYF29] 4.00
____Anakin Skywalker (Tatooine) [TYF30] 3.00
____Boba Fett [TYF31]...4.00
____Bosk [TYF32]..4.00
____C-3PO [TYF33] 4.00
____C-3PO and R2-D2 on platform [TYF34] 6.00
____Chewbacca [TYF35] 4.00

TYF21　TYF22　TYF23　TYF24　TYF25　TYF26　TYF27　TYF28　TYF29　TYF30　TYF31　TYF32　TYF33

TYF34　TYF35　TYF36　TYF37　TYF38　TYF39　TYF40　TYF41

TYF42　TYF43　TYF44　TYF45　TYF46　TYF47　TYF48　TYF49　TYF50　TYF51　TYF52　TYF53

TYF54 TYF55 TYF56 TYF57 TYF58 TYF59 TYF60 TYF61 TYF62 TYF63 TYF64

TYF65 TYF66 TYF67 TYF68 TYF69 TYF70 TYF71 TYF72 TYF73

TYF74 TYF75 TYF76

____Darth Maul [TYF36] 5.00
____Darth Vader [TYF37] 4.00
____Destroyer Droid [TYF38] 4.00
____Emperor Palpatine [TYF39] 4.00
____Greedo [TYF40] 4.00
____Han Solo and Jabba the Hutt [TYF41] 7.00
____Han Solo [TYF42] 4.00
____Jar Jar Binks [TYF43] 4.00
____Lando Calrissian [TYF44] 4.00
____Luke Skywalker [TYF45] 4.00
____Obi-Wan [TYF46] 5.00
____Obi-Wan Kenobi [TYF47] 4.00
____Obi-Wan Kenobi, spirit [TYF48] 4.00
____Pit Droid [TYF49] 4.00
____Princess Leia [TYF50] 4.00
____Queen Amidala (Naboo) [TYF51] 3.00
____Qui-Gon [TYF52] 5.00
____R2-D2 [TYF53] 4.00
____Snowtrooper [TYF54] 4.00
____Stormtrooper [TYF55] 4.00
____Tie Fighter Pilot [TYF56] 4.00
____Tusken Raider [TYF57] 4.00
____Wedge Antillies [TYF58] 4.00
____Yoda [TYF59] 4.00

Be@rbrick
____Wicket, wave 7 secret figure [TYF60] 265.00

Bimbo
Potmetal figures, approx. 1.5" in height. Chase figures, gold in color.
____Anakin Skywalker 16.00

TYF77 TYF78 TYF79 TYF80

TYF81 TYF82 TYF83 TYF84 TYF85

____Chewbacca 16.00
____Count Dooku 16.00
____Darth Vader 16.00
____General Grievous 16.00
____Obi-Wan Kenobi 16.00
____Palpatine 16.00
____Yoda 16.00

Potmetal figures, approx. 1.5" in height.
____Anakin Skywalker 8.00
____Chewbacca 8.00
____Count Dooku 8.00
____Darth Vader 8.00
____General Grievous 8.00
____Obi-Wan Kenobi 8.00
____Palpatine 8.00
____Yoda 8.00

Comics Spain
____C-3PO [TYF61] 12.00
____C-3PO, all gold colored [TYF62] 35.00
____Chief Chirpa [TYF63] 10.00
____Dulok [TYF64] 12.00
____Kez-Iban [TYF65] 10.00
____Kneesa [TYF66] 12.00
____Latara [TYF67] 10.00
____R2-D2 [TYF68] 12.00
____Teebo [TYF69] 10.00
____Wicket [TYF70] 10.00

DeAgostini
____01 Darth Vader 20.00
____02 Stormtrooper 20.00
____02 Yoda 20.00
____03 Han Solo 20.00
____04 Luke Skywalker 20.00
____05 Chewbacca 20.00
____06 TIE Advanced 20.00
____07 C-3PO 20.00
____08 Obi-Wan Kenobi 20.00
____09 Darth Maul 20.00
____10 Princess Leia 20.00
____11 Anakin Skywalker 20.00
____11 R2-D2 ....20.00
____12 Admiral Ackbar 20.00

____13 X-Wing Fighter 20.00
____14 Count Dooku 20.00
____15 Wicket the Ewok 20.00
____16 Jabba the Hutt 20.00
____17 Grand Moff Tarkin 20.00
____18 Imperial Royal Guard 20.00
____19 Anakin Skywalker 20.00
____20 Emperor 20.00
____21 Padme Amidala 20.00
____22 Boba Fett 20.00
____23 Clone Trooper 20.00
____24 Tion Medon 20.00
____25 Bib Fortuna 20.00
____26 Jango Fett 20.00
____27 Lando Calrissian 20.00
____28 AT-AT 20.00
____29 General Grirvous 20.00
____30 Greedo 20.00
____31 Jawa 20.00

Disney / MGM
____Artoo Detoo [TYF68] 8.00
____Chewbacca [TYF71] 8.00
____Darth Vader [TYF72] 8.00
____See Threepio [TYF73] 8.00
____Stormtrooper [TYF74] 8.00
____Wicket the Ewok [TYF75] 8.00
____Yoda [TYF76] 8.00

Blind packed in packets of three.
____Boba Fett 3.00
____C-3PO 3.00
____Captain Rex 3.00
____Chewbacca 3.00
____Darth Maul 3.00
____Darth Vader 3.00
____Ewok 3.00
____Jabba the Hutt 3.00
____Jar Jar Binks 3.00
____Jedi Mickey 3.00
____Mickey Mouse as Luke Skywalker 3.00
____Millennium Falcon 3.00
____Minnie Mouse as Princess Leia 3.00
____R2-D2 ....3.00
____Star Tours Starspeeder 3000 ....3.00
____Stormtrooper 3.00
____X-Wing Fighter 3.00
____Yoda 3.00

Kamiru
____Boba Fett with tin storage cylinder [TYF77] 15.00
____Boba Fett, single figure promotion 18.00
____Clone Set 1: 4 clones, clone commander [TYF78] 50.00
____Clone Set 1: 4 clones, clone pilot [TYF79] 50.00
____Han in Carbonite Block, single figure promotion [TYF80] 16.00

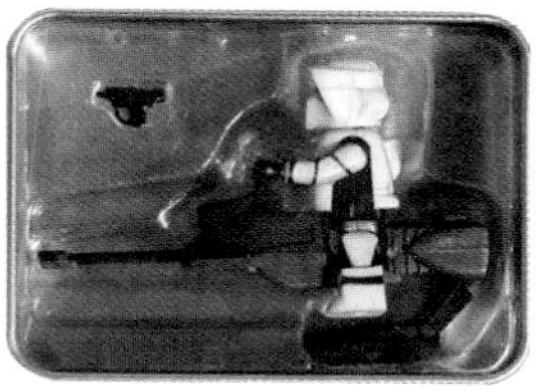
TYF86

TYF87

TYF88

TYF89

TYF90

TYF91

TYF92

TYF93

TYF94

TYF95

TYF96

TYF97

TYF98

TYF99

TYF100

TYF101

TYF102

____Set 1, ANH [TYF81] 45.00
____Set 2, ESB [TYF82]....52.00
____Set 3, ROTJ [TYF83] 45.00
____Set 4: Death Star Escape [TYF84]....45.00
____Set 5, EPI [TYF85] 25.00
____Speederbike trooper and speederbike with storage tin [TYF86] 35.00
____Stormtrooper [3:260] 10.00

Lego
Episode III.
____Anakin Skywalker with light-up lightsaber, 2004 gift 25.00

Maruka
____50-piece multi-pack....125.00
____C-3PO [TYF87] 9.00
____Darth Vader's Tie Fighter [TYF88]....9.00
____Landspeeder [TYF89] 9.00
____Millennium Falcon [TYF90] 9.00
____R2-D2 [TYF91] 9.00
____X-Wing Fighter [TYF92]....9.00
____Y-Wing Fighter [TYF93]....9.00

Tomy
____Anakin and Sebulba [TYF94] 4.00
____Anakin and Watto [TYF95] 4.00
____Battle Droid on Stap [TYF96] 4.00
____Darth Maul on Sith Speeder [TYF97] 4.00
____Destroyer Droid [TYF98] 5.00
____Nute Gunray and Senator Palpatine [TYF99]....4.00
____Obi-Wan and Darth Maul [TYF100] 4.00
____Obi-Wan and TC-14 [TYF101] 4.00
____Qui-Gon and Jar Jar Binks [TYF102] 4.00
____Qui-Gon with lightsaber and Jar Jar Binks 4.00

Toys: Figures – Mini, LEGO

The LEGO Group
Mini-figure 3-packs.
____#1 Emperor, Darth Vader, Darth Maul (3340) [2:124] 25.00
____#2 Han, Luke, Boba Fett (3341) [2:124]....25.00
____#3 Chewbacca, two biker scout troops (3342) [2:124] 25.00
____#4 OOM-9, two battle droids (3343) [2:124] 25.00

Toys: Figures – Mpire

Hasbro
2-packs with stands.
____Chewbacca and Master Windu [T2F01] 10.00
____Dooku and Maul [T2F02] 10.00
____Emperor and Anakin [T2F03] 10.00
____Grievous and Kenobi [T2F04] 10.00
____Luke and Leia [T2F05] 10.00
____Queen Amidala, R2-D2, and C-3PO [T2F06]....10.00
____Solo and Boba Fett [T2F07]....12.00
____Stormtrooper and Vader....12.00

2-packs with stands. Special Collector's Edition.
____Dooku and Maul....15.00
____Luke and Leia....15.00
____Queen Amidala, R2-D2, and C-3PO 15.00
____Solo and Boba Fett 15.00

Toys: Figures – Plastic / Resin

Belgium.
____Darth Vader....15.00

Deformed style figures, approximately 4" tall.
____Anakin Skywalker [2:267] 7.00
____Darth Maul [2:267] 9.00
____Sebulba, swivles at neck [2:267] 7.00
____Watto, swivles at waist [2:267] 7.00

Applause
Classic trilogy characters.
____Boba Fett [3:262] 30.00
____C-3PO [3:262]....15.00
____Chewbacca with C-3PO in cargo net [3:262] 18.00
____Darth Vader [3:262] 23.00
____Darth Vader with removable dome, limited edition [3:262]....48.00
____Darth Vader, cloth cape [3:262] 18.00
____Dash Rendar [3:262]....10.00
____Emperor Palpatine [3:262] 18.00
____Greedo [3:262] 18.00
____Han Solo in Stormtrooper disguise [3:262] 18.00
____Lando Calrissian in Skiff disguise [3:262] 18.00
____Leia as Jabba's Prisoner [3:262] 24.00
____Luke Skywalker in X-Wing Pilot Gear [3:262] 35.00
____Luke Skywalker, Jedi Training wih glow-in-dark lightsaber and removable blastshield helmet [3:262]....17.00
____Luke with Yoda in backpack [3:262] 12.00
____Luke with Yoda in backpack, pewter colored plastic [3:262]....24.00
____Obi-Wan Kenobi [3:262]....18.00
____Obi-Wan Kenobi, glow-in-dark [3:262] 20.00
____Prince Xizor [3:262] 26.00
____Princess Leia, Endor outfit [3:262]....18.00
____R2-D2 [3:262] 18.00
____Tie Fighter Pilot [3:262] 18.00
____Tusken Raider [3:262]....18.00
____Wedge Antillies [3:262]....20.00

EPI:TPM. "Collectible Character," approx. 10" tall.
____Darth Maul [2:267] 30.00
____Obi-Wan Kenobi [2:267]....18.00
____Queen Amidala [2:267]....15.00
____Qui-Gon Jinn [2:267] 18.00

EPI:TPM. "Mega Collectible," approx 14" with lighted saber in numbered package.
____Darth Maul [2:267] 50.00
____Obi-Wan Kenobi [2:267]....50.00
____Qui-Gon Jinn [2:267] 50.00

EPI:TPM. Approximately 7" tall. Some articulation
____Anakin Skywalker [3:262] 8.00
____Darth Maul with binoculars [3:262]....8.00
____Jar Jar Binks [3:262]....8.00
____Watto [3:262]....8.00

Daft Productions Ltd.
____Daft Duck "Luke" [FG01] 15.00

Decopac
EPI:TPM Cake top figures.
____Jar Jar Binks....4.00
____Watto....9.00

EPII:AOTC cake top figures.
____Darth Vader [2:267]....6.00
____Jango Fett [2:267]....6.00
____Obi-Wan Kenobi [2:267] 6.00

Fan Made
Deformed. JoeToy.com exclusive.
____Admiral Ackbar....24.00
____Boba Fett 24.00
____C-3PO....24.00
____Cantina Band Member....24.00
____Chewbacca [3:431] 24.00
____Darth Vader [3:431] 24.00
____Emperor 24.00
____Grand Moff Tarkin....24.00
____Han Solo [3:431]....24.00
____Han Solo in Carbonite 24.00
____Jabba's Dancer 24.00
____Jabba the Hutt 40.00
____Lando Calrissian....24.00
____Luke Skywalker [3:431] 24.00
____Obi-Wan Kenobi [3:431]....24.00
____Princess Leia and Salicious Crumb....24.00
____R2-D2 ....24.00
____Stormtrooper 24.00
____Wedge 24.00
____Wicket....24.00
____Yoda 24.00

Hasbro
____Anakin Skywalker [3:262] 12.00
____Darth Vader [3:262] 12.00
____Jango Fett [3:262] 12.00
____Mace Windu [3:262] 12.00

T2F01

T2F02

T2F03

T2F04

T2F05

T2F06

T2F07

Toys: Figures – Plastic / Resin

FG01

FG02-FG09 packaging

FG02

FG03

FG04

FG05

FG06

FG07

FG08

FG09

Itrangers Lab
Ciboy Star Wash (parody).

____Dark Vapor (Darth Vader) [FG02] 20.00
____Sh-it (Darth Maul) [FG03] 20.00
____Skywasher (Luke) [FG04] 20.00
____Soapie (Chewie) [FG05] 20.00
____Wash Trooper (stormtrooper) [FG06] 20.00
____Washer Master (Yoda) [FG07] 20.00
____WC30 (C-3PO) [FG08] 20.00
____WC30, silver (C-3PO; chase figure) [FG09] 25.00

Kinder
Hippo Star Wars parody figure accessories.

____Blue Star diorama [FG10] 35.00
____Hippo Landspeeder [FG11] 25.00
____Millennium Hippo [FG12] 4.00

Hippo Star Wars parody figures.

____Aubacca [FG13] 4.00
____Dark Laser [FG14] 4.00

____Dark Laser, black 65.00
____ER2WO Hippo [FG15] 4.00
____H-IPO [FG16] 4.00
____Happy Han [FG17] 4.00
____Hippoda [FG18] 4.00
____Jango Jett [FG19] 4.00
____Luke Eiwalker [FG20] 4.00
____Obi-Wan Hippobi [FG21] 4.00
____Prinzessin Hippeia [FG22] 4.00

Kurt S. Adler, Inc.
Christmas figures. 2005.

____C-3PO wrapped in lights [FG23] 20.00
____R2-D2 with presents [FG24] 20.00
____Santa Yoda [FG25] 20.00

Christmas figures. 2006.

____Darth Vader building Death Star in snow
[FG26] 20.00
____Santa Yoda [FG27] 20.00

M&M World
Approx. 6" tall with removable base. Limited to 2,500 each.

____Boba Fett 45.00
____Darth Maul 45.00
____Darth Vader 45.00
____Luke Skywalker 45.00
____Princess Leia 45.00

Medicom
Vinyl Collectible Dolls.

____501st Clone Trooper, Comicon exclusive 95.00
____Boba Fett, World Character Convention 18, limited to
2004 ....175.00
____Clone Trooper, limited to 2,006 ....75.00
____Darth Vader 75.00
____Stormtrooper 75.00
____TIE Pilot 75.00

Out of Character

____C-3PO [3:262] 19.00
____Chewbacca [3:262] 17.00
____Darth Vader [3:262] 18.00
____Han Solo [3:262] 17.00
____Luke Skywalker, Jedi [3:262] 17.00
____Luke Skywalker, X-wing pilot [3:262] 24.00
____Obi-Wan Kenobi [3:262] 18.00
____Princess Leia [3:262] 17.00
____R2-D2 [3:262] 19.00
____Stormtrooper [3:262] 18.00

Takara

____C-3PO [FG28] 245.00
____Chewbacca [FG29] 245.00
____Darth Vader [FG30] 245.00
____Stormtrooper [FG31] 245.00

FG10

FG11

FG12

FG13

FG14

FG15

FG16

FG17

FG18

FG19

FG20

FG21

FG22

FG23

FG24

FG25

FG26

FG27

FG28

FG29

FG30

FG31

FT101

FT102

FT103

FT104

FT105

FT106

FT107

FT108

FT109

FT110

FT111

FT112

FT113

FT114

FT115

Toys: Figures – Titanium

Hasbro
Color packaging. Includes a custom base and display case.

____Boba Fett	25.00
____Boba Fett, vintage finish [FT101]	30.00
____C-3PO [FT102]	25.00
____Clone Trooper [FT103]	30.00
____Clone Trooper, vintage finish [FT104]	30.00
____Darth Maul	175.00
____Darth Vader [FT105]	25.00
____Darth Vader, Mustafar armor, Target exclusive [FT106]	30.00
____Darth Vader, vintage finish [FT107]	30.00
____General Grievous [FT107]	25.00
____IG-88 [FT108]	30.00
____Luke Skywalker, snowspeeder pilot	165.00

Include a custom base and display case.

____Boba Fett [FT109]	25.00
____Boba Fett, vintage finish [FT110]	30.00
____Bossk [FT111]	20.00
____Bossk, vintage finish [FT112]	30.00
____Darth Vader [FT113]	20.00
____Darth Vader, vintage finish [FT114]	30.00
____Sandtrooper [FT115]	20.00
____Sandtrooper, vintage finish	30.00

Toys: Figures – Unleashed Battle Packs

Hasbro
Miniature static-posed figures.
Wave 1, Battle of Utapu.

____Attack Battalion (standing trooper positioned on right)	10.00
____Attack Battalion (standing trooper positioned second from left) [A1U01]	10.00
____Battle Droids (Battle Droids positioned on outside) [A1U02]	10.00
____Battle Droids (Battle Droids positioned on inside)	10.00
____Commanders[A1U03]	10.00
____Utapaun Warriors (kneeling warrior on left)	10.00
____Utapaun Warriors (kneeling warrior on right)	10.00

Wave 2, Battle of Felucia.

____Aayla Secura's Star Corps [A1U04]	10.00
____Kashyyyk and Felicua Heroes [A1U05]	10.00
____Wookiee Warriors [A1U06]	10.00
____Yoda's Elite Corps [A1U07]	10.00

Wave 3, Battle of Hoth.

____Imperial Encounter [A1U08]	10.00
____Imperial Invasion [A1U09]	10.00
____Imperial Snowtroopers [A1U10]	10.00
____Rebel Alliance Troopers [A1U11]	10.00
____Snowtrooper Battalion [A1U12]	10.00
____Wampa Assault [A1U13]	10.00

Wave 3, Deluxe.

____Evacuation at Echo Base [A1U14]	12.00
____Snowspeeder Assault [A1U15]	12.00

Wave 4, Order Sixty-Six.

____Jedi Masters [A1U16]	10.00
____Shock Trooper Battalioni [A1U17]	10.00
____The New Empire [A1U18]	10.00
____Vader's 501st Legion [A1U19]	10.00

Ultimate battle packs.

____Battle of Geonosis – The Clone Wars	20.00
____Battle of Hoth – Imperial Invasion	20.00
____Battle of Kashyyyk – Droid Invasion	20.00

A1U01

A1U02

A1U03

A1U04

A1U05

A1U06

A1U07

A1U08

A1U09

A1U10

A1U11

A1U12

A1U13

A1U14

A1U15

A1U16

A1U17

A1U18

A1U19

Toys: Figures – Unleashed

AFU01　　AFU02　　AFU03　　AFU04　　AFU05　　AFU06　　AFU07　　AFU08　　AFU09

AFU10　　AFU11　　AFU12　　AFU13　　AFU14　　AFU15　　AFU16　　AFU17　　AFU18

AFU19　　AFU20　　AFU21　　AFU22　　AFU23　　AFU24　　AFU25　　AFU26　　AFU27

Toys: Figures – Unleashed

Hasbro
Blue package.
____ Anakin Skywalker [AFU01] 45.00
____ Darth Maul [AFU02] 85.00
____ Darth Sidious [AFU03] 35.00
____ Darth Tyrannus [AFU04] 50.00
____ Darth Vader [AFU05] 100.00
____ Darth Vader (removable helmet) [AFU06] 265.00
____ Jango Fett and Boba Fett [AFU07] 60.00
____ Luke Skywalker, Jedi [AFU08] 70.00
____ Mace Windu [AFU09] 40.00
____ Obi-Wan Kenobi [AFU10] 40.00
____ Padme Amidala [AFU11] 70.00
____ Princess Leia [AFU12] 120.00

Color package.
____ Aayla Secura [AFU13] 40.00

____ Anakin Skywalker, EPIII [AFU14] 48.00
____ Asajj Ventress [AFU15] 15.00
____ Aura Sing [AFU16] 30.00
____ Boba Fett [AFU17] 120.00
____ Bossk [AFU18] 20.00
____ Chewbacca [AFU19] 40.00
____ Chewbacca on Kashyyyk [AFU20].....................30.00
____ Clone Commander [AFU21] 25.00
____ Clone Trooper [AFU22] 20.00
____ Count Dooku [AFU23] 50.00
____ Darth Sidious [AFU24] 40.00
____ Darth Vader (removable helmet) [AFU25]...........60.00
____ Darth Vader, EPIII [AFU26] 20.00
____ General Grievous [AFU27] 25.00
____ Han Solo [AFU28]...80.00
____ Han Solo in Stormtrooper outfit [AFU29]...........20.00
____ IG-88 [AFU30]..30.00
____ Luke Skywalker [AFU31] 60.00
____ Luke Skywalker, pilot [AFU32] 40.00
____ Mace Windu [AFU33] 40.00

____ Obi-Wan Kenobi [AFU34]....................................40.00
____ Obi-Wan Kenobi, EPIII [AFU35] 15.00
____ Princess Leia [AFU36] 70.00
____ Shock Trooper [AFU37].....................................20.00
____ Stormtrooper [AFU38].......................................80.00
____ Tusken Raider [AFU39].....................................20.00
____ Yoda [AFU40] 100.00
____ Yoda vs. Palpatine [AFU41] 35.00

Cylinder-shaped package.
____ Boba Fett, Target exclusive [AFU42] 30.00
____ Darth Vader, Best Buy exclusive [AFU43] 50.00
____ Darth Vader, Walmart exclusive 30.00
____ General Grievous, Target exclusive [AFU44] 30.00
____ Luke Skywalker, Walmart exclusive [AFU45]......30.00

Hasbro, Canada
Blue package.
____ Darth Maul [AFU46] 20.00
____ Jango Fett and Boba Fett [AFU47] 20.00

AFU28　　AFU29　　AFU30　　AFU31　　AFU32　　AFU33　　AFU34　　AFU35　　AFU36

AFU37　　AFU38　　AFU39　　AFU40　　AFU41　　AFU42　　AFU43　　AFU44　　AFU45

AFU46

AFU47

AFU48

AFU49

AFU50

YJ01

FR01

FRI02

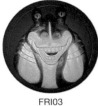
FRI03

FRI04

FRI05

FRI06

FRI07

FRI08

No SW Unleased logo on cardback.
____Anakin Skywalker [AFU48].................................25.00
____Darth Vader [AFU49] 35.00
____Padme Amidala [AFU50] 35.00

Toys: Flight Simulators

Kenner
____X-Wing Flight Simulator [YJ01] 24.00

Toys: Folding Picture Cubes

Disney / MGM
____Classic trilogy scenes [2:270]...........................9.00

Toys: Frisbees

Burger King
____Darth Vader frisbee [FRI01] 25.00

KFC
____Battle Droid flying bucket topper [FRI02]..............4.00
____Jar Jar Binks flying bucket topper [FRI03]...........4.00

Pine-Sol
Character line drawing and Star Wars logo, silver plastic frisbee, mail-in premium.
____C-3PO [FRI04] 16.00
____Chewbacca [FRI05] 16.00
____Darth Vader [FRI06] 16.00
____R2-D2 [FRI07] 16.00
____Stormtrooper [FRI08] 16.00

FRI09

FRI10

FRI11

FRI12

FR13

____X-Wing Fighter [FRI09]...................................16.00

Spectra Star
____Star Wars logo above raised images of Star Destroyer and Millennium Falcon [FRI10] 8.00

Worlds Apart
____Darth Maul E.Pix flying disc, glows in the dark [FRI11] 11.00
____Whizza Performance Disc, Star Wars logo and X-wings on colored sticker 18.00

Skimmer discs.
____Imperial Fighter [FRI12] 18.00
____Stormtrooper [FRI13] 18.00

Toys: Games – Board

Spain.
____La Guerre Des Etoiles 65.00

20th Century Fox
____EPII dice game with cloth pouch [3:267] 25.00

Avalon Hill
____The Queens Gambit [NB01]..............................60.00

Character Games, Ltd.
____Journey to Geonosis water maze [NB02] 10.00
____Rescue on Geonosis [NB03] 25.00

EG
____Star Wars The Game [2:272] 45.00

Gamma Two
____Star Wars [NB04] 55.00

Hasbro
____Battle for Naboo 3D action game [NB05] 20.00
____Galactic Battle, Episode I, electronic [NB06]......35.00
____Jar Jar Binks 3-D adventure game [NB07] 15.00
____Lightsaber Duel battle game [NB08] 20.00
____Simon space battle game [NB09] 34.00
____Star Wars Monopoly, Episode I edition [NB10]..35.00

Horn Abbott International
Australia.
____Trivial Pursuit, Star Wars Bite Size [NB11]..........25.00

NB01

NB02

NB03

NB04

NB05

NB06

NB07

NB08

NB09

NB10

NB11

NB12

NB13

NB14

NB15

NB16

NB17

NB18

NB19

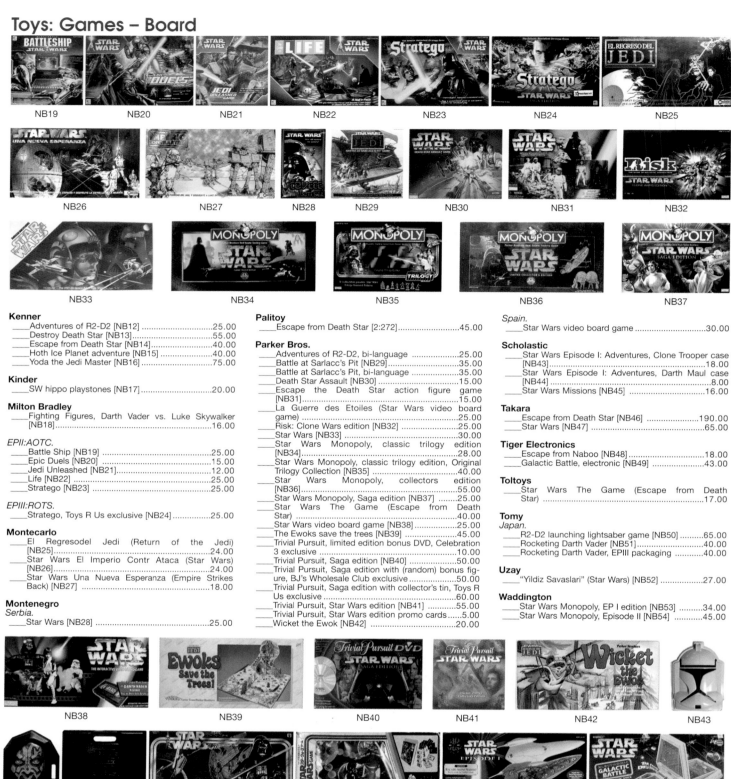
NB20

NB21

NB22

NB23

NB24

NB25

NB26

NB27

NB28

NB29

NB30

NB31

NB32

NB33

NB34

NB35

NB36

NB37

Kenner
____Adventures of R2-D2 [NB12] 25.00
____Destroy Death Star [NB13] 55.00
____Escape from Death Star [NB14] 40.00
____Hoth Ice Planet adventure [NB15] 40.00
____Yoda the Jedi Master [NB16] 75.00

Kinder
____SW hippo playstones [NB17] 20.00

Milton Bradley
____Fighting Figures, Darth Vader vs. Luke Skywalker [NB18] 16.00

EPII:AOTC.
____Battle Ship [NB19] 25.00
____Epic Duels [NB20] 15.00
____Jedi Unleashed [NB21] 12.00
____Life [NB22] 25.00
____Stratego [NB23] 25.00

EPIII:ROTS.
____Stratego, Toys R Us exclusive [NB24] 25.00

Montecarlo
____El Regresodel Jedi (Return of the Jedi) [NB25] 24.00
____Star Wars El Imperio Contr Ataca (Star Wars) [NB26] 24.00
____Star Wars Una Nueva Esperanza (Empire Strikes Back) [NB27] 18.00

Montenegro
Serbia.
____Star Wars [NB28] 25.00

Palitoy
____Escape from Death Star [2:272] 45.00

Parker Bros.
____Adventures of R2-D2, bi-language 25.00
____Battle at Sarlacc's Pit [NB29] 35.00
____Battle at Sarlacc's Pit, bi-language 35.00
____Death Star Assault [NB30] 15.00
____Escape the Death Star action figure game [NB31] 15.00
____La Guerre des Etoiles (Star Wars video board game) 25.00
____Risk: Clone Wars edition [NB32] 25.00
____Star Wars [NB33] 30.00
____Star Wars Monopoly, classic trilogy edition [NB34] 28.00
____Star Wars Monopoly, classic trilogy edition, Original Trilogy Collection [NB35] 40.00
____Star Wars Monopoly, collectors edition [NB36] 55.00
____Star Wars Monopoly, Saga edition [NB37] 25.00
____Star Wars The Game (Escape from Death Star) 40.00
____Star Wars video board game [NB38] 25.00
____The Ewoks save the trees [NB39] 45.00
____Trivial Pursuit, limited edition bonus DVD, Celebration 3 exclusive 10.00
____Trivial Pursuit, Saga edition [NB40] 50.00
____Trivial Pursuit, Saga edition with (random) bonus figure, BJ's Wholesale Club exclusive 50.00
____Trivial Pursuit, Saga edition with collector's tin, Toys R Us exclusive 60.00
____Trivial Pursuit, Star Wars edition [NB41] 55.00
____Trivial Pursuit, Star Wars edition promo cards 5.00
____Wicket the Ewok [NB42] 20.00

Spain.
____Star Wars video board game 30.00

Scholastic
____Star Wars Episode I: Adventures, Clone Trooper case [NB43] 18.00
____Star Wars Episode I: Adventures, Darth Maul case [NB44] 8.00
____Star Wars Missions [NB45] 16.00

Takara
____Escape from Death Star [NB46] 190.00
____Star Wars [NB47] 65.00

Tiger Electronics
____Escape from Naboo [NB48] 18.00
____Galactic Battle, electronic [NB49] 43.00

Toltoys
____Star Wars The Game (Escape from Death Star) 17.00

Tomy
Japan.
____R2-D2 launching lightsaber game [NB50] 65.00
____Rocketing Darth Vader [NB51] 40.00
____Rocketing Darth Vader, EPIII packaging 40.00

Uzay
____"Yildiz Savaslari" (Star Wars) [NB52] 27.00

Waddington
____Star Wars Monopoly, EP I edition [NB53] 34.00
____Star Wars Monopoly, Episode II [NB54] 45.00

NB38

NB39

NB40

NB41

NB42

NB43

NB44

NB45

NB46

NB47

NB48

NB49

NB50   NB51

NB52

NB53

NB54

NB55   NB56

NB57

NB58

| NC01 | NC02 | NC03 | NC04 | NC05 | NC06 | NC07 | NC08 | NC09 | NC10 |

| NC11 | NC12 | NC13 | NC14 | NC15 | NC16 | NC17 |

| NC18 | NC19 | NC20 | NC21 | NC22 | NC23 | NC24 |

West End Games

____Assault on Hoth [NB55] 30.00
____Battle for Endor [NB56] 30.00
____Escape from the Death Star [NB57] 26.00
____Lightsaber dueling pack [NB58].......................10.00
____Star Warriors – starfighter combat [2:273]..........25.00
____Starfighter battle book 10.00

German releases.
____Angriff Auf Hoth [3:269] 32.00

Toys: Games – Card

____Playing cards, Vader images [NC01] 8.00

Argentina.
____Burako [NC02] 20.00
____La Venganza De Los Sith [NC03].......................15.00
____Loteria Infantil..20.00

Australia.
____Feel the Force [NC04] 25.00

Brazil.
____Domino (flat cardboard) [NC05] 20.00
____Memotest [NC06] 20.00

Hungary.
____Return of the Jedi (matching) [NC07] 23.00

Character
____Feel the Force Hidden Powers Game 24.00

Copag
Brazil.
____Uno [NC08]..25.00

Cromy
____El Regresodel Jedi (Return of the Jedi) [NC09]..45.00

Decipher
____Empire Strikes Back 2 player introductory game
[NC10]..15.00
____Episode I Customizable Card Game, 160 cards in 4
decks plus rules [NC11]....................................14.00
____First Anthology Collectible Card Game (CCG) with 6
preview cards [NC12]...19.00
____Official Tournament Sealed Deck.......................43.00
____Young Jedi Collectible Card Game (CCG) 40 Card
Sample Pack (2 sample decks) "Not For Sale"
[NC13] 5.00

Hasbro
____Clash of the Lightsabers with mini-pewter Qui-Gon
Jinn and Darth Maul [NC14] 8.00

Heraclio Fournier
Spain
____Droids / Ewoks [NC15].......................................60.00

Nick Trost
____Star Wars Card Trick 30.00

Parker Bros.
____Ewoks: Favorite Five [NC16] 25.00
____Ewoks: Paw Pals [NC17] 20.00
____Ewoks: Say "Cheese" [NC18] 20.00
____Return of the Jedi: Play for Power [NC19] 15.00
____Top Trumps [NC20] 7.00

Ravensburger
Germany.
____Attack of the Clones, 110 cards and 25 pogs
[NC21]..25.00

Vintage Sports Cards
____Collectible Card Game, box of 14 CCG expansion
packs [NC22] 25.00

Winning Moves
____Top Trumps Specials, Star Wars Episodes I-III
[NC23]...12.00
____Top Trumps Specials, Star Wars Trilogy
[NC24]...12.00

Exclusive cards. Pre-order premiums.
____Biggs Darlighter 2.00
____Gamorrean Guard 2.00
____Grand Moff Tarkin 2.00
____Logray 2.00
____TIE Fighter Pilot 2.00

Toys: Games – Chess

A La Carte
Chess, sculpted plastic pieces.
____Red box [ND01] 65.00
____Yellow box [ND02] 85.00

Character Games, Ltd.
____EPII: Pewter and Bronze Effect [ND03] 50.00

Character
____Episode III...35.00

Danbury Mint
____Star Wars pewter pieces with playing board
[ND04] 980.00

Parker Bros.
____Episode II [ND05] 35.00
____Episode III [ND06]...35.00

Really Useful
____Episode I chess [ND07] 65.00

Tiger Electronics
____Galactic Chess, electronic [ND08] 79.00

Toys: Games – Electronic

____Episode I, handheld 8.00
____Star Wars, handheld 8.00

Hasbro
Episode I: The Phantom Menace.
____Sith Droid Attack Game [NE01] 22.00

Giga pets. Japan.
____R2-D2 [NE02] 15.00

Jakks Pacific, Inc.
Super gamekey combo packs.
____Darth Vader..35.00

TV Games. 5 games in one controller.
____Classic Trilogy Edition 25.00
____Darth Vader [NE03]..25.00
____General Grievous, Walmart exclusive 25.00
____R2-D2 [NE04] 25.00

| ND01 | ND02 | ND03 |

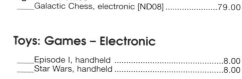

| ND04 | ND05 | ND06 | ND07 | ND08 |

Toys: Games – Electronic

NE01

NE02

NE03

NE04

NE05

NE06

NE07

NE08

NE09

NE10

NE11

NE12

NE13

NE14

NE15

NE16

NE17

NE18

NE19

NE20

TV Games. Super Value Power Packs. 5 games in one controller, game key, AC transformer.
____Yoda, Sams Club exclusive [NE05] 50.00

Wireless 2-piece sets.
____Darth Vader..45.00

Kenner
____Electronic Battle Command [NE06] 55.00
____Laser Battle [NE07] 85.00
____X-Wing Aces target game [NE08] 995.00

Micro Games of America
____Shakin' Pinball [NE09] 35.00
____Star Wars Intimidator, talking [NE10] 54.00

Handheld games.
____Empire Strikes Back, silver logo, blue controls...25.00
____Empire Strikes Back, silver logo, yellow controls...25.00
____Return of the Jedi, silver logo............25.00
____Return of the Jedi, stormtrooper art, red controls [NE11] 25.00
____Star Wars, character collage, yellow controls 25.00
____Star Wars, droid art, yellow controls 25.00
____Star Wars, silver logo, red controls..................25.00
____Star Wars, silver logo, yellow controls.............25.00

LCD games, boxed, character art with red controls.
____Empire Strikes Back..26.00
____Return of the Jedi [NE12].................................26.00
____Star Wars [NE13] 26.00

Palm games. Gray and white with black controllers.
____2-in-1 Star Wars game with Medallion [NE14] ..25.00
____Empire Strikes Back..20.00
____Return of the Jedi...20.00
____Star Wars [NE15] 20.00

Star Wars Wizard games.
____2-in-1 [NE16] 15.00
____3-in-1 [NE17] 17.00

Palitoy
____Destroy Death Star [NE18] 185.00

Thinkway
Episode I: The Phantom Menace.
____Dancing Jar Jar Binks [NE19] 18.00

Tiger Electronics
____Death Star Escape [NE20] 12.00
____Galactic Laser Pinball [NE21]...........................63.00
____Imperial Assault with Darth Vader joystick [NE22]...12.00
____Lightsaber Battle [NE23] 35.00
____Millennium Falcon "Sounds of the Force"..........18.00
____Millennium Falcon Challenge LCD game............16.00
____Quiz Whiz [NE24] 11.00
____R2-D2 Ditto Droid [NE25] 14.00
____R2-D2, clip-on [NE26]...6.00
____Rebel Forces Laser Game 26.00

EPII:AOTC.
____Anakin Skywalker's Lightsaber Duel [NE27] 25.00
____Jedi Starfighter Galactic Chase SFX Game........15.00

Episode I: The Phantom Menace.
____Battle of Naboo game with Capt. Tarples and Battle Droid joysticks [NE28] 12.00
____Battle Tank Attack game [NE29] 14.00
____Destroyer Droid game [NE30] 30.00
____Jedi Hunt game with Darth Maul and Qui-Gon Jinn joysticks [NE31] 12.00
____Lightsaber Duel game [NE32] 24.00
____Naboo Defense game [NE33] 21.00
____Naboo Escape game [NE34] 12.00
____Naboo Fighter game with exclusive Anakin Pilot figure (figure on center of card) 15.00
____Naboo Fighter game with exclusive Anakin Pilot figure (figure on right of card) [NE35].............................15.00
____Podrace Challenge game [NE36].........................15.00
____Podrace game [NE37]...24.00
____Sith Speeder game with Darth Maul action figure [NE38]...15.00
____Underwater Race to Theed game [NE39] 16.00

Giga pets.
____R2-D2 [NE40] 11.00
____Rancor [NE41] 11.00
____Yoda [NE42] 11.00

Keychain games, EPI:TPM.
____Droid Fighter Attack [NE43] 9.00
____Gian Speeder Chase [NE44]...............................7.00
____Gungan Sub Escape [NE45]................................7.00

Pen games, EPI:TPM.
____Lightsaber Duel [NE46] 9.00
____Sith Infiltrator [NE47]..9.00

NE21

NE22

NE23

NE24

NE25

NE26

NE27

NE28

NE29

NE30

NE31

NE32

NE33

NE34

NE35

NE36

NE37 NE38 NE39 NE40 NE41 NE42 NE43 NE44 NE45

NE46 NE47 NE48 NE49 NE50 NE51 NE52 NE53 NE54

R-Zone game consoles.
____Headgear with Jedi Adventure 18.00
____Headgear with Millennium Falcon Challenge [NE48] 18.00
____Xtreme pocket game with Jedi Adventure [NE49] 24.00

R-Zone xtreme pocket game cartridges.
____Imperial Assault [NE50] 8.00
____Jedi Adventure [NE51] 8.00
____Millennium Falcon Challenge [NE52] 8.00
____Rebel Forces [NE53] 8.00

Tsukuda
____Star Wars [NE54] 44.00

Toys: Games – Pinball

____Star Wars tabletop [AGP01] 35.00

Arco Falc
____Star Wars, 13"x24" [AGP02] 175.00

Toys: Helmets – Miniature

Riddell
____Boba Fett 175.00
____C-3PO 125.00
____Darth Vader 150.00
____Stormtrooper 150.00
____X-Wing Pilot 125.00

Tomy
Japan. Miniatures helmets blind-packed with display peg. Later produced as Master Replica products.
____C-3PO 45.00
____Darth Vader 45.00
____Rebel Trooper 45.00
____Stormtrooper 45.00
____Tie Pilot 45.00
____X-Wing Pilot Wedge / chase 50.00
____X-Wing Pilot 45.00

Toys: Hopper Balls

Kellytoy
____Darth Vader [HPB01] 10.00
____Yoda 10.00

Toys: Inflatables

Takara
____Inflatable X-Wing [ITN01] 325.00

Toys: Koosh Balls

Hasbro
____Captain Tarpals with Kaadu [KB01] 9.00
____Jar Jar Binks [KB02] 9.00
____Sebulba [KB03] 9.00
____Watto [KB04] 9.00

Toys: Light Bright Refills

Hasbro
____10 Sheets from SW Trilogy, and 8 freeform sheets with bonus pegs [LBR01] 5.00
____12 Sheets from SW Trilogy, and 8 freeform sheets [LBR02] 6.00
____Picture refill set, 8 classic trilogy characters 8.00

Toys: Marbles

Marble Vision
____Starbles, Limited 1st edition, boxed set of 12 [MRB01] 325.00

Starbles, 1.75" diameter. Front shows character or movie scene, back has collector information.
____C-3PO and R2-D2 on Hoth [3:285] 15.00
____Chewbacca [MRB02] 15.00

AGP01 AGP02

HN01 HN02 HN03 HN04 HN05 HN06 HN07 HN08 HN09 HN10 HN11

HPB01 ITN01 KB01 KB02 KB03 KB04 LBR01 LBR02

MRB01 closed and open MRB2-MRB7 rear MRB02 MRB03 MRB04 MRB05 MRB06 MRB07

Toys: Marbles

TYM01

TYM02

TYM03

TYM04

TYM05

TYM06

TYM07

TYM08

TYM09

TYM10

TYM11

TYM12

TYM13

TYM14

TYM15

____Darth Vader on Bespin gantry [MRB03]..............15.00
____Dogfight over Death Star [MRB04] 15.00
____Emperor Palpatine [3:285] 15.00
____Han Solo [3:285] 15.00
____Jabba the Hutt [MRB05] 15.00
____Luke Skywalker [3:285] 15.00
____Princess Leia (Jabba's prisoner) [3:285] 15.00
____Princess Leia and R2-D2 [MRB06] 15.00
____Wicket the Ewok [MRB07] 15.00
____Yoda [3:285] 15.00

Toys: Micro Collection Figures

Kenner
Bespin Control Room.
____Darth Vader lightsaber held ready [3:288] 5.00
____Darth Vader right arm fully extended [3:288] 5.00
____Luke Skywalker landing w/lightsaber [3:288].......5.00
____Luke Skywalker w/gun raised...............................5.00

Bespin Freeze Chamber.
____Boba Fett [3:288] 14.00
____Darth Vader hands on hips [3:288]..................5.00
____Han Solo in Carbonite [3:288] 10.00
____Han Solo in cuffs [3:288] 5.00
____Lando Calrissian with cape [3:288] 5.00
____Lobot [3:288] 5.00
____Stormtrooper gun pointing up [3:288] 5.00
____Stormtrooper with gun at waist [3:288] 5.00

Bespin Gantry.
____Darth Vader left arm extended [3:288] 5.00
____Darth Vader with cape blowing [3:288] 5.00
____Luke Skywalker lunging w/lightsaber [3:288].......5.00
____Luke Skywalker missing hand [3:288] 5.00

Build Your Armies mail away.
____Snowtrooper crawling [3:288].......................5.00
____Snowtrooper kneeling [3:288].......................5.00
____Snowtrooper with laser cannon [3:288] 6.00
____Soldier, gun pointing straight [3:288] 5.00
____Soldier, gun tilted down [3:288] 5.00
____Soldier, gun tilted up [3:288].....................5.00

Death Star Compactor.
____Darth Vader holding lightsaber to left [3:288]......5.00
____Han Solo in stormtrooper disguise [3:288]..........5.00
____Luke in stormtrooper disguise [3:288] 5.00
____Obi-Wan Kenobi [3:288] 5.00
____Princess Leia firing rifle [3:288].................5.00
____Stormtrooper firing forward [3:288] 5.00
____Stormtrooper firing up [3:288] 5.00
____Stormtrooper standing shot [3:288] 5.00

Death Star Escape.
____Chewbacca [3:288] 5.00
____Darth Vader right arm straight forward [3:288]......5.00
____Luke Skywalker [3:288] 5.00
____Princess Leia firing pistol [3:288] 5.00
____Stormtrooper advancing [3:288] 5.00
____Stormtrooper kneeling [3:288] 5.00

Hoth Generator Attack.
____Darth Vader walking [3:288] 5.00
____Snowtrooper crawling and firing [3:288] 5.00
____Snowtrooper firing from hip [3:288] 5.00
____Snowtrooper kneeling and firing [3:288] 5.00
____Snowtrooper standing and firing [3:288] 5.00
____Snowtrooper standing shot [3:288] 5.00

Hoth Ion Cannon.
____Han Solo on Tauntaun [3:288] 5.00
____Luke Skywalker shooting [3:288] 5.00
____Princess Leia [3:288] 5.00
____Soldier crawling and shooting [3:288] 5.00
____Soldier leaning forward and firing [3:288] 5.00
____Soldier standing, firing [3:288] 5.00
____Soldier with foot on larger mound [3:288] 5.00

Hoth Turret Defense.
____Han Solo standing and firing [3:288] 5.00
____Luke Skywalker on Tauntaun [3:288] 7.00
____Soldier crawling [3:288] 5.00
____Soldier kneeling and firing [3:288] 5.00
____Soldier with binoculars [3:288] 5.00
____Soldier with foot on mound [3:288] 5.00

Hoth Wampa Cave.
____Chewbacca hands up [3:288]..............................5.00

____Han Solo leaning forward and firing [3:288]..........5.00
____Luke Skywalker dangling [3:288] 5.00
____Probot [3:288] 3.00
____Wampa [3:288] 7.00

Millennium Falcon.
____C-3PO [3:288] 12.00
____Chewbacca with tool [3:288] 12.00
____Han Solo with gun pointing up [3:288] 12.00
____Lando Calrissian no cape [3:288] 12.00
____Luke Skywalker sitting relaxed [3:288] 12.00
____R2-D2 [3:288] 18.00

Snowspeeder.
____Gunner kneeling 25.00
____Pilot waving 25.00

Tie Fighter.
____Pilot...25.00

X-Wing Fighter.
____Pilot...25.00

Toys: Micro Collection

Kenner
____Bespin Control Room [TYM01] 35.00
____Bespin Freeze Chamber [TYM02] 75.00
____Bespin Gantry [TYM03] 35.00
____Bespin World [TYM04] 195.00
____Build Your Armys (Set of 6 troops) 45.00
____Death Star Compactor [TYM05] 75.00
____Death Star Escape [TYM06] 75.00
____Death Star World [TYM07]..........................175.00
____Hoth Generator Attack [TYM08] 35.00
____Hoth Ion Cannon [TYM09] 65.00
____Hoth Turret Defense [TYM10]........................35.00
____Hoth Wampa Cave [TYM11] 45.00
____Hoth World [TYM12] 120.00
____Imperial Tie Fighter, crash features [TYM13] 85.00
____Imperial Tie Fighter, crash features, Special
     offer [2:296] 110.00
____Imperial Tie Fighter, Special offer [2:296] 100.00
____Millennium Falcon, Sears excl. [TYM14] 410.00
____Snowspeeder, JC Penney exclusive
     [TYM15] 200.00
____X-Wing Fighter [2:296] 85.00
____X-Wing Fighter, crash features [2:296].............75.00
____X-Wing Fighter, Special offer [2:296] 95.00

Toys: MicroMachines

Galoob
Classic trilogy, "space" card.
____Imperial AT-AT [MCM01]..............................7.00
____Imperial Star Destroyer [MCM02].....................20.00
____Millennium Falcon [3:289] 7.00
____TIE Fighter [MCM03].................................7.00
____X-wing Starfighter [MCM04]..........................7.00

Classic trilogy, striped card.
____A-wing Starfighter [MCM05]..........................5.00
____Darth Vader's TIE Fighter [MCM06] 5.00
____Death Star II [MCM07] 5.00
____Imperial AT-AT 7.00
____Imperial Star Destroyer 20.00
____Landspeeder [MCM08].................................7.00
____Millennium Falcon..................................7.00

MCM01

MCM02

MCM03

MCM04

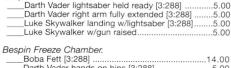

MCM05 MCM06 MCM07 MCM08 MCM09 MCM10

MCM11 MCM12 MCM13 MCM14 MCM15 MCM16 MCM17

MCM18 MCM19 MCM20 MCM21 MCM22 MCM23 MCM24 MCM25 MCM26

____Slave I [MCM09] 7.00
____Snowspeeder [MCM10] 7.00
____Super Star Destroyer Executor [MCM11]..............7.00
____TIE Bomber [MCM12]..9.00
____TIE Fighter...7.00
____X-Wing Starfighter 7.00
____Y-Wing Starfighter [MCM13]...................................7.00

Classic trilogy.
____Millennium Falcon, bagged [2:296] 12.00

EPI:TPM, boxed.
____Anakin's Podracer [MCM14]....................................5.00
____Gasgano's Podracer [MCM15] 5.00
____Gungan Sub (Bongo) [MCM16] 5.00
____Mars Guo's Podracer [MCM17] 10.00
____Naboo Fighter [MCM18].......................................10.00
____Sebulba's Podracer [MCM19] 10.00
____Sith Infilitrator [MCM20]..5.00
____Trade Federation MTT [MCM21] 10.00

MCM27 MCM28 MCM29 MCM30 MCM31 MCM32 MCM33

Galoob, Japan
2-packs: 1 vehicle, 1 figure; gray striped cards. Sold individually.
____Bespin Twin-Pod Cloud Car / Lando Calrissian [MCM22]...16.00
____Escape Pod / R2-D2 [MCM23] 16.00
____Imperial AT-AT / Stormtrooper [MCM24] 16.00
____Imperial AT-ST / Imperial Driver [MCM25] 16.00
____Imperial Star Destroyer / Darth Vader [MCM26]...16.00
____Millennium Falcon / Han Solo [MCM27] 16.00
____Rebel Blockade Runner / Princess Leia [MCM28]...16.00
____Shuttle Tydirium / Chewbacca [MCM29]............16.00
____Slave I / Boba Fett [MCM30] 16.00
____Snowspeeder / Rebel Pilot [MCM31] 16.00
____Tie Fighter / Imperial Pilot [MCM32] 16.00
____X-Wing Starfighter / Luke Skywalker [MCM33]...16.00

Toys: MicroMachines – Action Fleet Battle Pack

Galoob
1 – 8 released twice; once with an extra figure included.
____#1: Rebel Alliance [MMB01]...............................15.00
____#1: Rebel Alliance plus Yoda 25.00
____#2: Galactic Empire [MMB02] 15.00
____#2: Galactic Empire plus Royal Guard................25.00
____#3: Aliens and Creatures [MMB03]........................8.00
____#3: Aliens and Creatures plus Ponda Baba [MMB04]...25.00
____#4: Galactic Hunters [MMB05] 8.00
____#4: Imperial Hunters plus IG-88.........................25.00
____#5: Shadows of the Empire [MMB06] 20.00
____#5: Shadows of the Empire plus Chewbacca 25.00

MMB01 MMB02 MMB03

MMB04 MMB05 MMB06 MMB07 MMB08 MMB09 MMB10 MMB11 MMB12

MMB13 MMB14 MMB15 MMB16 MMB17 MMB18 MMB19 MMB20 MMB21

Toys: MicroMachines – Action Fleet Battle Pack

| MMO01 | MMO02 | MMO03 | MMO04 | MMO05 | MMO06 | MMO07 | MMO08 | MMO09 |

| MMO10 | MMO11 | MMO12 | MME01 | MME02 | MME03 |

| MME04 | MMF01 | MMF02 | MMF03 |

____#5: Shadows of the Empire plus Skahtul 25.00	
____#6: Dune Sea [MMB07] 20.00	
____#6: Dune Sea plus Barada [MMB08] 25.00	
____#7: Droid Escape [MMB09] 20.00	
____#7: Droid Escape, Avon exclusive, white box . .28.00	
____#7: Rebel Escape plus EG6 Power Droid.........25.00	
____#8: Desert Palace [MMB10] 15.00	
____#8: Desert Palace plus Weequay [MMB11] 27.00	
____#9: Endor Adventure [MMB12] 15.00	
____#10: Mos Eisley Spaceport [MMB13] 15.00	
____#11: Cantina Encounter [MMB14] 8.00	
____#12: Cantina Smugglers and Spies [MMB15] 30.00	
____#13: Hoth Attack [MMB16] 22.00	
____#14: Death Star Escape [MMB17] 20.00	
____#15: Endor Victory [MMB18] 20.00	
____#16: Lars Family Homestead [MMB19] 20.00	
____#17: Imperial Troops [MMB20]..........................20.00	
____#18: Rebel Troops [MMB21] 18.00	

Toys: MicroMachines –
Action Fleet Mini Scenes

Galoob

____#1 STAP Invasion [MMO01] 8.00
____#1 STAP Invasion, first edition 10.00
____#2 Destroyer Droid Ambush [MMO02] 8.00
____#2 Destroyer Droid Ambush, first edition 10.00
____#3 Gungan Assault [MMO03] 8.00
____#3 Gungan Assault, first edition.........................10.00
____#4 Sith Pursuit [MMO04] 8.00
____#4 Sith Pursuit, first edition 10.00
____#5 Trade Federation Raid [MMO05].....................15.00
____#6 Throne Room Reception [MMO06]...................15.00
____#7 Watto's Deal [MMO07] 15.00
____#8 Generator Core Duel [MMO08].....................20.00

Hasbro

____Dune Sea Ambush [MMO09] 20.00
____Imperial Endor Pursuit [MMO10] 20.00
____Mos Eisley Encounter [MMO11] 20.00
____Tatooine Droid Hunter [MMO12] 20.00

Toys: MicroMachines –
Adventure Gear

Galoob

Luke's Binoculars / Yavin Rebel Base,
____1st release w/Topps trading card [MME01]........20.00
____1st release without Topps trading card 15.00
____2nd release [MME02] 12.00
Vader's Lightsaber / Death Star Trench,
____1st release with Topps trading card
[MME03] 20.00
____1st release without Topps trading card 14.00
____2nd release [MME04] 12.00

Toys: MicroMachines – Boxed Sets

20th Century Fox

____10-pack of pewter colored ships, given away with
trilogy video sets in Mexico [MMF01] 35.00
____TIE Starfighter, pewter color, promo [2:298] 26.00

| MMF04 | MMF05 | MMF06 | MMF07 |

| MMF08 | MMF09 | MMF10 | MMF11 | MMF12 | MMF13 | MMF14 |

     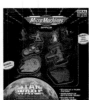

| MMF15 | MMF16 | MMF17 | MMF18 | MMF19 | MMF20 |

| MMJ01 | MMJ02 | MMJ03 | MMJ04 | MMJ05 | MMJ06 | MMK01 | MMK02 | MMK03 |

| MMK04 | MMK05 | MMK06 | MMK07 | MMK08 | MMK09 |

| MMK10 | MMK11 | MMK12 | MMK13 | MMK14 | MMK15 |

Galoob

____11-Piece Collector's Gift Set, KB Toys excl. 10.00
____3-pack: Micro 15.00
____Collector's Gift Set, bronze colored, Toys R Us exclusive [MMF02] 24.00
____Droids [MMF03] 10.00
____Galaxy Battle Collector's Set 1st edition, K-Mart exclusive with limited edition vehicle and 2 figures, limited edition sticker [MMF04] 10.00
____Galaxy Battle Collector's Set 2nd edition, K-Mart exclusive 10.00
____Imperial Forces Gift Set 1st edition, Target exclusive with exclusive Emperor figure [MMF05] 10.00
____Imperial Forces Gift Set 2nd edition, Target excl. introducing Darth Vader figure [MMF06] 10.00
____Master Collector's Edition 19-piece, Toys R Us exclusive with limited edition Super Star Destroyer Executor [MMF07] 25.00
____Master Collector's Edition 40-piece, Toys R Us exclusive [MMF08] 60.00
____Rebel Forces Gift Set 2nd edition, Target exclusive [MMF09] 10.00
____Rebel Forces Gift Set with exclusive Admiral Ackbar figure, Target exclusive [MMF10] 15.00
____Rebel vs. Imperial Gift Set introducing new Imperial Royal Guard with limited edition sticker [MMF11] 10.00

2-pack limited edition, Fan Club exclusives.
____Darth Vader / Star Destroyer, limited to 68,000 [MMF12] 10.00
____Han Solo / Millennium Falcon, limited to 26,000 [MMF13] 10.00

Collector's Editions, pewterized with limited edition sticker.
____A New Hope [MMF14] 7.00
____Empire Strikes Back [MMF15] 7.00
____Return of the Jedi [MMF16] 7.00

Galoob, UK

____16-pack, Trilogy Select Set [MMF17] 25.00
____3-pack: AT-AT, snowspeeder, X-wing, bronze colored [MMF18] 20.00
____3-pack: Star Destroyer, TIE Fighter, Millennium Falcon, bronze colored [MMF19] 20.00

Ideal

____Galaxy Battle Collector's Set 30.00
____Imperial Forces Gift Set 18.00
____Rebel Forces gift set [MMF20] 18.00

Toys: MicroMachines –
Epic Collections

Galoob

____I: Heir to the Empire [MMJ01] 5.00
____II: Jedi Search [MMJ02] 5.00
____III: Truce at Bakura [MMJ03] 5.00

Foreign exclusives.
____IV: Dark Apprentice [MMJ04] 90.00
____V: Dark Force Rising [MMJ05] 90.00
____VI: The Courtship of Princess Leia [MMJ06] 90.00

Toys: MicroMachines – Figures

Galoob

1994. Cards show rebel pilot, imperial pilot, stormtrooper, and ewok.
____Ewoks [MMK01] 18.00
____Imperial Pilots..18.00
____Imperial Stormtroopers [MMK02].....................18.00
____Rebel Pilots [MMK03].......................................18.00

1995. Cards show x-wing fighter with prominent MicroMachines Space logo.
____Echo Base Troops [MMK04] 12.00
____Ewoks [MMK05] 14.00
____Imperial Officers [MMK06] 12.00
____Imperial Pilots [MMK07] 12.00
____Imperial Stormtroopers [MMK08].....................14.00
____Jawas [MMK09] 12.00
____Rebel Pilots [MMK10].......................................12.00

1996. Cards show x-wing fighter with Star Wars logo.
____Classic Characters [MMK11] 10.00
____Echo Base Troops [MMK12] 10.00
____Ewoks [MMK13] 18.00
____Imperial Naval Troopers [MMK14] 10.00
____Imperial Officers [MMK15] 10.00
____Imperial Pilots [MMK16] 10.00
____Imperial Stormtroopers [MMK17].....................10.00
____Jawas [MMK18] 10.00
____Rebel Fleet Troopers [MMK19] 10.00
____Rebel Pilots [MMK20].......................................10.00
____Tusken Raiders [MMK21] 10.00

| MMK16 | MMK17 | MMK18 | MMK19 | MMK20 | MMK21 |

| MMK22 | MMK23 | MMK24 | MMK25 | MMK26 | MMK27 |

Toys: MicroMachines – Figures

MMK28

MMK29

MMK30

MMK31

MMK32

MMK33

MMK34

MMK35

MA701

M3M01

M3M02

M3M03

M3M04

M3M05

M3M06

M3M07

M3M08

1997. Cards are black and gray striped.
```
____Bounty Hunters [MMK22] .......................18.00
____Classic Characters [MMK23] ..................14.00
____Classic Characters (revised) [MMK24] ......11.00
____Echo Base Troops [MMK25] ....................7.00
____Endor Rebel Strike Team [MMK26] ...........20.00
____Imperial Naval Troopers [MMK27] ............7.00
____Imperial Officers [MMK28] .....................7.00
____Imperial Pilots [MMK29] ........................7.00
____Imperial Scout Troopers [MMK30] ...........20.00
____Imperial Stormtroopers [MMK31] .............10.00
____Jawas [MMK32] ..................................7.00
____Rebel Fleet Troopers [MMK33] ................7.00
____Rebel Pilots [MMK34] ...........................7.00
____Tusken Raiders [MMK35] ........................7.00
```

Ideal
1997. Cards are black and gray striped with orange background.
```
____Bounty Hunters ..................................11.00
```

```
____Classic Characters ............................11.00
____Classic Characters 2 .........................11.00
____Echo Base Troops .............................11.00
____Endor Rebel Strike Team ......................11.00
____Ewoks ...........................................11.00
____Imperial Naval Troopers ......................11.00
____Imperial Officers ..............................11.00
____Imperial Pilots .................................11.00
____Imperial Scout Troopers ......................11.00
____Imperial Stormtroopers .......................11.00
____Jawas ...........................................11.00
____Rebel Fleet Troopers .........................11.00
____Rebel Pilots ....................................11.00
____Tusken Raiders .................................11.00
```

Toys: MicroMachines –
Mega-Deluxe Playsets

Galoob
```
____Trade Federation MTT / Naboo Battlefield
     [MA701] ........................................38.00
```

Toys: MicroMachines – Micro Vehicles

Hasbro
2 vehicles and 2 figures.
```
____AT-RT and BARC Speeder with Clone Trooper and
     Chewbacca [M3M01] ...........................8.00
```

```
____Darth Vader's TIE fighter and an X-wing with Darth
     Vader and Luke Skywalker [M3M02] ............8.00
____Jedi Starfighter and ARC-170 with Obi-Wan Kenobi
     and Clone Pilot [M3M03] .......................8.00
____Jedi Starfighter and Droid Tri-Fighter with Anakin
     Skywalker and Battle Droid [M3M04] ...........8.00
____Millennium Falcon and B-Wing with Han Solo and
     Chewbacca [M3M05] ...........................8.00
____Sand Crawler and Landspeeder with Sandtrooper and
     Luke Skywalker [M3M06] .......................8.00
____Shuttle Tydirium and Slave I with Emperor and Boba
     Fett [M3M07] ..................................8.00
____Snowspeeder and Imperial AT-AT walker with
     Snowtrooper and Luke Skywalker ...............8.00
____TIE Fighter and A-Wing with TIE Fighter Pilot and
     A-Wing Pilot [M3M08] ..........................8.00
```

Toys: MicroMachines –
Mini-Action Sets

Collections:
1: Boba Fett, Admiral Ackbar, Gamorrean Guard
2: Nien Nunb, Greedo, Tusken Raider
3: Jawa, Yoda, Princess Leia as Boushh
4: Bib Fortuna, Figrin D'an, Scout Trooper
5: Bossk, Duros, Sandtrooper
6: 2-1B, Weequay, Emperor's Royal Guard
7: 4-LOM, Rebel Pilot, Snowtrooper
8: Wampa, Wicket, Tie Fighter Pilot
9: Salacious Crumb, Jabba the Hutt, AT-AT Driver

MMN01

MMN02

MMN03

MMN04

MMN05

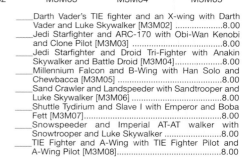
MMN06

MMN07

MMN08

MMN09

MMN10

MMN11

MMN12

MMN13

MMN14

MMN15

MMN16

MMN17

MMN18

MA401

MA402

MA403

MA404

MA405

MA406

MMP01

MMP02

MMP03

MMP04

MMP05

MMP06

MMP07

MMP08

MMP09

MMP10

Galoob / Gigi
1997. Italian. Gray bar packaging.
____Collection I 8.00
____Collection II 8.00
____Collection III [MMN01] 8.00
____Collection IV 8.00
____Collection V 8.00
____Collection VI 8.00
____Collection VII 8.00
____Collection VIII 8.00
____Collection IX 8.00

1997. Italian. Space packaging.
____Collection I [MMN02] 6.00
____Collection II 6.00
____Collection III 6.00
____Collection IV 6.00

Galoob
1st release.
____Collection I [MMN03] 5.00
____Collection II [MMN04] 5.00
____Collection III [MMN05] 5.00
____Collection IV [MMN06] 5.00

2nd release.
____Collection I [MMN07] 5.00
____Collection II [MMN08] 5.00
____Collection III [MMN09] 5.00
____Collection IV [MMN10] 5.00
____Collection V [MMN11] 40.00
____Collection VI [MMN12] 40.00

____Collection VII [MMN13] 125.00
____Collection VIII [MMN14] 40.00
____Collection IX [MMN15] 40.00

Individually bagged and distributed through Pizza Hut promotion.
____2-1B [2:299] 7.50
____Bossk [2:299] 7.50
____Duros [2:299] 7.50
____Imperial AT-AT Assault Pilot [2:299] 7.50
____Jabba The Hut [2:299] 7.50
____Royal Guard [2:299] 7.50
____Salacious Crumb [2:299] 7.50
____Stormtrooper [2:299] 7.50
____Tie Fighter Pilot [2:299] 7.50
____Wampa [2:299] 7.50
____Weequay [2:299] 7.50
____Wicket W. Warrick [2:299] 7.50

Mail-in exclusives.
____C-3PO, Walmart [3:291] 14.00

Mini-Action, boxed. 7 Figure Heads.
____C-3PO Set, foreign exclusive [MMN16] 295.00
____Yoda with trading card [MMN17] 12.00

Ideal
1997. UK. Gray bar packaging.
____Collection I 8.00
____Collection II 8.00
____Collection III [MMN18] 8.00
____Collection IV 8.00

Toys: MicroMachines – Platform Action Sets

Galoob
____Galactic Dogfight [MA401] 12.00
____Galactic Senate [MA402] 12.00
____Naboo Temple Ruins [MA403] 12.00
____Pod Race Arena [MA404] 20.00
____Tatooine Desert [MA405] 12.00
____Theed Rapids [MA406] 12.00

Toys: MicroMachines – Playsets

Galoob / Kidz Biz
Australia. Space / grid packaging. Micromachine poster offer sticker on front of box.
____Endor [MMP01] 15.00
____Ice Planet Hoth [MMP02] 15.00
____The Death Star 15.00

Galoob
1st release, space / grid packaging.
____Death Star [MMP03] 15.00
____Death Star Deluxe 38.00
____Endor Planetary Power Station [MMP04] 10.00
____Ice Planet Hoth [MMP05] 10.00
____Millennium Falcon carry playset, 24k gold Falcon offer [MMP06] 30.00

MMP11

MMP12

MMP13

MMP14

MMP15

MMP16

MMP17

MMP18

MMP19

Toys: MicroMachines – Playsets

MMP20

MMP21

MMP22

MMP23

MMP24

MMP25

MMDT01

MMDT02

MA201

MA202

MA203

MA204

MA205

MA206

MA207

____Millennium Falcon carry playset, 24k gold Star Destroyer offer [MMP07] 30.00
____Millennium Falcon carry playset [MMP08]..........25.00
____Planet Dagobah [MMP09] 10.00
____Planet Tatooine [MMP10] 10.00

2nd release, gray and black bar packaging.
____Cloud City [MMP11] 14.00
____Death Star [MMP12]..15.00
____Endor Planetary Power Station [MMP13] 15.00
____Ice Planet Hoth [MMP14] 10.00
____Millennium Falcon carry playset [MMP15]..........25.00
____Planet Dagobah [MMP16] 10.00
____Planet Tatooine [MMP17] 15.00
____Rebel Transport [MMP18] 20.00

Episode I: The Phantom Menace.
____Gian Speeder and Theed Palace [MMP19] 10.00
____Mos Espa Market [MMP20] 15.00
____Mos Espa Market, first edition 15.00
____Otoh Gunga [MMP21] 60.00
____Podracer Hanger Bay...20.00
____Podracer Hanger Bay, first edition [MMP22] 20.00
____Royal Starship Repair [MMP23]............................25.00
____Theed Palace [MMP24]...60.00
____Theed Palace Assault [MMP25] 150.00

Ideal
1st release, space / grid packaging.
____Death Star 18.00
____Endor Planetary Power Station 18.00
____Hoth Base...18.00
____Millennium Falcon carry playset 18.00

____Planet Dagobah 18.00
____Planet Tatooine..18.00

2nd release, gray and black bar packaging.
____Cloud City 25.00
____Death Star 20.00
____Endor Planetary Power Station 20.00
____Hoth Base...20.00
____Millennium Falcon carry playset 20.00
____Planet Dagobah 20.00
____Planet Tatooine..20.00
____Rebel Transport 25.00

Toys: MicroMachines – Playsets, Double-Takes

Galoob
____Death Star [MMDT01] 45.00
____Death Star, 24k Death Star offer [MMDT02] 95.00

Ideal
____Death Star 55.00

Toys: MicroMachines – Podracers

Galoob
Build Your Own Podracer sets.
____Blue [MA201]...9.00

____Red 7.00
____Teal 7.00
____Yellow 7.00

Podracer packs.
____I : Anakin Skywalker / Ratts Tyerell [MA202] 7.00
____II : Sebulba / Clegg Holdfast [MA203] 7.00
____III : Dud Bolt / Mars Guo [MA204] 7.00
____IV : Boles Roor / Neva Kee [MA205] 7.00

Racing sets.
____Arch Canyon Adventure [MA206]........................16.00
____Beggars Canyon Challenge [MA207]...................16.00
____Boonta Eve Challenge [MA208] 24.00

Turbo podracers.
____2-pack: Gasgano/Teemto Pagalies [MA209] 14.00
____Gasgano [MA210]...25.00
____Ody Mandrell [MA211] 12.00

Galoob, UK
Podracer packs.
____I : Anakin Skywalker / Ratts Tyerell 7.00
____II : Sebulba / Clegg Holdfast 7.00
____III : Dud Bolt / Mars Guo 7.00
____IV : Boles Roor / Neva Kee.....................................7.00

Hasbro
Build Your Own Podracer sets.
____Black 7.00
____Crystal blue...8.00
____Orange [MA212] 7.00
____Yellow 7.00

MA208

MA209

MA210

MA211

MA212

MMS01

MMS02

MMS03

MMS04

MMS05

MMS06

MMS07

MMS08

MMS09

MMS10

MMS11

MMS12

MMS13

MMS14

MMS15

MMS16

MMS17

MMS18

Toys: MicroMachines – Transforming Action Sets

Galoob

1st release, space / grid packaging.

____Boba Fett / Cloud City 25.00
____Boba Fett / Cloud City with Topps trading card...25.00
____C-3PO / Cantina [MMS01].................................19.00
____Chewbacca / Endor [MMS02] 16.00
____Darth Vader / Bespin [MMS03] 19.00
____R2-D2 / Jabba's Desert Palace [MMS04] 19.00
____Rebel Pilot / Hoth 16.00
____Rebel Pilot / Hoth with Topps trading card G1 [MMS05] 24.00
____Royal Guard / Death Star II [MMS06] 16.00
____Stormtrooper / Death Star [MMS07] 16.00
____Tie Pilot / Acadamy [MMS08] 16.00

2nd release, gray and black bar packaging.

____Boba Fett / Cloud City [MMS09] 16.00
____C-3PO / Cantina...16.00
____Darth Vader / Bespin [MMS10] 16.00
____Jabba / MosEisley Space Port [MMS11]............14.00
____Luke Skywalker / Hoth [MMS12] 16.00
____R2-D2 / Jabba's Desert Palace [MMS13] 16.00
____Royal Guard / Death Star II [MMS14] 16.00
____Slave I / Tatooine [MMS15].............................16.00
____Star Destroyer / Space Fortress [MMS16].........16.00
____Stormtrooper / Death Star [MMS17] 16.00
____Tie Fighter Pilot / Acadamy [MMS18] 16.00
____Yoda / Dagobah [MMS19] 16.00

Episode I: The Phantom Menace.

____Battle Droid / Trade Federation Control Ship [MMS20]...17.00
____Darth Maul / Theed Generator [MMS21] 28.00
____Gungan Sub / Otoh Gunga [MMS22] 28.00
____Jar Jar / Naboo [MMS23]..................................17.00

Hasbro

EPIII:ROTS Battle Sets.

____Kashyyyk Assault 15.00
____Mustafar Duel [MMS24] 15.00
____Sith Attack [MMS25] 15.00

Ideal

____1 Franc Bonus package add to any set...............7.00

1st release, space / grid packaging, silver logo.

____Boba Fett / Cloud City [MMS26] 18.00
____C-3PO / Bar [MMS27] 18.00
____Darth Vader / Bespin [MMS28] 18.00
____Rebel Pilot / Hoth [MMS29] 18.00
____Stormtrooper / Death Star [MMS30] 18.00

2nd release, space / grid packaging, gold logo.

____Boba Fett / Cloud City 18.00
____Chewbacca / Endor [MMS32] 18.00
____R2-D2 / Jabba's Palace [MMS33] 18.00

MMS19

MMS20

MMS21

MMS22

MMS23

MMS24

MMS25

MMS26

MMS27

MMS28

MMS29

MMS30

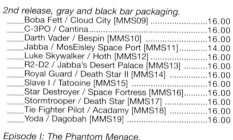

MMS31

MMS32

MMS33

MMS34

Toys: MicroMachines – Transforming Action Sets

MA301

MA302

MA303

MA304

MA305

MA306

MA307

MA308

MA309

MA310

MA311

MA312

MA313

MA314

MA315

MA316

MA317

3rd release, gray and black bar packaging.
____Jabba / Mos Eisley Space Port [MMS34] 18.00
____Royal Guard / Death Star II [MMS35] 18.00
____Tie Fighter Pilot / Acadamy 18.00
____Yoda / Dagobah 18.00

Toys: MicroMachines –

Vehicle / Figure Collections

Galoob
Episode I: The Phantom Menace.
____Collection 1, first edition 14.00
____Collection 1 [MA301] 7.00
____Collection 2, first edition [MA302] 14.00
____Collection 2 ....7.00
____Collection 3, first edition 14.00
____Collection 3 [MA303] 7.00

____Collection 4, first edition 14.00
____Collection 4 [MA304] 7.00
____Collection 5, first edition [MA305] 14.00
____Collection 5 ....7.00
____Collection 6, first edition [MA306] 14.00
____Collection 6 ....7.00
____Collection 7 [MA307] 15.00
____Collection 8 [MA308] 15.00
____Collection 9 [MA309] 15.00
____Collection 10 [MA310] 15.00

SOTE.
____Collection I 9.00
____Collection II 9.00
____Collection III 9.00

SOTE. Exclusive Micro Comic Inside.
____Collection I [MA311] 11.00
____Collection II [MA312] 11.00
____Collection III [MA313] 11.00

SOTE. Sticker covering Exclusive Micro Comic text.
____Collection I 11.00
____Collection II 11.00
____Collection III 11.00

Galoob, UK
____Trilogy Select Set [MA314] 18.00

Hasbro
Episode I: The Phantom Menace.
____Collection 11 [MA315] 35.00
____Collection 12 [MA316] 35.00
____Collection 13 [MA317] 35.00

Toys: MicroMachines –

Vehicle Collections

Galoob
1993. One set of vehicles per classic trilogy movie with holofoil logo.
____Star Wars [MMT01] 8.00
____Empire Strikes Back [MMT02] 8.00
____Return of the Jedi [MMT03] 8.00

1994. Cards show different ships in background.
____Collection I [MMT04] 14.00
____Collection II [MMT05] 14.00
____Collection III [MMT06] 14.00
____Collection IV [MMT07] 14.00

MMT01

MMT02

MMT03

MMT04

MMT05

MMT06

MMT07

MMT08

MMT09

MMT10

MMT11

MMT12

MMT13

MMT14

MMT15

MMT16

MMT17

MMT18

MMT19

MMT20

MMT21

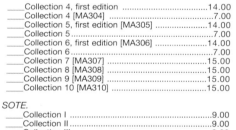
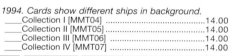

| MMT22 | MMT23 | MMT24 | MMT25 | MMT26 | MMT27 | MMT28 |

| MMT29 | MMT30 | MMT31 | MMT32 | MMT33 | MMT34 | MMT35 |

| MMT36 | MMT37 | MMT38 | MMT39 | MMT40 | MMT41 | MMT42 |

____Collection IX [MMT08] 14.00
____Collection V [MMT09]...........................14.00
____Collection VI [MMT10].........................14.00
____Collection VII [MMT11].........................14.00
____Collection VIII [MMT12]........................14.00

1994. Two sets of vehicles per classic trilogy movie.
____Empire Strikes Back [MMT13]...........8.00
____Empire Strikes Back II [MMT14]..............8.00
____Return of the Jedi [MMT15] 8.00
____Return of the Jedi II [MMT16]................8.00
____Star Wars [MMT17]............................8.00
____Star Wars II [MMT18]..........................8.00

1995. Cards show x-wing fighter with prominent MicroMachines Space logo.
____Collection I [MMT19] 12.00
____Collection II [MMT20]..........................12.00
____Collection III [MMT21] 12.00
____Collection IV [MMT22] 12.00
____Collection V [MMT23]..........................12.00
____Collection VI [MMT24] 12.00
____Collection VII [MMT25] 12.00
____Collection VIII [MMT26] 15.00
____Collection IX [MMT27] 12.00
____Collection X [MMT28]..........................12.00
____Collection XI [MMT29] 12.00

1996. Cards show x-wing fighter with prominent Star Wars logo.
____Collection I [MMT30] 10.00
____Collection II [MMT31] 10.00
____Collection III [MMT32] 10.00

____Collection IV [MMT33] 10.00
____Collection V [MMT34]..........................10.00
____Collection VI [MMT35] 10.00
____Collection VII [MMT36] 10.00
____Collection VIII [MMT37] 15.00
____Collection IX [MMT38] 10.00
____Collection X [MMT39] 10.00
____Collection XI [MMT40] 12.00
____Collection XII [MMT41] 12.00
____Collection XIII [MMT42] 12.00

1997. Cards are black and gray striped with orange background.
____Collection I [MMT43]............................8.00
____Collection II [MMT44]...........................8.00
____Collection III [MMT45].........................8.00
____Collection IV [MMT46] 8.00
____Collection V [MMT47]...........................8.00
____Collection VI [MMT48]..........................8.00
____Collection VII [MMT49] 8.00
____Collection VIII [MMT50] 25.00
____Collection IX [MMT51] 8.00
____Collection X [MMT52] 8.00
____Collection XI [MMT53] 20.00
____Collection XII [MMT54] 8.00
____Collection XIII [MMT55].........................8.00
____Collection XIV [MMT56] 16.00
____Collection XV 18.00

Ideal
1997. Cards are black and gray striped with orange background.
____Collection I 9.00

____Collection II 9.00
____Collection III 9.00
____Collection IV 9.00
____Collection V 9.00
____Collection VI 9.00
____Collection VII 9.00
____Collection VIII 9.00
____Collection IX 9.00
____Collection X 9.00
____Collection XI 9.00
____Collection XII 9.00
____Collection XIII 9.00
____Collection XIV 9.00
____Collection XV 9.00

One set of vehicles per classic trilogy movie with holofoil logo.
____Star Wars 24.00
____Empire Strikes Back 24.00
____Return of the Jedi.............................24.00

Toys: MicroMachines – Vehicles

Galoob / Gigi
1997. Italian. Gray bar packaging.
____Jawa Sandcrawler [MMZ01] 10.00

Galoob
24k prizes, limited to 30 of each.
____Imperial Star Destroyer [MMZ02] 250.00
____Millennium Falcon 250.00

| MMT43 | MMT44 | MMT45 | MMT46 | MMT47 | MMT48 | MMT49 |

| MMT50 | MMT51 | MMT52 | MMT53 | MMT54 | MMT55 | MMT56 |

Toys: MicroMachines – Vehicles

MMZ01

MMZ02

MMZ03

MMZ04

MMZ05

MMZ06

MMZ07

MMZ08

MMZ09

MMZ10

MMZ11

Classic trilogy. 24k gold plated 2-packs.

___Imperial Logo and Shuttle Tydirium [MMZ03] 35.00
___Millennium Falcon and Darth Vader's Tie Fighter [MMZ04] 35.00
___X-Wing and Slave I [MMZ05] 35.00

Classic trilogy. Round header with round bubble.

___Imperial Star Destroyer [MMZ06] 7.00
___Jawa Sandcrawler [MMZ07] 7.00
___Millennium Falcon [MMZ08] 7.00
___Tie Fighter [MMZ09] 7.00
___X-Wing Starfighter [MMZ10] 7.00
___Y-Wing Starfighter [MMZ11] 7.00

Classic trilogy.

___10-pack includes x-ray shuttle, JCPenney exlcusive, gold logo [MMZ12] 50.00
___10-pack includes x-ray shuttle, JCPenney exlcusive, silver logo [MMZ13] 50.00

___A-Wing Fighter [MMZ14] 70.00
___A-Wing Fighter, "special display stand" printed on bottom 70.00
___Death Star [MMZ15]................................24.00
___Death Star, "special display stand" printed on bottom 24.00
___Executor with Star Destroyer [MMZ16] 15.00
___Executor with Star Destroyer, "special display stand" printed on bottom 15.00
___Imperial Star Destroyer [MMZ17] 7.00
___Landspeeder [MMZ18]............................25.00
___Landspeeder, "special display stand" printed on bottom 25.00
___Millennium Falcon [MMZ19] 7.00
___Slave I [MMZ20] 65.00
___Slave I, "special display stand" printed on bottom 65.00
___Snowspeeder [MMZ21] 125.00
___Snowspeeder, "special display stand" printed on bottom 125.00

___Tie Bomber [MMZ22] 60.00
___Tie Bomber, "special display stand" printed on bottom 60.00
___Tie Fighter [MMZ23] 7.00
___X-Wing Fighter [MMZ24] 7.00
___Y-Wing Fighter [MMZ25]...........................7.00

Episode I: The Phantom Menace.

___Gian Speeder [MMZ26] 7.00
___Gian Speeder, first edition 9.00
___Republic Cruiser [MMZ27] 30.00
___Royal Starship [MMZ28] 7.00
___Royal Starship, first edition 9.00
___Sebulba's Podracer [MMZ29] 20.00
___Sith Infilterator [MMZ30].........................50.00
___Trade Federation Battleship [MMZ31] 7.00
___Trade Federation Battleship, first edition 9.00
___Trade Federation Droid Starfighter [MMZ32] 7.00
___Trade Federation Droid Starfighter, first edition 9.00
___Trade Federation Tank [MMZ33] 30.00

MMZ12

MMZ13

MMZ14

MMZ15

MMZ16

MMZ17

MMZ18

MMZ19

MMZ20

MMZ21

MMZ22

MMZ23

MMZ24

MMZ25

MMZ26

MMZ27

MMZ28

MMZ29

MMZ30

MMZ31

MMZ32

MMZ33

MMZ34

MMZ35

MMZ36 MMZ37 MMZ38 MMZ39

MMZ40 MMZ41 MMZ42 MMZ43 MMZ44 MMZ45 MMZ46 MMZ47 MMZ48 MMZ49 MMZ50 MMZ51 MMZ52 MMZ53 MMZ54 MMZ55

MMZ56 MMZ57 MMZ58 MMZ59 MMZ60 MMZ61 MMZ62 MMZ63 MMZ64 MMZ65 MMZ66 MMZ67 MMZ68 MMZ69 MMZ70 MMZ71 MMZ72

Galoob, Australia

____7-pack, boxed: X-Wing, Tie-Fighter, Death Star, Millennium Falcon, Y-Wing, Star Destroyer, Sandcrawler [MMZ34] 65.00

Galoob, Canada

____7-pack, boxed: X-Wing, Tie-Fighter, Death Star, Millennium Falcon, Y-Wing, Star Destroyer, Sandcrawler [MMZ35] 65.00

Hasbro

Titanium series 5-packs with raw metal (rm) *vehicle. Wal-mart exclusives.*

____Anakin's Jedi Starfighter, Republic Gunship, AT-RT (rm), Droid Tri-Fighter, Obi-Wan's Jedi Starfighter [MMZ36] 25.00
____Slave I, ARC-170, TIE Bomber (rm), X-Wing Fighter, Clone Swamp Speeder [MMZ37]....................25.00
____TIE Advanced, AT-AT, Death Star (rm), Star Destroyer, Imperial Shuttle [MMZ38]....................................25.00
____TIE Fighter, Landspeeder, Millennium Falcon (rm), X-Wing Fighter, Y-Wing Fighter [MMZ39] 25.00

Titanium series. Buy 1 Get 1 Free packaging.

____ARC-170 / X-Wing Fighter 8.00
____AT-RT / Slave I 8.00
____Millennium Falcon / Republic Gunship [MMZ40] 8.00
____TIE Fighter / Anakin's Jedi Starfighter 8.00

Titanium series. Ultimate Galactic Hunt.

____Slave I....................................15.00

Titanium series.

____2006 Darth Vader's TIE Fighter gold, Comic-Con exclusive [MMZ41] 65.00
____2006 Darth Vader's TIE Fighter gold, Toy Fair exclusive [MMZ42]....................................145.00
____A-Wing Fighter [MMZ43] 8.00
____A-Wing Starfighter [MMZ44]....................................8.00
____Anakin's Jedi Starfighter (Mustafar) [MMZ45] 8.00
____Anakin's Starfighter [MMZ46] 8.00
____ARC-170 [MMZ47] 8.00
____ARC-170, Clone Wars [MMZ48]..............................8.00
____AT-AT [MMZ49] 8.00
____AT-RT [MMZ50] 8.00
____AT-ST [MMZ51] 8.00
____B-Wing Fighter [MMZ52] 8.00
____Clone Turbo Tank [MMZ53] 8.00
____Darth Maul's Sith Speeder [MMZ54] 8.00
____Darth Vader's Sith Starfighter [MMZ55] 8.00
____Darth Vader's TIE Advanced [MMZ56] 8.00
____Death Star [MMZ57] 8.00
____Endor AT-AT [MMZ58]....................................8.00
____Federation Droid Vulture Starfighter [MMZ59] 8.00
____General Grievous' Starfighter [MMZ60] 8.00
____Imperial Shuttle, packaged nose forward 8.00
____Imperial Shuttle, packaged top up [MMZ61] 8.00
____Imperial Star Destroyer [MMZ62] 8.00
____Jedi Starfighter [MMZ63] 8.00
____Landspeeder [MMZ64] 8.00
____Leia's Speederbike [MMZ65] 8.00
____Mace Windu's Jedi Starfighter [MMZ66] 8.00
____Millennium Falcon [MMZ67] 8.00
____Millennium Falcon, Battle-Ravaged [MMZ68] 8.00
____Millennium Falcon, Episode III [MMZ69] 8.00
____Naboo Fighter [MMZ70] 8.00
____Naboo Patrol Fighter [MMZ71]..............................8.00
____Naboo Royal Starship [MMZ72]............................8.00
____Obi-Wan's Jedi Starfighter [MMZ73] 8.00
____Obi-Wan Kenobi's Jedi Starfighter [MMZ74] 8.00
____Rebel Blockade Runner [MMZ75] 8.00
____Republic Attack Cruiser [MMZ76] 8.00
____Republic Cruiser [MMZ77] 8.00
____Republic Gunship [MMZ78] 8.00
____Republic Gunship, Clone Wars markings, packaged nose down [MMZ79] 12.00
____Republic Gunship, Clone Wars markings, packaged nose up....................................12.00
____Sandcrawler [MMZ80] 8.00
____Sith Infiltrator [MMZ81]....................................8.00
____Slave I [MMZ82] 8.00
____Snowspeeder [MMZ83] 8.00
____Speeder Bike with Imperial Scout Trooper [MMZ84] 8.00
____Speeder Bike with Luke Skywalker [MMZ85] 8.00
____Star Destroyer Executor [MMZ86] 8.00
____Swamp Speeder [MMZ87] 8.00
____TIE Bomber [MMZ88] 8.00
____TIE Fighter [MMZ89] 8.00
____TIE Fighter, white [MMZ90] 18.00
____TIE Fighter, white with Titanium logo on wing 20.00
____TIE Interceptor [MMZ91]....................................8.00
____Trade Federation AAT [MMZ92] 8.00
____Tri-Fighter [MMZ93] 8.00
____Wookiee Flyer [MMZ94] 8.00
____X-Wing Fighter [MMZ95] 8.00
____X-Wing Fighter, gold, limited to 250 ....275.00
____Y-Wing Fighter [MMZ96]....................................8.00

Hasbro, UK

Episode I: The Phantom Menace.

____Gian Speeder 11.00
____Republic Cruiser....................................30.00
____Royal Starship 11.00
____Sebulba's Podracer 20.00
____Sith Infilterator 50.00
____Trade Federation Battleship...............................11.00
____Trade Federation Droid Starfighter......................30.00

Ideal

1997. Gray bar packaging.

____Jawa Sandcrawler [MMZ97] 12.00

Toys: MicroMachines – X-Ray Fleet

Galoob

____I: Darth Vader's TIE Fighter / A-Wing Starfighter [MMX01] 7.00
____I: Darth Vader's TIE Fighter / A-Wing Starfighter, 2nd release 65.00

MMZ73 MMZ74 MMZ75 MMZ76 MMZ77 MMZ78 MMZ79 MMZ80 MMZ81 MMZ82

MMZ83 MMZ84 MMZ85 MMZ86 MMZ87 MMZ88 MMZ89 MMZ90 MMZ91 MMZ92 MMZ93 MMZ94 MMZ95 MMZ96 MMZ97

MMX01

MMX02

MMX03

MMX04

MMX05

MMX06

MMX07

MMX08

MMX09

MMX10

TMS01

TMS02

TMS03

TMS04

MTR01

MTR02

MTR03

BPT01

BPT02

BPT03

BPT04

____II: X-Wing Starfighter / Imperial AT-AT [MMX02] 8.00
____II: X-Wing Starfighter / Imperial AT-AT, 2nd release 65.00
____III: Millennium Falcon / Jawa Sandcrawler [MMX03] 8.00
____III: Millennium Falcon / Jawa Sandcrawler, 2nd release 65.00
____IV: Boba Fett's Slave I and Y-Wing Starfighter [MMX04] 8.00
____IV: Y-Wing Starfighter / Boba Fett's Slave I, 2nd release [MMX05] 65.00
____V: B-Wing Starfighter / Tie-Bomber 62.00
____V: B-Wing Starfighter / Tie-Bomber, 2nd release [MMX06] 62.00
____VI: Landspeeder / TIE Fighter [MMX07] 62.00
____VI: Landspeeder / TIE Fighter, 2nd release [MMX08] 62.00
____VII: Snowspeeder / Imperial AT-ST [MMX09] 62.00
____VII: Snowspeeder / Imperial AT-ST, 2nd release [MMX10] 62.00

Toys: Miscellaneous

____Star Commanders, A-Wing [TMS01] 10.00
____Star Wars Episode III cellphone [TMS02] 16.00

Disney / MGM
____Robot Claw, C-3PO packaging [TMS03] 18.00

Izzy Bonkers
Crazy Bones.
____Leia look-alike [TMS04] 2.00

Toys: Motorcycle Toys

Hasbro
Star Wars "Customs" Choppers.
____Imperial, Darth Vader facing left [MTR01] 25.00
____Imperial, Darth Vader facing right 25.00
____Outlaw, Boba Fett facing left 25.00
____Outlaw, Boba Fett facing right [MTR02] 25.00

____Rebel, Luke Skywalker facing left 25.00
____Rebel, Luke Skywalker facing right [MTR03] 25.00

Toys: Organizers – Electronic

Tiger
____Jedi Dex [3:306] 25.00

Toys: Parachute

Unlicensed
2" figures with parachutes, available in: blue, green, orange, pink, purple, and yellow.
____C-3PO [BPT01] 3.00
____Chewbacca [BPT02] 3.00
____Greedo [BPT03] 3.00
____Leia, Hoth 3.00
____Luke / X-Wing pilot 3.00
____Stormtrooper [BPT04] 3.00

Toys: Play-Doh Sets

Kenner
____Attack the Death Star [YD01] 175.00
____ESB action set: Ice Planet Hoth [YD02] 55.00
____ESB action set: Yoda [YD03] 45.00
____ROTJ: Jabba the Hutt [YD04] 35.00
____SW action set [YD05] 45.00
____Wicket the Ewok [YD06] 40.00

Palitoy
____Star Wars Adventure Modeling Set [3:346] 155.00

Toys: Plush Toys and Dolls

Celebration 3.
____Yoda, limited to 500. Same as Pepsi Yoda but without hoverchair [TYN01] 185.00

Applause
____Jar Jar Binks 12" 12.00
____Jar Jar Binks 18" 29.00
____Jar Jar Binks 48", FAO Schwarz exclusive 95.00
____R2-D2 [TYN02] 18.00
____Watto 12" 12.00
____Watto 18" 29.00
____Wicket the Ewok 13", ltd. to 6,000 [TYN03] 75.00
____Yoda 18" [3:348] 40.00
____Yoda 24", FAO Schwarz excl. [TYN04] 120.00

Big Dog
Dog Wars, parody.
____Bark Maul [3:348] 14.00
____Luke Skybarker 14.00

Celebrity Bears
____Star Wars [2:350] 12.00

Disney / MGM
____Ewok, dark brown w/pink cowl, Ewoks tag........15.00
____Ewok, dark brown w/pink cowl, Mousketoys tag [TYN05]...12.00
____Ewok, light brown w/green cowl, Ewoks tag......18.00
____Ewok, light brown w/green cowl, Mousketoys tag [TYN06]...15.00
____Ewok, pink cowl, white face 20.00
____Yoda, 18" latex [TYN07].................................45.00

Star Wars Weekends.
____2004 Jedi Mickey, limited to 3,000 [TYN08] 25.00
____2005 Vader Mickey [TYN09]...........................25.00
____2006 Vader Goofy [TYN10] 30.00

Frito Lay
____Ewok 3' SW:SE promotion [TYN11] 335.00

Hasbro
____Jar Jar Binks Hungry Hero [2:350]....................24.00
____Jar Jar Binks, FAO Schwarz excl. [2:350] 22.00
____Watto, FAO Schwarz excl. [2:350] 22.00

Battle buddys.
____C-3PO...10.00
____Chewbacca [TYN12] 10.00
____Clone 10.00

YD01

YD02

YD03

YD04

YD05

YD06

TYN01 TYN02 TYN03 TYN04 TYN05 TYN06 TYN07 TYN08

TYN09 TYN10 TYN11 TYN12 TYN13 – TYN15 TYN16 TYN17

TYN18 TYN19 TYN20 TYN21 TYN22 TYN23

____R2-D2 ....10.00
____Yoda 10.00

Buddies. Episode I: The Phantom Menace.
____Darth Maul [2:123] 21.00
____Jar Jar Binks [2:123] 15.00
____Obi-Wan Kenobi [2:123] 15.00
____Padme Naberrie [2:123] 15.00
____Qui-Gon Jinn [2:123] 15.00
____Watto [2:123] 21.00

Lightsabers.
____Blue [TYN13] 12.00
____Green [TYN14] 12.00
____Red [TYN15] 12.00

Mpire buddies.
____Anakin Skywalker 10.00
____Boba Fett 15.00
____Chewbacca [TYN16] 10.00
____Count Dooku 12.00
____Darth Maul 12.00
____Darth Vader [TYN17] 10.00
____Emperor [TYN18] 10.00
____General Grievous 10.00
____Han [TYN19] 10.00
____Luke [TYN20] 10.00
____Mace Windu 10.00
____Obi-Wan [TYN21] 12.00
____Princess Leia [TYN22] 10.00
____Queen Amidala 10.00
____R2-D2 ....10.00
____Stormtrooper [TYN23] 10.00

Original Trilogy Collection (OTC)
____C-3PO 10.00
____Chewbacca 10.00
____R2-D2 ....10.00
____Wicket 10.00
____Yoda 10.00

Wrestling Buddy.
____Darth Vader [TYN24] 30.00
____R2-D2 [TYN25] 35.00

Idea Factory
Farce Wars.
____Anteater Dirtwalker [3:348] 7.00
____Dark Gator [2:350] 7.00
____Dark Mole [2:350] 7.00
____Goata [2:350] 7.00
____Queen Armadillo [2:350] 7.00
____Slabba the Mutt [2:350] 7.00

Idea Force International
____Yoda 15.00

Kenner
Vintage.
____Chewbacca [TYN26] 275.00
____R2-D2 [TYN27] 65.00

Buddies. Classic trilogy.
____C-3PO [2:123].................................10.00
____Chewbacca, black bandolier 10.00
____Chewbacca, brown bandolier [2:123] 22.00
____Figrin D'An [2:123] 10.00

____Jabba the Hutt [2:123] 8.00
____Jawa [2:123] 20.00
____Max Rebo [2:123] 8.00
____R2-D2 [2:123] 10.00
____Salacious Crumb [2:123] 10.00
____Wampa [2:123] 10.00
____Wicket the Ewok [2:123] 9.00
____Yoda [2:123] 25.00

Ewoks.
____Latara 29.00
____Paploo 85.00
____Princess Kneesaa 185.00
____Wicket 25.00

Woklings.
____Gwig 40.00
____Leeni 40.00
____Malani 40.00
____Mookiee 40.00
____Nippet 40.00
____Wiley [2:350] 40.00

Kenner, Canada
____The Ewok [2:350] 190.00

Kenneth Feld
____Yoda, plastic head, 12" tall 135.00

Kinder
Approximately 5.5" in height.
____Aubacca 18.00
____Hippoda 18.00

TYN24 TYN25 TYN26 TYN27 TYN28 TYN29 TYN30 TYN31

TYN32 TYN33 TYN34 TYN35 TYN36 TYN37 TYN38 TYN39

Toys: Plush Toys and Dolls

PCT01	PCT02	PCT03	PCT04	PCT05	PCT06	PCT07

PCT08	PCT09	PCT10	PCT11	PCT12	PCT13	PCT14

PCT15	PCT16	PCT17	PCT18	PCT19	PCT20	PCT21	PCT22	PCT23

Masterfoods USA
M&Ms 12" mail-in premiums.
____Darth Vader.............................35.00
____Emperor [TYN28]....................35.00
____Luke.....................................35.00

Palitoy
Ewoks, boxed.
____Leeni the Ewok 175.00
____Mookie the Ewok 175.00
____Princess Kneesa 175.00

Pepsi Cola
____Yoda, includes hoverchair [TYN29] 125.00
____Yoda, standing with cane [TYN30] 125.00

Quiron
____Kneesa, bagged.......................240.00
____Wicket, bagged 240.00
____Wicket, boxed 335.00

Regal
____Chewbacca, 15" 675.00
____Chewbacca, 4' 725.00
____Jawa, 12" [TYN31]...................340.00

Snap Toys
____Artoo-Detoo, talking.................35.00

Super Live Adventure
____Yoda [TYN32] 115.00

Takara
Oversized comic-style head, gold hang string. Approximately 7" tall.
____C-3PO [TYN33].......................25.00
____Chewbacca [TYN34] 25.00
____Darth Vader [TYN35] 30.00
____Luke Skywalker [TYN36] 25.00
____R2-D2, 5" [TYN37] 25.00

Tomy
Approximately 15" in height.
____Ewok [TYN38].........................45.00
____Jawa [TYN39] 45.00
____Yoda 45.00

Toys: Premiums

Barcel
Mexico. Mini-figures made of single-colored plastic.
____Battle Droid...........................5.00
____Clone Trooper 5.00
____Count Dooku..........................5.00
____Darth Sidious.........................5.00
____Darth Vader 5.00
____Darth Vader (Anakin) 5.00
____General Grievous 5.00
____Grievous' Bodyguard 5.00

Bimbo
Shooters target game pieces.
____Anakin Skywalker 5.00
____Count Dooku..........................5.00
____Darth Sidious.........................5.00
____Mace Windu 5.00
____Obi-Wan Kenobi 5.00
____Princess Leia 5.00
____Qui-Gon Jinn 5.00
____R2-D2 ....5.00
____Yoda 5.00

Burger King
EPIII:ROTS. Series I. Special.
____Darth Vader............................15.00

EPIII:ROTS. Series I. Image Viewers.
____C-3PO 5.00
____Darth Maul 5.00
____Luke Skywalker........................5.00
____Mace Windu 5.00
____Obi-Wan Kenobi 5.00
____Princess Leia Organa 5.00

EPIII:ROTS. Series I. Plush.
____Boga 5.00
____Chewbacca.............................5.00
____Jawa 5.00
____Tarfful...................................5.00
____Wampa 5.00
____Wicket 5.00

PCT24	PCT25	PCT26	PCT27	PCT28	PCT29	PCT30	PCT31	PCT32	PCT33

PCT34	PCT35	PCT36	PCT37	PCT38	PCT39	PCT40

PCT41

PCT42

PCT43

PCT44

PCT45

PCT46

PCT47

PCT48

PCT49

PCT50

PCT51

PCT52

PCT53

PCT54

PCT55

PCT56

PCT57

PCT58

PCT59

EPIII:ROTS. Series I. Pullbacks.

____Darth Vader's TIE fighter 5.00
____Jedi Starfighter 5.00
____Landspeeder 5.00
____Millennium Falcon [PCT01] 5.00
____Podracer 5.00
____X-Wing fighter [PCT02] 5.00

EPIII:ROTS. Series I. Water Squirters.

____Boba Fett 5.00
____Emperor Palpatine 5.00
____Jabba the Hutt [PCT03] 5.00
____Jar Jar Binks 5.00
____R2-D2 [PCT04] 5.00
____Super Battle Droid 5.00

EPIII:ROTS. Series I. Wind-Ups.

____Clone Trooper 5.00
____General Grievous 5.00
____Han Solo [PCT05] 5.00
____Padme Amidala 5.00
____Watto 5.00
____Yoda [PCT06] 5.00

EPIII:ROTS. Series II. Special.

____Darth Vader, breathing sound [PCT07] 5.00

EPIII:ROTS. Series II. Cosmic Cruisers.

____ARC Clone Fighter 5.00
____Naboo Starfighter 5.00
____Snowspeeder 5.00
____Vulture Droid 5.00

EPIII:ROTS. Series II. Galactic Spinners.

____Anakin Skywalker 5.00
____Chewbacca 5.00
____Emperor Palpatine 5.00
____Luke Skywalker 5.00

EPIII:ROTS. Series II. Jedi Wisdom.

____Kit Fisto 5.00
____Mace Windu 5.00
____Obi-Wan Kenobi 5.00
____Yoda 5.00

EPIII:ROTS. Series II. Shadow Casters.

____Bail Organa 5.00
____Queen Amidala 5.00
____R2-D2 .... 5.00
____Stormtrooper 5.00

Burger King, Argentina
EPIII:ROTS.

____C-3PO 10.00
____Chewbacca 10.00
____Darth Vader 10.00
____R2-D2 .... 10.00

Burger King, UK

____C-3PO 8.00
____Chewbacca 8.00
____Darth Vader 8.00
____Millennium Falcon 8.00
____R2-D2 .... 8.00
____Yoda 8.00

Frito Lay
3D Star Pics. Cheetos premiums. Red, blue, green, purple variations.

____Anakin Skywalker [PCT08] 1.00
____Clone Trooper, yellow only [PCT09] 3.00
____Count Dooku [PCT10] 1.00
____Jango Fett [PCT11] 1.00
____Mace Windu [PCT12] 1.00
____Obi-Wan Kenobi [PCT13] 1.00
____Padme Amidala [PCT14] 1.00
____R2-D2 and C-3PO [PCT15] 1.00
____Yoda [PCT16] 1.00
____Zam Wesell [PCT17] 1.00

Gamesa
Mini figures.

____Ben Kenobi 2.00
____C-3PO [PCT18] 2.00
____Chewbacca [PCT19] 2.00
____Darth Vader [PCT20] 2.00
____Han Solo [PCT21] 2.00
____Luke Skywalker [PCT22] 2.00
____Princess Leia [PCT23] 2.00

Hungry Jacks
EPIII:ROTS. Darth Vader assembly.

____Part 1 .... 3.00
____Part 2 .... 3.00
____Part 3 .... 3.00
____Part 4 .... 3.00

EPIII:ROTS finger puppets.

____Anakin 5.00
____Darth Sidious 5.00
____Obi-Wan 5.00
____Yoda 5.00

Kelloggs
Rebel Rocket cereal premiums from Kelloggs C-3PO's cereal.

____C-3PO and Darth Vader [PCT24] 35.00
____Chewbacca and Stormtrooper [PCT25] 25.00
____Luke Skywalker and R2-D2 [PCT26] 25.00

Kelloggs, Germany
Mini-statue scene viewers.

____Anakin Skywalker [PCT27] 4.00
____C-3PO and R2-D2 [PCT28] 4.00
____Darth Vader [PCT29] 4.00
____Jango Fett [PCT30] 4.00
____Obi-Wan Kenobi [PCT31] 4.00
____Padme Amidala [PCT32] 4.00

Kelloggs, Thailand
Gyros cereal premiums. Available in blue, red, yellow, green, purple, and pink.

____Anakin Skywalker [PCT33] 4.00
____Clone Tooper [PCT34] 4.00
____Darth Sidious [PCT35] 4.00
____Darth Vader [PCT36] 4.00
____General Grievous [PCT37] 4.00
____Obi-Wan Kenobi [PCT38] 4.00
____R2-D2 and C-3PO [PCT39] 4.00
____Yoda [PCT40] 4.00

Kelloggs, UK
EPIII:ROTS. Cereal and Milk bars sticker dispensers.

____Anakin Skywalker 8.00
____Darth Maul 8.00
____Darth Vader 8.00
____Luke Skywalker 8.00
____Princess Leia 8.00
____Yoda 8.00

EPIII:ROTS. Glow-in-the-dark lightsaber maze games.

____Anakin, blue 8.00
____Darth Vader, red 5.00
____Luke, green 5.00
____Mace Windu, purple 5.00
____Obi-Wan, blue 5.00
____Yoda, green 5.00

Statue with mini-scroll.

____10-piece set, boxed [PCT41] 45.00
____Anakin Skywalker [PCT42] 4.00
____Boss Nass [PCT43] 4.00
____C-3PO [PCT44] 4.00
____Darth Maul [PCT45] 4.00
____Darth Sidious [PCT46] 4.00
____Jar Jar Binks [PCT47] 4.00
____Obi-Wan Kenobi [PCT48] 4.00
____Queen Amidala [PCT49] 4.00
____Qui-Gon Jinn [PCT50] 4.00
____R2-D2 [PCT51] 4.00

KFC
Classic tilogy.

____AT-AT with snowtrooper on door [PCT53] 5.00
____AT-ST with walking action [PCT54] 5.00
____Balancing TIE figter & X-wing fighter [PCT55] 4.00
____Death Star shooter [PCT56] 4.00
____Sandcrawler with R2 [PCT57] 4.00
____Vader head spinner [PCT58] 4.00

Episode I: The Phantom Menace.

____Anakin Skywalker's Naboo fighter [2:412] 3.00
____Boss Nass squirter [2:412] 3.00
____Gungan Sub Squirter [2:412] 3.00
____Jar Jar Binks Squirter [2:412] 3.00
____Naboo ground battle [2:412] 3.00
____Opee Sea Creature Chaser [2:412] 3.00
____Planet Naboo [2:412] 3.00
____Queen Amidala's Hidden Identity [2:412] 3.00
____Swimming Jar Jar Binks [2:412] 3.00
____Trade Federation droid fighter [2:412] 3.00

KFC, Mexico
Episode I: The Phantom Menace.

____Collapsible Pit Droid 6.00
____Darth Mauls sith speeder with ripcord [2:412] 3.00
____Watto jumping, suction and spring [2:412] 6.00
____Yoda / Anakin illusion cube 4.00

Petroglyph

____Death Star desktop ball, pre-order for Empire at War game [PCT52] 8.00

Pizza Hut
Episode I: The Phantom Menace.

____Darth Maul's Sith Infilterator 3.00
____Jar Jar Binks Squishy [2:412] 3.00
____Lott Dod Walking Throne [2:412] 3.00
____Planet Coruscant 3.00
____Queen Amidala's Starship [2:412] 3.00
____R2-D2 .... 3.00
____Sith Holoprojector 3.00
____Yoda Jedi Destiny [2:412] 3.00

Pizza Hut, UK

____Death Star 3D puzzle [2:412] 6.00
____Han in Carbonite sliding puzzle [2:412] 6.00
____Millennium Falcon navigating asteroid field game [2:412] 6.00
____R2-D2 and C-3PO magnetic droid factory puzzle [2:412] 6.00

Taco Bell
Episode I: The Phantom Menace.

____Anakin's Podracer [2:412] 3.00
____Anakin Transforming Bank 3.00

Toys: Premiums

PST01

PST02

PST03

PST04

PST05

PST06

PST07

PST08

PST09

PST10

TYV01

TYV02

TYV03

TYV04

TYV05

TYV06

TYV07

TYV08

____Anakin Viewer [2:412] 3.00
____Darth Maul's Sith Speeder [2:412] 3.00
____Hovering Watto 3.00
____Joking Jar Jar [2:412] 3.00
____Levitating Queen's ship [2:412] 3.00
____Planet Tatooine [2:412] 3.00
____Sebulba's Podracer [2:412] 3.00
____Sith Probe Viewer 3.00
____Walking Sebulba [2:412] 3.00

Star Wars Special Edition / Feel the Force.
____Balancing Boba Fett 3.00
____Exploding Death Star 6.00
____Floating Cloud City 4.00
____Folding Picture Cube, Special Edition scenes 3.00
____Illusion Cube [2:412] 4.00
____Millennium Falcon with zip chord 4.00
____R2-D2 3-piece playset 4.00
____Yoda figure 5.00

Tambola
____AT-AT [2:413] 4.00
____AT-AT Attack, puzzle [2:413] 6.00
____C-3PO [2:413] 5.00
____Chewbacca [2:413] 5.00
____Darth Vader's Tie Fighter [2:413] 4.00
____Darth Vader [2:413] 5.00
____Darth Vader on Bespin, puzzle [2:413] 6.00
____Dogfight Above Death Star II, puzzle [2:413] 6.00
____Han Solo [2:413] 5.00
____Heroes on Hoth, puzzle [2:413] 6.00
____Imperial Shuttle [2:413] 4.00
____Luke Skywalker [2:413] 5.00
____Millennium Falcon [2:413] 4.00
____Princess Leia [2:413] 5.00
____R2-D2 [2:413] 5.00
____Stormtrooper [2:413] 5.00
____Tie Fighter [2:413] 4.00
____X-Wing Fighter [2:413] 4.00
____Yoda [2:413] 5.00
____Yoda, Puzzle [2:413] 6.00

Walkers
____Jar Jar Binks Sticky Tounge Toy, glows in dark
[PCT59]...11.00

Toys: Preschool Toys

Kenner
Ewoks.
____Family Hut [PST01]...85.00
____Fire Cart [PST02]..135.00
____Music Box Radio [PST03] 22.00
____Talking Telephone [PST04] 45.00
____Teaching Clock [PST05] 75.00
____Woodland Wagon [PST06] 95.00

Playskool
Mr. Potato Head.
____Darth Tater / Spud Trooper collector 2-pk. 35.00
____Darth Tater [PST07] 15.00
____R2-D2 Tater [PST08] 10.00
____SpudTrooper [PST09].......................................20.00
____Tater Trio set, Costco exclusive [PST10] 35.00

Toys: Projectors / Viewers

Chad Valley
____Slide Projector Set [2:361] 75.00

Harbert
____Star Wars movie strip viewer [2:361]...............150.00

Kenner
____Movie Viewer with "May The Force Be With You"
Cassette [TYV01] 100.00

Give-a-Show Projectors.
____ESB [TYV02] 95.00
____ESB with Scooby Doo Special Offer 2:361] 97.00
____SW [TYV04] 115.00
____Wicket the Ewok [2:361] 115.00

Movie Viewer cartridges.
____Assault on Death Star [TYV05]...........................50.00
____Battle in Hyperspace [TYV06] 50.00
____Danger at the Cantina [TYV07] 50.00
____Destroy Death Star [TYV08] 50.00

Meccano
____Minicinex 2:361]...185.00
____Star Wars Cinevue [2:361] 342.00
____Star Wars movie-frame cassette 87.00

Smith's Snackfood
____50 film cels, flashlight projector [3:357]...........166.00

Tiger Electronics
____Lightsaber Image Projector 16.00

Toltoys
____Give-A-Show projector [2:361] 115.00

Tomy
Mini-frame projectors.
____Boba Fett [3:357] 8.00
____Darth Maul [TYV03] 8.00
____Darth Vader [2:361] 8.00
____Yoda [2:361] 8.00

Toys: Puzzles

____Star Wars: Special Edition logo, 300 extra-large
pieces, 2'x3' [TYP01] 12.00

La Guerra de la Galaxias.
____Millennium Falcon cockpit [TYP02] 20.00

Character Games, Ltd.
____Heroes and Villains on Reflection Puzzle
[TYP03] 15.00
____Xtra Dimension 3D w/glasses [TYP04] 18.00

Episode II: AOTC.
____Double Vision [TYP05] 12.00

Character
____Darth Vader picture sculpture puzzle [TYP06]....25.00

42 chunky pieces.
____Darth Vader 15.00
____Wookiees and Clones 15.00

TYP01

TYP02

TYP03

TYP04

TYP05

TYP06

TYP07   TYP08   TYP09   TYP10   TYP11   TYP12

TYP13   TYP14   TYP15   TYP16   TYP17   TYP18   TYP19

TYP20   TYP21   TYP22   TYP23   TYP24   TYP25   TYP26   TYP27

Clementoni
France.
```
____250 pieces, Qui-Gon Jinn [TYP07] ....................18.00
____500 pieces, Episode I [TYP08]............................18.00
```

Craft Master
```
____B-Wing Fighters, 170 pieces [TYP09] ...............10.00
____Battle on Endor, 170 pieces [TYP10]..................10.00
____Death Star, 70 pieces [TYP11] .........................8.00
____Ewok Leaders, 170 pieces [TYP12]...................10.00
____Ewoks: Fishing, 35 pieces .............................7.00
____Ewoks: Lessons ........................................7.00
____Ewoks: Swimming Hole, 35 pieces [TYP13] .......7.00
____Jabba's Henchmen, 70 pieces [TYP14] ..............8.00
____Jabba's Throne Room, 70 pieces [TYP15]...........8.00
```

Tray puzzles.
```
____Darth Vader [TYP16] ...................................6.00
____Ewok Gliders [TYP17] ..................................6.00
____Ewok Village [TYP18] ...................................6.00
```

```
____Gamorrean Guard [TYP19] ..............................6.00
____Princess Kneesaa and Baga [TYP20]..................6.00
____Princess Leia and Wicket [TYP21] .....................6.00
____R2-D2 and Wicket [TYP22]...............................6.00
____Wicket the Ewok [TYP23] ...............................6.00
```

Cromy
El Regreso del Jedi.
```
____C-3PO and R2-D2 [TYP24] ..............................45.00
____Jabba's Palace .........................................45.00
____Luke Skywalker ........................................45.00
____Rebel Hanger ..........................................45.00
```

Hasbro
```
____TPM: teaser poster, 300 pieces [TYP25] ..............8.00
```

EPI:TPM 100 piece shaped puzzle, includes theme shaped pieces.
```
____Darth Maul [TYP26].....................................5.00
____Jar Jar Binks [TYP27] ..................................5.00
```

```
____R2-D2 [TYP28] ..........................................5.00
____Yoda [TYP29] ..........................................5.00
```

EPI:TPM 50 piece mini-puzzle, 5"x7".
```
____Jedi vs. Sith [TYP30]....................................2.00
____Pit Droids [TYP31].......................................2.00
____Queen Amidala [TYP32].................................2.00
____Sebulba [TYP33] ........................................2.00
```

EPI:TPM 540 pieces, movie maze puzzles.
```
____1 of 2 [TYP34]...........................................15.00
____2 of 2 [TYP35]...........................................15.00
```

EPI:TPM 750 pieces, puzzle printed on front and back.
```
____Bravo Squadron Assault [TYP36]........................7.00
____Gungan Sub Escape [TYP37].............................7.00
____Podrace Challenge [TYP38] ..............................7.00
```

EPI:TPM Slivers.
```
____Anakin Skywalker [TYP39] ...............................8.00
```

TYP28   TYP29   TYP30   TYP31   TYP32   TYP33   TYP34   TYP35

TYP36   TYP37   TYP38   TYP39   TYP40   TYP41   TYP42

TYP43   TYP44   TYP45   TYP46   TYP47   TYP48   TYP49

Toys: Puzzles

| TYP50 | TYP51 | TYP52 | TYP53 | TYP54 | TYP55 | TYP56 |

| TYP57 | TYP58 | TYP59 | TYP60 | TYP61 | TYP62 |

| TYP63 | TYP64 | TYP65 | TYP66 | TYP67 | TYP68 | TYP69 |

____Darth Maul [TYP40].............................8.00
____Jar Jar Binks [TYP41] 8.00

EPI:TPM. 200 pieces. Hidden image glows in the dark.
____Jedi vs. Sith [TYP42]............................7.00
____Mos Espa Podrace [TYP43] 7.00
____Opee Sea Creature [TYP44] 7.00

EPI:TPM. 3D mini-puzzles.
____Gungan Sub, 66 pieces [TYP45] 9.00

EPI:TPM. 73 pieces, 3D mini-puzzles.
____Sith Infilterator, 73 pieces [TYP46] 9.00

EPII:AOTC. 500 piece puzzle in tin storage box.
____Bounty Hunters 15.00
____Heroes 15.00
____Vehicles 15.00
____Villains..15.00

Hasbro, Canada
EPI:TPM. 100 piece shaped puzzle, includes theme shaped pieces. Bi-language.
____Darth Maul 5.00
____Jar Jar Binks [TYP47] 5.00
____R2-D2 ....5.00
____Yoda [TYP48] 5.00

Hasbro, Mexico
EPI:TPM. 50 piece mini-puzzle, 5"x7".
____Jedi vs. Sith [TYP49]............................2.00
____Pit Droids [TYP50]................................2.00
____Queen Amidala [TYP51] 2.00
____Sebulba [TYP52]..................................2.00

IN
EPIII:ROTS. Tray puzzles.
____Clone Trooper [TYP53] 8.00
____Darth Vader [TYP54] 8.00
____Darth Vader / Epic Duel [TYP55] 8.00

____Epic Duel / Yoda [TYP56] 8.00
____General Grievous and Darth Vader [TYP57]..........8.00
____General Grievous and Yoda [TYP58] 8.00
____Revenge of the Sith collage [TYP59] 8.00
____Yoda [TYP60] 8.00

Karnan
EPI:TPM. 50 pieces.
____Jedi Duel [TYP61]................................25.00

Kenner
____Aboard Millennium Falcon, 1000 pc [TYP62] 24.00
____Artoo-Detoo / See-Threepio, 140 pieces, black box [TYP63] 15.00
____Artoo-Detoo / See-Threepio, 140 pieces, blue box [TYP64] 24.00
____Bantha, 140 pieces [TYP65]................10.00
____Corridor of Lights, 1500 pieces [TYP66] 26.00
____Darth Vader and Obi-Wan Duel, 500 pieces [TYP67] 10.00

| TYP70 | TYP71 | TYP72 | TYP73 | TYP74 | TYP75 |

| TYP76 | TYP77 | TYP78 | TYP79 | TYP80 | TYP81 |

| TYP82 | TYP83 | TYP84 | TYP85 | TYP86 | TYP87 |

TYP88 TYP89 TYP90 TYP91 TYP92 TYP93 TYP94

TYP95 TYP96 TYP97 TYP98 TYP99 TYP100 TYP101 TYP102

TYP103 TYP104 TYP105 TYP106 TYP107 TYP108

____Han and Chewbacca, 140 pieces, black box [TYP68] 15.00
____Han and Chewbacca, 140 pieces, blue box [TYP69] 24.00
____Hildebrandt Movie Poster Art, 1000 pieces [TYP70] 17.00
____Jawas Capture R2-D2 [TYP71] 10.00
____Luke and Leia, 500 pieces [TYP72] 10.00
____Luke Meets R2-D2, 140 pieces [TYP73] 15.00
____Luke Skywalker, 500 pieces, black box [TYP74] 15.00
____Luke Skywalker, 500 pieces, purple box [TYP75] 12.00
____Millennium Falcon, 1500 pieces [TYP76]...........24.00
____Purchase of the Droids, 500 pieces [TYP77]......12.00
____Sandtroopers in Mos Eisley, 140 pieces [TYP78] 8.00
____Space Battle, 500 pieces, black box [TYP79] ...15.00
____Space Battle, 500 pieces, purple box [TYP80] ..24.00
____The Cantina Band, 500 pieces [TYP81]...........12.00

____Trapped in the Trash Compactor, 140 pieces, black box [TYP82] 8.00
____Tusken Raider, 140 pieces [TYP83] 8.00
____Victory Celebration, 500 pieces, correct image [TYP84] 10.00
____Victory Celebration, 500 pieces, wrong image, small correction sticker [TYP85] 65.00
____X-Wing Hanger tight view, 500 pieces...........10.00
____X-Wing Hanger wide view, 500 pieces [TYP86] 10.00

Kinder
____150 pieces, Hippo landspeeder scene 10.00

King International
____1,000 pieces, scenes from the classic trilogy [TYP87] 24.00

Lili Ledy
____Darth Vader, tray [TYP88]...........35.00

Milton Bradley
100 piece classic trilogy puzzles.
____C-3PO and R2-D2 in desert [TYP89] 8.00
____C-3PO, Chewbacca, Han, and Leia in Shuttle Tydirium [TYP90] 8.00
____Darth Vader [TYP91] 8.00
____Jabba's Dias [TYP92] 14.00
____POTF: Classic Trilogy [TYP93] 12.00
____POTF: Empire Strikes Back [TYP94] 12.00
____POTF: Return of the Jedi [TYP95] 12.00
____POTF: Star Wars [TYP96]...........12.00

221 piece mural puzzles.
____Scene 1: A New Hope [TYP97] 6.00
____Scene 2: Empire Strikes Back [TYP98] 6.00
____Scene 3: Return of the Jedi [TYP99] 6.00
____Scene 4: Trilogy [TYP100]...........6.00

3D sculpture puzzles.
____Darth Vader [TYP101]...........35.00

TYP109 TYP110 TYP111 TYP112 TYP113 TYP114 TYP115 TYP116

TYP117 TYP118 TYP119 TYP120 TYP121 TYP122 TYP123 TYP124 TYP125

TYP126 TYP127 TYP128 TYP129 TYP130 TYP131 TYP132 TYP133 TYP134 TYP135

Toys: Puzzles

TYP136

TYP137

TYP138

TYP139

TYP140

TYP141

TYP142

TYP143

TYP144

TYP145

TYP146

TYP147

TYP148

TYP149

____Darth Vader, tri-language [TYP102] 35.00
____Imperial Star Destroyer [TYP103].......................35.00
____Jar Jar Binks [TYP104]....................................25.00
____Jedi Starfighter [TYP105] 20.00
____Millennium Falcon [TYP106]..............................35.00
____R2-D2 with electronic sounds [TYP107] 35.00

550 pieces with foil highlights.
____Return of the Jedi [TYP108]...............................12.00
____Star Wars: A New Hope [TYP109] 12.00
____The Empire Strikes Back [TYP110] 12.00

60 piece classic trilogy puzzles.
____A New Hope [TYP111] 15.00
____Empire Strikes Back..15.00
____Return of the Jedi [TYP112]..............................15.00

EPII:AOTC. 50 piece mini-puzzle, 5"x7".
____Anakin Skywalker [TYP113] 3.00
____C-3PO and R2-D2 [TYP114]............................3.00
____Darth Vader [TYP115] 3.00
____Jango Fett [TYP116] 3.00
____Mace Windu [TYP117] 3.00
____Obi-Wan Kenobi [TYP118] 3.00
____Padme Amidala [TYP119] 3.00
____Zam Wesell [TYP120] 3.00

EPII:AOTC. 100 pieces.
____Anakin Skywalker [TYP121] 8.00
____Boba and Jango Fett [TYP122] 8.00
____Obi-Wan Kenobi [TYP123] 8.00
____Padme Amidala and Princess Leia [TYP124]........8.00

EPII:AOTC. 150 Metallix pieces.
____Anakin Skywalker [TYP125] 9.00
____Count Dooku 9.00
____Mace Windu [TYP126] 9.00
____Obi-Wan Kenobi 9.00

EPIII:ROTS. 50 piece mini-puzzle, 5"x7".
____Anakin [TYP127] 3.00
____C-3PO and R2-D2 [TYP128]............................3.00
____Darth Vader [TYP129] 3.00
____General Grievous [TYP130] 3.00
____Obi-Wan [TYP131] 3.00
____Padme [TYP132] 3.00
____Palpatine [TYP133] 3.00
____Yoda [TYP134] 3.00

EPIII:ROTS. 100 pieces.
____Anakin vs. Obi-Wan [TYP135] 10.00
____Darth Vader / Anakin [TYP136] 10.00
____Space Battle [TYP137] 10.00
____Wookiees [TYP138] 10.00

EPIII:ROTS. 500 pieces in tin storage box, 2-sided.
____Emperor, General Grievous, clone troopers / Anakin,
    Obi-Wan, Yoda, Mace Windu [TYP139].............15.00
____Obi-Wan Kenobi and Yoda / Darth Vader, Emperor,
    Count Dooku and Anakin Skywalker [TYP140] ..15.00

Parker Bros.
____Bantha, 140 pieces 35.00
____Battle above Death Star, 500 pieces
    [TYP141]...35.00

____C-3PO and R2-D2, 140 pieces [TYP142] 35.00
____Death Star II, 70 pieces [TYP143] 8.00
____Jabba's Henchmen, 70 pieces [TYP144] 8.00
____Light Saber Duel, 500 pieces...........................35.00
____Luke Meets R2-D2, 140 pieces 35.00
____Luke Skywalker, 500 pieces.............................35.00
____Rebel Base, 500 pieces [TYP145]........................35.00
____Sandtroopers in Mos Eisley, 140 pieces
    [TYP146]...8.00
____Selling of Droids, 500 pieces 35.00
____Stormtroopers, 140 pieces 35.00
____Trash Compactor, 140 pieces 35.00
____Victory, 500 pieces [TYP147]............................35.00

Kreig der Sterne mini-puzzles.
____Battle over Death Star 18.00
____Death Star Assault, art 18.00
____Han and Chewbacca 18.00
____Imperial Star Destroyer 18.00
____Obi-Wan Kenobi 18.00
____Princess Leia and R2-D2 ....18.00
____Stormtroopers 18.00
____Tusken Raider 18.00
____Vader confronts Leia 18.00

Party Express
____5 pieces, Darth Vader, 8-pack [TYP148] 5.00

Pizza Hut
Get Into It! Episode I Puzzle Games.
____Blue border 5.00
____Red border [TYP149] 5.00

TYP150

TYP151

TYP152

TYP153

TYP154

TYP155

TYP156

TYP157

TYP158

TYP159

TYP160

TYP161

TYP162

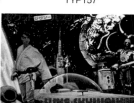
TYP163

TYP164

TYP165

TYP166

TYP167

TYP168

TYP169

TYP170

| TYP171 | TYP172 | TYP173 | TYP174 | TYP175 | TYP176 |

| TYP177 | TYP178 | TYP179 | TYP180 | TYP181 | PZB01 |

| PZB02 | PZB03 | PZB04 | PZB05 | PZB06 | PZB07 | PZB08 |

Ravensburger
France. Ewoks.
____Ewoks, 100 pieces 25.00
____Ewoks, 3x49 [TYP150] 25.00

Really Useful
3D miniature sculpture puzzles.
____Anakin Skywalker [TYP151] 14.00
____Darth Maul, color [TYP152] 25.00
____Darth Vader [TYP153] 14.00
____Jar Jar Binks [TYP154]...................32.00
____Obi-Wan Kenobi [TYP155] 14.00
____Qui-Gon Jinn [TYP156] 14.00

Rose Art Industries
100 pieces.
____Luke and Leia [TYP157] 8.00
____Star Wars poster art [TYP158] 8.00

550 pieces.
____1 Star Wars 8.00
____2 Empire Strikes Back 8.00
____3 Return of the Jedi 8.00

Schmid
Return of the Jedi 2-in-1.
____Darth Vader / Tyderium Cockpit [TYP159]..........36.00
____Jabba the Hutt and Luke in Jabbas Court 36.00

Springbok
____Empire Strikes Back, 1,000 pieces [TYP160] 24.00
____Star Wars, 1500 pieces [TYP161] 24.00

T. Theophanides and Son
____Mini-Puzzles, 63 pieces, 14x18cm, eight different pictures, each [TYP162] 24.00

Takara
60 pieces.
____C-3PO and R2-D2 ....35.00
____Chewbacca and Han Solo 35.00
____Darth Vader 35.00
____Luke Skywalker [TYP163] 35.00
____Space Battle....................................35.00
____Star Wars 35.00

Any of six scenes.
____100 pieces 45.00
____500 pieces 50.00
____700 pieces 50.00

Plastic framed tray puzzles.
____R2-D2 [TYP164] 45.00
____Victory Celebration [TYP165] 45.00

Tomy
____Anakin Skywalker, 56 pieces 15.00

Mini puzzles in tins.
____C-3PO and R2-D2 [TYP166]................7.00
____Darth Maul [TYP167] 7.00
____Yoda [TYP168] 7.00

Waddington / Capiepa
France. Guerre de Etoiles.
____Entree Dans la Ville [TYP169]...........36.00
____Yan Solo et Chiktabba [TYP170] 36.00

Waddington
150 pieces.
____C-3PO and R2-D2 [TYP171] 25.00
____Chewbacca and Han [TYP172] 25.00
____Darth Vader [TYP173]......................16.00
____Entering Mos Eisley [TYP174] 25.00
____Ewoks at home.................................14.00
____Ewoks in woods [TYP175] 14.00
____Ewoks sledding 14.00
____Ewoks swimming 14.00
____Inside the Millennium Falcon [TYP176] 25.00
____Jabba's Throne Room 16.00
____Luke with blaster 16.00

350 pieces. Action figure scenes.
____Land Speeder [TYP177].....................65.00
____Vehicles [TYP178]............................85.00

Wrebbit
3D sculpture puzzles.
____Millennium Falcon [TYP179]..............35.00
____R2-D2 [TYP180] 35.00
____Star Destroyer [TYP181]...................35.00

Toys: Puzzles – Block

Craft Master
____Ewoks, 9 block [PZB01]....................12.00
____Return of the Jedi characters, 9 block [PZB02]..12.00

Pepsi Cola
EPI:TPM. 36 piece promotional puzzles.
____Anakin Skywalker [PZB03] 7.00
____C-3PO [PZB04]..................................7.00
____Darth Maul [PZB05] 7.00
____Jar Jar Binks [PZB06] 7.00
____Obi-Wan Kenobi [PZB07] 7.00
____Queen Amidala [PZB08] 7.00

Takara
____C-3PO and R2-D2 ....45.00
____Character art 45.00
____Darth Vader 45.00
____Han Solo and Chewbacca 45.00
____Yavin Ceremony 45.00
____Yavin Hanger 45.00

Toys: Puzzles – Twisting

Harry N. Abrams, Inc.
____Dressing a Galaxy puzzle cube, book premium 18.00

Hasbro
____Darth Maul Rubik's Cube Puzzle [PZ01] 7.00

Kelloggs, Canada
EPII:AOTC. Cereal premium. Character sculpted on front and rear.
____Anakin Skywalker / Darth Vader [PZ02] 6.00
____C-3PO/ R2-D2 [PZ03]........................6.00
____Count Dooku / Darth Sidious [PZ04] 6.00
____Jango Fett / Clone trooper [PZ05] 6.00
____Obi-Wan Kenobi / Ben Kenobi [PZ06] 6.00
____Princess Leia / Padme Amidala [PZ07] 6.00

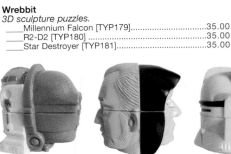

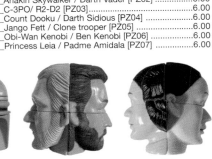

| PZ01 | PZ02 | PZ03 | PZ04 | PZ05 | PZ06 | PZ07 |

Toys: R2-D2

RBO01   RBO02   RBO03   RBO04   RBO05   RBO06   RBO07   RBO08   RBO09

RBO10   YF01   YL01   YL02   YL03

Toys: R2-D2

Hasbro
____Voice Command R2-D2 [RBO01] 135.00
____Voice Command R2-D2 in Saga Collection packaging [RBO02] 250.00
____Voice Command R2-D2 with bonus poster [RBO03] 200.00

Kinder
____R2-Hippo, pull-back friction [RBO04] 16.00

Micro Games of America
____Talking R2-D2, says four different phrases [RBO05] 14.00

Palitoy
____Talking R2-D2, says four different phrases [RBO06] 895.00

Takara
____Bump-and-Go battery powered R2-D2 [RBO07] 264.00
____Missile Firing R2-D2, die cast [RBO08]...........285.00
____Missile Firing R2-D2, plastic [RBO09] 175.00
____Missile Firing R2-D2, plastic in window box [RBO10] 175.00

Toys: Racing Sets

Fundimensions
____Duel at Death Star [YF01] 125.00

____Duel at Death Star, white line-art box [3:367] 165.00

Toys: Racing Vehicle Toys

Action / Revell
____"Pedal car bank" with trailer, 6.2" long; 2500 produced 55.00

Racing cars.
____1/18 scale, "standard limited edition" 45.00
____1/18 scale, 1,500 produced............................100.00
____1/18 scale, 4,000 produced............................250.00
____1/24 scale, "clear window bank", 8.3" long, 10,000 produced 75.00
____1/24 scale, "Elite" 26.00
____1/24 scale, "standard limited edition" 24.00
____1/24 scale, 12,500 produced [YL01] 36.00
____1/24, 8.3" long, 3,500 produced 42.00
____1/43 scale, 5,500 produced [YL02] 44.00
____1/64 scale diecast; 15,000 produced [YL03] 14.00
____1/64 scale, 20,000 produced 8.00

EPIII:ROTS.
____M&M 1/24 scale Elliott Sadler white gold, limited to 25 ....250.00

General Mills
Mail-away premiums. Car 43, 1/64 scale.
____Classic Trilogy [YL04] 15.00
____Episode I [YL05] 15.00
____Episode II [YL06] 15.00

Hasbro
EPI:TPM. Winner's Circle series.
____1/64 scale racing car with Jeff Gordon trading card [3:367]...12.00
____Pit Row [3:367] 17.00

Kenner
____Power Racing Speeder Bike [YL07]...................12.00

SSP vans.
____2 Vans, cones, obstacles [YL08] 995.00
____Darth Vader [YL09]......................................150.00
____Luke Skywalker [YL10] 150.00

Team Caliber
____1/24 scale 2002 John Andretti Star Wars Episode II Dark Chrome car, limited to 450 [3:367] 75.00
____1/64 scale 2002 John Andretti Star Wars Episode II car [YL11] 12.00

Toys: Radio Controlled Toys

____Cobot [YG01] 395.00

Foodland
____Mr. Grocer, licensed variation on the Cobot [1:308] 185.00

Hitari
____Darth Vader [YG02] 75.00

Kenner
____Imperial Speeder Bike [YG03] 50.00

YL04   YL05   YL06

YL07   YL08   YL09   YL10   YL11

YG01   YG02   YG03   YG04   YG05   YG06

YG07

YG08

YH01

YH02

YH03

PLS01

PLS02

PLS03

PLS04

PLS05

PLS06

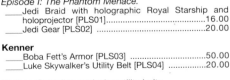
PLS07

YI01

YI02

YI03

YI04

YK01

TG01

____Speederbike with Luke Skywalker [YG04].........70.00

Vintage.
____R2-D2 [YG05].............................165.00
____R2-D2 with obstacle course [2:372] 3,850.00

Palitoy
____R2-D2 [3:367]..165.00

Takara
____R2-D2, fires toy discs and top of body turns [YG06] 425.00

Tomy
Astromech droids, control is lightsaber shaped.
____R2-D2 [YG07]...25.00
____R2-Q5 [YG08]...35.00
____R4-P17 ....35.00

Toys: Remote Controlled Toys

Banpresto
____Millennium Falcon [YH01] 23.00
____R2-D2 [YH02]..18.00

Kenner
____R2-D2 [YH03] 20.00

Toys: Role Playing Toys

Hasbro
Episode I: The Phantom Menace.
____Jedi Braid with holographic Royal Starship and holoprojector [PLS01].........................16.00
____Jedi Gear [PLS02] 20.00

Kenner
____Boba Fett's Armor [PLS03] 50.00
____Luke Skywalker's Utility Belt [PLS04] 20.00

Vintage Canadian exclusive utility belts.
____Darth Vader [PLS05] 340.00

____Luke Skywalker [PLS06] 365.00
____Princess Leia [PLS07] 375.00

Rubies
____Count Dooku accessory kit 15.00
____Jedi Knight accessory kit 15.00

Toys: Room Alerts

Kenner
____Boba Fett [YI01] 36.00
____Stormtrooper [YI02] 32.00

Tiger Electronics
____Destroyer Droid [YI03] 39.00
____Jango Fett [YI04] 39.00

Toys: Sit-and-Spins

Kenner
____Wicket the Ewok Sit'n Spin [YK01] 375.00

Toys: Space Shooters

Hasbro
____Naboo Fighter target game [TG01] 20.00

TG02

TG03

TG04

TG05

Milton Bradley
____Battle Belt with 32 foam disks [TG02] 11.00
____Imperial (Darth Vader's Tie Fighter) target game [TG03]...34.00
____Jango Fett's target game [TG04] 12.00
____Millennium Falcon target game [TG05] 34.00

Toys: Squeaky Toys

Brazil, unlicensed. Bagged with hang-card.
____Darth Maul [SQU01] 25.00
____Obi-Wan Kenobi [SQU02] 25.00
____Queen Amidala [SQU03] 25.00
____Qui-Gon Jinn [SQU04] 25.00

Toys: String / Streamer Canisters

Hasbro
Energy bem string refill canisters.
____Clone Trooper [SCS01].................................3.00
____General Grievous [SCS02] 3.00
____Super Battle Droid [SCS03] 3.00
____Yoda [SCS04] 3.00

Toys: Suction Cup

____Ben Kenobi [SCU01]......................................6.00

SQU01

SQU02

SQU03

SQU04

SCS01

SCS02

SCS03

SCS04

SCU01

SCU02

SCU03

SCU04

SCU05

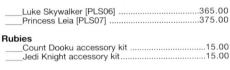

Toys: Suction Cup

| TST01 | TST02 | TST03 | TST04 | TST05 | TST06 | TST07 | TST08 |

| TST09 | TST10 | TST11 | TST12 | TTY01 | TSB01 | TSB02 | TSB03 |

| TSB04 | TSB05 | TSB06 | TSB07 | TSB08 | TSB09 | TSB10 | TSB11 |

____Chewbacca [SCU02] 6.00
____Darth Vader [SCU03] 6.00
____Luke Skywalker as X-Wing Pilot [SCU04] 6.00
____R5-D4 [SCU05] 6.00

Toys: Trucks

____Inter-Transmax Semi, Star Warrio [2:414] 46.00

Toys: Transforming

Hasbro
____Anakin Skywalker / Jedi Starfighter [TST01] 20.00
____Boba Fett / Slave I [TST02] 20.00
____Clone Pilot / ARC-170 Starfighter [TST03] 20.00
____Darth Maul / Sith Infilerator [TST04] 20.00
____Darth Vader / TIE Adv. Fighter [TST05] 20.00
____Emperor Palpatine / ImpZ. Shuttle [TST06]........20.00
____General Grievous / Wheel Bike [TST07] 20.00
____Han Solo and Chewbacca / Millennium Falcon
[TST08] 45.00
____Han Solo and Chewbacca / Millennium Falcon with
bonus Titanium vehicles [TST09] 50.00
____Jango Fett / Slave I [TST10]...........................20.00
____Luke Skywalker / X-Wing Fighter [TST11] 20.00
____Obi-Wan Kenobi / Jedi Starfighter [TST12] 20.00

30th anniversary packaging.
____Clone Pilot / ARC-170 Starfighter 20.00
____Darth Vader / Sith Starfighter.............................20.00

Takara
____Transforming X-Wing [TTY01] 535.00

Toys: Voice Changers

Hasbro
Darth Vader, 3 voice modifications, breathing, 5 pre-recorded phrases.
____AOTC packaging [TSB01] 40.00
____ROTS packaging [TSB02] 35.00
____ROTS packaging, bonus lightsaber [TSB03]......50.00
____ROTS packaging, ultimate with lightsaber and cape
[TSB04] 45.00

Hasbro, Japan
____C-3PO [TSB05]..16.00

Pepsi Cola
____C-3PO from TPM, promotional [TSB06] 15.00

Rubies
____Belt-clipped [TSB07] 20.00

Tiger Electronics
Authentic sounds plus speed adjustable record/playback.
____C-3PO [TSB08]..16.00

____Darth Vader [TSB09]..16.00
____Darth Vader, alters voice to Darth Vader's
[TSB10]...25.00
____Millennium Falcon [TSB11] 16.00

Toys: Water Guns

____Droid rifle on hanger card [2:422].........................6.00

Fun Favors
____4-pack party favors: vehicles [WG01]................24.00

Hasbro
Super soakers.
____Wookiee Water Blaster [WG02] 25.00

Kenner
____Water Blaster BlasTech DL-44 [WG03] 14.00

Larami
Power soakers.
____Battle Droid Rifle [WG04] 5.00
____Battle Mauser [WG05] 5.00
____Naboo Pistol [WG06] 5.00

Super soakers.
____Battle Droid Rifle [WG07] 18.00
____Naboo Pistol [WG08] 12.00
____Queen Amidala Pistol [WG09] 8.00

| WG01 | WG02 | WG03 | WG04 | WG05 |

| WG06 | WG07 | WG08 | WG09 |

TYW01 TYW02 TYW03 TYW04 TYW05

TYW06 TYW07 TYW08 TYW12 TYW22-23 TYW25 - 27 TYW28

TYW29 TYW35 TYW36 TYW37 TYW38

Toys: Weapons

____Episode I Electronic Sword [3:425] 25.00

Unlicensed. Diecast metal cap guns.
____Galaxi Spacial [2:424]............................65.00
____Galaxy Ray Gun 75.00

Unlicensed.
____Professional Computer Beam Gun, Han Solo graphics
       on box [3:425] 55.00
____Space sword, Star Destroyer on card [3:425] 5.00

Disney / MGM
Star Tours Power of the Jedi packaging.
____Galactic Empire Rifle E-11 [TYW01] 25.00
____Lightsaber..20.00
____Rebel Alliance Blaster [TYW02] 25.00
____Rebel Alliance Bowcaster [TYW03] 25.00

Star Tours Saga packaging.
____Rebel Alliance Blaster [TYW04] 25.00
____Stormtrooper Rifle [TYW05] 25.00

George Lucas Super Live Adventure Show
____Lightsaber..95.00

Harbert
____3-Position laser rifle 230.00
____Laser Pistol, SW 185.00
____Lightsaber with inflatable yellow blade 235.00

Hasbro
____Build Your Own Lightsaber [TYW06] 45.00
____Build Your Own Lightsaber with bonus
       DVD 45.00
____Laser Tag Naboo Accessory Set 135.00
____Naboo and Droid Fighter Laser Battle...............24.00
____Naboo Foam-Firing Blaster [TYW07]................15.00
____Tatooine Blaster Pistol, Electronic [TYW08]........22.00

Episode I lightsabers.
____Darth Maul's .0000 ....35.00
____Darth Maul's .0200 [TYW09] 30.00
____Obi-Wan's (blue) [TYW10] 26.00
____Qui-Gon's (green) [TYW11] 20.00

Episode I weapons.
____Battle Droid Blaster Rifle [TYW12] 20.00

Episode II electronic lightsabers.
____Anakin, blue [TYW13] 24.00
____Anakin Skywalker Interactive Jedi Training
       [TYW14] 35.00
____Count Dooku, red [TYW15] 24.00
____Darth Tyranus, red [TYW16] 25.00
____Jedi lightsaber, green [TYW17] 24.00
____Jedi lightsaber, orange [TYW18] 24.00
____Mace Windu, purple [TYW19] 24.00
____Obi-Wan, blue [TYW20] 26.00
____Yoda, green [TYW21] 24.00

TYW09 TYW10 TYW11 TYW13 TYW14 TYW15 TYW16 TYW17 TYW18 TYW19 TYW20 TYW21 TYW24 TYW30 TYW31

TYW32 TYW33 TYW34 TYW39 TYW40 TYW41 TYW42 TYW43 TYW44 TYW45 TYW46 TYW47 TYW48 TYW49 TYW50

Toys: Weapons

TYW53-54   TYW74   TYW77   TYW78   TYW79

TYW80   TYW81   TYW82   TYW83

TYW86   TYW87   TYW88   TYW89   TYW90

Episode II lightsabers.
____Blue 12.00
____Green [TYW22] 12.00
____Purple 12.00
____Red [TYW23] 12.00

Episode II weapons.
____Battle Droid Blaster Rifle, electronic 20.00
____Jango Fett's blasters 2-pack 20.00

Episode III lightsabers available in red, blue, purple, green.
____2-pack [TYW24] 18.00
____Obi-Wan handle [TYW25] 8.00
____Qui-Gon Jinn handle [TYW26] 8.00
____Vader handle [TYW27] 8.00

Force Action lightsabers. Spring loaded.
____Darth Vader.................................30.00
____Luke Skywalker 30.00
____Obi-Wan Kenobi...........................30.00

Light Saber Action Packs.
____Any colored saber with 3 random action figures [TYW28] 45.00

Lightsabers, The Saga Collection.
____Darth Maul 30.00

Revenge of the Sith electronic lightsabers.
____2-pack with 2 bonus figures and bonus poster [TYW29] 35.00
____Anakin Skywalker / Darth Vader, color-change blade [TYW30] 20.00
____Count Dooku [TYW31] 20.00
____Jedi 20.00
____Luke Skywalker 20.00
____Mace Windu [TYW32] 20.00
____Obi-Wan Kenobi, Force feedback vibration [TYW33] 20.00
____Yoda, training mode [TYW34] 20.00

ROTS. Energy beam blaster refill canisters.
____Clone Trooper 5.00
____General Grievous 5.00
____Super Battle Droid 5.00
____Yoda 5.00

ROTS.
____Chewbacca's Bowcaster [TYW35].....25.00
____Clone Trooper blaster [TYW36] 15.00
____Energy beam blaster [TYW37] 15.00
____General Grievous' Blaster [TYW38] ...25.00

Saga 2 electronic lightsabers.
____Anakin Skywalker [TYW39] 20.00
____Anakin Skywalker with bonus Lightsaber Action DVD 20.00
____Darth Vader [TYW40] 20.00
____Darth Vader with bonus Lightsaber Action DVD 20.00
____Mace Windu [TYW41] 20.00
____Obi-Wan Kenobi [TYW42] 20.00
____Obi-Wan Kenobi with bonus Lightsaber Action DVD 20.00
____Yoda [TYW43]..............................20.00

Saga 2 lightsabers, non-electronic. Blue, red, or green.
____2-packs, Jedi vs. Sith, Luke vs. Darth Vader......12.00
____2-packs, Jedi vs. Sith, Obi-Wan vs. Anakin ...12.00
____2-packs, Jedi vs. Sith, Yoda vs. Sidious 12.00
____Darth Vader handle 7.00
____Darth Vader handle with bonus Galactic Heroes figure 9.00
____Obi-Wan handle 7.00
____Obi-Wan handle with bonus Galactic Heroes figure 9.00
____Qui-Gon Jinn handle......................7.00
____Qui-Gon Jinn handle with bonus Galactic Heroes figure 9.00

Saga 2.
____Clone Trooper blaster....................15.00
____General Grievous' Blaster 25.00

Star Wars electronic lightsabers. Includes bonus Galactic Heroes figure(s).
____Original Trilogy Collection: Darth Vader, Vader and Kenobi [TYW44] 30.00
____Original Trilogy Collection: Luke Skywalker, Luke and R2-D2 ....30.00
____ROTS: Darth Vader (Anakin)...............25.00
____ROTS: Obi-Wan figure [TYW45] 25.00

Star Wars Original Trilogy Collection electronic lightsabers. Includes bonus DVD.
____Anakin Skywalker [TYW46] 30.00
____Darth Vader [TYW47] 30.00
____Obi-Wan Kenobi [TYW48] 30.00

Star Wars Original Trilogy Collection electronic lightsabers.
____Anakin Skywalker [TYW49] 25.00
____Darth Vader [TYW50] 25.00
____Luke Skywalker [TYW51] 25.00
____Yoda [TYW52]..............................25.00

Star Wars Original Trilogy Collection. Non-electronic.
____Blue [TYW53] 7.00
____Blue [TYW54] 7.00
____Green 7.00
____Green 7.00
____Purple 7.00
____Purple 7.00
____Red 7.00
____Red 7.00

Star Wars Saga electronic lightsabers.
AOTC.
____Yoda [TYW55]..............................25.00
Clone Wars.
____Anakin Skywalker [TYW56] 25.00
____Count Dooku [TYW57] 25.00
____Mace Windu, vert pkg [TYW58] 25.00
____Obi-Wan Kenobi [TYW59] 25.00
____Yoda [TYW60]..............................25.00
____Yoda, vert pkg [TYW61] 25.00

TYW51   TYW52   TYW55   TYW56   TYW57   TYW58   TYW59   TYW60   TYW61   TYW62   TYW63   TYW64   TYW65   TYW66

TYW91   TYW92   TYW93   TYW94   TYW95   TYW96   TYW97

TYW98   TYW99   TYW100   TYW101   TYW102   TYW103

ROTJ.
____Darth Vader [TYW62] 25.00
____Darth Vader, vert pkg [TYW63].................25.00
____Luke Skywalker [TYW64] 25.00
____Luke Skywalker, vert pkg [TYW65] 25.00

Hasbro, Canada
EPII electronic lightsabers. Tri-language packaging.
____Anakin's, blue [TYW66] 30.00
____Darth Tyranus, red [TYW67] 30.00
____Obi-Wan's, blue [TYW68].........................30.00

Original Trilogy Collection electronic lightsabers. Tri-language packaging.
____Darth Vader [TYW69] 20.00
____Luke Skywalker [TYW70] 20.00
____Yoda [TYW71]...20.00

Revenge of the Sith electronic lightsabers, tri-language packaging.
____Anakin Skywalker / Darth Vader, color-change blade...20.00
____Count Dooku 20.00
____Mace Windu, motion activated [TYW72] 20.00
____Obi-Wan Kenobi, Force feedback vibration [TYW73] 20.00
____Yoda, training mode 20.00

Hasbro, UK
Multi-language packaging.
____Naboo Foam-Firing Blaster [TYW74] 8.00

Kenner
POTF2 lightsabers.
____Luke Skywalker's [TYW75]........................55.00
Darth Vader's
____Green packaging [TYW76] 55.00
____Red packaging 60.00

POTF2.
____Chewbacca's Bowcaster [TYW77].....................18.00
Electronic Blaster Rifle
____Green package [TYW78] 45.00
____Orange package [TYW79] 50.00
Heavy blaster
____Camoflage [TYW80] 26.00
____Orange [TYW81]..22.00

Vintage lightsabers.
____Droids, collapsable blade, green [TYW82] 275.00
____Droids, collapsable blade, red [TYW83] 275.00
____ROTJ, red or green...................................45.00

TYW104   TYW105-106   TYW107   TYW108 TYW109 TYW110   TYW111   TYW112   TYW113

____SW with inflatable yellow blade......................275.00
____SW with inflatable yellow blade, SW Kenobi / Vader pkg. 275.00
____The Force, red [TYW84] 50.00
____The Force, yellow [TYW85] 50.00

Vintage.
____Biker Scout laser pistol [TYW86] 75.00
Laser rifle, 3 position [TYW87] 240.00
Electronic laser rifle
____ESB [TYW88] 275.00
____ROTJ, JC Penney exclusive [TYW89] 875.00
Laser Pistol
____SW [TYW90]..225.00
____ESB Han Solo photo [TYW91] 490.00
____ESB [TYW92] 155.00
____ROTJ [TYW93] 150.00

Kenner, UK
____Heavy blaster, orange [TYW94] 12.00

Larami
Electronic micro light and sound weapons. EPI:TPM.
____Battle Droid Rifle [TYW95] 7.00
____Battle Mouser [TYW96]...7.00
____Naboo Pistol [TYW97]..7.00

Electronic micro light and sound weapons. EPII:AOTC.
____Anakin Skywalker, lightsaber [TYW98] 6.00
____Jango Fett, blaster [TYW99] 6.00
____Zam Wesell, blaster [TYW100] 6.00

EPII:AOTC action sets.
____Jango Fett [TYW101] 20.00
____Jedi Knight [TYW102]...18.00

Sound and Light Blasters.
____Battle Droid [TYW103] 24.00
____Jango Fett [TYW104] 16.00

Maruka
____Lightsaber on Darth Vader header card..............77.00

Palitoy
____3-Position laser rifle...230.00
____Blaster Pistol, SW 180.00
____Lightsaber, inflatable blade, SW 195.00

Party Express
____Lightsaber, inflatable...8.00

Redondo
____Galaxia laser gun 79.00

Rubies
Colored lightsabers, extend to 36 inches.
____Blue 6.00
____Green [TYW105] 6.00
____Red 6.00
____White [TYW106] 6.00

Episode I lightsabers.
____Darth Maul, red..12.00
____Obi-Wan, blue 12.00
____Qui-gon, green 12.00

Episode II weapons.
____Anakin Skywalker Lightsaber [TYW107]................8.00
____Anakin Skywalker Lightsaber, hang-tab package [TYW108]...8.00
____Count Dooku Lightsaber [TYW109] 8.00
____Jango Fett Blaster [TYW110]..................................8.00
____Mace Windu Lightsaber [TYW111]........................8.00
____Padme Amidala Blaster [TYW112]....................20.00

ROTS.
____Darth Vader's Lightsaber [TYW113] 12.00

Super Live Adventure
Vintage lightsabers.
____Gold hilt 125.00
____Gray hilt 145.00

Super Sonic Toys
____SST Laser Sword, unlicensed [TYW114]............45.00

TYW67   TYW68   TYW69   TYW70   TYW71   TYW72   TYW73   TYW75   TYW76   TYW84-85 TYW114 TYW115   TYW116

Toys: Weapons

TW01 TW02 TW03 TW04 TW05 TW06 YM01 YM02 YM03 YM04 YM05 YM06

Takara
____Lightsaber [TYW115] 215.00

Tiger Electronics
Laser tag sets.
____Naboo Assault 34.00
____Star Wars 45.00

Toltoys
____Laser Pistol, SW 140.00

Tomy
____Lightsaber, deluxe electronic [TYW116] 45.00
____Lightsaber, inflatable 35.00

Weina
____SW Laser Space Pistol, released with Star Tours [2:424] 100.00

Toys: Wind-Up Toys

Kenner, Canada
____Wind-up walking R2-D2 [TW01] 2,250.00

Osaka
Tin Age Collection.
____Boba Fett [TW02]..185.00
____C-3PO [TW03] 185.00
____Darth Vader [TW04] 185.00
____R2-D2 [TW05] 225.00
____Stormtrooper [TW06] 185.00

Takara
____Wind-up walking R2-D2 ....265.00

Toys: Wind-Up Toys – Deformed

____Anakin Skywalker [TWD01]....................................6.00
____Anakin Skywalker, hands up [TWD02] 9.00
____Anakin Skywalker, slave [TWD03] 21.00
____Battle Droid, shot [TWD04]...................................7.00
____Battle Droid, silver [TWD05] 8.00
____Battle Droid, sliced [TWD06] 7.00
____C-3PO [TWD07] 15.00
____C-3PO, TPM [TWD08] 9.00
____Chewbacca [TWD09] 15.00
____Darth Maul empty handed [TWD10].......................8.00
____Darth Maul empty, gold [TWD11]..........................9.00
____Darth Maul with hooded cloak [TWD12] 9.00
____Darth Maul with saber [TWD13]..........................11.00
____Darth Vader [TWD14]..15.00
____Emperor Palpatine [TWD15]...............................23.00
____Jar Jar Binks [TWD16] 9.00
____Mace Windu [TWD17]..9.00
____Obi-Wan Kenobi [TWD18] 9.00
____OOM-9 [TWD19]..9.00
____Queen Amidala [TWD20] 9.00
____Queen Amidala, hands up [TWD21].......................7.00
____Qui-Gon Jinn [TWD22] 9.00
____R2-D2 [TWD23] 15.00
____Sebulba [TWD24]..9.00
____Stormtrooper [TWD25]...15.00
____Watto [TWD26] 9.00
____Yoda [TWD27]...15.00
____Yoda, brown [TWD28] 25.00

Toys: Wonder World

Kenner
____Create battle scenes in 3D [WW01]...................17.00

Toys: Yoyos

Spectra Star
3D character sculpt on sides.
____Darth Vader [YM01]..6.00
____Stormtrooper [YM02] 6.00

Tapper Candies
Lightsaber paper yo-yos.
____EPI:TPM, package of 4..4.00
____EPII:AOTC, package of 4 [YM03] 4.00

Tiger Electronics
Electronic yo-yos with sound FX and flashing lights.
____Destroyer Droid [YM04] 5.00
____Trade Federation Battle Ship [YM05] 6.00

Worlds Apart
____X-Wings and Tie Fighters [YM06] 14.00

Transfers

American Publishing
Presto Magix bagged sets.
____Astroids [CRT01]..7.00
____Beneath Cloud City [CRT02] 7.00
____Cloud City Battle [CRT03] 7.00
____Dagobah Bog Planet [CRT04] 7.00
____Death Star [CRT05]...7.00
____Deck of the Star Destroyer [CRT06].......................7.00
____Ewok Hut [CRT07] 9.00
____Ewok Village [CRT08] 7.00
____Ewoks at Play 9.00
____Hoth 7.00
____Jabba's Throne Room [CRT09] 7.00
____Rebel Base [CRT10] 7.00
____Sarlacc Pit [CRT11]...7.00

Presto Magix boxed sets.
____Battle on Endor [CRT12] 15.00
____Ewok Village 12.00
____Ewoks at Home [CRT13] 12.00
____Jabba's Throne Room [CRT14] 15.00
____Star Wars Activity set [CRT15]..............................20.00

BSB
____Death Star corridor [CRT16]..................................18.00

Kraft
Dairylea.
____Dagobag, Bog Planet [CRT17] 9.00
____ESB bumper transfer pack [CRT18] 65.00

Letraset
____01 Kidnap of Priness Leia [CRT19] 7.00
____02 Sale on Tatooine 7.00
____03 Action at Mos Eisley [CRT20] 7.00
____04 Escape from Stormtroopers 7.00
____05 Flight to Alderaan [CRT21] 7.00
____06 Inside the Death Star [CRT22]..........................7.00
____07 Prison Break [CRT23] 7.00
____08 Death Star Escape [CRT24].................................7.00
____09 Rebel Base [CRT25] 7.00
____10 Last Battle [CRT26] 7.00
____Part 1: Battle at Mos Eisley [CRT27] 16.00
____Part 2: Escape from the Death Star [CRT28]......16.00
____Part 3: Rebel Air Attack [CRT29] 16.00

Nabisco Shreddies premiums.
____C-3PO, stormtrooper, TIE, Chewbacca, R2-D2, Vader [CRT30]...15.00
____Han, R2-D2, X-wing, Obi-Wan, stormtrooper, C-3PO [CRT31]...15.00
____Leia, Luke, stormtrooper, TIE, Han, Chewbacca [CRT32]...15.00
____Luke, C-3PO, Obi-Wan, R2-D2, TIE, Vader [CRT33]..15.00

Rose Art Industries
Presto Magix.
____Stick 'n Lift [CRT34] 6.00

Thomas Salter
____Battle on Endor 12.00
____Ewok Village 10.00
____Ewoks [CRT35] 8.00
____Jabba's Throne Room 10.00
____Jabba the Hutt [CRT36] 8.00

TWD01 TWD02 TWD03 TWD04 TWD05 TWD06 TWD07

TWD08 TWD09 TWD10 TWD11 TWD12 TWD13 TWD14 TWD15 TWD16 TWD17 TWD18

TWD19 TWD20 TWD21 TWD22 TWD23 TWD24 TWD25 TWD26 TWD27 TWD28

CRT01 CRT02 CRT03 CRT04 CRT05 CRT06 CRT07 CRT08 CRT09 CRT10 CRT11 CRT12 CRT13

CRT14 CRT15 CRT16 CRT17 CRT18 CRT19 CRT20 CRT21 CRT22 CRT23 CRT24

CRT25 CRT26 CRT27 CRT28 CRT29 CRT30 CRT31 CRT32 CRT33 CRT34

CRT35 CRT36 CRT37 CRT38 CRT39 CRT40 CRT41 CRT42 CRT43 CRT44 CRT45 CRT46 CRT47 CRT48

CRT49 CRT50 CRT51 CRT52 CRT53

Bagged sets, multi-language packaging.
___Battle on Endor 12.00
___Ewok Village 10.00
___Ewoks [CRT37] 8.00
___Jabba's Throne Room 10.00
___Jabba the Hutt [CRT38] 8.00

Boxed sets.
___Ewok Village [CRT39] 18.00
___Sarlacc Pit [CRT40] 11.00

Italy.
___N. 21 – Il Ritorno Dello JEDI [CRT41] 18.00

Walls
Vintage, mail-away premiums.
___C-3PO [CRT42] 2.00
___Chewbacca [CRT43] 2.00
___Darth Vader [CRT44] 2.00
___Jawas [CRT45] 2.00
___Luke Skywalker [CRT46] 2.00
___Obi-Wan Kenobi [CRT47] 2.00
___Princess Leia [CRT48] 2.00
___R2-D2 [CRT49] 2.00
___Sandperson [CRT50] 2.00
___Stormtrooper [CRT51] 2.00
___Tie Fighter [CRT52] 2.00
___X-Wing Fighter [CRT53] 2.00

Travel Kits

Adam Joseph Industries
Princess Kneesaa personal care bags.
___Blue [3:414] 18.00
___Red [3:414] 18.00

Omni Cosmetics
___Luke Skywalker Belt Kit; clear vinyl with belt slots, bubble bath, shampoo, soap, comb, toothbrush [3:414] 26.00

___Princess Leia Beauty Bag; clear vinyl with straps, shampoo, rinse, cologne, soap, comb [3:414] 26.00

Sharper Image
___Zippered travel case with logo zipper keys and embossed rebel logo [3:414] 45.00

Trays

Chein Industries
___Ewoks animated scene tray 20.00
___ROTJ Logo and collage tray [TIT01] 24.00

Disney / MGM
___Star Wars artwork with Star Tours logo.............12.00

Umbrellas

Adam Joseph Industries
Clear plastic with characters on hood.
___C-3PO and R2-D2 ....18.00
___Darth Vader and Emperor's Royal Guards..........18.00

B/W Character Merchandising
___Empire Strikes Back Storm Stick 22.00

Happinet
Japan. Handle is replica Darth Vader lightsaber.
___Darth Vader [HOU01] 165.00
___Vader logo 165.00

Pyramid
Character represented on hood with sculpted figure on handle.
___Anakin Skywalker, podracing [HOU02] 8.00
___Darth Maul, gray, black, and red [HOU03] 8.00
___Darth Vader, gray and black [HOU04] 12.00

Vases

Sigma
___Yoda [3:416] 60.00

Vehicles: Display

Hasbro
___Millennium Falcon, 6' diameter [3:416] 1,400.00
___Naboo Fighter, 6' length [VDS01] 575.00
___Trade Federation droid fighter [3:416] 125.00

Vehicles: Propeller Driven

Estes / Cox
___Darth Vader's Tie Fighter kit with Cox engine 50.00
___Death Star Battle Station with X-Wing control line fighter kit, radio controller 160.00
___Landspeeder radio control vehicle kit with Cox engine [MIF01] 125.00
___Naboo Fighter [MIF02] 24.00

VDS01

TIT01

HOU01

HOU02 handle and open

HOU03 handle and open

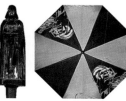

HOU04 handle and open

Vehicles: Propeller Driven

MIF01

MIF02

MIF03

MIF04

MIF05

PAV01

PAV02

____Snowspeeder Fighter kit [MIF03].......................50.00
____Star Wars Combat Set, X-Wing and TIE Fighter 120.00
____Trade Federation Droid Fighter [MIF04].............24.00
____X-Wing Fighter kit [MIF05] 50.00

Estes
____Naboo Fighter electronic remote control with display stand..18.00
____X-Wing Sterling Model Kit Control Line Fighter without engine..28.00
____Y-Wing Sterling Model Kit Control Line Fighter without engine [3:416] 35.00

Vehicles: Automobile

____Star Wars Hummer, grand prize in Taco Bell Feel the Force game [[3:278] ....N/V
____Vader Viper, Cingular Wireless grand prize ....N/V

Vending Machine Translites

Pepsi Cola
____Episode I Pod Racing [3:416] 95.00

Vitamins

Natural Balance
____3-tablet vitamin promotional sample [PAV01] 9.00
____60-tablet vitamin bottle and box [PAV02] 16.00

Wake-Up Systems

Thinkway
____Anakin's Pod Racer [3:417] 45.00
____Jar Jar Binks, includes pit-droid [3:417] 35.00
____Naboo Fighter [3:417] 45.00

Walkie-Talkies

Jollibee
____EPII. R2-D2 and C-3PO [WT01].........................25.00

Micro Games of America
____Darth Vader and Stormtrooper helmets designed to be clipped to belt [WT02] 24.00

Tiger Electronics
____Clone Trooper and Jango Fett [WT03]...............18.00
____Darth Vader voice changer, regular voice or altered [WT04]...28.00
____Imperial symbol over speaker with belt clips [WT05] 18.00
____Jedi Comlink [WT06] 10.00
____Rebel Alliance long-range, headset with sound effects function [WT07] 26.00

Titan
____Executive, shows R2-D2 and C-3PO on morse code pad [WT08]...85.00

Wall Decorations

Priss Prints
Border Stick Ups.
____Pod Race [1:359] 5.00
____Space Battle 5.00

Jumbo Stick-Ups.
____Podrace and Space Battle [1:359].......................14.00
____Podrace 10.00
____Space Battle...10.00

Wallets

____Return of the Jedi, nylon and velcro [PEX01] 10.00

EPIII:ROTS.
____Darth Vader / Epic Battle vinyl [PEX02] 8.00

Episode I, tri-fold.
____Darth Maul [PEX03]..7.00
____Jedi [PEX04] 7.00
____Jedi vs. Sith [PEX05]...7.00
____Pod Racing [PEX06] 7.00
____Queen Amidala [PEX07] 9.00

Episode I: The Phantom Menace.
____Darth Maul, zippered coin pouch [PEX08]..........12.00

Adam Joseph Industries
Billfolds, vinyl.
____Darth Vader [PEX09]...12.00
____Droids [PEX10] 12.00
____Yoda [PEX11] 12.00

Coin holders, nylon.
____Darth Vader [PEX12] 8.00
____Droids [PEX13] 8.00
____Yoda [PEX14] 8.00

Wallets, nylon.
____Darth Vader [PEX15] 8.00
____Darth Vader, ROTJ packaging band [PEX16] 25.00
____Droids [PEX17] 10.00
____Droids, ROTJ packaging band [PEX18].............25.00
____Yoda 10.00

Wallets, vinyl.
____Darth Vader...12.00
____Droids [PEX19] 12.00
____Princess Kneesaa [PEX20] 16.00
____Wicket the Ewok [PEX21]...................................14.00
____Yoda [PEX22] 12.00

Animations
____Darth Vader [PEX23] 6.00
____Darth Vader wallet and mini-flashlight gift set [PEX24] 8.00
____Darth Vader, crossed lightsabers [PEX25] 15.00
____Star Wars logo on black nylon [PEX26] 20.00

Disney / MGM
____Jedi Training Acadamy [PEX27] 14.00
____Star Tours logo 11.00

WT01

WT02

WT03

WT04

WT05

WT06

WT07

WT08

PEX01

PEX02

PEX03

PEX04

PEX05

PEX06

PEX07

PEX08

PEX09

PEX10

PEX11

PEX12

PEX13

PEX14

PEX15

PEX16

PEX17

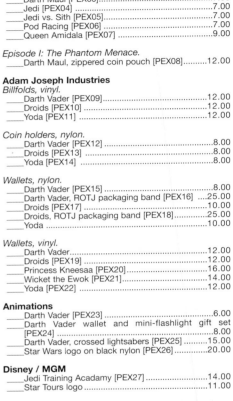

PEX18

PEX19

PEX20

PEX21 PEX22 PEX23 PEX24 PEX25 PEX26 PEX27 PEX28 PEX29

Industrias CYS

____Droids 25.00
____Star Wars 16.00

Mana

____Darth Vader, "There's a little good in everybody" Jedi Club [PEX28] 10.00
____Jedi Master / X-wing [PEX29] 10.00

Personajes Registrados

____Darth Vader...14.00
____R2-D2 ....14.00
____Wicket..12.00

Wallpaper

____Border: characters 24.00

Crown Wallcoverings Limited

10.05m rolls.

____Droids 32.00
____Ewoks 32.00

Imperial Chemicals

____ESB; alternating scenes: Falcon cockpit, Bespin, Vader Fett and Lando, Luke on Dagobah, asteroid battle, Hoth battle, Probot [WP01].....................34.00
____EWOKS border trim, Wicket swings from the vine while Kneesa and friends sit below [2:418] 19.00
____ROTJ border trim, alternating ovals with: 3 heroes, R2-D2, Chewbacca and C-3PO, Darth Vader, Ewoks, Rebo band [2:418] 25.00
____ROTJ; alternating scenes: Jabba and guards, Chewbacca and droids, Ewoks and speederbike, Darth Vader and guards, 3 heroes [WP02] 34.00
____SW; Vymura ready pasted wall vinyl, 21"x11 yard roll [WP03] 38.00

Waste Baskets

Chein Industries

Printed tin.

____Ewoks animated scene [TIW01]..........................14.00
____ROTJ characters [TIW02]...................................16.00

Jay Franco and Sons

Plastic.

____Naboo Space Battle [TIW03] 8.00
____Podracer 8.00

WP01 WP02 WP03 TIW01 TIW02 TIW03

Watches

____C-3PO and R2-D2 on round face [TAW01] 45.00
____C-3PO and R2-D2, round silver face with yellow inner border [TAW02]...75.00
____Darth Vader, round white face [TAW03] 35.00
____Episode I college [TAW04] 9.00
____Imperial Cog, stainless steel [TAW05] 35.00
____Lightsabers, black face on silver [TAW06]..........45.00
____Princess Leia and R2-D2, round face, no numbers [TAW07] 25.00
____Queen Amidala clip-on [TAW08] 19.00
____R2-D2, round white face [TAW09] 25.00
____Wicket Whistle Time watch 17.00
____Yoda [TAW10] 25.00

3D Arts

Orange hologram character, round black face, white numbers, black band, clear 3D Arts case.

____Boba Fett [TAW11] 45.00
____Darth Vader [TAW12] 40.00
____X-Wing Fighter [TAW13] 40.00
____Yoda [TAW14] 45.00

A.H. Prismatic

____Darth Vader, green hologram, round black face, white numbers, black band with "Star Wars" and "Darth Vader" [TAW15]..45.00

Armatron

____X-Wing [TAW16] 45.00

Avon

____Obi-Wan Kenobi, oval face, blue lightsaber second hand, plastic band [TAW17] 16.00

Bradley Time

____C-3PO and R2-D2 in desert, SW logo, round face, blue vinyl strap, gold casing, adult size 115.00
____C-3PO and R2-D2 in desert, SW logo, round face, blue vinyl strap, silver casing, child size [TAW18] 95.00
____C-3PO and R2-D2 in desert, SW logo, round face, blue vinyl strap, silver casing, child size, enhaced trademark 95.00
____C-3PO, R2-D2, SW logo, round black face, red second hand, numbers on outter silver ring [TAW19] 115.00
____C-3PO, R2-D2, SW logo, round black face, white hands and numbers [TAW20].............................85.00
____Darth Vader, SW logo, round gray face, planets on outter time ring, white hands, black-and-silver band [TAW21] 85.00
____Darth Vader, SW logo, round gray face, white hands, black band [TAW22] 78.00
____Darth Vader, SW logo, round white face, red hands, black band [TAW23] 65.00
____Ewok cartoon, round white face, stars and planet on outter time ring, red hands, black band [TAW24] 50.00
____Ewoks, ROTJ logo, round green face, black hands [TAW25] 45.00
____Jabba, ROTJ logo, round blue face, black band 60.00
____R2-D2, C-3PO, SW logo, round black face, white hands, black band [TAW26] 75.00
____Yoda, SW logo, round gray face, black hands, black band [TAW27] 65.00
____Yoda, SW logo, round white face, brown hands, brown leather band [TAW28] 80.00
____Yoda, SW logo, round white face, stars and planets on outter time ring, white hands, black-and-silver band [TAW29] 125.00

Bradley, Germany

____C-3PO and R2-D2, desert scene, octogonal face framed with screws [TAW30] 90.00
____C-3PO and R2-D2, desert scene, round dial on square face [TAW31] 85.00

TAW01 TAW02 TAW03 TAW04 TAW05 TAW06 TAW07 TAW08 TAW09 TAW10 TAW11 TAW12

TAW13 TAW14 TAW15 TAW16 TAW17 TAW18 TAW19 TAW20 TAW21 TAW22 TAW23 TAW24

TAW25 TAW26 TAW27 TAW28 TAW29 TAW30 TAW31 TAW32 TAW33 TAW34 TAW35 TAW36

Watches

TAW37 TAW38 TAW39 TAW40 TAW41 TAW42 TAW43 TAW44 TAW45 TAW46 TAW47 TAW48 TAW49

Disney / MGM
____Lightsabers face in round padded box 50.00

Star Wars Weekends.
____2003 Jedi Mickey and Yoda, limited to 250 [TAW32] 225.00
____2004 Mickey and Minnie, limited to 500 [TAW33] 175.00
____2005 Darth Vader / Mickey [TAW34] 75.00

Fantasma
____Battle of the Force, ltd. to 7,500 numbered 65.00
____Darth Vader, round black face, numbers on outter watch face, secondhand is Sci-Fi Channel logo, black band, limited to 7,500 numbered [TAW35] 85.00
____Darth Vader, round black face, numbers on outter watch face, secondhand is tie interceptor chasing x-wing, black band, limited to 7,500 numbered [TAW36] 85.00
____Millennium Falcon, flip-open cover reveals round face with sapce-battle scene, black band, limited to 10,000 numbered [TAW37] 75.00

Fossil, Inc.
____25th anniversary, classic scene, limited to 2,000 [TAW38] 175.00
____Artoo-Detoo and See Threepio, spiral background, blue and yellow highlights on face [TAW39] 135.00
____Boba Fett Collectors Watch, gold edition, limited to 1,000 numbered..125.00
____Boba Fett Collectors Watch, silver edition, limited to 10,000 numbered 86.00
____Boba Fett, brass finished face, brown strap, with matching storage box, limited to 10,000 [TAW40] 67.00
____C-3PO and R2-D2, limited to 500 numbered, includes sculpted R2-D2 case [TAW41].........................215.00
____C-3PO, gold finished face, brown strap, with matching storage box, limited to 10,000 [TAW42].............55.00
____Clone Wars, leather band [TAW43] 150.00
____Darth Vader (helmet) in flames, glowing face, black band, limited to 1,000 [TAW44] 175.00
____Darth Vader (helmet) in flames, glowing face, silver band, limited to 2,000 [TAW45] 170.00
____Darth Vader and his TIE, 23k gold plated, with Vader head storage box, limited to 1000 numbered..120.00
____Darth Vader and TIE, silver color all over, with Vader storage box, limited to 15,000 numbered 95.00
____Darth Vader and Imperial insignia, 23k gold case, black strap, with matching storage box, limited to 10,000 numbered [TAW46] 125.00
____Darth Vader DVD art face, limited to 300 [TAW47] 250.00
____Darth Vader, silver finish face, black strap, with matching storage box, limited to 10,000 [TAW48] 55.00
____Star Wars logo, hinged box features frame with five movie poster miniatures [TAW49] 115.00
____Stormtrooper, silver color all over, limited to 3,000 numbered [TAW50] 145.00
____Stormtrooper, silver color all over, with storage box, limited to 15,000 numbered 125.00
____SW logo, Rebel insignia, and Imperial insignia, with Death Star storage box, limited to 10,000 [TAW51] 95.00

Episode II: Attack of the Clones.
____Boba Fett etched on silver dial with Mandalorian etched metal band, dogtag, trading card, limited to 2,000 [TAW52] 95.00
____Gold logo on gunmetal face with black strap, limited to 2,500. [TAW53] 100.00

Hope Industries
Quartz analog, gold colored Death Star storage case.
____Return of the Jedi [TAW54] 32.00
____Star Wars: A New Hope......................................32.00
____The Empire Strikes Back [TAW55] 32.00

Quartz analog, gold tone buckle.
____Return of the Jedi [TAW56] 24.00
____Star Wars: A New Hope [TAW57]........................26.00
____The Empire Strikes Back [TAW58] 24.00

ILM
____Industrial Light and Magic employee watch 150.00

Nelsonic
Character watch with collectors storage tin.
____Anakin Skywalker podracer 16.00
____Darth Maul lightsaber [TAW59] 16.00
____Darth Maul sculpted case [TAW60] 18.00
____Jar Jar Binks rotating tounge............................17.00
____Jar Jar Binks water filled analog [TAW61] 28.00
____Queen Amidala [TAW62] 18.00
____Space Battle rotating starfighter disk [TAW63] 19.00

Character watches.
____C-3PO skeletal case [TAW64] 30.00
____Darth Maul holographic [TAW65] 34.00
____Darth Maul sculpted case [TAW66] 25.00
____Jar Jar Binks rotating tounge [TAW67] 24.00

Laser dial character watches with storage tin.
____Darth Maul [TAW68] 17.00
____Queen Amidala [TAW69] 17.00
____Qui-Gon Jinn [TAW70] 17.00

Pocket watches.
____Darth Maul Sith Probe Droid sound and lights effects [TAW71] 16.00
____Space Battle [TAW72] 18.00

Pepsi Cola
____"Feel the Force – Back on the big screen" [TAW73] 18.00

Skagen
Walt Disney Weekends 2006.
____Darth Vader with helmet box, ltd. to 500 ....175.00

Sony Ericsson
____Star Wars EPIII in steel canister [TAW74] 50.00

Star Movies
Attack of the Clones. Black stamped tin case.
____Anakin Skywalker [TAW75].................................35.00
____Padme Amidala [TAW76] 35.00

Super Live Adventure
____Darth Vader, same as Fantasma Vader on black coin dial, SLA box [TAW77] 145.00

Unlicensed
Starship, Yoda, logo, Anakin, clone commando on band. Orange hands with yellow sweep.
____Anakin Skywalker, blue band.............................10.00
____Darth Vader, red band 10.00
____EPIII Characters / Epic Duel, blue band 10.00
____Mace Windu, blue band.....................................10.00

Watchit
____C-3PO and R2-D2 [TAW78] 15.00
____Darth Vader face with stormtrooper band, analog [TAW79] 20.00
____Darth Vader face with stormtrooper band, relogio [TAW80] 20.00
____Star Wars movie poster face with logo band [TAW81] 17.00

Coin Watches. Character raised on brushed brass-tone face. Episode I storage tin included.
____Darth Maul [TAW82] 34.00
____Queen Amidala [TAW83] 34.00

World Wide Licenses Ltd.
Watches include round, padded storage tin.
____Darth Maul communicator [TAW84]...................35.00
____Droid Fighter, diecast with leather band [TAW85] 40.00
____Qui-Gon Jinn, hologram face, diecast with diecast band [TAW86] 45.00

Zeon
____Anakin Skywalker / Darth Vader lenticular [TAW87] 18.00
____Anakin Skywalker, lightsaber sweep hand 18.00

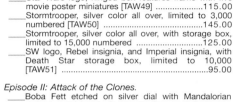

TAW50 TAW51 TAW52 TAW53 TAW54 TAW55 TAW56 TAW57 TAW58 TAW59 TAW60

TAW61 TAW62 TAW63 TAW64 TAW65 TAW66 TAW67 TAW68 TAW69 TAW70 TAW71 TAW72 TAW73

TAW74 TAW75 TAW76 TAW77 TAW78 TAW79 TAW80 TAW81 TAW82 TAW83 TAW84 TAW85 TAW86

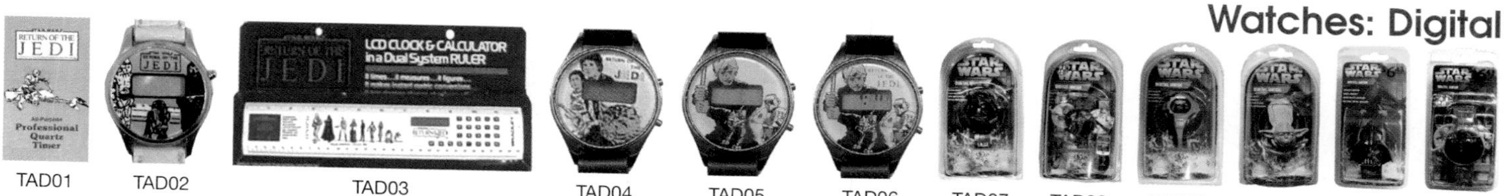

TAD01 TAD02 TAD03 TAD04 TAD05 TAD06 TAD07 TAD08 TAD09 TAD10 TAD11 TAD12

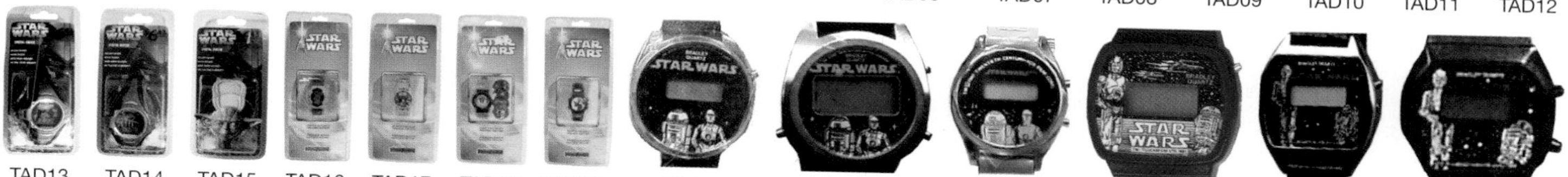

TAD13 TAD14 TAD15 TAD16 TAD17 TAD18 TAD19 TAD20 TAD21 TAD22 TAD23 TAD24 TAD25

Watches: Digital

____Biker Scout quartz stopwatch [TAD01] 75.00
____C-3PO left, R2-D2 below, Chewbacca right, ROTJ logo above display on white face, 1-button, white band [TAD02] 115.00
____Clock and calculator ruler [TAD03] 45.00
____Han, Leia, Jabba, Return of the Jedi on white face [TAD04] 60.00
____Luke, AT-ST, and Speederbike Trooper on white face [TAD05] 65.00
____Luke, AT-ST, and Speederbike Trooper, Return of the Jedi logo on white face [TAD06] 58.00
____R2-D2 watch face with alarm, timer, stopwatch, date indicator. Limited to 5,000. ....195.00

EPIII:ROTS. Dome shaped packaging.
____Darth Vader [TAD07]...10.00
____Darth Vader with changeable faces [TAD08] 10.00
____Jedi [TAD09] 10.00
____Yoda [TAD10] 10.00

EPIII:ROTS. Tin box packaging.
____Changeable faces 12.00

EPIII:ROTS.
____Darth Vader [TAD11]...10.00
____Darth Vader with changeable faces [TAD12] 10.00
____Jedi [TAD13] 10.00
____Sith [TAD14] 10.00
____Yoda [TAD15] 10.00

BNS Marketing Network, Inc.
Episode II
____Anakin Skywalker [TAD16] 15.00
____Anakin, Padme, Obi-Wan [TAD17].......................15.00
____Attack of the Clones, 5 interchangeable covers [TAD18] 15.00
____Jango Fett [TAD19]..15.00

Bradley Time
____C-3PO and R2-D2 below, SW logo above, round black face, 1-button, black band, blister packed [TAD20] 45.00
____C-3PO and R2-D2 below, SW logo above, round black face, 1-button, black band, clear case 60.00
____C-3PO and R2-D2 below, SW logo above, round black face, 1-button, black band, SW logo window box 65.00
____C-3PO and R2-D2 below, SW logo above, round black face, 3-button, black band [TAD21]...................50.00
____C-3PO and R2-D2 below, SW logo above, round starfield face, 2-button, blue band [TAD22]........46.00
____C-3PO left, R2-D2 right, 2 x-wings above, square starfield face, 1-button, black band [TAD23] 76.00
____C-3PO left, R2-D2 right, SW logo above, round starfield face, 1-button, black band...................60.00
____C-3PO left, R2-D2 right, SW logo above, round starfield face, 2-button, black band, musical 97.00
____C-3PO left, R2-D2 right, SW logo above, square starfield face, 1-button, black band [TAD24] 58.00
____C-3PO left, R2-D2 right, SW logo above, square starfield face, 2-button, black band, musical [TAD25]..135.00
____C-3PO left; R2-D2 right; x-wing, SW logo, tie fighter above, square blue face, 2-button, black band, musical [TAD26]..125.00
____C-3PO left; R2-D2 right; x-wing, SW logo; Vader's tie fighter above; musical alarm text below, square blue face, 3-button, black band, musical [TAD27]..135.00
____Darth Vader below, black SW logo above, round gray face, 1-button, black band [TAD28] 55.00
____Darth Vader below, black SW logo above, round gray face, 3-button, black band [TAD29] 55.00
____Darth Vader below, blue SW logo above, round gray face, 1-button, black band [TAD30] 55.00
____Darth Vader, red SW logo, white face, Vader holding time window, black vinyl band [TAD31] 55.00
____Darth Vader/SW logo changing image, round blue face, 1-button, black band [TAD32] 110.00
____Droids logo above, C-3PO right, R2-D2 below, square face, 1-button, black band [TAD33] 35.00
____Ewoks below, ROTJ logo above, round face, 1-button, black band [TAD34] 44.00
____Jabba below, ROTJ logo above, round face, 1-button, black band [TAD35] 47.00
____Jabba below, ROTJ logo above, square face, 1-button, black band [TAD36] 45.00
____SW silver logo below, blue face plate 65.00
____Yoda below, SW logo above, round white face, 1-button, black band [TAD37] 55.00
____Yoda below, SW logo above, square black-and-white face, 1-button, black band [TAD38]....................45.00

Radio watch with headphones.
____R2-D2, SW [TAD39] 95.00
____Wicket, ROTJ [TAD40] 85.00

Burger King
EPIII:ROTS DVD release promotion. Interchangable watches with a collector's tin.
____1 The Phantom Menace.......................................10.00
____2 Attack of the Clones 10.00
____3 Revenge of the Sith...10.00
____4 A New Hope 10.00
____5 The Empire Strikes Back...................................10.00
____6 Return of the Jedi 10.00

Casio
EPIII:ROTS.
____Darth Vader 300.00
____Star Wars logo 300.00

Disney / MGM
____Darth Vader helmet cover 25.00
____Star Tours, Disneyland [TAD41] 24.00

Duracell
____Digital Darth Vader SE art, promotional packaged with batteries [TAD42] 28.00

Ecclissi
____Death Star face, sterling silver [TAD43]............350.00

Hope Industries
____2-Pack Darth Maul flip top and Battle Droid flip top with collectors storage tin [TAD44] 26.00
____3-Pack Sculpted Collection: Anakin, Jar Jar, Darth Maul with lightsaber case [TAD45]......................16.00
____4-Pack diecast Battle Droid, Darth Maul, Pit Droid, R2-D2, boxed with magnet seal [TAD46] 65.00

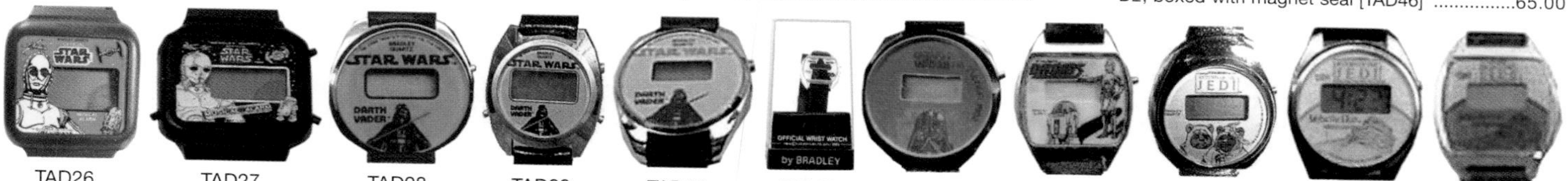

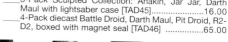

TAD26 TAD27 TAD28 TAD29 TAD30 TAD31 TAD32 TAD33 TAD34 TAD35 TAD36

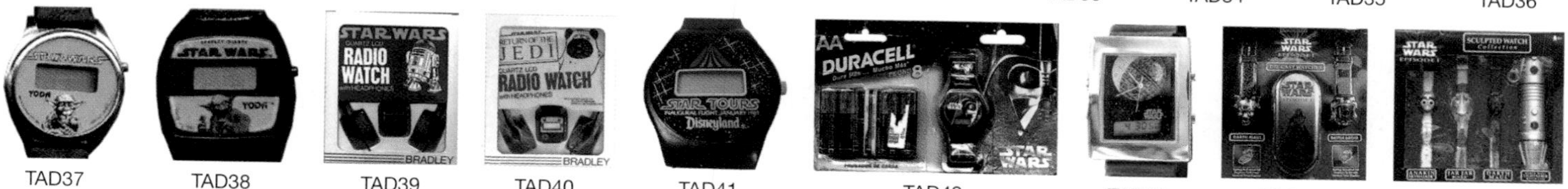

TAD37 TAD38 TAD39 TAD40 TAD41 TAD42 TAD43 TAD44 TAD45

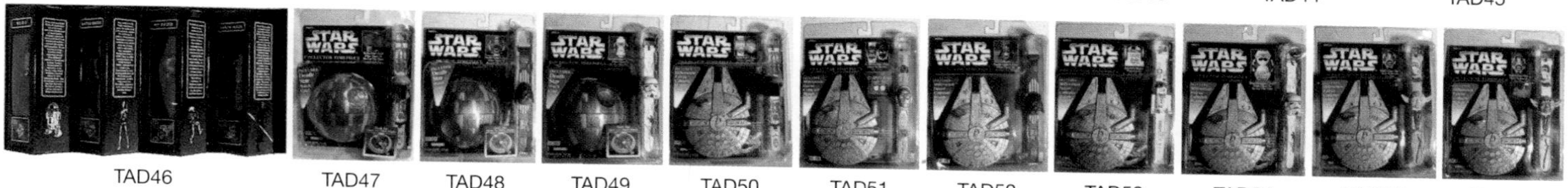

TAD46 TAD47 TAD48 TAD49 TAD50 TAD51 TAD52 TAD53 TAD54 TAD55 TAD56

Watches: Digital

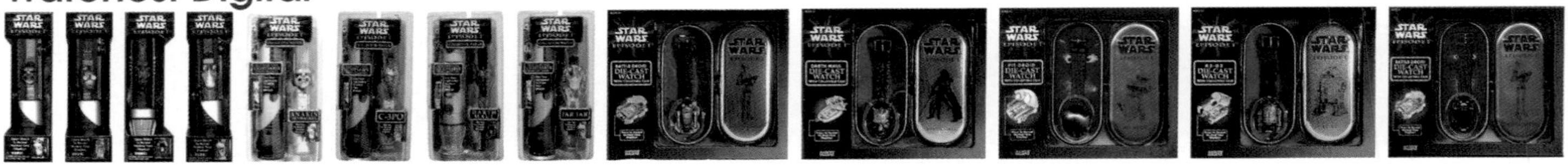

TAD57 - TAD60 TAD61 TAD62 TAD63 TAD64 TAD65 TAD66 TAD67 TAD68 TAD69

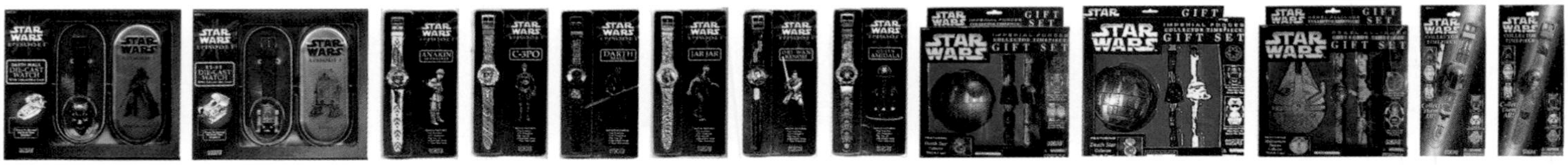

TAD70 TAD71 TAD72 TAD73 TAD74 TAD75 TAD76 TAD77 TAD78 TAD79 TAD80 TAD81 TAD82

Collector timepiece with plastic Death Star storage case.
____Boba Fett [TAD47] 20.00
____Darth Vader [TAD48] 20.00
____Stormtrooper [TAD49] 20.00

Collector timepiece with plastic Millennium Falcon storage case.
____Boba Fett [TAD50] 15.00
____C-3PO [TAD51] 15.00
____Darth Vader [TAD52] 15.00
____R2-D2 [TAD53] 15.00
____Stormtrooper [TAD54] 15.00
____Yoda [TAD55] 15.00
____Yoda, alternate coloring [TAD56] 15.00

Diecast watches in plastic case packaging.
____Battle Droid 10.00
____Darth Maul 10.00
____Pit Droid 12.00
____R2-D2 ....10.00

EPI Collector watch w/lighsaber case, box packaging.
____Anakin Skywalker [TAD57] 9.00
____C-3PO [TAD58] 9.00
____Darth Maul [TAD59] 9.00
____Jar Jar Binks [TAD60] 9.00

EPI Collector watch with lighsaber case, sealed bubble packaging.
____Anakin Skywalker [TAD61] 8.00
____C-3PO [TAD62] 8.00
____Darth Maul [TAD63] 8.00
____Jar Jar Binks [TAD64] 8.00

EPI Diecast watch with tin collector case, boxed, brass finish.
____Battle Droid [TAD65] 18.00
____Darth Maul [TAD66] 18.00
____Pit Droid [TAD67] 18.00
____R2-D2 [TAD68] 18.00

EPI Diecast watch with tin collector case, boxed, steel finish.
____Battle Droid [TAD69] 16.00
____Darth Maul [TAD70] 14.00
____Pit Droid 15.00
____R2-D2 [TAD71] 15.00

Flip top watches.
____Anakin Skywalker [TAD72] 7.00
____C-3PO [TAD73] 7.00
____Darth Maul [TAD74] 7.00
____Jar Jar Binks [TAD75] 7.00
____Obi-Wan Kenobi [TAD76] 7.00
____Queen Amidala [TAD77] 7.00

Imperial Forces collector timepiece giftset, character watches with plastic Death Star storage case.
____2-piece: Darth Vader and Boba Fett [TAD78] 18.00
____2-piece:Darth Vader and Stormtrooper [TAD79] 18.00
____3-piece: Boba Fett, Darth Vader, Stormtrooper 24.00

Rebel Alliance collector timepiece giftset, character watches with plastic Millennium Falcon storage case.
____2-piece: C-3PO and R2-D2 ....18.00
____2-piece: C-3PO and Yoda [TAD80] 18.00
____3-piece: C-3PO, R2-D2, Yoda 24.00

Sculpted classic trilogy character flip top watches.
____Boba Fett [TAD81] 7.00
____C-3PO [TAD82] 7.00
____Darth Vader [TAD83] 7.00
____R2-D2 [TAD84] 7.00
____Stormtrooper [TAD85] 7.00
____Yoda [TAD86] 7.00

Its About Time
____Battle Droid on Stap [TAD87] 8.00
____Destroyer droid transforming watch / clock [TAD88] 17.00
____Jar Jar Binks sticking out tounge [TAD89] 8.00
____Jar Jar Binks Talking watch [TAD90] 19.00
____Obi-Wan on battleship [TAD91] 8.00

Flip top watches.
____Anakin Skywalker [TAD92] 8.00
____Darth Maul, black band [TAD93] 8.00
____Darth Maul, red band [TAD94] 8.00
____Queen Amidala [TAD95] 8.00
____Queen Amidala interchangable [TAD96] 16.00

Nelsonic
____Podracer turbine [TAD97] 14.00

Character watch with collectors storage tin.
____Podracer watch with built-in compass [TAD98] 24.00

Talking watch with tin collector case.
____Darth Maul [TAD99] 28.00
____Jar Jar Binks [TAD100] 28.00

Playworks
____Darth Vader with Tie Fighters on wristband [TAD101] 7.00

Character head with face-cover.
____Boba Fett 7.00
____C-3PO 7.00
____Darth Vader [TAD102] 7.00
____Millennium Falcon [TAD103] 11.00
____R2-D2 [TAD104] 7.00
____Stormtrooper [TAD105] 7.00
____Yoda 7.00

Texas Instruments
____C-3PO and R2-D2 above, SW logo below, square blue starfield face, 2-buttons, black band, 10 decals 95.00
____C-3PO and R2-D2 above, SW logo below, square blue starfield face, 2-buttons, gray band [TAD106] 65.00
____C-3PO and R2-D2 above, X-Wings and Darth Vader below, square starfield face, 2 buttons, black band [TAD107] 95.00
____Darth Vader and x-wings above, SW logo below, square face, 2-buttons, black band, blister packed [TAD108] 95.00
____Darth Vader and x-wings above, SW logo below, square face, 2-buttons, black band, plastic case 85.00
____SW logo above and below, square silver face, 2-buttons, black band with R2-D2 and Darth Vader graphics [TAD109] 125.00

Toy Options
Silver metal flip-top watches.
____C-3PO [TAD110] 36.00
____Darth Vader [TAD111] 36.00
____Stormtrooper [TAD112] 36.00

Watchit
____Destroyer droid transforming watch / clock [TAD113] 14.00
____R2-D2, Light and Sound [TAD114] 16.00

Flip top watches.
____Boba Fett [TAD115] 9.00
____C-3PO [TAD116] 7.00
____Darth Maul [TAD117] 7.00
____Darth Vader, musical [TAD118] 11.00
____Millennium Falcon [TAD119] 10.00
____Queen Amidala [TAD120] 9.00
____Queen Amidala, interchangable [TAD121] 16.00
____R2-D2 [TAD122] 7.00

Novelty LCD watches. Classic trilogy.
____C-3PO [TAD123] 12.00

Novelty LCD watches. Episode I.
____Droid Fighter 14.00
____Sith Communicator 12.00

WatchWorks
____Battle Droid [TAD124] 6.00

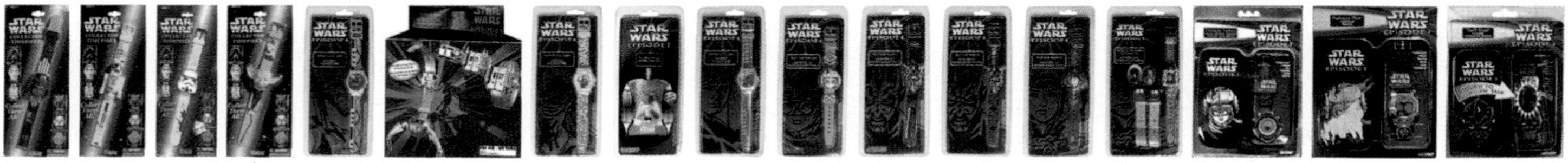

TAD83 TAD84 TAD85 TAD86 TAD87 TAD88 TAD89 TAD90 TAD91 TAD92 TAD93 TAD94 TAD95 TAD96 TAD97 TAD98 TAD99

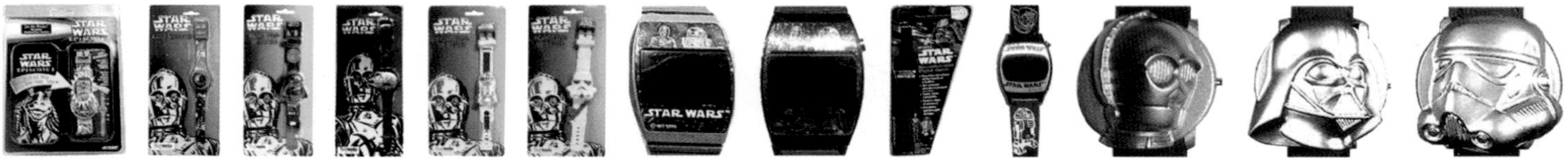

TAD100 TAD101 TAD102 TAD103 TAD104 TAD105 TAD106 TAD107 TAD108 TAD109 TAD110 TAD111 TAD112

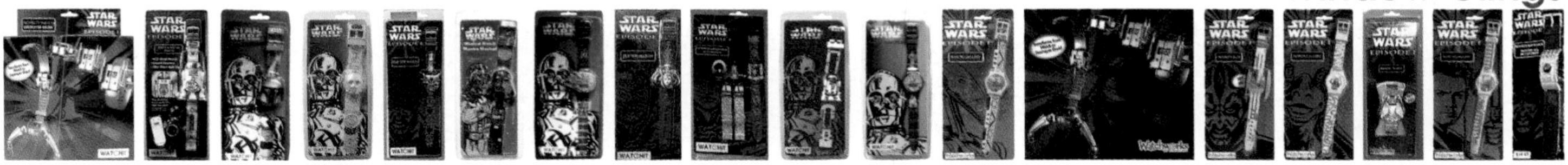

TAD113 TAD114 TAD115 TAD116 TAD117 TAD118 TAD119 TAD120 TAD121 TAD122 TAD123 TAD124 TAD125 TAD126 TAD127 TAD128 TAD129 TAD130

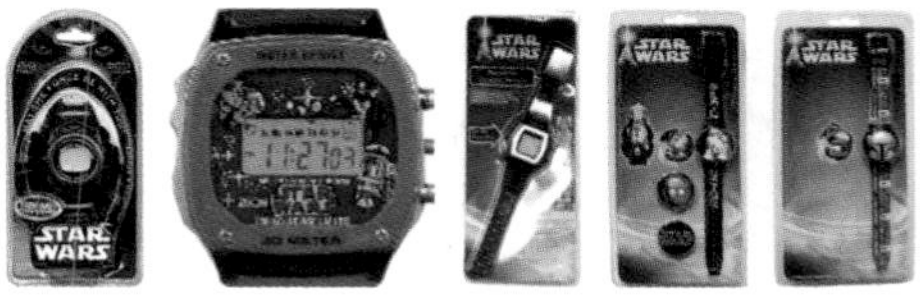

TAD131 TAD132 TAD133 TAD134 TAD135

____Destroyer droid transforming watch / clock [TAD125] 14.00
____Droid Fighter flip-up, sculpted [TAD126] 8.00
____Jar Jar Binks [TAD127] 6.00
____Jar Jar Binks Talking watch [TAD128] 19.00
____Obi-Wan Kenobi [TAD129] 8.00
____Sith Communicator [TAD130] 15.00

World Wide Licenses Ltd.
____Darth Maul sound and FX [TAD131] 29.00

Zeon
____C-3PO and R2-D2 on right, Millennium Falcon on left, Star Wars logo below display on blue face, 3-button, black band, water resistant [TAD132] 85.00

Episode II.
____Animated talking watch [TAD133] 18.00

Flip top watches.
____C-3PO / R2-D2 interchangable [TAD134] 15.00
____Jango Fett [TAD135] 15.00

Water Bottles

____Celebration 3 Anakin / Vader [SB01] 10.00

Disney / MGM
____Star Tours logo 5.00

Masterfoods USA
Metal canisters with M&M character graphics. Nylon bags. Hong Kong.
____Anakin Skywalker [SB02] 15.00
____General Grievous [SB03] 15.00

Pepsi Cola, Mexico
Episode I: The Phantom Menace.
____Jar Jar Binks [SB04] 5.00
____Qui-Gon vs. Darth Maul [SB05] 5.00

Star Wars: Special Edition.
____C-3PO [SB06] 10.00
____Darth Vader [SB07] 10.00
____R2-D2 [SB08] 10.00
____Stormtrooper [SB09] 10.00

Seneca Sports Inc.
____R2-D2 ....2.00

Spearmark Int.
____EPII Sports Bottle [SB10] 4.00

Watercolor Paint Sets

Craft House
____Star Wars watercolor by number [WPS01] 8.00

Fundimensions
____Ewok 18.00
____Ewok Glider 18.00
____Ewok Village 18.00

Kenner
____Dip Dots water color paint set [WPS02] 50.00

Window Clings

20th Century Fox
____EPII:AOTC Yoda, "Unlock the Saga" [3:427] 10.00

Blockbuster Video
____Win Yoda, video promotion 24.00

Disney / MGM
____Jedi Training Acadamy [3:427] 8.00

Fan Club
____Star Wars cling [WC01] 8.00

KFC
EPI character face with rectangle background.
____Jar Jar Binks [3:427] 19.00
____Queen Amidala 18.00

EPI full character figure 2-piece door cling.
____Queen Amidala 24.00
____Qui-Gon Jinn 24.00

Liquid Blue
____Anakin Skywalker 4.00
____Darth Maul with 2-sided saber 4.00
____Jedi vs. Sith 4.00
____Naboo space battle 4.00

Norben
Static cling decorations.
____Anakin Skywalker 3.00
____Darth Maul 3.00
____Jedi vs. Sith 3.00
____Space Battle 3.00

Pizza Hut
____"Don't Leave Coruscant Without Them." (toys, large rectangle) 10.00
____"Don't Leave Coruscant Without Them." (toys, small rectangle) 8.00
____"Welcome to Coruscant" 2-sided door cling 8.00
____Darth Maul life-size 2-piece door sticker 35.00
____Mace Windu and Yoda 22.00
____Qui-Gon Jinn and pink alien from jedi council ..17.00

Taco Bell
18"x24" advertising Star Wars Special Edition.
____Boba Fett, ESB [WC02] 10.00
____Chewbacca, SW [WC03] 10.00
____Darth Vader, ROTJ [WC04] 10.00
____Droids, ESB [WC05] 10.00
____Stormtrooper, SW [WC06] 10.00

6' tall door decals.
____C-3PO [WC07] 35.00
____Chewbacca [WC08] 35.00
____Stormtrooper [WC09] 35.00

Feel The Force promotion. Window promotions.
____Vader: Win Millions of Prizes! [3:427] 15.00
____Yoda: Play the Feel the Force game! [3:427] 15.00

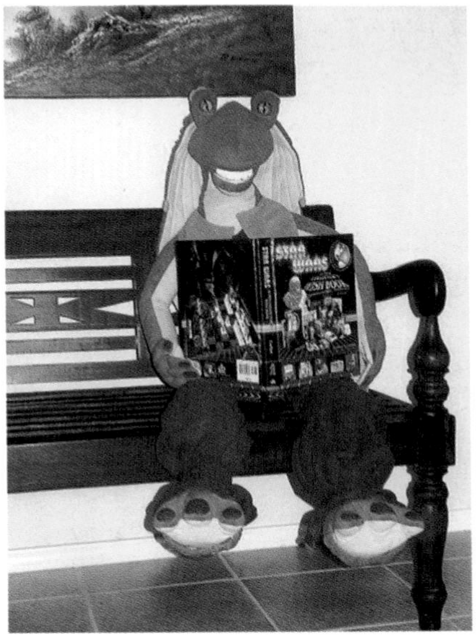

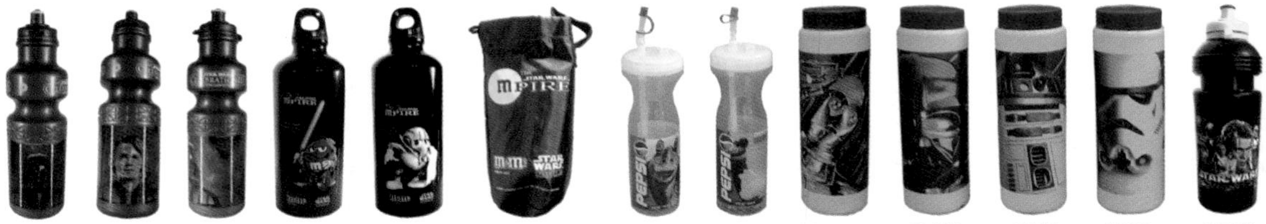

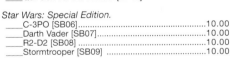

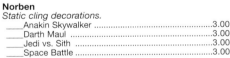

SB01 SB02 SB03 bottle and bag SB04 SB05 SB06 SB07 SB08 SB09 SB10

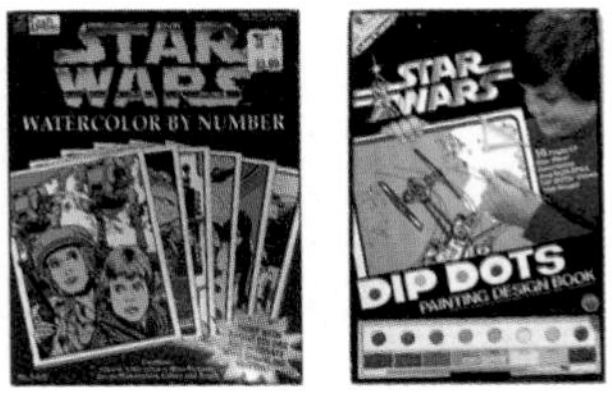

WPS01 WPS02

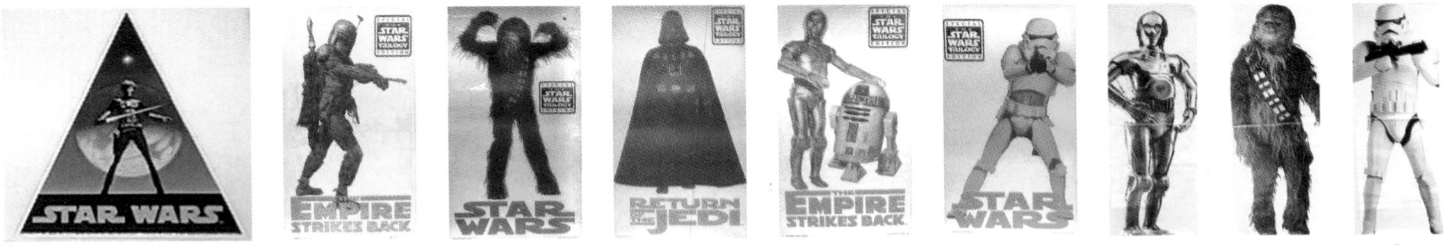

WC01 WC02 WC03 WC04 WC05 WC06 WC07 WC08 WC09

Super Collector's Scrapbook

A personal reflection by Geoffrey T. Carlton

The three photographs to the right are my current collection room. The photographs below are in order from 2001 (collection room construction in our new home one year before the first book release) to 2005 (Celebration III).

It has been an adventure evolving from a relatively unknown collector into the author of the *Star Wars Super Collector's Wish Book*, now in its fourth edition. Family, friends, clubs, and even the local community have embraced this journey and I owe it to them all to acknowledge that I do not walk alone. Support, encouragement, and ideas all flow from the people in my life.

This page is a tribute to many people, some of which I have never met in person, whom I owe a debt of thanks. It's also a brief glimpse into the antics of the communities I belong to, collectors, costumers, fans, and friends.

By myself, this would be no fun. Star Wars has brought us all together. May we never be apart.

Collection room: entry

Collection room: outer wall from hall 1

Collection room: back passage

Jack, helping to build collection shelves

Tamara's inlaid tile X-Wing

Back passage started

Lone Star Comics — 1st book signing

Friendly customers...

Guarded by Justin

Midnight madness 4/23/02

Midnight madness "initial damages"

Tamara's new creation

My wife and two of my children

Brian's new robes

501st Star Garrison (2nd book release)

Star Garrison vs. Dallas Fan Force — Clone Wars Celebration

Stormtrooper Jedi?? Holding his own!

3rd book release / Celebration III, Indianapolis

GSN interview

A Brief Star Wars Chronology

By Nathan P. Butler

"Novels and comics and video games . . . Oh my!"
- A certain overly-excited protocol droid

The Star Wars saga is now a vast, sprawling tale that spans over 5,135 years of recorded stories. Since 1997, Star Wars fan (and one time Star Wars Tales writer) Nathan P. Butler has been acting as a sort of historian for the saga, compiling his exhaustive, 1,300+ page Star Wars Timeline Gold (available for free online as an Adobe Acrobat .PDF document at http://www.starwarsfanworks.com/timeline and updated several times per year with new summaries, events, titles, and more).

What follows is not a complete list of every Star Wars story in existence. However, the following does serve as a guide to the chronological placement of the major tales within the Star Wars continuity.

Consider this a reference for the new or layman Star Wars fan, who might be looking to jump into the saga. Intermediate fans seeking summaries of just the major stories should check out Dan Wallace and Kevin J. Anderson's *New Essential Chronology*, available from Del Rey. More experienced fans, or those looking for a much more comprehensive guide should visit www.starwarsfanworks.com/timeline to check out Nathan P. Butler's Star Wars Timeline Gold.

COLOR KEY

Red = Comic Book / Comic Strip
Blue = Novel / Book / Graphic Novel
Purple = Video Game
Black = Film / Television Program / Etc.
Green = eBook

Titles in **bold** are series titles and will often include names of individual items in that series in an indented list immediately below the series title.

Stories are listed by when the majority of the "present" tale takes place, disregarding flashbacks. In cases where stories are broken somewhat evenly between time periods, multiple entries are listed for that title, followed by a (1), (2), and so on to keep track of that particular title. If a story spans several years, the title is given its own year listing under a heading of that time span, such as Rebel Dawn having a date of "3 - 0 BBY."

In some cases, stories will overlap, especially in the era of the Classic Trilogy. As such, titles are listed in approximate chronological placement, but some have been "tweaked" to make this listing easier on the reader.

All years are noted with the internal Star Wars dating convention of number of years "BBY" (Before the Battle of Yavin in A New Hope) or "ABY" (After the Battle of Yavin in A New Hope).

One should also note that in the case of the Star Wars films (and a few other stories), there are numerous adaptations available, whether in comic book, novel, video game, or other formats. These alternate presentations have been kept off of this list for the sake of clarity.

If you're not confused yet, let's proceed!

THE STAR WARS SAGA

5,000 BBY
Tales of the Jedi
    The Golden Age of the Sith
    The Fall of the Sith Empire

4,000 BBY
Tales of the Jedi
    Knights of the Old Republic

3,998 BBY
Tales of the Jedi
    The Freedon Nadd Uprising

3,997 BBY
Tales of the Jedi
    Dark Lords of the Sith

3,996 BBY
Tales of the Jedi
    The Sith War

3,986 BBY
Tales of the Jedi
    Redemption

3,964 BBY
Knights of the Old Republic
    Commencement
    Flashpoint

3,956 BBY
Knights of the Old Republic
    Knights of the Old Republic

3,951 BBY
Knights of the Old Republic
    The Sith Lords

3,937 BBY

Knights of the Old Republic
Current Untitled KOTOR #3
1,020 – 1,000 BBY
Path of Destruction
1,000 BBY
Jedi vs. Sith

89 BBY
Legacy / Secrets of the Jedi
    Legacy of the Jedi (1)

88 BBY
Republic
    Vow of Justice (1)

76 BBY
Legacy / Secrets of the Jedi
    Legacy of the Jedi (2)

67 BBY
Republic
    Vow of Justice (2)

58 – 31 BBY
Jango Fett: Open Seasons

circa 50 BBY
(Darth Plagueis Novel)

45 – 38 BBY
Jedi Apprentice
    The Rising Force
    The Dark Rival
    The Hidden Past
    The Mark of the Crown
    The Defenders of the Dead
    The Uncertain Path
    The Captive Temple
    The Day of Reckoning
Legacy / Secrets of the Jedi
    Legacy of the Jedi (3)
Jedi Apprentice
    The Fight for Truth
    The Shattered Peace
    The Deadly Hunter
    The Evil Experiment
    The Dangerous Rescue
Jedi Apprentice: Special Edition
    Deceptions (1)
Jedi Apprentice
    The Ties That Bind
    The Death of Hope
    The Call to Vengeance
    The Only Witness
    The Threat Within
Legacy / Secrets of the Jedi
    Secrets of the Jedi (1)
Jedi Apprentice: Special Edition
    The Followers (1)

38 BBY
Qui-Gon and Obi-Wan
    The Aurorient Express

37 BBY
Qui-Gon and Obi-Wan
    Last Stand on Ord Mantell

A Brief Star Wars Chronology

33 BBY
Jedi Council: Acts of War
Episode I Adventures
    The Death of Captain Tarpals
    Rescue in the Core
    Festival of Warriors
    Pirates from Beyond the Sea
    The Bongo Rally
Republic
    Prelude to Rebellion
Darth Maul
    Saboteur
Cloak of Deception
Darth Maul
Episode I Adventures
    Search for the Lost Jedi
    The Bartok Assassins
    The Fury of Darth Maul
    Jedi Emergency
    The Ghostling Children
    The Hunt for Anakin Skywalker
    Capture Arawynne
    Trouble on Tatooine
Obi-Wan

32 BBY
Darth Maul
    Shadow Hunter
Starfighter
    Starfighter
The Prequel Trilogy
    The Phantom Menace
Battle for Naboo
Episode I Adventures
    Danger on Naboo
    Podrace to Freedom
    The Final Battle
Episode I Adventures
Bounty Hunter
Republic
    Outlander
    Emissaries to Malastare
Bounty Hunters
    Aurra Sing

31 BBY
Republic
    Twilight
    Infinity's End
    Starcrash

30 BBY
Republic
    The Hunt for Aurra Sing
    Darkness
    The Stark Hyperspace War
    The Devaronian Version
    Rite of Passage

29 BBY
Rogue Planet
Jedi Apprentice: Special Edition
    Deceptions (2)
    The Followers (2)

28 BBY
Jedi Quest

The Path to Truth
Jedi Quest
Jedi Quest
    The Way of the Apprentice

27 BBY
Jedi Quest
    The Trail of the Jedi
Jango Fett
Zam Wesell
Outbound Flight

26 BBY
Jedi Quest
    The Dangerous Games
    The Master of Disguise
    The School of Fear
    The Shadow Trap
    The Moment of Truth
Starfighter
    Crossbones

25 BBY
Jedi Quest
    The Changing of the Guard
    The False Peace
    The Final Showdown

24 BBY
Republic
    Honor and Duty

23 BBY
Star Wars Adventures
    Hunt the Sun Runner
    The Cavern of Screaming Skulls
    The Hostage Princess
    Jango Fett vs. the Razor-Eaters
    The Shape-Shifter Strikes
    The Warlords of Balmorra

22 BBY
Starfighter
    Jedi Starfighter
The Approaching Storm
Boba Fett
    The Fight to Survive
The Prequel Trilogy
    Attack of the Clones
Republic Commando (1)
Boba Fett
    Crossfire
The Clone Wars
Boba Fett
    Maze of Deception
Republic
    Sacrifice
Boba Fett
    Hunted
Republic
    The Defense of Kamino
    The New Face of War
Jedi
    Mace Windu
Republic Commando
    Hard Contact
Republic
    Blast Radius

Clone Wars (1)
Clone Wars Adventures (1)
Jedi
    Shaak Ti
Legacy / Secrets of the Jedi
    Legacy of the Jedi (4)
Republic
    Double Blind
Shatterpoint
Jedi
    Aayla Secura
    Count Dooku

21 BBY
The New Droid Army
Republic
    Honor Bound
Clone Wars Adventures (2)
The Cestus Deception
The Hive
Republic Commando (2)
Republic Commando
    Triple Zero
Republic
    Last Stand on Jabiim
    Enemy Lines
    Hate and Fear
    Dead Ends
    No Man's Land
    Striking from the Shadows
    Show of Force
    Bloodlines
Jedi
    Yoda
Republic
    Forever Young

20 BBY
Republic
    Armor
Medstar
    Battle Surgeons
    Jedi Healer
General Grievous
Republic Commando (3)
Legacy / Secrets of the Jedi
    Secrets of the Jedi (2)
Jedi Trial
Dark Rendezvous
Clone Wars (2)
Republic
    Dreadnaughts of Rendili
    Trackdown
Obsession
Boba Fett
    A New Threat
    Pursuit

19 BBY
Labyrinth of Evil
Clone Wars (3)
Clone Wars Adventures (3)
Republic
    Siege of Saleucami
Evasive Action
    Reversal of Fortune
The Prequel Trilogy
    Revenge of the Sith

Republic
   Hidden Enemy
Dark Lord: The Rise of Darth Vader (1)
Republic
   Into the Unknown
   Loyalties
Legacy / Secrets of the Jedi
   The Last One Standing
Purge
Dark Times
   The Path to Nowhere
Dark Lord: The Rise of Darth Vader (2)
Evasive Action
   Recruitment
   Prey
Last of the Jedi
   The Desperate Mission
   Dark Warning
   Underworld
   Death on Naboo
   A Tangled Web
   Return of the Sith

19 – 0 BBY
Currently Untitled Death Star Novel

18 – 15 BBY
Coruscant Nights
   Jedi Twilight
   Currently Untitled CN Book #2
   Currently Untitled CN Book #3

15 BBY
Droids

10 BBY
The Han Solo Trilogy
   The Paradise Snare

5 BBY
The Han Solo Trilogy
   The Hutt Gambit
Droids
   The Kalarba Adventures

4 BBY
The Lando Calrissian Adventures
   Lando Calrissian and the Mindharp of
      Sharu
Jabba Hutt: The Art of the Deal
   The Gaar Suppoon Hit
   The Hunger of Princess Nampi
   The Dynasty Trap
Droids
   Rebellion
   Season of Revolt
The Protocol Offensive

3.5 BBY
Ewoks

3 BBY
The Lando Calrissian Adventures
   Lando Calrissian and the Flamewind
      of Oseon
   Lando Calrissian and the Starcave of
      ThonBoka

3 – 0 BBY
The Han Solo Trilogy
   Rebel Dawn
2 BBY
The Han Solo Adventures
   Han Solo at Star's End
   Han Solo's Revenge

1 BBY
The Han Solo Adventures
   Han Solo and the Lost Legacy
Boba Fett
   Enemy of the Empire
Dark Forces / Jedi Knight
   Soldier for the Empire
Dark Forces / Jedi Knight
   Dark Forces (1)
X-wing
   X-wing
Empire
   Betrayal
Underworld: The Yavin Vassilika
Empire
   What Sin Loyalty?
   Princess . . . Warrior
   The Short Happy Life of Roons Sewell
   Darklighter

circa 0
Anthology Series
   Tales from the Mos Eisley Cantina

0
The Classic Trilogy
   A New Hope

circa 0 – 4 ABY
Star Wars Galaxies
   An Empire Divided
   Jump to Lightspeed
   Rage of the Wookiees
   Trials of Obi-Wan
Allegiance

0 – 3 ABY
Rogue Squadron
   Rebel Strike (1)
Star Wars Missions
   Assault on Yavin IV
   Escape from Thyferra
   Attack on Delrakkin
   Destroy the Liquidator
   Darth Vader's Return
   Rogue Squadron to the Rescue
   Bounty on Bonadan
   Total Destruction
Rookies
   Rendezvous
   No Turning Back
Empire
   Sacrifice
   To the Last Man
Boba Fett
   Salvage
Science Adventures
   Emergency in Escape Pod Four
   Journey Across Planet X
Star Wars Missions

The Hunt for Han Solo
The Search for Grubba the Hutt
Ithorian Invasion
Togorian Trap
Revolt of the Battle Droids
Showdown in Mos Eisley
Bounty Hunters vs. Battle Droids
The Vactooine Disaster
The Bounty Hunter Wars Trilogy
   The Mandalorian Armor (1)
   Slave Ship (1)
   Hard Merchandise (1)
Classic Star Wars: A Long Time Ago...
   Doomworld
The Star Wars Holiday Special
Classic Star Wars
   The Early Adventures
Planet of Kadril
Empire
   A Little Piece of Home
   Alone Together
   The Bravery of Being Out of Range
   Idiot's Array
   "General" Skywalker
   Wreckage
Galaxy of Fear
   Eaten Alive
   City of the Dead
Empire
   In the Shadow of Their Fathers
   The Price of Power
   Model Officer
Galaxy of Fear
   Planet Plague
   The Nightmare Machine
   Ghost of the Jedi
   Army of Terror
Empire
   The Wrong Side of the War
Boba Fett
   Overkill
Rebellion
   My Brother, My Enemy
Galaxy of Fear
   The Brain Spiders
   The Swarm
   Spore
   The Doomsday Ship
Star Wars Galaxies
   Ruins of Dantooine
Galaxy of Fear
   Clones
   The Hunter
Classic Star Wars
   In Deadly Pursuit
   The Rebel Storm
Rogue Squadron
   Rogue Leader (1)
X-wing
   Imperial Pursuit
Vader's Quest
Classic Star Wars: A Long Time Ago...
   Dark Encounters
Shadow Stalker
Classic Star Wars
   Escape to Hoth
X-wing
   B-wing

A Brief Star Wars Chronology

Kenobi's Blade
Young Jedi Knights
Heirs of the Force
Shadow Academy
The Lost Ones
Lightsabers
Darkest Knight
Jedi Under Siege

24 ABY
Young Jedi Knights
Shards of Alderaan
Diversity Alliance
Delusions of Grandeur
Jedi Bounty
The Emperor's Plague
Return to Ord Mantell
Trouble on Cloud City
Crisis at Crystal Reef

25 ABY
A Practical Man
The New Jedi Order
Vector Prime
Chewbacca
The New Jedi Order
Dark Tide: Onslaught
Dark Tide: Ruin
Agents of Chaos: Hero's Trial
Agents of Chaos: Jedi Eclipse

26 ABY
The New Jedi Order
Balance Point
Recovery
Edge of Victory: Conquest
Edge of Victory: Rebirth

27 ABY
The New Jedi Order
Star by Star
Dark Journey
Enemy Lines: Rebel Dream
Enemy Lines: Rebel Stand
Traitor

28 ABY
The New Jedi Order
Destiny's Way
Ylesia
Force Heretic: Remnant
Force Heretic: Refugee
Force Heretic: Reunion
The Final Prophecy

29 ABY
The New Jedi Order
The Unifying Force

35 ABY
Dark Nest
The Joiner King

36 ABY
Dark Nest
The Unseen Queen
The Swarm War

40 ABY
Legacy of the Force
Betrayal
Bloodlines
Tempest

41 ABY
Legacy of the Force
Exile
Sacrifice
Currently Untitled LOTF Book #6

42 ABY
Legacy of the Force
Currently Untitled LOTF Book #7
Currently Untitled LOTF Book #8
Currently Untitled LOTF Book #9

130 ABY
Legacy
Broken (1)

137 ABY
Legacy
Broken (2)

MULTIPLE ERA ITEMS
Anthology Series
Tales from the Empire
Tales from the New Republic
Battlefront
Battlefront
Battlefront II
Empire at War
Empire at War
Forces of Corruption
Force Commander
Galactic Battlegrounds
Galactic Battlegrounds
Clone Campaigns
Official Star Wars Adventure Journal **
Star Wars Tales **
**(not all stories are in-continuity)*

A Brief Star Wars Chronology

Star Wars Visionaries
Tales from Mos Eisley

If the task of reading, viewing, or playing all of the materials listed above seems daunting . . . it should. Licensed Star Wars stories have been produced since the release of the novelization of the first Star Wars film back in 1976. Sure, the so-called "Official Continuity," the plan to actually create a cohesive universe from these continuation materials, didn't exist in print until Heir to the Empire and Dark Empire in 1991, but the universe was already growing by then, and the years since have seen an outright explosion of new Star Wars stories.

The best advice for a new "Expanded Universe" fan is still the simplest. Start with a story that sounds intriguing to you as a reader. Starting at the beginning will keep you away from many of the most impactful stories for a long while, whereas reading in the order these products were released will leave some of the most intriguing new stories (such as the Legacy of the Force novels or Legacy comic book series) out of reach for far too long.

The important thing is to simply pick up a story somewhere and start into the saga. If it gets confusing, just be sure to have a trusty guide, such as Wallace and Anderson's New Essential Chronology from Del Rey or Butler's Star Wars Timeline Gold on hand to sort out any missed details.

Just remember that any chronology, including this one, is almost immediately out of date, since new Star Wars stories are released on an almost weekly basis. Your best bet to keep track of these new releases and fill in the gaps in this and other printed resources is to use an online resource such as the Del Rey or Dark Horse Comics websites, The Star Wars Timeline Gold, or various other fan-made resources across the Internet.

To borrow the words of television news personality Bill O'Reilly, in Star Wars fandom, your fellow fans are often truly the ones "looking out for you."

Action Figure Short Term Storing and Moving Tip

Collectors move. Dealers pack up inventory for shows. Action figures need to be protected. Comic book boxes and plastic tubs are not optimal when it comes to packing uncased figures. A little pre-planning can prevent lifelong damage. A standard action figure's cardback is 6"x9". Loading figures into boxes with a 6"x9" *interior dimension* will keep them snug and secure for travel.

Shown here are two 6"x9"x24" boxes which each fit figures from vintage through 30th Anniversary. These brown corregated boxes are $0.82 each from *www.uline.com/ProductDetail.asp?model=S-4737*

Star Wars Combine

Reprinted with permission from http://www.SWCombine.com

The Star Wars Combine is a game set in the Star Wars Universe. The game has been online since 1998 and although it is technically a browser game, it sees itself rather as an MMORPG. It is programmed and run entirely by volunteers, so playing is free. There are no monthly charges and no premium features that are restricted to players who register a paid account.

The game is entirely player driven. All roles — from the emperor or commander of the Rebel Alliance to the fighter pilots — are open for player characters. The player driven economy offers many options to mine, trade, or build cities, facilities, and stations.

Any new player can create their individual character selecting from various skills and more than 50 different races from Star Wars (Wookiees, Twi'leks etc.). They can then join an existing group — from the infamous Empire to less famous smaller production, trading or even pirate groups — and later found their own company.

There are more than 5,000 planets that can be explored and colonized. Player characters can own their own ships, vehicles,

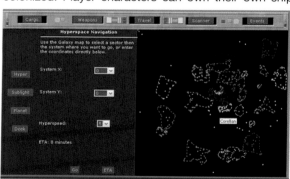

buildings, cities, or even companies. Also player groups ("factions") can be owners of anything, setting the Star Wars Combine apart from alliances and guilds in many other similar games.

The Star Wars Combine offers many roles to choose from and thus allows the player to not only live their own dream of being whatever they want in the Star Wars universe, but also to adapt the game to their favored style of play, playing the game as more of an adventure, a strategy game, a business simulation, or just enjoying the lively community of like minded gamers and Star Wars fans.

According to the main website, "The Star Wars Combine offers a complexity and variety rather unusual for free browser games. If you like Star Wars, you should really give it a go."

Main Features:

__Create Star Wars character, choose race, skills, background.

__Assign skill levels from 5 different areas.

__Join the Galactic Empire or the Rebel Alliance and enter the Galactic Civil War, or pursue a career in the backdrop in more than 50 other groups as a simple merchant, smuggler, pirate, pilot ... the possibilities are endless!

__Have a chance to be Force sensitive and become a soldier of the light or a lord of the dark!

__Buy and sell spaceships, space stations, vehicles, facilities, items, and weapons with other living players.

__Explore a vast galaxy of over 4,000 life-filled planets and visit the elegant cities of well-known localities like Corellia, Tatooine, Naboo, and more, using a unique real-time movement system for ground travel, air travel, subspace, and hyperspace travel.

__Use the graphical interface to move across the planet, moon, spaceship, or space station you are currently on and watch as your ship enters a planet's atmosphere.

__Prospect planets and mine their raw materials.

__Build your favorite ships, vehicles, space stations, droids, items, and weapons ... or recycle their wrecks into new raw materials.

__Post on the classified ads offering your services for all to see.

__Be a part of a vast community almost 3,000 members strong, visiting the message center, helping to shape the progress of the Star Wars Combine with suggestions, role playing your character with others in many unique scenarios, or visiting the chatrooms for general chit-chat with other members.

__Personalize the Darkness Interface

__Get a free, web-based holo-mail address to talk to your fellow combine members or anyone else on the Internet.

__With many more upcoming features such as combat, research and development, and creatures!

__Play the game, no matter whether you're on a Windows, Macintosh, or Linux/Unix computer.

Visit the Star Wars Combine today. Use your favorite Internet browser and go to: www.SWCombine.com.

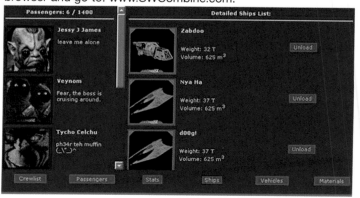

A History of JediTempleArchives.com

by Peter Hauerstein and Chuck Paskovics

JediTempleArchives.com is a website dedicated to creating high-resolution visual guides for the most commonly collected Star Wars merchandise in the universe. Although it was founded in early 2004, the history of the Visual Guides reaches back to the days when Paplatine seemed just your typical senator in the Republic. Chuck Paskovics had his own personal website and wanted to create a format for himself to document his passion for Star Wars: his vintage collection.

Chuck developed the current Visual Guide format in 2000 not only as a means of documenting his own collection, but also in a way that could be used as a wallpaper on his computer that would show off each figure, vehicle, beast, and playset in its full glory, all in one view. And so was born the very first Visual Guides.

It was not long before a popular fan site took notice of those ultra-cool guides, and Chuck signed on to offer his Visual Guides as one of the main features of the site. The whole collecting community was then able use them as a tool to aide them in their own collecting ventures.

The Droids Boba Fett is the same as all other released versions, except this one comes with a gold coin.

Right before the release of *Attack of the Clones*, a massive push formed to expand the Visual Guides from just the vintage line into the modern line. They were expanded to cover the immense amount of 3¾" product released for the movie, as well as items such as the brand new Unleashed, Playskool, 12" figures, and all the 3¾" product released since the mid-nineties.

After that initial push, the guides expanded even further to cover other fantastic lines that knocked collectors' socks off from companies such as Gentle Giant and Master Replicas, along with old time favorites like Hallmark and their fantastic holiday ornaments.

Peter Hauerstein quickly signed on to help build the Visual Guide library shortly after the release of *Attack of the Clones*. He had been so impressed with the Visual Guides that he wanted to work on them himself to give back to the archive of images which helped him so much with his collection.

The site hosting the guides eventually closed its virtual doors, but Chuck, Peter, and another heavy contributor, Mike Kelly, decided it was time to create a website dedicated to the massive guide library. They were extremely proud of the work that they had done and they simply had fun doing it so they wanted guide images to live on. That desire, coupled with a barrage of e-mails from fans all

over the world led to the creation of the Jedi Temple Archives. They wanted to provide a place where collectors from around the world could get visual information about Star Wars collectibles, so they decided to dedicate their website to providing just that: Visual Guides.

The Star Wars Visual Guides now cover a vast array of the most favorite collectibles from nearly every U.S.-released 3¾" scale figure, vehicle, beast, playset, and accessory set made since 1978, to the most sought after high-end items from Sideshow Collectibles, Gentle Giant, and Master Replicas. The guides are a reflection of not only the coolest Star Wars collectibles out there, but also Chuck and Pete's collection rooms. They also cover the fun items made just for kids (but loved by adults), such as the Galactic Heroes, Jedi Force, M&Ms, Star Wars Transformers, Titanium, Star Wars Miniatures, and more! Other Visual Guide sections from Medicom, Code 3, and documentation of the entire Kenner/Hasbro 12" line are all in the works as well.

Chuck and Pete remain in full force updating the site with new guides every single day! Just why do they create so many high resolution guide images every single day of the year? They enjoy making them and it is their special connection to a lifetime a love for the Star Wars saga. That so many people from all over the world enjoy them too just adds to the fun collecting Star Wars gives to both of them.

As Star Wars collectibles evolve, so have the photography and Visual Guide creation techniques of Jedi Temple Archives. The Visual Guides are constantly evolving as new collectibles are created to make sure that the item fans want to see is fully described in as few views as possible. Their big project for the near future will to upgrade all the older guides using the new techniques that have been developed. With over 3,500 guides currently online (and growing daily), this makes the Jedi Temple Archives the ultimate high resolution resource archive in the Star Wars galaxy.

The Best of the Online Star Wars Fan and Collector Resources

Compiled by Geoffrey T. Carlton

There is an abundance of experts who populate the Internet with golden nuggets of information just waiting to be picked up by those in need.

It is unfortunate that the most specialized of these bits of knowledge are so perfectly concise that they cannot warrant a successful single publication of their own. It is equally fortunate that the caretakers of this knowledge feel it is important enough to distribute it publicly so that others may in-the-know.

The Armory of the Jawas
www.loresdelsith.net/rincon/armeria/index2.htm

The Armory of the Jawas addresses a growing concern — the modern reproduction of weapons and accessories for vintage action figures. As technology progresses and the ability to reseal vintage figures to custom reproduced cardbacks using undistinguishable bubbles and reproduction accessories has created a gray market boom. An $8.00 loose figure expertly recarded for $20.00 worth of supplies can cost an uneducated collector $200.00 or more for the valueless forgery.

The Armory has a library of high resolution photographs of the front and back of every legitimate vintage action figure weapon and accessory. It also offers high resolution images of every known reproduction counterpart. Every legitimate variation and knock-off is accompanied by a text description of what to look for when authenticating or disputing pieces you encounter. The curator of the website maintains the completeness through frequent information contributions.

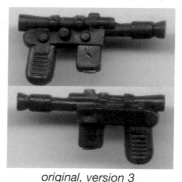
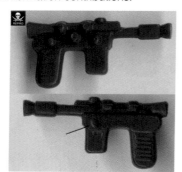

original, version 3   *reproduction*

Star Wars Trading Cards
www.StarWarsCards.net

Collectors of Star Wars trading cards (US and international) may need to locate an established site for current checklists and a support community that specializes in obscure sets and chase cards. Star Wars Trading Cards, the site operated by Cathy Kendrick at StarWarsCards.net, has checklists for cards and stickers from 1977 right up to the latest set.

The Jawa Trader
www.Jawa-Trader.co.uk

Trading card collectors who want look to for visual clues to their sets or to see images of wonderful rare cards and sets should bookmark the Jawa Trader. Andy Dukes has kept watch on the Star Wars trading cards from around the world and documented them visually, chronologically, and geographically at his site.

StarWarsCans.com
www.StarWarsCans.com

Niche collectors who find Star Wars beverage cans (and bottles!) to be of interest may be surprised that there is a dedicated resource to documenting and picturing every food and drink related Star Wars collectible. Almost 900 items have been added to their catalog so far.

Star Wars Origami
www.happymagpie.com/origami.html

In the second edition of the *Star Wars Super Collector's Wish Book* we featured a number of origami artists who all had taken to Star Wars folding. Chris Alexander, the individual who turned us on to it in the first place, ended up leading several life-sized origami folding demonstrations at Star Wars Celebration III in Indianapolis in 2005. (Watch for Chris's book at a bookstore near you to see his diagrams for creating the Star Wars universe in mini-paper replicas.)

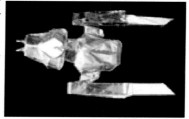

While you're waiting, you can hone up your mad paper skills by using online diagrams from Star Wars Origami. At the time of this writing, there are 14 different diagrams available.

Star Wars the Musical
www.infauxmedia.com/swmusical/control_room.htm

Fans of the Star Wars saga will appreciate the creative genius behind Star Wars the Musical! It's a serious effort behind a whimsical interpretation of Star Wars, designed to emulate a musical stage production. For those who are familiar with the award-winning fan film "One Season More," this musical project is its predecessor, comprised of 18 songs in two acts.

The composers invite any group to perform the musical, and assist such efforts with "karaoke tracks" for each song. For the fans who want nothing more than to enjoy the composition, links are also provided to track animations and alternate fan arrangements of several of the songs.

The Best of the Online Star Wars Fan and Collector Resources

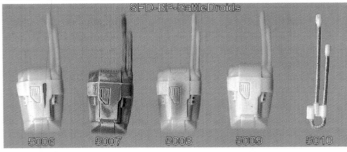

SW Inserts ...*formerly Gadders.com*
http://www.SWInserts.com

Reconstitute, reconstruct, restore. Whether it's your sideline hobby to give new life to abandoned vintage toys or just an idea that struck you on an idle Saturday, the ability to refurbish vehicles and playsets is only a couple of mouse-clicks away.

SW Inserts is a community contribution site in which you can post or download 1:1 scans of paper-pieces, inserts, and instruction sheets.

Originally created as SWInserts.com, the site has been moved to the domain "Gadders.com," but has now been revitalized under the original name.

Custom-carded hobbiests will be excited to find this site as the home for many high-resolution reproduction cardbacks.

For the less craft-phobic collectors, there is a treasure at this site in the form of 1:1 scans of the pieces that make up the vintage Palitoy cardboard Death Star playset. Print. Build. Play.

SW Collector
www.SWCollector.com

Checklists, variations, production changes, and manufacturing errors, all in high resolution. The "HD Photo Gallery" at SW Collector dates back to the original red card series of Power of the Force 2 action figures and the library is maintained up to and including the current wave of action figures.

The main page receives news updates on a nearly daily basis to keep collectors aware of release dates, new finds, and product announcements.

SWCollector.com was the primary contributor for the loose action figure guide in the 3rd edition of this book, and remains the visual authority for error and variation action figures / packaging.

SciFiDome
www.SciFiDome.com

Reproduction weapons and accessories aren't always "bad." They have a legitimate purpose in the world of collecting when acquired and used in their proper manor. Action figures cost significantly less when purchased without guns, capes, staves, helmets, or accessories. It is for the display of these otherwise incomplete figures that the "repro" market is embraced. The use of repro weapons and accessories is also convenient when in need of a wardrobe or armory expansion for diorama scenes.

Legitimate sellers identify their merchandise as being in the repro category when selling it. During the research for this article, the best site found online to acquire these items was the SciFiDome. SciFiDome seems to be on top of their game offering repro and original vintage weapons and accessories as well as modern action figure pieces and parts to action figure ships. Their online catalog offers a photograph of each piece and an identifying number with which to place the order.

Outside the realm of casting pastic parts, SciFiDome has covered the (repro) market for paper good parts as well. Decals for droids and ships included with playsets and vehicles are all available from the same site, making your shopping list for repair and replacement of toys, old and new, available from a single source.

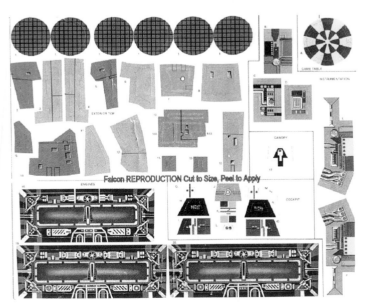

445

The Best of the Online Star Wars Fan and Collector Resources

Wookieepedia — Public Encyclopedia for All Things Star Wars
by Geoffrey T. Carlton

It shouldn't be surprising to realize that a bulk of the information for this article came from Wookieepedia; the subject of the page. To fully appreicate its concept you must first become familiar with Wikipedia, a publicly-editable online encyclopedia. The name Wookieepedia is a play on Wikipedia, because of the pronunciation similarity.

Wookieepedia is the Star Wars wiki for information on the Star Wars saga, including information on all six films, as well as the expanded universe of books, comics, video games, and literally any other licensed storyline product.

Wookieepedia was started on March 4, 2005, by Chad "White-Boy" Barbry. It strives to be the premier source for information on all aspects of the Star Wars universe. As of October 2006, the English language version of the wiki contains over 40,000 articles, making it the largest Wikia-hosted wiki in terms of article count. The Star Wars wiki is considered to be a branch of Wikipedia, but can expand on Star Wars information in greater detail and with more freedom than Wikipedia. Wookieepedia took form when Wikipedia users began to complain of the overabundance of material related to Star Wars appearing on Wikipedia.

The site's first editors were primarily users of Wikipedia who were frustrated by the requirements for articles there, and the debates over deletion of content that followed. Most of the founding articles were taken directly from Wikipedia under the GNU Free Documentation License.

As a fan-created encyclopedia, Wookieepedia is never intended to be a primary source for material, nor is it intended to become a replacement for the Star Wars Databank or any other official source. It serves as a fan effort to summarize aspects of the Star Wars universe in the best way possible, while directing the reader to official sources.

Beyond the scope of in-universe point-of-view entries, sections of the wiki cover actors, artists, real companies, and culture in an out-of-universe perspective.

Wikia also hosts Star Wars wikis in French, Hungarian, Polish, Portuguese, Russian, and Spanish. In addition, Wookieepedia coordinates efforts with Jedipedia, a German language wiki not hosted by Wikia.

To visit the Wookieepedia, connect an Internet browser to: *www.WookieePedia.com*

Dates of interest:

Wookieepedia was the most visited wiki hosted by Wikia as of July 2005.

On November 28, 2005, Wookieepedia was selected as the Sci Fi Channel's "Sci Fi Site of the Week."

In January 2006, the site was Wikia's featured wiki of the month.

Star Wars Attacktix

Most kids are familiar with the concept of standing up little green army men and shooting them down one-by-one with a BB gun. It's classic backyard fun from the past.

Hasbro incorporated that concept into their tabletop Star Wars game Attacktix. The goal of the game is simple: the last team to have any pieces left standing is the winner.

Part of the attraction to the game is that it targets both miniature tabletop gamers and collectors. For collectors Hasbro has integrated many of the traits that encourage sales. Every set of figures has a number assigned to each piece, and a level of rarity. Every piece is also available as a chase piece (more rare) which is distinguished by a chrome base. The movement abilities and any special skills are all available for quick review on the figure's base.

Figures included in special multi-packs are distinguished with a yellow base.

With the exception of starter packs and multi-packs, the figures are all sold in blind booster packs.

Standard pieces have black bases.
Chase pieces have chromed bases.

No special board, area, or surface is needed and any number of players can play at once.

Individual pieces are assigned values for worth and movement. Players choose their squads based upon the total number of figure points agreed upon for that game.

Most pieces have spring loaded projectiles with which to attack. Some specialized pieces have close range attacks instead, such as some of the Jedi who are armed with long lightsabers attached to their spring tension arms. The figure's value is related to the strength of the weapon they carry, and how difficult it is to knock them over (shape and center of gravity).

Once killed (knocked over) there's a possibility of a special event or attack based upon a randomizer wheel on the bottom of the figure that changes with every movement.

Attacktix has grown beyond the Star Wars universe with other licenses having compatible attacks and point systems. For instance, it is possible to pit a Star Wars squad against a squad of Transformer figures.

With the possibility of trading figures like bubblegum cards, having to buy blind packs hoping for something good, an economical price (around $6.00 for two random figures), and frankly a game anybody can play and everybody enjoys, Star Wars fans and collectors have all found a favorite with this line of figures. Thank you, Hasbro. A great line of toys with mass appeal.

Star Wars Denizen's Tusken Raider Costume

By Geoffrey T. Carlton

After successfully creating her Jawa costume, my wife's second endeavor at a from-scratch Star Wars costume was to assemble a Tusken Raider for me to wear.

We attempted to cheat the system by buying a pre-made Tusken head mask off of an auction site. After it became apparent that it wasn't going to fit my face properly we dissected it to see how it was made. Fearful we were going to have to learn to sculpt and create the pieces; we were shocked to find that most of the complex parts were actually available at our local dollar store.

In fact, once we got started we were further surprised at how "not difficult" the entire Tusken project turned out to be. Costuming is never easy, but given the proper amount of time and liberal creativity to track down parts, the Tusken Raider is a costume that can be created by most fans with very few skills required.

Our assembly time was five days, and (excluding the $100 mask we bought to get started) the completed costume cost us less than $100, including the making of our own mask!

After we were well on our way, we turned to the Internet for reference materials to get the look just right.

When using Internet tutorials to create costumes, the uninitiated usually follow the instructions step-by-step and to the letter. As costuming skills evolve, new ideas come to mind. Sometimes a little extra experimentation can lead to improvements through a more complex and detailed construction. Sometimes that same experimentation can lead to easier, better looking (or more comfortable!) designs. The mask we had purchased had a rigid flat face that rubbed my nose raw when I tried to wear it. Our own mask was created by molding stiff window screen over a mannequin head, using unsharpened pencils taped in position to get the shape right for the mouth area. The flexibility of the screen allowed us to adjust it for comfort before finalizing its permanent shape.

Our Internet research of the Gaffi stick lead us down the road of searching for an obscure Hershey's Kisses® candy holder and making a plaster cast of it for the weapon's head. After tracking down said dish, plaster casting was a whole-day learning experience and the plaster turned out to be heavy and relatively fragile. Not every idea on the Internet works for every person.

DZ-190, the Fighting 501st's designation for my Tusken raider, is three years old now. As I returned to the Internet for references to re-create and chronicle of how he was built, I came across a website which was titled, The Definitive How To — Tusken Raider Costume.

I approached the site with caution. Visions of paying $100 for dollar store supplies, plaster weapons that could seriously hurt somebody and completely demolish your costume in one fell swoop, and searching the web for long forgotten glass candy dishes wasn't the type of resource I wanted to refer readers to. After following through the website step-by-step as a first time costumer might, I was relived to find their approach practical, easy to understand, and well documented with lots of photography.

The Definitive Guide is broken up into seven chapters:

Creating the Head, The Robes, The Respirator, The Bandoliers, The Leggings, The Gaffi Stick, and The Tusken Rifles.

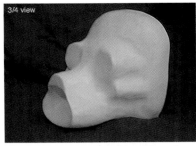
A simple pre-made face mold could save hours

Each chapter is a single page of detailed instructions reinforced with a combination of photography and illustrations. The head chapter is a little longer weighing in at nine pages due the level of detail required to get the identifying features of the Tusken raider right.

The only tip I might offer to improve the experience of assembling a new raider based upon this site is in the chapter on the head. The website author says, "The teeth are vacuum formed plastic painted to look like metal." Since not many costumers have access to vacuuform tables, it might be easier to use a solid foam rubber ball and a serrated knife to create this piece of the mask.

The material list below demonstrates how economical it can be to create your own professional costume. Give it a try; you might just surprise yourself with a new hobby.

Studio Creations
The Definitive How To — Tusken Raider Costume
www.studiocreations.com/howto/tuskenraider/main.html

Tools:
Hot glue gun, scissors, box knife, drill, rivets

Cloth:
4 yards of 48 inch wide tan robe cloth
3 yards of tan cloth for the bandages
12" x 12" leather scrap
24" x 10" burgundy vinyl
4 yards of leather looking vinyl
2' of $1/2$" inch wide foam padding
18" Velcro or cloth snap-button strip

Hardware:
12" of $1/2$" diameter aluminum rod
24" of $1/4$" diameter aluminum rod
30" of $1 1/4$" PVC pipe
24" of $3/4$" PVC pipe
1" to $1/2$" PVC reducer coupling

Specialty:
Base face mold ($20 online)
Automotive fuel filter
Medium sized magic markers
Medium sized plastic bowl
4 plastic fins
Tan cloth gloves
Rain boots

Expressions

Through a Collector's Eye

Every image used above may be found elsewhere within this book.

Star Wars Toy Collecting…A Long Time Ago

By Cole Houston

The Everclear song AM Radio waxes nostalgic about the world I grew up in, that of the seventies. While it makes mention of the technological distractions of our modern world it does not so much decry the loss of an innocent age as it recalls the way things were in what now seems a bygone era. Such is the nature of this memoir of the early days of Star Wars toy collecting, from 1977 to 1985, the "vintage" years. In that time long past, my lifelong love of obtaining mementos of George Lucas's intergalactic saga in action figure form began.

It was the infamous Early Bird Set that started the ball rolling for both Kenner's Star Wars action figure line and my own collecting passion. A thin, lightweight rectangle surrounded in festive foil paper awaited me under the tree that Christmas morning in 1977, courtesy of my older brother. Though Wal-Mart brought us a contemporary version of this unique marketing concept in 2005, the wait for those first four action figures to arrive in the mail was certainly far more grueling. They were, after all, the first Star Wars figures ever! It may be difficult to imagine what it was like to look at that cardboard backdrop with the plastic foot pegs sitting on a shelf as the requisite six to eight weeks slowly passed. Awaiting Luke, Leia, R2, and Chewie was something of an exercise in patience that was beyond the capacity of the average 12 year-old. And needless to say, that quartet of figures got quite a workout during the months that would pass until they were joined by the now-classic first 12 figures released.

In time the first line of Star Wars figures began to appear. Oddly enough it was the Jawa and Death Squad Commander that proved the most elusive and prompted a habit that would hold true for my Star Wars figure collecting well into Return of the Jedi. In those days we did not have the Internet, of course, and though many stores stocked Star Wars figures, their stock was sporadic and fluctuating. So I began keeping a phone number list for all of the stores that I knew carried the much-desired figures. There was not a Toys R Us in the immediate area until the mid-eighties, but we did have Sears, JC Penny, Best Products, and Circus World, an in-the-mall toy store. Within a few months of constant calls to find the figures I sought, I had the better part of all of their phone numbers memorized. I had even begun to work out when some stores received new toys. My mother has told me that I was an established eccentric by the age of eight so it is of little wonder that I would take such an approach to my collecting passion. But then, I must admit that my mother played an even larger role in this pursuit.

I've often told fellow collectors (especially those who started in the seventies) that I am "one of the lucky ones." My mother realized the cultural impact of Star Wars from day one. She encouraged my brothers and me to take good care of our Star Wars toys. Though my brothers eventually lost interest in their figures, none ever met with a post Fourth of July explosive demise or faced the "Dread Lawnmower of Dantooine" fates all too common for vintage collections. Most of my vintage collection consists of the actual figures and vehicles I collected as they were released. And to that end equal credit must go to my father, who was known to find an excuse to run an errand miles out of the way so I could obtain a figure or playset that just could not be found locally. Many were the miles that were logged on behalf of my collection well into the eighties.

Perhaps the most unusual instance of my collecting passion knowing no boundaries was my discovery of the AT-AT at a mall in Baton Rouge, Louisiana, when visiting a friend there. Not content to hope to find this Holy Grail of the Empire line when I returned to Texas, I purchased it there, repacked it the night before I left, and checked the box as baggage (with a handle of twine taped to the box suitcase style)! I do not believe that my father was too surprised to see a huge Star Wars box glide out of the chute and onto the baggage carousel when he picked me up at the airport. No lengths were too great when it came to owning every single figure and vehicle in the Star Wars line! I vividly recall a day when my best friend and I followed a couple with a toddler around Best Products' toy department for nearly an hour knowing full well that they were not going to purchase the Romba figure he clutched in his hand, but being too embarrassed as teenagers to request that he might be persuaded to relinquish his prize. Eventually the family left and the abandoned figure was obtained and, absent its package, stands proudly with his fellow Ewoks to this day.

Making a pest of myself to the less than enthusiastic denizens of toy departments in a 40 mile radius became something of a hobby of mine. This was secondary to Star Wars collecting, but no less vital to the cause. One had to suffer the uneducated in the ways of Star Wars, like an elderly employee reading names off cards like "Gringo" or having assure the person on the other end of the line to hold the figures you were seeking at the counter under impassioned assurances that you would pick them up within the hour. Back then my collecting was something of a quest, ever on the lookout for the latest releases. The ability to coordinate with fellow collectors was limited at best back then and action figures had not yet become one of the major cash cows of the convention dealer's room scene. Conventions were few and far between and price guides were a rarity as well. In those days it was difficult to keep up to date on upcoming releases. The Internet was some years in the future, but then so too were magazines committed to toy collecting. Your best resource was the pamphlets that Kenner placed in the boxes of vehicles and playsets, which outlined upcoming releases and were updated from time to time. The most curious of these were produced in advance of the release of Return of the Jedi and had all images of the Ewoks and Jabba the Hutt blacked out, undoubtedly at the bequest of LucasFilm. Even then folks were mindful of spoilers!

There were the occasional hints at things to come. Much like the Episode I and III Sneak Preview action figure releases from Hasbro, the Kenner mail-away figures were a glimpse into the next film. Boba Fett blazed this trail, though he had to lose his missile-firing backpack in the process, a change that made for a better figure in the long run. A personal favorite sneak preview was Admiral Ackbar, a character of enough importance to make a worthy figure, but minor enough in the grand scheme to be allowed an early release. I recall the long weeks awaiting the arrival of this curious, fish-faced figure and the thrill of opening the nondescript white mailing box. There was nothing quite like obtaining a figure that you knew would be available on the card in a few months without having to wait and then face a relentless search to find one of your own. Especially given that the practice of keeping Star Wars figures eternally carded had not yet come into common coinage. Back then most collectors were kids or young adults. We were the pioneers of Star Wars action figure collecting. Much of what Star Wars toy collectors enjoy today, like Star Cases or the perpetuation of the line by Hasbro, is a result of we kids of the 70s and 80s never quite growing up.

Star Wars as Muse

By Bill Cable

I've been a recreational artist pretty much my entire life. When I was in high school I was drawing comic books. When I was in college I drew for the newspaper. I always loved it, but I never had any real aspirations of doing it for a living. It was a hobby. My art continues to be a hobby, but it has become much more prominent in my life because of the inspiration of Star Wars.

Let me begin by stating that I never intended to draw Star Wars art for money. I just collected the toys. The idea of drawing commissioned art was forced (ha ha... forced!) on me by a fellow Star Wars fan. I started out just wanting to design club T-shirts. I became a freshly-minted member of the Ohio Star Wars Collectors Club shortly after graduating college, and one of my first contributions was to propose a club T-shirt. The other members loved the idea, so I put together three possible concepts. Yoda won out, but one of the members was so impressed by the art (a rough sketch, honestly) I did of Boba Fett that he offered to buy it. And the next month he came to me with a business plan on how to sell more of this Star Wars art to collectors. He even researched the legality of selling original art based on copyrighted characters, assuaging my biggest concern. I was hesitant to jump in, but finally he pressed me enough that I agreed to try it out.

I never expected that collectors would pay good money for my art. I mean... I wouldn't buy any of it myself. There are just so many better artists out there... I'm just an amateur now and I was REALLY rough around the edges back then. But for whatever reason, collectors did. It started out as a trickle within OSWCC, but I slowly began to generate a following, and I'd find myself with three or four commissions lined up. I eventually created a website to promote my art. After I built a gallery of around 30 commissions, I was finding a simple online art gallery not nearly fulfilling enough to satisfy my Star Wars appetite. Then, like a bolt from the heavens it hit me... I should be in comedy. Thus I undertook my greatest Star Wars project to date: CreatureCantina.com. I'd have a place to promote my art, a place to write (or attempt to write) humorous news stories, and a place to draw my own weekly comic strip. At last I'd be fulfilled.

I don't know what it is about Star Wars that inspires such creativity and fervor. Maybe it's the mystical, fantastical concept of an invisible power we can tap into to control the universe. Perhaps it's the powerful, primal themes... good versus evil, father versus son, damnation and redemption. Maybe it's just the bad-ass dudes with lightsabers, metal bikinis, and freaky aliens. Whatever it is, it's an inspiration across all mediums. It inspires musicians and poets. It inspired entrepreneurs and webmasters to design all manner of fantastic and useful web sites. I've had the great privilege of working with many contributors on CreatureCantina.com, but few as dedicated or as zealous as two of my current staffers. Dan "Darth Danno" Dudych has written a news story every single week since he joined the site, some of the most clever prose and hilarious ideas I've ever read. And "Tresob Yr" is a master of multimedia, contributing everything from weekly action figure photo comics to Flash movies to an extensive Customizable Card Games he designed from scratch. These are real guys with real, demanding lives, yet they pour untold hours into these projects, simply because George Lucas's creation has fomented a passion that cannot be quenched.

You could say that Star Wars is my muse... inciting all manner of creativity in media both electronic and tactile. I've evolved from drawing T-shirts to pen & ink art to being hired to design a Christmas card. But one of my favorite projects has really brought me full circle... from someone who bought Star Wars collectibles to someone who creates Star Wars collectibles! Yeah, I know many of my patrons consider my portraits to be "collectibles," the business plan was designed to nurture such thoughts; but I'm talking *real* collectibles. Back in 2003 I was pondering what sort of replica proof card I should design for the Pennsylvania (yes, I moved to Pennsylvania) Star Wars Collecting Society summer social, when yet again I was inspired! In past years we'd just slapped a photo onto a template in Photoshop and there was our commemorative proof. But that year I decided to try something completely original. I drew the cardback artwork in the style of the Vintage Droids cartoon toys. The reaction was so amazingly positive that I decided to create a small run of custom carded Vintage figures using that cardback. And those sold so well that I've tried to make it an annual tradition... creating a new custom carded Droids-style figure every summer.

  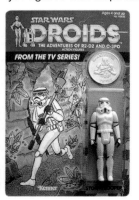

Evolution from original Cable art to a limited edition Cable custom carded action figure

Were it not for my love of Star Wars I'd never have had the opportunity to do all these rewarding projects. I'm very thankful to have it. It brings out a lot in me that I otherwise wouldn't have the chance to express and share. And it has given me the the chance to grow and improve to where even I think my art is respectable. The Star Wars universe has such breadth and depth that I could continue in these endeavors for the rest of my life. Granted, it's still just a hobby, but it's a hobby I wouldn't sacrifice for the world.

"Cable Original" art from http://CreatureCantina.com

Star Wars Action News

By Arnie and Marjorie Carvalho

When we met, it was one of the first things we discovered about each other. As we continued our relationship, our love for all things Star Wars brought and kept us close. We even had a Star Wars wedding where Arnie donned an $800 (at that time) Icons Obi-Wan Kenobi saber replica as an accessory to his wedding attire.

(She got the diamond ring, he got the saber, it was all fair.)

Soon our collection was big. And I mean big. We bought a house with the collection in mind. The collection, now dubbed The Sithsonian, has its own floor. Then Arnie had an idea: We should do a podcast. This podcast should be all about Star Wars collecting, and it should showcase how collecting both obsesses us and brings us closer together. So on August 29, 2005, we launched Star Wars Action News.

Star Wars Action News quickly became popular beyond our wildest dreams. We have listeners all over the world and on popular ranking sites Star Wars Action News has consistently been the top Star Wars podcast. We have conducted panels on collecting and traveled from coast to coast, all in the name of Star Wars collecting.

And we've had the time of our life.

Together.

You can listen to Star Wars Action News at www.swaction-news.com

Listen to each new Podcast, released every Monday.

The Carvalho's collection being prepared for the move into the new Sithsonian

Selling Collections and Buying the Best Pieces

By Geoffrey T. Carlton

The original concept for the *Star Wars Super Collector's Wish Book* was to be a visual encyclopedia of the tens of thousands of Star Wars collectibles produced around the globe that most casual collectors are unfamiliar with. In its current incarnation it is a beautiful color glossy book which has the additional benefit of doing an amazing job at keeping current values up-to-date.

There are many questions posed to me as the author, but two of them stand out, and they are on linear opposite ends of the collecting spectrum. The first: "where can I sell my collection for the values listed in the book?" The second: "where can I buy all of the unusual stuff that the book has chronicled?"

The first question is a difficult question when posed to me. The values listed in the book are replacement value. They're how much collectors should expect to pay to acquire the pieces if their own were to become lost or damaged. In order to receive that value, they must become an established dealer and hold onto the collectibles at the stated value until a collector "in need" comes along and is willing to pay for the piece (assuming it's in the condition they're seeking). Collectors seeking to sell usually don't have months or years to wait around with inventories posted at book value prices. They want to turn their hard won treasures back into cash fast... and that's a convenience that will be costly.

Higher value pieces are risky on auction sites. If they don't get the attention they warrant, they could go for much less than they're worth. Also, the more experienced collectors all watch the auction sites for bargains so the auction audience may already have that most desirable piece and not be inclined to own another. If the best pieces from a collection do sell on auction sites, that leaves only the common pieces in the collection left to move, and common pieces by themselves don't sell quickly. Nobody really wants the responsibility for a lot of common pieces unless they're offered for bottom-dollar investment.

To move an entire collection in a reasonable amount of time and not get left holding the remains after it's been picked clean of the best pieces, sellers need to find the right buyer and be ready to accept the right clearance price. (Remember all those bargains at the store that go on close-out? Now it's time to follow suit.)

Prepare inventory count sheets. To get the most money for a collection, an exact listing of every piece and its condition is mandatory. Spreadsheets work best for this since data can be entered in multiple columns, and unnecessary information can be omitted when it comes time to print the distribution copy.

Sort by categories. Buyers will appraise the list based upon groups of most interest. If the list is too difficult to follow, they'll just pick a low price that they know they can recoup from, and let the chips fall where they may, or decline to offer all together.

Avoid stating grades for individual pieces. Simply use a column to list damage, defects, or specific conditions. Let the buyer decide condition based upon the description.

Do not print individual values in the list unless the buyer is allowed to pick pieces out of the collection. To a buyer, items may have a different value in the markets they serve.

Two words should describe the list: specific and concise. When submitting an inventory to a potential buyer, that inventory is the only tool to accurately convey the seriousness of collection, and knowledge that went into building it.

Once the list reflects a true understanding of what is for sale (most people have no idea exactly what they've got until they're forced to recount it all), determine the value for each piece for its condition. Deduct liberally for defects; the buyer will. Take the sum of the value of the collection and *divide by three*. If the accuracy and grading values are honest, that total divided by three is what the collector is looking at reaping to make a quick sale. After seeing that number, many collectors decide it's not worth it to dump their collection, and have enjoyed inventorying it so much, their desire to collect is renewed.

For the purposes of this article, we'll continue with the sale. Take the sum and divide it by two this time. That number should be your initial asking price, open to negotiation. Send the inventory out to the potential buyers, asking them to make a reasonable offer for the lot. For local comic book stores and hobby shops, invite their buyer to schedule a time to come and see the collection. For Internet outlets, sending along some digital photos of random group shots and detailed close-ups of higher valued items may help the cause.

When the replies arrive (make sure to get them all), don't become greedy. If the highest offer comes in between the two calculated numbers, it's a good bet that the sale is about to be made. If the offers are below the lowest calculated number, some tact is required to get it bumped up. Explain to the seller that the number in mind is... (use the sum divided by two) and see if they are willing to negotiate a higher amount. Like an auction, the buyer is always trying to pay the least. If they cannot meet the minimum amount, it's time to settle for less or thank them and move along to the next potential buyer.

It is at this point that our two original questions meet, "where to sell a collection?" and "where to buy the neatest stuff listed?"

Collectors don't usually buy other collectors' collections. The purchase amount is outside of most collectors' budgets, and then the problem of what to do with all the extras and duplicates would simply be passed along to the next guy. It happens, but it's rare.

I personally dislike promoting the auction sites, but one can usually find the best collectibles at immorally low prices from fellow down-on-their luck collectors there. Likewise, a down-on-their-luck collector can ditch most of a collection for pennies on the dollar there, too.

The method that has been proven to be the most profitable for those selling collections and best choice of collectibles for buyers wanting to expand their collection is to go to the dealers with the highest turn-over of inventory of the type that is of interest.

James Boryla at *www.SWSeller.com* is definitely on the list for buyers and sellers alike. SWSeller.com offers an extensive inventory of Star Wars merchandise and has thousands of items in stock at all times. He adds new inventory weekly, priming his site for both audiences. SWSeller.com is a Star Wars collectibles virtual super store. Many of the odd, obscure, or difficult pieces pictured in this book came though James's hands.

If the focus is Star Wars action figures, creatures, vehicles, and play sets, then Dave Roberts at *www.DNSToys.com* is the site to look into. DNS Toys has a wide range of affordable Star Wars products, and can help fill in holes in collections at very reasonable prices.

Another reliable outlet that offers fair prices for a broad variety of Star Wars goods is the Intergalactic Trading Company, found on the web at *www.InterGalacticTrading.com*. Their website proclaims an inventory having over 10,000 pieces in it. Their variety of offerings is certain to tempt.

For high-end pieces, vintage and rare in particular, Cloud City Collectibles *www.CloudCity.com* is the place to contact.

Mainly modern and common vintage action figures can be sought and sold at Brian's Toys *www.BriansToys.com*. Brian's Toys offers frequent newsletters and catalogs, and publishes a regular "buy list" posting bounties for pieces in demand.

Collectors looking to unload their collections or those who wish to spice their holdings up should both be able to find some measure of satisfaction with the sites and dealers listed above.

Library of "Must Have" Reference Books

The following books are found in the author's own personal library. Unless specifically listed, Collector Books has no association with, or endorsement for these titles. The author believes you'd be impressed if you picked them up to read.

Irwin Toys — The Canadian Star Wars Connection

James T. McCallum
2000 CG Publishing, Ltd., London
No values listed

Comment: The author explains the relationship Kenner had with Irwin Toys in Canada. Clarifies the role vintage Canadian toys play in today's U.S. collecting market. Information not available elsewhere.

(La Guerre des Etoiles) Meccano to TriLogo

Stéphane Faucourt
2006 Stéphane Faucourt, France
No values listed

Comment: The first book ever to detail the French and European vintage toy releases. Big, clear photographs of nearly the entire line. Timeless and complete. This book will never be replaced by any other on the subject.

Star Heroes Collector

Axel Hennel
2006 Fantasia Verlag Dreieich, Germany
2006 European Values

Comment: Annual pocket-sized book. Great for matching up accessories to loose figures and on learning about specific packaging variations. US, EU, and Canadian content.

Star Wars Action Figure Database Vol. 1 — (current)

Takuya Kubo
2006 Hobby Japan Co., Ltd., Tokyo, Japan
No values listed

Comment: Text is entirely in Japanese, but that's of no concern. The multi-angle photographs and modern layout are sure to please any action figure collector. One production series per volume.

Star Wars Poster Book

Stephen J. Sansweet and Peter Vilmur
2006 Chronicale Books, LLC, San Francisco, CA
No values listed

Comment: Huge beautiful photographs and exact measurement listings will make identification and authentication a breeze. A pleasure just to gaze through.

Star Wars Super Collector's Wish Book Editions 1 – 4

Geoffrey T. Carlton
2001 – 2007 Collector Books, Paducah, KY
Values Listed

Comment: Each book has a different emphesis on content and features. Photo selections are made book-by-book. All four books are recommended to combine into a complete detailed reference.

Star Wars Vintage Action Figures

John Kellerman
2003 Frontback Books, San Rafael, CA
2003 Values

Comment: The analysis of the production of vintage action figures and the variations available of figure-to-cardback alone make this book a requirement to own. No other vintage guide anywhere is as detailed.

Tomart's Price Guide to Worldwide Star Wars Collectibles

Stephen J. Sansweet and T.N. Tumbusch
1997 Tomart Publications, Dayton, OH
1997 Values

Comment: Not the first Star Wars price guide ever, but it set the standard by which all other Star Wars price guides are judged to this day. Even with aged values, this is still a "must have" guide for identifiaction.

Index

Index

Index

Index

A Closing Note:

ToysRGus.com has been forced out of their 10-year old online home.

After successfully challenging a cease and desist letter from lawyers for Toys R Us in 1999, the controversy was reignited in late 2006. Nearly 10 years of peaceful online existence ended as Toys R Us went after Gus's toy information archive again, unprovoked.

Gus Lopez, the operator of the oldest, best Star Wars toy documentation site, faced facts that no matter how many times he repelled the toy giant's aggressions, their legal team would always be ready to pick another fight over the clever, well established domain name.

Since ToysRGus.com was a site focused solely upon recording the history of the most rare of Star Wars collectible toys and proto-types and was not a money making venture, Gus decided it was easier and less costly to surrender to industry and just pick another name.

To find the new location of this priceless museum of knowledge, you must now point your browser at www.TheSWCA.com (which stands for The Stars Wars Collector's Archive).

While TheSWCA.com doesn't exactly have the classic ring as ToysRGus had, it is a relief to collectors around the world that Gus's ordeal is finally at an end and the archive is safe in its new home.

Carlton Family Biography

Geoffrey Carlton lives in Arlington, Texas, where he is a communications engineer for a financial news and analysis firm.

When not writing the *Super Collector's Wish Book*, Geoffrey develops his personal website StarWarsGuide.net to keep the collecting community informed about Star Wars collectibles. Additionally, he is a member of the Star Garrison of the Fighting 501st Imperial cos-tuming club.

Geoffrey's wife Tamara is the design editor for the original *Wish Book* manuscript, prior to submitting it to the publisher, and Geoffrey's partner and lookout on toy runs and at conventions. Tamara is an active duty member in the Star Garrison and belongs to the Dallas chapter of Fan Force.

Kay (Nelson) and Patricia are Geoffrey's daughters who are certain he already has everything for sale at the store, but love to go shop-ping "for him" all the same. Kay livies in Michigan, and Patricia is preparing to go off to college, giving Geoffrey hope that a larger geo-graphical area can now be covered to help him find the more difficult pieces still missing from his collection.

During the flood of Revenge of the Sith merchandise, Geoffrey's mother Casey and his son Lawrence picked up his camera and togeth-er they shot several hundred photographs for this fourth edition of the book, rounding it out to be a true family project.

Contributors

"Que the Credits!" Here is the fourth edition of the *Star Wars Super Collector's Wish Book*. All information is up-to-the-moment when it goes to press, because I don't really work alone. The contributors' acknowledgements have grown to two pages! Because information for each edition is used from book-to-book, every person and group listed is of equal importance, whether they were a one-time contributor who helped to send the first edition off to the press, or if I hear from them with weekly updates. (There are a few!)

Star Wars collecting is my full time hobby, and in the capacity of a collector, I owe an additional debt of thanks to the many dealers, fans, and fellow collectors who have given generously of their time, knowledge, and images of their own memorabilia to make this book the accomplished work that it has become.

Thank you. You have all made a difference.

If you are reading this and have not yet made your impact on the collecting community, it's not too late for next time. If you have access to information or an image taken from your own collection that would improve the next edition, please e-mail: info@StarWarsGuide.net.

Chris Albright
Collector, Costumer

Jeff Allen
Costumer

John Allen
Collector

Victor Arriaga
Collector (Mexico)

Scott Baker
Toy Customizer

Pedro Barrios
Collector (Mexico)

Jonathon Bearrie
Collector: Action Figures

Daniel Berghelli
Collector (Argentina)

James Boryla
Collector / Dealer

Chris Brennan
Collector (Australia)

Sharon Bronson
Collector

Neil Brown
Collector: Autographs

Nathan P. Butler
Timeline Archive

Bill Cable
Collector, Artist

Jose Antonio Macias Ceron
Collector (Mexico)

John Caboco
Collector

Brian Callahan
Collector: Vintage and Glass

Arnaldo Carvalho
Collector, Podcast Host

Marjorie Carvalho
Collector, Podcast Host

Gordon Chan
Collector (Hong Kong)

Mike Chockley
Collector

Jeff Craycraft
Disney Collector

Wayne Crews
Collector: LEGOs

Chris Da Costa
Collector (Canada)

Justin Dalby
Collector, Costumer

Anthony Damata
Collector: Vintage & Variations

Andrew Davison
Collector (United Kingdom)

Chris Dent
Collector

Thomas Derby IV
Collector: Vintage

Sophie Dessiméon
Collector (Belgium)

James Dollins
Collector, Costumer

Andy Dukes
Collector (United Kingdom)

John Eck
Collector

David Elliott
Collector: Cards (Australia)

Monty Elliott
Collector

Dan Emmons
Collector

Jeff Ensor
Collector

Jereomy Faber
Collector, Costumer

Chris Fawcett
Collector: Vintage

Guy Fernous
Collector

Jack Flukinger
Collector, Costumer

Dave Fox
Collector: Patches

Edgard Villasenor Franco
Collector (Mexico)

Matthew Frey
Collector: Visual Media

Davis Fuller
Owner: Star Wars Hummer

Lori Gifford
Fan

Mike Glover
Costumer

Brian Graham
Collector

Contributors

Evan Grant
Collector (Australia)

Marilyn Guyote
Collector - In Memoriam

Jay Harris
Collector

Peter Hauerstein
Collector

Kevin Heffner
Collector (Canada)

Brian Heiar
Collector, Costumer

Jeff Hendrickson
Collector

Kevin & Tanja Horn
Fans

Cole & Catherine Houston
Organizers: Fandom@Random

Shawn Houze
Collector: Beverage Packaging

Mark Huff
Gamer

David Humphries
Collector: Bootleg Figures

Mark Ivy
Collector

Keith Jakubowski
Collector

Bryan Janorske
Collector

Stephen Jones
Collector (United Kingdom)

Dan Joplin
Collector: Replicas, Costumer

Cathy Kendrick
Collector: Cards / Stickers

Deborah Kittle
Collector

"Brother Dave" Krempasky
Collector

Jason Krueger
Collector

Martin Lacy
Collector (United Kingdom)

Richard Leigh
Collector

Tait Lifto
Collector

Becky Lockerby
Collector

Brian Long
Collector

Joe Lynch
Collector: Micromachines

Charles Marcus
Collector

Jim McCallum
Collector (Canada), Author

Marcella McCuiston
Collector

Michael & Karen McGoldrick
Collectors (Australia)

Chuck & Barbara McLaughlin
Fans

Andrew McLennan
Dealer (New Zealand)

Dennis McLeod
Collector

Marc Miller
Collector, Costumer

Peter Mittag
Collector (Germany)

Phil Mizzi
Collector (Australia)

Lance Moran
Collector, Costumer

Scot Alan Morrison
Collector

Glen Mullaly
Collector (Canada)

Philip Murphy
Collector (United Kingdom)

Douglas Neman
Collector

Anne Newmann
Collector, Historical Archives

Barbara Ownbey
Fan

Mark Palmer
Collector (United Kingdom)

Cory Parker
Costumer, Fan

Chuck Paskovics
Collector

Peter Payne
Collector (Japan)

Steven Peacock
Collector

Ryan Peterman
Collector

Kristi Pointer
Collector, Costumer

Gary Price
Celebrity Promotions

Shannon Reynolds
Collector - In Memoriam

Mark Richert
Collector

Sandy Rivers
Collector: Martigras Coins

Dave Roberts
Collector, Dealer

Bill Rodgers
Collector (United Kingdom)

Mark Rodnitzky
eBay ID: Playeramusement

Ross Rosemurgy
Collector

Oscar Saenz
Collector

Buddy Saunders
Owner, Lone Star Comics

Gary Saunders
Collector (United Kingdom)

Tom Schaefer
Collector

Chris Seabolt
Collector, Costumer

George Seeds IV
Collector

Joseph Setele
Collector

Helen Silver
Collector

Mark Simonetti
Collector

Jeff Stagner
Collector

Ben Stevens
Celebrity Promotions

Tré Stratton
Collector

Adam Sylvester
Collector

Jason Thompson
Collector (United Kingdom)

Wayne Thompson
Collector

Martin Thurn
Historical Archives

Chris Toki
Collector (New Zealand)

Curt Vigneri
Collector: Store Displays

Charles Walker
Collector: Replicas, Costumer

Trent White
Collector: Replicas, Costumer

Scott Will
Costumer

Stuart Wilkshire
Collector (Japan)

Philip Wise
Collector, Celebrity Promoter

DOLLS & FIGURES

6315	American Character Dolls, Izen	$24.95
6317	Arranbee Dolls, The Dolls That Sell on Sight, DeMillar/Brevik	$24.95
6319	Barbie Doll Fashion, Volume III, 1975 – 1979, Eames	$29.95
6221	Barbie, The First 30 Years, 2nd Edition, Deutsch	$24.95
6134	Ency. of Bisque Nancy Ann Storybook Dolls, 1936 – 1947, Pardee/Robertson. $29.95	
6825	Celluloid Dolls, Toys & Playthings, Robinson	$29.95
6451	Collector's Ency. of American Composition Dolls, Vol. II, Mertz	$29.95
6546	Collector's Ency. of Barbie Doll Exclusives, 3rd Ed., Augustyniak	$29.95
6636	Collector's Ency. of Madame Alexander Dolls, 1948 – 1965, Crowsey	$24.95
6473	Collector's Ency. of Vogue Dolls, 2nd Ed., Izen/Stover	$29.95
6563	Collector's Guide to Ideal Dolls, 3rd Ed., Izen	$24.95
6456	Collector's Guide to Dolls of the 1960s and 1970s, Vol. II, Sabulis	$24.95
6944	Complete Gde. to Shirley Temple Dolls and Collectibles, Bervaldi-Camaratta. $29.95	
7028	Doll Values, Antique to Modern, 9th Ed., Edward	$14.95
7360	Madame Alexander Collector's Dolls Price Guide #32, Crowsey	$14.95
6929	Official Precious Moments Collector's Guide to Figurines, 2nd Ed., Bomm. $16.95	
6467	Paper Dolls of the 1960s, 1970s, and 1980s, Nichols	$24.95
6642	20th Century Paper Dolls, Young	$19.95

TOYS & MARBLES

2333	Antique & Collectible Marbles, 3rd Ed., Grist	$9.95
6649	Big Book of Toy Airplanes, Miller	$24.95
4945	G-Men and FBI Toys, Whitworth	$18.95
6633	Hot Wheels, The Ultimate Redline Guide, 2nd Ed., Clark/Wicker	$29.95
6466	Matchbox Toys, 4th Ed., 1947 to 2003, Johnson	$24.95
6638	The Other Matchbox Toys, 1947 to 2004, Johnson	$19.95
6840	Schroeder's Collectible Toys, Antique to Modern Price Guide, 10th Ed.	$17.95
6650	Toy Car Collector's Guide, 2nd Ed., Johnson	$24.95

FURNITURE

6928	Early American Furniture: A Guide to Who, When, and Where, Obbard $19.95	
3906	Heywood-Wakefield Modern Furniture, Rouland	$18.95
7038	The Marketplace Guide to Oak Furniture, 2nd Edition, Blundell	$29.95

JEWELRY & ACCESSORIES

4704	Antique & Collectible Buttons, Volume I, Wisniewski	$19.95
5903	Antique & Collectible Buttons, Volume II, Wisniewski	$24.95
6122	Brilliant Rhinestones, Aikins	$24.95
6323	Christmas Pins, Past & Present, 2nd Edition, Gallina	$19.95
4850	Collectible Costume Jewelry, Simonds	$24.95
5675	Collectible Silver Jewelry, Rezazadeh	$24.95
6453	Collecting Costume Jewelry 101, Carroll	$24.95
7025	Collecting Costume Jewelry 202, Carroll	$24.95
6468	Collector's Ency. of Pendant & Pocket Watches, 1500 – 1950, Bell	$24.95
6554	Coro Jewelry, A Collector's Guide, Brown	$29.95
4940	Costume Jewelry, A Practical Handbook & Value Guide, Rezazadeh	$24.95
6027	The Esteé Lauder Solid Perfume Compact Collection, 1967 to 2001	$24.95

5812	Fifty Years of Collectible Fashion Jewelry, 1925 – 1975, Baker	$24.95
6330	Handkerchiefs: A Collector's Guide, Guarnaccia/Guggenheim	$24.95
6833	Handkerchiefs: A Collector's Guide, Volume 2	$24.95
6464	Inside the Jewelry Box, Pitman	$24.95
7358	Inside the Jewelry Box, Volume 2, Pitman	$24.95
5695	Ladies' Vintage Accessories, Bruton	$24.95
1181	100 Years of Collectible Jewelry, 1850 – 1950, Baker	$9.95
6645	100 Years of Purses, Aikins	$24.95
6942	Rhinestone Jewelry: Figurals, Animals, and Whimsicals, Brown	$24.95
6038	Sewing Tools & Trinkets, Volume 2, Thompson	$24.95
6039	Signed Beauties of Costume Jewelry, Brown	$24.95
6341	Signed Beauties of Costume Jewelry, Volume II, Brown	$24.95
6555	20th Century Costume Jewelry, 1900 – 1980, Aikins	$24.95
4850	Unsigned Beauties of Costume Jewelry, Brown	$24.95
4878	Vintage & Contemporary Purse Accessories, Gerson	$24.95
4955	Vintage Hats & Bonnets, 1770 –1970, Langley	$24.95
5923	Vintage Jewelry for Investment & Casual Wear, Edeen	$24.95

PAPER COLLECTIBLES & BOOKS

6623	Collecting American Paintings, James	$29.95
7039	Collecting Playing Cards, Pickvet	$24.95
6826	Collecting Vintage Children's Greeting Cards, McPherson	$24.95
6553	Collector's Guide to Cookbooks, Daniels	$24.95
1441	Collector's Guide to Post Cards, Wood	$9.95
6627	Early 20th Century Hand-Painted Photography, Ivankovich	$24.95
6936	Leather Bound Books, Boutiette	$24.95
7036	Old Magazine Advertisements, Clear	$24.95
6940	Old Magazines, 2nd Ed., Clear	$19.95
3973	Sheet Music Reference & Price Guide, 2nd Ed., Guiheen/Pafik	$19.95

GLASSWARE & POTTERY

6326	Collectible Cups & Saucers, Book III, Harran	$24.95
6331	Collecting Head Vases, Barron	$24.95
6830	Collector's Encyclopedia of Depression Glass, 17th Ed., Florence	$19.95
6629	Collector's Encyclopedia of Fiesta, 10th Ed., Huxford	$24.95
5609	Collector's Encyclopedia of Limoges Porcelain, 3rd Ed., Gaston	$29.95
5677	Collector's Encyclopedia of Niloak, 2nd Edition, Gifford	$29.95
5842	Collector's Encyclopedia of Roseville Pottery, Vol. 2, Huxford/Nickel	$24.95
6646	Collector's Ency. of Stangl Artware, Lamps, and Birds, 2nd Ed., Runge	$29.95
7029	Elegant Glassware of the Depression Era, 12th Edition, Florence	$24.95
6126	Fenton Art Glass, 1907 – 1939, 2nd Edition, Whitmyer	$29.95
6320	Gaston's Blue Willow, 3rd Edition	$19.95
6127	The Glass Candlestick Book, Vol. 1, Akro Agate to Fenton, Felt/Stoer	$24.95
6648	Glass Toothpick Holders, 2nd Edition, Bredehoft	$29.95
6329	Glass Tumblers, 1860s to 1920s, Bredehoft/Sanford	$29.95
6562	The Hazel-Atlas Glass Identification and Value Guide, Florence	$24.95
5840	Heisey Glass, 1896 – 1957, Bredehoft	$24.95
5913	McCoy Pottery, Volume III, Hanson/Nissen	$24.95
6135	North Carolina Art Pottery, 1900 – 1960, James/Leftwich	$24.95
6335	Pictorial Guide to Pottery & Porcelain Marks, Lage	$29.95
6925	Standard Encyclopedia of Carnival Glass, 10th Ed., Edwards/Carwile	$29.95
6476	Westmoreland Glass, The Popular Years, 1940 – 1985, Kovar	$29.95